P. Enjalbert   E. W. Mayr   K. W. Wagner   (Eds.)

STACS 94

11th Annual Symposium
on Theoretical Aspects of Computer Science
Caen, France, February 24-26, 1994
Proceedings

Springer-Verlag

Berlin Heidelberg New York
London Paris Tokyo
Hong Kong Barcelona
Budapest

Series Editors

Gerhard Goos
Universität Karlsruhe
Postfach 69 80
Vincenz-Priessnitz-Straße 1
D-76131 Karlsruhe, Germany

Juris Hartmanis
Cornell University
Department of Computer Science
4130 Upson Hall
Ithaca, NY 14853, USA

Volume Editors

Patrice Enjalbert
Laboratoire d'Informatique, Université de Caen
F-14132 Caen Cedex, France

Ernst W. Mayr
Institut für Informatik, Technische Universität München
Arcisstraße 21, D-80290 München, Germany

Klaus W. Wagner
Lehrstuhl für Theoretische Informatik, Universität Würzburg
Am Exerzierplatz 3, D-97072 Würzburg, Germany

CR Subject Classification (1991): F, D.1, D.4, G.1-2

ISBN 3-540-57785-8 Springer-Verlag Berlin Heidelberg New York
ISBN 0-387-57785-8 Springer-Verlag New York Berlin Heidelberg

CIP data applied for

© Springer-Verlag Berlin Heidelberg 1994
Printed in Germany

Typesetting: Camera-ready by author
SPIN: 10131926   45/3140-543210 - Printed on acid-free paper

Lecture Notes in Computer Science

Edited by G. Goos and J. Hartmanis

Advisory Board: W. Brauer   D. Gries   J. Stoer

775

Foreword

The Symposium on Theoretical Aspects of Computer Science is an annual conference organised jointly by the Special Interest Group for Fundamental Computer Science of AFCET and the Special Interest Group for Theoretical Computer Science of Gesellschaft für Informatik (GI). It is held in alternating years in France and in Germany.

This year, 234 papers were submitted by authors from 38 countries. Of these submissions, 60 were selected after competitive and thorough refereeing process. Thus STACS maintains the high scientific level and continues the success achieved by this series of symposia in the past years.

The conference took place in Caen (France) on February 24-26, 1994. Three invited talks were given: *Hypertransition Graphs* by André Arnold (Bordeaux, France), *Towards a Theory of Recursive Structures* by David Harel (Rehovot, Israel), and *The Meaning and Nature of Perturbations in Geometric Computing* by Raymund Seidel (Berkeley, USA). As in earlier years, some research computer systems were presented on invitation by Program Committee members. Organised in parallel, the first International Conference *Verification and Validation of Systems and Software* proposed tutorials and conferences in this field of increasing interest, often related with advances in theoretical computer science.

The Program Committee of STACS'94 consisted of:

J.L. Balcazar (Barcelona), M. Crochemore (Marne la Vallée), V. Diekert (Stuttgart), P. Enjalbert (Caen, chair), R. Klein (Hagen), P. McKenzie (Montréal), E.W. Mayr (Munich, co-chair), L. Pacholski (Wroclaw), R. Pinzani (Firenze), D. Richard (Clermont-Ferrand), B. Rozoy (Orsay), M. Rusinowitch (Nancy), L. Staiger (Aachen), J.V. Tucker (Swansea), K.W. Wagner (Würzburg, co-chair).

We wish to thank AFCET and the local Committee in Caen for their organisational support, EATCS and INRIA for their cooperation, and the sponsors of the symposium:

Human Capital Mobility program of the European Community, University of Caen, ISMRA (ENSI de Caen), SEPT, PRC "Mathématiques et Informatique", University of Paris 11, OPL, France Télécom, Conseil Régional de Basse Normandie, City of Caen, SYNERGIA (Technopole de Caen).

December 1993

Patrice Enjalbert
Ernst W. Mayr
Klaus W. Wagner

List of Reviewers

ABDULRAB H.
ABITEBOUL S.
ABOULHAMID M.
ABRAHAMSON K.
ACETO L.
AGUZZI G.
ALEXANDRE F.
ALLENDER E.
ALT R.
ALT H.
AMBOS-SPIES K.
AMBROISE D.
ANANTHARAMAN S.
ANGLUIN D.
ARNBORG S.
ARNOLD A.
AUTEBERT J.-M.
AVENHAUS K.
AZEMA P.

BAADER F.
BADOUEL E
BANDT C.
BARCUCCI E.
BEAUDRY M.
BEAUQUIER D.
BEAUQUIER J.
BERARD B.
BERGERON F.
BERGERON A.
BERGSTRA J.A.
BERLINE C.
BERRE D.
BERSTEL J.
BERTHOME P.
BERTOL M.
BIDOIT N.
BIRGET J.-C.
BOASSON L.
BODLAENDER H.-L.

BOLDI P.
BOUABDALLAH A.
BOUCHERON S.
BOUDET A.
BOUDJLIDA N.
BOUDOL G.
BOUGE L.
BOUHOULA A.
BOUSSINOT F.
BOUZIANNE Z.
BOYAR J.
BRANDENBURG F.
BRANDST A.
BRANDSTÄDT A.
BREVIGLIERI L.
BRLEK S.
BRONSARD F.
BRUYERE V.
BRÜGGEMANN-
    KLEIN A.

BUCIARELLI A.
BUHRMAN H.
BUNTROCK G.
BURTSCHICK H.-J.

CARDONE F.
CASPI P.
CAVALLI A.
CECE G.
CEGIELSKI P.
CESARINI F.
CEZERO A.
CHARATONIK W.
CHARRETTON C.
CHISCI L.
CHOFFRUT Ch.
CHRETIENNE Ph.
CHRISTEN C.
CLERBOUT M.
CLOTE P.

COLLAVIZZA H.
COLMERAUER A.
COMON H.
CONDON A.
CONTEJEAN E.
COOPERMAN G.
CORI R.
COSNARD M.
COURCELLE B.
COUSINEAU G.
COUSOT R.
COUSOT P.
CREPEAU C.
CRESPI-REGHIZZI S.
CZUMAJ A.

DARONDEAU P.
DASSOW J.
DAWAR A.
DE GROOTE Ph.
DE ROUGEMONT M.
DE SIMONE R.
DECKER H.
DEL BIMBO A.
DEL LUNGO A.
DELAET S.
DELAHAYE J.-P.
DELORME C.
DELPORTE C.
DESARMENIEN J.
DESEL J.
DIAZ J.
DIETZFELBINGER M.
DIKS K.
DJELLOUL S.
DOSCH W.
DOSSY S.
DOWEK G.
DUCHAMP G.
DUJOLS R.

DULUCQ S.
DUNNE P.E.

EBINGER W.
ENGBERG U.
ENGELFRIET J.
ESBELIN H.-A.
ESPARZA J.
ETIEMBLE D.

FANCHON J.
FARINAS L.
FAUCONNIER H.
FEELEY M.
FEREIRA J.
FERNANDEZ DE LA
    VEGA W.
FERNAU H.
FERRAGINA P.
FERRAND G.
FERREIRA M.
FISCHER P.
FLAJOLET
FLEURY G.
FORTNOW L.
FRANHÖFER B.
FREIVALD R.
FREUND R.
FRIBOURG L.
FURBACH U.

GABARRO J.
GAMATIE B.
GARDY D.
GASTIN P.
GAUDEL M.-C.
GAVALDA R.
GHAVAMIZADEH R.
GIAVITTO J.-L.
GIESSMANN E.-G.

GIOVANNETTI E.
GOERDT A.
GOETZE B.
GOLD R
GORI M.
GOURGAND M.
GOUYOU-
    BEAUCHAMPS D.
GRAEDEL E.
GRANDJEAN E.
GRAZZINI E.
GRIGORIEFF S.
GROSSI R.
GUESSARIAN I.
GUILLAUME M.
GUREVICH Y.
GUTLEBEN N.
GÜNDEL S.

HABEL A.
HAGERUP T.
HAINS G.
HAMMER D.
HANATANI Y.
HANCART Ch.
HARIHARAN R.
HARMAN N.A.
HEBRARD J.-J.
HEINEMANN B.
HEMASPAANDRA
    L.-A.
HEMMERLING A.
HERMANN N.
HERTRAMPF U.
HEUN V.
HINDLEY R.
HINTERMEIER C.
HOFFMANN F.
HOFMEISTER T.
HOHBERG W.
HOLLUNDER B.
HOOGEBOOM H.-J.
HROMKOVIC J.
HUFFLEN J.-M.

ICKING Ch.
IDURY R.
IMBERT J.-L.

JANTZEN M.
JENNER B.
JERON T.
JIANG T.
JOHNEN C.
JURDZINSKI T.
JURIE P.-F.

KANAREK P.
KANNAN S.
KEIL M.
KHELLADI A.
KIEHN A.
KONIG J.-C.
KOPPENHAGEN U.
KOSCIELSKI A.
KRATSCH D.
KRAUSE M.
KREOWSKI H.-J.
KRIVINE J.-L.
KRIZANC D.
KROB D.
KUCHEROV G.
KUDLEK M
KUNDE M.
KUTYLOWSKI M.

LAGERGREN J.
LAMBERT J.-L.
LANDAU G.
LANGE K.J.
LAPLANTE S.
LATTEUX M.
LE N.-M.
LE GALL P.
LEMIEUX F.
LENHART B.
LEROUX P.
LESCANNE P.
LESTREE L.

LESVENTES G.
LEVY F
LI M.
LISCHKE G.
LISKIEWICZ M.
LONGO G.
LORHO B.
LORYS K.
LOZANO A.
LUGIEZ D.
LUKASZEWICZ W

MA L.
MACIEL A.
MAGGS B.
MALENFANT J.
MALER O.
MALGOUYRES R.
MALUCELLI F.
MANNOUSSAKIS Y.
MARCINKOWSKI J.
MARQUIS P.
MARRE B.
MARTINEZ C.
MASINI G.
MAZOYER J.
MEINEL C
MELTON A.
MERY D.
MERZENICH W.
MICHEL P.
MIDDELDORP A.
MIRKOWSKA G.
MODIGLIANI U.
MOHRI M.
MORE M.
MORO A.
MULLINS J.
MUNDHENK M.
MUSCHOLL A.
MYOUPO J.-F.
MÜCK A.
MÜLLER H.

NARENDRAN P.
NERAUD J.
NICKAU H.
NICKELSEN A.
NICOLLIN X.
NIELSEN M.
NIEUWENHUIS R.
NIPKOW T.
NIWINSKI D.
NUTT W.

ÖHRING S.
OLDEROG R.
OLSEN H.
OREJAS F
OTTO F.

PAGLI L.
PANANGADEN P.
PARROW J.
PECUCHET J.-P.
PELADEAU P.
PELZ E.
PENAUD J.-G.
PERRIN D.
PETERSEN H.
PETIT A.
PETRENKO A.
PIGHIZZINI G.
PIOTROW M.
PIPPENGER N.
PIPPOLINI F.
PLATEAU G.
PLUMP D.
PUDLAK P.

QUEINNEC Ch.

RAHBAR H.
RAUZY A.
RAZBOROV A.
REGAN K.
REGNIER M.
REINHARDT K.

REISCHUK R.
REISSENBERGER W.
REMY D.
REVUZ D.
REYNAUD J.-C.
RINDONE G.
RINGEISSEN C.
ROBERT Y.
ROOSS D.
ROTH P.
ROYER V.
RUBIO A.
RUZZO L.

SALOMAA K.
SALWICKI A.
SALZER G.
SANCHEZ-
    LEIGHTON V.
SANDKOFF D.
SANSONNET J.-P.
SANTHA M.
SAQUET J.
SCHEWE K.-D.
SCHINDELHAUER C.

SCHIRRA ST.
SCHNEIDER M.
SCHNOEBELEN Ph.
SCHNORR C.-P.
SCHREIBER G.
SCHULZ K.
SCHWIND C.
SCHÖNING U.
SCOTT Ph.
SEIDL H.
SENIZERGUES G.
SIEGEL P.
SIMON D.
SODA G.
SONG X.
SOTTEAU D.
SPRUGNOLI R.
SREEDHAR V.-C.
STACHOWIAK G.
STEFANI J.-B.
STEFFEN B.
STERN J.
STEWART I.A.
STRAUBING H.
SZALAS A.

TAHHAN BITTAR E.
THALHEIM B.
THERIEN D.
THIAGARAJAN P.S.
THIBON J.-Y.
THIERAUF Th.
THIMONIER L.
THOMAS W.
THOMPSON B.C.
TISON S.
TIURYN J.
TOFTS C.
TOMAZIK J.
TORAN J.
TREHEL M.
TRYSTRAM D.
TUCKER J.V.

VALIANT L.
VALKEMA E.
VALLEE B.
VAUCHER J.
VAUZEILLES J.
VERDIER I.
VIDAL-NAQUET G.

VITANYI P.
VOELKEL L.
VOGEL J.
VOGLER W.
VOLLMER H.

WAGENER H.
WALUKIEWICZ I.
WANKE E.
WEGENER I.
WEIHRAUCH K.
WEIL P.
WENGER R.
WIEHAGEN R.
WILKE T.
WOHLFEIL S.
WOLPER P.

YUNES J.-B.

ZAPPA G.
ZIELONKA W.
ZIMMERMANN P.
ZISSIMOPOULOS V.
ZVONKIN A.

Table of Contents

EFFICIENT ALGORITHMS

Invited Lecture

The Nature and Meaning of Perturbations in Geometric Computing

RAIMUND SEIDEL*

Computer Science Division, 571 Evans
University of California Berkeley
Berkeley CA 94720, USA
email: seidel@cs.berkeley.edu

Abstract. This note addresses some fundamental questions concerning perturbations as they are used in computational geometry: How does one define them? What does it mean to compute with them? How can one compute with them? Is it sensible to use them?
We define perturbations to be curves, point out that computing with them amounts to computing with limits. and (re)derive some methods of computing with such limits automatically. In principle a line can always be used as a perturbation curve. We discuss a generic method for choosing such a line that is applicable in many situations.

1 Introduction

When faced with the problem of geometric degeneracy, a typical computational geometry paper, talk, or lecture will simply appeal to "standard perturbation methods." This may be followed by a reference, such as [5], [16], or [6], but usually not much more discussion is offered. This may be okay, were there not the curious fact that when one asks a typical computational geometer for a precise definition of "perturbation," one will usually not receive a satisfactory answer (*'You perturb the input a little bit.' 'You move the input points by an infinitesimal amount.'* etc.). Consulting the main references does not guarantee satisfaction either. Usually one finds a lengthy discussion on "degeneracies" and the distinction between "problem induced" and "algorithm induced" ones, and then perturbations are defined, either by what properties they are supposed to have (and not by what they are supposed to be), or as sequences satisfying some technical, rather unintuitive conditions.

Why this peculiar situation? The answer, I believe, lies in the somewhat dubious motivation for using perturbations: Here I have a program that solves some problem on all non-degenerate instances (whatever non-degenerate means). Give me some automatic, strictly syntactic method that transform my program into one that solves the problem on all instances.

A reasonably cautious researcher will almost immediately raise his (or her) eyebrows. How can one transform a program that does not always work into one

---

* Supported by NSF Presidential Young Investigator award CCR-9058440

that always works by purely syntactic means? This seems like wishful thinking and is very unlikely to succeed in general. But as it turns out, the method of perturbations comes surprisingly close to achieving just that. The transformed program always "works." However, it does not always solve the original problem, but is solves some related problem. The exact nature of this related problem, though, and its relationship to the original problem is usually left unclear.[2] But exactly here seems to be the crux of the difficulty of understanding, definining, and using perturbations.

It is the goal of this note to elucidate some of these issues. In Section 2 we define perturbations (for us they are just curves). Before ever mentioning algorithms or programs, we show how a perturbation scheme can be used to transform a *problem mapping* into a *perturbed problem mapping* via a simple limit construction. We consider under what circumstances the original mapping F and and the perturbed mapping $\overline{F}$ agree and hence computing $\overline{F}$ gives the same result as computing F. Finally we discuss how for certain models of computation any program that computes F "almost everywhere" can be purely syntactically transformed into a program that computes $\overline{F}$ everywhere (which is great if F and $\overline{F}$ agree).

Section 3 considers the choice of perturbation curves. It comes as no big suprise that the simplest of all possible nontrivial curves, namely a straight line, can always be chosen to do the job. A somewhat surprising finding though shows that, considering almost any geometric problem, essentially the same line can be used for all possible inputs. The finding can be paraphrased as *"if you know one non-degenerate input, then you have a good perturbation for all inputs."* We discuss the ramifications of this insight, in particular the problem of producing non-degenerate input.

In Section 4 we discuss previous perturbation schemes and how they fit into our framework. This is almost immediate for the SoS scheme of Edelsbrunner and Mücke [5] and for the efficient linear scheme of Canny and Emiris [6, 7]. It is slightly more involved for the symbolic scheme of Yap [16, 17], however leads to a consistency proof that is maybe simpler than the ones offered in the original papers.

The last section deals with the shortcomings of the perturbation method and to some extent questions the wisdom of using it.

This note does not contain many new results. It is rather meant mainly as an elucidation and clarification of previous ideas. The topic of perturbations is one of the very few ones that, in my experience, can cause heated, opinionated discussions among computational geometers. Thus I apologize in advance if some of my statements should have turned out more pointed than they should be. I would like to acknowledge lengthy discussions with John Canny, Herbert Edelsbrunner, Ioannis Emiris, Jeff Erickson, Kurt Mehlhorn, and Chee Yap. Finally, my apologies to Richard Dedekind for stealing the title.

---

[2] For instance it is a priori not clear whether the transforms of two different programs for the same original problem solve the same related problem.

2 The Framework

2.1 Perturbations

In this section we consider the computation of functions F from some *input space* $\mathcal{I}$ to some *output space* $\mathcal{O}$. We will assume that $\mathcal{I}$ as well as $\mathcal{O}$ is endowed with some topology, which allows for the notion of a limit. Typically $\mathcal{I}$ will be $\mathbb{R}^N$ with the usual euclidean topology; $\mathcal{O}$ will be $\mathbb{R}^M$ with euclidean topology, or some finite set with the discrete topology, or the product or direct sum of such spaces.

As typical examples consider CHS, the *convex hull sequence* function, which given the coordinates of a sequence S of n points $(x_1, y_1), \ldots, (x_n, y_n)$ in the plane asks for the sequence of indices of the points that constitute the vertices of the convex hull of S, and consider CHA, the *convex hull area* function, which, given the sequence S just asks for a single real number, namely the area of the convex hull of S. For both functions the input space $\mathcal{I}$ is $\mathbb{R}^{2n}$ with its usual topology, where the input sequence S is encoded as the $(2n)$-tuple $q = (x_1, y_1, \ldots, x_n, y_n)$. For CHA the output space $\mathcal{O}$ is just $\mathbb{R}$ with the usual topology. For CHS the output space $\mathcal{O}$ is the (finite) set of all sequences of distinct integers from $\{1, \ldots, n\}$ of length at most n with the discrete topology.

Definition 1. For a point $q \in \mathcal{I}$ we define a *perturbation of q* to be any curve $q()$ beginning in q, in other words the image of a continuous mapping $q() : [0, \infty) \mapsto \mathcal{I}$ with $q(0) = q$. A *perturbation scheme* Q assigns to every point $q \in \mathcal{I}$ a perturbation $q()$. [3]

Definition 2. A perturbation scheme Q induces for every function $F : \mathcal{I} \mapsto \mathcal{O}$ a *perturbed function* $\overline{F}^Q : \mathcal{I} \mapsto \mathcal{O}$, defined by

$$\overline{F}^Q(q) = \lim_{\varepsilon \to 0+} F(q(\varepsilon)).$$

We will assume that this limit exists. Since the scheme Q is often clear form context, we will sometimes omit the superscript Q and just write $\overline{F}$ for the perturbed function. Keep in mind, though, that the perturbed function does depend on the scheme Q. In general for two different perturbation schemes Q and Q' the perturbed functions $\overline{F}^Q$ and $\overline{F}^{Q'}$ will be different.

When do F and its perturbed function $\overline{F}$ agree? Here is a simple and obvious, but useful condition:

Lemma 3. *If F is continuous at q, then $F(q) = \overline{F}(q)$*

Note that the statement in the lemma holds for any perturbation scheme. Also note, that if F is not continuous at q, very little, if anything at all, can be said in general about the relationship between $F(q)$ and $\overline{F}(q)$. Of course our

---

[3] For the sake of better readability we forego a more precise notation where a perturbation scheme π assign to each point q a curve π_q.

hope is that there is some reasonable relationship, because the whole idea of using the "perturbation method" is to compute $\overline{F}(q)$ instead of $F(q)$.

Why is this useful? Frequently, instead of writing a program that compute F for all inputs, it is much easier to write a program Π that correctly computes F for *almost all* inputs (ignore the special, "degenerate" cases!). This partially working program Π can then rather straightforwardly be transformed into a program $\overline{\Pi}$ that computes $\overline{F}$ for all inputs. In other words, in order to make Π work for all inputs one simply redefines the problem that it is supposed to solve.

This certainly seems like a dubious way of proceeding, but is often less crazy than it looks. If, for instance, F is continuous everywhere, then $\overline{F} = F$ everywhere and the program $\overline{\Pi}$ computes the correct thing. This happens for instance in the convex hull area function CHA mentioned above. But even if F is not continuous for some input q, computing $\overline{F}(q)$ can yield enough information to recover $F(q)$ relatively easily. For instance, the convex hull sequence function CHS mentioned above is discontinuous for inputs q representing planar point sets that have more than two points colinear on a convex hull edge. However, it is easy to see that in that case $CHS(q)$ must be a subsequence of $\overline{CHS}(q)$; the extra elements correspond to vertices in the middle of edges and can be discovered and removed easily in a postprocessing step.

Not all discontinuous functions admit such an easy postprocessing step. We will dwell no further on this now, but discuss this issue in Section 5. For now we will concentrate on the problem of computing $\overline{F}$.

2.2   Computing the perturbed function $\overline{F}$

First we have to settle on the model of computation — what kind of algorithms do we consider? Most algorithms in computational geometry can be modeled by so-called *extended algebraic decision trees* [12]. These are ternary trees, where each interior node v is labeled by a test function $f_v : \mathbb{R}^N \mapsto \mathbb{R}$ and its branches labeled -1, 0, and $+1$, respectively; each leaf v is labeled with a result function $r_v : \mathbb{R}^N \mapsto \mathcal{O}$ (we are now assuming that $\mathcal{I} = \mathbb{R}^N$). Computation with such a tree works as follows: upon input $q \in \mathbb{R}^N$ the function $\text{sign} f_v(q)$ is evaluated, where v is the root node; the branch labeled by the outcome of this evaluation is taken, and the computation is continued in that subtree; if a leaf ℓ is reached, then $r_\ell(q)$ is evaluated and returned as the "output" of the computation. It is assumed here that the test functions f_v and the result functions r_ℓ are defined and continuous for each q that "reaches" their node v or ℓ. Moreover, each test function f_v must be "easily computable." This is the case, for instance, if it is a small degree polynomial.

There is a slightly more powerful model, called *algebraic computation trees* [12], which we will not consider in this paper. Extended algebraic decision trees abstract away all book-keeping and storage details. They model many geometric algorithms well, since such algorithms often rely exclusively on a small set of so-called geometric primitive tests (see [9]) for their geometric content. These tests supply the test functions f_v in the tree model.

For the planar convex hull examples, typical primitives will be coordinate comparisons, $x_i \lessgtr x_j$ or $y_i \lessgtr y_j$, yielding test functions $f_v(q) = x_i - x_j$ and $f_v(q) = y_i - y_j$, and so-called sidedness tests, that determine the relative orientation of three points (x_i, y_i), (x_j, y_j), (x_k, y_k), in particular whether they are colinear; this is expressed by the test function

$$f_v(q) = \begin{vmatrix} 1 & x_i & y_i \\ 1 & x_j & y_j \\ 1 & x_k & y_k \end{vmatrix}.$$

Other geometric primitives tests that typically arise are so-called in-circle or in-sphere tests, the higher-dimensional version of the sidedness test, distance comparisons, and others. They can all be expressed by suitable, relatively simple test functions f_v.

Now assume I have an extended algebraic decision tree T that computes some function $F : \mathbb{R}^N \mapsto \mathcal{O}$. How can I compute the perturbed function $\overline{F}^Q$ for some perturbation scheme Q? It is easy to see that all I need to do is the following *perturbed evaluation of T*: at each internal node v, instead of $s_v(q) = \text{sign} f_v(q)$, evaluate the "perturbed test function" $\overline{s_v}^Q(q) = \lim_{\varepsilon \to 0^+} \text{sign} f_v(q(\varepsilon))$; for each leaf ℓ compute and return $\overline{r_\ell}^Q(q) = \lim_{\varepsilon \to 0^+} r_\ell(q(\varepsilon))$.

Let us ignore for the time being how the new perturbed test and result functions involving the limits can be evaluated.

Definition 4. Let $f : \mathbb{R}^N \mapsto \mathbb{R}$ be continuous, let $q \in \mathbb{R}^N$, and let $q()$ be a perturbation (curve) of q. We say that $q()$ is *valid for f* iff $\lim_{\varepsilon \to 0^+} \text{sign} f(q(\varepsilon))$ exists and is not zero. A perturbation scheme Q is valid for f iff $q()$ is valid for f for each $q \in \mathbb{R}^N$. If $\mathcal{F}$ is a family of functions f, then we say that a perturbation or a perturbations scheme is valid for $\mathcal{F}$ if it is valid for each $f \in \mathcal{F}$.

Let T be a tree for computing F as above and let Q be a perturbation scheme that is valid for $\mathcal{F}$, the set of all test functions f_v appearing in that tree. If we now use the method outlined above for using T to compute the perturbed function $\overline{F}^Q$, then, as is easy to see, no branch labeled 0 will ever be followed during a computation. Thus these branches could all be pruned away. Even better, if T was incomplete and had some of the 0-branches missing, it still can be used to compute $\overline{F}^Q$. And this is the observation that lies at the heart of the whole perturbation method. Even if I have an incomplete program that computes F for most q but misses parts that deal with inputs q that make some geometric primitive tests evaluate to 0 (and are hence deemed "degenerate"), I can still make this program compute $\overline{F}^Q$ for all q. This is all expressed by the following theorem:

Theorem 5. *Let T be a correct extended algebraic decision tree computing some function $F : \mathbb{R}^N \mapsto \mathcal{O}$, and let Q be a perturbation scheme that is valid for the set of test functions appearing in T.*

1. *A perturbed evaluation of T computes the perturbed function $\overline{F}^Q$.*
2. *If F is continuous at q, then the perturbed evaluation of T with input q yields $F(q)$.*
3. *The above statements remain true, if some, or all, of the 0-branches of T are removed.*

Note one interesting fact: The method prescribes that the perturbed test function $\overline{s_v}^Q$ has to be evaluated for *all* v along the computation path. This means that if I have a program that has some "degenerate cases" programmed and others missing, and I introduce the perturbation method, then I have to discard the programmed "degenerate" cases (unless there is some additional information and reasoning available)! This may seem counterintuitive, but here is example situation that can arise in a planar convex hull computation. Say, I have a program that has dealt with all three cases for coordinate comparisons, but only with the two "non-degenerate" cases for the sidedness tests, and I apply perturbation only to the sidedness tests. If now three input points lie on a common vertical line, then the program might detect their colinearity because of coordinate comparisons, but also non-colinearity because of a perturbed sidedness test. Needless to say, this can lead to severe consistency problems within the program.

In order to apply the perturbation method to some incomplete program we need three things: (1) a valid perturbation scheme, or at least a way to come up with a valid perturbation for each input; (2) a way to evaluate the perturbed test functions; (3) a way to evaluate the perturbed result functions $\overline{r_\ell}^Q$.

Points (1) and (2) we will deal with in the following sections. About (3) we will just offer a few comments. Let ℓ be a leaf of T that is reached from the root by following only non-zero branches. Let X_ℓ be the set of inputs q that reach ℓ upon normal evaluation of T, and let $\overline{X_\ell}$ be the set of inputs that reach ℓ upon perturbed evaluation. Assuming reasonably behaved test functions, X_ℓ will be an open subset of $\mathbb{R}^N$, and $\overline{X_\ell}$ will contain X_ℓ plus some boundary points. (Although the notation may suggest it, $\overline{X_\ell}$ will in general not be the topological closure of X_ℓ.) Perturbed evaluation of T requires the evaluation of the perturbed result function $\overline{r_\ell}$ for $q \in \overline{X_\ell}$. This is no problem if $q \in X_\ell$, since by assumption r_l is continuous for such q, and hence $\overline{r_\ell}(q) = r_\ell(q)$. Problems can only arise with boundary points; for instance $\overline{r_\ell}(q)$ might not even be defined for such points q (although this means that $\overline{F}(q)$ is not defined either). However, in many cases there will not be a problem at all. It may be that r_ℓ is constant for all $q \in X_\ell$, and hence $\overline{r_\ell}(q)$ is the same constant for boundary points q. This happens, for instance in the convex hull sequence problem. It may also happen that the expression computing r_ℓ actually yields a function that is continuous for all of $\mathbb{R}^N$, in which case we have $\overline{r_\ell}(q) = r_\ell(q)$. This happens for instance in the convex hull area problem, where r_l will typically be the sum of the areas of triangles or trapezoids spanned by various input points. At this point the astute reader will certainly have noticed that the result functions r_ℓ are one of the weak spots of the extended algebraic decision tree model.

3   Linear Perturbations

A perturbation $q()$ of a point $q \in \mathbb{R}^N$ is called *linear* if $q(\varepsilon) = q + \varepsilon a_q$, where a_q is some direction, i.e. non-zero vector in $\mathbb{R}^N$. A perturbation scheme Q is called *linear* if $q()$ is linear for each q.

Linear perturbations are interesting because they tend to allow relatively easy evaluation of perturbed functions.

Theorem 6. *Let $f : \mathbb{R}^N \mapsto \mathbb{R}$ be a multivariate polynomial of total degree at most Δ, and let B_f be a "black box algorithm" computing f. Let $q()$ be a linear perturbation of q that is valid for f. Then*

$$\lim_{\varepsilon \to 0^+} \operatorname{sign} f(q(\varepsilon))$$

can be determined using at most $\Delta + 1$ calls to B_f plus some small overhead.

Proof. Since $q()$ is linear $f(q(\varepsilon))$ is a polynomial $p(\varepsilon)$ of degree at most Δ. The desired limit is given by the sign of the smallest degree non-zero coefficient of p (which exists because of validity of the perturbation). But the coefficients of p can be determined by computing $p(\varepsilon) = f(q + \varepsilon a_q)$ for $\varepsilon = 0, 1, \dots, \Delta$ using the black box B_f, and using polynomial interpolation.

Note that if $p(0)$ evaluates to non-zero, nothimg more needs to be done, since it is the smallest degree coefficient of p. □

A similar theorem can be proven if f is, say, the quotient of two multivariate polynomials of bounded degree.

This theorem makes the perturbation method readily applicable to a large class of programs computing geometric functions. Almost all geometric primitive tests seem to be expressible by test functions that are small degree multivariate polynomials. This is certainly true for all the ones mentioned before, such as co-ordinate comparisons, sidedness tests, in-sphere tests, and distance comparisons. We are still not home free, though, since the theorem makes the assumption that a valid linear perturbation is available. How can we obtain such a perturbation?

3.1   A random construction

Let us first consider the geometric meaning of validity. Let f be some continuous real valued function on $\mathbb{R}^N$. Then $f^{-1}(0)$, the zero set of f, forms a hypersurface σ in $\mathbb{R}^N$. Let $q()$ be some curve starting in the point q. If some open initial segment of $q()$ does not intersect σ, i.e. $f(q(\varepsilon)) \neq 0$ for $0 < \varepsilon < \varepsilon_1$ for some $\varepsilon_1 > 0$, then for all points $x = q(\varepsilon)$ on this segment $f(x)$ must have the same non-zero sign s. This follows from applying the mean value theorem to the continuous function $g(\varepsilon) = f(q(\varepsilon))$. But this immediately implies that $\lim_{\varepsilon \to 0^+} \operatorname{sign} f(q(\varepsilon)) = s$, i.e. the limit exists and is non-zero. In other words, if some open initial segment of the curve $q()$ fails to intersect the surface σ, then $q()$ is valid for f.

Now let $q()$ be a linear perturbation, i.e. a line, or more precisely, a ray starting at some point q, and let σ be some surface. How could $q()$ not be valid, i.e. how could every open initial segment of this ray intersect σ? Certainly there is no problem if q does not lie in σ. Otherwise, if q lies in σ, validity may fail because either (1) σ contains some entire initial segment or even all of the ray, or (2) σ is very badly behaved (e.g. some analogue of a space filling curve, or of $x \sin(1/x)$). Let us ignore (2) and assume that σ is well behaved, in a sense "smooth." (For practically all interesting functions f, such as for instance polynomials, $\sigma = f^{-1}(0)$ is "smooth.") In that case "most" rays starting in q will be okay; the set A of all directions a so that the perturbation $q(\varepsilon) = q + \varepsilon a$ is not valid will be of measure 0. This means that if we pick a direction a from $\mathbb{R}^N$ at random with probability 1 the resulting linear perturbation of q will be valid for σ. It follows that this "random" linear perturbation of q is also valid with probability 1 for any finite set Σ of smooth surfaces (or any finite set $\mathcal{F}$ of functions whose zero sets form smooth surfaces).

This method of selecting a valid perturbation is less attractive than it looks at first, since it is not clear how to randomly select a random direction a from $\mathbb{R}^N$ within reasonable time. So the question arises whether one can choose a randomly form a much smaller, finite set. This is possible and was first analyzed in [7] for polynomial and rational surfaces of bounded degree. We present a somewhat modified version here, just dealing with the polynomial case. The rational case is similar.

Let T be some extended algebraic decision tree, where each test function is a multivariate polynomial of total degree at most d. Let $\mathcal{F}$ be the set of test functions in T, and let $S = |\mathcal{F}|$. Certainly $S \leq 3^t$, where t is the height of T (in other words, the worst case running time of the program modeled by T). In many cases, however, S will be much smaller; for instance for a tree modeling a typical planar convex hull algorithm $S = O(n^3)$, since n planar points allow only this many different sidedness tests. Let $[m]$ denote $\{1, 2, \ldots, m\}$. Let $q \in \mathbb{R}^N$ be some fixed input to T. The question now is: what is the probability that for a direction a chosen from $[m]^N$ uniformly at random the perturbation $q(\varepsilon) = q + \varepsilon a$ is valid for all[4] S test functions in $\mathcal{F}$. Moreover, how large does one need to make m so that this probability becomes suitably small?

Theorem 7. *Let T be an extended algebraic decision tree with a set $\mathcal{F}$ of S different test functions, each a multivariate polynomial of total degree at most d, and let $q \in \mathbb{R}^N$ be a fixed input to T. If direction a is chosen uniformly at random from $[m]^N$, then the linear perturbation $q(\varepsilon) = q + \varepsilon a$ fails to be valid with probability at most dS/m.*

Proof. If for any $f \in \mathcal{F}$ the probability that some random $a \in [m]^N$ does not yield a linear perturbation of q valid for f is upper bounded by some number p, then the probability of non-validity of such a random a for all of $\mathcal{F}$ is upper bounded by $p|\mathcal{F}| = pS$. Now it only remains to show that one can use $p = d/m$.

---

[4] One would think that validity for the at most t test functions encountered by q on its path down the tree during a perturbed evaluation would be good enough. However, this path is not well defined, since it depends on the choice of a.

The perturbation $q(\varepsilon) = q + \varepsilon a$ is not valid for some polynomial f means $f(q(\varepsilon)) = 0$ for all ε, in particular for $\varepsilon = 1$, i.e. $f(q + a) = 0$ has to happen. The function $g(a) = f(q + a)$ is a multivariate polynomial in a of total degree at most d. Assuming that f does not vanish everywhere, g does not either. For such a g a lemma due to J. Schwartz [13] now says that if a is chosen uniformly at random from $[m]^N$ the probability that $g(a) = 0$ is at most d/m. $\qquad\square$

Of course, if such a randomly chosen a turns out to be bad, i.e. during the perturbed evaluation of T a 0-branch is to be taken, one simply aborts and restarts with linear perturbation given by a new randomly chosen a.

3.2 A deterministic construction

Deterministic construction of a valid linear perturbation seems to be rather difficult for the general case. However, for most of the important special arising in computational geometry interesting things can be said.

Definition 8. Let $\sigma = f^{-1}(0)$ be the surface formed by the zero set of some continuous function $f : \mathbb{R}^N \mapsto \mathbb{R}$.

We call σ and f *well behaved* iff every straight line L is either contained in σ or every bounded segment of L intersects σ in at most finitely many points.

We call σ and f *scale invariant* iff $a \in \sigma$ implies $\lambda a \in \sigma$ for all $\lambda \in \mathbb{R}$.

Many functions are well behaved; for instance, polynomials, rational functions, and even analytic functions.

Practically all primitive test functions arising in geometric algorithms are scale invariant. The reason can be exemplified by the sidedness test: if applied to three planar points such a test evaluates to zero, then these points must be colinear, and this happens irrespective of the scale of the coordinate system.

Some natural geometric tests are not scale invariant because they involve constants, for instance the test whether the triange spanned by three planar points has area 1. However, usually such a test can be transformed into a scale invariant one, as in our example, where on can replace the constant 1 by the expression u^2, and make u another parameter of the test function.

Lemma 9. *Let $f : \mathbb{R}^N \mapsto \mathbb{R}$ be continuous, well behaved, and scale invariant, and let a be a direction in $\mathbb{R}^N$ be such that $f(a) \neq 0$.*

Then for every $q \in \mathbb{R}^N$ the linear perturbation $q(\varepsilon) = q + \varepsilon a$ is valid for f.

Proof. If $f(q) \neq 0$ then every linear perturbation of q is valid for f, in particular the one with direction a. So assume $f(q) = 0$ Since f is well behaved, validity of the perturbation $q(\varepsilon) = q + \varepsilon a$ can only fail because the line spanned by the perturbation is contained in the zero-surface of f, i.e. $f(q + \varepsilon a) = 0$ for all $\varepsilon \in \mathbb{R}$. But this cannot happen. For in that case scale invariance of f implies that $f(\lambda(q + \varepsilon a)) = 0$ for all λ, in particular for $\lambda = 1/\varepsilon$, i.e. we would have $f((1/\varepsilon)q + a) = 0$ for all ε. But taking the limit as $\varepsilon \to \infty$ and appealing to the continuity of f we would get $f(a) = 0$, contradicting the assumption $f(a) \neq 0$. $\qquad\square$

This immediately yields the following important theorem.

Theorem 10. *Let T be an extended algebraic decision tree algorithm and $\mathcal{F}$ be its set of test functions. Assume that all $f \in \mathcal{F}$ are well behaved and scale invariant.*

Then, if a is a direction in $\mathbb{R}^N$ such that $f(a) \neq 0$ for all $f \in \mathcal{F}$, then for every $q \in \mathbb{R}^N$ the perturbation $q(\varepsilon) = q + \varepsilon a$ is valid for $\mathcal{F}$.

This theorem can be paraphrased as *"if you know just one non-degenerate input, then you can use it for a valid linear perturbation for every possible input."*

As we already mentioned the set $\mathcal{F}$ of test functions that appear in algorithms in computational geometry is usually quite limited. An algorithm computing some function on n points in $\mathbb{R}^d$ will typically use geometric primitives such as the $d\binom{n}{2}$ coordinate comparisons, the $\binom{n}{d+1}$ sidedness tests, the $\binom{n}{d+2}$ in-sphere tests, and maybe the $O(n^4)$ possible interpoint distance comparisons. In order to apply our theorem one now needs to come up with a set S of n points in $\mathbb{R}^d$ that are non-degenerate with respect to these primitives, i.e. (1) no two points in S agree in any coordinate, (2) no $d+1$ points in S lie on the same hyperplane, (3) no $d+2$ points lie on the same sphere, and (4) all the interpoint distances are distinct.

If one chooses n points from the moment curve $\gamma(t) = (t, t^2, \ldots, t^d)$, then (1) is obviously satisfied and because of the non-vanishing of the Vandermonde determinant (2) is satisfied. Using Descartes' Rule of Sign for polynomials it is easy to show that the positive branch of the moment curve (i.e. consider only $t > 0$) intersects no sphere in more than $d+1$ points; thus choosing the n points from the positive branch ensures (3) also hold. Whether (4) is also satisfied clearly depends on which points are actually chosen from $\gamma()$. This becomes particularly challenging if one insists on points with integral coordinates. It may be that $\{\gamma(1), \gamma(2), \ldots, \gamma(n)\}$ actually satisfies (4) but I have been unable to prove it. (The fact that for $d = 2$ the points $\gamma(20)$ and $\gamma(-16)$ are equidistant from $\gamma(18)$ provides some negative evidence.) However, note that k points on $\gamma()$ can make at worst the first k^2 integral places on $\gamma()$ ineligible for placing a $(k+1)$-st point. Performing a greedy construction this implies that there always is a set I of n integers between 0 and n^2 such that $S = \{\gamma(i) | i \in I\}$ satisfies (4) besides (1),(2), and (3).

Although the moment curve construction yields non-degenerate point sets for the most commonly occuring geometric primitive test functions it is certainly not a panacea that can be applied as easily to other primitives. Moreover, even for the test functions considered here it is not completely satisfying, since integral points are used with rather large coordinates. The question naturally arises how small an integer m one can use so that the grid $\{1, 2, \ldots, m\}^d$ contains a set S of n points non-degenerate with respect to various geometric primitives.

Let $\gamma_p(t) = (t \bmod p, t^2 \bmod p, \ldots, t^d \bmod p)$ a "modular" moment curve, where p is prime. If one uses $S = \{\gamma_p(1), \ldots, \gamma_p(n)\}$ it is not too hard to see that this will satisfy (2) if $p > n$, and hence we get $m = O(n)$. This choice will not neccesarily satisfy the disjoint coordinate condition (1), since $t^j \bmod p = c$

this in $O(n)$ time; if linear perturbation is applied to those points with the directions chosen from the moment curve as in Section 3, then the convex hull of the perturbed set will be a cyclic polytope with $O(n^{\lfloor d/2\rfloor})$ facets, and any algorithm will need $\Omega(n^{\lfloor d/2\rfloor})$ time to compute that.

One may be content with computing $\overline{F}$ instead of F. However, this may lead to problems when F (or $\overline{F}$) is part of a larger system. Even if for all the functions that appear in this system one uses a perturbed version it will be rather difficult to make the perturbations interact in a graceful manner.

But the severest shortcoming of the perturbation method may actually be something that we have swept under the rug completely so far: The perturbation method relies on and assumes the availability of exact arithmetic. Whether such an assumption is viable in real world computing remains to be seen.

References

1. C. Burnikel, K. Mehlhorn, and S. Schirra, On Degeneracy in Geometric Computations. *Proc. 5th Annual ACM-SIAM Symp. on Discrete Algorithms (1994).*
2. J. Canny, *Private Communication.*
3. G.B. Dantzig, **Linear Programming and Extensions.** Princeton Univ. Press, Princeton, 1963.
4. K. Dobrindt, Algorithmen für Polyeder. *Diplomarbeit, FB 14, Informatik, Univ. des Saarlandes, Saarbrücken (1990).*
5. H. Edelsbrunner and E.P. Mücke, Simulation of Simplicity: A technique to Cope with Degenerate Cases in Geometric Algorithms. *ACM Trans. Graphics, 9(1), (1990), 67–104.*
6. I. Emiris and J. Canny, A General Approach to Removing Degeneracies. *Proc. 32nd Annual IEEE Symp. FOCS (1991), 405–413.*
7. I. Emiris and J. Canny, An Efficient Approach to Removing Geometric Degeneracies. *Proc. 8th Annual ACM Symp. on Comp. Geom. (1991), 74–82.*
8. A. Griewank and G.F. Corliss, **Automatic Differentiation of Algorithms: Theory, Implementation, and Applications.** SIAM (1991).
9. L.J. Guibas and J. Stolfi, Primitives for Manipulation of General Subdivisions and Computation of Voronoi Diagrams. *ACM Trans. Graphics, 4(2), (1985), 74–123.*
10. S.G. Krantz and H.R. Parks, **A Primer of Real Analytic Functions.** Birkhäuser Verlag (1992).
11. C. Monma, M. Paterson, S. Suri, and F. Yao, Computing Euclidean Maximum Spanning Trees. *Proc. 4th Annual ACM Symp. on Comp. Geom. (1988), 241–251.*
12. F.P. Preparata and M.I. Shamos, **Computational Geometry, An Introduction.** Springer Verlag (1985).
13. J.T. Schwartz, Fast Probabilistic Algorithms for Verification of Polynomial Identities. *JACM 27(4), (1980), 701–717.*
14. R. Seidel, Output-Size Sensitive Algorithms for Constructive Problems in Computational Geometry. *PhD thesis, Computer Science Dept., Cornell Univ., (1986).*
15. T. Thiele, *Private Communication.*
16. C.-K. Yap, Symbolic Treatment of Geometric Degeneracies, *J. Symbolic Computation 10 (1990), 349–370.*
17. C.-K. Yap, A Geometric Consistency Theorem for a Symbolic Perturbation Scheme. *J. Computer and Systems Science 40 (1990), 2–18.*

Logic

One Binary Horn Clause is Enough

Philippe Devienne, Patrick Lebègue, Jean–Christophe Routier
Laboratoire d'Informatique Fondamentale de Lille – CNRS UA 369
Université des Sciences et Technologies de Lille
Cité Scientifique, 59655 Villeneuve d'Ascq Cedex, France
devienne,lebegue,routier@lifl.fr,

Jörg Würtz
Deutsches Forschungszentrum für Künstliche Intelligenz – DFKI,
Stuhlsatzenhausweg 3, 66123 Saarbrücken 11, Germany
wuertz@dfki.uni-sb.de

Topics : Logic in Computer Science, Theory of Programming Languages.

Abstract. This paper proposes an equivalent form of the famous Böhm-Jacopini theorem for declarative languages. C. Böhm and G. Jacopini [1] proved that all programming can be done with at most one single while-do. That result is cited as a mathematical justification for structured programming. A similar result can be shown for declarative programming. Indeed the simplest class of recursive programs in Horn clause languages can be defined by the following scheme :

$$\begin{cases} \mathcal{A}_1 \leftarrow . \\ \mathcal{A}_2 \leftarrow \mathcal{A}_3. \quad \text{that is} \quad \forall x_1 \cdots \forall x_m [\mathcal{A}_1 \wedge (\mathcal{A}_2 \vee \neg \mathcal{A}_3) \wedge \neg \mathcal{A}_4] \\ \leftarrow \mathcal{A}_4. \end{cases}$$

where $\mathcal{A}_i$ are positive first–order literals. This class is shown here to be as expressive as Turing machines and all simpler classes would be trivial. The proof is based on a remarkable and not enough known codification of any computable function by unpredictable iterations proposed by [5]. Then, we prove effectively by logical transformations that all conjunctive formulas of Horn clauses can be translated into an equivalent conjuctive 4–formula (as above). Some consequences are presented in several contexts (mathematical logic, unification modulo a set of axioms, compilation techniques and other program patterns).

1 Introduction

This paper is about the computational power of classes of quantificational formulas specified by restrictions on the number of atomic subformulas. Important works have been done about decision problems for such classes. W. Goldfarb and H.R. Lewis in [10] established the undecidability of the class of those formulas containing five atomic formulas as follows

$$\forall x \exists w \forall z_1 \cdots \forall z_m [(\neg \mathcal{A}_1 \vee \mathcal{A}_2 \wedge \mathcal{A}_3) \vee (\neg \mathcal{A}_4 \wedge \mathcal{A}_5)]$$

Indeed, the satisfiability of such a class is equivalent to the halting problem for two–counter machines which is undecidable [16]. H.R. Lewis tried to solve the 4–subformulas case, but without success. This problem remained open until last year and was shown to be undecidable too by two independant ways ([12] and [9]). The main result of this paper is obtained by merging these two proofs and we establish that this undecidability is of the maximal degree, in other words, this class of formulas has, in fact, the same expressive power than Turing machines. Moreover, this class can be reduced to Horn clause formulas :

$$(\mathcal{HC}) \quad \forall x_1 \cdots \forall x_m [(\mathcal{A} \vee \neg \mathcal{A}_1 \vee \cdots \vee \neg \mathcal{A}_n)] \qquad \text{(denoted } \mathcal{A} \leftarrow \mathcal{A}_1 \cdots \mathcal{A}_n.)$$

Such clauses, useful in logic programming, contain at most one positive subformula (or literal).

Within this particular class, related decision problems have been also studied. For instance, *Implication of Horn clauses*, denoted "$\mathcal{HC}_1 \Rightarrow \mathcal{HC}_2$", also called generalized subsumption, is an important notion in learning theory and compilation. It was shown decidable if clause $\mathcal{HC}_1$ is binary (two–literal) [19] and has been shown recently undecidable if $\mathcal{HC}_1$ is ternary [15].

More precisely, our paper is devoted to establish that all computation on Minsky machines can be expressed as the checking of consistency of the 4–formulas of the following form :

$$\forall x_1 \cdots \forall x_m [\mathcal{A}_1 \wedge (\mathcal{A}_2 \vee \neg \mathcal{A}_3) \wedge \neg \mathcal{A}_4] \qquad \text{that is} \qquad \begin{cases} \mathcal{A}_1 \leftarrow . \\ \mathcal{A}_2 \leftarrow \mathcal{A}_3. \\ \leftarrow \mathcal{A}_4. \end{cases}$$

where, because of the existence of universal Minsky Machines, the three first subformulas, $\mathcal{A}_1$, $\mathcal{A}_2$ and $\mathcal{A}_3$ can be fixed in a constructible way and $\mathcal{A}_4$ corresponds to the input datum. This very restrictive class is Turing–complete.

The proof is based on two different techniques. The first part (Section 2) is an encoding of periodically linear functions whose iterations have been proved to be equivalent to Minsky machines by [5]. Standard methods for decision problems and computational power use Minsky or Turing machines. It seems to be surprising that the remarkable result proposed by Conway was rarely used. Its formalism is of higher level and much easier to encode. The second part (Section 3) is based on logical transformations using meta–programs and meta–interpreters.

This theorem is clearly equivalent to the famous Böhm–Jacopini theorem to declarative languages. In 1966, they had proven that within imperative languages, every flowchart is equivalent to a while–program with one occurrence of while–do, provided auxiliary variables are allowed. This proof is constructive and usually cited as the mathematical justification for structured imperative programming (see also [13]). We show that in Horn clause languages, any program can be automatically transformed to another one composed of one binary Horn clause and two unit clauses. This transformation preserves both termination and the answer–substitutions (on the original variables). This shows the expressive power of a single Horn clause and can be used as a theoretical tool for decision problems in theorem proving. Some applications on other notions or structures are presented in the last section.

2   An Original Codification of the Conway Functions

Here we present an original proof method, previously defined in [8, 9] where it was the main basis of the proofs of the undecidability of the halting and emptiness problem for one binary recursive Horn clause. It is based on an original codification of some work by J.H. Conway[5], which we will present briefly here.

2.1   The Conway Unpredictable Iterations

J.H. Conway considers the class of periodically piecewise linear functions g : $\mathbb{N} \to \mathbb{N}$ having the structure :

$$\forall\, 0 \leq k \leq d-1, \text{ if } (n \bmod d) = k \text{ , then } g(n) = a_k n \ .$$

where $a_0, \cdots, a_{d-1}$ are rational numbers such that $g(n) \in \mathbb{N}$. These are exactly the functions $g : \mathbb{N} \to \mathbb{N}$ such that $\frac{g(n)}{n}$ is periodic. Conway studies the behaviour of the iterates $g^{(k)}(n)$ and he states the following theorem :

Theorem 1. (Conway). *If f is any partial recursive function, there is a Conway function g such that :*

1. *$\forall\, n \in \mathbb{N}, n \in Dom(f)$ iff $\exists (k, j) \in \mathbb{N}^* \times \mathbb{N}, g^{(k)}(2^n) = 2^j$.*
2. *$g^{(k)}(2^n) = 2^{f(n)}$ for the minimal $k \geq 1$ such that $g^{(k)}(2^n)$ is a power of 2.*

where $\mathbb{N} = \mathbb{N}^* \cup \{0\}$. This result is based on a direct and clever translation of the behavior of Minsky machines [16] (having the same computational power than Turing machines) into Conway functions. Conway and Guy proposed an instance of such Conway functions which produces all the prime number [11]. A more complex characterization of prime numbers had been done within diophantine equations [16].

In the next proofs, we will need to transform Conway iterations "$n \to g(n)$" to Conway equivalences "$n \leftrightarrow g(n)$" by using Corollary 2. Considering the particular partial recursive functions f such that :

$$\forall\, n \in Dom(f) \supset \{0\}, f(n) = 0$$

and their associated Conway functions (we called them *null Conway functions*) we can define some *Conway equivalence relations* $\equiv_g$, which mean that we do not only consider positive iterates $g^k(2^n)$ resulting in $2^0 (= 2^{f(n)})$ but also negative iterates $g^{-k}(2^0)$ resulting in 2^n where $g^{-k}(n) = \{m \in \mathbb{N} \mid g^k(m) = n\}$. Thus we establish the following corollary :

Corollary 2. *For every recursively enumerable set Σ containing $\{0\}$, there exists a Conway equivalence relation $\equiv_g$ such that $\Sigma = \{n \in \mathbb{N} \mid 2^n \equiv_g 1\}$*

2.2 Conway Functions and Conjuctive 4–formulas

Let us recall some definitions and notations about Horn clauses. A Horn clause is a disjunction of atomic formulas (called literals) of which at most one is positive.

$$(\mathcal{HC}) \quad \forall x_1 \cdots \forall x_m [(\mathcal{A} \vee \neg \mathcal{A}_1 \vee \cdots \vee \neg \mathcal{A}_n)] \qquad \text{(denoted } \mathcal{A} \leftarrow \mathcal{A}_1 \cdots \mathcal{A}_n.)$$

$\mathcal{A}$ is called the head part of the clause, and the other literals the body part. A fact (resp. a goal) is a clause whose body part (resp. the head part) is empty. A Horn clause is said to be binary if it is a composition of only two literals. As an example consider :

$$\begin{cases} append([\,], L, L) \leftarrow . & \textit{fact} \\ append([X \mid L], LL, [X \mid LLL]) \leftarrow append(L, LL, LLL). & \textit{binary clause} \\ \leftarrow append(L, LL, [a, b]). & \textit{goal.} \end{cases}$$

A Horn clause program is a conjunction of Horn clauses universally quantified. The procedural semantics of such programs is based on the SLD–resolution [14] derived from the refutation procedure of Robinson [18]. According to the Edinburgh syntax ([4]), variables $(X, L, LL, ...)$ are written using capital letters and function symbols (a, b, c) with small letters. $[X_1, X_2 \mid L]$ denotes a list of which X_1, X_2 are the two first elements and L the tail of the list. The SLD resolution, possibly infinite, computes all answer–substitutions ($\{L = [\,], LL = [a, b]\}$, $\{L = [a], LL = [b]\}$, $\{L = [a, b], LL = [\,]\}$ in our example).

The variables occurring in Horn clauses are renamed into fresh variables during the resolution. The simplest way to do is to attach an additional index to the variable, denoted by subscripts as in X_i . Since we only consider one binary Horn clause, we can choose this index to correspond to the number of inferences using this clause.

In [8, 9], using this renaming of variables, we have explicitly described how relations of the form $X_n = X_{g(n)}$, where g is any null Conway function, can be expressed by a Horn Clause of the form :

$$p(left(X)) \leftarrow p(right(X)).$$

where $left(X)$ and $right(X)$ are terms with variable X occurring in it. Thus, considering the case where n is a power of 2, this corresponds to a codification of the Conway equivalence relations into a binary Horn clause ($X_{2^n} = X_{g(2^n)} = X_{2^0} = X_1$).

Indeed, in the following program :

$$\begin{aligned} p([\overbrace{Z, \_, \cdots, \_}^{a} \mid L], [X \mid LL]) &\leftarrow p(L, LL). \\ \leftarrow p([\underbrace{\_, \cdots, \_}_{b} \mid L], L). \end{aligned}$$

the size of the first variable of the Horn clause decreases by a while the size of the second decreases by one, so we have (the trees denote lists) :

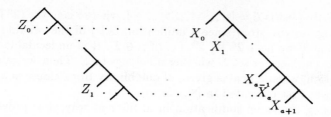

If there $b = 0$ in the goal, the equality of the two arguments would have generate :
$Z_i = X_{ai}$, the b shifts this equation then we have : $Z_i = X_{ai+b}$.

By composition of two programs like this one, we obtain :

$$p([\overbrace{Z, \_, \cdots, \_}^{a}|L1], [X|L2], [\overbrace{Z, \_, \cdots, \_}^{a'}|L3], [X|L4]) \leftarrow p(L1, L2, L3, L4).$$
$$\leftarrow p([\underbrace{\_, \cdots, \_}_{b}|L], L, [\underbrace{\_, \cdots, \_}_{b'}|LL], LL).$$

It involves the equalities :

$$X_{ai+b} = Z_i \qquad \text{and} \qquad X_{a'i+b'} = Z_i .$$

It is clear now that as many as needed equalities of the form $X_{ai+b} = X_{a'i+b'}$ can be expressed in one binary Horn clause and one goal.

Let g be a periodically piecewise linear function defined by $d, a_0, \cdots, a_{d-1}$. For all $n = \alpha d + k$ $(0 \le k \le d)$, we have $g(n) = g(\alpha d + k) = a_k n = (a_k d)\alpha + ka_k$, with $(a_k d, ka_k) \in \mathbb{N}^2$. Then $(X_n = X_{g(n)})_{n \in \mathbb{N}}$ can be decomposed into a finite number of equivalence relations in the form $(X_{ai+b} = X_{a'i+b'})_{i>0}$. All the right–linear binary clauses and goals which characterized these relations (as explained above) can be merged in one right–linear binary clause and one goal by merging their arguments. Thus it is clear that for any Conway function, there exist a particular binary Horn clause and a goal.

Consequently, according to the previous corollary, for every recursively enumerable set Σ, containing 0, there exists a binary Horn clause (associated with the corresponding g) which build a list $\mathcal{L} = [X_1, X_2, \cdots, X_n, \cdots]$ with all the X_i linked by relations $X_i = X_{g(i)}$. Thus we can characterize Σ as :

$$\Sigma = \{n \in \mathbb{N} \mid X_{2^n} \equiv_g X_1\}$$

Moreover, if at startup X_1 is marked by $\sharp$, then this mark will be propagated to every X_{2^n} such that n belongs to Σ. Thus the clause can be considered as a process of enumeration of the elements of Σ. An element of $\mathcal{L}$ will be instantiated to $\sharp$ iff it is a pure power of 2 and this power belongs to Σ, that is iff $2^n \equiv_g 2^0$.

The following program is an example in the case where Σ is $\mathbb{N}$:

$$p([X|L], [Y, X|LL]) \leftarrow p(L, LL) .$$
$$\leftarrow p([\sharp|L], [\sharp|L]) .$$

This program puts a $\sharp$ in every n^{th} position of the list $[\sharp|L]$ iff $n = 2^p$.

If the starting list is $\mathcal{L} = [\natural, \_, \cdots, \_, \flat, \_, \cdots]$, where $\flat$ is in the $(2^n)^{th}$ position, then the program will stop (since a unification fails) iff the equality $X_1 = X_{2^n}$ occurs, that is iff we have $2^n \equiv_g 2^0$, i.e. iff $n \in \Sigma$. It is undecidable for every n and recursive enumerable set Σ whether n belongs to Σ. Thus, we can prove that the termination, when a goal is given, of one binary Horn clause is undecidable. This result was first presented in [8].

In [9], using the same codification in a different way, it is proved that the satisfiability problem is undecidable too. In this proof, a linear propagation of the mark $\natural$ is created and the existence of solutions for our minimal program structure is shown to be equivalent to the fact that Σ is not total.

2.3 The Main Lemma

Using the above codification, we establish the following lemma which is required to prove the main theorem of this paper. In the following statement, the term "program" corresponds to the intuitive meaning. You can consider, if you prefer, it denotes "a machine (in sense of Turing machine) which computes a partial recursive function". This lemma needs a sharp analysis of how the codification of Conway functions works. The proof is technical, therefore we will not present it here. It will appear soon in a extended report.

Main Lemma 3. *For every program Π with input I, there exists a binary Horn clause $\mathcal{R}_\Pi$ such that there exists a goal, depending on I, such that $\mathcal{R}_\Pi$ stops after at least n iterative applications iff Π stops after n elementary steps with input I, and does not stop otherwise.*

Proof. To appear soon, it can already be communicated to every interested person.

3 Logical transformations

In the previous section, we have presented how to express Minsky machines into binary Horn clauses. In this part, we show that there exists a constructible reduction from the Horn clause programs into the 1–binary Horn clause programs. This result is obtained by a combination of the proof techniques of [12] and [8, 9]. The first one is used to generate the SLD resolution, the second to assure the halting of the build meta–interpreter.

3.1 A Word Generator

In this section we show how to generate all words over the alphabet $\{a, b\}$. The codification is similar to the one used in [12] to encode the Post Correspondence Problem:

$$gen([W \mid R] - RR, W) \leftarrow .$$
$$gen([W \mid R] - [[a \mid W], [b \mid W] \mid RR], AW) \leftarrow gen(R - RR, AW).$$
$$\leftarrow gen([[] \mid R] - R, Word).$$

where $R - RR$ denotes a difference list [3, 6].

By unifying the goal and the fact we obtain the solution $Word = []$. Using the binary clause once, results in the new goal

$$gen([[a], [b] \mid RR^1] - RR^1, AW^1)$$

producing the solution $Word = [a]$. Resolving this new goal with the binary clause instead of the fact results in the goal

$$gen([[b], [aa], [ba] \mid RR^2] - RR^2, AW^2)$$

resulting in the solution $Word = [b]$ etc. Observe that a and b serve as prefixes of two new words such that the suffix of these words is the first element of the list generated so far [1]. These two words are concatenated to the tail of the list generated so far. In other words, the difference–list can be seen as a LIFO (Last In First Out) stack.

3.2 A First Meta–Interpreter

Let Π be a set of Horn clauses $\{clause_1, \cdots, clause_n\}$, and "$\leftarrow g_1 \cdots g_n$." be a goal, the following meta–program generates the same answer–substitutions in the same order as a standard SLD interpreter :

$$solve([], []) \leftarrow .$$
$$solve([Goal \mid R_1], [[Goal \mid R_2] - R_1 \mid L]) \leftarrow solve(R_2, \mathcal{P}).$$
$$solve(Goals, [Clause \mid Rest]) \leftarrow solve(Goals, Rest).$$
$$\leftarrow solve(\mathcal{G}, \mathcal{P}).$$

$\mathcal{G}$ denotes list $[g_1, g_2, ...g_n]$ and $\mathcal{P}$ is the list of encoded clauses of a program Π, i.e., $\mathcal{P} = [clause_1, \cdots, clause_n]$. A clause $a \leftarrow b_1, \ldots, b_n$ of Π is encoded by the difference list $[a, b_1, \ldots, b_n \mid R] - R$. The first binary clause serves for choosing the first clause in the current clause list for reduction. The second clause discards the first clause in the current clause list. The complexity of the meta–program have been shown to be linearly dependent on that of the original program (see [17]).

For encoding an arbitrary program Π only the first binary and the goal have to be adapted in a appropriate way. Let us suppose now that Π is one of known Horn clause meta–interpreters (i.e. a universal Horn clause program), then this codification defines a constructible meta–interpreter in the form :

$$\begin{cases} \mathcal{A}_1 \leftarrow . \\ \mathcal{A}_2 \leftarrow \mathcal{A}_3. \\ \mathcal{A}_4 \leftarrow \mathcal{A}_5. \\ \leftarrow \mathcal{A}_6. \end{cases} \text{ or } \forall x_1 \cdots \forall x_m [\mathcal{A}_1 \wedge (\mathcal{A}_2 \vee \neg \mathcal{A}_3) \wedge (\mathcal{A}_4 \vee \neg \mathcal{A}_5) \wedge \neg \mathcal{A}_6]$$

---

[1] Note that this generator can be easily extended for any finite alphabet.

3.3 A Binary Meta–Interpreter

In this section we combine the two programs of Section 3.1 and 3.2.

Assume a program Π consisting of the two binary clauses $left_1 \leftarrow right_1$ and $left_2 \leftarrow right_2$, one goal $goal$, and one fact $fact$. Consider the word–generator where $\mathcal{A} = right_1, left_1$ and $\mathcal{B} = right_2, left_2$.

$$meta([\,W \mid R\,] - RR\,,\,W) \leftarrow .$$
$$meta([\,W \mid R] - [[\mathcal{A} \mid W], [\mathcal{B} \mid W] \mid RR], [H \mid RRR])$$
$$\leftarrow meta(R - RR, [H, X, X \mid RRR]).$$
$$\leftarrow meta([[goal \mid L\,] \mid R] - R, [fact \mid LL\,]).$$

After n times using the binary clause for resolving we obtain as second argument of the new goal the list

$$[fact, X_1, X_1, X_2, X_2, \ldots, X_n, X_n \mid T\,].$$

Furthermore, we obtain after some iterations as the head of the first argument (cf. Section 3.1)

$$[right_{i_m}, left_{i_m}, \ldots, right_{i_1}, left_{i_1}, goal \mid T\,].$$

By resolving a current meta–goal with the fact of the meta–program above we obtain the unification problem

$$right_{i_m} \doteq fact, left_{i_m} \doteq right_{i_{m-1}}, \ldots, left_{i_1} \doteq goal.$$

Note that by construction it is assured that the list containing the fact is of sufficient length to obtain these equations. This set is solvable if and only if there exists a corresponding refutation of the original program Π using the resolution order imposed by the equations.

Since the meta–interpreter of Section 3.2 is such a program Π, it is possible to associate to any logic program an equivalent program (i.e., with the same solutions) containing a binary clause and two unit clauses. Unfortunately, this codification does not preserve termination. In the next section we will show how to construct from this non–terminating interpreter a terminating one.

Let $solve$ be the first meta–interpreter (Section 3.2) and all SLD derivation whose length is n w.r.t. $solve$ is evaluated w.r.t. its meta–program before at most 2^n resolution steps. In other words, all answer–substitution computed after n resolution steps w.r.t. $solve$ will be computed before 2^n resolution steps w.r.t. its meta–program.

3.4 A Technical Preliminary

MP_{nS} denotes the non–stopping meta–interpreter defined in Section 3.2. Let us consider the following program Π, with input a Horn clause program P :

1. input P
2. evaluate P by a breadth–first strategy and keep the solutions in $\mathcal{S}_1$

TRANSFORMING CONSTRAINT LOGIC PROGRAMS

N. Bensaou - I. Guessarian*

Abstract

We study "à la Tamaki–Sato" transformations of constraint logic programs. We give an operational and fixpoint semantics of our constraint logic programs, show that the operational semantics is sound and complete with respect to the fixpoint semantics; we then extend the Tamaki–Sato transformation system into a fold-unfold transformation system which can take care of constraints and we give a direct proof of its correctness which is simpler than the Tamaki–Sato proof.

1 INTRODUCTION

Logic programming has been extended to constraint logic programming to integrate the resolution of numerical, boolean or set-theoretical constraints together with symbolic evaluation methods. Program transformations have been introduced to improve efficiency of programs; the usual strategy is to first write a simple, but may be non efficient program, which can easily be proved correct, and to then improve its efficiency by applying to it program transformations which preserve correctness. For logic programs, a well-known such system is the one introduced by Tamaki–Sato [17], following a methodology first defined by Burstall–Darlington [2]. Other transformation systems have been proposed in different frameworks and properties of these transformations, e.g. the associativity of the unfolding rule, have been proved in [3].

In the framework of Prolog, such transformation methods and their correctness with respect to the operational or denotational semantics have been studied. In [14], transformations preserving the solutions of programs together with their computation times (in a linear ratio) are given, while in [16] syntactical conditions have been defined to ensure that the transformations preserve the sequence of answer substitutions semantics for Prolog.

In [12] a transformation system for logic programs with a stronger form of correctness (but, according to the author, less practicable for automatic transformation systems than the Tamaki-Sato system) is proposed and it is adapted to constraint logic programs in [13].

A sequence of program transformations is correct if the final program is equivalent to the original one, namely the two programs have the same semantics, cf. Section 3.2. Usually, we will be given a basic program P, together with new predicates defined in terms of the predicates of P, and the goal of the program transformations will be to find direct definitions, more efficiently computable, of these new predicates. We will then say that a constraint logic program has been successfully transformed when the sequence of transformations ends with a folding which gives a direct definition of the new predicates and the final program is equivalent to the original one. We here extend the Tamaki–Sato fold-unfold program transformations to constraint logic programs.

We first recall the similarities and differences between logic programming and constraint logic programming.

*LITP - Université Paris 6 - email: ig@litp.ibp.fr, bensaou@litp.ibp.fr

a) both have an operational semantics based on the notion of refutation and a fixpoint semantics based on an immediate consequence operator T_P.

b) logic programs compute answer substitutions while constraint logic programs compute answer constraints together with answer substitutions

c) the tranformation rules which will transform a constraint logic program will have to take into account the constraints both to be applicable and to suitably modify them.

The main contributions of our paper are the following

1) we define fold-unfold program transformations for constraint logic programs, and give the conditions under which fold is correct,

2) we give an operational and fixpoint semantics of our constraint logic programs, show that the operational semantics is sound and complete with respect to the fixpoint semantics,

3) we prove the correctness of our transformation system; our proof is simpler than the Tamaki–Sato proof, since we use only the semantics of the programs, via a suitably defined immediate consequence operator T_P. As a consequence, we obtain a different proof of the correctness of the Tamaki–Sato transformation system in the strongest form of correctness [11].

The paper is organized as follows: we recall the basic definitions about constraint logic programs (in short CLP programs) and we define the transformation rules in the next section; in section 3 we define the semantics of our programs, show the soundness and completeness of the operational semantics with respect to the fixpoint semantics, and prove the correctness of the proposed transformation system with respect to the defined semantics; technical proofs are omitted for lack of space and can be found in the full paper.

2 CLP PROGRAMS AND THEIR TRANSFORMATION RULES

2.1 CLP programs

We assume the framework of a constraint logic programming language CLP [6]. A CLP program is a set of definite clauses, of the following form:

$$p_0(\vec{t_0}) \longleftarrow p_1(\vec{t_1}), \ldots, p_n(\vec{t_n}) : c_1(\vec{u_1}), \ldots, c_m(\vec{u_m}) \tag{1}$$

where for $0 \leq i \leq n$, p_i is a predicate symbol, for $j = 1, \ldots, m$, c_j is a constraint, and for $k = 1, \ldots, m$, $i = 0, \ldots, n$, $\vec{t_i}, \vec{u_k}$ are vectors of terms, n and m can be equal to 0.

In the sequel, clauses will be written in the following form:

$$p_0(\vec{t_0}) \longleftarrow p_1(\vec{t_1}) : d_1, \ldots, p_n(\vec{t_n}) : d_n \tag{2}$$

where for $k = 1, \ldots, n$, $i = 0, \ldots, n$, $\vec{t_i}$ are terms, and d_k are constraints. Both forms 1 and 2 are equivalent; this is shown below.

For technical reasons the form 2 is better suited for program transformations: when proving the correctness of the fold-unfold transformation, we will have to show that, if a constrained atom in the head of a rule is provable, then the corresponding constrained atoms in the body of the rule are all provable; to this end we have to share out the global constraints of the rule (given in 1) among the atoms of the body (resulting in a rule with distributed constraints given in 2). We might of course just allocate the global constraint to each individual atom in the body, but this would result in uselessly big constraints. The form 2 that we give is an optimized form which can be obtained at the cost of a very easy analysis of the program: intuitively, it allocates to each atom in the body of a rule only the constraints which are relevant to that particular atom, together with global constraints (which are relevant e.g. only to the head of the rule, and thus must not be left out, but which cannot be attributed to any particular atom in the body because they share no common variable with the body of the rule).

Let Φ be the set of constraints, Θ be the set of terms, V a denumerable set of variables, and

$$Var : \Phi \cup \Theta \longmapsto V$$

the function associating with each constraint ϕ (resp. set of terms $\vec{t}$), the set of variables occurring in ϕ (resp. $\vec{t}$). The rules $p_0(\vec{t_0}) \longleftarrow p_1(\vec{t_1}), \ldots, p_n(\vec{t_n}) : \phi_1, \ldots, \phi_m$ and $p_0(\vec{t_0}) \longleftarrow p_1(\vec{t_1}) : d_1, \ldots, p_n(\vec{t_n}) : d_n$ are equivalent as soon as

$$d_1 \wedge \cdots \wedge d_n = \phi_1 \wedge \cdots \wedge \phi_m \qquad (3)$$

3 is satisfied if e.g. $d_j = \bigcup_{m \geq k \geq 1}\{\phi_k \mid Var(\phi_k) \cap Var(\vec{t_j}) \neq \emptyset\} \cup \bigcup_{m \geq k \geq 1}\{\phi_k \mid Var(\phi_k) \cap (\bigcup_{n \geq i \geq 1} Var(\vec{t_i})) = \emptyset\}$.

Example 2.1 Let the predicate p be defined by the clause:
$$p(y_1, y_2, x_1, x_2) \longleftarrow q(y_1, y_2), r(y_1, x_1), r(y_2, x_2) : x_1 < x_2.$$
This clause is equivalent to:
$$p(y_1, y_2, x_1, x_2) \longleftarrow q(y_1, y_2), r(y_1, x_1) : x_1 < x_2, r(y_2, x_2) : x_1 < x_2.$$

Example 2.2 The clause: $\quad p(x, y, z) \longleftarrow A(x), B(y) : (x \geq 0, y \geq x, y = 5)$
is equivalent to: $\quad p(x, y, z) \longleftarrow A(x) : (x \geq 0, y \geq x)$, $B(y) : (y \geq x, y = 5)$;
while: $\quad p(x, y, z) \longleftarrow A(x), B(x, y) : (x \geq 0, y \geq x, y = 5)$
is equivalent to:
$$p(x, y, z) \longleftarrow A(x) : (x \geq 0, y \geq x) , B(x, y) : (x \geq 0, y \geq x, y = 5)$$
the condition $d_1 \wedge \cdots \wedge d_n = \phi_1 \wedge \cdots \wedge \phi_m$ is indeed satisfied.

2.2 The transformation rules

The transformation process consists in applying an arbitrary number of times the transformation rules which are: definition, unfolding and folding as in the Tamaki–Sato system [17]. The basic difference between the Tamaki–Sato system and the Burstall–Darlington system [2] is in folding, which cannot be arbitrary in the Tamaki–Sato system: only specific clauses defining new predicates, hereafter called definition clauses, can be used as folders, and definition clauses are not foldable, while most other clauses are foldable; if a clause can be folded, it is labeled as such. Definition clauses introduce new predicates, and the goal of the program transformation is to find a simpler form, e.g. a synthetic form, or a direct recursion, for these new predicates. The reason why arbitrary folding is not allowed is to preserve total correctness of the transformation system; unfolding is always totally correct (cf. Corollary 3.19) but arbitrary folding is well known to be only partially correct in the absence of constraints, and is not even partially correct for constraint logic programs (cf. Example 2.7).

Each transformation step transforms a program P_i, together with definition clauses D_i into P_{i+1}, D_{i+1}. Let P be an initial program and D the set of new predicates. Initially, $P_0 = P$, $D_0 = D$ is empty, and all clauses of P are marked foldable.

Moreover, at each transformation step, the constraints can be simplified as follows: if (ρ) is a clause of the form

$$p_0(\vec{t_0}) \longleftarrow p_1(\vec{t_1}) : d_1, \ldots, p_n(\vec{t_n}) : d_n$$

then we can substitute for (ρ) any clause (ρ')

$$p_0(\vec{t_0}) \longleftarrow p_1(\vec{t_1}) : d'_1, \ldots, p_n(\vec{t_n}) : d'_n$$

such that d'_j is a simplified constraint logically equivalent to d_j. (cf. Definition 3.1).

In the rest of this section, we will define the syntax of the transformation rules. The semantics will be given formally in Section 3.1; however, we will allow for informal references to the yet–to–be–defined semantics in intuitive explanations.

2.3 Definition rule

Introduce a clause of the form

$$(\delta) \quad p(x_1, x_2, \ldots, x_n) \longleftarrow A_1 : c_1, \ldots, A_m : c_m$$

where p is a new predicate name not appearing in P_i or D_i, $x_1, x_2, \ldots, x_n$ are pairwise distinct variables, $A_1, A_2, \ldots, A_m$ are predicates appearing in the initial program P, $c_1, c_2, \ldots, c_m$ are (possibly empty) constraints.

(δ) is *not* marked foldable. The clause (δ) is added to P_i and D_i, so that $P_{i+1} = P_i \cup \{(\delta)\}$, $D_{i+1} = D_i \cup \{(\delta)\}$. This implies that, for each given new predicate p, there can be at most one definition clause in D_i with head p.

Example 2.3 Let P be the following program, defining the length of a list and the matching of two lists, with initially $D = \emptyset$:

$$long([], X) \longleftarrow \qquad\qquad : X = 0 \qquad\qquad (4)$$
$$long([N|Y], X) \longleftarrow \quad long(Y, X') : X = X' + 1 \qquad\qquad (5)$$
$$match([], Y_2) \longleftarrow \qquad\qquad\qquad\qquad\qquad (6)$$
$$match([N_1|Y_1], [N_2|Y_2]) \longleftarrow \quad match(Y_1, Y_2), N_1 = N_2 \qquad\qquad (7)$$

Let the predicate $mtlg$ define the matching of two lists, such that the length of the first list is shorter than the length of the second list; $mtlg$ is defined by:

$$mtlg(Y_1, Y_2, X_1, X_2) \longleftarrow \quad match(Y_1, Y_2), long(Y_1, X_1) : X_1 < X_2,$$
$$long(Y_2, X_2) : X_1 < X_2 \qquad\qquad (8)$$

$P_1 = P \cup \{8\}$ and $D_1 = \{8\}$.

2.4 Unfolding rule

Let (ρ) be a clause in program P_i.

$$(\rho) \quad A \longleftarrow A_1 : c_1, \ldots, A_q : c_q, \ldots, A_n : c_n$$

Let (π_k), for $k = 1, \ldots, m$, be *all* the clauses in P the head of which can be unified with A_q:

$$(\pi_k) \quad T_k \longleftarrow T_{k1} : c'_1, \ldots, T_{kj} : c'_j$$

The unfolding of ρ by these m clauses at the constraint atom $(A_q : c_q)$ is obtained by unifying A_q with each of the T_k's.

Let the substitution μ_k $(k = 1, \ldots, m)$ be an m.g.u. of A_q and T_k, hence: $\mu_k(A_q) = \mu_k(T_k)$ and substitute for $\mu_k(A_q : c_q)$

$$\mu_k(T_{k1} : c'_1 \wedge c_q, \ldots, T_{kj} : c'_j \wedge c_q),$$

for $k = 1, \ldots, m$. Let now clauses (τ_k) be defined by, for $k = 1, \ldots, m$:

$$(\tau_k) \quad \mu_k(A) \longleftarrow \mu_k(A_1 : c_1, \ldots, A_{q-1} : c_{q-1}, T_{k1} : (c'_1 \wedge c_q), \ldots,$$
$$T_{kj} : (c'_j \wedge c_q), A_{q+1} : c_{q+1}, \ldots, A_n : c_n)$$

clause (ρ) is replaced by the set of clauses (τ_k), for $m \geq k \geq 1$, which are all marked foldable, and $P_{i+1} = (P_i - \rho) \cup \{\tau_1, \ldots, \tau_m\}$, $D_{i+1} = D_i$.

Proof: Since unfold is correct, $M(P') = M(unfold(P'))$; $\mathcal{R}$ is correct if and only if $M(P) = M(P')$, and this is equivalent to $M(P) = M(unfold(P'))$. □

Example 3.21 (Example 2.8 revisited) We can apply the above Corallary to show that the folding rule proposed in Example 2.8 is not correct. Unfolding (τ) by (δ) gives $s(x,y) \longleftarrow q(x,z)$, $q(z,y)$, which is no longer equivalent to (ρ).

Lemma 3.22 *If P is transformed into P' via one unfold transformation, then, for all interpretations I, $T_{P'}(I) \subseteq T_P(I \cup T_P(I))$.*

The reverse inclusion is false, but we have the

Lemma 3.23 *If P is transformed into P' via one unfold transformation, then, $\forall n$, $\exists k$, $T_P \uparrow n \subseteq T_{P'} \uparrow k$.*

Proof of Proposition 3.18: Since the T_P and $T_{P'}$ operators are monotone, we can prove by induction on n that, for all n, $T_P \uparrow n \subseteq T_P \uparrow (n+1)$, whence $T_P(T_P \uparrow n \cup T_P \uparrow (n+1)) = T_P(T_P \uparrow (n+1)) = T_P \uparrow (n+2)$.

We then can conclude by induction on n that

$$T_{P'} \uparrow n \subseteq T_P \uparrow (2n) \tag{15}$$

This is clearly true for $n = 0$; assuming $T_{P'} \uparrow (n-1) \subseteq T_P \uparrow (2n-2)$, we obtain $T_{P'} \uparrow n = T_{P'}(T_{P'} \uparrow (n-1)) \subseteq T_{P'}(T_P \uparrow (2n-2))$, and applying Lemma 3.22 with $I = T_P \uparrow (2n-2)$, we obtain $T_{P'}(T_P \uparrow (2n-2)) \subseteq T_P(T_P \uparrow (2n-2) \cup T_P(T_P \uparrow (2n-2))) = T_P(T_P \uparrow (2n-1)) = T_P \uparrow (2n)$. Whence the inductive step and the inclusion 15.

Combining the inclusion 15 with Lemma 3.23 yields Proposition 3.18. □

Proposition 3.18 showed that unfold transformations preserve total correctness. In the case when P is transformed into P' via one fold transformation we can no longer prove "locally" the correctness of the transformation (see the full paper for technical details), we must prove the following "global correctness" result

Lemma 3.24 *If P_0 is transformed into P_N via a sequence of fold-unfold transformations, then, $\forall i = 1, \ldots, N$, $\bigcup_{n \in \mathbb{N}} T_{P_i} \uparrow n = \bigcup_{n \in \mathbb{N}} T_{P_0} \uparrow n$.*

Theorem 3.17 then immediately follows since $M(P_0) = \bigcup_{n \in \mathbb{N}} T_{P_0} \uparrow n$ and $M(Tr(P_0)) = \bigcup_{n \in \mathbb{N}} T_{P_N} \uparrow n$.

4   CONCLUSION

We gave in this paper a transformation system for constraint logic programs and proved its correctness. This system is an extension of the Tamaki-Sato system to constraint logic programs; its correctness proof, which is based on the T_P operator, is simpler than their proof: this simplicity stems from the naturalness of the T_P operator, and it will still hold even if we extend the transformation system with other rules such as the replacement rule, etc. We prove the strongest form of correctness from which one can deduce simply other equivalences with respect to weaker semantics, while conserving the advantage to propose a practical tool for automatic transformation system.

References

[1] A. Bossi; N. Cocco; S. Dulli. A method for specializing logic programs. *ACM Trans. on programming langages and systems*, Vol.12, 2, April 1990, 253-302.

[2] R.M. Burstall; J. Darlington. A transformation system for deriving recursive programs, *JACM*, Vol. 24, 1, 1977.

[3] F. Denis, J.P. Delahaye. Unfolding, procedural and fixpoint semantics of logic programs *Proc. STACS'1991*, LNCS 480, 1991, 511-522.

[4] M. Falaschi; G. Levi; M. Martelli; C. Palamidessi. Declarative Modeling of the Operational Behavior of Logic Languages, *Theoretical Computer Science* 69 , 1989, 289-318.

[5] M Gabbrielli ; G. Levi. Modeling answer constraints in Constraint Logic Programs. *Proc. eight int. conf. on Logic Programming*, eds. Koichi & Furukawa, 1991, 238-252.

[6] J. Jaffar; J.L. Lassez. Constraint logic programming, *Proc. fourteenth ACM symp. on principles of programming languages*, 1987, 111-119.

[7] J. Jaffar; J.L. Lassez. Constraint logic programming, Tech. report, Department of Computer Science, Monash university, June 1986.

[8] P. Kanellakis; G. Kuper; P. Revesz. Constraint Query Languages, Tech. report, Department of Computer Science, Brown university, November 1990.

[9] G. Levi. Models, unfolding rules and fixpoint semantics, *Proc.of the fifth international conf. on Logic programming*, 1988, 1649-1665.

[10] J.W. Lloyd. *Foundations of logic programming*, Springer-Verlag, Berlin, 1987.

[11] M.J.Maher. Equivalences of logic programs, *Fondations of Deductive Databases and Logic Programming*, J.Minker Ed., Morgan-Kaufmann, Los Altos, 1988, 627-658.

[12] M.J.Maher. Correctness of a logic program transformation system, IBM Research Report RC 13496, T.J. Watson Research center, 1987.

[13] M.J.Maher, A transformation system for deductive database modules with perfect model semantics. *Theoretical Computer Science* 110, 1993, 377-403.

[14] A. Parrain; P. Devienne; P. Lebegue. Techniques de transformations de programmes généraux et validation de meta-interpréteurs, *BIGRE 1991*.

[15] M. Proietti, A. Pettorossi. An abstract strategy for transforming logic programs, *Fundamenta Informaticae*, Vol. 18, 1993, 267-286.

[16] M. Proietti, A. Pettorossi. Semantics preserving transformation rules for Prolog, *Proc. PEPM'91*, ACM-SIGPLAN 9, 1991, 274-284.

[17] H. Tamaki; T. Sato. Unfold/Fold transformation of logic programs, *Proc. 2nd logic programming conference*, Uppsala, Sweden, 1984.

A Hierarchy of Temporal Logics with Past
(Extended Abstract)

F. Laroussinie* and Ph. Schnoebelen*
LIFIA-IMAG, Grenoble, France

Abstract

We extend the classical hierarchy of branching-time temporal logics between UB and CTL^* by studying which additional expressive power (if any) stems from the incorporation of past-time modalities. In addition, we propose a new temporal combinator, N for "Now", that brings new and interesting expressive power. In several situations, non-trivial translation algorithms exist from a temporal logic with past to a pure-future fragment. These algorithms have important practical applications e.g. in the field of model-checking.

Introduction

Temporal logics have long been recognized as a very convenient formalism in which to reason about concurrent and reactive systems [Eme90, MP92]. In computer science, most theoretical studies of temporal logics only use future-time constructs. This is in contrast with the temporal logics studied by linguists, philosophers, ..., where past-time and future-time have been on an equal footing.

Past-time constructs can be very useful when it comes to express certain properties. For example, using "□" for "at all future moments" and "◇⁻¹" for "at some past moment", a formula like

$$□(\text{problem} \Rightarrow ◇^{-1}\text{cause}) \tag{1}$$

states that in all cases the occurrence of a problem must have been preceded by a cause, that is, no problem will ever occur without a cause. It is a natural (and important) safety property that one often use (in some form) when formally specifying the correct behavior of reactive systems.

Finally, the usefulness of past-time constructs is most apparent in the classification of temporal properties [Zuc86, MP90, CMP92].

However, it has been shown that formulas using past-time constructs can be replaced by equivalent formulas without past-time constructs [GPSS80, LPZ85]. For example, (1) is equivalent to

$$\neg(\neg\text{cause U problem}) \tag{2}$$

which uses the "Until" construct U. (The two formulas are equivalent because we use an *anchored* version of temporal logic [MP89], that is, a version where properties apply at some initial state of a system. This is a very natural approach when reasoning about computer systems.)

*LIFIA-IMAG, 46 Av. Félix Viallet, F-38031 Grenoble Cedex, FRANCE. Email:{fl,phs}@lifia.imag.fr

The underlying motto is that *past-time brings additional expressivity from a practical, but not from a theoretical viewpoint.* Clearly, a formulation like (1) is much more natural than the clumsier (2). This is even more obvious when one try to express a statement like □(problem ⇒ (◇⁻¹cause1 ∧ ◇⁻¹cause2)) without past-time.

Another reason why past-time is often omitted in theoretical studies is that model-checking is very easy for state-based logics like CTL while it is not clear how to efficiently do model-checking for logics with past.

When we surveyed the available *past-elimination results* in the literature, we found:

- PTL + Past can be translated into PTL [GPSS80, Gab87]. This is the standard result in the field. (Gabbay's combinatorial proof greatly simplified the theorem originally due to Kamp.)

- The linear-time propositional μ-calculus, $L\mu$ + Past can be translated into the usual pure-future μ-calculus [Var88]. In fact, [Var88] gives a translation from some kind of backward-and-forward Büchi automata into usual Büchi automata, so that one has to translate from the μ-calculus into Büchi automata, and backward.

- CTL^* + Past can be translated into CTL^* [HT87]. This is a simple corollary of Gabbay's proof for PTL.

- $PTL \setminus X$ + Past can be translated into $PTL \setminus X$ [MMKR93]. This uses rewrite rules similar to Gabbay's rules.

However these results certainly do not answer all questions. For example, if we want to add past-time constructs to a branching-time temporal logic like CTL, we only know how to translate CTL + Past into CTL^*. This is not satisfactory if we consider CTL precisely because it admits a very efficient model-checking procedure, while this is not the case with CTL^*. Therefore, knowing that CTL + Past can be translated into CTL would be, from a practical viewpoint, a very interesting addition to the results we mentioned.

This is exactly what we investigate in this paper. The general questions we address have the form *Which past-time combinators can be added to branching-time temporal logics like CTL, ECTL, ... without compromising the possibility to translate back into CTL, ECTL, ... ?* We considered the classical branching-time hierarchy from UB to CTL^* [EH85, EH86] and systematically tried to add past-time constructs.

A second motivation for this study is the introduction of a new temporal combinator, "N" for "Now". N is very useful in some situations where we want to restrict the extent to which past-time combinators may refer. This new combinator can also be eliminated (that is, translated into pure-future constructs) in some situations.

Here is the plan of the paper: we define $PCTL^*$ (CTL^* + Past) in Section 1, and the relevant fragments (PTL, CTL, ...) in Section 2. Section 3 discusses and motivates *initial equivalence*, the correctness criterion we use for our expressivity problems. Then Section 4 and Section 5 state fundamental expressivity results of past-time combinators in branching-time logics. The new "Now" combinator is motivated and introduced in Section 6 where our expressivity results are extended. Most proofs are omited in this extended abstract. The longer version of this paper can be obtained by anonymous ftp, on machine `ftp.imag.fr`, in directory `pub/CONCUR` (or by writing to the authors).

1 Temporal logics with Past

1.1 Syntax

We define $PCTL^*$ (for "CTL^* with Past") as an extension of CTL^* [EH86] with past-time combinators. (Our definition differs slightly from the $PCTL^*$ used in [HT87] as we explain later.) We assume a given set $Prop = \{a, b, \ldots, \texttt{problem}, \texttt{cause}, \ldots\}$ of *atomic propositions*.

Definition 1.1 *(Syntax of $PCTL^*$)* *The formulas of $PCTL^*$ are given by the following grammar*

$$PCTL^* \ni f, g ::= a \mid f \wedge g \mid \neg f \mid Ef \mid f\,U\,g \mid Xf \mid f\,S\,g \mid X^{-1}f$$

where $a \in Prop$.

Here S is the "Since" combinator, a past-time variant of U ("Until"). X^{-1} is "Previously", a past-time variant of X ("Next"). We use the standard abbreviations $\top$, $\bot$, $f \vee g$, $f \Leftrightarrow g$, ... and

$$
\begin{aligned}
Ff &\overset{\text{def}}{=} \top\,U\,f & F^{-1}f &\overset{\text{def}}{=} \top\,S\,f & Af &\overset{\text{def}}{=} \neg E\neg f \\
Gf &\overset{\text{def}}{=} \neg F\neg f & G^{-1}f &\overset{\text{def}}{=} \neg F^{-1}\neg f & \overset{\infty}{F} f &\overset{\text{def}}{=} GFf \\
& & & & \overset{\infty}{G} f &\overset{\text{def}}{=} FGf
\end{aligned}
\tag{3}
$$

F and G corresponds to the $\Diamond$ and $\Box$ notation sometimes used in modal logics. In $PCTL^*$, (1) is written $G(\texttt{problem} \Rightarrow F^{-1}\texttt{cause})$.

$PCTL^*$ includes as fragments the CTL and CTL^* branching-time temporal logics, as well as the PTL linear-time temporal logic. In all the following, "a logic" means "a fragment of $PCTL^*$".

A *pure-future formula* is a formula in which no X^{-1} and S occur. Then CTL^* is the fragment of $PCTL^*$ containing all pure-future formulas. A *state formula* is a pure-future formula that starts with a A or E quantifier. A *linear-time formula* is a formula without any E (or A) quantifier.

1.2 Semantics

Temporal logics are interpreted in Kripke structures:

Definition 1.2 *A Kripke structure S is a tuple $S = \langle Q_S, R_S, l_S \rangle$ where $Q_S = \{p, q, \ldots\}$ is a set of states, $R_S \subseteq Q \times Q$ is a total [1] accessibility relation, and $l_S : Q_S \to 2^{Prop}$ is a labeling of the states with propositions.*

A *run* in a structure S is any infinite sequence of states $q_0.q_1 \ldots$ s.t. $q_i R q_{i+1}$ for $i = 0, \ldots$. We write $\Pi_S(q) = \{\pi, \ldots\}$ for the set of all runs (in S) starting from q, and $\Pi(S)$ for the set of all runs in S. For

---

[1] Restricting to structures with a total accessibility relation is a technical simplification that does not change any of our expressivity results.

any i, $\pi(i)$ $(\overset{\text{def}}{=} q_i)$, π^i $(\overset{\text{def}}{=} q_i.q_{i+1}\ldots)$, and $\pi_{|i}$ $(\overset{\text{def}}{=} q_0.q_1\ldots q_{i-1})$ are resp. the i-th state, the i-th suffix and the i-th prefix of π.

A $PCTL^*$ formula expresses properties of a moment in a run. Formally, we define, for any $\pi \in \Pi(S)$ and any $n = 0, 1, 2, \ldots$ when a formula $f \in PCTL^*$ is true of run π at time n, written $\pi, n \models_S f$. We often drop the "S" subscript when it is clear from the context.

Definition 1.3 *(Semantics of $PCTL^*$) We define $\pi, n \models_S f$ by induction on the structure of f:*

$$
\begin{aligned}
\pi, n &\models a && \textit{iff} && a \in l(\pi(n)), \\
\pi, n &\models f \wedge g && \textit{iff} && \pi, n \models f \text{ and } \pi, n \models g, \\
\pi, n &\models \neg f && \textit{iff} && \pi, n \not\models f, \\
\pi, n &\models Ef && \textit{iff} && \text{there exists a } \pi' \in \Pi(S) \text{ with } \pi'_{|n} = \pi_{|n} \text{ s.t. } \pi', n \models f, \\
\pi, n &\models f \, U \, g && \textit{iff} && \text{there is a } k \geq n \text{ s.t. } \pi, k \models g \text{ and } \pi, i \models f \text{ for all } n \leq i < k, \\
\pi, n &\models Xf && \textit{iff} && \pi, n+1 \models f, \\
\pi, n &\models f \, S \, g && \textit{iff} && \text{there is a } 0 \leq k \leq n \text{ s.t. } \pi, k \models g \text{ and } \pi, i \models f \text{ for all } k < i \leq n, \\
\pi, n &\models X^{-1}f && \textit{iff} && n > 0 \text{ and } \pi, n-1 \models f.
\end{aligned}
$$

Informally, $\pi(i)$ is the present state. The prefix $\pi_{|i}$ is the past and π^i is a selected future. a means "a holds now", $f \, U \, g$ means "g will hold at some point in the (selected) future, and f holds in the meantime", Xf means "f holds at the next moment", $X^{-1}f$ means "f did hold at the previous moment", $f \, S \, g$ means "g did hold in the past and f has been holding ever since that moment", Ef means that "the present admits another possible future for which f holds", $\overset{\infty}{F} f$ means that "f will hold infinitely many times in the (selected) future" and $\overset{\infty}{G} f$ means that "f will hold at all but finitely many times in the (selected) future".

Remark 1.4 *Observe that our definition differs from [HT87] where one has*

$$\pi, n \models Ef \text{ iff there is a } \pi' \in \Pi(\pi(n)) \text{ s.t. } \pi', 0 \models f$$

None of these two definitions is a special case of the other. We believe our definition is more natural and we present in Section 6 a larger logic, $NCTL^*$, which includes both constructs.

Now for a formula f we define derived truth concepts:

$$
\begin{aligned}
\pi \models_S f &\overset{\text{def}}{\Leftrightarrow} \pi, 0 \models_S f && \text{reads} && \textit{"run } \pi \textit{ satisfies } f\textit{"} \\
q \models_S f &\overset{\text{def}}{\Leftrightarrow} \pi \models_S f \text{ for all } \pi \in \Pi(q) && && \textit{"state } q \textit{ satisfies } f\textit{"} \\
S \models f &\overset{\text{def}}{\Leftrightarrow} \pi \models_S f \text{ for all } \pi \in \Pi(S) && && \textit{"structure } S \textit{ satisfies } f\textit{"} \\
\models_g f &\overset{\text{def}}{\Leftrightarrow} \pi, n \models_S f \text{ for all } (\pi, n) \text{ in all Kripke structures } S && && \textit{"f is (globally) valid"} \\
\models_i f &\overset{\text{def}}{\Leftrightarrow} S \models f \text{ for all Kripke structures } S && && \textit{"f is (initially) valid"}
\end{aligned}
$$

$\models_g f$ entails $\models_i f$ but the converse is not true, and in fact $\models_g f$ iff $\models_i Gf$. As indicated by our definition of $S \models f$, it is the "$\models_i$", so-called anchored [MP89], notion of validity that interests us here, as is usual in computer science [Eme90].

Definition 1.5 *1. We say that two formulas f and g are equivalent, written $f \equiv g$, when for all (π, n) in all structures, $\pi, n \models f$ iff $\pi, n \models g$.*

2. *We say that f and g are* initially equivalent, *written $f \equiv_i g$, when for all π in all structures,* $\pi \models f$ *iff* $\pi \models g$.

Thus $f \equiv g$ when $\models_g f \Leftrightarrow g$, and $f \equiv_i g$ when $\models_i f \Leftrightarrow g$. Clearly, $f \equiv g$ entails $f \equiv_i g$ but the converse is not true. Here is a simple example: $\mathsf{X}^{-1}\mathsf{T} \equiv_i \perp$ because no run satisfies $\mathsf{X}^{-1}\mathsf{T}$ at its starting point. But of course $\mathsf{X}^{-1}\mathsf{T} \not\equiv \perp$ because for any run π with length at least 2, we have $\pi, 1 \models \mathsf{X}^{-1}\mathsf{T}$. Similarly, $\mathsf{G}(\text{problem} \Rightarrow \mathsf{F}^{-1}\text{cause})$ is initially equivalent and not globally equivalent to (2). [2]

When we use temporal logics to reason about programs, it is customary to consider initial validity as the basic concept. Specifications refer to the runs of a program, starting from some initial states. Therefore, we are content to replace a given formula f by an equivalent f', using "initial equivalence" as the relevant notion. The interest with global equivalence is that it is substitutive: if $f \equiv f'$ then f can be replaced by f' in any temporal context, yielding equivalent formulas. That is, $\equiv$ is a congruence w.r.t. all temporal combinators. On the other hand, $\equiv_i$ is only a congruence w.r.t. boolean combinators (and X^{-1} and S).

Considering initial equivalence as the correctness criterion allows to eliminate past-time combinators, according to

$$\mathsf{X}^{-1}f \equiv_i \perp,$$
$$f \mathsf{S} g \equiv_i g. \tag{4}$$

but, because $\equiv_i$ is not substitutive in temporal contexts, these simplification rules cannot be used in all situations.

2 A menagerie of temporal logics

Many fragments of CTL^* have been used and investigated. In fact, CTL^* was first proposed as a logic which included all other previously proposed temporal logics. Emerson and Halpern introduced a very convenient device to denote such fragments. Following them, we write $B(C, \ldots)$ the fragment of CTL^* where $C, \ldots$ are the only allowed linear-time combinators, and where every occurrence of a linear-time combinator must be under the immediate scope of an E or A quantifier (the "B" is for "branching"). For example:

- $B(\mathsf{X}, \mathsf{F})$ is the UB logic from [BPM83]. $\mathsf{AFX}a$ is not in UB while $\mathsf{AFAX}a$ is.

- $B(\mathsf{X}, \mathsf{U})$: This is the CTL logic from [CE81]. $\mathsf{A}[a \mathsf{U} \mathsf{EX}b]$ is in CTL but not in UB where only F and X can be used.

- $B(\mathsf{X}, \mathsf{U}, \overset{\infty}{\mathsf{F}})$: This is the $ECTL$ ("Extended CTL") logic from [EH86]. $\mathsf{E} \overset{\infty}{\mathsf{F}} a$ is in $ECTL$ but not in CTL.

$B(C, \ldots, \neg, \wedge)$ denotes a fragment enlarging $B(C, \ldots)$ inasmuch as it allows boolean combinators to appear between the linear-time combinators $C, \ldots$ and the branching-time quantifier on top of it. For example:

- $B(\mathsf{X}, \mathsf{F}, \neg, \wedge)$ (also called UB^+) allows $\mathsf{E}[\mathsf{F}a \wedge \mathsf{F}b \Rightarrow \mathsf{X}c]$.

- $B(\mathsf{X}, \mathsf{U}, \neg, \wedge)$ (also called CTL^+) allows $\mathsf{A}[(a \mathsf{U} b) \vee \mathsf{X}c]$.

---

[2] To be precise (2) is not sufficient. $\mathsf{G}(\text{problem} \Rightarrow \mathsf{F}^{-1}\text{cause}) \equiv_i \neg(\neg\text{cause} \mathsf{U} (\text{problem} \wedge \neg\text{cause}))$ is correct.

- $B(X, U, \overset{\infty}{F}, \neg, \wedge)$ is the $ECTL^+$ logic that roughly corresponds to the CTF logic introduced in [EC80].

This classification of relevant fragments of $PCTL^*$ can be linked to some semantic notions through the following

Definition 2.1 • *A formula f is a* future-formula *iff the truth of f at (π, n) only depends on the future $\pi(n)\pi(n+1)\ldots$, i.e. if $\pi^n = \pi'^m$ implies $\pi, n \models f \Leftrightarrow \pi', m \models f$.*

- *f is a* present-formula *iff the truth of f at (π, n) only depends on the current state, i.e. if $\pi(n) = \pi'(m)$ implies $\pi, n \models f \Leftrightarrow \pi', m \models f$*

- *f is a* branching-time formula *iff the truth of f at (π, n) does not depend of the selected future, i.e. if $\pi(0)\ldots\pi(n) = \pi'(0)\ldots\pi'(m)$ implies $\pi, n \models f \Leftrightarrow \pi', m \models f$.*

Clearly, any present-formula is a future-formula and a branching formula.

Proposition 2.2 *1. Any pure-future formula is a future-formula.*

2. Any state formula is a present-formula.

Proposition 2.3 *A logic of the form $B(C, \ldots, \neg, \wedge)$ only contains branching-time formulas.*

3 Compared expressivity

When we discuss comparative expressivity between two temporal logics L_1 and L_2, two notions can be used:

Definition 3.1 *1. L_1 is less [3] expressive than L_2, written $L_1 \preceq_g L_2$, if for any $f_1 \in L_1$ there is a $f_2 \in L_2$ s.t. $f_1 \equiv f_2$.*

2. L_1 is initially less expressive than L_2, written $L_1 \preceq_i L_2$, if for any $f_1 \in L_1$ there is a $f_2 \in L_2$ s.t. $f_1 \equiv_i f_2$.

Clearly $L_1 \subseteq L_2$ implies $L_1 \preceq_g L_2$. Also, $L_1 \preceq_g L_2$ implies $L_1 \preceq_i L_2$. In both cases the converse is not true in general. As usual we denote by "$\prec_*$" and "$\equiv_*$" the strict ordering and the equivalence relation induced by "$\preceq_*$".

Also, for pure-future logics, both "$\preceq_g$" and "$\preceq_i$" coincide. For pure-future logics, the classical hierarchy result has been established in [EH85, EH86]:

$$UB \prec UB^+ \prec CTL \equiv CTL^+ \prec ECTL \prec ECTL^+ \prec CTL^*$$

When logics with past-time are considered, the most relevant result is the Separation Theorem for PTL:

Theorem 3.2 *[GPSS80] Any $PPTL$ formula can be rewritten into an equivalent separated formula (that is, a boolean combination of pure-past and pure-future $PPTL$ formulas.)*

---

[3] or equally ...

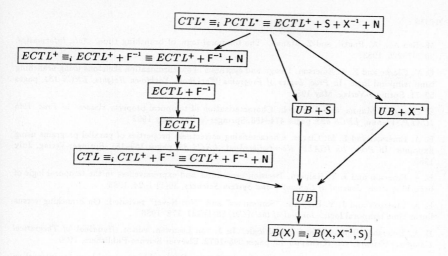

Figure 1: A hierarchy of temporal logics with past

Topics deserving further studies are (among others):

Axiomatizations for temporal logics with N: Given a complete axiomatizations for CTL^*, it is easy to get complete axiomatizations for $NCTL^*$ by providing axioms for the separation of formulas. But it would be interesting to study axiomatizations capturing natural way of reasoning with past-time combinators and N.

Complexity issues: The general question when we have a translation from L_1 to L_2 is "what is the size of the L_2 formula equivalent to a given L_1 formula ?". We already implemented our translations and it appears that some of them may exhibit a non-polynomial behaviour.

Practical use of $CTL^+ + F^{-1} + N$: It would be interesting to investigate, through a set of case studies, how much the specification of "real" systems is simplified and made more natural when using $CTL^+ + F^{-1} + N$ rather than just CTL.

Extensions of the separation methods: The separation methods we developed for branching-time logics should be investigated in the contexts of non-interleaving temporal logics, of interval temporal logics, of real-time temporal logics, ...

Modal logics of reactive systems: We already investigated in [LPS93] how these methods can be used for modal logics characterizing behavioral equivalences of reactive systems. This research direction has many possible prolongations.

Acknowledgments

We would like to thank S. Pinchinat for her many helpful comments on this work.

References

[BPM83]   M. Ben-Ari, A. Pnueli, and Z. Manna. The temporal logic of branching time. *Acta Informatica*, 20:207–226, 1983.

[CE81]   E. M. Clarke and E. A. Emerson. Design and synthesis of synchronization skeletons using branching time temporal logic. In *Proc. Logics of Programs Workshop, Yorktown Heights, LNCS 131*, pages 52–71. Springer-Verlag, May 1981.

[CMP92]   E. Chang, Z. Manna, and A. Pnueli. Characterization of temporal property classes. In *Proc. 19th ICALP, Vienna, LNCS 623*, pages 474–486. Springer-Verlag, July 1992.

[EC80]   E. A. Emerson and E. M. Clarke. Characterizing correctness properties of parallel programs using fixpoints. In *Proc. 7th ICALP, Noordwijkerhout, LNCS 85*, pages 169–181. Springer-Verlag, July 1980.

[EH85]   E. A. Emerson and J. Y. Halpern. Decision procedures and expressiveness in the temporal logic of branching time. *Journal of Computer and System Sciences*, 30(1):1–24, 1985.

[EH86]   E. A. Emerson and J. Y. Halpern. "Sometimes" and "Not Never" revisited: On branching versus linear time temporal logic. *Journal of the ACM*, 33(1):151–178, 1986.

[Eme90]   E. A. Emerson. Temporal and modal logic. In J. van Leeuwen, editor, *Handbook of Theoretical Computer Science, vol. B*, chapter 16, pages 995–1072. Elsevier Science Publishers, 1990.

[Gab87]   D. Gabbay. The declarative past and imperative future: Executable temporal logic for interactive systems. In *Proc. Temporal Logic in Specification, Altrincham, UK, LNCS 398*, pages 409–448. Springer-Verlag, April 1987.

[GPSS80]   D. Gabbay, A. Pnueli, S. Shelah, and J. Stavi. On the temporal analysis of fairness. In *Proc. 7th ACM Symp. Principles of Programming Languages, Las Vegas, Nevada*, pages 163–173, January 1980.

[HT87]   T. Hafer and W. Thomas. Computation tree logic CTL* and path quantifiers in the monadic theory of the binary tree. In *Proc. 14th ICALP, Karlsruhe, LNCS 267*, pages 269–279. Springer-Verlag, July 1987.

[LPS93]   F. Laroussinie, S. Pinchinat, and Ph. Schnoebelen. Translation results for modal logics of reactive systems. In *Proc. AMAST'93, Enschede, NL*, pages 299–310. Springer-Verlag, June 1993.

[LPZ85]   O. Lichtenstein, A. Pnueli, and L. Zuck. The glory of the past. In *Proc. Logics of Programs Workshop, Brooklyn, LNCS 193*, pages 196–218. Springer-Verlag, June 1985.

[MMKR93]   L. E. Moser, P. M. Melliar-Smith, G. Kutty, and Y. S. Ramakrishna. Completeness and soundness of axiomatizations for temporal logics without next. *Fundamenta Informaticae*, 1993. To appear.

[MP89]   Z. Manna and A. Pnueli. The anchored version of the temporal framework. In *Linear Time, Branching Time and Partial Order in Logics and Models for Concurrency, Noordwijkerhout, LNCS 354*, pages 201–284. Springer-Verlag, 1989.

[MP90]   Z. Manna and A. Pnueli. A hierarchy of temporal properties. In *Proc. 9th ACM Symp. Principles of Distributed Computing, Quebec City, Canada*, pages 377–408, August 1990.

[MP92]   Z. Manna and A. Pnueli. *The Temporal Logic of Reactive and Concurrent Systems*, volume I: Specification. Springer-Verlag, 1992.

[Var88]   M. Vardi. A temporal fixpoint calculus. In *Proc. 15th ACM Symp. Principles of Programming Languages, San Diego, CA*, pages 250–259, January 1988.

[Zuc86]   L. Zuck. *Past Temporal Logic*. PhD thesis, Weizmann Institute, Rehovot, Israel, August 1986.

The Complexity of Resource-Bounded First-Order Classical Logic

Jean Goubault

Bull Corporate Research Center, rue Jean Jaurès, Les Clayes sous Bois
Jean.Goubault@frcl.bull.fr

Abstract. We give a finer analysis of the difficulty of proof search in classical first-order logic, other than just saying that it is undecidable. To do this, we identify several measures of difficulty of theorems, which we use as resource bounds to prune infinite proof search trees.

In classical first-order logic without interpreted symbols, we prove that for all these measures, the search for a proof of bounded difficulty (i.e, for a simple proof) is Σ_2^p-complete. We also show that the same problem when the initial formula is a set of Horn clauses is only NP-complete, and examine the case of first-order logic modulo an equational theory. These results allow us not only to give estimations of the inherent difficulty of automated theorem proving problems, but to gain some insight into the computational relevance of several automated theorem proving methods.

Topics: computational complexity, logics, computational issues in AI (automated theorem proving).

1 Introduction

First-order classical logic proofs are hard to find. The undecidability of this logic [6, 7] if only a superficial justification. It has never deterred researchers from inventing new automated deduction methods. Moreover, it is generally felt that some undecidable problems are harder than others, for example, proof search in full first-order logic vs. for a set of Horn clauses. We attempt here to give a rigorous justification of such feelings, measuring hardness by complexity classes.

The complexity of a computational problem is usually defined as a function of the size of its input. But, whatever the definition of size of the input of a proof search problem, if it is computable (number of atomic subformulas, or of variables, for instance), then no decidable complexity class can characterize the problem. Hence some kind of uncomputable notion of size must be introduced.

To get a useful notion of size, we define it in terms of the *degree of difficulty*, or non-obviousness of the outcome, typically a minimal length of a proof in the given logic. This difficulty shall be finite if and only if the input proposition is provable. In particular, it will also be uncomputable. But it will be related to our intuition closely enough to be meaningful.

In this paper, we tackle the problem of analyzing the complexity of proof search problems of skolemized formulas, in classical first-order logics — possibly with interpreted symbols —, where proofs must consume no more than a given amount of resources corresponding to an a priori bound on the difficulty of the input logical sentence. We assume that the reader is familiar with basic logic and abstract complexity theory [13].

The plan of the paper is as follows. In Section 2, we review related approaches to the analysis of the complexity of theorem proving problems and procedures. In Section 3, we define some measures of difficulty for theorem proving in first-order logic without interpreted symbols, and relate them to each other. These difficulties are then considered the resources to bound. In Section 4, we determine the complexity classes of the proof search problems of bounded difficulties. After having proved the main theorem (Theorem 2), which in particular gives the answer in first-order logic without interpreted symbols, we examine the particular case of Horn clauses (Prolog programs), and give a view of first-order logic with symbols interpreted in an equational theory. Section 5 is the conclusion.

2   Related works

One approach to the analysis of proof search complexity is to determine the complexity of the so-called decidable classes of first-order logic [10, 18], which has been worked out by Lewis [22]. These classes provide hard decision problems: the monadic, Gödel, and Schönfinkel-Bernays classes cannot be decided in less than deterministic subexponential or exponential time, and the decision problem for Ackermann's class is PSPACE-hard. Kozen [21] has shown that first-order logic without negation, even with equality, in NP-complete, and Stockmeyer and Meyer [33] have shown that pure first-order logic with equality is PSPACE-complete. Decidability, in particular, does not mean tractability. Unfortunately, this approach gives no intuition on the complexity of undecidable classes.

To get a finer analysis, the idea of bounding resources (lengths of authorized proofs, number of times that certain logical rules can be used, etc.) has been used by others. A precursor is Parikh [27], who reduced the problem of finding proofs with a bounded number of steps in second-order Peano arithmetic to that of second-order unifiability. The latter problem, unfortunately, turned out to be undecidable, making the construction unfruitful [15]. Bounding the number of uses of the contraction and weakening rules of classical logic leads to fragments of linear logic [14]. Propositional linear logic with exponentials, i.e, unbounded uses of these rules, is undecidable [23], though classical propositional logic is only NP-complete [8]. Bounding the uses of these rules regains decidability, but even the small multiplicative propositional fragment without variables is NP-complete [25]. The decidability is maintained when lifting the multiplicative-additive fragment to first-order logic, although the problem is NEXPTIME-hard, thus provably intractable [24].

Finally, a complementary approach to our work is to compare the minimal lengths of proofs that different calculi allow for, which is the subject of Eder's work [11] in first-order logic. As Eder notes in his introduction, the length of a shortest proof always gives a lower bound on the complexity of any theorem-

5 Conclusion

We have presented an approach to the practical analysis of the computational complexity of an undecidable problem, classical first-order theorem proving. For this, we needed to define suitable notions of difficulties (or resource bounds), and transform the problem of proof-search into that of bounded proof-search.

Although the problem has a complicated structure (it is not likely to be in NP, contradicting the common idea that proof search is just another combinatorial problem), it lies in the polynomial hierarchy, and usually not higher than level 2, even with interpreted symbols. Hence, mechanized classical first-order proving is not utopic. In contrast, linear logic, although based on resource-bounding ideas, is unsuited to automatic proof discovery.

The analysis of bounded proof search has also led us to examine the computational relevance of several methods (leading us to think that tableaux may not be ideal, or justifying the fact that AC-unification should not be performed naively). This approach promises to guide us effectively in our search for better automatic proof methods.

This paper is a first step towards a finer, practical analysis of the structure of undecidable (or decidable) problems. As a first step, still in the automated proving realm, first-order logic with equality is a subject of choice; results on this topic [16] will be the subject of a forthcoming paper.

References

1. P. B. Andrews. Theorem proving via general matings. *J. ACM*, 28(2):193–214, 1981.
2. D. Benanav, D. Kapur, and P. Narendran. Complexity of matching problems. *J. Symb. Computation*, 3:203–216, 1987.
3. W. Bibel. *Automated Theorem Proving*. Vieweg, second, revised edition, 1987.
4. A. Boudet. A new combination technique for AC-unification. Technical Report 494, LRI, Orsay, France, Juin 1989.
5. C.-L. Chang and R. C.-T. Lee. *Symbolic Logic and Mechanical Theorem Proving*. Computer Science Classics. Academic Press, 1973.
6. A. Church. A note on the Entscheidungsproblem. *J. Symb. Logic*, 1:40–41, 1936.
7. A. Church. A note on the Entscheidungsproblem (correction). *J. Symb. Logic*, 1:101–102, 1936.
8. S. A. Cook. The complexity of theorem-proving procedures. In *3rd STOC*, pages 151–158, New York, 1971. ACM.
9. W. F. Dowling and J. H. Gallier. Linear time algorithms for testing the satisfiability of propositional Horn formulae. *J. Logic Programming*, 3:267–284, 1984.
10. B. Dreben and W. D. Goldfarb. *The Decision Problem — Solvable Classes of Quantificational Formulas*. Addison–Wesley, Reading, Massachussetts, 1979.
11. E. Eder. *Relative Complexities of First-Order Calculi*. Artificial Intelligence. Vieweg Verlag, Wiesbaden, Germany, 1992.
12. M. C. Fitting. *First-Order Logic and Automated Theorem Proving*. Springer-Verlag, 1990.

13. M. R. Garey and D. S. Johnson. *Computers and Intractability — A Guide to the Theory of* NP-*Completeness.* W.H. Freeman and Co., San Francisco, 1979.

14. J.-Y. Girard. Linear logic. *TCS*, 50:1–102, 1987.

15. W. D. Goldfarb. The undecidability of the second-order unification problem. *TCS*, 13:225–230, 1981.

16. J. Goubault. *Démonstration automatique en logique classique : complexité et méthodes.* PhD thesis, École Polytechnique, Palaiseau, France, September 1993.

17. J. Goubault. Syntax independent connections. In *Workshop on Theorem Proving with Analytic Tableaux and Related Methods*, number MPI-I-93-213 in Max-Planck-Iinstitut für Informatik, pages 101–111, Marseille, France, avril 1993.

18. Y. Gurevich. On the classical decision problem. *Bulletin of the EATCS*, 42:140–150, October 1990.

19. D. Kapur and P. Narendran. Matching, unification and complexity. *SIGSAM Bulletin*, October 1987.

20. D. Kapur and P. Narendran. Double-exponential complexity of computing a complete set of AC-unifiers. In *7th LICS*, pages 11–21, , 1992.

21. D. Kozen. Positive first-order logic is NP-complete. *IBM J. Res. and Development*, 25(4):327–332, 1981.

22. H. R. Lewis. Complexity of solvable cases of the decision problem for the predicate calculus. In *19th FOCS*, pages 35–47, 1978.

23. P. Lincoln, J. Mitchell, A. Scedrov, and N. Shankar. Decision problems for propositional linear logic. In *32nd FOCS*, pages 662–671, 1990.

24. P. Lincoln and A. Scedrov. First order linear logic without modalities is nexptime-hard. Available through anonymous ftp from ftp.csl.sri.com, 1992.

25. P. Lincoln and T. Winkler. Constant-only multiplicative linear logic is NP-complete. Available through anonymous ftp from ftp.csl.sri.com, file /pub/lincoln/comultnpc.dvi, 1992.

26. M. Minoux. LTUR: A simplified linear-time unit resolution algorithm for Horn formulæ and computer implementation. Technical Report 206, Laboratoire MASI, CNRS UA 818, Université Pierre et Marie Curie, janvier 1988.

27. R. Parikh. Some results on the lengths of proofs. *Trans. AMS*, 177:29–36, 1973.

28. M. Paterson and M. Wegman. Linear unification. *J. Comp. Sys. Sciences*, 16:158–167, 1978.

29. G. Plotkin. Building in equational theories. *Machine Intelligence*, 7:73–90, 1972.

30. J. Posegga. *Deduction with Shannon Graphs or: How to Lift BDDs to First-order Logic.* PhD thesis, Institut für Logik, Komplexität und Deduktionssysteme, Uni. Karlsruhe, FRG, 1993.

31. D. Prawitz. An improved proof procedure. *Theoria*, 26:102–139, 1960.

32. D. Prawitz. Advances and problems in mechanical proof procedures. *Machine Intelligence*, 4:59–71, 1969.

33. L. J. Stockmeyer and A. R. Meyer. Word problems requiring exponential time. In *5th STOC*, pages 1–9, New York, NY, USA, 1973. ACM.

34. G. Tseitin. On the complexity of proofs in propositional logics. *Seminars in Mathematics*, 8:466–483, 1970.

35. C. Wrathall. Complete sets and the polynomial-time hierarchy. *TCS*, 3:23–33, 1976.

Two proof procedures for a cardinality based language in propositional calculus [*]

Belaid Benhamou, Lakhdar Sais and Pierre Siegel

L.I.U.P. Case Ater, UFR-MIM - Université de Provence,
3,Place Victor Hugo - F13331 Marseille cedex 3, France
phone number : 91.10.61.08
e-mail : [Benhamou, Sais, Siegel]@gyptis.univ-mrs.fr

Abstract. In this paper we use the cardinality to increase the expressiveness efficiency of propositional calculus and improve the efficiency of resolution methods. Hence to express propositional problems and logical constraints we introduce the pair formulas $(\rho, \mathcal{L})$ which mean that "at least ρ literals among those of a list $\mathcal{L}$ are true". This makes a generalization of propositional clauses which express "At least one literal is true among those of the clause". We propose a cardinality resolution proof system for which we prove both completenesss and decidability. A linear proof for Pigeon-hole problem is given in this system showing the advantage of cardinality.

On other hand we provide an enumerative method (DPC) which is Davis and Putnam procedure adapted with Cardinality. Good results are obtained on many known problems such as Pigeon-hole problem, Queenes and some other instances derived from mathematical theorems (Ramsey, Schur's lemma) when this method is augmented with the principle of symmetry.

Key words: theorem proving, propositional calculus, symmetry and cardinality.

1 Introduction

Determining an appropriate language for the representation of knowledge, requires a good compromise between expressiveness of the language and efficiency of the deduction methods. With increased interest in theorem proving procedures, a collection of proof systems and constraint logic programming languages CLP [4,7,11] have been proposed to handle a variety of logical theories. The cardinality operator [8] is a new logical connective for constraint logic programming. It provides CLP users with a new way of combining (primitive) constraints to build non-primitive ones. It also implements the principle "infer simple constraints from difficult ones" which is actually the basic principle behind the design of CLP over finite domains, and would be appropriate to build non-primitive constraints as well.

[*] This work is supported by the PRC-GDR Intelligence Artificielle, the project *BAHIA* and the MRE-INTER-PRC project *CLASSES POLYNOMIALES*

In this paper we introduce the pair formulas which are cardinality formulas, to express logic problems. In Section 2 we introduce the necessary terminology and notations. In Sections 3, 4 and 5 we study a resolution method for which we prove both completeness and decidability.

In sections 6 we describe the DPC method which is Davis and Putnam procedure adapted with cardinality. The property of symmetry [3] (section 7) is combined with the method DPC to provide short proofs for some problems showing the efficiency of our method. Finally we give computation times for the method DPC with the advantage of symmetry on some known benchmarks.

2 Definition and notations

We shall assume some familiarities with the propositional calculus. A propositional variable is called a variable, and we distinguish it from a literal, which is a variable together with a parity-positive or negative. A formula means a well formed propositional formula using one of the binary connectives. The connectives of primary interest are: AND ($\wedge$), OR ($\vee$), NOT ($\neg$). The constants TRUE and FALSE will be represented by 1 and 0, respectively.

2.1 Syntax

A pair formula is a statement $(\rho, \mathcal{L})^2$ in which ρ is a positive integer and $\mathcal{L}$ a list of literals with eventual repetitions. The pair formula $(\rho, \mathcal{L})$ expresses the constraint "At least ρ literals among those of the list $\mathcal{L}$ are true". In the following we use pair instead of pair formula.

Example 1. $-$ $(1, abc)$ is logically equivalent to the clause $a \vee b \vee c$
 $-$ $(2, abc)$ is logically equivalent to the set of clauses $\{a \vee b, a \vee c, b \vee c\}$
 $-$ $(2, aabc)$ is logically equivalent to the set of clauses $\{a \vee a \vee b, a \vee a \vee c, a \vee b \vee c\}$
   which is equivalent to $\{a \vee b, a \vee c\}$

It is interesting to note at this point that pairs are quite expressive. A conjunction of literals $\psi_1 \wedge \psi_2 \ldots \wedge \psi_n$ can be expressed by $(n, \psi_1 \psi_2 \ldots \psi_n)$, a disjunction $\psi_1 \vee \psi_2 \ldots \vee \psi_n$ by $(1, \psi_1 \psi_2 \ldots \psi_n)$ and a negation $\neg \psi$ by $(1, \neg \psi)$. In the sequel we prove that a pair $(\rho, \mathcal{L})$ represents a set of propositional clauses.

2.2 Semantics

A classical truth assignment I satisfies a pair $(\rho, \mathcal{L})$ if and only if at least ρ literals among those of $\mathcal{L}$ are assigned to the value true in I. It is obvious that a pair

---

^{2} Two additional cardinality formulas can be considered : "At most ρ literals among those of $\mathcal{L}$ are true", and " Exactly ρ literals among those of $\mathcal{L}$ are true", however, in practice they can be expressed using pairs.

$(\rho, \mathcal{L})$ such that $\rho >| \mathcal{L} |^3$ is unsatisfiable (contradictory). On the other hand, each pair $(0, \mathcal{L})$ is a tautology. The assignment I satisfies a set S of pairs if it satisfies all of its pairs (I is a model of S). Henceforth we will assume that the formulas are given in pair formula representation. We observe that in the case of sets containing only pairs of kind $(1, \mathcal{L})$ the definition of a truth assignment is the same as in propositional calculus.

Example 2. The truth assignment I, such that $I[a] = 1$, $I[b] = 0$ and $I[c] = 0$ satisfies the pairs $(1, abc)$ and $(2, ab\neg c)$, but does not satisfy the pair $(2, abc)$.

3 Proof system

Let S be a set of pairs. We give two basic inference rules to define a resolution method. We also prove both completeness and decidability for this method.

3.1 Resolution rule

Let $(\alpha, \ell_1 \ell_2 \ldots \ell_n.\mathcal{L})$ and $(\beta, \neg \ell_1 \neg \ell_2 \ldots \neg \ell_n.\acute{\mathcal{L}})$ be two pairs of the set S such that $n \geq 1$, then we can deduce the pair $(\alpha + \beta - n, \mathcal{L}.\acute{\mathcal{L}})$. This is,

$$\frac{(\alpha, \ell_1 \ell_2 \ldots \ell_n.\mathcal{L}),\ (\beta, \neg \ell_1 \neg \ell_2 \ldots \neg \ell_n.\acute{\mathcal{L}})}{(\alpha + \beta - n, \mathcal{L}.\acute{\mathcal{L}})}$$

Example 3. If $S = \{(2, abc), (1, \neg a \neg b)\}$, then a single application of the previous rule is enough to obtain the pair $(1, c)$.

However the previous rule is not sufficient to prove the unsatisfiability of the set $S = \{(2, aay), (2, \neg a \neg ax)\}$. To get a complete system, we need to introduce the following merging rule as it is done in classical resolution.

3.2 Merging rule

If $c = (\alpha, \ell^k \mathcal{L})^4$ is a consistent pair of S such that $| \ell^k \mathcal{L} |= \theta$ and k a positive integer, then for every sublist φ of $\mathcal{L}$ such that $| \varphi |= max\{0, \theta - \alpha + 1 - k\}$ we infer the pair $(1, \ell\varphi)$ and the pair $(max\{0, \alpha - k\}, \mathcal{L})$. This is :

$$\frac{(\alpha, \ell^k \mathcal{L}), \forall \varphi \subseteq \mathcal{L} :| \varphi |= max\{0, \theta - \alpha + 1 - k\}}{(1, \ell\varphi), (max\{0, \alpha - k\}, \mathcal{L})}$$

Note that when $k \geq \theta - \alpha + 1$ the pair $(1, \ell)$ is deduced. This means that when the number of redundancy k of the literal ℓ is greater than or equal to $\theta - \alpha + 1$ we prove the literal ℓ. The number of pairs $(1, \ell\varphi)$ to be generated becomes smaller when $\theta - \alpha + 1$ gets close to zero. In general the number of pairs we generate is not important.

---

[3] $| \mathcal{L} |$ denotes the number of literals in $\mathcal{L}$
[4] ℓ^k means k times the literal ℓ

The proof of the previous example $S = \{(2, aay), (2, \neg a \neg ax)\}$ becomes now obvious. Indeed the pairs $(1, a)$ and $(1, \neg a)$ are infered by the merging rule. Applying the resolution rule on them we deduce the unsatisfiable pair $(1, \emptyset)$.

In the case of a pair $(1, \ell^k \mathcal{L})$, the rule has the same behavior as the merging rule in propositional calculus.

Proposition 1. *Both previous rules are sound.*

Proof. Due to the semantics defined before, the soundness of the previous rules becomes evident.

3.3 Subsumption rules

To make the system decidable and more efficient, we have to add subsumption rules.

1. Let $(\alpha, \mathcal{L})$ and $(\beta, \acute{\mathcal{L}})$ be two satisfiable pairs of S such that $\alpha \geq \beta$ and $\mathcal{L} \subseteq \acute{\mathcal{L}}$, then the pair $(\alpha, \mathcal{L})$ subsumes the pair formula $(\beta, \acute{\mathcal{L}})$ in S.

   Example. $(3, a\ b\ c\ d)$ subsumes $(2, a\ b\ c\ d\ e)$

2. Let $(\alpha, \mathcal{L})$ and $(\beta, \acute{\mathcal{L}})$ be two satisfiable pairs of S such that $\beta \leq \alpha$, $\acute{\mathcal{L}} \subseteq \mathcal{L}$ and $\beta \leq \alpha - (\mid \mathcal{L} \mid - \mid \acute{\mathcal{L}} \mid)$, then the pair formula $(\alpha, \mathcal{L})$ subsumes the pair $(\beta, \acute{\mathcal{L}})$ in S.

   Example. $(2, a\ b\ c\ d)$ subsumes $(1, a\ b\ c)$

4 Resolution method

In the following we shall give some analogs of the classical resolution properties. A resolvant pair is :

- Either the pair r obtained by applying the resolution rule on pairs c_1 and c_2, which contains at least two opposite literals.
  If $c_1 = (\alpha, \ell_1 \ell_2 \ldots \ell_n . \mathcal{L})$ and $c_2 = (\beta, \neg \ell_1 \neg \ell_2 \ldots \neg \ell_n . \acute{\mathcal{L}})$, then
  $r = (\alpha + \beta - n, \mathcal{L}.\acute{\mathcal{L}})$
- Or the pair r obtained by applying the merging rule on a pair $c = (\alpha, \ell^k \mathcal{L})$, then $r = (1, \ell \varphi)$ with $\mid \varphi \mid = max\{0, \theta - \alpha + 1 - k\}$ or $r = (max\{0, \alpha - k\}, \mathcal{L})$

The soundness of the proof system is straightforward, for each of the inference rules soundness can be eazily checked. Thus, if cr is a resolvant pair obtained from a set S of pairs, then $S \models cr$.

Proposition 2. *If S is a set of pairs and Cr a set of resolvant pairs obtained from S, then $S \equiv^5 S \cup Cr$.*

Proof. This is a direct consequence of the Proposition 1.

Definition 3. A resolution method defined on a sytem S of pairs is a map R which associates with each subset C of S a subset $R(C)$ such that:

1. $C \subset R(C)$

2. Each pair in $R(C)$ which does not appear in C is logically equivalent to a resolvant pair of C.

By vertue of proposition 2 we get,

Proposition 4. $R(C) \equiv C$

If $R(C)$ contains the unsatisfiable pair, then C is unsatisfiable. Let C be a subset of S, we denote $R^0(C) = C, R^{n+1}(C) = R^n(R(C))$, and $R^*(C) = \cup_{n \in N} R^n(C)$. By construction of $R^*(C)$ we see that if c is a pair of C, then c belongs to $R^*(C)$ iff there exists $n \in N$ such that $c \in R^n(C)$.

Applying Proposition 4 we obtain the following property.

Proposition 5. $C \equiv R^*(C)$

It is obvious that if $R^*(C)$ includes the unsatisfiable pair, then C will be contradictory. A resolution method R defined on a set S of pairs is complete iff for all contradictory subset C of S, the unsatisfiable pair belongs to $R^*(C)$. This means that there exists an integer n such that the unsatisfiable pair belongs to $R^n(C)$. We say that the method R is decidable if it is complete and for each subset C of S there exists an integer n such that $R^n(C) = R^{n+1}(C)$. Thus $R^n(C) = R^*(C)$.

Definition 6. A set of pairs S is saturated if all of its resolvant pairs that are not tautologies are subsumed by other pairs of S.

Definition 7. If $\mathcal{L}$ is a list of literals such that $| \mathcal{L} | = n$, and m an integer such that $m \leq n$ then $C_n^m \{\mathcal{L}\}$ denotes the set of propositional clauses obtained by considering all the disjunctions formed by the combinations of m literals among those of the list $\mathcal{L}$.

Proposition 8. *Let $c = (\alpha, \mathcal{L})$ be a pair such that $| \mathcal{L} | = \theta$ then we have the following logical equivalence : $c \equiv C_\theta^{\theta - \alpha + 1} \{\mathcal{L}\}$*

Proof. Let I be a model of c. Thus at least α literals among those of $\mathcal{L}$ are satisfied by I. In other words, I satisfies at most $\theta - \alpha$ literals among the negation literals of $\mathcal{L}$. This implies that I satisfies each clause of the set $C_\theta^{\theta - \alpha + 1} \{\mathcal{L}\}$. This

---
[5] $\equiv$ denote the semantic equivalence

is so, because each clause of the set $\mathcal{C}_{\theta}^{\theta-\alpha+1}\{\mathcal{L}\}$ contains exactly $\theta - \alpha + 1$ literals. To prove the converse, we show that if $(\alpha, \mathcal{L})$ has no model then $\mathcal{C}_{\theta}^{\theta-\alpha+1}\{\mathcal{L}\}$ has no model too. Suppose that $(\alpha, \mathcal{L})$ has no model, then any truth assignment I, satisfies less than α literals among those of $\mathcal{L}$ (at most $\alpha - 1$); That is, I satisfies more than $\theta - \alpha$ literals among the negation literals of $\mathcal{L}$ (at least $\theta - \alpha + 1$). It is not hard to see that the clause of $\mathcal{C}_{\theta}^{\theta-\alpha+1}\{\mathcal{L}\}$ which is formed with the negations of the $\theta - \alpha + 1$ literals with the value true in I, is not satisfied by I. We conlude that I is not a model of $\mathcal{C}_{\theta}^{\theta-\alpha+1}\{\mathcal{L}\}$.

As a consequence of proposition 8, we obtain the following lemma.

Lemma 9. *If $S = \cup_{i=1,k}\{(\alpha_i, \mathcal{L}_i)/ \mid \mathcal{L}_i \mid = \theta_i\}$ is a set of k pairs, and S_p a set of propositional clauses, such that $S_p = \cup_{i=1,k}\mathcal{C}_{\theta_i}^{\theta_i-\alpha_i+1}\{\mathcal{L}_i\}$, then $S \equiv S_p$.*

Proof. The proof is a direct consequence of the proposition 8.

It is interesting to see that for each set S of pairs there exists an equivalent set S_p of propositional clauses and vice versa. It is obvious that in general the number of clauses in S_p is greater than the number of pairs in S.

Lemma 10. *Let S be a set of pairs, and S_p the corresponding set of propositional clauses, then S is saturated iff S_p is saturated.*

Proof. C.f. [2].

Now we can conclude :

Theorem 11. (completeness) A saturated set S of pairs is contradictory iff it contains the unsatisfiable pair.

Note that if R is a resolution method defined on a set S of pairs, such that for all subset C of S, $R^*(C)$ is saturated, then R is complete. The proof of the theorem is based on the two previous lemmas. Indeed completeness property is a known result for saturated propositional clauses systems. On the other hand we deduce from lemma 9 and lemma 10 that all saturated set S of pairs can be transformed into an equivalent system S_p of propositional clauses which is also saturated. It is obvious that the property of completeness is verified for the set S.
Many improvement can be done for this method as it has been done for classical resolution.

5 A proof for Pigeon-Hole problem

The problem consists in putting n pigeons in $n - 1$ holes such that each hole holds at most one pigeon. We show here how cardinality leads to a linear proof for Pigeon-Hole problem. This problem is described with the following set of pairs.

1    $(1, p_{1(1)} p_{1(2)} \cdots p_{1(n-1)})$
2    $(1, p_{2(1)} p_{2(2)} \cdots p_{2(n-1)})$

$\vdots$

n $(1, p_{n(1)} p_{n(2)} \cdots p_{n(n-1)})$

n+1 $(n - 1, \neg p_{1(1)} \neg p_{2(1)} \cdots \neg p_{n(1)})$
n+2 $(n - 1, \neg p_{1(2)} \neg p_{2(2)} \cdots \neg p_{n(2)})$

$\vdots$

2n-1 $(n - 1, \neg p_{1(n-1)} \neg p_{2(n-1)} \cdots p_{n(n-1)})$

Note that $p_{i(j)}$ means that the the pigeon-hole j holds the pigeon i. The problem is expressed with only $2n - 1$ pairs, however the same problem requires $n + n(n - 1)^2/2$ propositional clauses.

One way to prove the unsatisfiability of the problem is to use a linear resolution method. It consist to apply at each step the resolution rule on the current resolvant and another pair of the remaining pair formulas. The proof is given by the following steps:

Proof. By application of the resolution rule on the formulas (1) and $(n + 1)$ we deduce the pair $(n - 1, p_{1(2)} \cdots p_{1(n-1)} \neg p_{2(1)} \cdots \neg p_{n(1)})$. We continue the resolution on the $n - 2$ first positive literals of the previous pair. Thus by $n - 2$ applications of the resolution rule we get the pair:
$((n-1)+(n-2)(n-1)-(n-2), \neg p_{2(1)} \cdots \neg p_{n(1)} \neg p_{2(2)} \cdots \neg p_{n(2)} \cdots \neg p_{2(n-1)} \cdots \neg p_{n(n-1)})$
in which only negative literals appear. It is obvious now that with $n - 1$ applications of the resolution rule on the literals $\neg p_{2(1)}, \neg p_{2(2)}, \ldots, \neg p_{2(n-1)}$ we obtain the pair $((n - 1) + (n - 2)(n - 1) - (n - 2) - (n - 1)(n - 2), \emptyset)$ which is identical to the unsatisfiable pair $(1, \emptyset)$.Therefore the unsatisfiability of the problem is shown using only $2n - 2$ applications of the resolution rule. Thus we find a linear proof for the pigeon-hole problem which is not possible in classical resolution.

6   The method DPC

Lemma 9 permits the translation of resolution tools from propositional logic to pair formula representation. On the other hand, by few elementary transformations we obtain the corresponding method of Davis and Putnam [6] in the pair formulas representation. We describe it below and give some results and applications for some interesting problems.

Given a set S of pair formulas and a literal p of S, we will denote by $S_{p \leftarrow 1}(S_{p \leftarrow 0})$ the set obtained by the following two rules :

1. Striking out all the pairs of cardinality one, that contain $p(\neg p)$ respectively. Deleting all occurences of $p(\neg p)$ and decreasing the cardinality by one from the remaining pairs.

2. deleting all occurences of $\neg p(p)$ from the remaining pair formulas without decreasing the cardinality.

Proposition 12. *Let S be a set of pair formulas and let p be a literal of S, then S is satisfiable if and only if $S_{p \leftarrow 1}$ or $S_{p \leftarrow 0}$ is satisfiable.*

The Davis and Putnam is based on the previous proposition. To define the procedure we use two other rules:

1. *Unit pair rule.* If the set S of pairs contains a unit pair, *i.e.* a pair $(n, \mathcal{L})$, such that $\mid \mathcal{L} \mid = n$, then assign all the literals in $\mathcal{L}$ the value TRUE.
2. *Pure literal rule.* If there exists a literal p in S such that $\neg p$ does not appear in S, then strick it in all pairs and decrease the cardinality. Thus we obtain the system $S_{p \leftarrow 1}$ which is satisfiable if and only if S is satisfiable.

We present in Figure 1, Davis and Putnam procedure with cardinality (DPC) using the two previous rules :

DPC Procedure

Given a set S of pairs defined over a set of variables V.

- If S is empty, return "satisfiable".
- If S contains an unsatisfiable pair, return "unsatisfiable".
- (Unit pair rule) If S contains a unit pair c, assign all the literals mentioned the value TRUE and return the result of calling DPC on the simplified set of pairs.
- (Pure literal rule) If there exists a pure literal in S, assign it a value TRUE, and return the result of calling DPC on the simplified set of pairs.
- (Splitting rule) Select from V some unvalued variable v. Assign it a value, and call DPC on the simplified set of pairs. If this call returns "satisfiable", then return "satisfiable". Otherwise, set v to the opposite value, and return the result of calling DPC on the re-simplified set of pairs.

Figure 1: The Davis and Putnam procedure with cardinality.

7 Symmetries in cardinality formulas

The principle of symmetry is originaly suggested by Krishnamurty [13], he showed that it is a powerful augmentation to resolution. On the other hand, Benhamou and Sais in [3] discusses detection an use of symmetry in some automated deduction methods, such as Sl-resolution [12], Davis and Putname procedure and Semantic Evaluation [14].

First of all, let us define the concepts of permutations and symmetry, and prove significant properties that will enable us to improve algorithms efficiency, for more details we refer the reader to [3,2].

If V is a set of propositional variables then a bijection map $\sigma : V \rightarrow V$ is called a permutation of variables. If S is a set of pairs, c a pair of S and σ a permutation of variables occuring in S, then $\sigma(c)$ is the pair obtained by applying σ to each variable of c and $\sigma(S) = \{\sigma(c)/c \in S\}$

Definition 13. A set P of literals is called complete if $\forall \ell \in P$; then $\neg \ell \in P$

Definition 14. Let P be a complete set of literals and S a set of pairs of which all literals are in P. Then a permutation σ defined on P ($\sigma : P \to P$) is called a symmetry of S if it satisfies the following conditions:

1. $\forall \ell \in P, \sigma(\neg \ell) = \neg \sigma(\ell)$
2. $\sigma(S) = S$

Two literals (variables)ℓ and $\acute{\ell}$ are symmetrical in S (notation $\ell \sim \acute{\ell}$) if there exists a symmetry σ of S such that $\sigma(\ell) = \acute{\ell}$. A tuple $(\ell_1, \ell_2, \ldots, \ell_n)$ of literals is called a cycle of symmetry in S if there exists a symmetry σ defined on S, such that $\sigma(\ell_1) = \ell_2, \ldots \sigma(\ell_{n-1}) = \ell_n, \sigma(\ell_n) = \ell_1$.

Remark. All the literals in a cycle of symmetry are symmetrical two by two. The symmetry detection method is not discribed here, it is very closed to the one given in [2] .

Theorem 15. *Let ℓ and ℓ' be two literals of S. If $\ell \sim \ell'$ in S, then ℓ has a model [6] in S if and only if ℓ' has a model in S .*

Proof. C.f. [3].

This theorem expresses an important property that we use in to make prune the proof tree. Indeed if ℓ has no model in S and $\ell \sim \ell'$, then ℓ' will have no model in S, thus we prune the branch which corresponds to the assignment of ℓ' in the resolution tree. Therefore, if there are n symmetrical literals we can cut $n - 1$ branches in the proof tree.

The DPC method is increased with the previous property and applied for the following problems.

7.1 Description of the benchmarks

- Queens. Placing N queens in $N \times N$ chessboard such that there is no couple of queens attacking each other.
- Erdös's theorem. Find the permutation σ of N first numbers such that for each 4-tuple $1 \le i < j < k < l \le$ N none of the two relations $\sigma(i) < \sigma(j) < \sigma(k) < \sigma(l)$ and $\sigma(l) < \sigma(k) < \sigma(j) < \sigma(i)$ is verified.
  This problem is modeled by creating for each couple (i,j) a variable $f_{i,j}$ which means $\sigma(i) < \sigma(j)$. The rules express the associativity of the relation $<$, and prohibit the misplaced 4-tuples.
  For $N \le 9$ the problem admits solutions, beyond it doesn't.
- Schur's lemma: How to distribute N counters numbred from 1 to N into 3 boxes A, B, C in accordance with the following rules:
  1) A box can't contain both the counters numbered i and $2 * i$
  2) A box can't contain the counters numbered i, j and $i + j$
  This problem is modeled simply by creating one variable by counter and by box.For $N \le 13$ the problem admits solutions, beyond it doesn't.

---

[6] ℓ has a model in S iff there exists a model I of S such that $I[\ell] = 1$

– Ramsey problem's: Color the edges of a complete graph on N vertices with three different colors such that no monochromatic triangle appears. For $N \leq 16$ the problem admits solutions, beyond it doesn't.

Below we present in Tables 1 and 2 some results for different problems obtained by DPC with the advantage of symmetry. The most satisfying results is that we

Problems	Size formula		DPC+Sym	
	pairs	Variables	Steps	Times
Queens 8	50	64	47	0.06"
Queens 10	64	100	85	2.04"
Erdös 9	420	36	35	0.36"
Erdös 10	660	45	914	8.21"
Schur13	152	39	42	0.05"
Schur14	175	42	249	1.33"
Ramsey14	1274	273	273	2.82"
Ramsey15	1575	315	723	50.73"
Ramsey16	1920	360	2957	1'.25"
Ramsey17	2312	408	27000	30'

Table 1. Schur's Lemma, Ramsey's problem, Erdös and Queens

Number of pigeons	Size formula		DPC+Sym	
	Pairs	Variables	Steps	Times
10	19	90	61	0.183"
15	29	210	131	0.950"
20	39	380	226	3.350"
25	49	600	346	9.950"
30	59	870	491	25.133"
35	69	1190	661	57.333"
40	79	1560	673	1'57"
45	89	1980	781	3'35"
50	99	2450	897	4'57"

Table 2. Pigeon hole problems

have proved for the first time the unsatisfiability of Ramsey problem $R(3,3,3)$ with 17 vertices. This result is given by our algorithm, implemented in Pascal, 30 min CPU on a SUN4/110. The Semantic Evaluation algorithm has run 15 h CPU and more than 1400000 steps on a HP 9000/350 without success. Note that the complexity of pigeon-hole problem, in number of steps becomes linear. Pigeon-Hole and Ramsey problems are solved in [3] using only symmetries. Howover with the advantage of cardinality we get best times : with cardinality we solve Pigeon-Hole until 50 pigeons, while in [3] it is solved until 30 pigeons.

8 Related works

- Hooker [10] has established the connection between resolution method for logic and cutting plane methods for integer programming[5,9]. In his work he gives a generalized resolution procedure for clauses that asserts that at least a certain number of their literals are true.

- The cardinality operator [8] implements the principle "infer simple constraints from difficult ones" which is actually the basic principle behind the design of CLP over Finite Domains, and would be appropriate to build non-primitive constraints as well
- Four types of constrains are defined in [1] to express naturally propositional problems and a generalization for model partition theorem is given.

9 Conclusion

In this paper, we have introduced the pair formulas to express problems in a more natural way and inprove the efficiency of resolution methods in propositional calculus. The pair formulas have a simple semantic and let to get a generalization of the conjunctive normal form (CNF). A proof system which is at once complete and decidable is given. Thanks to cardinality, the detection of symmetries seems to be less expensive. Symmetries are applied to Davis and Putnam procedure with cadinality and satisfactory CPU times are obtained on different problems. We intend to generalize Sl-resolution method to pair formulas, some properties of cardinality seems to be particularly useful when dealing with this method.

References

1. A. S. M. Aguirre. *How to use symmetries in boolean constraints solving.* PhD thesis, GIA - Luminy (Marseille), 1992.
2. B. Benhamou and L. Sais. Cardinality formulas in propositional calculus. Technical Report 1, Université de provence, 1992.
3. B. Benhamou and L. Sais. Theoretical study of symmetries in propositional calculus and application. *Eleventh International Conference on Automated Deduction, Saratoga Springs,NY, USA,* 1992.
4. A. Colmerauer. An introduction to prolog III. *CACM,* 4(28):412–418, 1990.
5. C. C. cook, W. and Gy. Turan, on the complexity of cutting-planes proofs, working paper, cornell university, ithaca, ny. 1985.
6. M. Davis and H. Putnam. A computing procedure for quatification theory. *JACM,* (7):201–215, 1960.

7. M. Dincbas, P. V. Hentenryck, H. Simonis, A. Aggoun, T. Grof, and F.Berthier. The constraint logic programing language CHIP. In *the International Conference on Fifth Generation Computer Systems, Tokyo, Japon,* December 1988.

8. P. V. Hentenryck and Y. Deville. The cardinality operator: A new logical connective for constraint logic programming. Technical report, CS Departement, Brown University, Technical Report, october, 1990.

9. J. N. Hooker. Generalized resolution and cutting planes. *Approches to Intelligent Decision Suport, a volume in Annals of Operations Researchs series.*

10. J. N. Hooker. A quantitive approach to logical inference. *Decision Suport Systems,* (4):45–69, 1988.

11. J. Jaffar and J. L. Lassez. Constraint logic programing. *POPL-87,Munich, FRG,* January 1988.

12. R. Kowalski and D. Kuehner. Linear resolution with selection function. *Artificial Intelligence,* (2):227–260, 1971.

13. B. Krishnamurty. Short proofs for tricky formulas. *Acta informatica,* (22):253–275, 1985.

14. L. Oxusoff and A. Rauzy. *L'évaluation sémantique en calcul propositionnel.* PhD thesis, GIA - Luminy (Marseille), 1989.

Complexity Classes

The Alternation Hierarchy for Machines with Sublogarithmic Space is Infinite

Burchard von Braunmühl, Romain Gengler
and Robert Rettinger

Institut für Informatik I, Universität Bonn
Römerstraße 164, D-53117 Bonn, Germany
bvb@cs.uni-bonn.de   gengler@cs.uni-bonn.de

Abstract. The alternation hierarchy for Turing machines with a space bound between loglog and log is infinite. That applies to all common concepts, especially a) to two-way machines with weak space-bounds, b) to two-way machines with strong space-bounds, and c) to one-way machines with weak space-bounds. In all of these cases the Σ_k- and Π_k- classes are not comparable for $k \geq 2$. Furthermore the Σ_k-classes are not closed under intersection and the Π_k-classes are not closed under union. Thus these classes are not closed under complementation. The hierarchy results also apply to classes determined by an alternation depth which is a function depending on the input rather than on a constant.

1 Introduction

Only a few results are known about the various hierarchies defined in the structural complexity theory and normally, if known, they are negative, i.e., the considered (infinite) hierarchy does not exist. It is well known that the strong exponential time hierarchy SEH collapses to P^{NE} (see [Hem87]) and the hierarchy IP(k) of interactive proof systems does so to IP(2) (see [BM88]). Concerning strong space-complexity, [Imm88] and [Sze88] independently showed that strong–NSPACE(s) is closed under complementation for $s \geq$ log. As a consequence of this all oracle hierarchies and all alternation hierarchies related to space-bounded machines collapse, provided that we consider strong space-complexity and space-bounds in $\Omega(\log)$.

But the more common concept is the weak space-complexity. A weakly space-bounded machine has to observe the space bound in at least one of the possible successful computations, whereas a strongly space-bounded machine has to observe the space bound in all cases. No statement on the complementation of weak–NSPACE(s) can be made if s is not space-constructable. The Immerman–Szelepcsényi–theorem definitely does not hold for weak space-bounds below log, since the language $L_= := \{ a^n b^n \mid n \in \mathbb{N} \}$ is not in weak–NSPACE(log) but its complement $L_{\neq}$ is in weak–DSPACE(loglog) (see [Fre79]). Moreover, for this reason there cannot be a function s between loglog and log which is fully space-constructable by a nondeterministic Turing machine, since otherwise a NSPACE(s)-TM would be able to recognize $L_=$ (see [Bra91] or [LR93a]). It is known that no function $s \in o(\log\log)$ can be fully space-constructable, not even by an alternating Turing machine, since otherwise an alternating Turing machine with a space bound below loglog would be able to recognize a non-regular language, which is impossible [Iwa86]. Curiously enough, there are some "pathological" functions below log which are fully space-constructable even by deterministic Turing machines. But these are functions whose values fall below a constant bound an infinite number of times and reach loglog infinitely often. So we see that it is much more relevant to distinguish between weak and strong below log than above log. Weak complexity makes machines much more powerful. There exist deterministic, weakly loglog–space-bounded machines, that cannot be simulated even by alternating, strongly $o(\log)$–space-bounded Turing machines (see [LR93a]).

Now, the question arises — what holds in the area of space bounds between loglog and log, especially for the alternating hierarchies? In what follows it is proven:

The alternation hierarchy for Turing machines with a space bound between loglog and log is infinite. This holds for weak as well as for strong complexity.

We consider two types of machines, those with a one-way input tape and those with a two-way input tape. These two differ considerably. So it can be shown that even the weakly $o(\log)$–space-bounded, alternating one-way machines cannot simulate all strongly loglog–space-bounded, two-way machines, not even those with at most one alternation (see [IIT87]).

All languages recognized by any alternating one-way machine with a strong space-bound below log are regular. Thus strong complexity makes no sense in the case of one-way machines. But there are non-regular languages recognized by nondeterministic one-way machines with the weak space-bound loglog (see [Iwa86]). So we can ask the above question for one-way machines again. In [Bra91] it is proven that the alternation hierarchy related to one-way machines with a space bound below log is infinite. This result can also be derived from the Main Theorem of this paper.

1.1 The results

If the state changes from universal to existential or vice versa, we say that the computation path has an alternation at this point. Let us call M a weak–$2\Sigma_k[f]$–Turing machine if M is an alternating Turing machine with a two-way input-tape, with a weak space-bound f, with an existential start situation, and with at most $k-1$ alternations per computation path. If we write strong instead of weak, one-way instead of two-way, Π instead of Σ, the corresponding meaning should be clear. An A replacing Σ_k or Π_k means unrestricted alternation.

In this paper we will prove:

Theorem 1 (Main Theorem). *There are languages* $\mathrm{L}_k^{\exists}$ *and* $\mathrm{L}_k^{\forall}$ *for* $k \geq 2$ *such that for all arithmetical functions* f *with* $\liminf\limits_{n \to \infty} f(n)/\log(n) = 0$

$$\mathrm{L}_k^{\exists} \in \text{weak–}1\Sigma_k[\log\log] \cap \text{strong–}2\Sigma_k[\log\log] \setminus \text{weak–}2\Pi_k[f],$$
$$\mathrm{L}_k^{\forall} \in \text{weak–}1\Pi_k[\log\log] \cap \text{strong–}2\Pi_k[\log\log] \setminus \text{weak–}2\Sigma_k[f].$$

As a consequence of this theorem we conclude that the following hierarchies are infinite:

(a) that related to one-way machines with a weak space-bound below log,

(b) that related to two-way machines with a weak space-bound below log,

(c) that related to two-way machines with a strong space-bound below log.

We will even show that the classes weak–$2\Sigma_k[f]$ and weak–$2\Pi_k[f]$, and even weak–$2\Sigma_k[f]$ and weak–$1\Pi_k[f]$, as well as weak–$1\Sigma_k[f]$ and weak–$2\Pi_k[f]$ are not comparable for $k \geq 2$; the same holds for two-way machines in the case of strong complexity.

We can even extend the hierarchy beyond constant alternation depth. If we replace the constant k by an arithmetical function f in Σ_k or Π_k, we mean that the alternation depth is bounded by this function f instead of the constant k.

Theorem 2. *Let f and g be arithmetical functions, let g be monotone and computable within linear space, let $h := g \circ \mathrm{loglog}$, and let $h(N) = h(\sqrt{N})$ and $f(N)(h(N))^2 \leq \delta \log N$, for all $\delta \in \mathbb{R}$ and for infinitely many $N \in \mathbb{N}$. Then there are languages $\mathrm{L}_h^{\exists}$ and $\mathrm{L}_h^{\vee}$ such that*

$$\mathrm{L}_h^{\exists} \in \mathrm{weak}\text{–}1\Sigma_h[\mathrm{loglog}] \cap \mathrm{strong}\text{–}2\Sigma_h[\mathrm{loglog}] \setminus \mathrm{weak}\text{–}2\Pi_h[f],$$

$$\mathrm{L}_h^{\vee} \in \mathrm{weak}\text{–}1\Pi_h[\mathrm{loglog}] \cap \mathrm{strong}\text{–}2\Pi_h[\mathrm{loglog}] \setminus \mathrm{weak}\text{–}2\Sigma_h[f].$$

Several closure results can be proven using our techniques.

Theorem 3. *The following Table 1 states the closure properties of space classes with a space bound s between loglog and $\log$, for two-way strongly bounded, for two-way weakly bounded and for one-way weakly bounded machines. The entry $+$ indicates that the class is closed, $-$ indicates that it is not closed under the operation, and $?$ indicates that the question is open.*

	two-way strong						two-way weak						one-way weak				
	D	Σ_1	Π_1	Σ_k	Π_k	A	D	Σ_1	Π_1	Σ_k	Π_k	A	Σ_1	Π_1	Σ_k	Π_k	A
Intersection	+	+	+	−	+	+	+	+	+	−	+	+	+	+	−	+	+
Union	+	+	?	+	−	+	+	+	?	+	−	+	+	−	+	−	+
Complement	+	?	?	−	−	?	−	−	−	−	−	?	−	−	−	−	?

Table 1: Closure properties for sublogarithmic space, for $k \geq 2$.

We would like to comment on the related work of other authors. In [LR93b] and in [Gef93] the authors independantly found another proof for the hierarchy and the closure properties concerning strongly space bounded two-way machines. Their methods cannot be generalized to the case of weak space-bounds, and thus to one-way machines. For more details of the history see [Wag93].

Finally we want to remark that actually there are two infinite alternation hierarchies of somewhat different natures: that of Turing machines with a random-access input tape and a logarithmic time bound, which in reality is the hierarchy AC_k^0 of Boolean circuits with unbounded fan-in, polynomial size, and constant depth (see [Sip83]); and that of the reversal-bounded one-tape Turing machines (without an extra input tape) which is reduced to the hierarchy of nondeterministic space classes by mutual simulation (see [LL89]).

1.2 Open problems

In [Bra91] it is shown that the classes weak–$1\Sigma_1[f]$ and weak–$1\Pi_1[f]$ are not comparable if $f \in o(\log)$. Surprisingly we know nothing about the relationship between the classes $2\Sigma_1[f]$ and $2\Pi_1[f]$ in the case of weak and strong space complexity. The relationship between the co–Σ_k-classes and the Π_k-classes is not known as well. By [Bra91], $L_{\neq} \in$ weak–$1\Sigma_1[\log\log] \cap$ weak–2D[loglog] and $L_= \notin$ weak–$1\Pi_3[o(\log) \cup$ weak–$2\Sigma_2[o(\log)]$. Thus the classes co–Σ_k and Π_k at the level one and two are different in the case of weak complexity (for one-way machines this applies to the first three levels).

Weakly space-restricted machines are more powerful than strongly space-restricted ones. Even if one were to use more space and the power of alternation, one could not make up for this discrepancy. So we know from [LR93a] that weak–2D[loglog] $\nsubseteq$ strong–2A[$o(\log)$] and weak–$1\Sigma_1[\log\log] \nsubseteq$ strong–2A[$o(\log)$]. It is well known that all languages in weak–1D[$o(\log)$] are regular. Vice versa we will show in this paper that the weak concept is not powerful enough to make up for the loss of alternation power: strong–$2\Sigma_k[f] \nsubseteq$ weak–$2\Sigma_{k-1}[f]$ and weak–$1\Sigma_k[f] \nsubseteq$ weak–$2\Sigma_{k-1}[f]$ if $f \in o(\log)$. Two-way machines are more powerful than one-way machines. Using even more space and even more alternation power, even in the weak mode, cannot make up for this difference. So [IIT87] showed that strong–$2\Sigma_2[\log\log] \nsubseteq$ weak–1A[$o(\log)$] and strong–$2\Pi_2[\log\log] \nsubseteq$ weak–1A[$o(\log)$]. On the other hand in [CIRB87] it is shown that weak–$2\Sigma_1[f] \subseteq$ weak–1A[f] for $f \in o(\log)$. So the question arises whether weak–$2\Sigma_1[f]$ is contained in weak–$1\Sigma_k[f]$ for some k, or at least in weak–$1\Sigma_*[f]$. In [Bra91] is shown that even the small class strong–2D[loglog]–bounded of bounded languages cannot be simulated by so strong–2D[loglog]–bounded $\nsubseteq$ weak–$1\Pi_2[o(\log)]$. This leads us to the question of whether even bounded languages are sufficient to bear witness to the infiniteness of the alternation hierarchy of two-way machines with a weak space-bound below log. And does this hold true in the case of one-way machines? Up to now we know from [Bra91] that the following can be proven using bounded languages: the alternation hierarchy of one-way machines with a weak space-bound below log does not collapse below level four and the alternation hierarchy of two-way machines with a weak space-bound below log does not collapse below level three. In [LR93a] is shown using bounded languages that the alternation hierarchy of two-way machines with a strong space-bound below log does not collapse below level four.

2 The proofs

Notations. Let M be a two-way alternating Turing machine. A *configuration* of M is determined by the state of M and by the content and head position of its working tape. A situation $s = (c, p)$ is a configuration c together with the input head position p.

T is a *computation tree* of M on input w if T is a labelled tree such that:

1. the root is labelled by the start situation of M on w,
2. if a node r is labelled by a situation s and $s_1, \ldots, s_k$ are the situations immediately succeeding s, then r has exactly k sons $r_1, \ldots, r_k$ labelled by $s_1, \ldots, s_k$.

A finite subtree T' of T is a *success tree* of M on w *rooted* in the situation s, if

1. its root is labelled by s and every leaf is labelled by an accepting situation;
2. if r is a node in T' labelled by an $\forall$–situation, then all sons of r in T are also sons in T'; and
3. if r is a node in T' labelled by an $\exists$–situation, then exactly one son of r in T is also a son in T'.

We call a situation s in a computation path or in a success tree an *alternation* if the state changes from universal to existential or vice versa in the last computation step leading to s. A path π is *alternation-free* if no node of π is an alternation except possibly the start and end node. A path or a success tree is b–bounded if no situation of it takes more than b space. A situation s is b–successful on w for some b in $\mathbb{N}$ if there is a b–bounded success tree on w rooted in s. A (computation) path π is b–successful on w if it ends in a b–successful situation. Note that a path may be a subpath of another path. M *accepts* an input w if the start situation is b–successful on w for some b in $\mathbb{N}$.

Let r be in $\{1, 2\}$, k be in $\mathbb{N}$ and f be an arithmetical function. M is a strong–$iA_k[f]$–Turing machine if M has an i–way input tape and if for every input w all paths of the computation tree of M on w are $f(|w|)$–bounded and contain at most $k-1$ alternations. M is a weak–$iA_k[f]$–Turing machine if M has an i–way input tape and if for every input w accepted by M there is a success tree whose paths are all $f(|w|)$–bounded and contain at most $k-1$ alternations. We write Σ_k or Π_k instead of A_k if the start situation is existential or universal, respectively.

The witness languages. We will define our witness languages which enable us to separate the different classes. For every i in $\mathbb{N}$ we have a special symbol $\overset{i}{\#}$. Let $\Sigma := \{0, 1\}$ and $\Sigma_r := \Sigma \cup \{\#\} \cup \{\overset{i}{\#} \mid 1 \le i \le r\}$ and u a word in $\{0, 1\}^*$. Let

$$D_1 := \Sigma^* \qquad \text{and} \qquad D_{i+1} := (D_i\{\overset{i}{\#}\})^* \cdot D_i \quad (i \ge 1),$$
$$\exists D_1(u) := \Sigma^* \setminus \{u\} \qquad \text{and} \qquad \forall D_1(u) := \{u\} \qquad \text{and, for } i \ge 1,$$
$$\exists D_{i+1}(u) := \{W_1 \overset{i}{\#} \ldots \overset{i}{\#} W_m \in D_{i+1} \mid \exists j \; W_j \in \forall D_i(u), \; m \in \mathbb{N}\} \quad \text{and}$$
$$\forall D_{i+1}(u) := \{W_1 \overset{i}{\#} \ldots \overset{i}{\#} W_m \in D_{i+1} \mid \forall j \; W_j \in \exists D_i(u), \; m \in \mathbb{N}\}.$$

Further let b_i be the reversal of the binary representation of i and $\mathrm{BIN}(n) := b_n\#b_{n-1}\#\ldots\#b_2\#b_1$. Note that $|b_i| = \log i + 1$ and $|\mathrm{BIN}(n)| := \log 1 + \cdots + \log n + 2n - 1 < n \log n + 2n + 1 < 2n \log n$ if $n > 8$. Now, let us define:

$$L_k^{\exists} := \bigcup \{\exists D_k(u) \cdot \{\#u\#\mathrm{BIN}(n)\}\{\#\}^* \mid u \in \Sigma^{\log n - 1}, \; n \in \mathbb{N}\} \quad (k \ge 2)$$
$$L_k^{\forall} := \bigcup \{\forall D_k(u) \cdot \{\#u\#\mathrm{BIN}(n)\}\{\#\}^* \mid u \in \Sigma^{\log n - 1}, \; n \in \mathbb{N}\} \quad (k \ge 2)$$

Example.

$$\mathrm{L}_2^{\exists} = \{w_1 \overset{1}{\#} \ldots \overset{1}{\#} w_m \# u \# \mathrm{BIN}(n) \#^* |$$
$$u \in \Sigma^{\log n - 1}; \, n, m \in \mathbb{N}; \, \forall i \, (w_i \in \Sigma^*), \, \exists i \, (w_i = u) \}.$$

We will prove Theorem 1 using the witness languages $\mathrm{L}_k^{\exists}$ and $\mathrm{L}_k^{\forall}$ defined above. The proof of the next theorem, which states the upper bounds, is straightforward and left to the reader (for details see [BGR93]):

Theorem 4 (Upper Bounds). *For $k \geq 2$ the following holds:*

(1) $\mathrm{L}_k^{\exists} \in$ weak-$1\Sigma_k[\log\log]$, $\mathrm{L}_k^{\forall} \in$ weak-$1\Pi_k[\log\log]$,

(2) $\mathrm{L}_k^{\exists} \in$ strong-$2\Sigma_k[\log\log]$, $\mathrm{L}_k^{\forall} \in$ strong-$2\Pi_k[\log\log]$.

Theorem 5 (Lower bounds). *Let $k \geq 2$ and f be an arithmetical function with $\liminf_{n \to \infty} f(n)/\log(n) = 0$. Then $\mathrm{L}_k^{\exists} \notin$ weak-$2\Pi_k[f]$ and $\mathrm{L}_k^{\forall} \notin$ weak-$2\Sigma_k[f]$.*

We will prove both assertions in parallel. Consider a weak-$2A_k[f]$–Turing machine M with $\liminf_{n \to \infty} f(n)/\log(n) = 0$. W.l.o.g. we assume that M is a *normal* machine, i.e., 1) a maximal computation path terminates only on the blank symbol right of w; 2) there is no infinite alternation-free computation path that has all its situations at the same position; and 3) all maximal computation paths beginning in the start situation of M contain exactly $k-1$ alternations.

We will prove that M does not recognize $\mathrm{L}_k^{\exists}$ if M is a Π_k–machine, and that M does not recognize $\mathrm{L}_k^{\forall}$ if M is a Σ_k–machine. At this point we will need a technical definition as well as a technical lemma.

Definition (Table). *Let C_M^b be the set of the configurations of M using at most space b. For every w in $(\Sigma \cup \#)^*$ and every b in $\mathbb{N}$ we can define the* table *$T_M^b(w) \subseteq (C_M^b \times \{l, r\}) \times (C_M^b \times \{l, r\} \cup \{\infty, \perp\})$ of w with respect to b and M (let $p(s) = 1$ if $s = l$, $p(s) = |w|$ otherwise; $p'(s) = 0$ if $s = l$, $p'(s) = |w| + 1$ otherwise):*

- $((c, s), (c', s')) \in T_M^b(w)$ *if there is an alternation-free computation path (on w) leading from $(c, p(s))$ to $(c', p'(s'))$ which is b–bounded and does not leave w in between,*

- $((c, s), \infty) \in T_M^b(w)$ *if there is an alternation-free path starting at $(c, p(s))$ which is infinite or not b–bounded, and does not leave w,*

- $((c, s), \perp) \in T_M^b(w)$ *if there is a b–bounded path starting at $(c, p(s))$ which has an alternation and does not leave w.*

Note that for $c_M = 2 \log |\Gamma| + |Q| + 1$ there are at most 2^{bc_M} configurations in C_M^b and at most $2^{(2 \cdot 2^{bc_M})(2 \cdot 2^{bc_M} + 2)} \leq 2^{2^{3bc_M}}$ different tables $T_M^b(w)$ with w in $(\Sigma \cup \#)^*$. Given a word $W = w_1 \# \ldots \# w_n$ where w_i in Σ^* for $i = 1, \ldots, n$, we call $\{w_1, \ldots, w_n\}$ the content of W. In $G_n = (\Sigma^{\log n - 1} \{\overset{1}{\#}\})^{n-1} \Sigma^{\log n - 1}$ there are $2^{2^{\log n - 1}} - 1$ equivalence classes of words with the same content. Thus if $3bc_M < \log n - 1$, there are two words in G_n with the same table but different contents. For given M, b and n we specify two of these words, to be called $U(n, b, M)$ and $V(n, b, M)$, together with a distinguishing subword $u(n, b, M)$

in such a way that $u(n, b, M)$ is in the content of $U(n, b, M)$ but not in the content of $V(n, b, M)$. Note that $|U(n, b, M)| = |V(n, b, M)| = n \log n - 1$ and $|u(n, b, M)| = \log n - 1$.

Lemma 6 (Table Lemma). *Let U and V be words in $(\Sigma \cup \frac{1}{\#})^*$ with the same length and the same table, i.e., $|U| = |V|$ and $T_M^b(U) = T_M^b(V)$, and let $W = X_1 W_1 \ldots X_n W_n X_{n+1}$ and $W' = X_1 W_1' \ldots X_n W_n' X_{n+1}$ be words in Σ_k^* with the subwords W_i, W_i' in $\{U, V\}$ beginning at the positions $p_i := |X_1 W_1 \ldots X_i| + 1$ for $i = 1, \ldots, n$. Then for all situations s with position not in $\bigcup_{i=1}^{n}[p_i + 1, \; p_i + |W_i| - 2]$ and all situations s' with position not in $\bigcup_{i=1}^{n}[p_i, \; p_i + |W_i| - 1]$ the following holds:*

- *if there is an alternation-free b–bounded path on W leading from s to s' then this also holds for W',*
- *if there is an alternation-free path on W starting at s which is infinite or not b-bounded then this also holds for W',*
- *if there is a b–bounded path on W starting at s with alternations then this also holds for W'.*

The proof is essentially straightforward using cut-and-paste arguments although several cases have to be considered. It can be found in [Bra91].

For arbitrary ε and n we define $m(n) := 2 \cdot n^\varepsilon + 1$ and $l_i(n) := n \log n \cdot m(n)^{i-1} - 1$ for $i = 2, \ldots, k$. We choose $\varepsilon < 1$ such that $l_k(n) + \log n + 1 + |\mathrm{BIN}(n)| \leq n^2$ for all $n \geq n_o$ where n_o is sufficiently large. Let $\delta := \varepsilon / (3c_M(p+1))$. We take an N in $\mathbb{N}$ (which will be the input length) with $(n_o)^2 \leq N$ and $f(N) < \delta \cdot \log N$ (remember that $\liminf_{n \to \infty}(f(n)/\log(n)) = 0$). For this N we choose an $n > n_o$ such that $n^2 \leq N < n^3$. For this n, now, we set $m := m(n)$, $l_i := l_i(n)$, $z_i := m^{k-i}$ for $i = 2, \ldots, k$ and $b := f(N)$. Then we have $3c_M b < \varepsilon \log n$. Thus

- the number $|C_M^b|$ of b–bounded configurations of M is less than n^ε,
- for these chosen n, b and M the words $U := U(n, b, M)$ and $V := V(n, b, M)$ in G_n, and the word $u := u(n, b, M))$ in $\Sigma^{\log n - 1}$ with the properties mentioned above exist.

We define inductively the sets E_i of words with $E_1 := \{U, V\}$ and $E_{i+1} := \{X_1 \# \ldots \# X_m | X_j \in E_i$ for $j = 1, \ldots, m\}$ for $i = 1, \ldots, k-1$. The words of E_i have the length $l_i = n \cdot \log n \cdot m^{i-1}$ for $i \leq k$.

Let $S := \# u \# \mathrm{BIN}(n) \#^t$, where $t := N - (l_k + \log n + 1 + |\mathrm{BIN}(n)|)$. Then all the words in $E_k S$ have length N. (We simply write $E_k S$ instead of $E_k \cdot \{S\}$.)

Let W be a word in $E_k S$. An *r–block* of W is a part of W delimited by two neighboring marks in $\{\frac{i}{\#} \mid i \geq r\}$ (for $r = 1$ we consider only $\frac{1}{\#}$–marks with positions on $\nu \cdot n \log n$ where ν is in $\mathbb{N}$, for $r = k$ we regard the first $\#$ in S as well as the blank symbol immediately before the input word W as an $\frac{k}{\#}$–mark). We call these two marks the *borders* of the r–block and the subword between these two borders the *content* of the r–block. Note that the number of r–blocks in an $(r+1)$–block is m. The number of r–blocks in W is $z_r = m^{k-r}$. Particularly W has just one k–block.

Let W_0 be the word in $E_k S$ whose 1–blocks all contain U , and let W_1 be the word in $E_k S$ whose 1–blocks all contain V . Now we define again inductively the words W_i in E_k for $i = 2, \ldots, k$. Assume we have defined the word W_r for an r in $\{1, \ldots, k-1\}$.

The free r–blocks in W_r . In every $(r+1)$–block B in W_r we specify a special r–block which we will call the free r–subblock of B . Consider a b-bounded situation c with input position on one of the marks bordering on B . (Note that there are at most n^ε b–bounded configurations and thus less than $m = 2n^\varepsilon + 1$ such situations.)

If c is an $\exists$–situation and has at least one alternation-free path on W_r lying in B (with input position in B) and leading from c to a b-bounded $\forall$–situation in B which is b–successful on W_r , then we specify one of these paths and mark the r–subblock of B which contains the $\forall$–situation at the end of this path.

If c is an $\forall$–situation and has at least one alternation-free path on W_r lying in B and leading from c to a b-bounded $\exists$–situation in B which is *not b–successful on W_r* , then we specify one of these paths and mark the r-subblock of B containing the final $\exists$–situation of this path.

By doing so for all b-bounded situations bordering on B we mark less than m r-subblocks in B . Therefore there is at least one unmarked r–block in B . We specify one of them and call it *the free r-subblock of B* . Let $\mathcal{B}_r$ be the set of the free r–blocks in W_r . Now, we can state the following fact:

Lemma 7. *Let c be a b-bounded situation on a border of an $(r+1)$–block and let π be an alternation-free path on W_r from c to an alternation c', where c' is b–successful on W_r if c is an $\exists$–situation, and c' is not b–successful on W_r if c is an $\forall$–situation. Then there is also an alternation-free path on W_r from c ending in such an alternation, which does not lie in any free r–block of W_r .*

The word family W_i . Now we are able to define the words W_i in E_i for $i = 2, \ldots, k$. We have already described the words W_0 and W_1 . Assume that we have defined the words $W_0, \ldots, W_r$ for $r < k$. Let α be a subset of $\mathcal{B}_r$. We get the word $W_r \alpha$ from W_r by replacing the content of each free r–block in α with the content of the corresponding r–block of W_{r-1} . This is to say that $W_r \alpha$ equals W_r in all r–blocks except for the free r–blocks in α which are taken over from W_{r-1} . If we take over all free r–blocks of W_r from W_{r-1} , then we get W_{r+1} , i.e., $W_r \alpha = W_{r+1}$ if $\alpha = \mathcal{B}_r$. Note the following simple but helpful aspect:

Lemma 8. *For each subset α of $\mathcal{B}_r$ there is a subset β of $\mathcal{B}_{r-1}$ such that $W_r \alpha = W_{r-1} \beta$.*

We need some further technical notations. A situation c is called a (Qj)–*situation*, where Q in $\{\forall, \exists\}$ and j in $\{1, \ldots, k\}$, if its state is a Q-state, and all maximal paths starting at c have at most $j-1$ alternations (note that M is a normal machine). It is called a (rQj)–*situation*, where Q in $\{\forall, \exists\}$ and r, j in $\{1, \ldots, k\}$, if it is a (Qj)–situation and its input position is situated on a border of an r–block.

The following lemma is the basis of our proof.

Lemma 9 (Main Lemma). *Let α, α' be subsets of $\mathcal{B}_r$ and r in $\{1, \ldots, k-1\}$.*

(I) If an $(r+1\exists r+1)$–situation is b–successful on W_r, then it is b–successful on $W_r\alpha$, too.

(II) If an $(r+1\forall r+1)$–situation is not b–successful on W_r, then it is not b–successful on $W_r\alpha$, too.

(III) An $(r+1Qr)$–situation is b–successful on $W_r\alpha$ if and only if it is b–successful on $W_r\alpha'$.

From this lemma we can immediately derive Theorem 5:

- $L_k^{\vee} \notin \text{weak-}2\Sigma_k[f]$.

  Proof. Assume that M is a Σ_k–Turing machine accepting all the words in $L_k^{\vee}$, particularly the word W_{k-1} in $L_k^{\vee}$. Since the start situation of M is a $(k\exists k)$–situation and b–successful on W_{k-1}, the start situation is also b–successful on W_k which is not in $L_k^{\vee}$. Thus M does not recognize $L_k^{\vee}$.

- $L_k^{\exists} \notin \text{weak-}2\Pi_k[f]$.

  Proof. Assume that M is a Π_k–Turing machine rejecting all the words not in $L_k^{\exists}$, particularly the word W_{k-1} not in $L_k^{\exists}$. Since the start situation of M is a $(k\forall k)$–situation and not b–successful on W_{k-1}, the start situation is not b–successful on W_k either, eventhough W_k is in $L_k^{\exists}$. Thus M does not recognize $L_k^{\exists}$.

So, all that we have left to prove is the Main Lemma.

Proof of the Main Lemma. We prove (I)–(III) by induction on r.

Note. Let W and W' be in $E_k S$, and let c be a situation on a border of an r–block. If c is an $\exists$–situation b–successful on W and if π is an alternation-free b–bounded path from c which ends in an accepting situation, then there is also such a path from c on W' by the Table Lemma (note that M is a normal machine), i.e., c is b–successful on W', too. If c is an $\forall$–situation b–successful on W and if π is an alternation-free path starting at c which is infinite, or not b–bounded, or ends in a rejecting situation, then there is also such a path from c on W' by the Table Lemma (note that M is a normal machine), i.e., c is not b–successful on W', too. After we have stated that, we can limit our considerations to such b–successful $\exists$–situations which do not have an alternation-free path ending in an accepting situation, and to such $\forall$–situations which are not b–successful and which do not have an alternation-free path that is infinite, or not b–bounded, or ending in a rejecting situation.

Induction basis. $(r = 1)$

Ad (I). Let c be a $(2\exists 2)$–situation which is b–successful on W_2. Then there is an alternation-free b–bounded path from c to an $(\forall 1)$–situation c'. By Lemma 7 we can assume that c' does not lie in an free 1–block of W_2. By the Table Lemma c' is successful on $W_2\alpha$. (Remember that we get $W_2\alpha$ from W_2 by replacing the U of the free 1–blocks that lie in the free 2–blocks of α with V.) By the Table Lemma there exists an alternation-free b–bounded path from c to c' on $W_2\alpha$, too. Therefore c is also b–successful on $W_2\alpha$.

Ad (II). Let c be a $(2\forall 2)$–situation which is *not* b–successful on W_2. Then there is an alternation-free path π from c to an $(\exists 1)$–situation c' (remember the note). Again, by Lemma 7, c' does not lie in a free 1–block of W_2. By the Table Lemma c' is not b–successful on $W_2\alpha$. Since on $W_2\alpha$ there is also an alternation-free b–bounded path from c to c', c' is not b–successful on $W_2\alpha$ either.

Ad (III). Let c be a $(2Q1)$–situation b–successful on $W_2\alpha$. By the Table Lemma, c is b–successful on $W_2\alpha'$, too.

Induction hypothesis. Let us assume that assertions (I) to (III) hold for $r-1$ where $r<k$.

Induction step. We will show that this is true for r, too. Before starting the actual proof of the assertions (I)–(III), let us show that the assertions stated below follow from the induction hypothesis.

(IVa) Let β and β' be subsets of $\mathcal{B}_{r-1}$, and c be a $(Qr-1)$–situation lying in an r–block B of W_{r-1}, such that $W_{r-1}\beta$ equals $W_{r-1}\beta'$ in B. Then c is b–successful on $W_{r-1}\beta$ if and only if it is b–successful on $W_{r-1}\beta'$.

(IVb) Let α and α' be subsets of $\mathcal{B}_r$, and c be a $(Qr-1)$–situation lying in an r–block B of W_r, such that $W_r\alpha$ equals $W_r\alpha'$ in B. Then c is b–successful on $W_r\alpha$ if and only if it is b–successful on $W_r\alpha'$.

(V) Let α and α' be subsets of $\mathcal{B}_r$ with $\alpha \supseteq \alpha'$, and c an $(r\exists r)$–situation. If c is b–successful on $W_r\alpha$, then it is b–successful on $W_r\alpha'$, too.

(VI) Let α and α' be subsets of $\mathcal{B}_r$ with $\alpha \supseteq \alpha'$, and c an $(r\forall r)$–situation. If c is not b–successful on $W_r\alpha$, then it is not b–successful on $W_r\alpha'$ either.

Proof of (IVa). Let c be a $(Qr-1)$–situation, b–successful on $W_{r-1}\beta$ and lying in an r–block B, such that $W_{r-1}\beta$ and $W_{r-1}\beta'$ do not differ in B. All maximal paths of the success tree Γ of c on $W_{r-1}\beta$ which do not leave B, are also b–successful on $W_{r-1}\beta'$. A path of Γ which leaves B has a first $(r\overline{Q}j)$–situation c' on a border of B for a $j<r-1$ with $\overline{Q}$ in $\{\exists,\forall\}$. By the induction hypothesis (III) c' is b–successful on $W_{r-1}\beta'$. Overall we conclude that c is b–successful on $W_{r-1}\beta'$.

Proof of (IVb). (IVb) is an immediate consequence of (IVa) and Lemma 8.

Proof of (V). Let c be an $(r\exists r)$–situation b–successful on $W_r\alpha$. Then there is an alternation-free b–bounded path from c to an $(\forall r-1)$–situation c' b–successful on $W_r\alpha$ (remember the note). Let B be the r–block containing c'.

(a) Let B be in both α and α', or in neither. Then $W_r\alpha$ equals $W_r\alpha'$ in B. Thus c' is b–successful on $W_r\alpha'$, according to (IVb), and by the Table Lemma c is as well.

(b) Let B be in α but not in α'. Then $W_r\alpha$ equals W_{r-1} in B. By Lemma 8 there is a subset β of $\mathcal{B}_{r-1}$ with $W_r\alpha = W_{r-1}\beta$. According to (IVa), c' is b–successful on W_{r-1}, and, by the Table Lemma, so does c. By Lemma 8 there is a subset β' of $\mathcal{B}_{r-1}$ for α', such that $W_r\alpha' = W_{r-1}\beta'$. By the induction hypothesis (I) c is also b–successful on $W_{r-1}\beta' = W_r\alpha'$.

Proof of (VI). This proof is very similar to that of (IV). We get it from the proof of (IV) by doing the following textual replacements: "$(r\exists r)$" with "$(r\forall r)$",

"($\forall r-1$)" with "($\exists r-1$)", "b–successful" with "not b–successful" and "(I)" with "(II)".

Now we are prepared to show the actual assertions (I)–(III).

Proof of (I). Let c be an $(r+1\exists r+1)$–situation, b–successful on W_r. Then there is an alternation-free b–bounded path π from c to an $(\forall r)$–situation c' b–successful on W_r. By Lemma 7 we can assume that c' does not lie in any r–block of α, i.e., W_r equals $W_r\alpha$ in the r–block containing c'.

We will show that c' is b–successful on $W_r\alpha$ and thus, by the Table Lemma, c is as well. We assume that c' is not b–successful on $W_r\alpha$. Then there is an alternation-free path π' on $W_r\alpha$ from c' to an $(\exists r-1)$–situation c'' not b–successful on $W_r\alpha$ (remember the note). Let B be the r–block containing c''.

(a) If B is not in α, then W_r equals $W_r\alpha$ in B, and, therefore c'' is *not* b–successful on W_r, according to (IVb), and thus this is true for c' by the Table Lemma. That contradicts our assumption.

(b) Let B be in α, and c''' the first $(r\forall r)$–situation in π'. By (VI) c''' is not b–successful on W_r, and c' is not either, again contradicting our assumption.

Proof of (II). Again we get the proof of (II) from that of (I) by the following textual replacements: "b–successful" with "not b–successful" and vice versa, "$(r+1\exists r+1)$" with "$(r+1\forall r+1)$", "($\forall r$)" with "($\exists r$)", "$(\exists r-1)$" with "$(\forall r-1)$", and "(VI)" with "(V)".

Proof of (III). If c is an $(r+1\exists r)$–situation (and thus an $(r\exists r)$–situation) b–successful on $W_r\alpha$, then c is b–successful on W_r, according to (V), and thus b–successful on $W_r\alpha'$, according to (I).

If c is an $(r+1\forall r)$–situation (and thus an $(r\forall r)$–situation) not b–successful on $W_r\alpha'$, then c is not b–successful on W_r, according to (VI), and thus not b–successful on $W_r\alpha$, according to (II). $\qquad\qquad\square$

Proof of Theorem 1. Theorem 1 follows from Theorem 4 and Theorem 5. $\quad\square$

Proof of Theorem 2. We define the languages $L_h^\exists$ and $L_h^\forall$ analogously to the languages $L_k^\exists$ and $L_k^\forall$ for $k\in\mathbb{N}$: the marks $\overset{i}{\#}$ are replaced with strings $\#\mathrm{bin}(i)\#$, where $\mathrm{bin}(i)$ is the binary representation of the number i, and we have r–blocks for $r=1,\ldots,h(n)$, where n is the number represented in the suffix of the input. The proof is analogous to the proof of the Main Theorem. $\qquad\qquad\square$

Proof of Theorem 3. We sketch only a proof of the closure results for the Σ_k– and Π_k–classes for $k\geq 2$. For proof sketches of the other results see [BGR93]. For $k\geq 2$ let $\Delta_k := \{0,1,\overset{1}{\#},\ldots,\overset{k-1}{\#}\}$, and

$$S_k^\exists := \bigcup\{\,\Delta_k^*\cdot\{\overset{k}{\#}\}\cdot\exists D_k(u)\cdot\{\#u\#\mathrm{BIN}(n)\}\cdot\{\#\}^* \mid u\in\Sigma^{\log n-1},\ n\in\mathbb{N}\,\},$$

$$R_k^\exists := \bigcup\{\,\exists D_k(u)\cdot\{\overset{k}{\#}\}\cdot\Delta_k^*\cdot\{\#u\#\mathrm{BIN}(n)\}\cdot\{\#\}^* \mid u\in\Sigma^{\log n-1},\ n\in\mathbb{N}\,\}.$$

The languages $S_k^\exists$ and $R_k^\exists$ are in weak-$1\Sigma_k[\mathrm{loglog}]$ and in strong-$2\Sigma_k[\mathrm{loglog}]$. But using the methods of the proof of the Main Theorem one can show that $S_k^\exists\cap R_k^\exists$ is not in weak-$2\Sigma_{k+1}$. (Note that only two k–blocks are necessary for the proof. If we specify the free k–block we consider only the start situation, so we mark just one k–block.) Thus weak–$2\Sigma_k[s]$, strong–$2\Sigma_k[s]$ and weak–$1\Sigma_k[s]$ cannot be closed under intersection.

The non-closure of the Π_k–classes under union follows analogously. The Σ_k–classes are trivially closed under union and the Π_k–classes under intersection. Non-closure under complementation follows by de Morgan's rules. □

Acknowledgement: The authors would like to thank M. Liśkiewicz for discussions about the closure properties.

References

[BGR93] B. von Braunmühl, R. Gengler, and R. Rettinger. The alternation hierarchy with sublogarithmic space is infinite. *Computational Complexity*, 3/3:207–230, 1993. To appear.

[BM88] L. Babai and S. Moran. Arthur-Merlin games: a randomized proof-system, and a hierarchy of complexity classes. *Journal of Computer and System Sciences*, 36:254–276, 1988.

[Bra91] B. v. Braunmühl. Alternationshierarchien von Turingmaschinen mit kleinem Speicher. Informatik Berichte 83, Inst. f. Informatik, Universität Bonn, 1991.

[CIRB87] J. H. Chang, O. H. Ibarra, B. Ravikumar, and L. Berman. Some observations concerning Turing machines using small space. *Information Processing Letters*, 25:1–9, 1987. Erratum, *Information Processing Letters*, 25:53, 1988.

[Fre79] R. Freivalds. On time complexity of deterministic and nondeterministic Turing machines. *Latvijski Mathematičeskij Eshegodnik*, 23:158–165, 1979. In Russian.

[Gef93] V. Geffert. A hierarchy that does not collapse: Alternations in low level space. Research report, Šafárik University, Košice, 1993.

[Hem87] L. A. Hemachandra. The strong exponential hierarchy collapses. In *Proc. 19th. STOC Conference*, pages 110–122, 1987.

[IIT87] A. Ito, K. Inoue, and I. Takanami. A note on alternating Turing machines using small space. *The Trans. of the IEICE*, E 70 no. 10:990–996, 1987.

[Imm88] N. Immerman. NSPACE is closed under complement. *SIAM J. Comput.*, 17:935–938, 1988.

[Iwa86] K. Iwama. ASPACE(o(log log)) is regular. Research report, KSU/ICS Kyoto Sangyo University, Kyoto, 603, Japan, March 1986. See also *SIAM J. Comput.* 22:136–146, 1993.

[LL89] M. Liśkiewicz and K. Loryś. On reversal complexity for alternating Turing machines. In *Proc. 30st FOCS*, pages 618–623, 1989.

[LR93a] M. Liśkiewicz and R. Reischuk. Separating the lower levels of the sublogarithmic space hierarchy. In *Proc. 10. STACS, LNCS 665*, pages 16–28, 1993.

[LR93b] M. Liśkiewicz and R. Reischuk. The sublogarithmic space world. Technical report, Institut für Theoretische Informatik, TH Darmstadt, 1993.

[Sip83] M. Sipser. Borel sets and circuit complexity. In *Proc 15. Ann. ACM Symp. on Theory of Computing*, pages 330–335, 1983.

[Sze88] R. Szelepcsényi. The method of forced enumeration for nondeterministic automata. *Acta Informatica*, 26:279–284, 1988.

[Wag93] K. W. Wagner. The alternation hierarchy for sublogarithmic space: an exciting race to STACS'93 (Editorial note). In *Proc. 10. STACS, LNCS 665*, pages 2–4, 1993.

Quasilinear Time Complexity Theory

Ashish V. Naik*
SUNY Buffalo
avnaik@cs.buffalo.edu

Kenneth W. Regan†
SUNY Buffalo
regan@cs.buffalo.edu

D. Sivakumar
SUNY Buffalo
sivak-d@cs.buffalo.edu

Abstract

This paper furthers the study of quasi-linear time complexity initiated by Schnorr [Sch76] and Gurevich and Shelah [GS89]. We show that the fundamental properties of the polynomial-time hierarchy carry over to the quasilinear-time hierarchy. Whereas all previously known versions of the Valiant-Vazirani reduction from NP to parity run in quadratic time, we give a new construction using error-correcting codes that runs in quasilinear time. We show, however, that the important equivalence between search problems and decision problems in polynomial time is unlikely to carry over: if search reduces to decision for SAT in quasi-linear time, then all of NP is contained in quasi-polynomial time. Other connections to work by Stearns and Hunt [SH86, SH90, HS90] on "power indices" of NP languages are made.

1. Introduction

The notion of "feasible" computation has most often been identified with the concept of polynomial time. However, an algorithm which runs in time n^{100} or even time n^2 may not really be feasible on moderately large instances. Quasi-linear time, namely time $qlin := n \cdot (\log n)^{O(1)}$, reduces the problem of the exponent of n. Let DQL and NQL stand for time $qlin$ on deterministic and nondeterministic Turing machines. Schnorr [Sch76, Sch78] showed that SAT is complete for NQL under DQL many-one reductions ($\leq_m^{ql}$). Together with Stearns and Hunt [SH86, SH90], it was shown that many known NP-complete problems also belong to NQL and are complete for NQL under $\leq_m^{ql}$, so that the NQL vs. DQL question takes on much the same shape as NP vs. P. Related classes within P are studied by Buss and Goldsmith [BG93].

One theoretical difficulty with the concept of quasilinear time is that it appears not to share the degree of independence on particular machine models that makes polynomial time such a *robust* concept. Gurevich and Shelah [GS89] showed that a wide variety of models related to the RAM under log-cost criterion [CR73] accept the same class of languages in quasilinear time—we call this class DNLT. They also showed that nondeterministic $qlin$ time for these machines, namely NNLT, equals NQL. However, currently it appears that DNLT is larger than DQL, and that for all $d > 1$, Turing machines with d-dimensional tapes accept more languages in time $qlin$ than do TMs with $(d-1)$-dimensional tapes (cf. [WW86]). Our constructions all work for DQL as well as DNLT.

*Supported in part by NSF grant CCR-9002292.
†Supported in part by NSF grant CCR-9011248.

Our main motivation is to ask: How much of the known theory of complexity classes based on polynomial time carries over to the case of quasilinear time? Section 2 observes that the basic results for the polynomial hierarchy and PSPACE hold also for the quasilinear hierarchy (QLH) and QLSPACE.

Section 3 shows that the randomized reduction from NP to parity given by Valiant and Vazirani [VV86] and used by Toda [Tod91], previously proved by constructions which run in quadratic time (see [VV86, Tod91, CRS93, Gup93]), can be made to run in time $qlin$. Our construction also markedly improves both the number of random bits needed and the success probability, and uses error-correcting codes in an interesting manner first noted in [NN90].

Section 4 studies what may be the major difference between polynomial and quasilinear time: the equivalence between functions and sets seems no longer to hold. It has long been known that any function can be computed in polynomial time using some set as an oracle. In contrast, we show that there exist functions which cannot be computed in quasilinear time using any set as an oracle whatsoever. Many natural problems in NP have associated $search$ $functions$ which reduce to the decision problems in polynomial time, and in most cases, quadratic time (cf. [Sel88, JY90]). We show that for SAT, search does not reduce to decision in quasilinear time, unless all of NP is contained in DTIME$[2^{\text{polylog}\,n}]$. We also give a sense in which the quadratic bound is optimal, one connected to the conjecture of Stearns and Hunt [SH90] that the $power$ $index$ of SAT equals 1.

2. Notation and Basic Results

Let $\Sigma := \{0,1\}$. Given strings $y_1, \dots y_m \in \Sigma^*$, each y_i of length n_i, let $y = \langle y_1, \dots y_m \rangle$ stand for the binary string of length $2r + 2m$ obtained by translating 0 to 00, 1 to 11, and 'comma' to 01, with an extra 01 at the end. For any language B we often write $B(x, y)$ in place of '$\langle x, y \rangle \in B$' and consider B as a predicate. For convenience we call q a $quasilinear$ $function$ if there are constants $k, c, d \geq 0$ such that for all n, $q(n) = cn(\log^k n) + d$. Where n is understood we write q as short for $q(n)$, and also write $(\exists^q y)$ for $(\exists y \in \{0,1\}^{q(n)})$, $(\forall^q y)$ for $(\forall y \in \{0,1\}^{q(n)})$. The notation $(\#^q y : B(x, y))$ means "the number of strings $y \in \{0,1\}^{q(|x|)}$ such that $B(x, y)$ holds."

Definition 2.1. If $A \in$ NP, $B \in$ P, and p is a polynomial such that for all x, $x \in A \iff (\exists^p y)\, B(x, y)$, then we call B a $witness$ $predicate$ for A, with the length bound p understood. We use the same terms in the context of NQL and DQL.

We note the following provision about oracle Turing machines M made standard in [WW86] (see also [LL76, Wra77, Wra78]): Whenever M enters its query state $q_?$ with the query string z on its query tape, z is $erased$ when the oracle gives its answer. If the oracle is a function g, we suppose that $g(z)$ replaces z on the query tape in the next step. If A and B are languages such that $L(M^B) = A$ and M^B runs in quasilinear time, then we write $A \leq^{\text{ql}}_{\text{T}} B$. As usual we may also write $A \in \text{DQL}^B$ or $A \in \text{DQL}(B)$, and if M is nondeterministic, $A \in \text{NQL}^B$ or $A \in \text{NQL}(B)$. Henceforth our notations and definitions of complexity classes are standard, with 'P' replaced by 'QL', except that we use square brackets for "class operators":

Definition 2.2. For any languages A and B,

(a) $A \in \text{NQL}[B]$ if there is a quasilinear function q such that for all $x \in \Sigma^*$, $x \in A \iff (\exists^q y)\, B(x, y)$.

(b) $A \in \text{UQL}[B]$ if there is q such that for all $x \in \Sigma^*$, $x \in A \implies (\#^q y : B(x, y)) = 1$, and $x \notin A \implies (\#^q y : B(x, y)) = 0$.

(c) $A \in \oplus \text{QL}[B]$ if there is q such that for all x, $x \in A \iff (\#^q y : B(x, y))$ is odd.

(d) $A \in \text{BQL}[B]$ if there is a quasilinear function q such that for all $x \in \Sigma^*$, $x \in A \implies (\#^q y : B(x, y))/2^q > 2/3$, and $x \notin A \implies (\#^q y : B(x, y))/2^q < 1/3$.

(e) $A \in \text{RQL}[B]$ if there are q and $\epsilon > 0$ such that for all $x \in \Sigma^*$, $x \in A \implies (\#^q y : B(x, y))/2^q > 2/3$, and $x \notin A \implies (\#^q y : B(x, y)) = 0$.

For any class $\mathcal{C}$ of languages, $\text{NQL}[\mathcal{C}]$ equals $\cup_{B \in \mathcal{C}} \text{NQL}[B]$, and similarly for the other operators. With $\mathcal{C} = \text{DQL}$ these classes are simply written NQL, UQL, $\oplus$QL, BQL, and RQL. It is easy to check that "machine definitions" of these classes are equivalent to the above "quantifier definitions"; e.g. UQL is the class of languages accepted by unambiguous NTMs which run in quasilinear time. By standard "amplification by repeated trials," for any function $r = O(\log^k n)$, the classes BQL and RQL remain the same if '1/3' is replaced by $2^{-r(n)}$ and '2/3' by $1 - 2^{-r(n)}$; and similarly for $\text{BQL}[\mathcal{C}]$ and $\text{RQL}[\mathcal{C}]$ provided $\mathcal{C}$ is closed under "polylogarithmic majority truth table reductions." This is also enough to give $\text{BQL}[\text{BQL}[\mathcal{C}]] = \text{BQL}[\mathcal{C}]$.

Definition 2.3. The *quasilinear time hierarchy* is defined by: $\Sigma_0^{ql} = \Pi_0^{ql} = \Delta_0^{ql} = \text{DQL}$, and for $k \geq 1$,

$$\Sigma_k^{ql} = \text{NQL}[\Pi_{k-1}^{ql}], \quad \Pi_k^{ql} = \text{co-}\Sigma_k^{ql}, \quad \Delta_k^{ql} = \text{DQL}^{\Sigma_{k-1}^{ql}}.$$

Also $\text{QLH} := \cup_{k=0}^{\infty} \Sigma_k^{ql}$, and $\text{QLSPACE} := \text{DSPACE}[qlin]$. By the results of [GS89], all these classes from NQL upward are the same for Turing machines and log-cost RAMs. Next we observe the following concavity property of quasilinear functions. Part (a) is an instance of *Jensen's inequality*.

Lemma 2.1. (a) Let $q(n) = cn \log^k n$, let $n_1, \ldots n_m$ be nonnegative real numbers, and let $\sum_{i=1}^m n_i \leq r$. Then $\sum_{i=1}^m q(n_i) \leq q(r)$.

(b) If $q(n) = cn \log^k n + d$, each $n_i \geq 1$, and the bound r in (a) is given by a quasilinear function $r(n)$, then $\sum_{i=1}^m q(n_i)$ is bounded by a quasilinear function. $\square$

Corollary 2.2. The relation $\leq_T^{ql}$ is transitive.

Proof. Let $A = L(M_0^B)$ and $B = L(M^C)$, where M runs in time $q(n)$ and M_0 in time $r(n)$. Define M_1 on any input x to simulate $M_0(x)$ but use M to answer the queries $y_1, \ldots, y_m$ made by M_0. For each query y_i let $n_i := \max\{|y_i|, 1\}$. Then $\sum_i n_i$ is bounded by $r(n)$, $q(n_i)$ bounds the runtime of M on input y_i, and Lemma 2.1(b) bounds the total runtime of M_1. $\square$

With this in hand it is straightforward to show that the most fundamental properties of the polynomial hierarchy (from [Sto77, Wra77]) carry over to QLH.

Theorem 2.3.

(a) *(Equivalence of oracles and quantifiers): For all* $k \geq 1$, $\Sigma_k^{ql} = \mathrm{NQL}^{\Sigma_{k-1}^{ql}}$.

(b) *(Downward separation): For all* $k \geq 0$, *if* $\Sigma_k^{ql} = \Pi_k^{ql}$ *then* $\mathrm{QLH} = \Sigma_k^{ql}$.

(c) *(Turing closure): For all* $k \geq 0$, $\Sigma_k^{ql} \cap \Pi_k^{ql}$ *is closed downward under* $\leq_{\mathrm{T}}^{\mathrm{ql}}$. *In particular, DQL and NQL $\cap$ co-NQL are closed under* $\leq_{\mathrm{T}}^{\mathrm{ql}}$.

(d) *For each* $k \geq 1$, *the language* B_k *of quantified Boolean formulas in prenex form with at most k alternating quantifier blocks beginning with '$\exists$' is complete for* Σ_k^{ql} *under DQL many-one reductions.*

(e) $\mathrm{QLH} \subseteq \mathrm{QLSPACE}$.

The case $k = 1$ of (d) is Schnorr's seminal result, and the higher cases follow quickly from this and (a). It is worth sketching Schnorr's construction (see also [BG93]): Take a time-$t(n)$ DTM M which decides a witness predicate $B(x, y)$ for the given language $A \in \mathrm{NQL}$. Convert M into $O(t(n) \log t(n))$-sized circuits C_n of fan-in 2 in variables $x_1, \ldots, x_n$ and $y_1, \ldots, y_q$ such that for all x, $x \in A \iff (\exists y_1, \ldots, y_q) \, C_n(x_1, \ldots, x_n, y_1, \ldots, y_q) = 1$. Then assign a dummy variable to each of the $O(n \log n)$ wires in C_n and write a 3-CNF formula which expresses that each output wire has the correct value given its input wires. This reduces A to SAT and is computable in time $O(n \log n)$.

Let QBF stand for $\cup_k B_k$. QBF belongs to linear space, but we do not know whether it is complete under (quasi-)linear time reductions. The standard reduction in [HU79], when applied to a given set A in $\mathrm{DSPACE}[O(n)]$, has a quadratic blowup in size. This seems related to the issue of whether Savitch's simulation of nondeterministic space $s(n) = \Omega(\log n)$ by deterministic space $O(s(n)^2)$ *must* have quadratic blowup. By the same token, the familiar "one-line proof" $\mathrm{NP}^{QBF} \subseteq \mathrm{NPSPACE} = \mathrm{PSPACE} = \mathrm{P}^{QBF}$ is not valid for QL. However, the result (a) below is still true:

Proposition 2.4. (a) $\mathrm{NQL}^{QBF} = \mathrm{DQL}^{QBF}$.
(b) *There is an oracle B such that NQL^B is not contained in* $\mathrm{DTIME}[2^{o(n)}]$.

The proof of (a) uses Schnorr's construction and Lemma 2.1, and in fact the DQL machine need only make one query to QBF. Statement (b) holds for the standard oracle B separating NP^B from P^B in [HU79].

The result of [PZ83] that $\oplus \mathrm{P}^{\oplus \mathrm{P}} = \oplus \mathrm{P}$ also carries over because of the quasilinear bound on the total length of all queries in an oracle computation: $\oplus \mathrm{QL}^{\oplus \mathrm{QL}} = \oplus \mathrm{QL}$. However, it is unclear whether the theorem $\mathrm{BPP}^{\mathrm{BPP}} = \mathrm{BPP}$ [Ko82] carries over, because the amplification of success probability to $1 - 2^{-\,\mathrm{polylog}}$ obtainable for BQL seems insufficient. However we are able to show, in the next section, that the well-known $\mathrm{NP} \subseteq \mathrm{BP}[\oplus \mathrm{P}]$ lemma from [VV86] and [Tod91] *does* carry over by a new construction, where all previous known constructions were quadratic or worse.

3. Quasilinear-Time Reduction to Parity

Let $A \in$ NP with witness predicate $B(x, y)$ and length bound $q = q(n)$, and for any x let $S_x := \{ y \in \{0,1\}^q : B(x, y) \}$ be the corresponding witness set, so that $x \in A \iff S_x \neq \emptyset$. Valiant and Vazirani [VV86] constructed a probabilistic NTM N which on any input x of length n first flips q^2-many coins to form q-many vectors $w_1, \ldots, w_q$ each of length q. N also flips coins to form a number j, $0 \leq j \leq q$. Then N guesses $y \in \{0,1\}^q$ and accepts iff $B(x, y)$ and for each i, $1 \leq i \leq j$, $y \cdot w_i = 0$, where $\cdot$ is inner product of vectors over GF(2). Let $N_{w,j}$ stand for the NTM N with $w = w_1, \ldots, w_q$ and j fixed. Clearly whenever $x \notin A$, for all w and i, the number $\#acc(N_{w,j}, x)$ of accepting computations of $N_{w,j}$ on input x is zero. The basic lemma of [VV86] states that whenever $x \in A$, $\Pr_w[(\exists j)\#acc(N_{w,j}, x) = 1] \geq 1/4$. In particular, $\Pr_{w,j}[\#acc(N_{w,j}, x)$ is odd$] \geq 1/4(q + 1)$. A "product construction" yields an N' which flips coins to form just w, guesses strings $y_0, \ldots, y_q$, and achieves

$$x \in A \implies \Pr_w[\#acc(N_w', x) \text{ is odd}] \geq 1/4,$$
$$x \notin A \implies \Pr_w[\#acc(N_w', x) \text{ is odd}] = 0$$

for all x. In symbols, this says that NP $\subseteq$ RP[$\oplus$P] (cf. [Tod91]).

However, in the case $A = SAT$ addressed by [VV86], with $q(n) = n$, N' runs in quadratic time—in fact, N' flips quadratically many coins and makes quadratically many nondeterministic moves. It was well known that by using small families $\mathcal{H} = \{ H_k \}$ of universal$_2$ hash functions [CW79] $h_k : \{0,1\}^q \to \{0,1\}^k$ ($1 \leq k \leq q + 1$) cuts the number $r(n)$ of random bits used to $2q(n)$. The construction of [CRS93] achieves the same effect, still with quadratic runtime when $q(n) = n$. Gupta [Gup93] gives a randomized reduction to parity which achieves constant success probability $3/16$ with only $\nu(n) = q(n)$ nondeterministic moves, but still using q^2-many random bits and quadratic time. The only previous construction which ours does not improve by an order of magnitude in these measures is by Naor and Naor [NN90, NN93], which in this setting boils down to the following: Using $2q + 2$ coin flips, their N determines, for each $k \leq q(n)$, a hash function $h_k \in H_k$. Next N flips $q + 1$ more coins to form $u \in \{0,1\}^{q+1}$. Then N nondeterministically guesses $y \in \{0,1\}^q$ and k, $1 \leq k \leq q + 1$, and accepts iff $B(x, y) \land h_k(y) = 0 \land u_k = 1$. This uses $3q + 3$ random bits, achieves success probability at least $1/8$, and runs in the time to compute h_k, which is $O(q \log q \log\log q)$. Our construction achieves better constants than this and avoids the extra guess of k.

Naor and Naor also mention the idea of using error-correcting codes for similar purposes, ascribing the idea to Bruck with a reference to [ABN$^+$92]. However, using the codes in [ABN$^+$92] appears to require computing exponentiation in finite fields GF(2^m) where the size m of field elements is polynomial in n. This is not known to be possible in quasilinear time, even by randomized algorithms; the sequential method of von zur Gathen [vzG91] takes quadratic time on TMs. The main point of our construction is that by scaling down the size of the field, and using multi-variable polynomials, one can achieve quasi-linear runtime. Our code is similar to those used in recent improvements of "holographic proof systems" [BFLS91, Sud92], and is only inferior to that of [ABN$^+$92] in using $2q - o(q)$ rather than $q + O(1)$ random bits.

Let Γ be an alphabet of size 2^l. We can give Γ the structure of the field $F = \mathrm{GF}(2^l)$; then Γ^n becomes an n-dimensional vector space over F. An $[N, K, D]$ *code* over F is a set $C \subseteq \Gamma^n$ which forms a vector subspace of dimension K (so $\|C\| = 2^K$), such that for all distinct $x, y \in C$, $d_H(x, y) \geq D$, where d_H is Hamming distance. Since C is closed under addition (i.e., a *linear* code), the *minimum distance* D equals the minimum *weight* (i.e., number of non-zero entries over F) of a non-zero codeword. The *rate* of the code is $R = K/N$, and the *density* is given by $\delta = D/N$. Any basis for C forms a $K \times N$ *generator matrix* for the code. If $F = \mathrm{GF}(2)$ we speak of a *binary* code.

The *idea* is to take a $2^q \times 2^{r(n)}$ generator matrix G for a binary code C of constant density $\delta = 1/2 - \epsilon$, and have the probabilistic NTM N work as follows:

1. Flip $r(n)$ coins to choose a column j.

2. Guess a row i, $1 \leq i \leq 2^q$, identified with a possible witness string $y_i \in \{0, 1\}^q$.

3. Accept iff $B(x, y_i) \wedge G(i, j) = 1$.

Suppose $S = S_x$ is nonempty. Then to S there corresponds the unique non-zero codeword $w_S := \sum_{y \in S} G(y, \cdot)$, where the sum is over $\mathrm{GF}(2)$. Then $\#acc(N_j, x)$ is odd iff the jth entry of w_S is a '1'. Since the proportion of non-0 entries of w_S is at least δ, $\Pr_j[\#acc(N_j, x) \text{ is odd}] > \delta$; that is, N reduces A to parity with success probability at least δ. And if S is empty, N has no accepting computations at all. Thus to show $\mathrm{NQL} \subseteq \mathrm{RQL}[\oplus\mathrm{QL}]$, we need to construct C so that $G(i, j)$ is computable in quasilinear time. Our C is the *concatenation* of two simpler codes:

• The *Hadamard code* $\mathcal{H}_k$ over $\{0, 1\}$ of length $n = 2^k$ has n codewords. The codewords can be arranged into an $n \times n$ array with rows and columns indexed by strings $u, v \in \{0, 1\}^k$, and entries $u \cdot v$, where $\cdot$ is inner product over $\mathrm{GF}(2)$. $\mathcal{H}_k$ has distance $d_k = 2^{k-1}$, so $\delta_k = 1/2$ is constant.

• The *full 2^k-ary generalized Reed-Muller code* $\mathcal{R}_{2^k}(d, m)$ of order d, where $d < m(2^k - 1)$, has length $N = 2^{km}$ over the field $F = \mathrm{GF}(2^k)$.[1] Each polynomial $f(x_1, \ldots x_m)$, in m variables over F of total degree at most d, defines the codeword with entries $f(a_1, \ldots, a_m)$, where $\vec{a} = (a_1, \ldots, a_m)$ ranges over all sequences of arguments in F. In the important case $d \leq 2^k - 1$ a generator matrix for this code is easy to describe: it has one row for each monomial $x_1^{i_1} x_2^{i_2} \cdots x_m^{i_m}$ such that $i_1 + i_2 + \ldots + i_m \leq d$. Since $d \leq 2^k - 1$ these monomials are all distinct, and they are all linearly independent, so the dimension is $K = \binom{m+d}{d}$. The well-known property on which these codes are based (cf. [BFLS91, Sud92]) is that for every two distinct polynomials f and g over F of total degree at most d, and for every $I \subseteq F$,

$$|\{ \vec{a} \in I^m : f(\vec{a}) = g(\vec{a}) \}| \leq d|I|^{m-1}. \tag{1}$$

With $I = F$, it follows that the density Δ is at least $1 - d/|F|$.

If we simply regarded $\mathcal{R}_{2^k}(d, m)$ as a binary code of length kN, we would only be able to assert that the density is at least $1/2k$, because two distinct elements $a_1, a_2 \in \mathrm{GF}(2^k)$ might differ in only one out of k places as binary strings. But if we

---

[1] The standard notation is $\mathcal{R}_q(r, m)$ as in [TV91], where q is a prime power and $r < m(q - 1)$. Below, $d = d_0 m$.

apply the Hadamard code to a_1 and a_2, the two resulting strings, though of length 2^k, differ in at least $1/2$ their places, yielding our code C of length $2^k N$ and density $1/2 - \epsilon$, where $\epsilon = d/2|F|$. This is done by step 11. of our construction of N:

1. Input x and ϵ; $n := |x|$, $q := q(n)$

2. $b := \lceil \log_2 q \rceil$ /*block length for exponents*/

3. $d_0 := 2^b - 1$ /*maximum degree in each variable*/

4. $m := \lceil q/b \rceil$ /*number of variables*/

5. $k := \lceil \log_2 d_0 + \log_2 m + \log_2(1/\epsilon) - 1 \rceil$

6. Calculate an irreducible polynomial α of degree k over GF(2)

7. Flip $mk + k$ coins to form $j = \langle a_1, \ldots, a_m, v \rangle$, where $v \in \{0,1\}^k$

8. Guess $y \in \{0,1\}^q$

9. Taking b bits of y at a time, form integers $i_1, i_2, \ldots i_{m-1}, i_m \in \{0, \ldots, d_0\}$. (It is OK for i_m to be truncated.)

10. Compute $u := a_1^{i_1} \cdot a_2^{i_2} \cdots a_m^{i_m}$

11. Compute $G(y,j) := u \cdot v$

12. Accept iff $B(x,y) \wedge G(y,j) = 1$.

Let t_B be the time to compute the witness predicate $B(x,y)$, and let $\log^+ n$ abbreviate $\log n \log\log n \log\log\log n$.

Theorem 3.1. *For any fixed $\epsilon < 1/2$, N accepts A with success probability $1/2 - \epsilon$, making q nondeterministic moves and running in time $O(q \log^+ q)$ (apart from the time to recognize B), and uses a number of random bits bounded by*

$$r = 2q - q \log\log q / \log q + (1 + \log(1/\epsilon))q / \log q + O(\log q).$$

Proof Sketch. Step 10 dominates the running time. To multiply two polynomials of degree $k-1$ over GF(2) and reduce them modulo α in the field GF(2^k) takes time $t_1 = O(k \log k \log\log k)$ on standard Turing machine models (see [AHU74] and [Rab80]). The time to compute a^i in GF(2^k) where $i \leq n$ is $t_2 = O(\log n \cdot 2k \log k \log\log k)$ via repeated squaring. Hence the time to evaluate the monomial is at most $O(mt_2 + mt_1) = O(m \log(n) k \log k \log\log k) = O(n \log^+ n)$, since $m = O(n/\log n)$ and $k = O(\log n)$. $\square$

Corollary 3.2. NQL $\subseteq$ RQL[$\oplus$QL]. $\square$

The first open problem is whether two or more alternations can be done in quasilinear time; that is, whether NQL$^{\text{NQL}} \subseteq$ BQL[$\oplus$QL]. The obstacle is the apparent need to amplify the success probabilities of the second level to $1 - 2^{-q}$, for which straightforward "amplification by repeated trials" takes time q^2. The second is whether the code can be improved and still give quasi-linear runtime. Our codes have rate

$R = K/N = 2^q/2^{(2q-\cdots)}$, which tends to 0 as q increases. Families of codes are known for which R (as well as δ) stays bounded below by a constant; such (families of) codes are called *good*. Good codes require only $q + O(1)$ random bits in the above construction. The codes in [ABN$^+$92, JLJH92, She93] are good, but do not seem to give quasi-linear runtime here.

4.   Search Versus Decision in Quasilinear Time

The classical method of computing partial, multivalued functions using sets as oracles is the *prefix-set* method (cf. [Sel88]). To illustrate, let f be an arbitrary length-preserving, partial function from Σ^* to Σ^*. Define:

$$L_f = \{x\#w \mid w \text{ is a prefix of some value of } f(x)\}.$$

Clearly f is computable in quadratic time using L_f as an oracle. First we observe that for "random" functions f, quadratic time is best possible.

Theorem 4.1. *There exist length-preserving functions $f : \Sigma^* \to \Sigma^*$ with the property that there does not exist an oracle set B relative to which f is computable in less than $n^2 - n$ steps.*

Proof. Let B and an OTM M such that $M^B(x) = f(x)$ on all strings $x \in \{0,1\}^n$ be given, and suppose M^B runs in time $g(n)$. Then the following is a description of f on $\{0,1\}^n$:

- The finite control of M, plus finite descriptions of the function $g(n)$ and "this discussion" (see [LV90]). This has total length some constant C.

- A look-up table for all the strings of length $< n$ which belong to B—this is specifiable by a binary string of length $\sum_{i=0}^{n-1} 2^i = 2^n - 1 < 2^n$.

- For each $x \in \{0,1\}^n$, the answers given by B to those queries z made by M on input x such that $|z| \geq n$. There are at most $g(n)/n$ such queries. All of this is specifiable by a binary string of length $2^n g(n)/n$.

Now let K_f be the *Kolmogorov complexity* of f, relative to some fixed universal Turing machine. Then $C + 2^n + 2^n g(n)/n \geq K_f$, so $g(n) \geq nK_f/2^n - n - nC/2^n$. Since functions $f : \{0,1\}^n \to \{0,1\}^n$ are in 1-1 correspondence with binary strings of length $n2^n$, and (by simple counting) some such strings have Kolmogorov complexity at least $n2^n$, there exist f with $K_f \geq n2^n$. Then $g(n) \geq n^2 - n$. $\qquad\square$

(Remarks: The $n^2 - n$ is close to tight—an upper bound of $g(n) \leq n^2 + 2n \log n$ is achievable by a modification of L_f. By diagonalization one can also construct such functions f which are computable in exponential time.)

Hence the equivalence between functions and sets does not carry over to quasilinear time complexity in general. Theorem 4.1 can be read as saying that Kolmogorov-random functions have so much information that large query strings are needed to encode it. We are interested in whether natural functions in NP, such as witness functions for NP problems, pack information as tightly.

Let L be a language in NP and let B be some polynomial-time witness predicate for L. Define the partial multivalued function f_B by:

$$f_B(x) \mapsto y, \text{if } |y| = q(|x|) \text{ and } B(x, y).$$

Then f_B is called a *search function* for L. The following is a straightforward extension of the standard notion of search reducing to decision in polynomial time [BD76, BBFG91, NOS93] to other time bounds $t(n)$.

Definition 4.1. Let $L \in$ NP and a time bound $t(n)$ be given. Then we say that *search reduces to decision for L in time $t(n)$* if there exists a witness predicate B for L and a $t(n)$ time-bounded deterministic oracle TM M such that for all inputs x, if $x \in L$ then $M^L(x)$ outputs some y such that $f_B(x) \mapsto y$, and if $x \notin L$ then $M^L(x) = 0$.

Let polylog n abbreviate $(\log n)^{O(1)}$ as before. Then DTIME$[2^{\text{polylog}\, n}]$ is often referred to as *quasi-polynomial* time (cf. [Bar92]).

Theorem 4.2. Let $L \in$ NP. If search reduces to decision for L in quasilinear time, then $L \in$ DTIME$[2^{\text{polylog}\, n}]$.

Proof. Let M be the oracle TM from Definition 4.1, and let c and k be constants such that M runs in time $cn \log^k n$. We may suppose that M itself verifies that its output y satisfies $B(x, y)$. Let $f(n) := n/\log n$. Let n_0 be an appropriately chosen constant number; on inputs x of length $< n_0$, whether $x \in L$ is looked up in a table.

Now we define a TM M' which operates as follows on any input x of length $n \geq n_0$: M' simulates M. Whenever M makes a query z and $|z| < n_0$, M' answers from the table. If $|z| > f(n)$, we call z a "large query." Here M' branches, simulating both a "yes" and a "no" answer to z. Finally, if $n_0 \leq |z| \leq f(n)$, then M' calls itself recursively on input z to answer the query. The above is a recursive description of what M' does. The actual machine M' simulates both the recursion and the branching on large queries using a stack, and halts and accepts iff at least one of the simulations of M outputs a string y such that $B(x, y)$ holds. Clearly M' accepts L.

Let $t_{M'}(n)$ denote the running time of M' on inputs of length n. We show that for all n, $t_{M'}(n) \leq 2^{c \log^{k+2} n}$. Since table-lookup takes only linear time, this holds for $n < n_0$. Now consider the binary tree T whose nodes are large queries made by M, and whose edges represent computation paths by M' between large queries. Then T has depth at most $c \log^{k+1} n$ and at most $2^{c \log^{k+1} n}$ branches. The number of small queries on each branch is at most $cn \log^k n$, and each such query has length at most $n/\log n$. Hence the time taken by M' to traverse all branches, namely $t_{M'}(n)$, satisfies the following condition:

$$t_{M'}(n) \leq 2^{c \log^{k+1} n} \cdot cn \log^k n \cdot t_{M'}(n/\log n). \qquad (2)$$

By induction hypothesis, $t_{M'}(n/\log n) \leq 2^{c(\log(n/\log n))^{k+2}}$. Substitution into (2) and some elementary calculation gives

$$t_{M'}(n) \leq 2^{c \log^{k+1} n} \cdot cn \log^k n \cdot 2^{c(\log n - \log\log n)^{k+2}} \leq 2^{c \log^{k+2} n}. \qquad \square$$

Corollary 4.3. *If search reduces to decision for SAT is quasilinear time, then*

$$\text{NP} \subseteq \text{DTIME}[2^{\text{polylog}\, n}].$$

The technique of Theorem 4.2 extends (again with $f(n) = n/\log n$) to show that the quadratic bound on the search-to-decision reduction for SAT is likely to be optimal.

Corollary 4.4. *If there exists an $\epsilon > 0$ such that search reduces to decision for SAT in* $\text{DTIME}[n^{1+\epsilon}]$, *then* $\text{NP} \subseteq \text{DTIME}[2^{n^{\epsilon}}]$.

Stearns and Hunt [SH90] define a language $L \in \text{NP}$ to have *power index* ϵ if ϵ is the infimum of all δ such that $L \in \text{DTIME}[2^{n^{\delta}}]$. They classify familiar NP-complete problems according to known bounds on their power indices, and conjecture that SAT has power index 1. In this setting, Corollary 4.4 can be restated as:

Corollary 4.5. *If there exists an $\epsilon > 0$ such that search reduces to decision for SAT in* $\text{DTIME}[n^{1+\epsilon}]$, *then SAT has power index at most ϵ.*

This establishes a relation between reducing search to decision and the power index of an NP language. However, we now show that the converse is unlikely to be true.

Let EE stand for $\text{DTIME}[2^{2^{O(n)}}]$, and NEE for its nondeterministic counterpart. The classes EE and NEE were considered by Beigel, Bellare, Feigenbaum, and Goldwasser [BBFG91], and there are reasons for believing it unlikely that NEE = EE.

Theorem 4.6. *Suppose* NEE $\neq$ EE. *Then for all $k > 0$ there is a tally language in NP whose power index is at most $1/k$, but for which search does not reduce to decision in polynomial time.*

Proof Sketch. Let T be the tally set constructed in [BBFG91] such that search does not reduce to decision for T in polynomial time, unless NEE = EE. Suppose p is a polynomial such that for all n, all witnesses of the string 0^n are of length $p(n)$. Define:

$$T^k = \{0^{p(n)^k} \mid 0^n \in T\}.$$

It is easy to see that T^k has power index at most $1/k$, since an exhaustive search algorithm recognizes T^k in time $2^{n^{1/k}}$. However if search reduces to decision in polynomial time for T^k, then it does so for T, which is a contradiction. $\qquad\square$

Finally, it is interesting to ask whether there are length-preserving 1-1 functions f which are computable in *qlin* time but not invertible in *qlin* time. Homer and Wang [HW89] construct, for any $k \geq 1$, functions computable in quadratic time which are not invertible in time $O(n^k)$, but their methods seem not to apply for *qlin* time or length-preserving functions. If DQL $\neq$ UQL, then such "quasilinear one-way" functions exist, but unlike the polynomial case (assuming P $\neq$ UP), the converse is not known to hold. We look toward further research which might show that length-preserving functions with certain "pseudorandom" properties cannot be inverted in *qlin* time, unless unlikely collapses of quasilinear classes occur.

References

[ABN+92] N. Alon, J. Bruck, J. Naor, M. Naor, and R. Roth. Construction of asymptotically good low-rate error-correcting codes through pseudo-random graphs. *IEEE Trans. Info. Thy.*, 38(2):509–512, March 1992.

[AHU74] A. Aho, J. Hopcroft, and J. Ullman. *The Design and Analysis of Computer Algorithms.* Addison-Wesley, Reading, Mass., 1974.

[Bar92] D. Mix Barrington. Quasipolynomial size circuit classes. In *Proc. 7th Structures,* pages 86–93, 1992.

[BBFG91] R. Beigel, M. Bellare, J. Feigenbaum, and S. Goldwasser. Languages that are easier than their proofs. In *Proc. 32nd FOCS*, pages 19–28, 1991.

[BD76] A. Borodin and A. Demers. Some comments on functional self-reducibility and the NP hierarchy. Technical Report TR 76-284, Cornell Univ. Comp. Sci. Dept., 1976.

[BFLS91] L. Babai, L. Fortnow, L. Levin, and M. Szegedy. Checking computations in polylogarithmic time. In *Proc. 23rd STOC*, pages 21–31, 1991.

[BG93] J. Buss and J. Goldsmith. Nondeterminism within P. *SIAM J. Comp.*, 22:560–572, 1993.

[CR73] S. Cook and R. Reckhow. Time bounded random access machines. *J. Comp. Sys. Sci.*, 7:354–375, 1973.

[CRS93] S. Chari, P. Rohatgi, and A. Srinivasan. Randomness-optimal unique element isolation, with applications to perfect matching and related problems. In *Proc. 25th STOC*, pages 458–467, 1993.

[CW79] J. Carter and M. Wegman. Universal classes of hash functions. *J. Comp. Sys. Sci.*, 18:143–154, 1979.

[GS89] Y. Gurevich and S. Shelah. Nearly-linear time. In *Proceedings, Logic at Botik '89*, volume 363 of *LNCS*, pages 108–118. Springer Verlag, 1989.

[Gup93] S. Gupta. On isolating an odd number of elements and its applications to complexity theory. Technical Report OSU-CISRC-6/93-TR24, Dept. of Comp. Sci., Ohio State University, 1993.

[HS90] H. Hunt III and R. Stearns. The complexity of very simple Boolean formulas, with applications. *SIAM J. Comp.*, 19:44–70, 1990.

[HU79] J. Hopcroft and J. Ullman. *Introduction to Automata Theory, Languages, and Computation.* Addison–Wesley, Reading, MA, 1979.

[HW89] S. Homer and J. Wang. Absolute results concerning one-way functions and their applications. *Math. Sys. Thy.*, 22:21–35, 1989.

[JLJH92] J. Justesen, K. Larsen, H.E. Jensen, and T. Hoholdt. Fast decoding of codes from algebraic plane curves. *IEEE Trans. Info. Thy.*, 38(1):111–119, January 1992.

[JY90] D. Joseph and P. Young. Self-reducibility: the effects of internal structure on computational complexity. In A. Selman, editor, *Complexity Theory Retrospective*, pages 82–107. Springer Verlag, 1990.

[Ko82] K. Ko. Some observations on the probabilistic algorithms and NP-hard problems. *Inf. Proc. Lett.*, 14:39–43, 1982.

[LL76] R. Ladner and N. Lynch. Relativization of questions about log-space computability. *Math. Sys. Thy.*, 10:19–32, 1976.

[LV90]   M. Li and P. Vitányi. Applications of Kolmogorov complexity in the theory of computation. In A. Selman, editor, *Complexity Theory Retrospective*, pages 147–203. Springer Verlag, 1990).

[NN90]   J. Naor and M. Naor. Small-bias probability spaces. In *Proc. 22nd STOC*, pages 213–223, 1990.

[NN93]   J. Naor and M. Naor. Small-bias probability spaces: efficient constructions and applications. *SIAM J. Comp.*, 22:838–856, 1993.

[NOS93] A. Naik, M. Ogiwara, and A. Selman. P-selective sets, and reducing search to decision vs. self-reducibility. In *Proc. 8th Structures*, pages 52–64, 1993.

[PZ83]   C. H. Papadimitriou and S. Zachos. Two remarks on the power of counting. In *The 6th GI Conference on Theoretical Computer Science*, Lecture Notes in Computer Science No. 145, pages 269–276. Springer Verlag, 1983.

[Rab80] M. Rabin. Probabilistic algorithms in finite fields. *SIAM J. Comp.*, pages 273–280, 1980.

[Sch76] C. Schnorr. The network complexity and the Turing machine complexity of finite functions. *Acta Informatica*, 7:95–107, 1976.

[Sch78] C. Schnorr. Satisfiability is quasilinear complete in NQL. *J. ACM*, 25:136–145, 1978.

[Sel88] A. Selman. Natural self-reducible sets. *SIAM J. Comp.*, 17:989–996, 1988.

[SH86]   R. Stearns and H. Hunt III. On the complexity of the satisfiability problem and the structure of NP. Technical Report 86–21, Dept. of Comp. Sci., SUNY at Albany, 1986.

[SH90]   R. Stearns and H. Hunt III. Power indices and easier hard problems. *Math. Sys. Thy.*, 23:209–225, 1990.

[She93] B.-Z. Shen. A Justesen construction of binary concatenated codes than asymptotically meet the Zyablov bound for low rate. *IEEE Trans. Info. Thy.*, 39(1):239–242, January 1993.

[Sto77] L. Stockmeyer. The polynomial time hierarchy. *Theor. Comp. Sci.*, 3:1–22, 1977.

[Sud92] M. Sudan. *Efficient checking of polynomials and proofs and the hardness of approximation problems*. PhD thesis, University of California, Berkeley, 1992.

[Tod91] S. Toda. PP is as hard as the polynomial-time hierarchy. *SIAM J. Comp.*, 20:865–877, 1991.

[TV91]   M. Tsfasman and S. Vladut. *Algebraic-Geometric Codes*, volume 58 of *Mathematics and Its Applications (Soviet Series)*. Kluwer Academic, Dordrecht, 1991.

[VV86]   L. Valiant and V. Vazirani. NP is as easy as detecting unique solutions. *Theor. Comp. Sci.*, 47:85–93, 1986.

[vzG91] J. von zur Gathen. Efficient exponentiation in finite fields. In *Proc. 32nd FOCS*, pages 384–391, 1991.

[Wra77] C. Wrathall. Complete sets and the polynomial-time hierarchy. *Theor. Comp. Sci.*, 3:23–33, 1977.

[Wra78] C. Wrathall. Rudimentary predicates and relative computation. *SIAM J. Comp.*, 7:194–209, 1978.

[WW86]   K. Wagner and G. Wechsung. *Computational Complexity*. D. Reidel, 1986.

Space-efficient deterministic simulation of probabilistic automata

(extended abstract)

Ioan I. Macarie
Department of Computer Science
University of Rochester
Rochester, NY 14627

Abstract

Given a description of a probabilistic automaton (one-head probabilistic finite automaton or probabilistic Turing machine) and an input string x of length n, we ask how much space does a deterministic Turing machine need in order to decide the acceptance of an input string by that automaton?

The question is interesting even in the case of one-head one-way probabilistic finite automata. We call *(rational) stochastic languages* ($S_{rat}^{>}$) the class of languages recognized by these devices with rational transition probabilities and rational cutpoint. Our main results are as follows:

- The (proper) inclusion of $S_{rat}^{>}$ in Dspace(log n), which is optimal (i.e. $S_{rat}^{>} \not\subset$ Dspace(o(log n))). The previous upper bounds were Dspace(n) [Dieu 1972], [Wang 1992] and Dspace(log n log log n) [Jung 1984].

- The inclusion of the languages recognized by $S(n) \in O(\log n)$ space-bounded probabilistic Turing machines in Dspace(min($2^{S(n)} \log n$, log n(S(n)+ log log n))). The previous upper bound was Dspace(log n(S(n) + log log n)) [Jung 1984].

Of independent interest is our technique to compare numbers given in terms of their values modulo a sequence of primes, $p_1 < p_2 < \cdots < p_n = O(n^a)$ (where a is some constant) in $O(\log n)$ deterministic space.

1   Background

In this section, we present the definitions of the concepts used in this paper and some basic theorems about probabilistic automata.

Definition 1 [Rabin 1963] A *(one-way one-head) probabilistic finite automaton* (PFA) A is a 5-tuple:

$$A = (Q, \Sigma, \pi, \{M(x)|x \in \Sigma\}, F),$$

where:

Q is the (finite) set of states,

Σ is the alphabet of input symbols,

π is the initial state-distribution vector

F is the set of final states, $F \subseteq Q$,

$M(x)$ is a stochastic matrix of order $n = |Q|$, whose component $m_{ij}(x)$ is the probability of transition from the state s_i into the state s_j under the input x and $\sum_{j=1}^{n} m_{ij}(x) = 1$.

Definition 2 [Tur 1968] A *generalized (one-way one-head) probabilistic finite automaton* (GPFA) is a 5-tuple as above with the distinction that π in a n-dimensional real vector (and not a distribution vector) and the transition matrices $M(x), \forall x \in \Sigma$, are real matrices (not constrained to be stochastic). This concept is also known as *weighted finite automaton*.

Let Σ^* the set of words over the alphabet Σ , and let ϵ be the empty word. A word matrix $M(y), y \in \Sigma^*$ is defined $M(\epsilon) = I$, I being the identity matrix of order n and $M(y) = M(x_1) \cdots M(x_k)$, where $y = x_1 \ldots x_k$, $x_i \in \Sigma$.

The distribution of a probabilistic automaton A after scanning the word $y \in \Sigma^*$ is $r_A(y) = \pi M(y)$. The probability that A accepts y is $p_A(y) = \pi M(y)\eta^F$ where η^F is the column vector whose i-th component is equal to 1 or 0 depending if the i-th state is final or not.

For a GPFA A, we define the acceptance function p_A in a similar way, but in this case $p_A : \Sigma^* \to R$ and it is not a probability function anymore.

Definition 3 [Rabin 1963] The class of *stochastic languages* (S$^>$) is defined as containing the languages of the form:

$$T(A, \lambda) = \{y \in \Sigma^* | p_A(y) > \lambda\}$$

where A is a PFA and λ is a real number in [0,1], called *cutpoint*. If $\forall y \in \Sigma^* \Rightarrow |p_A(y) - \lambda| > \epsilon$, then λ is called *isolated cutpoint*.

Definition 4 [Starke 1966]The class of languages S$^=$ is defined as containing the languages of the form $T^=(A, \lambda) = \{y \in \Sigma^* | P_A(y) = \lambda\}$ where A is a PFA and λ is a cutpoint in [0,1].

Definition 5 The class of languages S$^{\neq}$ is defined as containing the languages of the form $T^{\neq}(A, \lambda) = \{y \in \Sigma^* | P_A(y) \neq \lambda\}$, where A is a PFA and λ is a cutpoint in [0,1].

Definition 6 [Tur 1969b] A *rational stochastic language* for the class S^a (where $a \in \{>, =, \neq\}$) is a language $L = T_{rat}^a(A, \lambda)$ where A is a PFA with the elements of its stochastic matrices and of its initial state-distribution vector all rationals and λ is a rational cutpoint. We have defined in this way S$^>_{rat}$, S$^=_{rat}$, S$^{\neq}_{rat}$.

We use the notations 2U-PFA$_{rat}$ (2-PFA$_{rat}$) for the class of languages recognized by one-head (isolated cutpoint) two-way probabilistic finite automata with rational transition probabilities.

The definition for probabilistic Turing machine (PTM) can be found in [Gill 1977]. We use the notations PrSpace(f(n)) for the classes of languages recognized by PTM in $f(n)$ space with unbounded-error. The computation of a space-bounded PTM or of a probabilistic finite automaton on an input string can be viewed as a Markov process that is defined by its configuration transition matrix. This approach is developed in Section 3.

Finally, we explain some of the notations we use in this paper:

- $\subsetneq$ means proper inclusion,

- $\subset$ means inclusion (not necessarily proper),

- $|x|$ represents the length of x if x is a string, or the absolute value of x if x is a number, or the number of elements of x if x is a set,

- $\|X\|$ is the norm of the matrix X defined by $\|X\| = \max_i(\sum_j |x_{ij}|)$.

In what follows, we call $S_{rat}^>$, $S_{rat}^=$ and $S_{rat}^{\neq}$ (rational) stochastic classes. All the probabilistic automata, used in this paper have rational transition probabilities, so we can drop the word "rational" without creating misunderstanding.

We mention some closure properties of these classes and we present relations between these classes and the Chomsky's hierarchy.

Proposition 1 *[Dieu 1971a] The classes* $S_{rat}^=$ *and* $S_{rat}^{\neq}$ *are closed under intersection and union, but are not closed under complement. The complement of each class is the other class.*

Theorem 1 *[Tur 1969a]* $S_{rat}^{\neq}$ *and* $S_{rat}^=$ *are properly included in* $S_{rat}^>$.

Proposition 2 *[Buk 1967] The class of regular languages is properly included in* $S_{rat}^= \bigcap S_{rat}^{\neq}$.

The stochastic classes contain languages which are not context free; but, on the other hand, there are context free languages which are not contained in none of the stochastic classes. One example for the second claim is $\{x1y|\, x, y \in (0+1)^*, |x| = |y|\} \in CFL - S_{rat}^>$. In fact this language is not even in S$^>$ [DwSt 1990],[Rav 1992]. Using the closure properties of $S_{rat}^=$, we can prove that $\{a^n b^n | n \in N\}$, $\{a^n b^n c^n | n \in N\} \in S_{rat}^=$ [Ma 1993]. We arrive at the conclusion that the stochastic classes do not fit in the Chomsky's hierarchy. The next step is to compare them with the deterministic space-bounded complexity classes. This problem will be investigated in section 2.

We mention now a result relating complexity classes defined by one-way and two-way probabilistic finite automata.

Theorem 2 *[Ka 1989]* $S_{rat}^> = $2U-PFA$_{rat}$.

2 Space-efficient deterministic simulation of stochastic languages

In this section we compare the stochastic complexity classes we have defined so far ($S^=_{rat}$, $S^{\neq}_{rat}$, $S^>_{rat}$) with the deterministic space-bounded complexity classes. The main result is the $O(\log n)$ deterministic space simulation of the class $S^>_{rat}$. Lemma 3, used to compare integers given in terms of their residue representations, is of independent interest.

Let A be a PFA. Its transition probabilities are rational numbers. In constant space we can find the least common multiple (call it b) of the denominators of the transition probabilities and of the components of the initial-distribution vector π. Without loss of generality, we suppose $\pi = (1, 0, \cdots, 0)$. We compute the accepting probability for the input string $w = w_1 \cdots w_n$ of length n:

$$p(w) = \pi M(w_1) \cdots M(w_n) \eta_F^T$$

$$= (1/b^n)\pi M'(w_1) \cdots M'(w_n)\eta_F^T$$

where each matrix $M'(w_i) = bM(w_i)$ has integer elements in the interval [0,b]. Every element of $M'(w_i)$ can be computed in constant space. We have $p(w) = (1/b^n)p'(w)$ where $p'(w)$ is the word function generated by a GPFA having $M'(w_i)$ as transition matrices ($p'(w) = \pi M'(w_1) \cdots M'(w_n)\eta^T$).

Comparing $p(w)$ with $1/2$ is equivalent to compare the integers $2p'(w)$ and b^n. We pick a constant c such that

$$\prod_{i=1}^{cn} p_i > 2^{cn} > 4b^n$$

and p_i is the i-th prime starting with $p_1 = 3$. (The fact that we do not use the prime 2 is not compulsory because we can avoid using Lemma 1 but we have to modify Lemmas 2 and 3 accordingly [DMS 1993].) Then both $2p'(w)$ and b^n are natural numbers smaller than $\prod_{i=1}^{cn} p_i - 1$. We compute these numbers modulo $p_1, \cdots, p_{cn}$. The advantage to use the multiple residue representation is that, at any given time, we do not have to store all the residues, but only a finite number of them. Of course, we have to be able to compute each such residue in a small amount of space when we need it. In this way we use only $O(\log p_{cn}) = O(\log n)$ deterministic space. Note that the i-th prime can be found in $O(\log i)$ deterministic space. The computation of $2p'(w) \pmod{p_k}$ for each $k = 1, \cdots, cn$ requires $O(\log p_k) \in O(\log n)$ space. It is enough to keep all the elements of the partial product matrix

$$M'(w_1 \ldots w_j) = \prod_{i=1}^{j} M'(w_i) \bmod p_k$$

(for $j = 1, \ldots, n$) in the working space. We remark that their number is constant. The computation of $b^n \bmod p_k$ for each $k = 1, \cdots, cn$ also requires only $O(\log n)$ space.

In what follows, the representation of a number modulo a set of primes (that is determined by the context) will be called *residue representation*. We conclude that we can compute the residue representations of $2p'(w)$ and b^n in $O(\log n)$ space, for one prime at a time. Now we turn to the presentation of the main results of this section.

Theorem 3 $S_{rat}^{=} \subsetneq Dspace(\log n);\ S_{rat}^{\neq} \subsetneq Dspace(\log n)$ *and both inclusions are optimal.*

Proof. We prove the first relation. Because $Dspace(\log n)$ is closed under complementation [Sip 1980] and $S_{rat}^{\neq}$ is the complement of $S_{rat}^{=}$, it results the second relation.

Let L belongs to $S_{rat}^{=}$ and let A be a PFA that recognizes L and computes the probability p. Let w be an input word of length n.

$$w \in L \Longleftrightarrow 1/2 = p(w) \Longleftrightarrow 2p'(w) = b^n.$$

We check the last equality (whose members are integers) modulo the first cn primes. If $2p'(w) \bmod p_i = b^n \bmod p_i$ for all $i = 1, \ldots, cn$ then $w \in L$ else $w \notin L$. We have obtained that the acceptance or rejection of w can be done deterministically in $O(\log n)$ space. It results $L \in Dspace(\log n)$. The time required by this simulation is $O(n^2)$.

Both inclusions are proper because the classes $S_{rat}^{=}$ and $S_{rat}^{\neq}$ are not closed under complementation. Using the relation $\{a^n b^n \mid n \in N\} \in Dspace(\Omega(\log n))$ [LeStHa65] we obtain that both inclusions are optimal (i.e. it is not possible to include $S_{rat}^{=}$ and $S_{rat}^{\neq}$ in $Dspace(o(\log n))$). $\square$

In what follows, we present a deterministic space simulation for $S_{rat}^{>}$. The difference from the proof of Theorem 3 is that, at a given moment, we have to compare the numbers $2p'(w)$ and b^n after computing their residue representations. The standard procedure is to recompute the numbers from their residue representations (using the Chinese Remainder Theorem), and to compare them bit by bit. This approach was used by Jung [Jung 1984] who made crucial use of the results of Reif [Reif 1986] and Borodin [Bo 1977]. Using this technique we obtain only $S_{rat}^{>} \subsetneq Dspace(\log n \log \log n)$.

The main remark about the technique mentioned above is that we do not need to recompute the numbers (whose residue representations we already have) in order to decide which is bigger. The comparison can be done working directly on their residue representations. In what follows we focus on this idea and we prove $S_{rat}^{>} \subsetneq Dspace(\log n)$ (Theorem 4). We describe first a technique to compare numbers (whose residue representations can be deterministically obtained in $O(\log n)$ space) using only $O(\log n)$ space. This result is contained in Lemmas 1-3.

Lemma 1 *If N is an odd integer and $X, Y \in [0, N-1]$ are also integers then $X \geq Y$ iff $(X - Y)$ has the same parity as $(X - Y) \bmod N$.*

Proof. It results from the fact that N is odd and

$$(X - Y) \bmod N = \begin{cases} (X - Y) & if \quad X \geq Y \\ N + (X - Y) & if \quad X < Y \end{cases}$$

□

Lemma 2 *For every finite ascending sequence of primes $p_1, \cdots, p_n$, for every integer $X \in [0, \prod_{i=1}^{n} p_i)$, if we can compute the residue representation of X (modulo these primes) in $O(\log p_n)$ deterministic space, then for every positive integer N we can compute $X \bmod N$ in $O(\log p_n + \log N)$ deterministic space.*

Proof. Let $X = (x_1, \cdots, x_n)$ the residue representation of $X \in [0, \prod_{i=1}^{n} p_i)$ modulo $p_1, \cdots, p_n$ and let $M_n = \prod_{i=1}^{n} p_i$. Using the Chinese Remainder Theorem we have:

$$X = \sum_{i=1}^{n} (x_i c_i)_{p_i} \frac{M_n}{p_i} - r \cdot M_n,$$

where $r \in [0, n]$, $c_i \frac{M_n}{p_i} = 1 \pmod{p_i}$ and $(x_i c_i)_{p_i}$ means $x_i c_i \bmod p_i$. It results

$$r = \sum_{i=1}^{n} \frac{(x_i c_i)_{p_i}}{p_i} - \frac{X}{M_n},$$

where $0 \leq \frac{X}{M_n} < 1$ and $r = \sum_{i=1}^{n} \frac{(x_i c_i)_{p_i}}{p_i} \in [0, n)$.
In what follows, we will show how to compute r using small space. We compute each $\frac{(x_i c_i)_{p_i}}{p_i}$ with $(k+1)\log n$ exact digits and then we sum them up. We get the number $A_0.A_1 \cdots A_k A_{k+1}$ where $A_i, i = 0, k+1$ are blocks of $\log n$ digits, and $A_0 \in [0, n)$ is the integer part of the sum. The value k is obtained from the condition:

$$\frac{M_n}{n^k} < \frac{M_{n-1}}{4} \iff n^k > 4 \cdot p_n, \text{ for all } n \in N \text{ greater than a threshold.}$$

(For example, if the sequence $(p_i), i = 1, n$ contains the first n odd primes then we can take $k = 2$.) It is possible to have $(n-1)$-unit carry from the right of the A_{k+1} block in an exact computation. Furthemore, the block A_k can get at most one unit carry from the block A_{k+1}. It results that the bits in the blocks $A_i, (i = 0, k)$ are exact or are affected by one-unit carry to the block A_k. In fact our computation error is $1/n^k$. If we can compute exactly A_0 then $r = A_0$ and we are done. If all the blocks $A_i, i = 1, k$ have all their bits equal to 1, then a carry from the block A_{k+1} can increment A_0 and this is the only case when A_0 is affected by our computation error. In conclusion we test if all the blocks $A_i, (i = 1, k)$ have all their bits equal to 1, if not we stop returning $r = A_0$ else we continue with our investigation to decide whether $r = A_0$ or $r = A_0 + 1$. In this case we have:

$$X \in [M_n - \frac{M_n}{n^k}, M_n] \text{ or } X \in [0, \frac{M_n}{n^k}]$$

because our computation error is $< 1/n^k$. In order to treat both variants in a uniform way, we consider a number in the interval $(M_n/2, M_n)$ negative and a number in the interval $[0, M(n)/2)$ positive.

For every prime $p > 2$, we define the integer function $(smod \ p)$ defined on integers and with values in the interval $(-p/2, p/2]$ by:

$$(X \ smod \ a) \ \text{mod} \ a = X \ \text{mod} \ a,$$

for every integer X. The function $smod \ p$ is similar with the standard $mod \ p$ function but its values are in the interval $(-p/2, p/2]$. The previous inclusion relations are equivalent to:

$$X \ smod \ M_n \in (-\frac{M_n}{n^k}, \frac{M_n}{n^k}).$$

Now, our goal is to find the sign of $X \ smod \ M_n$.

We solve this problem recursively. If $Y \ smod \ M_{n-1}$ is the number having the residue representation $(x_1, \cdots, x_{n-1})$ then we have the recurrence:

$$X \ smod \ M_n = Y \ smod \ M_{n-1} + \alpha M_{n-1},$$

where α is integer in the interval $(-p_n/2, \cdots, p_n/2]$. From the fact that $X smod \ M_n \in (-\frac{M_n}{n^k}, \frac{M_n}{n^k}) \subset (-\frac{M_{n-1}}{4}, \frac{M_{n-1}}{4})$, (the value k has been computed in order to make this last inclusion relation true) and $Y \ smod \ M_{n-1} \in (-\frac{M_{n-1}}{2}, \frac{M_{n-1}}{2})$ it results $\alpha = 0$ in the previous recurrence. (This observation belongs to Dietz [Dietz 1993].) It results:

$$X \ smod \ M_n = Y \ smod \ M_{n-1} \in (-\frac{M_{n-1}}{4}, \frac{M_{n-1}}{4}),$$

and we have to compute the sign of $Y \ smod \ M_{n-1}$.

In conclusion, we have to decide whether $Y \ smod \ M_{n-1} \in [0, \frac{M_{n-1}}{4})$ and to return $r = A_0 + 1$ in this case, or if $Y smod \ M_{n-1} \in (-\frac{M_{n-1}}{4}, 0)$ and then $r = A_0$. We continue the recursion as above.

After computing r, using the Chinese Remainder Theorem, we can easily compute X mod N using only multiplications and additions modulo N.$\Box$

Lemma 3 *Consider* $p_1, p_2 \cdots, p_n$ *strictly increasing odd primes and* $M_n = \prod_{i=1}^{n} p_i$. *If for two integers* $X, Y \in [0, M_n - 1]$ *we can compute their residue represen-tation in* $O(\log p_n)$ *deterministic space then we can decide* $X > Y, X = Y$ *or* $X < Y$ *in* $O(\log p_n)$ *deterministic space.*

Proof. Let $X = (x_1, \cdots, x_n)$, $Y = (y_1, \cdots, y_n)$ the residue representation of X and Y and let

$$Z = ((x_1 - y_1) \ \text{mod} \ p_1, \cdots, (x_n - y_n) \ \text{mod} \ p_n)$$

$$= (X - Y) \ \text{mod} \ M_n.$$

We compute the parity of X, Y, and Z using Lemma 2 (with $N = 2$), we check if $Z = 0$ and we apply Lemma 1 to find the order relation between X and Y. Every operation is done in $O(\log p_n)$ deterministic space. □

This lemma has a crucial importance in proving the most important results of this paper. It gives us a cheap tool (from the point of view of space complexity) to compare numbers having their residue representations. Other applications of this technique can be found in [DMS 1993]. Davida and Litow, independently, propose another method to efficiently compare numbers given their residue representations [DL 1991]. The two method turn out to have similar strength. Although one was expressed in the setting of deterministic space and the other in the setting of parallel time, they can easily be adapted to the other context. A more detailed comparison between them can be found in [DMS 1993].

Theorem 4 $S^{>}_{rat} \subsetneq \text{Dspace}(\log n)$ *and the inclusion is optimal.*

Proof. We work with odd primes and we follow the method presented at the begining of this section until the moment when we have to compare two integers having their residue representations. Then, we use the result from Lemma 3. The time required by this simulation is $O(n^3)$.

The inclusion is proper ($\{x1y | x, y \in (0+1)^*, |x| = |y|\} \in \text{Dspace}(\log n) - S^{>}_{rat}$) and it is optimal ($S^{=}_{rat}$ is optimally included in $\text{Dspace}(\log n)$ and $S^{=}_{rat} \subsetneq S^{>}_{rat}$). □

This theorem improves the result of Dieu [Dieu 1972] ($S^{>}_{rat} \subsetneq \text{Dspace}(n)$).

Corollary 1 $2\text{U-PFA}_{rat} \subsetneq \text{Dspace}(\log n)$ *and the inclusion is optimal.*

Proof. We use the equality $S^{>}_{rat} = 2\text{U-PFA}_{rat}$. □

This corolary improves the result of Wang [Wang 1992] ($2\text{U-PFA} \subsetneq \text{Dspace}(n)$) and the result of Jung [Jung 1984] ($\text{PrSpace}(O(1)) \subsetneq \text{Dspace}(\log n \log \log n)$).

3   Space-efficient deterministic simulations of $O(\text{lo}$ space-bounded probabilistic Turing machines

The main result of this section is a space-efficient deterministic simulation of small-space-bounded probabilistic Turing machines.

Theorem 5 *For any probabilistic space-constructible functions* $S(n) \in O(\log n)$, $\text{PrSpace}(S(n))$ *is included in*

$$\text{Dspace}(\min(2^{S(n)} \log n, \log n(S(n) + \log \log n))).$$

Proof. Let A be an $S(n) \in O(\log n)$ space-bounded PTM, and x an input word of length n. Without loss of generality, we suppose that A has only one accepting configuration, one rejecting configuration and that the computation

- Probabilistic Turing machines with space bound $S(n) \in o(\log\log\log n)$ can be simulated deterministically in $O(2^{S(n)} \log n)$ space.The existance of languages with probabilistic space complexities at this level was pointed out by Freivalds [Fre 1981]. In the nondeterministic case, on the other hand, there are no such languages, since there is a space complexity gap below $\log\log n$.

Our main tool for proving these results is a new technique to deterministically compare numbers (given in terms of their residue representations) in small space. We turn now to some open problems.

The main limitation in the proof of Theorem 5 is that we are able to use only the bandwidth of the matrix, but not its sparse structure, within the bandwidth. We are looking for more sophisticated algorithms for inverting matrices, able to take advantage of the bandwidth combined with the sparsity.

Another question is how to take further advantage of the fact that we can do small modifications on the configuration transition matrices when we try to invert them.

5 Acknowledgments

I am very grateful to Joel Seiferas and Paul Dietz for many and valuable discussions about this subject as well as for reading an earlier version of this paper and suggesting significant improvements. I also thank Helmut Jurgensen for his comments on a recent version of this paper and Marius Zimand and Bruce Litow for bringing to my attention the paper by Davida and Litow [DL 1991].

References

[Bo 1977] Borodin, A. On relating time and space to size and depth. SIAM J. Comput. 6, 1977, pp. 733-744.

[Buk 1967] Bukharaev R. On the representability of events in probabilistic automata. Prob. methods and Cybernetics, V, Kazan, 1967, pp. 7-20 (in Russian).

[DL 1991] Davida, G.I., and Litow, B. Fast parallel arithmetic via modular representation. SIAM J. Comput. 20, 1991, pp. 756-765.

[Dietz 1993] Dietz, P. Personal communication. April 1993.

[DMS 1993] Dietz, P., Macarie, I., and Seiferas, J. Bits and Relative Order from Residues, Space Efficiently. TR 464, July 1993, Dept. of Computer Science, Univ. of Rochester.

[Dieu 1971a] Dieu, P.D. On a Class of Stochastic Languages. Zietschr. f. math. Logik und Grundlagen d. Math. 17, 1971, pp. 421-425.

[Dieu 1972] Dieu, P.D. On a Necessary Condition for Stochastic Languages. Electronische Informationsverarbeitung und Kybernetik EIK 8, 10, 1972, pp. 575-588.

[DwSt 1990] Dwork, C., and Stockmeyer, L. A time complexity gap for two-way Probabilistic Finite-state Automata. Siam J. Comput. Vol. 19, No. 6, pp 1011-1023, December 1990.

[Fre 1981] Freivalds, R. Probabilistic two-way machines. Proceedings, Int. Sympos. Math. Found. of Comput. Sci., Lecture Notes in Computer Science Vol. 118, Springer, 1981, pp. 33-45.

[Gill 1977] Gill, J. Computational complexity of probabilistic Turing machines. SIAM J. Comput. 6,No 4, 1977, pp. 675-695.

[GoVL 1983] Golub, G., and Van Loan, C. Matrix Computations. The Johns Hopkins University Press, Baltimore, Maryland, 1983.

[Jung 1984] Jung, H. On probabilistic tape complexity and fast circuits for matrix inversion problems. Proc. ICALP 1984, LNCS 172, pp. 281-291.

[Ka 1989] Kaneps, J. Stochasticity of the languages recognizable by 2-way finite probabilistic automata. Diskretnaya Matematika, Vol. 1, No 4, 1989, pp. 63-77 (Russian).

[LeStHa65] Lewis II, P.M., Stearn, R., and Hartmanis, J. Memory bounds for recognition of context-free and context-sensitive languages. IEEE Conference Record on Switching Circuit Theory and Logical Design, 1965, pp. 191-202.

[Ma 1993] Macarie, I. Closure properties of stochastic languages. TR441, Jan 1993, Dept. of Comp. Science, Univ. of Rochester

[MoSu 1982] Monien, B. and Sudborough I. H. On eliminating nondeterminism from Turing machines which use less than logarithm worktape space. Theoretical Computer Science 21, 1982, pp. 237-253.

[Rabin 1963] Rabin, M.O. Probabilistic automata. Information and control, 6, 1963, pp. 230-244.

[Reif 1986] Reif, J. Logarithmic depth circuits for algebraic functions. SIAM J. Comput., 15, No 1, 1986, pp. 231-242.

[Rav 1992] Ravikumar, B. Some Observations on 2-way Probabilistic Finite Automata. TR92-208, May 1992, Dept. of Comp. Science and Statistics, Univ. of Rhode Island.

[RuSiTo82] Ruzzo, W., Simon, J.,and Tompa, M. Space-bounded hierarchies and probabilistic computation. 14th Annual ACM Symposium on Theory of Computing, 1982, pp. 215-223.

[Sim 1977] Simon, J. On the difference between one and many. 4th Coll. on Automata,Languages and Programming, 1977, LNCS 52, pp. 480-491.

[Sip 1980] Sipser, M. Halting space-bounded Computation. Theoretical Computer Science 10, 1980, pp. 335-338.

[Starke 1966] Starke, P. Stochastische Ereignisse und Wortmengen. Zietschr. f. math. Logik und Grundlagen d. Math. 12, 1966, pp. 61-68.

[Stone 1973] Stone, H. An efficient parallel algorithm for the solution of a tridiagonal linear system of equations. JACM 20, No 1, 1973, pp. 27-38.

[Tur 1968] Turakainen, P. On Stochastic Languages. Information and Control 12, 1968, pp. 304-313.

[Tur 1969a] Turakainen, P. On languages representable in rational probabilistic automata. Ann. Acad. Sci. Fenn. Ser. A I 439, 1969.

[Tur 1969b] Turakainen, P. Generalized automata and stochastic languages. Proc. Amer. Math. Soc. 21, 1969, pp. 303-309.

[Wang 1992] Wang, J. A note on two-way probabilistic automata. IPL 43, 1992, pp. 321-326.

$$G_n \models \varphi(\bar{c}, \bar{d}) \quad \Leftrightarrow \quad G_n \models \varphi(\pi_i(\bar{c}), \pi_i(\bar{d})) \tag{2.8}$$

It follows from Equation 2.8 that if $G_n \models \varphi_d(\bar{c}, \bar{d})$ and $\bar{d}$ includes a vertex with subscript i, then so does $\bar{c}$. (Otherwise, $\pi_i(\bar{c}) = \bar{c}$, but, $\pi_i(\bar{d}) \neq \bar{d}$ and thus $\bar{c}$ has two outgoing φ-edges.)

It follows that over the graphs $G_n, n = 1, 2, \ldots$ DTC(φ) is equivalent to a first-order formula. Thus over these graphs, (FO + DTC) = (FO). Of course reachability is not first-order expressible over the G_n's. (This follows for example from Gaifman's theorem, see Theorem 4.2.)

To show that reachability is not expressible in (FO + COUNT + DTC), we first note that the above argument shows that on the G_n's, (FO + COUNT + DTC) is equal to (FO + COUNT). It now remains to show that (FO + COUNT) cannot express reachability over the G_n's.

The automorphism of the G_n's rendered the DTC operator useless. Now that DTC is gone we lose no generality in considering slightly simpler graphs. Let D_n be the induced subgraph of G_n restricted to the vertices $\{a_1, a_2, \ldots, a_{2n}\}$. In D_n, let $s = a_1$, and $t = a_n$, so that t is reachable from s in D_n. Let D'_n be the same graph but with $t = a_{2n}$, so t is not reachable from s in D'_n. We prove:

Lemma 2.9 *No sentence from (FO + COUNT) is true for all the D_n's and false for all the D'_n's.*

Proof We just have room for a sketch: We use the Ehrenfeucht-Fraïssé counting game of [CFI92] to prove that D_n and D'_n agree on all sentences from (FO + COUNT) of quantifier-rank $\lfloor \lg(n) - 1 \rfloor$. We must show that Player II – the Duplicator – wins the $\lfloor \lg(n) - 1 \rfloor$-move counting game on D_n and D'_n. Consider the standard winning strategy for the Duplicator in the game without counting. This induces a 1:1 correspondence between points that could be chosen at any move by Player I – the Spoiler – and the appropriate response in that game by the Duplicator. Thus, in the counting game the Duplicator can safely match any set chosen by the Spoiler by a set of the same cardinality. $\square$

This completes the proof of Theorem 2.7. $\square$

Note that this theorem is not very satisfying because rather than proving that L $\neq$ NL, it just shows the weakness of the model: It is easy for (FO + DTC) to express reachability over the G_n's in the presence of ordering: Let

$$N(x, x') \equiv E(x, x') \wedge (\forall z)(E(x, z) \rightarrow x' \leq z), \qquad \text{then,}$$
$$\text{PATH}(u, v) \equiv (\exists w)[\text{DTC}(N(x, x'))(u, w) \wedge (v = w \vee E(w, v))]$$

This definition also works in the presence of a local ordering, cf. Definition 3.1.

3 The JAG Model: Locally Ordered Graphs

In this section we define the JAG model. We will see that the JAG model is somewhat weaker than (FO + DTC) over locally ordered graphs, cf. Theorem 3.5. When the JAG is applied to ordered graphs it has the same power as (FO + DTC) on ordered graphs, i.e. exactly L, cf. Proposition 3.6.

As we have indicated, an important issue concerning the power of JAGs is that they take as input locally ordered graphs. We thus first define:

Definition 3.1 Local Ordering. Consider a graph

$$G = \langle \{0, 1, \ldots, n-1\}, \{v_0, v_1, \ldots, v_{n-1}\} \leq, 0, \mathbf{m}, E, F, s, t \rangle$$

in which F is a ternary relation on vertices. Suppose that for each vertex, v, $F(v, \cdot, \cdot)$ is a total ordering on the vertices w for which there is an edge from v to w. Then F is called a *local ordering* on (the outgoing edges of) G, and G is called a *locally ordered* graph.

The following observation gives an alternate way to view local orderings:

Observation 3.2 *In $(FO + DTC)$ one can express for locally ordered graphs the relation $E_i(v, w)$ meaning that vertex w is the head of the ith edge out of v. (Here i is a number variable, not a constant.)*

Proof Using (FO + DTC) we can express the 1:1 correspondence between the numbers $0, 1, \ldots, i$ and the first $i + 1$ edges out of v. We first say that a vertex z is the head of the zeroth edge out of v:

$$\zeta(z) \equiv (E(v, z) \wedge (\forall w)(E(v, w) \to F(v, z, w))$$

Then we say that there is a φ-path from the pair $\langle j, x \rangle$ to the pair $\langle j + 1, y \rangle$ iff y is the head of the next edge out of v after x:

$$\varphi(j, x, k, y) \equiv (k = j + 1) \wedge x \neq y \wedge F(v, x, y) \wedge (\forall u)[(F(v, x, u) \wedge F(v, u, y)) \to (x = u \vee y = u)]$$

Finally,

$$E_i(v, w) \equiv (\exists z)(\zeta(z) \wedge (\mathrm{DTC}_{jxky}\varphi)(0, z, i, w))$$

□

We now define the JAG. Note that the JAG defined in [CR80] is a non-uniform model. We modify the definition here exactly so that the model is uniform:

Definition 3.3 JAG. A uniform *Jumping Automaton on Graphs* (JAG) is a logspace Turing machine that accesses its input via a bounded number of pebbles. Input to a JAG is a locally ordered graph with two specified vertices, s and t. Initially, all the pebbles are on an initial vertex, s. At each move, the JAG can detect which of its pebbles coincide, and which are on s or t. Based on this information, besides making its usual Turing machine moves, it may jump any pebble to the location of another specified pebble, or, it may slide a pebble currently at vertex v along a specified edge out of v.. Edges are specified by their number in the local ordering $F(v, \cdot, \cdot)$. If there is no such edge, then the pebble remains where it is.

As an example, we prove the following

Proposition 3.4 *The GAP problem for the set of graphs G_n of Figure 1, is solvable by a JAG.*

Proof Define the JAG, J_0 as follows: J_0 needs two pebbles: p_0, p_1; and, doesn't use its work tape. J_0 begins with its pebbles on vertex s. If $s = t$, then J_0 accepts. Otherwise, at the first move J_0 moves p_0 along the 0 edge out of the current vertex, and p_1 along the 1 edge. If either pebble is on t, J_0 accepts, otherwise it jumps p_1 to p_0, and repeats. J_0 can detect if its current vertex has no outgoing edge because after it tried to slide p_0 along the 0 edge, p_0 and p_1 would still coincide. In this case it should reject.
□

We now prove that over locally ordered graphs, JAGs are strictly weaker than (FO + DTC). First we show:

Theorem 3.5 *Over locally ordered graphs,* $JAG \subseteq (FO + DTC)$

Proof Let J be an arbitrary JAG. We must show that there is a sentence $\chi_J \in (FO + DTC)$ such that the set accepted by J is exactly the set of locally ordered graphs that satisfy χ_J.

This is similar to the proof that $L \subseteq (FO + DTC)$ over ordered structures [I87]. We will use a bounded number of numeric variables to codes J's $O(\log n)$ bit work tape. We will use a vertex variable v_i to denote the vertex on which pebble p_i sits. Thus jumping, and coincidence of pebbles is first-order. The movement along edges is expressible in (FO + DTC) by Observation 3.2. Thus, the relation $\text{NEXT}_J(\text{ID}_1, \text{ID}_2)$, meaning that ID_2 follows from ID_1 in one move of J, is expressible. Finally, the acceptance condition is given by

$$\chi_J \equiv \text{DTC}(\text{NEXT}_J)(\text{ID}_0, \text{ID}_f)$$

$\square$

When a JAG is given an ordered graph we assume that it has a pebble placed on 0 and that it may slide any pebble from vertex i to vertex $i + 1$. It is interesting to note that in this case:

Proposition 3.6 *The JAG model over ordered graphs is equivalent to $(FO + DTC)$ over ordered graphs, i.e., it exactly captures L.*

Proof The easiest way to see this is to observe that over ordered graphs the JAG model is equivalent to $(FO + DTC)$. This can be seen as follows: We use one pebble to simulate each first-order variable. Quantification can be simulated by cycling through all vertices in numeric order. Furthermore, DTC can be simulated by starting at a tuple $\bar{u}$, and cycling through all tuples $\bar{v}$ in lexicographical order. If it is discovered that there is a unique $\bar{v}$ such that $\varphi(\bar{u}, \bar{v})$ holds, the JAG shifts the $\bar{u}$ pebbles to $\bar{v}$ and repeats. $\square$

3.1 Reachability on Trees with DTC

Now we show that in $(FO + DTC)$ a total ordering is expressible on locally ordered trees. It follows from the proof that reachability on trees is expressible as a DTC of a first-order formula. It is interesting to contrast this with Theorem 5.3 which shows that such DTC's can not express reachability on locally ordered DAGs.

Theorem 3.7 *There is a formula $\gamma(x, y) \in (FO + DTC)$ which, over locally-ordered connected trees, expresses a linear ordering of the vertices of the tree. Furthermore, γ is expressible as a single DTC of arity 2 (plus booleans).*

Proof We do a preorder traversal of the tree. The formula π below expresses the next step in this preorder traversal. Then we define $\gamma(x, y)$ to mean that we can get from x to y in this traversal, i.e. x precedes y.

In our definition of π and γ we make use of boolean variables i and j. This is so that the arity of the vertex variables can be kept down to two. In the definition of the preorder traversal, π, when we enter a vertex v for the first time, we will actually enter $(v, 0)$. When we want to leave v for the last time after visiting all of v's children, we will enter the dummy node, $(v, 1)$. Thus the traversal of $V \times \{0\}$ is the preorder traversal, and the vertices $V \times \{1\}$ are just used for bookkeeping.

Let the formula $\sigma(u, v)$ mean that v is u's next sibling:

$$\sigma(u, v) \equiv u \neq v \wedge (\exists p)[F(p, u, v) \wedge (\forall w)(F(p, u, w) \rightarrow (u = w \vee F(p, v, w)))]$$

The preorder traversal, π, and the ordering, γ, are defined as follows:

$$\pi(x, i, x', i') \equiv \delta_0 \vee \delta_1 \vee \delta_2 \vee \delta_3 \qquad \text{where,}$$

$$\delta_0 \equiv (i = 0 \wedge i' = 0 \wedge E(x, x') \wedge \forall z(\neg \sigma(z, x')))$$
$$\delta_1 \equiv (i = 0 \wedge i' = 1 \wedge x = x' \wedge (\forall z)\neg E(x, z))$$
$$\delta_2 \equiv (i = 1 \wedge i' = 0 \wedge \sigma(x, x'))$$
$$\delta_3 \equiv (i = 1 \wedge i' = 1 \wedge E(x', x) \wedge (\forall z)\neg \sigma(x, z))$$

$$\gamma(a, b) \equiv \text{DTC}(\pi(x, i, x', i'))(a, 0, b, 0)$$

$\square$

One can easily modify the above formula for linear ordering to obtain a formula for s-t-Reachability, just by conjoining π with $\neg(x = s \wedge i = 1)$. This guarantees that π does not ascend from s, and thus that $\gamma(s,t)$ holds iff t is a descendant of s.

In fact, Reachability on directed trees is expressible in (FO + DTC) even without local ordering. This is because each vertex besides the root has a unique edge to it. Thus we can use DTC to walk backwards. Thus the following formula expresses reachability for directed trees:

$$\text{Reach}(s,t) \quad \equiv \quad \text{DTC}_{xx'}(E(x',x))(t,s)$$

This proves:

Proposition 3.8 *Reachability on trees (even without local ordering) is expressible in $(FO + DTC)$. In fact, it is expressible as a single DTC of arity 2.*

3.2   Local Ordering and (FO + TC)

The empty set is a local ordering for any graph with no edges. It follows that:

Proposition 3.9 *Over locally ordered graphs, having an odd number of vertices is not expressible in $(FO + TC)$.*

However, the more interesting situation is when the graph is connected:

Theorem 3.10 *Over locally ordered graphs, there is a formula $\lambda(x,y) \in (FO + TC)$ that describes a total ordering on the vertices reachable from s.*

Proof   We only consider those vertices reachable from s. We first construct a formula $\delta(x,y,i)$ which means that the distance from x to y is i. This is done below as follows: σ identifies a single step; $\mu(u,v,i)$ takes the transitive closure of σ, asserting that there is a path from u to v of length i; and, then δ is defined using μ:

$$\sigma(w,j,w',j') \equiv (j' = j + 1) \wedge E(w,w')$$
$$\mu(u,v,i) \equiv \text{TC}(\sigma)(u,0,v,i)$$
$$\delta(x,y,i) \equiv \mu(x,y,i) \wedge (\forall k < i)(\neg\mu(x,y,k))$$

Next, we construct a formula $\alpha(z,x)$ which means that z occurs on the lexicographically first, shortest path from s to x. This is done again by taking single steps: $\rho(u,i,u',i')$ means that if u occurs on the lexicographically first, shortest path from s to x and is distance i from x, then u' is the next vertex on this path and is distance $i' = i - 1$ from x:

$$\rho(u,i,u',i') \quad \equiv \quad \big(i' = i - 1 \wedge E(u,u') \wedge \delta(u',x,i') \wedge (\forall v)[(F(u,v,u') \wedge \delta(v,x,i')) \rightarrow v = u']\big)$$

and α is a transitive closure of ρ:

$$\alpha(z,x) \quad \equiv \quad (\exists d)(\delta(s,x,d) \wedge (\exists i)\text{TC}(\rho)(s,d,z,i))$$

Now, define the total ordering $\lambda(x,y)$ to mean that the distance from s to x is less than the distance from s to y, or the distances are equal, but the lexicographically first, shortest path from s to x precedes the lexicographically first, shortest path from s to y:

$$\lambda(x,y) \equiv (\exists ij)\Big(\delta(s,x,i) \wedge \delta(s,y,j) \wedge (i < j \ \vee$$
$$(i = j \ \wedge \ (\exists zuvk)(\alpha(z,x) \wedge \alpha(z,y) \wedge \alpha(u,x) \wedge \alpha(v,y) \wedge F(z,u,v) \wedge u \neq v)))\Big)$$

In the above, z is the last vertex on which those two lexicographically first, shortest paths agree. □

Theorem 3.10 shows that for the interesting case, ordering is definable from local ordering in (FO + TC). We are fairly sure that the following conjecture holds, although it remains open at this writing:

Conjecture 3.11 *Over locally ordered graphs,*

$$(FO + TC + COUNT) = NL$$

Note that by Proposition 3.9, counting is necessary in Conjecture 3.11. Furthermore, note that Theorem 3.10 cannot be extended to define a total ordering on the whole graph because locally ordered graphs can admit nontrivial automorphisms. What remains to be shown to prove this conjecture is that the language (FP + TC + COUNT) canonizes all trees, cf. [IL90, L92].

4 Two Way Local Graphs

The feature of the JAG model that makes it unrealistically weak is its inability to back up. This is the reason why JAGs can't search trees as they should be able to, unlike the language (FO + DTC) which can: Proposition 3.8.

In (FO + DTC) we can usually back up. Namely, if we are at a vertex a that has an edge coming into it from vertex b and vertex b has some special property (such as being the only vertex x such that the 17th edge out of x is to a) then we can back up to b. On the other hand, we can construct our graphs so that all vertices of interest have duplicate, "shadow" predecessors that look locally identical to each real predecessor. In this way we can force the language (FO + DTC) to be artificially weak. We will exploit this idea to get a general lower bound for (FO + DTC) for one-way local graphs: Theorem 5.3.

For this reason, we feel that it is more reasonable to consider graphs equipped with a two-way local ordering:

Definition 4.1. A *two-way local ordering* is just a local ordering, H, on the incoming edges to each vertex, in addition to the the local ordering, F, on the outgoing edges. There is no assumption about consistency between F and H.

A *two-way JAG* is a JAG that takes as input graphs with a two-way local ordering. At each move, the JAG may choose a specified incoming or outgoing edge and move a pebble along it. From now on, we will refer to the usual JAG model as a *one-way JAG*.

4.1 (FO + DTC) and Two Way JAGs

Now we show that the language DTC(FO) – the restriction of (FO + DTC) to single DTC's of first order formulas – over two-way locally ordered structures is essentially equivalent to the two-way JAG. The first observation we make is the well known fact that fixed first-order statements are essentially local in nature. This is stated nicely, for example, in the following theorem of Gaifman. Any logical structure $\mathcal{A}$ may be thought of as a generalized graph in which an edge exists between two points a and b iff a and b occur together in some tuple of a relation in $\mathcal{A}$. The distance between a and b (dist(a, b)) is the minimum number of such edges that must be traversed to get from a to b.

If we restrict all quantifiers in a formula φ to the union of the balls of distance d around a set of points, $\bar{v}$, then we get a local formula, denoted $\varphi^d(\bar{v})$. Gaifman's theorem says that a first-order formula may describe the local neighborhood around its free variables and constants (1), and it may describe the existence of certain landmarks (2), and that is all:

Fact 4.2 ([Ga81]) *Let φ be a first-order formula whose free variables and constants are in the tuple $\bar{u}$. Then there exists a distance d depending only on φ such that φ is equivalent to a boolean combination of*

1. *a finite set of formulas, $\alpha_i^d(\bar{u})$, and,*

2. *a finite set of sentences (in which no constants nor free variables occur),*

$$\beta_j \equiv (\exists v_1, \ldots, v_s)[\bigwedge_{i=1}^{s} \psi^d(v_i) \wedge \bigwedge_{i<j\leq s} dist(v_i, v_j) > 2d]$$

We now use Fact 4.2 to analyze the computation performed by the expression $DTC[\varphi(\bar{x}, \bar{x}')](\bar{c}, \bar{e})$, where φ is an arbitrary first-order formula.

We know that φ is equivalent to a boolean combination of some β_j's asserting the existence of some distant landmarks; and, some α_i's which are local facts about $\bar{x}, \bar{x}'$, and the only constants available: s and t. We may assume that all of the β_j's are satisfiable because any unsatisfiable ones are just superfluous. It follows that there is a locally ordered graph L_φ that contains neither s nor t, but does satisfy all of the β_j's; i.e., L_φ contains all the relevant landmarks. By only considering graphs that include a copy of L_φ disjoint from everything else, we reduce φ to a boolean combination of α_i's which is thus equivalent to one fixed formula,

$$\varphi(\bar{x}, \bar{x}') \equiv \alpha^d(\bar{x}, \bar{x}', s, t)$$

Now, consider a $DTC(\varphi)$ walk. Call the step from $\bar{a}$ to $\bar{b}$ *d-local* (or just *local* if d is understood) if every point b_i in $\bar{b}$ is within the d-neighborhood of some point in $\bar{a} \cup \{s, t\}$. If the step is not local because of b_i, then the point b_i must have been the unique point in the graph with some special property. Suppose now, that we add a new, disjoint copy of the graph (with the vertices s and t not labelled in the new copy). Then in this expanded graph there are two equally valid points b_i that we could move to. Thus, in the expanded graph all steps are local.

We summarize the above discussion in the following definition, observation, and lemma:

Definition 4.3. Let φ be a fixed first-order formula as in the above discussion. We will call a graph G *adequate for* φ (or just *adequate* if φ is understood) iff G satisfies all the β_i's of Fact 4.2; and, for every point $a \in V_G$, G contains another point b where $dist(a, b) > 2d$ and b's d-local neighborhood is isomorphic to a's.

The following observation shows that without loss of much generality we can restrict our attention to adequate graphs.

Observation 4.4 *Let G be any graph containing the constants s and t. Let $adq(G)$ be the disjoint union of four locally ordered graphs: G, G_1, H_0, H_1 where $G \cong G_1$, and $H_0 \cong H_1 \cong L_\varphi$. Then $adq(G)$ is adequate for φ. Furthermore, in terms of reachability from s to t and as inputs to JAG-like automata, G and $adq(G)$ are indistinguishable.*

Lemma 4.5 *Let $\varphi(\bar{x}, \bar{x}'; \bar{p})$ be a first-order formula where $\bar{p}$ is the set of parameters, i.e., constants and free variables besides $\bar{x}, \bar{y}$. Then there exists a constant d depending only on φ and there exists a d-local formula $\alpha^d(\bar{x}, \bar{x}', \bar{p})$ such that for every graph G that is adequate for φ, we have,*

1. *In G, α is equivalent to φ.*

2. *Every step in every $DTC(\varphi)$ walk in G is d-local.*

A consequence of Lemma 4.5 is that the two-way JAG is very similar to the language (FO + DTC) on two-way local graphs. In particular, a lower bound in one of these models translates to a lower bound in the other:

Theorem 4.6 *Let $\mathcal{G}$ be a class of two-way locally ordered graphs with numbers that is closed under the adq operation of Observation 4.4. Then the following two statements are equivalent:*

1. *For some first-order formula φ, $DTC[\varphi(\bar{x}, \bar{x}')](\bar{s}, \bar{t})$ expresses reachability from s to t for $\mathcal{G}$.*

2. *There exists a two-way JAG that recognizes reachability from s to t for $\mathcal{G}$.*

*On the other hand, if $\mathcal{G}$ is as above but **without numbers**, then condition (1) is equivalent to*

3. *There exists a finite state, two-way JAG that recognizes reachability from s to t for $\mathcal{G}$.*

Proof [Sketch] One direction of this follows from Theorem 3.5. In the other direction, the JAG can simulate the DTC because it can exhaustively visit all vertices of distance at most d and thus choose the correct tuple to go to next. Note that arity$(\varphi) = k$ suffices to simulate a k-pebble JAG. □

5 Lower Bound: (FO + DTC) on One-Way Locally Ordered Graphs

We now use Theorem 4.6, together with two previous lower bounds, to prove two lower bounds on the descriptive power of (FO + DTC) first for locally ordered graphs, and then for two-way locally ordered graphs. We first recall a theorem of Cook and Rackoff that we have previously mentioned:

Fact 5.1 ([CR80]) *No one-way JAG can solve the s to t reachability problem on all finite trees.*

As we mentioned at the beginning of Section 4, a weakness of one-way JAGs is that they can't back up. We can however similarly prevent DTC walks from backing up by replacing a tree T by a *shadowed* counterpart T', where for each edge $\langle v, w \rangle$ we introduce a new vertex v' and edge $\langle v', w \rangle$ that will be locally indistinguishable from $\langle v, w \rangle$. Next we replace each old or new edge by a path of length d. Since one-way local ordering only posits an ordering on the out-going edges, we can show, in the form of the following lemma, that over such shadowed trees[1] DTC is essentially as weak as JAGs. Due to the page limit, we have omitted the proof of the following.

Lemma 5.2 *Let ψ be any formula $\psi(\bar{s}, \bar{t}) \equiv DTC[\varphi(\bar{x}, \bar{y})](\bar{s}, \bar{t})$ of arity $2k$ and quantifier depth r. Then there is a $k + 4$ pebble JAG, J, such that for any tree T, the computation $J(T)$ "simulates" the computation $\psi(T')$ where T' is the shadowed tree of T (with d appropriately chosen).*

From this and Fact 5.1 it follows that

Theorem 5.3 *For any first-order formula, φ, $DTC[\varphi](\bar{s}, \bar{t})$ does not express s to t reachability for all one-way locally ordered, directed acyclic graphs.*

---

[1] Note that a "shadowed tree" is a DAG, not a tree.

6 Lower Bound: (FO + DTC) on Two-Way Locally Ordered Graphs

It is harder to prove a lower bound on two-way locally ordered graphs. (For example, reachability for the shadowed trees in the above lower bound is expressible with $DTC(\varphi)(\bar{s}, \bar{t})$, given two-way local ordering.) To prove such a lower bound we use a theorem of Blum and Sakoda [BS77]. They showed that no finite automata (or in fact any finite set of finite automata) can search all finite three dimensional mazes. A three dimensional maze is a special kind of two-way locally ordered graph: Each vertex is an element of $\mathbf{Z}^3$ and has six potential neighbors: those to the north, south, east, west, up, and down. Thus the automata of Blum and Sakoda are finite state, two-way JAGs, with only one pebble. By Theorem 4.6, these JAGs correspond to formulas of the form $DTC[\varphi(x, \bar{b}, x', \bar{b}')](s, \bar{0}, t, \bar{1})$, were $\bar{b}$ is a tuple of booleans, cf. Theorem 3.7. It thus follows that

Theorem 6.1 *Reachability is not expressible as an arity two DTC, for finite two-way locally ordered graphs, in fact not even for finite three dimensional mazes.*

A language that is strictly stronger than arity two DTCs is Second Order, Existential, Monadic logic (SO∃(arity1)), studied by Ajtai and Fagin [AF90]. Ajtai and Fagin show that reachability over unordered graphs is not expressible in SO∃(arity1). However, their proof does not go through in the presence of a local ordering and thus it does not imply Theorem 6.1. Furthermore, they observe that unlike arity two DTCs, SO∃(arity1) does express reachability on bounded degree graphs.

7 Conclusion

We have begun an investigation of transitive closure logics applied to locally ordered graphs. We have shown that the JAG model is intimately related to these logics. We have indicated why the JAG model is unreasonably weak and should, wherever possible, be replaced by the two-way JAG model. Furthermore, we have shown that the language (FO + DTC) over two-way locally ordered graphs is more robust than even the two-way JAG model, and yet lower bounds remain accessible.

We have proved an interesting upper bound on the power of TC over locally ordered graphs (Theorem 3.10), and three lower bounds on DTC (Theorems 2.7, 5.3, and 6.1).

We hope that we have given convincing evidence that further study of the relationship between (FO + DTC) and (FO + TC) is both feasible and important for understanding the relationship between L and NL.

The following topics merit further study:

1. Blum and Sakoda [BS77] proved their lower bound not only for one finite automaton, but for any finite number. However, that does not immediately translate to an improvement of Theorem 6.1 to arbitrary arity. To do so, we would need a lower bound on a more general model. Namely, the automata in [BS77] can only communicate with each other by literally bumping into each other. Consider a model called, "Maze Automata with Walkie Talkies," in which at each step the automata can poll the states of all the other automata and decide on a next move accordingly. We conjecture that the [BS77] lower bound can be extended to these stronger automata. A consequence would be Theorem 6.1 for arbitrary arity.
2. A trick that Blum and Sakoda use to fool their finite automata, is that a finite automaton can't tell how far it has walked, even in a straight direction. Thus, even if we proved the walkie talkie conjecture of (1.), the lower bound that would follow would be for two-way locally ordered graphs **without numbers**. (Note that whether or not we had numbers is not an issue when the arity is only two, because it is never useful to remove our single pebble from the vertex domain in order to count something.) It would be very interesting to know whether two-way JAGS, or (FO + DTC) **with numbers**, can search all three dimensional mazes. In particular, to our knowledge it is open whether this can be done in L; or, on the other hand whether this problem is complete for NL.

3. The lower bounds of Theorems 5.3 and 6.1 prove the impossibility of expressing reachability by formulas of the form $DTC[\varphi](\bar{s}, \bar{t})$, where φ is first-order. We conjecture that the lower bound of Theorem 5.3 holds for all of (FO + DTC). In the presence of ordering, there is a normal form theorem which says that every formula in (FO + DTC) can be written in the form $DTC[\varphi](\bar{s}, \bar{t})$ where φ is not only first-order, but quantifier-free, [I87]. This normal form theorem is false without ordering, even with two way local ordering. However, we feel that a generalization of the proof of Theorem 5.3 will extend to a lower bound on all of (FO + DTC).

4. We have argued that (FO + COUNT + DTC) over two-way locally ordered graphs is a robust approximation to L and yet admits tractable approaches to lower bounds. Much further study is needed. In particular, lower bounds on (FO + COUNT + DTC) are very desirable. Such a lower bound would at least show us a deficiency of this language which we could then fix. At best, such a lower bound could prove that L $\neq$ NL.

5. Related to 4 is the following challenge: Find a set of graphs for which reachability is in L but not in (FO + DTC) with two-way local ordering.

References

[AF90] M. Ajtai and R. Fagin, "Reachability is Harder for Directed than for Undirected Graphs," *J. Symb. Logic*, **55** (1990), 113-150.

[A-R79] R. Aleliunas, R.M. Karp, R.J. Lipton, L. Lovasz, and C. Rackoff, "Random Walks, Universal Traversal Sequences, and the Complexity of the Maze Problem," *Proceedings of the 20th annual IEEE Found. of Comp. Sci. Symp.*, pages 218-223, October 1979.

[BB90] P. Beame, A. Borodin, P. Raghavan, W. Ruzzo, and M. Tompa, "Time-Space Tradeoffs for Undirected Graph Traversal," *Proceedings of the 31st Annual IEEE Found. of Comp. Sci. Symp.*, pages 429-438, St. Louis, MO, October 1990.

[BK78] M. Blum and D. Kozen, "On the Power of the Compass," *Proceedings of the 19th Annual IEEE Found. of Comp. Sci. Symp.*, pages 132-142, Ann Arbor, MI, October 1978.

[BS77] M. Blum and W.J. Sakoda, "On the Capability of Finite Automata in 2 and 3 Dimensional Space," *Proceedings of the 18th Annual IEEE Found. of Comp. Sci. Symp.*, pages 147-161, October 1977.

[CFI92] J. Cai, M. Fürer, N. Immerman, "An Optimal Lower Bound on the Number of Variables for Graph Identification," *Combinatorica* **12** (4) (1992) 389-410.

[CR80] S. A. Cook and C. W. Rackoff, "Space Lower Bounds for Maze Threadability of Restricted Machines," *SIAM J. Comput.*, 9(3):636-652, Aug 1980.

[Ed93] J. Edmonds, "Time-Space Tradeoffs for Undirected ST-Connectivity on a JAG," *Proceeding of the 25th Annual ACM Symp. Theory Of Comput.*, pages 718-727, May 1993.

[Ga81] H. Gaifman, "On Local and Non-Local Properties," *Proc. Herbrand Logic Colloq.*, Marseille, 1981, pages 105-135.

[GM92] E. Grädel and G. McColm, "Deterministic vs. Nondeterministic Transitive Closure Logic," In *Proceedings of the 7th IEEE Conference on Logic in Computer Science*, 1992.

[I82] N. Immerman, "Upper and Lower Bounds for First Order Expressibility," *JCSS* **25**, No. 1 (1982), 76-98.

[I87] N. Immerman, "Languages that Capture Complexity Classes," *SIAM J. Comput.*16:4 (1987), 760-778.

[I88] N. Immerman, "Nondeterministic Space is Closed Under Complementation," *SIAM J. Comput.* 17: 5 (1988), 935-938.

[I89] N. Immerman, "Descriptive and Computational Complexity," in *Computational Complexity Theory*, ed. J. Hartmanis, *Proc. Symp. in Applied Math.*, 38, American Mathematical Society (1989), 75-91.

[I89a] N. Immerman, "Expressibility and Parallel Complexity," *SIAM J. of Comput* **18** (1989), 625-638.

[IL90] Neil Immerman and Eric S. Lander, "Describing Graphs: A First-Order Approach to Graph Canonization," in *Complexity Theory Retrospective*, Alan Selman, ed., Springer-Verlag (1990), 59-81.

[L92] Steven Lindell, "A Logspace Algorithm for Tree Canonization," *ACM Symp. Theory Of Comput.*(1992), 400-404.

Are Parallel Machines Always Faster than Sequential Machines?

(Preliminary Version)

Louis Mak*

University of Illinois at Urbana-Champaign, Urbana, IL 61801, USA

Abstract. We demonstrate that parallel machines are always faster than sequential machines for a wide range of machine models, including tree Turing machine (TM), multidimensional TM, log-cost random access machine (RAM), and unit-cost RAM. More precisely, we show that every sequential machine M (in the above list) that runs in time T can be sped up by a parallel version M' of M that runs in time $o(T)$. All previous speedup results either rely on the severe limitation on the storage structure of M (e.g., M is a TM with linear tapes) or require that M' has a more versatile storage structure than M (e.g., M' is a parallel RAM (PRAM), and M is a TM with linear tapes). It is unclear whether it is the parallelism, or the restriction on the storage structures, or the combination of both that realizes such speedup. We remove all the above restrictions on storage structures in previous results. We present speedup theorems where both M and M' use the same kind of storage medium, which is not linear tapes. Thus, we prove conclusively that parallelism alone suffices to achieve the speedup.

1 Introduction and Motivation

For many problems, there exist parallel algorithms which run asymptotically faster than the best known sequential algorithms. Sorting, minimum spanning tree, and connected components are but a few examples [1, 8]. But is it always the case? In other words, given a sequential algorithm for a problem, does there always exist a parallel algorithm for the same problem that runs asymptotically faster? In more formal terms, this question can be phrased as follows. Consider a class of sequential machines S and their "parallel" counterparts P. Is it true that each machine in the class S that runs in time T can be simulated by a machine in the class P that runs in time $o(T)$? In order to discuss this question rigorously, we need to fix S and P. To facilitate our discussion, we call the simulating machine the *host* and the machine being simulated the *guest*.

The deterministic Turing machine (DTM) is one of the standard models of sequential computation. Chandra et al. [2] introduced a parallel version of the DTM, which has become known as the alternating Turing machine (ATM). Paul and Reischuk [12] established that every DTM running in time T can

---
* Supported by the National Science Foundation under Grant CCR-8922008. Author's address: Coordinated Science Laboratory, 1308 W. Main St., Urbana, IL 61801, USA.

be simulated by an ATM that runs in time $O(T \log \log T / \log T)$. Using a two-person pebble game, Dymond and Tompa [5] improved the simulation time to $O(T / \log T)$. Together with the alternating time hierarchy theorem [3], this result implies that the class of languages accepted by ATM's in time $O(T)$ strictly includes the class of languages accepted by DTM's in time $O(T)$. Thus, parallel time is strictly more powerful than deterministic time for TM's.

However, it is unclear whether this relationship between parallel time and deterministic time is just an "artifact" of the TM, because the proofs of both Paul and Reischuk [12] and Dymond and Tompa [5] rely heavily on the linearity of the tapes of the TM. We demonstrate that this relationship between parallel time and deterministic time also holds for TM's with tree-structured tapes and multidimensional tapes and random access machines (RAM's) under both log-cost and unit-cost measures. Thus, the statement "Parallel time is strictly more powerful than deterministic time" is neither an "artifact" of the linearity of tapes nor an "idiosyncrasy" of the Turing type of machine models. Instead, we believe that it is an intrinsic property of the nature of computation.

Dymond and Tompa [5] gave further evidence to our belief by showing that every DTM that runs in time T can be simulated by a CREW PRAM in time $O(T^{1/2})$. Nevertheless, the random access memory of the PRAM is much more flexible than the linear tapes of the DTM. It is questionable whether it is the parallelism, or the more flexible storage mechanism of the host, or the combination of both that makes such speedup possible. We settle this question conclusively by establishing speedup theorems where the guest uses the same type of storage mechanism as the host. Hence, parallelism alone suffices to achieve the speedup.

In previous speedup results [5, 11, 12], the guest is limited to the DTM. All previous results depend on the fact that the changes in the configuration of a DTM in t steps are localized to the $2t - 1$ cells around each tape head. In contrast, the random access storage of a unit-cost RAM allows the RAM to change the contents of registers with widely different addresses in consecutive steps. The versatility of the random access memory of a unit-cost RAM has defied all prior attempts to speed up a unit-cost RAM by a PRAM. As one of the major contributions of this paper, we show that every unit-cost RAM that runs in time T can be simulated by a CREW PRAM in time $O(T^{1/2} \log T)$.

Reif [14] demonstrated that every probabilistic unit-cost RAM that runs in time T can be simulated by a probabilistic CREW PRAM in time $t(T, L) = O((T \log T \log(LT))^{1/2})$, where L is the largest integer manipulated by the probabilistic RAM during its computation. It is straightforward to modify Reif's proof to show that every unit-cost RAM running in time T can be simulated by a CREW PRAM in time $t(T, L)$. With unit-time addition, however, a RAM can generate integers as large as $2^{O(T)}$ in time T. Reif's result does not guarantee a speedup, since $t(L, T) = O(T(\log T)^{1/2})$ when $L = 2^{O(T)}$. Our result (Theorem 1) gives a definite speedup of unit-cost RAM's by PRAM's.

Parberry and Schnitger [11] considered the WRAM, a variant of the CRCW PRAM, and showed that every DTM can be simulated in constant time by a WRAM. Nonetheless, the WRAM is too strong to be considered reasonable [10].

The *parallel computation thesis* [7] asserts that the class of languages accepted by any reasonable parallel machine model in polynomial time is equivalent to *PSPACE*, where *PSPACE*, as usual, denotes the class of languages accepted by DTM's in polynomial space. The WRAM violates the parallel computation thesis and is considered unreasonably powerful [10]. In contrast, all parallel models used in this paper (ATM, alternating log-cost RAM, and PRAM) are considered reasonable because they satisfy the parallel computation thesis [2, 6].

We state our results in Sect. 2 and discuss their significance in Sect. 3. In Sect. 4, we define precisely the machine models we use. In Sects. 5, 6, 7, and 8, we sketch of the proofs of our theorems. All logarithms are taken to base 2.

2 Summary of Results

Fortune and Wyllie [6] introduced the parallel random access machine (PRAM), which comprises an infinite collection of processors, all sharing a global memory. The global memory is an infinite sequence of registers (g_i), where $i \geq 0$. A d-dimensional PRAM is one with global memory $(g_{i_1 \cdots i_d})$, where $i_1, \ldots, i_d \geq 0$.

Theorem 1. *Every unit-cost RAM that runs in time T can be simulated by a CREW PRAM in time $O(T^{1/2} \log T)$.*

Theorem 2. *Every d-dimensional CREW PRAM that runs in time T can be simulated by a 1-dimensional CREW PRAM in time $O(T)$. The same result also holds for CRCW PRAM's.*

A tree TM is one whose work "tapes" are infinite rooted complete binary trees; a d-dimensional TM is one whose work "tapes" are d-dimensional lattices. Reischuk [15] described these machines in more detail.

Theorem 3. *Every tree ATM running in time T can be simulated by a 1-dimensional ATM in time $O(T)$.*

Theorem 4. *Every d-dimensional ATM running in time T can be simulated by a 1-dimensional ATM in time $O(T)$.*

By Theorems 3 and 4, we may, without loss of precision, talk about ATM's without mentioning the storage structure.

Theorem 5. *Every tree DTM that runs in time T can be simulated by an ATM in time $O(T/\log T)$.*

Theorem 6. *Every d-dimensional DTM that runs in time T can be simulated by an ATM in time $O(T 5^{d \log^* T}/\log T)$.*

Cook and Reckhow [4] defined the log-cost RAM. An alternating RAM (ARAM) is a RAM equipped with existential and universal choices. Like an ATM, an ARAM can branch out existentially and universally. The definition of acceptance for an ARAM is analogous to that of an ATM [2].

Theorem 7. *Every log-cost RAM that runs in time T can be simulated by a log-cost ARAM in time $O(T \log \log T/\log T)$.*

3   Significance of Results

3.1   Parallel Time Is More Powerful Than Deterministic Time

We have shown that for nearly all common models of computation, parallel machines are indeed faster than their sequential counterparts (Theorems 1, 5, 6, and 7). Theorem 1, together with the time hierarchy theorem for unit-cost RAM's [4], shows that the class of languages accepted by PRAM's in time $O(T)$ strictly includes the class of languages accepted by unit-cost RAM's in time $O(T)$. Since the alternating time hierarchy is sharp [3], as a corollary of Theorems 5 and 6, we conclude that the class of languages accepted by ATM's in time $O(T)$ strictly includes the class of languages accepted by DTM's in time $O(T)$, regardless of the type of storage structure. By Theorem 7 and the time hierarchy theorem for log-cost RAM's [4], we deduce that the class of languages accepted by log-cost ARAM's in time $O(T)$ strictly includes the class of languages accepted by log-cost RAM's in time $O(T)$. We conclude that parallel time is strictly more powerful than deterministic time as a resource of computation.

3.2   A Second Parallel Computation Thesis

Fortune and Wyllie [6], Savitch and Stimson [17], and Savitch [16] showed that the classes of languages accepted by various parallel machine models in polynomial time are all equal to *PSPACE*. These results, among others, prompted Goldschlager [7] to promulgate the celebrated *parallel computation thesis*, which asserts that the class of languages accepted by any "reasonable" parallel machine model in polynomial time is equivalent to *PSPACE*. The parallel computation thesis provides a criterion to judge whether a parallel machine model is reasonable. Encouraged by our results, we propose the following *second parallel computation thesis*.

> The class of languages accepted by any "reasonable" parallel machine model $\mathcal{P}$ in time $O(T)$ strictly includes the class of languages accepted by the "sequential counterpart" of $\mathcal{P}$ in time $O(T)$.

Hence, a "parallel" machine model which cannot speedup its sequential counterpart is too weak to be called a parallel machine model. Contrarily, a "sequential" machine model which cannot be sped up by its parallel counterpart is too strong to be called a sequential model. The second parallel computation thesis provides an additional criterion to gauge the reasonableness of a parallel machine model.

3.3   Effects of Storage Structure on Parallel Machines

We proved that a more flexible storage structure does not increase the computing power of an ATM (Theorems 3 and 4). Similarly, having multidimensional memories does not increase the computing power of a CREW or CRCW PRAM (Theorem 2). Thus, the class of languages accepted by a parallel machine model in time $O(T)$ seems to be invariant under different storage structures. In other words, the power of parallelism is strong enough to overcome the handicap in the

Table 1. Instructions of a RAM

Instruction	Meaning
$r_i \leftarrow r_j$	r_i gets $\langle r_j \rangle$.
$r_i \leftarrow (r_0)$	r_i gets $\langle r_j \rangle$, where $j = \langle r_0 \rangle$.
$(r_0) \leftarrow r_i$	r_j gets $\langle r_i \rangle$, where $j = \langle r_0 \rangle$.
$r_i \leftarrow r_i + r_j$	r_i gets $\langle r_i \rangle + \langle r_j \rangle$.
$r_i \leftarrow r_i - r_j$	r_i gets $\langle r_i \rangle - \langle r_j \rangle$.
BRANCH q	If $\langle r_0 \rangle \geq 0$, then pass control to the qth instruction.
ACCEPT	Accept and halt.
REJECT	Reject and halt.

storage medium. This observation suggests a further criterion that a reasonable parallel machine model should satisfy: for a reasonable parallel machine model, a modest change in its storage structure should not affect its computing power.

4 Definitions

A RAM R consists of a memory, and a program. The memory is an infinite sequence of registers (r_i), $i \geq 0$. The *address* of r_i is the integer i. Each register can hold an integer. Denote by $\langle r_i \rangle$ the content of r_i. The program consists of a finite number of instructions, numbered $1, \ldots, Q$. Table 1 shows the allowed instructions. The input of R is a binary number $\alpha = a_0 \cdots a_{n-1}$; each $a_i \in \{0, 1\}$. Initially, $r_0, \ldots, r_{K-1}$ hold some constant values required in the computation of R, where K is a constant that depends on R; r_{K+i} holds a_i for $0 \leq i < n$, and r_{K+n} holds -1 to mark the end of the input. All other registers contain zero. A unit-cost RAM executes each instruction in one step. Each step takes one time unit. The running time of a unit-cost RAM is the number of steps performed.

A PRAM comprises a collection of processors $P_0, P_1, \ldots$, which communicate via a global memory. Each processor is a unit-cost RAM with its own local memory. Initially, only P_0 is active. When a processor executes a FORK instruction, an idle processor is activated. Henceforth, we restrict our attention to CREW PRAM's. Unless otherwise stated, our results also hold for CRCW PRAM's.

5 Speedup of RAM by PRAM

In this section, we prove that PRAM's are always faster than unit-cost RAM's. First, we state two lemmas. It is convenient to interpret integers as logical values. We interpret a nonzero integer as true and zero as false.

Lemma 8 (folklore). *Suppose in a PRAM P, the global memory registers g_1, $\ldots, g_N$ store N integers $n_1, \ldots, n_N$. Then P can find the sum and logical AND of these N integers in $O(\log N)$ time.*

Lemma 9 (folklore). *A PRAM with time complexity T and k global memories $(g_i^1), \ldots, (g_i^k)$ can be simulated in time $O(T)$ by a PRAM with one global memory.*

We now sketch the proof of Theorem 1. Let R be a unit-cost RAM with memory (r_i) and time complexity $T = T(n)$. We devise a CREW PRAM P with multiple memories that simulates R in time $O(T^{1/2} \log T)$. Theorem 1 then follows from Lemma 9. Let the input be $\alpha = a_0 \cdots a_{n-1}$. Initially, $r_0, \ldots, r_{K-1}$ holds some constant values, r_{K+i} holds a_i for $0 \le i < n$, and r_{K+n} holds -1.

5.1   Configuration of R

Consider the computation of R on α. The *configuration* of R at time t consists of the addresses and contents of all nonzero registers and the instruction number of R at time t. Denote by $\mathit{config}(t)$ the configuration of R at time t. Initially, all registers of R contain zero, except for $r_0, \ldots, r_{K+n}$. For $0 \le i \le K + n$, let u_i denote r_i. For $i > K + n$, let u_i denote the register of R that is first written to in step $i - K - n$. By convention, the first step of R is step 1, and $r_0, \ldots, r_{K+n}$ are first written to in step 0 (i.e., they are initialized at time 0). Thus, to describe the configuration of R at time t, it suffices to specify the instruction number of R at time t and the address and content at time t of u_i for $0 \le i \le t + K + n$. P uses a data structure CONFIG to represent the configuration of R. CONFIG consists of three global memories (a_i), (b_i), and (c_i). Register b_0 holds the instruction number of R, whereas a_i and c_i respectively hold the address and content of u_i.

5.2   Overview of Simulation

The computation of P comprises two phases. In phase I, P uses $O(T^{1/2} \log T)$ time to activate $T^{1/2}$ groups of $T^{O(T^{1/2})}$ processors. For $1 \le m \le T^{1/2}$, the processors in group m perform some preprocessing such that after the preprocessing, $\mathit{config}(mT^{1/2})$ can be computed from $\mathit{config}((m-1)T^{1/2})$ in $O(\log T)$ time. In phase II, P finds $\mathit{config}(T)$ as follows. The initial configuration of R ($\mathit{config}(0)$) can be determined trivially. For $m = 1, \ldots, T^{1/2}$, P computes $\mathit{config}(mT^{1/2})$ from $\mathit{config}((m-1)T^{1/2})$ in $O(\log T)$ time. P accepts if and only if the instruction number in $\mathit{config}(T)$ is that of an ACCEPT instruction. Both phases take $O(T^{1/2} \log T)$ time. It remains to provide the details of phases I and II.

5.3   Phase I

We fix m and describe the processors in group m. Divide the instructions of R into four types:

1. ACCEPT and REJECT
2. BRANCH q
3. direct/indirect load and store instructions ($r_i \leftarrow r_j, r_i \leftarrow (r_0)$, and $(r_0) \leftarrow r_i$)
4. arithmetic operations ($r_i \leftarrow r_i + r_j$ and $r_i \leftarrow r_i - r_j$)

config(a), and $\Psi_a(q')$ be a procedure that accepts if and only if q' is true at time a. Thus, Ψ_a specifies *config*(a) by answering questions about *config*(a). Procedure $\Phi[\Psi_a, c](q)$ uses a specification Ψ_a of *config*(a) to answer a question q about *config*(c) and accepts if and only if q is true at time c. Notice that $\Phi[\Psi_a, c]$ is one way to implement Ψ_c. Let q_0 be the question: "Is M in an accepting state?" To determine whether M accepts the input, M' simply calls $\Phi[\Psi_0, T](q_0)$. Let $f(\Psi_a)$ be the maximum (over all questions q' about *config*(a)) running time of Ψ_a. The running time of M' is therefore at most $f(\Phi[\Psi_0, T])$. We give three different strategies to implement Φ.

Strategy 1. Strategy 1 is a direct step by step simulation of M. Starting from *config*(a), specified by Ψ_a, $\Phi[\Psi_a, c](q)$ simulates M for $(c - a)$ steps to obtain *config*(c), and accepts if and only if q is true at time c. The running time of Strategy 1 is $O(c - a) + X$, where $X = O(\log T) + f(\Psi_a)$ is the time required to extract from Ψ_a the information about *config*(a) necessary for the simulation.

Strategy 2. Define b to be $(a + c)/2$. Let $\widehat{\Psi}_b$ be the procedure $\Phi[\Psi_a, b]$. For Strategy 2, $\Phi[\Psi_a, c](q)$ recursively calls $\Phi[\widehat{\Psi}_b, c](q)$. The running time of Strategy 2 is $f(\Phi[\widehat{\Psi}_b, c]) + O(\log T)$, where the $O(\log T)$ term accounts for the time required to set up the parameters for the recursive call.

Strategy 3. Let Q be the set of questions q' that Φ asks Ψ_b during the invocation of $\Phi[\Psi_b, c](q)$ such that q' is true at time b if and only if q' is false at time a. Let Γ be a table that specifies, for each q' in Q, whether q' is true at time b. Define a procedure $\widetilde{\Psi}_b(q')$ as follows. On input q', if q' is in Q, then $\widetilde{\Psi}_b(q')$ accepts if and only if, according to Γ, q' is true at time b; else, $\widetilde{\Psi}_b(q')$ calls $\Psi_a(q')$.

For Strategy 3, $\Phi[\Psi_a, c](q)$ first guesses Γ and then universally chooses to do (i) verifies Γ and (ii) recursively calls $\Phi[\widetilde{\Psi}_b, c](q)$. To verify Γ, Φ universally chooses a question q' in Q and recursively calls $\Phi[\Psi_a, b](q')$. Let $|\Gamma|$ denote the size of Γ. The running time of Strategy 3 is $O(|\Gamma|) + \max\{f(\Phi[\Psi_a, b]), f(\Phi[\widetilde{\Psi}_b, c])\} + O(\log T)$, where the $O(\log T)$ term represents the time to set up the parameters of the recursive calls.

Procedure Φ existentially chooses which strategy to use. The running time of Φ is thus the minimum among the three strategies. Solving the recurrence relation $f(\Phi[\Psi_a, c]) = O(\log T) + \min\{O(c - a) + f(\Psi_a), f(\Phi[\widehat{\Psi}_c, b]), O(|\Gamma|) + \max\{f(\Phi[\Psi_a, b]), f(\Phi[\widetilde{\Psi}_b, c])\}\}$, we get $f(\Phi[\Psi_0, T]) = O(T/\log T)$. $\square$

Lemma 11 [15]. *Every d-dimensional DTM that runs in time T can be simulated by a tree DTM in time $O(T5^{d \log^* T})$.*

Proof of Theorem 6. Immediate from Theorem 5 and Lemma 11. $\square$

Lemma 12 [13]. *Every log-cost RAM that runs in time T can be simulated by a tree DTM in time $O(T)$.*

Lemma 13 [9]. *Every DTM with time complexity T can be simulated by a log-cost RAM in time $O(T \log \log T)$.*

Proof of Theorem 7 (sketch). Let R be a log-cost RAM that runs in time T. By Lemma 12, there exists a tree DTM M that simulates R in time $O(T)$. Then Theorem 5 implies that there is a 1-dimensional ATM M' that simulates M in time $O(T')$, where $T' = T/\log T$. Without loss of generality, we may assume that the computation of M' consists of two phases: an initial phase during which M' makes all the necessary alternating choices and a second phase with only deterministic computation. We construct a log-cost ARAM R' that simulates M', and hence R, as follows. R' emulates the initial phase of M' by direct simulation. By Lemma 13, R' can simulate the second phase of M' in time $O(T' \log \log T')$. Hence, the running time of R' is $O(T \log \log T / \log T)$. □

References

1. S. G. Akl. *The Design and Analysis of Parallel Algorithms.* Prentice Hall, Englewood Cliffs, New Jersey, 1989.
2. A. K. Chandra, D. C. Kozen, and L. J. Stockmeyer. Alternation. *J. Assoc. Comput. Mach.*, 28:114–133, 1981.
3. A. K. Chandra and L. J. Stockmeyer. Alternation. In *Proc. 17th Ann. IEEE Symp. on Foundations of Computer Science*, pages 98–108, 1976.
4. S. A. Cook and R. A. Reckhow. Time bounded random access machines. *J. Comput. System Sci.*, 7:354–375, 1973.
5. P. W. Dymond and M. Tompa. Speedups of deterministic machines by synchronous parallel machines. *J. Comput. System Sci.*, 30:149–161, 1985.
6. S. Fortune and J. Wyllie. Parallelism in random access machines. In *Proc. 10th Ann. ACM Symp. on Theory of Computing*, pages 114–118, 1978.
7. L. M. Goldschlager. A universal interconnection pattern for parallel computers. *J. Assoc. Comput. Mach.*, 29:1073–1086, 1982.
8. R. M. Karp and V. Ramachandran. Parallel algorithms for shared-memory machines. In J. van Leeuwen, editor, *Handbook of Theoretical Computer Science*, volume A, chapter 17, pages 869–941. MIT Press, Cambridge, Massachusetts, 1990.
9. J. Katajainen, J. van Leeuwen, and M. Penttonen. Fast simulation of Turing machines by random access machines. *SIAM J. Comput.*, 17:77–88, 1988.
10. I. Parberry. Parallel speedup of sequential machines: a defense of the parallel computation thesis. *ACM SIGACT News*, 18:54–67, 1986.
11. I. Parberry and G. Schnitger. Parallel computation with threshold functions. *J. Comput. System Sci.*, 36:278–302, 1988.
12. W. Paul and R. Reischuk. On alternation II. *Acta Inform.*, 14:391–403, 1980.
13. W. Paul and R. Reischuk. On time versus space II. *J. Comput. System Sci.*, 22:312–327, 1981.
14. J. H. Reif. On synchronous parallel computations with independent probabilistic choice. *SIAM J. Comput.*, 13:46–56, 1984.
15. K. R. Reischuk. A fast implementation of a multidimensional storage into a tree storage. *Theoret. Comput. Sci.*, 19:253–266, 1982.
16. W. J. Savitch. Parallel random access machines with powerful instruction sets. *Math. Systems Theory*, 15:191–210, 1982.
17. W. J. Savitch and M. J. Stimson. Time bounded random access machines with parallel processing. *J. Assoc. Comput. Mach.*, 26:103–118, 1979.

Term Rewriting and Unification

Ground Reducibility and Automata with Disequality Constraints

Hubert Comon and Florent Jacquemard
Laboratoire de Recherche en Informatique. CNRS URA 410
Univ. Paris-Sud, Bât. 490
91405 Orsay cedex. France

Abstract

Using the automata with constraints, we give an algorithm for the decision of ground reducibility of a term t w.r.t. a rewriting system $\mathcal{R}$. The complexity of the algorithm is doubly exponential in the maximum of the depths of t and $\mathcal{R}$ and the cardinal of $\mathcal{R}$.

Introduction

Ground reducibility of a term t w.r.t. a term rewriting system $\mathcal{R}$ is the property that all ground instances (i.e. instances without variables) of t are reducible by $\mathcal{R}$. This property, which is also known as "quasi-reducibility" and "inductive reducibility", has been used by several authors for proving properties of algebraic specifications (the *sufficient completeness*) as well as in inductive theorem proving (see [2, 4, 7–13] among others).

Ground reducibility has been shown to be decidable for an arbitrary rewrite system by D. Plaisted [13]. Further decidability proofs where given by Kapur, Narendran and Zhang [9] and Kounalis [11]. These three proofs are based on a "test set" method: they show that there is a bound $B(\mathcal{R})$ such that, if all instances of t obtained by substituting ground terms of depth smaller than $B(\mathcal{R})$ are reducible, then t is ground reducible. Only Kapur et al. [9] give an explicit bound in their paper which is five times exponential in the depth of $\mathcal{R}$.

The three aforementioned decidability proofs all rely on a "pumping" property: if a ground term is irreducible and large enough there should be a smaller irreducible ground term. This suggests a formulation of the problem in formal language theory. That is what one of the authors did in his thesis [4], introducing *ground normal form grammars*. This was however not satisfactory because the emptiness test for these grammars is multiply exponential in the worst case (although, in contrast to the other methods, the bound needs not to be reached even when the term is indeed ground reducible). Recently, Caron, Coquidé and Dauchet come up with a very elegant proof: they show that the first-order theory of *encompassment* is decidable [3]. More precisely, they consider unary predicates

encomp$_t$ which hold on u when some instance of t is a subterm of u. They use a technique à la Büchi for the decidability of first order theories (see e.g. [14, 15] for surveys on these techniques). They define tree automata on tuples which test equalities and disequalities between subterms. The class of automata has the desired closure properties. Then, the decidability of the theory reduces to the emptiness decision for the corresponding language, which is shown thanks to a pumping property. Finally, it turns out that ground reducibility is expressible in the first-order theory of encompassment: if $l_1, \ldots, l_n$ are the left hand sides of the rewrite system $\mathcal{R}$, t is ground reducible iff the following formula holds.

$$\forall x. \, \mathbf{encomp}_t(x) \, \rightarrow \, (\mathbf{encomp}_{l_1}(x) \vee \ldots \vee \mathbf{encomp}_{l_n}(x))$$

In this paper, we give another decidability proof for ground reducibility. For, we consider a subclass of Caron et al. automata which is large enough so as to express the language of irreducible ground instances of a term. Then, deciding ground reducibility amounts to decide emptiness for our class of tree automata. Our emptiness decision proof differs from former ones. Therefore the complexity of the ground reducibility decision is reduced to a double exponential w.r.t. the depth and cardinality of the rewrite system.

Pumping properties can be stated as follows: an automaton $\mathcal{A}$ is associated with a bound $\mathcal{B}(\mathcal{A})$ such that every ground term recognized by $\mathcal{A}$ and minimal w.r.t. to a given *well-founded ordering* is smaller in depth than $\mathcal{B}(\mathcal{A})$. Then, emptiness decision can be done in $O(\alpha^{\mathcal{B}(\mathcal{A})})$ where $\alpha \geq 2$. Indeed, it suffices to check the recognizability by $\mathcal{A}$ of all ground terms of depth smaller than $\mathcal{B}(\mathcal{A})$. In the proofs for standard finite bottom-up tree automata [6] and for Caron et al. class, the well-founded ordering is the transitive closure of the *pumping* reduction, which consists in replacing a subterm by one of its proper subterms. Here, we generalize the notion of pumping, considering combinations of pumpings and "inverse pumpings" on different subterms. This new transformation allows us to derive a smaller bound $\mathcal{B}(\mathcal{A}) = O(|\mathcal{A}|.2^{c(\mathcal{A}).\ln(c(\mathcal{A}))})$, where $|\mathcal{A}|$ is the size of $\mathcal{A}$ and $c(\mathcal{A})$ the maximal size of one of its constraints.

Then we show how to compute an automaton $\mathcal{A}_{\mathcal{R},t}$ of our class which recognizes the set of $\mathcal{R}$-irreducible ground instances of t. This automaton has a size $|\mathcal{A}_{\mathcal{R},t}| = O(\alpha^{\max(d(\mathcal{R}),d(t))})$ and $c(\mathcal{A}_{\mathcal{R},t}) = O(\max(d(\mathcal{R}),d(t)) \times \mathrm{card}(\mathcal{R}))$. It can be constructed in time $O(\alpha^{\max(d(\mathcal{R}),d(t)) \times \mathrm{card}(\mathcal{R})})$. Altogether, we prove that the ground reducibility of t w.r.t. $\mathcal{R}$ can be decided in time:

$$O(\alpha^{\alpha^{\max(d(\mathcal{R}),d(t)) \times \mathrm{card}(\mathcal{R})}})$$

This result is optimal: there is an example of a rewrite system $\mathcal{R}_n$ ($n > 0$) such that $\mathrm{card}(\mathcal{R}) = n$ and the smallest $\mathcal{R}$-irreducible ground instance of a given t has a depth larger than 2^n which is of the same magnitude as $\mathcal{B}(\mathcal{A}_{\mathcal{R},t})$.

Moreover we claim that our bound $\mathcal{B}(\mathcal{A})$ well behaves in practice:

- when there is no constraint (which corresponds to left-linear rewrite systems), the bound is linear w.r.t. the number of states in the automaton. This is the well known pumping property of recognizable tree languages [6].

- when the disequality constraints are only performed between brother positions[1], the bound is polynomial w.r.t. the number of states and rules and the maximal number of disequality constraints that can be performed by the automaton during a transition. This corresponds to the bound for (deterministic) automata with disequality constraints between brothers, as defined in [1].

The paper is organized as follows: in section 1 we give the basic definitions of tree automata (with constraints). In section 2 comes the main result: a simply exponential bound for the emptiness decision in our class of constraints automata. We sketch here the proof and explain the trick which allows to reduce the complexity[2]. In section 3 we give the construction of $\mathcal{A}_{\mathcal{R},t}$ from which the ground reducibility test complexity is derived.

1 Notations, definitions

Concerning rewrite systems, we use mainly the definitions of [5]. Let us only recall that a *position* in a term is a string of natural numbers; Λ is the empty string and $\leq_{pref}$ the prefix ordering on strings. The relation $/$ on pairs of positions is defined by $p \cdot q / p := q$. $Pos(t)$ is the set of all positions of a term t. The depth $d(t)$ of a term t is the maximal length of the positions of $Pos(t)$. $d(\mathcal{R})$ is the depth of the rewriting system $\mathcal{R}$ which is the maximal depth of its left members. For every $p \in Pos(t)$, the subterm of t at position p is denoted $t|_p$ and the term obtained by replacing $t|_p$ with u is denoted $t[u]_p$. The alphabet $\mathcal{F}$ of function symbols (together with their arity) is fixed through all the paper. It is assumed to contain a symbol of arity ≥ 2. $\mathcal{F}_0$ is its subset of constant symbols. A non-ground term may also contain variable symbols out of a set X. We start with the definition of constrained bottom-up tree automata.

Definition 1.1 *A constrained automaton (CA for short) consists of a tuple* $(Q, Q_f, \mathcal{P})$ *where*

- Q *is a finite set of* state symbols.

- $Q_f \subseteq Q$ *is a set of* final states.

- $\mathcal{P}$ *is a ground constrained rewrite system over* $\mathcal{F} \cup Q$; *each rule has the form:*

$$f(q_1, \ldots, q_n) \xrightarrow{c} q$$

with $f \in \mathcal{F}$, $q, q_1, \ldots, q_n \in Q$ *and* c *is either the trivial constraint* $\top$ *or a Boolean combination without negation of unary predicates* $p_1 = p_2$ *or* $p_1 \neq p_2$ *with* $p_1, p_2 \in \mathbb{N}^+$.

---

[1] and if there are no equality constraints

[2] We cannot show here the proof in details, because of space limitations. The reader who is interested can get a full version of the paper via anonymous ftp on lri.lri.fr, directory /LRI/articles/comon, file pumping.dvi.Z.

The above predicate symbols are interpreted on ground terms as follows: $\top$ is always true and $(p_1 = p_2)(t)$ (resp. $(p_1 \neq p_2)(t)$) is true iff $p_1, p_2 \in Pos(t)$ and $t|_{p_1} = t|_{p_2}$ (resp. $t|_{p_1} \neq t|_{p_2}$).

The *target* of a rule $f(q_1, \ldots, q_n) \xrightarrow{c} q$ in $\mathcal{P}$ is the state symbol q. Given a CA $\mathcal{A} = (Q, Q_f, \mathcal{P})$, $t \xrightarrow{c}_{\mathcal{P}} t'$ if there is a rule $f(q_1, \ldots, q_n) \xrightarrow{c} q$ in $\mathcal{P}$ and a position p in t such that $t|_p = f(q_1, \ldots, q_n)$, $t' = t[q]_p$ and c holds on $t|_p$.

A run $t \xrightarrow{+}_{\mathcal{P}} t'$ (t is a ground term) is *successful* if $t' \in Q$ and *final* if $t' \in Q_f$. In the second case, we say moreover that t is *recognized* by $\mathcal{A}$. The language recognized by $\mathcal{A}$, (denoted $L(\mathcal{A})$) is the set of ground terms recognized by $\mathcal{A}$.

A CA $\mathcal{A}$ is *deterministic* when there is at most one run of $\mathcal{A}$ on each ground term. It is *completely-defined* when all runs are successful.

A successful run $t \xrightarrow{*}_{\mathcal{P}} t'$ is represented by a labeled tree r with the same set of positions as t and whose labels are rules of $\mathcal{P}$. The position $p \in Pos(t)$ of r is labeled by $\rho \in \mathcal{P}$ if, along the reduction, ρ is applied at position p.

If $\mathcal{R}$ is a left-linear rewriting system and t is a linear term, there is an automaton $\mathcal{A}_{\mathcal{R},t}$ without constraints (for which all constraints are $\top$) which fulfills the properties announced in introduction. But this is no longer true for non-left-linear systems. Consider for example $\mathcal{R} = \{x + x \to 0\}$ and $t = x + y$. Then for every ground term $g_1 + g_2$, the automaton $\mathcal{A}_{\mathcal{R},t}$ recognizing irreducible ground instances of t will have to check whether $g_1 \neq g_2$. Moreover, if $t = f(y, y)$, $\mathcal{A}_{\mathcal{R},t}$ will have to check whether $g_1 = g_2$ on $f(g_1, g_2)$. It is well known that standard *finite* tree automata are not able to perform such tests, because g_1, g_2 may be arbitrarily deep. This is why we will have to use constrained automata.

Example 1.2 Consider $\mathcal{F} = \{0, s, m\}$ where 0 is a constant, s is unary and m is ternary. Let $Q = \{q_0, q_1, q_2, q\}$ and $Q_f = \{q\}$. The automaton $\mathcal{A}$ is now defined by the set of constrained rules:

$$\rho_1, \rho_2: \quad 0 \;\to\; q_0 \mid q \qquad\qquad \rho_6, \rho_7: \quad m(q, q, q) \xrightarrow{\;1 \neq 2 \wedge 1 \neq 3 \wedge 2 \neq 3\;} q_m \mid q$$

$$\rho_3, \rho_4: \quad s(q_0) \;\to\; q_1 \mid q \qquad\qquad \rho_8, \rho_9: \quad s(q_m) \xrightarrow{\qquad\qquad} q_m \mid q$$

$$\rho_5: \quad s(q_1) \;\to\; q$$

This (non-deterministic) automaton recognizes the set of all ground terms which are not reducible by a rewrite system whose left hand sides are $\{s(s(s(0))), m(x, x, y), m(x, y, x), m(y, x, x)\}$. For example, the term $s(m(0, s(0), s(s(0))))$ is recognized by $\mathcal{A}$, through the run $r = \rho_9(\rho_6(\rho_2, \rho_4(\rho_1), \rho_5(\rho_3(\rho_1))))$. This run fits the definition: for example, the targets of $r(11), r(12)$ and $r(13)$ are q, q and q respectively and $r(1) = \rho_6$, Moreover, $t|_{11} \neq t_{12}, t_{11} \neq t_{13}, t_{12} \neq t|_{13}$. On the contrary, $m(0, 0, s(0))$ is not recognized since the constraint $1 \neq 2$ of ρ_7 is not satisfied.

2 Two pumping properties for subclasses of CA

Emptiness is undecidable for the whole class CA. As Caron et al. did, we have to impose some additional restrictions on the automata. We will show that, under these restrictions, emptiness is decidable and that the class is still general enough for expressing the ground reducibility problem. We investigate first in section 2.1 automata which do not involve equality constraints and in section 2.2 automata allowing some restricted kind of equality constraints.

As stated in introduction, we are looking for minimal terms recognized by the automaton. Our notion of minimality is not given by the subterm relation. We rather use the ordering on ground terms defined by $s \ll_{mul} s'$ iff $\mathcal{M}(s) \ll \mathcal{M}(s')$ where $\mathcal{M}(s)$ is the multiset of the lengths of leaves positions in s and $\ll$ is the multiset extension of the ordering on natural numbers. According to this notion of minimality, we define a more general notion of pumping, which is the key for reducing the complexity.

2.1 Automata with disequality constraints (ADC)

We assume in this section that $\mathcal{A} = (Q, Q_f, \mathcal{P})$ is a CA without equality constraints. For sake of simplicity, we assume moreover until section 2.3, that there are no disjunction in the constraints of the rules of $\mathcal{A}$.

Let us recall the main components of our proof: we want to compute $\mathcal{B}(\mathcal{A})$ such that if $s \in L(\mathcal{A})$ and $d(s) \geq \mathcal{B}(\mathcal{A})$ then there is a $s' \in L(\mathcal{A})$ such that $s' \ll_{mul} s$. From now on , we assume given a term $s \in L(\mathcal{A})$ and a final run r of $\mathcal{A}$ on s. We first try the classical pumping relation:

Definition 2.1 A lifting *on s is a pair $(p, p') \in Pos(s)^2$ such that $p <_{pref} p'$ and the target states of $r(p)$ and $r(p')$ are identical.*

We could obviously remark that if $d(s) \geq |Q| + 1$ then there is at least one lifting (on s) in $Pos(s)^2$. The term $s' := s[s|_{p'}]_p$ is the term obtained from s by the lifting (p, p'). It is clear that $s[s|_{p'}]_p \ll_{mul} s$. However, there is not necessary any final run on s' since the constraints of the rules applied "above" p in r might be no longer satisfied. Let us illustrate the problem on an example:

Example 2.2 Let $Q = \{q_1, q\}$ and $Q_f = \{q\}$. The rules in $\mathcal{A}$ are $\rho_1 : a \to q_1, \rho_2 : g(q_1) \to q_1$, $\rho_3 : f(q_1, q_1) \xrightarrow{1 \neq 2} q$. Consider now the term $s = f(g(g(a)), g(a))$ and the run $\rho_3(\rho_2(\rho_2(\rho_1)), \rho_2(\rho_1))$. This is indeed a run since $s|_1 \neq s|_2$. However, lifting $(1, 1 \cdot 1)$ (these two subterms are associated with the same rules in the run) results in $s' = f(g(a), g(a))$ which is not accepted by the automaton since $s'|_1 = s'|_2$.

In this case, we say that the lifting *creates an equality* between subterms. As in former works on ground reducibility[3], we distinguish three kinds of equalities that are created by a lifting (p, p'):

---

[3] This distinction was not always formulated this way in former works, but we believe that this was always underlying the method.

- equalities which do not disturb the run of the automaton

- *close equalities* which falsify a disequality test "close" to the lifting position p. Formally, this means that there are p_0, p_2, p'_2, p_3 such that $p_0 <_{pref} p \leq_{pref} p_0 \cdot p_2 = p \cdot p'_2$, $p \not\leq_{pref} p_3$, the rule $r(p_0)$ checks a disequality $p_2 \neq p_3$ (i.e. $s|_{p_0 \cdot p_2} \neq s|_{p_0 \cdot p_3}$) and $s|_{p' \cdot p'_2} = s|_{p_0 \cdot p_3}$.

- *remote equalities* which falsify a "remote" disequality test. Formally, there are p_0, p_2, p_3 such that $p_0 \cdot p_2 <_{pref} p$, the rule $r(p_0)$ checks a disequality $p_2 \neq p_3$ (i.e. $s|_{p_0 \cdot p_2} \neq s|_{p_0 \cdot p_3}$) and $s[s|_{p'}]_p|_{p_0 \cdot p_2} = s|_{p_0 \cdot p_3}$.

Now, $s' \in L(\mathcal{A})$ if the lifting does not create any close equality nor any remote equality. Our goal is to find sufficiently many lifting positions on some path, so as to be able to choose one of them following these requirement.

Close equalities   It is not very difficult to see how to deal with close equalities. Indeed, "close" means that the first lifting position p is at a distance bounded independently of s of the position of the rule whose constraint is falsified by the lifting. Thus, the maximal number of close equalities that could be created by any fixed lifting (p, p') only depends of $\mathcal{A}$. Let us illustrate the situation using a significant example.

Example 2.3   Assume that f is ternary and that we have some constrained rule $\rho_0 : f(q_1, q_2, q) \xrightarrow{1 \neq 31 \wedge 1 \neq 32} q$. Consider now a term $s = f(s_0, u_0, f(s_1, u_1, f(s_2, u_2, f(s_3, u_3, f(s_4, u_4, f(s_5, u_5, f(s_6, u_6, v)))))))$ (see figure 1)
and a run assigning ρ_0 to all positions 3^i, $0 \leq i \leq 4$ and any rule whose target is the same target as ρ_0 for positions 3^j, $j \geq 5$. Let $p_i = 3^i$, $1 \leq i \leq 6$. If each lifting (p_1, p_i), $2 \leq i \leq 6$ creates a close equality, we have $\bigwedge_{i=2}^{6}(s_0 = s_i \vee s_0 = u_i)$ i.e. for each lifting, either we create the equality $1 = 3 \cdot 1$ or $1 = 3 \cdot 2$. Since there are 5 liftings, three of them should create the same equality. Assume for example that $s_0 = s_2$ and $s_0 = s_4$ and $s_0 = s_6$ (the equality $1 = 3 \cdot 1$ is created three times). Now, we extract the subsequence $p_{i_1} = 3^2, p_{i_2} = 3^4, p_{i_3} = 3^6$. If the two liftings (p_{i_1}, p_{i_2}) and (p_{i_1}, p_{i_3}) create a close equality, we must have $s_1 = u_4 = u_6$ (corresponding to the equality $1 = 3 \cdot 2$). Indeed, we know that $s_1 \neq s_2$ (because the automaton accepts s) and $s_2 = s_4 = s_6$, hence the close equality created by the two liftings cannot be $s_1 = s_4$ nor $s_1 = s_6$: it must be the other one. Next, we again extract the sequence $p_{j_1} = 3^4, p_{j_2} = 3^6$, the lifting (p_{j_1}, p_{j_2}) cannot create any close equality because $s_3 \neq s_4$ and $s_3 \neq u_4$ on one hand, and $s_4 = s_6, u_4 = u_6$ on the other hand. This implies $s_3 \neq s_6$ and $s_3 \neq u_6$.

The following lemma shows that the situation described in example 2.3 is actually the worse one. We use some characteristics of $\mathcal{A}$: K is the maximal number of conjunctions in a constrained rule of $\mathcal{A}$, D is the maximal length of a position p_1 or p_2 in any predicate $p_1 \neq p_2$ of any constraint of a rule, C is the number of pairs of paths (p_1, p_2) that can *cross* a position π of some term s w.r.t. some run r of $\mathcal{A}$ on s. (p_1, p_2) crosses π if there are p_0, p' such that

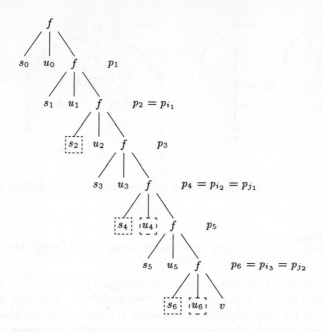

Figure 1: Close equalities that are created by liftings on s (example 2.3)

$\pi = p_0 \cdot p_1$ and there is a disequation $p_1 \cdot p_2 \neq p'$ in the constraint of $r(p_0)$ such that $p_1 \not\leq_{pref} p'$.

Lemma 2.4 *Given $k \leq 1$ if θ is a maximal length path in s whose length is larger or equal to*

$$\mathcal{B}_k(\mathcal{A}) = (1 + K^C \times C! \times k \times \sum_{i=0}^{C} \frac{1}{i!}) \times |\mathcal{P}|^D \times |Q| \times (D+1) + 1$$

then there are k liftings $(p, p_1), \ldots, (p, p_k)$ on s which do not create any close equality and such that $p \leq_{pref} p_1 \leq_{pref} \cdots \leq_{pref} p_n$ are on the path θ and $|p_{i+1}| - |p_i| > D$.

Remote equalities Now, we differ significantly from other methods in the treatment of remote equalities. Indeed, in contrast to other techniques, considering remote equalities only increases the complexity by a linear factor. Let us show first the problem of remote equalities.

Example 2.5 Consider the automaton whose states are $\{q, q'\}$, function symbols are a (constant), g, h (unary), f (binary), m (ternary) and the rules:

$\rho_1 : a \rightarrow q'$, $\rho_2 : g(q') \rightarrow q'$, $\rho_3 : h(q') \rightarrow q$, $\rho_4 : f(q, q) \xrightarrow{1 \neq 2} q$, $\rho_5 :$

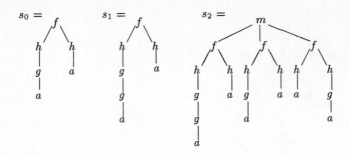

Figure 2: Remote equality and transformations (example 2.5)

$m(q, q, q) \xrightarrow{\;1 \neq 2 \wedge 1 \neq 3\;} q$. Consider now the term $s_0 = f(h(g(a)), h(a))$ (see also figure 2).

The run r of the automaton on s_0 is $\rho_4(\rho_3(\rho_2(\rho_1)), \rho_3(\rho_1))$. The lifting $(1^2, 1^3)$ creates a remote equality at the root position. The first idea would be to proceed as for close equalities: consider a longer path on which we find sufficiently many liftings. At least one of them should not create the remote equality under consideration. For, consider the term $s_1 = f(h(g(g(a))), h(a))$ (see also the figure). There are two liftings: $(1^2, 1^4)$ and $(1^2, 1^3)$. Indeed, the first one creates a remote equality and not the other one.

Now, how long should be the path? Actually, there is no upper bound which guarantees that some lifting does not create any remote equality upper in the term, since this remote equality may occur arbitrarily "far" from the liftings. Let us illustrate this on our example. Consider the term $s_2 = m(s_1, s_0, f(h(a), h(g(a))))$. We know that there are two liftings on the leftmost branch: $(1^3, 1^5)$ and $(1^3, 1^4)$. However, the first one creates a remote equality at position 1, and the second one creates a remote equality at the root.

Former algorithms consider the length of the lifting positions in order to bound the number of possible remote equalities that are created. This leads to very complex algorithms. Let us explain our trick which avoids this combinatorial explosion. If some remote equality is created by a lifting, this means that, on another branch of the tree, we have "almost the same" tree as on the lifting path. The idea is then to work on this other branch too.

On the example, the lifting $(1^3, 1^5)$ on s_2 creates a remote equality $1 \cdot 1 = 1 \cdot 2$. This means that we may put at positions $1 \cdot 1$ and $1 \cdot 2$ any different terms among $g(a)$, a, obtained from $g(g(a))$ by liftings. Unfortunately, the two possibilities create equalities $1 = 2$ or $1 = 3$. But this means that, choosing a, $g(a)$ for $1 \cdot 1$, $1 \cdot 2$, we can replace at positions 2 and 3 (possibly same) subterms obtained from $s_2|_1$ by the above operations, e.g. s_0 twice. Thus, we get a recognized term smaller than s_2 w.r.t. $\ll_{mul}$.

This suggests how to inductively define new reductions which generalize liftings:

Definition 2.6 *A* transformation *of s is a term s' which is constructed in one of the following ways:*

- *either there is a lifting (p, p') on s such that $|p'| - |p| > D$ and $s' = s[t|_{p'}]_p$*

- *or else, there are $n + 1$ incomparable positions $p_0, \ldots, p_n$ of s such that for every $i \leq n$, $||p_i| - |p_0|| \leq D - 1$ and there are n transformations $s_1, \ldots, s_n$ of $s|_{p_0}$ such that $s' = s[s_1]_{p_1} \cdots [s_n]_{p_n}$.*

$s' \ll_{mul} s$ will be guaranteed by the hypotheses on lengths. Using the inductive definition, we can also associate a transformation of r with each transformation of s: $r' := r[r_1]_{p_1} \cdots [r_n]_{r_n}$ corresponds to $s' = s[s_1]_{p_1} \cdots [s_n]_{p_n}$. The definition of close (resp. remote) equalities created by a lifting carry over (non lifting) transformations replacing the lifting position p with one of the p_i's.

Our goal is now to inductively construct a transformation which does not create any close nor remote equality. One construction step is given by the following "propagation lemma". It uses a classification of remote equalities created by any transformation into three parts (w.r.t. $p \in Pos(s)$):

- *remote equalities below p which verify $p \leq_{pref} p_0 <_{pref} p_0 \cdot p_2 <_{pref} p_i$ (for some p_i)*

- *remote equalities crossing p: $p_0 <_{pref} p <_{pref} p_0 \cdot p_2 <_{pref} p_i$*

- *remote equalities above p: $p_0 \cdot p_2 \leq_{pref} p$ ($<_{pref} p_i$)*

Lemma 2.7 *Assume $n = 2KD + 1$ and let $p \in Pos(s) \setminus \{\Lambda\}$ a prefix position of a path of maximal length in $Pos(s)$.*

Assume moreover that there are n distinct transformations $s_1, \ldots, s_n$ of s such that (a) for all $i \leq n$ $s_i|_p$ is also a transformation of $s|_p$ according to definition 2.6; (b) each transformation s_i does not create any close equality nor any remote equality below p; (c) each transformation s_i does not create any remote equality crossing p; (d) $d(s_1) = d(s_2) = \ldots = d(s_n)$ and (e) $\forall i \leq n$, $s_i \ll_{mul} s$.

Then there is a strict prefix p' of p, and n distinct transformations $s'_1, \ldots, s'_n$ of s satisfying the same properties (with p').

Then we can iterate this operation up to the root where no remote equality can be created any more. The base case of induction will be a lifting, more precisely the right number $(2KD + 1)$ of liftings which satisfies the above properties.

Lemma 2.8 *Assume $d(s) > 2D$ and $p \in Pos(s)$ such that $|p| \geq 2D - 1$. Assume moreover that there are $n' = 6KD$ liftings $(p, p_1), \ldots, (p, p_{n'})$ which do not create any close equality and which satisfy $p \leq_{pref} p_1 \leq_{pref} \cdots \leq_{pref} p_n$ are prefix to a maximal length path and $|p_{i+1}| - |p_i| > D$ for all $i \leq n' - 1$.*

Then there exists $p_0 <_{pref} p$ and $n = 2KD + 1$ distincts transformations $s_1, \ldots, s_n$ of s such that $s_i \ll_{mul} s$ and

- *either $p_0 = \Lambda$ and each transformation is recognized by $\mathcal{A}$.*

- *or p_0, s and $s_1, \ldots, s_n$ satisfy the hypotheses of lemma 2.7.*

Now, using lemmas 2.7, 2.8 and 2.4, we can state the main result:

Theorem 2.9 *If the language recognized by $\mathcal{A}$ is not empty, then it contains a tree of depth strictly smaller than $\mathcal{B}_{6KD}(\mathcal{A})$.*

As announced, remote equalities do not introduce any significant overhead. If the bound of lemma 2.4 is enhanced in some way, then the bound of theorem 2.9 will be enhanced accordingly.

2.2 Automata with "few" equality constraints

The above class ADC is no longer sufficient to catch all automata $\mathcal{A}_{\mathcal{R},t}$. We have to generalize a little bit in order to capture the non-linearities of the term t we want to recognize the ground instances.

Definition 2.10 *A semi-ADC is the union of an ADC $(Q, Q_f, \mathcal{P})$ and a triple $(\{q'\}, \{q'\}, \{f(q_1, \ldots, q_n) \xrightarrow{c \wedge c'} q' \mid f(q_1, \ldots, q_n) \xrightarrow{c} q' \in \mathcal{P}\})$ where c' is a conjunction of "equality" predicates $p_1 = p_2$.*

The emptiness is still decidable for semi-ADCs. In fact, we can use the results of the above section, provided that all transformations are performed at positions deeper than $d(s)$ and simultaneously on equals subterms. The bound for this class depends on characteristics of semi-ADCs that are characteristics of its "ADC-parts" (K, D and C) and D', the maximal length of a path which is involved in an equality constraint, o_c, the maximal number of equality constraints with a common path plus one.

Theorem 2.11 *If the language recognized by a semi-ADC $\mathcal{A}'$ is not empty, then it contains a tree of depth strictly smaller than $\mathcal{B}_{m'+D'}(\mathcal{A}')$ where $m' = max(6KD, K(o_c.D' + 4D))$.*

2.3 Handling disjunctions

Given an automaton $\mathcal{A}$, a term s and a run r of the automaton on s, if $r(\pi) = \rho$ is a rule whose constraint is a conjunction of disjunctions, there should be at least one disequality which is satisfied for each disjunct. Hence, the automaton behaves as if ρ were replaced with a rule without disjunction, choosing carefully which disequality tests are kept. This means that we can apply the results of the former sections, replacing the number $|\mathcal{P}|$ of rules with the *weight* of $\mathcal{P}$ which is defined as follows:

$$W(\mathcal{P}) = |\mathcal{P}_l| + \sum_{d_1 \wedge \ldots \wedge d_m = \mathcal{C}(\rho), \rho \in \mathcal{P}} |d_1| \times \ldots \times |d_m|$$

where $|d|$ is the number of atomic formulae in d, $\mathcal{C}(\rho)$ is the constraint of the rule ρ in c.n.f. and $\mathcal{P}_l$ is the set of unconstrained rules in $\mathcal{P}$.

Of course, this increases the complexity, but this is quite different from considering the equivalent automaton where disjunctions have been removed, since such an automaton would be non-deterministic even if the original automaton is deterministic. Then when deciding the emptiness of the language, we would have to consider *all* possible runs of the automaton, which is not the case if we keep disjunctions in the constraints as we do.

3 Decision of ground reducibility

We now show how to construct a semi-ADC $\mathcal{A}_{\mathcal{R},t}$, recognizing the expected language. The construction we will briefly show is far from being the most efficient one (it cannot be implemented).

Let "Ω" be a new constant (which will represent a "hole" in a term). Let T be the set of all terms in $T(\mathcal{F} \cup \{\Omega\})$ of depth smaller than $d(\mathcal{R})$ and such that Ω only occurs at depth $d(\mathcal{R})$ and this is the only symbol occurring at such a depth. (T has a size bounded by $\alpha^{1+d(\mathcal{R})}$, where $\alpha = a \times |\mathcal{F}|$ and a is the maximal arity of a function symbol). Let Q be the set of all q_s such that $s \in T$ cannot be reduced by a linear left hand side of a rule. Intuitively, the set of terms accepted in state q_s is the set of all terms that match s and that are irreducible by $\mathcal{R}$. In order to make it precise,

Definition 3.1 *A term u matches a term $s \in T$, if u is obtained by replacing each occurrence of Ω in s with some term. (All occurrences of Ω need not to be replaced with the same term).*

Then, the set $\mathcal{P}$ is constructed as follows: if $q_{f(s_1,\ldots,s_m)}, q_{u_1}, \ldots, q_{u_m} \in Q$ are such that $u_1, \ldots, u_m$ match respectively $s_1, \ldots, s_m$, we add the following constrained rule:

$$f(q_{u_1}, \ldots, q_{u_m}) \xrightarrow{c} q_{f(s_1,\ldots,s_m)}$$

where c is the conjunction for all non linear left hand side l whose $f(u_1, \ldots, u_m)$ is an instance, of the disjunction for each two distinct occurrences p_1, p_2 of the same variable x in l of the constraint $p_1 \neq p_2$.

The language accepted by the constrained automaton $(Q, Q_f := Q, \mathcal{P})$ is the set of all $\mathcal{R}$-irreducible ground terms.

The semi-ADC $\mathcal{A}_{\mathcal{R},t}$ that recognized the $\mathcal{R}$-irreducible ground instances of t is given by $\mathcal{A}_{\mathcal{R},t} := (Q, Q_f, \mathcal{P}) \cup (\{q'\}, \{q'\}, \mathcal{P}')$ where $\mathcal{P}'$ is a set of constrained rules of the form $f(q_{u_1}, \ldots, q_{u_m}) \xrightarrow{c \wedge c'} q'$ where $f(u_1, \ldots, u_m)$ matches t_Ω (the term t in which all variables are replaced with Ω), c' is the conjunction of the constraints $p_1 = p_2$ for each two occurrences of some non linear variable in t and c is the constraint of the rule $f(q_{u_1}, \ldots, q_{u_m}) \xrightarrow{c} q \in \mathcal{P}$ (if any).

The characteristics of this automaton are (roughly) bounded as expected in introduction: (we don't write below the tedious verifications) $C \leq 1 + n(\mathcal{R})d(\mathcal{R})$,

$K \leq n(\mathcal{R})$, $D \leq d(\mathcal{R})$, $D' \leq d(t)$ and $\mathcal{W}(\mathcal{P}) \leq \alpha^{3+(2n(\mathcal{R})+1)d(\mathcal{R})}$, $|Q| \leq \alpha^{1+d(\mathcal{R})}$, $o_c \leq \alpha^{d(\mathcal{R})}$ ($n(\mathcal{R})$ is the number of non-linear left sides of $\mathcal{R}$).

Then, deciding the ground reducibility of a term t w.r.t. a rewrite system $\mathcal{R}$ can be done in time: (writing d for $\max(d(t), d(\mathcal{R}))$ and n for $n(\mathcal{R})$)

$$O(\exp(d^2 \times n^{2+nd} \times \alpha^{2+3d(1+n)}))$$

References

[1] B. Bogaert and S. Tison. Equality and disequality constraints on brother terms in tree automata. In A. Finkel, editor, *Proc. 9th Symp. on Theoretical Aspects of Computer Science*, Paris, 1992. Springer-Verlag.

[2] R. Bündgen and W. Küchlin. Computing ground reducibility and inductively complete positions. Universitaet Tübingen, Oct. 1988.

[3] A.-C. Caron, J.-L. Coquidé, and M. Dauchet. Encompassment properties and automata with constraints. In *Proc. RTA 93*, 1993.

[4] H. Comon. Unification et disunification: Théorie et applications. Thèse de Doctorat, Institut National Polytechnique de Grenoble, France, 1988.

[5] N. Dershowitz and J.-P. Jouannaud. Notations for rewriting. *EATCS Bulletin*, 43:162–172, 1990.

[6] M. Gécseg and M. Steinby. *Tree Automata*. Akademia Kiadó, Budapest, 1984.

[7] J.-P. Jouannaud and E. Kounalis. Automatic proofs by induction in theories without constructors. *Information and Computation*, 82(1), July 1989.

[8] D. Kapur, P. Narendran, D. Rosenkrantz, and H. Zhang. Sufficient completeness, ground reducibility and their complexity. *Acta Inf.*, 28:311–350, 1991.

[9] D. Kapur, P. Narendran, and H. Zhang. On sufficient completeness and related properties of term rewriting systems. *Acta Inf.*, 24(4):395–415, 1987.

[10] E. Kounalis. Completeness in data type specifications. In *Proc. EUROCAL 85, Linz, LNCS 204*, pages 348–362. Springer-Verlag, Apr. 1985.

[11] E. Kounalis. Testing for the ground (co)-reducibility in term rewriting systems. *Theoretical Comput. Sci.*, 106(1):87–117, 1992.

[12] T. Nipkow and G. Weikum. A decidability result about sufficient completeness of axiomatically specified abstract data types. In *Proc. 6th GI Conf.* Springer-Verlag, 1982.

[13] D. Plaisted. Semantic confluence tests and completion methods. *Information and Control*, 65:182–215, 1985.

[14] M. Rabin. Decidable theories. In J. Barwise, editor, *Handbook of Mathematical Logic*, pages 595–629. North-Holland, 1977.

[15] W. Thomas. Automata on infinite objects. In J. van Leeuwen, editor, *Handbook of Theoretical Computer Science*, pages 134–191. Elsevier, 1990.

Perpetuality and Strong Normalization in Orthogonal Term Rewriting Systems

Zurab Khasidashvili

School of Information Systems, UEA
Norwich NR4 7TJ England
zurab@sys.uea.ac.uk

Abstract. We design a strategy that for any given term t in an Orthogonal Term Rewriting System (OTRS) constructs a longest reduction starting from t if t is strongly normalizable, and constructs an infinite reduction otherwise. For some classes of OTRSs the strategy is easily computable. We develop a method for finding the least upper bound of lengths of reductions starting from a strongly normalizable term. We give also some applications of our results.

1 Introduction

It is shown in O'Donnell [12] that the innermost strategy is perpetual for orthogonal term rewriting systems (OTRSs). That is, contraction of innermost redexes gives an infinite reduction of a given term whenever such a reduction exists. In fact, a strategy that only contracts redexes that do not erase any other redex is perpetual. Moreover, one can even reduce redexes whose erased arguments are strongly normalizable (Klop [10]). For the lambda-calculus, a more subtle perpetual strategy was invented in Barendregt et. al. [1]. However, none of these strategies are general enough to capture perpetuality in all Orthogonal Combinatory Reduction Systems (OCRSs), i.e., OTRSs with bound variables (Klop [9]).

Perpetual reductions are interesting because termination of a perpetual reduction starting from a term t implies strong normalization of t (i.e., termination of all reductions starting from t). Our aim is not only to construct an infinite reduction of any given term t whenever it exist, but also to construct a longest reduction if all reductions starting from t are finite. Thus we will be able to characterize the complexity of computations of terms. The idea is that in order to construct a perpetual reduction one should try to avoid erasure of (infinite) redexes. On the other hand, in order to construct a longest possible reduction, one should delay contraction of a redex until it will no longer be possible to duplicate it by reducing an outer redex. The two conditions agree if in each term s one contracts a *limit* redex, which is defined as follows: choose in s an *unabsorbed* redex u_1, i.e., a redex whose descendants never appear inside arguments of other redexes; choose an erased argument s_1 of u_1 that is not in normal form; choose in s_1 an unabsorbed redex u_2, and so on, as long as possible. The last chosen redex is a limit redex of s. It is shown in [8] that the limit strategy is perpetual also in OCRSs.

An unabsorbed redex exists in any term not in normal form, but there is no general algorithm to find one. However, for some classes of OTRSs, such as persistent, inside-creating, non-absorbing, non-left-absorbing, and non-right-absorbing systems, the unabsorbed redexes are easy to find. For example, in non-left-absorbing systems, where no subterm can be absorbed to the left of the contracted redex, the leftmost-outermost redexes are unabsorbed (the λ-calculus and the Combinatory Logic are non-left-absorbing). Unabsorbed redexes can easily be found also in the wide class of strongly sequential OTRSs [4].

We develop a method for proving that the reductions constructed according to our perpetual strategy are indeed the longest, and for finding their lengths. Our method is similar to Nederpelt's method [11] by which proving strong normalization in a typed λ-calculus gets reduced to proving weak normalization (i.e., existence of a normal form). Nederpelt's method was reinvented and used by Klop [9] for OCRSs. For any OTRS R, we define the corresponding non-erasing OTRS R_μ which contain special function symbols μ^n and show that the least upper bound of lengths of R-reductions starting from a term o coincides with the number of μ-occurrences in the R_μ-normal form of o. To find this number, sometimes it is not necessary to do actual transformation of t. We show this for the case of persistent TRSs.

Further, a term t is strongly normalizable in R iff it is weakly normalizable in R_μ; this result holds also on the level of OTRSs: an OTRS R is strongly normalizing iff its μ-extension R_μ is weakly normalizing [9]. Therefore, for any class of OTRSs that is closed under μ-extension, i.e., contains the μ-extension of each of its elements, one can prove undecidability of weak normalization if undecidability of strong normalization is known, and prove decidability of strong normalization if decidability of weak normalization is known. For example, all the above classes of OTRSs are closed under μ-extension.

We describe some applications of our results in section 3. The main results are obtained in section 2. Complete proofs can be found in [7].

2 Perpetual strategies in OTRSs

We recall some basic notions of TRS theory; one can find comprehensive introductions to the subject in [3] and [10]. A *TRS* is a pair (Σ, R), where the alphabet Σ consists of variables and function symbols and R is a set of rewrite rules r of the form $t \rightarrow s$. The left-hand side t is any term different from a variable, and the term s may only contain variables that occur in t. An *r-redex* u is obtained from t by substituting arbitrary terms for the variables in t, and the corresponding instance of s is the *contractum* of u. *Arguments* of u are subterms of u that correspond to variables of t, and the rest is the *pattern* of u. Subterms of u rooted at the pattern are called the *pattern-subterms* of u. The arguments, pattern, and pattern-subterms are defined analogously in the contractum of u. A TRS is *orthogonal* if it is left-linear and non-ambiguous, i.e., patterns of redexes can never overlap in a term.

A one step *reduction* in which a redex u in a term o is contracted is written $o \xrightarrow{u} e$ or $o \to e$. We write $P : o \twoheadrightarrow e$ if P is a *reduction* of o to e comprising 0 or more steps. A term t is called *weakly* (resp. *strongly*) *normalizable* if t has a normal form (resp. if any reduction starting from t is terminating). An OTRS R is *weakly* (resp. *strongly*) *normalizing* if any term in R is weakly (resp. strongly) normalizable. We use t, s, e, o for terms, u, v, w for redexes, and P, Q for reductions. $|P|$ denotes the length of P. We write $s \subseteq t$ if s is a subterm of t.

For a given OTRS R we now define its "μ-extension" R_μ: for each R-rule $t \to s$, we have a set of R_μ-rules of the form $t' \to \mu^l(\mu^0, \ldots, \mu^0, x_{i_1}, \ldots, x_{i_k}, s)$, where μ^n is a fresh n-ary function symbol; t is obtained from t' by removing all except the last arguments of μ-symbols occurring in t' (we write $t = [t']_\mu$); and $x_{i_1}, \ldots, x_{i_k}$ are all variables of t that do not occur in s. If a term e has a normal form in R_μ, then all R_μ-reductions of e are finite, since their lengths can not exceed the number $\|o\|_\mu$ of μ-occurrences in the R_μ-normal form o of e. (Indeed, for any R_μ-reduction $P : e \twoheadrightarrow e'$, we have $e' \twoheadrightarrow o$; hence $|P| \leq \|e'\|_\mu \leq \|o\|_\mu$.) For any R-reduction $Q : t_1 \to t_2 \to \ldots \to t_n$ we construct a corresponding R_μ-reduction $Q_\mu : s_1 = t_1 \to s_2 \to \ldots \to s_n$ such that $[s_i]_\mu = t_i$. So in order to prove that a term t in R is strongly normalizable it is enough to prove that t has a normal form in R_μ. This is the idea of Nederpelt's method. Now if s_n is an R_μ-normal form of s_1, then $\|s_n\|_\mu$ is an upper bound of lengths of R-reductions starting from t_1. Thus the length of Q is maximal if s_n is the R_μ-normal form of s_1 whenever t_n is the normal form of t_1, and $|Q_\mu| = \|s_n\|_\mu$, i.e., each step of Q_μ increases the number of μ-occurrences exactly by 1. This is achieved by contracting the limit redexes only. Indeed, in this case the old μ-occurrences do not duplicate, and the only new μ-symbol created in each step is the head symbol of the contractum. (In [7], we give a simple direct proof of the fact that limit reductions are the longest.)

Definition 2.1 The *μ-extension* (Σ_μ, R_μ) of an OTRS (Σ, R) is defined as follows:

1. $\Sigma_\mu = \Sigma \cup \{\mu^n \mid n = 0, 1, \ldots\}$, where μ^n is a fresh n-ary function symbol. For any subterm $s = \mu^{n+1}(t_1, \ldots, t_n, t_0)$ of a term t over Σ_μ, the arguments $t_1, \ldots, t_n$, as well as subterms and symbols in $t_1, \ldots, t_n$ and the head-symbol μ itself, are called *μ-erased* or more precisely *μ'-erased*, where μ' is the occurrence of the head symbol of s in t. The argument t_0 is called *μ'-main*. Symbols and subterms in t that are not μ-erased are called *μ-main*. We denote by $[t]_\mu$ the term obtained from t by removing all μ-erased symbols.

2. R_μ is the set of all rules of the form $r_\mu : t' \to s'$ such that

(a) there is a rule $r : t \to s$ in R such that $[t']_\mu = t$;

(b) the term t' is linear (i.e., no variable appears twice or more in t');

(c) the head symbol of t' is not a μ-symbol, i.e., it coincides with the head symbol of t;

(d) the μ-erased arguments of each occurrence μ' of a μ-symbol in t' are variables, and the μ'-main argument is not a variable (i.e., it contains a function symbol from Σ or a μ-symbol);

(e) if $x_1, \ldots, x_n$ are all μ-main variables of t' (from left to right), $y_1, \ldots, y_m$ are all μ-erased variables of t', and $x_{i_1}, \ldots, x_{i_p}$ are all variables among $x_1, \ldots, x_n$ that do not occur in s, then

$$s' = \mu^l(\overbrace{\mu^0, \ldots, \mu^0}^{k}, y_1, \ldots, y_m, x_{i_1}, \ldots, x_{i_p}, s),$$

where k is the number of occurrences of μ-symbols in t' and $l = k+m+p+1$. For any r_μ-redex $u = t'\theta$, we call arguments that correspond to $x_{i_1}, \ldots, x_{i_l}$ *quasi-erased* arguments of u, and call the arguments that correspond to other variables from $x_1, \ldots, x_n$ *quasi-main*. R_μ and R are called μ-corresponding OTRSs (the orthogonality of R_μ is easy to check), and r_μ and r are called corresponding rules in R_μ and R.

Example 2.1 Let $R = \{r : f(a, x) \to b\}$. Then R_μ-rules have the form

$$f(\mu^k(x_1, \ldots, x_{k-1}, \mu^l(y_1, \ldots, y_{l-1}, \ldots \mu^m(z_1, \ldots, z_{m-1}, a) \ldots)), x) \to$$
$$\mu(\mu^0, \ldots, \mu^0, x_1, \ldots, x_{k-1}, y_1 \ldots, y_{l-1}, \ldots, z_1 \ldots, z_{m-1}, x, b)$$

For example, r_μ : $f(\mu^2(y, \mu^2(z, a), x) \to \mu^6(\mu^0, \mu^0, y, z, x, b))$ is an R_μ-rule. For any r_μ-redex $t = f(\mu^2(o, \mu^2(s, a)), \epsilon)$, $[t]_\mu = f(a, \epsilon)$ is an r-redex, $t' = \mu(\mu^0, \mu^0, o, s, \epsilon, b)$ is the contractum of t, and $[t']_\mu = b$ is the contractum of $f(a, \epsilon)$.

Lemma 2.1 Let t be a term over Σ_μ the head-symbol of which is not a μ-symbol, and let $[t]_\mu = s$. Then t is an r_μ-redex iff s is an r-redex, where r_μ and r are corresponding rules in R_μ and R, respectively. Moreover, if t' is the contractum of t in R_μ and s' is the contractum of s in R, then $[t']_\mu = s'$.

Proof. From Definition 2.1 (see also Example 2.1).

Corollary 2.1 Let R be an OTRS and $s_0 \xrightarrow{u_0} s_1 \xrightarrow{u_1} \ldots$ be a reduction in R. Then, for any term t_0 in R_μ such that $[t_0]_\mu = s_0$, there is a reduction $t_0 \xrightarrow{v_0} t_1 \xrightarrow{v_1} \ldots$ in R_μ such that $[t_i]_\mu = s_i$ and u_i and v_i are corresponding subterms in s_i and t_i $(i = 0, 1, \ldots)$.

Notation $\|t\|_\mu$ denotes the number of occurrences of μ-symbols in t.

Lemma 2.2 Let t be a term in an OTRS R. If t is weakly normalizable in R_μ, then t is strongly normalizable in R_μ and R.

Proof. Let s be an R_μ-normal form of t and $t \to t_1 \to \ldots$ be an R_μ-reduction. By the Church-Rosser theorem, $t_i \twoheadrightarrow s$ for all $i = 1, 2, \ldots$ It is easy to see that $i \leq \|t_i\|_\mu \leq \|s\|_\mu$. So t is strongly normalizable in R_μ. Hence, by Corollary 2.1, t is strongly normalizable in R.

Definition 2.2 Let $t \xrightarrow{u} s$ and let e be the contractum of u in s. For each argument o of u there are 0 or more arguments of e. We call them $(u\text{-})descendants$ of o. Correspondingly, subterms of o have 0 or more *descendants*. An argument of u is called $(u)\text{-}erased$ if it does not have a descendant, and is called $(u)\text{-}main$ otherwise. By definition, the *descendant* of each pattern-subterm of u is e. Descendants of all redexes of t except u are also called *residuals*. By definition, u does not have residuals in s. A redex of s is said to be *created* by contracting u or to be an $(u)\text{-}new$ redex if it is not a residual of a redex of t. It is clear what is to be meant by *descendants* of subterms that are not in u. The notions of *descendant* and *residual* extend naturally to arbitrary reductions. The *ancestor* relation is the inverse of the descendant relation.

Definition 2.3 We call a redex u *complete* (resp. $\infty\text{-}complete$) if the erased arguments of u are in normal form (resp. are strongly normalizable). A reduction is *complete* (resp. $\infty\text{-}complete$) if it only contracts complete (resp. $\infty\text{-}complete$) redexes.

Lemma 2.3 Let $P : t_0 \xrightarrow{u_0} t_1 \xrightarrow{u_1} \ldots \to t_n$ be a complete reduction in an OTRS (Σ, R), and let $P_\mu : s_0 \xrightarrow{v_0} s_1 \xrightarrow{v_1} \ldots \to s_n$ be a corresponding R_μ-reduction such that all R_μ-redexes in s_0 are μ-main. Then

(1) for each k $(0 \leq k \leq n)$, we have $(b)_k$: any R_μ-redex in s_k is μ-main.

(2) if P is normalizing, then so is P_μ.

Proof. (1) By induction on k. $(b)_0$ is obvious. Suppose that $(b)_k$ holds and let us show $(b)_{k+1}$. Let $u_k = C[o_1, \ldots, o_m]$ and $v_k = C'[e_1, \ldots, e_m, e'_1, \ldots, e'_p]$, where $e_1, \ldots, e_m$ are μ-main arguments of v_k, which correspond to arguments $o_1, \ldots, o_m$ of u_k, and $e'_1, \ldots, e'_p$ are μ-erased arguments of v_k. Then the contractum of v_k in R_μ has the form $o' = \mu(\mu^0, \ldots, \mu^0, e'_1, \ldots, e'_p, e_{i_1}, \ldots, e_{i_l}, o)$, where o is the contractum of $C[e_1, \ldots, e_m]$ in (Σ_μ, R) and, for each j, o_{i_j} is u_k-erased. Since v_k and u_k are corresponding subterms of s_k and t_k, and e_i and o_i are corresponding arguments, we have that (α): $[e_i]_\mu = o_i$, $i = 1, \ldots, m$. Since $o_{i_1}, \ldots, o_{i_l}$ are u_k-erased and u_k is complete, we have that (β): $o_{i_1}, \ldots, o_{i_l}$ are R-normal forms. It follows from $(b)_k$ that in $e'_1, \ldots, e'_p$ there are no R_μ-redexes and that R_μ-redexes in s_{k+1}, that are not in o' or are in o, are μ-main. It follows from $(b)_k$, (α), (β), and Lemma 2.1 that $e_{i_1}, \ldots, e_{i_l}$ are R_μ-normal forms. Thus $(b)_{k+1}$ holds and (1) is proved.

(2) By Lemma 2.1 and $(b)_n$.

Recall that a (*sequential*) *strategy* selects a redex to be contracted in any given term. A *complete* (resp. $\infty\text{-}complete$) *strategy* contracts a complete (resp. an ∞-complete) redex in each step. A strategy is *perpetual* if it constructs an infinite reduction of any given term whenever such a reduction exists.

Theorem 2.1 A complete strategy is perpetual in OTRSs.

Proof. It is enough to show that if t has a normalizing complete reduction $P : t \twoheadrightarrow t'$, then t is strongly normalizable. Indeed, by Lemma 2.3, the corresponding R_μ-reduction of P is also normalizing. Hence, by Lemma 2.2, t is strongly normalizable in R.

As a corollary, one has that a non-erasing OTRS is weakly normalizing iff it is strongly normalizing (Church), and that the innermost strategy is perpetual in OTRSs (O'Donnell [12]).

Theorem 2.2 (Klop [10]) An ∞-complete strategy is perpetual in OTRSs.

Proof. It is enough to prove that if t_0 has a normalizing ∞-complete reduction $P : t_0 \xrightarrow{u_0} t_1 \xrightarrow{u_1} \ldots \rightarrow t_n$, then t_0 is strongly normalizable in R. Since u_i is ∞-complete, there is a complete normalizing reduction $Q : t_0 \twoheadrightarrow t_1 \twoheadrightarrow \ldots \twoheadrightarrow t_n$. Now by Theorem 2.1, t_0 is strongly normalizable.

The following propositions are obtained in Klop [9]. The proof of Proposition 2.2 is, however, not correct — a proof of Proposition 2.1 is presented as a proof of Proposition 2.2, while the former establishes weak normalization of R_μ only for terms of R, not for all terms of R_μ. The difference is significant for the applications presented below.

Proposition 2.1 (Klop [9]) A term t in an OTRS R is strongly normalizable iff t is weakly normalizable in R_μ.

Proof. ($\Rightarrow$) From Lemma 2.3. ($\Leftarrow$) From Lemma 2.2.

Proposition 2.2 (Klop [9]) An OTRS R is strongly normalizing iff R_μ is weakly normalizing.

Proof. ($\Rightarrow$) Let t' be a term in R_μ. We prove that t' is weakly normalizable by induction on the length of t'. By the induction assumption, all μ-erased subterms of t' are weakly normalizable in R_μ. Let t^* be obtained from t' by their reduction to normal forms. By Lemma 2.3, t^* is weakly normalizable in R_μ, since $[t^*]_\mu$ is strongly normalizable in R. Hence, t' is weakly normalizable. ($\Leftarrow$) From Lemma 2.2.

Definition 2.4 (1) ([5]) We call a subterm s of a term t *unabsorbed in a reduction* $P : t \twoheadrightarrow e$ if the descendants of s do not appear inside redex-arguments of terms in P, and call s *absorbed in P* otherwise. We call s *unabsorbed in t* if it is unabsorbed in any reduction starting from t, and *absorbed in t* otherwise.

(2) Let u_l be a redex in a term t defined as follows: choose an unabsorbed redex u_1 in t; choose an erased argument s_1 of u_1 that is not in normal form (if any); choose in s_1 an unabsorbed redex u_2, and so on, as long as possible. Let $u_1, s_1, u_2, \ldots, u_l$ be such a sequence. Then we call u_l a *limit redex* and call $u_1, s_1, u_2, \ldots, u_l$ a *limit sequence* of t.

In [4], Huet and Lévy introduced the notion of *external redex* of a term and proved that each term not in normal form possesses an external redex. It is easy to show that a redex $u \subseteq t$ is unabsorbed iff u is external in t. A direct short proof of the existence of an unabsorbed redexes in any term not in normal form can be found in [5]. Thus in any term not in normal form there is a limit redex.

We call a reduction *limit* if each contracted redex in it is limit, and call a strategy *limit* if in any term not in normal form it contracts a limit redex.

Lemma 2.4 Let u be a limit redex in t and $P : t \twoheadrightarrow e$. Then there is no new redex in e that contains a descendant of u in its argument.

Proof. Let $u_1, s_1, u_2, \ldots, u_l$ be the limit sequence of t with $u_l = u$. We prove by induction on $|P|$ that (a): descendants of redexes $u_1, \ldots, u_l$ do not appear inside arguments of new redexes. If $|P| = 0$, then (a) is obvious. So let $P : t \twoheadrightarrow e' \xrightarrow{v} e$, let o be a descendant of u in e, and let o' be its ancestor in e'. It follows from the induction assumption that each redex u_i ($i = 1, \ldots, l-1$) has exactly one residual u'_i in e' (because contraction of a residual of any of the redexes $u_1, \ldots, u_{l-1}$ erases the descendant of u), there is no new redex in e' that contains o' in its argument, and o is the only descendant of u. Thus if there is a new redex w in e that contains the residual u''_i of some u_i in its argument, then it must be created by v. If $v \not\subseteq u'_1$, then w contains u''_i in its argument iff it contains the residual of u'_1 in its argument, but this is impossible since u_1 is unabsorbed. Thus $v \subseteq u'_1$. Let k be the maximal number such that v is in u'_k and let s'_k be the descendant of s_k in e'. Then v is in s'_k and contains u'_{k+1}. Let $Q : s_k \twoheadrightarrow s''_k$ consist of steps of P that are made in descendants of s_k. Then the residual of u_{k+1} is in an argument of the new redex $w \subseteq s''_k$. But this is impossible since u_{k+1} is unabsorbed in s_k. Thus (a) is valid and the lemma is proved.

Lemma 2.5 Let (Σ, R) be an OTRS, $P : t_0 \xrightarrow{u_0} t_1 \xrightarrow{u_1} \ldots \rightarrow t_n$ be a limit reduction in R and $P_\mu : s_0 = t_0 \xrightarrow{v_0} s_1 \xrightarrow{v_1} \ldots \rightarrow s_n$ be its corresponding reduction in R_μ.

(1) For each k ($0 \leq k \leq n$) the following holds:

$(a)_k$: $\|s_k\|_\mu = k$;

$(b)_k$: each redex $v'_k \subseteq s_k$ is μ-main in s_k;

$(c)_k$: in quasi-main arguments of any redex v''_k in s_k there are no μ-symbols.

(2) If P is normalizing, then so is P_μ.

Proof. (1) $(a)_0 - (c)_0$ are obvious. Suppose that $(a)_k - (c)_k$ hold and let us show $(a)_{k+1} - (c)_{k+1}$. Let $u_k = C[o_1, \ldots, o_q]$ and $v_k = C'[\epsilon_1, \ldots, \epsilon_q, \epsilon'_1, \ldots, \epsilon'_m]$, where $\epsilon_1, \ldots, \epsilon_q$ are μ-main arguments of v_k (which correspond to arguments $o_1, \ldots, o_q$ of u_k respectively) and $\epsilon'_1, \ldots, \epsilon'_m$ are μ-erased arguments of v_k. Since u_k and v_k are corresponding redexes in t_k and s_k, we have $[v_k]_\mu = u_k$ and hence (α): $[\epsilon_i]_\mu = o_i$ for all $i = 1, \ldots, q$. Let $o_{i_1}, \ldots, o_{i_l}$ be u_k-erased arguments and $o_{j_1}, \ldots, o_{j_p}$ be u_k-main arguments. Then the contractum of v_k in R_μ has the following form: $o' = \mu(\mu^0, \ldots, \mu^0, \epsilon'_1, \ldots, \epsilon'_m, \epsilon_{i_1}, \ldots, \epsilon_{i_l}, o)$, where o is the contractum of $C[\epsilon_1, \ldots, \epsilon_n]$ in (Σ_μ, R). Since u_k is limit, (β): $o_{i_1}, \ldots, o_{i_l}$ are in R-normal form. By $(c)_k$, (γ): there are no occurrences of μ-symbols in $\epsilon_{j_1}, \ldots, \epsilon_{j_p}, o$. (Hence o coincides with the contractum of u_k.) It follows from (α), (β), $(b)_k$, and Lemma 2.1 that (δ): $\epsilon_{i_1}, \ldots, \epsilon_{i_l}$ are in R_μ-normal form.

By (γ), $\|o'\|_\mu = \|v_k\|_\mu + 1$. Hence $\|s_{k+1}\|_\mu = \|s_k\|_\mu + 1 = k + 1$, i.e., $(\alpha)_{k+1}$ holds.

If $v'_{k+1} \not\subseteq o'$, then $(b)_k$ implies that v'_{k+1} is μ-main. If $v'_{k+1} \subseteq o'$, then, by $(b)_k$, $v'_{k+1} \not\subseteq \epsilon'_1, \ldots, \epsilon'_m$ (since ancestors of $\epsilon'_1, \ldots, \epsilon'_m$ are μ-erased arguments of

v_k) and, by (δ), $v'_{k+1} \not\subseteq \epsilon_{i_1}, \ldots, \epsilon_{i_l}$. Hence $v'_{k+1} \subseteq o$ and v'_{k+1} is μ-main by (γ). Now $(b)_{k+1}$ is proved.

If $o' \cap v''_{k+1} = \emptyset$, then $(c)_{k+1}$ follows immediately from $(c)_k$. If $v''_{k+1} \subseteq o'$, then as we have shown above (for v'_{k+1}), $v''_{k+1} \subseteq o$ and $(c)_{k+1}$ follows from (γ). Suppose now that o' is a proper subterm of v''_{k+1} and v''_{k+1} has an v_k-ancestor v_k^* in s_k for which v''_{k+1} is a residual. Let u_k^* be the corresponding redex of v_k^* in t_k (it exists, because, by $(b)_k$, v_k^* is μ-main). Obviously, u_k is a proper subterm of u_k^* and since u_k is limit, it must be in an erased argument of u_k^*. Hence v_k is in a quasi-erased argument of v_k^*. Therefore o' is in a quasi-erased argument of v''_{k+1} and the quasi-main arguments of v''_{k+1} coincide with the corresponding quasi-main arguments of v_k^*. Thus, by $(c)_k$, in the quasi-main arguments of v''_{k+1} there are no occurrences of μ-symbols. To prove $(c)_{k+1}$, it remains to consider the case when o' is a proper subterm of v''_{k+1} and v''_{k+1} is created by v_k. If in quasi-main arguments of v''_{k+1} there are μ-symbols, then in main arguments of corresponding redex u''_{k+1} in s_{k+1}, which is also a u_k-new redex, there are descendants of redexes contracted in P. (Since v_k is μ-main, o' and hence u_{k+1} are also μ-main.) But each redex contracted in P is a limit redex. Thus, by Lemma 2.4, their descendants can not occur in arguments of new redexes. Hence, also in this case, there are no μ-symbols in quasi-main arguments of v''_{k+1}, and $(c)_{k+1}$ is valid. Now (1) is proved.

(2) By Lemma 2.1 and $(b)_n$.

Theorem 2.3 A limit strategy is perpetual in OTRSs. Moreover, if a term t in an OTRS R is strongly normalizable, then a limit strategy constructs a longest normalizing reduction starting from t, and its length coincides with the number of μ-occurrences in an R_μ-normal form of t.

Proof. If a limit R-reduction P starting from t is normalizing, then by Lemma 2.5 its corresponding R_μ-reduction also is normalizing. Hence, by Lemma 2.2, t is strongly normalizable in R. Thus, the limit strategy is perpetual. Now, if t is strongly normalizable, Q is a normalizing R-reduction, and s is an R_μ-normal form of t, then $|Q| =$(by Corollary 2.1)$= |Q_\mu| \leq$ (by the CR property of R_μ)$\leq \|s\|_\mu =$(by Lemma 2.5)$= |P|$. Thus, P has the maximal length among all reductions of t to normal form.

3 Applications

3.1 Recursive perpetual strategies for some classes of OTRSs

We now define some classes of OTRSs, introduced in [5], for which the limit strategy is efficient.

Definition 3.1 (1) Let $t \xrightarrow{u} s$ in an OTRS R, and let $v \subseteq s$ be a new redex. We call v *generated* if its pattern is in the pattern of the contractum of u. We call an OTRS R *persistent* (PTRS) if, for each reduction step in R, any created redex is generated.

(2) We call an OTRS *outside-creating* if, for any reduction step $t \xrightarrow{u} s$, any new redex in s contains at least one symbol above the contractum of u.

(3) We call an OTRS *non-absorbing* if, for any reduction step $t \xrightarrow{u} s$, the arguments of any new redex in s are in the contractum of u.

(4) We call an OTRS *non-left-absorbing* (resp. *non-right-absorbing*) if, for any reduction step $t \xrightarrow{u} s$, any argument of a created redex in s is inside the contractum of u or to the right (resp. to the left) of it.

It is easy to see [5] that outermost redexes in non-absorbing OTRSs, leftmost-outermost redexes in non-left-absorbing OTRSs, and rightmost-outermost redexes in non-right-absorbing OTRSs are unabsorbed. Thus a limit redex can be found efficiently in these systems. Note that left-normal OTRSs [12] (where in left-hand sides of rules function symbols precede variables), and Combinatory Logic in particular, are non-left-absorbing. Persistent systems are non-absorbing.

Proposition 3.1 Outside-creating OTRSs are strongly normalizing.

Proof. It is easy to see that if R is an outside-creating OTRS, then so is R_μ. Thus, by Lemma 2.2, it is enough to prove that R is weakly normalizing. Let P be an innermost reduction in which any created redex is contracted immediately after creation (each step creates at most one redex). Since a created redex is strictly above the contractum of a contracted redex, the number of redexes of terms in P is decreasing. Thus P is terminating.

Remark 3.1 Proposition 3.1 is equivalent to Corollary 4.10 of van Raamsdonk [13] stating that all "superdevelopments" in OTRSs are finite.

3.2 On decidability of weak and strong normalization

Definition 3.2 We call a class $\mathfrak{R}$ of OTRSs *closed under μ-extension* if $\mathfrak{R}$ contains the μ-extension of each of its elements.

Proposition 3.2 Let $\mathfrak{R}$ be a class of OTRSs closed under μ-extension. Then decidability of weak normalization for OTRSs in $\mathfrak{R}$ implies decidability of strong normalization for OTRSs in $\mathfrak{R}$.

Proof. For any $R \in \mathfrak{R}$, weak normalization is decidable for $R_\mu \in \mathfrak{R}$. Hence, by Proposition 2.2, strong normalization is decidable for R.

It is easy to see that all classes of OTRSs, defined in Definition 3.1, and the class of strongly sequential OTRSs [4] are closed under μ-extension. Note that although, for any OTRS R, R_μ contains infinitely many rules, it is decidable whether a term in R_μ is an R_μ-redex. Thus the decidability question makes sense for R_μ. We show in [5] that weak normalization is decidable in Persistent TRSs. Hence, by Proposition 3.2, strong normalization is also decidable for Persistent TRSs. For inside-creating TRSs, decidability of weak and strong normalization is open. For OTRSs in general, undecidability of strong normalization follows from undecidability of the (uniform) halting problem. Thus, weak normalization is also undecidable.

3.3 The least upper bound of lengths of reductions in persistent TRSs

We now present an algorithm for finding the least upper bound of lengths of co-initial reductions in persistent TRSs, which does not need to make an actual transformation of an input term. In particular, Recursive Program Schemes [2] are persistent. Developments also can be represented as reductions in persistent TRSs. We first recall some results from [6].

Definition 3.3 We call a redex in a PTRS R *trivial* if it is a left-hand side of a rewrite rule in R. We call redexes u and v *similar* if they are instances of the left-hand side of a same rule $r \in R$. We call u *finite* if its similar trivial redex is strongly normalizable. We call an *r-tree* the maximal tree with rules as nodes and r as the root, such that a redex corresponding to a node has an occurrence in the right-hand side of its ancestor node.

Lemma 3.1 ([6]) (1) An r-redex u in a PTRS R is finite iff the r-tree is finite.
(2) A term t in a PTRS is strongly normalizable iff any redex in t is finite.

Definition 3.4 Let R be a PTRS.
(1) Let t be a term in R_μ, let $s \subseteq t$, and let $P : t \twoheadrightarrow \epsilon$ be the rightmost innermost normalizing R_μ-reduction. Then, by definition, $Mult_\mu(s,t)$ is the number of P-descendants of s in ϵ
(2) Let $u = C[\epsilon_1, \ldots, \epsilon_n]$ be an r-redex in R_μ, let $s' \subseteq \epsilon_i$, let $v = C[o_1, \ldots, o_n]$ be an r-redex similar to u with arguments $o_1, \ldots, o_n$ in R_μ-normal form, and let $Q : v \twoheadrightarrow o$ be the rightmost innermost normalizing R_μ-reduction. Then, by definition, $mult_\mu(u,i) = mult_\mu(u,s') = mult_\mu(r,i) = Mult_\mu(o_i,v)$, and $mult_\mu(u) = mult_\mu(r)$ is the number of μ-subterms in o that appear during Q, i.e., that are not descendants of subterms with head-symbol μ from (arguments of) u. Numbers $mult_\mu(u,i)$ and $mult_\mu(r,i)$ are *proper μ-indices* of u and r, and numbers $mult_\mu(u)$ and $mult_\mu(r)$ are *μ-indices* of u and r.

The correctness of Definition 3.4.(2) can be shown by induction on $|Q|$.

Lemma 3.2 Let t be a normalizable term in a PTRS R_μ, let $\epsilon \subseteq s \subseteq t$, and let s be in R_μ-normal form. Then $Mult_\mu(s,t) = Mult_\mu(\epsilon,t)$.

Proof. An easy application of Definition 3.4.

Notation $L(t)$ denotes the least upper bound of lengths of reductions starting from t.

Lemma 3.3 Let t be a strongly normalizable term in a PTRS R and $u_1, \ldots, u_n$ be all redexes in t. Then

$$L(t) = \sum_{i=1}^{n} Mult_\mu(u_i, t) mult_\mu(u_i).$$

Proof. Let $P : t \twoheadrightarrow o$ be the rightmost innermost normalizing R_μ-reduction and let $u_1, \ldots, u_n$ be the enumeration of redexes in t from right to left. In the fragment of P where u_i is reduced to R_μ-normal form, $mult_\mu(u_i)$ new μ-symbols appear (in the beginning of the fragment, all arguments of u_i are in R_μ-normal form). By Lemma 3.2, during the rest of P each of these $mult_\mu(u_i)$ μ-occurrences is duplicated $Mult_\mu(u_i, t)$-times. Hence $\|o\|_\mu = \sum_{i=1}^{n} Mult_\mu(u_i, t) mult_\mu(u_i)$ and the lemma follows from Theorem 2.3.

Lemma 3.4 Let t be a strongly normalizable term in a PTRS R_μ, let $s \subseteq t$, and let $u_1, \ldots, u_n$ be all redexes in t that contain s in their arguments. Suppose that s is in m_i-th argument of u_i ($i = 1, \ldots, n$). Then

$$Mult_\mu(s, t) = \prod_{i=1}^{n} mult_\mu(u_i, s) = \prod_{i=1}^{n} mult_\mu(u_i, m_i).$$

Proof sketch From Definition 3.4 and Lemma 3.2.

Lemma 3.5 Let $u = C[\epsilon_1, \ldots, \epsilon_k]$ be an r-redex with arguments $\epsilon_1, \ldots, \epsilon_k$ in normal form in a PTRS R_μ. Then for all $j = 1, \ldots, k$:

$$mult_\mu(u, j) = mult_\mu(r, j) = \sum_{i=1}^{m_j} Mult_\mu(\epsilon_{j_i}, o),$$

$$mult_\mu(u) = mult_\mu(r) = \sum_{i=1}^{m} Mult_\mu(u_i, o) mult_\mu(u_i) + 1,$$

where o is the contraction of u in R_μ, $\epsilon_{j_1}, \ldots, \epsilon_{j_{m_j}}$ are all descendants of ϵ_j in o, and $u_1, \ldots, u_m$ are all redexes in o.
Proof sketch From Definition 3.4.

Theorem 3.1 Let t be a term in a PTRS R. Then the least upper bound $L(t)$ of lengths of reductions starting from t can be found by the following

Algorithm 3.1 Let $r_1, \ldots, r_n$ be all rules in R such that an r_i-redex has an occurrence in t ($i = 1, \ldots, n$). If the r_i-tree is not finite for at least one i, then $L(t) = \infty$. Otherwise, using Lemmas 3.5 and 3.4, find μ-indices and proper μ-indices of all rules r_i. Finally, using Lemmas 3.3 and 3.4, find $L(t)$.

Proof sketch From Theorem 2.3 and Lemmas 3.1 and 3.3-3.5.

3.4 The least upper bound of lengths of developments

Let $R = \{r_i : t_i \rightarrow s_i\}$ be an OTRS and let $\underline{R} = \{\underline{r_i} : \underline{t_i} \rightarrow s_i\}$, where $\underline{t_i}$ is obtained from t_i by underlining its head-symbol; *terms* in $\underline{R}$ are constructed in the usual way with the restriction that underlined symbols may only occur as head-symbols of redexes. Then, for each development $P : \epsilon_0 \rightarrow \epsilon_1 \rightarrow \ldots \rightarrow \epsilon_n$ of ϵ_0 in R, there is a reduction $P' : \epsilon'_0 \rightarrow \epsilon'_1 \rightarrow \ldots \rightarrow \epsilon'_n$ in $\underline{R}$ such that ϵ'_i is obtained from e_i by underlining head-symbols of residuals of redexes from e_0. Obviously, $\underline{R}$ is persistent, since no creation of redexes is possible in it. Thus, to find least upper bounds of developments in R, one can use Algorithm 3.1, which becomes simpler in this case. For any rule $\underline{r} : C[x_1, \ldots, x_n] \rightarrow s \in \underline{R}$, $mult_\mu(\underline{r}) = 1$, $mult_\mu(\underline{r}, i) = 1$ if x_i does not occur in s, and $mult(\underline{r}, i)$ coincides with the number of occurrences of x_i in s otherwise.

Acknowledgments I enjoyed discussions with H. Barendregt, J. W. Klop, J.-J. Lévy, L. Maranget, G. Mints, Sh. Pkhakadze, Kh. Rukhaia, and V. Sazonov. I also would like to thank G. Gonthier, J. R. Kennaway, G. Tagviashvili, K. Urbaitis, and F. J. de Vries for their help in preparation of this paper.

References

1. Barendregt H. P., Bergstra J., Klop J. W., Volken H. Some notes on lambda-reduction, in: Degrees, reductions and representability in the lambda calculus. Preprint no.22, University of Utrecht, Department of mathematics, p. 13-53, 1976.
2. Courcelle B. Recursive Applicative Program Schemes. In: J.van Leeuwen ed. Handbook of Theoretical Computer Science, Chapter 9, vol.B, 1990, p. 459-492.
3. Dershowitz N., Jouannaud J.-P. Rewrite Systems. In: J.van Leeuwen ed. Handbook of Theoretical Computer Science, Chapter 6, vol.B, 1990, p. 243-320.
4. Huet G., Lévy J.-J. Computations in Orthogonal Rewriting Systems. In Computational Logic, Essays in Honour of Alan Robinson, ed. by J.-L. Lassez and G. Plotkin, MIT Press, 1991.
5. Khasidashvili Z. Optimal normalization in orthogonal term rewriting systems. In: Proc. of the fifth International Conference on Rewriting Techniques and Applications, Springer LNCS, vol. 690, C. Kirchner, ed. Montreal, 1993, p. 243-258.
6. Khasidashvili Z. On the equivalence of persistent term rewriting systems and recursive program schemes. In: Proc. of the second Israel Symposium on Theory and Computing Systems, Natanya, 1993, p. 240-249.
7. Khasidashvili Z. Perpetual reductions and strong normalization in orthogonal term rewriting systems. CWI Report CS-R9345, Amsterdam, July 1993.
8. Khasidashvili Z. Perpetual reductions in orthogonal combinatory reduction systems. CWI Report CS-R9349, Amsterdam, July 1993.
9. Klop J. W. Combinatory Reduction Systems. Mathematical Centre Tracts n. 127, CWI, Amsterdam, 1980.
10. Klop J. W. Term Rewriting Systems. In: S. Abramsky, D. Gabbay, and T. Maibaum eds. Handbook of Logic in Computer Science, vol. II, Oxford University Press, 1992, p. 1-116.
11. Nederpelt R. P. Strong normalization for a typed lambda-calculus with lambda structured types. Ph. D. Thesis, Eindhoven, 1973.
12. O'Donnell M. J. Computing in systems described by equations. Springer LNCS 58, 1977.
13. Van Raamsdonk F. A simple proof of confluence for weakly orthogonal combinatory reduction Systems. Report CS-R9234, CWI Amsterdam, 1992.

About Changing the Ordering During Knuth-Bendix Completion

Andrea Sattler-Klein

Fachbereich Informatik, Universität Kaiserslautern,
D-67653 Kaiserslautern, Germany

Abstract. We will answer a question posed in [5], and will show that Huet's completion algorithm [9] becomes incomplete, i.e. it may generate a term rewriting system that is not confluent, if it is modified in a way that the reduction ordering used for completion can be changed during completion provided that the new ordering is compatible with the actual rules. In particular, we will show that this problem may not only arise if the modified completion algorithm does not terminate: Even if the algorithm terminates without failure, the generated finite noetherian term rewriting system may be non-confluent. Most existing implementations of the Knuth-Bendix algorithm provide the user with help in choosing a reduction ordering: If an unorientable equation is encountered, then the user has many options, especially, the one to orient the equation manually. The integration of this feature is based on the widespread assumption that, if equations are oriented by hand during completion and the completion process terminates with success, then the generated finite system is a maybe nonterminating but locally confluent system (see e.g. [11]). Our examples will show that this assumption is not true.

1 Introduction

The Knuth-Bendix completion procedure [12] is an important deduction tool for term rewriting systems. Given a (finite) set of equations $\mathcal{E}$ and a reduction ordering $>$ as input, the Knuth-Bendix completion procedure tries to generate a complete (confluent and terminating) term rewriting system $\mathcal{R}$ that presents the same equational theory as $\mathcal{E}$. The basic steps of the completion procedure are the computation of certain equational consequences and the generation of rewrite rules by orienting equations according to the given reduction ordering. The completion procedure may either terminate with success, i.e. it generates a finite complete term rewriting system $\mathcal{R}$ equivalent to $\mathcal{E}$, or with failure, or it may not terminate. In the latter case it computes successive approximations $\mathcal{R}_0, \mathcal{R}_1, \mathcal{R}_2, \ldots$ of an infinite complete system $\mathcal{R}$ which is equivalent to $\mathcal{E}$. If the completion procedure terminates with success, then the generated finite complete system $\mathcal{R}$ can be used to decide the word problem of $\mathcal{E}$, since then two terms are equivalent if and only if their normal forms w.r.t. $\mathcal{R}$ are the same.

In general, it is not easy to choose an appropriate reduction ordering for a set $\mathcal{E}$ of equations. A completion procedure will fail if it tries to orient an equation and the corresponding terms are incomparable w.r.t. the given reduction ordering. Sometimes failure cannot be avoided, e.g. if $\mathcal{E}$ cannot be presented by a complete term rewriting system. But even if failure can be avoided, completion may fail. If an equation cannot be oriented w.r.t. the given ordering, then in many cases this problem could be circumvented by choosing another ordering.

But instead restarting the completion process for $\mathcal{E}$ with a new reduction ordering, one would prefer to carry out the completion process in an incremental fashion, i.e. to continue completion with the new ordering without recomputing critical pairs between rules that have been previously considered. Which requirements are needed to ensure that completion remains correct under these modifications? Obviously, the new ordering should be compatible with the actual term rewriting system in order to guarantee that the system is terminating. Is this requirement strong enough to guarantee correctness of this procedure?

In practice, the Knuth-Bendix algorithm is usually used interactively. One reason for human interaction is to specify incrementally the reduction ordering during completion, i.e. to stepwise refine the reduction ordering given as input if needed. In current implementations of completion based methods, like for example in the system RRL [11], the user cannot only refine the actual reduction ordering during completion, but also orient equations that are not comparable w.r.t. the actual ordering by hand. This feature allows to delay testing for termination until all critical pairs have been considered as proposed e.g. in [4]. In that case it is no longer guaranteed that the resulting system as well as the intermediately generated systems are terminating, and hence, a completion process may not terminate due to the computation of an infinite reduction sequence. Methods that can be used to detect certain kinds of non-termination in rewriting have been proposed by Plaisted [13] and Purdom [14]. However, what about a successful computation in case that the termination test is delayed? Is the resulting term rewriting system confluent if it is noetherian, i.e. is it locally confluent, as often implicitly used in the literature (see e.g. [4], [14]) and explicitly stated for example in [11]? Of course, this is true if interreduction is not used during completion, since then a critical pair that is joinable in an intermediate system will be joinable in the resulting system as well. In practice, interreduction is essential for reasons of efficiency. But, if interreduction is used, then a rule that is used to resolve a critical pair during completion may not exist in the final system. Will the final system yet be confluent?

In this paper we will consider these questions and analyse which problems may arise if a completion algorithm is modified in the ways described. Doing this we will focus our attention on string rewriting systems. String rewriting systems can be viewed as special term rewriting systems, namely such term rewriting systems where only unary function symbols occur. (For the notions of string rewriting systems we refer to [1], [2] and [10].) Usually, in order to complete a string rewriting system, a total reduction ordering is used. Hence, in this case failure cannot arise, and a completion procedure will generate a (maybe infinite) complete string rewriting system. But also if a string rewriting system is completed, it would be desirable to have the possibility to change the ordering during completion in an incremental fashion, since in this way divergence of completion, i.e. non-termination of completion, may sometimes be avoided too [7]. In this paper we will consider the following class of wellfounded orderings: Let Σ be a finite alphabet, $>$ be a total ordering on Σ called *precedence* and let for $u \in \Sigma^*$, $max(u)$ denote the largest letter with respect to the precedence $>$ that occurs in u. Then the induced *syllable ordering* $>_{syl}$ on Σ^* is defined as follows: $u >_{syl} v$ iff $((\mid u \mid_{max(uv)} > \mid v \mid_{max(uv)})$ or $(max(uv) = a, \mid u \mid_a = \mid v \mid_a = n, u = u_1 a \ldots u_n a u_{n+1}, v = v_1 a \ldots v_n a v_{n+1},$ and $\exists i \in \{1, \ldots, n+1\} : u_i >_{syl} v_i$ and $u_j = v_j$ for all $j \in \{i+1, \ldots, n+1\}))$. (Note, ε (the empty word) is the smallest element w.r.t. any syllable ordering.) This syllable ordering corresponds to the well-known recursive path ordering for monadic terms [16].

2 Modified Completion

In order to complete a term rewriting system a fixed reduction ordering is used. This ensures that any of the successively generated term rewriting systems $\mathcal{R}_0, \mathcal{R}_1, \mathcal{R}_2, \ldots$ is terminating. One may wonder if a completion procedure remains correct if it is only required that the systems $\mathcal{R}_0, \mathcal{R}_1, \mathcal{R}_2, \ldots$ are noetherian, instead of requiring that the termination of these systems can be proved using the same reduction ordering. In the following we will call a corresponding algorithm *modified completion algorithm* and a corresponding process *modified completion* in short.

In the present paper we will consider this problem by studying Huet's completion algorithm [9], and analyse whether or not it remains correct, if it is allowed to change the reduction ordering during a completion process provided that the new ordering is compatible with the actual term rewriting system. More precisely, we will analyse the correctness of the following algorithm.

MODIFIED COMPLETION ALGORITHM CA_MOD1 :
Initial data: a (finite) set of equations $\mathcal{E}$, and
                  a family of (recursive) reduction orderings $(>_i)_{i \in \mathbb{N}}$.
$\mathcal{E}_0 := \mathcal{E}$; $\mathcal{R}_0 := \emptyset$; $i := 0$; $p := 0$;
loop
  while $\mathcal{E}_i \neq \emptyset$ **do**
    Reduce equation : Select equation $M = N$ in $\mathcal{E}_i$.
    Let $M\downarrow$ (resp. $N\downarrow$) be an $\mathcal{R}_i$-normal form of M (resp. N) obtained by applying rules of $\mathcal{R}_i$ in any order, until none applies.
    if $M\downarrow = N\downarrow$ **then** $\mathcal{E}_{i+1} := \mathcal{E}_i - \{M = N\}$; $\mathcal{R}_{i+1} := \mathcal{R}_i$; $i := i + 1$;
    else if $>_i$ is compatible with $\mathcal{R}_i$ **then**
        if $(M\downarrow >_i N\downarrow)$ **or** $(N\downarrow >_i M\downarrow)$ **then**
        begin
        if $M\downarrow >_i N\downarrow$ **then** $\lambda := M\downarrow$; $\rho := N\downarrow$
                else $\lambda := N\downarrow$; $\rho := M\downarrow$
(*)   *Add new rule*: Let K be the set of labels k of rules of $\mathcal{R}_i$ whose
(*)   left-hand side λ_k is reducible by $\lambda \to \rho$, say to λ'_k.
(*) $\mathcal{E}_{i+1} := \mathcal{E}_i - \{M = N\} \cup \{\lambda'_k = \rho_k \mid k : \lambda_k \to \rho_k \in \mathcal{R}_i \text{ with } k \in K\}$;
(*) $p := p + 1$;
(*) $\mathcal{R}_{i+1} := \{j : \lambda_j \to \rho'_j \mid j : \lambda_j \to \rho_j \in \mathcal{R}_i \text{ with } j \notin K\} \cup \{p : \lambda \to \rho\}$,
(*)   where ρ'_j is a normal form of ρ_j, using rules from $\mathcal{R}_i \cup \{\lambda \to \rho\}$.
        The rules coming from $\mathcal{R}_i$ are marked or unmarked as they were
        in $\mathcal{R}_i$, the new rule $\lambda \to \rho$ is unmarked.
        $i := i + 1$
        end
      else exitloop (*failure*) **endif**
    else exitloop (*failure*) **endif**
  endwhile ;
Compute critical pairs: If all rules in $\mathcal{R}_i$ are marked, **exitloop** ($\mathcal{R}_i$ *canonical*).
Otherwise, select an unmarked rule in $\mathcal{R}_i$, say with label k. Let $\mathcal{E}_{i+1}$ be the set of all critical pairs computed between rule k and any rule of $\mathcal{R}_i$ of label not greater than k. Let $\mathcal{R}_{i+1}$ be the same as $\mathcal{R}_i$, except that rule k is now marked.
$i := i + 1$
endloop

The starting point of this work was the following problem which is stated in the list of 'open problems' collected by Dershowitz et al. in [5] (see also [6]):

Problem 35. *Huet's proof [9] of the "completeness" of completion is predicated on the assumption that the ordering supplied to completion does not change during the process. Assume that at step i of completion, the ordering used is able to order the current rewriting relation $\rightarrow_{R_i}$, but not necessarily $\rightarrow_{R_k}$ for $k < i$ (since old rules may have been deleted by completion). Is there an example showing that completion is then incomplete (the persisting rules are not confluent)?*

The formulation of problem 35 points out that the use of interreduction might play an essential role in that context. Hence, the question arises whether or not the algorithm CA_MOD1 is correct, if interreduction is not used, i.e. if we replace the lines marked with ($*$) by the following ones:

$$\mathcal{E}_{i+1} := \mathcal{E}_i - \{M = N\};$$
$$p := p + 1 ;$$
$$\mathcal{R}_{i+1} := \mathcal{R}_i \cup \{p : \lambda \rightarrow \rho\}$$

In the present paper we also will analyse the correctness of this algorithm which we will denote CA_MOD2. For both algorithms we will adopt the fairness of selection hypothesis given in [9]. This hypothesis states that for every rule label k, there is an iteration i such that either the rule of label k is deleted from $\mathcal{R}_i$, or the rule of label k is selected at "compute critical pairs". Moreover, we will assume that the algorithms CA_MOD1 and CA_MOD2 use the following simple strategies: In order to compute critical pairs, the unmarked rule with the least label is selected. Furthermore, the sets $\mathcal{E}_i$ are implemented as queues. If a rule is overlapped with a set of rules, this also will be done according to the labels of the rules, i.e. in the set of rules to be considered the rule with least label has highest priority. (For the notions of term rewriting systems and more information about completion we refer to the literature (see e.g. [4], [9]).)

In case that the algorithm CA_MOD1 (CA_MOD2) terminates with success, say with the pair $(\mathcal{R}_n, \mathcal{E}_n)$, we define for any $j > n$, $\mathcal{R}_j := \mathcal{R}_n$ and $\mathcal{E}_j := \mathcal{E}_n$. In the following $\mathcal{R}_\infty$ denotes the set of persisting rules, i.e. $\mathcal{R}_\infty = \cup_{i \geq 0} \cap_{j \geq i} \mathcal{R}_j$.

2.1 Modified Completion without Interreduction

If interreduction is not used during completion, then the generated term rewriting systems $\mathcal{R}_0, \mathcal{R}_1, \mathcal{R}_2, \ldots$ form an increasing chain, i.e. $\mathcal{R}_0 \subseteq \mathcal{R}_1 \subseteq \mathcal{R}_2 \subseteq \ldots$ holds, and we have $\mathcal{R}_\infty = \cup_{i \in \mathbb{N}} \mathcal{R}_i$. Moreover, since only equational consequences are added during completion, $\mathcal{R}_\infty$ is equivalent to the input system $\mathcal{E}$.

Obviously, these properties are independent of the fact that a fixed reduction ordering is used during completion. Thus, they also hold for modified completion. In modified completion it only is allowed to change the reduction ordering if the new ordering is compatible with the actual rewrite system. Hence, it is guaranteed that any of the intermediately generated systems $\mathcal{R}_i$ is noetherian if modified completion is used. Moreover, since the successive term rewriting systems $\mathcal{R}_0, \mathcal{R}_1, \mathcal{R}_2, \ldots$ generated by modified completion form an increasing chain, a critical pair that is joinable w.r.t. $\mathcal{R}_i$ for some i is also joinable w.r.t. any $\mathcal{R}_j$ with $j \geq i$. Hence, since it is assumed that a fair strategy is used, $\mathcal{R}_\infty$ is locally confluent. Now consider the case that modified completion stops with success. In that case we have that the generated finite system $\mathcal{R}_\infty$ is noetherian in addition. Thus, modified completion is partially correct in that it generates a complete system equivalent to the input system $\mathcal{E}$ whenever it terminates with success.

But, what about those cases when modified completion does not terminate? Is the generated infinite system $\mathcal{R}_\infty$ complete in those cases too? We will consider this case in the following.

The union of a family of noetherian term rewriting systems that form an increasing chain need not be noetherian, and in fact, the systems $\mathcal{R}_\infty$ generated by modified completion without interreduction can be non-noetherian.

Example 1. Let $\mathcal{R} = \{wa \to ab, ac \to abc\}$.
Obviously, $\mathcal{R}$ is noetherian and there is an overlap between the first rule and the second one. The corresponding critical pair is: $(abc, wabc)$. While abc is irreducible, $wabc$ can be reduced to the irreducible string $abbc$. Hence, $\mathcal{R}$ is not confluent and a Knuth-Bendix completion procedure will generate either the rule $abc \to abbc$ or the rule $abbc \to abc$, depending on the ordering used for completion. Consider the first case: If the rule $abc \to abbc$ is added, then the resulting system $\mathcal{R}_0 = \{wa \to ab, ac \to abc, abc \to abbc\}$ will be noetherian, too. But, there will be a new overlap between this new rule and the first one: We have $wabc \to abbc$ and $wabc \to wabbc \to abbbc$. Thus, a further rule has to be added. If we add the rule $abbc \to abbbc$, then the situation will be similar to the one before: The resulting system $\mathcal{R}_1 = \{wa \to ab, ac \to abc, abc \to abbc, abbc \to abbbc\}$ will be noetherian, but there will be a new overlap between the rule added and the first one. Going on in the way described, we will generate an infinite sequence of noetherian string rewriting systems $\mathcal{R}_0$, $\mathcal{R}_1$, $\mathcal{R}_2$, ... satisfying $\mathcal{R}_i = \{wa \to ab\} \cup \{ab^n c \to ab^{n+1}c \mid 0 \le n \le i+1\}$ $(i \in \mathbb{N})$. Since interreduction has not been used during the described process, we have $\mathcal{R}_\infty = \cup_{i \in \mathbb{N}} \mathcal{R}_i = \{wa \to ab\} \cup \{ab^n c \to ab^{n+1}c \mid n \in \mathbb{N}\}$. Hence, $\mathcal{R}_\infty$ is not noetherian.

Thus, in general modified completion is not correct, since it may generate a non-noetherian system. As mentioned above, the generated systems $\mathcal{R}_\infty$ are always locally confluent. Are they confluent too? Note that the system $\mathcal{R}_\infty$ of example 1 is confluent since it is strongly confluent [8]. For non-noetherian string rewriting systems local confluence and confluence do not coincide. Hence, modified completion might generate also non-confluent systems.

We know that the reduction induced by $\mathcal{R}_\infty$ is acyclic, since all the intermediate systems $\mathcal{R}_i$ are noetherian. Nevertheless, as the following example will show, $\mathcal{R}_\infty$ can indeed be non-confluent.

Example 2. Let $\mathcal{R} = \{1 : uv \to xA, 2 : vbc \to W, 3 : uW \to o, 4 : Abc \to abbc, 5 : wa \to Ab, 6 : wA \to ab, 7 : xa \to o, 8 : ob \to o, 9 : oc \to o, 10 : xA \to O, 11 : Ob \to O, 12 : Oc \to O\}$.
$\mathcal{R}$ is noetherian. There are 3 overlaps: Rule 1 overlaps with rule 2, and rule 4 overlaps with rule 6 and 10. Overlapping rule 1 with rule 2 yields the critical pair $(xAbc, uW)$, which is joinable in the following way: $xAbc \to xabbc \to obbc \to obc \to oc \to o \leftarrow uW$. Overlapping rule 4 with rule 6 yields the critical pair $(abbc, wabbc)$. While $abbc$ is irreducible, $wabbc$ will be reduced to the irreducible string $Abbbc$ using rule 5. Adding the rule $abbc \to Abbbc$ will result in the noetherian system $\mathcal{R}_0 = \mathcal{R} \cup \{abbc \to Abbbc\}$. Overlapping rule 4 with rule 10 results in the critical pair $(Obc, xabbc)$, which is joinable, since $Obc \leftarrow Obbc \leftarrow Obbbc \leftarrow xAbbbc \leftarrow xabbc$. The rule added overlaps with rule 5 and with rule 7. The corresponding critical pairs are $(Abbbc, wAbbbc)$ and $(obbc, xAbbbc)$. $Abbbc$ is irreducible and $wAbbbc$ can be reduced to $abbbbc$, which

is irreducible too. Adding the rule $Abbbc \to abbbbc$ will result in the system $\mathcal{R}_1 = \mathcal{R} \cup \{abbc \to Abbbc, Abbbc \to abbbbc\}$, which is noetherian. In $\mathcal{R}_1$ the critical pair $(obbc, xAbbbc)$ is joinable: $obbc \leftarrow obbbc \leftarrow obbbbc \leftarrow xabbbbc \leftarrow xAbbbc$. Thus in the next step the new rule $Abbbc \to abbbbc$ will be overlapped with the other rules. In this way the infinite, locally confluent system $\mathcal{R}_\infty = \mathcal{R} \cup \{ab^n c \to Ab^{n+1}c \mid n \geq 2, n \text{ even} \} \cup \{Ab^n c \to ab^{n+1}c \mid n \geq 3, n \text{ odd}\}$ will be generated. Since $o \leftarrow uW \leftarrow uvbc \to xAbc \to Obc \to Oc \to O$, and o and O are $\mathcal{R}_\infty$-irreducible, $\mathcal{R}_\infty$ is not confluent.

In the examples 1 and 2 we have used a very simple modified completion algorithm. It can be easily checked that the algorithm CA_MOD2 will generate the same infinite systems in these cases if appropriate reduction orderings are chosen. Thus, the algorithm CA_MOD2 is not correct in general.

Usually, the reduction orderings used for completion belong to the class of simplification orderings [3]. Termination of the systems $\mathcal{R}_i$ that have been constructed in the previous examples cannot be proved using simplification orderings: In example 1 the initial system $\mathcal{R}$, and hence, any of the successively generated systems $\mathcal{R}_i$, is self-embedding and thus not compatible with a simplification ordering. In example 2 any of the systems $\mathcal{R}_i$ contains the set $\{Abc \to abbc, abbc \to Abbbc\}$. Since any simplification ordering contains the homeomorphic embedding relation, we have that the string $Abbbc$ is greater than the string Abc w.r.t. any simplification ordering. Hence any string rewriting system containing the rules $Abc \to abbc, abbc \to Abbbc$ is not compatible w.r.t. a simplification ordering.

One class of orderings often used to complete string rewriting systems is the class of syllable orderings. Since syllable orderings are simplification orderings, they cannot be used to prove termination in the previous examples. Thus, the question arises whether or not similar phenomena may occur, if we restrict the reduction orderings that may be used during modified completion to the class of syllable orderings.

If $\mathcal{R}$ is a finite string rewriting system and Σ the underlying alphabet, then there are only finitely many, namely $|\Sigma|!$, different syllable orderings on Σ^*. But, if the family $(>_i)_{i \in \mathbb{N}}$ of reduction orderings used during a modified completion process is restricted to a finite set and if in addition interreduction is not used, then one of these orderings is compatible with any of the successively generated systems $\mathcal{R}_i$ and thus with the set $\mathcal{R}_\infty$. Hence, modified completion without interreduction is correct if the reduction orderings $>_i$ ($i \in \mathbb{N}$) given as input belong to a finite set.

We conclude this section with the following theorem that summarizes the main results obtained so far.

Theorem 1. *For the algorithm CA_MOD2 holds:*

1. *The algorithm CA_MOD2 is not correct in general: If it terminates on input $(\mathcal{E}, (>_i)_{i \in \mathbb{N}})$, then the generated finite system $\mathcal{R}_\infty$ is complete and equivalent to $\mathcal{E}$, but otherwise it may generate an equivalent infinite system $\mathcal{R}_\infty$ that is neither noetherian nor confluent.*

2. *The algorithm CA_MOD2 is correct for string rewriting systems and the class of syllable orderings: If it is started on input $(\mathcal{E}, (>_i)_{i \in \mathbb{N}})$ where $\mathcal{E}$ is a string rewriting system and $(>_i)_{i \in \mathbb{N}}$ is a family of syllable orderings, then the generated system $\mathcal{R}_\infty$ is noetherian, confluent and equivalent to $\mathcal{E}$.*

2.2 Modified Completion with Interreduction

As shown in the previous section Huet's completion algorithm remains correct if it is allowed to change the reduction ordering during completion (provided that the new ordering is compatible with the actual set of rules) if interreduction is not used and in addition, the orderings used belong to the class of syllable orderings. Example 2 has illustrated that the second condition, i.e. the restriction of the reduction orderings to the class of syllable orderings, is essential for the correctness of this modified completion algorithm. What about the first condition not to use interreduction during completion? Is this requirement essential for the correctness of the algorithm, too?

In this section we will consider this question and analyse the correctness of the algorithm CA_MOD1. But before investigating this special algorithm, let us first consider example 1 again and analyse what will happen if interreduction is incorporated in the simple algorithm used there.

Example 3. Let $\mathcal{R} = \{wa \rightarrow ab, ac \rightarrow abc\}$.
As mentioned in example 1 a Knuth-Bendix algorithm may generate the rule $abc \rightarrow abbc$ by overlapping. Now, this new rule could be used to reduce the right hand side of the second rule. In this way we obtain the noetherian system $\mathcal{R}_0 = \{wa \rightarrow ab, ac \rightarrow abbc, abc \rightarrow abbc\}$. Again, there is an overlap between the new rule, and the first one and the rule $abbc \rightarrow abbbc$ may be generated. If interreduction is used, then this rule will be used to reduce the right hand sides of the second and the third rule. This yields $\mathcal{R}_1 = \{wa \rightarrow ab, ac \rightarrow abbbc, abc \rightarrow abbbc, abbc \rightarrow abbbc\}$. The new rule overlaps with the first rule too, and this overlap may result in the rule $abbbc \rightarrow abbbbc$, which could be used for interreduction. Using the strategy described, we may generate an infinite sequence of noetherian string rewriting systems $\mathcal{R}_0, \mathcal{R}_1, \mathcal{R}_2, \ldots$ satisfying $\mathcal{R}_i = \{wa \rightarrow ab\} \cup \{ab^n c \rightarrow ab^{i+2} c \mid 0 \leq n \leq i+1\}$ ($i \in \mathbb{N}$). Since the right hand side of any rule different from $wa \rightarrow ab$ will be modified infinitely many times by interreduction, we have $\mathcal{R}_\infty = \{wa \rightarrow ab\}$. Hence, in this case $\mathcal{R}_\infty$ is noetherian and confluent, but it is not equivalent to $\mathcal{R}$.

Thus, if interreduction is used during modified completion, then the system $\mathcal{E}$ that has been given as input and the limit system $\mathcal{R}_\infty$ that will be generated can be non-equivalent. This phenomenon is due to the facts that the set $\cup_{i \in \mathbb{N}} \mathcal{R}_i$ may be non-noetherian and that the interreduction process in some sense simulates the computation of certain reduction sequences with respect to $\cup_{i \in \mathbb{N}} \mathcal{R}_i$. Of course, any of the intermediate systems $\mathcal{R}_i$ ($i \in \mathbb{N}$) is noetherian, and hence, any reduction process that will be performed will terminate. But, if $\cup_{i \in \mathbb{N}} \mathcal{R}_i$ is not noetherian, then the computation of a certain infinite reduction sequence w.r.t. $\cup_{i \in \mathbb{N}} \mathcal{R}_i$ may be simulated stepwise by interreduction in the following way: A rule $l \rightarrow r$ may be simplified to another rule which will be simplified to another one later on, and so on. Hence, neither the original rule $l \rightarrow r$ nor one of its simplified forms will belong to the limit system $\mathcal{R}_\infty$. Therefore, $\mathcal{R}_\infty$ may be non-equivalent to $\mathcal{R}$.

Example 3 differs from our intended one in the way that no syllable ordering is compatible with $\mathcal{R}$. But, the next example shows that even if syllable orderings are used during modified completion, it is no longer guaranteed that the initial system and the generated limit system are equivalent.

Example 4. Let $\mathcal{R} = \{1 : X \to egabc, 2 : QH \to ga, 3 : QA \to Eega, 4 : Qh \to ga, 5 : qH \to a, 6 : qA \to q, 7 : qd \to q, 8 : qc \to o, 9 : qh \to a, 10 : qb \to q, 11 : WH \to Hbb, 12 : WA \to Add, 13 : wh \to hdd, 14 : wA \to Abb, 15 : eE \to \varepsilon, 16 : Eego \to go, 17 : Hbc \to Addc, 18 : hddc \to Abbbc\}$.

Moreover, let $\succ_1$ be the syllable ordering induced by the precedence $X > W > w > Q > q > H > h > b > d > a > c > g > e > A > E > o$ and $\succ_2$ the syllable ordering induced by the precedence $X > W > w > Q > q > H > h > d > b > a > c > g > e > A > E > o$, and let $(>_i)_{i \in \mathbb{N}}$ be defined by: $>_i = \succ_1$ for $0 \le i \le 39$, $>_{40+14j+k} = \succ_2$ for $j \in \mathbb{N}$ and $0 \le k \le 6$, and $>_{40+14j+k} = \succ_1$ for $j \in \mathbb{N}$ and $7 \le k \le 13$.

Claim: Given $\mathcal{R}$ and $(>_i)_{i \in \mathbb{N}}$ as input, the algorithm CA_MOD1 will generate an infinite sequence $(\mathcal{R}_0, \mathcal{E}_0), (\mathcal{R}_1, \mathcal{E}_1), (\mathcal{R}_2, \mathcal{E}_2), \dots$ such that for all $j \in \mathbb{N}$ the following holds:

1) $\mathcal{E}_{40+14j} = \emptyset$

2) $\mathcal{R}_{40+14j} = \tilde{\mathcal{R}}_j$ where

$$
\begin{aligned}
\tilde{\mathcal{R}}_j = (\mathcal{R} - & \{1 : X \to egabc\}) \\
\cup\ & \{1 : X \to egad^{2j+2}c\} \\
\cup\ & \{Hb^n c \to Ad^{n+1}c \mid n \text{ odd and } 1 \le n \le 2j+1\} \\
\cup\ & \{ab^n c \to o \mid n \text{ odd and } 1 \le n \le 2j\} \\
\cup\ & \{hd^n c \to Ab^{n+1}c \mid n \text{ even and } 2 \le n \le 2j\} \\
\cup\ & \{ad^n c \to o \mid n \text{ even and } 2 \le n \le 2j\} \\
\cup\ & \{l_{j,1} : hd^{2j+2}c \to Ab^{2j+3}c\} \\
\cup\ & \{l_{j,2} : ab^{2j+1}c \to o\} \\
\cup\ & \{l_{j,3} : Hb^{2j+3}c \to Ad^{2j+4}c\} \\
\cup\ & \{l_{j,4} : Eegad^{2j+2}c \to go\}
\end{aligned}
$$

where $l_{j,1}, l_{j,2}, l_{j,3}, l_{j,4} \in \mathbb{N}$ with $l_{j,1} < l_{j,2} < l_{j,3} < l_{j,4}$ and all rules except the rules $l_{j,1}$, $l_{j,2}$, $l_{j,3}$ and $l_{j,4}$ are marked.

Proof. For the proof we refer to the full version of this paper [15]. $\quad\Box$

The above claim implies that for the set $\mathcal{R}_\infty$ of persisting rules the following holds:

$$
\begin{aligned}
\mathcal{R}_\infty = (\mathcal{R} - & \{1 : X \to egabc\}) \\
\cup\ & \{Hb^n c \to Ad^{n+1}c \mid n \text{ odd and } 1 \le n\} \\
\cup\ & \{ab^n c \to o \mid n \text{ odd and } 1 \le n\} \\
\cup\ & \{hd^n c \to Ab^{n+1}c \mid n \text{ even and } 2 \le n\} \\
\cup\ & \{ad^n c \to o \mid n \text{ even and } 2 \le n\}
\end{aligned}
$$

Since the orderings $\succ_1$ and $\succ_2$ are both used infinitely many times during the described process, $\mathcal{R}_\infty$ is compatible with both of them. Thus, $\mathcal{R}_\infty$ is noetherian. But, $\mathcal{R}_\infty$ is not equivalent to the initial system $\mathcal{R}$: $X \to egabc$ is an initial rule, but X and $egabc$ are obviously not congruent modulo $\mathcal{R}_\infty$.

It can easily be checked that the limit system $\mathcal{R}_\infty$ generated in the last example is confluent. Hence, the algorithm CA_MOD1 has generated a noetherian and confluent system in that case. But, as mentioned before $\mathcal{R}_\infty$ is not equivalent to $\mathcal{R}$. This is due to the following facts: The right hand side of rule 1 is simplified infinitely many times during the process described ($egabc \to^* egad^2c \to^* egab^3c \to^* egad^4c \to^* egab^5c \to^* \dots$). Hence neither the original form of rule 1 nor one of its simplified forms belong to $\mathcal{R}_\infty$. On the other hand, none of these rules is redundant w.r.t. $\mathcal{R}_\infty$.

Obviously, if a non-redundant rule is simplified infinitely many times, then the generated limit system may also be non-confluent, since the crucial non-redundant rule may have been used to resolve critical pairs. For instance, consider the following modification of example 4. Extend the precedences used by $U >$ $V > Y > Z > F > X$, and let $\succ_1$ and $\succ_2$ be the syllable orderings induced. Moreover, add the rules $UV \rightarrow Y, VZ \rightarrow Fgabc, YZ \rightarrow X, UF \rightarrow e$ in a way that the overlap between the rules $UV \rightarrow Y$ and $VZ \rightarrow Fgabc$ is the first to be considered. If the algorithm CA_MOD1 is started on this input, then the following will happen: At the moment the rules $UV \rightarrow Y$ and $VZ \rightarrow Fgabc$ are overlapped the corresponding critical pair $(YZ, UFgabc)$ is joinable in the following way: $YZ \rightarrow X \rightarrow egabc \leftarrow UFgabc$. Since the symbols of the left hand sides of the rules added are 'new' ones, the new rules will not have any further influence on the execution of the algorithm CA_MOD1, i.e. the limit system that will be generated is the union of the limit system of example 4 and the set $\{UV \rightarrow Y, VZ \rightarrow Fgabc, YZ \rightarrow X, UF \rightarrow e\}$. Thus, the critical pair $(YZ, UFgabc)$ will not be joinable w.r.t. the limit system, i.e. the limit system is not confluent in that case.

This example already gives an answer to the problem 35 of [5], but we can even give an example where the algorithm generates an *equivalent*, noetherian system that is not confluent. For this purpose let us consider example 4 again, and see what will happen if we remove the crucial rule $X \rightarrow egabc$. Since this rule has neither been used for overlapping nor for reduction, the algorithm CA_MOD1 will generate the same limit system as before. Hence, in that case the generated limit system is complete and equivalent to the input system. But nevertheless, there is still a rule in the set $\cup_{i \in \mathbb{N}} \mathcal{R}_i$ that is simplified infinitely many times during this modified completion process: The rule $gabc \rightarrow Eegad^2c$ generated by overlapping is simplified to the equation $go = Eegad^2c$, which will be oriented to the rule $Eegad^2c \rightarrow go$, which will be simplified to the equation $EeEegab^3c = go$, which will yield the rule $Eegab^3c \rightarrow go$, which will be simplified to the equation $go = EeEegad^4c$, which will yield the rule $Eegad^4c \rightarrow go$, and so on. But, in this case this infinite simplification does not affect the equational theory presented by the limit system, since the rules and equations generated during this simplification process are redundant: In $\mathcal{R}_\infty$ the following reduction steps can be performed: $EeEegab^nc \rightarrow Eegab^nc \rightarrow Eego \rightarrow go$ if n is odd, and $EeEegad^nc \rightarrow Eegad^nc \rightarrow Eego \rightarrow go$ if n is even and greater than 1.

The proof of the above claim shows that the rule $Eego \rightarrow go$ will never be used for reductions during the execution of the algorithm CA_MOD1. Moreover, it shows that this rule will be overlapped only once and the corresponding critical pair is trivial in that case. Hence, if we remove the rule $Eego \rightarrow go$ as well as the rule $X \rightarrow egabc$ from the input system of example 4, the algorithm CA_MOD1 will generate the limit system $\mathcal{R}'_\infty = \mathcal{R}_\infty - \{Eego \rightarrow go\}$ where $\mathcal{R}_\infty$ is the limit system generated in example 4. Again the rule $gabc \rightarrow Eegaddc$ will be generated by overlapping and it will be simplified infinitely many times as in example 4. But the limit system $\mathcal{R}'_\infty$ that will be generated is a superset of the input system and hence, both systems are equivalent. In $\mathcal{R}'_\infty$ the following reduction steps can be performed: $go \leftarrow gabc \leftarrow QHbc \rightarrow QAddc \rightarrow Eegaddc \rightarrow Eego$. Hence we have $go \leftrightarrow^*_{\mathcal{R}'_\infty} Eego$. Thus, $\mathcal{R}'_\infty$ is noetherian and equivalent to the input system, but it is not confluent. (For a more detailed discussion of this example we refer to the full version of this paper [15].)

There remains to check whether the algorithm CA_MOD1 at least is partially correct, i.e. if it always generates correct results whenever it terminates with success. If the algorithm CA_MOD1 terminates with success, then the finite system is noetherian and equivalent to the input system. But even in this case, the generated system may be non-confluent.

Example 5. Let $\mathcal{R} = \{1 : xwef \rightarrow xweg, 2 : egc \rightarrow dgc, 3 : xwd \rightarrow xwi, 4 : ubc \rightarrow o, 5 : xwigc \rightarrow o, 6 : xwa \rightarrow u, 7 : abc \rightarrow efc, 8 : zf \rightarrow \varepsilon, 9 : hz \rightarrow we, 10 : yb \rightarrow g, 11 : iy \rightarrow a\}$.

Moreover, let $\succ_1$ be the syllable ordering induced by the precedence $z > x > y > a > f > g > b > w > e > d > c > i > o > h > u$ and $\succ_2$ be the syllable ordering induced by the precedence $z > x > y > g > a > f > b > w > e > d > c > i > o > h > u$, and let $(>_i)_{i \in \mathbb{N}}$ be a family of syllable orderings satisfying: $>_i = \succ_1$ for $0 \leq i \leq 24$ and $>_i = \succ_2$ for $25 \leq i \leq 30$. Since $\mathcal{R}$ is compatible with $\succ_1$ and $\mathcal{R}$ is interreduced, the algorithm $\overline{\text{CA\_MOD1}}$ will generate the sets $\mathcal{R}_{11} = \mathcal{R}$, $\mathcal{E}_{11} = \emptyset$, where all rules in $\mathcal{R}_{11}$ are unmarked. Since there are no overlaps between rules of $\mathcal{R} - \{7 : abc \rightarrow efc, 8 : zf \rightarrow \varepsilon, 9 : hz \rightarrow we, 10 : yb \rightarrow g, 11 : iy \rightarrow a\}$, we have $\mathcal{R}_{17} = \mathcal{R}$, $\mathcal{E}_{17} = \emptyset$, where all rules of $\mathcal{R}_{17}$ except the rules 7, 8, 9, 10 and 11 are marked. Hence, in the next step the rule 7 will be marked and all critical pairs between the rule 7 and the rules 1-7 will be computed. Rule 7 only overlaps with rule 6. The corresponding critical pair is $(ubc, xwefc)$. Thus we obtain $\mathcal{R}_{18} = \mathcal{R}$, where all rules except the rules 8-11 are marked, and $\mathcal{E}_{18} = \{ubc = xwefc\}$. Since the critical pair $(ubc, xwefc)$ is joinable ($ubc \rightarrow o \leftarrow xwigc \leftarrow xwdgc \leftarrow xwegc \leftarrow xwefc$) the following holds: $\mathcal{R}_{19} = \mathcal{R}$ and $\mathcal{E}_{19} = \emptyset$. In the next step rule 8 will be marked and the corresponding critical pairs will be computed. Since there are no overlaps between rule 8 and the rules 1-8, we obtain $\mathcal{R}_{20} = \mathcal{R}$, $\mathcal{E}_{20} = \emptyset$, where all rules except the rules 9-11 are marked. Rule 9 overlaps only with rule 8. The corresponding critical pair is (wef, h). Thus, we have $\mathcal{R}_{21} = \mathcal{R}$ and $\mathcal{E}_{21} = \{wef = h\}$. Since wef and h are irreducible w.r.t. $\mathcal{R}_{21}$ and $wef \succ_1 h$, the rule $12 : wef \rightarrow h$ will be added. Now this new rule will be used to reduce the left hand side of the first rule. This gives $\mathcal{R}_{22} = (\mathcal{R} - \{1 : xwef \rightarrow xweg\}) \cup \{12 : wef \rightarrow h\}$ and $\mathcal{E}_{22} = \{xweg = xh\}$. Since $xweg$ and xh are irreducible w.r.t. $\mathcal{R}_{22}$ and $xweg \succ_1 xh$, the rule $13 : xweg \rightarrow xh$ will be added. This yields: $\mathcal{R}_{23} = (\mathcal{R} - \{1 : xwef \rightarrow xweg\}) \cup \{12 : wef \rightarrow h, 13 : xweg \rightarrow xh\}$ and $\mathcal{E}_{23} = \emptyset$, where all rules except the rules 10-13 are marked. Since there are no overlaps between rule 10 and the rules 1-10, the sets $\mathcal{R}_{24} = \mathcal{R}_{23}$ and $\mathcal{E}_{24} = \emptyset$ will be generated. In the next step rule 11 will be overlapped with rule 10. This gives $\mathcal{R}_{25} = \mathcal{R}_{23}$ and $\mathcal{E}_{25} = \{ab = ig\}$. $\mathcal{R}_{25}$ is compatible with $\succ_2$. Hence, $\succ_2$ can be used for the next step. Since ab and ig are $\mathcal{R}_{25}$-irreducible and $ig \succ_2 ab$, the rule $14 : ig \rightarrow ab$ will be generated. This new rule will be used to reduce the left hand side of rule 5. In this way we obtain $\mathcal{R}_{26} = \{2 : egc \rightarrow dgc, 3 : xwd \rightarrow xwi, 4 : ubc \rightarrow o, 6 : xwa \rightarrow u, 7 : abc \rightarrow efc, 8 : zf \rightarrow \varepsilon, 9 : hz \rightarrow we, 10 : yb \rightarrow g, 11 : iy \rightarrow a, 12 : wef \rightarrow h, 13 : xweg \rightarrow xh, 14 : ig \rightarrow ab\}$ and $\mathcal{E}_{26} = \{xwabc = o\}$. Since $xwabc \rightarrow ubc \rightarrow o$, the sets $\mathcal{R}_{27} = \mathcal{R}_{26}$ and $\mathcal{E}_{27} = \emptyset$ will be generated. Rule 12 does not overlap with any of the rules 1-12. Therefore we obtain $\mathcal{R}_{28} = \mathcal{R}_{26}$ and $\mathcal{E}_{28} = \emptyset$, where all rules except the rules 13 and 14 are marked. Next, rule 13 will be marked. Rule 13 only overlaps with rule 2. The corresponding critical pair $(xhc, xwdgc)$ is joinable in the following way: $xwdgc \rightarrow xwigc \rightarrow xwabc \rightarrow xwefc \rightarrow xhc$. Hence, we have $\mathcal{R}_{29} = \mathcal{R}_{26}$ and $\mathcal{E}_{29} = \emptyset$. Since rule 14 does not overlap with any of the other rules, the algorithm $\overline{\text{CA\_MOD1}}$ will stop with the sets $\mathcal{R}_{30} = \mathcal{R}_{26}$ and $\mathcal{E}_{30} = \emptyset$. Hence, $\mathcal{R}_\infty = \mathcal{R}_{26}$. But $\mathcal{R}_{26}$ is not confluent: $o \leftrightarrow^* xhc$ (since $o \leftarrow ubc \leftarrow xwabc \rightarrow xwefc \rightarrow xhc$), and o and xhc are $\mathcal{R}_{26}$-irreducible.

In order to illustrate this phenomenon, let us consider how the relationship between the strings ubc and $xwefc$ (which form a critical pair) changes during the described process: At the moment of the process when this critical pair is considered it is joinable (see figure 5.1). Later on, the rule $1 : xwef \rightarrow xweg$ that has been used to solve the critical pair $(ubc, xwefc)$ is simplified. Therefore, the critical pair is no longer joinable, but it is connected below $xwabc$ with respect to $\succ_1$ as illustrated in figure 5.2.

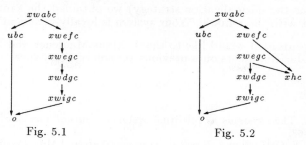

Fig. 5.1   Fig. 5.2

In one of the further steps the ordering used is changed such that ig is greater than ab with respect to the new ordering. In order to illustrate this fact, we have rewritten the graph of figure 5.2 to the one of figure 5.3. During the following steps the rule $ig \rightarrow ab$ will be generated by overlapping. Thus, the rule $5 : xwigc \rightarrow o$ will be deleted, and the situation illustrated in figure 5.4 arises. In the graph of figure 5.4 there are two 'peaks'. For the corresponding critical pairs the following holds: The critical pair $(ubc, xwefc)$ has already been considered and the critical pair $(xwdgc, xhc)$ is joinable. But, nevertheless the critical pair $(ubc, xwefc)$ is not joinable any more.

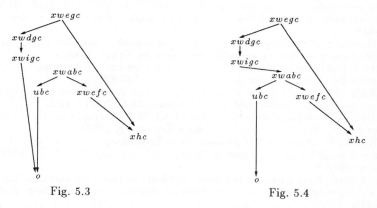

Fig. 5.3   Fig. 5.4

Concluding our analysis of the correctness of the algorithm CA_MOD1 we summarize the results obtained.

Theorem 2. *The algorithm CA_MOD1 is not correct:*
1. *If it does not terminate on input $(\mathcal{E}, (>_i)_{i \in \mathbb{N}})$, then the generated infinite system $\mathcal{R}_\infty$ may be non-equivalent to $\mathcal{E}$. In addition, $\mathcal{R}_\infty$ may or may not be confluent.*
2. *If it terminates on input $(\mathcal{E}, (>_i)_{i \in \mathbb{N}})$, then the generated finite system $\mathcal{R}_\infty$ is noetherian and equivalent to $\mathcal{E}$, but it may be non-confluent.*

3 Concluding Remarks

The results presented here may affect the correctness of existing implementations of completion that provide the option to orient equations by hand. For example, we have run example 5 with the system RRL (version 4.1) [11] using the option to orient equations manually. By choosing the parameters 'option critical pick f', 'option norm m' (which determine the strategy used for computing critical pairs as well as the normalization strategy) we obtained the same result as in example 5 but with the remark: "Your system is locally-confluent".

Acknowledgement: I would like to thank Klaus Madlener and Birgit Reinert for their valuable comments on a previous version of this paper.

References

1. R.V. Book. Thue systems as rewriting systems. *Journal Symbolic Computation* 3 (1987), 39-68.
2. R.V. Book, F. Otto. *String-Rewriting Systems.* Texts and Monographs in Computer Science (Springer, New York, 1993).
3. N. Dershowitz. Orderings for term-rewriting systems. *Theoretical Computer Science* 17(3) (1982), 279-301.
4. N. Dershowitz. Completion and its applications. In: H. Ait-Kaci and M. Nivat (eds.): *Resolution of Equations in Algebraic Structures, Vol. II: Rewriting Techniques* (Academic Press, New York, 1989), 31-86.
5. N. Dershowitz, J.-P. Jouannaud, J.W. Klop. Open Problems in Rewriting. In: *Proc. Fourth International Conference on Rewriting Techniques and Applications,* Como, Italy, Lecture Notes in Computer Science 488 (Springer, Berlin, 1991), 445-456.
6. N. Dershowitz, J.-P. Jouannaud, J.W. Klop. More Problems in Rewriting. In: *Proc. Fifth International Conference on Rewriting Techniques and Applications,* Montreal, Canada, Lecture Notes in Computer Science 690 (Springer, Berlin, 1993), 468-487.
7. M. Hermann. *Vademecum of divergent term rewriting systems.* CRIN Report 88-R-082 (Centre de Recherche en Informatique de Nancy, 1988).
8. G. Huet. Confluent reductions: Abstract properties and applications to term rewriting systems. *Journal of the ACM* 27(4) (1980), 797-821.
9. G. Huet. A complete proof of correctness of the Knuth-Bendix completion algorithm. *Journal Computer and System Science* 23(1) (1981), 11-21.
10. M. Jantzen. *Confluent String Rewriting.* EATCS Monographs on Theoretical Computer Science Vol. 14 (Springer, Berlin - Heidelberg, 1988).
11. D. Kapur, H. Zhang. *RRL: Rewrite Rule Laboratory - User's Manual,* GE Corporate Research and Development Report, Schenectady, New York, 1987 (revised version: May 1989).
12. D.E. Knuth, P. Bendix. Simple word problems in universal algebras. In: J. Leech (ed.): *Computational Problems in Abstract Algebra* (Pergamon, New York, 1970), 263-297.
13. D.A. Plaisted. A simple non-termination test for the Knuth-Bendix method. In: *Proc. Eighth International Conference on Automated Deduction,* Oxford, England, Lecture Notes in Computer Science 230 (Springer, Berlin, 1986), 79-88.
14. P. Purdom. Detecting loop simplifications. In: *Proc. Second International Conference on Rewriting Techniques and Applications,* Bordeaux, France, Lecture Notes in Computer Science 256 (Springer, Berlin, 1987), 54-61.
15. A. Sattler-Klein. *About changing the ordering during Knuth-Bendix completion.* Internal report (Universität Kaiserslautern, 1993). To appear.
16. J. Steinbach. *Comparing on Strings: Iterated Syllable Ordering and Recursive Path Orderings.* SEKI Report SR-89-15 (Universität Kaiserslautern, 1989).

Example 1. Assume $E_1 = \{x + x = x\}$ and E_2 is the empty theory with $\mathcal{F}_2 = \{f\}$. $(f(x) + f(x + x))^{\pi_1} = X + X$ provided $X = \pi(f(x) \downarrow_R) = \pi(f(x + x) \downarrow_R)$.

3.2 Solving in one component

Solutions of a i-left pure match-equation $s \leq^?_E t$ may be found by solving $s \leq^?_{E_i} t^{\pi_i}$ but the i-abstraction of the right-hand side t must be performed carefully because $t =_E t'$ does not imply $t^{\pi_i} =_{E_i} t'^{\pi_i}$.

Example 2. Assume $E_1 = \{x + x = x\}$ and E_2 is the empty theory with $\mathcal{F}_2 = \{f\}$. The match-equation $f(f(x)) \leq^?_E f(f(a) + f(a))$ is equivalent to $f(f(x)) \leq^?_E f(f(a))$. But $f(f(x)) \leq^?_{E_2} f(C)$ has no solution whereas $f(f(x)) \leq^?_{E_2} f(f(a))$ has a unique solution $\{x \mapsto a\}$.

We show in this section that solving $s \leq^?_E t^{\pi_i}$ in one component is correct and complete provided t is in layers reduced form.

Definition 6. A term t is in *layers reduced form* if t is a variable or if $t(\epsilon)$ and $t \downarrow_R (\epsilon)$ are symbols in the same theory and the alien subterms of t are in layers reduced form.

The notion of layers reduced form is clearly related to the word-problem.

Lemma 7. *If s is in layers reduced form and $s \to_R t$ then t is in layers reduced form and $s^{\pi_i} =_{E_i} t^{\pi_i}$.*

Corollary 8. *Let s, t be two terms in layers reduced form. Then $s =_E t \iff s^{\pi_i} =_{E_i} t^{\pi_i}$.*

Proof. $s^{\pi_i} =_{E_i} (s \downarrow_R)^{\pi_i} = (t \downarrow_R)^{\pi_i} =_{E_i} t^{\pi_i}$.

The computation of a layers reduced form is possible and an algorithm can be derived from the below definitions since matching (and thus word-problem) is decidable in each theory.

Definition 9. An alien subterm or a variable u of a i-term t is *collapsing* for t if $t^{\pi_i} =_{E_i} u^{\pi_i}$.

The related E_i-theorem is collapsing since u^{π_i} is a variable.

Example 3. Assume $E_1 = \{x + x = x\}$ and E_2 is the empty theory with $\mathcal{F}_2 = \{f\}$. $f(a)$ is collapsing for $f(a) + f(a)$.

Definition 10. let $t_i[s_1, \ldots, s_m]$ be the i-term t where $s_1, \ldots, s_m$ denotes alien subterms and variables. $t \Downarrow$ denotes the term defined as follows:
$v \Downarrow = v$ if v is a variable.
$(t_i[s_1, \ldots, s_m]) \Downarrow = t_i[s_1 \Downarrow, \ldots, s_m \Downarrow]$ if no collapsing term exists for $t_i[s_1 \Downarrow, \ldots, s_m \Downarrow]$.
$(t_i[s_1, \ldots, s_m]) \Downarrow = u$ if u is collapsing for $t_i[s_1 \Downarrow, \ldots, s_m \Downarrow]$.

Proposition 11. *If the word-problem in E_i ($i = 1, 2$) is decidable then $t \Downarrow$ is a computable term in layers reduced form and E-equal to t.*

Note that the existence of a collapsing term for $t_i[s_1 \Downarrow, \ldots, s_m \Downarrow]$ is decidable since alien subterms are already in layers reduced form.

Example 4. Assume $E_1 = \{x + x = x\}$ and E_2 is the empty theory with $\mathcal{F}_2 = \{f\}$. Let s be the term $f(a, y) + (f(a, y) + f(a, y))$ and t the term $f(a + a, y)$. We have $s =_E t$ since $(s \Downarrow)^{\pi_2} = s \Downarrow = f(a, y) = t \Downarrow = (t \Downarrow)^{\pi_2}$.

Corollary 12. *The word-problem in $E_1 \cup E_2$ is decidable iff the word-problem in E_i ($i = 1, 2$) is decidable.*

Lemma 13. *Let $(s \leq^? t)$ be a i-left pure match-equation, σ a R-normalized substitution and t a term in layers reduced form. Then $s\sigma =_E t \Longleftrightarrow (s\sigma)^{\pi_i} =_{E_i} t^{\pi_i}$.*

Proof. Since σ is R-normalized, it is easy to prove [1] that $(s\sigma)^{\pi_i} =_{E_i} ((s\sigma) \downarrow_R)^{\pi_i}$. Since t and $t \downarrow_R$ are in layers reduced form, $t^{\pi_i} =_{E_i} (t \downarrow_R)^{\pi_i}$ with $(s\sigma) \downarrow_R = t \downarrow_R$.

Note that $(s\sigma)^{\pi_i}$ is identical to $s\sigma^{\pi_i}$ and $\sigma^{\pi_i} \leq^{\mathcal{X}}_E \sigma$. Lemma 13 is similar to the one given in [1] for unification.

According to this lemma, an (E_1, E_2)-extended matching problem Γ is transformed into a conjunction $\Gamma_1 \wedge \Gamma_2$ of two pure unification problems by applying as long as possible the following rule:

Right Purification

$$\frac{\Gamma \wedge s \leq^? t}{\Gamma \wedge s =^? (t \Downarrow)[\omega_1 \hookleftarrow v_1][\ldots][\omega_m \hookleftarrow v_m] \wedge \bigwedge_{k=1}^{m} v_k \leq^? (t \Downarrow)_{|\omega_k}}$$

where

- $s \in T(\mathcal{F}_i, \mathcal{X})$,
- $\{\omega_1, \ldots, \omega_m\} = AlienPos(t)$ if $t \Downarrow (\epsilon) \in \mathcal{F}_i$, otherwise $\{\omega_1, \ldots, \omega_m\} = \{\epsilon\}$,
- $\{v_1, \ldots, v_m\}$ is a set of new variables.

Definition 14. $\mathcal{GSV}(\Gamma_i)$ is the union of $\mathcal{GV}(\Gamma)$ and the set of variables introduced by Right Purification and occurring as a member of an equation in Γ_i.

New variables introduced in right-hand sides of i-left pure match-equations are included in $\mathcal{GSV}(\Gamma_j)$, $j \neq i$, and will be skolemized in E_i as shown next.

3.3 Combining solutions from each equational theory

As in the context of unification, the main difficulty is to combine the solutions of each pure unification problem.

The first reason is that a same variable may be simultaneously instantiated in both theories. The method initiated in [10] consists of choosing nondeterministically for each variable x a single theory, say E_i, in which x will be instantiated and skolemize x in the other theory E_j, $j \neq i$, so that there is no more conflict of theories.

Second, the conjunction of two solutions does not always give a solved form since a compound cycle can appear, for example $x =^? t_1[y] \wedge y =^? t_2[x]$. For breaking such a cycle, the idea is to choose, again in a nondeterministic way, a linear ordering on variables, for example $x < y$ (or $y < x$). In each theory, pure problems are solved according to this linear restriction where alien variables are considered as free constants and thus unification with *linear constant restriction* is needed. Let us briefly recall this notion introduced in [1].

Consider that terms are built over the signature $\mathcal{F} \cup C$, where C denotes a set of additional free constants. Any constant $c \in C$ is equipped with a set $\eta(c)$ of variables. A unification problem (Γ, C) w.r.t. a *constant restriction* (C, η) is denoted (Γ, C, η). A E-solution σ of (Γ, C, η) is a E-solution such that $\forall c \in C$, $c\sigma = c$ and $\forall x \in \eta(c)$, $c \notin x\sigma$. It is enough to deal with *linear* constant restriction, which means: for a given linear ordering $<$ on $\mathcal{X} \cup C$, the sets $\eta(c)$ are defined as $\eta(c) = \{x \mid x \in \mathcal{X}$ and $x < c\}$. The set of E-solutions (resp. a complete set of E-solutions) w.r.t. a linear constant restriction $<$ is denoted $SU_E^<(\Gamma, C)$ (resp. $CSU_E^<(\Gamma, C)$)). In practice, we have to choose all possible linear orderings $<$ on $V_1 \oplus V_2 = (V_1 \cup V_2) \backslash (V_1 \cap V_2)$ where V_1 denotes the variables instantiated in E_1 (skolemized in E_2) and V_2 denotes the set of variables instantiated in E_2 (skolemized in E_1).

Combined solutions A *combined* solution is obtained from two pure solutions with respect to the same linear restriction by transforming a dag solved form into a tree solved form where replacement has been performed.

Definition 15. The *combined solution* $\sigma = \sigma_1 \odot \sigma_2$ of $(\Gamma_1, V_2, <)$ and $(\Gamma_2, V_1, <)$ obtained from $\sigma_1 \in SU_{E_1}^<(\Gamma_1, V_2)$ and $\sigma_2 \in SU_{E_2}^<(\Gamma_2, V_1)$ is defined as follows: let x be a variable in V_i and $\{y_1, \ldots, y_n\}$ be the set of (smaller) variables in V_j, $j \neq i$, occurring in $x\sigma_i$. Then $x\sigma = x\sigma_i[y_k \hookleftarrow y_k\sigma]_{k=1,\ldots,n}$.

The set of combined solutions denoted $SU_{E_1}^<(\Gamma_1, V_2) \odot SU_{E_2}^<(\Gamma_2, V_1)$ is obviously included in $SU_{E_1 \cup E_2}(\Gamma_1 \wedge \Gamma_2)$. For the completeness part, we need the fact that combining solutions from complete sets of solutions provides a complete set of combined solutions. This result can be easily derived from [1].

Extended matching problems with constant restriction The Right Purification rule introduces new variables in right-hand sides of i-left pure match-equations but these variables are necessarily instantiated by ground terms in E_j ($j \neq i$), i.e. $V_j \supseteq \mathcal{GSV}(\Gamma_j)$, and so are skolemized in E_i. Therefore, (Γ_1, V_2) and (Γ_2, V_1) are pure extended matching problems. Again, we would like to be able to solve this kind of problems w.r.t. a linear constant restriction. As for unification, a constant elimination algorithm is of greatest interest for taking into account the linear constant restriction.

Definition 16. A unification problem w.r.t. constant restriction $(\hat{\sigma}, C, \eta)$ such that $\forall c \in C$, $\eta(c) \subseteq \mathcal{D}om(\sigma)$ is called a *constant elimination problem*.

Theorem 17. *Extended matching (resp. unification) with constant restriction is finitary iff matching (resp. unification) and constant elimination problem are finitary.*

The matching algorithm is devoted to the solving process and the constant elimination algorithm is used for taking into account the constant restriction. This can be done for unification [1] as well as for matching.

Identifications Two variables instantiated with a same solution in one theory, say E_1, must be skolemized into the same free constant in E_2.

Example 5. If $+$ is idempotent, then solving $x + c \leq^? c'$ yields no solution but $x + c \leq^? c$ has the unique solution $\{x \mapsto c\}$. The identification $c = c'$ is necessary in order to obtain a solution.

As a consequence of skolemization, we have to consider each unification problem $\Gamma_1 \wedge \Gamma_2 \wedge \hat{\xi}$ where $\hat{\xi}$ denotes a conjunction of equations between variables which are pure in both theories.

Definition 18. Let V and W two sets of variables. An identification ξ of V on W is an idempotent substitution such that $\mathcal{D}om(\xi) \subseteq V$ and $\mathcal{R}an(\xi) \subseteq W$. The set of identifications on V to W is denoted by ID_V^W or ID_V if $W = V$. An identification $\xi \in ID_{V_1 \cup V_2}$ is compatible with a linear ordering $<$ on $V_1 \oplus V_2$ if

- $\forall x, y \in \mathcal{D}om(\xi), \ x\xi = y\xi \Rightarrow x, y \in V_i$ for $i = 1, 2$,
- $x\xi < y\xi \Rightarrow x < y$.

The identification $\xi_{|V_i}$ is denoted by ξ_i.

The union of all $CSU_{E_1}^{\leq}(\Gamma_1 \xi_2 \wedge \hat{\xi}_1, V_2) \odot CSU_{E_2}^{\leq}(\Gamma_2 \xi_1 \wedge \hat{\xi}_2, V_1)$ is a $CSU_{E_1 \cup E_2}(\Gamma_1 \wedge \Gamma_2)$. One can now ask: are $(\Gamma_1 \xi_2 \wedge \hat{\xi}_1, V_2)$ and $(\Gamma_2 \xi_1 \wedge \hat{\xi}_2, V_1)$ solvable thanks to (extended) matching algorithms? If $\Gamma_1 \wedge \Gamma_2$ is a conjunction of two pure matching problems then $\Gamma_1 \xi$ and $\Gamma_2 \xi$ remain (pure) matching problems for any identification ξ. This leads to this first result:

Theorem 19. *A conjunction of left pure matching problems is decidable (resp. finitary) if E_i-matching ($i = 1, 2$) with linear constant restriction is decidable (resp. finitary).*

Identification of extended matching problems Unfortunately, an identified extended matching problem $(\Gamma_1 \xi_2 \wedge \hat{\xi}_1, V_2)$ or $(\Gamma_2 \xi_1 \wedge \hat{\xi}_2, V_1)$ is no more an extended matching since an identification of two variables skolemized in E_i may produce a unification in E_j of two non ground terms abstracted by the identified variables. For instance, after identification one may get the following situations:
1) In a match-equation $l \leq^?_{E_i} r$, a skolemized variable occurs twice in l and does not occur in r.
2) In a solved equation $l =^?_{E_i} x$, the skolemized variable x occurs twice in l.
These identifications can be dropped if we can assume without loss of generality that
1) a variable can be eliminated from a linear term,
2) collapse theorems are linear.
The notion of partially linear theories formalizes this idea.

4 Partially linear theories

We give a condition on theorems of the equational theory in order to express the idea that a variable can be eliminated or collapsing without any identification. This is possible for instance in a theory that contains both theorems $x \star x = 0$ and $x \star y = 0$ since the second theorem generalizes the first one and may replace its application.

Definition 20. A term r eliminates a set of variables V of l if $\forall x \in V$, $x \in V(l)$ and $x \notin V(r)$. An equational theory E is *partially linear* if for each linear term l, and any identification $\xi \in ID_{V(l)}$, we have
1) for each term r such that $l\xi =_E r$ and r eliminates $V\xi$ of $l\xi$, then there exists d such that $l =_E d$ and d eliminates V of l,
2) $l\xi =_E x$ implies $l =_E x$ if $x\xi = x$.

Linear theories and collapse-free regular theories satisfy the above definition but there are also other theories which are partially linear.

Example 6.

$$DA = \begin{cases} x + (y+z) = (x+y)+z \\ x * (y+z) = x*y + x*z \\ (x+y) * z = x*z + y*z \end{cases} \quad Z = \begin{cases} x + \bot = \bot \\ x * \bot = \bot \end{cases}$$

If $\bot$ occurs in $l\xi$ then $\bot$ occurs also in l and $l =_{DAZ} \bot$. Otherwise $l\xi$ is equal to another term modulo DA which is a collapse-free regular theory. Therefore, DAZ is partially linear but neither regular nor linear. A DAZ-matching algorithm is easily derived from a DA-matching algorithm. The constant elimination problem is equivalent to match on $\bot$. Then, DAZ-extended matching is finitary, although DAZ-unification is infinitary since DA-unification is infinitary [11].

The class of partially linear theories is closed under disjoint union.

4.1 Extended matching vs unification

We are mostly interested in extended matching with linear constant restriction which is strongly related to extended matching with free symbols. In the following, $\emptyset$ denotes the empty theory and $E \cup \emptyset$ the equational theory generated by $(\mathcal{F} \cup \mathcal{F}_\emptyset, E)$ where $\mathcal{F}_\emptyset$ is a set of additional function symbols.

Definition 21. A *E-freely extended matching problem* is a unification problem $(\Gamma \wedge \hat{\sigma}_\emptyset, C)$ where (Γ, C) is an E-extended matching problem and $\sigma_\emptyset$ an idempotent substitution of terms built over free symbols such that for each $x, y \in \mathcal{D}om(\sigma_\emptyset)$, $x \neq y$, $x\sigma_\emptyset =_\emptyset^? y\sigma_\emptyset$ has no solution.

Variables in $\mathcal{D}om(\sigma_\emptyset)$ are necessarily instantiated in $\emptyset$ and cannot be identified.

Proposition 22. *If E-freely extended matching is decidable (resp. finitary) then E-extended matching with linear constant restriction is decidable (resp. finitary).*

Proof. According to [1], just consider $\sigma_\emptyset = \{c \mapsto f_c(x_1, \ldots, x_m) \mid \{x_1, \ldots, x_m\} = \eta(c)\}$, where $\eta(c) = \{x \in \mathcal{X} \mid x < c, \ c \in C\}$ and f_c is a free function symbol associated to c.

The next result states that there exist theories for which the introduction of unification problems cannot be avoided.

Proposition 23. *If E is not partially linear then $E \cup \emptyset$-freely extended matching is decidable (resp. finitary) iff $E \cup \emptyset$-unification is decidable (resp. finitary).*

Proof. (Sketch) Free symbols are used to introduce alien subterms which are unified since they are abstracted by variables which are identified. Three cases must be considered according to three different reasons for which an identification is needed. The first one is due to an identification of eliminated variables. The second one is due to an identification of persistent variables which helps to eliminate another variable. The last one is due to the identification of a collapsing variable.

After this negative result, the combination problem is solved for partially linear theories.

4.2   Combined matching algorithm

The idea of the nondeterministic combined matching algorithm is to perform only admissible identifications, that are those which do not lead to a unification problem. This restriction preserves the completeness of the returned set of solutions when theories are partially linear.

Proposition 24. *(Match-Combi Algorithm) Let E_1 and E_2 be two partially linear theories and Γ be an (E_1, E_2)-extended matching problem. The following decomposition algorithm provides a $CSU_{E_1 \cup E_2}(\Gamma)$:*

1. Purification: *Transform Γ into a conjunction $\Gamma_1 \wedge \Gamma_2$ of two pure unification problems thanks to* Right Purification.
2. Choose ordering and theory indices: *Consider all possible linear orderings $<$ on $V_1 \oplus V_2 = \mathcal{V}(\Gamma_1 \wedge \Gamma_2) \backslash \mathcal{GV}(\Gamma)$ s.t. $V_1 \supseteq \mathcal{GSV}(\Gamma_1)$ and $V_2 \supseteq \mathcal{GSV}(\Gamma_2)$.*
3. Variable identification: *Consider all possible identifications ξ compatible with $<$ s.t. $\xi_i \in ID^{\mathcal{GSV}(\Gamma_i)}_{V_i \backslash \mathcal{SV}(\Gamma_j)} \circ ID^{V_i}_{\mathcal{SV}(\Gamma_j)}$ for $i, j = 1, 2, i \neq j$.*
4. Solve: *Compute all combined solutions $\sigma_1 \odot \sigma_2$ s.t. $\sigma_1 \in CSU^{\leq}_{E_1}(\Gamma_1 \xi_2 \wedge \hat{\xi}_1, V_2)$ and $\sigma_2 \in CSU^{\leq}_{E_2}(\Gamma_2 \xi_1 \wedge \hat{\xi}_2, V_1)$.*

Note that the variables in $\mathcal{GV}(\Gamma) = \mathcal{GSV}(\Gamma_1) \cap \mathcal{GSV}(\Gamma_2) = V_1 \cap V_2$ are skolemized in both E_1 and E_2.

Proposition 25. *Pure unification problems obtained at the step* Solve *of the* Match-Combi *algorithm are equivalent to extended matching problems.*

Proof. Identifications in $ID^{V_i}_{\mathcal{SV}(\Gamma_j)}$ yield new solved equations which transform the extended matching problem (Γ_i, V_j) into another one since $\mathcal{SV}(\Gamma_1) \cap \mathcal{SV}(\Gamma_2) = \emptyset$.

Identifications in $ID^{\mathcal{GSV}(\Gamma_i)}_{V_i \backslash \mathcal{SV}(\Gamma_j)}$ yield match-equations since variables in $\mathcal{GSV}(\Gamma_i)$ are equal to ground terms in E_i. Then, $(x =^? s \wedge y \leq^? t \Downarrow) \wedge (x =^? y)$ is equivalent to $(s \leq^? t \Downarrow \wedge y \leq^? t \Downarrow) \wedge (x =^? y)$.

5   Discussion

The combined matching algorithm can be used to compute finite complete sets of solutions or to solve the decision problem. From Proposition 24, one can deduce the following results:

Theorem 26. *If E_1 and E_2 are two partially linear theories then (E_1, E_2)-extended matching is decidable (resp. finitary) if E_i-extended matching with linear constant restriction $(i = 1, 2)$ is decidable (resp. finitary).*

This theorem can be easily lifted since the combined matching algorithm is able to solve freely extended matching.

Theorem 27. *If E_1 and E_2 are two partially linear theories then $E_1 \cup E_2$-freely extended matching is decidable (resp. finitary) iff E_i-freely extended matching $(i = 1, 2)$ is decidable (resp. finitary).*

Proof. The combined matching problem can be applied by a straightforward generalization to the union of three partially linear theories E_1, E_2 and $\emptyset$. Then, pure and satisfiable unification problems to solve in each theory are still extended matching problems since identification of variables in $\mathcal{D}om(\sigma_\emptyset)$ yields no solution.

This result is now applied to the combination of a partially linear theory with the empty theory $\emptyset$ which is also a partially linear theory. The second point comes from Proposition 23.

Corollary 28. *(1) If E is a partially linear theory then $E \cup \emptyset$-freely extended matching is decidable (resp. finitary) iff E-freely extended matching is decidable (resp. finitary). (2) If E is not a partially linear theory then $E \cup \emptyset$-freely extended matching is decidable (resp. finitary) iff $E \cup \emptyset$-unification is decidable (resp. finitary).*

Theorem 26 allows solving unification problems more general than $E_1 \cup E_2$-matching. If we restrict to this last kind of problems we can get rid of the linear constant restriction since solving matching problems cannot create a compound cycle and partially linear theories generalize in this sense regular theories.

Theorem 29. *If E_1 and E_2 are two partially linear theories then $E_1 \cup E_2$-matching is decidable (resp. finitary) iff E_i-matching $(i = 1, 2)$ is decidable (resp. finitary).*

Proof. Consider a conjunction of pure extended matching problems $(\Gamma_1 \wedge \hat{\sigma}_1, V_2, <)$ and $(\Gamma_2 \wedge \hat{\sigma}_2, V_1, <)$ obtained at the step Solve. The unification problem $\hat{\sigma}_1 \wedge \hat{\sigma}_2$ is necessarily in dag solved form thanks to performed identifications. Solving (Γ_1, V_2) and (Γ_2, V_1) does not introduce a compound cycle. Consequently, there exists a linear ordering $<$ for which $(\Gamma_1 \wedge \hat{\sigma}_1, V_2, <)$ and $(\Gamma_2 \wedge \hat{\sigma}_2, V_1, <)$ are satisfiable if (Γ_1, V_2) and (Γ_2, V_1) are satisfiable.

For instance, we are now able to combine matching algorithms for the union of a linear theory and a collapse-free regular theory.

Example 7. Assume $E_1 = \{f(x, y) = y\}$ and $E_2 = \{x \star y = y \star x\}$ the commutativity. The heterogeneous match-equation $f(y \star y, y \star z) \leq^? a \star b$ is equivalent to $(f(v, w) \leq^? c) \wedge (v =^? y \star y \wedge w =^? y \star z \wedge c \leq^? a \star b)$ by purification, where variables v, w, c are skolemized in E_1 since E_2 is collapse-free. The identification $\{v \mapsto c\}$ leads to a failure in E_1. Nevertheless, the match-equation $f(v, w) \leq^? c$ becomes true with the identification $\{w \mapsto c\}$. This identification leads to $y \star z \leq^? a \star b$ in E_2, which is then solved and yields a complete set of solutions: $\{y \mapsto a, z \mapsto b\}$ and $\{y \mapsto b, z \mapsto a\}$.

6 Conclusion

We have solved in this paper the combined matching problem for the so-called partially linear theories. There is no hope to extend this result to non partially linear theories since combination techniques need then unification instead of matching.

Extending combination techniques for non disjoint theories is now in progress. For instance, combining unification algorithms in equational theories sharing only constants is also possible [8] and this can be directly applied to matching algorithms.

Acknowledgements: I would like to thank Hélène Kirchner for many helpful comments, and the PROTHEO group at Nancy for fruitful discussions. I am grateful to Alexandre Boudet for pointing out a mistake in a previous version of this paper and the referees for their pertinent and constructive remarks.

References

1. Franz Baader and Klaus Schulz. Unification in the union of disjoint equational theories: Combining decision procedures. In *Proceedings 11th International Conference on Automated Deduction, Saratoga Springs (N.Y., USA)*, pages 50–65, 1992.
2. A. Boudet. Unification in a combination of equational theories: An efficient algorithm. In M. E. Stickel, editor, *Proceedings 10th International Conference on Automated Deduction, Kaiserslautern (Germany)*, volume 449 of *Lecture Notes in Computer Science*. Springer-Verlag, July 1990.
3. H.-J. Bürckert. Matching — A special case of unification? *Journal of Symbolic Computation*, 8(5):523–536, 1989.
4. A. Herold. Combination of unification algorithms. In J. Siekmann, editor, *Proceedings 8th International Conference on Automated Deduction, Oxford (UK)*, volume 230 of *Lecture Notes in Computer Science*, pages 450–469. Springer-Verlag, 1986.
5. J.-P. Jouannaud and Claude Kirchner. Solving equations in abstract algebras: a rule-based survey of unification. In Jean-Louis Lassez and G. Plotkin, editors, *Computational Logic. Essays in honor of Alan Robinson*, chapter 8, pages 257–321. MIT Press, Cambridge (MA, USA), 1991.
6. Claude Kirchner. *Méthodes et outils de conception systématique d'algorithmes d'unification dans les théories équationnelles*. Thèse de Doctorat d'Etat, Université de Nancy I, 1985.
7. T. Nipkow. Combining matching algorithms: The regular case. *Journal of Symbolic Computation*, pages 633–653, 1991.
8. Ch. Ringeissen. Unification in a combination of equational theories with shared constants and its application to primal algebras. In *Proceedings of LPAR'92*, volume 624 of *Lecture Notes in Artificial Intelligence*, pages 261–272. Springer-Verlag, 1992.
9. Ch. Ringeissen. Combination of matching algorithms (extended version). Research report, INRIA, Inria-Lorraine & CRIN, 1994. Also as: Internal report 93-R-197, CRIN.
10. M. Schmidt-Schauß. Combination of unification algorithms. *Journal of Symbolic Computation*, 8(1 & 2):51–100, 1989. Special issue on unification. Part two.
11. P. Szabó. *Unifikationstheorie erster Ordnung*. PhD thesis, Universität Karlsruhe, 1982.
12. E. Tidén. Unification in combinations of collapse-free theories with disjoint sets of functions symbols. In J. Siekmann, editor, *Proceedings 8th International Conference on Automated Deduction, Oxford (UK)*, volume 230 of *Lecture Notes in Computer Science*, pages 431–449. Springer-Verlag, 1986.
13. K. Yelick. Unification in combinations of collapse-free regular theories. *Journal of Symbolic Computation*, 3(1 & 2):153–182, April 1987.

Parallel Algorithms 1

Parallel Algorithms 1

Periodic constant depth sorting networks[*]

Marcin Kik   Mirosław Kutyłowski   Grzegorz Stachowiak

Institute of Computer Science, University of Wrocław,
ul. Przesmyckiego 20, PL-51-151 Wrocław, Poland,
email: kik,mirekk,gst@ii.uni.wroc.pl

Abstract. Comparator networks of constant depth can be used for sorting in the following way. The computation consists of a number of iterations, say t, each iteration being a single run through the comparator network. The output of iteration j ($j < t$) is used as the input for iteration $j + 1$. The output of the iteration t is the output of the computation. In such a way, it is possible to apply a network with a small number of comparators for sorting long input sequences. However, it is not clear how to make such a computation fast.

Odd-Even Transposition Sort gives a periodic sorting network of depth 2, that sorts n numbers in $n/2$ iterations. The network of depth 8 proposed by Schwiegelshohn [8] sorts n numbers in $O(\sqrt{n}\log n)$ iterations. Krammer [5] modified the algorithm and obtained a network of depth 6 sorting in $O(\sqrt{n}\log n)$ iterations.

For a fixed but arbitrary $k \in \mathbb{N}$, we present a periodic sorting network of depth $O(k)$ that sorts n input numbers in $O(k^2 \cdot n^{1/k})$ steps.

1 Introduction

Comparator networks are widely used for sorting sequences of numbers. A comparator network of depth d sorting n input numbers may be viewed as a set of n registers and a set of communication links between the registers divided into d so called levels. Each level can be represented by a directed graph of degree one, i.e. a single register may be connected to at most one other register at a given level. At step $i \leq d$ of the computation, all links of the ith level are used in parallel to perform comparison-exchange operations between the elements stored in different registers: For a given link (R, R'), if numbers x and x' are stored in R and R', respectively, then after the compare-exchange operation R stores $\min(x, x')$ and R' stores $\max(x, x')$.

A large number of sorting comparator networks has been proposed in the literature. The networks proposed by Batcher [2] are regarded as most successful in practice. They are very elegant in design and have depth $\frac{1}{2}(\log n)^2$. There has been a lot of effort to reduce the depth of sorting comparator networks to $\log n$. This was achieved by the famous AKS network of depth $O(\log n)$ [1]. However, the result is of purely theoretical importance, because of large constants involved.

[*] supported by KBN grant 2 1197 91 01 and Volkswagen Foundation, Project "Paralleles Rechnen: Theoretische und experimentelle Untersuchungen zu parallelen Rechnenmodellen und systemnahen Algorithmen", partially this work was done while the first and the second author visited Heinz–Nixdorf-Institut, Universität Paderborn

Except for relatively large depth, the networks of Batcher have yet another disadvantage. Every level is different from another. Therefore, if the sorting network is directly wired in a VLSI chip, then there is a large number of wires put into circuitry, making the chip large and expensive. If the comparator network is emulated by a set of processors, then there is a lot of overhead due to routing along many different paths at different times. One may try to overcome these difficulties by applying periodic sorting algorithms [3]. We may use a single comparator network (presumably of a small depth) repeatedly: after getting output that is still not sorted, we put it as an input to the network again. We stop once the output is sorted. The total computation time is therefore $\delta \cdot T$, where δ is the depth of the network and T is the number of iterations. Dowd *et al* [3] proposed a network of depth $\log n$ that sorts in $\log n$ iterations. All communication links of this network are those of an $\log n$-dimensional hypercube.

To achieve low cost sorting circuits for large inputs it would be desirable to reduce the depth of comparator networks used for periodic sorting to a constant while preserving a small number of iterations. The question whether such networks exist has been raised by Meyer auf der Heide [7]. For example, Odd-Even Transposition Sort leads to a network of depth 2 that sorts in $n/2$ iterations, i.e. n parallel steps [6]. Schwiegelshohn's network of depth 8 sorts n elements in $O(\sqrt{n} \log n)$ iterations [8]. Krammer [5] modified the construction of Schwiegelshohn and obtained a network of depth 6 sorting in $O(\sqrt{n \log n})$ iterations. We prove the following theorem.

Theorem 1. *Let $k \in \mathbb{N}$ be an arbitrary constant. Let $n \in \mathbb{N}$. There is a comparator network of depth $O(k)$ that sorts n numbers in $O(k \cdot n^{1/k})$ iterations, i.e. in time $O(k^2 \cdot n^{1/k})$.*

The proof of Theorem 1 is constructive – we show how to build the required network using ε-halver networks of Ajtai, Komlós and Szemerédi. However, our network is not applicable directly in practice, since the constants seem to be not small enough and wiring due to ε-halvers might be complicated.

Due to space limitations, some proofs in this paper are only sketched. More technical details can be found in [4].

2 Preliminaries

Definition 2. A *comparator network* $N = (V, C_1, \ldots, C_d)$ for input sequences of n numbers consists of a set V of n registers $R_1, \ldots, R_n$ and d directed graphs $C_1, \ldots, C_d$, each of degree 1, with vertices in V. For $i \le d$, C_i is called the ith *level* of N; d is called the *depth* of N. Network N works as follows. Initially, the input numbers are stored in the registers, the ith number in the register R_i. At step t ($t \le d$), for each arc $(R_j, R_{j'}) \in C_t$ the numbers stored in R_j and $R_{j'}$ are compared. The minimum of them is put into R_j, the maximum into $R_{j'}$. (Since C_t has degree 1, there is at most one arc incident to a given vertex and the definition is unambiguous.) For an input sequence $\mathbf{x} = (x_1, \ldots, x_n)$, by the output of N on $\mathbf{x}$, $N(\mathbf{x})$, we mean the sequence $(x_{j_1}, \ldots, x_{j_n})$, where x_{j_i} denotes the contents of R_i after step d.

A comparator network N is *monotonic* if $j < j'$ for every arc $(R_j, R_{j'}) \in C_t, t \le d$. (All comparator networks considered in this paper are monotonic).

Definition 3. Let $N^1(\mathbf{x}) = N(\mathbf{x})$ and $N^{j+1}(\mathbf{x}) = N(N^j(\mathbf{x}))$ for $i \geq 1$. We say that network N sorts a sequence $\mathbf{x}$ in at most t iterations, if the sequence $N^t(\mathbf{x})$ is sorted.

To prove that a comparator network sorts one can use well known 0–1 *Principle* (see [6]). Clearly, iterating computation of a comparator network is equivalent to a single computation on a comparator network with iterated layers.

Lemma 4. (0–1 Principle) *A comparator network correctly sorts every input sequence if and only if it correctly sorts every input consisting of 0's and 1's.*

3 Construction of the network

In our construction we use ε-halver networks introduced in [1]. We recall their definition and basic properties.

Definition 5. Let $\varepsilon \geq 0$. A comparator network N is an *ε-halver* for inputs of size n if the following holds:

(i) The set of registers of N consists of two subsets V_1 and V_2 of cardinality $n/2$, and all comparison arcs point from V_1 to V_2.
(ii) Let the input for N contain k ones and $n-k$ zeroes. If $k \leq n/2$, then the output of N contains at most $\varepsilon \cdot k$ ones stored in V_1. If $k \geq n/2$, then the output of N contains at most $\varepsilon \cdot (n-k)$ zeroes stored in V_2.

We shall also say that N is a (V_1, V_2, ε)-halver.

Lemma 6. [1] *For each $\varepsilon > 0$ and $n \in \mathbb{N}$, there exists an ε-halver for inputs consisting of n numbers which has depth $O(1/\varepsilon \cdot \log(1/\varepsilon))$.*

The construction of ε-halver networks is based on expander graphs [1].

Definition 7. Let $N = (V, C_1, \ldots, C_d)$ and $N' = (V', C'_1, \ldots, C'_{d'})$ be comparator networks. Then $N|N'$ denotes the network $(V \cup V', C_1, \ldots, C_d, C'_1, \ldots, C'_{d'})$. If $V \cap V' = \emptyset$ and $d = d'$, then $N \cup N'$ is the network $(V \cup V', C_1 \cup C'_1, \ldots, C_d \cup C'_d)$.

(ε, m)-blocks that we define below are key components of our sorting networks.

Definition 8. An (ε, m)-*block* built on registers $R_1, \ldots, R_n$ is defined as follows. Let $l = \lceil \frac{n}{m} \rceil$. For $i < l$, let $K_i = \{R_{m \cdot (i-1)+1}, \ldots, R_{m \cdot i}\}$, and $K_l = \{R_{m \cdot (l-1)+1}, \ldots, R_n\}$. Let E_i be an $(K_i, K_{i+1}, \varepsilon)$-halver. (If K_l consists of less than m registers, then we add dummy registers to make K_l contain m registers, we take an $(K_{l-1}, K_l, \varepsilon)$-halver and remove all arcs pointing to the dummy registers; E_{l-1} consists of the arcs that remain.) Let $P = (E_1 \cup E_3 \cup E_5 \cup \cdots)$ and $N = (E_2 \cup E_4 \cup E_6 \cup \cdots)$. Then the network $P|N$ is called an (ε, m)-block. P is called the first layer and N is called the second layer of the (ε, m)-block. In particular, a $(0, 1)$-block is a network $(\{R_1, \ldots, R_n\}, C_1, C_2)$, where $C_1 = \{(R_1, R_2), (R_3, R_4), \ldots\}$ and $C_2 = \{(R_2, R_3), (R_4, R_5), \ldots\}$

We can imagine the registers of an (ε, m)-block to be arranged in an $m \times l$-matrix, with K_i being the ith column of the matrix. Between each pair of columns we put an ε-halver . During the first part of computation corresponding to P we apply ε-halvers for the pair of columns K_1 and K_2, K_3 and K_4, ... During the second part of the computation corresponding to N, we use ε-halvers for the pairs of columns K_2 and K_3, K_4 and K_5, ... The crucial property of (ε, m)-blocks is that in $O(l)$ iterations each element is moved to a column not far from the column of its final destination in the sorted sequence (to be proved in Section 4).

Now we complete the construction of our comparator network that sorts n numbers in $O(k \cdot n^{1/k})$ iterations:

Definition 9. For $n, k \in \mathbb{N}$, let $I_{n,k}$ be a comparator network of the form

$$I_{n,k} = F_1 | F_2 | \cdots | F_k | F_{k+1}$$

where F_{k+1} is a $(0, 1)$-block, and F_i is an $(\varepsilon, n^{(k-i)/k} \cdot (c \cdot \log n)^{i-1})$-block for $i = 1, \ldots, k$. (The constants c and ε $(0 < \varepsilon < \frac{1}{2})$ will be determined later.)

It follows from the definition that $I_{n,k}$ has depth $2\delta k + 2$, where $\delta = O(\frac{1}{\varepsilon} \cdot \log(\frac{1}{\varepsilon}))$ denotes the depth of the ε-halvers used in the construction.

4 The time bounds

This section is organized as follows. First we analyze computation of a single (ε, m)-block. In Subsection 4.1 we formulate the main lemma and make some straightforward observations. Subsections 4.2, 4.3, 4.4 are devoted to the proof of the main lemma. Finally, in Subsection 4.5 we use the main lemma to estimate the number of iterations required by the network $I_{n,k}$.

4.1 Main lemma

Let B be an (ε, m)-block consisting of registers $R_1, \ldots, R_n$, $l = \lceil \frac{n}{m} \rceil$. Let $K_i = K_i(B, m)$ denote the ith column of B of height m, i.e., $K_i = \{R_{m(i-1)+1}, \ldots, R_{mi}\}$, for $i < l$, and $K_l = \{R_{m(l-1)+1}, \ldots, R_n\}$. We shall use this notation throughout the whole section.

Definition 10. Let $C = X_1 | B | X_2$ and let the registers of C store 0's and 1's, only. Then we say that network C is at most (p, m)-dirty, if there is j such that the columns $K_1, \ldots, K_j$ contain only zeroes, and the columns $K_{j+p+1}, \ldots, K_l$ contain only ones.

Lemma 11. (Main Lemma) *Let B' be a comparator network such that $B' = X_1 | B | X_2$ for some monotonic comparator networks X_1, X_2 and the (ε, m)-block B. There are constants $\alpha \in \mathbb{N}$ and $\beta \in \mathbb{R}$, such that if initially B' stores 0's and 1's and is at most (p, m)-dirty, then after $\alpha \cdot p$ iterations, B' is at most $(\beta \cdot \log(p \cdot m), m)$-dirty.*

It is convenient to reduce Main Lemma using three following observations:

Proposition 12. *It suffices to prove Main Lemma for $l = p$ and for the case when the last column of B consists of m registers.*

The first claim is obvious. The second claim can be proved by adding lacking registers containing ones to the last column.

Proposition 13. *If Main Lemma holds for the case when the number of ones is an odd multiple of m, then it holds in general.*

Sketch of the proof. If $x_1, x_2 \in \{0,1\}^n$, then we write $x_1 \subseteq x_2$ if x_2 contains a 1 at each position where x_1 contains a 1. One can easily prove the following claim:
Claim. [5] *If $x_1 \subseteq x_2$ and F is a comparator network, then $F(x_1) \subseteq F(x_2)$.*
Let x be an arbitrary input to B'. Consider x_1, x_2 such that $x_1 \subseteq x \subseteq x_2$ and for some odd r, x_1 contains $r \cdot m$ ones and x_2 contains $(r+2) \cdot m$ ones. For $i = 1, 2$, assume that $(B')^{\alpha l}(x_i)$ is $(\beta \log(lm), m)$-dirty. The dirty columns of $(B')^{\alpha l}(x_2)$ contain less than $m \cdot \beta \log(lm)$ zeros. The remaining 0's occupy all positions in the first $l - (r+2) - \beta \log(lm)$ columns (and may be some other columns, too). Similarly, the last $r - \beta \log(lm)$ columns of $(B')^{\alpha l}(x_1)$ contain only 1's. By the claim, $(B')^{\alpha l}(x_1) \subseteq (B')^{\alpha l}(x) \subseteq (B')^{\alpha l}(x_2)$. It follows that $(B')^{\alpha l}(x)$ is at most $(2\beta \log(lm) + 2, m)$-dirty.□
A particular case of Main Lemma has been proved in [5]:

Lemma 14. *Suppose that B' is a comparator network of the form $X_1|B|X_2$, where X_1, X_2 are monotonic and B is the Odd-Even Transposition Sort network (i.e. B is a $(0,1)$-block). Assume that the contents of B is at most $(p, 1)$-dirty. Then after at most $\lceil p/2 \rceil$ iterations the contents of B is sorted.*

4.2 Dominance relation

We consider the number of 1's in each column K_i during the computation on inputs consisting of 0's and 1's. This motivates the definitions that follow.

Definition 15. Let $a = (a_1, \ldots, a_l)$, $b = (b_1, \ldots, b_l)$, where $a_i, b_i \in [0, m]$ ($a_i, b_i \in \mathbb{R}$), for $i \leq l$. Let $\text{head}_i(a) = \sum_{j=1}^{i} a_j$ for $i \leq l$. We say that a *dominates* b (denoted by $a \succeq b$), if $\text{head}_l(a) = \text{head}_l(b)$ and $\text{head}_k(a) \leq \text{head}_k(b)$ for every $k < l$.

Intuitively, a_i, b_i denote the number of ones in K_i. If $a \succeq b$, then the sequence of 0's and 1's corresponding to a is closer to the sorted sequence than the sequence corresponding to b. Equivalently, for $a, b \in \{0,1\}^l$, we could define: $a \succeq b$ if a and b contain the same number of 1's, and for every i, the ith one in b occurs no later than the ith one in a (cf. [5]). The following properties follow directly from the definition:

Proposition 16. *The relation $\succeq$ is a partial order.*

Proposition 17. Let X be an arbitrary monotonic network on the registers $R_1, \ldots, R_n$. Consider an input consisting of 0's and 1's; let e_i denote the number of 1's in K_i and $e = (e_1, \ldots, e_l)$. Let x_i denote the number of 1's in K_i after applying X to the input and $x = (x_1, \ldots, x_l)$. Then $x \succeq e$.

Definition 18. Let B' be the network defined in Main Lemma. Let the input of the network B' consist of 0's and 1's. Then $a_{2t,i}$ denotes the number of ones in the column K_i of (ε, m)-block B immediately after iteration t of B', and $a_{2t+1,i}$ denotes the number of ones in K_i after applying the first layer P of B at iteration $t + 1$ of B'. Let $\mathbf{a}_t = (a_{t,1}, \ldots, a_{t,l})$.

The vectors $\mathbf{a}_t$ might be very difficult to determine. Even if we fix ε-halvers used to build B, there are many different distributions of 0's and 1's corresponding to the same vector $\mathbf{a}_0$, and each of them influences $\mathbf{a}_t$ in some way. Therefore, we look for simpler vectors $\mathbf{b}_t$ such that $\mathbf{a}_t \succeq \mathbf{b}_t$ for each t. The key point is to define $\mathbf{b}_{t+1}$ from $\mathbf{b}_t$ without loosing the property that $\mathbf{a}_{t+1} \succeq \mathbf{b}_{t+1}$. For this purpose we define functions $f_1^\varepsilon, f_2^\varepsilon$ that estimate how a single ε-halver works.

Definition 19. Let $\varepsilon \in [0, \frac{1}{2})$. We define

$$f_1^\varepsilon(x) = \begin{cases} \varepsilon x & \text{for } x \le m, \\ m - (1 - \varepsilon)(2m - x) & \text{for } x > m. \end{cases}$$

and $f_2^\varepsilon(x) = x - f_1^\varepsilon(x)$.

Note that f_1^ε and f_2^ε are nondecreasing functions and by the definition of ε-halvers the following holds:

Fact 20. *Assume that H is a (V_1, V_2, ε)-halver and an input $\mathbf{x}$ to H contains x ones. Then $H(\mathbf{x})$ contains at most $f_1^\varepsilon(x)$ ones in V_1 and at least $f_2^\varepsilon(x)$ ones in V_2.*

In order to define the sequence $\{\mathbf{b}_t\}_{t \ge 0}$ we define two operations on vectors in $[1, m]^l$. These operations correspond to the layers P and N of (ε, m)-block B.

Definition 21. Let $\mathbf{b} = (b_1, b_2, b_3, \ldots) \in [0, m]^l$. We define $P^\varepsilon(\mathbf{b}), N^\varepsilon(\mathbf{b}) \in [1, m]^l$ as follows:

$$P^\varepsilon(\mathbf{b}) = (f_1^\varepsilon(b_1 + b_2), f_2^\varepsilon(b_1 + b_2), f_1^\varepsilon(b_3 + b_4), f_2^\varepsilon(b_3 + b_4), f_1^\varepsilon(b_5 + b_6), \ldots),$$
$$N^\varepsilon(\mathbf{b}) = (b_1, f_1^\varepsilon(b_2 + b_3), f_2^\varepsilon(b_2 + b_3), f_1^\varepsilon(b_4 + b_5), f_2^\varepsilon(b_4 + b_5), f_1^\varepsilon(b_6 + b_7), \ldots).$$

The relationship between $P^\varepsilon, N^\varepsilon$ and layers P, N of (ε, m)-block is given by the following lemma.

Lemma 22. *Let $\mathbf{b} = (b_1, \ldots, b_l)$ where b_i is the number of ones in K_i. Let $\mathbf{b}^P = (b_1^P, \ldots, b_l^P)$ and $\mathbf{b}^N = (b_1^N, \ldots, b_l^N)$ where b_i^P (b_i^P) is the number of ones in K_i after applying network P (N) to the sequence described by $\mathbf{b}$. Then $P^\varepsilon(\mathbf{b}) \preceq \mathbf{b}^P$ and $N^\varepsilon(\mathbf{b}) \preceq \mathbf{b}^N$.*

Proof. The lemma follows from Fact 20. $\square$

Lemma 23. *If $\mathbf{a} \succeq \mathbf{b}$, then $P^\varepsilon(\mathbf{a}) \succeq P^\varepsilon(\mathbf{b})$ and $N^\varepsilon(\mathbf{a}) \succeq N^\varepsilon(\mathbf{b})$.*

Proof. We prove the lemma for P^ε (for N^ε the proof is similar). Let $\mathbf{a} = (a_1, \ldots, a_l)$ and $\mathbf{b} = (b_1, \ldots, b_l)$. We have to show that $\mathrm{head}_h(P^\varepsilon(\mathbf{a})) \leq \mathrm{head}_h(P^\varepsilon(\mathbf{b}))$ for $h \leq l$. If h is even, then obviously $\mathrm{head}_h(\mathbf{x}) = \mathrm{head}_h(P^\varepsilon(\mathbf{x}))$, hence the claimed inequality holds. For h odd we consider two cases:

Case 1. $a_h + a_{h+1} \geq b_h + b_{h+1}$. Then $\mathrm{head}_h(P^\varepsilon(\mathbf{a})) = \mathrm{head}_{h+1}(P^\varepsilon(\mathbf{a})) - f_2(a_h + a_{h+1}) \leq \mathrm{head}_{h+1}(\mathbf{a}) - f_2(b_h + b_{h+1}) \leq \mathrm{head}_{h+1}(\mathbf{b}) - f_2(b_h + b_{h+1}) = \mathrm{head}_{h+1}(P^\varepsilon(\mathbf{b})) - f_2(b_h + b_{h+1}) = \mathrm{head}_h(P^\varepsilon(\mathbf{b}))$.

Case 2. $a_h + a_{h+1} \leq b_h + b_{h+1}$. Then $\mathrm{head}_h(P^\varepsilon(\mathbf{a})) = \mathrm{head}_{h-1}(P^\varepsilon(\mathbf{a})) + f_1(a_h + a_{h+1}) \leq \mathrm{head}_{h-1}(\mathbf{a}) + f_1(b_h + b_{h+1}) \leq \mathrm{head}_{h-1}(\mathbf{b}) + f_1(b_h + b_{h+1}) = \mathrm{head}_{h-1}(P^\varepsilon(\mathbf{b})) + f_1(b_h + b_{h+1}) = \mathrm{head}_h(P^\varepsilon(\mathbf{b}))$. □

To estimate vector $\mathbf{a}_t$ according to relation $\preceq$ we need some vector $\mathbf{b}_0$ dominated by any vector $\mathbf{a}_0$ representing an input sequence with a given number of ones.

Definition 24. Let $m|s$. Then $\mathbf{b}_0 = (b_1, \ldots, b_l)$ is the *worst vector for s ones*, if $b_i = m$ for $i \leq s/m$, and $b_i = 0$, otherwise.

From now on, we consider only inputs to network B' that contain 0's and 1's, only, and contain exactly $r \cdot m$ ones for some fixed but arbitrary odd number r.

Definition 25. For $i \in \mathbb{N}$, let $\mathbf{b}_i^\varepsilon$ be defined as follows: $\mathbf{b}_0^\varepsilon = \mathbf{b}_0$, $\mathbf{b}_{i+1}^\varepsilon = N^\varepsilon(\mathbf{b}_i^\varepsilon)$, if $i + 1$ is odd, and $\mathbf{b}_{i+1}^\varepsilon = P^\varepsilon(\mathbf{b}_i^\varepsilon)$, if $i + 1$ is even.

Lemma 26. $\mathbf{b}_i^\varepsilon \preceq \mathbf{a}_t$, *for every* t.

Lemma 26 follows from Proposition 17, Lemma 22 and 23.

For $\varepsilon = 0$, we get vectors $\mathbf{b}_i^0$ that are closely related to the sequences of 0's and 1's occurring during Odd-Even Transposition Sort. Namely, let $\tilde{b}_i^0$ be the sequence obtained from $\mathbf{b}_i^0$ by replacing every m by 1.

Lemma 27. $\tilde{b}_i^0$ *is the sequence obtained after i steps of Odd-Even Transposition Sort, when started with $\tilde{b}_0$. In particular, for $t \geq l - 1$, $\mathbf{b}_t^0 = (0, \ldots, 0, m, \ldots, m)$. For $t < l - 1$, $\mathbf{b}_t^0$ contains only 0's in positions 1 through $(l - r) - (l - 1 - t)$ and contains only m's in positions $(l - r + 1) + (l - 1 - t)$ through l.*

Hints for the proof. Since r is odd, Odd-Even Transposition Sort sorts $\tilde{b}_0^0$ in exactly $l - 1$ steps. At step $t \leq l - 1$ every element must be at a distance not larger than $l - 1 - t$ from its final destination. □

4.3 Convex estimates

The vectors b_i^ε defined in the previous section are much easier to estimate than the vectors $\mathbf{a}_t$, however they are still difficult to handle. For this reason we introduce *convex estimates* of the vectors b_i^ε.

Recall that for $\alpha_1, \ldots, \alpha_k \geq 0$ such that $\sum_{i=1}^k \alpha_i = 1$, the vector $\alpha_1 \mathbf{e}_1 + \cdots + \alpha_k \mathbf{e}_k$ is a *convex combination of* $\mathbf{e}_1, \ldots, \mathbf{e}_k$. First, we prove the following property of the operators N^ε and P^ε on convex combinations:

Lemma 28. *Let $\alpha_1, \ldots, \alpha_k \geq 0$, $\sum_{i=1}^{k} \alpha_i = 1$ and $e_1, \ldots, e_k \in [0, m]^l$. Then*

$$\sum_{i=1}^{k} \alpha_i P^\varepsilon(e_i) \preceq P^\varepsilon(\sum_{i=1}^{k} \alpha_i e_i) \quad and \quad \sum_{i=1}^{k} \alpha_i N^\varepsilon(e_i) \preceq N^\varepsilon(\sum_{i=1}^{k} \alpha_i e_i)$$

Proof. It follows from the definition of f_1^ε that $f_1^\varepsilon(\alpha x + \beta y) \leq \alpha f_1^\varepsilon(x) + \beta f_1^\varepsilon(y)$ if $\alpha, \beta \geq 0$, $\alpha + \beta = 1$, and $x, y \in [0, 2m]$.

We prove the lemma for $k = 2$. The generalization for an arbitrary k is standard. Also, we consider only P^ε. We have to show that $\text{head}_h(\alpha P^\varepsilon(\mathbf{x}) + \beta P^\varepsilon(\mathbf{y})) \geq \text{head}_h(P^\varepsilon(\alpha\mathbf{x} + \beta\mathbf{y}))$ for every $h \leq l$.

Obviously, $\text{head}_h(\alpha\mathbf{x}) = \alpha\text{head}_h(\mathbf{x})$, and $\text{head}_h(\mathbf{x} + \mathbf{y}) = \text{head}_h(\mathbf{x}) + \text{head}_h(\mathbf{y})$ for every $\alpha, h, \mathbf{x}, \mathbf{y}$. For every even h, $\text{head}_h(\mathbf{x}) = \text{head}_h(P^\varepsilon(\mathbf{x}))$. It follows easily that $\text{head}_h(\alpha P^\varepsilon(\mathbf{x}) + \beta P^\varepsilon(\mathbf{y})) = \text{head}_h(P^\varepsilon(\alpha\mathbf{x} + \beta\mathbf{y}))$ for even h.

If h is odd, then $\text{head}_h(\alpha P^\varepsilon(\mathbf{x}) + \beta P^\varepsilon(\mathbf{y})) = \alpha(f_1^\varepsilon(x_h + x_{h+1}) + \text{head}_{h-1}(P^\varepsilon(\mathbf{x}))) + \beta(f_1^\varepsilon(y_h + y_{h+1}) + \text{head}_{h-1}(P^\varepsilon(\mathbf{y}))) \geq f_1^\varepsilon(\alpha(x_h + x_{h+1}) + \beta(y_h + y_{h+1})) + \alpha\text{head}_{h-1}(\mathbf{x}) + \beta\text{head}_{h-1}(\mathbf{y}) = f_1^\varepsilon(\alpha(x_h + x_{h+1}) + \beta(y_h + y_{h+1})) + \text{head}_{h-1}(\alpha\mathbf{x} + \beta\mathbf{y}) = f_1^\varepsilon(\alpha(x_h + x_{h+1}) + \beta(y_h + y_{h+1})) + \text{head}_{h-1}(P^\varepsilon(\alpha\mathbf{x} + \beta\mathbf{y})) = \text{head}_h(P^\varepsilon(\alpha\mathbf{x} + \beta\mathbf{y}))$. □

Lemma 29. *Let $0 \leq i \leq l - 2$. If i is even, then*

$$N^\varepsilon(\mathbf{b}_i^0) = N^\varepsilon(\mathbf{b}_{i+1}^0) = \varepsilon\mathbf{b}_i^0 + (1 - \varepsilon)\mathbf{b}_{i+1}^0.$$

If i is odd, then

$$P^\varepsilon(\mathbf{b}_i^0) = P^\varepsilon(\mathbf{b}_{i+1}^0) = \varepsilon\mathbf{b}_i^0 + (1 - \varepsilon)\mathbf{b}_{i+1}^0.$$

Moreover, $P^\varepsilon(\mathbf{b}_0^0) = \mathbf{b}_0^0$; $P^\varepsilon(\mathbf{b}_{l-1}^0) = \mathbf{b}_{l-1}^0$, if l is even; $N^\varepsilon(\mathbf{b}_{l-1}^0) = \mathbf{b}_{l-1}^0$, if l is odd.

Lemma 29 follows easily from Lemma 27 by examining the vectors $\tilde{b}_i^0$. We may apply Lemma 28 and 29 as follows. Assume that $\mathbf{b} \succeq \alpha_0\mathbf{b}_0^0 + \cdots + \alpha_{l-1}\mathbf{b}_{l-1}^0$. Then

$$N^\varepsilon(\mathbf{b}) \succeq N^\varepsilon(\alpha_0\mathbf{b}_0^0 + \cdots + \alpha_{l-1}\mathbf{b}_{l-1}^0) \succeq \alpha_0 N^\varepsilon(\mathbf{b}_0^0) + \cdots + \alpha_{l-1}N^\varepsilon(\mathbf{b}_{l-1}^0) =$$
$$\varepsilon(\alpha_0 + \alpha_1)\mathbf{b}_0^0 + (1 - \varepsilon)(\alpha_0 + \alpha_1)\mathbf{b}_1^0 + \varepsilon(\alpha_2 + \alpha_3)\mathbf{b}_2^0 + (1 - \varepsilon)(\alpha_2 + \alpha_3)\mathbf{b}_3^0 + \cdots.$$

Similarly,

$$P^\varepsilon(\mathbf{b}) \succeq \alpha_0\mathbf{b}_0^0 + \varepsilon(\alpha_1 + \alpha_2)\mathbf{b}_1^0 + (1 - \varepsilon)(\alpha_1 + \alpha_2)\mathbf{b}_2^0$$
$$+ \varepsilon(\alpha_3 + \alpha_4)\mathbf{b}_3^0 + (1 - \varepsilon)(\alpha_3 + \alpha_4)\mathbf{b}_4^0 + \cdots.$$

Definition 30. *Convex estimate $\alpha_0^t\mathbf{b}_0^0 + \cdots + \alpha_{l-1}^t\mathbf{b}_{l-1}^0$ of $\mathbf{b}_t^\varepsilon$ is defined as follows:*

(i) for $t = 0$, the convex estimate equals $\mathbf{b}_0^0$ (i.e. $\alpha_0^0 = 1$ and $\alpha_i^0 = 0$ for $i \neq 0$),

(ii) if t is even, then the convex estimate of $\mathbf{b}_{i+1}^\varepsilon$ equals
$\alpha_0^t N^\varepsilon(\mathbf{b}_0^0) + \cdots + \alpha_{l-1}^t N^\varepsilon(\mathbf{b}_{l-1}^0)$, that is,
$\alpha_i^{t+1} = \varepsilon(\alpha_i^t + \alpha_{i+1}^t)$ if i is even and $0 \leq i < l-1$, $\quad \alpha_i^{t+1} = (1-\varepsilon)(\alpha_{i-1}^t + \alpha_i^t)$ if i is odd and $0 \leq i \leq l-1$, $\quad \alpha_i^{t+1} = \alpha_{i-1}^t$ if $i = l - 1$ and $l - 1$ is even.

(iii) if t is odd, then the convex estimate of $\mathbf{b}_{i+1}^\varepsilon$ equals
$\alpha_0^t P^\varepsilon(\mathbf{b}_0^0) + \cdots + \alpha_{l-1}^t P^\varepsilon(\mathbf{b}_{l-1}^0)$, that is,

$$\alpha_i^{t+1} = \alpha_0^t \text{ if } i = 0, \quad \alpha_i^{t+1} = \varepsilon(\alpha_i^t + \alpha_{i+1}^t) \text{ if } i \text{ is odd and } 0 \le i < l - 1,$$
$$\alpha_i^{t+1} = (1 - \varepsilon)(\alpha_{i-1}^t + \alpha_i^t) \text{ if } i \text{ is even and } 0 \le i \le l - 1, \quad \alpha_i^{t+1} = \alpha_{l-1}^t$$
$$\text{if } i = l - 1 \text{ and } l - 1 \text{ is odd.}$$

By Lemma 23 and 28, for every t, $\mathbf{b}_t^\varepsilon$ dominates its convex estimate. The coefficients α_j^t are relatively easy to compute. Moreover, we shall see that the coefficients of $\mathbf{b}_i^0$, for a small i, quite fast begin to decrease exponentially when t grows. Once they become very small, then $\mathbf{b}_t^\varepsilon$ is "almost sorted".

4.4 Flow of coefficients

It would be tiresome to estimate the coefficients α_i^t directly. Instead, we use a method based on the concept of *flow of coefficients*:

Definition 31. For $i, t \in \mathbb{N}$, $i \le l - 1$, let $\text{flow}_t(i) = \alpha_i^t - \alpha_i^{t-1}$, if t and i have the same parity, and $\text{flow}_t(i) = 0$, otherwise.

Intuitively, $\text{flow}_t(i)$ describes the increase of α_i at expense of α_{i-1} at step t. Indeed, if t and i have the same parity, then $\alpha_i^t = (1 - \varepsilon) \cdot (\alpha_i^{t-1} + \alpha_{i-1}^{t-1})$, $\alpha_{i-1}^t = \varepsilon \cdot (\alpha_i^{t-1} + \alpha_{i-1}^{t-1})$, hence $\alpha_i^t + \alpha_{i-1}^t = \alpha_i^{t-1} + \alpha_{i-1}^{t-1}$. So $\alpha_{i-1}^t = \alpha_{i-1}^{t-1} - \text{flow}_t(i)$.

Lemma 32. *Let $i < l$ and let $t+1$ and i have the same parity. Then for $1 < i < l-1$,*

$$\text{flow}_{t+1}(i) = (1 - \varepsilon) \cdot \text{flow}_t(i - 1) + \varepsilon \cdot \text{flow}_t(i + 1).$$

For $i = 1$ and $i = l - 1$ we have:

$$\text{flow}_{t+1}(1) = \varepsilon \cdot \text{flow}_t(2), \qquad \text{flow}_{t+1}(l - 1) = (1 - \varepsilon) \cdot \text{flow}_t(l - 2).$$

Proof. By the construction of convex estimates, $\alpha_i^{t-1}/\alpha_{i-1}^{t-1} = (1 - \varepsilon)/\varepsilon$. Hence

$$(1 - \varepsilon)\alpha_{i-1}^{t-1} = \varepsilon\alpha_i^{t-1}. \tag{1}$$

Let $\text{flow}_t(i - 1) = x$ and $\text{flow}_t(i + 1) = y$. So $\alpha_{i-1}^t = \alpha_{i-1}^{t-1} + x$ and $\alpha_i^t = \alpha_i^{t-1} - y$. Hence, $\alpha_i^{t+1} = (1 - \varepsilon)(\alpha_{i-1}^{t-1} + x + \alpha_i^{t-1} - y) = \alpha_i^{t-1} + (1 - \varepsilon)x - (1 - \varepsilon)y$ (the second equality follows from (1)). So $\text{flow}_{t+1}(i) = \alpha_i^{t+1} - (\alpha_i^{t-1} - y) = (1 - \varepsilon)x + \varepsilon y$. The formulas for $\text{flow}_{t+1}(1)$ and $\text{flow}_{t+1}(l - 1)$ can be obtained in a similar way. $\square$

Clearly, $\text{flow}_1(1) = 1 - \varepsilon$ and $\text{flow}_i(1) = 0$ for $i \ne 1$. Hence by Lemma 32 we get:

Corollary 33. $\text{flow}_t(i) \ge 0$ *for every t, i.*

To get an upper bound on flows we define $\text{upflow}_t(i)$ for $i \in \mathbb{Z}$. Namely, for $t = 1$ we put $\text{upflow}_1(1) = 1$, and $\text{upflow}_1(i) = 0$ for $i \ne 1$. (We put $\text{upflow}_1(1) = 1$ instead of $\text{upflow}_1(1) = 1 - \varepsilon$ in order to simplify some expressions.) To define upflow_{t+1} from upflow_t, we use a formula based on the formula for flows given in Lemma 32:

$$\text{upflow}_{t+1}(i) = (1 - \varepsilon) \cdot \text{upflow}_t(i - 1) + \varepsilon \cdot \text{upflow}_t(i + 1),$$

if $t + 1$ and i have the same parity, and $\text{upflow}_{t+1}(i) = 0$ otherwise. The following lemmas can be easily proved by induction on t:

Lemma 34. $\mathrm{upflow}_t(i) \geq 0$ *and* $\mathrm{upflow}_t(i) \geq \mathrm{flow}_t(i)$ *for every* $t, i \in \mathbf{N}$, $i < l-1$. $\sum_{i \in \mathbf{Z}} \mathrm{upflow}_t(i) = 1$, *for every* $t \in \mathbf{N}$.

Lemma 35. *If* t *and* i *have the same parity,* $-t+2 \leq i \leq t$, *then*

$$\mathrm{upflow}_t(i) = \binom{t-1}{\frac{t+i}{2}-1} \varepsilon^{\frac{t-i}{2}}(1-\varepsilon)^{\frac{t+i}{2}-1}. \tag{2}$$

For the rest of the proof we fix constants $d, c_0 \in \mathbf{R}$ such that

(i) $d > \frac{1}{1-2\varepsilon}$ and dl is an even natural number,
(ii) $c_0 = \frac{(d+1)\varepsilon}{(d-1)(1-\varepsilon)}$.

Corollary 36. *If* $0 < i < l$ *and* i *is even, then*

$$\frac{\mathrm{upflow}_{dl}(i)}{\mathrm{upflow}_{dl}(i+2)} \leq c_0 < 1. \tag{3}$$

Proof. The first inequality may be easily obtained using equality (2). The second one holds since $d > \frac{1}{1-2\varepsilon}$. We leave details to the reader. $\square$

Corollary 37. *If* i *is even,* $0 < i < l$, *then* $\mathrm{upflow}_{dl}(i) \leq c_0^{\lceil (l-i)/2 \rceil}$.

Proof. By inequality (3), we get $\mathrm{upflow}_{dl}(i) \leq c_0^j \cdot \mathrm{upflow}_{dl}(i+2j)$, for $i+2j \leq l+1$. Let $s = \lceil (l-i)/2 \rceil$. Then $i + 2s \leq l+1$. By Lemma 34, $\mathrm{upflow}_{dl}(i+2s) \leq 1$. Hence $\mathrm{upflow}_{dl}(i) \leq c_0^s$. $\square$

Lemma 38. *There is a constant* c_1 *such that for every odd* i, $0 < i < l$,

$$\alpha_{i-1}^{dl-2} + \alpha_i^{dl-2} < c_1 \cdot c_0^{(l-i)/2}.$$

Proof. Let $i < l$ be odd. We define $x_j = \alpha_{j-1}^{dl-2} + \alpha_j^{dl-2}$, for $j < l$. Then $\alpha_{i-1}^{dl-1} = \varepsilon x_i$ and $\alpha_i^{dl-1} = (1-\varepsilon)x_i$. For $j < l$, let y_j denote $\mathrm{flow}_{dl}(j)$. Then $\alpha_i^{dl} = \alpha_i^{dl-1} - y_{i+1}$ and $\alpha_{i+1}^{dl} = \alpha_{i+1}^{dl-1} + y_{i+1}$. On the other hand, $\alpha_i^{dl}/\alpha_{i+1}^{dl} = \varepsilon/(1-\varepsilon)$. Hence

$$\frac{(1-\varepsilon)x_i - y_{i+1}}{\varepsilon x_{i+2} + y_{i+1}} = \frac{\varepsilon}{1-\varepsilon},$$

or equivalently,

$$x_i = \frac{\varepsilon^2}{(1-\varepsilon)^2} \cdot x_{i+2} + \frac{1}{(1-\varepsilon)^2} \cdot y_{i+1}. \tag{4}$$

(Note that $\frac{\varepsilon^2}{(1-\varepsilon)^2} < 1$, since $\varepsilon < \frac{1}{2}$.) By Lemma 34 and Corollary 37, $y_{i+1} \leq c_0^{(l-i-1)/2}$, so we get easily

$$x_i \leq R + \frac{1}{(1-\varepsilon)^2} \cdot \sum_{j=0}^{\lfloor (l-i)/2 \rfloor} \left(\frac{\varepsilon}{1-\varepsilon}\right)^{2j} c_0^{(l-i-1)/2-j} \leq R + \frac{1}{(1-\varepsilon)^2} \cdot c_0^{(l-i-1)/2} \cdot \sum_{j=0}^{\infty} \left(\left(\frac{\varepsilon}{1-\varepsilon}\right)^2 \cdot \frac{1}{c_0}\right)^j.$$

where $R = \left(\frac{\varepsilon}{1-\varepsilon}\right)^{2\lfloor (l-i)/2 \rfloor}$. Note that $\left(\frac{\varepsilon}{1-\varepsilon}\right)^2 \cdot \frac{1}{c_0} \leq \frac{\varepsilon}{1-\varepsilon} < 1$. Hence

$$x_i \leq \left(\frac{\varepsilon}{1-\varepsilon}\right)^{2\lfloor (l-i)/2 \rfloor} + \frac{1}{(1-\varepsilon)(1-2\varepsilon)} \cdot c_0^{(l-i-1)/2}. \tag{5}$$

Since $(\frac{\varepsilon}{1-\varepsilon})^2 < c_0$, the last term in (5) dominates the first one and therefore $x_i \leq c_1 \cdot c_0^{(l-i)/2}$ for some constant c_1. $\square$

We are now looking for an η such that $\sum_{i=0}^{l-\eta} \alpha_i^{dl-2} < \frac{1}{ml}$, i.e., up to $\alpha_{l-\eta}^{dl-2}$, the coefficients α_i^{dl-2} are very small (which means that the vectors $\mathbf{b}_i^0$ contribute very little to the convex estimation of $\mathbf{b}_{dl-2}^{\varepsilon}$).

Lemma 39. *There is a $c_2 > 0$ such that $\sum_{i=0}^{l-\eta} \alpha_i^{dl-2} < \frac{1}{ml}$ for $\eta = c_2 \cdot \log(m \cdot l)$.*

Proof. We consider η such that $l - \eta$ is odd. Then by Lemma 38,

$$\sum_{i=0}^{l-\eta} \alpha_i^{dl-2} \leq c_1 \cdot c_0^{\eta/2} \cdot \sum_{s=0}^{\infty} c_0^s = \frac{c_1}{1-c_0} \cdot c_0^{\eta/2}.$$

For an $\eta = O(\log(ml))$ appropriately chosen (namely, for $\eta > \frac{2}{-\log c_0}(\log(ml) + \log \frac{c_1}{1-c_0})$), the last expression is smaller than $\frac{1}{ml}$. $\square$

Proof of Main Lemma. Recall that $\mathbf{a}_t \succeq \mathbf{b}_t^{\varepsilon} \succeq \sum_{i=0}^{l-1} \alpha_i^t \cdot \mathbf{b}_i^0$. It follows that for every $h \leq l$, $\mathrm{head}_h(\mathbf{a}_t) \leq \mathrm{head}_h(\sum_{i=0}^{l-1} \alpha_i^t \cdot \mathbf{b}_i^0)$. Let $\eta = c_2 \cdot \log(m \cdot l)$ and $h = l - r - \eta - 1$. Then

$$\mathrm{head}_h(\mathbf{a}_{dl-2}) \leq \sum_{i=0}^{l-1} \alpha_i^{dl-2} \cdot \mathrm{head}_h(\mathbf{b}_i^0).$$

By Lemma 27, $\mathbf{b}_i^0$ contains only zeroes up to position $(l-r)-(l-1-i)$. For $i > l-\eta$, $(l-r)-(l-1-i) > h$, hence $\mathrm{head}_h(\mathbf{b}_i^0) = 0$. So

$$\mathrm{head}_h(\mathbf{a}_{dl-2}) \leq \sum_{i=0}^{l-\eta} \alpha_i^{dl-2} \cdot \mathrm{head}_h(\mathbf{b}_i^0) \leq ml \cdot \sum_{i=0}^{l-\eta} \alpha_i^{dl-2}.$$

Hence by Lemma 39, $\mathrm{head}_h(\mathbf{a}_{dl-2}) < 1$. Since $a_{t,i} \in \mathbb{N}$ for every t and i, it follows that $a_{dl-2,1}, \ldots, a_{dl-2,l-r-\eta-1} = 0$.

The proof that $a_{dl-2,h}, \ldots, a_{dl-2,l} = m$, for $h = (l-r+1)+\eta+1$, is similar. (We change the directions of all comparators and obtain an (ε, m)-block that works in opposite direction. Ones in this (ε, m)-block behave exactly like zeroes in the original (ε, m)-block.) It follows that after iteration $(dl-2)/2$, the contents of the network is at most $(2\eta + 2, m)$-dirty. Since $\eta = O(\log(m \cdot l))$, Main Lemma follows. $\square$

4.5 Analysis of the algorithm

We shall show that the network $I_{n,k}$ sorts in $\alpha k n^{1/k} + (c \log n)^k$ iterations, where the constants α, β are from Main Lemma while $c = \beta + 1$ is a parameter from the definition of $I_{n,k}$. By 0-1 Principle, it suffices to consider inputs consisting of 0's and 1's. We divide the iterations into $k+1$ phases. Each of the first k phases consists of $\alpha n^{1/k}$ iterations; the last phase consists of the last $(c \log n)^k$ iterations. In order to analyze phase i, for $i \leq k$, we use the fact that $I_{n,k}$ is of the form $X_1|F_i|X_2$, where X_1, X_2 are some monotonic networks. Let m_i denote the size of the columns of F_i, that is, $m_i = n^{(k-i)/k} \cdot (c \log n)^{i-1}$ and $m_{k+1} = 1$.

Claim 40. *For $i \leq k$, at the beginning of phase i, the network $I_{n,k}$ is at most $(n^{1/k}, m_i)$-dirty. At the beginning of phase $k+1$, $I_{n,k}$ is at most $((c \log n)^k, 1)$-dirty.*

Proof. The proof is by induction on i. By definition, every input sequence is at most $(n^{1/k}, n^{(k-1)/k})$-dirty. Hence the lemma holds for $i = 1$. By Main Lemma, if the input of phase i is at most $(n^{1/k}, m_i)$-dirty, then the output of phase i is at most $(\beta \log(n^{1/k} \cdot m_i), m_i)$-dirty. Since $n^{1/k} \cdot m_i \leq n$, the output is at most $(\beta \log n, m_i)$-dirty, as well. This means that the number of registers from the first register containing a 1 to the last register containing a 0 is at most $m_i \cdot \beta \log n$. For $i < k$, these registers are contained in at most $\lceil \frac{m_i \cdot \beta \log n}{m_{i+1}} \rceil + 1 = \lceil n^{1/k} \frac{\beta}{\beta+1} \rceil + 1$ adjacent columns of (ε, m_{i+1})-block F_{i+1}. We may assume that n is sufficiently large so that $\lceil n^{1/k} \frac{\beta}{\beta+1} \rceil + 1 \leq n^{1/k}$. Hence the input of phase $i+1$ is at most $(n^{1/k}, m_{i+1})$-dirty. If $i = k$, then $m_i \cdot \beta \log n \leq (c \log n)^k$, hence the output of stage k is at most $((c \log n)^k, 1)$-dirty. $\square$

The output of phase k is at most $((c \log n)^k, 1)$-dirty. $I_{n,k} = X | F_{k+1}$, where X is some monotonic network, so by Lemma 14, after $\lceil (c \log n)^k / 2 \rceil$ iterations at stage $k + 1$ the sequence stored by $I_{n,k}$ is sorted.

The total time for sorting a sequence of n elements on $I_{n,k}$ is the depth of the network multiplied by the number of necessary iterations, that is, at most $(2\delta k + 2)(k\alpha n^{1/k} + (c \log n)^k) = O(k^2 \cdot n^{1/k})$, where $\delta = O(\frac{1}{\varepsilon} \cdot \log \frac{1}{\varepsilon})$ is the depth of an ε-halver. This completes the proof of Theorem 1. $\square$

Acknowledgment

We thank Friedhelm Meyer auf der Heide for presenting us the problem of periodic sorting networks of constant depth. Many ideas leading to the solution presented in the paper have been contributed by Friedhelm Meyer auf der Heide, Juraj Hromkovič, Krzysztof Loryś and Rolf Wanka.

Added in proof: Very recently, in Wrocław and Paderborn, the results of this paper have been significantly improved giving more practical solutions.

References

1. M. Ajtai, J. Komlós and E. Szemerédi. Sorting in $c \log n$ parallel steps. *Combinatorica* **3** (1983) 1-19.
2. K. E. Batcher. Sorting networks and their applications. In *AFIPS Conf. Proc. 32*, pp. 307–314, 1968.
3. M. Dowd, Y. Perl, M. Saks, and L. Rudolph. The periodic balanced sorting network. *J. ACM* **36** (1989) 738–757.
4. M. Kik, M. Kutyłowski, G, Stachowiak. *Periodic constant depth sorting networks.* Tech. Report tr-rf-93-007, Heinz-Nixdorf-Institut, Universität Paderborn, September 1993.
5. J. G. Krammer. *Lösung von Datentransportproblemen in integrierten Schaltungen.* Ph.D. Dissertation, Technical University Munich, 1991.
6. F. T. Leighton. *Introduction to Parallel Algorithms and Architectures: Arrays, Trees, Hypercubes* (Morgan Kaufmann, San Mateo, 1992).
7. F. Meyer auf der Heide. *Personal communication*, 1991.
8. U. Schwiegelshohn. A shortperiodic two-dimensional systolic sorting algorithm. In *IEEE International Conference on Systolic Arrays*, pp. 257-264, 1988.

Optimal Pattern Matching on Meshes

Bogdan S. Chlebus and Leszek Gąsieniec

Instytut Informatyki, Uniwersytet Warszawski, Banacha 2, 02-097 Warszawa, Poland.

Abstract. Parallel pattern matching on a mesh-connected array of processors is considered. The problem is to find all occurrences of a pattern in a text. The input text is a string of n symbols placed in a $\sqrt{n} \times \sqrt{n}$ mesh, each processor storing one symbol. The pattern is stored similarly in a contiguous portion of the mesh. An algorithm solving the problem in time $O(\sqrt{n})$ is presented. It applies a novel technique to design parallel pattern-matching algorithms based on the notion of a *pseudo-period*.

1   Introduction

The problem of pattern matching is to find all occurrences of a given pattern in a given text. A parallel algorithm solving this problem on a mesh-connected computer is presented. This parallel computer is a $\sqrt{n} \times \sqrt{n}$ array of n processors interconnected according to a grid pattern.

Suppose a text t is a string of n symbols taken from some alphabet, and a pattern p is a string of m symbols, $m \leq n$, from the same alphabet (no restrictions on the size of alphabets are assumed). The input words t and p are assumed to have already been allocated in the processors in such a way that each processor stores a single text symbol, and some processors additionally a single pattern symbol. The input words are stored symbol-by-symbol in consecutive processors numbered according to the snake-like indexing, that is, the processors in the odd-numbered rows 1, 3, 5, ... are numbered from left to right, and in the even-numbered rows from right to left. (The first symbols of t and p are in processor 1, the next in processor 2, and so on.) This allocation scheme places symbols adjacent in the text or pattern in adjacent processors. The problem is to find all occurrences of p in t. After an algorithm solving this problem has been completed, each processor is to be marked as either being a starting position of an occurrence of p in t or not.

The main result of this paper is a new pattern matching algorithm, which is shown to be implementable on a $\sqrt{n} \times \sqrt{n}$ mesh so as to run in time $O(\sqrt{n})$. The time bound is optimal, because $2 \cdot \sqrt{n} - 2$ is the diameter of the network. The presented algorithm is the first optimal pattern-matching algorithm developed on a mesh-connected computer.

Many parallel algorithms for the pattern matching problem have been designed on the PRAM model. The first such optimal algorithm was given by Galil [10] under the assumption that the alphabet is of constant size. Vishkin [19] developed an optimal algorithm running in time $O(\log m)$ for arbitrary alphabets, where m is the pattern length. Breslauer and Galil [4] designed an optimal algorithm running in time $O(\log \log m)$ and proved in [5] a matching lower bound.

More references to the literature on pattern matching on PRAMs can be found in the book [12] by JáJá. Recently, in [7, 8], a constant time CRCW-PRAM algorithm finding all occurrences of a pattern in a text has been developed, after a deterministic $O(\log \log m)$ preprocessing phase on the pattern. These two papers also include a constant expected-time randomized algorithm to preprocess the pattern. Optimal pattern-matching algorithms the CREW-PRAM, the EREW-PRAM, and the hypercube, have been developed in [9].

Our model of computation is a mesh-connected computer (see [14]). This is a two-dimensional $\sqrt{n} \times \sqrt{n}$ array of n processors connected according to the pattern of a grid: each processor $\mathcal{P}(i, j)$ in row i and column j is connected by direct links to processors $\mathcal{P}(i - 1, j)$, $\mathcal{P}(i, j + 1)$, $\mathcal{P}(i + 1, j)$, and $\mathcal{P}(i, j - 1)$, assuming they exist. Every processor has a constant number of registers, each capable of storing $O(\log n)$ bits. This means that a processor can store a constant number of symbols, boolean values or numbers, and is capable of performing standard operations on the contents of these registers in constant time. Processors communicate with their neighbors by exchanging packets. It is assumed that a processor can send to its neighbor a packet with the contents of one register in constant time. More sophisticated communication schemes among processors resort to algorithms of packet routing or sorting, which can be performed in time $O(\sqrt{n})$, see [6, 14, 15, 18].

The recent research concerning meshes has concentrated on such communication problems as routing or sorting (see [14]). There is however a growing body of results concerning other algorithmic problems, like graph problems [2, 3, 17], search problems [1, 13], computational-geometry problems [16], and image-processing [11]. This paper contributes to this line of research, and, by presenting an optimal algorithm for the classical problem of pattern matching, it shows the viability of the mesh architecture.

2   Preliminaries

In this section some definitions are recalled and the needed terminology is fixed. A text t is a sequence of n symbols $t_1 t_2 \ldots t_n$. The notation $|w| = k$ means that k is the length of word w. A pattern $p = p_1 p_2 \ldots p_m$ is a string of length $|p| = m$, where $m \leq n$. Pattern p is said to *occur* at position i in t, for $0 \leq i \leq n - m$, if $p_j = t_{i+j}$, for $1 \leq j \leq m$. The notation w^k means k concatenated copies of word w. A subword w_p of w is a *period* of w if both the equality $w = w_p w'$ holds and w' is a prefix of w (maybe empty). Hence every word has at least one period. The shortest period of a word w is *the period* of w. A word w is *periodic* if its period w_p satisfies the inequality $|w_p| \leq \lfloor |w|/2 \rfloor$. A periodic word w is of the form $w_p^k w_r$, where $k \geq 2$ and w_r is a prefix of w_p, possibly empty. Certain properties of words are listed in Lemma 1 for further reference.

Lemma 1. *Let x be the length of the period of a word w, and let t be an arbitrary word of length $|t| \geq |w|$. Then the following two facts hold:*
1. If c is any period of w such that $|c| \leq |w| - x$, then $|c|$ is a multiple of x.

2. *If w occurs in t at positions i and j, $i < j$, then $j - i \geq x$. If moreover $j - i \leq |w| - x$, then the number $j - i$ satisfies the inequality $j - i \geq x$, and w occurs in t at positions $i + k \cdot x$, for any integer k such that $i + k \cdot |x| \leq j$.* ☐

Proofs of these statements may be found in [12].

Consider a copy $\hat{p}$ of p placed on top of p such that the first position of $\hat{p}$ and the i-th position of p are aligned. There could be two aligned positions (say, j of p and $j - i + 1$ of $\hat{p}$) at which the two words differ. The number j is called a *witness* for position i of p. There can be certain positions in p for which there are no witnesses: these are exactly the first position and the multiples of the length of the period of p, as follows from Lemma 1.

3   Line of Processors

In this section three text algorithms on a line of processors are described. These algorithms are used as subroutines in the pattern-matching algorithm on a two-dimensional mesh.

A line of n processors is built from processors $\mathcal{P}_1, \ldots, \mathcal{P}_n$, where $\mathcal{P}_i$ is connected to $\mathcal{P}_{i-1}$ and $\mathcal{P}_{i+1}$, if they exist. The text is assumed to have been already allocated in the processors, such that the processor $\mathcal{P}_i$ stores the ith symbol of text $t = t_1 \ldots t_n$. The pattern $p = p_1 \ldots p_m$ is an input to the line, the symbols are fed into $\mathcal{P}_m$ and then transmitted through the line. The order of the input symbols is p_m through p_1, see Figure 1.

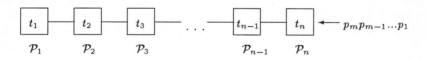

Fig. 1. A line of n processors $\mathcal{P}_1$ through $\mathcal{P}_n$.

In the next subsection an algorithm to search a text for a pattern on a line of processors is presented. This algorithm, called LINE PATTERN MATCHING (LPM in short), is often used in what follows. Two other algorithms for a line of processors are developed: one finds the period of a pattern, the other the witnesses of a pattern. Both of them are modifications of LPM. All of these algorithms together are referred to as LPM.

3.1   Finding Occurrences of a Pattern

The transmission of information through the line of processors is described in terms of routing packets, each of which carries a pattern symbol and some attached messages.

CASE 1: Processor $\mathcal{P}_j$ receives the pattern symbol p_m.

The packet with p_m does not include any attached messages. The received pattern symbol p_m is compared with t_j, and an attached message AM is created. If $p_m = t_j$, then AM is "POSSIBLE MATCHING", otherwise it is "MISMATCH DETECTED". Next, the symbol p_m is forwarded to $\mathcal{P}_{j-1}$, if $j > 1$, while AM remains stored at $\mathcal{P}_j$.

CASE 2: Processor $\mathcal{P}_j$ receives the symbol p_k, for $1 \le k < m$.

The packet carrying p_k brings an attached message, say $\mathrm{AM_{new}}$. There is also another attached message, say $\mathrm{AM_{old}}$, residing at P_j. If $\mathrm{AM_{new}}$ is "POSSIBLE MATCHING", then t_j is compared with p_k, and if $t_j \ne p_k$, then $\mathrm{AM_{new}}$ is changed to "MISMATCH DETECTED", otherwise it remains the same. Next, a packet storing p_k and $\mathrm{AM_{old}}$ is broadcast to P_{j-1}, provided that $j > 1$, while $\mathrm{AM_{new}}$ remains stored at P_j. It will be treated as $\mathrm{AM_{old}}$ after the symbol p_{k-1} has been received, for $k > 1$. If $k = 1$ then it is decided whether p_j is the beginning of an occurrence of the pattern in the text or not. How this is done is described after the next lemma, from which the correctness of the algorithm follows.

Lemma 2. *Suppose a packet received by processor P_j brings a pattern symbol p_k and an attached message "POSSIBLE MATCHING". If $t_j = p_k$ then $t_{j+l} = p_{k+l}$ for any integer l such that both the inequalities $1 \le j + l \le n$ and $1 \le k + l \le m$ hold.*

Proof. Induction on k, starting from $k = m$ and then down to $k = 1$. $\qquad\square$

Now consider again the case when processor P_j receives the packet carrying the pattern symbol p_1 and an attached message AM. If both AM is "POSSIBLE MATCHING" and the equality $t_j = p_1$ holds, then, by Lemma 2, the equalities $p_l = t_{j+l-1}$ hold for every integer l such that $1 \le l \le m$ and $j + l - 1 \le n$. If this happens then it is said that pattern p is *consistent* with text t at position j. Clearly, a position j is the beginning of an occurrence of p in t if both p is consistent with t at j and $j + m - 1 \le n$. Hence, when the last packet with p_1 travels through the line, all the occurrences of the pattern p in the text t can be detected by verifying those two conditions. This completes the proof of the next result:

Lemma 3. *Algorithm LPM finds all the occurrences of pattern p in text t on a line of $n = |t|$ processors in time $O(n)$.* $\qquad\square$

3.2 Finding the Period of a Pattern

Given a pattern p of length $m = |p|$, a line of m processors is used to determine its period. To this end run the LPM algorithm on text p and pattern p. Find all the positions where p is consistent with itself. The smallest such a position gives the period, if any exists, otherwise p is its own period.

Lemma 4. *The period of a pattern p of length m can be found in time $O(m)$ on a line of m processors.* $\qquad\square$

3.3 Finding Witnesses for a Pattern

A witness for a position i of a pattern p, where $1 < i \leq |p| = m$, is such a number j, for $1 < j \leq m - i + 1$, that $p_j \neq p_{i+j-1}$. It will be shown how to find witnesses, for all positions in p for which they exist, on a line of m processors. To this end the algorithm LPM from Subsection 3.1 is adapted.

Run LPM on text p with pattern p. When processor $\mathcal{P}_m$ forwards a symbol p_i, then let it add the message "WITNESS FOR POSITION $m - i + 1$" to the packet. This message and the symbol p_i will be always carried together by a packet. Notice that for every number k, such that $1 \leq k \leq m$, there is an attached packet carrying the message "WITNESS FOR POSITION k". The flow of packets and comparisons of text and pattern symbols are governed by the same rules as in LPM of Subsection 3.1, but instead of changing the message "POSSIBLE MATCHING" to "MISMATCH DETECTED", set it equal to "WITNESS VALUE IS j", where j is the number of processor performing this instruction. In other words, the position where the first mismatch is detected is stored. In this variant of the LPM algorithm, a packet carries two attached messages: one is "WITNESS FOR POSITION x", the other is either "POSSIBLE MATCHING" or "WITNESS VALUE IS y".

The processing terminates when the packet carrying p_1 arrives at $\mathcal{P}_1$. Consider the smallest integer $k > 1$ such that there is a packet with the messages "WITNESS FOR POSITION k" and "POSSIBLE MATCHING", if there is any. It follows from the analysis of LPM that k is the length of the period of p. For every integer in the range $1 < i < k$ there is a packet with the message "WITNESS FOR POSITION i". Its other message "WITNESS VALUE IS $\hat{i}$" gives witness $\hat{i}$ for position i. If there is no such integer $k > 1$, then p itself is the period of p, and there is a witness for every position $1 < i \leq m$. This proves:

Lemma 5. *Given a pattern p, witnesses for all positions in p, for which there is a witness in p, can be computed on a line of $m = |p|$ processors in time $O(m)$.*
□

4 Pattern Preprocessing

The pattern-matching algorithm developed in this paper consists of two phases: first is preprocessing of a pattern, next is searching a text. In the preprocessing part the periodic structure of a pattern is examined. The way the algorithm operates depends on whether a pattern has a "short" period or not. The short-period case is handled in a straightforward way, the long-period case is the key part of the algorithm.

4.1 Short Period of a Pattern

The first thing checked about a pattern p is if it has a period of length at most $\sqrt{n}$. To this end consider the prefix w of p of length $2 \cdot \sqrt{n}$. Find the period of

w applying the algorithm LPM for a line of processors. It is run on the two top rows of the mesh interpreted as a line of length $2 \cdot \sqrt{n}$. Suppose a word c is found to be the period of w. The next observation follows from Lemma 1.

Lemma 6. *If the period of pattern p has length at most $\sqrt{n}$, then the word c defined above is the period of p.* □

Next, check if c is indeed the period of the whole pattern. Every processor which stores a pattern symbol sends a packet to the processor of distance $|c|$ ahead in the snake-like ordering, asking if it contains the same symbol. The word c is a period only if all processors reply with confirming answers. This proves:

Lemma 7. *If the length of the period c of the pattern p is at most $\sqrt{n}$, then c can be found in time $O(\sqrt{n})$.* □

4.2 Long Period of a Pattern

In this subsection the case when the period of p is longer than $\sqrt{n}$ is considered.

An Aperiodic Subword First find an aperiodic subword p_s of p, of length $2 \cdot \sqrt{n}$. Consider the prefix w of p of length $2 \cdot \sqrt{n}$. If w is not periodic, then this $2 \cdot \sqrt{n}$-length prefix of p can be taken as p_s. Otherwise, let c be the period of w. The word c is not a period of p because $|c| \leq \sqrt{n}$. Consider the word c^k, for k such that $|c^k| \geq |p|$, and let $i \leq m$ be the first position where p and c^k differ. Take the position $i - 2 \cdot \sqrt{n} + 1$ in p as the beginning of p_s. The next fact follows from Lemma 1.

Lemma 8. *The word p_s defined above is not periodic.* □

The word p_s can be found quickly as follows. First compute the period c of w by the LPM algorithm. If $|c| > \sqrt{n}$, then take the $\sqrt{n}$-length prefix of p as p_s. Otherwise, let each processor send an inquiry to the processor of distance $|c|$ ahead in the snake-like ordering. The smallest position (that is, snake-like index) of that processor which sends back a negative answer is the required number i. This proves:

Lemma 9. *If the period of p is longer than $\sqrt{n}$, then an aperiodic subword p_s of p, such that $|p_s| = 2 \cdot \sqrt{n}$, can be found in time $O(\sqrt{n})$.* □

Pseudo-Period of a Pattern Let $\hat{p}$ be the word obtained from p by replacing each symbol by either 1, if this is a beginning of an occurrence of p_s, otherwise by 0. The period q of $\hat{p}$ is called the *pseudo-period* of p (with respect to p_s). The usefulness of a pseudo-period follows from the following fact, which follows from Lemma 1.

Lemma 10. *1. The length of a pseudo-period is greater or equal to $\sqrt{n}$.*
2. The length of the period c of p is greater or equal to the length of a pseudo-period q of p. Moreover, number c is a multiple of $|q|$, provided the inequality $|c| \le |p| - |q|$ holds.   □

Since p_s is aperiodic, there is at most one occurrence of p_s in a segment of p of size $\lfloor \sqrt{n} \rfloor$. Hence the word $\hat{p}$ is sparse in the sense that there is at most one occurrence of 1 in each row of the mesh. This can be used to find the period of $\hat{p}$ quickly.

Lemma 11. *The pseudo-period of p can be found in time $O(\sqrt{n})$.*

Proof. First find all the occurrences of p_s in p. To this end divide p into segments of size $\lfloor \sqrt{n} \rfloor$ and apply LPM in each double segment. Collect the information about the portion of $\hat{p}$ which is in a row in the leftmost column. This information is just the position of 1 in the row, if there is any. Call LPM in the column and find the period of $\hat{p}$. Actually the algorithm LPM needs to be adjusted to the specific form of the data, the details are omitted.   □

Finding the Period of a Pattern In this subsection it is shown how a long period of a pattern can be found efficiently on a mesh, what is one of the main applications of the notion and properties of a pseudo-period. Let q be a pseudo-period of a pattern p. Visualize the word p as divided into k segments R_1, R_2, ..., R_k of length $|q|$ each, and then the segments put on top of each other, as in Figure 2.

The last segment R_k may be of length smaller than $|q|$. This creates an array of size $|q| \times k$, it is called *the pattern array*. Notice that $k \le \sqrt{n}$. The pattern array has columns $K_1, \ldots, K_{|q|}$, each of length k, depicted also in Figure 2. Let the words $c_1, \ldots, c_{|q|}$ be the periods of the columns. The next observation follows from Lemma 1.

Lemma 12. *If the least common multiple LCM of the numbers $|c_1|, \ldots, |c_{|q|}|$ satisfies the inequality $LCM < |p|/|q|$, then the length of the period of p is equal to $|q| \cdot LCM$.*   □

To find the periods c_i, allocate the columns of the pattern arrays so that they are placed one after the other along the global snake-like ordering. Run the period-finding algorithm LPM on each column in parallel. Mark each position of the

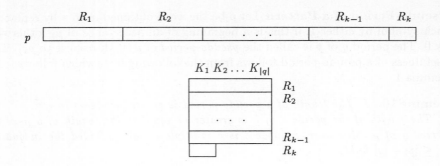

Fig. 2. A pseudo-period q of a pattern p determines a pattern array.

pattern array with 1 if this is a beginning of an occurrence of the period of the column, otherwise by 0. The least common multiple of the numbers $|c_1|, \ldots, |c_{|q|}|$ is the first row position of the pattern array in which there are only occurrences of 1. To find it, reallocate the pattern array so that the rows are placed one after the other along the global snake, next check the rows to find the first one with only 1's. This proves:

Lemma 13. *If the period of p has length greater than $\sqrt{n}$, then it can be found in time $O(\sqrt{n})$.* □

Let c be the just found period of p. In what follows witnesses for c will be needed, but only for positions of the form $i \cdot |q|$. They can be found during processing the pattern array to determine c.

Lemma 14. *Witnesses for the period c of p for positions of the form $i \cdot |q|$ can be found in time $O(\sqrt{n})$.*

Proof. Notice that shifting p by $|q|$ positions corresponds to shifting the pattern array by one row, that is, every row by one position. Find witnesses in every column of the pattern array, for every position for which a witness exists. To this end apply the algorithm LPM. Next, select a witness from each row, if there is any. □

5 Text Processing

The text-processing phase depends on the size of the period of the pattern p.

5.1 Short Period of the Pattern

Suppose pattern p has been found to have a period c of length at most $\sqrt{n}$. The word p is of the form $p = c'c^k$, for an integer $k \geq 2$, where c' is a suffix of c. Denote by $\bar{c}$ the word c without its first symbol, if $|c| > 1$, otherwise pattern matching is straightforward. There is at most one occurrence of $\bar{c}c$ in every segment of the text t of size $|c|$. Divide t into segments of that size and find occurrences of $\bar{c}c$ in each segment by running LPM on each double segment. Put a 1 at a position in t at the end of each occurrence of $\bar{c}c$, and put 0 at the remaining positions of t, denote the obtained word by $\hat{p}$. To identify an occurrence of p in t, k consecutive 1's in $\hat{p}$ must be found, of distance $|c|$ apart, followed by an occurrence of c' in t. Process the subword of $\hat{p}$ in each row, collecting the information in the leftmost column, next process the column, finally switch back to the rows, all the time counting the number of occurrences of 1's and the distances. Finish up by checking for occurrences of c' in the required places. The overall time is $O(\sqrt{n})$.

5.2 Long Period of the Pattern

Now a more difficult case is considered, when the pattern p has a long period c. If c is long then it is not even clear how to verify directly and efficiently whether there is an occurrence of c at a given position of the text t. Instead, the pseudo-period structure of p is resorted to, which is defined by occurrences of a "short" aperiodic subword p_s of p (here "short" means $O(\sqrt{n})$). This enables us to find occurrences of p_s by calling LPM on adjacent rows of the mesh.

Suppose first that pattern p is periodic. Now use Lemma 10. If the period of p is of length greater than $\sqrt{n}$, then an aperiodic subword p_s of p of length $2 \cdot \sqrt{n}$ is found during the pattern-preprocessing phase, together with the pseudo-period q corresponding to p_s, and the period c of p. Having this information, start by identifying all the occurrences of p_s in text t: divide t into segments of length $\sqrt{n}$ and apply LPM on each double segment. Mark the occurrences of p_s by 1, and the remaining positions by 0, thus creating word $\hat{t}$. The next step is to find all occurrences of the pseudo-period q in $\hat{t}$. Notice that $\hat{t}$ is sparse, in the sense that there is at most one occurrence of 1 in a segment of length $\sqrt{n}$, the remaining symbols are 0's. Collect the information about the consecutive $\sqrt{n}$-length subwords of $\hat{t}$ in the leftmost column of the mesh and call LPM there to find occurrences of the pseudo-period q. Actually LPM needs to be adjusted to handle the specific form of the data, namely a processor knows just the position of an occurrence of 1 in the row, if there is any.

At this point one apparently cannot decide directly which occurrences of q in $\hat{t}$ correspond to occurrences of c in t, because there could possibly be still too many occurrences of q. Hence the number of occurrences of q must be reduced to be manageable. This is done in two stages. The first is by restricting our attention to q-chains of sufficient length. Define, for a pattern w, text s, and a positive integer k, an occurrence of w in s to be *in a w-chain of length k*, if this w can be extended in s to an occurrence of w^k. Identify all the q-chains in $\hat{t}$ and eliminate those of length smaller than $|c|/|q|$. In the second stage divide the surviving q-chains into *blocks*, which are adjacent subwords of size $\min(|c|, \lfloor |p|/2 \rfloor)$. There may be at most one occurrence of the period c in t in the region corresponding to such a block in $\hat{t}$. Recall that, during the pattern-preprocessing phase, witnesses for c have been found, for these positions which are multiples of $|q|$. Now it is the time when they can be used to eliminate all but one (if not all) occurrences of q in a block. To this end, for any two occurrences of q in a block arrange a *duel* between them, that is, verify which one of them survives a comparison with p at the witness position. More precisely, given two occurrences of q at positions i and j in a block, where $i < j$, let k be the witness for position $j - i$. Compare the symbol t_{i+k-1} with the symbols $x = p_{i+k-1}$ and $y = p_{j+k-1}$. Number k is a witness, hence $x \neq y$. If $t_{i+k-1} \neq x$, then i is killed, and if $t_{i+k-1} \neq y$, then j is killed. In any case, at most one of the numbers i and j survives this duel. Since this happens for any pair of numbers i and j, there is at most one survival in every chain block.

Lemma 15. *All the duels can be performed in time $O(\sqrt{n})$.*

Proof. The occurrences of q are at least $\sqrt{n}$ positions apart, hence the number of 1's is at most $\sqrt{n}$ and the number of duels is at most n. For each duel create a packet storing all the information about this duel. More precisely, if the duel is between positions i and j, where $i < j$, and k is the witness for $j - i$, put the numbers i, j, and k in a packet. Call the number $i + k - 1$ the *inquiry address* of the packet. Sort the packets in the snake-like order by their inquiry addresses. The first packet in a block of packets with the same inquiry address creates a packet with this destination address. All such packets are routed to their destination processors to collect the text symbol, and then are routed back. The packet who receives this information, propagates it to all the packets with the same destination address. In a similar way each duel packet storing numbers i, j, and k receives the symbols p_{i+k-1} and p_{j+k-1}. This is all that is needed to decide the result of a duel. Next, the packets with surviving numbers are sorted on this key, the first packet in a block of packets with the same key generates a packet with the good news and routes it to the surviving processor. Since both sorting and routing can be done in time $O(\sqrt{n})$, the total time is $O(\sqrt{n})$. □

Now, when the words $\hat{t}$ and the pseudo-period q have done their job, switch back to the pattern p and its cycle c, found during preprocessing. Let $p = c'c^k$, where c' is a suffix of c. The positions that have survived duels are at least of distance $|c|$ apart. Broadcast the word $c'c$ to all of them and verify directly whether $c'c$ occurs there. The rest of the text-processing phase is similar as in the case of a short period of p described in Subsection 5.1.

The remaining case is $|c| > |p|/2$. First find all occurrences of sufficient length q-chains in $\hat{t}$. Then make duels between all survived positions in every $|p|/2$ segment of $\hat{t}$. Afterwards in each segment of t of length $|p|/2$ there is at most one possible occurrence of p, check this directly.

This completes a proof of the following main result.

Theorem 16. *All occurrences of a pattern in a text of length n can be found in time $O(\sqrt{n})$ on a $\sqrt{n} \times \sqrt{n}$ mesh-connected computer.* □

6 Remarks

An optimal pattern-matching algorithm on a mesh-connected architecture has been developed. It is suitable to be implemented on MIMD meshes.

The algorithm is in two phases: pattern preprocessing and text processing. The case when a pattern has a short period, that is of length $O(\sqrt{n})$, is handled directly. The other case of a long period of the pattern is the key part of the algorithm, where the notion of a pseudo-period of a pattern is applied. This approach makes possible to find efficiently the required information about the periodic structure of the pattern on an array of processors.

Usually, in pattern matching algorithms, preprocessing and searching phases are performed with the number of processors corresponding to the length of the pattern p and the text t. The presented algorithm uses the same mesh for both preprocessing and searching. It is possible to modify the preprocessing phase so that it is performed on a $\sqrt{m} \times \sqrt{m}$ mesh.

Acknowledgement: Kunsoo Park has read a preliminary version of this manuscript, and his numerous comments helped considerably to improve the quality of the paper.

References

1. M.J. Atallah, F. Dehne, R. Miller, A. Rau-Chaplin, and J.-J. Tsay, Multisearch techniques for implementing data structures on a mesh-connected computer, in *Proc. 3rd Annual ACM Symposium on Parallel Algorithms and Architectures*, 1991, pp. 204-214.
2. M.J. Atallah, and S. Hambrush, Solving tree problems on a mesh-connected processor array, *Information and Control* 69 (1986) 168-186.
3. M.J. Atallah, and S. Rao Kosaraju, Graph problems on a mesh-connected processor array, in *Proc. 14th Annual ACM Symposium on Theory of Computing*, 1982, pp. 345-353.
4. D. Breslauer, and Z. Galil, An optimal $O(\log \log n)$ time parallel string matching algorithm, *SIAM J. Computing* 19 (1990) 1051-1058.
5. D. Breslauer, and Z. Galil, A lower bound for parallel string matching, *SIAM J. Computing* 21 (1992) 856-862.
6. B.S. Chlebus, M. Kaufmann, and J. Sibeyn, Deterministic permutation routing on meshes, in *Proc. 5th IEEE Symp. on Parallel and Distributed Processing*, 1993.
7. R. Cole, M. Crochemore, Z. Galil, L. Gąsieniec, R.Hariharan, S. Muthukrishnan, K. Park and W. Rytter, Optimally fast parallel algorithms for preprocessing and pattern matching in one and two dimensions, in *Proc. 34th Annual IEEE Symposium on Foundations of Computer Science*, pp. 248-258, 1993.
8. M. Crochemore, Z. Galil, L. Gąsieniec, K. Park, and W. Rytter, Constant-time deterministic sampling and its applications, 1993, Manuscript.
9. A. Czumaj, Z. Galil, L. Gąsieniec, and W. Plandowski, From the CRCW-PRAM to the hypercube, via the CREW-PRAM and the EREW-PRAM (or In the Defense of the PRAM), 1993, manuscript.

10. Z.Galil, Optimal parallel algorithms for string matching, *Information and Control* 67 (1985) 144-157.

11. S. Hambrush, X. He, and R. Miller, Parallel algorithms for gray-scale image component labeling on a mesh-connected computer, in *Proc. 4th Annual ACM Symposium on Parallel Algorithms and Architectures*, 1992, pp. 100-108.

12. J.JáJá, "Introduction to Parallel Algorithms", 1992, Addison-Wesley, Reading, Massachusetts.

13. C. Kaklamanis, and G. Persiano, Branch-and-bound and backtrack search on mesh-connected arrays of processors, in *Proc. 4th Annual ACM Symposium on Parallel Algorithms and Architectures*, 1992, pp. 118-126.

14. F.T. Leighton, "Introduction to Parallel Algorithms and Architectures: Arrays, Trees, Hypercubes", 1992, Morgan Kaufmann, San Mateo, California.

15. F.T. Leighton, F. Makedon, and I.G. Tollis, A $2n - 2$ step algorithm for routing in an $n \times n$ array with constant size queues, in *Proc. 1st Annual ACM Symposium on Parallel Algorithms and Architectures*, 1989, pp. 328-335.

16. R. Miller, and Q.F. Stout, Mesh computer algorithms for computational geometry, *IEEE Trans. Comp.* 38 (1989) 321-340.

17. D. Nassimi, and S. Sahni, Finding connected components and connected ones on a mesh-connected parallel computer, *SIAM J. Computing* 9 (1980) 744-757.

18. C.P. Schnorr, and A. Shamir, An optimal sorting algorithm for mesh connected computers, in *Proc. 18th Annual ACM Symposium on Theory of Computing*, 1986, pp. 255-263.

19. U.Vishkin, Optimal parallel matching in strings, *Information and Control* 67 (1985) 91-113.

Faster Sorting and Routing on Grids with Diagonals

Manfred Kunde   Rolf Niedermeier[1]   Peter Rossmanith[1]

Fakultät für Informatik, Technische Universität München,
Arcisstr. 21, 80290 München, Fed. Rep. of Germany
kunde/niedermr/rossmani@informatik.tu-muenchen.de

Abstract. We study routing and sorting on grids with diagonal connections. We show that for so-called h-h problems faster solutions can be obtained than on comparable grids without diagonals. In most of the cases the number of transport steps for the new algorithms are less than half the on principle smallest number given by the bisection bound for grids without diagonals.

1   Introduction

Over the last decade a well-studied topic of parallel algorithmics was sorting and routing on fixed-size networks of processors. A lot of papers presented optimal and nearly optimal solutions for the conventional two-dimensional $n \times n$ grid (or mesh) with four-neighborhood. In many cases algorithms for tori of processors (meshes with wrap-around connections) derive from algorithms for ordinary meshes. The additional amount of hardware for the wrap-arounds leads in many cases to solutions twice as fast. Meshes with diagonals (with eight-neighborhood) have twice the number of data channels. In spite of the fact that meshes with diagonals are well-known and have been used for some applications like matrix multiplication and LU decomposition [6], near to nothing is known how to exploit the additional communication links for faster sorting and routing. For mesh-connected arrays with diagonals we present deterministic routing and sorting algorithms that often halve the number of parallel data transfers compared to the best possible solutions on grids without diagonals. In some cases the number of transport steps is strictly smaller than the half. On the other hand, in a fixed period of time we sort and route *always* strictly more than the double amount of data compared to grids without diagonals.

A two-dimensional *processor grid with diagonals* is a network of n^2 processors arranged in an $n \times n$ array. Processor (r, c) in row r and column c on the grid is directly connected by a bi-directional communication channel to processor (r', c') if $\max\{|r - r'|, |c - c'|\} = 1$. For grids with wrap-arounds (tori) the processors in the two border rows and two border columns are also connected to a processor in the opposite border. In this way each processor is the center of an eight-neighborhood.

---

[1] Work supported by the Deutsche Forschungsgemeinschaft, SFB 342, A4 "KLARA."

For an *h-h routing problem* each processor contains at most h packets initially. Each packet has a destination address specifying the processor to which it must travel. Each processor is destination of at most h packets. The routing problem is to transport each packet to its destination address. For the sorting problem we need some more details. We assume that each packet in a processor P lies in a (memory) place (P, j), where $0 \leq j < h$. For a given j the set of places $\{ (P, j) \mid P$ is a processor $\}$ is called the jth layer. There are exactly h disjoint layers, numbered from 0 to $h - 1$. The places are indexed by an index function g that is a one-to-one mapping from the places onto $\{0, \ldots, hn^2 - 1\}$. Then the sorting problem (with respect to g) is to transport the ith smallest element to the place indexed with $i - 1$. For a *full h-h* routing problem where a processor contains exactly h packets initially one can supply each packet with an index of its destination processor. In this manner the full h-h routing problem becomes an h-h sorting problem.

The model of computation is the conventional one [7], where only nearest neighbors exchange data. In one step a communication channel can transport at most one packet (as an atomic unit) in each direction. Processors may store more than h packets, but the number has to be bounded by a *constant* that is independent of the number of processors. For complexity considerations we count only communication steps; we ignore operations within a processor, especially between different layers.

For two-dimensional $n \times n$ meshes without diagonals 1-1 problems have been studied for more than twenty years. The so far fastest solutions for 1-1 problems and for h-h problems with small $h \leq 9$ are summarized in Table 1. In that table we also present our new results on grids with diagonals and compare them with those for grids without diagonals. The table contains results obtained by deterministic as well as by randomized algorithms that work with high probability (the latter ones are marked with an asterisk). We omit all sublinear terms, which are of no importance for the asymptotic complexity.

On meshes with diagonals for h-h problems we have $hn/2$ steps as a simple lower bound, the bisection bound. Recently this lower bound was asymptotically reached by randomized algorithms [2, 3] as well as by deterministic algorithms [5]. These results are optimal for this type of architecture. On meshes with diagonals we reach $2hn/9 + O(hn^{2/3})$ steps for deterministic h-h sorting and routing, provided that $h \geq 9$. This gives an acceleration factor of 2.25. (In the paper we deal only with the 9-9 problem. The algorithm easily generalizes to $h > 9$.) Note that the bisection bound for meshes with diagonals is $hn/6$.

For wrap-around meshes (or tori) without diagonals the respective bisection bound is $hn/4$, which was also matched by algorithms recently: with high probability [3] and deterministically [5]. If we add diagonals to tori, we can sort and route in only $hn/10 + O(hn^{2/3})$ steps if $h \geq 10$. That means we get a speedup of 2.5. Though the diameter of a torus with diagonals is $n/2$ and the bisection bound is $hn/12$, our best algorithm for the h-h problem with $h \leq 10$ needs still $n + o(n)$ steps.

Table 1. Comparison of results between grids with and without diagonals.

Problem	New results with diagonals	Without diagonals	
1-1 routing	$1.11n$	$2n$	Leighton et al. [8]
1-1 sorting	$1.33n$	$2.5n$	Kunde [4]
		$2n^*$	Kaklamanis and Krizanc [1]
2-2 routing	$1.67n$	$3n$	Park and Balasubramanian [9]
		$2.67n^*$	Sibeyn and Kaufmann [3]
2-2 sorting	$1.67n$	$3n$	Park and Balasubramanian [9]
4-4 routing	$2n$	$4n$	Kunde [4]
		$2n^*$	Kaufmann et al. [2]
4-4 sorting	$2n$	$4n$	Kunde [4]
		$3n^*$	Sibeyn and Kaufmann [3]
8-8 sorting		$4n$	Kunde [5]
9-9 sorting	$2n$		

*randomized algorithm

The results of this paper demonstrate that grids with diagonals are a promising architecture, because they improve the times for sorting and routing. Note that grids with diagonals are not substantially more complicated than plain grids: They have constant degree and are scalable.

We use a sorting method that is based on all-to-all mappings [5]. Roughly speaking, this method consists of two kinds of operations: local sorting in blocks of processors (cheap) and global communication in a regular communication pattern (expensive). The sorting algorithm performs the global communication, called all-to-all mapping, twice.

Due to the lack of space several details and proofs had to be omitted. A full paper is available from the authors.

2 Sorting and Routing with All-to-all Mappings

In this section we briefly describe how to sort the elements on a grid with the help of an all-to-all mapping that distributes data uniformly all over the mesh. You can find a more detailed description in the paper that introduced all-to-all mappings [5].

For sorting we divide the $n \times n$-mesh into m^2 quadratic $n/m \times n/m$-submeshes, called blocks. We further divide each block into m^2 subblocks and call a layer of such a subblock a *brick*. That means each block contains hm^2 bricks arranged in h layers. We number the blocks from 0 to $m^2 - 1$ where block i and block $i + 1$ are neighbors. We must choose the indexing g in such a way that all places in block i have smaller indices than all places in block $i + 1$. We call such an indexing continuous. To see the correctness of the following sorting method we use the 0-1 principle (see for example [7]).

In a first step we sprinkle all data all over the mesh in order to get approximately *the same number of ones* into each block. We start by sorting each block individually as follows. The ith brick gets elements i, $i + m^2$, $i + 2m^2$, and so on. In this way the number of ones in each brick differs at most by 1. Next we send from every block exactly h bricks to every block on the mesh as illustrated in Fig. 1. Now each block contains almost the same number of ones (the difference is at most hm^2). We call such a global distribution of data an *all-to-all mapping* [5].

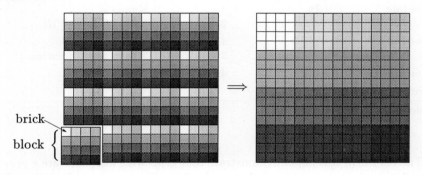

Fig. 1. The standard all-to-all mapping on a mesh with 16 blocks

In a second step we sort each block in such a way that the first brick contains the smallest elements and the last brick the largest ones. So at most one brick contains zeros *and* ones. Let us call it the *dirty brick*. Since each block contains almost the same *number* of ones, the position of the dirty brick is also almost the same in each block: The positions of the dirty bricks differ at most by one, say, the position is either the kth or $(k + 1)$st brick, provided that a brick contains at least hm^2 elements.

Now an all-to-all mapping sends the first h bricks of each block to the first block, the second h bricks of each block to the second block, and so on. Afterwards all dirty bricks are in the $\lfloor k/h \rfloor$th or $\lfloor (k + 1)/h \rfloor$th block, so the whole mesh is nearly sorted. To finish, we sort all adjacent pairs of blocks. Herein adjacent refers to any given continuous block indexing.

We choose $m \leq \sqrt[3]{n/h}$ such that $m = \Theta(\sqrt[3]{n/h})$. In total the complexity of the all-to-all mapping asymptotically governs the time of our method.

The above sorting algorithm directly applies to full h-h routing. For partial h-h routing, say with a load of 75 percent, the above method also works, provided some additional tricks are used (see Kunde [5]). Algorithms for partial routing are used as subprocedures for algorithms in this paper. See the full paper for a detailed discussion.

3   Sorting for Loads of Four and Nine Elements

In this section we start with an algorithm for the 4-4 sorting problem to present the basic ideas.

Theorem 1 *The 4-4 sorting problem requires at most $2n + o(n)$ steps on a mesh with diagonals.*

Proof. We show how to solve the all-to-all mapping for the 4-4 problem in n steps. Let us divide the mesh into four equally sized submeshes, called A, B, C, and D. The four layers of A are A_A, A_B, A_C, and A_D. By the all-to-all mapping each block gets $h = 4$ bricks from each other block. So each brick has a source block, from where it comes and a target block, where it goes. The position of a brick within each block is at the moment of no importance.

Our strategy is divide and conquer: We recursively perform an all-to-all mapping on all four submeshes individually. We do this in such a way that in submesh A every brick already reaches its target block relative within submesh A. As a consequence each brick with destination address within A already has reached its final position. To complete the all-to-all mapping on the whole grid, we move all bricks into the proper submesh preserving their relative positions. We perform this final transportation in exactly $n/2$ steps as follows: All packets in A that preserve their location move to the first layer A_A, packets whose target block is in B move to A_B, and so on. All these movements take place within processors and thus do not count for the time bound. Then layer A_B moves as a whole to B, A_C moves to C, and A_D moves to D. This takes exactly $n/2$ steps.

Summing up the time requirements of all recursive calls yields the total running time. The final transportation as described takes $n/2$ steps on an $n \times n$-grid. In general a transportation step on an $n/2^i \times n/2^i$-grid takes $n/2^{i+1}$ steps. Altogether we need $\sum_{i=1}^{k} \frac{n}{2^i} < n$ steps for the whole recursive method, if there are $2^k \times 2^k$ blocks in the grid. Independent of the block-size we need always less than n steps for a 4-4 all-to-all mapping. $\qquad\square$

Before we attack the more complicated 9-9 problem, let us look at the 4-4 sorting algorithm from a different point of view. Recall what an all-to-all mapping should do. There are m^2 blocks arranged in m columns and m rows. Each of those m^2 blocks contains hm^2 bricks. It seems natural to address blocks by pairs $(x, y) \in \{1, \ldots, m\} \times \{1, \ldots, m\}$, where x denotes the column and y the row. Each brick has a *source block* and a *target block*. Each block is target of hm^2 bricks; from each block it receives exactly h bricks. Our task is to move all bricks to their target block. From the source and target blocks of a brick we can compute the path it travels, assuming that we use the above stated recursive algorithm. For this end we better use a slightly different scheme to address blocks. We use a *quaternary* number system to address blocks using the four symbols ⊡, ⊟, ⊞, and ⊟ as digits. An example reveals best how to apply this number system.

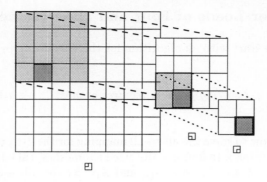

Fig. 2. The quad coordinates are (⊟,⊟,⊟)

In Fig. 2 we consider a grid containing 8×8 blocks. We want to address
the block in the fourth row and second column, i.e., the block whose Cartesian
coordinates are $(4, 2)$. If we divide the grid into four equal squares, our brick is
located in the upper-left one. Therefore the most significant digit is ⊟, a symbol
meaning "upper-left." If we extract the upper-left subgrid and divide it again in
four squares, our block is now in the lower-left one. This corresponds to ⊟, which
is the next digit. We can subdivide once more and get ⊟ as the rightmost digit.
The address is (⊟,⊟,⊟). We will subsequently call this kind of address the *quad
coordinate* of a block. What is the connection between the quad coordinates of
a brick's source and target block and the path on which it travels?

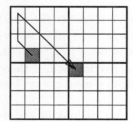 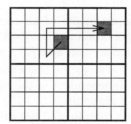 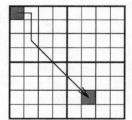

Fig. 3. Three examples of paths on which bricks travel to their destination

Figure 3 contains examples for bricks that move from (⊟,⊟,⊟) to (⊟,⊟,⊟),
from (⊟,⊟,⊟) to (⊟,⊟,⊟), and from (⊟,⊟,⊟) to (⊟,⊟,⊟).

A packet's path always consists of three shifts. Each of these shifts is either
horizontal, vertical, or diagonal. The lengths of the shifts are 1, 2, and finally 4
blocks wide. If a source block of a packet is (s_1, s_2, s_3) and the destination block is
(d_1, d_2, d_3), then the first shift leads to (s_1, s_2, d_3), the second one to (s_1, d_2, d_3),
and the third one to the final destination (d_1, d_2, d_3). So the ith shift depends
only on s_i and d_i. We compute the path of a brick by subtracting its destination

231

address from its source address using componentwise subtraction from Table 2. This is a special way of subtraction: The difference between two coordinates is a path between them.

Table 2. Computing the path between two quad coordinates.

−	◰	◳	◱	◲
◰	·	↓	→	↘
◳	↑	·	↗	→
◱	←	↙	·	↓
◲	↘	←	↑	·

We compute the paths in Fig. 3 as $(◲,◱,◰) - (◰,◲,◲) = (↘, ↑, ↘)$, $(◲,◰,◳) - (◰,◳,◱) = (→, ↑, ↗)$, and $(◲,◲,◲) - (◰,◱,◳) = (↘, ↓, →)$.

Our findings yield the following algorithm:

Algorithm F. (All-to-all mapping for load four)
for $i = 1$ **to** k **do**
  for all $(s_1, \ldots, s_k)$, $(d_1, \ldots, d_k)$ **do in parallel**
    Shift the brick with source address $(s_1, \ldots, s_k)$ *and destination address* $(d_1, \ldots, d_k)$ *in direction* $d_i - s_i$ *for* $n/2^i$ *steps.*

By an *i-shift* we understand to route all bricks in direction $d_i - s_i$, subtracting according to Table 2. The distance of the transport is 2^{n-i} for a $2^n \times 2^n$ grid. An i-shift changes exactly the ith component of a quad coordinate from source to destination. We realize an all-to-all mapping by performing i-shifts for all i. The order of these i-shifts is arbitrary.

The ideas of the above discussion will now be used to solve the 9-9 problem. After Theorem 2 we will sketch the main algorithmic ideas.

Theorem 2 *The 9-9 sorting problem requires at most $2n + o(n)$ steps on a mesh with diagonals.*

Divide the grid into *nine* subgrids, called *ninths*. Transport one layer from each ninth to each ninth in order to mix data among them. Then complete the all-to-all mapping by applying this procedure recursively on each ninth, just like Algorithm F did. We can describe this method by *ninth-coordinates* (using symbols ◰, ◳, ...) in analogy to quad coordinates. Assume that the $n \times n$ grid consists of $3^k \times 3^k$ blocks. Every block contains $3^k \times 3^k \times 9$ bricks. Each block has its unique ninth-coordinate $(s_1, \ldots, s_k)$. From each block exactly nine bricks must travel to each other block. The following algorithm transports a brick from its *source block* $(s_1, \ldots, s_k)$ to its *destination block* $(d_1, \ldots, d_k)$. The transport consists of k phases. In each phase a brick moves a certain distance in some direction. Here a "direction" is not as simple as in Algorithm F. Besides the nine directions ($\cdot$, $\uparrow$, $\nearrow$, $\rightarrow$, $\searrow$, $\downarrow$, $\swarrow$, $\leftarrow$, $\nwarrow$) from Algorithm F, Algorithm N uses some more directions, directions that *change* in exactly the middle of the journey: $\nearrow$, $\swarrow$, $\leftarrow$, and so on. Direction $\nearrow$, for example, means "travel the first half of the time upwards and the second half of the time to the northeast." There is also $\swarrow$, which means "stay were you are during the first half of time and travel then to the southwest" and $\leftarrow$, which means "travel to the west during the first half of time and stay then where you are." In the ith phase Algorithm N computes a new direction by subtracting the ith component of the destination address from the ith component of the source address in ninth coordinates. It subtracts according to Table 3.

Table 3. Computing the path between two ninth-coordinates.

$-$	⊡	⊟	⊡	⊡	⊡	⊡	⊡	⊡	⊡
⊡	$\cdot$	$\uparrow$	$\uparrow$	$\leftarrow$	$\nwarrow$	$\nwarrow$	$\leftarrow$	$\nwarrow$	$\nwarrow$
⊟	$\updownarrow$	$\cdot$	$\uparrow$	$\nwarrow$	$\leftarrow$	$\nwarrow$	$\swarrow$	$\leftarrow$	$\nwarrow$
⊡	$\downarrow$	$\downarrow$	$\cdot$	$\swarrow$	$\swarrow$	$\leftarrow$	$\swarrow$	$\swarrow$	$\leftarrow$
⊡	$\leftrightarrow$	$\nearrow$	$\nearrow$	$\cdot$	$\uparrow$	$\uparrow$	$\leftrightarrow$	$\nwarrow$	$\nwarrow$
⊡	$\searrow$	$\leftrightarrow$	$\nearrow$	$\updownarrow$	$\cdot$	$\uparrow$	$\swarrow$	$\leftrightarrow$	$\nwarrow$
⊡	$\searrow$	$\searrow$	$\leftrightarrow$	$\downarrow$	$\downarrow$	$\cdot$	$\swarrow$	$\swarrow$	$\leftrightarrow$
⊡	$\rightarrow$	$\nearrow$	$\nearrow$	$\rightarrow$	$\nearrow$	$\nearrow$	$\cdot$	$\uparrow$	$\uparrow$
⊡	$\searrow$	$\rightarrow$	$\nearrow$	$\searrow$	$\rightarrow$	$\updownarrow$	$\cdot$	$\uparrow$
⊡	$\searrow$	$\searrow$	$\rightarrow$	$\searrow$	$\searrow$	$\rightarrow$	$\downarrow$	$\downarrow$	$\cdot$

Algorithm N. (All-to-all mapping for load nine)
for $i = 1$ to k do
    for all $(s_1, \ldots, s_k)$, $(d_1, \ldots, d_k)$ do in parallel
       Shift the brick with source address $(s_1, \ldots, s_k)$ and destination
       address $(d_1, \ldots, d_k)$ in direction $d_i - s_i$ for $2n/3^i$ steps.

We check the correctness by verifying that shifts in direction $d_i - s_i$ route a brick from block $(d_1, \ldots, d_{i-1}, s_i, s_{i+1}, \ldots, s_k)$ to block $(d_1, \ldots, d_{i-1}, d_i, s_{i+1}, \ldots, s_k)$. Let us consider for example $d_i = \Box$ and $s_i = \Box$. From Table 3 we get $d_i - s_i = \nwarrow$. So the brick is transported $n/3^i$ steps to the northwest and then $n/3^i$ steps upward.

In the same way we can verify the whole Table 3 and then we know that Algorithm N does the right thing. We have to check carefully, whether all these shifts can be performed *in parallel*. Each shift itself is easy, but superimposing all shifts could lead to overloaded communication lines. Superimposing all shifts of the first $n/3^i$ steps leads to a special routing problem shown in Fig. 4. We obtain the same figure also for the second $n/3^i$ steps.

You can read Fig. 4 as follows: There are two arrows from ninth B to ninth A. That means that Algorithm N attempts to move two full layers of data from B

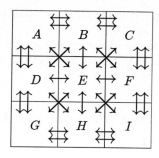

Fig. 4. All shifts at once

to A. Why? Well, all bricks in ninth B have ⊡ as part of their source address and this component will be changed to one of the nine possible addresses. One ninth of the bricks in B have □ as their destination address. They will move in direction ← according to Table 3. This corresponds to one full layer moving from B to A. Another ninth of B's bricks has destination address ⊡. They travel in direction ↙. In the first $n/3^i$ steps they contribute another full layer that travels from B to A.

How can we transport *two* layers at once horizontally? At first glance, this is easy: One layer uses horizontal lines ▫→▫→▫→▫→▫→▫→▫ and the other layer performs a *shiver shift* using diagonal lines ▫⌃⌄▫⌄⌃▫⌄▫. This simple solution, however, does not work in our setting, since we additionally have to move data from B to D and from E to A. These transports must use the diagonal lines that we wanted to reserve for the shiver shift.

We solve the problem by a generalization of shiver shifts as shown in Fig. 5.

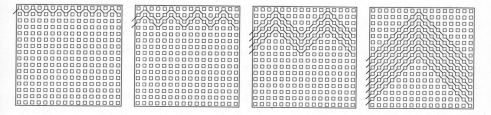

Fig. 5. A generalized shiver shift that transports one layer horizontally to the left at the upper border of a (sub)grid

The zig-zag movement has different amplitude and period-length for different packets. In Fig. 5 we show only the routes of the *rightmost* packets. All other packets move in the same fashion as the rightmost packet in the same row. We can think of this movement as rectangles moving to the northeast and bouncing at the upper border. The first rectangle is the lower half of the ninth. It bounces only once. The next rectangle is again the lower half of the rest of the ninth. It bounces twice.

Figure 5 explains the case of ninths whose length is a power of two, but in general the length of a ninth is 3^k times the length of a block. See the full paper for details and the proof of correctness.

4   Sorting and Routing for Loads of One and Two Elements

Let us begin with the 1-1 routing and sorting problems. The 1-1 problem is special in the sense that we can solve the routing problem faster than the sorting problem. We handle first the routing.

Theorem 3 *The 1-1 routing problem requires at most $10/9n + o(n)$ steps on a mesh with diagonals.*

Proof. Each packet has, in ninth-coordinates, a source address $(s_1, \ldots, s_m)$ and a target address $(d_1, \ldots, d_m)$. These addresses consist of processor coordinates, i.e., are on the lowest level. We start by routing each element to address $(s_1, d_2, s_3, \ldots, s_m)$ by a 2-shift, which adjusts the second component of each element's address. This changes the 1-1 problem into a partial 9-9 problem and needs $2/9n$ steps. Next, we route to address $(s_1, d_2, d_3, \ldots, d_m)$ by using the 9-9 sorting algorithm as an routing algorithm in all eighty-one $n/9 \times n/9$-submeshes. This takes $2/9n$ steps according to Theorem 2. Finally, we perform a 1-shift and route thus from $(s_1, d_2, \ldots, d_m)$ to $(d_1, d_2, \ldots, d_m)$ in $2/3\, n$ steps. Altogether the algorithm needs $10/9n$ steps. $\qquad\square$

Theorem 4 *The 1-1 sorting problem requires at most $4/3n + o(n)$ steps on a mesh with diagonals.*

Proof. We divide the mesh into nine squares and move the outer squares into the middle. Then we sort the middle square in $2/3n$ steps (Theorem 2) and move eight squares back to their outer positions. $\qquad\square$

There is another algorithm for the 1-1 sorting problem that does not build upon the 9-9 sorting of Theorem 2. It has the same time complexity as above and can be found in the full paper.

Theorem 5 *The 2-2 sorting problem requires at most $5/3n + o(n)$ steps on a mesh with diagonals.*

Proof. We use essentially the same trick as for the 1-1 sorting problem, but we divide the mesh into only four squares. All that is left to do is to shift the four quarters as fast as possible into the center of the mesh and back.

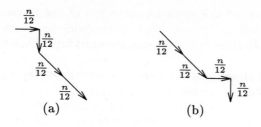

Fig. 6. Interleaved diagonal transports

The upper left quarter has to travel $n/4$ steps to the southeast. According to Fig. 6 (a), one layer goes first $n/12$ steps east, then $n/12$ steps south, and finally $n/6$ steps southeast.

The second layer travels first southeast, then east, and at the end south (see Fig. 6 (b)). The other squares behave symmetrically. □

5 Sorting and Routing on Tori with Diagonals

Theorem 6 *The 10-10 sorting problem requires at most $n + o(n)$ steps on a torus with diagonals.*

Proof. Instead of a subdivision into nine submeshes as in Theorem 2, we rather use *twentyfive* submeshes. If we transport one layer to each "twentyfifth," we perform an all-to-all mapping for a 25-25 problem. Unfortunately, it is hard to do this fast. We are humble and stick to simple routing scheme and see how much data we can transport within the distance bound. First, in $n/5$ steps we move eight layers in all eight directions (Fig. 7 (a)).

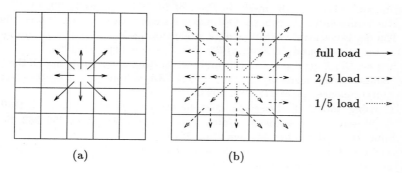

full load ——→
2/5 load - - - -→
1/5 load ·······→

(a)   (b)

Fig. 7. Standard routing scheme for all-to-all mappings on tori

Second, in another $n/5$ steps we move $2/5$ of one of the inner layers into each outer layer according to Fig. 7 (b). At the same time each inner twentyfifth receives another $1/5$ layer from the central twentyfifth. That fills it out to a $2/5$ layer.

Up to now all algorithms we considered moved *full* layers. At this point we start to consider shifting *partial* layers. Shifting a half layer, for example, means to transport one packet from every second processor. To perform an all-to-all mapping for a 10-10 problem means that every twentyfifth has to send a $2/5$ layer to each other twentyfifth. The situation is symmetric for all twentyfives, because a torus has no "center."   □

6   Conclusion

Meshes with diagonals are simple, scalable parallel architectures. Compared to meshes with four-neighborhood the distance bound is two times smaller and the bisection bound is three times smaller. We developed algorithms with small constant buffer size for sorting and routing on grids and tori with diagonals that come close to the lower bounds. The algorithmic methods are generalizable to higher dimensional grids.

Some open questions remain. Is there a 1-1 routing algorithm that needs only n steps, matching the distance bound? Is there a 12-12 sorting algorithm that needs only $2n$ steps? More general, is there a sorting algorithm that matches the bisection bound for some bigger load h?

References

1. C. Kaklamanis and D. Krizanc. Optimal sorting on mesh-connected processor arrays. In *Proc. of 3d SPAA*, pages 50–59, 1992.
2. M. Kaufmann, S. Rajasekaran, and J. F. Sibeyn. Matching the bisection bound for routing and sorting on the mesh. In *Proc. of 3d SPAA*, pages 31–40, 1992.
3. M. Kaufmann and J. F. Sibeyn. Optimal k-k sorting on meshes and tori. 1993.
4. M. Kunde. Concentrated regular data streans on grids: Sorting and routing near to the bisection bound. In *Proc. of 32d FOCS*, pages 141–150, 1991.
5. M. Kunde. Block gossiping on grids and tori: Sorting and routing match the bisection bound deterministically. In *Proc. of 1st ESA*, volume 726 of Lecture Notes in Computer Science, pages 272–283, 1993.
6. H. T. Kung and C. E. Leiserson. Systolic arrays (for VLSI). In I. S. Duff and G. W. Stewart, editors, *Sparse Matrix Proceedings 1978*, pages 256–282. Society for Industrial and Applied Mathematics, 1979.
7. T. Leighton. *Introduction to Parallel Algorithms and Architectures: Arrays, Trees, Hypercubes*. Morgan Kaufmann, 1992.
8. T. Leighton, F. Makedon, and I. Tollis. A $2n - 2$ step algorithm for routing in an $n \times n$ array with constant size queues. In *Proc. of 1st SPAA*, pages 328–335, 1989.
9. A. Park and K. Balasubramanian. Reducing communication costs for sorting on mesh-connected and linearly connected parallel computers. *Journal of Parallel and Distributed Computing*, 9:318–322, 1990.

Deterministic 1-k Routing on Meshes

With Applications to Worm-Hole Routing

Jop F. Sibeyn*   Michael Kaufmann†

Abstract

In 1-k routing each of the n^2 processing units of an $n \times n$ mesh connected computer initially holds 1 packet which must be routed such that any processor is the destination of at most k packets. This problem has great practical importance in itself and by its implications for hot-potato worm-hole routing.

We present a near-optimal deterministic algorithm running in $\sqrt{k} \cdot n/2 + \mathcal{O}(n)$ steps, and an algorithm with slightly worse routing time but working queue size three. Nontrivial extensions are given to l-k routing, and for routing on higher dimensional meshes. We show that under a natural condition 1-k routing can be performed in $\mathcal{O}(n)$ steps. Finally we show that k-k routing can be performed in $\mathcal{O}(k \cdot n)$ steps with working queue size four. Hereby hot-potato worm-hole routing can be performed in $\mathcal{O}(k^{3/2} \cdot n)$ steps.

Keywords: theory of parallel and distributed computation, meshes, packet routing, hot-potato worm-hole routing.

1   Introduction

Various models for parallel machines have been considered. One of the best studied machines with a fixed interconnection net-

work, is the MIMD mesh. In this model the processing units, **PUs**, form an array of size $n \times n$ and are connected by a two-dimensional grid of communication links (see Section 2 for details).

The problems concerning the exchange of packets among the PUs are called **routing problems**. Here the destinations of the packets are known beforehand. The packets must be send to their destination such that at most one packet passes through any wire during a single step. The quality of a routing algorithm is determined by (1) its **running time**, the maximum time a packet may need to reach its destination, and (2) its **queue length**, the maximum number of packets any PU may have to store.

A special case of the routing problem is **permutation routing**. In permutation routing, each PU is the origin of at most one packet and each PU is the destination of at most one packet. Permutation routing has been considered extensively. Optimal algorithms were found [15, 10, 2].

When the size of the packets is so large that they cannot be transferred over a connection in a single step, the packets have to be split into several flits. The routing of these flits is considered in the k-k routing problem: each PU is assumed to send and receive at most k packets. If the flits are routed independently of each other we speak of **multi-packet routing**. Multi-packet routing is also important when the PUs have to route packets to several destinations. Multi-packet routing algorithms [6, 9, 7] solve this task much faster than routing the packets one-by-one. Alternatively, the flits can be routed as a kind of worm such that con-

*Max-Planck-Institut für Informatik, Im Stadtwald, 66123 Saarbrücken, Germany. E-mail: jopsi@mpi-sb.mpg.de. This research was partially supported by EC Cooperative Action IC-1000 (Project ALTEC: Algorithms for Future Technologies).

†Wilhelm-Schickard-Institut für Informatik, Universität Tübingen, Sand 13, 72076 Tübingen, Germany. E-mail: mk@informatik.uni-tuebingen.de

secutive flits of a packet reside in adjacent PUs during all steps of the routing: cut-through routing [6]. If there is the additional condition that the worms may be expanded and contracted only once, then this variant is called worm-hole routing [5, 12]. Unlike the other more theoretical models, worm-hole routing has direct applications in many parallel machines [1, 13, 18, 3].

We consider an original variant of the routing problem: the routing of 1-k distributions, under which every PU is sending at most one packet, but may be the destination of up to k packets. 1-k routing reflects practical purposes better than the routing of permutations: if the PUs are working independently of each other and generate packets that have to be transferred to other PUs, then it is unrealistic to assume that every PU is the destination of at most one packet. The parameter k, $1 \leq k \leq n^2$, need not to be known by the PUs, but is needed for stating the complexity of the problem. The 1-k routing problem also has implications for hot-potato worm-hole routing. Hot-potato routing is a routing paradigm in which packets may never be queued at a PU but have to keep moving at all times until they reach their destination [4]. Like worm-hole routing, this model is used in many systems. In a recent paper of Newman and Schuster [12] it is demonstrated that under a light condition any efficient 1-k routing algorithm with working queue size at most four is useful as a subroutine for the hot-potato worm-hole routing problem. We are among the first to perform a detailed analysis of the 1-k routing problem for meshes. In [11] Makedon and Symvonis independently consider the problem. Their algorithm has running time $\mathcal{O}(\sqrt{k} \cdot n)$. Furthermore, for certain expander networks, Peleg and Upfal have studied in [14] the related l-k routing problem.

In the algorithms of Section 3 and Section 4 a packet is routed either row-first: along the row to its destination column and then along this column to its desti-nation; or column-first: first along the column and then along the row. The central point is the decision which packets will be routed row-first and which packets will be routed column-first. Straightforward strategies result in algorithms requiring $\Omega(k \cdot n)$ steps, much more than the lower bound of $\sqrt{k} \cdot n/2$. The essential idea which makes possible the breakthrough to a $\mathcal{O}(\sqrt{k} \cdot n)$ time algorithm, is to count the numbers of packets with destination in every row and column, and to make the decision on basis of these data: if many packets are going to a row, it is better to route most of the packets row-first. Most easily this idea is worked out by tossing a biased coin, but we can do it deterministically as well. The obtained algorithms require $\sqrt{k} \cdot n/2 + \mathcal{O}(n)$ steps with queues of maximal length $2 \cdot k + 2$. One of the algorithms can be applied to the l-k routing problem. This is the problem of routing l-k distributions, under which every PU sends at most l packets and receives at most k packets. This problem is interesting because of its generality but also because it appears as a subproblem of 1-k routing on higher dimensional meshes. When $l = o(k)$ the algorithm is near-optimal: the leading term of its runtime matches the leading term of a lower bound.

It turns out (Section 5) that under a natural condition l-k distributions can be routed in $\mathcal{O}(l \cdot n)$ time for l upto $n \cdot k$. Informally, the condition is that the 'density of the destinations increases gradually', excluding large areas in which all PUs receive k packets.

In Section 6 we aim for a working queue size four or less, in order to create a subroutine for the hot-potato worm-hole routing algorithm of [12]. This is achieved with routing time $5 \cdot \sqrt{k} \cdot n + o(\sqrt{k} \cdot n)$. In the algorithm the mesh is subdivided into k squares of size $n/\sqrt{k} \times n/\sqrt{k}$ and the packets are redistributed such that every square holds at most one packet for each destination. Then these squares are rotated along a Hamiltonian cycle and after each $n/\sqrt{k}$ steps the packets that reached their destination square are routed to their destination. A theorem of [12] implies that using this algorithm as a subroutine, the hot-potato worm-hole routing problem for worms of maximal length k can be solved in $\mathcal{O}(k^2 \cdot n)$ steps, coming close to the obvious lower bound of $\Omega(k \cdot n)$.

Finally (Section 7) we apply the new techniques to the problem of k-k routing with short queues. With a *randomized* algorithm this is rather easy. With a minor extension of the model, k-k distributions can even be routed with a *deterministic* algorithm in $\mathcal{O}(k \cdot n)$ steps and with working queue size four. This reduces the routing time for the hot-potato worm-hole routing problem to $\mathcal{O}(k^{3/2} \cdot n)$.

Due to a lack of space many details had to be omitted in this paper. The section on generalizations of the algorithms to higher dimensional meshes is reduced to stating its main results. Details can be found in the full version [17].

2 Preliminaries

Machine Model. As computer model we assume a two-dimensional $n \times n$ MIMD mesh without wrap-around connections. We refer to this machine simply by **mesh**. It consists of n^2 PUs, each of which is connected to (at most) four other PUs by a regular square grid. The PU at position (i,j) is referred to by $P_{i,j}$, and $(0,0)$ is in the lower-left corner.

The PUs are synchronized. In a single **step** each PU can perform arbitrary internal computation and communicate with all its neighbors. The only restriction is that each PU can send and receive at most one packet of bounded length per edge and per step. Thus a PU may send and receive during a step (at most) four packets.

Each PU has a **working queue**, in which packets are stored temporarily, and an **internal queue** in which packets are stored that do not yet move or that have

reached their destination. Only packets in the working queue can be transferred to a neighboring PU. On the packets in the internal queues any operation can be performed and new packets can be generated. The operations that can be performed on the packets in the working queues are limited to checking and comparing their keys. This allows sorting and routing operations.

Basics of Routing. We speak of **edge contention** when several packets residing in a PU have to be routed over the same connection. Contentions are resolved using a priority scheme. The **farthest-first strategy** gives priority to the packet that has to go farthest.

For the analysis of the routing on higher dimensional meshes we need the 'routing lemma' for routing a distribution of packets on a one dimensional mesh [6]. Define for a given distribution of packets over the PUs $h_{\text{right}}(i,j) = \#\{$*packets passing from left to right through both P_i and $P_j\}$, where P_i denotes the PU with index i. Define $h_{\text{left}}(j,i)$ analogously.

Lemma 1 *Routing a distribution of packets on a linear array with n PUs, using the farthest-first strategy, takes* $\max_{i<j}\{\max\{h_{\text{right}}(i,j), h_{\text{left}}(j,i)\} + j - i - 1\}$ *steps. This bound is sharp.*

Lower Bounds. Considering the maximal distance a packet may have to travel, it follows that $d \cdot n - d$ is a lower bound for routing on d dimensional meshes: the **distance bound**. For routing k-k distributions on a mesh $k \cdot n/2$ steps are required when all packets residing in the lower half of the mesh have destination in the upper half: the **bisection bound**.

For l-k distributions we can apply a more general bisection argument, also considering the number of packets that may have to move into or out-of a corner region. This gives

Lemma 2 *The l-k routing problem requires at least* $\max\{\frac{k}{2} \cdot (\frac{l}{l+k})^{1/2}, \frac{l \cdot k}{l+k}, \frac{l}{2} \cdot (\frac{k}{l+k})^{1/2}\} \cdot n$ *steps.*

In the extreme cases the bound becomes very simple:

Corollary 1 *When $l = o(k)$, or $k = o(l)$, then routing l-k distributions requires at least $(1 - o(1)) \cdot \sqrt{l \cdot k} \cdot n/2$ steps.*

3 Randomized Algorithm

One might think that the following algorithm has good performance:

1. Send all packets to a random destination.

2. Route the packets to their destinations: with probability 1/2 row-first, and with probability 1/2 column-first.

However, algorithms of this type require $\Omega(k \cdot n)$ time for a distribution of packets under which all packets have destination in the highest n/k rows. Such a distribution can be routed in $\mathcal{O}(n)$ steps when all packets are routed row-first. This illustrates the utmost importance of the decision along which axis a packet is routed first. Clearly such a decision cannot be based only on information that is available locally: the 1-k routing problem is essentially more difficult than the permutation routing problem, for which the greedy algorithm has optimal routing time.

The following randomized algorithm for the 1-k routing problem has near-optimal performance:

Algorithm RANDROUTE
1. Send one copy of the routing information of each packet along the row to its destination column, and one copy along the column to its destination row.

2. For all $0 \leq i, j < n$, determine the numbers r_i and c_j of packets that have to move along row i and column j, respectively. Broadcast these numbers.

3. If a PU P holds a packet p with destination $P_{i,j}$, then P takes r_i and c_j out of the stream. p is colored white with probability $r_i/(r_i + c_j)$, and black otherwise.

4. Randomize the white (black) packets within their columns (rows).

5. Route the white (black) packets along the rows (columns) to their destination columns (rows).

6. Route the white (black) packets along the columns (rows) to their destinations.

Randomizing a packet p within its column means that the packet is routed to a randomly and uniformly selected position within its column. The randomization is intended to bound the size of the queues.

RANDROUTE works *without knowing k*. In [17] we prove that the following theorem holds for all k:

Theorem 1 *Routing 1-k distributions by* RANDROUTE *takes $\sqrt{k} \cdot n/2 + 5 \cdot n + \mathcal{O}((\sqrt{k} \cdot n \cdot \log n)^{1/2})$ steps.*

4 Deterministic Algorithm

Randomization enables us to formulate RANDROUTE concisely and without loosing many routing steps. However, both steps involving randomization can be replaced by deterministic steps with the same effect.

At first glance coloring the packets deterministically appears to be difficult. However, this can be achieved by sorting the packets on their destination PU and coloring for every destination regularly interspaced packets white and black. The sorting can be performed in $2 \cdot n + o(n)$ steps. By rounding errors at most $n/2$ extra packets may move through any row or column during the last routing phase (compared to the $\mathcal{O}((\sqrt{k} \cdot n \cdot \log n)^{1/2})$ of the randomized algorithm).

The randomization of the packets can be replaced by sorting the packets that are going to be routed row-first (the white packets) in column-major order, and the packets that are going to be routed column-first (the black packets) in row-major order. This idea goes back on Kunde [8].

An additional idea, by which the routing time can be reduced, is to divide the mesh regularly in $n' \times n'$ submeshes and to route the packets first to any destination within their destination squares. From there the packets are routed to their destinations. n' rows (columns) spanning n/n' submeshes are called a **bundle** of rows (columns).

4.1 Algorithm

In the algorithm we take care that the lengths of the queues never exceed $\mathcal{O}(k)$. For the sake of a simple exposition we choose $n' = \sqrt{n}$.

Algorithm DETROUTE

1. Count in every submesh how many packets are going to any bundle of rows (columns), and store the number going to row (column) bundle i in the PU at position (i, i). Perform a routing along row (column) and column (row) in order to obtain the total number r_i (c_i) of packets going to row (column) bundle i, for all $0 \leq i \leq \sqrt{n} - 1$, in position (i, i) of all submeshes.

2. Sort the packets on the indices of their destination submeshes.

3. The numbers r_i and c_j are broadcast within every $\sqrt{n} \times \sqrt{n}$ submesh. A PU P_h holding a packet p with destination in submesh (i, j) picks r_i and c_j out of the stream. Let $\alpha_{i,j} = r_i/(r_i + c_j)$. If $h \bmod (1/\alpha_{i,j}) < 1$, then p is colored white, else p is colored black.

4. Let $m = n/\sqrt{k}$. Divide the mesh in $m \times m$ squares. Sort in each square the white (black) packets in column-major (row-major) order on their destination column (row) bundles.

5. Route the white (black) packets along the row (column) to the first PU in their destination column (row) bundle holding less than $k + 1$ white (black) packets.

6. In every submesh, sort the white (black) packets in row-major (column-major) order on their row (column) bundle.

7. Route the white (black) packets along the column (row) to the first PU in their destination submesh holding less than $k + 1$ white (black) packets.

8. Route the packets within the submeshes to their destinations.

If the value of k is unknown, then in Step 4 we should use some lower estimate of it, e.g. obtained from the maximum of the r_i and the c_j.

4.2 Analysis

We analyze the correctness and the routing time of DETROUTE. Step 1 takes $2 \cdot n + \mathcal{O}(\sqrt{n})$ steps. After Step 1, the r_i and c_j are locally available in all submeshes. Step 2 can be overlapped almost perfectly:

Lemma 3 *Step 1 and Step 2, can be performed in* $2 \cdot n + \mathcal{O}(n^{2/3})$ *steps.*

The sorting in Step 2 is for rearranging the packets such that the packets going to the same submesh stand in positions with consecutive indices. Then, in Step 3 the correct fractions of them can be selected. Notice that Step 3 works in a distributed fashion without knowing where the packets going to a certain submesh reside or how many packets are going to a submesh. It seems hard to compute these numbers. Step 4 is performed in order to bound the queues at the end of Step 5.

Lemma 4 *Step 3 takes* $\mathcal{O}(\sqrt{n})$ *steps; Step 4 takes* $\mathcal{O}(n/\sqrt{k})$ *steps; and Step 5 takes* n *steps.*

The most important point in the analysis is the proof of the following

Lemma 5 *Step 5 can be performed correctly, i.e. no PU holds more than k white (black) packets afterwards. Step 5 takes* $\mathcal{O}(k \cdot \sqrt{n})$ *steps. After Step 6 no column (row) holds more than* $\sqrt{k} \cdot n/2 + \mathcal{O}(\sqrt{n})$ *white (black) packets.*

Proof: Denote the number of packets going to submesh (i, j) by $a_{i,j}$. For S_j, the number of packets that will move through column bundle j, we now get $S_j \leq \sum_i \lceil a_{i,j} \cdot r_i/(r_i + c_j) \rceil < \sum_i a_{i,j} \cdot r_i/(r_i + c_j) + \sqrt{n}$. Considering the restrictions on the $a_{i,j}$, r_i and c_j, this can be shown to imply $S_j < \sqrt{k} \cdot n^{3/2}/2 + \sqrt{n}$. These packets are distributed over at least $m \cdot \sqrt{n}$ PUs. Hence at most $\lceil k + \sqrt{k}/n \rceil = k+1$ packets have to be stored in any PU. After the sorting in Step 5 the S_j packets are almost perfectly distributed over the $\sqrt{n}$ columns of the bundle: at most $\sqrt{k} \cdot n/2 + \mathcal{O}(\sqrt{n})$ packets end in every column. □

Comparable to Lemma 5 but easier is

Lemma 6 *Step 7 can be performed correctly in $\sqrt{k} \cdot n/2 + n - n/\sqrt{k} + \mathcal{O}(\sqrt{n})$ steps. I.e. afterwards no PU holds more than $k+1$ white (black) packets. Step 8 takes $\mathcal{O}(k \cdot \sqrt{n})$ steps.*

Proof: If S_j assumes its maximum then the packets in the column bundle j (that may have to go all to the highest or lowest rows) are spread out over at least m rows. Now Lemma 1 gives the maximum routing time. By the sorting in Step 7 the packets going to a submesh are well distributed over the columns. By 'rounding errors' there may be in a column at most $\sqrt{n}$ packets too much. They can be spread out over the $\sqrt{n}$ rows of the destination submesh. Step 8 is a $(2 \cdot k + 2)$-k routing in $\sqrt{n} \times \sqrt{n}$ meshes. The algorithm of [7] can be used. □

Summing all routing times we find

Theorem 2 DETROUTE *takes $\sqrt{k} \cdot n/2 + 4 \cdot n - n/\sqrt{k} + \mathcal{O}(k \cdot \sqrt{n})$ steps. The size of the queues is bounded by $2 \cdot k + 2$.*

Corollary 2 *For $k = o(n^{1/3})$, DETROUTE takes less than $\sqrt{k} \cdot n/2 + 4 \cdot n$ steps.*

4.3 Large k

Corollary 2 expresses that our choice $n' = \sqrt{n}$ is particularly good for $k = o(n^{1/3})$.

For $k = n^\alpha$, $1/3 \leq \alpha < 2$, the additive term can be bounded to $o(n)$ by taking $n' = n^{1/2 - \alpha/4}$. However, for these k we are willing to spend $\mathcal{O}(n)$ extra steps in order to obtain a much simpler algorithm:

Algorithm LARGEKROUTE

1. Sort the packets on the indices of their destinations.

2. Make two copies of the routing information. Send one copy to the destination row and one to the destination column. Count the copies within rows and columns. Broadcast the numbers r_i and c_j back. A PU P_h with a packet going to $P_{i,j}$ picks out r_i and c_j. Let $\alpha_{i,j} = r_i/(r_i + c_j)$. If $h \bmod (1/\alpha_{i,j}) < 1$, then p is colored white, else p is colored black.

3. Sort the white (black) packets in column-major (row-major) order on their destination columns (rows).

4. Route the white (black) packets to their destination columns (rows).

5. Route the white (black) packets along the columns (rows) to their destinations,

Analogously to the lemmas of the previous section we can prove

Lemma 7 *Step 1 takes less than $3 \cdot n$ steps; Step 2 takes $3 \cdot n$ steps; Step 3 takes $6 \cdot n$ steps; Step 4 takes n steps; Step 5 takes $\sqrt{k} \cdot n/2 + n$ steps.*

Theorem 3 LARGEKROUTE *routes 1-k permutations in $\sqrt{k} \cdot n/2 + 14 \cdot n$, for all k. The size of the queues is bounded by $2 \cdot k + 2$.*

We believe that by its simplicity and its generality LARGEKROUTE is a very practical algorithm.

Generalizations. Many of the ideas presented in this paper are suitable for generalization to other networks that have some similarity with meshes. Also, these ideas might successfully be applied to related problems. Easiest are generalizations for d-dimensional meshes:

Lemma 12 *If $k \leq n/2$, then the packets with color c, $0 \leq c \leq 2 \cdot k - 1$, constitute a slice.*

Proof: Let $X(i,s) = X_{n-1}(i,s)$ be the number of packets in row i with destination in $\mathcal{M}_s$. In total at most $\sum_{i=0}^{n-1} \lceil X(i,s)/(2 \cdot k) \rceil < n + \sum X(i,s)/(2 \cdot k) = n + n^2/(2 \cdot k)$ of these packets get color c, for any c. If $k \leq n/2$, then $n + n^2/(2 \cdot k) \leq n^2/k$. □

A small problem with the constructed coloring is that a PU may hold several packets with the same color. However, this is not serious:

Lemma 13 *If $k \leq n/2$, then there are at most n packets with color c, $0 \leq c \leq 2 \cdot k - 1$, in any row.*

Proof: In total at most $\sum_{s=0}^{k-1} \lceil X(i,s)/(2 \cdot k) \rceil < k + \sum X(i,s)/(2 \cdot k) = k + k \cdot n/(2 \cdot k) = k + n/2$ of the packets in row i get color c, for any c. □

Corollary 4 *The packets with color c, $0 \leq c \leq 2 \cdot k - 1$, can be redistributed within their rows such that every PU holds at most one packet of color c. This takes $2 \cdot n$ steps and working queue size one.*

Proof: By Assumption 1, within every row the rank of the packets with color c can be determined in $n - 1$ steps. Then the packet with rank r moves to P_r. If it has to travel d steps, it starts to move after $2 \cdot n - d$ steps. □

Now k-k distributions can be routed by first applying DETCOLOR and then $2 \cdot k$ times SLICEROUTE preceded by the redistribution step.

Theorem 15 *Under Assumption 1, k-k routing can be performed by a deterministic algorithm in $\mathcal{O}(k \cdot n)$ time and with working queue size three, for all $k \leq n/2$.*

Proof: Use Lemma 10, Lemma 12 and Corollary 4. □

Combining Theorem 12 and Theorem 15 gives

Theorem 16 *Under Assumption 1, hot-potato worm-hole routing for worms of maximal length $k \leq n/2$, can be performed in $\mathcal{O}(k^{3/2} \cdot n)$ steps.*

Acknowledgement

We thank Assaf Schuster for triggering our interest in the 1-k routing problem. The idea to route in stages originated from a shared work together with Andrea Pietracaprina and Geppino Pucci.

8 Conclusion

We analyzed the 1-k routing problem, and presented a deterministic near-optimal algorithm for it. We also presented an algorithm with very short working queue size, which is useful as a subroutine for hot-potato worm-hole routing. The results were extended to l-k routing, to routing on higher dimensional meshes, and to k-k routing with short working queues.

We developed several ideas that may be further exploited. The most important are: (1) the information gathering, which can be used for coloring the packets in an intelligent way; (2) a deterministic selection procedure based on local sorting; (3) routing packets along a Hamiltonian cycle, by which a 1-k problem reduces to repeatedly routing permutations.

Future research might consider dynamic variants of the problem and the algorithms. Somehow one must assure that the number of active packets remains n^2. This is the case when it is assumed that only a PU that received a packet generates a new packet. Our near-optimal time algorithm can be adapted to this model. It seems more difficult to handle dynamically generated packets in an algorithm with very short working queues. Another open problem is whether deterministic k-k routing with short working queues can be performed without any assumptions.

References

[1] Athas, W.C., 'Physically Compact, High Performance Multicomputers,' *MIT Conference on Advanced Research in VLSI*, pp. 302-313, 1990.

[2] Chlebus, B.S., M. Kaufmann, J.F. Sibeyn, 'Deterministic Permutation Routing on Meshes,' *Proc. 5th Symp. on Parallel and Distributed Proc.*, IEEE, 1993, to appear.

[3] Dally, W.J., 'Virtual Channel Flow Control,' *17th Symp. on Computer Architecture*, pp. 60-68, ACM, 1990.

[4] Feige, U., P. Raghavan, 'Exact Analysis of Hot-Potato Routing,' *Proc. 33rd Symp. on Foundations of Computer Science*, pp. 553-562, IEEE, 1992.

[5] Felperin, S., P. Raghavan, E. Upfal, 'A Theory of Wormhole Routing in Parallel Computers,' *Proc. 33rd Symp. on Foundations of Computer Science*, pp. 563-572, IEEE, 1992.

[6] Kaufmann, M., S. Rajasekaran, J.F. Sibeyn, 'Matching the Bisection Bound for Routing and Sorting on the Mesh,' *Proc. 4th Symposium on Parallel Algorithms and Architectures*, pp. 31-40, ACM, 1992.

[7] Kaufmann, M., J.F. Sibeyn, T. Suel, 'Derandomizing Algorithms for Routing and Sorting on Meshes,' *Proc 5th Symposium on Discrete Algorithms*, ACM-SIAM, 1994, to appear.

[8] Kunde, M., 'Routing and Sorting on Mesh Connected Processor Arrays,' *Proc. VLSI Algorithms and Architectures*, Lecture Notes in Computer Science, 319, pp. 423-433, Springer-Verlag, 1988.

[9] Kunde, M., 'Block Gossiping on Grids and Tori: Deterministic Sorting and Routing Match the Bisection Bound,' *Proc. European Symp. on Algorithms*, 1993.

[10] Leighton, T., F. Makedon, Y. Tollis, 'A $2n-2$ Step Algorithm for Routing in an $n \times n$ Array with Constant Size Queues,' *Proc. Symposium on Parallel Algorithms and Architectures*, pp. 328-335, ACM, 1989.

[11] Makedon, F., A. Symvonis, 'Optimal Algorithms for the Many-to-One Routing Problem on 2-Dimensional Meshes,' *Microprocessors and Microsystems*, 17, pp. 361-367, 1993.

[12] Newman, I., A. Schuster, 'Hot-Potato Worm Routing as almost as easy as Store-and-Forward Packet Routing,' *Proc. ISTCS*, 1993.

[13] Noakes, M., W.J. Dally, 'System Design of the J-Machine,' *MIT Conference on Advanced Research in VLSI*, pp. 179-194, 1990.

[14] Peleg, D., E. Upfal, 'The Generalized Packet Routing Problem,' *Theoret. Computer Sc.*, 53, pp. 281-293, 1987.

[15] Rajasekaran, S., Th. Tsantilas, 'Optimal Routing Algorithms for Mesh Connected Processor Arrays', *Algorithmica*, 8, pp. 21-38, 1992.

[16] Schnorr, C.P., A. Shamir, 'An Optimal Sorting Algorithm for Mesh Connected Computers,' *Proc. 18th Symposium on Theory of Computing*, pp. 255-263, ACM, 1986.

[17] Sibeyn, J.F., M. Kaufmann, 'Deterministic 1-k Routing on Meshes, with Applications to Worm-Hole Routing,' *Techn. Rep. MPI-I-93-163*, Max-Planck Institut für Informatik, Saarbrücken, Germany, 1993.

[18] Seitz, et al., 'The Architecture and Programming of the Ametek Series 2010 Multicomputer', *3rd Conference on Hypercube Concurrent Computers and Applications*, pp. 33-36, ACM, 1988.

Semantics and Specifications

A Unifying Type-Theoretic Framework for Objects

Martin Hofmann[*]   Benjamin Pierce[†]

Abstract: We give a direct type-theoretic characterization of the basic mechanisms of object-oriented programming, objects, methods, message passing, and subtyping, by introducing an explicit *Object* type constructor and suitable introduction, elimination, and equality rules. The resulting abstract framework provides a common basis for justifying and comparing previous encodings of objects based on recursive record types [7, 9], F-bounded quantification [4, 13, 19], and existential types [23].

1 Introduction

Research on the foundations of object-oriented programming languages has produced a number of attempts to capture the static typing properties of "well-behaved programs" in conventional object-oriented languages [7, 9, 13, 19, 4, 12, 23]. These proposals have focused on encodings of high-level syntax for objects into more primitive constructions in various typed lambda-calculi, the semantics of objects being understood simply as the semantics of their encodings. Our goal here is to use the tools of type theory to give a more direct account of the syntax and semantics of objects and message passing, with the aim of isolating high-level axioms for reasoning about objects.

An *object* in the sense of Simula [14] or Smalltalk [16] can be thought of as a *state component* of some hidden *representation type* together with a collection of *methods* that are used to analyze or modify the state. For example, consider simple one-dimensional point objects with the operations setX and getX, where setX is expressed in a functional style, returning an object with an updated state component rather than modifying the state in-place.[1] Such objects can be implemented by choosing a representation type, say Int, a state component, say 5, and

---

[*]Department of Computer Science, University of Edinburgh, The King's Buildings, Edinburgh, EH9 3JZ, U.K. Electronic mail: mxh@dcs.ed.ac.uk.

[†]Same postal address. Email: bcp@dcs.ed.ac.uk.

[1]Because we are mainly concerned here with the typing properties of object-oriented features, this very simple example will suffice for our purposes throughout the paper. The applicability of these techniques to larger examples and to objects with mutable state are discussed in [23].

two method implementations, say `setX = fun(state:Int) fun(newX:Int) newX` and `getX = fun(state:Int) state`, and packaging them together so that the state component is protected from external access except through the methods.

Unlike the elements of ordinary abstract data types, different point objects may have different internal representations; every point comes with its own implementation of the `setX` and `getX` methods, appropriate to its internal representation type. Thus, another implementation of point objects might use the representation type `{x:Int,other:Int}`, the initial state `{x=5,other=8}`, and the methods

```
setX = fun(state:{x:Int,other:Int}) fun(i:Int) {x=i, other=state.other}
getX = fun(state:(x:Int,other:Int}) state.x
```

This flexibility is central to the spirit of object-oriented programming. Although it is not present in its most general form in some object-oriented languages (e.g. Smalltalk and C++, which do not allow multiple implementations of a class), equivalent mechanisms like "virtual classes" are used in its place. The crucial point is that when a message is sent to an object, the identity of the object itself determines what code is executed in response. Thus, a program manipulating a point object must do so "generically" — by calling the point's methods to analyze and update its state as necessary — rather than concretely, by direct operations on the state. In other words, it uses a uniform function `Point'setX : Point -> Int -> Point` that, given a point, invokes its internal `setX` method and packages the resulting concrete representation into a new `Point`, and another function `Point'getX : Point -> Int` that uniformly invokes internal the `getX` method of any point and returns the resulting integer.

Our purpose here is to study the mechanisms of encapsulation and message passing (and, in less detail, their interaction with subtyping) in a type-theoretic setting. In Section 2, we introduce the basic constructions of our abstract framework. We state a simple syntactic condition on object types, capturing the intuition that methods can only access the state of one object at a time, and show that this yields a natural definition of uniform method invocation. In Section 3, we extend this framework to include subtyping. Section 4 justifies our framework by showing that the familiar encoding of object types as recursive records satisfies the axioms, including the special case of F-bounded quantification. Section 5 shows that a simple encoding of objects in terms of existential types also satisfies our axioms. Section 6 offers concluding remarks. An expanded version with more detailed treatment of the technical material is available as [17].

2 Objects

The representation type of an object is hidden from external view: its *interface* is just the types of its methods. Type-theoretically, the interface can be modeled as a type operator with one argument, thought of as a type with one free variable that stands for the hidden representation type. For example, the interface of point objects is described by the operator `PointM =`

Fun(X) {setX: X->Int->X, getX: X->Int}. For now, we leave unspecified the "ambient type theory" in which our definitions are embedded. In Sections 4 and 5 we will be using two extensions of the higher-order polymorphic λ-calculus, System F^ω [15]. The calculus under consideration will determine the precise force of the equational constraints expressed by the diagrams.

To characterize the set of objects sharing a common interface, we introduce a new type constructor *Object*, which turns an interface specification (a type operator of kind $\star\to\star$, i.e. a map from types to types) into a type. The type of point objects is Point = Object(PointM).

Elements of an object type are created using the term constructor *object*. Given an interface specification M, a concrete representation type R, a collection m of methods, and an initial value s of the representation type, we use *object* to package them together into an element $object_M (R, s, m) \in Object(M)$. The *object* constructor has the following typing rule (we will alter it slightly later on):

$$\frac{\Gamma \vdash M \in \star\to\star \qquad \Gamma \vdash s \in R \qquad \Gamma \vdash m \in M(R)}{\Gamma \vdash object_M (R, s, m) \in Object(M)}$$

For the elimination of elements of object types, we might use an unpacking rule in the style of the existential elimination rule of Mitchell and Plotkin [21]. But this runs counter to the spirit of object-style programming, in which objects are never "opened" but are acted on externally by sending messages to invoke their internal methods. We want to capture this mechanism directly.

Since every point object must implement the setX method, there should be a uniform function Point'setX : Point -> Int -> Point that, given a point, invokes its setX method. More generally, for each operator M representing the interface of an object type, we introduce a term constant GM_M denoting the "generic method" for objects with interface M:

$$\frac{\Gamma \vdash M \in \star\to\star}{\Gamma \vdash GM_M \in M(Object(M))}$$

Then GM_Point : {setX: Point->Int->Point, getX: Point->Int} and Point'setX = GM_Point.setX.

Such uniform functions do not necessarily exist. For example, we can extend our first implementation of points with an equality method eq = fun(state1:Int) fun(state2:Int) (state1 = state2), but we cannot expect to be able to invoke this eq uniformly — that is, we cannot expect to write a function Point'eq : Point -> Point -> Bool that calls the eq method of its first parameter and passes it the internal representations of both parameters: such an invocation of the low-level eq function would only be well typed when the two points passed as arguments to Point'eq happen to have *identical* representation types, which Point'eq is clearly unable to check. Of course, this does not mean that comparisons between points cannot be implemented. We can write an external equality *function* (as opposed to an equality *method* local to one of the points) using the getX method of both points generically . Indeed, we can easily provide special methods that allow the implementation of eqPoint to query parts of the internal state of the two points and then protect these methods from public access using a bounded existential quantifier [11]; this construction is developed in [24].

The difficulty illustrated by this example corresponds to a well-known limitation of object-style encapsulation [26]. In most object-oriented languages, there is no way to write a method that has concrete access to the internal state of more than one object at a time. This limitation can be modeled abstractly as a syntactic restriction on the form of M, capturing the intuition that the methods should all be "essentially unary functions" of the representation type. A "unary" operator M is one of the form $M(X) = \{l_1{:}X{\to}N_1(X), \dots, l_n : X{\to}N_n(X)\}$or, more simply, $M(X) = X \to N(X)$ for $N(X) = \{l_1{:}N_1(X), \dots, l_n{:}N_n(X)\}$, where N_1 through N_n contain X only in positive positions.[2] We write $co(Fun(A)\,T)$ in formulas to assert that the parameter A only appears positively in the body T of the operator $Fun(A)\,T$.

We will henceforth assume that every M under consideration has this form. To simplify the development, we take N rather than M as the interface of an object type, so that, for example, `Point = Object(PointN)`, where `PointN = Fun(X) {setX: Int->X, getX: Int}`. This means that we need to change our typing rules for the *object* constructor and the generic method:[3]

$$\frac{\Gamma \vdash N \in \star{\to}\star \quad co(N) \quad \Gamma \vdash s \in R \quad \Gamma \vdash m \in R{\to}N(R)}{\Gamma \vdash object_N\,(R,\,s,\,m) \in Object(N)}$$

$$\frac{\Gamma \vdash N \in \star{\to}\star \quad co(N)}{\Gamma \vdash GM_N \in Object(N) \to N(Object(N))}$$

Next, we need a suitable axiomatization of the behavior of generic methods. This should reflect the intuition that a generic method should be a "packaged version of" the method that was originally used to build an object. More precisely, the result of applying the generic method to a newly built object should be the same as the result of applying the concrete method to the object's state and then "repacking" the result — i.e., the informal diagram

$$Object(N) \xrightarrow{\;GM_N\;} N(Object(N))$$

$$object_N\,(R,\,-,\,m)\Big\uparrow \qquad\qquad \Big\uparrow \text{"repack"}$$

$$R \xrightarrow{\quad m \quad} N(R)$$

should commute, where $object_N\,(R,\,-,\,m)$ stands for the packing function $fun\,(x\,:\,R)\;object_N\,(R,\,x,\,m)$. The repacking function can be defined using

---

[2] A variable appears only positively in a type if every occurrence is on the left hand side of an even number of arrows. For polymorphic types, recursive types, and type operators, some additional considerations apply. C.f. [17].

[3] It would be cleaner here to allow the formation of $Object\,(N)$ only when N is functorial, and to state the other rules only for well-formed object types. But stating the rules in this way would require, in Section 3, that we be able to quantify over covariant operators. The study of a refined type theory in which this would be possible is an interesting topic for future research.

the notion of functorial strength: A type operator $N \in \star{\to}\star$ is *functorial* if there exists a function $strength_N \in All(X)\, All(Y)\, (X{\to}Y) \to (N(X){\to}N(Y))$ such that if $f \in S{\to}T$ and $g \in T{\to}U$, then $strength_N\,[S]\,[U]\,(f;g) = strength_N\,[S]\,[T]\,(f)\,;\,strength_N\,[T]\,[U]\,(g)$, where "$f;g = \lambda x.\ g(f(x))$" denotes composition in diagrammatic order, and such that $strength_N\,[S]\,[S]\,(id[S]) = id\,[N(S)]$.

For the type systems used in Sections 4 and 5, the action of a positive type operator N on a function $f \in X{\to}Y$ can be interpreted as "applying f to each occurrence of X in $N(X)$" — that is, given an element $n \in N(X)$, decompose n, apply f to each component of type X, and use the results to rebuild an element of $N(Y)$.[4] In the type theories under consideration, every positive operator is functorial and its strength can be defined by induction on its structure (see [17]). We henceforth use the terms "positive," "covariant," and "functorial" interchangeably.

Using this definition, we can specify the behavior of generic methods for an arbitrary positive operator N. Given a representation type R, a state $s \in R$, and a concrete method $m \in R{\to}N(R)$, we require that the diagram

$$
\begin{array}{ccc}
Object(N) & \xrightarrow{\ GM_N\ } & N(Object(N)) \\
\big\uparrow{\scriptstyle object_N} & & \big\uparrow{\scriptstyle strength_N} \\
{\scriptstyle (R, -, m)} & & {\scriptstyle [R]\,[Object(N)]} \\
& & {\scriptstyle object_N} \\
& & {\scriptstyle (R, -, m)} \\
R & \xrightarrow{\quad m \quad} & N(R)
\end{array}
\qquad (\dagger)
$$

commute, or equivalently that the equation $GM_N(object_N\,(R, s, m)) = strength_N\,[R]\,[Object(N)]\,(object_N\,(R, -, m))\,(m\ s)$ be satisfied. Indeed, if we orient this equation from left to right, we obtain a natural computation rule for objects.

Note that the specification ($\dagger$) constrains only the behavior of those elements of $Object(N)$ that lie in the image of the packing function $object_N\,(R, -, m)$. Operationally this is sufficient, since every object occurring in a program must at some stage have been constructed with the packing function. However, it may be desirable to internalize this observation by imposing an additional η-like equation:

$$
\frac{\Gamma \vdash x \in Object(N)}{\Gamma \vdash x = object_N\,(Object(N), x, GM_N) \in Object(N)}
$$

We prefer to regard this axiom as optional, since it places a strong constraint on the encodings we discuss below. But in [17] we prove that under certain uniformity assumptions, (η) is actually implied by ($\dagger$), up to observational equivalence.

---

[4] The term "strength" is borrowed from category theory [18], where an endofunctor $N \in C{\to}C$ on a cartesian closed category C is called "strong" if its action on morphisms can be internalized, i.e., if there exists a natural transformation $str_{X,Y} : (X \Rightarrow Y) \to (N(X) \Rightarrow N(Y))$, that captures the action of N.

It is interesting to note that our abstract specification of objects defines $Object(N)$ as a weakly terminal co-algebra for the functor N. Indeed, our encoding of objects using existential types in Section 5 corresponds exactly to the impredicative coding of weakly terminal co-algebras proposed by Wraith [27]. It is worth considering modeling objects by (strongly) terminal co-algebras instead. The introduction rule and generic method would remain unchanged in this case, but we would have, in addition, a stronger proof principle for objects based on bisimulation equivalence.

3   Objects and Subtyping

Next, we consider extending our abstract characterization of objects and message passing to include another important concept from object-oriented programming languages: subtyping. Our conclusions in this section are more tentative, both because the formal metatheory (in particular, the equational theory) of the type systems we use is not yet fully understood and because we are not yet confident that we have arrived at a "canonical" formulation of the laws of subtyping for objects. Nevertheless, the extended framework allows a closer comparison of the object encodings using existential and recursive types. Various extensions of F^ω with subtyping have been proposed [8, 5, 22, 23]; we choose the simplest [22]. The formulation of this system, called $F^\omega_\leq$, follows the pattern used by Cardelli and Wegner to obtain $F_\leq$ from the pure polymorphic lambda-calculus [15, 25].

With these extensions of the base calculus, we are ready to deal with object types. We want the *Object* constructor to be monotone in the subtype relation, so that CPoint = Object(CPointN) < Object(PointN) = Point, where CPointN = Fun(X) {setX: Int->X, getX: Int, setC: Color->X, getC: Color}. (c.f. [8, 23]). This leads to the following subtyping rule for object types:

$$\frac{\Gamma \vdash N' \leq N \qquad \Gamma \vdash Object(N') \in \star \qquad \Gamma \vdash Object(N) \in \star}{\Gamma \vdash Object(N') \leq Object(N)}$$

The monotonicity of the *Object* constructor captures the intuition that whenever the interface N' of an object type $Object(N')$ is more refined than the interface N of an object type $Object(N)$, elements of $Object(N')$ should be allowed in contexts where elements of $Object(N)$ are expected.

Next, we consider generic methods. Observe that if we simply apply the generic setX of points to an element of CPoint (which is valid by the rule of subsumption), the result will be an element of Point, not of CPoint: in the presence of subtyping, our generic methods are insufficiently polymorphic. More generally, suppose that N is a functorial operator and $N' \leq N$.[5] The application of GM_N to an element of $Object(N')$ should yield an element of $N(Object(N'))$, not $N(Object(N))$ as above. This suggests a change in the type of GM (c.f. [11]):

$$\frac{\Gamma \vdash N \in \star \rightarrow \star \qquad co(N)}{\Gamma \vdash GM_N \in All(N' \leq N) \; Object(N') \rightarrow N(Object(N'))}$$

---

[5] Note that this does not imply that N' is also functorial.

The interaction between the subtype relation and the term constructors *object* and *GM* is axiomatized by a rule stipulating that they should commute when all the operators involved are functorial.(More generally, we might require that every well-typed equation whose type-erasure is a syntactic identity should be provable in the equational theory; c.f. [10, 20].)

$$\frac{\Gamma \vdash N' \leq N \quad \Gamma \vdash Object(N') \in \star \quad co(N') \quad co(N)}{\Gamma \vdash R' \leq R \quad \Gamma \vdash s \in R' \quad \Gamma \vdash m \in R \to N'(R')}$$
$$\frac{}{\Gamma \vdash object_{N'}(R', s, m) = object_N(R, s, m) \in Object(N)}$$

$$\frac{\Gamma \vdash N' \leq N \in \star \longmapsto \star \quad co(N') \quad co(N)}{\Gamma \vdash GM_{N'} = GM_N \in All(N'' \leq N') \; Object(N'') \to N(Object(N''))}$$

These conditions imply an equation similar to one appearing in Mitchell's treatment of method specialization and inheritance via natural transformations [19]:

$$Object(N) \xrightarrow{\quad GM_N[N] \quad} N(Object(N))$$
$$\leq\uparrow \qquad\qquad\qquad \uparrow\leq$$
$$Object(N') \xrightarrow[\quad GM_{N'}[N'] \quad]{} N'(Object(N'))$$

Combining this diagram with the specification (†), we obtain the following generalized characterization of the behavior of the generic method, capturing the idea that it does nothing but invoke the concrete methods of the object to which it is applied:

$$Object(N') \xrightarrow{\quad GM_N[N'] \quad} N(Object(N'))$$
$$\uparrow \qquad\qquad \uparrow \leq$$
$$object_{N'}(R, -, m) \qquad\qquad N'(Object(N'))$$
$$\qquad\qquad\qquad \uparrow \; strength_{N'}\,[R]\,[Object(N')] \atop object_{N'}(R, -, m)$$
$$R \xrightarrow[\quad m \quad]{} N'(R) \qquad\qquad (\dagger_{\leq})$$

4 Objects as Recursive Records

Next we show that the familiar encoding of objects as recursive records [7, 9, 4, 19, etc.] satisfies the abstract specification developed in Sections 2 and 3. This justifies both the abstract framework itself (by showing that a familiar construction is a specific instance of it) and the encoding (by showing that some of its tricky aspects, e.g. the creation of objects, can be explained from general considerations).

We extend pure $F_{\leq}^{\omega}$ with a recursive type constructor μ, which obeys the subtyping laws [2]:

$$\frac{\Gamma \vdash \mu(A)T \in \star}{\Gamma \vdash \mu(A)T \sim [(\mu(A)T)/A]T}$$

$$\frac{\Gamma, B \leq Top(\star), A \leq B \vdash S \leq T}{\Gamma \vdash \mu(A)S \leq \mu(B)T}$$

We also assume the existence of a fixed-point combinator $fix \in All(A \leq Top(\star))(A \to A) \to A$. This does not add any computational power, since fix can be defined using contravariant μ-types [2].

Our type constructor $Object$ can be encoded in this calculus by taking $Object(N) = \mu(X)\,N(X)$, reflecting the intuition that the extension of an object comprises the potential results of all methods applicable to it. This is analogous to the observation that the extension of a function is its input-output behavior.

The $object$ constructor is implemented by using the equational specification (†) as a recursive definition: $object_N\,(R,\,s,\,m) = obj\,s$, where

$$
\begin{aligned}
obj \;=\; & fix\,[R \to Object(N)] \\
& fun\,(f{:}R \to Object(N)) \\
& fun\,(s{:}R) \\
& \quad (fold \in N(Object(N)) \to Object(N)) \\
& \quad (strength_N\,[R]\,[Object(N)]\,f\,(m\,s))
\end{aligned}
$$

(The function $fold$ is actually an implicit coercion; we write it explicitly here as an aid to the reader.) Finally, since $Object(N) \sim N(Object(N))$, (by S-Mu) the generic method is just an identity function:

$$
\begin{aligned}
GM_N \;=\;\; & fun\,(N' \leq N)\;\; id\,[Object(N')] \\
\in\;\; & All(N' \leq N)\;\; Object(N') \to Object(N') \\
\sim\;\; & All(N' \leq N)\;\; Object(N') \to N'(Object(N')) \\
\leq\;\; & All(N' \leq N)\;\; Object(N') \to N(Object(N')).
\end{aligned}
$$

For example, suppose we are given the representation type `Int` and the following implementation of the point methods: `m = fun(r:Int) {getX = r, setX = fun(i:Int) i} : Int -> PointN(Int)` Then by unravelling the definition of $object$, we obtain a function `mkpoint` mapping internal states to point objects as follows: `mkpoint = fix [Int->Point] fun(mkp: Int->Point) fun(s:Int) (fold {getX = s, setX = fun(i:Int) mkp i})`.

If objects are modeled using recursive types, the higher-order quantification in the type of the generic method can be eliminated in favor of a specialized form of second-order quantification called *F-bounded quantification* [6, 13], where the type variable introduced by a quantifier may appear free in its bound. Cardelli and Mitchell have observed that F-bounded quantification can be expressed in terms of higher-order quantification and recursive types [1, 4]: $All(A \leq F(A))\,S \approx All(G \leq F)\,[(\mu(A)G(A))/A]S$. Indeed, it follows from an observation by Abadi [1] that, in many models, these two types denote the same collection. Using this correspondence, we can recast the type of our generic method as $GM_N \in All(A \leq N(A))\ A \to N(A)$ to match the specification of object interfaces given in [13].

5 Objects as Packages

We now consider a specific encoding of objects, where existential types are used to achieve the hiding of the internal states of objects [23]:[6] $Object(N) = Some(A)\ \{state : A, methods : A \to N(A)\}$, or, in the more familiar notation: $Object(N) = \exists A.\ A \times (A \to N(A))$. We denote the associated (standard) introduction and elimination operators by pack and open (see [21]). The type-theoretic encoding of objects in $F_{\leq}^{\omega}$ using existentials is given by:

$$Object(N) \quad = \quad Some(A)\ \{state : A, methods : A \to N(A)\}$$

$$object_N\ (R, s, m) \quad = \quad pack\ \{state = s, methods = m\}\ as\ Object(N)\\ hiding\ R$$

$$GM_N \quad = \quad fun\ (N' \leq N)\\ fun\ (x : Object(N'))\\ open\ x\ as\ [R, r]\ in\\ (strength_N\ [R]\ [Object(N')]\\ object_{N'}\ (R, —, r.methods))\\ (r.methods\ r.state)$$

Note that the encoding of object types and the packing function *object* make sense for arbitrary N — indeed, even for the non-unary interface types we excluded in Section 2 — but the definition of the generic method relies on the functoriality of N. Conversely, the definition $Object(N) = \mu(X)\ N(X)$ and the use of identity functions for the generic method make sense for mixed-variance N. However, it is not possible to define the packing function *object* uniformly in this case. Thus, the encodings using existentials and recursive types offer complementary ways of extending our account to mixed-variance method signatures. We conjecture that the arguments in [3] and in Freyd's email notes on "Structors" can be generalized to show that, in the Bruce/Mitchell model [5], the encodings using recursive types and existential types are isomorphic for covariant N. This encoding is interesting both because it works in a fairly simple calculus — pure $F_{\leq}^{\omega}$ enriched with existential types, which, indeed, can be encoded in pure $F_{\leq}^{\omega}$ — and because it avoids introducing the possibility of nontermination in situations where fixed points are not strictly required.

---

[6] Also c.f. [4], which is mainly based on recursive records, but where existential types are used to implement hidden instance variables.

6   Conclusions

We have presented a direct, high-level axiomatization of objects and their types in a higher-order polymorphic λ-calculus with subtyping. This framework yields a natural high-level syntax for sending messages to objects and allows several previously studied encodings of objects to be presented in a common setting.

In [17] we show how the object axioms in Section 2 can be justified in terms of more fundamental mathematical considerations, using an argument based on parametricity; [17] also extends this framework to mixed-variance method signatures, illustrating the correspondence between our approach and previously studied encodings of mixed-variance objects. In the mixed-variance case, the extra power of recursive types gives rise to a more flexible encoding, since it correctly captures subtyping while the encoding in terms of existential types does not. This flexibility can be used, for example, to assign types to *binary methods* such as equality functions. An alternative treatment of binary methods that does not require mixed-variance signatures is described in [23].

We have dealt here only with the basic mechanisms of objects and subtyping (a relation between specifications of objects) and not with *inheritance* (a mechanism for deriving the implementation of one class of objects by incrementally modifying the implementation of another class; c.f. [13]). It has been argued [23] that, once the fundamental mechanisms of encapsulation and subtyping are accounted for and their interactions properly handled, inheritance becomes "just a matter of programming." This leads us to believe that it would be a straightforward matter to extend the abstract framework developed here to include an implementation of inheritance.

Another application of our framework may lie in suggesting appropriate proof rules for the verification of object-oriented programs. Here, existing work on implementations of inheritance does not seem sufficiently abstract to yield useful *high-level* rules for reasoning about programs involving inheritance. Instead, the process we have described here for objects and subtyping — finding a direct axiomatization and showing that existing implementations can be derived as instances of it — must be repeated for inheritance as well.

Acknowledgements

David N. Turner joined in many discussions and helped formalize the definitions of positivity and strength in Section 5. Marcelo Fiore pointed out a relationship between terminal algebras and recursive types that led to the axiomatization of mixed-variance methods (described in [17]). Phil Wadler posed the problem of relating the encoding of objects using recursive records and the one using existential types. Martín Abadi, Eugenio Moggi, and Andre Scedrov supplied pointers to relevant literature. Terry Stroup gave us helpful suggestions on an earlier draft. This research was mainly carried out at the University of Edinburgh's Lab for Foundations of Computer Science.

References

[1] Martín Abadi. Doing without F-bounded quantification. Message to Types electronic mail list, February 1992.

[2] Roberto M. Amadio and Luca Cardelli. Subtyping recursive types. In *Proceedings of the Eighteenth ACM Symposium on Principles of Programming Languages*, pages 104–118, Orlando, FL, January 1991. Also available as DEC Systems Research Center Research Report number 62, August 1990. To appear in TOPLAS.

[3] S. Bainbridge, P. Freyd, A. Scedrov, and P. Scott. Functorial polymorphism. *Theoretical Computer Science*, 70:35–64, 1990.

[4] Kim B. Bruce. Safe type checking in a statically typed object-oriented programming language. In *Proceedings of the Twentieth ACM Symposium on Principles of Programming Languages*, 1993. To appear in *Journal of Functional Programming*.

[5] Kim Bruce and John Mitchell. PER models of subtyping, recursive types and higher-order polymorphism. In *Proceedings of the Nineteenth ACM Symposium on Principles of Programming Languages*, Albequerque, NM, January 1992.

[6] Peter Canning, William Cook, Walter Hill, Walter Olthoff, and John Mitchell. F-bounded quantification for object-oriented programming. In *Fourth International Conference on Functional Programming Languages and Computer Architecture*, pages 273–280, September 1989.

[7] Luca Cardelli. A semantics of multiple inheritance. *Information and Computation*, 76:138–164, 1988. Preliminary version in *Semantics of Data Types*, Kahn, MacQueen, and Plotkin, eds., Springer-Verlag LNCS 173, 1984.

[8] Luca Cardelli. Notes about $F^{\omega}_{<:}$. Unpublished notes, October 1990.

[9] Luca Cardelli. Extensible records in a pure calculus of subtyping. Research report 81, DEC Systems Research Center, January 1992. Also in Carl A. Gunter and John C. Mitchell, editors, *Theoretical Aspects of Object-Oriented Programming: Types, Semantics, and Language Design* (The MIT Press; to appear, 1993).

[10] Luca Cardelli, Simone Martini, John C. Mitchell, and Andre Scedrov. An extension of system F with subtyping. In T. Ito and A. R. Meyer, editors, *Theoretical Aspects of Computer Software (Sendai, Japan)*, number 526 in Lecture Notes in Computer Science, pages 750–770. Springer-Verlag, September 1991.

[11] Luca Cardelli and Peter Wegner. On understanding types, data abstraction, and polymorphism. *Computing Surveys*, 17(4), December 1985.

[12] G. Castagna, G. Ghelli, and G. Longo. A calculus for overloaded functions with subtyping. In *ACM conference on LISP and Functional Programming*, pages 182–192, San Francisco, July 1992. ACM Press. Also available as Rapport de Recherche LIENS-92-4, Ecole Normale Supérieure, Paris.

[13] William R. Cook, Walter L. Hill, and Peter S. Canning. Inheritance is not subtyping. In *Seventeenth Annual ACM Symposium on Principles of Programming Languages*, pages 125–135, San Francisco, CA, January 1990. Also in Carl A. Gunter and John C. Mitchell, editors, *Theoretical Aspects of Object-Oriented Programming: Types, Semantics, and Language Design* (The MIT Press; to appear, 1993).

[14] O. J. Dahl and K. Nygaard. SIMULA–An ALGOL-based simulation language. *Communications of the ACM*, 9(9):671–678, September 1966.

[15] Jean-Yves Girard. *Interprétation fonctionelle et élimination des coupures de l'arithmétique d'ordre supérieur.* PhD thesis, Université Paris VII, 1972.

[16] Adele Goldberg and David Robson. *Smalltalk-80: The Language and Its Implementation.* Addison-Wesley, Reading, MA, 1983.

[17] Martin Hofmann and Benjamin Pierce. An abstract view of objects and subtyping (preliminary report). Technical Report ECS-LFCS-92-226, University of Edinburgh, LFCS, 1992.

[18] A. Kock. Strong functors and monoidal monads. *Various Publications Series 11, Aarhus Universitet*, 1970.

[19] John C. Mitchell. Toward a typed foundation for method specialization and inheritance. In *Proceedings of the 17th ACM Symposium on Principles of Programming Languages*, pages 109–124, January 1990. Also in Carl A. Gunter and John C. Mitchell, editors, *Theoretical Aspects of Object-Oriented Programming: Types, Semantics, and Language Design* (The MIT Press; to appear, 1993).

[20] John C. Mitchell. A type-inference approach to reduction properties and semantics of polymorphic expressions. In Gérard Huet, editor, *Logical Foundations of Functional Programming*, University of Texas at Austin Year of Programming Series, pages 195–212. Addison-Wesley, 1990.

[21] John Mitchell and Gordon Plotkin. Abstract types have existential type. *ACM Transactions on Programming Languages and Systems*, 10(3), July 1988.

[22] Benjamin C. Pierce and Robert Pollack. Higher-order subtyping. Unpublished manuscript, August 1992.

[23] Benjamin C. Pierce and David N. Turner. Simple type-theoretic foundations for object-oriented programming. *Journal of Functional Programming*, 1993. To appear; a preliminary version appeared in Principles of Programming Languages, 1993, and as University of Edinburgh technical report ECS-LFCS-92-225, under the title "Object-Oriented Programming Without Recursive Types".

[24] Benjamin C. Pierce and David N. Turner. Statically typed friendly functions via partially abstract types. Technical Report ECS-LFCS-93-256, University of Edinburgh, LFCS, April 1993. Also available as INRIA-Rocquencourt Rapport de Recherche No. 1899.

[25] John Reynolds. Towards a theory of type structure. In *Proc. Colloque sur la Programmation*, pages 408–425, New York, 1974. Springer-Verlag LNCS 19.

[26] John C. Reynolds. User defined types and procedural data structures as complementary approaches to data abstraction. In David Gries, editor, *Programming Methodology, A Collection of Articles by IFIP WG2.3*, pages 309–317. Springer-Verlag, New York, 1978. Reprinted from S. A. Schuman (ed.), *New Advances in Algorithmic Languages 1975*, Inst. de Recherche d'Informatique et d'Automatique, Rocquencourt, 1975, pages 157-168. Also in Carl A. Gunter and John C. Mitchell, editors, *Theoretical Aspects of Object-Oriented Programming: Types, Semantics, and Language Design* (The MIT Press; to appear, 1993).

[27] Gavin C. Wraith. A note on categorical datatypes. Number 389 in Lecture Notes in Computer Science. Springer-Verlag, 1989.

Operational Specifications with Built-Ins

Jürgen Avenhaus and Klaus Becker *

Universität Kaiserslautern, Fachbereich Informatik
Postfach 3049, 67663 Kaiserslautern, Germany
email: {avenhaus,klbecker}@informatik.uni-kl.de

Abstract

We present a framework for studying equational specifications that partially specify functions over built-in structures. Using an order-sorted approach we are able to suitably assign semantics to such specifications in a denotational as well as an operational way. The operationalization, based on a combination of order-sorted and constraint based reasoning, enables us to generalize some basic results from classical rewrite theory.

1 Introduction and motivation

Conditional equational specifications can be regarded as the programs of a programming language that combines a clear, logic based semantic foundation with a simple, functional style operationalization, using conditional rewriting as its computation mechanism. Whereas built-in concepts are available in common programming languages, they usually are missing in rewrite based specification environments. The reason for this lack is that built-in structures destroy the balance between the syntactic and the semantic equality induced by the specification (as stated in Birkhoff's theorem) and thus complicate the programming paradigm. However, built-in concepts are attractive due to the fact that they provide the "basic world of interest", which thus need not be constructed.

This paper provides an approach of how to enrich equational specifications with built-in concepts, the latter being represented by a built-in algebra. Similar to the CLP-scheme [JaLa87], this approach is a general one, as any algebra $\mathcal{A}$ is allowed to be built in. In order to be of practical interest, the functions in $\mathcal{A}$ should be computable of course. Consider as an example the following equations:

$$
\begin{array}{llll}
(1) & g(x,0) & = & x \\
(2) & g(0,y) & = & y \\
(3) & g(x+y,y) & = & g(x,y) \\
(4) & g(x,x+y) & = & g(x,y)
\end{array}
$$

---

*This research was supported by the Deutsche Forschungsgemeinschaft, SFB 314, Proj. D4.

These equations are to define the greatest common divisor function over the natural numbers. However, they are not "executable" in most specification environments as the symbols 0 and + are not defined. The situation changes if there is given a built-in algebra that provides built-in definitions for the base symbols. Concerning the present example, the natural number algebra $\mathcal{N}$ can be used to assign meaning to the constants $0, 1, 2, \ldots$ and the symbol + in a canonical way.

Built-ins thus allow one to program at a higher level of abstraction. Evenmore, they may lead to a gain of efficiency if suitable algorithms are available to treat the built-in operations. There is another reasons in favour of built-in concepts. Built-ins may increase the expressive power of the programming language. In the equational specification case built-in structures, being "non-constructive" in the sense that the built-in domain cannot be characterized equationally, make more powerful the programming language. Real numbers provide an example for such a domain. Hence there is some interest in enriching equational specifications with built-in structures. In the sequel we informally describe how this can be done.

The specifications to be considered are hierarchic. They consist of a base part, given by a built-in algebra $\mathcal{A}$ over a base signature Σ_0, and a top part, consisting of a set $\mathcal{E}$ of conditional equations over Σ, where Σ is an enrichment of Σ_0. We are faced with several problems when assigning semantics to such a specification in a denotational as well as an operational way. The intuition to be modelled is that the semantics of the base symbols is fixed by the built-in algebra $\mathcal{A}$ and that the new symbols are to be partially defined over the predefined domain by the equations from $\mathcal{E}$. In order to be consistent, the equations from $\mathcal{E}$ should not identify different elements in $\mathcal{A}$.

The notion of partiality to be modelled is very comon in natural specifications, either because of the intended meaning of the function (e.g. $div(x, 0)$ is usually not defined for the division function div over $\mathcal{N}$), or because the specification is incomplete in the sense that it may be extended later on [KaMu86]. However, partial algebra semantics based on the notion of strong equality (as used in [BPW84, Wi90], saying that two terms are (semantically) equal if either they are both defined and equal in the algebra, or else they are both undefined), is not suited for our purposes due to the fact that it is not monotonic wrt. extending the specification. Consider as an example the following specification over the natural number algebra $\mathcal{N}$ with $\mathcal{E}$ consisting of the two equations

(1) $f(x, 0) = x$ (2) $f(x + 1, y + 1) = f(x, y)$.

These equations partially define $f(x, y) = x \dot{-} y$, the subtraction over $\mathcal{N}$, but also $f(x, y) = |x - y|$. Note that terms like $f(2, 5)$ or $f(3, 5)$ are junk terms. Thus $f(2, 5) = f(3, 5)$ assuming strong equality. But adding the equation

(3) $f(0, y) = y$

results in a total definition of f (namely $f(x, y) = |x - y|$) with $f(2, 5) \neq f(3, 5)$.

Instead of dealing with partial algebras we use an order-sorted construction (see [SNGM89]) to model partiality. This construction provides a junk sort for every base sort and thus enables one to introduce auxiliary objects in order to denote junk terms. Hence we are able to semantically reflect the structure that is induced by $\mathcal{E}$ on the junk terms instead of identifying all junk terms. In order to reflect the auxiliary character of the non-predefined objects, we assume that there exist no variables for the junk sorts. Thus variables must be instantiated by base objects only.

In order to operationalize semantics we define a suitable notion of rewriting modulo the given built-in algebra. Due to the variable restriction, which we model by using the order-sorted setting, this rewrite relation has a different behaviour compared with rewriting modulo an equational theory as introduced in [JoKi86, BaDe89] for the "flat" case. As a consequence, matching and unification problems reduce to pure constraint solving problems (i.e. solving equations in the built-in algebra). This allows one to construct semantic rpo-like orderings for proving termination [AvBe92]. Furthermore it enables one to prove ground confluence, provided the constraints induced by the specification are solvable. Ground confluence is a key notion in our approach as it can be used to guarantee the soundness (i.e. consistency) of the specification.

So, the major contribution of this paper is the indication of a way to operationally handle specifications with built-in structures using a suitable combination of order-sorted and constraint based equational reasoning.

There has been done some related work on integrating predefined structures into algebraic specifications in [BPW84]. However, this work is not concerned with an operationalization via rewriting. Concerning the integration of predefined structures into rewrite based reasoning there exist approaches by Vorobyov [Vo89], who deals with the special case of built-in arithmetic, and Kaplan&Choppy [KaCh89], who concentrate more on implementational aspects. Kirchner&Kirchner&Rusinowitch [KKR90] develop an approach of constrained equational deduction that is similar to constraint logic programming [JaLa87]. Our approach differs from the latter mainly due to the order-sorted framework we use to separate syntactic and semantic problems.

The paper is organized as follows. In section 2 we make precise our notion of specification with built-in algebra. Section 3 provides the order-sorted setting that is used to assign semantics to the specifications. In section 4 we present suitable notions of rewriting. Section 5 finally is devoted to critical pair criteria that allow one to show ground confluence of the rewrite relation. For more details see [AvBe92].

2 Specifications with built-in algebras

We assume that the reader is familiar with the basic notions of algebraic specification and term rewriting (see e.g. [AvMa90, DeJo90, Wi90]).

The specifications to be considered are hierarchic, consisting of two parts. Whereas the "base part" is given semantically by an algebra, the "top part" is mere syntactic, consisting of (directed) conditional equations. This separation is reflected by the kind of signature that provides the vocabulary of the specification language.

A *many-sorted signature* (S, F, D) consists of a set S of sort symbols, a set F of function symbols and a set D of declarations $f : s_1, \ldots, s_n \to s$ for the function symbols $f \in F$. (Order-sorted signatures are introduced in Section 3.) A *hierarchic signature* Σ over the *base signature* $\Sigma_0 = (S_0, F_0, D_0)$ has the form $\Sigma = (S_0, F_0 + F_1, D_0 + D_1)$. Here '+' denotes the disjoint union of sets. So a hierarchic signature is a signature enrichment of Σ_0 in the usual sense with the restriction that no new sorts are added. This restriction is motivated by the point of view we adopt here. It can be removed without conceptual difficulties.

Given a hierarchic signature Σ, we assume that there is given a family $\{V_s \mid s \in S_0\}$ of variables with $x \in V_s$ of sort s. Let V denote the union of all these V_s. Let $TERM(\Sigma, V)$ be the set of Σ-terms and $TERM(\Sigma)$ the set of (variable-free) Σ-ground terms. A conditional equation over Σ has the form $\Gamma \Rightarrow u = v$, where Γ is a (finite) conjunction of equations over Σ.

Definition 2.1 *A specification with a built-in algebra is a triple* $SP = (\Sigma, \mathcal{E}, \mathcal{A})$ *where*
(a) $\Sigma = (S_0, F_0 + F_1, D_0 + D_1)$ *is a hierarchic signature,*
(b) $\mathcal{E}$ *is a set of conditional equations over* Σ *and*
(c) $\mathcal{A}$ *is a term-generated* Σ_0-*algebra, where* $\Sigma_0 = (S_0, F_0, D_0)$.

We call $\mathcal{A}$ the *base algebra* of the specification $SP = (\Sigma, \mathcal{E}, \mathcal{A})$. It can either be given explicitly as in the examples of Section 1 ($\mathcal{A}$ is the algebra of natural numbers there) or implicitly by a ground confluent and terminating base rewrite system $\mathcal{R}_0$ over Σ_0. In the latter case, $\mathcal{A}$ is the canonical term algebra $\mathcal{T}_{(\Sigma_0, \mathcal{R}_0)}$ defined by $\mathcal{R}_0$ on $TERM(\Sigma_0)$. The symbols $f \in F_0$ then are called constructors and the rules in $\mathcal{R}_0$ constructor rules.

The intuition to be associated with such a specification is that the predefined algebra $\mathcal{A}$ fixes the base structure and that $\mathcal{E}$ (partially) defines the "new" functions over $\mathcal{A}$. Such specifications, with canonical constructor algebras as built-in algebras, are in the spirit of Kapur&Musser [KaMu86]. They as well form the basis of an operational treatment of positive/negative conditional specifications in [WiGr92].

3 Order-sorted algebra semantics

Semantics associated with a specification with a built-in algebra should reflect the fact that the intended domain of computation is given by an algebra and thus is fixed. Furthermore it should be monotonic wrt. enrichment of the equational part of the specification. Note that the latter requirement is not satisfied by a partial algebra semantics based on the notion of strong equality, as discussed in the introduction. In order to adequately capture our intuition, we use as in [SNGM89] an order-sorted construction that allows one to semantically reflect the structure that operationally is induced by the equations on the ground terms. Note that a similar construction using generalized partial algebras can be found in [BrWi83].

Informally, one introduces auxiliary elements, not given by the built-in algebra, in order to denote the junk terms. Technically this can be done by introducing a junk sort $s^\wedge$ for each base sort $s \in S_0$ and relating them by a subsort declaration $s \trianglelefteq s^\wedge$. An algebra for such a situation has a carrier set for the base sort that is part of a greater carrier set for the non-base sort.

Definition 3.1 *Let* $\Sigma = (S_0, F_0 + F_1, D_0 + D_1)$ *be a hierarchic signature. The order-sorted signature* $\Sigma^\wedge = (S^\wedge, F^\wedge, D^\wedge)$ *induced by* Σ *is defined as follows:*
(a) $S^\wedge = S_0 + S_0^\wedge$, *where* $S_0^\wedge = \{s^\wedge \mid s \in S_0\}$
(b) $F^\wedge = F_0 + F_1$
(c) $D^\wedge = D_0 + D_0^\wedge + D_1^\wedge + D_s$, *where*
$$D_0^\wedge = \{f : s_1^\wedge, \ldots, s_n^\wedge \to s^\wedge \mid f \in F_0, \; f : s_1, \ldots, s_n \to s \; \in D_0\}$$
$$D_1^\wedge = \{f : s_1^\wedge, \ldots, s_n^\wedge \to s^\wedge \mid f \in F_1, \; f : s_1, \ldots, s_n \to s \; \in D_1\}$$
$$D_s = \{s \trianglelefteq s^\wedge \mid s \in S_0\}.$$

If $\Sigma^\wedge$ is the order-sorted signature induced by Σ, then we assume that the family of variables associated with $\Sigma^\wedge$ is just the same as the family associated with Σ. Hence $V_{s^\wedge}$ is empty for all $s^\wedge \in S_0^\wedge$. As a result, variables range over the elements of the base part of an algebra only.

The set of order-sorted terms of some sort $s \in S^\wedge$ is defined in the usual way (see e.g. [SNGM89]). The order-sorted signatures used here are well-behaved in the sense that they allow to equip every order-sorted term t with a least sort s — which we denote by $sort(t)$ — such that t is of sort s. Due to the construction we have $sort(t) \in S_0$ iff t contains base symbols and variables only, and $sort(t) \in S_0^\wedge$ iff t contains at least one non-base symbol from F_1.

As a consequence of this construction there exists a direct correspondence between the many-sorted Σ-terms and the order-sorted $\Sigma^\wedge$-terms. Literally they are just the same: $TERM(\Sigma^\wedge, V) = TERM(\Sigma, V)$. However, there is a difference between the many-sorted and the order-sorted setting concerning the substitutions to be used for equational reasoning. In both settings a variable $x \in V_s$ may be replaced by a term $\sigma(x)$ of sort s. In the many-sorted setting this means $\sigma(x) \in TERM(\Sigma, V)$. In the order-sorted case however we have $\sigma(x) \in TERM(\Sigma_0, V)$ because x is of a base sort $s \in S_0$ and a term of a base sort must not contain a function symbol $f \in F_1$. Since we use the order-sorted setting throughout this paper one should keep in mind that any substitution σ is a Σ_0-substitution, i.e. $\sigma(x) \in TERM(\Sigma_0, V)$ for all $x \in dom(\sigma)$.

Next we make precise our notion of an order-sorted algebra. Note that we use a restricted notion compared with [SNGM89] which is suited to model the special situations we are interested in.

Definition 3.2 *Let* Σ *be a hierarchic (many-sorted) signature. Let* $\Sigma^\wedge$ *be the order-sorted signature induced by* Σ. *An order-sorted* $\Sigma^\wedge$-algebra $\mathcal{B}$ *consists of a family* $\{B_s \mid s \in S^\wedge\}$ *of sets and a family* $\{f^{\mathcal{B}} \mid f \in F\}$ *of functions such that* $B_s \subseteq B_{s^\wedge}$ *for all* $s \in S_0$ *and such that the following conditions are satisfied: (i) If* $f \in F_0$ *and* $f : s_1, \ldots, s_n \to s \; \in D_0$, *then* $f^{\mathcal{B}} : B_{s_1^\wedge} \times \cdots \times B_{s_n^\wedge} \to B_{s^\wedge}$. *Furthermore* $f^{\mathcal{B}}(b_1, \ldots, b_n) \in B_s$ *if* $b_i \in B_{s_i}$ *for all* i. *(ii) If* $f \in F_1$ *and* $f : s_1, \ldots, s_n \to s \; \in D_1$, *then* $f^{\mathcal{B}} : B_{s_1^\wedge} \times \cdots \times B_{s_n^\wedge} \to B_{s^\wedge}$.

Let $OALG(\Sigma)$ denote the class of order-sorted $\Sigma^\wedge$-algebras, where $\Sigma^\wedge$ is induced by Σ.

In order to give meanings to the syntactic constructs, we use the model notation for order-sorted equational logic. For semantic considerations the syntactic constructs thus implicitly are to be considered as constructs over the order-sorted signature.

Now let $SP = (\Sigma, \mathcal{E}, \mathcal{A})$ be a specification with built-in algebra. Let $\Sigma^\wedge$ be the order-sorted signature induced by Σ. Note that every order-sorted $\Sigma^\wedge$-algebra $\mathcal{B}$ can be restricted to a flat Σ_0-algebra by forgetting about the non-base part. We say that a $\Sigma^\wedge$-algebra $\mathcal{B}$ *contains* $\mathcal{A}$ iff there exists a homomorphism from $\mathcal{A}$ to the restriction $\mathcal{B}|_{\Sigma_0}$. Further, $\mathcal{B}$ is said to be a *model* of $SP = (\Sigma, \mathcal{E}, \mathcal{A})$ iff $\mathcal{B}$ contains $\mathcal{A}$ and $\mathcal{B}$ is a model of $\mathcal{E}$. Now let

$$\mathcal{K}_{SP} = \{\mathcal{B} \in OALG(\Sigma) \mid \mathcal{B} \text{ is a model of } SP\}.$$

In order to single out the most representative model of a specification $SP = (\Sigma, \mathcal{E}, \mathcal{A})$, we next construct the canonical term algebra induced by SP. Let $E_\mathcal{A} = \{u = v \mid u, v \in TERM(\Sigma_0) \text{ and } \mathcal{A} \models u = v\}$ be the equational ground theory of $\mathcal{A}$. Further let $INST_0(\mathcal{E})$ denote the set of all ground instantiations $\tau(E)$, where E is an equation of $\mathcal{E}$ and τ is a Σ_0-ground substitution (with $var(E) \subseteq dom(\tau)$). The set $E_\mathcal{A} \cup INST_0(\mathcal{E})$ of conditional ground equations (over $\Sigma^\wedge$) induces a congruence relation $\sim_{SP}$ on the order-sorted $\Sigma^\wedge$-ground terms and henceforth a canonical $\Sigma^\wedge$-ground term algebra $\mathcal{T}_{SP}$. This algebra $\mathcal{T}_{SP}$ is to assign semantics to the specification SP, provided the specification is consistent in the following sense:

Definition 3.3 *A specification SP is said to be* consistent *iff $\mathcal{T}_{SP}|_{\Sigma_0}$ is isomorhic to $\mathcal{A}$.*

Hence we require the equations from $\mathcal{E}$ to produce no confusion on the base structure induced by $\mathcal{A}$. The following result shows that this construction provides an initial algebra semantics. As a consequence, an equation is valid in $\mathcal{T}_{SP}$ iff it is valid in all $\mathcal{B} \in \mathcal{K}_{SP}$.

Theorem 3.1 *Let $SP = (\Sigma, \mathcal{R}, \mathcal{A})$ be a consistent specification. Then $\mathcal{T}_{SP}$ is initial in the class $\mathcal{K}_{SP}$.*

4   Rewriting modulo a built-in algebra

The main goal of this section is to generalize syntactic rewriting to a kind of semantically enriched rewriting by taking into account the built-in structures.

Term rewriting provides a mechanism for operationalizing an equational specification. For that purpose the conditional equations have to be turned into rewrite rules. A *conditional rule over* Σ (or simply a rule) is a formula $\Gamma \Rightarrow u = v$ where Γ is a finite set of Σ-equations and $u = v$ is a directed Σ-equation such that all variables occuring in Γ or v occur in u as well. Such a rule is said to be *hierarchic* iff the left hand side u contains at least one symbol of F_1 (i.e. $u \notin TERM(\Sigma_0, V)$).

In the sequel we assume that $\mathcal{R}$ denotes the set of rules that is obtained from the set $\mathcal{E}$ of conditional equations when imposing directionality on the conclusion equations. We always assume that $\mathcal{R}$ is hierarchic. The latter condition is to preserve base terms from being reducible by the rules listed in the specification.

In order to integrate $\mathcal{A}$ into the rewrite relation, let $\sim_\mathcal{A}$ be the congruence relation on $TERM(\Sigma, V)$ generated by $\{(u, v) \mid u, v \in TERM(\Sigma_0, V)$ and $\mathcal{A} \models u = v\}$. Note that $\sim_\mathcal{A}$ extends structure axioms in a weak fashion only. For instance, if the commutativity axiom $x + y = y + x$ holds in $\mathcal{A}$, then $f(y + x, y) \sim_\mathcal{A} f(x + y, y)$ is true whereas the relation $x + f(y, z) \sim_\mathcal{A} f(y, z) + x$ does not hold (f denotes a new operation here). This kind of behaviour of course can be obtained in any framework (like OBJ3) that models order-sorted equational logic.

The rewrite relation $\longrightarrow_{R/A}$ to be defined next is a relation on $\sim_\mathcal{A}$-congruence classes mainly. We use the notation $a \downarrow b$ in order to denote joinability wrt. $\longrightarrow$ (where $\longrightarrow$ is some binary relation), i.e. $a \downarrow b$ iff $a \xrightarrow{*} c$ and $b \xrightarrow{*} c$ for some c.

Definition 4.1 *For $s, t \in TERM(\Sigma, V)$ let $s \longrightarrow_{R/A} t$ iff there exist terms $s', t' \in TERM(\Sigma, V)$, a position $p \in O(s')$, a Σ_0-substitution τ and a rule $\Gamma \Rightarrow u = v$ in $\mathcal{R}$ such that the following conditions are satisfied:*
(a) $s \sim_\mathcal{A} s'$, $s' \equiv s'[\tau(u)]_p$, $s'[\tau(v)]_p \equiv t'$, $t' \sim_\mathcal{A} t$
(b) $a \downarrow_{R/A} b$ for all $a = b \in \Gamma$.

Here $\xrightarrow{*}_{R/A}$ is the familiar iteration of $\longrightarrow_{R/A}$ starting with $\xrightarrow{0}_{R/A} = \sim_\mathcal{A}$.

Note that the variable restriction induces a kind of innermost rewriting. For special purposes like inductive theorem proving one can define more general rewrite relations with the variable restriction being weakened.

As with rewriting modulo a theory [JoKi86, BaDe89] it is convenient to consider a weaker notion of rewriting that allows one to localizes the equivalence step to the matching terms. Whereas $\longrightarrow_{R/A}$ is of interest for conceptual reasons, the weaker relation is of practical interest due to the fact that it is easier to compute.

Definition 4.2 *For $s, t \in TERM(\Sigma, V)$ let $s \longrightarrow_{R \backslash A} t$ iff there exists a position $p \in O(s)$, a Σ_0-substitution τ and a rule $\Gamma \Rightarrow u = v$ in $\mathcal{R}$ such that the following conditions are satisfied:*
(a) $s/p \sim_\mathcal{A} \tau(u)$, $s[\tau(v)]_p \equiv t$
(b) $a \downarrow_{R \backslash A} b$ for all $a = b \in \Gamma$.

Here $\xrightarrow{*}_{R \backslash A}$ is the iteration of $\longrightarrow_{R \backslash A}$ starting with $\xrightarrow{0}_{R/A}$ being the syntactic identity $\equiv$.

Contrary to rewriting modulo a theory [JoKi86, BaDe89], the two rewrite relations do not differ essentially in our setting. Hence, changing the rewrite relation does not involve new problems.

Lemma 4.1 *Let $s, t \in TERM(\Sigma, V)$. Then $s \xrightarrow{*}_{R/A} t$ iff there exists $t' \in TERM(\Sigma, V)$ such that $s \xrightarrow{*}_{R \backslash A} t' \sim_\mathcal{A} t$.*

In order to show this result one easily verifies that the following implication is true in our approach: Whenever $s \sim_{\mathcal{A}} s' \equiv s'[\tau(u)]_p$ for some $s, s' \in TERM(\Sigma, V)$ and $\Gamma \Rightarrow u = v \in \mathcal{R}$, then $s/p \sim_{\mathcal{A}} \tau(u)$ and $s[\tau(v)]_p \sim_{\mathcal{A}} s'[\tau(v)]_p$.

Next we briefly comment on the decidability of rewriting with $\longrightarrow_{R\backslash A}$. As in the syntactic case one has to impose a kind of decreasingness restriction on $\mathcal{R}$ (see [DeOk90]) in order to guarantee that there exists no infinite recursive descent when checking a condition. This can be done using appropriate orderings (see [AvBe92]). In addition, the operations used to define $\longrightarrow_{R\backslash A}$ must be decidable. In general, however, neither the $\mathcal{A}$-match nor the $\mathcal{A}$-equivalence check is decidable.

For the former let $\mathcal{Z}$ be the integer number algebra with addition and multiplication. One easily verifies that if $\mathcal{Z}$-matching were decidable, then Hilbert's 10th problem were too. The undecidability of the $\mathcal{A}$-equivalence check follows from the fact that one can construct a base rewrite system $\mathcal{R}_0$ such that the inductive theory induced by this base rewrite system is not recursively enumerable. If we take the canonical term algebra $\mathcal{T}_{(\Sigma_0, \mathcal{R}_0)}$ as base algebra $\mathcal{A}$, then $\sim_{\mathcal{A}}$ is not decidable.

But there exist positive results too. For special (classes of) algebras the notions are decidabe, at least if restricted to ground terms. In [DMS92] there is developed a decision procedure for semantic matching which applies to canonical constructor term algebras that are induced by ground convergent rewrite systems with some extra conditions imposed on the rules. Another way to obtain a decidable $\mathcal{A}$-match is to restrict the form of the rules. For instance, in order to obtain a decidable $\mathcal{Z}$-match, one may restrict the rules to have a linear arithmetic structure only. Such rules are e.g. $even(2 * x) = t$ and $even(2 * x + 1) = f$ (for more details consider [AvBe92]).

5 Critical pair criteria

We are particularily interested in ground confluence of the rewrite relation $\longrightarrow_{R/A}$ due to the following obvious results.

Lemma 5.1 *Let $SP = (\Sigma, \mathcal{R}, \mathcal{A})$ be a specification with built-in algebra. If the relation $\longrightarrow_{R/A}$ is ground confluent, then $\sim_{SP} = \downarrow_{\mathcal{R}/A}$.*

Lemma 5.2 *Let $SP = (\Sigma, \mathcal{R}, \mathcal{A})$ be a specification with built-in algebra such that $\mathcal{R}$ is hierarchic. If the relation $\longrightarrow_{R/A}$ is ground confluent, then SP is consistent.*

Thus, ground confluence of $\longrightarrow_{R/A}$ can be considered as a kind of correctness property of the specification SP. Before we develop some criteria for ground confluence, we review some notions and results (see [Hu80]).

A relation $\longrightarrow$ (over some given set) is said to be *confluent* iff $\xleftarrow{*} \circ \xrightarrow{*} \subseteq \xrightarrow{*} \circ \xleftarrow{*}$. It is said to be *locally confluent* iff $\longleftarrow \circ \longrightarrow \subseteq \xrightarrow{*} \circ \xleftarrow{*}$. Finally it is said to be *strongly confluent* iff $\longleftarrow \circ \longrightarrow \subseteq \xrightarrow{*} \circ \xleftarrow{\leq 1}$ and

$\longleftarrow \circ \longrightarrow \ \subseteq \ \xrightarrow{\leq 1} \circ \xleftarrow{*}$, where $\xrightarrow{\leq 1} = \xrightarrow{0} \cup \longrightarrow$. If the set to be considered is the set of ground terms induced by some signature, then we speak of ground confluence instead of confluence.

The following results are well-known. If $\longrightarrow$ is terminating and locally (ground) confluent, or, if $\longrightarrow$ is strongly (ground) confluent, then $\longrightarrow$ is (ground) confluent. Our interest in the latter result stems from the fact that termination of $\longrightarrow_{R/A}$ might be difficult to verify or that $\longrightarrow_{R/A}$ even might not be terminating. Below we show a criterion for (ground) confluence based on this result that uses no termination requirement.

An equation $s = t$ is *joinable wrt.* $\longrightarrow$ iff $s \xrightarrow{*} \circ \xleftarrow{*} t$. We say that $s = t$ is *strongly joinable wrt.* $\longrightarrow$ iff $s \xrightarrow{*} \circ \xleftarrow{\leq 1} t$ and $s \xrightarrow{\leq 1} \circ \xleftarrow{*} t$. A conditional equation $\Gamma \Rightarrow u = v$ is said to be *(strongly) joinable* wrt. $\longrightarrow$ iff $u = v$ is (strongly) joinable whenever all $s = t \in \Gamma$ are joinable. Finally, a (conditional) equation is *(strongly) ground joinable wrt.* $\longrightarrow$ iff every ground instance of the (conditional) equation is (strongly) joinable wrt. $\longrightarrow$. Remember that ground instances are induced by Σ_0-ground substitutions in our setting.

In order to show ground confluence one usually represents all (non-variable) overlaps bewteen the rules by so-called critical pairs. In the syntactic case, the notion of most general unifier (mgu) is used for a finite representation of all overlaps. In general such a finite, substitution based representation does not exist in the semantic case. But there is a way to replace the notion of mgu by a suitable notion of constraint in our approach.

Definition 5.1 *A Σ-constraint is a finite conjunction of Σ_0-equations, or one of the (meta-)symbols $\top$ and $\bot$.*

We say that a Σ_0-substitution τ is an $\mathcal{A}$-solution of an equation $s = t$ resp. a constraint γ iff $\tau(s) \sim_{\mathcal{A}} \tau(t)$ resp. $\mathcal{A} \models \tau(\gamma)$. We assume that every Σ_0-substitution is an $\mathcal{A}$-solution of $\top$, but not an $\mathcal{A}$-solution of $\bot$.

The following lemma provides a key result in our approach. Due to the order-sorted construction, a unification problem concerning the whole language can be transformed into a related constraint problem, the latter concerning the base specification only. Hence the difficult (possibly undecidable) semantic part of the unification problem can be separated from the mere syntactic part. Using a constraint logic as in [KKR90], the semantic part then can be treated in a lazy fashion.

Lemma 5.3 *Let $s = t$ be a Σ-equation. Then there exists a constraint $\gamma_{s=t}$ such that $s = t$ and $\gamma_{s=t}$ have the same $\mathcal{A}$-solutions.*

The transformation of $s = t$ into $\gamma_{s=t}$ can be considered as a kind of partial unification. One proceeds by syntactic decomposition until one arrives either at equations over Σ_0 only, or at a clash resulting from an equation with one term being a base term and the other term being a non-base term, or resulting from an equation with both terms being non-base terms and having different top symbols. In the latter two cases the resulting constraint is $\bot$. Concerning the introductory example, the equation $g(x + y, y) = g(x', 0)$ is decomposed into the constraint $x + y = x', y = 0$. The equation $x = g(x', 0)$ produces a clash and so is transformed into the constraint $\perp$.

Now we define the notion of critical pairs in our context.

Definition 5.2 *Let* $\Gamma \Rightarrow u = v$ *and* $\Gamma' \Rightarrow u' = v'$ *be two rules from* $\mathcal{R}$ *that have no variables in common. Let* $p \in O(u)$ *be such that* $\gamma_{u/p=u'} \neq \perp$. *Then*

$$\gamma_{u/p=u'}, \Gamma, \Gamma' \Rightarrow u[v']_p = v$$

is said to be a (conditional) *critical pair induced by the two rules. Let* $CRIT(\mathcal{R})$ *denote the set of all critical pairs induced by the rules from* $\mathcal{R}$.

Note that $\gamma_{u/p=u'} = \perp$ implies that u/p and u' are not unifiable modulo $\mathcal{A}$. This is true in particular if u/p is a variable. So variable overlaps do not exist in our approach.

The following theorem generalizes the usual syntactic critical pair lemma.

Theorem 5.1 *Let* $\longrightarrow_{R/A}$ *be terminating. If* $CRIT(\mathcal{R})$ *is ground joinable wrt.* $\longrightarrow_{R/A}$, *then* $\longrightarrow_{R/A}$ *is ground confluent.*

This theorem requires the rewrite relation to be terminating only, which is in contrast to the usual syntactic case (see [DeOk90]), where one has to require for decreasingness. The reason for this difference is that there exist no variable overlaps in our setting. However, showing termination is still a non-trivial problem in our approach as one has to construct orderings that are compatible with the congruence relation $\sim_{\mathcal{A}}$. We do not proceed in this direction here. The reader is referred to [AvBe92] for the construction of a recursive path ordering that integrates predefined structures. Instead we proceed along the lines of the field of "programming with equations" by showing how to obtain ground confluence without any termination requirement.

Theorem 5.2 *If* $CRIT(\mathcal{R})$ *is strongly ground joinable wrt.* $\longrightarrow_{R/A}$, *then* $\longrightarrow_{R/A}$ *is ground confluent.*

Note that the condition in the theorem implies that $\longrightarrow_{R/A}$ is strongly ground confluent. The proof of this implication is straightforward because there exist no variable overlaps in our approach. This is in contrast to the result in [Hu80], where linearity requirements are needed to treat variable overlaps.

We finish this section with some remarks about how to prove (strong) ground joinability of critical pairs.

Firstly, it may be convenient to propagate or solve the constraint part of a condition. This enables one to make more explicit the representation of the critical overlaps. Furthermore, checking the constraint part for satisfiability wrt. the base algebra may reveal a critical pair to be unfeasible.

Secondly, one can define — as in the syntactic case — a suitable notion of contextual rewriting. An even more general method can be designed along the lines of [Be93] leading to a prover for ground joinability.

The following considerations are to illustrate the remark about constraint based reasoning. First we continue the introductory example concerning the greatest common divisor. Note that $\longrightarrow_{R/N}$ is not terminating. For instance $g(1,0) \sim_N g(1+0,0)$ and thus $g(1,0) \longrightarrow_{R/N} g(1,0)$. Thus Theorem 5.1 is not applicable. In order to show ground confluence of $\longrightarrow_{R/N}$ we verify strong ground joinability of $CRIT(\mathcal{R})$. We treat the following three critical pairs only, the other cases can be done analogously.

$$
\begin{aligned}
(1,4) \quad & x = x', 0 = x' + y' & \Rightarrow \quad & x = g(x', y') \\
(3,3) \quad & x + y = x' + y', y = y' & \Rightarrow \quad & g(x,y) = g(x', y') \\
(3,4) \quad & x + y = x', y = x' + y' & \Rightarrow \quad & g(x,y) = g(x', y')
\end{aligned}
$$

The constraint part of $C_{(1,4)}$ has the solution representation $\sigma : \{x \mapsto 0, x' \mapsto 0, y' \mapsto 0\}$. Thus $C'_{(1,4)} : 0 = g(0,0)$. This equation is strongly ground joinable as $g(0,0) \longrightarrow_{R/N} 0$. The constraint part of $C_{(3,3)}$ has the solution representation $\sigma : \{x' \mapsto x, y' \mapsto y\}$. The propagated critical pair $C'_{(3,3)} : g(x,y) = g(x,y)$ is trivially strongly ground joinable. The constraint part of $C_{(3,4)}$ has the solution representation $\sigma : \{x \mapsto 0, y \mapsto x', y' \mapsto 0\}$. The propagated critical pair thus is $C'_{(3,4)} : g(0, x') = g(x', 0)$. Using the reduction steps $g(0, x') \longrightarrow_{R/N} x'$ and $g(x', 0) \longrightarrow_{R/N} x'$ we get the desired result in that case too. It thus follows that $\longrightarrow_{R/N}$ is ground confluent.

As a second example consider the following conditional equations (rules) that define division over the natural numbers (enriched with a standard boolean part).

$$
\begin{aligned}
(1) \quad & y > x = t & \Rightarrow \quad & div(x,y) & = \quad & 0 \\
(2) \quad & y > 0 = t & \Rightarrow \quad & div(x+y, y) & = \quad & div(x,y) + 1
\end{aligned}
$$

Now we only consider the critical pair

$$
(1,2) \quad x = x' + y', y = y', y > x = t, y' > 0 = t \Rightarrow 0 = div(x', y') + 1.
$$

Using a suitable constraint checker one may verify that the constraint part of the critical pair has no $\mathcal{N}$-solution. Thus $C_{(1,2)}$ is unfeasible. It follows that $\longrightarrow_{R/N}$ is ground confluent.

Acknowledgements: We would like to thank the referees for their helpful suggestions.

References

[AvBe92]   J. Avenhaus and K. Becker, Conditional rewriting modulo a built-in algebra, SEKI Report SR-92-11.

[AvMa90]   J. Avenhaus and K. Madlener, Term rewriting and equational reasoning, in: R. B. Banerji, ed., *Formal Techniques in Artificial Intelligence* (Amsterdam, 1990) pp. 1-43.

[BaDe89]   L. Bachmair and N. Dershowitz, Completion for rewriting modulo a congruence, *Theor. Comp. Science* 67 (1989) pp. 173-201.

[Be93]   K. Becker, Proving ground confluence and inductive validity in constructor based equational specifications, *TAPSOFT '93*, LNCS 668 (Berlin, 1993) pp. 46-60.

[BrWi83]   M. Broy and M. Wirsing, Generalized heterogenous algebras and partial interpretations, in: *Proc. 8th CAAP*, LNCS 159 (Berlin, 1983) pp. 1-34.

[BPW84]   M. Broy, C. Pair and M. Wirsing, A systematic study of models of abstract data types, *Theor. Comp. Science* 33 (1984) pp. 139-174.

[DeJo90]   N. Dershowitz and J. P. Jouannaud, Rewriting systems, in: J. van Leeuwen, ed., *Handbook of Theoretical Computer Science, Vol. B* (Amsterdam, 1990) pp. 241-320.

[DeOk90]   N. Dershowitz and M. Okada, A rationale for conditional equational rewriting, *Theoret. Comput. Science* 75(1/2) (1990) pp. 111-137.

[DMS92]   N. Dershowitz, S. Mitra and G. Sivakumar, Decidable matching for convergent systems, in: *CADE 11*, LNCS 607 (Berlin, 1992) pp. 589-602.

[Hu80]   G. Huet, Confluent reductions: abstract properties and applications to term rewriting systems, *J. of the ACM* 27 (1980) pp. 797-821.

[JaLa87]   J. Jaffar and J.-L. Lassez, Constraint logic programming, in *ACM Symp. on Principles of Progr. Languages '87* (1987) pp. 111-119.

[JoKi86]   J.-P. Jouannaud and H. Kirchner, Completion of a set of rules modulo a set of equations, *SIAM J. on Comp.* 15 (1986) pp. 1155-1194.

[KaCh89]   S. Kaplan and C. Choppy, Abstract rewriting with concrete operators, in: *3rd RTA '89*, LNCS 355, (Berlin, 1989) pp. 178-185.

[KaMu86]   D. Kapur and D.R. Musser, Inductive reasoning for incomplete specifications, in: *Proc. IEEE Symposium on LICS* (Cambridge MA, 1986) pp. 367-377.

[KKR90]   C. Kirchner, H. Kirchner and M. Rusinowitch, Deduction with symbolic constraints, *Revue d'Intelligence Artificielle* 4 (1990) pp. 9-52.

[SNGM89]   G. Smolka, W. Nutt, J.A. Goguen and J. Meseguer, Order-sorted equational computation, in: *CREAS* (San Diego, 1989) pp. 297-367.

[Vo89]   S.G. Vorobyov, Conditional rewrite rule systems with built-in arithmetic and induction, in: *3rd RTA '89*, LNCS 355, (Berlin, 1989) pp. 492-512.

[Wi90]   M. Wirsing, Algebraic specification, in: J. van Leeuwen, ed., *Handbook of Theoretical Computer Science, Vol. B* (Amsterdam, 1990) pp. 675-788.

[WiGr92]   C.-P. Wirth and B. Gramlich , A constructor-based approach for positive/negative conditional equational specifications, *CTRS 92*, LNCS 656 (Berlin, 1993) pp. 198-212.

Reactive variables for system specification and design

E. Pascal Gribomont[*]   Jacques Hagelstein

University of Liège, Belgium   Sema Group Belgium

Abstract. A reactive system takes action when some event (induced by the environment) occurs. It is not easy to transform informal requirements about such a system into formal specifications, nor to refine these specifications into a correct design. The notion of *reactive variable*, introduced in this paper, can make the specification-design process easier.

1 Introduction

Numerous languages have been proposed to represent formal specifications of programs and more general systems. (See for instance [4] for an overview.) Specification languages are often *declarative*, i.e. logic-based, to reach a sufficiently abstract level of description. However, the declarative style is not so well-adapted to the specification of reactive systems, since logical formulas have to specify not only what modifications are induced by some event occurrence, but also that many things are not affected by this occurrence; besides, it is not only necessary to specify that the causes induce the event, but also that the event does not happen when none of these causes occurs. In the operational, assignment-based style often used to write programs, there is no such problem. If the conditional assignment '*if C then x := a*' is executed, the fact that variable y is not modified is implicit; so is the fact that nothing happens if C is false. However, even if modelling a reactive system as a set of conditional assignments can be concise, it is also error-prone and lacks modularity; a change in the requirements usually induces several changes in the operational code. The language introduced in this paper has both operational and declarative features, leads to more modular code and easier consistency verification.

1.1 Transparent variables

The notion of *transparent variable* has been proposed for the design of concurrent systems; we first briefly recall the basics of the language UNITY used in [3]. As a toy example, here is a simple program, computing the integer square root of a natural number n.

> **declare** x, y : integer
>
> **initially** $x = 0 \ \wedge \ y = 0$
>
> **assign** $\langle$ IF $y + 2x + 1 \leq n \ \longrightarrow \ (x, y) := (x + 1, y + 2x + 1)$
>
> $[\!] \ y + 2x + 1 > n \ \longrightarrow \ $ skip FI $\rangle$

A computation of a UNITY program is obtained by repeatedly executing an arbitrary statement of the **assign** section; in this program, there is only one

---

[*] Partially supported by FNRS (National Fund for Scientific Research, Belgium) under grant number 84536.94.

statement.[1] The formula $(y = x^2) \wedge (x^2 \leq n)$ is an invariant of the program. When $y+2x+1 > n$ holds, the subsequent steps do not change the state any more and the formula $x^2 \leq n < (x+1)^2$ holds. We observe that $y+2x+1$ is computed twice in the statement; it is therefore convenient to name this expression by introducing a *transparent variable* $z = y + 2x + 1$. Here is the revised version of the example.

> **declare** x, y : (ordinary) integer; z : transparent integer
> **initially** $x = 0 \wedge y = 0$
> **always** $z = y + 2x + 1$
> **assign** $\langle$ IF $z \leq n \longrightarrow (x,y) := (x+1,z)$ ▯ $z > n \longrightarrow$ skip FI $\rangle$

The behaviour of a transparent variable z is specified by an equation $z = f(x,y)$ where x and y are ordinary variables or previously introduced transparent variables. Every time the value of (x,y) is modified, the value of z is updated in order to satisfy again its definition. The transparent variable z makes the program slightly more efficient, since z is evaluated only when x, y are modified (once per iteration, whereas it is used twice). However, we intend to use (generalized) transparent variables not for programming but for specification; in this framework, efficiency is less important than clarity and simplicity; this could lead us to transform y into a transparent variable, since it functionally depends on the variable x. We obtain the following program.

> **declare** x : integer; y, z : transparent integer; $y \prec z$
> **initially** $x = 0$
> **always** $y = x^2 \wedge z = y + 2x + 1$
> **assign** $\langle$ IF $z \leq n \longrightarrow x := x + 1$ ▯ $z > n \longrightarrow$ skip FI $\rangle$

The notation $y \prec z$ (read "y precedes z") means that y is updated before z. Every iteration is therefore a three-step cycle: the statement is executed,[2] y is updated, and then z is updated. Transparent variables are simply names for expressions so this notion is little more than an abbreviation mechanism; nevertheless several examples given in [3] demonstrate the usefulness of this concept for the design of concurrent programs.

1.2 Transparent variables for specification ?

Transparent variables cannot be used as such to represent the reactions of a system to events induced by the environment, since these reactions usually are nondeterministic. We propose in the sequel a nondeterministic variant of the transparent variable, namely the *reactive variable*, that leads to an appropriate language for the specification of reactive systems.

---

[1] In [3], statements are (multiple, conditional) assignments but, in this context, every failure-free, always-terminating program can be viewed as a statement; nondeterministic statements and specification assignments are allowed. Angle brackets can be used to delimit programs viewed as statements. See [9] for more details about generalized assignments used in specifications.

[2] Only ordinary variables can be modified by a statement.

The language RSS (Reactive System Specification) is presented in Section 2, with a formal semantics. The consistency problem and the verification problem are addressed in Section 3 and examples are considered in Section 4. Comparison with related work and conclusions are in the last section.

2 The specification language

2.1 Structure of an RSS text

A specification in RSS is structured like a UNITY program and contains four parts.

The **declare** section of an RSS text enumerates the disjoint lists A and R of typed *active* and *reactive* variables, and describes the acyclic precedence relation $\prec$ on R, as a set ρ of couples (the partial order $\prec$ is the reflexive transitive closure of ρ). The **initially** section is an assertion that specifies which values are acceptable as initial values of the active variables. No initial condition is given for reactive variables, that are bound to verify their defining assertions (see below) in every state, including the initial one. The **action** section is a set of failure-free, always-terminating statements. Only active variables are modified by them, but statements may refer to active and reactive variables. The **reaction** section is a set of couples $u : E$, where u is a reactive variable and E is an assertion that may contain active variables, variable u, and any reactive variable v such that $v \prec u$.
Comment. A reactive variable u reduces to a transparent variable when its only defining assertion E is an equation $u = e$, where u does not occur in e.

A *state* is a function that maps each variable of $A \cup R$ on a value of the appropriate type; the set of states is Σ; the type of a variable x is $type(x)$. If $\sigma \in \Sigma$ and $x \in V$, then $x_\sigma \in type(x)$ denotes the value of x for state σ. A *computation*, or a *model*, is an infinite sequence of states.

We view a reactive system interacting with its environment as a computation generator,[3] so a specification of such an interacting pair is interpreted as a set of (acceptable) computations.

2.2 Operational semantics of RSS

Let $\mathcal{S}$ be an RSS-specification where the list of active variables is denoted by $A = \mathbf{x}$ and the reactive ones by $R = \mathbf{u}$. The list $\mathbf{u} = (u_1, \ldots, u_n)$ is such that $u_i \prec u_j$ can occur only for $i < j$ (this is always possible : every partial order can be extended into a total order). Each u_i is defined in the reaction-section by a single[4] assertion E_i which may refer to another u_k only if $u_k \prec u_i$.

The operational semantics of an RSS specification $\mathcal{S}$ is a rule that determines whether some sequence of states is a computation, i.e. a model of S. This rule is :[5]

A sequence $(\sigma_i : i \in \mathbf{N})$ is a model for the specification $\mathcal{S}$ if σ_0 satisfies the initially-section and the reaction-section, and if the following conditions hold for

---

[3] An RSS specification is not necessarily executable, but we often refer to a model of the specification, that is, an acceptable sequence of states, as a computation.

[4] This is not a real restriction; $x : E_1$ and $x : E_2$ can be replaced by $x : E_1 \wedge E_2$.

[5] This rule depends on the partial order $\prec$, but not on the total extension used only for exposition purpose.

any two successive states $\sigma_i = \sigma$ and $\sigma_{i+1} = \sigma'$:

- There is a state $\rho_0 \in \Sigma$ and a statement $S \in \textbf{action}$ such that S leads from σ to ρ_0; notice that ρ_0 can differ from σ in the active variables only.
- There is a sequence of states $\rho_1, \ldots, \rho_n$, where $\rho_n = \sigma'$, such that
  - ρ_j ($j > 0$) differs from ρ_{j-1} at most in the value assigned to u_j;
  - if the assertion E_j evaluates to *true* in state ρ_{j-1}, then $\rho_j = \rho_{j-1}$, else $(u_j)_{\rho_j}$ is any value such that E_j is true at state ρ_j.

To distinguish σ and σ' from the states ρ_i which do not belong to the model of the specification, we call the former *observable* states and the latter *transient* states. State σ' is an *observable successor* of state σ, whereas ρ_j is a *transient successor* of state ρ_{j-1}.

Note that ρ_j satisfies E_k for all $k \leq j$. As a result $\rho_n = \sigma'$ satisfies the whole reaction-section. This has a very important consequence: the assertions in the reaction-section hold in any observable state, and may be used for deducing additional properties. The reaction-section can be viewed as declarative semantics for the reactive variables.[6] Also observe that modifications of reactive variables are *minimized*: a change is allowed (and enforced) for a reactive variable u only when it is needed, that is, when a defining assertion of u has been falsified.[7]

The semantics of a specification determines the set of its models and contains only infinite sequences of states. However, if the specification is seen as a highly non-deterministic program and "executed" blindly, it might well be blocked in some transient state where a reactive variable cannot be consistently changed to restore its defining assertion(s). As we are not interested in specifying systems ending in blocked states, the semantics do not include such finite sequences, and this kind of "inconsistent" specification is viewed as incorrect (see Section 3).

2.3 Two additional features

In order to specify reactive systems more comfortably, two features are introduced: events and the temporal operator '•'.

Events are found in many specification languages, simply because early and informal specifications are often sentences of the form: "when this event occurs, then this reaction should take place". The notion of event can be simulated by means of variables, but it is neater to just include it in the language. In RSS, an event ev is modelled by a special kind of active boolean variable, possibly with parameters. It can only be explicitly set to true by the special statement 'ev!' (event occurrence). It is implicitly reset to false by any other statement (including other event occurrences), so that it holds in just one state. Finally, it is necessarily false in the initial state. Event occurrences are statements, so only one event can occur at a time; besides, an event cannot occur while an ordinary statement is executed. The semantics of RSS is affected in four ways by the introduction of events. First, the declaration of an event ev extends the state by the boolean variable ev. Second, the only statement allowed to explicitly modify

---

[6] The reaction-section retains the main part of the role of the always-section in unity.

[7] Declarative temporal specification languages have no minimization mechanism, and this results in longer and less modular specification; examples will be given in the sequel.

this variable is 'ev!', interpreted as '$ev := \mathrm{true}$'. Thirdly, the interpretation of all statements is extended by setting to false all events (except the one, if any, that the statement explicitly sets to true). Finally, all events are false in the initial state. Let us emphasize that events are no more than syntactic sugaring; they can be eliminated in a straightforward mechanic way.

The second feature is the use of the temporal operator '•', which may prefix any term or assertion. The use of such operators is naturally suggested by the fact that RSS specifications admit sequences of states as models. The evaluation of '•α' in a given state is equivalent to the one of α in the previous *observable* state. In particular, '•α' in one of the transient states leading from observable state σ to observable state σ' is evaluated like α in σ. To interpret '•' in the first state, we assume that the sequence of states is extended to the left (past) by an infinite repetition of the first state.

The operator • is useful in the reaction section. If for instance u and v are reactive variables with $u \prec v$, an assertion defining u cannot evoke v, but can evoke •v, and also •u. Once again, this feature is little more than syntactic sugaring. The use of • can be avoided if each variable x (active or reactive) is "doubled" with another variable that records the value of •x. Otherwise stated, •x can be viewed as an additional variable, whose value is updated every time the value of x is updated. With this point of view (adopted in the sequel of this paper), defining assertions appear as formulas of classical logic.

With notation introduced in paragraph 2.2, we have $(•x)_{\sigma'} = (•x)_{\rho_j} = x_\sigma$, where x is any (active or reactive) variable, for all $j = 0, \ldots, n$.

2.4 A toy example

The following example demonstrates both events and temporal operators. The device we consider can be toggled by pressing a button, but can also be broken:

declare   toggle, break: event; device: reactive {on, off, broken}
action   toggle!
              break!
reaction device: toggle ⇒ device = reverse(•device)
              break ⇒ device = broken

The function 'reverse' swaps 'on' and 'off' and maps 'broken' to itself.

Checking consistency is trivial here. In any observable state, except the initial one, either 'toggle' or 'break' (but not both) holds. If it is 'toggle', the identity 'device = reverse(•device)' must hold; there is no problem since 'reverse' is a total function. Otherwise, the value of 'device' is 'broken'. In the initial state, the antecedents of both defining assertions are false.

The equivalent specification using the classical temporal logic interpretation of assertions without minimisation, would explicitly state that 'device' does not change in absence of events:

toggle ⇒ device = reverse(•device)
break ⇒ device = broken
(¬ toggle ∧ ¬ break) ⇒ device = •device

The absence of minimization in classical specification languages based on temporal logic prevents modularity in specification design. Indeed, if a third event 'new' is introduced that may alter 'device', it is not sufficient to add an assertion describing the effect of this new event; the last assertion has to be rewritten as

$$(\neg \text{ toggle} \wedge \neg \text{ break} \wedge \neg \text{ new}) \Rightarrow \text{device} = \bullet\text{device}$$

3   Consistency and correctness

Formal specifications cannot be proved correct since the requirements they have to satisfy are usually expressed in an informal way. However, specifications ought to be checked for consistency, that is, for model existence. Besides, when an RSS text S is transformed, the new version S' should be a refinement of the old one (the set of S-models has to be included in the set of S'-models), or at least preserve some user-specified properties. These problems will be briefly addressed in this section.

3.1   Consistency

The consistency of a program, that is, the existence of a legal computation, is usually a trivial problem. This is the case for UNITY programs, even when transparent variables are used (one has to check that the right member of every defining equation is always defined). On the contrary, this is not true for specifications, and the experience shows that it is too easy to write inconsistent specifications. Besides, in the framework of reactive systems, proving the existence of a model is not sufficient, and consistency means here that any reachable observable state has an observable successor.

LTL (linear temporal logic) has often been proposed as an adequate language for reactive system specification. A non trivial example is given in [2]. A specification is simply a set of formulas. The consistency problem for full propositional linear temporal logic is known to be solvable, but of P-space complexity. A more serious drawback in practice is that, when inconsistency is detected, there is no systematic way to discover which part of the specification has to be modified. The problem is, specifications in LTL are global, even if the set of formulas is informally divided into subsets, to make the presentation easier.

The consistency problem, and especially the elimination of detected inconsistencies, is easier for RSS specifications. Here is now the (rather elementary) theoretical result. The notation introduced in paragraph 2.2 is used, with an additional convention: for all $j = 1, \ldots, n$, if $\mathbf{v}$ is $(v_1, \ldots, v_n)$, then $\mathbf{v}_{i..j}$ denotes $(v_i, \ldots, v_j)$.

Theorem. The specification S is consistent if for all states σ and ρ_0 such that σ satisfies the reaction section and such that there is a statement in the action section leading from σ to ρ_0, the following formula holds for all $j = 1, \ldots, n$, and for all $a_1, \ldots, a_{j-1}$ such that $a_k \in type(u_k)$:

$$
\begin{aligned}
(\bullet\mathbf{x} = \mathbf{x}_\sigma \wedge \mathbf{x} = \mathbf{x}_{\rho_0} \wedge \bullet\mathbf{u} = \mathbf{u}_\sigma \wedge \mathbf{u}_{1..j-1} = \mathbf{a}_{1..j-1} \wedge u_j = (u_j)_\sigma \\
\wedge E_{u_1} \wedge \cdots \wedge E_{u_{j-1}} \wedge \neg E_{u_j}) \\
\Rightarrow \\
\exists a_j \, (\bullet\mathbf{x} = \mathbf{x}_\sigma \wedge \mathbf{x} = \mathbf{x}_{\rho_0} \wedge \bullet\mathbf{u} = \mathbf{u}_\sigma \wedge \mathbf{u}_{1..j} = \mathbf{a}_{1..j} \wedge E_{u_j})
\end{aligned}
\tag{1}
$$

Proof. Consistency means that every observable state σ has some observable successor σ'. In paragraph 2.2 we have expressed how σ' can be obtained from σ. First, the execution of an arbitrary statement of the action section leads from σ to an auxiliary, transient state ρ_0. Then, the reactive variables $u_1, \ldots, u_n$ are updated (if needed) in sequence; these updates generate a sequence of transient states $\rho_1, \ldots, \rho_{n-1}$, ending in the next observable state $\rho_n = \sigma'$. So consistency means that the sequence $(\rho_0, \rho_1, \ldots, \rho_n)$ always exists. As we have required that statements never fail and always terminate ($\S$ 1.1), the existence of ρ_0 is trivial. Now we suppose that ρ_{j-1} is given and use formula (1) to deduce that ρ_j exists. We choose $a_k = (u_k)_{\rho_{j-1}}$ for all $k = 1, \ldots, j-1$. All terms of the antecedent of formula (1) are true at state ρ_{j-1}, except maybe the last one. If E_{u_j} holds at state ρ_{j-1}, then ρ_j is simply ρ_{j-1}. Otherwise, the antecedent is true and so should be the consequent. If a_j is an appropriate value, then ρ_j is the same state as ρ_{j-1}, except that the value of u_j is now a_j.

Comments.
The condition expressed by formula (1) is sufficient, but not necessary.
The theorem is expressed here for finite-state systems; otherwise, if Φ is formula (1), it has to be replaced by $(\forall a_1 \in type(u_1)) \ldots (\forall a_{j-1} \in type(u_{j-1})) \Phi$.
It was mentioned in paragraph 2.3 that the use of the symbol $\bullet$ does not prevent defining assertions, and also formula (1), from being formulas of classical logic. As a result, the notion of reactive variable allows us to stay within classical logic instead of temporal logic. If all (active and reactive) variables are of finite type (Σ is finite), the complexity of the consistency problem is reduced from P-space to NP. Another advantage is that RSS specifications are structured. In case of inconsistency, one can detect which reactive variable is "immediately responsible" for it; it is u_j, if j is the least value for which formula (1) can be false.

3.2 Correctness

If requirements are expressed in a formal way (say in LTL), correctness of an RSS specification w.r.t. the requirements can be proved in the same way as program correctness. Indeed, RSS specifications are computation (model) generators, just as programs. The only difference is nondeterminism but that does not prevent the use of Hoare's logic [1].

4 Examples

In this section, we illustrate the use of RSS on two examples. The first one is elementary, the second one, although rather short, shows that care and formality are needed in specification, and how RSS can make specification design easier.

4.1 Television control

The sound volume of a television set can be changed by pressing the VoluUp and VoluDown buttons. The volume is initialised to a predefined value v_0 when the television is switched on. Whenever the volume changes, the new value is displayed on top of the screen. This display is removed by pressing the OsdOff (on screen display off) button.

Although rather simple, this example is sufficient to illustrate some useful features of RSS. On the one hand, some effects like Osd disappearance may have several causes, namely hitting OsdOff or switching off. On the other hand, some causes like pressing VoluUp start a chain of effects, namely raising the volume, thereby causing the display of the new value.

Before starting the specification, we note that the informal text contains ambiguities, and even errors, if interpreted literally. For instance, it is not strictly correct that *whenever the volume changes, the new value is displayed on top of the screen*. This is certainly not true when the volume changes because the television is switched off. Similarly, despite what is stated, the buttons VoluUp, VoluDown, and OsdOff certainly have effect only if the television is on. Also, the volume must have some minimum and maximum values for which VoluDown and VoluUp respectively have no effect.

The first step in handling this example in RSS is the identification of appropriate state components. The inputs of the television, i.e. the variables whose change is outside of its control, are the users actions of switching on and off, changing volume, and cancelling the Osd. We model them by active variables. The outputs are the variables controlled by the television. The sound volume is modelled by a variable 'Volu' of type 'Vol'. This type is the range of integers between 0 and 'max', with two functions 'sub1' and 'add1' which are the obvious ones, except that $sub1(0) = 0$ and $add1(max) = max$. The on screen display is modelled by the variable 'Osd' which may take Vol-values and a distinguished value 'none' for when there is no display:

> **declare** VoluUp, VoluDown, OsdOff : active event;
> on : active boolean;
> Volu : reactive Vol; Osd : reactive Vol $\cup$ { none };
> Volu $\prec$ Osd

The ordering of reactive variables reflects their dependencies. In this case, changes of 'Osd' may result from changes of 'Volu', but the opposite never occurs.

We now turn to the definition of the acceptable initial states of the system:

> **initially** $\neg$ on

The action-section formalizes the user-induced changes:

> **action** on := $\neg$ on
> VoluUp!
> VoluDown!
> OsdOff!

The assertions in the reaction-section describe the input/output dependencies that the television is supposed to maintain. They may be specified as follows:

> **reaction** Volu : (on $\wedge$ VoluUp) $\Rightarrow$ Volu = add1($\bullet$Volu)
> (on $\wedge$ VoluDown) $\Rightarrow$ Volu = sub1($\bullet$Volu)
> (on $\wedge$ $\bullet\neg$ on) $\Rightarrow$ Volu = v_0
> $\neg$ on $\Rightarrow$ Volu = 0
> Osd : $\neg$ on $\Rightarrow$ Osd = none
> (on $\wedge$ Volu $\neq$ $\bullet$Volu) $\Rightarrow$ Osd = Volu
> OsdOff $\Rightarrow$ Osd = none

To illustrate how the operational semantics specifies successive states, consider the situation where we have 'on $\wedge$ Volu $= 5 \wedge$ Osd $=$ none', and the event VoluDown occurs. We consider the first reactive variable 'Volu' and notice that its second defining assertion is false. The only change of 'Volu' restoring its assertions is to set it to 4. The variable 'Osd' is considered next. Its second assertion is violated and can only be restored by setting 'Osd' to 4. After these reactions, the next observable state satisfies 'on $\wedge$ Volu $= 4 \wedge$ Osd $= 4$'.

As soon as the precedence relation between reactive variables is not empty, consistency can be checked in a modular way. Two steps are needed here, one for 'Volu' and one for 'Osd'. Both are trivial here. For 'Volu', there are four assertions but exactly one antecedent holds in any observable state, so adaptation is always possible. For 'Osd', the antecedent of the second assertion is incompatible with the antecedent of both other assertions, so the update is always possible: the new value of 'Osd' is either 'none' or 'Volu'.

4.2 Telephone network

We consider now a more substantial problem, first proposed in [8].

Consider a very simple telephone network in which connections may be established between pairs of telephones. A request may be made for the connection of a given phone to any other. If the request cannot be satisfied immediately (because the other is engaged), it will be stored by the network and satisfied if possible at some later time.

We assume a type 'phone' and define two predicates (boolean arrays) applicable to pairs of phones: 'engaged' and 'request'. The former, which is symmetric, holds between two connected phones. The latter is dissymmetric: 'request[p_1,p_2]' holds if p_1 requests a connection with p_2. To ease the specification, we add an auxiliary predicate 'free' applicable to phones. A phone is free if it is not engaged and is not requesting another phone. Note that arrays are simply sets of variables with the same precedence, whose behaviour exhibit symmetry, that are considered together only for simplifying the notation; a declaration like 'engaged $\prec$ free' will stand for 'engaged[p_1,p_2] $\prec$ free[p]', for all p, p_1, p_2.

The predicate 'request' is active, as users create requests (by dialling) and destroy them (by hanging up) outside of the control of the network. The reactive variables are 'engaged' and 'free'; their variations are determined by those of the active predicate 'request' and by the assertions in the reaction-section.

The initial state of the system is supposed to be one where there is no request. The possible actions are (1) requesting a connection, and (2) cancelling this request by hanging up. These actions are conditional: a phone may create a request only if it is free; it can request only phones other than itself; it may cancel a request only if there is one.

A simple specification is as follows:

declare   request: active array [phone,phone] of boolean
                 engaged: reactive array [phone,phone] of boolean
                 free: reactive array [phone] of boolean
                 engaged $\prec$ free

initially $\neg$ request[p_1,p_2]

action   free[p] $\wedge$ p $\neq$ p_1 $\rightarrow$ request[p,p_1] := true

request[p_1,p_2] $\rightarrow$ request[p_1,p_2] := false

reaction engaged: engaged[p_1,p_2] $\Rightarrow$ (request[p_1,p_2] $\vee$ request[p_2,p_1])

engaged[p_1,p_2] $\Rightarrow$ engaged[p_2,p_1]

(engaged[p_1,p_2] $\wedge$ engaged[p_1,p_3]) $\Rightarrow$ $p_2 = p_3$

(request[p_1,p_2] $\wedge$ $\bullet$ free[p_2]) $\Rightarrow$ engaged[p_1,p_2]

free: free[p] $\equiv$ $\forall$ p_1 ($\neg$ request[p,p_1] $\wedge$ $\neg$ engaged[p,p_1])

Comment. There is an implicit universal quantification for all statements.

The first three assertions defining 'engaged' formalize the *safety* properties of the network; the last assertion above 'engaged' enforces phone engagement.

Consistency is checked in a modular way. Let us consider first the case of the reactive variable 'engaged'. An inconsistency is detected, due to the fourth assertion: if both p_1 and p_3 request communication with p_2 when p_2 becomes free, at most one of them will become engaged. So the assertion is weakened into

reaction engaged: ($\exists p_1$ request[p_1,p_2] $\wedge$ $\bullet$ free[p_2]) $\Rightarrow$ $\exists p_1$ engaged[p_1,p_2]

Observe that this assertion now simply says "p_2 becomes engaged again". It does say neither that it is engaged only once, nor that the engagement is with a requesting station. These relevant additional pieces of information are deduced from other assertions. It can be verified that this weakening restores consistency.

This example illustrates some benefits the usage of RSS brings about:
− The **reaction** part provides a declarative specification, without the formulas normally needed to circumvent the "no cause, no effect" problem.
− The subdivision between the action-section and the reaction-section allows to distinguish 'input events', which may not be forced to happen, from 'outputs', which are forced reactions. This useful separation is not explicit in purely declarative approaches.
− Auxiliary predicates have a standard handling which requires no invention.
− Assertions in the reaction-section can be violated only in transient states; they are safely assumed in writing initial conditions and guards of *actions*.

Notice that the detection of inconsistencies like the aforementioned one is not evident (otherwise, requirement and specification engineering would be a simple matter!). However, a formalism like RSS should make easier the detection and even the prevention of inconsistencies; the behaviour of the system in particular and not intuitive situations can be formally determined. For instance, 'request[p_1,p_2] := false' can be executed if 'engaged[p_1,p_2]' and 'request[p_2,p_1]' are true; 'engaged[p_1,p_2]' and 'engaged[p_2,p_1]' remain true in this case. This corresponds to the exchange of the roles of the caller and the callee.

Comment. The fact that the reaction-section can be interpreted as an invariant of the system is very helpful, but this invariant is concerned only with the behaviour of reactive variables. Just as for programming, it is recommended that the designer specifies and proves additional properties of the system, about active variables; one can add for instance the following "documentation" section:

invariant (request[p_1,p_2] $\wedge$ request[p_1,p_3]) $\Rightarrow$ $p_2 = p_3$

$\bullet$ (request[p_1,p_2] $\wedge$ free[p_2]) $\Rightarrow$ $\neg$ (request[p_1,p_2] $\wedge$ free[p_2])

The first property specifies that a phone p_1 can call only one other phone at a time. The second property asserts that a phone that gets free while another is calling for it would become engaged again at the next step.

5   Comparison and conclusion

This section investigates the advantages of the specification of the television control in RSS over two classical specifications: a purely operational one, and a purely declarative one.

The essence of an operational approach is to describe state changes by means of statements, with the hypothesis that unassigned variables are left unchanged. Each input event somehow triggers a routine modifying the reactive variables. For example, the program triggered by 'VoluUp' may be written as follows:

> **if** on **then** old_Volu := Volu
> Volu := add1(Volu)
> **if** Volu $\neq$ old_Volu **then** Osd := Volu

The use of 'old_Volu' could have been avoided by checking whether 'Volu' had the value 'max' before attempting to increase it and display the new value, but this would have been less clear.

A first difference between the operational and declarative approach is that this program must consider all possible consequences of VoluUp, be they direct (the change of volume) or indirect (the on screen display). In comparison, the RSS approach identifies chains of consequences and cuts them into separate assertions: one saying that VoluUp causes a volume change; another to say that a volume change causes a display.

The weaker separation of concerns in the operational approach not only reduces the clarity, but also leads to longer specifications. The assertion about Osd change is only given once in RSS, whereas in the operational specification, the corresponding assignment must be written three times: in the programs triggered by VoluUp, VoluDown, and the change of 'on'. This redundancy also makes the specification difficult to maintain and update. If the display of the volume is suppressed, or replaced by some other form of feedback, the operational specification must be changed in three places, instead of one for RSS. These drawbacks are of course amplified when the size of the specification grows.

Besides, the operational style suffers from its inherent inability to directly state crucial properties like 'there is no Osd when the television is off'. Such properties can only be deduced from a careful analysis of the specification.

On the other hand, a purely declarative specification written in first order logic contains the same statements as the RSS reaction-section, plus those required to explicitly circumvent the "frame problem" (no effect without a cause). These statements are:

$$(\neg \text{ VoluUp} \wedge \neg \text{ VoluDown} \wedge \text{on} \wedge \bullet \text{on}) \Rightarrow \text{Volu} = \bullet \text{Volu} ,$$
$$(\neg \text{ OsdOff} \wedge \text{Volu} = \bullet \text{Volu} \wedge \text{on}) \Rightarrow \text{Osd} = \bullet \text{Osd} .$$

Each is devoted to a specific reactive variable, and states that it may not change outside of the conditions known to require a change.

The possibility given by RSS to omit these statements has several benefits. Of course, it exempts the user from finding these assertions, which is often not too easy. It also reduces the total size of the specification, which is always a win. Finally, it improves the incrementality of the specification, i.e. its ability to be easily changed. Suppose indeed that we add an input event 'mute', which resets the volume to 0. In RSS, this would only amount to add the following reaction:

Volu : (on $\wedge$ mute) $\Rightarrow$ Volu = 0

In the first-order logic approach, the mere adjunction of this statement leads to an inconsistent specification. Indeed, it is contradictory with the first frame assertion above, that has to be replaced by:

$(\neg$ VoluUp $\wedge \neg$ VoluDown $\wedge$ on $\wedge$ $\bullet$on $\wedge \neg$ mute $) \Rightarrow$ Volu = $\bullet$Volu

This makes any change rather difficult, especially if the specification is large.

A declarative (logic-based) specification has advantages over an operational (assignment-based) one, in terms of modularity and expressiveness. The former suffers, however, from a drawback sometimes called the *frame problem* (by analogy with a similar problem occurring in AI), i.e. the need to explicitly state what may not change in addition to saying what must change. In both styles, formal specifications tend to be lengthy.

In an attempt to free the declarative style from the frame problem, we found that the programming language UNITY is an appropriate starting point, as it already combines an operational component with a declarative one. The strengthening of the latter has led to a new language called RSS, which we presented and applied to simple, but revealing case studies; the gain in clarity and concision is important when the specified system has a strong concurrent and/or non-deterministic flavour; besides, checking consistency becomes easier.

References

1. K.R. Apt, "Ten years of Hoare logic, part II: Nondeterminism", *Theoret. Comput. Sci.* **28** (1984) 83-109.
2. H. Barringer, "Up and Down The Temporal Way", *The Computer Journal*, **10**, pp. 134-148.
3. K.M. Chandy and J. Misra, "Parallel Program Design: a Foundation", Addison-Wesley, 1988.
4. N. Gehany and A.D. McGettrick (Eds.), "Software Specification Techniques", Addison-Wesley, 1986.
5. P. Gribomont, "Stepwise refinement and concurrency: the finite-state case", *Science of Computer Programming*, **14**, pp. 185-228, 1990.
6. P. Gribomont, "A programming logic for formal concurrent systems", *CONCUR 90 (Amsterdam), Lect. Notes in Comput. Science*, **458**, pp. 298-313, Springer, 1990.
7. M. Minsky, "A Framework for Representing Knowledge" MIT, Artificial Intelligence Memo 306, 1974.
8. C. Morgan, "Telephone Network" *in* I. Hayes, "Specification Case Studies", Prentice Hall International, Englewood Cliff, 1987, pp. 73-87.
9. C. Morgan, "The Specification Statement", *ACM Trans. on Progr. Lang. Syst.* **10** (1988) 403-419

Complexity: NC Hierarchy

A New Parallel Vector Model, with Exact Characterization of NC^k

Kenneth W. Regan*

State University of New York at Buffalo

Abstract

This paper develops a new and natural parallel vector model, and shows that for all $k \geq 1$, the languages recognizable in $O(\log^k n)$ time and polynomial work in the model are exactly those in NC^k. Some improvements to other simulations in parallel models and reversal complexity are given.

1. Introduction

This paper studies a model of computation called the *Block Move* (BM) model, which makes two important changes to the Pratt-Stockmeyer vector machine (VM). It augments the VM by providing bit-wise *shuffle* in one step, but restricts the *shifts* allowed to the VM. Computation by a BM is a sequence of "block moves," which are finite transductions on parts of the memory. Each individual finite transduction belongs to uniform NC^1 and is computable in at most logarithmic time on the common parallel machine models. Hence counting the number of block moves is a reasonable measure of parallel time. It is also natural to study restrictions on the kinds of finite transducers S a BM can use. We write BM(gh) for the model in which every S must be a *generalized homomorphism* (gh), and BM(ap) for the restriction to S such that the monoid of transformations of S is *aperiodic*. Every gh is an NC^0 function, and Chandra, Fortune, and Lipton [6] showed that every aperiodic transduction belongs to AC^0. The object is to augment the the rich theory of classes within NC^1 and algebraic properties of automata which has been developed by Barrington and others [2, 5, 4, 15, 3].

Karp and Ramachandran [14] write EREW^k, CREW^k, CRCW^k, and VM^k for $O(\log^k n)$ time and polynomial work on the three common forms of PRAM and the VM, respectively, and cite the following results:

- For all $k \geq 1$, $\mathrm{NC}^k \subseteq \mathrm{EREW}^k \subseteq \mathrm{CREW}^k \subseteq \mathrm{CRCW}^k = \mathrm{AC}^k$ [23].
- For all $k \geq 2$, $\mathrm{NC}^k \subseteq \mathrm{VM}^k \subseteq \mathrm{AC}^k$ [24].

Now write BM^k, $\mathrm{BM}^k(\mathrm{gh})$, and $\mathrm{BM}^k(\mathrm{ap})$ for $O(\log^k n)$ time and polynomial work on the BM forms above. The main result of this paper is:

- For all $k \geq 1$, $\mathrm{NC}^k = \mathrm{BM}^k(\mathrm{gh})$.

We also observe that $\mathrm{BM}^k \subseteq \mathrm{NC}^{k+1}$ and $\mathrm{BM}^k(\mathrm{ap}) \subseteq \mathrm{AC}^k$. The main theorem is noteworthy for being an exact characterization by a simple machine without using alternation. From its proof we derive several technical improvements to results on Turing machine reversal complexity, with reference to [7] and [16]. Sections 2-4 define the model and give fairly full sketch proofs of the main results, and Section 5 gives other results and open problems.

*The author was supported in part by NSF Research Initiation Award CCR-9011248
Author's current address: Computer Science Department, 226 Bell Hall, UB North Campus, Buffalo, NY 14260-2000. Email: *regan@cs.buffalo.edu*, tel.: (716) 645-3189, fax: (716) 645-3464.

2. The BM Vector Model

The model of finite transducer we use is the *deterministic generalized sequential machine* (DGSM), as formalized in [12] (see also [9]). A DGSM S is like a Mealy machine, but with the ability to output not just one but zero, two, three, or more symbols in any one transition. A special case is when a finite function $h : \Sigma^d \to \Gamma^e$ $(d, e > 0)$ is extended to a function $h_* : \Sigma^* \to \Gamma^*$ as follows: (1) for all $x \in \Sigma^*$ with $|x| < d$, $h_*(x) = \lambda$ (the empty string), and (2) for all $x \in \Sigma^*$ and $w \in \Sigma^d$, $h_*(wx) = h(w)h_*(x)$. Then h_* is called a *generalized homomorphism* (gh) with *ratio* $d : e$. Three important examples with $\Sigma = \Gamma = \{0, 1\}$ are $A(x)$, which takes the AND of each successive pair of bits and thus is 2:1, $O(x)$ similarly for OR, and bit-wise negation $N(x)$, which is 1:1. Another is *dilation* $D(x)$, which doubles each bit of x and is 1:2; e.g., $D(101) = 110011$.

The BM model has a single tape, and an alphabet Γ in which the blank B and endmarker \$ play special roles. A BM M has four "pointers" labeled a_1, b_1, a_2, b_2, and some number $m \geq 4$ of "pointer markers." The finite control of M consists of "DGSM states" $S_1, \ldots S_r$ and finitely many "move states." Initially, the input x is left-justified in cells $0 \ldots n-1$ of the tape with \$ in cell n and all other cells blank, one pointer marker with b_1 and b_2 assigned to it is in cell n, and cell 0 holds all other pointer markers with a_1 and a_2 assigned there. The *initial pass* is by S_1. The computation is a sequence of passes, and if and when M halts, the content of the tape up to the first \$ gives the output $M(x)$. In a move state, each pointer marker on some cell a of the tape may be moved to cell $\lfloor a/2 \rfloor$, $2a$, or $2a + 1$ or left where it is. Then the four pointers are redistributed among the m markers, and control branches according to the symbol in the cell now occupied by pointer a_1. Each move state adds 1 to both the *work* $w(x)$ and the *pass count* $R(x)$ of the computation. A GSM state S executes the *block move*

$$S[a_1 \ldots b_1] \; into \; [a_2 \ldots b_2]$$

defined as follows: Let z be the string held in locations $[a_1 \ldots b_1]$—if $b_1 < a_1$, then z is read right-to-left on the tape. Then $S(z)$ is written into locations $[a_2 \ldots b_2]$, overwriting any previous content, *except* that any blank B appearing in $S(z)$ leaves the symbol in its target cell unchanged. Control passes to a unique move state. We may also suppose wlog. that each move state sends control to some DGSM state. If $a_1 \leq b_1$ and $a_2 \leq b_2$, the pass is called *left-to-right*. It falls out of our main theorem that left-to-right passes alone suffice for all NC^1 computations, extending the known observation that strings can be reversed in $O(\log n)$ vector operations (see [11]).

The work in the move is defined to be $|z|$, i.e. $|b_1 - a_1| + 1$. The *validity condition* is that the intervals $[a_1 \ldots b_1]$ and $[a_2 \ldots b_2]$ must be disjoint, and the *strict boundary condition* is that the output must exactly fill the target interval; i.e., that $|S(z)| = |b_2 - a_2| + 1$. The former can always be met at constant-factor slowdown by buffering outputs to an unused portion at the right end of the tape, and so we may ignore it. We leave the reader to check that the strict boundary condition is observed in our simulations—in most moves, a_1, b_1, a_2, b_2 are multiples of powers of two.

The original vector model of Pratt and Stockmeyer [19] is a RAM M with arbitrarily many arithmetical registers R_i and some number k of "vector registers" (or tapes) V_j, each of which holds a binary string. M uses standard RAM operations on the arithmetical registers, bitwise AND, OR, and negation on (pairs of) vector tapes, and *shift* instructions of the form $V_k := R_i \uparrow V_j$, which shift the contents of tape V_j by an amount equal to the integer n_i in R_i and store the result in V_k. If n_i is positive, n_i-many 0's are prepended, while if n_i is negative (a left shift), the first n_i-many bits of V_j are discarded.[1] These shift instructions essentially provide "random access" to the vector tapes. The two *main points* of the BM as opposed to the VM are the realistic provision of constant-time *shuffle*, and the constraint on random-access. Having the former improves the bounds given by Hong [11] for many basic operations, and these operations seem not to be helped by full random-access anyway. The main theorem of this paper is that these adjustments lead to exact characterizations of the classes NC^k.

3. Basic List Operations

Much of the following is standard, but there are several innovations from Lemma 3.5 onward. These innovations come in situations where previous cited work used quantities which are powers of 2, and where our work seems to require double powers of 2; i.e., that lengths be normalized to numbers of the form 2^{2^b}. All logs below are to base 2. To save space we introduce a useful shorthand for hierarchical lists.

We call a sequence $(x_1, x_2, \ldots, x_l)$ of nonempty binary strings a *list*, and represent it by the string $X = x_1^{\#} x_2^{\#} \cdots x_l^{\#}$. Here $x^{\#}$ means that the last symbol of x is a "compound symbol," either $(0, \#)$ or $(1, \#)$, and similarly for the other *list separator symbols* $\$, \%, @$. Informally, the separators have "precedence" $\% < \# < @ < \$$. The *length* of the list is l, and the *bit-length* is $\sum_{j=1}^{l} |x_i|$. If each string x_i has the same length s, then the list X is *normal*, a term used by Chen and Yap [7] when also l is a power of 2 (see below). A normal list represents an $l \times s$ Boolean matrix in row-major order. Many of the technical lemmas concern larger objects we call *vectors of lists*, with the general notation

$$\begin{aligned} \mathcal{X} &= X_1^{\$}; X_2^{\$}; \ldots; X_m^{\$} \\ &= x_{11}^{\#} x_{12}^{\#} \cdots x_{1l_1}^{\$} x_{21}^{\#} x_{22}^{\#} \cdots x_{2l_2}^{\$} \cdots x_{m-1,l_{m-1}}^{\$} x_{m1}^{\#} \cdots x_{ml_m}^{\$}. \end{aligned}$$

If each list X_i is normal with string length s_i, then $\mathcal{X}$ is a vector of Boolean matrices. If also $s_1 = s_2 = \ldots = s_m = s$ and $l_1 = l_2 = \ldots = l_m = l$, we call $\mathcal{X}$ *fully normal*. Finally, if s and l are also powers of 2 (notation: $s = 2^b$, $l = 2^c$), then $\mathcal{X}$ is *supernormal*. We often treat vectors of lists as simple lists subdivided by $\$$, and even as single strings. Let the bits of x be $a_1 a_2 \ldots a_s$:

Basic string operations

- R stands for "replicate string": $R(x) = xx$.
- D stands for "dilate" as above: $D(x) = a_1 a_1 a_2 a_2 \ldots a_s a_s$.
- H splits x into two halves $H_1(x) = a_1 \ldots a_{s/2}$, $H_2(x) = a_{s/2+1} \ldots a_s$ (s even).

---

[1] It has been observed that the distinction between arithmetic and vector registers is inessential, shifts being the same as multiplication and division by powers of 2, and that left shifts are unnecessary—see [21, 1, 25, 14, 24] for these observations and alternate forms of the VM. The original form makes the clearest comparison to the BM.

- J joins two strings together: $J(H_1(x), H_2(x)) = x$.

- S shuffles the first and second halves of a string x of even length; i.e., $S(x) = a_1 a_{s/2+1} a_2 a_{s/2+2} \cdots a_{s/2} a_s$. Note that SJ shuffles two strings of equal length.

- U is "unshuffle," the inverse of S: $U(x) = a_1 a_3 a_5 \cdots a_{s-1} a_2 a_4 \cdots a_s$.

List operations

- $D_\#$ duplicates list elements: if $X = x_1^\# x_2^\# \ldots x_l^\#$, then $D_\#(X) = x_1^\% x_1^\# x_2^\% x_2^\# \ldots x_l^\% x_l^\#$. Note $D_\#^2(x) = x_1^\% x_1^\% x_1^\% x_1^\# x_2^\% x_2^\% x_2^\% x_2^\# \ldots x_l^\% x_l^\% x_l^\% x_l^\#$.

- $S_\#$ shuffles lists element-wise: $S(X) = x_1^\# x_{l/2+1}^\# x_2^\# x_{l/2+2}^\# \ldots x_{l/2}^\# x_l^\#$, defined when l is even. $S_\# J$ shuffles two lists of the same length l element-wise.

- $U_\#$ is the inverse of $S_\#$; $HU_\#$ breaks off odd and even sublists.

- $T_\#(a_{11} \cdots a_{1s}^\#, a_{21} \cdots a_{l1} \cdots a_{ls}^\#) = a_{11} a_{21} \cdots a_{l1} a_{12} \cdots a_{l2} \cdots a_{1s}^\# a_{2s}^\# \cdots a_{ls}^\#$.

- $B_{\%\#}$ places a % halfway between every two #s in a list, when all such distances are even. $B_{\#\#}$ inserts more #s instead.

When applied to a vector list $\mathcal{X}$, these operations treat $\mathcal{X}$ as a single list of strings subdivided by #, but preserve the higher-level \$ separators. The operations $D_\$$, $S_\$$, $U_\$$, $T_\$$, and $B_{\$\$}$, however, treat $\mathcal{X}$ as a list of strings subdivided by \$. Note that we have allowed for marked symbols being displaced in matrix transpose $T_\#$. All the string and list operations op above may be *vectorized* via the general notation

$$\vec{op}(\mathcal{X}) = op(X_1)^\$ op(X_2)^\$ \ldots op(X_m)^\$.$$

A convenient general property is that $(op_1 \vec{\circ} op_2)(\mathcal{X}) = \vec{op}_1(\vec{op}_2(\mathcal{X}))$. Sometimes we omit the $\circ$ and compose operators from right to left. We note that for any $\mathcal{X}$, $\vec{D}_\#(\mathcal{X}) = D_\#(\mathcal{X})$, but for instance with $l = m = 8$:

$$\vec{U}_\#(\mathcal{X}) = x_{11}^\# x_{13}^\# x_{15}^\# x_{17}^\# x_{12}^\# \ldots x_{18}^\$ x_{21}^\# x_{23}^\# \ldots x_{26}^\# x_{28}^\$ \ldots x_{81}^\# x_{83}^\# \ldots x_{86}^\# x_{88}^\$,$$

while

$$U_\#(\mathcal{X}) = x_{11}^\# x_{13}^\# x_{15}^\# x_{17}^\# x_{21}^\# x_{23}^\# x_{25}^\# x_{27}^\# \ldots x_{85}^\# x_{87}^\# x_{12}^\# x_{14}^\# x_{16}^\# x_{18}^\# x_{22}^\$ \ldots x_{86}^\# x_{88}^\$.$$

Note the displacement of \$ signs in the latter. For Lemma 3.2 below we want instead $U'_\#(\mathcal{X}) = x_{11}^\# x_{13}^\# x_{15}^\# x_{17}^\# x_{21}^\$ x_{23}^\# x_{25}^\# x_{27}^\$ \ldots x_{85}^\# x_{87}^\$ x_{12}^\# x_{14}^\# x_{16}^\# x_{18}^\$ x_{22}^\# \ldots x_{86}^\# x_{88}^\$$. However, our BMs need not rely on the markers, but can use counters for b and c (prepended to the data) to compute the long expressions given below. We omit the details of these counters here, but note some places where $B_{\#\#}$ and $B_{\%\#}$ are explicitly used.

Lemma 3.1. *Let X be a normal list with $s = 2^b$ and l even. Then*

(a) $B_{\%\#}(X) = S^{b-1} \circ$ (*mark every 2nd bit of the first $2l$ with %*) $\circ U^{b-1}(X)$.

(b) $T_\#(X) = U^b(X)$.

(c) *For any $a \geq 1$, $D_\#^a(X) = T_\#^{-1} D^a(T_\#(X)) = S^b D^a U^b(X)$.*

(d) $S_\#(X) = S^{b+1}(J(U^b H_1(X), U^b H_2(X)))$.

(e) $U_\#(X) = J(S^b(H_1 U^{b+1}(X)), S^b(H_2 U^{b+1}(X)))$.

Item (c) technically needs a final application of $B_{\%\#}$. Alternatively, the % markers can be introduced during the D^a part. The key point of the next lemma and its sequel is that the number of passes to compute $\vec{S}_\#(\mathcal{X})$ and $\vec{U}_\#(\mathcal{X})$ is independent of m. Analogous operations given by Hong on pp111–115 of [11] for the Pratt-Stockmeyer model have an $O(\log m)$ term in their time.

Lemma 3.2. *Let $\mathcal{X}$ be super-normal with $s = 2^b$, $l = 2^c$, and m even. Then*

(a) $\vec{U}_\#(\mathcal{X}) = S_\$(U_\#'(\mathcal{X})) = S^{b+c+1}(J(U^c H_1(U^{b+1}(\mathcal{X})), U^c H_2(U^{b+1}(\mathcal{X}))))$.

(b) $\vec{S}_\#(\mathcal{X}) = S_\#(U_\$(\mathcal{X})) = S^{b+1}(J(S^c(H_1 U^{b+c+1}(\mathcal{X})), S^c(H_2(U^{b+c+1}(\mathcal{X})))))$.

Lemma 3.3. *Assuming good initial pointer and marker placements,*

(a) *Each of the string operations is computable in $O(1)$ passes by a $BM(gh)$.*

(b) *With reference to Lemma 3.1, $D_\#^a(X)$ is computable in $O(a+b)$ passes, and the other four list operations in $O(b)$ passes.*

(c) *The two vector operations in Lemma 3.2 are computable in $O(b+c)$ passes.*

The product of two Boolean matrices X and Y of size $2^b \times 2^b$ is computed by

$$M(X, Y) = O^b ASJ(D_\#^b(X), R^b T_\#(Y)).$$

Define the *outer-product* of two strings $x = a_1 \ldots a_2$ and $y = b_1 \ldots b_s$ by $V(x, y) = a_1 b_1 a_1 b_2 \cdots a_1 b_s a_2 b_1 \ldots a_2 b_s \ldots a_s b_1 \ldots a_s b_s$. Then $V(x, y) = SJ(D^b(x), R^b(y))$, and $AV(x, y)$ gives the $s \times s$ Boolean outer-product matrix. The corresponding list operation is applied to adjacent pairs of strings in a list, viz.: $V_\#(X) = V(x_1, x_2)^\# V(x_3, x_4)^\# \ldots V(x_{l-1}, x_l)^\#$. We also vectorize these operations:

Lemma 3.4. *For super-normal vector lists $\mathcal{X}$ with $l = 2^c$, $s = 2^b$:*

(a) $\vec{V}_\#(\mathcal{X}) = SJ(D^b H_1(U_\# \mathcal{X}), D_\#^b H_2(U_\# \mathcal{X}))$, *and is computable in $O(b)$ passes.*

(b) $\vec{M}(\mathcal{X}, \mathcal{X}) = O^b ASJ(D_\#^b H_1(D_\# U_\#(\mathcal{X})), D_\$ T_\# H_2((D_\# U_\#(\mathcal{X}))))$ *provided that $b = c$, and is then computable in $O(b)$ passes.*

The following way to do vectorized conversion from binary to unary notation works for binary numbers whose lengths are powers of 2. Let $X = n_1^\# n_2^\# \ldots n_m^\#$, where each n_i is a string of length $s = 2^b$ in binary notation (thus $0 \le n_i \le 2^s - 1$), with the most significant bit first. The object is to convert each n_i to $0^{2^s - n_i - 1} 10^{n_i}$. Call the resulting vector $W_b(X)$. Note that $W_0(X)$ is just the homomorphism which maps $0 \to 01$ and $1 \to 10$ (or technically, $0^\# \to 01^\#$ and $1^\# \to 10^\#$).

Lemma 3.5. *For all $b > 0$, $W_b(X) = AV_\# W_{b-1} B_{\#\#}(X)$, and is computable in $O(s)$ passes.*

Proof. Consider any item $n_i = a$ on the list X. $B_{\#\#}$ converts that item to $a_1^\# a_2^\#$, such that $a = a_1 2^{s/2} + a^2$. Arguing inductively, suppose that W_{b-1} then converts $a_1^\# a_2^\#$ to $0^{2^{s/2} - a_1 - 1} 10^{a_1}{}^\# 0^{2^{s/2} - a_2 - 1} 10^{a_2}{}^\#$. Then the outer-product of adjacent pairs of elements produces $O^{2^s - a} 10^a$ as needed, and by Lemma 3.4(a), is computed in $O(s)$ passes. The time t_b to compute W_b has the recursion $t_b = O(b) + t_{b-1} + O(2^b)$, with solution $t_b = O(2^b) = O(s)$. $\square$

Lemma 3.6. *The list I_b of all strings of length $s = 2^b$ in order can be generated in $O(s)$ passes by a BM(gh).*

Proof. $I_0 = 0^\# 1^\#$, and for $b \geq 1$, $I_b = S_\# J(D^s(I_{b-1}), R^s(I_{b-1}))$. The timing recursion is similar to before. □

Next, given a single-tape Turing machine M with state set Q and work alphabet Γ, define the *ID alphabet* of M to be $\Gamma_I := (Q \times \Gamma) \cup \Gamma$. A valid ID of M has the form $I = x(q, c)y$ and means that M is in state q scanning character c. The *next move* function steps M through to the next ID.

Lemma 3.7. *The next move function of a single-tape TM T can be extended to a total function $\delta_M : \Gamma_I^* \to (\Gamma_I \cup \{+, -, !\})^*$, and there is a 2:1 generalized homomorphism $h : (\Gamma_I \cup \{+, -, !\})^* \to (\Gamma_I \cup \{+, -, !\})^*$ such that*

(a) *δ_T is the composition of three 3:3 generalized homomorphisms.*

(b) *Consider strings $I \in \Gamma_I^*$ of length 2^b. If I is a valid ID and T goes from I to an accepting (resp. rejecting) ID within t steps, staying within the 2^b allotted cells of the tape, then $h^b(\delta_T^t(I)) = +$ (resp. $-$). Else $h^b(\delta_T^t(I)) = !$.*

(c) *The above properties can be obtained with Γ_I re-coded over $\{0, 1\}$.*

Proof Sketch. One of the three gh's updates cells $0, 3, 6, \ldots$ of the tape of T, one does $1, 4, 7, \ldots$, and the last does $2, 5, 8 \ldots$ If T halts and accepts, the homomorphisms detect this and replace the symbol (q, c) by $+$, and similarly with $-$ for rejection. If T is detected to move its head off the tape, the homomorphisms introduce a ! symbol. The same happens if T "crashes" in I or if I is a string over Γ_I with more than one "head" and two of these "heads" come within two cells of each other. Finally h is written so that it preserves a $+$ or $-$ under iteration iff every other character it reads belongs to Γ. □

We note a trick needed to extend the above idea for multitape TMs. For alternating TMs, it appears that the k-to-1 tape reduction theorem of Paul, Prauss, and Reischuk [17] holds even for log-time bounds, but we still allow for multiple tapes.

Lemma 3.8. *Let T be a TM with $k \geq 2$ tapes, which is constrained to operate within space $s = 2^b$ on each tape. Then b moves by T can be simulated in $O(b)$ passes by a BM(gh). Furthermore, this operation can be vectorized; i.e., applied to a list of IDs of T.*

Proof Sketch. The contents and head position for each tape are represented as described before Lemma 3.7, and then IDs of T are encoded by shuffling these representations. The difficulty in simulating one move by T is that heads of T on different tapes may be up to s cells apart, and it is impossible to record and propagate the information about the character each head is scanning in one pass by a gh. Let $g = |\Gamma|$. The solution is to do g^k passes, one for each k-tuple of symbols that the heads could possibly be scanning. The simulating BM M has a special character for each k-tuple over Γ, and all symbols in the output of each pass are marked by the special character for the tuple assumed in that pass. Each such pass appends its output to the right end of the tape. After the g^k passes, we have g^k candidates for the next move by T. The process is repeated on the list of candidates until it produces a tree of depth b with g^{bk} leaves, where each branch is a possible b moves by T. Then with b passes by a 2:1 gh on a spare copy of the tree, M can verify for each node whether the tuple assumed for it was correct. In $O(bg^k) = O(b)$ more passes, M can propagate the marking of bad nodes from parents to all descendents, leaving just one correct branch. In $O(b)$ more passes, this information is transferred back to the original copy of the tree. $\qquad\square$

Remarks for later reference: For simulating the next b steps by T, it is not necessary to erase all the bad leaves—the '!' markings of bad IDs can be copied forward in later passes. Now suppose $g = |\Gamma|$ is a power of 2. When the next-move operation is vectorized and applied once to a level of nodes $N_1, \ldots, N_j$ of the tree, the next level comes out in the order

$$[\text{child 1 of } N_1]^\# \ldots [\text{child 1 of } N_j]^\$ [\text{child 2 of } N_1]^\# \ldots [\text{child } g^k \text{ of } N_j]^\$.$$

Now applying $S_\#$ $(k \log g)$-many times would bring all the children of each node together. However, since the list elements are $s = 2^b$ symbols long, this would take $O(b)$ passes, and since later we will have $n = 2^s$, this would make the overall pass count $O(\log n \log\log n)$. Instead we wait until the bottom-level IDs have been converted to single-symbol values $+$, $-$, or $!$ (or 0, 1, $!$) by b-many applications of a 2:1 gh. Then children can be brought together at each level via the string operation $S^{k \log g}$, and since k and g are independent of n, the number of passes per level is constant. This will be used when T is an alternating TM with binary branching.

4. Main Theorem

Cook [8] made it standard to refer to the U_{E^*} uniformity condition of Ruzzo [20] in defining the classes NC^k and AC^k for $k \geq 1$. For AC^1 and higher this is equivalent to older conditions of log-space uniformity, and we use this for NC^k with $k \geq 2$ below. Using U_{E^*} uniformity gives the identity $NC^k = \text{ATISP}(O(\log^k n), O(\log n))$ for all $k \geq 1$ [20], where ATISP refers to simultaneously time- and space-bounded alternating Turing machines. Thus NC^1 is also called ALOGTIME. A circuit is *leveled* if its nodes can be partitioned into $V_0, \ldots, V_d$ such any wire from a node in some V_i goes to a node in some V_{i+1}. The *width* of a leveled circuit equals $\max_i |V_i|$. The circuit is *layered* if in addition the input level V_0 consists of inputs x_i and their negations, and the remaining levels alternate AND and OR gates. For all $k \geq 1$, an NC^k circuit can be converted to an equivalent layered NC^k circuit, within the same condition of uniformity.

Theorem 4.1. *For all $k \geq 1$, $BM^k(gh) = NC^k$.*

Proof. (Sketches) (1) $BM^k(gh) \subseteq NC^k$. Let M have m markers, DGSM states $S_1, \ldots S_r$, and a tape alphabet Γ of size g. Let $p(n)$ be a polynomial which bounds the work, and also the space, used by M on inputs of length n. The simulating circuit C_n is organized vertically into *blocks*, each of which simulates $b(n) = \epsilon \log n$ moves by M. Each block is organized horizontally into *segments*, each of which has $p(n)+1$ inputs and outputs. The extra input/output is a "flag," where '1' stands for "good" and '0' for "bad." For simplicity we describe C_n as though gates compute finite functions over the tape alphabet of M; conversion to a Boolean circuit expands size and depth by only a constant.

A *setting* consists of a positioning of the m markers, an assignment of the four pointers to the markers, and the current GSM. This makes $p(n)^m m^4 r$ possible settings. Given a setting before a pass, the total number of possible settings after the pass and subsequent move state is at most g, one for each tape character pointer a_1 might scan. Thus the total number of possible sequences of settings in the course of $b(n)$ moves is $B(n) := g^{b(n)} = n^{\epsilon \log g}$, which is polynomial. This is the point of constraining the machine's "random access."

Each block has $p(n)^m m^4 B(n)$ segments operating in parallel. Each individual segment corresponds to a different initial setting and one of the $B(n)$ sequences which can follow. Each segment is leveled with width $p(n) + 1$, and has $b(n)$ "pass slices," each representing $p(n)$ tape cells plus the flag. Each pass slice corresponds to a setting and has the "hard wiring" for the block move $S_i[a_1 \ldots b_1]$ *into* $[a_2 \ldots b_2]$ carried out in the DGSM state S_i of that setting. Since S_i is one of finitely many gh's, each slice has constant depth. The flag gate in a pass slice is hard-wired to check that, based on the character scanned by a_1, the subsequent move state sets the pointers according to the setting in the next slice. If not, the flag is set to 0, and this is propagated downward.

The circuit carries the invariant that at the beginning of the ith block, there are $p(n)^m m^4 B(n)$ copies of the correct configuration of the tape of M after $b(n) \cdot i$ moves. Of these, those whose initial setting is incorrect already have the flag of their top slice set to 0; only the $B(n)$-many segments with the correct setting have flag 1. After $b(n)$ pass slices, *exactly one* of the segments has flag 1, namely the one whose sequence of settings M actually followed on the particular input. The other $p(n)^m m^4 B(n) - 1$ segments have flag 0. The rest of the block must locate the segment with flag 1 and route $B(n)$ copies of its $p(n)$ outputs among those segments in the next block whose initial setting matches the final setting of the source. This is standard: in $O(\log n)$ depth the segments with flag 0 are zeroed out, then bitwise comparison in an $O(\log n)$ depth butterfly pattern automatically replicates the correct one. The interconnect pattern is explicitly defined and regular enough to make the circuit U_{E^*} uniform.

(2) $NC^k \subseteq BM^k$ for $k \geq 2$: Let $\epsilon > 0$ and a log-space uniform family $[C_n]_{n=1}^\infty$ of layered circuits of depths $d(n)$ be given. We claim there is an equivalent family $[C_n']_{n=1}^\infty$ of circuits which have the following properties:

(a) C_n' is broken into *blocks*, each of depth $b(n) = \lceil \epsilon \log_2 n \rceil$. Let $w(n)$ be the next power of 2 higher than the width of C_n. Each block describes a circuit with $w(n)$ outputs, and is broken in parallel into $w(n)$ *formulas*, one for each output. Each formula has alternating levels of AND and OR with negations at the inputs. The formula has input variables $u_1, \ldots, u_{w(n)}$, some of which are dummy variables, together with their negations. (The negations are needed only in the first block.)

(b) C'_n has a special encoding E_n as a vector of lists, where each list represents a block and has $w(n)$ elements denoting the formulas in that block. The formulas are written in infix notation, and since they are full binary trees in which levels of AND and OR alternate, only the variables need be written. Each variable u_i is represented by the string $0^{w(n)-i}10^{i-1}\%$; its negation $\bar{u}_i$ by $0^{w(n)-i}-10^{i-1}\%$

(c) There is a log-space Turing machine which on input 0^n outputs the string E_n.

The proof of this claim is similar to proofs that log-space uniformity is preserved under other circuit normalizations, and omitted here. To finish part (2) we need to build a BM(gh) M such that on any input x of length n, M constructs E_n in $O(\log^2 n)$ passes and polynomial work, and evaluates E_n in $O(d_n)$ passes.

Since the formulas have size $2^{b(n)}$ which is polynomial, there is a polynomial $r(n)$ which bounds the length of E_n. It is well known that having E_n computable from 0^n in logspace is the same as having a log-space machine T which given 0^n and $i \le r(n)$ decides the ith bit of E_n. We may then eliminate the input tape and make T start with i and n in binary notation on a single worktape with explicit endmarkers constraining T to logarithmic space $s_0(n)$. Let $s = s(n)$ be the next highest power of 2 after $s_0(n) \cdot C$, where C is the constant implied by the transformation from the ID alphabet of T to $\{0, 1\}$ in Lemma 3.7. Then T always halts within 2^s steps. Put $b = \log_2 s$.

The BM M first calculates n from $|x|$ and generates the list I of all binary strings of length $s(n)$ in lex order via Lemma 3.6. Each element in I is a potential ID of T. M then applies the next move function of T *once* to every element. The resulting list of strings of length s is no longer in lex order. Now this list can be converted to a Boolean matrix which represents the next-move function by running binary-to-unary on the list. This takes $O(s)$ passes. Then the matrix is raised to the power of 2^s by iterated squaring, in $O(s^2)$ passes. After conversion from unary back to binary, this produces a list of the final IDs reached from each given ID by T. Finally, $r(n)$ copies are made of this list by $O(\log n)$ replications. Then the numbers i from 1 to $r(n)$ are generated and aligned with successive copies. The answer given by T for each i can be computed by iterating a 2:1 gh h like that in Lemma 3.7 which preserves $+$ or $-$ in a final ID iff the corresponding starting ID held i, n. Iterating h $2s$-many times, and then changing $+$ to 1 and $-$ to 0, yields exactly the string E_n.

The circuit is evaluated by replicating the output of the previous block, and shuffling this with the list of unary variable identifiers $\pm u_j = 0^{w(n)-j} \pm 10^{j-1}$. The single '1' (or -1) then pulls off the input value of u_j from the previous block. The remainder of the block is evaluated by alternating $A(\cdot)$ and $O(\cdot)$.

(3) $\mathrm{NC}^1 \subseteq \mathrm{BM}^1(\mathrm{gh})$. Here we use the identity $\mathrm{NC}^1 = \mathrm{ALOGTIME}$. Let T be an ALOGTIME machine which accepts some language A. It is well known (see [22, 4]) that T can be converted to an ALOGTIME machine T' with the following properties: T' alternates existential and universal steps, and each non-terminal configuration has exactly two successors (called "right" and "left"). Each branch ignores the input tape until it reaches a terminal configuration, at which point the contents of a designated "address tape" specify in binary an integer i, $1 \le i \le n$, and the configuration accepts or rejects depending only on the value of the ith input. (Our simulation appears not to require the additional feature that every branch records

its own sequence of left-right choices.) Now let n' be the next number above n of the form 2^{2^b}; then $n < n' \leq n^2$. We may further modify T' so that each of its k-many worktapes is constrained to $s = 2^b$ cells, each branch runs for exactly t steps, where $t = O(s)$ and t is a multiple of b, and each branch writes $n' - i$ right-justified on the address tape instead of i. Let Γ be the alphabet of T' and let $g := |\Gamma|$; we may suppose that g is a power of 2 (or even that $g = 2$).

The simulation begins with the single blank initial worktape ID I_λ. The computation by T' is simulated in block of b moves by the process of Lemma 3.8, but modified to produce both successors of every ID. Thus with reference to the proof, every ID has $2g^k$ children, two of which are legitimate—it is important that one good ID is in the first g^k and the other in the second g^k when the tree is flattened into a list. After t steps, there are $(2g^k)^t$ IDs, of which 2^t are legitimate. Since the tapes of T' are shuffled, one pass by a $k{:}1$ gh leaves just the address tape contents in these IDs, written in binary with extra trailing 0s out to length exactly $s = 2^b$. Then the unary-to-binary conversion of Lemma 3.5 is applied, with a slight change to preserve '!' markings in bad IDs. Now there is a polynomial-sized list of elements of the form $!^{n'}$ or $0^{i-1}10^{n'-i}$; the latter comes out that way because T' wrote $n' - i$ to address the ith bit. Then trailing dummy symbols are appended to pad the input x out to length n', and this is replicated and shuffled bit-wise with the list. One pass then picks up the input bit x_i addressed by each good terminal ID, and writes the value, 0 or 1, given by T' to that ID. Then s more passes by a $2{:}1$ gh leave just the values 0, 1, or '!' of each terminal ID, bad ones included. The resulting string z has length $(2g^k)^t$ and contains exactly 2^t 0 or 1 symbols. Per remarks following Lemma 3.8, applying $S^{1+k\log g}$ to z brings the children of each bottom node together, and by the "important" note above, among each $2g^k$ children of a good node, exactly one symbol in the left-hand g^k is Boolean, and similarly for the right-hand g^k.

Now let $Er_!$ be the partially defined $2{:}1$ gh which maps

$$!! \mapsto ! \qquad !0 \mapsto 0 \qquad 0! \mapsto 0 \qquad !1 \mapsto 1 \qquad 1! \mapsto 1, $$

Let $A_!$ be the total extension of $Er_!$ which behaves like AND on 00,01,10, and 11, and let $O_!$ be similar for OR. For argument's sake, suppose the last alternation by T' in each branch is AND. After $k\log g$ applications of $Er_!$ to $S^{1+k\log g}(z)$, the two Boolean values under each of these nodes are brought together, and then one application of $A_!$ evaluates this level. Under bad nodes, every character remains '!'. The next level is similarly evaluated by applying $O_! Er_!^{k\log g} S^{1+k\log g}$, in $O(1)$ passes. Doing this for $O(t) = O(s) = O(\log n)$ total passes evaluates the entire tree. $\qquad\square$

Corollary 4.2. (to (1) and [6]): *For all $k \geq 1$, $\mathrm{BM}^k(ap) \subseteq \mathrm{AC}^k$.*

Let "BM_0" stand for BMs which are provided with any finite set of NC^0 operations to use in block moves, and which may have more than one tape. In general a machine is *oblivious* if the movements of its tape heads depend only on the length of the input.

Corollary 4.3. *Every BM_0 which runs in polynomial work and $R(n) = \Omega(\log n)$ passes, can be simulated in polynomial work and $O(R(n))$ passes by a $\mathrm{BM}(gh)$ with a single tape which is oblivious and only makes left-to-right passes.* $\qquad\square$

5. Other Results and Conclusion

There are several definitions of *reversal complexity* for multitape Turing machines, where in a given transition, each head may stay stationary (S) as well as move left (L) or right (R). The older "strict" criterion of Kameda and Vollmer [13] is the same as counting any S move as a reversal. The newer one [18, 11, 16, 7] counts a reversal only when a head moves L which has previously moved R, or vice-versa. (Some other sources do not count reversals on the input tape.)

Lemma 5.1. *Every BM M which makes $R(n)$ passes can be simulated by a 2-tape TM T which makes $O(R(n))$ reversals.*

Proof Sketch. The first tape of T equals the tape of M, while the second tape is used to buffer the output in block moves. The second tape also helps T move the m markers to new positions in at most $2m$ reversals. □

For a BM(gh), or more generally when every GSM in M translates input symbols to output symbols in some finite ratio $d:e$, $R(n)$ corresponds in this simulation to a notion of reversal complexity which is intuitively midway between the "strict" and the standard one: in every interval between reversals, each tape head must operate at some "fixed stride."

Parberry [16] showed that TMs which run in space $s(n)$ and $r(n)$ reversals can be simulated by uniform circuits of depth $O(r(n)\log^2 s(n))$ and width polynomial in $s(n)$. Chen and Yap [7] showed that any $r(n)$ reversal bounded multitape TM can be simulated by a 2-tape TM in $O(r(n)^2)$ reversals. In the case where the TM runs in polynomial space we obtain an inprovement:

Corollary 5.2. *A multitape TM which runs in polynomial space and $r(n)$ reversals can be simulated by a 2-tape TM in $O(r(n)\log^2 r(n))$ reversals.*

Finally, we term a BM M to be a *cascading finite automaton* (CFA) if M consists of a single DGSM S which is iterated left-to-right on its own output. (The validity condition is ignored.) For instance, the language D_1 of balanced parentheses is acceptable by a CFA S which skips the leading '('—writing '!' to reject if the first symbol is ')'—and thereafter translates

$$((\mapsto (\qquad)) \mapsto) \qquad () \mapsto \lambda \qquad)(\mapsto \lambda.$$

Then for all $x \neq \lambda$, either $S(x) = !$ or $x \in D_1 \iff S(x) \in D_1$, and always $|S(x)| \leq |x|/2$. Hence iterating S recognizes D_1 in $O(\log n)$ passes and linear work.

Open Problem 1. Does every language accepted by a CFA in $O(\log n)$ passes belong to NC^1? (Such languages do belong to one-way logspace [10].)

Open Problem 2. For $k \geq 1$, is $AC^k = BM^k(ap)$? In general, how do conditions on the structure of GSMs allowed to a BM correspond to circuit classes?

To conclude, the BM is a natural model which offers finer complexity analyses, and we look toward its further use on basic open problems in the NC hierarchy.

References

[1] J. Balcázar, J. Díaz, and J. Gabarró. *Structural Complexity Theory*. Springer Verlag, 1988.

[2] D. Mix Barrington. Bounded-width polynomial-size branching programs recognize exactly those languages in NC^1. *J. Comp. Sys. Sci.*, 38:150–164, 1989.

[3] D. Mix Barrington, K. Compton, H. Straubing, and D. Thérien. Regular languages in NC^1. *J. Comp. Sys. Sci.*, 44:478–499, 1992.

[4] D. Mix Barrington, N. Immerman, and H. Straubing. On uniformity within NC^1. *J. Comp. Sys. Sci.*, 41:274–306, 1990.

[5] D. Mix Barrington and D. Thérien. Finite monoids and the fine structure of NC^1. *J. ACM*, 35:941–952, 1988.

[6] A. Chandra, S. Fortune, and R. Lipton. Unbounded fan-in circuits and associative functions. *J. Comp. Sys. Sci.*, 30:222–234, 1985.

[7] J. Chen and C. Yap. Reversal complexity. *SIAM J. Comp.*, 20:622–638, 1991.

[8] S. Cook. A taxonomy of problems with fast parallel algorithms. *Info. Control*, 64:2–22, 1985.

[9] T. Harju, H.C.M. Klein, and M. Latteux. Deterministic sequential functions. *Acta Informatics*, 29:545–554, 1992.

[10] J. Hartmanis, N. Immerman, and S. Mahaney. One-way log tape reductions. In *Proc. 19th FOCS*, pages 65–72, 1978.

[11] J.-W. Hong. *Computation: Similarity and Duality*. Research Notes in Theoretical Computer Science. Wiley, 1986.

[12] J. Hopcroft and J. Ullman. *Introduction to Automata Theory, Languages, and Computation*. Addison–Wesley, Reading, MA, 1979.

[13] T. Kameda and R. Vollmar. Note on tape reversal complexity of languages. *Info. Control*, 17:203–215, 1970.

[14] R. Karp and V. Ramachandran. Parallel algorithms for shared-memory machines. In J. Van Leeuwen, editor, *Handbook of Theoretical Computer Science*, pages 871–941. Elsevier and MIT Press, 1990.

[15] P. McKenzie, P. Péladeau, and D. Thérien. NC^1: The automata-theoretic viewpoint. *Computational Complexity*, 1:330–359, 1991.

[16] I. Parberry. An improved simulation of space and reversal bounded deterministic Turing machines by width and depth bounded uniform circuits. *Inf. Proc. Lett.*, 24:363–367, 1987.

[17] W. Paul, E. Prauss, and R. Reischuk. On alternation. *Acta Informatica*, 14:243–255, 1980.

[18] N. Pippenger. On simultaneous resource bounds. In *Proc. 20th FOCS*, pages 307–311, 1979.

[19] V. Pratt and L. Stockmeyer. A characterization of the power of vector machines. *J. Comp. Sys. Sci.*, 12:198–221, 1976.

[20] W. Ruzzo. On uniform circuit complexity. *J. Comp. Sys. Sci.*, 22:365–373, 1981.

[21] J. Simon. *On some central problems in computational complexity*. PhD thesis, Cornell University, 1975.

[22] M. Sipser. Borel sets and circuit complexity. In *Proc. 15th STOC*, pages 61–69, 1983.

[23] L. Stockmeyer and U. Vishkin. Simulations of parallel random access machines by circuits. *SIAM J. Comp.*, 13:409–422, 1984.

[24] J. Trahan, M. Loui, and V. Ramachandran. Multiplication, division, and shift instructions in parallel random access machines. *Theor. Comp. Sci.*, 100:1–44, 1992.

[25] P. van Emde Boas. Machine models and simulations. In J. Van Leeuwen, editor, *Handbook of Theoretical Computer Science*, pages 1–66. Elsevier and MIT Press, 1990.

On Adaptive Dlogtime and Polylogtime Reductions*

(Extended Abstract)

Carme Àlvarez [†]

Dept. L.S.I.
Universitat Politècnica de Catalunya
Pau Gargallo 5, E–08028 Barcelona, Spain

Birgit Jenner [‡]

Fakultät für Informatik
Technische Universität München
D–80290 München, Germany

Abstract

We investigate properties of the relativized NC and AC hierarchies in their DLOGTIME-, respectively, ALOGTIME-uniform setting and show that these hierarchies can be characterized in terms of adaptive reducibility in deterministic (poly)logarithmic time, i.e. in time $O(\log n)^i$ for $i \geq 0$. Using this characterization, we substantially generalize various previous results concerning the structure of the NC and AC hierarchies.

1 Introduction

The concept of reducibility is a central one in complexity theory. Intuitively, a problem A is reducible to a problem B when an algorithm for B can be efficiently transformed into an algorithm for A. Loosely speaking, the complexity of A is bounded by the complexity of B "plus" the complexity of the reduction. Here, a natural assumption is that the complexity of the reduction should not be greater than the complexity of the problem we are reducing to. With the study of smaller and smaller complexity classes finer and finer reductions using lesser and lesser resources have become neccessary. At the extreme end, we have reducibilities via constant depth circuits [14] or LOGTIME reducibility [10], suitable for studying completeness for classes such as (uniform) AC^0 and NC^1.

Reducibilities can also be used to characterize complexity classes. For example, the classes Δ_2^P [21] and Θ_2^P [23] are, respectively, the closure of NP under polynomial-time Turing and truth-table reducibility. Θ_2^P has a variety of

*Partially supported by DAAD and Spanish Government (Acción Integrada 131–B, 313–AI–e–es/zk).

[†]Research supported by the ESPRIT Basic Research Actions Program of the EC under contract No. 7141 (project ALCOM II). E-mail address: alvarez@lsi.upc.es

[‡]On leave until March 1995, visiting Dept. L.S.I. of Univ. Politècnica de Catalunya supported by a Habilitationsstipendium of Deutsche Forschungsgemeinschaft (DFG-Je 154 2/1). E-mail address: jenner@lsi.upc.es

further characterizations by other types of reducibilities, e.g., logspace Turing reducibility or reducibility via (uniform) AC^0 circuits (for an overview see [17]).

A further recent example are the NC and AC hierarchies. Wilson shows that any class of these hierarchies can be characterized by applying AC^i or, alternatively, NC^{i+1} reducibility to lower classes [25]. Hence, when applied to classes in the NC and AC hierarchies, AC^i and NC^{i+1} reducibility coincide. More precisely, it holds for $i, j \geq 0$:

$$\begin{aligned} AC^{i+j} &= AC^i(AC^j) &= NC^{i+1}(AC^j), \\ NC^{i+j+1} &= AC^i(NC^{j+1}) &= NC^{i+1}(NC^{j+1}). \end{aligned}$$

Wilson argued in [25] that a further investigation of the circumstances under which AC^i and NC^{i+1} reducibility coincide may be helpful in understanding the relationship between the classes AC^i and NC^{i+1}. His results are not completely satisfying for the following two principal reasons:

- (1) Wilson's proofs do not relativize, and hence it was left open whether AC^i and NC^{i+1} reducibility also coincide when applied to classes not in the NC or AC hierarchy. For the classes L and NL (deterministic and nondeterministic logspace) this question was solved positively in [3] with the help of adaptive logspace Turing reductions. But unfortunately, the proof techniques apply only to these two particular cases.

- (2) The techniques used in [25, 3] essentially presuppose logspace uniformity of the circuits, which is unsatisfactory for the low level classes AC^0 and NC^1, since then the complexity of the circuit constructor exceeds the complexity of the circuit. Here DLOGTIME-uniformity [8, 11] and ALOGTIME-uniformity [19, 10] is preferable.

In this article, we show how the above mentioned two problems can be overcome by introducing the notion of *adaptive* reducibility in deterministic logarithmic and polylogarithmic time, i.e. in time $O((\log n)^i)$ for $i \geq 0$ (DLOG^{i}TIME reducibility). This reducibility is *not* the same as the usual *non-adaptive* (poly)logarithmic-time reducibility. For example, any class AC^i, NC^{i+1} is closed under the deterministic logtime reducibility of Buss [10], but closure under DLOG^{1}TIME reducibility would collapse the AC and NC hierarchies: Our main theorem shows that adaptive DLOG^{i}TIME reductions are strong enough to decompose (or build up) the relativized AC and NC hierarchies. Any set in the class NC^{i+j+1} can be characterized by applying adaptive DLOG^{i}TIME reducibility to a function in the class FNC^{j+1}, and, analogously, any set in the class AC^{i+j} by applying DLOG^{i}TIME reducibility to a function in FAC^j for $i, j \geq 0$. (Since DLOG^{i}TIME reducibility for technical reason reduces to functions, here FAC^j and FNC^{j+1} denote the classes of functions (rather than the class of languages) corresponding to AC^j and, respectively, NC^{j+1} circuits.) More precisely, it holds for $i, j \geq 0$ and arbitrary function class $\mathcal{F}$:

$$\begin{aligned} AC^{i+j}(\mathcal{F}) &= DLOG^iTIME(FAC^j(\mathcal{F})) &= AC^i(FAC^j(\mathcal{F})), \\ NC^{i+j+1}(\mathcal{F}) &= DLOG^iTIME(FNC^{j+1}(\mathcal{F})) &= NC^{i+1}(FNC^{j+1}(\mathcal{F})), \end{aligned}$$

where it suffices to assume DLOGTIME- and, respectively, ALOGTIME-uniformity rather than logspace uniformity for the AC and NC circuits. As a corollary, the relationship between AC^i and NC^{i+1} reducibility is clarified by the following result that strengthens a similiar result for logspace-uniform circuits announced in [6]: AC^i and NC^{i+1} reducibility coincide for all $i \geq 0$ when applied to a function class $\mathcal{F}$ if they coincide on $\mathcal{F}$ for $i = 0$, i.e., if $AC^0(\mathcal{F}) = NC^1(\mathcal{F})$. In particular, this is the case if $\mathcal{F}$ is closed under NC^1 reducibility. Hence, the drawbacks stated in (1) and (2) above are completely overcome. First, our results do not only apply to the special cases L and NL, but are so general as to apply to any class known to be closed under NC^1 reducibility, like LOGCFL [22, 9] or optL [4]. Secondly, our results hold for uniformities below logspace.

Furthermore, we also show that $DLOG^i TIME$ reducibility has other interesting properties. Besides decomposing parallel classes, this reducibility also decomposes classes that may rather be called "sequential": firstly, "small" simultaneously space and time bounded classes, and, secondly, classes defined via polynomial-time bounded oracle Turing machines that may query $O(\log^i n)$ times an oracle function.

Our paper is organized as follows. In Section 2 we define $DLOG^i TIME$ reducibility and the uniformity conditions for circuits with arbitrary functional oracle gates. In Section 3 we show the decomposition results for "sequential" classes obtainable with $DLOG^i TIME$ reductions. In Section 4, we state some normal form lemmas for AC^i and NC^{i+1} circuits, and finally, in Section 5, we present the main result concerning the decomposition of the NC and AC hierarchies by $DLOG^i TIME$ reductions, using the normal forms obtained before. Due to space restrictions, we only make brief comments on the proofs. For more detailed proofs we refer to [5].

2 $DLOG^i TIME$-Reducibility and Circuit Classes

In this section, we define the notion of adaptive $DLOG^i TIME$ reducibility and the uniform circuit classes that we will consider. Throughout this paper $\log^i n$ means the function $max(1, \lceil \log_2 n \rceil^i)$. All logarithms are to the base two. We treat sets of words over a finite, fixed alphabet which when required we will identify with the set $\{0, 1\}$. The empty word is denoted by λ. Functions map $\{0, 1\}^*$ into $\{0, 1\}^*$, and they satisfy that (i) all the values $f(x)$ have the same length for all x of the same length (a condition implicitly given if the function belongs to a circuit class), and (ii) they are polynomially-length bounded, i.e., that for all x, $|f(x)| \leq |x|^k$ for some constant k.

2.1 *Adaptive* $DLOG^i TIME$ *Reducibility*

For polylogarithmic-time bounded classes, the standard Turing machine model with its sequential input access does not make sense, since only a prefix of the input could be read. To enable access to any bit of the input, we will use a known variant of the standard model (see e.g. [19, 10, 7]).

An *indirect-access machine* is an usual Turing machine that additionally has a special tape (input index tape) to access the input and four distinguished states ("read input", "input 1", "input 0", "input undefined"). When a string i is written in the input index tape and the machine is in the special state "read input" then it enters either the "input 1" or "input 0" state, depending on the ith bit of the input. We assume that the input is written in the leftmost cells of the input tape. If an input position greater than the input length is queried, then the machine enters an special state "input undefined". We will further assume that the content of the input index tape is not erased after querying the input. (The latter two assumptions allow to compute the input length in logarithmic time (see [10], where this was credited to Dowd).)

Definition 2.1 *Using the machine model described above we define the complexity classes* DTIME($O(\log^i n)$) *for* $i \geq 0$. *We denote* DTIME($O(\log n)$) *by* DLOGTIME.

These complexity classes are language classes (classes of 0–1 functions). The corresponding function classes FDTIME($O(\log^i n)$) are defined in the obvious way by supplying the indirect-access machine with an additional output tape. Note that such functions have "small" outputs of length $O(\log^i n)$ for inputs of length n.

By introducing nondeterminism or alternation the machine model described above gives rise to the classes NLOGTIME or, respectively, ALOGTIME (see [19] for such machines).

The concept of adaptive polylogtime reducibility is defined by attaching a functional oracle to the indirect-access machine in the following way.

An *indirect-access machine with adaptive oracle queries to an oracle function* is an indirect-access machine with three additional tapes, (oracle) query tape, (oracle) answer tape, answer index tape, and five distinguished states ("query oracle", "read answer", "answer 1", "answer 0", "answer undefined"). As for the input index tape, we assume that querying any bit position greater than the length of the oracle answer is notified by transition to a special state "answer bit undefined". Similarly, we assume that the answer index tape is not erased after querying.

The machine may construct queries on the (one-way write-only) oracle query tape and will receive the answer (the value of the function) on the oracle answer tape. To access the kth bit of the answer, the answer index tape is used in the same fashion as the input index tape: When a string k is written in the answer index tape and the machine is in the special state "read answer", it enters either the "answer 0", "answer 1", or the "answer undefined" state depending on the kth bit of the answer.

We assume that the input is always a prefix of the query, and that it is written initially in the oracle query tape. Furthermore, to obtain adaptivity, the last oracle answer will always be part of the query (following the input, but separated by a \$-symbol). Both input and last oracle answer are prevented to be overwritten by the machine, by letting the write-head for the new part of the query be positioned immediately after them. Whenever the machine is in the special state "query oracle", we assume the following to happen in one step: The contents of both query and answer tape are erased and the oracle answer appears on the answer tape as well as on the query tape. In the query tape, it is preceded by the input (separated by a \$-symbol and followed by a \$-symbol in order to separate it from the new part of the following query). The write head of the oracle query tape is positioned immediately after the second \$-symbol.

Definition 2.2 *For $i \geq 0$, DLOG^{i}TIME($\mathcal{F}$) is the class of languages that can be computed by $O(\log^i n)$-time bounded indirect-access machines with adaptive oracle queries to a function in $\mathcal{F}$. If $\mathcal{F}$ is a language class (i.e. a class of 0–1 functions), then we obtain with the above model a DLOG^{i}TIME Turing reducibility.*

Since the oracle has always access to the complete input, it makes sense to consider constant time-bounded base machines that give rise to the class DLOG^{0}TIME. Let A be a language and c_A its characteristic function. Then it holds: $A \subseteq$ DLOG^{0}TIME(c_A).

2.2 Boolean Circuits

Boolean circuits with *bounded fan-in* are finite directed acyclic graphs with nodes or gates up to indegree 2 with a certain label or type. Nodes of indegree zero are the input nodes $x_0, x_1, \ldots, x_{n-1}$ or nodes labelled 0 or 1; nodes with indegree one are labelled $\neg$ or *id* (the identity function), and nodes with indegree two are labelled $\wedge$ or $\vee$. Some of the nodes are specified as output nodes $y_0, y_1, \ldots, y_{m-1}$. In circuits with *unbounded fan-in* there is no restriction on the indegree of the $\vee$ and $\wedge$ nodes. In this case these nodes are also called existential and universal, respectively.

A *circuit family* $\{C_n\} := (C_1, C_2, \ldots)$ computes a function f, if the output of C_n on input x of length n is the same as $f(x)$ for all x. If $f(x) \in \{0, 1\}$ for all x, i.e., there is only one output node in each circuit of the family, then we can also say that $\{C_n\}$ accepts the set of all x for which $f(x) = 1$. For a circuit C, the size of C *size*(C), is the number of nodes C contains. The depth of C, *depth*(C), is the length of the longest path from some input node to some output node.

We will allow our circuits to have access to *oracle gates*, which compute the value $f(x)$ of x for a functional oracle $f : \{0, 1\}^l \rightarrow \{0, 1\}^m$ (see [15]). Note that usually oracle nodes determine the membership of a string x in an oracle set; this corresponds in our approach to taking $m = 1$, i.e. using a 0–1 valued function f instead of the set $L_f := \{x \mid f(x) = 1\}$ (see e.g. [24, 25]). For unbounded fan-in circuits, oracle nodes have depth 1. In the case of bounded fan-in circuits an oracle gate with k inputs and k' outputs contributes $\log(k \cdot k')$ to the depth of the circuit. This is the standard way of counting the depth of oracle nodes (see e.g. [15]).

2.3 *Uniformity*

We restrict ourselves to *uniform circuit families* for which the codification of the nth circuit may be "easily" determined from n. There exists a variety of such uniformity conditions (see e.g. [19, 10, 8, 11]). For AC^i or NC^{i+1} with $i \geq 1$, most of these uniformities result in the same class, namely the commonly considered logspace uniform AC^i or NC^{i+1}. For $i = 0$ there are differences and much effort has been devoted in particular to develop uniformity conditions for which $AC^0 =$ LH, (LH is the logtime hierarchy of Sipser [20]) and $NC^1 =$ ALOGTIME [19, 10, 8].

In the following we generalize the notions of extended and direct connection language [19] to be applicable to circuits with oracle gates of arbitrary fan-in and fan-out. For both bounded fan-in or unbounded fan-in circuits we assume that each oracle gate number is a 3-tuple (o, k, k'), that contains the fan-in k and fan-out k' of gate o. (Here suffices any codification for which the fan-in and fan-out of any oracle gate can be determined in DLOGTIME.) To be able to refer to the input gates $x_1, x_2, \ldots, x_n$ and output gates $y_1, y_2, \ldots, y_m$ of a circuit C_n in DLOGTIME, we assume that the input gates are numbered $0, 1, \ldots, n-1$ and the output gates are numbered $2^{|size(C_n)|}, \ldots, 2^{|size(C_n)|} + m - 1$. (Here again suffices any convention that allows to compute the number of any of the input or output gates in DLOGTIME.)

For a bounded fan-in circuit C with or without oracle gates for a function f, let g be a gate and let $p \in ([0], [1], [k, k', i, j])^*$ such that $k, k', i, j \in \{0, 1\}^*$. Then $g(p)$ (for $p \neq \lambda$) is the gate reached when p is followed as a path towards the inputs of C by starting at g, going left (or right) when $[0]$ (or $[1]$) appears and following input $i+1$ when $[k, k', i, j]$ appears. $[k, k', i, j]$ stands for an oracle gate with fan-in k, fan-out k' that is reached via its $j + 1$st output and left via its $i + 1$st input, $0 \leq i \leq k - 1$, $0 \leq j \leq k' - 1$. For example, $g([1])$ is the right input gate of g, and $g([0][11, 1, 10, 0])$ is the 3rd input of an oracle gate (with fan-in 3 and fan-out 1 that has been reached via its first output) of the left input to g.

For a bounded fan-in circuit family $\{C_n\}$ with or without oracle gates, the *extended connection language* ECL_C, consists of all 4-tuples (x, g, p, y), where $|x| = n$, $g \in \{0, 1\}^*$ (g is the gate number), $y \in \{input, 0, 1, output, \neg, id, \wedge, \vee, oracle\} \cup \{0, 1\}^*$ (y is either gate type or gate number), and $p \in ([0], [1], [k, k', i, j])^*$ with $|p| \in O(\log(size(C_n)))$ such that (i) if $p = \lambda$ then y is the type of gate g, and (ii) if $p \neq \lambda$ then y is the gate number of $g(p)$, including, if $g(p)$ is oracle gate, the number of $g(p)$'s output.

ECL_C encodes local information about the wiring of C_n within distance $O(\log(size(C_n)))$. For unbounded fan-in circuits, we are only interested in the information about direct wiring between two gates.

We define for an unbounded fan-in circuit family $\{C_n\}$ with or without oracle gates the *direct connection language* DCL_C, as above, except $p \in \{\lambda, [0], [k, k', i, j]\}$ such that (i) if $p = \lambda$ then y is the type of gate g, (ii) if $p = [0]$ then y is the gate number of an input to g, (iii) if $p = [k, k', i, j]$ then g is an oracle gate (with fan-in k and fan-out k') and y is the $i + 1$st input to g, including if y is oracle gate, the number of y's output. (j is redundant in this case.)

Definition 2.3 *An unbounded fan-in circuit family with or without oracle gates*
$\{C_n\}$ *is DLOGTIME-DCL-uniform if there is a DLOGTIME machine that rec-*
ognizes DCL_C. *A bounded fan-in circuit family with or without oracle gates*
$\{C_n\}$ *is DLOGTIME-ECL-uniform (ALOGTIME-ECL-uniform) if there is a*
DLOGTIME (ALOGTIME) machine that recognizes ECL_C.

Note that for circuits without oracle gates DLOGTIME-*DCL*-uniformity coincides with DLOGTIME-*DCL*-uniformity of [8] (see also [11]) and ALOGTIME-
ECL-uniform NC^1 (DLOGTIME-*ECL*-uniformity) coincides with U_{E^*}-uniform
NC^1 (U_E-uniformity) of [19].

Definition 2.4 *We denote by* FAC^i *for* $i \geq 0$ *and by* FNC^i *for* $i \geq 1$ *the class of*
functions computable by DLOGTIME-DCL-uniform unbounded fan-in and, re-
spectively, ALOGTIME-ECL-uniform bounded fan-in circuit families $\{C_n\}$ *of*
polynomial size, $size(C_n) = n^{O(1)}$, *and polylogarithmic depth,* $depth(C_n) =$
$O(\log^i n)$. *The corresponding classes of languages (0–1 functions) are denoted*
by AC^i *and* NC^i, *respectively. If the circuits contain functional oracle nodes for*
a function f *in a function class* $\mathcal{F}$, *we will refer to* $FAC^i(\mathcal{F})$ *and* $FNC^i(\mathcal{F})$, *or*
in the case of languages, to $AC^i(\mathcal{F})$ *and* $NC^i(\mathcal{F})$.

Note that by [1, 16], PARITY separates the two classes $AC^0=$LH [8] and
$NC^1=$ALOGTIME[19].

3 Some Properties of $DLOG^iTIME$ Reducibility

In Section 5 we will see that for any (function) class $\mathcal{F}$ closed under FAC^0 (FNC^1)
reducibility, like the functional versions of the classes mentioned above, there is
a precise characterization of $DLOG^iTIME(\mathcal{F})$ in terms of unbounded (bounded)
fan-in circuits of depth $O(\log^i n)$ ($O(\log^{i+1} n)$) with oracle gates for $\mathcal{F}$. In this
section, we obtain characterizations of the class $DLOG^iTIME(\mathcal{F})$ for function
classes $\mathcal{F}$ that are not known to be closed under FAC^0 or FNC^1 reducibility.
The two results presented below may be interpreted as decomposition results of
"sequential" classes by $DLOG^iTIME$-reducibility.

Denote by DSPACE,TIME($O(\log^k n), O(\log^l n)$), for $k, l \geq 0$, the class of
languages that are accepted by simultaneously $O(\log^k n)$-space bounded and
$O(\log^l n)$-time bounded Turing machines.

Proposition 3.1 *For all* $0 \leq i \leq j$ *it holds*
DSPACE,TIME $(O(\log^j n), O(\log^{i+j} n)) = DLOG^iTIME(FDTIME(O(\log^j n))$.

Our second example of a decomposition result for sequential classes concerns
the class $P_{\log^k}(\mathcal{F})$ of languages that are accepted by polynomial-time bounded
oracle Turing machines that may query $O(\log^k n)$ times, $k \geq 0$, an oracle function
in the function class $\mathcal{F}$.

Proposition 3.2 *Let $\mathcal{F}$ be an arbitrary class of functions. Then,*
$$P_{\log^{i+j}}(\mathcal{F}) = \mathrm{DLOG}^i\mathrm{TIME}(FP_{\log^j}(\mathcal{F})) \quad \text{for } i, j \geq 0.$$

In particular, we obtain $P_{\log^i}(\mathrm{NP}) = \mathrm{DLOG}^i\mathrm{TIME}(\mathrm{FP}_1(\mathrm{NP}))$ (compare [12]) and a new characterization of $\Theta_2^P = \mathrm{DLOGTIME}(\mathrm{FP}_1(\mathrm{NP}))$. $\mathrm{DLOG}^i\mathrm{TIME}$-reducibility here nicely separates the logarithmic adaptiveness and "sequential" computation power of $P_{\log^i}(\mathcal{F})$ computations into the complexity of the base machine on the one hand, and, the computational power of its oracle, on the other. Results similiar to Proposition 3.2 hold also for adaptive logspace reductions (see [2], where the relationship between adaptive $\mathrm{DLOG}^i\mathrm{TIME}$ reducibility and adaptive logspace reductions has been investigated).

4 Normal form circuits for $\mathrm{NC}^{i+1}(\mathcal{F})$ and $\mathrm{AC}^i(\mathcal{F})$

In this section we state two normal form lemmas for circuits. We will use these lemmas in the proof of our main theorem in the next section. The first lemma states that any AC^i or NC^{i+1} circuit can be transformed such that it becomes "easily" divisible into subcircuits of the same depth, where "easily" means that the number of the subcircuit a gate g of C belongs to depends only on g's gate number. The second lemma states that any of such subcircuits can be resolved by one oracle node, and hence the whole circuit by a chain of oracle nodes. In both lemmas ALOGTIME-*ECL*-uniformity (or even DLOGTIME-*ECL*-uniformity) of the NC circuits and DLOGTIME-*DCL*-uniformity of the AC circuits is preserved. Similar lemmas for logspace-uniform circuits without oracle gates are implicit in [25], but for the most parts the proofs do not carry over because new subtleties arise if oracles are present in the circuits and the circuits are logtime-uniform.

Let C be a circuit. For any gate g of C, let $level(g) = 0$, if g has indegree 0, and let $level(g)$ be the maximal number of nodes on a path from some node with indegree 0 to g, otherwise. C is *levelled*, if (1) for any gate g of C, $level(\mathrm{g})$ is part of the gate name of g, and (2) no gate at any level p is connected with some gate at level less than $p - 1$ in C. C is *divisible*, if C is (1) levelled, and (2) for all gates of C, $depth(g) \leq 2 \cdot level(g)$.

For AC circuits, the depth of the oracle gates contributes 1 to the circuit. Hence all gates g of such a circuit satisfy $level(g) = depth(g)$, and when the circuit is levelled it is easily divisible into subcircuits of the same depth by looking at the gate numbers only. Difficulties arise for NC circuits. Here the depth of a gate g essentially depends on the fan-in and fan-out of the oracle gates that occur on paths between the inputs and g. For an NC circuit, $level(g)$ and $depth(g)$ of a gate g may differ by up to a logarithmic factor, i.e., $level(g) \leq depth(g) \leq O(\log n) \cdot level(g)$, for example, when C_n has on its first level an oracle gate with fan-in n. The following lemma shows that we can bound the difference between level and depth of an NC circuit by a factor of 2, which is the case for divisible circuits.

Lemma 4.1 *Let f be a function. Then it holds for $i \geq 0$;*
For any $NC^{i+1}(f)$ (or, respectively, $AC^i(f)$) circuit family there is an equivalent
divisible $NC^{i+1}(f)$ ($AC^i(f)$) circuit family that obeys the same uniformity.
(We may even assume DLOGTIME-ECL-uniformity for the NC circuits.)

For the AC case, as argued above, any levelled AC circuit is also divisible.
For levelling, we refine a technique of [9] used by Wilson for his decomposibility
results ([25], Theorem 3.2) to become applicable in the case of DLOGTIME-
uniformity.

For the NC case, we first transform a given circuit C_n so as to ensure that
level and depth of all gates differ at most by a factor of 2. For this we use an
idea of Peter Rossmanith (see [6]). We add for each oracle gate g_i in C_n a chain
of length $\log(\text{fan-in}(g) \cdot \text{fan-out}(g))$ of identity gates between g and each of g's
input gates. This yields a circuit C_n' that satisfies $depth(g) \leq 2 \cdot level(g)$ for
all gates g, since the depth of each gate increases at most by a factor of 2, but
the level of each gate g increases by the sum of the depths of the oracle gates
on a path with maximal depth leading to g. The numbering of the gates in C_n'
will be such that the name of a gate g that has a "copy" in C_n contains the
number of that copy, and if g is a new identity gate, then g's name indicates
that it is the lth element in the chain that was added between the jth input
gate of the corresponding oracle gate in C_n. ALOGTIME- (or, respectively,
DLOGTIME-) ECL-uniformity of C_n' follows basically from the fact that paths
without oracle nodes are the same in C_n and C_n', and in the description of paths
that contain oracle gates the parts corresponding to added chains of identity
gates can be easily identified and deleted, since the fan-in and fan-out of the
oracle gate forms part of the path description. Equally, if a path leads to an
added identity gate, the corresponding gate number is computable from the last
oracle gate in the path and the number of ([0], [1]) elements following it; and if
a path starts from an added identity gate g, then the corresponding oracle gate
can be detected from the name of g. To obtain a levelled circuit, we apply the
refined levelling technique mentioned in the AC case to C_n'.

Lemma 4.2 *Let f be a function. Then it holds for $i, j \geq 0$:*
For any $FNC^{i+j+1}(f)$ ($FAC^{i+j}(f)$) circuit family there exists an equivalent cir-
cuit family, where each circuit is a chain of length $O(\log^i n)$ of $FNC^{j+1}(f)$
($FAC^j(f)$) oracle gates.
(We may even assume DLOGTIME-ECL-uniformity for the NC circuits.)

The proof of the AC case follows the same lines as the one for the NC case.
We sketch the latter. Let $\{C_n\}$ be a NC^{i+j+1} circuit family with oracle gates
for a function f obtained from applying Lemma 4.1. We will divide C_n into
subcircuits L_n^k of depth $O(\log^j n)$, consisting of $2^{j \cdot \log\log n}$ consecutive levels of
C_n each. The input of L_n^0 is the input of C_n, and each L_n^k receives as input the
output of L_n^{k-1}. By Lemma 4.1, C_n has a very regular structure, in fact, each of
its levels, but the input level, differ only in the level number in the gate names.
Hence we only have to distinguish two types of subcircuits, L_n^0 and L_n^1, and can

define an oracle function h with $h(x\$z) = \begin{cases} L^0_{|x|}(x)\$z + 1, & \text{if } z = 0; \\ L^1_{|x|}(x)\$z + 1, & \text{otherwise.} \end{cases}$

h can be computed by a FNC^{j+1} circuit family $\{H_n\}$ with oracle nodes for f, which ALOGTIME- (or DLOGTIME-) ECL-uniformity follows basically from the fact the subcircuits L^0_n or L^1_n are ALOGTIME- (DLOGTIME-) ECL-uniform. Now consider the circuit family $\{C'_n\}$, where C'_n consists of a chain of length $O(\log^i n)$ of oracle nodes that compute h, where the input to the first node is $x\$0$. Clearly, $\{C'_n\}$ is equivalent to $\{C_n\}$.

5 Decomposing $\text{NC}^{i+1}(\mathcal{F})$ and $\text{AC}^i(\mathcal{F})$

The main result of this section is the decomposition of the relativized NC - and AC - hierarchies in terms of adaptive DLOG^iTIME reductions. More specifically we show the following:

(Main)Theorem 5.1 *Let $\mathcal{F}$ be an arbitrary function class. It holds for $i, j \geq 0$:*
(i) $\text{NC}^{i+j+1}(\mathcal{F})=\text{DLOG}^i\text{TIME}(\text{FNC}^{j+1}(\mathcal{F}))=\text{NC}^{i+1}(\text{FNC}^{j+1}(\mathcal{F}))$,
(ii) $\text{AC}^{i+j}(\mathcal{F})=\text{DLOG}^i\text{TIME}(\text{FAC}^j(\mathcal{F}))= \text{AC}^i(\text{FAC}^j(\mathcal{F}))$.

As a corollary we obtain an answer to the question raised by Wilson in [25] "Under which circumstances do relativized NC^{i+1} and AC^i coincide?" that generalizes previous answers to this question [3, 6].

Corollary 5.1 *Let $\mathcal{F}$ be an arbitrary function class.*
If $\text{AC}^0(\mathcal{F}) = \text{NC}^1(\mathcal{F})$, then $\text{AC}^i(\mathcal{F}) = \text{NC}^{i+1}(\mathcal{F})$ for all $i \geq 0$.

The proof of the main theorem follows the same lines for (i) and (ii). It consists of three lemmas that we present for the NC case only (which is a little more involved than (ii)). The main theorem follows from Lemma 5.2 and Lemma 5.3 for the left to right inclusions, and Lemmas 5.4 and 5.2 for the right to left inclusions.

The first lemma states that an NC^{i+j+1} circuit can be decomposed using DLOG^iTIME reducibility.

Lemma 5.2 $\text{NC}^{i+j+1}(\mathcal{F}) \subseteq \text{DLOG}^i\text{TIME}(\text{FNC}^{j+1}(\mathcal{F}))$ *for $i, j \geq 0$.*
(We may even assume DLOGTIME-ECL-uniformity of the NC circuits.)

The proof uses the normal form lemma 4.2 of the previous section that provides a representation of an $\text{NC}^{i+j+1}(\mathcal{F})$ circuit as a chain of oracle nodes for a function in $\text{NC}^{j+1}(\mathcal{F})$. It remains to modify the oracle function in such a way that it can be used as functional oracle of a DLOG^iTIME machine. To achieve this, the oracle function not only evaluates a sequence of levels of the original circuit, but it also increments a counter of the number of queries. The base machine first initializes the queries counter and then queries the functional oracle $O(\log^i n)$ times.

The second lemma shows that adaptive DLOG^iTIME reductions can be simulated by NC^{i+1} circuits.

Lemma 5.3 $DLOG^i\mathrm{TIME}(\mathcal{F}) \subseteq NC^{i+1}(\mathcal{F})$ *for* $i \geq 0$.
(We may even assume DLOGTIME-*ECL-uniformity of the* NC *circuits.)*

The proof follows Ladner's simulation of a sequential machine by a boolean circuit [18] that can be modified to integrate the indirect access to input and answer oracle tape.

The third lemma shows how to join the circuits of the oracle gates to one circuit.

Lemma 5.4 *Let* $\mathcal{F}$ *be an arbitrary function class. Then,*
$NC^{i+1}(FNC^{j+1}(\mathcal{F})) \subseteq NC^{i+j+1}(\mathcal{F})$ *for* $i, j \geq 0$.

In this case we are not able to prove the result conserving DLOGTIME-*ECL*-uniformity, but are forced to use ALOGTIME-*ECL*-uniformity instead. Consider that we are given a path in a circuit C_n that results from substituting the oracle gates by their corresponding subcircuits. Then we are confronted with the problem of decomposing the path into parts that correspond to former subcircuits. The only solution to achieve this deterministically seems to be in following the path step by step. But this consumes up to time $O(\log^2 n)$. Hence we use nondeterminism for guessing the different parts of the path, and, afterwards, we verify the guesses using the ALOGTIME algorithms for the *ECL* of the original circuit family and the circuit family of the oracle function.

Acknowledgement

We thank Ricard Gavaldà and Jacobo Torán for many helpful comments.

References

1. M. Ajtai, Σ_1^1 formulae on finite structures, *Ann. Pure Appl. Logic*, **24** (1983), 1–48.

2. C. Àlvarez, Polylogtime and Logspace Adaptive Reductions, Tech. Report LSI–93–42–R, Dept. LSI, Universitat Politècnica de Catalunya, 1993.

3. C. Àlvarez, J.L. Balcázar and B. Jenner, Adaptive logspace reducibility and parallel time, to appear in *Math. Systems Theory.* (preliminary version in Proc. 8th STACS, *LNCS* **480** (Springer, Berlin, 1991), 422–433.)

4. C. Àlvarez and B. Jenner, A very hard log-space counting class, *Theoret. Computer Science* **107** (1993), 3–30.

5. C. Àlvarez and B. Jenner, On adaptive dlogtime and polylogtime Reductions, Tech. Report LSI–93–41–R, Dept. LSI, Universitat Politècnica de Catalunya, 1993.

6. J.L. Balcázar, Adaptive logspace and depth-bounded reducibilities, Proc. 6th Structure in Complexity Theory Conference (1991), 240–254.

7. J.L. Balcázar, A. Lozano, J. Torán, The Complexity of Algorithmic Problems on Succinct Instances, R. Baeza-Yates, U. Manber (eds.), *Computer Science*, Plenum Press, New York, (1992), 351–377.

8. D.A. Mix Barrington, N. Immerman, H. Straubing, On uniformity within NC^1, *J. of Comp. and System Sci.* **41**,3 (1990), 274–306.

9. A. Borodin, S.A. Cook, P.W. Dymond, W.L. Ruzzo, M. Tompa, Two applications of inductive counting for complementation problems, *SIAM J. of Comput.* **18**,3 (1989), 559–578.

10. S.R. Buss, The formula value problem is in ALOGTIME, Proc. 19th ACM STOC Symp., 1987, 123–131.

11. S. Buss, S. Cook, A. Gupta, V Ramachandran, An optimal parallel algorithm for formula evaluation, typescript, Univ. of Toronto, 1989.

12. J. Castro, C. Seara, Characterizations of some complexity classes between Θ_2^p and Δ_2^p, Proc. 9th STACS, *LNCS* **577** (Springer, Berlin, 1992), 305–319.

13. A.K. Chandra, D. Kozen, L.J. Stockmeyer, Alternation, *J. of the ACM* **28** (1981), 114–133.

14. A.K. Chandra, L.J. Stockmeyer, U. Vishkin, Constant depth reducibility, *SIAM J. of Comput.* **13** (1984), 423–439.

15. S.A. Cook, A taxonomy of problems, with fast parallel algorithms, *Information and Control* **64** (1985), 2–22.

16. M. Furst, J.B. Saxe, M. Sipser, Parity, circuits, and the polynomial-time hierarchy, *Math. Systems Theory* **17** (1984), 13–27.

17. B. Jenner, J. Torán, Parallel queries to NP, Proc. 8th Structure in Complexity Theory Conference (1993), 280–291. (to appear in *Theoret. Computer Science*)

18. R. Ladner, The circuit value problem is log space complete for P, *SIGACT News* **7** (1975), 18–20.

19. W.L. Ruzzo, On uniform circuit complexity, *J. of Comput. and System Sci.* **22** (1981), 365–383.

20. M. Sipser, Borel sets and circuit complexity, Proc. 15th ACM STOC Symp. (1983), 61–69.

21. L. Stockmeyer, The polynomial-time hierarchy, *Theoret. Computer Science* **3** (1977), pp 1–22.

22. I.H. Sudborough, On the tape complexity of deterministic context-free languages, *J. of the ACM* **25** (1978), 405–414.

23. K.W. Wagner, Bounded Query Classes, *SIAM J. of Comput.* **19**,5 (1990), 833–846.

24. C.B. Wilson, Relativized NC, *Math. Systems Theory* **20** (1987), 13–29.

25. C.B. Wilson, Decomposing NC and AC, *SIAM J. of Comput.* **19**,2 (1990), pp. 384–396.

$\mathrm{NC}^k(\mathrm{NP}) = \mathrm{AC}^{k-1}(\mathrm{NP})$

Mitsunori Ogiwara*

Abstract

It is shown for any $k \geq 1$, that the closure of NP under NC^k reducibility coincides with that of NP under AC^{k-1} reducibility, thereby giving an answer to a basic question that has been open for a long time. A similar result is shown for $\mathrm{C}_{=}\mathrm{P}$.

1   Introduction

Resource-bounded reducibility is one of the most important concepts in complexity theory. Resource-bounded reducibilities are classified into two types: (1) time- and/or space-bounded reducibilities [12,11,7], which are defined in terms of Turing machines, and (2) size- and/or depth-bounded reducibilities [9,6,8, 17,18], which are defined in the context of circuit theory. One of the most important subjects of the study of resource-bounded reducibility would be to distinguish or equate reducibilities, in particular, to find relationships between Turing machine-based reducibilities and circuit theory-based reducibilities (for such results, see for example [3,16]). Questions arising in the subject, however, in many cases, turn out to be too general or too difficult. So, we often attempt to find relationships between reducibilities with a restriction that the oracle sets are in a certain complexity class.

For that reason, reducibilities of sets to NP have been widely discussed in many ways. This is partly because that NP is the most fundamental and the most important class. Above all, Θ_2^p, the closure of NP under polynomial-time truth-table reducibility has been widely discussed [1,4,5,15]. It has been proven by Buss and Hay[4] and by Wagner [15] that many time-bounded and/or

*Department of Computer Science, University of Rochester, Rochester, NY 14627, USA. email: ogiwara@cs.rochester.edu. Supported in part by the JSPS under grant NSF-INT-9116781/JSPS-ENG-207.

space-bounded reducibilities to NP coincide with polynomial-time truth-table reducibility to NP. Among such reducibilities, there are logspace reducibility, polynomial-time $\mathcal{O}(\log n)$ Turing reducibility, polynomial-time Boolean formula reducibility, and so on.

On the other hand, concerning circuit theory-based reducibilities, one of the most basic question is whether polynomial-time truth-table reducibility to NP is equivalent to NC^1-reducibility to NP. Roughly speaking, a set L is NC^k-reducible [8,17] to a set A if a membership question for L can be determined by a family of Boolean circuits with access to B, in $\mathcal{O}(\log^k n)$ parallel time and with a polynomial number of gates. From the above mentioned equivalence result, it follows that Θ_2^p is included in $NC^1(NP)$, the closure of NP under NC^1-reducibility. The converse inclusion, however, has been left open for a long time (for results related to this question, see [1,5]). In this paper, we prove that the inclusion does hold; that is, we show that $NC^1(NP) = \Theta_2^p$.

Our result is presented as a more general statement; that is, we show for any $k \geq 1$, that $NC^k(NP) \subseteq P^{NP[\log^k]}$—the class of sets polynomial time reducible to NP via $\mathcal{O}(\log^k n)$ adaptive queries. Castro and Seara[5] have proven that $P^{NP[\log^k]}$ coincides with $AC^{k-1}(NP)$—the closure of NP under AC^{k-1} reductions, where AC^k [18] is defined similarly to NC^k with only exception that AND and OR gates can have unlimited number of inputs, whereas the number is bounded by 2 in NC^k. It is well-known for any class of sets $\mathcal{C}$ and $k \geq 1$, that $AC^{k-1}(\mathcal{C}) \subseteq NC^k(\mathcal{C}) \subseteq AC^k(\mathcal{C})$. Also, it is known that $AC^{k-1}(\mathcal{C}) = NC^k(\mathcal{C})$ holds for NL[2] and for both NC^j and AC^j for any j[18]. By combining the result in [5] with our result, we get a simple classification of hierarchies of $NC^k(NP)$, $AC^k(NP)$, and $P^{NP[\log^k]}$; namely, we show for any $k \geq 1$, that $NC^k(NP) = AC^{k-1}(NP) = P^{NP[\log^k]}$.

We note here that the above equivalence can be derived as a corollary of a result by Gottlob [10], proven independently. He showed that TREES(NP), the class of sets recognized by polynomial-size trees with queries to SAT, coincides with Θ_2^p. Given an NC^1 circuit C with queries to SAT and an input x to C, one can easily construct a polynomial-size tree which represents the computation of the circuit. So, we have $NC^1(NP) \subseteq \Theta_2^p$.

Our proof technique can be applied to any class that is closed under $\leq_{ctt}^{NP}$-reductions. An example of such classes is $C_=P$ [14]. A set L is in $C_=P$ if there is a polynomial time-bounded nondeterministic Turing machine M such that for every x, $x \in L$ if and only if M on x has the same number of accepting computation paths and rejecting computation paths. Since $coC_=P$, the class of sets whose complements are in $C_=P$, is closed under $\leq_{ctt}^{NP}$-reductions [13], we have for any $k \geq 1$, that $NC^k(C_=P) = AC^{k-1}(C_=P) = P^{C_=P[\log^k]}$.

2 Preliminaries

In this section, we set down the notations and notions we will use throughout. The alphabet we will use is $\{0,1\}$, which is denoted by Σ. All languages are subsets of Σ^*. For an element $x \in \Sigma^*$, $|x|$ denotes its length. We will use $\mathbf{N}$ to denote the set of all nonnegative integers. All logarithms will be base 2.

Our model of parallel computation is the Boolean circuit. For more details, the reader may refer to [17,8,3]. A Boolean circuit can be considered as an acyclic directed graph with labelled nodes representing gates of the type AND, OR, NOT, which compute, *and* of two Boolean values, *or* of two Boolean values, and the *negation* of a Boolean value, respectively. Thus, the *fan-in* of these gates are bounded by two. Since we wish Boolean circuits to compute characteristic functions of sets, they have some n inputs, but have only one output. We distinguish those inputs and the output by INPUT gates and by an OUTPUT gate, respectively. Furthermore, we will endow Boolean circuits with access to oracles, by introducing a type of gates called ORACLE gates. An ORACLE gate has some k inputs and one output. Given an oracle set X, an oracle gate, on an input x, outputs the value 1, if x is in the set X, and 0 otherwise. Without loss of generality, we assume that the number of inputs to an ORACLE gate is larger than 1.

The complexity of a Boolean circuit is measured by its size and depth. The size of a Boolean circuit C, denoted by $size(C)$, is the number of edges in it. The depth of a circuit C, denoted by $depth(C)$, is the length of the longest directed path from some INPUT gate to the OUPUT gate, where an ORACLE gate of k inputs contributes $\lceil \log k \rceil$ to the path length. More precisely, for a gate g in a Boolean circuit C, define the length of g, denoted by $|g|$, to be 0 if g is an INPUT gate, 1 if g is neither an INPUT gate nor an ORACLE gate, and $\lceil \log k \rceil$ if g is an ORACLE gate with k inputs. For a directed path $\pi = (g_1, \cdots, g_m)$ in C, define the length of π, denoted by $|\pi|$ to be $|g_1| + \cdots + |g_m|$. Then $depth(C) = \max\{|\pi| : \pi \text{ is a directed path from an INPUT gate to the OUTPUT gate in } C\}$.

Let $\mathcal{F} = \{C_n\}_{n \geq 1}$ be a family of Boolean circuits, where C_n has exactly n

INPUT gates for all $n \geq 1$. We say that $\mathcal{F}$ *accepts* a set A with oracle B if for any $n \geq 1$ and $x \in \Sigma^n$, $x \in A$ if and only if C_n on input x with oracle B outputs 1.

For a function $s : \mathbf{N} \mapsto \mathbf{N}$, we say that $\mathcal{F}$ is $s(n)$ size-bounded if for all n, $size(C_n) \leq s(n)$. For a function $d : \mathbf{N} \mapsto \mathbf{N}$, we say that $\mathcal{F}$ is $d(n)$ depth-bounded if for all n, $depth(C_n) \leq d(n)$. We say that a family of Boolean circuits $\mathcal{F} = \{C_n\}_{n \geq 1}$ is *uniform* if there is a logarithmically space-bounded Turing machine that, on input 0^n, outputs C_n for any n.

Definition 2.1 *For any $k \geq 0$, a set A is NC^k reducible to a set B if there is a uniform family of Boolean circuits $\mathcal{F}$ such that*

1. *$\mathcal{F}$ accepts A with oracle B;*

2. *there is a polynomial p such that $\mathcal{F}$ is $p(n)$ size-bounded; and*

3. *there is a constant $c > 0$ such that $\mathcal{F}$ is $c \log^k n$ depth-bounded.*

Definition 2.2 *For any $k \geq 0$ and a class of sets $\mathcal{C}$, $\mathrm{NC}^k(\mathcal{C})$ denotes the class of all sets L that are NC^k-reducible to some set in $\mathcal{C}$.*

We also consider a slightly different computation model, which is called unbounded fan-in circuits[18]. In the model, there is no restriction on the number of inputs to AND gates and OR gates. The size and the depth of AC circuits are measured similarly, except $|g|$ is defined to be 1 even for oracle gates.

Definition 2.3 *For any $k \geq 0$, a set A is AC^k reducible to a set B if there is a uniform family of unbounded fan-in Boolean circuits $\mathcal{F}$ such that*

1. *$\mathcal{F}$ accepts A with oracle B;*

2. *there is a polynomial p such that $\mathcal{F}$ is $p(n)$ size-bounded; and*

3. *there is a constant $c > 0$ such that $\mathcal{F}$ is $c \log^k n$ depth-bounded.*

Definition 2.4 *For any $k \geq 0$ and class of sets $\mathcal{C}$, $\mathrm{AC}^k(\mathcal{C})$ denotes the class of all sets L that are AC^k-reducible to some set in $\mathcal{C}$.*

It is well-known [18] for any class $\mathcal{C}$ and for any $k \geq 0$ that, $\mathrm{AC}^k(\mathcal{C}) \subseteq \mathrm{NC}^{k+1}(\mathcal{C}) \subseteq \mathrm{AC}^{k+1}(\mathcal{C})$.

Next we define reducibility notions we will use throughout.

Definition 2.5   *1. [12] A set A is $\leq_{tt}^p$-reducible to a set B if there exists a polynomial time-bounded deterministic oracle Turing machine M such that for every x,*

- *$x \in A$ if and only if M on x with oracle B accepts; and*
- *M on x computes all the queries to B in advance.*

2. [15,5] A set A is $\leq_{\mathcal{O}(\log^k n)\text{-}T}^p$-reducible to a set B, if there is a polynomial time-bounded oracle Turing machine M that for all x,

- *$x \in A$ if and only if M on x with oracle B accepts; and*
- *M on x makes at most $\mathcal{O}(\log^k |x|)$ adaptive queries to its oracle.*

For a class of sets $\mathcal{C}$, we write $P_{tt}^{\mathcal{C}}$ ($P^{\mathcal{C}[\log^k]}$) to denote the class of sets that are $\leq_{tt}^p$-reducible ($\leq_{\mathcal{O}(\log^k n)\text{-}T}^p$-reducible) to some set in $\mathcal{C}$. We also use Θ_2^p to denote P_{tt}^{NP}. It is known that many reduction classes of NP coincide with Θ_2^p [4,15]. In particular, $\Theta_2^p = P^{NP[\log]}$. It is also known that $\Theta_2^p \subseteq NC^1(NP)$ (see [1]). Castro and Seara have proven that for any $k \geq 1$, it holds that $P^{NP[\log^k]} = AC^{k-1}(NP)$.

Proposition 2.6

$$
\begin{aligned}
\Theta_2^p &= AC^0(NP) = P^{NP[\log]} \subseteq NC^1(NP) \subseteq AC^1(NP) = P^{NP[\log^2]} \subseteq \cdots \\
&\subseteq AC^{k-1}(NP) = P^{NP[\log^k]} \subseteq NC^k(NP) \\
&\subseteq AC^k(NP) = P^{NP[\log^{k+1}]} \subseteq NC^{k+1}(NP) \\
&\subseteq \cdots \subseteq P^{NP}.
\end{aligned}
$$

3   The Main Theorem

Theorem 3.1 *For any $k \geq 1$, $NC^k(NP) \subseteq P^{NP[\log^k]}$.*

Proof   Let L be accepted by a uniform family of Boolean circuits $\mathcal{F} = \{C_n\}_{n \geq 1}$ with oracle $A \in NP$. Let p be a polynomial and $c > 0$ be a constant such that $size(C_n) \leq p(n)$ and $depth(C_n) \leq c \log^k n$ for all n. Let x denote the string whose membership in L we are testing.

Let g be any gate in $C_{|x|}$. By $\pi_{in}(g)$ and $\pi_{out}(g)$, we denote the number of directed paths from INPUT gates to g in $C_{|x|}$ and that of directed paths from g to the OUTPUT gate in $C_{|x|}$. It clearly holds that $\pi_{in}(h)$, where h is the OUTPUT gate, is an upper bound on the value of $\pi_{out}(g)$ for any gate g.

Fact 1 *For any gate g in $C_{|x|}$, $\pi_{in}(g) \leq 2^{depth(C_n)}$.*

Proof of Fact 1   For each gate $g \in C_{|x|}$, let $\delta(g)$ denote the length of the longest directed paths from some INPUT gate to g. Since for any gate g in $C_{|x|}$, $\delta(g) \leq depth(C_{|x|})$, it suffices to show for any gate $g \in C_{|x|}$, that $\pi_{in}(g) \leq 2^{\delta(g)}$. Note for any gate g in $C_{|x|}$, that if there is an edge (h, g) in $C_{|x|}$, then $\delta(h) \leq \delta(g) - |g|$.

The proof is by an induction on $\delta(g)$. For the base case, let $\delta(g) = 0$. Clearly, g is an INPUT gate, and there is only one path from an INPUT gate to g (the path consisting only of g). So, $\pi_{in}(g) = 1 = 2^0$, and the claim holds.

For an induction step, let $\delta(g) = l > 0$, and suppose that the claim holds for every $l' < l$. Let g be a gate with $\delta(g) = l$. Clearly, g is not an INPUT gate. So, we have only to consider the following three cases.

(Case 1) g is a NOT gate: There uniquely exists a gate h connected to g, and $\delta(h) \leq \delta(g) - 1$. So, $\pi_{in}(g) = \pi_{in}(h)$, and by our induction hypothesis, $\pi_{in}(h) \leq 2^{\delta(h)}$. Therefore, $\pi_{in}(g) \leq 2^{\delta(g)}$.

(Case 2) g is either an AND gate or an OR gate: g has exactly two inputs, which are connected to outputs of gates h and h'. By definition, $|g| = 1$, so, $\delta(h), \delta(h') \leq \delta(g) - 1$. Clearly, $\pi_{in}(g) = \pi_{in}(h) + \pi_{in}(h')$. By our induction hypothesis, it holds that $\pi_{in}(h) \leq 2^{\delta(h)} \leq 2^{\delta(g)-1}$ and that $\pi_{in}(h') \leq 2^{\delta(h')} \leq 2^{\delta(g)-1}$. Therefore, $\pi_{in}(g) \leq 2^{\delta(g)}$.

(Case 3) g is an ORACLE gate: Let $m \geq 2$ be the number of inputs to g. Let $h_1, \cdots, h_m$ be the gates such that for each $i, 1 \leq i \leq m$, the i-th input of g is the output of h_i. It holds that $\pi_{in}(g) = \sum_{i=1}^{m} \pi_{in}(h_i)$ and for every $i, 1 \leq i \leq m$, $\delta(h_i) \leq \delta(g) - |g|$. Since $|g| = \lceil \log m \rceil$, by our induction hypothesis, it holds that

$$
\begin{aligned}
\pi_{in}(g) \quad &\leq \quad \sum_{i=1}^{m} 2^{\delta(h_i)} \\
&\leq \quad m 2^{\delta(g)-|g|} \\
&\leq \quad 2^{\log m + \delta(g) - \lceil \log m \rceil} \\
&\leq \quad 2^{\delta(g)}.
\end{aligned}
$$

Thus, the claim holds for this case, too.

By the above discussions, the claim holds for every l. This proves the fact.

■ **Proof of Fact 1**

By the above fact, there are at most $2^{depth(C_{|x|})}$ paths from some INPUT gate to the OUTPUT gate in $C_{|x|}$, and thus, for any gate g in $C_{|x|}$, $\pi_{out}(g) \leq 2^{depth(C_{|x|})}$. Let S denote the set of all ORACLE gates in $C_{|x|}$. For distinct $g, h \in S$, we say that g is *connected* to h, if there is a directed path from g to h in $C_{|x|}$. Furthermore, we say that g is *strongly connected* to h, if (1) g is connected to h and (2) there exist no directed paths from g to h having ORACLE gates in between. For each $g \in S$, let $D(g)$ and $E(g)$ denote the set of all $h \in S$ to which g is connected and g is strongly connected, respectively, and let $D^*(g)$ denote the set of all $h \in S$ to which there is a path from g. It is not hard to see that the following fact holds:

Fact 2 *For any $g \in S$,*

(a) $D^*(g) - E(g) \subseteq \cup_{h \in E(g)} D^*(h)$; *and*

(b) $\pi_{out}(g) \geq \sum_{h \in E(g)} \pi_{out}(h)$.

For each $g \in S$, define the level of g, denoted by $\lambda(g)$, in the following inductive way:

- Define $\lambda(g) = 0$ if and only if $E(g) = \emptyset$.

- For $l \geq 1$, define $\lambda(g) = l$ if and only if there is some $h \in E(g)$ such that $\lambda(h) = l - 1$ and for all $h \in E(g)$, $\lambda(h) \leq l - 1$.

Define $\hat{l}$ to be the maximum of all $\lambda(g)$, and for each $l, 0 \leq l \leq \hat{l}$, let $S_l = \{g \in S : \lambda(g) = l\}$. Obviously, $\hat{l} \leq depth(C_{|x|})$.

For each $g \in S$, we define the weight assigned to g, denoted by $w(g)$, in the following inductive way:

- If $\lambda(g) = 0$, then define $w(g) = 1$.

- If $\lambda(g) = l > 0$, then define $w(g) = 1 + \sum_{h \in D^*(g)} w(h)$.

It is not hard to see that, given x, one can compute $\hat{l}$ and $S_0, \cdots, S_{\hat{l}}$ in time polynomial in $|x|$. So, there is a polynomial time algorithm that, given x and $g \in C_{|x|}$, computes $w(g)$.

Fact 3 *For any $g \in S$, $w(g) \leq 2^{2\lambda(g)} \pi_{out}(g)$.*

Proof of Fact 3 The proof is by induction on $\lambda(g)$. For the base case, let $\lambda(g) = 0$. Then $w(g) = 1 = 2^0 \cdot 1 \leq 2^{\lambda(g)} \pi_{out}(g)$, so the claim holds.

For an inductive step, let $l \geq 1$ and suppose that the claim holds for all $l' < l$. By definition, it holds that $w(g) = 1 + \sum_{h \in D^*(g)} w(h) = 1 + \sum_{h \in D^*(g) - E(g)} w(h) + \sum_{h \in E(g)} w(h)$. By Fact 2 (a), $D^*(g) - E(g) \subseteq \cup_{h \in E(g)} D^*(h)$. So, $\sum_{h \in D^*(g) - E(g)} w(h) \leq \sum_{h \in E(g)} \sum_{u \in D^*(h)} w(u) \leq \sum_{h \in E(g)} w(h)$. Thus, $w(g) \leq 1 + 2 \sum_{h \in E(g)} w(h) \leq 4 \sum_{h \in E(g)} w(h)$. For any $h \in E(g)$, $\lambda(g) \leq l - 1$. So, by our induction hypothesis, for any $h \in E(g)$, $w(h) \leq 2^{2\lambda(g)-2} \pi_{out}(h)$. Moreover, by Fact 2 (b), $\pi_{out}(g) \geq \sum_{h \in E(g)} \pi_{out}(h)$. Therefore, $w(g) \leq 2^{2\lambda(g)} \sum_{h \in E(g)} \pi_{out}(h) \leq 2^{2\lambda(g)} \pi_{out}(g)$, and thus, the claim holds for l. This proves the fact. ∎ **Proof of Fact 3**

Note, since for any $g \in S$, $\lambda(g) \leq depth(C_{|x|}) \leq c \log^k |x|$ and $\pi_{out}(g) \leq 2^{depth(C_{|x|})}$, from the fact above, for any $g \in S$, we have $w(g) \leq 2^{a \log^k |x|}$ for some constant a.

Now let $r(\leq p(n))$ denote the number of ORACLE gates in $C_{|x|}$ and $g_1, \cdots, g_r$ be an enumeration of all ORACLE gates in $C_{|x|}$. For $b \in \Sigma^r$, consider a simulation of $C_{|x|}$ on x assuming the output of g_i to be 1 if and only if $b(i) = 1$, where $b(i)$ is the ith bit of b. Given such a b, the input to g_i for each $i, 1 \leq i \leq r$, and the output of $C_{|x|}$ can be computed in time polynomial in n. By $Q(x, b, i)$, we denote the input to g_i and by $R(x, b)$, we denote the output. Call b *legal* if for all $i, 1 \leq i \leq r$, with $b(i) = 1$, it holds that $Q(x, b, i) \in A$, and call b *accepting* if $R(x, b) = 1$. Define $W(x, b)$ to be the sum of all $w(g_i)$ with $b(i) = 1$. Clearly, $W(x, b) \leq 2^{a \log^k |x|} p(|x|)$.

Now define

$$B_1 = \{(x, m) : (\exists b \in \Sigma^r) W(x, b) = m \text{ and } b \text{ is legal}\}$$

and

$$B_2 = \{(x, m) : (\exists b \in \Sigma^r) W(x, b) = m, R(x, b) = 1, \text{ and } b \text{ is legal}\}$$

Clearly, $B_1, B_2 \in NP$. Let $m_{\max}$ denote the largest m such that $(x, m) \in B_1$.

Fact 4 $x \in L$ *if and only if* $(x, m_{\max}) \in B_2$.

Proof of Fact 4 Let $\tilde{b} \in \Sigma^r$ be such that for all $i, 1 \leq i \leq r$, the output of g_i is in A if and only if $\tilde{b}(i) = 1$, and let $m_0 = W(x, \tilde{b})$. Obviously, $\tilde{b}$ is legal, so $(x, m_0) \in B$. Furthermore, x is in L if and only if $\tilde{b}$ is accepting. Below, we show for any legal b other than $\tilde{b}$, that $W(x, b) < m_0$. If this holds, then $m_0 = m_{\max}$, and $\tilde{b}$ is the unique legal b such that $W(x, b) = m_{\max}$. Therefore, $x \in L$ if and only if $\tilde{b}$ is accepting, and thus, $x \in L$ if and only if $(x, m_{\max}) \in B_2$.

Let $b \in \Sigma^r - \{\tilde{b}\}$ be legal and let I be the set of all $i, 1 \le i \le r$, such that $b(i) \ne \tilde{b}(i)$. Let I_0 be the set of all $i \in I$ such that $g_i \notin D^*(g_j)$ for any $j \in I$ and $I_1 = I_0 \cup \{i : 1 \le i \le r, g_i \in D^*(g_j) \text{ for some } j \in I\}$. Clearly, it holds that $I_0 \subseteq I \subseteq I_1$ and that for any $i \in I_1 - I_0$, $g_i \in D^*(g_j)$ for some $j \in I_0$.

We claim that for any $i \in I_0$, $b(i) = 0$ and $\tilde{b}(i) = 1$. This is seen as follows: Let $i \in I_0$. By definition, for any j such that $g_i \in D^*(g_j)$, $b(j) = \tilde{b}(j)$. Since $Q(x, b, i)$ is determined from x and from b_j with $g_i \in D^*(g_j)$, it holds for any $i \in I_0$, that $Q(x, b, i) = Q(x, \tilde{b}, i)$. By definition, $b(i) \ne \tilde{b}(i)$, $\tilde{b}(i) = 1$ if and only if $Q(x, \tilde{b}, i) \in A$, and $b(i) = 1$ implies $Q(x, b, i) \in A$. So, $b(i) = 0$ and $\tilde{b}(i) = 1$.

Now we evaluate $W(x, \tilde{b}) - W(x, b)$. By definition, the difference is equal to

$$\sum_{i \in I} \tilde{b}(i) w(g_i) - \sum_{i \in I} b(i) w(g_i).$$

By the above claim, the first sum is at least $\sum_{i \in I_0} w(g_i)$ and the second sum is at most $\sum_{i \in I - I_0} w(g_i) \le \sum_{i \in I_1 - I_0} w(g_i)$. Since for any $i \in I_1 - I_0$, $g_i \in D^*(g_j)$ for some $j \in I_0$, we have

$$\sum_{i \in I} b(i) w(g_i) \le \sum_{i \in I_0} \sum_{h \in D^*(g_i)} w(h).$$

By the definition of $w(g)$, for any $i \in I_0$, it holds that $w(g_i) > \sum_{h \in D^*(g_i)} w(h)$. Therefore,

$$W(x, \tilde{b}) - W(x, b) \ge \sum_{i \in I_0} \left(w(g_i) - \sum_{h \in D^*(g_i)} w(h) \right) > 0.$$

Thus, $W(x, \tilde{b}) > W(x, b)$. This proves the fact. ■ **Proof of Fact 4**

By the above discussions, one can determine whether $x \in L$ in the following way: (1) by using a binary search method on $[1, 2^{a \log^k |x|} p(|x|)]$ compute $m_{\max} = \max\{i : (x, i) \in B_1\}$, and (3) accepts x if and only if $(x, m_{\max}) \in B_2$. The number of queries to be made is $\mathcal{O}(\log(2^{a \log^k |x|} p(|x|))) = \mathcal{O}(\log^k |x|)$. So, L is in $\mathrm{P}^{\mathrm{NP}[\log^k]}$. This proves the theorem. ■

Corollary 3.2 *For any $k \ge 1$, $\mathrm{AC}^{k-1}(\mathrm{NP}) = \mathrm{NC}^k(\mathrm{NP}) = \mathrm{P}^{\mathrm{NP}[\log^k]}$. Especially, $\mathrm{P}_{tt}(\mathrm{NP}) = \mathrm{AC}^0(\mathrm{NP}) = \mathrm{NC}^1(\mathrm{NP}) = \mathrm{P}^{\mathrm{NP}[\log]}$.*

A set A is $\le_{ctt}^{NP}$-reducible to a set B [12] if there exists a polynomial time-bounded nondeterminstic Turing machine M such that for every x, $x \in A$ if and only if M on x outputs a tuple $(y_1, \cdots, y_m)$ such that $y_1, \cdots, y_m \in B$ for some computation path. From the proof of Theorem 3.1, one can deduce the following lemma.

322

Lemma 3.3 *For any $k \geq 1$, if $L \in \mathrm{NC}^k(A)$, then there is some B such that* $L{\leq}^p_{\mathcal{O}(\log^k n)\text{-}T} B$ *and* $B \leq^{NP}_{ctt} A$.

Moreover, by using the techniques developed in [15,4,5], one can show the following.

Lemma 3.4 *For any $k \geq 1$, if $L{\leq}^p_{\mathcal{O}(\log^k n)\text{-}T} A$, then there is some B such that such that $L \in \mathrm{AC}^{k-1}(B)$ and $B \leq^{NP}_{ctt} A$.*

Thus, we have the following theorem.

Theorem 3.5 *Let $\mathcal{C}$ be a class closed under $\leq^{NP}_{ctt}$-reductions. For any $k \geq 1$,* $\mathrm{NC}^k(\mathcal{C}) = \mathrm{P}^{\mathcal{C}[\log^k]} = \mathrm{AC}^{k-1}(\mathcal{C})$.

Now we apply the above result to a class called $\mathrm{C}_=\mathrm{P}$. A set L is in $\mathrm{C}_=\mathrm{P}$[14] if there is a polynomial time-bounded nondeterministic Turing machine M such that for every x, $x \in L$ if and only if exactly a half of the computation paths of M on x is accepting. It is well-known that $\mathrm{coC}_=\mathrm{P} = \{A : \overline{A} \in \mathrm{C}_=\mathrm{P}\}$ is closed under $\leq^{NP}_{ctt}$-reductions [13]. So, the equivalence similar to that of NP holds for $\mathrm{C}_=\mathrm{P}$.

Corollary 3.6 *For any $k \geq 1$, $\mathrm{AC}^{k-1}(\mathrm{C}_=\mathrm{P}) = \mathrm{NC}^k(\mathrm{C}_=\mathrm{P}) = \mathrm{P}^{\mathrm{C}_=\mathrm{P}[\log^k]}$. Especially, $\mathrm{P}_{tt}(\mathrm{C}_=\mathrm{P}) = \mathrm{AC}^0(\mathrm{C}_=\mathrm{P}) = \mathrm{NC}^1(\mathrm{C}_=\mathrm{P}) = \mathrm{P}^{\mathrm{C}_=\mathrm{P}[\log]}$.*

Acknowledgement The author would like to thank Eric Allender, Seinosuke Toda, and Chris Wilson for useful discussions, Richard Beigel for letting him know the existence of Gottlob's paper, and Georg Gottlob for kindly sharing his results with him. The author would like to thank an anonymous referee for valuable suggestiolns.

References

[1] E. Allender and C. Wilson. Width-bounded reducibility and binary search over complexity classes. In *Proceedings of the 5th Conference on Structure in Complexity Theory*, pages 122–129. IEEE Computer Society Press, 1990.

[2] C. Alvarez, J. Balcazar, and B. Jenner. Functional oracle queries as a measure of parallel time. In *Proceedings of the 8th Symposium on Theoretical Aspects of Computer Science*, pages 422–433. Springer-Verlag *Lecture Notes in Computer Science #480*, 1991.

[3] A. Borodin. On relating time and space to size and depth. *SIAM Journal on Computing*, 6(4):733–744, December 1977.

[4] S. Buss and L. Hay. On truth-table reducibility to SAT and the difference hierarchy over NP. In *Proceedings of the 3rd Conference on Structure in Complexity Theory*, pages 224–233. IEEE Computer Society Press, 1988.

[5] J. Castro and C. Seara. Characterizations of some complexity classes between Θ_2^p and Δ_2^p. In *Proceedings of the 9th Symposium on Theoretical Aspects of Computer Science*, pages 305–317. Springer-Verlag *Lecture Notes in Computer Science #577*, 1992.

[6] A. Chandra, L. Stockmeyer, and U. Vishkin. Constant depth reducibility. *SIAM Journal on Computing*, 13(2):423–439, May 1984.

[7] S. Cook. The complexity of theorem proving procedures. In *Proceedings of the 3rd Symposium on Theory of Computing*, pages 151–158. ACM Press, 1971.

[8] S. Cook. A taxonomy of problems with fast parallel algorithms. *Information and Computation*, 64:2–22, 1985.

[9] M. Furst, J. Saxe, and M. Sipser. Parity, circuits, and the polynomial-time hierarchy. *Mathematical Systems Theory*, 17:13–27, 1984.

[10] G. Gottlob. NP trees and Carnap's modal logic. In *Proceedings of the 34th Symposium on Foundations of Computer Science*. IEEE Computer Society Press, 1993. to appear.

[11] R. Ladner and N. Lynch. Relativization of questions about logspace computability. *Mathematical Systems Theory*, 10:19–32, 1976.

[12] R. Ladner, N. Lynch, and A. Selman. A comparison of polynomial time reducibilities. *Theoretical Computer Science*, 1(2):103–123, 1975.

[13] M. Ogiwara. Generalized theorems on the relationships among reducibility notions to certain complexity classes. *Mathematical Systems Theory*. to appear.

[14] K. Wagner. The complexity of combinatorial problems with succinct input representation. *Acta Informatica*, 23:325–356, 1986.

[15] K. Wagner. Bounded query classes. *SIAM Journal on Computing*, 19(5):833–846, October 1990.

[16] C. Wilson. Relativized circuit complexity. *Journal of Computer and System Science*, 31:169–181, 1985.

[17] C. Wilson. Relativized NC. *Mathematical Systems Theory*, 20:13–29, 1987.

[18] C. Wilson. On the decomposability of NC and AC. *SIAM Journal on Computing*, 19(2):384–296, April 1990.

Invited Lecture

Hypertransition systems

André Arnold

LaBRI [*]
Université Bordeaux I

Abstract. Hypertransition systems are extensions of transition systems
in the same way as tree automata are extensions of word automata and
hypergraphs are extensions of graphs. In this paper we explain why we
need such an extension in order to model nondeterminism and refinements in systems of concurrent processes.

1 Introduction

Transition systems are a well known and widely spread model for representing
concurrent systems. Formally a (labeled) transition system over an alphabet A
of *actions* or *events* is a tuple $\mathcal{A} = \langle S, T, \alpha, \beta, \lambda \rangle$ where

- S is a set of *states*,
- T is a set of *transitions*,
- α and β are two mappings from T to S, associating with a transition t its
  source state $\alpha(t)$ and its *target* state $\beta(t)$,
- $\lambda : T \to A$ associates with t the action or event $\lambda(t)$ having caused this
  transition.

Moreover, we assume that the triple $\langle \alpha, \lambda, \beta \rangle : T \to S \times A \times S$ is one-to-one
so that, as usual, T can be considered as a subset of $S \times A \times S$, and a transition
t can be pictured as

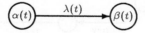

It turns out that this model is, in some cases, not precise enough to capture
some relevant features of a sytem one wishes to model, thus we are led to propose
an extension of this model.

Free will and Contingency When, in a given transition system, a state s is the
source of two distinct transitions t and t', this may mean two different things:

- the process represented by this transition system, when it is in state s, is
  allowed to perform the two transitions t and t', according to its "free will",

[*] Unité de Recherche associée au Centre National de la Recherche Scientifique n° 1304

- or it can be forced, by its environment, to execute either t or t', in a "contingent" way.

For instance, I can use the telephone to call Mr. A or Mr. B. This is represented by the two transitions

and I choose whom I call.

On the other hand, I can be called by Mr. A or Mr. B.

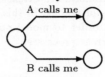

Here I cannot choose who calls me.

The two above transition systems, although formally identical, can bear a quite different meaning.

Another famous example is the "vending machine" [8, 9]. After having put a coin in the machine, the consumer chooses to get coffee or tea by hitting the adequate button (free will).

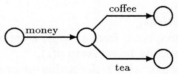

With a variant of this machine, the consumer puts in coin and the machine gets in a state where it can deliver only coffee, or in a state where it can deliver only tea, whatever the preference of the consumer is (contingency).

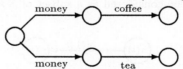

To model such a situation, the effect of putting a coin will be represented by only one transition (instead of two), having *two target states* expressing that the resulting state of the machine can be any of them, but the consumer has no effect on the choice of the machine. Then, the previous system will be pictured as

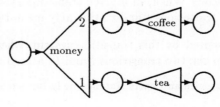

Such transitions, with several target states, will be called *hypertransitions*, by analogy with the notion of a hyperedge in a hypergraph.

Action refinement Another reason why it is interesting to consider hypertransitions is the definition of an action refinement [1, 6, 10]. Roughly speaking, a refinement amounts to substituting a more or less complex transition system for a single transition; for instance, a transition can represent a procedure call and a refinement consists in replacing the call by the body of the procedure.

The point is that in some cases transitions labelled by different actions cannot be independently refined, because they are different realizations of a contingently non deterministic action. For instance, one may refine the system

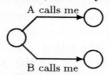

by giving more details on the succession of events involved in a call, getting

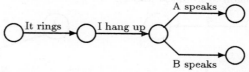

Obviously, the two actions *A calls me* and *B calls me* have to be refined together. This is made obvious if the system to be refined is represented by

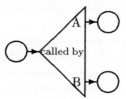

This paper is organized as follows. In Section 2 we define the notion of a hypertransition system. In section 3 we define synchronization constraints on hypertransition systems and their synchronized product with respect to these constraints; we also define the notion of a globally deterministic system. In Section 4 we define a notion of refinement for hypertransition systems and we study how a refinement behaves with respect to synchronization constraints.

2 Hypertransition systems

A *ranked alphabet* A is a finite set of symbols, denoting actions, together with a mapping $\rho : A \rightarrow \mathbb{N}$. For an action a in A, the natural number $\rho(a)$ is the *arity* of the symbol a. It represents the number of different results the action a may have, depending on the context in which it is applied.

A *hypertransition system* over a ranked alphabet A is a tuple $\mathcal{A} = \langle S, T, \alpha, \beta, \lambda \rangle$ where

- S is a set of *states*,
- T is a set of *hypertransitions*,
- λ is a mapping from T into A; if $t \in T$, the symbol $\lambda(t)$ is called the *label* of the hypertransition t,
- α is a mapping from T into S; if $t \in T$, the state $\alpha(t)$ is the *source* of t,
- β is a mapping from T into the set of finite sequences over S; if $t \in T$, then $\beta(t) \in S^n$ where $n = \rho(\lambda(t))$ is the arity of the label of t; $\beta(t)$ is called the *target sequence* of t.

In case the arity of any action a is 1, β is a mapping from T into S, and we get the usual notion of a transition system. In case $n = \rho(a) > 1$, a hypertransition t labeled by a has a target sequence $\beta(t) = s_1 s_2 \cdots s_n$, which means that, depending on the environment, t can put the system in any of the states $s_1, s_2, \ldots, s_n$. The case $\rho(a) = 0$ is also allowed; this may be used to express the fact that a is a nonterminating action. Then, if t is labeled by a, the target sequence $\beta(t)$ is empty and t will never put the transition system in a new state.

As an example consider the alphabet $\{a, b\}$ with $\rho(a) = 1, \rho(b) = 0$ and the two hypertransition systems $\mathcal{A}$ and $\mathcal{B}$.

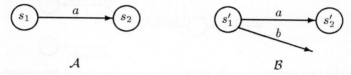

$$\mathcal{A} \qquad\qquad\qquad \mathcal{B}$$

In the state s_1 of $\mathcal{A}$, the action b cannot be executed; in the state s_1' of $\mathcal{B}$ it can, but does not terminate. In both cases, only a allows the system to enter a new state.

Finally, when several hypertransitions have the same source state, it corresponds to a "free will" choice of the process. Therefore there is no real need to assume that a process has to choose between several transitions labelled with the same action. Thus, we can restrict ourself to consider *deterministic* hypertransition systems: for every state s and every action a there is at most one hypertransition of source S and label a.

Example 1. Let us consider the program `while b=0 do b:=1; b:=0;`

We model it by an hypertransition system with three hyperactions: *test* of rank 2, *asg0* and *asg1* of rank 1, pictured as follows.

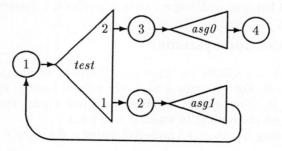

The variable b may be modeled as a system with two states, 0 and 1, and two hyperactions $a0$ and $a1$ of rank 3:

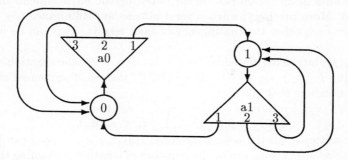

The three target states of each of these actions correspond respectively to the cases where the variable is read, is set to 0, or set to 1 by the "user" of the variable.

3 Synchronized products of hypertransition systems

In this section we generalize to hypertransition systems the notion of a synchronization constraint, and the definition of the synchronized product [3, 5] that formalizes the behaviour of several hypertransition systems interacting together.

We begin with the case where there is no interaction at all.

3.1 Free product of hypertransition systems

For $i = 1, \ldots, n$, let $\mathcal{A}_i = \langle S_i, T_i, \alpha_i, \beta_i, \lambda_i \rangle$ be a hypertransition system over the ranked alphabet (A_i, ρ_i).

Let us consider the alphabet $A = A_1 \times A_2 \times \cdots \times A_n$ with the mapping $\rho : A \to \mathbb{N}$ defined by $\rho(\langle a_1, a_2, \ldots, a_n \rangle) = \rho_1(a_1) \times \rho_2(a_2) \times \cdots \times \rho_n(a_n)$. The *free product* of the $\mathcal{A}_i$'s is the system $\langle S, T, \alpha, \beta, \lambda \rangle$ where

- $S = S_1 \times \cdots \times S_n$,
- $T = T_1 \times \cdots \times T_n$,
- $\lambda(t_1, \ldots, t_n) = \langle \lambda_1(t_1), \ldots, \lambda_n(t_n) \rangle$,
- $\alpha(t_1, \ldots, t_n) = \langle \alpha_1(t_1), \ldots, \alpha_n(t_n) \rangle$,
- $\beta(t_1, \ldots, t_n)$ is the sequence of all n-tuples $\langle s_{j_1}^{(1)}, \ldots, s_{j_n}^{(n)} \rangle$ such that $1 \leq j_k \leq m_k = \rho(\lambda_k(t_k))$ (there are $m_1 \times \cdots \times m_n = \rho(\lambda(t_1, \ldots, t_n))$ such n-tuples), where the states $s_j^{(k)}$ are given by $\beta_k(t_k) = \langle s_1^{(k)}, \ldots, s_{m_k}^{(k)} \rangle$.

Let us remark that when each letter is of rank 1, we get the usual free product of transition systems [3].

3.2 Synchronization constraints

A synchronization constraint explains how the contingent choice between the different results of an action can be restricted by the environmemt in which it is executed. More precisely, when several actions are simultaneously executed, they restrict each other the contingency of their results. This can be formalized as follows:

Let (A_i, ρ_i) be ranked alphabets for $i = 1, \ldots, n$. A synchronisation constraint is a mapping $I : A_1 \times A_2 \times \cdots \times A_n \to (\mathbb{N}^n)^*$, the set of sequences of n-tuples of natural numbers that satisfies:
if $\langle i_1, \ldots, i_j, \ldots, i_n \rangle$ occurs in $I(a_1, \ldots, a_j, \ldots, a_n)$ then
$1 \le i_1 \le \rho_1(a_1), \ldots, 1 \le i_j \le \rho_j(a_j), \ldots, 1 \le i_n \le \rho_n(a_n)$.

In case arities of all the actions are one, $I(a_1, \ldots, a_j, \ldots, a_n)$ can have only two values: the empty sequence or the sequence of length n containing the n-tuple $\langle 1, \ldots, 1 \rangle$.

We also may consider that I defines a new ranked alphabet $(A_1 \times \cdots \times A_n, \rho_I)$ where $\rho_I(a_1, \ldots, a_n)$ is equal to the length of the sequence $I(a_1, \ldots, a_n)$.

3.3 Synchronized products

For $i = 1, \ldots, n$, let $\mathcal{A}_i = \langle S_i, T_i, \alpha_i, \beta_i, \lambda_i \rangle$ be a hypertransition system over the ranked alphabet (A_i, ρ_i). and let I be a synchronization constraint. The synchronized product of the $\mathcal{A}_i$'s with respect to I, denoted by $\prod_I(\mathcal{A}_1, \ldots, \mathcal{A}_n)$ is a hypertransition system $\langle S_1 \times \cdots \times S_n, T_1 \times \cdots \times T_n, \alpha, \beta, \lambda \rangle$ over the ranked alphabet $(A_1 \times \cdots \times A_n, \rho_I)$ defined by

- $\alpha(t_1, \ldots, t_n) = \langle \alpha_1(t_1), \ldots, \alpha_n(t_n) \rangle$,
- $\lambda(t_1, \ldots, t_n) = \langle \lambda_1(t_1), \ldots, \lambda_n(t_n) \rangle$, considered as a member of $(A_1 \times \cdots \times A_n, \rho_I)$,
- $\beta(t_1, \ldots, t_n)$ is the sequence

$$\langle s_{j_{1,1}}^{(1)}, \ldots, s_{j_{1,i}}^{(i)}, \ldots, s_{j_{1,n}}^{(n)} \rangle \cdots \langle s_{j_{k,1}}^{(1)}, \ldots, s_{j_{k,i}}^{(i)}, \ldots, s_{j_{k,n}}^{(n)} \rangle$$

of length k such that
- $\beta_i(t_i) = s_1^{(i)} \ldots s_{m_i}^{(i)}$ with $m_i = \rho_i(\lambda_i(t_i))$,
- $I(\lambda_1(t_1), \ldots, \lambda_i(t_i), \ldots, \lambda_n(t_n)) =$
$$\langle j_{1,1}, \ldots, j_{1,i}, \ldots, j_{1,n} \rangle \cdots \langle j_{k,1}, \ldots, j_{k,i}, \ldots, j_{k,n} \rangle.$$

Example 2. Let us consider the hypertransition systems in Example 1. We define the following synchronisation constraint:

$I(test, a0) = (\langle 1, 3 \rangle)$
$I(test, a1) = (\langle 2, 3 \rangle)$
$I(asg0, a0) = (\langle 1, 2 \rangle)$
$I(asg0, a1) = (\langle 1, 1 \rangle)$
$I(asg1, a0) = (\langle 1, 1 \rangle)$
$I(asg1, a1) = (\langle 1, 2 \rangle)$

The first two lines mean that the result of a test depends on the action that is simultaneously executed by the variable, which, itself, depends only on the state of the variable. The other ones mean that the new value assigned to the variable depends on the assignment performed by the program.

One can check that their synchronized product, with respect to the above constraint, is

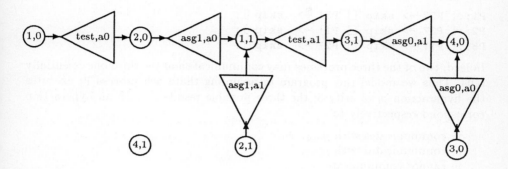

3.4 Global determinism

In [7], the authors distinguish between two kinds of nondeterminism in CSP programs:

- the *local* nondeterminism occurring when a process "decides *on its own* for which communication to wait" is clearly our notion of free will;
- the *global* nondeterminism "is resolved by inspecting the other processes w.r.t. their willingness to communicate."

More generally, global nondeterminism is related to the quantity of contingency remaining when each process of a system operates in the environment provided by the other processes of the system. Thus, it is a property of the synchronization constraint, and we say that a synchronisation constraint $I : A_1 \times A_2 \times \cdots \times A_n \to (\mathbb{N}^n)^*$ is *globally deterministic* if

$$\forall(a_1, \ldots, a_n), \ \mathrm{card}(I(a_1, \ldots, a_n)) \leq 1.$$

The fact that $\mathrm{card}(I(a_1, \ldots, a_n)) = 1$ means that the simultaneous execution of $a_1, \ldots, a_n$ by n processes leads each process to a unique new state, even if each action a_i may have several target states, thus the effect of the global action $(a_1, \ldots, a_n)$ is deterministic. The fact that $\mathrm{card}(I(a_1, \ldots, a_n)) = 0$ means that the global action cannot be executed, or is deadlocking.

If the latter case never appears, i.e.,

$$\forall(a_1, \ldots, a_n), \ \mathrm{card}(I(a_1, \ldots, a_n)) = 1,$$

we say that the synchronization constraint is *implementable.* We choose this term because in this case it is indeed easy to implement the synchronization constraint. Each process decides which action it will execute and it broadcasts this information to all other processes; when a process knows what the other processes intend to do, it also knows, by I, in which state to go (a similar mechanism was described in [4]).

Example 3. Let us consider the CSP program `[P1||P2||P3]` where

```
P1::[ P2? -> skip [] P3! ->  skip ];
P2::[ P3? -> skip [] P1! ->  skip ];
P3::[ P1? -> skip [] P2! ->  skip ];
```

Indeed, two of the three processes may communicate and the third one essentially fails. Thus we model this program in assuming thate ach process Pi executes the hyperaction p_i of arity 3; the three possible results of such an hyperaction correspond respectively to

p_i communicates with $p_{i\oplus 1}$,
p_i communicates with $p_{i\ominus 1}$,
p_i cannot communicate.

The synchronisation constraint is defined by

$$I(p_1, p_2, p_3) = (\langle 1, 2, 3\rangle\langle 2, 3, 1\rangle\langle 3, 1, 2\rangle).$$

This constraint is not globally deterministic in our sense and this fits with the intuition that this kind of rendez-vous cannot be implemented without additional mechanisms to deal with global nondeterminism.

4 Refinements

4.1 Definitions

A *refinement* of a ranked alphabet A over a ranked alphabet B is a mapping ϕ that associates an hypertransition system $\phi(a)$ over B with any letter a of A, submitted to the following restriction:

(i) $\phi(a)$ has $n + 1$ distinguished states s_0, $s_1, \ldots, s_n$, where $n = \rho(a)$ is the rank of a. s_0 is called the *entry state* of $\phi(a)$ and $s_1, \ldots, s_n$ are the *exit states* of $\phi(a)$,
(ii) the entry state is not a target of an hypertransition of $\phi(a)$,
(iii) no exit state is the source of an hypertransition of $\phi(a)$.

We shall show later on why we need the restrictions (ii) and (iii) in the definition of a refinement.

If ϕ is a refinement of A over B and if $\mathcal{A} = \langle S, T, \alpha, \beta, \lambda\rangle$ is an hypertransition system over A then $\phi(\mathcal{A})$ is the hypertransition system obtained by replacing each hypertransition t of $\mathcal{A}$ by $\phi(\lambda(t))$.

Formally, $\phi(\mathcal{A})$ is the hypertransition system $\langle S', T', \alpha', \beta', \lambda'\rangle$ defined in the following way. For each letter a, let us consider

- $\langle S_a, T_a, \alpha_a, \beta_a, \lambda_a \rangle$, the hypertransition system $\phi(a)$,
- $s_0(a)$, the entry state of $\phi(a)$,
- $s_1(a), \ldots, s_{\rho(a)}(a)$, the sequence of exit states of $\phi(a)$,
- $S'_a = S_a - \{s_0(a), s_1(a), \ldots, s_{\rho(a)}(a)\}$, the set of other states.

Let us also recall that, for any $a \in A$, $\lambda^{-1}(a)$ is the set of hypertransitions of $\mathcal{A}$ labelled by a.

Then S', the set of states of $\phi(\mathcal{A})$, is $S \cup \bigcup_{a \in A}(\lambda^{-1}(a) \times S'_a)$, and T', the set of hypertransitions of $\phi(\mathcal{A})$, is $\bigcup_{a \in A}(\lambda^{-1}(a) \times T_a)$. The mappings α', β', and λ' are defined, for $t \in T$, and $t' \in T'_a$, with $a = \lambda(t)$, by

- $\alpha'(t, t') = \begin{cases} \alpha(t) & \text{if } \alpha_a(t') = s_0(a), \\ (t, \alpha_a(t')) & \text{if } \alpha_a(t') \in S'_a. \end{cases}$
  Note that $\alpha_a(t')$ cannot be in $\{s_1(a), \ldots, s_{\rho(a)}(a)\}$ because of (iii) above.
- if $\beta(t) = s_1 s_2 \cdots s_{\rho(a)}$ and $\beta_a(t') = s'_1 s'_2 \cdots s'_k$, then $\beta'(t, t') = q_1 q_2 \cdots q_k$
  where $q_i = \begin{cases} s_j & \text{if } s'_i = s_a(j), \\ (t, s'_i) & \text{if } s'_i \in S'_a. \end{cases}$
  Note that s'_i cannot be equal to $s_0(a)$, because of (ii) above.
- $\lambda'(t, t') = \lambda_a(t')$.

Example 4. Let us consider the system $\mathcal{A}$

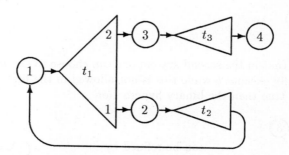

with three hypertransitions t_1, t_2, and t_3 respectively labelled by a, b, and b. The hyperactions a and b are refined by

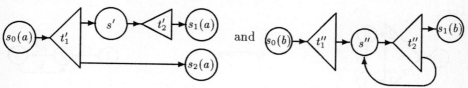

with $\lambda_a(t'_1) = a_1, \lambda_a(t'_2) = a_2$ and $\lambda_b(t''_1) = b_1, \lambda_b(t''_2) = b_2$.
  Then $\phi(\mathcal{A})$ is

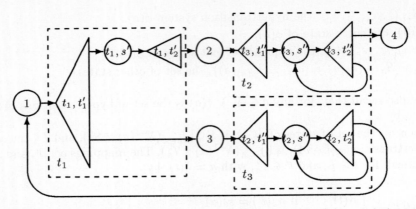

Now we can explain why we assume the restrictions (ii) and (iii) above. If (ii) is not true, the unary hyperaction a can be refined by

then, the refinement of

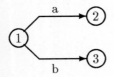   becomes

and one can see that in the second system one can choose to execute a and then one can eventually execute b while this is not allowed in the first system.

If (iii) is not true then the binary hyperaction

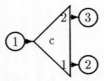   can be refined by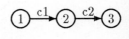

Then

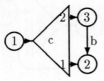   becomes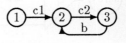

thus b can be executed at most once in the first system and any number of times in the second one.

4.2 Synchronization and refinement

Let $\mathcal{A}_1$, $\mathcal{A}_2$,...,$\mathcal{A}_n$ be hypertransition systems over the alphabets A_1, A_2,..., A_n, and let I be a synchronization constraint defined on $A_1 \times A_2 \times \cdots \times A_n$. Let $\mathcal{A}$ be the synchronized product of the $\mathcal{A}_i$'s with respect to I, which is a hypertransition system over the ranked alphabet $(A_1 \times \cdots \times A_n, \rho_I)$.

For $i = 1, \ldots, n$, let $\phi_i : A_i \to B_i$ be a refinement and let $\mathcal{B}_i$ be the hypertransition system $\phi_i(\mathcal{A}_i)$. Let J be a synchronization constraint over $B_1 \times B_2 \times \cdots \times B_n$ and let $\mathcal{B}$ be the synchronized product of the $\mathcal{B}_i$'s with respect to J.

We want to compare $\mathcal{A}$ and $\mathcal{B}$.

Let us consider, for any $(a_1, a_2, \ldots, a_n) \in A_1 \times A_2 \times \cdots \times A_n$, the synchronized product of the hypertransition systems $\phi_i(a_i)$'s with respect to J, and let $\psi(a_1, a_2, \ldots, a_n)$ be its restriction to the states reachable from $s_0(a_1, a_2, \ldots, a_n) = \langle s_0(a_1), s_0(a_2), \ldots, s_0(a_n) \rangle$. Let us assume that the set of states of $\psi(a_1, a_2, \ldots, a_n)$ has the following properties

(i) it contains $\langle s_0(a_1), s_0(a_2), \ldots, s_0(a_n) \rangle$ and $\langle s_{i_1}(a_1), s_{i_2}(a_2), \ldots, s_{i_n}(a_n) \rangle$ for any $\langle i_1, i_2, \ldots, i_n \rangle \in I(a_1, a_2, \ldots, a_n)$,
(ii) all its other states are in $S'(a_1) \times S'(a_2) \times \cdots \times S'(a_n)$.

Then it is easy to show

Proposition 1. $\psi : (A_1 \times \cdots \times A_n, \rho_I) \to (B_1 \times B_2 \times \cdots \times B_n, \rho_J)$ *is a refinement and* $\psi(\mathcal{A}) = \mathcal{B}$.

An example Let $\mathcal{A}_1$, $\mathcal{A}_2$,...,$\mathcal{A}_n$ be hypertransition systems over the alphabets A_1, A_2,..., A_n, and let I be a synchronization constraint defined on $A_1 \times A_2 \times \cdots \times A_n$.

For each alphabet A_i let us consider the alphabet

$$B_i = \{\gamma\} \cup \{(a, j) \mid a \in A_i, 1 \leq j \leq \rho(a)\}$$

where γ is a new letter and each letter of B_i has rank 1.

For every $a \in A_i$ define $\phi_i(a)$ as the hypertransition system

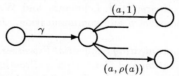

Let us define the synchronisation constraint J over $B_1 \times B_2 \times \cdots \times B_n$ by

$$J(\gamma, \gamma, \ldots, \gamma) = \{\langle 1, 1, \ldots, 1 \rangle\}$$

$$J((a_1, i_1), \ldots, (a_n, i_n)) = \begin{cases} \{\langle 1, \ldots, 1 \rangle\} & \text{if } \langle i_1, \ldots, i_n \rangle \in I(a_1, \ldots, a_n) \\ \emptyset & \text{otherwise} \end{cases}$$

One can easily see that the synchronized product of the $\phi_i(a_i)$ with respect to J has the following form

338

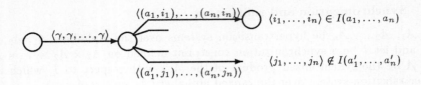

$$\langle i_1, \ldots, i_n \rangle \in I(a_1, \ldots, a_n)$$

$$\langle j_1, \ldots, j_n \rangle \notin I(a_1', \ldots, a_n')$$

Thus we can apply Proposition 1: the mapping ψ, such $\psi(a_1, \ldots, a_n)$ is the above hypertransition system is a refinement and $\psi(\mathcal{A})$ is equal to the synchronized product of the $\phi_i(\mathcal{A}_i)$ with respect to J.

Indeed this construction allows us to represent hypertransition systems by usual transition systems provided a special action γ representing the internal choice (free will) of the processes and an indexing of all possible realizations of a hyperaction.

References

1. L. Aceto and M. Hennessy. Towards action-refinement in process algebras. In: *Proc. 4th LICS*, pages 138–145, IEEE Comp. Soc. 1989.
2. A. Arnold. Transition systems and concurrent processes. In *Mathematical problems in Computation Theory*, pages 9–20, Banach Center Publication 21, 1987.
3. A. Arnold. *Systèmes de transitions finis. Sémantique des processus communicants.* Masson, 1992.
4. A. Arnold and P. Guitton. Un modèle de description de protocoles: les réseaux fermés d'automates triphasés. In M. Paul and B. Robinet, editors, *6th International Symposium on Programming, Toulouse, 1984*, pages 1–12, Lect. Notes Comput. Sci. 167, 1984.
5. A. Arnold and M. Nivat. Comportements de processus. In *Les Mathématiques de l'Informatique*, pages 35–68, Colloque AFCET, Paris, 1982.
6. R. van Glabbeek and U. Goltz. Refinement of actions in causality based models. In J. W. de Bakker, W.-P. de Roever, G. Rozenberg, editors, *Stepwise Refinements of Distributed Systems*, pages 267–300, Lect. Notes Comput. Sci. 430, 1989.
7. N. Francez, C. A. R. Hoare, D. J. Lehmann, and W. P. de Roever. Semantics of nondeterminism, concurrency, and communication. *J. Comput. Syst. Sci.*, 19:290–308, 1979.
8. C. A. R. Hoare. *Communicating Sequential Processes.* Prentice Hall, 1985.
9. R. Milner. *Communication and Concurrency.* Prentice Hall, 1989.
10. W. Vogler. Failures semantics based on interval semiwords is a congruence for refinement. *Distributed Computing*, 4:139–162, 1991.

Formal Languages

On the Star Operation
and
the Finite Power Property
in
Free Partially Commutative Monoids [*]

(Extended Abstract)

Yves Métivier and Gwénaël Richomme

LaBRI, Université Bordeaux I, ENSERB,
351 cours de la Libération, 33405 Talence, France

Abstract. We prove that if it is decidable whether X^* is recognizable for a recognizable subset X of a free partially commutative monoid, then it is decidable whether a recognizable subset of a free partially commutative monoid possesses the finite power property. We prove that if every trace of a set X is connected, we can decide whether X possesses the finite power property. Finally, it is also shown that if X is a finite set containing at most four traces, it is decidable whether X^* is recognizable.

Keywords : trace monoids, recognizability, finite power property.

1 Introduction

Free partially commutative monoids have been introduced by Cartier and Foata [1] for the purposes of combinatorics. They have been intensively studied since Mazurkiewicz [15] proposed these monoids, also called trace monoids, to modelize the behaviour of concurrent processes .

Among these studies, many deal with the problem of recognizability of a set of traces. The family of recognizable trace languages of a free partially commutative monoid is closed under union, intersection, complementation and concatenation [3, 6]. But as soon as the trace monoid is not a free monoid, this family is not closed under star operation.

Hence, many studies concern the decidability of the Star Problem : *"if L is a recognizable trace language, is L^* recognizable ?"*. In the general case, the decidability of the Star Problem remains open. Many methods have been used in order to decide this problem. Sufficient conditions assuring the recognizability of L^* have been found [2, 7, 13, 17, 18]. In the case of finite sets, necessary conditions have been given [19]. The decidability also exists in the extremal case of free monoids and of totally commutative monoids [9, 10]. Since [22], the decidability of the Star Problem is known in case of free product of free commutative monoids. Since [8], the decidability of Star Problem is known in $A^* \times b^*$.

[*] This work has been supported by Esprit Basic Research Actions ASMICS II.

To get new results, we study two problems. The first one is the Finite Power Property Problem and the second one is the star of finite sets containing an increasing number of traces. A set X has the finite power property, if there exists an integer p such that $X^* = \bigcup_{i \leq p} X^i$. The Finite Power Property Problem is "given a recognizable set of traces; does it then possess the finite power property?".

Note that the study of the Finite Power Property Problem is natural when studying the Star Problem. If a recognizable set possesses the finite power property, then its star is also recognizable since the family of recognizable subsets of a free partially commutative monoid is closed under union and concatenation.

We prove that if the Star Problem is decidable in any free partially commutative monoid then the Finite Power Property Problem is also decidable.

We prove also that, for a set X such that each element of X is connected, it is decidable whether X has the finite power property.

Finally, considering some finite sets containing an increasing number of traces or an increasing number of connected traces, we establish some necessary conditions of recognizability. These conditions show the decidability of the Star Problem for sets containing at most four traces and give answers to some questions formulated in [8] and [21].

This paper is organized as follows. In Section 2, we introduce notation and recall some notions concerning free partially commutative monoids and automata and some results concerning the Star Problem. In Section 3, we define the Finite Power Property Problem and show that if the Star Problem is decidable in every free partially commutative monoid, it is also the case for the Finite Power Property Problem. We also prove the decidability of the Finite Power Property Problem in case of a set containing only connected traces. In Section 4, we give necessary conditions of the recognizability of the star of a recognizable set. In Section 5, using results of the previous one, it is shown that the Star Problem is decidable for finite sets containing at most four traces.

The complete proofs can be found in [20].

2   Basic Notions and Notation

2.1   Free Partially Commutative Monoid

We assume that the reader is familiar with the notions of free partially commutative monoid. Here we use the notation of [19].

2.2   Recognizable Subsets of $M(A, \Theta)$

By analogy with the theory of formal languages the subsets of $M(A, \Theta)$ are called trace languages. We recall the following basic facts from [5].

Let X be a set of $M(A, \Theta)$ and let $m \in M(A, \Theta)$. The left quotient of X by $m \in M(A, \Theta)$ is the set :

$$m^{-1}X = \{m' \in M(A, \Theta) | mm' \in X\}.$$

A set X is recognizable if and only if the set $\{m^{-1}X | m \in M\}$ is finite. We have :

Proposition 1. *A subset X of $M(A, \Theta)$ is recognizable if and only if $[X]_\Theta^{-1}$ is a recognizable subset of A^*.*

So X is recognizable if and only if there is an automaton which recognizes $[X]_\Theta^{-1}$.

The family of recognizable subsets of a trace monoid is closed under union, intersection, complementation and concatenation but as soon as the alphabet contains at least two independent letters, this family is not closed under the star operation. For example, if a and b commute, $\{ab\}^*$ is not recognizable.

The Star Problem is :

> *given a recognizable set of traces, is X^* recognizable ?*

Since every recognizable trace languages is rational, the Star Problem is clearly related to the recognizability problem :

> *given a rational set of traces, is it recognizable ?.*

Recently Sakarovitch [22] has proved that the recognizability problem is decidable in free product of free commutative monoids. Consequently, the Star Problem is decidable in such monoids. In [8], it is shown that the Star Problem is of a different nature than the recognizability problem since the Star Problem is decidable in $A^* \times b^*$ where A is an alphabet and b is a letter not in A.

Sufficient conditions ensuring the recognizability of L^* can be found in [2, 7, 13, 17, 18]. We will use the following one [18] :

Proposition 2. *If X is a recognizable subset of $M(A, \Theta)$ such that each trace of X is connected then X^* is recognizable.*

2.3   Automata and Distance Functions

We now recall notions about automata which will be useful in Subsection 3.2.

A finite automaton $\mathcal{A}$ is a quintuple $< A, Q, I, F, \Delta >$ where A is the input alphabet, Q is the finite set of states, I is the set of initial states, F is the set of final states and $\Delta \subseteq Q \times A \times Q$ is the set of transitions.

A path in the automaton $\mathcal{A}$ is a sequence $\mathcal{C} = (f_1, \ldots, f_n)$ of consecutive transitions $f_i = (q_i, a_i, q_{i+1})$ $(1 \le i \le n)$. The integer n is called the length of the path $\mathcal{C}$. The word $w = a_1 \ldots a_n$ is the label of $\mathcal{C}$. The state q_1 is the origin of the path and the state q_{n+1} its end. By convention, there is for each state $q \in Q$ a path of length 0 from q to q. Its label is the empty word ε.

A path $\mathcal{C}$ from q to q' is successful if $q \in I$ and $q' \in F$. The set recognized by $\mathcal{A}$, denoted by $\mathcal{L}(\mathcal{A})$ is defined as the set of labels of successful paths.

A distance function over the automaton $\mathcal{A} = < A, Q, I, F, \Delta >$ is a function :

$$d : Q \times A \times Q \longrightarrow \{0, 1, \infty\}$$

where ∞ denotes infinity and d satisfies for any $(q, a, q') \in Q \times A \times Q$, $d(q, a, q') = \infty$ if and only if $(q, a, q') \notin \Delta$.

For a path $\mathcal{C}$, we note $d(\mathcal{C}) = \sum_{i=1}^{n} d(q_i, a_i, q_{i+1})$. The function d is extended on $Q \times A^* \times Q$ by : $d(q, w, q')$ being the minimum of the $d(\mathcal{C})$ for all the path $\mathcal{C}$ from q to q' labeled by w. If there does not exist such a path, $d(q, w, q') = \infty$.

The automaton $\mathcal{A}$ with the function distance d (denoted by $(\mathcal{A}, d)$) is limited in distance if there exists an integer k such that for any $w \in \mathcal{L}(\mathcal{A})$, $d(q, w, q') \leq k$ for some $q \in I$ and $q' \in F$.

The following result [12] will be used in Subsection 3.2 :

Theorem 3. *For a finite automaton $(\mathcal{A}, d)$ with a function distance, it is decidable whether it is limited in distance.*

3 The Finite Power Property Problem

In this section, we study the Finite Power Property Problem. In Subsection 3.1, we present this problem and show how its decidability is related to the decidability of the Star Problem. In Subsection 3.2, we prove that for a set containing only connected traces, the Finite Power Property Problem is decidable.

3.1 Presentation

A subset X of a monoid possesses the finite power property if there exists an integer k such that :

$$X^* = \bigcup_{i=0}^{k} X^i.$$

We call then the Finite Power Property Problem, the question :

given a recognizable set, does it possess the finite power property ?

The Finite Power Property Problem is decidable in a free monoid [11, 23, 24] but the problem has never been approached in general free partially commutative monoids.

The following lemma holds :

Lemma 4. *Let X be a subset of $M(A, \Theta)$. If $[X]_{\Theta}^{-1}$ possesses the finite power property in A^* then X possesses the finite power property in $M(A, \Theta)$.*

Proof. Let $L = [X]_{\Theta}^{-1}$. Suppose that $L^* = \bigcup_{i \leq k} L^i$. Let $x \in X^n$, with $n > k$. There exists $w_1, \dots, w_n$ words of L such that $x = [w_1 \dots w_n]$. Since L possesses the finite power property, there exists $u_1, \dots, u_j$ words of L with $j \leq k$ such that $w_1 \dots w_n = u_1 \dots u_j$. Then $x = [u_1] \dots [u_j]$ and $X^* = \bigcup_{i \leq k} X^i$.

The converse of Lemma 4 does not hold :

Example 1. Let $A = \{a, b\}$, $a\Theta b$ and $X = (a^2)^* + (b^2)^* + ab$.

We have : $L = [X]_{\Theta}^{-1} = (a^2)^* + (b^2)^* + ab + ba$. This set does not possess the finite power property since for all integer n, $(ab)^n$ belongs to L^n but not to $\bigcup_{i<n} L^i$.

Nevertheless, the subset X of $M(A, \Theta)$ verifies : $X^* = X^3$.

Proposition 5. *If the Star Problem is decidable in any free partially commutative monoid, then the Finite Power Property Problem is decidable in any free partially commutative monoid.*

In fact, we have the more precise result :

Lemma 6. *Let $M(A, \Theta)$ be a free partially commutative monoid, and let b be a letter which does not belong to A.*

If the Star Problem is decidable in $M(A, \Theta) \times b^*$
then the Finite Power Property Problem is decidable in $M(A, \Theta)$.

Since the Star Problem is decidable in free commutative monoids, we have :

Corollary 7. *The Finite Power Property Problem is decidable in a free commutative monoid.*

Lemma 6 is a direct corollary of the following one :

Lemma 8. *Let X be a recognizable subset of $M(A, \Theta)$, b be a letter not in A and $Y = X.b^+$:*

X possesses the finite power property in $M(A, \Theta)$
if and only if
Y^* is recognizable in $M(A, \Theta) \times b^*$.

Proof. Suppose that X possesses the finite power property in $M(A, \Theta)$. There exists an integer p such that :

$$X^+ = \bigcup_{i=1}^{p} X^i.$$

In $M(A, \Theta) \times b^*$, $\forall a \in A$, a and b commute. Then :

$$Y^* = \bigcup_{i=1}^{p} X^i b^i b^* \cup \{\varepsilon\}$$

Since X is recognizable, for all i X^i is recognizable. So $\bigcup_{i=1}^{p} X^i b^i b^*$ is recognizable. Finally Y^* is recognizable.

Conversely, suppose now that Y^* is recognizable in $M(A, \Theta) \times b^*$. Let n be the number of states of the minimal automaton recognizing Y^*, let $m > n$ and $x \in X^m$. By definition of Y, $xb^m \in Y^*$. Using the iteration lemma for Y^*, there exists an integer $k \leq n$ such that $xb^k \in Y^*$, so there exists $i \leq n$ such that $x \in X^i$. Finally :

$$X^* = \bigcup_{i \leq n} X^i.$$

In [8], the decidability of the Star Problem in $A^* \times b^*$ uses implicitly the fact that if X and X^* are recognizable then $Conn(X)^* \cup NConn(X)$ possesses the finite power property. The following example shows that this property is false in a general free partially commutative monoid.

Example 2. If we consider an alphabet $A = \{a, b, c\}$ with the relation Θ defined by $a\Theta c$, the trace $t = ac$, the sets $Y = \{a^2, c^2, b\}$ and $X = Y \cup \{t\}$, we have $[X^*]_\Theta^{-1} = (((a + c)^2)^* b^*)^*$, then X^* is recognizable.
But for all positive integers n, $(acb)^n \in (t \cup Y^*)^{2n}$ and $\forall i < 2n \ (acb)^n \notin (t \cup Y^*)^i$.

3.2 One Sufficient Condition of Decidability

In this subsection, we prove the following :

Theorem 9. *Let X be a recognizable subset such that each element of X is connected.*

  1 . X^* is recognizable.
  2 . It is decidable whether X possesses the finite power property.

The first part of Theorem 9 was already known in [18]. We give here explicitly the construction of an automaton which recognizes X^*. We add to this automaton a distance function such that X has the finite power property if and only if the automaton is limited in distance.
Before constructing the automaton, let us remark :

Lemma 10. *Let $t_i \in M(A, \Theta)$ $(1 \le i \le n)$ and u, v be some traces such that $uv = t_1 \ldots t_p$.*
  Then there exist unique traces $t'_1, \ldots, t'_p, t''_1, \ldots, t''_p$ such that :

$$\begin{cases} u = t'_1 \ldots t'_p, \\ v = t''_1 \ldots t''_p, \\ t_i = t'_i t''_i \ (1 \le i \le n), \\ t''_i \Theta(t'_{i+1} \ldots t'_p) \ (1 \le i < n). \end{cases}$$

  Furthermore, if $v = av'$, let $u' = ua$ then the traces $x'_1, \ldots, x'_p, x''_1, \ldots, x''_p$ such that

$$\begin{cases} u' = x'_1 \ldots x'_p, \\ v' = x''_1 \ldots x''_p, \\ t_i = x'_i x''_i \ (1 \le i \le n), \\ x''_i \Theta(x'_{i+1} \ldots x'_p) \ (1 \le i < n), \end{cases}$$

verify :
  $\exists k \in [1..p]$ such that

$$\begin{cases} x'_k = t'_k a, \ t''_k = a x''_k \ and \\ \forall j \ne k, \ x'_j = t'_j \ and \ x''_j = t''_j. \end{cases}$$

Moreover, if we suppose each t_i $(1 \leq i \leq n)$ to be connected then

$$card\{i|t_i \neq t_i' \text{ and } t_i \neq t_i''\} \leq card(A).$$

The first part of the lemma is in [3]. By iterating it, we obtain the other part of the lemma.

Remark. Completing the second point of Lemma 10, we can consider four cases :

1 : $t_k' \neq \varepsilon$ and $x_k'' \neq \varepsilon$: adding a to u, we continue an existing 'open' trace in the decomposition, without closing it.

2 : $t_k' \neq \varepsilon$ and $x_k'' = \varepsilon$: adding a to u, we close a trace in the decomposition.

3 : $t_k' = \varepsilon$ and $x_k'' \neq \varepsilon$: adding a to u, we 'open' a new trace in the decomposition.

4 : $t_k' = \varepsilon$ and $x_k'' = \varepsilon$: a is a trace of X and adding a to u makes appear a new complete trace in the decomposition.

Remark. As a corollary of points 1 and 3 in Lemma 10, we have Lemma 2.7 in [18] :

Lemma 11. *Let X be a subset of $M(A, \Theta)$ such that each element of X is connected. Then the product of two traces u, v of $M(A, \Theta)$ belongs to X^* if and only if $\exists n \geq 0$, $y_i, z_i \in X^*$ $(0 \leq i \leq n)$ and $u_i, v_i \in M(A, \Theta)$ $(1 \leq i \leq n)$ with*

(1) $u = y_0 u_1 y_1 \ldots u_n y_n$,
(2) $v = z_0 v_1 z_1 \ldots v_n z_n$,
(3) $u_i v_i \in X$,
(4) $z_i \Theta(u_{i+1} y_{i+1} \ldots u_n y_n)$ $(0 \leq i \leq n)$
(5) $v_i \Theta(y_i u_{i+1} y_{i+1} \ldots u_n y_n)$ $(1 \leq i \leq n)$
(6) $alph(u_i) \neq alph(u_j)$ $(1 \leq i < j \leq n)$

The two previous remarks are the key points of the construction of the following automaton. After the construction, we will prove that this automaton recognizes X^* and that we can define a distance function such that X has the finite power property if and only if the automaton is limited in distance.

With all traces u of $M(A, \Theta)$, we can associate the set of factorizations of the form :

$$u = y_0 u_1 y_1 \ldots u_n y_n$$

with

$$\begin{cases} y_i \in X^* \ (0 \leq i \leq n), \\ u_i \neq \varepsilon \ (1 \leq i \leq n) \text{ and} \\ alph(u_i) \neq alph(u_j) \ (1 \leq i < j \leq n). \end{cases}$$

We call such a factorization : Pref-factorization.

For each Pref-factorization, we can associate a tuple $(\beta_0, \ldots, \beta_n)$ with

$$\begin{cases} \beta_0 = (A, X, A), \\ \beta_i = (alph(u_i), u_i^{-1} X, alph(y_i)) \ (1 \leq i \leq n). \end{cases}$$

Then we define the set

$$E = \{(alph(u), u^{-1}X, C) | u \in M(A, \Theta), u \neq \varepsilon, C \subseteq A\}$$

and the set Q_* of the states of the automaton $\mathcal{A}_*$ as the set of all $(n+1)$ tuples $(\beta_0, \ldots, \beta_n)$ such that

$$\begin{cases} n \geq 0, \\ \beta_0 = (A, X, A), \\ \beta_i = (B_i, u_i^{-1}X, C_i) \in E \ (1 \leq i \leq n) \\ B_i \neq B_j \ (1 \leq i < j \leq n). \end{cases}$$

We can note that since $i \neq j$ leads to $B_i \neq B_j$, thus $n \leq 2^{card(A)}$ and Q_* is finite. So to each Pref-factorization of a trace u, we can associate a state in Q_*.

To the trace ε, we can associate only one Pref-factorization and then we define the state (β_0) as the unique initial state of $\mathcal{A}_*$.

To any trace $x \in X^*$, we can associate the state (β_0). Then, we define this state as the unique final state.

Now, we define the transitions of the automaton. Let u be a trace and a be a letter. Let $u = y_0 u_1 y_1 \ldots u_n y_n$ be a Pref-factorization of u.

One can remark that the relations between the y_i, u_i and the t_i', t_i'' of Lemma 10 are : y_i is a product of traces t_j already recognized and u_i is a prefix of one trace t_i. The transitions are given to obtain the Pref-factorization induced by Lemma 10.

Considering some Pref-factorizations of the trace ua, we define four kinds of transitions which correspond to the four cases of Remark 3.2.

1 : If $a\Theta(y_i u_{i+1} \ldots y_n)$ then $y_0 u_1 \ldots y_{i-1}(u_i a)y_i \ldots y_n$ can be a Pref-factorization of ua. For this case being possible, we must have $\forall j \neq i$, $alph(u_i a) \neq alph(u_j)$. If this last condition is verified, we define a transition from the state associated with $y_0 u_1 \ldots y_n$ to the state associated with $y_0 u_1 \ldots y_{i-1}(u_i a)y_i \ldots y_n$. Such a transition continues an 'open' trace in the Pref-factorization. We denote by Δ_1 the set of such transitions.

2 : If $a\Theta(y_i u_{i+1} \ldots y_n)$ and if $u_i a$ is a trace of X, then $y_0 u_1 \ldots u_{i-1} y_{i-1}' u_{i+1} \ldots y_n$ with $y_{i-1}' = y_{i-1} u_i a y_i$ is a Pref-factorization of ua. We define a transition from the state associated with $y_0 u_1 \ldots y_n$ to the state associated with the trace $y_0 u_1 \ldots u_{i-1} y_{i-1}' u_{i+1} \ldots y_n$. Such a transition closes an 'open' trace in the Pref-factorization. We denote by Δ_2 this set of transitions.

3 : If $a\Theta(y_i u_{i+1} \ldots y_n)$, $y_0 u_1 \ldots y_{i-1} u_i \varepsilon a y_i \ldots y_n$ can be a Pref-factorization of ua. For being possible, we must have $\forall j$, $alph(a) \neq alph(u_j)$. If this last condition is verified we define a transition from the state associated with $y_0 u_1 \ldots y_n$ to the state associated with $y_0 u_1 \ldots y_{i-1} u_i \varepsilon a y_i \ldots y_n$.
If $a\Theta u_{i+1} \ldots y_n$ and if $\forall j$, $alph(a) \neq alph(u_j)$, we define a transition from the state associated with the trace $y_0 u_1 \ldots y_n$ to the state associated with the trace $y_0 u_1 \ldots y_i a \varepsilon u_{i+1} y_{i+1} \ldots y_n$.
Such a transition 'opens' a new trace in the Pref-factorization.
We denote by Δ_3 the set of transitions obtained by case 3.

4 : Finally, if a belongs to X and $a\Theta(u_{i+1}\ldots u_n y_n)$, we define a transition from the state associated with the trace $y_0 u_1 \ldots y_n$ to the state associated with the trace $y_0 u_1 \ldots u_i(y_i a)u_{i+1}\ldots y_n$. Such a transition 'makes appear a new complete trace' in the Pref-factorization.

We denote by Δ_4 the set of transitions obtained in this case.

One can remark that we have forgotten the case where the letter a opens a new trace and this one 'cuts' a y_i i.e. $y_i = y_i' y_i''$ with $y_i' \in X^*$, $y_i'' \in X^*$ and the final trace $t = u y_i' v y_i'' w$ with u, v, w in X^*. But since $y_i' y_i''$ had been recognized before v, $v\Theta y_i''$. Thus $t = u y_i' y_i'' v w$. Then this case has already been treated by Case 3 or Case 4.

We verify that :

Proposition 12. *The automaton $\mathcal{A}_*$ recognizes the set X^*.*

We define now the distance function d_* over $\mathcal{A}_*$ by :

$$\begin{cases} d_*(\tau) = 0 \text{ if } \tau \in \Delta_1 \text{ or } \tau \in \Delta_3 \text{ and} \\ d_*(\tau) = 1 \text{ if } \tau \in \Delta_2 \text{ or } \tau \in \Delta_4. \end{cases}$$

We have :

Proposition 13. *The set X has the finite power property if and only if $(\mathcal{A}_*, d_*)$ is limited in distance.*

Proof of Theorem 9. Now, Theorem 9 appears as a direct corollary of Proposition 12, Proposition 13 and Theorem 3.

4 Necessary Conditions

In this section, we give some necessary conditions for the recognizability of the star of finite sets. These results will be used in the next section to study the recognizability of the star of finite sets containining at most four traces.

4.1 A Relation Between Iterative Factors and Connected Traces

A trace t is said to be an iterative factor of a subset T of $M(A,\Theta)$ if there exist two traces t_1 and t_2 such that $t_1 t^* t_2$ is a subset of T.

The following proposition shows that if X is finite and X^* is recognizable then X must contain a minimal number of connected traces and those connected traces are related to the iterative factors of X^*.

Proposition 14. *Let X be a finite subset of $M(A,\Theta)$ such that X^* is recognizable. Let h be a trace such that a power of h is an iterative factor of X^*, and let a be a letter of $alph(h)$.*
Then there exists a connected trace $x \in X$ such that $a \in alph(x) \subseteq alph(h)$.

Since all elements of X^* are iterative factors of X^*, using Proposition 14, we have :

Corollary 15. *Let X be a finite subset of $M(A, \Theta)$ such that X^* is recognizable. Let h be a non-connected element of X^*. We denote $h = h_1 \ldots h_n$ with :*

$\forall i \in [1..n], \forall j \in [1..n], i \neq j \Longrightarrow h_i \Theta h_j$
$\forall i \in [1..n], h_i$ *is connected and* $h_i \neq \varepsilon.$

Then there exist some not empty connected traces of X, $x_1, \ldots, x_n$ such that :

$\forall i \in [1..n], alph(x_i) \subseteq alph(h_i).$

The proof of Proposition 14 is an iteration on connected iterative factors using the following results ([19]2.1, [19]3.2) :

Theorem 16. *Let X be a finite subset of $M(A, \Theta)$, let h be a connected iterative factor of X^*. Then there exist a positive integer k, a trace t belonging to X^* and a trace λ in $M(A, \Theta)$ such $h^k \lambda = \lambda t$ (h^k and t are said to be conjugate).*

Lemma 17. *Let X be a subset of $M(A, \Theta)$ such that X^* is recognizable, let h be an iterative factor of X^*, if $h = uv$ with $u \Theta v$ then there exists a positive integer k such that u^k is an iterative factor of X^*.*

4.2 On Non Connected Traces

Lemma 18. *Let X be a subset of $M(A, \Theta)$ such that X^* is recognizable. There exists an integer k such that for each non connected element x of X^* there exists an integer $0 < i \leq k$ such that $x^i \in (X \setminus x^*)^*$.*

The proof of Lemma 18 uses the following one :

Lemma 19. *In $M(A, \Theta)$, if $x^k = uxv$ then $x^{k-1} = uv$.*

This lemma can be easily proved in free monoids by using the Lévi's Lemma. To prove it in all free partially commutative monoids, since for all letters a in A, $|x^{k-1}|_a = |uv|_a$, it suffices to prove that the lemma is verified by the projections of the traces x, u, v on $\{a, b\}^*$ for all non commuting letters a and b. The proof ends by using the following result :

Proposition 20. *Let u and v be two traces. Then $u = v$ if and only if :*

(i) $\forall a \in A \qquad : |u|_a = |v|_a,$
(ii) $\forall (a, b) \notin \Theta \quad : \Pi_{\{a,b\}}(u) = \Pi_{\{a,b\}}(v).$

Proof of Lemma 18. Let $x = uv$ with $u \Theta v$, $u \neq \varepsilon$ and $v \neq \varepsilon$ being a non connected trace of X^*.

Since X^* is recognizable, $\{(u^k)^{-1} X^* | k \in \mathbb{N}\}$ is a finite set (let n be its order). There exist two different integers k and l such that $(u^k)^{-1} X^* = (u^l)^{-1} X^*$. Since $u \Theta v$, $v^k \in (u^k)^{-1} X^*$. So $v^k \in (u^l)^{-1} X^*$ and $u^l v^k \in X^*$. In the same way, $u^k v^l \in X^*$. Let $x_1, \ldots, x_i, y_1, \ldots, y_j$ traces of X such that :

$u^k v^l = x_1 \ldots x_i$
$u^l v^k = y_1 \ldots y_j$
thus $x^{k+l} = (uv)^{k+l} = x_1 \ldots x_i y_1 \ldots y_j$

Since $k \neq l$, one of the traces $x_1, \ldots, x_i$ does not belong to x^*. By applying Lemma 19 on x^{k+l}, there exists an integer $0 < p \leq k + l$, such that $x^p \in (X \setminus x^*)^+$.

We end the proof of Lemma 18 noting that k and l can be chosen between 1 and $n + 1$. Then, since $p \leq k + l$, we obtain that for each non connected element of X^* there exists an integer $0 < i \leq 2n + 1$ such that $x^i \in (X \setminus x^*)^*$.

5 Applications

Using the previous necessary conditions, we can show that it is decidable whether X^* is recognizable for a set X containing 2, 3 or 4 connected traces. One of the referees noted that this result has been announced independently by Ochmański.

For a set containing only one trace, the result was already known (see [2] and [13]). *The set w^* is recognizable if and only if the trace w is connected.*

In fact, for a set containing less than four traces, we have the following results :

Fact 21. *Let X be a subset of $M(A, \Theta)$ containing one or two traces. Then X^* is recognizable if and only if all traces of X are connected.*

Proposition 22. *Let $X \subseteq M(A, \Theta)$ containing three traces :*

$$X^* \text{ is recognizable}$$
$$\text{if and only if}$$
$$(1) \ \forall x \in NConn(X), \quad \exists k \text{ such that } x^k \in Conn(X)^*.$$

Moreover, if X^* is recognizable, $X = Conn(X)$ or $X = \{u^{p_1}, v^{q_1}, u^{p_2}v^{q_2}\}$ where p_1, p_2, q_1 and q_2 are strictly positive integers, $u\Theta v$, u and v are connected.

Proposition 23. *Let X be a subset of $M(A, \Theta)$ containing four traces .*

$$X^* \text{ is recognizable}$$
$$\text{if and only if}$$
$$X \text{ can be written in one of the five following ways :}$$

(1) $X = \{x, y, z, t\}$ with x, y, z, t connected.
(2) $X = \{x^i, y^j, x^{l_1}y^{l_2}, x^{k_1}y^{k_2}\}$ with x, y connected , $x\Theta y$ and i, j non zero.
(3) $X = \{x^i, y^j, z^k, x^{l_1}y^{l_2}z^{l_3}\}$ with x, y, z connected , $x\Theta y$, $y\Theta z$, $z\Theta x$ and i, j, k non zero.
(4) $X = \{x^i, y^j, z^k, x^{l_1}y^{l_2}\}$ with x, y, z connected, $x\Theta y$, $y\cancel{\Theta}z$, $z\cancel{\Theta}x$ and i, j, k non zero.
(5) $X = \{x^i, y^j, z^k, uy^l\}$ with x, y, z connected, $x\Theta y$, $y\Theta z$, $z\cancel{\Theta}x, u\Theta y, i, j, k$ non zero and $\{x^i, z^k\}^* \cup \{u\}$ has the finite power property.

Acknowledgements. Authors are grateful to Paul Gastin, who found an error in the original proof of Lemma 8 and provided useful comments. They also thank anonymous referees for helpful remarks.

References

1. P. Cartier and D. Foata, *Problèmes combinatoires de commutation et réarrangements*, Lecture Notes in Math. 85, 1969.
2. R. Cori and Y. Métivier, *Recognizable subsets of some partially abelian monoids*, Theoret. Comput. Sci. 35, p179-189, 1985.
3. R. Cori and D.Perrin, *Automates et commutations partielles, Sur la reconnaissabilité dans les monoïdes partiellement comutatif libres*, RAIRO, Theoretical Informatics and Applications 19, p 21-32, 1985.
4. C. Duboc, *On some equations in free partially commutative monoids*, Theoret. Comput. Sci. 46, p159-174, 1986.
5. S.Eilenberg, *Automata, Languages and Machines*, Academic Press, New York, 1974.
6. M. Fliess, *Matrices de Hankel*, J. Math Pures et Appl. 53, p197-224, 1974.
7. M.P. Flé and G. Roucairol, *Maximal seriazibility of iterated transactions*, Theoret. Comput. Sci. 38, p1-16, 1985.
8. P. Gastin, E. Ochmański, A. Petit, B. Rozoy, *Decidability of the Star Problem in $A^* \times \{b\}^*$*, Inform. Process. Lett. 44, p65-71, 1992.
9. S. Ginsburg and E. Spanier, *Semigroups, presburger formulas and languages*, Pacific journal of mathematics 16, p285-296, 1966.
10. S. Ginsburg and E. Spanier, *Bounded regular sets*, Proceedings of the AMS, vol. 17(5), p1043-1049, 1966.
11. K. Hashigushi, *A decision procedure for the order of regular events*, Theoret. Comput. Sci. 8, p69-72, 1979.
12. K. Hashigushi, *Limitedness Theorem on Finite Automata with Distance Functions*, J. of Computer and System Science24, p233-244, 1982.
13. K. Hashigushi, *Recognizable closures and submonoids of free partially commutative monoids*, Theoret. Comput. Sci. 86, p233-241, 1991.
14. M. Linna, *Finite Power Property of regular languages*, Automata, Languages and Programming, 1973.
15. A. Mazurkiewicz, *Concurrent program schemes and their interpretations*, Aarhus university, DAIMI rep. PB 78, 1977.
16. A. Mazurkiewicz, *Traces, Histories, Graphs : instances of a process monoid*, Lecture Notes in Computer Science 176, p254-264, 1984.
17. Y. Métivier, *Une condition suffisante de reconnaissabilité dans un monoïde partiellement commutatif*, RAIRO Theoretical Informatics and Applications 20, p121-127, 1986.
18. Y. Métivier, *On recognizable subset of free partially Commutative Monoids*, Theoret. Comput. Sci. 58, p201-208, 1988.
19. Y. Métivier and B. Rozoy, *On the star operation in free partially commutative monoids*, International Journal of Foundations of Computer Science 2, p257-265, 1991.
20. Y. Métivier and G. Richomme, *On the star operation and the finite power property in free partially commutative monoid*, Internal Report LaBRI-Université Bordeaux I 93-15, 1993.
21. E. Ochmański , *Notes on a star mystery*, Bulletin of EATCS 40, p252-257, February 1990.
22. J. Sakarovitch, *The "last" decision problem for rational trace languages*, Proceedings of LATIN'92, Lecture Notes in Computer Science 583, p460-473, 1992.
23. A. Salomaa, *Jewels of formal languages theory*, PITMAN eds.
24. I. Simon, *Limited subsets of a free monoid*, Proceedings of th 19th FOCS, p143-150, 1978.

Coding with Traces

Véronique Bruyère*, Clelia De Felice** and Giovanna Guaiana***

Abstract. We prove that the existence of a coding between two trace monoids is decidable for some families of trace monoids. Decidability heavily depends on the structure of the dependence graphs. The concept of coding is based on the new notion of strong morphism between trace monoids.

1 Introduction

The theory of traces has encountered continuous interest since the works of Mazurkiewicz and Cartier, Foata [CF69, Ma77]. Mazurkiewicz introduced the concept of traces as a suitable semantics for concurrent processes, while Cartier and Foata studied mathematical aspects of trace monoids as a tool in enumerative combinatorics. We refer to the surveys [Ch86, Ma87, AR88, Pe89] or to the monograph [Di90b] for more background information on the theory of traces. A book on traces and their generalizations is in preparation [DR93].

In this paper we study how coding with traces works.

Coding in trace monoids is much more tricky than in the case of free monoids. Indeed, in free monoids codings are injective morphisms $F : A_1^* \to A_2^*$ and each letter a of A_1 is coded by the code-word $F(a) \in A_2^*$ [BP85]. In this context, any alphabet A_1 can be trivially coded using only two symbols. After the works of Sardinas and Patterson [SP53], several authors designed efficient algorithms to test whether a given morphism $F : A_1^* \to A_2^*$ is a coding [Ro82, AG84, Ca86].

When working with traces, "coding" is understood as an injective morphism between two trace monoids. The works of Chrobak, Rytter and Ochmanski pointed out the complex behaviour of codings with traces [CR87, Oc88]. They gave interesting but partial answers to the two questions naturally raised for the free case [Oc88, Di90a] : for two given trace monoids, (1) is the existence of an injective morphism between them decidable, (2) given a morphism between them, is there an algorithm to test its injectivity ?

---

* Université de Mons-Hainaut, 15 Avenue Maistriau, B-7000 Mons, Belgium. This work was partially supported by ESPRIT-BRA Working Group 6317 *ASMICS*.

** Dipartimento di Informatica ed Applicazioni, Università di Salerno, I-84081 Baronissi (SA), Italy. Partially supported by ESPRIT-BRA Working Group 6317 *ASMICS* and Project 40% MURST *Algoritmi, Modelli di Calcolo e Strutture Informative*.

*** L.I.T.P., Institut Blaise Pascal, Université Paris 7, 2 place Jussieu, F-75251 Paris cedex 05, France and Dipartimento di Matematica e Applicazioni, Università di Palermo, via Archirafi 34, I-90123 Palermo, Italy. Partially supported by a C.N.R. fellowship and Cooperation Project C.G.R.I.-C.N.R.S. *Théorie des Automates et Applications*.

We focus here on the first question which was only solved in the extreme cases of free and free commutative monoids. We prove decidability for some families of trace monoids. The decision algorithm is based on graph-theoretical characterizations of dependence graphs.

We have adopted a new notion of trace morphism F, called "strong" morphism : when a, b are independent, we prefer the independence $F(a)$ I $F(b)$ to the property of commutation $F(a)F(b) = F(b)F(a)$. This notion is perhaps restrictive but seems a more natural definition when coming back to the original motivations of the theory of traces. Indeed, in a common mathematical approach to parallelism, the actions of a concurrent process are modelized by letters, and two actions performed concurrently are represented by independent letters. Suppose now that the execution of any action a in a concurrent process is realized by a microprocess P_a (see [Pre85]). On a certain level of abstraction, P_a may be interpreted as a coding $F(a)$ of the action a. Our concept of strong morphism F requires that the microprocesses P_a and P_b are performed completely concurrently for any pair of concurrent actions a and b (condition $F(a)$ I $F(b)$), whereas the original definition of trace morphism also allows P_a and P_b to share some identical microactions (condition $F(a)F(b) = F(b)F(a)$). The performance of a and b in this latter case is no more completely concurrent (see [GPS91]).

By studying Problem 1 in trace monoids, we have discovered a strong relation between the decidability question and the property for a graph G_2 to be a "splitting" of another graph G_1. Roughly G_2 is a copy of G_1 except that vertices of G_1 are split into several ones to build up vertices of G_2. On the other hand, we have designed a tool based on codings in free monoids to produce trace codings : we locally define codings on cliques of M_1, seen as free monoids, and arrange them in a suitable way to build a trace coding F from M_1 into M_2.

With the previous techniques, we achieve a decidability result when the dependence graph of M_1 has no triangle, i.e. no clique of size 3 (Proposition 14). The existence of an injective strong morphism F from M_1 into M_2 is then equivalent to the existence, inside the dependence graph of M_2, of an induced graph which is a splitting of the dependence graph of M_1. The decidability still holds when a certain quotient of the dependence graph of M_1 is without triangle (Theorem 15). In this more general case, the decision condition is again a splitting, with in addition some technical requirements for equivalence classes with at least 2 elements.

This paper is divided in 5 sections. After the introduction, Section 2 recalls basic definitions and properties of traces monoids and graphs. Section 3 introduces the notion of strong morphism between trace monoids and states Question 1. In Section 4, we first give sufficient conditions and then necessary conditions for the existence of a trace coding between two given trace monoids. Section 4 also details how to construct trace codings from classical codings in free monoids. Finally, Section 5 collects the main decidability results based on the notion of splitting of a graph.

In this paper we do not give all the proofs. A forthcoming paper will contain detailed proofs together with further results [BDG93].

2 Preliminaries

Let A be a finite alphabet and A^* the free monoid generated by A. Let $I \subseteq A \times A$ be a symmetric irreflexive relation, called *commutation relation* or *independence relation*. The complement of I, $D = A \times A \setminus I$, is called *dependence relation*.

Consider the congruence on A^* generated by the set of pairs (ab, ba) for $(a, b) \in I$. The quotient of A^* by this congruence is denoted by $M(A, D)$ and is called the *free partially commutative monoid* generated by A, or shortly *trace monoid*. The elements of $M(A, D)$ which are equivalence classes of words of A^*, are called *traces*. In particular, if $I = \emptyset$, then $M(A, D)$ is the free monoid A^* and if $I = A \times A \setminus \{(a, a) | a \in A\}$, then $M(A, D)$ is the free commutative monoid generated by A (with respect to I).

We denote by $alph(u)$, for $u \in M(A, D)$, the set of letters appearing in u. Two traces u and v are *independent* , denoted by uIv, if $alph(u) \times alph(v) \subseteq I$, or equivalently,

$$uv = vu \quad \text{and} \quad alph(u) \cap alph(v) = \emptyset. \qquad (*)$$

Conversely we write uDv if there exist $a \in alph(u), b \in alph(v)$ such that $(a, b) \in D$. In the same way, for $X, Y \subseteq A$, we write $X \ I \ Y$ if aIb for any $a \in X, b \in Y$, and $X \ D \ Y$ otherwise.

Next Proposition 1 is fundamental to characterize the elements of $M(A, D)$, namely to verify the equality of two traces. Before to state it, we need to recall some notions about graph theory.

We can view the relation D as an undirected graph, called the *dependence graph*, where the vertices are the letters of A and the edges are drawn between all different dependent letters. This graph, corresponding to $(A, D \setminus \{(a, a) | a \in A\})$ is simply denoted by (A, D). For $B \subseteq A$, we set $D_B = D \cap (B \times B)$ and we denote $M(B, D_B)$ the submonoid of $M(A, D)$ generated by B. Thus (B, D_B) is the subgraph of (A, D) induced by B.

A subset C of A is a *clique* of the graph (A, D) if the induced subgraph (C, D_C) is complete, i.e. aDb for any $a, b \in C$. In the following, a clique C is considered either as a subset of A or as a graph, depending on the context. A *n-clique* denotes a clique of cardinality n. Thus a 2-clique is an *edge* and a 3-clique is a *triangle*. A family of cliques $(C_i)_{i=1,...,n}$ is called a *clique-covering* of the graph (A, D) if for all $a, b \in A$

$$aDb \quad \Leftrightarrow \quad \exists i \in \{1, \ldots, n\} \quad \{a, b\} \subseteq C_i.$$

Any graph has at least a clique-covering, namely all n-cliques with $n \leq 2$.

Let π_B be the projection morphism of $M(A, D)$ onto $M(B, D_B)$ defined by $\pi_B(a) = a$ if $a \in B$ and $\pi_B(a) = 1$ if $a \in A \setminus B$. We can now state the announced proposition [CP85, Du86a]:

Proposition 1. *Let $M(A, D)$ be a trace monoid and $(C_i)_{i=1,...,n}$ be a clique-covering of the graph (A, D). Let $u, v \in M(A, D)$. Then*

$$u = v \quad \Leftrightarrow \quad \forall i \in \{1, \ldots, n\} \quad \pi_{C_i}(u) = \pi_{C_i}(v).$$

□

This statement is slightly more general than the result proved in [CP85] where the clique-covering of (A, D) is constituted by 1-cliques and 2-cliques only.

3 Coding Morphisms

In this section, we define the concept of injective strong morphism between two trace monoids. We also introduce the decidability problem studied in this paper with its partial known answers.

Let $M_1 = M(A_1, D_1)$ and $M_2 = M(A_2, D_2)$ be trace monoids. A *trace morphism* from M_1 to M_2 is a monoid morphism induced by a map $F : A_1 \rightarrow M_2$ such that [Ch86]

$$\forall a, b \in A_1 \quad a I_1 b \Rightarrow F(a)F(b) = F(b)F(a).$$

A natural notion of trace morphism arises by requesting that the images of independent letters not only commute but are also independent traces.

Definition 2. A trace morphism $F : M_1 \rightarrow M_2$ is *strong* if

$$\forall a, b \in A_1 \quad a I_1 b \Rightarrow F(a) I_2 F(b).$$

Using (*), it is easy to prove that F is strong if and only if

$$\forall a, b \in A_1 \quad a I_1 b \quad \Rightarrow \quad alph F(a) \cap alph F(b) = \emptyset.$$

Definition 3. A morphism $F : M_1 \rightarrow M_2$ is *injective* if

$$\forall u, v \in M_1 \quad u \neq v \Rightarrow F(u) \neq F(v).$$

Injective trace morphisms generalize the injective morphisms between free monoids, also known as coding functions. The theory of variable-length codes studies properties of *codes* defined as sets $\{F(a)|a \in A_1\}$ with $F : A_1^* \rightarrow A_2^*$ an injective morphism [BP85].

Injective trace morphisms are thus codings with traces. Ochmanski studied them in [Oc88] where he proposed some necessary conditions for a trace morphism to be injective. The equation $xy = yx$ in trace monoids plays a fundamental role in his study. The characterization of the solutions of this equation has been obtained by Duboc [Du86b], and also by Cori, Métivier [CM85].

Injectivity and strongness are two distinct notions for trace morphisms.

Example 1. Let M_1, M_2 be with dependence graphs :

(A_1, D_1) a———b———c (A_2, D_2) α———β———γ

Consider the morphism $F : M_1 \rightarrow M_2$ defined by $F(a) = \alpha, F(b) = \beta, F(c) = \alpha\gamma$. It can be easily proved that F is injective but not strong.

An interesting class of trace morphisms studied in [Oc88] is that of connected morphisms. A morphism is *connected* if the image of any connected trace in M_1 is a connected trace in M_2. Recall that $u \in M(A, D)$ is connected if the graph (B, D_B) with $B = alph(u)$ is connected. Proposition 4 and Example 2 show that injective strong morphisms generalize injective connected morphisms.

Proposition 4 [Oc88]. *Let $F : M_1 \to M_2$ be a trace morphism. If F is injective and connected, then F is strong.*   □

Example 2. Let M_1, M_2 be with dependence graphs :

(A_1, D_1) $a \underline{\hspace{1cm}} b \underline{\hspace{1cm}} c$ (A_2, D_2) $\alpha \underline{\hspace{1cm}} \beta \quad \delta \underline{\hspace{1cm}} \gamma$

The morphism $F : M_1 \to M_2$ defined by $F(a) = \alpha, F(b) = \beta\delta, F(c) = \gamma$ is strong and injective (injectivity is proved by Proposition 10 in the next section), but it is not connected.

Whereas deciding the existence of a strong morphism between two trace monoids is trivial, the following problem seems hard to solve.

Problem 5. Given two trace monoids M_1, M_2, is the existence of an injective strong morphism $F : M_1 \to M_2$ decidable ?

This problem has been raised by Ochmanski in [Oc88] (see also [Di90a]) for injective trace morphisms in general. It is already solved in the extreme cases of free monoids and free commutative monoids. Indeed given two free monoids M_1, M_2, two letters in A_2 are enough to construct an injective morphism between them (folklore) [BP85]. The existence of an injective morphism between two free commutative monoids is equivalent to the condition $|A_1| \le |A_2|$ (basic results from linear algebra) [Oc88].

In this paper we take into account strong morphisms and we obtain a decidability condition for some families of trace monoids, depending on the structure of the dependence graphs (Sections 4 and 5).

Another related problem is to decide whether a trace morphism $F : M_1 \to M_2$ is injective or not. Chrobak and Rytter proved that this problem heavily depends on the structure of the commutation graph of M_2 [CR87]. It is undecidable for graphs containing an induced square, it is decidable for "simple" graphs, particularly for graphs with at most 3 vertices (see also [AH89]).

For strong morphisms we can also give a positive answer to a third problem raised in [Oc88, Di90a]. To any trace morphism $F : M_1 \to M_2$, we can associate the set of morphisms between free monoids $f_i : A_1^* \to A_2^*$ defined by choosing a word $f_i(a)$ in the equivalence class $F(a)$. It is not hard to prove that if F is an injective strong morphism, then any morphism f_i is also injective [BDG93].

The following lemma will be useful in the sequel. Its proof is not difficult. Roughly this lemma means that to any pair of dependent letters $a, b \in A_1$ corresponds a pair of dependent letters respectively in $alph F(a), alph F(b)$.

Lemma 6. *Let $F : M_1 \to M_2$ be an injective morphism. For any $a, b \in A_1, a \ne b$, if $a D_1 b$, then there exist $\alpha_{a,(a,b)} \in alph F(a), \alpha_{b,(a,b)} \in alph F(b)$ such that $\alpha_{a,(a,b)} \ne \alpha_{b,(a,b)}$ and $\alpha_{a,(a,b)} D_2 \alpha_{b,(a,b)}$.*

With the notation $\alpha_{a,(a,b)}$, we want to point out that this is the letter associated to a in reference to the edge (a, b) of (A_1, D_1). This will be useful later on.

In investigating solutions to Problem 5, we can reduce ourselves to the case of connected graphs (A_1, D_1). This possibility is inherently due to strongness : the images by F of distinct connected components of (A_1, D_1) have disjoint alphabets. Formally we can state the following proposition.

Proposition 7. *Let M_1, M_2 be two trace monoids and $B_1, \ldots, B_n$ be the subsets of A_1 corresponding to the connected components of (A_1, D_1). There exists an injective strong morphism $F : M_1 \rightarrow M_2$ iff*
1. *$\exists B'_1, \ldots, B'_n \subseteq A_2$ such that $\forall i, j \in \{1, \ldots, n\}, i \neq j$, we have $B'_i \ I_2 \ B'_j$,*
2. *there exist n injective strong morphisms $F_i : M(B_i, (D_1)_{B_i}) \rightarrow M(B'_i, (D_2)_{B'_i})$.*
$\square$

Hence, in the next sections, we will always consider (A_1, D_1) as a connected graph. We will also assume that it has at least two vertices.

4 Some Conditions for Existence

In this section we give a necessary condition and a sufficient condition for the existence of an injective strong morphism between two trace monoids. Proposition 8 says that for an injective strong morphism to exist, it is necessary to have "enough" edges in (A_2, D_2). The minimum number of necessary edges is linked to the size of the clique-coverings of (A_1, D_1). Corollary 11 states that this lower bound is also sufficient, under the additional hypothesis that these edges are all independent. In that case, we construct an injective strong morphism by mixing, in a suitable way, codes defined on some cliques of (A_1, D_1).

Proposition 8. *Let M_1, M_2 be two trace monoids. Let n be the minimum size of the clique-coverings of (A_1, D_1) and m be the number of edges of (A_2, D_2). If there exists an injective strong morphism $F : M_1 \rightarrow M_2$, then $n \leq m$.*

Proof.   Let $F : M_1 \rightarrow M_2$ be an injective strong morphism.

(1) By Lemma 6 we associate with any edge (a, b) in (A_1, D_1) a (fixed) edge $(\alpha_{a,(a,b)}, \alpha_{b,(a,b)})$ in (A_2, D_2) with $\alpha_{a,(a,b)} \in alphF(a)$, $\alpha_{b,(a,b)} \in alphF(b)$.

(2) For any edge (a, b) in (A_1, D_1), there exists a clique C in (A_1, D_1) containing all edges (x, y) such that $\alpha_{x,(x,y)} = \alpha_{a,(a,b)}$, $\alpha_{y,(x,y)} = \alpha_{b,(a,b)}$.
Indeed, denote C the set of these edges (x, y). If x, x' are two vertices in C, then there exist, by definition of C, some elements $y, y' \in A_1$ such that $\alpha_{x,(x,y)} \in alphF(x) \cap \{\alpha_{a,(a,b)}, \alpha_{b,(a,b)}\}$ and $\alpha_{x',(x',y')} \in alphF(x') \cap \{\alpha_{a,(a,b)}, \alpha_{b,(a,b)}\}$. Consequently $\alpha_{x,(x,y)} D_2 \alpha_{x',(x',y')}$. Then $F(x) D_2 F(x')$ and $x D_1 x'$ as F is strong. This proves that C is a clique.

(3) The set of C's obtained in (2) is a clique-covering of (A_1, D_1). By (2) its size is less than or equal to the cardinality of the set

$$\{(\alpha_{a,(a,b)}, \alpha_{b,(a,b)}) \mid (a, b) \text{ in } (A_1, D_1)\}.$$

$\square$

In order to prove a counterpart to Proposition 8, we need a technique for constructing some injective strong morphisms. Proposition 10 states that, starting by local codings on cliques, we can construct an injective strong morphism on trace monoids.

Definition 9. A trace morphism $F: M_1 \to M_2$ is *constructed by codes* if there exist a clique-covering of (A_1, D_1) by n cliques $(C_i)_{i=1,\dots,n}$, a set of n cliques $(C_i')_{i=1,\dots,n}$ of (A_2, D_2) and n injective morphisms $F_i: C_i^* \to C_i'^*$ between free monoids such that $alpha F(A_1) \subseteq \bigcup_{i=1,\dots,n} C_i'$ and

$$\forall i \in \{1, \dots, n\}, \forall a \in A_1, \quad \pi_{C_i'}(F(a)) = F_i(\pi_{C_i}(a)).$$

Example 3. Let M_1, M_2 be with dependence graphs :

(A_1, D_1) [dependence graph with vertices a, b, c, d, e, f]
    (A_2, D_2) α——β γ——δ ε——η

Consider the morphism $F: M_1 \to M_2$ defined by :

$F(a) = \beta$, $F(b) = \alpha\beta\delta$, $F(c) = \alpha^2\beta\eta$, $F(d) = \gamma\delta$, $F(e) = \gamma^2\delta\varepsilon\eta$, $F(f) = \varepsilon^2\eta$.

F is constructed by codes. Indeed the set of cliques $C_1 = \{a, b, c\}$, $C_2 = \{b, d, e\}$ and $C_3 = \{c, e, f\}$ is a clique-covering of (A_1, D_1) and the morphisms

$$F_1: C_1^* \to C_1'^* = \{\alpha, \beta\}^* \quad a \to \beta, \ b \to \alpha\beta, \ c \to \alpha^2\beta$$
$$F_2: C_2^* \to C_2'^* = \{\gamma, \delta\}^* \quad b \to \delta, \ d \to \gamma\delta, \ e \to \gamma^2\delta$$
$$F_3: C_3^* \to C_3'^* = \{\varepsilon, \eta\}^* \quad c \to \eta, \ e \to \varepsilon\eta, \ f \to \varepsilon^2\eta$$

are injective.

Proposition 10. *Let $F : M_1 \to M_2$ be a trace morphism. If F is constructed by codes, then F is an injective strong morphism.* $\square$

The proof of this proposition is based on Proposition 1, it is not hard. Note that there are injective strong morphisms which are not constructed by codes (see Example 4).

Now, suppose $(C_i)_{i=1,\dots,n}$ is a clique-covering of (A_1, D_1) and there are in (A_2, D_2) n edges $(\alpha_i, \beta_i)_{i=1,\dots,n}$ which are pairwise independent. Then the construction of injective morphisms $F_i : C_i^* \to \{\alpha_i, \beta_i\}^*$ is straightforward: any binary coding F_i works. Then F, defined by $F(a) = \prod_{\{i | a \in C_i\}} F_i(a)$ is a strong morphism constructed by codes (see Example 3). So we have the following corollary.

Corollary 11. *If n is the minimum size of the clique-coverings of (A_1, D_1) and if (A_2, D_2) contains n independent edges, then there exists an injective strong morphism $F: M_1 \to M_2$.* $\square$

5 Decidability for Skeletons Without Triangle

In this section we give a positive answer to Problem 5 for graphs (A_1, D_1) without triangle (Proposition 14) and more generally when their "skeleton" has no triangle (Theorem 15). Roughly the skeleton of (A_1, D_1) is the graph obtained by merging any two vertices in (A_1, D_1) with the same neighbourhoods. In both cases, the existence of an injective strong morphism is related to the existence inside (A_2, D_2) of a "splitting" of (A_1, D_1), i.e. a copy of (A_1, D_1) whose vertices have been split.

We start with precise definitions of splitting and skeleton. These two operations on graphs have some connections with the "substitution" operation in graph theory [Lo72, Bo78].

Definition 12. Let $G_1 = (A_1, D_1)$, $G_2 = (A_2, D_2)$ be two graphs. We say that G_2 is a *splitting* of G_1 if there exists a partition $(V_a)_{a \in A_1}$ of A_2 such that

$$\forall a, b \in A_1 \quad a\, D_1\, b \quad \Leftrightarrow \quad V_a\, D_2\, V_b.$$

Definition 13. The *skeleton*, $Skel(A, D)$, of a graph (A, D) is its quotient graph $(A_{/\sim}, D_{/\sim})$ under the equivalence relation $\sim$ defined on A by

$$a \sim b \quad \Leftrightarrow \quad \{\forall c \in A \quad aDc \Leftrightarrow bDc\}.$$

In particular, $a \sim b$ implies aDb. We denote $[a]$ the equivalence class of $a \in A$ under $\sim$. We have $[a]\, D_{/\sim}\, [b]$ if and only if for any $a' \in [a]$, $b' \in [b]$, $a'Db'$. In this case we shortly set $[a]D[b]$.

Next proposition deals with graphs (A_1, D_1) without triangle. It is the first step towards the main result stating that the existence of an injective strong morphism is decidable when $Skel(A_1, D_1)$ has no triangle (Theorem 15).

Proposition 14. *Let M_1, M_2 be two trace monoids such that (A_1, D_1) has no triangle. There exists an injective strong morphism $F: M_1 \to M_2$ if and only if (A_2, D_2) has an induced subgraph which is a splitting of (A_1, D_1).*

Proof. Assume that $F : M_1 \to M_2$ is an injective strong morphism. By Lemma 6 we associate with any edge (a, b) in (A_1, D_1) an edge $(\alpha_{a,(a,b)}, \alpha_{b,(a,b)})$ in (A_2, D_2) with $\alpha_{a,(a,b)} \in alphF(a)$, $\alpha_{b,(a,b)} \in alphF(b)$. We set for any $a \in A_1$

$$V_a = \{\alpha_{a,(a,b)} \mid (a, b) \text{ in } (A_1, D_1)\}.$$

Then $V_a \subseteq alphF(a)$. We are going to prove that the subgraph of (A_2, D_2) induced by $(V_a)_{a \in A_1}$ is a splitting of (A_1, D_1).
First, we prove that for all $a, b \in A_1$, we have $aD_1b \Leftrightarrow V_a\, D_2\, V_b$.

$$aI_1b \Rightarrow (F \text{ is strong}) \quad alphF(a)\, I_2\, alphF(b) \qquad\qquad \Rightarrow V_a\, I_2\, V_b,$$
$$aD_1b \Rightarrow \exists \alpha_{a,(a,b)} \in V_a, \exists \alpha_{b,(a,b)} \in V_b : \quad \alpha_{a,(a,b)}\, D_2\, \alpha_{b,(a,b)} \Rightarrow V_a\, D_2\, V_b.$$

Second, we show that for any $a, b \in A_1, a \neq b$, then $V_a \cap V_b = \emptyset$. Assume that for some $a \neq a'$, there exists $\alpha_{a,(a,b)} \in V_a \cap V_{a'}$. Then let $b' \in A_1$ such that $\alpha_{a,(a,b)} = \alpha_{a',(a',b')}$. We have $a D_1 b$, $a' D_1 b'$, we have also $a D_1 a'$ as $V_a D_2 V_{a'}$. By definition, $b \neq a$, $b' \neq a'$. Moreover, either $b \neq a'$ or $b' \neq a$ by Lemma 6. Consequently

$$\alpha_{a,(a,b)} = \alpha_{a',(a',b')} \ D_2 \ \alpha_{b',(a',b')} \Rightarrow V_a \ D_2 \ V_{b'} \Rightarrow a D_1 b'.$$
$$\alpha_{a',(a',b')} = \alpha_{a,(a,b)} \ D_2 \ \alpha_{b,(a,b)} \ \Rightarrow V_{a'} \ D_2 \ V_b \Rightarrow a' D_1 b.$$

Then $\{a, a', b\}$ and $\{a, a', b'\}$ are cliques and at least one of them has size three, which is a contradiction.

For the converse, let us now suppose that (A_2, D_2) contains a splitting of (A_1, D_1) induced by a family $(V_a)_{a \in A_1}$ of disjoint subsets of A_2 . Then, for any pair of letters $a, b \in A_1$, we have

$$a D_1 b \quad \Leftrightarrow \quad \exists \alpha_{a,(a,b)} \in V_a, \exists \alpha_{b,(a,b)} \in V_b \quad \alpha_{a,(a,b)} \ D_2 \ \alpha_{b,(a,b)}. \qquad (**)$$

It is easy to define a morphism F constructed by codes. Indeed the set of edges (a, b) of (A_1, D_1) is a clique-covering of (A_1, D_1) and any morphism

$$F_{(a,b)} : \{a, b\}^* \to \{\alpha_{a,(a,b)}, \alpha_{b,(a,b)}\}^* \quad \text{defined by} \quad a \to \alpha_{a,(a,b)}, \quad b \to \alpha_{b,(a,b)}$$

is an injective morphism between free monoids. Then morphism F is injective and strong using Proposition 10 and $(**)$. $\qquad\qquad\square$

Example 2 (continued). Let $V_a = \{\alpha\}, V_b = \{\beta, \delta\}, V_c = \{\gamma\}$. This partition of A_2 induces the graph (A_2, D_2) which is a splitting of (A_1, D_1).

The next example suggests, through different situations, how Proposition 14 has to be adapted to obtain Theorem 15.

Example 4. Let M_1 be with dependence graph and skeleton

(A_1, D_1)

$Skel(A_1, D_1)$

$\{a_1, a_2, a_3\} \ \text{------} \ \{b\} \ \text{------} \ \{c\}$

So $Skel(A_1, D_1)$ has no triangle. Suppose (A_2, D_2) is the graph

$$\alpha \underline{\qquad} \beta \underline{\qquad} \gamma$$

which is a splitting of $Skel(A_1, D_1)$. There is no injective strong morphism F : $M_1 \to M_2$. Indeed $\{a_1, a_2, a_3\} I_1 c$, then $alphF(a_i) \ I_2 \ alphF(c)$, $i = 1, 2, 3$, as F is strong, but we need two letters of A_2 to "encode" $\{a_1, a_2, a_3\}$. The splitting is not rich enough.

Suppose now that (A_2, D_2) is the splitting

$$\alpha \underline{\qquad} \beta \ \delta \underline{\qquad} \gamma$$

of $Skel(A_1, D_1)$ ($V_b = \{\beta, \delta\}$). An injective strong morphism F exists defined by

$$F(a_1) = \alpha\beta, \; F(a_2) = \alpha^2\beta, \; F(a_3) = \alpha^3\beta, \; F(b) = \beta\delta, \; F(c) = \gamma.$$

Indeed the two letters α, β, independent of γ are used to encode a_1, a_2, a_3 independently of the letter c. One can verify that F is constructed by codes.

A morphism F also exists if (A_2, D_2) is the splitting

$$\alpha\underline{\quad\quad}\beta\underline{\quad\quad}\gamma$$

$$\overset{|}{\underset{\delta}{}}$$

($V_a = \{\alpha, \delta\}$). Now the pair α, δ independent of γ is used to encode a_1, a_2, a_3 :

$$F(a_1) = \alpha\delta, \; F(a_2) = \alpha^2\delta, \; F(a_3) = \alpha^3\delta, \; F(b) = \beta, \; F(c) = \gamma.$$

This morphism is no more constructed by codes. However, one can prove that F is an injective strong morphism (see the next proof).

Theorem 15. *Let M_1, M_2 be trace monoids such that the skeleton $Skel(A_1, D_1)$ of (A_1, D_1) has no triangle. There exists an injective strong morphism $F : M_1 \rightarrow M_2$ if and only if there exists a subgraph of (A_2, D_2) induced by $(V_{[a]})_{[a] \in A_1/\sim}$ which is a splitting of $Skel(A_1, D_1)$ and such that*

1. *a pair $\{\alpha, \alpha'\}$ is associated with any $[a]$ having size ≥ 2, such that $\alpha D_2 \alpha'$ and $\alpha \in V_{[a]}$, $\alpha' \in V_{[b]}$ for some $[a] \; D_1 \; [b]$*

2. *$[a] \; I_1 \; [b] \quad \Rightarrow \quad lett([a]) \; I_2 \; lett([b])$,*
   where $lett([a]) = V_{[a]}$ \qquad if $[a]$ has size 1
   $\qquad\qquad\quad = V_{[a]} \cup \{\alpha, \alpha'\}$ otherwise.

Proof. The proof is difficult. We only give a sketch of proof illustrated by an example.

We first assume the existence of an injective strong morphism $F : M_1 \rightarrow M_2$. The restriction of F to the induced subgraph $Skel(A_1, D_1)$ of (A_1, D_1) is still an injective strong morphism and Proposition 14 states that (A_2, D_2) contains a splitting of $Skel(A_1, D_1)$. On the other hand, for any equivalence class $[a]$ whose size is ≥ 2, there exists at least one pair $\{\alpha, \alpha'\}$ in A_2 such that $\alpha D_2 \alpha'$ (Lemma 6). The splitting is then enriched by judiciously chosen pairs $\{\alpha, \alpha'\}$ in a way that the hypotheses are satisfied. This is possible as the morphism F is strong.

For the converse, the proof is in the same spirit as in Proposition 14. However it is more complex due to the equivalence classes $[a]$ with size ≥ 2, the associated pair $\{\alpha, \alpha'\}$ will be used to "encode" the elements of $[a]$.

The trace morphism F is defined such that :

(1) $alph F(a) \subseteq lett([a])$ for any $a \in A_1$. This insures that F is strong.

(2) First, for any class $[a]$ with more than one element, F uses a code over the alphabet $\{\alpha, \alpha'\}$. Second, F is "nearly" constructed by codes : there are a clique-covering $(C_i)_{i=1,...,n}$ of (A_1, D_1), n edges $(C'_i)_{i=1,...,n}$ of (A_2, D_2) and n morphisms $F_i : C_i^* \rightarrow {C'_i}^*$ such that

$$\pi_{C'_i} F(u) = F_i(\pi_{C_i} u).$$

several initial states) as follows: The state set of $\mathcal{A}$ is Q, a state q is initial if some tile $\boxed{(\#, q) | (a, q')}$ occurs in Δ, a state q is final if some tile $\boxed{(a, q) | (\#, q')}$ occurs in Δ, and (q, a, q') is a transition of $\mathcal{A}$ if some tile $\boxed{(a', q) | (a, q')}$ occurs in Δ.

We will refer to the triple (Σ, Q, Δ) as a *tiling system* while the language L recognized by such a tiling system will be denoted $L = L(\Sigma, Q, \Delta)$.

We denote by REC the family of all recognizable picture languages. The proofs of the following theorems can be found in [6].

Theorem 3. *The family* REC *is closed under row and column concatenation.*

Theorem 4. *The family* REC *is closed under union and intersection.*

In a different set-up, it was proved by K. Inoue and I. Takanami (cf. [13], [10], [11]) that REC is not closed under complementation. Their proof refers to two other definitions of the recognizable picture languages, using "on-line tessellation automata" and and is quite complicated. In [7] a short combinatorial proof of this fact is given which refers directly to tiling systems. We report here the most interesting part of this proof.

Theorem 5. *The family* REC *is not closed under complement.*

Proof. Let $L = \{p \in \Sigma^{**} \mid p = s \ominus s$ where s is a square$\}$ where $\Sigma =$ is an alphabet with two letters. In other words, L contains the pictures of size $(2n, n)$ for every n such that the top and the bottom square halves are identical.

By using closure properties of REC under concatenation it can be proved that the complement language ^cL belongs to REC. We now show that $L \notin$ REC.

Suppose that $L \in$ REC, that is L is a projection of a local language L' over an alphabet Γ. A counting argument will show that this leads to a contradiction. Let σ and γ be the sizes of the alphabets Σ and Γ respectively.

For $n \geq 1$ let $L_n = \{p \in \Sigma^{**} \mid p = s \ominus s$ where s is a square of size $(n, n)\}$. The number of pictures in L_n is σ^{n^2}. Let L'_n be the set of rectangles in L' (over Γ) whose projections are in L_n. For the stripe rectangles over Γ of size $(2, n)$ consisting of the n-th and $(n+1)$-st rows in the rectangles of L'_n there are at most γ^{2n} possibilities. For n sufficiently large, we have $\sigma^{n^2} \geq \gamma^{2n}$. Therefore, for n sufficiently large, there will be two different pictures $p = s_p \ominus s_p$, $q = s_q \ominus s_q \in L_n$ (with $s_p \neq s_q$) such that the corresponding pictures $p' = s'_p \ominus s''_p$, $q' = s'_q \ominus s''_q \in L'_n$ over the tiling alphabet Γ have the same stripes consisting of the n-th and $(n+1)$-st rows. This implies that, by definition of local languages, also the pictures $v' = s'_p \ominus s''_q$ and $w' = s'_q \ominus s''_p$ belong to L'_n and therefore the pictures $\pi(v') = s_p \ominus s_q$ and $\pi(w') = s_q \ominus s_p$ belong to L_n. This gives a contradiction. $\square$

Another property of recognizable sets of words, besides closure under complement, which fails to be preserved in the context of pictures is decidability of the emptiness problem. Using a reduction to the halting problem for Turing machines, the following theorem is proved in [6]:

Theorem 6. *The emptiness problem is undecidable for the family* REC.

2.2 Logical definability

We will give now definitions of logical definability of pictures and picture languages. As mentioned above, we will identify a picture $p \in \Sigma^{**}$ with the model $\underline{p} = (dom(p), S_1, S_2, (P_a)_{a \in \Sigma})$ where $dom(p) = \{1, \ldots, \ell_1(p)\} \times \{1, \ldots, \ell_2(p)\}$. Properties of pictures will be described by first-order and monadic second-order formulas, using first-order variables $x, y, z, x_1, x_2, \ldots$ for points of $dom(p)$, i.e. "positions", and monadic second-order variables $X, Y, Z, X_1, X_2, \ldots$ for sets of positions.

Atomic formulas are of the form $x S_i y$ (where $i \in \{1, 2\}$), $X(x)$, and $P_a(x)$, interpreted in the natural way by $(x, y) \in S_i$, $x \in X$, $x \in P_a$, respectively. *Formulas* are built up from atomic formulas by means of the Boolean connectives $\neg, \wedge, \vee, \rightarrow, \leftrightarrow$ and the quantifiers $\exists, \forall$, applicable to first-order as well as to second-order variables. A formula without free variables is called a *sentence*. The language $L(\varphi)$ defined by a sentence φ is the set of all pictures $p \in \Sigma^{**}$ such that $\underline{p}$ satifies φ.

Definition 7. A picture language L is called *monadic second-order definable* ($L \in$ MSO) if there is a monadic second-order sentence φ with $L = L(\varphi)$.

L is *first-order definable* ($L \in$ FO) if there is a sentence φ containing only first-order quantifiers (i.e., ranging over positions only) such that $L = L(\varphi)$.

L is *existential monadic second-order definable* ($L \in$ EMSO), if there is a sentence of the form $\varphi = \exists X_1, \ldots, \exists X_n \psi(X_1, \ldots, X_n)$ where ψ contains only first-order quantifiers, such that $L = L(\varphi)$.

Let us mention some technically useful formulas. An upper border position x of a picture, i.e. a position $x = (1, j)$ for some j, is described by the formula $\varphi_{top}(x) := \neg \exists y\, y S_1 x$. Similarly, the other borders can be described by corresponding formulas $\varphi_{left}(x), \varphi_{right}(x), \varphi_{bottom}(x)$. The four corner positions (top-left, top-right, bottom-left, bottom-right) are defined by appropriate conjunctions of these formulas.

As an example of a picture language in EMSO let us mention the set of square pictures over a given alphabet: In a defining formula, it suffices to postulate a set of positions which (1.) contains the left upper corner, (2.) is "closed under diagonal successors" (i.e. passing from (i, j) to $(i+1, j+1)$), and (3.) does not hit the bottom or right border, excepting the bottom right corner. Applying Theorem 10 of the subsequent section one can show that no first-order sentence defines the set of square pictures.

3 Equivalence theorem

In this section we give the main result of the present paper.

Theorem 8. *For any picture language L: $L \in$ REC iff $L \in$ EMSO.*

We shall start by showing how to describe recognizability by a finite tiling system using an existential monadic second-order formula (Section 3.1). For the reverse direction (Section 3.2), we will use the notion of a locally threshold testable picture language as an intermediate stage. First we will show that a picture language in EMSO is a projection of a locally threshold testable language. Then, in two more steps, we will prove that locally threshold testable picture languages are recognizable. This completes the proof of the theorem since REC is clearly closed under projections.

3.1   From tiling systems to existential monadic second-order logic

Proposition 9. *For any picture language L: If $L \in$ REC then $L \in$ EMSO.*

Proof. Let $L \subseteq \Sigma^{**}$ be recognizable, say defined by the finite tiling system (Σ, Q, Δ), where Δ is a set of 2×2–pictures over $\Sigma \times Q \cup \{\#\}$. Then we have $p \in L$ iff there is a picture $c \in Q^{**}$ of the same size as p such that $\widehat{p \times c}$ is tilable by Δ.

We have to formalize the right-hand side by an EMSO-formula to be interpreted in p. Given $Q = \{q_1, \ldots, q_k\}$, we shall do this using set variables $X_1, \ldots, X_k$ where $X_l(x)$ is intended to mean $c(x) = q_l$. Thus $p \in L$ iff $\underline{p}$ satisfies

$\exists X_1 \ldots \exists X_k$ [$X_1, \ldots, X_k$ form a partition of $dom(p)$ and for the picture c
$\qquad$ given by $c(i,j) = q_l$ iff $(i,j) \in X_l$ the picture $\widehat{p \times c}$ is tilable by Δ].

We have to express the condition $[\ldots]$ in first-order logic. It is easy to write down a formula $\varphi_{partition}(X_1, \ldots, X_k)$, expressing that $X_1, \ldots, X_k$ is a partition. In order to express that each sub-picture of size $(2, 2)$ of $\widehat{p \times c}$ (where c is defined by a given partition $X_1, \ldots, X_k$ as above) belongs to Δ, we numerate each tile $\delta \in \Delta$ in the form

$$\delta = \begin{array}{|c|c|} \hline \delta_1 & \delta_2 \\ \hline \delta_3 & \delta_4 \\ \hline \end{array}$$

also written as $(\delta_1, \delta_2, \delta_3, \delta_4)$, where $\delta_i \in (\Sigma \times Q) \cup \{\#\}$ for $i \in \{1, \ldots 4\}$.
We divide Δ into nine disjoint sets:

$$\Delta = \Delta_m \,\dot{\cup}\, \Delta_t \,\dot{\cup}\, \Delta_b \,\dot{\cup}\, \Delta_l \,\dot{\cup}\, \Delta_r \,\dot{\cup}\, \Delta_{tl} \,\dot{\cup}\, \Delta_{tr} \,\dot{\cup}\, \Delta_{bl} \,\dot{\cup}\, \Delta_{br}$$

where e.g. Δ_m contains all "middle tiles", i.e. those without $\#$, Δ_t contains the "top tiles" $(\#, \#, \delta_3, \delta_4)$ with $\delta_3, \delta_4 \in \Sigma \times Q$, and so on. By nine corresponding first-order formulas $\psi_m, \psi_t, \ldots, \psi_{br}$ one can describe in each case which of the four positions $x_1, \ldots, x_4$ of a tile should match the picture, excluding the boundary $\#$. (For example, ψ_t expresses that x_1, x_2 have no S_1-predecessors.) If for a tile δ we have $\delta_i = (a, q_l)$, where $i \in \{1, \ldots, 4\}$, let $\varphi_{\delta_i}(x)$ be an abbreviation for $P_a(x) \wedge X_l(x)$. Now let

$\chi_m : \psi_m(x_1, \ldots, x_4) \to \bigvee_{(\delta_1, \ldots, \delta_4) \in \Delta_m} (\varphi_{\delta_1}(x_1) \wedge \varphi_{\delta_2}(x_2) \wedge \varphi_{\delta_3}(x_3) \wedge \varphi_{\delta_4}(x_4))$

$\chi_t : \psi_t(x_3, x_4) \to \bigvee_{(\#, \#, \delta_3, \delta_4) \in \Delta_t} (\varphi_{\delta_3}(x_3) \wedge \varphi_{\delta_4}(x_4))$

etc., up to

$\chi_{br} : \psi_{br}(x_1) \to \bigvee_{(\delta_1, \#, \#, \#) \in \Delta_{br}} \varphi_{\delta_1}(x_1)$

Then the following existential monadic second-order sentence defines L:

$\exists X_1 \ldots \exists X_k (\varphi_{partition} \wedge \forall x_1 \ldots \forall x_4 \, (\chi_m \wedge \chi_t \wedge \chi_b \wedge \chi_l \wedge \chi_r \wedge \chi_{tl} \wedge \chi_{tr} \wedge \chi_{bl} \wedge \chi_{br}))$ $\quad\square$

3.2   From existential monadic second-order logic to tiling systems

For the reverse direction of Theorem 8, we introduce an auxiliary notion which generalizes the local picture languages: the *locally threshold testable picture languages*. As in string language theory, not only the existence of a tiling is required here, but also extra conditions on the occurrences of tiles (counted up to a fixed threshold) should be satisfied. Given a *threshold number* $t \geq 1$ and a square dimension $d \geq 1$, we say that two pictures p and p' are (d, t)-equivalent (short: $p \sim_{d,t} p'$) if for each quadratic picture σ of dimension $\leq d$, there are either at least t occurrences of σ in $\widehat{p}$ and $\widehat{p'}$, or the numbers $(\leq t)$ of occurrences of σ in $\widehat{p}$ and $\widehat{p'}$ coincide. The relation $\sim_{d,t}$ is an equivalence relation. A picture language L is called *locally d-testable with threshold t* if L is a union of $\sim_{d,t}$-equivalence classes. If for some d and t, L is locally d-testable with threshold t, we say L is *locally threshold testable*.

Let Σ_d^{**} be the set of pictures of size (m, n) with $m \geq d$ and $n \geq d$ over Σ. When discussing locally d-testable sets we henceforth restrict to pictures in Σ_d^{**} only, in order to simplify the presentation. Within this restriction, one may refer in the previous definition only to tiles of dimension d exactly, without changing the notion of d-testability. In the sequel we will use this variant of the definition. The same is usually assumed in the theory of string languages ([2]).

Theorem 10. *A picture language is first-order definable iff it is locally threshold testable.*

In this extended abstract, we omit the proof for lack of space. The direction from right to left is almost straightforward. For the reverse direction we use some notions and results from model theory involving the Ehrenfeucht-Fraïssé technique. For more details the reader may consult the textbook [3] or the survey paper [15], applied to the special case where all models under consideration are picture models p. The next step of the reverse direction of Theorem 8 is provided by the following proposition.

Proposition 11. *If $L \in$ EMSO then L is a projection of a locally threshold testable picture language.*

Proof. Assume the picture language $L \subseteq \Sigma^{**}$ is defined by the existential monadic second-order sentence $\exists X_1 \ldots \exists X_k \psi(X_1, \ldots, X_k)$ where ψ is a first-order formula. The formula $\psi(X_1, \ldots, X_k)$ is satisfied in picture models of the form $(p, Q_1, \ldots, Q_k)$ with $Q_i \subseteq dom(p)$ for $i = 1, \ldots, k$. Such an expanded picture model corresponds to a picture over the extended alphabet $\Sigma \times \{0, 1\}^k$ where the m-th additional component is 1 at point (i, j) iff $(i, j) \in Q_m$ (otherwise 0). Let π be the canonical projection from $\Sigma \times \{0, 1\}^k$ to Σ. Then L is the projection under π of the picture language $L' \subseteq (\Sigma \times \{0, 1\}^k)^{**}$ defined by $\psi(X_1, \ldots, X_k)$ in the sense explained above. By Theorem 10, the picture language L' is locally threshold testable. $\square$

Let d be a positive integer. To prove the main result, starting from Proposition 11, we shall simulate threshold counting of sub-blocks of size $d \times d$ by a tiling system with tiles of size $d \times d$, and then reduce the tiles under consideration to size 2×2.

Definition 12. *A language $L \subseteq \Sigma_d^{**}$ is d-local if there exists a set $\Delta^{(d)}$ of pictures of size (d, d) (or "d-tiles") over $\Sigma \cup \{\#\}$, such that $L = \{p \in \Sigma^{**} | T_{d,d}(\widehat{p}) \subseteq \Delta^{(d)}\}$.*

In other words, if a rectangle belongs to a *d-local* picture language then it can be recognized by looking at its sub-blocks of size (d, d).

Proposition 13. *A locally threshold testable picture language is a projection of a d-local language for some integer $d \geq 2$.*

Proof. Let L be a locally threshold testable language over an alphabet Σ. By definition, L is a union of $\sim_{d,t}$-equivalence classes for some threshold t and some dimension d. Without loss of generality, we consider $d \geq 3$.

Let $k = (|\Sigma \cup \{\#\}|)^{d^2}$ and let $\sigma_1, \sigma_2, \ldots, \sigma_k$ be the different $d \times d$-pictures over $\Sigma \cup \{\#\}$. Then every $\sim_{d,t}$-class can be represented by a k-tuple $(t_1, t_2, \ldots, t_k)$ of integers, where $0 \leq t_i \leq t$ and t_i gives the number of occurrences of σ_i, counted up to the threshold t, in the pictures of that class. Thus we think the language L as given by a set of *accepting k-tuples* corresponding to the $\sim_{d,t}$-classes contained in L.

We will describe a procedure to define a d-local language L' over an appropriate alphabet $\Sigma \times \mathcal{C}$ whose projection to Σ is the language L. We start by giving the idea of the construction. When we are given a picture p, we can decide whether p belongs to L as follows. We perform a scanning of p using a square window of size $d \times d$ and count, up to the threshold t, how many times we see, through the window, each of the σ_i's $(i = 1, \ldots, k)$. The scanning is carried out along all horizontal stripes of height d and explores them independently from left to right. By an additional component (a k-tuple) within the tiles, the intermediate results of the threshold counting are recorded. By scanning the rightmost tiles from top to bottom, the threshold counting over the whole picture is completed. The picture will belong to the language L if and only if this procedure leads to an accepting k-tuple at the bottom-right corner.

In the formal construction (see [8] for details) we define the d-local language L' by presenting the set $\Delta^{(d)}$ of d-tiles. Let $\mathcal{C}$ be the set of all k-tuples $(t_1, t_2, \ldots, t_k)$, $0 \leq t_i \leq t$ for $i = 1, \ldots, k$. The d-local language L' will be defined over the alphabet $\Sigma \times \mathcal{C}$, and the generic element of $\Delta^{(d)}$ will be of the form $\sigma \times c$, where $\sigma \in (\Sigma \cup \{\#\})^{d \times d}$, and $c \in (\mathcal{C} \cup \{\#\})^{d \times d}$. (Strictly speaking, we use $(\#, \#)$ as the present border symbol and postulate that σ and c have the same occurrences of $\#$, i.e. $\sigma(i, j) = \# \Leftrightarrow c(i, j) = \#$.) We define the d-tiles to enforce a "local compatibility" that makes them describing the scanning procedure. More precisely, position $(d-1, d-1)$ of the d-tiles will keep track of a counting from left to right in each horizontal stripe of height d. Since we have assumed $d \geq 3$, this position contains a symbol different from $\#$.

The set $\Delta^{(d)}$ defines a language L' such that given $p \in \Sigma^{**}$, the existence of $p' \in L'$ with $p = \pi(p')$ is equivalent to the existence of a scanning for p which performs the counting procedure and arrives at an accepting k-tuple. $\qquad \square$

We can now finish the proof of Theorem 8 by the following proposition:

Proposition 14. *A d-local picture language is a projection of a local language.*

Proof. Let $L \subseteq \Sigma_d^{**}$ be a d-local picture language and let $\Delta^{(d)} = \{\sigma_1, \sigma_2, \ldots, \sigma_h\}$ be the set of d-tiles over $\Sigma \cup \{\#\}$ that defines it. We have to define a local language L' over a larger alphabet $\Gamma = \Sigma \times \mathcal{C}$ such that $\pi(L') = L$, by specifying its set $\Delta^{(2)}$ of tiles.

The idea of the construction is to add for each letter of a picture p the information by which d-tiles it is covered in the original $\Delta^{(d)}$-tiling. Since every d-tile is a $d \times d$-matrix of letters, and a letter in a picture generally has to occur for each position $(i, j) \in (\{1, \ldots, d\})^2$ as $\sigma(i, j)$ for some $\sigma \in \Delta^{(d)}$, we represent this information in a $d \times d$-matrix $(m(i, j))$ of tile numbers. Thus, given a position (i_0, j_0) of a picture p $(1 \leq i_0, j_0 \leq d)$, a matrix $(m(i, j))_{i,j=1}^{d}$ will be appended to the value $a = p(i_0, j_0)$, building the extension c of p at this position, i.e. $(a, m) = (p \times c)(i_0, j_0)$. The entry $m(i, j)$ will be the index k of that d-tile, in a tiling of $\hat{p}$, whose position (i, j) matches (i_0, j_0). Clearly, for a matrix m appended to a, every tile $\sigma_{m(i,j)}$ has to carry letter a at position (i, j). We will fix this condition in the definition of the enlarged alphabet below.

For $d > 2$ there will occur the case that a position (i_0, j_0) is near to the border of $\widehat{p \times c}$, so that e.g. $i > i_0 + 1$ for some $i \leq d$. In this case no d-tile can occur as sub-block of $\hat{p}$ whose position (i, j) matches (i_0, j_0). We will denote this case by 0 in the matrix, and have to take care in the construction that 0 occurs at the correct positions.

In the formal construction (see [8]) we define a new alphabet Γ as a subset of $\Sigma \times \{0, \ldots, h\}^{d \times d}$ and specify a set of tiles $\Delta^{(2)} \subseteq (\Gamma \cup \{\#\})^{2 \times 2}$ to define the desired local language L'. $\qquad\square$

4 Concluding Remarks

In this paper we have proved that the family REC of picture languages recognized by finite tiling systems coincides with the family EMSO of picture languages definable in existential monadic second-order logic. This result indicates that the notion of recognizability presented in this paper is a robust one in the sense that at the same time it has a natural logic meaning and generalizes in a straightforward way the automaton recognizability for sets of strings.

In developing a theory of recognizability for picture languages a general task is to individuate interesting sub-families of recognizable picture languages and to state relationships between them. A first possible approach takes into account the closure operations of recognizable picture languages. The family REC contains all finite sets and is closed (cf. [7]) under row and column concatenation, denoted by $\ominus$ and Φ respectively, row and column Kleene closure, denoted by $*\ominus$ and $*\Phi$ respectively, union and intersection. However, REC is not closed under complementation (cf. Theorem 5). So one can introduce some regular-like expressions and define sub-families of REC. In more specific way, given the set $\Theta = \{\ominus, \Phi, *\ominus, *\Phi, \cup, \cap, {}^c\}$ of operations and a subset $X \subseteq \Theta$, the family REG(X) is defined as the smallest family of picture languages containing all finite sets and closed under the operations of X. If X does not contain the complement, REG(X) is a subfamily of REC. The cases in which X contains the complement lead to some interesting open problems, concerning the inclusion of REG(X) in REC. Two cases play a special role: $X = \Theta$, REG(Θ), denoted shortly by REG, defines the family of (generalized) *regular picture languages*; for $X = \{\ominus, \Phi, \cup, \cap, {}^c\}$, REG$(X)$ defines the family of *star-free picture languages* and is denoted by SF.

In the context of another approach, one can introduce sub-families of REC (=EMSO) by taking into account specific sub-logics of existential monadic second-order logic. An interesting example is first-order logic where the two successor relations S_1 and S_2 are replaced by the corresponding orderings $\leq_1$ and $\leq_2$ (defined by $(i, j) \leq_1 (i', j)$ iff $i \leq i'$, resp. $(i, j) \leq_2 (i, j')$ iff $j \leq j'$).

A third approach is to study and compare restricted versions of recognizability, for instance in terms of "nonambigous tiling systems" (allowing at most one tiling on a given picture) or suitable versions of "deterministic" tiling systems (similar to the tessellation automata of [10]).

A general problem is then to compare the families of picture languages obtained by particular regular-like expressions, by specific sublogics, as well as by restricted types of tiling systems.

References

1. M. Blum and C. Hewitt. Automata on a two-dimensional tape. *IEEE Symposium on Switching and Automata Theory*, 1967,pp. 155–160.
2. D. Beauquier and J.E. Pin. Factors of words, In *Proc. 16th Int. Colloquium on Automata, Languages and Programming*, G. Ausiello et al., (eds.), Lecture Notes in Computer Science, 372, Springer-Verlag, Berlin 1989, pp. 190–200.
3. H.D. Ebbinghaus and J. Flum and W. Thomas. *Mathematical Logic*, Springer-Verlag, Berlin, Heidelberg, New York 1984.
4. R. Fagin Monadic generalized spectra, *Z. math. Logik Grundl. Math.* 21, 1975, pp.89-96.
5. Fagin, R., Stockmeyer, L., Vardi, M.Y.: On monadic NP vs. monadic co-NP. Proc. *8th IEEE Conf. on Structure in Complexity Theory*, 1993, pp. 19-30.
6. D. Giammarresi and A. Restivo. Recognizable picture languages. In *Proc. First International Colloquium on Parallel Image Processing*, 1991. International Journal Pattern Recognition and Artificial Intelligence. Vol. 6, No. 2& 3, 1992.
7. D. Giammarresi and A. Restivo. On recognizable two-dimensional languages. Tech. Report Dipartimento di matematica ed applicazioni, Università di Palermo.
8. D. Giammarresi, A. Restivo, S. Seibert, W. Thomas. *Monadic second-order logic over pictures and recognizability by tiling systems.* Tech. Report 9318 Institut für Informatik und Praktische Mathematik, Christian-Albrechts-Universität Kiel.
9. J. E. Hopcroft, and J. D. Ullman. *Introduction to Automata Theory, Languages and Computation.* Addison-Wesley, Reading, MA, 1979.
10. K. Inoue and A. Nakamura. Some properties of two-dimensional on-line tessellation acceptors. *Information Sciences*, Vol. 13, 1977, pp. 95–121.
11. K. Inoue and A. Nakamura. Nonclosure properties of two-dimensional on-line tessellation acceptors and one-way parallel/sequential array acceptors. *Transaction of IECE of Japan*, Vol. 6, 1977, pp.475–476.
12. K. Inoue and I. Takanami. A survey of two-dimensional automata theory. In *Proc. 5th Int. Meeting of Young Computer Scientists*, J. Dasson and J. Kelemen (Eds.), Lecture Notes in Computer Science 381, Springer-Verlag, Berlin 1990, pp. 72–91.
13. K. Inoue and I. Takanami. A characterization of recognizable picture languages. In *Proc. Second International Colloquium on Parallel Image Processing*, A. Nakamura et al. (Eds.), Lecture Notes in Computer Science 654, Springer, Berlin 1992.
14. W. Thomas. On Logics, Tilings, and Automata. In *Proc. 18th Int. Colloquium on Automata, Languages and Programming*, Lecture Notes in Computer Science, 510, Springer-Verlag, Berlin 1991, pp. 441–453.
15. W. Thomas. On the Ehrenfeucht-Fraissé Game in Theoretical Computer Science. In *Proc. TAPSOFT '93*, M.C. Gaudel, J.P. Jouannaud (Eds.) Lecture Notes in Computer Science, 668, Springer-Verlag, Berlin 1993, pp. 559 – 568.

q-Grammars : Results, Implementation[*]

Maylis Delest[1] and Jean-Philippe Dubernard[2]

[1] LaBRI - Université Bordeaux I, 351 Cours de la Libération,
33405 TALENCE CEDEX FRANCE

[2] LIUP- Université de Poitiers, 40 Avenue du Recteur Pinaud,
86022 POITIERS CEDEX FRANCE

Abstract. This paper deals with an extension of the Schützenberger's methodology in which algebraic grammars are used in order to enumerate combinatorial objects. The extension allows us to make computation with q-series. We present here some results and a computer algebra system QGRAM for the resolution of such equations.

1 Introduction

Symbolic manipulation languages allow us to make some usual operations as factorization, differentiation or solving linear or algebraic system. The precursor in this field was the language Macsyma [11] developed by the MIT since 1975. Maple [8] is also a well-known language of this type. It has been developed by the University of Waterloo since 1983. Now many different types of this software are being used. All of them are good tools and show good results when applied to combinatorial problems, though Maple seems to be the most used. On the other hand in certain fields some software system were created more specifically adapted to the fields in question. For example in Combinatorics, the system Darwin [2] allows us to compute using the species theory defined by Joyal. In our current approach in Combinatorics, we deal with M.P. Schützenberger methodology.

Let Ω be a class of combinatorial objects. Suppose that they are enumerated by integers a_n according to the value n of a statistic p and that the corresponding generating function

$$f(t) = \Sigma_{n \geq 0} \, a_n \, t^n$$

is algebraic. The methodology of M.P. Schützenberger [10] which consists in first constructing a bijection between the objects Ω and words of an algebraic language, and then takes the "commutative image", produces, when it exists, the algebraic generating function and also explains this algebraicity. The q-grammars were introduced by Delest and Fedou [4] in order to get some non algebraic equations by means of attribute grammars. In some sense, they extend the previous methodology. The q-equations which in general are not algebraic, can be obtained by this method

[*] With the support of the PRC Mathématiques et Informatique.
[1] maylis@labri.u-bordeaux.fr
[2] dubernar@matpts.univ-poitiers.fr

even if the initial encoding by algebraic language yielded only algebraic results. The reader not familiar with q-series will find a complete survey in the book by Andrews [1]. This new method led to new results enumerating "polyominoes" according to the area [3, 5].

The software which is described here is based on some theoretical results on the q-grammars which are developed in sections 2 and 3.

As a very simple example of a result given by this program, let us consider the combinatorial functional equation associated to the q-grammar for binary trees weighted by the sum of the heights of the leaves :

$$C(x,\bar{x},t;q)=qxt\bar{x} + qxt\bar{x}C(x,\bar{x},t;q) + x\,C(x,\bar{x},qt;q)\,\bar{x} + x\,C(x,\bar{x},qt;q)\,\bar{x}\,C(x,\bar{x},t;q).$$

This equation means that the weight on trees is recursively computed from the height of the leaves by means of Dyck words. The QGRAM package is written in Maple and allows us to obtain such equations automatically from the description of the grammar. This is due to the results of section 3. When computing an equation, QGRAM constructs a representation giving the coefficients of the generating power series and others relevant results. The software is described in section 4.

2 Series and q-grammars

We will consider here attribute grammars in a very simplified way. A complete description can be found in [7].

An attribute grammar is an algebraic grammar $G= <V,X,\mathcal{P},S>$ with a finite attribute set $A(Y)$ associated to every non terminal symbol Y of V. Each attribute τ is an application from V to a range D_τ. An attribute τ is said to be synthesized if, for every rule of $\mathcal{P}$ of the form

$$Y \rightarrow u_1Y_1u_2Y_2..... Y_nu_{n+1}$$

where u_i is in X^*, $\tau(Y)$ can be computed in the following way

$$\tau(Y) = f(\gamma_1(Y_1), ..., \gamma_n(Y_n))$$

where for every k in [1,n], γ_k is in $A(Y_k)$ and f is an application from $D_{\gamma_1}\times ...$ $\times D_{\gamma_n}$ in D_τ . The image of a word w by τ is equal to the value of $\tau(S)$ in the derivation $S \xrightarrow{*} w$ of w in G.

In the following, when a non terminal symbol appears several times in the right-hand side of a rule in $\mathcal{P}$, we will number each occurrence in order to distinguish them. For example, an attribute associated with a rule

$$D \rightarrow x\,D\,\bar{x}\,D$$

will be written as

$$\tau(D) = f(\tau(D_1),\tau(D_2))$$

where D_1 (resp. D_2) is the first (resp. second) non-terminal letter D in (4).

Definition 1. A q-grammar is an attribute grammar (G,τ) satisfying the following conditions :
(i) $G = <V,X,\mathcal{P},S>$ is an unambiguous algebraic grammar,
(ii) τ is a synthesized attribute with value in $\mathbb{C}[X\cup\{q\}]$,
(iii) for every letter x in X and every word w in $\mathcal{B}(G)$ we have $|\tau(w)|_x = |w|_x$.

The translation $\tau(w)$ which is an element of $(X\cup\{q\})^*$ is called q-analog of the word w and is denoted by (w;q). As usual in Schützenberger methodology, we will denote by the same letter Y in V :
- the language of the words derivated from Y,
- the non-commutative power series $\displaystyle\sum_{Y \overset{*}{\to} w} w$.

Definition 2. Let $^qG = (G,\tau)$ a q-grammar. The q-analog $^q\mathcal{B}(G)$ of the language S is defined by

$$^q\mathcal{B}(G) = \sum_{w\in\mathcal{B}(G)} (w;q).$$

Note that by the previous notation, we have $S=\mathcal{B}(G)$. We will denote by χ_0 the morphism which commutes the letters and which in the Schützenberger's methodology is said to be "taking the commutative images" of the word that is

$$\chi_0(w) = \prod_{x\in X} x^{|w|_x}.$$

Then, the commutative generating function of S (i.e. $\mathcal{B}(G)$), denoted by the lower case s, is given by

$$s = \sum_{w\in\mathcal{B}(G)} \chi_0(w) .$$

Definition 3. Let $^qG = (G,\tau)$ be a q-grammar. The q-generating function of the q-analog of the language S is defined by

$$^qs = \sum_{w\in\mathcal{B}(G)} \chi_1(\tau(w)) \chi_0(w)$$

where χ_1 is the morphism which deletes all the letters of X in a word of $(X\cup\{q\})^*$.

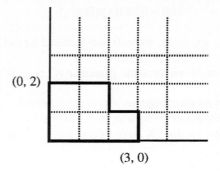

$(0, 2)$

$(3, 0)$

Fig. 1. Ferrers diagram of 5 units encoded by aabab.

Thus, let $X=\{x_1, x_2, ..., x_k\}$, as usual ^qs stands for $^qs(x_1, x_2, ..., x_k)$, so the variables are omitted when they are not useful.

Example. Let $G = <\{S,L\},\{a,b\},\{S \to aLb, L \to aL; L \to bL; L \to \varepsilon\}S\}$ and τ be defined by

$$\tau(S) = q^{|\tau(L)|_a + |\tau(L)|_b + 1} \, a \, \tau(L) \, b \,, \qquad \text{(associated to } S \to a \, L \, b)$$

$$\tau(L) = q^{|\tau(S)|_b} \, a \, \tau(L), \qquad \text{(associated to } L \to a \, L)$$

$$\tau(L) = \ b \, \tau(L) \,, \qquad \text{(associated to } L \to b \, L)$$

$$\tau(L) = \ \varepsilon. \qquad \text{(associated to } L \to \varepsilon)$$

The language S is equal to $a \, (a+b)^*b$ which encodes the paths of $\mathbb{N} \times \mathbb{N}$ going from $(y,0)$ to $(0,x)$ making only East and South steps, which defines a Ferrers diagram [11] (see figure 1). Then $w = aabab$ is a word of S. We have

$$(w;q) = q^4 \, a \, q \, a \, b \, a \, b,$$

$$^q\mathfrak{S}(G) = \varepsilon + qab + q^2aab + q^2 \, abb + q^3aaab + q^3aqabb + q^3abab + q^3abbb + ...,$$

$$\chi_0(w) = a^3b^2,$$

$$s = \frac{ab}{1-a-b},$$

$$^qs = \varepsilon + qab + q^2a^2b + q^2ab^2 + q^3a^3b + (q^4+q^3) \, a^2b^2 + q^3ab^3 + ...$$

3 Main Results on q-grammars

In this section, we present three theorems which allow us to write out a q-equation from a q-grammar in such a way that one of the solutions of this q-equation is the q-generating function associated to the q-grammar. We do not give in this short version the proofs of these theorems but only their application to the example of the previous section.

Let X be the alphabet $\{x_1, x_2, ..., x_k\}$. In the following, the symbol G will denote a non ambiguous algebraic grammar $<V,X,\mathcal{P},S>$.

Theorem 4. *Let* (G,τ) *be a q-grammar, let* Y, U, W *belong to* V. *Suppose that* $\mathcal{P}$ *contains only the following rule on Y*

$$R : Y \rightarrow UW.$$

Let $\eta_R(q)$ *be a q-series; if* τ *is defined on* R *by*

$$\tau(Y) = \eta_R(q) \; q^{\sum\limits_{i=1}^{k} \alpha_i |\tau(U)|_{x_i}} \; q^{\sum\limits_{i=1}^{k} \beta_i |\tau(W)|_{x_i}} \; \tau(U) \, \tau(W)$$

then

$$qY = \eta_R(q) \, \hat{U} \, \hat{W}$$

where $\hat{U}$ *(resp.* $\hat{W}$*) is the q-generating function* qU *(resp.* qW*) in which we replace every letter* x_i *by* $q^{\alpha_i} x_i$ *(resp.* $q^{\beta_i} x_i$*).*

Proof. Let Y the set of words generated from the rule R. Let v a word of Y, it can be factorized in the form

$$v = uw$$

where u is in U and w is in W. Let us compute now qY,

$$qY = \sum_{u \in U, w \in W} (uw; q),$$

thus by definition, we have

$$qY = \sum_{u \in U, w \in W} \tau(uw) ,$$

Using the definition of τ and the fact that G is unambigous, we get

$$qY = \sum_{u \in U, w \in W} \eta_R(q) \; q^{\sum\limits_{i=1}^{k} \alpha_i |\tau(u)|_{x_i}} \; q^{\sum\limits_{i=1}^{k} \beta_i |\tau(w)|_{x_i}} \tau(u) \, \tau(w)$$

$$^q Y = \sum_{u\in U, w\in W} \eta_R(q)\, q^{\sum_{i=1}^{k} \alpha_i |\tau(u)|_{x_i}}\, q^{\sum_{i=1}^{k} \beta_i |\tau(w)|_{x_i}} (u;q)(w;q).$$

Then we can factorize this expression according to the words u and w

$$^q Y = \eta_R(q) \left(\sum_{u\in U} q^{\sum_{i=1}^{k} \alpha_i |\tau(u)|_{x_i}} (u;q) \right) \left(\sum_{w\in W} q^{\sum_{i=1}^{k} \beta_i |\tau(w)|_{x_i}} (w;q) \right)$$

which gives the result.

A very particular case of this theorem occurs when $U=x_i$ where $x_i \in X$, in this case we have

$$^q S = \eta_R(q)\, q^{\alpha_i}\, x_i\, \hat{W}.$$

Of course a similar case takes place when $W=x_i$.

Theorem 5. *Let* (G,τ) *be a q-grammar, let* Y, U, Z *belong to* V. *Suppose that* $\mathcal{P}$ *contains only the following rules on* Y

$$R_1 : Y \to U \quad and \quad R_2 : Y \to Z$$

Let $\eta_{R_1}(q)$ *and* $\eta_{R_2}(q)$ *be two q-series; if* τ *is defined on* R_1 *by*

$$\tau(Y) = \eta_{R_1}(q)\, q^{\sum_{i=1}^{k} \alpha_i |\tau(U)|_{x_i}}\, \tau(U)$$

and on R_2 *by*

$$\tau(Y) = \eta_{R_2}(q)\, q^{\sum_{i=1}^{k} \gamma_i |\tau(Z)|_{x_i}}\, \tau(Z)$$

then

$$^q Y = \eta_{R_1}(q)\, \hat{U} + \eta_{R_2}(q)\, \hat{Z}$$

where $\hat{U}$ *(resp.* $\hat{Z}$*) is the q-generating function* $^q U$ *(resp.* $^q Z$*) in which we replace every letter* x_i *by* $q^{\alpha_i} x_i$ *(resp.* $q^{\gamma_i} x_i$*).*

Proof. Let Y the set of words generated from the rule R. Let v a word of Y, because G is unambigous, the word v belongs to U or Z. Let us compute now $^q Y$,

$$^q Y = \sum_{v\in U} (v;q) + \sum_{v\in Z} (v;q),$$

thus by definition, we have

$$qY = \sum_{v \in U} \tau(v) + \sum_{v \in Z} \tau(v),$$

Using the definition of τ, we get

$$qY = \sum_{v \in U} \eta_{R_1}(q) \, q^{\sum_{i=1}^{k} \alpha_i |\tau(v)|_{x_i}} \tau(v) + \sum_{v \in Z} \eta_{R_2}(q) \, q^{\sum_{i=1}^{k} \gamma_i |\tau(v)|_{x_i}} \tau(v),$$

then factorizing we have

$$qY = \eta_{R_1}(q) \sum_{v \in U} q^{\sum_{i=1}^{k} \alpha_i |\tau(v)|_{x_i}} (v;q) + \eta_{R_2}(q) \sum_{v \in Z} q^{\sum_{i=1}^{k} \gamma_i |\tau(v)|_{x_i}} (v;q)$$

from which it is easy to get the theorem.

The next theorem is easy to prove

Theorem 6. *Let (G,τ) be a q-grammar, let* u *be a word of* X^*. *Suppose that* $\mathcal{P}$ *contains only the following rules on Y*

$$R : Y \to u$$

Let $\eta_R(q)$ *be a q-series; if* τ *is defined on* R *by*

$$\tau(Y) = \eta_R(q) \, u$$

then

$$qY = \eta_R(q) \, u.$$

Example. The grammar G of section 2 can be written in the form

$$G' = \langle\{S, S',L,L'\},\{a,b\},\{S \to aS'; \, S' \to Lb; \, L \to aL; \, L \to L';L' \to bL; \, L' \to \varepsilon\}, S\rangle.$$

Then, the attribute τ can be written in the form

$$\tau(S) = q^{|\tau(L)|_a + 1} \, a \, \tau(S'),$$ \qquad\qquad (associated to $S \to a \, S'$)

$$\tau(S') = q^{|\tau(L)|_b} \, \tau(L) \, b,$$ \qquad\qquad (associated to $S' \to Lb$)

$$\tau(L) = q^{|\tau(S)|_b} \, a \, \tau(L),$$ \qquad\qquad (associated to $L \to a \, L$)

$$\tau(L) = \tau(L') , \qquad\qquad \text{(associated to } L \rightarrow L')$$

$$\tau(L') = \varepsilon. \qquad\qquad \text{(associated to } L' \rightarrow \varepsilon)$$

Then, using the theorems, we deduce the following set of equations:

$$^q S(a,b) = q\, a\ ^q S'(aq,b),$$

$$^q S'(a,b) = \ ^q L(a,bq)\, b ,$$

$$^q L(a,b) = a\ ^q L(a,bq) + \ ^q L'(a,b) ,$$

$$^q L'(a,b) = b\ ^q L(a,b) + \varepsilon .$$

These equations can be reduced to :

$$^q S(a,b) = q\, a\ ^q L(aq,bq)\, b,$$

$$^q L(a,b) = a\ ^q L(a,bq) + b\ ^q L(a,b) + \varepsilon ,$$

and then solved, thus giving the well known generating function for Ferrers diagrams according to the area and the perimeter

$$q_S(z) = \sum_{n\geq 1} \frac{z^{n+1} q^n}{(1-qz)(1-q^2 z)...(1-q^n z)} .$$

4   The Maple Package QGRAM

The package contains functions for manipulating either the classical Schützenberger methodology or the q-grammars. It is based on the classical functions of Maple dealing with commutative and non-commutative algebra. Almost all the functions of the package are working in linear time according to the length of the data. We describe here only the main functions. The reader will find a table giving their complexity in figure 2.

The CONSGRAM function allows the user to declare a grammar to Maple. The result is a table with the following fields: a list of q-variables, the q-variable associated to the grammar axiom, a table containing the q-equations.

In all the computations we need to know how to truncate the series and to obtain their fixed point. Such criterion are called *weight*. The ITERE function gives the first terms of the language generated by a grammar using the user criterion defined by weight. The complexity of this function depends strongly on the weight which is declared by the user. In the general case, iterating a grammar leads to the construction of an infinite labelled tree. The weight which is introduced in the computation allows to stop the iteration when the branches of the tree have a given length. The implementation is made in a firdt depth left order on the infinite tree.

Name of the function	Complexity	Datas
CONSGRAM	$O(|V|+|\mathcal{P}|)$	$G=<V,X,\mathcal{P},S>$
COMMUTE	o(mnk)	m: number of words to compress n : average length of the words k : number of commutation rules
COMPRIME	o(mn)	m: number of words to compress n : average length of the words
CALCULE_Q_EQUATION	$o(|\mathcal{P}|r)$	$G=<V,X,\mathcal{P},S>$, τ r=average number of non terminal symbol in a rule of $\mathcal{P}$.

Fig. 2. Complexity of the main functions of QGRAM .

Two functions, COMMUTE and COMPRIME, allows to compute on a partial commutative generating function. The COMMUTE function uses the algorithm of Perrin [9].

The CALCULE_Q_EQUATION function takes as parameter a q-grammar. Using the theorems of the previous section, it gives the corresponding q-equation.

Other functions which we do not list here for now allows manipulation and computation on the truncated series and on the q-equation.

For example, let us see how the system deduces the equation on trees given in the introduction. In this case, we use the q-grammar (G,τ) where

$$G=<\{D\},\{x,\bar{x},t\},\{D\to x\,t\,\bar{x}\,;D\to x\,t\,\bar{x}\,D\,;D\to x\,D\,\bar{x}\,;D\to x\,D\,\bar{x}\,D\}, D>$$

and the attribute τ is defined by

$$\tau(D) = q\,x\,t\,\bar{x} \qquad\qquad \text{(associated to } D\to x\,t\,\bar{x})$$

$$\tau(D) = q\,x\,t\,\bar{x}\,\tau(D) \qquad\qquad \text{(associated to } D\to x\,t\,\bar{x}\,D)$$

$$\tau(D) = q^{|\tau(D)|}\,t\,x\,\tau(D)\,\bar{x} \qquad\qquad \text{(associated to } D\to x\,D\,\bar{x})$$

$$\tau(D) = q^{|\tau(D_1)|}\,t\,x\,\tau(D_1)\,\bar{x}\,\tau(D_2) \qquad\qquad \text{(associated to } D\to x\,D_1\,\bar{x}\,D_2).$$

Many new results may be derived from this equation or others which are close to it with the help of the system especially for skew Ferrers diagrams which are in bijection with trees. Some are given in [6].

Here below are the details of a Maple session.

```
# give the grammar G
> G:=consgram({x,y,t},{C},C,C=xty+xtyC+xCy+xCyC);

        G := table([
               alph_non_term = {C}
               alphterm = {t, y, x}
```

386

```
            produc = table([
                    C = xty + xtyC + xCy + xCyC
                ])
            axiome = C
        ])
# Define the weight
> poids:=<taille(mot,x)|mot>:
# words having at most 4 letters x
> serie:=itere(G,[poids,`+`,4]);
 serie := xty + xtyxty + xtyxtyxty + xtyxtyxtyxty + xtyxtyxxtyy + xtyxxtyy

    + xtyxxtyxtyy + xtyxxxtyyy + xtyxxtyyxty + xxtyy + xxtyxtyy + xxtyxtyxtyy

    + xxtyxxtyyy + xxxtyyy + xxxtyxtyyy + xxxxtyyyy + xxxtyyxtyy + xxtyyxty

    + xxtyyxtyxty + xxtyyxxtyy + xxtyxtyyxty + xxxtyyyxty

# compress the series output
> comprime(serie);
   xty + xtyxty + xtyxtyxty + xtyxtyxtyxty + xtyxtyx^2ty^2 + xtyx^2ty^2

    + xtyx^2tyxty^2 + xtyx^3ty^3 + xtyx^2ty^2xty + x^2ty^2 + x^2tyxty^2

    + x^2tyxtyxty^2 + x^2tyx^2ty^3 + x^3ty^3 + x^3tyxty^3 + x^4ty^4

    + x^3ty^2xty^2 + x^2ty^2xty + x^2ty^2xtyxty + x^2ty^2x^2ty^2

    + x^2tyxty^2xty + x^3ty^3xty
# non-commutative substitution
> subst(x=aa,y=epsilon,serie);
   aat + aataat + aataataat + aataataataat + aataataaaat + aataaaat

    + 2 aataaaataat + aataaaaaat + aaaat + 2 aaaataat + 3 aaaataataat

    + 2 aaaataaaat + aaaaaat + 3 aaaaaataat + aaaaaaaat
# 2nd arg = letters in commutative
# 3rd arg = commutation rules
> commute(serie,{},{{x,t}});
 txy + txytxy + txytxytxy + txytxytxytxy + txytxytxxyy + txytxxyy + txytxxytxyy

    + txytxxxyyy + txytxxyytxy + txxyy + txxytxyy + txxytxytxyy + txxytxxyyy

    + txxxyyy + txxxytxyyy + txxxxyyyy + txxxyytxyy + txxyytxy + txxyytxytxy

    + txxyytxxyy + txxytxyytxy + txxxyyytxy
# t is commuting with x and y
> commute(serie,{t});
          2          3          4            3          2
    t xy + t  xyxy + t  xyxyxy + t  xyxyxyxy + t  xyxyxxyy + t  xyxxyy
```

$$+ t^3 xyxxyxyy + t^2 xyxxxyyy + t^3 xyxxyyxy + t xxyy + t^2 xxyxyy$$

$$+ t^3 xxyxyxyy + t^2 xxyxxyyy + t xxxyyy + t^2 xxxyxyyy + t xxxxyyyy$$

$$+ t^2 xxxyyxyy + t^2 xxyyxy + t^3 xxyyxyxy + t^2 xxyyxxyy + t^3 xxyxyyxy$$

$$+ t^2 xxxyyyxy$$

```
# all the letters are commuting
> commute(serie);
      2 2 2   3 3 3   4 4 4    4 3 4     3 2 3    4 2 4
  x t y + x  t  y + x  t  y + x  t  y + 6 x  t  y + 3 x  t  y + 6 x  t  y

      2  2    3  3    4  4
    + x  t y + x  t y + x  t y
# definition of the q-grammar
> qsyst:=calcule_q_equation(G,[q],[q,0],[epsilon,lg_to(C,t)],
>                    [epsilon,lg_to(C,t),0]);
 qsyst :=

    table([
       q_axiome = G[axiome](t, y, x)
       q_eq = table([
               C(t, y, x) = qxty + qxty.(C(t, y, x)) + .x.(C(qt, y, x)).y

                    + ..x.(C(qt, y, x)).y.(C(t, y, x))
           ])
       ens_qvar = {C(t, y, x)}
    ])
# defining a new weight
> qpoids:=proc(mot)
> local i,poids;
> poids:=0;
> for i from 1 to nops(mot) do
>        if type(op(i,mot),`function`)
>        then poids:=poids+1
>        fi
> od;
> poids
> end:
# computing the first terms of the q-serie
> q_itere(qsyst,[qpoids,`+`,3]);
bytes used=5001860, alloc=1179432, time=22.13
bytes used=6002784, alloc=1244956, time=25.60
```

qxty + qxtyqxty + qxtyqxtyqxty + qxtyqxtyqxtyqxty + qxtyqxtyxqxqtyy

  + qxtyxqxqtyy + qxtyxqxqtyqxqtyy + qxtyxxqxqqtyyy + qxtyxqxqtyyqxty

  + xqxqtyy + xqxqtyqxqtyy + xqxqtyqxqtyqxqtyy + xqxqtyxqxqqtyyy

  + xxqxqqtyyy + xxqxqqtyqxqqtyyy + xxxqxqqqtyyyy + xxqxqqtyyqxqtyy

  + xqxqtyyqxty + xqxqtyyqxtyqxty + xqxqtyyxqxqtyy + xqxqtyqxqtyyqxty

  + xxqxqqtyyyqxty

References

1. G.E. ANDREWS, q-series : their development and applications in analysis, number theory, combinatorics, physics and computer algebra, AMS library of congress, Cataloging in publication data (1986).
2. F. BERGERON, G. CARTIER, DARWIN : Computer Algebra and enumerative combinatorics, Proc. STACS 88, Eds. R. Cori et M. Wirsing, Springer Lectures Notes in Computer Science, **294** (1988), 393-394.
3. M. BOUSQUET-MELOU, q-énumération de polyominos convexes, Thèse de l'Université de Bordeaux 1, (1991).
4. M. DELEST, J.M. FEDOU, Attribute grammars are useful for combinatorics, Theor. Comp. Sci. **98**, (1992) 65-76.
5. M. DELEST, J.M. FEDOU, Enumeration of skew Ferrers diagrams, Discrete Maths (to appear).
6. J.P. DUBERNARD, q-grammaires et polyominos parrallélogrammes, Thèse Université Bordeaux I, 1993.
7. F. ENGELFRIED, G. FILE, Formal power of attribute grammars, Acta Informatica **16** (1981) 275-302.
8. K.O. GEDDES, G.H. GONNET, B.W. CHAR, Maple, User's Manual, Research report CS-83-41, University of Waterloo, 1983.
9. D. PERRIN, Words of partially commutative alphabet, Eds. A. Apostolico, Z. Galil, Combinatorial algorithm on words, NATO ASI-series, **F12** (1985), 329-340.
10. M.P. SCHUTZENBERGER, Certain elementary families of automata, in Proc. Symp. on Mathematical Theory of Automata, Polytechnic Institute of Brooklyn, 1962, 139-153.
11. SYMBOLICS INC., Macsyma reference manual, version 10, 3rd edition, 1984.
12. X. VIENNOT, A survey of polyominoes enumeration, Proceedings of FPSAC'92, Montréal, Eds. P. Leroux, C. Reutenauer (1992), 399-420.

A topology for complete semirings

Georg Karner

Alcatel Austria Forschungszentrum, Ruthnergasse 1–7, A-1210 Wien, Austria
email: `G.Karner@aaf.alcatel.at`

Abstract. It is shown that every (algebraically) complete semiring has a "natural" topology associated with it. We discuss the relation between algebraic properties of the summation and separation axioms for the topology. This leads to a topological characterization of finitary semirings. The relation with the well-known Scott topology for complete partial orders (CPOs) is also discussed.

Introduction

The theory of formal power series in non-commuting variables (with coefficients in a semiring) was developed as a generalization of formal language theory. Considering non-negative integers or reals as coefficients allows one to deal with multiplicities and probabilities (weighted grammars), respectively, in the same notational framework (see e.g. [10]). When transferring the notion of a rational transduction to formal power series, difficulties arise from the fact that infinite sums of coefficients occur (corresponding to forming infinite unions of languages). For similar reasons, the behaviour of a finite automaton (i.e. the power series it defines) is not well-defined, in general. This led (among other approaches) to introducing complete semirings [1, 2]. Here arbitrary infinite sums of elements are defined.

Later authors considered additional axioms for complete semirings (an overview is given in [6]). In particular, Krob [7, 8] studied the relation of the purely algebraic definition of summability with a topological one (called t-complete semirings). Whereas topological sums always obey the algebraic laws, the reverse implication remained an open problem. (Krob solved a very special case, cf. Sect. 3). Our approach can be sketched as follows. We first weaken Krob's definition, leading to st-complete semirings which are still complete in the algebraic sense. Next we construct a topology in an arbitrary complete semiring. This topology has some very nice properties: addition and multiplication are argumentwise continuous. Moreover, some algebraic properties of the summation correspond to separation axioms for the topology. This leads then to our main result. An important class of complete semirings (the finitary ones, cf. Sect. 2) can be characterized topologically. Krob's result mentioned above turns out to be a special case of our construction.

By choosing appropriate categories, some of our results can be restated as properties of certain functors. In particular, adjoining "our" topology to a complete semiring may be seen as the left adjoint to a suitable forgetful functor.

The topology we define formally resembles the well-known Scott topology for complete partial orders (CPOs). We also make this correspondence more explicit. A "natural" sub-class of the above mentioned finitary semirings are also CPOs, and in this case our topology is strictly finer than the Scott topology.

The paper is organized as follows. After giving the preliminaries, we introduce *st*-complete semirings in Sect. 2. The subsequent sections then introduce our topology. This leads to the main result in Sect. 4. Then we deal with "categorical" aspects of our construction. We finally discuss the relation with CPOs and the Scott topology.

1   Some basic facts about complete semirings

The reader is assumed to be familiar with the basics of complete semirings (cf. e.g. [2, 6]) and of point set topology. We only write A for a semiring $(A, +, .)$ since the semiring operations are always clear from the context. We need the following notions. A semiring A is called *partially ordered (p.o.)* by $\leq$ if $\leq$ is a partial order on A with least element 0 and $a \leq b$ implies $a + c \leq b + c$, $ca \leq cb$, and $ac \leq bc$. Open or half-open intervals defined by the order will be denoted as $(a, b)_\leq$ or $(a, b]_\leq$, respectively. The subscript $\leq$ may be omitted if it is clear from the context. A is called *naturally ordered (n.o.)* if the relation $\sqsubseteq$ defined by $a \sqsubseteq b$ iff $a + c = b$ for some $c \in A$ is a partial order on A. $(A, \sqsubseteq)$ is then a p.o. semiring. In an *idempotent* semiring (i.e. $a + a = a$ for all $a \in A$) there is exactly one partial order defined by $a \leq b$ iff $a + b = b$. In a complete semiring $(A, \sum)$, we will find it very convenient to reserve the letters E and F (possibly provided with indices) to denote *finite* index sets. A p.o. complete semiring $(A, \sum, \leq)$ is called *finitary (w.r.t. $\leq$)* if

$$\sum_{i \in I} a_i = \sup_{F \subseteq I} \sum_{i \in F} a_i \tag{1}$$

for all families $(a_i, i \in I)$ in A. The term "finitary w.r.t the natural order" is often abbreviated as "continuous". We will not use the latter term to avoid confusion with topological notions.

Proposition 1. *The following conditions are equivalent for a complete semiring A and families $(a_i, i \in I)$ in A.*

(i) If, for all $i \in I$, $a + x_i = a$ then $a + \sum_{i \in I} x_i = a$.
(ii) If, for some fixed F_0 and $F_0 \subseteq E \subseteq I$, $\sum_{i \in E} a_i = a$ then $\sum_{i \in I} a_i = a$.
(iii) If for some fixed $a \in A$ and for all $F \subseteq I$ there is a finite $E(F)$ with $F \subseteq E(F) \subseteq I$ and $\sum_{i \in E(F)} a_i = a$ then $\sum_{i \in I} a_i = a$.

Proof. We first consider the implication (i) $\Rightarrow$ (iii). Every semiring satisfying (i) is n.o. by [6, Props. 3.1 and 3.2]. Consider now a family $(a_i, i \in I)$ satisfying the preconditions of (iii). We set $F = E(\emptyset)$ and $a = \sum_{i \in F} a_i$. Then we obtain, for $j \in I \setminus F$, $a \leq a + a_j = \sum_{i \in F \cup \{j\}} \leq \sum_{i \in E(F \cup \{j\})} = a$ and thus $a + a_j = a$. Hence $\sum_{i \in I} a_i = a + \sum_{i \in I \setminus F} = a$ by (i). The implication (iii) $\Rightarrow$ (ii) is trivial, and (ii) $\Rightarrow$ (i) follows as in the proof of [6, Prop. 3.2]. $\square$

Since condition (ii) deals with nets that converge w.r.t. the discrete topology, we call a semiring satisfying any of (i)–(iii) $\bar{d}$-*complete*. As was already used in the proof, this generalizes the notion "d-complete" introduced in [3].

2 Semitopological complete semirings

A concept of topological summability for semirings can be defined as follows (cf. [7]). For any family $(a_i, i \in I)$ of elements of A, the net

$$\left(\sum_{i \in F} a_i \mid F \subseteq I, F \text{ finite} \right) \tag{2}$$

is defined by addition. (Here the family $(F, F \subseteq I)$ is directed by set inclusion. The frequent use of such nets is the reason for our convention that E and F always denote finite index sets.) If there is a T_2 topology on A such that every net of the form (2) converges, we may set

$$\sum_{i \in I} a_i = \lim_{F \subseteq I} \sum_{i \in F} a_i . \tag{3}$$

(The T_2 axiom implies that the limit is unique.) Thus for every neighbourhood V of $\sum_{i \in I} a_i$ there is a finite $F_0 \subseteq I$ such that

$$\sum_{i \in F} a_i \in V \qquad \text{for } F \supseteq F_0 . \tag{4}$$

In general, this does not yield a complete semiring in the sense of Sect. 1. An *st-complete (semitopological complete)* semiring is a pair (A, τ) where A is a semiring and τ is a T_2 topology on A such that every net (2) converges and addition and multiplication are argumentwise continuous, i.e. for fixed $a \in A$, the mappings from A into itself where $x \mapsto x + a$, $x \mapsto ax$, and $x \mapsto xa$ are continuous. We will denote them by t_a, l_a, and r_a, respectively. This generalizes the t-complete semirings introduced in [7], where the semiring operations are jointly continuous. Prop. 3 justifies our more general definition. We need an auxiliary result.

Lemma 2. *If A is st-complete, $(a_i, i \in I)$ a family in A, and $I = \bigcup_{j \in J} I_j$ is a partition with J finite then $\sum_{i \in I} a_i = \sum_{j \in J} \left(\sum_{i \in I_j} a_i \right)$.*

Proof. Assume first that $J = \{1, 2\}$. We set $s = \sum_{i \in I} a_i$, $a = \sum_{i \in I_1} a_i$, $b = \sum_{i \in I_2} a_i$. If $s \neq a + b$, then there are disjoint neighbourhoods V of s and W of $a + b$ with V closed. Since t_b is continuous, $U = t_b^{-1}(W)$ is a neighbourhood of a. Thus by [7, Lemme II.4] there are $F_0 \subseteq I$ and $F_1 \subseteq I_1$ with $\sum_{i \in I'} a_i \in V$ for $F_0 \subseteq I' \subseteq I$ and $\sum_{i \in F} a_i \in U$ for $F_1 \subseteq F \subseteq I_1$. If now I_2 is finite, we obtain $\sum_{i \in F_0 \cup F_1 \cup I_2} a_i = b + \sum_{i \in (F_0 \setminus I_2) \cup F_1} \in V \cap t_b(U) \subseteq V \cap W$ (*) which contradicts our assumption. If I_2 is infinite, observe that the equality in (*) now holds by the very special case of Lemma 2 just established. So the argument from above can literally be used to prove the case with I_2 infinite. Finally, the statement for arbitrary finite J follows by induction on the cardinality of J. $\qquad\square$

Proposition 3. *Every st-complete semiring* (A, τ) *is also a complete semiring* $(A, \sum)$ *if* $\sum$ *is defined by (3).*

Proof. Similar to that of [7, Prop. III.4], using Lemma 2. □

The next example shows that an st-complete semiring is not t-complete, in general.

Example 1. Consider $\mathbf{Q}_+^\infty$, the non-negative rational numbers together with an element ∞ satisfying $a + \infty = \infty + a = \infty$ for all $a \in \mathbf{Q}_+^\infty$, $0.\infty = \infty.0 = 0$, and $a.\infty = \infty.a = \infty$ for $a \neq 0$. A subbase for the topology τ is given by $\{\{a\} | a \in \mathbf{Q}_+\} \cup \{\mathbf{Q}_+^\infty \setminus \{a\} | a \in \mathbf{Q}_+\}$. Thus every point in $\mathbf{Q}_+$ is isolated, and the neighbourhoods of ∞ are the co-finite sets. It is straightforward to verify that this defines an st-complete semiring, where

$$\sum_{i \in I} a_i = \begin{cases} \sum_{a_i \neq 0} a_i & \text{if } \{i | a_i \neq 0\} \text{ is finite,} \\ \infty & \text{otherwise.} \end{cases} \qquad (5)$$

It has been shown in [6, Example 5.3] that $(\mathbf{Q}_+^\infty, \sum)$ cannot be made a t-complete semiring. One can also show that there is no other summation $\sum'$ such that $(\mathbf{Q}_+^\infty, \sum')$ is a complete semiring. (We give the proof in the Appendix.) Thus $(\mathbf{Q}_+^\infty, \tau)$ is an st-complete semiring that is not t-complete. □

Proposition 4. *Assume that* (A, τ_A) *and* (B, τ_B) *are st-complete semirings. Then every continuous semiring morphism* $h : A \to B$ *is complete.*

Proof. Assume on the contrary that there is a family $(a_i, i \in I)$ with $\sum_{i \in I} h(a_i) = b \neq h(\sum_{i \in I} a_i)$. Then there are disjoint neighbourhoods V of b and W of $h(\sum_{i \in I} a_i)$. By (4) and the continuity of h, $h(\sum_{i \in F} a_i) = \sum_{i \in F} h(a_i)$ is finally in $V \cap W$, which is a contradiction. □

Remark. The T_2 axiom was necessary only for B. Moreover, we only needed that h is additive, i.e. h commutes with the addition. Similar generalizations will also be possible for some subsequent results. We will not mention them for the sake of conciseness and readability.

The following result generalizes [8, Prop. III.5 ii] and uses exactly the same proof.

Proposition 5. *Assume that* $(A, \leq, \tau)$ *is a p.o. st-complete semiring. If all intervals* $[0, a]_\leq$, $a \in A$, *are closed (w.r.t. τ), then* $(A, \leq)$ *is finitary.*

3 The summation topology

In the previous section, we used a topology to define infinite summation. Now we deal with the converse. To this end, we consider a fixed complete semiring $(A, \sum)$. We consider the collection τ_Σ of *all* sets V satisfying (4). It is straightforward to verify that this indeed defines a topology. As is also indicated by the title of this section, we call τ_Σ the *summation topology (on A)*. Examples of open sets are $\{0\}$ and, more generally, for every $a \in A$ the set $\{b \in A | \exists c \in A \text{ with } b + c = a\}$. Similarly, if A is p.o., then all intervals $[0, a]_{\leq}$ are open.

Example 2. The summation topology on $\mathbf{Q}_+^\infty$ is given as follows. All $a \in \mathbf{Q}^+$ are isolated, and a set X with $\infty \in X \subseteq \mathbf{Q}_+^\infty$ is open iff $\mathbf{Q}_+^\infty \setminus X$ is well-ordered by $\geq$ (the reverse of the usual order $\leq$). We leave the proof to the reader. $\square$

Example 3. The summation topology on $\mathbf{R}_+^\infty$ is given by the base $\mathcal{B} = \{\{0\}\} \cup \{(\alpha, \beta] | \alpha, \beta \in \mathbf{R}_+^\infty\}$. It is clear that the base sets are actually open. We have to show that for $x \in X \in \tau_\Sigma$ there is $a < x$ with $(a, x] \subseteq X$. Assume on the contrary that for all $a < x$ there is $b(a)$ with $a < b(a) < x$ and $b(a) \notin X$. Choose a strictly monotonic sequence c_n, $n \in \mathbf{N}$, with $\sup_{n \in \mathbf{N}} c_n = a$. Then define $a_0 = b_0 = c_0$, $b_{n+1} = b(\max(b_n, c_n)) > b_n$, $a_{n+1} = b_{n+1} - b_n$. Then $\sum_{i \in \mathbf{N}} a_i = a$, but $\sum_{0 \leq i \leq n} a_i = b(\max(b_n, c_n)) \notin X$ for $n \geq 1$. This contradicts (4). $\square$

The summation topology has a lot of nice properties which we will discuss in the sequel. From now on, we will always consider complete semirings with their summation topology, unless stated otherwise. Note that by definition τ_Σ is the *finest* topology such that (4) holds. Now we present a converse to Prop. 4.

Lemma 6. *Let* (A, Σ_1) *and* (B, Σ_2) *be two complete semirings and* $f : A \to B$ *a mapping satisfying* $f(\sum_{i \in I} a_i) = \sum_{i \in I} f(a_i)$ *for all non-empty families* $(a_i, i \in I)$ *in* A. *Then* $f : (A, \tau_{\Sigma_1}) \to (B, \tau_{\Sigma_2})$ *is continuous. Moreover, the operations* t_a, l_a, *and* $r_a : A \to A$ *are continuous.*

Proof. We only consider t_a since the other statements are handled similarly. Consider a fixed $Y \in \tau_{\Sigma_2}$ and $X := t_a^{-1}(Y)$. Assume that $x = \sum_{i \in I} x_i \in X$. Define the family $(y_i, i \in I \cup \{j_0\})$ with $j_0 \notin I$, $y_{j_0} = a$, and $y_i = x_i$ for $i \in I$. Then for $j_0 \in F$, $\sum_{i \in F} y_i = t_a\left(\sum_{i \in F \setminus \{j_0\}} x_i\right)$. The statement now follows directly from the definition of τ_{Σ_1}. $\square$

If necessary, τ_{Σ_2} can be replaced by any weaker topology. This is not true for τ_{Σ_1}. Both observations are used in Sect. 5. The above result is very important since it solves all problems concerning continuity. Note that usually an order relation is required to prove similar properties.

Corollary 7. *Every complete isomorphism between complete semirings is also a homeomorphism.*

Such isomorphisms, like e.g. $(A \ll M \gg)^{I \times I} \simeq A^{I \times I} \ll M \gg$ or $(A^{I \times I})^{J \times J} \simeq A^{(I \times I) \times (J \times J)}$, are widely used in an axiomatic approach to automata theory. See [10] for more information.

The remainder of this section deals with direct products, subsemirings and homomorphic images.

Let $(A_i, i \in I)$ be a family of complete semirings. The product topology τ_π is the weakest topology on $A = \prod_{i \in I} A_i$ such that the projections are continuous. Since the projections are continuous w.r.t. the summation topologies on A and A_i by Lemma 6, we have $\tau_\pi \subseteq \tau_\Sigma$. The summation topology is strictly finer, in general. Consider $A' = \mathbf{Q}_+^\infty \times \mathbf{Q}_+^\infty$ and $+ : A' \to \mathbf{Q}_+^\infty$. Then $+$ is continuous w.r.t. τ_Σ on A' by Lemma 6, but $+$ is not continuous w.r.t. τ_π by the proof of [6, Ex. 5.1].

Next we deal with (complete) subsemirings. The summation topology is finer than the subspace topology, the argument being similar to that for products of semirings above. Again, we do not have equality of the topologies, in general. Consider $A = \{0\} \cup [1, \infty] \subseteq \mathbf{R}_+^\infty$. Then all points in $A \setminus \{0, 1, \infty\}$ are isolated in the summation topology, but not in the subspace topology.

We finally consider homomorphic images.

Proposition 8. *Assume that $h : A \to A'$ is a surjective complete morphism. Then the summation topology τ_Σ' on A' coincides with the final topology τ_h generated by h.*

Proof. By definition, τ_h is the finest topology on A' such that h is continuous. Since h is continuous w.r.t. τ_Σ' by Lemma 6, we have $\tau_\Sigma' \subseteq \tau_h$. The reverse inclusion follows straightforwardly from the definition of τ_Σ'. $\qquad\square$

4 Separation axioms

Recall that our final goal is to show that certain semirings are st-complete. Thus τ_Σ should ideally satisfy T_2. In this section we discuss the relations between the algebraic notions from Sect. 1 and the axioms T_i, $i = 0, 1, 2$. This also leads to our main result: a topological characterization of finitary semirings.

We conjecture that in general τ_Σ does not even satisfy T_0, though we have not found an explicit example. A sufficient condition for T_0 is that A be p.o. If $a, b \in A$ with $a \neq b$, say $a \not\leq b$, then $a \notin [0, b]_\leq \in \tau_\Sigma$.

The conditions T_1 and T_2 both admit a nice algebraic characterization.

Proposition 9. τ_Σ *satisfies T_2 (T_1) iff A is st-complete ($\bar{d}$-complete).*

Proof. Recall that the summation topology τ_Σ is always the finest topology on A such that (4) holds. So if (A, τ) is st-complete, τ satisfies T_2 and the same holds for the finer topology τ_Σ. On the other hand, if τ_Σ satisfies T_2, then (A, τ_Σ) is an st-complete semiring by Prop. 6. T_1 is equivalent to the fact that, for all $a \in A$, $\{a\}$ is closed, i.e. $X_a := A \setminus \{a\}$ is open. The result now follows straightforwardly from the definition of τ_Σ and Prop. 1. $\qquad\square$

Thus the question of the existence of a topology that makes a complete semiring A st-complete can be answered by just looking at the summation topology on A. The distinguished role of τ_Σ will further be highlighted by categorical considerations in Sect. 5.

As a corollary, we note that whenever τ_Σ satisfies T_1, A must be naturally ordered. In particular, this holds for every st-complete semiring.

Recall that in a finitary semiring the summation is determined by addition and partial order. Thus we will use the short phrase "$(A, \leq)$ is finitary" to mean that all the sups required by (1) exist and that $(A, \sum)$ thus defined is a complete semiring.

Theorem 10. *Let $(A, \leq)$ be a p.o. semiring. Then the following statements are equivalent.*

(i) $(A, \leq)$ is finitary.
(ii) A is also a complete semiring $(A, \sum)$, and all intervals $[0, a]_\leq$, $a \in A$, are closed in τ_Σ.
(iii) A is also st-complete with all intervals $[0, a]_\leq$, $a \in A$, closed.

Proof. $(i) \Rightarrow (ii)$. We have to show that $V_a := A \setminus [0, a]_\leq$ is open. Assume that $\sum_{i \in I} a_i = b \in V_a$. If we had $\sum_{i \in F} a_i \leq a$ for all $F \subseteq I$, then also $b \leq a$, since A is finitary. So there must be F_0 with $\sum_{i \in F_0} a_i \in V_a$. Since, for $F \supseteq F_0$, $\sum_{i \in F} a_i \geq \sum_{i \in F_0} a_i$, the former sum must also be in V_a.

$(ii) \Rightarrow (iii)$. We consider the summation topology. Recall that all intervals $U_a = [0, a]_\leq$ are open. $V_a = A \setminus U_a$ is open by (ii). If now $a \neq b$, say $a \nleq b$, then $a \in V_b$, $b \in U_b$. This shows that T_2 is satisfied. The rest follows by Lemma 6.

$(iii) \Rightarrow (i)$. This is Prop. 5. $\qquad\qquad\qquad\qquad\qquad\qquad\qquad\qquad\qquad$ $\square$

The equivalence of (i) and (iii) is our main result. The more technical condition (ii) will be needed in the next section.

The following diagram relates properties of a complete semiring and of its summation topology. All implications are strict (see the examples in [6]).

$$
\begin{array}{cccc}
\text{finitary} & \Rightarrow st\text{-complete} \Rightarrow \bar{d}\text{-complete} \Rightarrow & \text{p.o.} \\
\Updownarrow & \Updownarrow \qquad\qquad \Updownarrow & \Downarrow \\
T_2 \text{ and} & T_2 \qquad\qquad T_1 & T_0 \\
[0, a]_\leq \text{ closed} & &
\end{array}
$$

Fig. 1. Properties of a complete semiring and its summation topology

5 Applications and "categorical" remarks

We now consider the relationship with Krob's work. We can show that the two constructions yield the same topology.

Proposition 11 (Krob, [8, Cor. III.4]). *If A is finitary w.r.t. the natural order $\sqsubseteq$ and also totally ordered by $\sqsubseteq$, then (A, τ) is t-complete, where a base for τ is given by $\{\{0\}\} \cup \{(\alpha, \beta]_\sqsubseteq | \alpha, \beta \in A\}$.*

Proposition 12. *Under the assumptions of Prop. 11, τ coincides with τ_Σ.*

Proof. Since (A, τ) is t-complete, it is also st-complete. As τ_Σ is the finest topology with this property, we have $\tau \subseteq \tau_\Sigma$. To establish the reverse inclusion, we need some results from [8]. (Only throughout the following proof, the notions "morphism" and "congruence" will refer to addition and summation only, but not to multiplication.) $A \setminus \{0\}$ can be partitioned as $\bigcup_{i \in I} S_i$ where I is a totally ordered index set and all $S_i \cup \{0\}$ are complete subsemigroups of $(A, +)$, each of which is (completely) isomorphic to one of the following: $\mathbf{N}^\infty$, $\mathbf{N}^\infty / \equiv_j$, $j \in \mathbf{N}$, $\mathbf{R}_+^\infty$, $\mathbf{R}_+^\infty / \equiv_1$, $\mathbf{R}_+^\infty / \equiv_1'$. Here $\equiv_j$ and $\equiv_j'$ are the congruences identifying all elements $\geq j$ or $> j$, respectively. Since all S_i are naturally ordered, the isomorphisms also respect the order. Moreover, if $x \in S_i$, $y \in S_j$ with $i < j$ then $x + y = y$ (∗). Note that each S_i has a maximal element (w.r.t. the natural order). Assume now that $x \in X \in \tau_\Sigma$. We then have to find $\alpha \sqsubset x$ with $(\alpha, x] \subseteq X$. We have $x \in S_j$ for some j. If x has a predecessor x' in S_j then $(x', x] = \{x\} \subseteq X$. If x does not have a predecessor but x is not the least element of S_j, then α can be found as in the proof of Ex. 3. So we assume now that $x = \min S_j$ and consider $s = \sum_{y \sqsubset x} y$. Every such y is contained in some S_i with $i < j$, and so is every finite sum of such y's by (∗). Thus $s \sqsubseteq x$ since A is finitary. If $s \sqsubset x$ then $(s, x] = \{x\} \subseteq X$ and we are done. So we assume that $s = x$. Since $X \in \tau_\Sigma$, there is some finite F_0 with $\sum_{y \in F} y \in X$ for $F \supseteq F_0$. Let $\sum_{y \in F_0} y \in S_{i_0}$ (with $i_0 < j$) and set $\alpha = \max S_{i_0}$. Then for $z \in (\alpha, x)$, we have $z = z + \sum_{y \in F_0} y = \sum_{y \in F_0 \cup \{z\}} y \in X$ by (∗). Thus $(\alpha, x] \subseteq X$ as required. □

Proposition 13. *Every idempotent $\bar{d}$-complete semiring A is finitary w.r.t. the natural order. Every finite p.o. semiring $(A, \leq)$ is finitary.*

Proof. Recall that the only order on an idempotent semiring is given by $a \leq b$ iff $a + b = b$. Consider now τ_Σ and $c \in A$. By Prop. 9, $\{c\}$ is closed. Thus $[0, c]_\leq = t_c^{-1}(\{c\})$ is closed as well. The result now follows by Th. 10. On a finite A, we consider the discrete topology τ_d. Clearly the semiring operations are continuous, T_2 is satisfied and all sets $[0, c]_\leq$ are closed. Since every finite directed set has a maximum, every net of the form (2) converges w.r.t. τ_d. The result again follows by Th. 10. □

As a corollary, we note that every idempotent st-complete semiring is finitary w.r.t. the natural order. This generalizes [6, Props. 7.1 and 7.3].

In the remainder of the section, we assume the reader to be familiar with the basics of category theory, cf. e.g. [11]. Some of our results can conveniently be restated using the following categories. (For foundational issues concerning classes of complete semirings see [3, 5].)

CSR... complete semirings with complete semiring morphisms

STSR... semitopological semirings with continuous semiring morphisms

STCSR... st-complete semirings with continuous complete semiring morphisms

(The term "semiring morphism" has no unique meaning. It may refer to addition and multiplication only, it may include 0, or it may include both 0 and 1. Our considerations hold for each of the three choices.)

By Prop. 4 the condition "complete" for morphisms in **STCSR** may be dropped. Thus **STCSR** is a full subcategory of **STSR**. Moreover, the embedding **STCSR** → **CSR** is a faithful functor U which is forgetful in the sense that the topology defining the summation is lost. We may restrict the "codomain" of U to the full subcategory **CSR**$_\tau$ of complete semirings whose summation topology satisfies T_2 (cf. Prop. 9). We denote this functor by U_τ.

On the other hand, assigning to every complete semiring its summation topology is a functor V from **CSR** to **STSR**. This functor is both full and faithful. If we restrict the "domain" of V to **CSR**$_\tau$, we obtain a functor V_τ from **CSR**$_\tau$ to **STCSR** which is a left adjoint for the (forgetful) functor U_τ.

Finally, we introduce the category **STCSR**$_{\tau_\Sigma}$ of complete semirings with their summation topology. This category has products by Lemma 6. (The same holds directly for **CSR** and **STCSR**.) Moreover, **STCSR**$_{\tau_\Sigma}$ is a coreflective subcategory of **STCSR**.

6 Relationship with the Scott topology

We refer to [4] for all unexplained notions. The definition of the summation topology on a complete semiring formally resembles the definition of the Scott topology for complete partial orders. The latter topology can be described as follows. Let $(V, \leq)$ be a CPO. An *upper set* U is a subset of V such that $y \geq x$ and $x \in U$ implies $y \in U$. A directed set can be viewed as a net indexed by itself. The Scott topology on V is then the finest topology such that (i) every directed set converges to its sup, and (ii) only upper sets are open.

Theorem 14. *Assume that A is finitary w.r.t. the natural order $\leq$. Then $(A, \leq)$ is also a CPO.*

Proof. By a result of Markovsky [12], it suffices to show that every chain X in A has a sup. Using transfinite induction, we construct a family whose sum is the desired sup. Since every chain has a well-ordered confinal subset, we may assume w.l.o.g. that X itself is well-ordered by $\leq$. We define a family $(a_x, x \in X)$ satisfying the condition $\sum_{y \leq x} a_y = x$ (*). For our induction we assume that $a_{x'}$ is already defined for $x' \leq x$ and that (*) holds for these x'. We first consider $Y = \{y | y < x\}$ and $s = \sum_{y \in Y} a_y$ and claim that $s = \sup Y$. Indeed, we have $y = \sum_{y' \leq y} a_{y'} \leq s$ for $y \in Y$. Moreover, if t is an upper bound of Y and $F \subseteq Y$ then $\sum_{y \in F} a_y \leq \sum_{y \leq \max F} = \max F \leq t$ and so $s \leq t$ since A is finitary. Thus also $s = \sup Y \leq x$, and there is z with $s + z = x_1$ since A is n.o. Then (*) holds with $a_{x_1} = z$. A similar argument shows that $\sum_{x \in X} a_x = \sup X$ as intended. $\square$

Remark. The theorem does not hold if the natural order is replaced by an arbitrary one. Consider the semiring $A_1 = \{0, \infty\} \cup ([1, \infty) \cap \mathbf{Q}) \subseteq \mathbf{Q}_+^\infty$. Since the finite partial sums of an infinite family (of non-zero elements) grow without bound, A_1 is finitary w.r.t. the usual order $\leq$. As this is a total order, every subset of A_1 is directed but there are clearly subsets without sup.

The theorem also cannot be strengthened in the other direction. More precisely, the CPO is neither algebraic nor an (upper or lower) semi-lattice, in general. In $\mathbf{R}_+^\infty$ the only compact element is 0. Thus $\mathbf{R}_+^\infty$ is not algebraic as a CPO. Consider now the monoid $M = \mathbf{N}^\infty / \equiv_2$ where $\equiv_2$ is defined in the proof of Prop. 12. From this we construct the monoid $M_1 = M \times M / \sim$ where $\sim$ is the congruence identifying $(0, 2)$ and $(2, 0)$. We consider the natural order $\sqsubseteq$. Then there is no l.u.b. for $(1, 0)$ and $(0, 1)$, and no g.l.b. for $(2, 0)$ and $(1, 1)$. To make M_1 a semiring A_1, we simply use the trivial multiplication, i.e. $ab = ba = 0$ for all $a, b \in A_1$. Since A_1 is finite, $(A_1, \sqsubseteq)$ is finitary by Prop. 13. Finally, we obtain a complete semiring which is neither algebraic nor a semilattice by simply considering the direct product $\mathbf{R}_+^\infty \times A_2$.

The characterization of the Scott topology given above immediately yields the next result.

Proposition 15. *If A is finitary w.r.t the natural order, the summation topology on A is finer than the Scott topology.*

In the rest of the section, we will only consider complete semirings that are finitary w.r.t. the natural order. There are further analogies with the Scott topology. One can show that if f is monotone and continuous, it has a least fix-point. Thus we have the following statements for semiring morphisms h: h is continuous iff it is complete (i.e. h respects the infinite summation); if h is continuous, it has a least fix-point. One can also show that polynomial functions $A^n \to A^n$ are indeed continuous (the proof is similar to that of Prop. 6). This provides an alternative proof of the existence of the "strong solution" of algebraic systems as they occur e.g. in formal language theory, cf. [10, 9].

The above considerations suggest to define a topology for arbitrary CPOs by using only clause (i) in the characterization of the Scott topology given above. This indeed defines a T_2 topology (the argument is similar to that for finitary semirings). Moreover, we have the following statements for *monotone* functions f: f is continuous iff it preserves sups; f has a least fix-point whenever it is continuous. (The proofs are completely similar to the standard ones using the Scott topology.) Unfortunately, all the fs that are thus shown to have a least fixpoint are also Scott-continuous, so this provides nothing essentially new. However, it does show (as one of the referees pointed out) that there is a useful topology on CPOs that is finer than the Scott topology.

An important application of CPOs is the construction of solutions to domain equations. Unfortunately, this cannot be carried over to complete semirings. The main reason for this is that the category **CSR** (and all its subcategories we have considered in this paper) are not Cartesian closed since the hom-sets do not posess the structure of a complete semiring.

Conclusions

For the sake of simplicity, we restricted our presentation to complete semirings. The concepts can easily be applied in a more general setting. In particular, the definition of the summation topology can be transferred to countably complete semirings (cf. e.g. [7]). The a-complete semirings of [13] can also be handled. (Here sums are defined only for families whose cardinality does not exceed the given infinite cardinal a.) Finally, the concepts also apply to complete monoids [7], as was already indicated in Sect. 2.

We have defined a topology for arbitrary complete semirings. This was done without reference to the structure of the semiring. The reader my compare this to the limit concepts defined to handle infinite sums in [10]. We discussed the connection between algebraic properties of the summation and separation axioms for the topology. This led to a topological characterization of finitary semirings. Thus we settled the main open problem of [8, 6]. We also showed that infinite summation can be put on a topological basis. This can be compared to the fact that morphims between CPOs can also be defined topologically. We also highlightened the distinguished role of the summation topology in a "categorical" context. We further elaborated on the connection with CPOs and discussed an alternative to the Scott topology. Future research may consider applying topological concepts to other parts of the theory of complete semirings. A minor open problem is also the following: find other sufficient conditions on the summation guaranteeing that τ_Σ satisfies T_2. Another interesting question is the existence of free objects in the categories considered in Sect. 5.

Acknowledgement. The author would like to thank the anonymous referees for their comments which significantly helped in improving the presentation of the paper.

A Appendix

Proposition 16. *The only summation on $A = \mathbf{Q}_+^\infty$ is given by (5).*

Proof. Assume that there is another summation on A. We denote it by $\sum^{\mathbf{Q}}$ to distinguish it from the usual summation on $B = (\mathbf{R}_+^\infty, \leq, \sum^{\mathbf{R}})$ defined according to (1). Note that $\sum^{\mathbf{R}}$ coincides with the usual sum of absolutely convergent series in the case of countable index sets. Without loss of generality we only consider families $(x_i, i \in I)$ in $\mathbf{Q}_+^\infty$ with $x_i \neq 0$ for all $i \in I$. We first establish two auxiliary claims.

$$\sum_{i \in I}^{\mathbf{R}} x_i \leq \sum_{i \in I}^{\mathbf{Q}} x_i \tag{6}$$

If I is uncountable then $$\sum_{i \in I}^{\mathbf{R}} x_i = \sum_{i \in I}^{\mathbf{Q}} x_i = \infty . \tag{7}$$

We have $\sum_{i \in F}^{\mathbf{R}} x_i = \sum_{i \in F}^{\mathbf{Q}} x_i \leq \sum_{i \in I}^{\mathbf{Q}} x_i$ for all $F \subseteq I$. Thus (6) holds since $\mathbf{R}_+^\infty$ is finitary. In (7) there must be an $a \in A$ with $I_1 = \{i \in I | x_i = a\}$ uncountable since I is uncountable. Recall that $a \neq 0$ by our initial assumption. Then $\sum_{i \in I}^{\mathbf{Q}} x_i \geq \sum_{i \in I}^{\mathbf{R}} x_i \geq \sum_{i \in I_1}^{\mathbf{R}} x_i = \sup_{n \in \mathbf{N}} n.a = \infty$ by (6).

Now we continue the proof of Prop. 16. Since we assume that $\sum^{\mathbf{Q}}$ is different from $\sum$, there must be an infinite family $(a_i, i \in I)$ with $\sum_{i \in I}^{\mathbf{Q}} a_i < \infty$. By (7) we assume $I = \mathbf{N}$. We construct a "quickly decreasing" family $(b_j, j \in \mathbf{N})$. We set $n_0 = 0$. For any $j \geq 1$ there is $n_j > n_{j-1}$ with $\sum_{i \geq n_j}^{\mathbf{R}} a_i \leq b_{j-1}/2$. This holds since $\lim_{n \to \infty} \sum_{i \geq n}^{\mathbf{R}} a_i = 0$ by (6). Then we set $b_j = a_{n_j}$. Observe that by construction $b_j \geq 2 \sum_{i \geq n_j}^{\mathbf{R}} a_i \geq 2 \sum_{k \geq j+1}^{\mathbf{R}} b_k \geq 2b_{j+1}$ $(*)$. Next we consider the sums $c_K = \sum_{j \in K}^{\mathbf{R}} b_j$ and $d_K = \sum_{j \in K}^{\mathbf{Q}} b_j$ for all subsets $K \subseteq \mathbf{N}$. A standard argument using $(*)$ shows that $c_K \neq c_{K'}$ whenever $K \neq K'$. Since there are uncountably many K's we may choose a K_0 with c_{K_0} irrational. Thus we have $c_{K_0} < d_{K_0}$ by (6). This implies that $\alpha = d_{\mathbf{N}} - c_{\mathbf{N}} > 0$. So we have, for all $n \in \mathbf{N}$, $\sum_{j \geq n}^{\mathbf{Q}} b_j = d_{\mathbf{N}} - \sum_{j < n}^{\mathbf{Q}} b_j = d_{\mathbf{N}} - \sum_{j < n}^{\mathbf{R}} b_j \geq \alpha$. From $(*)$ we have $b_j \geq 2^k b_{j+k}$ for all $j, k \in \mathbf{N}$. So $d_{\mathbf{N}} = \sum_{j \geq 0}^{\mathbf{Q}} b_j \geq 2^k \sum_{j \geq 0}^{\mathbf{Q}} b_{j+k} \geq 2^k \alpha$ for all k which implies $d_{\mathbf{N}} = \infty$. Note that the second inequality holds since $\mathbf{Q}_+^\infty$ is *naturally* ordered. Finally, we obtain $\sum_{i \in I}^{\mathbf{Q}} a_i \geq \sum_{j \geq 0}^{\mathbf{Q}} a_{n_j} = \infty$ which contradicts our initial assumption about the family $(a_i, i \in I)$. $\qquad \square$

References

1. J. H. Conway. *Regular Algebra and Finite Machines*. Chapman and Hall, 1971.
2. S. Eilenberg. *Automata, Languages, and Machines*, Vol. A. Academic Press, 1974.
3. M. Goldstern. Vervollständigung von Halbringen. Master's thesis, Technische Universität Wien, 1986.
4. C. A. Gunter and D. S. Scott. Semantic domains. In J. van Leeuwen, editor, *Handbook of Theoretical Computer Science*, Vol. B, Ch. 12, pp. 635–674. North-Holland, 1990.
5. U. Hebisch. Zur algebraischen Theorie unendlicher Summen in Halbgruppen und Halbringen. Habilitationsschrift, Technische Universität Clausthal-Zellerfeld, 1990.
6. G. Karner. On limits in complete semirings. *Semigroup Forum*, 45:148–165, 1992.
7. D. Krob. Monoides et semi-anneaux complets. *Semigroup Forum*, 36:323–339, 1987.
8. D. Krob. Monoides et semi-anneaux continus. *Semigroup Forum*, 37:59–78, 1987.
9. W. Kuich. Automata and languages generalized to ω-continuous semirings. *Theoretical Comput. Sci.*, 79:137–150, 1991.
10. W. Kuich and A. Salomaa. *Semirings, Automata, Languages*. Springer, 1986.
11. S. MacLane. *Categories for the Working Mathematician*. Springer, 1988.
12. G. Markovsky. Chain-complete posets and directed sets with applications. *Algebra Universalis*, 6:53–68, 1976.
13. H. J. Weinert. Generalized semialgebras over semirings. *Lecture Notes in Mathematics*, 1320:380–416, 1988.

Structural Complexity
and Recursivity

The Global Power of Additional Queries to Random Oracles

Ronald V. Book*
Department of Mathematics
University of California
Santa Barbara, CA   93106
U.S.A.

Jack H. Lutz†
Department of Computer Science
Iowa State University
Ames, IA   50011
U.S.A.

David M. Martin Jr.†‡
Department of Computer Science
Boston University
Boston, MA   02215
U.S.A.

Abstract. It is shown that, for every $k \geq 0$ and every fixed algorithmically random language B, there is a language that is polynomial-time, truth-table reducible in $k + 1$ queries to B but not truth-table reducible in k queries in *any* amount of time to *any* algorithmically random language C. In particular, this yields the separation $P_{k-tt}(\text{RAND}) \subsetneq P_{(k+1)-tt}(\text{RAND})$, where RAND is the set of all algorithmically random languages.

1   Introduction

Will an algorithm have increased computational power when it is modified to be able to ask additional questions? One way of making this question precise is to consider it in the context of reducibilities computed by algorithms with bounds on their computational resources. In this paper, we investigate the phenomenon of increased access to oracle sets lending increased computational power for bounded truth-table reducibilities computed in polynomial time. We show that, in a strong global sense, if just one more question can be asked of sets with "maximum information content," then the class of problems that can be solved will indeed grow.

For each $k \geq 0$ and each language A, let $P_{k-tt}(A)$ denote the class of languages that are polynomial time truth-table reducible in k queries to A. It is well-known that there are languages A such that for every $k \geq 0$, $P_{k-tt}(A)$ is properly included in $P_{(k+1)-tt}(A)$. If the language A is restricted to the class of those having very low information content, say tally languages (languages over

---

*This research was supported in part by National Science Foundation Grant CCR-8913584.

†This research was supported in part by National Science Foundation Grant CCR-9157382, with matching funds from Rockwell International and Microware Systems Corporation.

‡This research was carried out while the third author was at Iowa State University.

a one letter alphabet), or to the class of those having very high information content, say the "algorithmically random" languages (in the sense of Martin-Löf [13]), then this same phenomenon holds (see [19, 3]). (The definition and some basic properties of algorithmic randomness are given in Section 3.)

The property of gaining more computational power by making additional queries can be extended from a "local" property of individual languages to a "global" property of classes of languages. For each $k \geq 0$ and each class $\mathcal{C}$ of languages, let $P_{k-tt}(\mathcal{C})$ be the class of languages B such that for some $A \in \mathcal{C}$, B is polynomial-time truth-table reducible in k queries to A. In the case of languages with small information content, Book and Ko [2] showed that for every $k \geq 0$, $P_{k-tt}(\text{SPARSE})$ is properly included in $P_{(k+1)-tt}(\text{SPARSE})$, where SPARSE denotes the class of all languages with some polynomial bound on the number of strings of each length. In the case of languages with high information content, the main result of the present paper shows the parallel result for the case of RAND, the class of algorithmically random languages (the class of languages with essentially maximum information content): for every $k \geq 0$, $P_{k-tt}(\text{RAND})$ is properly included in $P_{(k+1)-tt}(\text{RAND})$. The proof of the main result establishes an even stronger property: for every $k \geq 0$ and every $A \in \text{RAND}$, there is a language B in $P_{(k+1)-tt}(A)$ with the property that B is *not* k-truth table reducible to any language in RAND in any amount of time, that is, $P_{(k+1)-tt}(A) \not\subseteq \text{REC}_{k-tt}(\text{RAND})$.

A note of caution is in order. Languages in the class SPARSE and also languages in the class RAND have the *local* property that increasing the number of queries to an individual language A in the class allows more computational power (i.e., $P_{k-tt}(A) \subsetneq P_{(k+1)-tt}(A)$). In addition, the classes themselves have this property as a *global* property. This might suggest that for any class $\mathcal{C}$ of languages, if $\mathcal{C}$ has the local property, then $\mathcal{C}$ also has the corresponding global property. But this is known to be false. As noted above, the class of all tally languages, denoted TALLY, has the local property, but it is known (see [2, 1]) that TALLY does not have the global property: for every $k \geq 1$, $P_m(\text{TALLY}) = P_{k-tt}(\text{TALLY}) = P_{btt}(\text{TALLY})$.

It is important to note that while for each $k \geq 1$, there is a recursive witness to the separation of $P_{(k+1)-tt}(\text{SPARSE})$ from $P_{k-tt}(\text{SPARSE})$ [2], the separation of $P_{(k+1)-tt}(\text{RAND})$ from $P_{k-tt}(\text{RAND})$ can have no recursive witness. This is because $P_{(k+1)-tt}(\text{RAND}) \cap \text{REC} = P$ [4].

Section 2 is devoted to preliminary definitions. In Section 3, algorithmic randomness and the class RAND are considered and some useful properties are reviewed. The main result is presented in Section 4.

2 Preliminaries

The *Boolean value* of a condition ψ is

$$[\![\psi]\!] = \begin{cases} 1 & \text{if } \psi \\ 0 & \text{if not } \psi. \end{cases}$$

We write $\mathbf{N}$ for the set of nonnegative integers and $\mathbf{Z}^+$ for the set of positive integers.

We write $\{0,1\}^*$ for the set of all (finite, binary) *strings* and $\{0,1\}^\infty$ for the set of all (infinite, binary) *sequences*. The length of (number of bits in) a string $x \in \{0,1\}^*$ is denoted by $|x|$. The length of a sequence $x \in \{0,1\}^\infty$ is ∞. The *empty string* is the unique string λ of length 0 and, for $k \in \mathbf{N}$, $\{0,1\}^k = \{\, x \in \{0,1\}^* \mid |x| = k \,\}$. Finally, $\{0,1\}^+ = \{0,1\}^* - \{\lambda\}$.

If x is a string or sequence and $0 \le i \le j < |x|$, then $x[i..j]$ is the string consisting of the ith through j^{th} bits of x. In particular, if x is a string, then $x = x[0..|x|-1]$. We write $x[i]$ for $x[i..i]$, the ith bit of a string or sequence x. A *prefix* of a sequence $x \in \{0,1\}^\infty$ is a string of the form $x[0..n-1]$, where $n \in \mathbf{N}$. For $w \in \{0,1\}^*$ and $x \in \{0,1\}^\infty$, we write $w \sqsubseteq x$ to indicate that w is a prefix of x.

The *standard enumeration* of $\{0,1\}^*$ is the sequence $s_0 = \lambda, s_1 = 0, s_2 = 1, s_3 = 00, s_4 = 01, \cdots$. More generally, the *standard enumeration* of an infinite set $X \subseteq \{0,1\}^*$ is the sequence $x_0, x_1, \cdots$ in which the elements of X appear first in order of length, then in lexicographic order.

A *language* is a set $A \subseteq \{0,1\}^*$. The *characteristic sequence* of a language A is the sequence $\chi_A \in \{0,1\}^\infty$ defined by $\chi_A[n] = [\![s_n \in A]\!]$ for all $n \in \mathbf{N}$.

We fix a one-to-one pairing function $\langle , \rangle$ from $\{0,1\}^* \times \{0,1\}^*$ onto $\{0,1\}^*$ that is computable in polynomial time. Then we extend this function to k-tuples for all k so that $\langle , \rangle : (\{0,1\}^*)^k \to \{0,1\}^*$.

Given a number $k \in \mathbf{N}$, a *k-query function* is a function f with domain $\{0,1\}^*$ such that, for all $x \in \{0,1\}^*$,

$$f(x) = \langle f_0(x), ..., f_{k-1}(x) \rangle \in \{0,1\}^*.$$

Each $f_i(x)$ is called a *query* of f on input x, and the k-tuple $f(x)$ is called a *k-query list* on input x. A *k-truth table function* is a function g with domain $\{0,1\}^*$ such that, for each $x \in \{0,1\}^*$, $g(x)$ is the encoding of a k-input, 1-output Boolean circuit. We write $g(x)(w)$ for the output of this circuit on input $w \in \{0,1\}^k$. A $\le^{\mathrm{P}}_{k-tt}$-*reduction* is an ordered pair (f,g) such that f is a k-query function, g is a k-truth table function, and f and g are computable in polynomial time.

Let $A, B \subseteq \{0,1\}^*$. A $\le^{\mathrm{P}}_{k-tt}$-*reduction of A to B* is a $\le^{\mathrm{P}}_{k-tt}$-reduction (f,g) such that, for all $x \in \{0,1\}^*$,

$$[\![x \in A]\!] = g(x)([\![f_0(x) \in B]\!] \cdots [\![f_{k-1}(x) \in B]\!]).$$

In this case we say that $A \le^{\mathrm{P}}_{k-tt} B$ via (f,g). We say that A is $\le^{\mathrm{P}}_{k-tt}$-*reducible to B*, and write $A \le^{\mathrm{P}}_{k-tt} B$, if there exists (f,g) such that $A \le^{\mathrm{P}}_{k-tt} B$ via (f,g). For a language $A \subseteq \{0,1\}^*$ and a class $\mathcal{C}$ of languages,

$$\mathrm{P}_{k\text{-}tt}(A) = \{\, B \subseteq \{0,1\}^* \mid B \le^{\mathrm{P}}_{k-tt} A \,\}$$

and

$$\mathrm{P}_{k\text{-}tt}(\mathcal{C}) = \bigcup_{A \in \mathcal{C}} \mathrm{P}_{k\text{-}tt}(A).$$

We also use general k-truth-table reductions, which only require the functions f and g to be computable. A $\leq_{k-tt}$-*reduction* is an ordered pair (f, g) such that f is a k-query function, g is a k-truth table function, and f and g are computable. For a language $A \subseteq \{0, 1\}^*$ and a class $\mathcal{C}$ of languages, define

$$\text{REC}_{k-tt}(A) = \{\, B \subseteq \{0, 1\}^* \mid B \leq_{k-tt} A \,\}$$

and

$$\text{REC}_{k-tt}(\mathcal{C}) = \bigcup_{A \in \mathcal{C}} \text{REC}_{k-tt}(A).$$

Finally, let REC denote the class of all recursive (i.e., decidable) languages.

3   Randomness, 1-Reductions, and Normality

In this section we review Martin-Löf's definition of algorithmic randomness, along with two well-known properties of random sequences that are used in this paper.

Recall that the *characteristic sequence* of a language $A \subseteq \{0, 1\}^*$ is the infinite binary sequence

$$\chi_A = [\![s_0 \in A]\!][\![s_1 \in A]\!][\![s_2 \in A]\!] \cdots,$$

where $s_0, s_1, s_2, \cdots$ is the standard enumeration of $\{0, 1\}^*$.

Definition. The *cylinder generated by* a string $w \in \{0, 1\}^*$ is

$$\mathbf{C}_w = \{\, A \subseteq \{0, 1\}^* \mid w \sqsubseteq \chi_A \,\}.$$

The *cylinder generated by* the special symbol $\top$ is

$$\mathbf{C}_\top = \emptyset.$$

Definition. For $w \in \{0, 1\}^* \cup \{\top\}$, the *probability* (or *measure*) of the cylinder $\mathbf{C}_w$ is

$$\Pr(\mathbf{C}_w) = \begin{cases} 2^{-|w|} & \text{if } w \in \{0, 1\}^* \\ 0 & \text{if } w = \top. \end{cases}$$

Remark 3.1. Note that $\Pr(\mathbf{C}_w)$ is the probability that $A \in \mathbf{C}_w$ when a language $A \subseteq \{0, 1\}^*$ is chosen probabilistically according to a random experiment in which an independent toss of a fair coin is used to decide whether $x \in A$ for each $x \in \{0, 1\}^*$.

Definition (Martin-Löf [13]). A *constructive null cover* of a set Y of languages is a computable function

$$G : \mathbf{N} \times \mathbf{N} \to \{0, 1\}^* \cup \{\top\}$$

such that, for each $k \in \mathbf{N}$,

(i) $Y \subseteq \bigcup_{l=0}^{\infty} \mathbf{C}_{G(k,l)}$ (the *covering condition*); and

(ii) $\sum_{l=0}^{\infty} \Pr(\mathbf{C}_{G(k,l)}) \leq 2^{-k}$ (the *measure condition*).

A *constructive null set* is a set of languages that has a constructive null cover.

Remark 3.2. Conditions (i) and (ii) of the above definition imply that the event $A \in Y$ occurs with probability at most 2^{-k} in the random experiment of Remark 3.1. Since this holds for all k, every constructive null set is a probability 0 event in this random experiment. The computability requirement on G then means that a constructive null set is a set of languages that "has probability 0 in a constructively specifiable sense."

Intuitively, membership in a constructive null set is a very special (unusual) property for a language to have, and random languages should not have such properties.

Definition (Martin-Löf [13]). A language is *algorithmically random* (or, briefly, *random*) if it is not an element of any constructive null set. We write RAND for the set of all algorithmically random languages.

It is well known that the above definition is robust, in the sense that it is equivalent to subsequent definitions given by Levin [11], Schnorr [15], Chaitin [5], Solovay [18], and Shen' [16, 17].

Remark 3.3. Algorithmically random languages exist. In fact, it is easy to see [13] that RAND is a probability 1 event in the random experiment of Remark 3.1.

Now we discuss an important closure property of RAND that we use in this paper.

Definition (Post [14]). A *1-reduction* is a function $h : \{0,1\}^* \to \{0,1\}^*$ that is one-to-one and computable. If A and B are languages, then a *1-reduction of A to B* is a 1-reduction h such that $[\![x \in A]\!] = [\![h(x) \in B]\!]$ for all $x \in \{0,1\}^*$. We write $A \leq_1 B$ via h to indicate that h is a 1-reduction of A to B. We say that A is *1-reducible to B*, and write $A \leq_1 B$, if there exists h such that $A \leq_1 B$ via h.

The following well-known fact follows directly from the definitions of algorithmic randomness and 1-reducibility.

Lemma 3.4. RAND is downward closed under 1-reductions. That is, if $A \leq_1 B \in$ RAND, then $A \in$ RAND.

We also use the fact that random languages are *normal*. This notion, which is a minor variant of a property investigated by Borel, is developed in the following definitions.

Definition. For all $x \in \{0,1\}^\infty$, $w \in \{0,1\}^+$, and $n \in \mathbf{Z}^+$, define the nth *frequency of w in x* by

$$\text{freq}^{w,n}\, x = \frac{1}{n}\left|\{\, i \mid 0 \le i < n \text{ and } x[i|w|..(i+1)|w|-1] = w\,\}\right|,$$

where $|S|$ denotes the cardinality of S. That is, $\text{freq}^{w,n}\, x$ is the frequency with which the string w occurs in the first n nonoverlapping blocks of length $|w|$ in x.

Definition. For $x \in \{0,1\}^\infty$ and $w \in \{0,1\}^+$, the *limiting frequency of w in x* is

$$\text{freq}^w\, x = \lim_{n \to \infty} \text{freq}^{w,n}\, x,$$

provided that this limit exists.

Definition. Let $k \in \mathbf{Z}^+$. A language $A \subseteq \{0,1\}^*$ is *k-normal*, and we write $A \in \text{NORM}_k$, if for all $w \in \{0,1\}^k$,

$$\text{freq}^w\, \chi_A = 2^{-k}.$$

A language $A \subseteq \{0,1\}^*$ is *normal*, and we write $A \in \text{NORM}$, if A is k-normal for all $k \in \mathbf{Z}^+$. That is,

$$\text{NORM} = \bigcap_{k=1}^{\infty} \text{NORM}_k.$$

Remark 3.5. Several properties similar to that defined above have been investigated under various terminologies over the years. Knuth [9] surveys much of this work. The k-normality property defined above is the special case $j = 0$ of Knuth's "(k, k)-distributivity."

We use the following well-known fact.

Theorem 3.6. RAND $\subseteq$ NORM.

We do not know a single, direct reference for this fact, but it is well-known that every algorithmically random language is Church-random [10] and that every Church-random sequence is normal [9].

In addition, the Champernowne sequence

$$x = 0\,1\,00\,01\,10\,11\,000\,001\,010\,011\,100\cdots,$$

formed by concatenating the elements of $\{0,1\}^*$ in standard order, is known to be normal [7]. Since x is clearly computable, it cannot be random, so RAND is a *proper* subset of NORM.

4   Main Result

In this section we prove our main result, namely, that for every $k \in \mathbf{N}$ and every language $A \in$ RAND, there exists a language B with the following two properties.

(i) $B \leq^{\mathrm{P}}_{(k+1)-tt} A$.

(ii) For every language $A' \in$ RAND, $B \not\leq_{k-tt} A'$.

That is, $B \in \mathrm{P}_{(k+1)\text{-}tt}(A) - \mathrm{REC}_{k\text{-}tt}(\mathrm{RAND})$.

Our principal tool for proving this result is the notion of k-resolvability, which we now develop.

Definition. The *limiting frequency* of a language $A \subseteq \{0,1\}^*$ is

$$\mathrm{freq}\, A = \mathrm{freq}^1 \chi_A,$$

i.e., the limiting frequency of the string 1 in the sequence χ_A, as defined in section 3.

Definition. Let $k \in \mathbf{N}$. A language $A \subseteq \{0,1\}^*$ is *k-resolvable* if there is a language $B \leq_1 A$ such that $2^k \cdot \mathrm{freq}\, B \in \mathbf{N}$.

That is, A is k-resolvable if there is a 1-reduction h such that the inverse image $B = h^{-1}(A)$ has a limiting frequency that can be written as a rational number with denominator 2^k. It is clear that if A is k-resolvable and $k \leq k'$, then A is also k'-resolvable. Intuitively, we regard a language that is k-resolvable as being "coarse at level k." The smaller the parameter k is, the coarser the k-resolvable language must be. (Similarly, 30-grit sandpaper is coarser than 60-grit sandpaper!)

The following fact is obvious but useful.

Lemma 4.1. For each $k \in \mathbf{N}$, the collection of k-resolvable languages is upward closed under 1-reductions. That is, if $A \leq_1 B$ and A is k-resolvable, then B is k-resolvable.

The following two easy lemmas illustrate the notion of k-resolvability.

Lemma 4.2. Every recursive language is 0-resolvable.

Lemma 4.3. Every algorithmically random language is 1-resolvable, but not 0-resolvable.

The following terminology simplifies our discussion.

Definition. For languages $B, X \subseteq \{0,1\}^*$ with X infinite, the *X-selection* of B is the language
$$\sigma_X(B) = \{ s_i \mid x_i \in B \},$$
where $s_0, s_1, \cdots$ is the standard enumeration of $\{0,1\}^*$ and $x_0, x_1, \cdots$ is the standard enumeration of X.

Observation 4.4. Let $B, X \subseteq \{0,1\}^*$. If X is recursive and infinite, then $\sigma_X(B) \leq_1 B$ and $\sigma_X(B) \leq_1 B \cap X$.

Now we move to the central part of our argument.

Lemma 4.5 (Main Lemma). Let $k \in \mathbf{N}$ and $A, B \subseteq \{0,1\}^*$. If $A \in \text{RAND}$ and $B \leq_{k-tt} A$, then B is k-resolvable.

Proof. We proceed by induction on k.

Basis The case $k = 0$ follows immediately from Lemma 4.2.

Induction Step Assume that the statement holds for k, where $k \in \mathbf{N}$, that $\overline{A \in \text{RAND}}$, and that $B \leq_{(k+1)-tt} A$ via (f, g).

For each $x \in \{0,1\}^*$, let
$$Q(x) = \{f_0(x), f_1(x), \cdots, f_k(x)\}$$
be the set of queries of f on input x. Define the sets
$$H = \left\{ x \in \{0,1\}^* \,\middle|\, |Q(x)| \leq k \right\}$$
and, for each $y \in \{0,1\}^*$,
$$V_y = \{ x \in \{0,1\}^* \mid y \in Q(x) \}.$$

Thus H is the set of inputs on which f repeats a query and V_y is the set of inputs on which f queries y. Note that the sets H and V_y are all recursive.

It suffices to prove that B is $(k+1)$-resolvable in each of the following three cases.

CASE 1. H is infinite
CASE 2. V_y is infinite for some $y \in \{0,1\}^*$.
CASE 3. The sets H and V_y, for $y \in \{0,1\}^*$, are all finite.

In Case 1, the reduction (f, g) can clearly be modified to make do with one fewer query on inputs in H, so $B \cap H \leq_{k-tt} A$. It follows by Observation 4.4 that $\sigma_H(B) \leq_{k-tt} A$, whence $\sigma_H(B)$ is k-resolvable by the induction hypothesis. By Observation 4.4 and Lemma 4.1, it follows that B is k-resolvable, hence certainly $(k+1)$-resolvable.

In Case 2, fix $y \in \{0,1\}^*$ such that V_y is infinite. The answer to the query "$y \in A$?" is constant, so the reduction (f, g) can be modified to make do with one fewer query on elements of V_y. Thus $B \cap V_y \leq_{k-tt} A$. It follows by Observation 4.4 that $\sigma_{V_y}(B) \leq_{k-tt} A$. By the induction hypothesis, this implies that $\sigma_{V_y}(B)$ is k-resolvable. Thus, by Observation 4.4 and Lemma 4.1, B is k-resolvable, hence $(k+1)$-resolvable.

Finally, assume that Case 3 holds. Then for each finite set $S \subseteq \{0,1\}^*$, the set

$$\tilde{S} = H \cup \left(\bigcup_{x \in S} \bigcup_{y \in Q(x)} V_y \right)$$

is finite. Fix a truth table $\tau : \{0,1\}^{k+1} \to \{0,1\}$ such that the set

$$T = \{ x \in \{0,1\}^* \mid g(x) = \tau \}$$

is infinite. For each finite set $S \subseteq \{0,1\}^*$, let $u(S)$ be the first element of the infinite set $T - \tilde{S}$ in the standard enumeration of $\{0,1\}^*$. Define a language $U = \bigcup_{i=0}^{\infty} U_i$ by the recursion

$$U_0 = \emptyset, \qquad U_{i+1} = U_i \cup \{u(U_i)\}.$$

It is easy to check that U has the following properties.

(i) U is infinite and recursive.

(ii) $U \subseteq T$.

(iii) $U \cap H = \emptyset$.

(iv) For all $x, y \in U$, if $x \neq y$, then $Q(x) \cap Q(y) = \emptyset$.

Let $u_0, u_1, \cdots$ be the standard enumeration of U. Define the language

$$D = \{ s_n \mid f_r(u_q) \in A \},$$

where q and r are the quotient and remainder, respectively, when n is divided by $k+1$. That is, for $q \in \mathbf{N}$ and $0 \leq r \leq k$, $s_{q(k+1)+r}$ is an element of D if and only if the rth query of f on input u_q is an element of A. Properties (i), (iii), and (iv) above ensure that the function $s_n \mapsto f_r(u_q)$ is one-to-one and recursive, so $D \leq_1 A$. Since $A \in \text{RAND}$, it follows by Lemma 3.4 and Theorem 3.6 that $D \in \text{RAND} \subseteq \text{NORM}_{k+1}$. Let $W \subseteq \{0,1\}^{k+1}$ be the support of the truth table τ, i.e.,

$$W = \{ w \in \{0,1\}^{k+1} \mid \tau(w) = 1 \}.$$

Intuitively, the membership (or nonmembership) of each string s_i in $\sigma_U(B)$ is determined, via the truth table τ, by the membership (or nonmembership) in D of the elements of the ith nonoverlapping block of $k+1$ consecutive strings in the standard enumeration of $\{0,1\}^*$. That is, for all $i \in \mathbf{N}$, property (ii) tells us that

$$s_i \in \sigma_U(B) \quad \Longleftrightarrow \quad u_i \in B$$

$$\Longleftrightarrow \quad \tau(\llbracket f_0(u_i) \in A \rrbracket \cdots \llbracket f_k(u_i) \in A \rrbracket) = 1$$
$$\Longleftrightarrow \quad \llbracket f_0(u_i) \in A \rrbracket \cdots \llbracket f_k(u_i) \in A \rrbracket \in W$$
$$\Longleftrightarrow \quad \llbracket s_{i(k+1)} \in D \rrbracket \cdots \llbracket s_{i(k+1)+k} \in D \rrbracket \in W$$
$$\Longleftrightarrow \quad \chi_D[i(k+1)..i(k+1)+k] \in W.$$

Recalling that D is $(k+1)$-normal, it follows that

$$\operatorname{freq} \sigma_U(B) = \sum_{w \in W} \operatorname{freq}^w \chi_D = |W| \cdot 2^{-(k+1)}.$$

It follows by property (i) above and Observation 4.4 that B is $(k+1)$-resolvable. This completes the proof of the Main Lemma. $\qquad \square$

Recall that our objective is to prove that, for every $k \in \mathbf{N}$ and $A \in \text{RAND}$, there is a language $B \in \text{P}_{(k+1)\text{-}tt}(A) - \text{REC}_{k\text{-}tt}(\text{RAND})$. By Lemma 4.5, this can be achieved by exhibiting a language $B \leq^{\text{P}}_{(k+1)\text{-}tt} A$ that is not k-resolvable. The following definition provides such a language.

Definition. For $k \in \mathbf{N}$, the *k-fold conjunction* of a language $A \subseteq \{0,1\}^*$ is the language
$$\wedge^{(k)} A = \left\{ x \in \{0,1\}^* \mid (\forall 0 \leq i < k)\, x 10^i \in A \right\}.$$
(Note that, vacuously, $\wedge^{(0)} A = \{0,1\}^*$.)

We need just one more lemma.

Lemma 4.6. Let $k \in \mathbf{N}$. If $A \in \text{RAND}$ and $C \leq_1 \wedge^{(k)} A$, then $\operatorname{freq} C = 2^{-k}$.

Proof. If $k = 0$, then $\wedge^{(k)} A = \{0,1\}^*$ and this is trivial, so assume that $k > 0$. Assume that $C \leq_1 \wedge^{(k)} A$ via h and define the language

$$D = \left\{ s_n \in \{0,1\}^* \mid h(s_q) 10^r \in A \right\},$$

where q and r are the quotient and remainder obtained when n is divided by k. Then $D \leq_1 A$, so D is k-normal by Lemma 3.4 and Theorem 3.6. In particular, this implies that

$$\operatorname{freq}^{1^k} \chi_D = 2^{-k}.$$

Also, for all $i \in \mathbf{N}$,

$$
\begin{aligned}
\llbracket s_i \in C \rrbracket &= \llbracket h(s_i) \in \wedge^{(k)} A \rrbracket \\
&= \llbracket (\forall 0 \leq r < k)\, h(s_i) 10^r \in A \rrbracket \\
&= \llbracket (\forall 0 \leq r < k)\, s_{ki+r} \in D \rrbracket \\
&= \llbracket \chi_D[ki..k(i+1)-1] = 1^k \rrbracket,
\end{aligned}
$$

so

$$\operatorname{freq} C = \operatorname{freq}^{1^k} \chi_D = 2^{-k}. \qquad \square$$

Now we have our main result.

Theorem 4.7 (Main Theorem). For all $k \in \mathbf{N}$ and $A \in \mathrm{RAND}$,

$$\mathrm{P}_{(k+1)\text{-}tt}(A) \not\subseteq \mathrm{REC}_{k\text{-}tt}(\mathrm{RAND}).$$

Thus, for all $k \in \mathbf{N}$,

$$\mathrm{P}_{k\text{-}tt}(\mathrm{RAND}) \subsetneq \mathrm{P}_{(k+1)\text{-}tt}(\mathrm{RAND}).$$

Proof. Let $k \in \mathbf{N}$ and $A \in \mathrm{RAND}$. Let $B = \wedge^{(k+1)}(A)$. It is clear that $B \in \mathrm{P}_{(k+1)\text{-}tt}(A)$. On the other hand, Lemma 4.6 tells us that, for all $C \leq_1 B$, $2^k \cdot \mathrm{freq}\, C = 2^k \cdot 2^{-(k+1)} = 1/2 \notin \mathbf{N}$, so B is not k-resolvable. It follows by the Main Lemma that $B \notin \mathrm{REC}_{k\text{-}tt}(\mathrm{RAND})$. Thus $B \in \mathrm{P}_{(k+1)\text{-}tt}(A) - \mathrm{REC}_{k\text{-}tt}(\mathrm{RAND})$. $\square$

In the course of proving the above result, we have shown that, for $k \in \mathbf{N}$ and $A \in \mathrm{RAND}$, the language $\wedge^{(k+1)}A$ is $(k+1)$-resolvable but not k-resolvable. It is interesting to note that, when $k = 0$, this is precisely Lemma 4.3.

Acknowledgments

We thank Charles Bennett and Steve Kautz for helpful discussions.

References

[1] J. L. Balcázar, J. Díaz, and J. Gabarró, *Structural Complexity I*, Springer-Verlag, 1988.

[2] R. Book and K.-I Ko, On sets truth-table reducible to sparse sets, *SIAM Journal on Computing* **17** (1988), pp. 903–919.

[3] R. V. Book, Additional queries and algorithmically random languages, In K. Ambos-Spies, S. Homer, and U. Schöning, editors, *Complexity Theory*. Cambridge University Press, 1993, to appear.

[4] R. V. Book, J. H. Lutz, and K. Wagner, An observation on probability versus randomness with applications to complexity classes, *Mathematical Systems Theory* (1993), to appear.

[5] G. J. Chaitin, A theory of program size formally identical to information theory, *Journal of the Association for Computing Machinery* **22** (1975), pp. 329–340.

[6] G. J. Chaitin, Incompleteness theorems for random reals, *Advances in Applied Mathematics* **8** (1987), pp. 119–146.

[7] D. G. Champernowne, Construction of decimals normal in the scale of ten, *J. London Math. Soc.* **2** (1933), pp. 254–260.

[8] T. Hagerup and C. Rüb, A guided tour of Chernoff bounds, *Information Processing Letters* **33** (1990), pp. 305–308.

[9] Donald E. Knuth, *The Art of Computer Programming*, volume 2, Addison-Wesley, 1966.

[10] A. N. Kolmogorov and V. A. Uspenskii, Algorithms and randomness, translated in *Theory of Probability and its Applications* **32** (1987), pp. 389–412.

[11] L. A. Levin, On the notion of a random sequence, *Soviet Mathematics Doklady* **14** (1973), pp. 1413–1416.

[12] J. H. Lutz, Almost everywhere high nonuniform complexity, *Journal of Computer and System Sciences* **44** (1992), pp. 220–258.

[13] P. Martin-Löf, On the definition of random sequences, *Information and Control* **9** (1966), pp. 602–619.

[14] E. L. Post, Recursively enumerable sets of positive integers and their decision problems, *Bulletin of the American Mathematical Society* **50** (1944), pp. 284–316.

[15] C. P. Schnorr, Process complexity and effective random tests, *Journal of Computer and System Sciences* **7** (1973), pp. 376–388.

[16] A. Kh. Shen', The frequency approach to the definition of a random sequence, *Semiotika i Informatika* (1982), pp. 14–42, in Russian.

[17] A. Kh. Shen', On relations between different algorithmic definitions of randomness, *Soviet Mathematics Doklady* **38** (1989), pp. 316–319.

[18] R. M. Solovay, 1975, reported in [6].

[19] S. Tang and R. Book, Polynomial-time reducibilities and "almost-all" oracle sets, *Theoretical Computer Science* **81** (1991), pp. 35–47.

[20] M. van Lambalgen, *Random Sequences*, PhD thesis, Department of Mathematics, University of Amsterdam, 1987.

[21] M. van Lambalgen, Von Mises' definition of random sequences reconsidered, *Journal of Symbolic Logic* **52** (1987), pp. 725–755.

Cook Versus Karp-Levin: Separating Completeness Notions if NP Is not Small

(Extended Abstract)

Jack H. Lutz[*]

Dept. of Computer Science
Iowa State University
Ames, Iowa 50011,
U.S.A.

Elvira Mayordomo[†]

Dept. L.S.I.
Univ. Politècnica de Catalunya
Pau Gargallo 5
08028 Barcelona, Spain

Abstract

Under the hypothesis that NP does not have p-measure 0 (roughly, that NP contains more than a negligible subset of exponential time), it is shown that there is a language that is $\leq_T^P$-complete ("Cook complete"), but not $\leq_m^P$-complete ("Karp-Levin complete"), for NP. This conclusion, widely believed to be true, is not known to follow from P $\neq$ NP or other traditional complexity-theoretic hypotheses.

Evidence is presented that "NP does not have p-measure 0" is a reasonable hypothesis with many credible consequences. Additional such consequences proven here include the separation of many truth-table reducibilities in NP (e.g., k queries versus $k+1$ queries), the class separation E $\neq$ NE, and the existence of NP search problems that are not reducible to the corresponding decision problems.

1 Introduction

The NP-completeness of decision problems has two principal, well-known formulations. These are the polynomial-time Turing completeness ($\leq_T^P$-completeness) introduced by Cook [5] and the polynomial-time many-one completeness ($\leq_m^P$-completeness) introduced by Karp [8] and Levin [11]. These two completeness notions, sometimes called "Cook completeness" and "Karp-Levin completeness," have been widely conjectured, but not proven, to be distinct. The main purpose of this paper is to exhibit a reasonable complexity-theoretic hypothesis that implies the distinctness of these two completeness notions.

In general, given a polynomial-time reducibility $\leq_r^P$ (e.g., $\leq_T^P$ or $\leq_m^P$), a language (i.e., decision problem) C is $\leq_r^P$-complete for NP if $C \in$ NP and, for all $A \in$ NP, $A \leq_r^P C$. The difference between $\leq_T^P$-completeness and $\leq_m^P$-completeness (if any) arises from the difference between the reducibilities $\leq_T^P$ and

---

[*]This author's research was supported in part by National Science Foundation Grant CCR-9157382, with matching funds from Rockwell International and Microware Systems Corporation.

[†]This author's research, performed while visiting Iowa State University, was supported in part by the ESPRIT EC project 3075 (ALCOM), in part by National Science Foundation Grant CCR-9157382, and in part by Spanish Government Grant FPI PN90.

$\leq_m^P$. If A and B are languages, then A is *polynomial-time Turing reducible to B*, and we write $A \leq_T^P B$, if A is decided in polynomial time by some oracle Turing machine that consults B as an oracle. On the other hand, A is *polynomial-time many-one reducible to B*, and we write $A \leq_m^P B$, if every instance x of the decision problem A can be transformed in polynomial time into an instance $f(x)$ of the decision problem B with the same answer, i.e., satisfying $x \in A$ iff $f(x) \in B$.

It is clear that $A \leq_m^P B$ implies $A \leq_T^P B$, and hence that every $\leq_m^P$-complete language for NP is $\leq_T^P$-complete for NP. Conversely, all known, natural $\leq_T^P$-complete languages for NP are also $\leq_m^P$-complete. Nevertheless, it is widely conjectured (e.g., [10, 29, 12, 6]) that Cook completeness is more general than Karp-Levin completeness:

CvKL Conjecture. ("Cook versus Karp-Levin"). There exists a language that is $\leq_T^P$-complete, but not $\leq_m^P$-complete, for NP.

The CvKL conjecture immediately implies that $P \neq NP$, so it may be very difficult to prove. We mention five items of evidence that the conjecture is reasonable.

1. Selman [24] proved that the widely-believed hypothesis $E \neq NE$ implies that the reducibilities $\leq_T^P$ and $\leq_m^P$ are distinct in NP $\cup$ co$-$NP. That is, if DTIME(2^{linear}) $\neq$ NTIME(2^{linear}), then there exist $A, B \in$ NP $\cup$ co$-$NP such that $A \leq_T^P B$ but $A \not\leq_m^P B$. Under the stronger hypothesis $E \neq NE \cap$ co$-$NE, Selman proved that the reducibilities $\leq_T^P$ and $\leq_m^P$ are distinct in NP.

2. Ko and Moore [9] constructed a language that is $\leq_T^P$-complete, but not $\leq_m^P$-complete, for E. Watanabe [26, 27] refined this by separating a spectrum of completeness notions in E.

3. Watanabe and Tang [28] exhibited reasonable complexity-theoretic hypotheses implying the existence of languages that are $\leq_T^P$-complete, but not $\leq_m^P$-complete, for PSPACE.

4. Watanabe [27] and Buhrman, Homer, and Torenvliet [4] constructed languages that are $\leq_T^P$-complete, but not $\leq_m^P$-complete, for NE.

5. Longpré and Young [12] showed that, for every polynomial time bound t, there exist languages A and B, both $\leq_T^P$-complete for NP, such that A is $\leq_T^P$-reducible to B in linear time, but A is not $\leq_m^P$-reducible to B in $t(n)$ time.

Item 1 above indicates that the reducibilities $\leq_T^P$ and $\leq_m^P$ are likely to differ in NP. Item 3 indicates that the CvKL conjecture is likely to hold with NP replaced by PSPACE. Items 2 and 4 indicate that the CvKL Conjecture definitely holds with NP replaced by E or by NE. Item 5 would imply the CvKL Conjecture, were it not for the dependence of A and B upon the polynomial t. Taken together, these five items suggest that the CvKL Conjecture is reasonable.

The CvKL Conjecture is very ambitious, since it implies that $P \neq NP$. The question has thus been raised [10, 24, 6, 4] whether the CvKL Conjecture can be derived from some reasonable complexity-theoretic hypothesis, such as $P \neq NP$ or the separation of the polynomial-time hierarchy into infinitely many levels.

To date, even this more modest objective has not been achieved.

The Main Theorem of this paper, Theorem 3.1 below, says that the CvKL Conjecture follows from the hypothesis that "NP does not have p-measure 0". This hypothesis, whose formulation involves *resource-bounded measure* [13, 14] (a complexity-theoretic generalization of Lebesgue measure), is explained in detail in section 2 below. *Very* roughly speaking, the hypothesis says that "NP is not small," in the sense that NP contains more than a negligible subset of the languages decidable in exponential time.

In section 2 below it is argued that "NP does not have p-measure 0" is a reasonable hypothesis for two reasons: First, its negation would imply the existence of a surprisingly efficient algorithm for betting on all NP languages. Second, the hypothesis has a rapidly growing body of credible consequences. We summarize recently discovered such consequences [16, 7, 15] and prove two new consequences, namely the class separation $E \neq NE$ and (building on recent work of Bellare and Goldwasser [1]) the existence of NP search problems that are not reducible to the corresponding decision problems.

In section 3 we prove our Main Theorem. In section 4, we prove that, if NP is not small, then many truth-table reducibilities are distinct in NP.

Taken together, our results suggest that "NP does not have p-measure 0" is a *reasonable scientific hypothesis*, which may have the *explanatory power* to resolve many questions that have not been resolved by traditional complexity-theoretic hypotheses.

2   If NP Is Not Small

In this section we discuss the meaning and reasonableness of the hypothesis that NP is not small. Inevitably, our discussion begins with a review of measure in complexity classes.

Resource-bounded measure [13, 14] is a very general theory whose special cases include classical Lebesgue measure, the measure structure of the class REC of all recursive languages, and measure in various complexity classes. In this paper we are interested only in measure in $E = \text{DTIME}(2^{\text{linear}})$ and $E_2 = \text{DTIME}(2^{\text{polynomial}})$, so our discussion of measure is specific to these classes. The interested reader may consult section 3 of [13] for more discussion and examples. We also refer to [13] for a full introduction of the notation used in the next pages.

Throughout this section, we identify every language $A \subseteq \{0,1\}^*$ with its characteristic sequence $\chi_A \in \{0,1\}^\infty$, defined as usual (see for instance [13]).

The *cylinder generated by* a string $w \in \{0,1\}^*$ is
$$\mathbf{C}_w = \{x \in \{0,1\}^\infty \mid w \sqsubseteq x\} = \{A \subseteq \{0,1\}^* \mid w \sqsubseteq \chi_A\}.$$

Notation The classes $p_1 = p$ and p_2, both consisting of functions $f : \{0,1\}^* \to \{0,1\}^*$, are defined as follows.

$$p_1 = p = \{f \mid f \text{ is computable in polynomial time}\}$$
$$p_2 = \{f \mid f \text{ is computable in } n^{(\log n)^{O(1)}} \text{ time}\}$$

The measure structures of E and E_2 are developed in terms of the classes p_i, for $i = 1, 2$.

Definition. A *density function* is a function $d : \{0,1\}^* \to [0, \infty)$ satisfying

$$d(w) \geq \frac{d(w0) + d(w1)}{2} \tag{3.1}$$

for all $w \in \{0,1\}^*$. The *global value* of a density function d is $d(\lambda)$. The *set covered by* a density function d is

$$S[d] = \bigcup_{\substack{w \in \{0,1\}^* \\ d(w) \geq 1}} C_w. \tag{3.2}$$

A density function d *covers* a set $X \subseteq \{0,1\}^\infty$ if $X \subseteq S[d]$.

For all density functions in this paper, equality actually holds in (3.1) above, but this is not required. Consider the random experiment in which a language $A \subseteq \{0,1\}^*$ is chosen by using an independent toss of a fair coin to decide whether each string $x \in \{0,1\}^*$ is in A. Taken together, parts (3.1) and (3.2) of the above definition imply that $\Pr[A \in S[d]] \leq d(\lambda)$ in this experiment. Intuitively, we regard a density function d as a "detailed verification" that $\Pr[A \in X] \leq d(\lambda)$ for all sets $X \subseteq S[d]$.

More generally, we will be interested in "uniform systems" of density functions that are computable within some resource bound.

Definition. An n-dimensional *density system* (n-*DS*) is a function
$$d : \mathbf{N}^n \times \{0,1\}^* \to [0, \infty)$$
such that $d_{\vec{k}}$ is a density function for every $\vec{k} \in \mathbf{N}^n$. It is sometimes convenient to regard a density function as a 0-DS.

Definition. A *computation* of an n-DS d is a function $\widehat{d} : \mathbf{N}^{n+1} \times \{0,1\}^* \to \mathbf{D}$ (where $\mathbf{D} = \{m2^{-n} \mid m \in \mathbf{Z}, n \in \mathbf{N}\}$ is the set of *dyadic rationals*) such that
$$\left| \widehat{d}_{\vec{k},r}(w) - d_{\vec{k}}(w) \right| \leq 2^{-r}$$
for all $\vec{k} \in \mathbf{N}^n$, $r \in \mathbf{N}$, and $w \in \{0,1\}^*$. For $i = 1, 2$, a p_i-*computation* of an n-DS d is a computation $\widehat{d}$ of d such that $\widehat{d} \in p_i$. An n-DS d is p_i-*computable* if there exists a p_i-computation $\widehat{d}$ of d.

We now come to the key idea of resource-bounded measure theory.

Definition. A *null cover* of a set $X \subseteq \{0,1\}^\infty$ is a 1-DS d such that, for all $k \in \mathbf{N}$, d_k covers X with global value $d_k(\lambda) \leq 2^{-k}$. For $i = 1, 2$, a p_i-*null cover* of X is a null cover of X that is p_i-computable.

In other words, a null cover of X is a uniform system of density functions that cover X with rapidly vanishing global value. It is easy to show that a set $X \subseteq \{0,1\}^\infty$ has classical Lebesgue measure 0 (i.e., probability 0 in the above coin-tossing experiment) if and only if there exists a null cover of X.

Definition. A set X has p_i-*measure 0*, and we write $\mu_{p_i}(X) = 0$, if there exists a p_i-null cover of X. A set X has p_i-*measure 1*, and we write $\mu_{p_i}(X) = 1$, if $\mu_{p_i}(X^c) = 0$.

Thus a set X has p_i-measure 0 if p_i provides sufficient computational resources to compute uniformly good approximations to a system of density functions that cover X with rapidly vanishing global value.

We now turn to the internal measure structures of the classes $E = E_1 = DTIME(2^{linear})$ and $E_2 = DTIME(2^{polynomial})$.

Definition. A set X has *measure 0 in* E_i, and we write $\mu(X \mid E_i) = 0$, if $\mu_{p_i}(X \cap E_i) = 0$. A set X has *measure 1 in* E_i, and we write $\mu(X \mid E_i) = 1$, if $\mu(X^c \mid E_i) = 0$. If $\mu(X \mid E_i) = 1$, we say that *almost every* language in E_i is in X.

We write $\mu(X \mid E_i) \neq 0$ to indicate that X does *not* have measure 0 in E_i. Note that this does *not* assert that "$\mu(X \mid E_i)$" has some nonzero value.

The following is obvious but useful.

Fact 2.1. For every set $X \subseteq \{0,1\}^\infty$,

$$\mu_p(X) = 0 \quad \Longrightarrow \quad \mu_{p_2}(X) = 0 \quad \Longrightarrow \quad \Pr[A \in X] = 0$$
$$\Downarrow \qquad\qquad\qquad \Downarrow$$
$$\mu(X \mid E) = 0 \qquad\quad \mu(X \mid E_2) = 0,$$

where the probability $\Pr[A \in X]$ is computed according to the random experiment in which a language $A \subseteq \{0,1\}^*$ is chosen probabilistically, using an independent toss of a fair coin to decide whether each string $x \in \{0,1\}^*$ is in A.

It is shown in [13] that these definitions endow E and E_2 with internal measure structure. This structure justifies the intuition that, if $\mu(X \mid E) = 0$, then $X \cap E$ is a *negligibly small* subset of E (and similarly for E_2). The next two results state aspects of this structure that are especially relevant to the present work.

Theorem 2.2 ([13]). For all cylinders C_w, $\mu(C_w \mid E) \neq 0$ and $\mu(C_w \mid E_2) \neq 0$. In particular, $\mu(E \mid E) \neq 0$ and $\mu(E_2 \mid E_2) \neq 0$.

Regarding deterministic time complexity classes, the following fact is an easy exercise. (It also follows immediately from Theorem 4.16 of [13].)

Fact 2.3. For every fixed $c \in \mathbf{N}$,

$$\mu(DTIME(2^{cn}) \mid E) = \mu_p(DTIME(2^{cn})) = 0, \text{ and}$$

$$\mu(DTIME(2^{n^c}) \mid E_2) = \mu_{p_2}(DTIME(2^{n^c})) = 0.$$

$\square$

Figure 1 summarizes known implications among various conditions asserting the non-smallness of NP. (These implications follow from Facts 2.1 and 2.3.) Lutz has conjectured that the strongest conditions in Figure 1, namely, $\mu(NP \mid E_2) \neq 0$ and $\mu(NP \mid E) \neq 0$, are true. Most of the results of the present paper involve the weakest measure-theoretic hypothesis in Figure 1, namely the hypothesis that NP does not have p-measure 0. The rest of this section discusses the reasonableness and consequences of this particular hypothesis.

$$\mu(\text{NP} \mid \text{E}_2) \neq 0 \qquad\qquad\qquad \mu(\text{NP} \mid \text{E}) \neq 0$$
$$\Updownarrow \qquad\qquad\qquad\qquad\qquad \Downarrow$$
$$\mu_{\text{p}_2}(\text{NP}) \neq 0 \qquad \Longrightarrow \qquad \mu_{\text{p}}(\text{NP}) \neq 0$$
$$\Downarrow \qquad\qquad\qquad\qquad\qquad \Downarrow$$
$$(\forall k)\, \text{NP} \not\subseteq \text{DTIME}(2^{n^k}) \quad \Longrightarrow \quad (\forall c)\, \text{NP} \not\subseteq \text{DTIME}(2^{cn})$$
$$\Downarrow$$
$$\text{P} \neq \text{NP}$$

Figure 1: Non-smallness conditions

The hypothesis that $\mu_{\text{p}}(\text{NP}) \neq 0$ is best understood by considering the meaning of its negation, that NP has p-measure 0. A particularly intuitive interpretation of this latter condition is in terms of certain algorithmic betting strategies, called martingales.

Definition. A *martingale* is a density function d that satisfies condition (3.1) with equality, i.e., a function $d : \{0,1\}^* \to [0, \infty)$ such that

$$d(w) = \frac{d(w0) + d(w1)}{2} \tag{3.3}$$

for all $w \in \{0,1\}^*$. A martingale d *succeeds* on a language $A \subseteq \{0,1\}^*$ if

$$\limsup_{n \to \infty} d(\chi_A[0..n-1]) = \infty.$$

Intuitively, a martingale d is a betting strategy that, given a language A, starts with capital (amount of money) $d(\lambda)$ and bets on the membership or nonmembership of the successive strings $s_0, s_1, s_2, \cdots$ (the standard enumeration of $\{0,1\}^*$) in A. Prior to betting on a string s_n, the strategy has capital $d(w)$, where

$$w = [\![s_0 \in A]\!] \cdots [\![s_{n-1} \in A]\!].$$

After betting on the string s_n, the strategy has capital $d(wb)$, where $b = [\![s_n \in A]\!]$. Condition (3.3) ensures that the betting is fair. The strategy succeeds on A if its capital is unbounded as the betting progresses.

Martingales were used extensively by Schnorr [20, 21, 22, 23] in his investigation of random and pseudorandom sequences. Recently, martingales have been shown to characterize p-measure 0 sets:

Theorem 2.4 ([13, 14]). A set X of languages has p-measure 0 if and only if there exists a p-computable martingale d such that, for all $A \in X$, d succeeds on A. $\qquad\qquad\qquad\qquad\qquad\qquad\qquad\qquad\qquad\qquad\qquad\qquad\qquad\qquad\square$

In the case $X = \text{NP}$, Theorem 2.4 says that NP has p-measure 0 if and only if there is a single p-computable strategy d that succeeds (bets successfully) on every language $A \in \text{NP}$. The fact that the strategy d is p-computable means that, when betting on the condition "$x \in A$", d requires only $2^{c|x|}$ time for some fixed constant c. (This is because the running time of d for this bet is polynomial in the number of predecessors of x in the standard ordering of $\{0,1\}^*$.) On the other hand, for all $k \in \mathbf{N}$, there exist languages $A \in \mathrm{NP}$ with the property that the apparent search space (space of witnesses) for each input x has $2^{|x|^k}$ elements. Since c is fixed, we have $2^{cn} \ll 2^{n^k}$ for large values of k. Such a martingale d would thus be a very remarkable algorithm! It would bet successfully on *all* NP languages, using far less than enough time to examine the search spaces of most such languages. It is reasonable to conjecture that no such martingale exists, i.e., that NP does not have p-measure 0.

Since $\mu_{\mathrm{p}}(\mathrm{NP}) \neq 0$ implies $\mathrm{P} \neq \mathrm{NP}$, and $\mu_{\mathrm{p}}(\mathrm{NP}) = 0$ implies $\mathrm{NP} \neq \mathrm{E}_2$, we are unable to prove or disprove the $\mu_{\mathrm{p}}(\mathrm{NP}) \neq 0$ conjecture at this time. Until such a mathematical resolution is available, the condition $\mu_{\mathrm{p}}(\mathrm{NP}) \neq 0$ is best investigated as a *scientific hypothesis*, to be evaluated in terms of the extent and credibility of its consequences.

We now mention three recently discovered consequences of the hypothesis that NP does not have p-measure 0. The first concerns P-bi-immunity.

Definition. A language $A \subseteq \{0,1\}^*$ is P-*immune* if, for all $B \in \mathrm{P}$, $B \subseteq A$ implies that B is finite. A language $A \subseteq \{0,1\}^*$ is P-*bi-immune* if A and A^c are both P-immune.

Theorem 2.5 (Mayordomo [16]). The set of P-bi-immune languages has p-measure 1. Thus, if NP does not have p-measure 0, then NP contains a P-bi-immune language. □

The next known consequence of $\mu_{\mathrm{p}}(\mathrm{NP}) \neq 0$ involves complexity cores of NP-complete languages.

Definition. A language $A \subseteq \{0,1\}^*$ is *dense* if there is a real number $\epsilon > 0$ such that $|A_{\leq n}| \geq 2^{n^\epsilon}$ for all sufficiently large n.

Definition. Given a machine M and an input $x \in \{0,1\}^*$, we write $M(x) = 1$ if M accepts x, $M(x) = 0$ if M rejects x, and $M(x) = \bot$ in any other case. If $M(x) \in \{0,1\}$, we write $\mathrm{time}_M(x)$ for the number of steps used in the computation of $M(x)$. If $M(x) = \bot$, we define $\mathrm{time}_M(x) = \infty$. We partially order the set $\{0, 1, \bot\}$ by $\bot < 0$ and $\bot < 1$, with 0 and 1 incomparable. A machine M is *consistent with* a language $A \subseteq \{0,1\}^*$ if $M(x) \leq [\![x \in A]\!]$ for all $x \in \{0,1\}^*$.

Definition. Let $K, A \subseteq \{0,1\}^*$. Then K is an *exponential complexity core* of A if there is a real number $\epsilon > 0$ such that, for every machine M that is consistent with A, the "fast set"

$$F = \left\{ x \,\middle|\, \mathrm{time}_m(x) \leq 2^{|x|^\epsilon} \right\}$$

satisfies $|F \cap K| < \infty$.

Theorem 2.6 (Juedes and Lutz [7]). If NP does not have p-measure 0, then every $\leq_m^{\mathrm{P}}$-complete language A for NP has a dense exponential complexity core. □

Thus, for example, if NP is not small, then there is a dense set K of Boolean formulas in conjunctive normal form such that every machine that is consistent with SAT performs exponentially badly (either by running for more than $2^{|x|^\epsilon}$

steps or by failing to decide) on all but finitely many inputs $x \in K$. (The weaker hypothesis P $\neq$ NP was already known [19] to imply the weaker conclusion that every $\leq_m^P$-complete language for NP has a nonsparse polynomial complexity core.)

The third consequence of $\mu_p(NP) \neq 0$ to be mentioned here concerns the density of hard languages for NP. Ogiwara and Watanabe [18] recently showed that P $\neq$ NP implies that every $\leq_{btt}^P$-hard language for NP is non-sparse (i.e., is not polynomially sparse). More recently, it has been proven that the $\mu_p(NP) \neq 0$ hypothesis yields a stronger conclusion:

Theorem 2.7 (Lutz and Mayordomo [15]). If NP does not have p-measure 0, then for every real number $\alpha < 1$ (e.g., $\alpha = 0.99$), every $\leq_{n^\alpha-tt}^P$-hard language for NP is dense.

We conclude this section by noting some new consequences of the hypothesis that $\mu_p(NP) \neq 0$. The following lemma involves the exponential complexity classes E = DTIME(2^{linear}) and NE = NTIME(2^{linear}), and also the doubly exponential complexity classes, EE = $\bigcup_{c=0}^\infty$ DTIME($2^{2^{n+c}}$) and NEE = $\bigcup_{c=0}^\infty$ NTIME($2^{2^{n+c}}$).

Lemma 2.8.

1. If NP contains a P-bi-immune language, then E $\neq$ NE and EE $\neq$ NEE.
2. If NP $\cap$ co$-$NP contains a P-bi-immune language, then E $\neq$ NE $\cap$ co$-$NE and EE $\neq$ NEE $\cap$ co$-$NEE.

Theorem 2.9.

1. If NP does not have p-measure 0, then E $\neq$ NE and EE $\neq$ NEE.
2. If NP $\cap$ co$-$NP does not have p-measure 0, then E $\neq$ NE $\cap$ co$-$NE and EE $\neq$ NEE $\cap$ co$-$NEE.

Proof. This follows immediately from Theorem 2.5 and Lemma 2.8. □

Corollary 2.10. If NP does not have p-measure 0, then there is an NP search problem that does not reduce to the corresponding decision problem.

Proof. Bellare and Goldwasser [1] have shown that, if EE $\neq$ NEE, then there is an NP search problem that does not reduce to the corresponding decision problem. The present corollary follows immediately from this and Theorem 2.9. □

3 Separating Completeness Notions in NP

In this section we prove our main result, that the CvKL Conjecture holds if NP is not small:

Theorem 3.1 (Main Theorem). If NP does not have p-measure 0, then there is a language C that is $\leq_T^P$-complete, but not $\leq_m^P$-complete, for NP.

In fact, the language C exhibited will be $\leq_{2-T}^P$-complete, hence also $\leq_{3-tt}^P$-complete, for NP.

Our proof of Theorem 3.1 uses the following definitions and lemma.

Definition. The *tagged union* of languages $A_0, \cdots, A_{k-1} \subseteq \{0,1\}^*$ is the language

$$A_0 \oplus \cdots \oplus A_{k-1} = \left\{ x10^i \mid 0 \le i < k \text{ and } x \in A_i \right\}.$$

Definition. For $j \in \mathbf{N}$, the jth *strand* of a language $A \subseteq \{0,1\}^*$ is

$$A_{(j)} = \left\{ x \mid x10^j \in A \right\}.$$

Lemma 3.2 (Main Lemma). For any language $S \subseteq \{0,1\}^*$, the set

$$X = \left\{ A \subseteq \{0,1\}^* \mid A_{(0)} \le_m^P A_{(4)} \oplus (A_{(4)} \cap S) \oplus (A_{(4)} \cup S) \right\}$$

has p-measure 0.

The proof of the Main Lemma is omitted from this extended abstract.

Proof of Theorem 3.1 Assume that NP does not have p-measure 0. Let

$$X = \left\{ A \mid A_{(0)} \le_m^P A_{(4)} \oplus (A_{(4)} \cap \mathrm{SAT}) \oplus (A_{(4)} \cup \mathrm{SAT}) \right\}.$$

By the Main Lemma, X has p-measure 0, so there exists a language $A \in \mathrm{NP} - X$. Fix such a language A and let

$$C = A_{(4)} \oplus (A_{(4)} \cap \mathrm{SAT}) \oplus (A_{(4)} \cup \mathrm{SAT}).$$

Since $A \in \mathrm{NP}$, we have $A_{(0)}, A_{(4)} \in \mathrm{NP}$. Since $A_{(4)}, \mathrm{SAT} \in \mathrm{NP}$ and NP is closed under $\cap$, $\cup$, and $\oplus$, we have $C \in \mathrm{NP}$. Also, the algorithm

begin
input x;
if $x1 \in C$
then if $x10 \in C$ **then** accept
              else reject
else if $x100 \in C$ **then** accept
              else reject
end

clearly decides SAT using just two (adaptive) queries to C, so $\mathrm{SAT} \le_{2\text{-}T}^P C$. Thus C is $\le_{2\text{-}T}^P$-complete, hence certainly $\le_T^P$-complete, for NP. On the other hand, $A \notin X$, so $A_{(0)} \not\le_m^P C$. Since $A_{(0)} \in \mathrm{NP}$, it follows that C is not $\le_m^P$-complete for NP. □

4   Separating Reducibilities in NP

In this section, assuming that NP is not small, we establish the distinctness of many polynomial-time reducibilities in NP. Proofs are omitted.

The first two such results build on work of Selman [25].

Theorem 4.1. Assume that NP does not have p-measure 0.
1. There exist $A, B \in \mathrm{NP} \cup \mathrm{co-NP}$ such that $A \le_T^P B$, but $A \not\le_{\mathrm{pos-T}}^P B$.
2. There exist $A, B \in \mathrm{NP} \cup \mathrm{co-NP}$ such that $A \le_{tt}^P B$, but $A \not\le_{\mathrm{pos-}tt}^P B$.

Theorem 4.2. Assume that $\mathrm{NP} \cap \mathrm{co-NP}$ does not have p-measure 0.
1. There exist $A, B \in \mathrm{NP}$ such that $A \le_T^P B$ but $A \not\le_{\mathrm{pos-T}}^P B$.
2. There exist $A, B \in \mathrm{NP}$ such that $A \le_{tt}^P B$ but $A \not\le_{\mathrm{pos-}tt}^P B$.

The rest of our results concern the separation of various polynomial-time truth-table reducibilities in NP, according to the number of queries. Theorem 4.3 separates $\leq^{\mathrm{P}}_{(k+1)-tt}$ reducibility from $\leq^{\mathrm{P}}_{k-tt}$, for any constant k, while Theorem 4.4 separates $\leq^{\mathrm{P}}_{q-tt}$ reducibility from $\leq^{\mathrm{P}}_{r-tt}$, for $q(n) = o(\sqrt{r(n)})$ and $r(n) = O(n)$.

Theorem 4.3. If NP does not have p-measure 0, then for all $k \in \mathbf{N}$ there exist $A, B \in \mathrm{NP}$ such that $A \leq^{\mathrm{P}}_{(k+1)-tt} B$ but $A \not\leq^{\mathrm{P}}_{k-tt} B$.

For non constant query-bounds, we have the following result.

Theorem 4.4. If NP does not have p-measure 0 and $q, r : \mathbf{N} \to \mathbf{N}$ are polynomial-time computable query-counting functions satisfying the conditions $q(n) = o(\sqrt{r(n)})$ and $r(n) = O(n)$, then there exist $A, B \in \mathrm{NP}$ such that $A \leq^{\mathrm{P}}_{r-tt} B$ but $A \not\leq^{\mathrm{P}}_{q-tt} B$.

The query bounds of Theorems 4.3 and 4.4 can be relaxed if we make the stronger assumption that $\mu(\mathrm{NP} \mid \mathrm{E}_2) \neq 0$.

Theorem 4.5. If $\mu(\mathrm{NP} \mid \mathrm{E}_2) \neq 0$ and q is a polynomial-time computable query-counting function such that $q(n) = O(\log n)$, then there exist $A, B \in \mathrm{NP}$ such that $A \leq^{\mathrm{P}}_{(q+1)-tt} B$ but $A \not\leq^{\mathrm{P}}_{q-tt} B$.

Theorem 4.6. If $\mu(\mathrm{NP} \mid \mathrm{E}_2) \neq 0$ and $q, r : \mathbf{N} \to \mathbf{N}$ are polynomial-time computable query-counting functions satisfying $q(n) = o(\sqrt{r(n)})$, then there exist $A, B \in \mathrm{NP}$ such that $A \leq^{\mathrm{P}}_{r-tt} B$ but $A \not\leq^{\mathrm{P}}_{q-tt} B$.

5   Conclusion

We have shown that the hypothesis "NP does not have p-measure 0" resolves the CvKL Conjecture affirmatively. We have also shown that this hypothesis resolves other questions in complexity theory, including the class separation $\mathrm{E} \neq \mathrm{NE}$, the existence of NP search problems not reducible to the corresponding decision problems, and the separation of various truth-table reducibilities in NP. For each of these questions, the hypothesis gives the answer that seems most likely, relative to our current knowledge. Further investigation of this hypothesis and its power to resolve other questions is clearly indicated.

The most immediate open problem involves the further separation of completeness notions in NP. We have shown that the hypothesis $\mu_{\mathrm{p}}(\mathrm{NP}) \neq 0$ separates $\leq^{\mathrm{P}}_{\mathrm{T}}$-completeness ("Cook completeness") from $\leq^{\mathrm{P}}_{m}$-completeness ("Karp-Levin completeness") in NP. However, there is a large spectrum of completeness notions between $\leq^{\mathrm{P}}_{\mathrm{T}}$ and $\leq^{\mathrm{P}}_{m}$. Watanabe [26, 27] and Buhrman, Homer, and Torenvliet [4] have shown that nearly all these completeness notions are distinct in E and in NE, respectively. In light of the results of sections 3 and 4 above, it is reasonable to conjecture that the hypothesis "NP does not have p-measure 0" yields a similarly detailed separation of completeness notions in NP. Investigation of this conjecture may shed new light on NP-completeness phenomena.

Acknowledgments. We thank Alan Selman, Mitsunori Ogiwara, and Osamu Watanabe for helpful remarks.

References

1. M. Bellare and S. Goldwasser, The complexity of decision versus search, *SIAM Journal on Computing*, to appear. See also MIT Laboratory for Computer Science Technical Memorandum MIT/LCS/TM 444.

2. L. Berman and J. Hartmanis, On isomorphism and density of NP and other complete sets, *SIAM Journal on Computing* **6** (1977), pp. 305–322.

3. R. V. Book, Tally languages and complexity classes, *Information and Control* **26** (1974), pp. 186–193.

4. H. Buhrman, S. Homer, and L. Torenvliet, Completeness for nondeterministic complexity classes, *Mathematical Systems Theory* **24** (1991), pp. 179–200.

5. S. A. Cook, The complexity of theorem proving procedures, *Proceedings of the Third ACM Symposium on the Theory of Computing*, 1971, pp. 151–158.

6. S. Homer, Structural properties of nondeterministic complete sets, *Proceedings of the Fifth Annual Structure in Complexity Theory Conference*, 1990, pp. 3–10.

7. D. W. Juedes and J. H. Lutz, The complexity and distribution of hard problems, *Proceedings of the 34th IEEE Symposium on Foundations of Computer Science*, 1993, pp. 177-185. *SIAM Journal on Computing*, to appear.

8. R. M. Karp, Reducibility among combinatorial problems, In R. E. Miller and J. W. Thatcher, editors, *Complexity of Computer Computations*, pp. 85–104. Plenum Press, 1972.

9. K. Ko and D. Moore, Completeness, approximation and density, *SIAM Journal on Computing* **10** (1981), pp. 787–796.

10. R. Ladner, N. Lynch, and A. Selman, A comparison of polynomial-time reducibilities, *Theoretical Computer Science* **1** (1975), pp. 103–123.

11. L. A. Levin, Universal sequential search problems, *Problems of Information Transmission* **9** (1973), pp. 265–266.

12. L. Longpré and P. Young, Cook reducibility is faster than Karp reducibility in NP, *Journal of Computer and System Sciences* **41** (1990), pp. 389–401.

13. J. H. Lutz, Almost everywhere high nonuniform complexity, *Journal of Computer and System Sciences* **44** (1992), pp. 220–258.

14. J. H. Lutz, Resource-bounded measure, in preparation.

15. J. H. Lutz and E. Mayordomo, Measure, stochasticity, and the density of hard languages, *SIAM Journal on Computing*, to appear.

16. E. Mayordomo, Almost every set in exponential time is P-bi-immune, *Seventeenth International Symposium on Mathematical Foundations of Computer Science*, 1992, pp. 392–400. Springer-Verlag. *Theoretical Computer Science*, to appear.

17. A. R. Meyer, 1977, reported in [2].

18. M. Ogiwara and O. Watanabe, On polynomial bounded truth-table reducibility of NP sets to sparse sets, *SIAM Journal on Computing* **20** (1991), pp. 471–483.

19. P. Orponen and U. Schöning, The density and complexity of polynomial cores for intractable sets, *Information and Control* **70** (1986), pp. 54–68.

20. C. P. Schnorr, Klassifikation der Zufallsgesetze nach Komplexität und Ordnung, *Z. Wahrscheinlichkeitstheorie verw. Geb.* **16** (1970), pp. 1–21.

21. C. P. Schnorr, A unified approach to the definition of random sequences, *Mathematical Systems Theory* **5** (1971), pp. 246–258.

22. C. P. Schnorr, Zufälligkeit und Wahrscheinlichkeit, *Lecture Notes in Mathematics* **218** (1971).

23. C. P. Schnorr, Process complexity and effective random tests, *Journal of Computer and System Sciences* **7** (1973), pp. 376–388.

24. A. L. Selman, P-selective sets, tally languages, and the behavior of polynomial time reducibilities on NP, *Mathematical Systems Theory* **13** (1979), pp. 55–65.

25. A. L. Selman, Reductions on NP and P-selective sets, *Theoretical Computer Science* **19** (1982), pp. 287–304.

26. O. Watanabe, A comparison of polynomial time completeness notions, *Theoretical Computer Science* **54** (1987), pp. 249–265.

27. O. Watanabe, *On the Structure of Intractable Complexity Classes*, PhD thesis, Tokyo Institute of Technology, 1987.

28. O. Watanabe and S. Tang, On polynomial time Turing and many-one completeness in PSPACE, *Theoretical Computer Science* **97** (1992), pp. 199–215.

29. P. Young, Some structural properties of polynomial reducibilities and sets in NP, *Proceedings of the Fifteenth ACM Symposium on Theory of Computing*, 1983, pp. 392–401.

On Sets Bounded Truth-Table Reducible to P-selective Sets *

Thomas Thierauf**   Seinosuke Toda***   Osamu Watanabe[†]

Abstract. We show that if every NP set is $\leq_{btt}^P$-reducible to some P-selective set, then NP is contained in $\text{DTIME}(2^{n^{O(1/\sqrt{\log n})}})$. The result is extended for some unbounded reducibilities such as $\leq_{polylog-tt}^P$-reducibility.

1   Introduction

One of the important questions in structural complexity theory is whether every NP problem is solvable by polynomial-size circuits, i.e., NP $\subseteq$? P/poly. Furthermore, it has been asked what the deterministic time complexity of NP problems is (e.g., NP $\subseteq$ P) if NP $\subseteq$ P/poly. That is, if NP is easy in the nonuniform complexity measure, how easy is NP in the uniform complexity measure? We study such type of questions in this paper.

Let $R_T^P(\text{SPARSE})$ be the class of languages that are polynomial-time Turing reducible to some sparse set. (In general, let $R_r(\text{SPARSE})$ be the class of languages that are polynomial-time r reducible to some sparse set. Since we consider only polynomial-time reducibilities, we often omit "polynomial-time" in the following.) In other words, L is in $R_T^P(\text{SPARSE})$ if and only if L is recognizable by some polynomial-time deterministic Turing machine using some sparse set as an oracle. Since P/poly = $R_T^P(\text{SPARSE})$, the above question is equivalent to the following one: For which uniform complexity class $\mathcal{C}$ do we have NP $\subseteq R_T^P(\text{SPARSE}) \Longrightarrow$ NP $\subseteq \mathcal{C}$? While no nontrivial answer is known to this question[5], we have obtained several interesting results under the stronger assumptions that NP is contained in certain subclasses of $R_T^P(\text{SPARSE})$.

Since $R_T^P(\text{SPARSE})$ is the class of languages that are Turing reducible to some sparse set, one way of obtaining subclasses of $R_T^P(\text{SPARSE})$ is to consider some restriction on the reducibility. For example, Mahaney [Mah82] showed that if all NP sets are many-one reducible to some sparse set, then P = NP. That is,

$$\text{NP} \subseteq R_m^P(\text{SPARSE}) \implies \text{NP} \subseteq \text{P}.$$

* Part of the work was done while the authors were visiting the University of Rochester, Department of Computer Science. This research is supported in part by JSPS/NSF International Collaboration Grant JSPS-ENGR-207/NSF-INT-9116781, DFG Postdoctorial Stipend Th 472/1-1, and NSF grant CCR-8957604.
** Abteilung für Theoretische Informatik, Universtät Ulm.
*** Department Computer Science, Univiversity Electro-Communications.
† Deptartment Computer Science, Tokyo Institute of Technology.
5 We should note here that we have some evidence indicating that NP $\subseteq$ P/poly is unlikely. That is, it has been proved that NP $\subseteq$ P/poly $\Longrightarrow$ PH $\subseteq \Sigma_2^P$ [KL82]. However, although PH $\subseteq \Sigma_2^P$ indirectly shows that NP is not as difficult as we expect, it does not give any specific upper deterministic time bound for NP.

Ogiwara and Watanabe [OW91] proved a similar result for bounded truth-table reducibility, one restriction of the Turing reducibility which is more general than the many-one reducibility. They extended Mahaney's result by showing that

$$\text{NP} \subseteq \text{R}^{\text{P}}_{\text{btt}}(\text{SPARSE}) \implies \text{NP} \subseteq \text{P}.$$

This result has been improved further more recently; see [AHH+93]. However, it is open whether the result can be improved for $b(n)$-bounded truth-table reducibility for some nonconstant function $b(n)$. Indeed, Saluja [Sal92] showed that such an improvement is impossible with any relativizable technique.

Other subclasses of $\text{R}^{\text{P}}_{\text{T}}(\text{SPARSE})$ are obtained by considering P-selective sets introduced by Selman [Sel79]. A set A is P-selective, if there exists a polynomial-time computable function that selects one of two given input strings such that if any of the two strings is in A, then also the selected one. Let SELECT denote the class of P-selective sets, and for any polynomial-time reducibility r, let $\text{R}_r(\text{SELECT})$ denote the class of languages that are r reducible to some P-selective set. It follows from Theorem 12 of [Sel82b] and Theorem 3 of [Ko83] that $\text{R}^{\text{P}}_{\text{T}}(\text{SELECT}) = \text{R}^{\text{P}}_{\text{T}}(\text{SPARSE})$. Thus, by using a restricted reducibility r, we define some subclass $\text{R}_r(\text{SELECT})$ of $\text{R}^{\text{P}}_{\text{T}}(\text{SPARSE})$ that can be different from $\text{R}_r(\text{SPARSE})$. (For example, $\text{R}^{\text{P}}_{\text{tt}}(\text{SELECT}) \neq \text{R}^{\text{P}}_{\text{tt}}(\text{SPARSE})$ because $\text{R}^{\text{P}}_{\text{tt}}(\text{SPARSE}) = \text{R}^{\text{P}}_{\text{T}}(\text{SPARSE})$ but $\text{R}^{\text{P}}_{\text{tt}}(\text{SELECT}) \subsetneq \text{R}^{\text{P}}_{\text{T}}(\text{SELECT})$ [Wat90].)

For some of those $\text{R}_r(\text{SELECT})$ subclasses, we have been able to solve our question. Selman [Sel79] proved that no NP set is many-one reducible to a P-selective set unless P = NP. Furthermore, by extending this argument slightly, one can also prove that no NP set is 1-truth table reducible to a P-selective set unless P = NP [HHO+93]. That is,

$$\text{NP} \subseteq \text{R}^{\text{P}}_{\text{1-tt}}(\text{SELECT}) \implies \text{NP} \subseteq \text{P}.$$

For a more general type of reducibility, Toda [Tod91] and Beigel [Bei88] proved the following.

$$\text{NP} \subseteq \text{R}^{\text{P}}_{\text{tt}}(\text{SELECT}) \implies \text{NP} \subseteq \text{R}. \tag{1}$$

Note that the last upper bound of NP (namely, the class R) is a randomized complexity class. Thus, one interesting question is to show some deterministic upper bound from a more general assumption than "NP $\subseteq \text{R}^{\text{P}}_{\text{1-tt}}(\text{SELECT})$". In this paper, we study this question and obtain the following result.

$$\text{NP} \subseteq \text{R}^{\text{P}}_{\text{btt}}(\text{SELECT}) \implies \text{NP} \subseteq \text{DTIME}(2^{n^{O(1/\sqrt{\log n})}}). \tag{2}$$

The result is extended to $\text{R}^{\text{P}}_{b(n)\text{-tt}}(\text{SELECT})$ for some polynomial-time computable function $b(n)$, e.g., $b(n) = (\log n)^{O(1)}$.[6]

Jenner and Torán [JT93] obtained a weaker subexponential upper bound for NP (from a weaker assumption) by a very different technique. However, it seems impossible [Tor93] to obtain the same upper bound by their technique.

---

[6] The authors have been informed by Mitsunori Ogiwara that he has quite recently improved the result to NP $\subseteq \text{R}^{\text{P}}_{\text{btt}}(\text{SELECT}) \implies \text{NP} = \text{P}$.

In the following, we briefly explain the outline of our proof, but let us first review the proof of (1). First note the following fact [Tod91, Bei88]:

$$\text{UP} \subseteq \text{R}_{tt}^{P}(\text{SELECT}) \implies \text{UP} \subseteq \text{P},$$

where UP is the class of languages recognized by polynomial-time nondeterministic Turing machines that have at most one accepting path on each input. Indeed, from $\text{NP} \subseteq \text{R}_{tt}^{P}(\text{SELECT})$, one can deduce a slightly stronger consequence: $(*)$ for any polynomial-time nondeterministic computation, if it has *exactly one* accepting path, then the path is computable in deterministic polynomial time. This is used to show $\text{NP} \subseteq \text{R}$. For any polynomial-time nondeterministic machine and any input, its nondeterministic computation on the input can be regarded as a tree T. Roughly speaking, by using Valiant-Vazirani's randomized hashing technique [VV86], we can define subtrees $T_1, ..., T_m$ of T so that if T has some accepting path, then, say, $1/4$ of $T_1, ..., T_m$ has exactly one accepting path. (These subtrees share the same root with T, and hence, each subtree's accepting path is also T's accepting path.) Then from $(*)$, for such T_k with exactly one accepting path, one can compute the accepting path. Thus, by choosing T_k randomly for several times, one can compute some accepting path of T with high probability if T indeed has an accepting path. This is the idea of showing $\text{NP} \subseteq \text{R}$.

We also use $(*)$ for proving (2). Consider again any nondeterministic computation tree T. From our assumption, namely, $\text{NP} \subseteq \text{R}_{btt}^{P}(\text{SELECT})$, we can define subtrees $T_1', ..., T_n'$ of T such that if T has some accepting path, then some T_k has exactly one accepting path. Again from $(*)$, if T_k has exactly one accepting path, then it is verified by some polynomial-time deterministic machine M. Thus, the NP question "Does T have an accepting path?" is reduced to another NP question "Is there any k such that M verifies that T_k' has an accepting path?". The important point here is that n can be taken fairly small compared with the number of paths in T. (*Cf.* The randomized hashing technique needs to define large number of subtrees.) Hence, for solving the reduced NP question, one need a smaller number of nondeterministic guesses. Therefore, iterating this process, we can finally solve the original problem deterministically. This is the outline of obtaining our *deterministic* upper bound.

2 Preliminaries

In this abstract, we follow the standard definitions and notations in computational complexity theory (see, e.g., [BDG88, BDG91]).

Throughout this abstract, we fix our alphabet to $\Sigma = \{0, 1\}$. For any set X, we denote the complement of X as $\overline{X}$. Natural numbers are encoded in Σ^* in an ordinary way. For any string x, let $|x|$ denote the length of x, and for any set X, let $\|X\|$ denote the cardinality of X. We consider a standard one-to-one pairing function from $\Sigma^* \times \Sigma^*$ to Σ^* that is computable and invertible in polynomial time. For inputs x and y, we denote the output of the pairing function by (x, y); this notation is extended to denote any n tuple. For a function f, we simply write $f(x, y)$ instead of $f((x, y))$. A set S of strings is called *sparse* if for some polynomial p and for all n, $\|S^{\leq n}\| \leq p(n)$, where $S^{\leq n}$ is the set of strings $x \in S$ of length $\leq n$.

We use the standard Turing machine as our computation model. P (resp., NP) denotes the class of languages that can be recognized by some polynomial-time deterministic (resp., nondeterministic) Turing machine. We assume that for any nondeterministic computation, every nondeterministic configuration of a Turing machine has exactly two succeeding ones, and hence, each nondeterministic computation corresponds naturally to a binary tree.

For any sets A and B, we say that A is *many-one reducible to* B (and write $A \leq_m^P B$) if there is some polynomial-time computable function f, the *reduction*, such that for any $x \in \Sigma^*$, we have $x \in A \iff f(x) \in B$. A set C is called *NP-complete* if (i) every NP set is many-one reducible to C, and (ii) C itself is in NP. The reducibility notions that we are interested in are generalization of this "many-one reducibility". We say that A is *truth-table reducible to* B (and write $A \leq_{tt}^P B$) if there are two polynomial-time computable functions, *generator* g that, for a given $x \in \Sigma^*$, produces a set of strings, and *evaluator* e that, when knowing which of the strings produced by g are in B, decides membership of x in A. That is, for any $x \in \Sigma^*$,

$$x \in A \iff e(x, g(x), g(x) \cap B) = 1,$$

where we assume that $g(x)$ (resp., $g(x) \cap B$) is encoded as a string by some appropriate coding method. For any $b(n) \geq 0$, we say that A is $b(n)$-*truth-table reducible to* B (and write $A \leq_{b(n)\text{-}tt}^P B$) if the generator g produces at most $b(n)$ strings for each input of length n. If A is $\leq_{k\text{-}tt}^P$-reducible to B for some constant $k \geq 0$, we say that A is *bounded-truth-table reducible to* B (and write $A \leq_{btt}^P B$). A set H is $\leq_{b(n)\text{-}tt}^P$-*hard* (resp., $\leq_{btt}^P$-*hard*) for NP if every NP set is $\leq_{b(n)\text{-}tt}^P$- (resp., $\leq_{btt}^P$-) reducible to H.

P-selective sets were introduced by Selman [Sel79] as the polynomial-time analog of semi-recursive sets [Joc68]. A set A is *P-selective*, if there exists a polynomial-time computable function f, called a *P-selector for A*, such that for all $x, y \in \Sigma^*$,

1. $f(x, y) \in \{x, y\}$, and
2. if $x \in A$ or $y \in A$, then $f(x, y) \in A$.

Intuitively, f selects the one of two given strings that is "more likely" to be in A. More formally, if $f(x, y) = x$ and $y \in A$, then $x \in A$.

Ko [Ko83] showed that from the P-selector function f of a P-selective set A, one can define a linear ordering on a quotient of Σ^* such that A is the union of an initial segment of this ordering. Toda [Tod91] modified this to an ordering on a given finite set Q (instead of Σ^*). Here, we use this ordering. That is, the relation $\preceq_{f,Q}$ on Q is defined as follows: For all $x, y \in Q$,

$$x \preceq_{f,Q} y \iff \exists z_1, \ldots, z_n \in Q : f(z_i, z_{i+1}) = z_i \text{ for } i = 1, \ldots, n-1,$$
$$f(x, z_1) = x, \text{ and } f(z_n, y) = z_n.$$

Define $x \cong_{f,Q} y \iff x \preceq_{f,Q} y \wedge y \preceq_{f,Q} x$. Then $\cong_{f,Q}$ is an equivalence relation on Q, and $\preceq_{f,Q}$ induces a linear ordering on the quotient $Q/\cong_{f,Q}$. This is reflected by the following partial ordering $\prec_{f,Q}$ on Q:

$$x \prec_{f,Q} y \iff x \preceq_{f,Q} y \wedge x \not\cong_{f,Q} y.$$

For simplicity, we omit the subscripts f and Q when both are clear from the context. For technical reasons, we introduce a minimum and a maximum element, denoted as $\bot$ and $\top$ respectively, such that $\bot \prec x \prec \top$, for all $x \in Q$.

It is easy to see that the relations $\prec$ and $\cong$ are decidable in polynomial time in $\sum_{x \in Q} |x|$. The crucial point is that $A \cap Q$ is an initial segment of Q with respect to $\preceq$. That is, we have

(*) $\exists z \in Q \cup \{\bot\}: Q \cap A = \{y \in Q \mid y \preceq z\}$ and $Q \cap \overline{A} = \{y \in Q \mid y \succ z\}$.

We call a string z witnessing (*) a *cutpoint* of A in Q (with respect to $\preceq$). A consequence of this property is that $\forall x, y \in Q: x \preceq y \land y \in A \implies x \in A$.

3 Main Result

Here, we state the proof of our main result. We begin by recalling some notion and result that will be used in our proof.

Definition 1. [ESY84] A *promise problem* is a pair of sets (Q, R). A set L is called a *solution* of the promise problem (Q, R), if for all $x \in Q$ we have $x \in R \iff x \in L$.

Toda [Tod91] showed that if all NP sets are $\leq_{tt}^P$-reducible to some P-selective set, then the promise problem $(1SAT, SAT)$ has a solution in P, where $1SAT$ is the set of Boolean formulas that have at most one satisfying assignment. We restate his theorem in a slightly more general form.

Theorem 2. *[Tod91] If* NP $\subseteq$ R$_{tt}^P$(SELECT)*, then, for any NP machine N the promise problem $(1L(N), L(N))$ has a solution in P, where $1L(N)$ is the set of strings x such that N has at most one accepting path on input x. Furthermore, if N is $p(n)$-time bounded, then the solution is in* DTIME$(q_T(p(n)))$*, for some fixed polynomial q_T.*

Now, we prove our main theorem.

Theorem 3. *If there exists a P-selective set that is $\leq_{btt}^P$-hard for NP, then* NP $\subseteq$ DTIME$(2^{n^{O(1/\sqrt{\log n})}})$*.*

Remark *The following proof also works for some "unbounded" reducibility. For example, the theorem is provable for $\leq_{polylog\text{-}tt}^P$-reducibility.*

Proof. Let us first define two NP sets. The first one is similar to the canonical universal NP complete set except that the number of nondeterministic steps is stated explicitly.

$UNIV = \{ (M, x, 0^d, 0^t) \mid$ there exists $w \in \Sigma^d$ such that the deterministic machine M accepts input (x, w) in at most t steps $\}$.

A string $w \in \Sigma^d$ is called a *nondeterministic path* of $(M, x, 0^d, 0^t)$, and if w witnesses $(M, x, 0^d, 0^t) \in UNIV$, it is called an *accepting path* of $(M, x, 0^d, 0^t)$. Obviously, $UNIV$ is NP complete.

Our second set is defined similarly except that it has, as an additional component, the prefix of an accepting path for the considered machine.

$$PrefixPATH = \{ (M, x, 0^d, 0^t, u) \mid \text{there exists } v \in \Sigma^{d-|u|} \text{ such that}$$
$$\text{the deterministic machine } M \text{ accepts input } (x, uv)$$
$$\text{in at most } t \text{ steps } \}.$$

Consider any instance $\tau = (M, x, 0^d, 0^t)$ for $UNIV$, and let it be fixed for a while. We can regard τ's nondeterministic paths as paths in some binary tree T. That is, T is a binary tree whose nodes are of the form (τ, u), for $u \in \Sigma^{\leq d}$. T's root is (τ, λ) (where λ is empty string), and T's leaves are nodes (τ, u) such that $|u| = d$. A binary string $u \in \Sigma^{\leq d}$ is regarded as a path from the root to (τ, u). A string $w \in \Sigma^d$ is called an *accepting path* of T if M accepts input (x, w). Clearly, $\tau \in UNIV$ if and only if there exists an accepting path in T.

Let c and e be some integers that will be specified later. Below, we define $c^{\lceil d/e \rceil}$ subtrees T_k of T in such a way that if there is an accepting path in T, then there exist a subtree T_k that has *exactly one* accepting path. That is,

$$\tau \in UNIV \iff \exists w \in \Sigma^d : w \text{ is an accepting path in } T \qquad (3)$$
$$\iff \exists k \leq c^{\lceil d/e \rceil} : T_k \text{ has exactly one accepting path.} \qquad (4)$$

At this point, we can explain our proof idea; that is, the strategy of deciding whether $\tau \in UNIV$ in deterministic subexponential-time. Consider a promise problem $(1SubTREE, SubTREE)$, where $1SubTREE$ is the set of T_k with at most one accepting path, and $SubTREE$ is the set of T_k with an accepting path. Then since we are assuming that $\text{NP} \subseteq \text{R}^{\text{P}}_{tt}(\text{SELECT})$, by Theorem 2, this promise problem has a solution in P. Thus if T_k has exactly one accepting path, we can verify it in polynomial time. Hence, both condition (3) and (4) are NP-type predicates for deciding whether $\tau \in UNIV$. While there are 2^d possibilities for w, we can reduce the scope of k by choosing e large; in other words, while d (binary) nondeterministic guesses are necessary for the first NP-type predicate, $\dfrac{d \log c}{e}$ guesses are enough for the second. On the other hand, enlarging e will increase the time to decide the promise problem. We will see below that by appropriately choosing e (i.e., $e \approx \log c \log n$), we can reduce the number of nondeterministic guesses by a factor of about $1/\log n$, without increasing the time to decide the promise problem too much. That is, the original NP-type predicate is reduced to a simpler one. By iterating this process, we can finally solve the problem without using guesses, i.e., deterministically, and we will see that the whole process can be done in subexponential time.

Let us define the subtrees more precisely. For this, we divide T into "blocks" of depth e. In other words, for each h, where $0 \leq h \leq \lceil d/e \rceil - 1$, and $u \in \Sigma^{h \cdot e}$, we consider a set $X(\tau, u) = \{ (\tau, uv) \mid v \in \Sigma^e \}$ of nodes in T, which is regarded as a block of depth e.[7] Notice that if $(\tau, u) \in PrefixPATH$, then some elements of $X(\tau, u)$ also belong to $PrefixPATH$. Here, for the decomposition of T satisfying (4), we would like to divide $X(\tau, u)$ into $X_1(\tau, u), \ldots, X_r(\tau, u)$ so that (if $(\tau, u) \in PrefixPATH$ then) some $X_i(\tau, u)$ has exactly one element in $PrefixPATH$. Key point of our proof is that

---

[7] Precisely speaking, when $|u| = (\lceil d/e \rceil - 1)e$ (i.e., $h = \lceil d/e \rceil - 1$), $X(\tau, u)$ should be $\{ (\tau, uv) \mid v \in \Sigma^{d-|u|} \}$. In the following, we omit explaining such exceptional cases.

this is possible by using the assumption that *PrefixPATH* ($\in$ NP) is $\leq^{P}_{btt}$-reducible to some P-selective set. That is, we have the following lemma.

Key Lemma. *Let $b > 0$ and let L be any set that is $\leq^{P}_{b\text{-}tt}$-reducible to some P-selective set. Then for any set X of strings of length n, there exist r disjoint subsets $X_1, \ldots, X_r$ of X, where $r \leq 6(\lfloor b/2 \rfloor + 1) - 1$, with the following property.*

$$X \cap L \neq \emptyset \iff \exists i \in \{1, \ldots, r\} : \| X_i \cap L \| = 1.$$

Furthermore, we can compute $X_1, \ldots, X_r$ in polynomial time w.r.t. n and $\| X \|$.

Since *PrefixPATH* is in NP, for some $b > 0$ it is $\leq^{P}_{b\text{-}tt}$-reducible to some P-selective set by assumption. Thus, from this lemma (with $L = PrefixPATH$ and $X = X(\tau, u)$) we can divide each $X(\tau, u)$ into c disjoint subsets $X_1(\tau, u), \ldots, X_c(\tau, u)$ of $X(\tau, u)$ such that

$$(\tau, u) \in PrefixPATH \iff$$
$$\exists j \in \{1, \ldots, c\} : X_j(\tau, u) \text{ has exactly one element in } PrefixPATH,$$

where $c = 6(\lfloor b/2 \rfloor + 1) - 1$. (For simplifying our discussion, we assume that $X(\tau, u)$ is always divided into exactly c subsets; we may assume this by defining $X_j(\tau, u) = \emptyset$, for all j, where $r < j \leq c$.) An important point to note here is that c does not depend on e.

In order to define subtrees T_k of T, we assign an integer label k to each node (τ, u), where $u = v_1 v_2 \cdots v_h$ for some $1 \leq h \leq \lceil d/e \rceil$ and $v_1, \ldots, v_h \in \Sigma^e$. The label of (τ, u) is determined by the *history* $(j_1, \ldots, j_h)$ of indices, where each j_i $(1 \leq i \leq h)$ is the index such that $(\tau, v_1 \cdots v_i) \in X_{j_i}(\tau, v_1 \cdots v_{i-1})$. Since the sets $X_1(\tau, v_1 \cdots v_{i-1})$, $\ldots$, $X_c(\tau, v_1 \cdots v_{i-1})$ are pair-wise disjoint, each node has an unique history and label. Note that each history is expressed as a path (from the root to some node) of a c-ary tree. We give numbers to nodes of the c-ary tree as in Figure 1 and regard them as history labels. Then each node of T is given the label associated with its history.

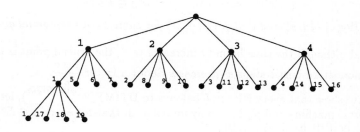

Fig. 1. Tree with branching factor 4 and its labeling.

Define *history*(τ, u) to be the history $(j_1, \ldots, j_h)$ of (τ, u), and define *label*$(j_1, \ldots, j_h)$ to be the label of the history $(j_1, \ldots, j_h)$ in the c-ary tree. Then

$label(\tau, u)$ is defined as $label(history(\tau, u))$. It is easy to see that the label of (τ, u) is bounded by c^{h+1}; that is, no node in T is assigned a label $> c^{\lceil d/e \rceil}$. Now, for each k, where $1 \le k \le c^{\lceil d/e \rceil}$, define T_k as the subtree of T consisting of all nodes with label k and their father nodes. Then we have the following.

Claim 1 *There exists an accepting path in T if and only if for some k, $1 \le k \le c^{\lceil d/e \rceil}$, T_k has exactly one accepting path.*

Next, consider the following set.

$$SubTREE_e \;=\; \{\, (M, x, 0^d, 0^t, k) \mid 1 \le k \le c^{\lceil d/e \rceil} \text{ and } T_k \text{ has an accepting path,}$$
$$\text{where } T_k \text{ is the subtree of } T \text{ defined by } (M, x, 0^d, 0^t) \,\}.$$

For each e, clearly $SubTREE_e$ is in NP and thus we could now solve the promise problem $(1SubTREE_e, SubTREE_e)$ deterministically in polynomial time (Theorem 2). But we should be careful about the polynomial-time bound, which depends on the choice of e. Precisely speaking, $(1SubTREE_e, SubTREE_e)$ has the following upper bound.

Claim 2 *For some polynomial q_S and for all $e \ge 1$, there exists a deterministic machine M_e such that (i) M_e is $q_S(n + 2^e)$-time bounded, and (ii) $L(M_e)$ is a solution of $(1SubTREE_e, SubTREE_e)$. (That is, for every input $\eta = (M, x, 0^d, 0^t, k)$, (i) M_e halts in $q_S(|\eta| + 2^e)$ steps, and (ii) if $\eta \in 1SubTREE_e$, then $\eta \in SubTREE_e \iff M_e$ accepts η.)*

Thus, we reached our goal to reduce the scope of the existential quantifier; that is, $(\tau \in UNIV \iff) \exists w \in \Sigma^d : w$ is an accepting path in $T \iff \exists k \le c^{\lceil d/e \rceil} : (\tau, k) \in L(M_e)$. Here, notice that we can easily translate our reduced problem to a new instance for $UNIV$. Then we can apply the above construction recursively!

Claim 3 *For any e, there exists some $\tilde{M}_e$ such that for every input $\tau = (M, x, 0^d, 0^t)$,*

$$\tau \in UNIV \iff (\tilde{M}_e, \tau, 0^{d'}, 0^{t'}) \in UNIV,$$

where $d' = \lceil \log c \rceil \cdot \lceil d/e \rceil$ and $t' = q_U(|\tau| + 2^e)$ for some fixed polynomial q_U.

Note that although the time bound t increases to t', the crucial point is that the number of nondeterministic steps d' decreases about a factor $\dfrac{\log c}{e}$.

Finally, to show that every NP set L belongs to $\mathrm{DTIME}(2^{n^{O(1/\sqrt{\log n})}})$, let M_L be a deterministic machine and p_L be a polynomial such that for every $x \in \Sigma^*$, $x \in L \iff (M_L, x, 0^{p_L(|x|)}, 0^{p_L(|x|)}) \in UNIV$.

Let x be any string for which we want to decide membership in L. Let $n = |x|$, and we define $e = \lceil 3\delta(n) \log c \rceil$, where function δ will be chosen appropriately at the end of the proof. (We assume that n is large enough so that $e \ge 3$.) First, define $x_0 = x$, $d_0 = p_L(n)$, $t_0 = p_L(n)$, and $\tau_0 = (M_L, x_0, 0^{d_0}, 0^{t_0})$. For each $i \ge 1$, define inductively $x_i = \tau_{i-1}$, $d_i = \lceil \log c \rceil \cdot \lceil d_{i-1}/e \rceil$, $t_i = q_U(|\tau_{i-1}| + 2^e)$, and $\tau_i = (\tilde{M}_e, x_i, 0^{d_i}, 0^{t_i})$, until $d_i < e$ (= $\lceil 3\delta(n) \log c \rceil$). Let m be the first integer such that $d_m < e$. Then from Claim 3, we have $\tau_0 \in UNIV \iff \tau_1 \in UNIV \iff \cdots \iff \tau_m \in UNIV$. On the other hand, $x \in L \iff \tau_0 \in UNIV$. Hence, $x \in L \iff \tau_m \in UNIV$. That is, the problem of deciding $x \in L$ is reduced to that of deciding $\tau_m \in UNIV$.

Let us evaluate the deterministic computation time for deciding $\tau_m \in UNIV$. First, we give an upper bound for t_m. Note that for some polynomial p_1, we have $|\tau_i| \leq p_1(t_i)$. Thus, $t_i = q_U(|\tau_{i-1}| + 2^e) \leq q_U(p_1(t_{i-1}) + 2^e) \leq q_U(p_1 \circ q_U(\cdots(p_1 \circ q_U(p_L(n) + 2^e))\cdots) + 2^e$. Hence, for some constant c_1 and c_2, we have $t_m \leq n^{(c_1)^m} 2^{(c_1)^m e} = 2^{(c_1)^m (e + \log n)} \leq 2^{(c_1)^m (c_2 \delta(n) \log c + \log n)}$. On the other hand, note that for any $d \geq e \geq 3$, $d' = \lceil \log c \rceil \cdot \lceil d/e \rceil \leq (3d \log c)/e \leq d/\delta(n)$. Thus, $m \leq \log_{\delta(n)} d_0 \leq c_3 \log n / \log \delta(n)$, for some constant c_3. Therefore, for some c_4,

$$t_m \leq 2^{((c_1)^{\frac{c_3 \log n}{\log \delta(n)}})(c_2 \delta(n) \log c + \log n)} \leq 2^{(n^{\frac{c_4}{\log \delta(n)}})(c_2 \delta(n) \log c + \log n)},$$

which takes the smallest order when $\delta(n) = n^{1/\sqrt{\log n}}$. Thus, we define $\delta(n) = n^{1/\sqrt{\log n}}$; then for some constant c_5, we have $t_m \leq 2^{n^{c_5/\sqrt{\log n}}}$.

Clearly, "$\tau_m \in UNIV$?" is deterministically decidable in polynomial time w.r.t. $|\tau_m|$. Also τ_m is deterministically computable in polynomial time w.r.t. $|\tau_m|$. Recall that $|\tau_m| \leq p_1(t_m)$. Thus, the deterministic computation time for computing τ_m and deciding $\tau_m \in UNIV$ is polynomially bounded by t_m. Therefore, with some constant c_0, it is bounded by $2^{n^{c_0/\sqrt{\log n}}}$. That is, $x \in L$ is deterministically decidable in $2^{n^{c_0/\sqrt{\log n}}}$ steps. $\qquad\square$

It remains to prove the Key Lemma.

Proof of the Key Lemma. Let $b > 0$ and let g and e be the generator and the evaluator of a $\leq^{P}_{b\text{-tt}}$-reduction from L to a P-selective set A, and let f be a P-selector for A. Define Q to be the set of queries to A for all $x \in X$; that is, $Q = \bigcup_{x \in X} g(x)$. Let $\preceq$ denote $\preceq_{f,Q}$. Notice that $\preceq$ is polynomial-time decidable w.r.t. n and $\|X\|$.

For any $u, v \in Q \cup \{\perp, \top\}$, an *interval* $[u, v)$ is a set $\{w \in Q \mid u \preceq w \prec v\}$. For any set $\mathcal{I}$ of intervals, we simply write $\bigcup \mathcal{I}$ for $\bigcup_{I \in \mathcal{I}} I$.

For each $x \in X$, we can define an associated set of intervals in Q that characterizes the membership of x in L according to a cutpoint of A in Q. More formally, letting $g(x) = \{y_1 \preceq \cdots \preceq y_h\}$ (where $h \leq b$), $y_0 = \perp$, and $y_{h+1} = \top$, we define

$$\mathcal{I}_x = \{[y_i, y_{i+1}) \mid e(x, g(x), \{y_1, \ldots, y_i\}) = 1, \text{ where } i \in \{0, \ldots, h\}\}.$$

If two adjacent intervals, i.e., $[y_i, y_{i+1})$ and $[y_{i+1}, y_{i+2})$, belong to $\mathcal{I}_x$, we regard them as one interval $[y_i, y_{i+2})$. Note that each $\mathcal{I}_x$ has at most $\lfloor b/2 \rfloor + 1$ intervals.

Let $J_x = \bigcup \mathcal{I}_x$, $J = \bigcup_{x \in X} J_x$, and let z_* be a cutpoint of A in Q. Then, for all $x \in X$, we have $x \in L \iff z_* \in J_x$, and hence, $X \cap L \neq \emptyset \iff z_* \in J$.

By the Combinatorial Lemma stated below, we can select r subsets $X_1, \ldots, X_r$ of X such that

$$\forall z \in J, \exists i \in \{1, \ldots, r\}, \exists x! \in X_i : z \in J_x,$$

where $r \leq 6(\lfloor b/2 \rfloor + 1) - 1$.

Now, we show that $X_1, \ldots, X_r$ have the property claimed in the lemma. It suffices to consider the if direction. Suppose that $X \cap L \neq \emptyset$. Hence, $z_* \in J$. Then, from the above property of $X_1, \ldots, X_r$, there exists some X_i that has exactly one x such that

$z_* \in J_x$. This means that X_i has exactly one element (namely, x) in L. (Recall that $x \in L \iff z_* \in J_x$.) Therefore, $\|X_i \cap L\| = 1$. □ Key Lemma

Combinatorial Lemma. *Let $\{\mathcal{I}_x\}_{x \in X}$ be any family of sets of intervals in Q, where the index set X is finite, and each $\mathcal{I}_x$ consists of at most ℓ intervals. Let $\mathcal{I}$ be the set of intervals appearing in $\mathcal{I}_x$ for some $x \in X$; i.e., $\mathcal{I} = \{I \mid I \in \mathcal{I}_x \text{ for some } x \in X\}$. Let $J = \bigcup \mathcal{I}$ and $J_x = \bigcup \mathcal{I}_x$. Then there exist $r \leq 6\ell - 1$ disjoint subsets $X_1, \ldots, X_r$ of X such that*

$$\forall z \in J, \exists i \in \{1, \ldots, r\}, \exists! x \in X_i : z \in J_x.$$

Furthermore, if $\preceq$ is polynomial-time computable w.r.t. $\sum_{u \in Q} |u|$, then the selection of $X_1, \ldots, X_r$ can be done in polynomial time w.r.t. ℓ, $\|X\|$, and $\sum_{u \in Q} |u|$.

Proof. First we construct a minimum size cover of $\mathcal{I}$. We say that $\hat{\mathcal{I}}$ is a *minimum size cover* of $\mathcal{I}$ if (i) $\hat{\mathcal{I}} \subseteq \mathcal{I}$, (ii) $\bigcup \hat{\mathcal{I}} = J$, and (iii) no $\mathcal{I}'$ such that $\|\mathcal{I}'\| < \|\hat{\mathcal{I}}\|$ satisfy both (i) and (ii). From $\mathcal{I}$, we can construct such a set in polynomial-time by a greedy algorithm.

Next, we define a graph from $\hat{\mathcal{I}}$. For each $I \in \hat{\mathcal{I}}$, define $support(I)$ to be an index x such that $I \in \mathcal{I}_x$, and let $support(\hat{\mathcal{I}}) = \{support(I) \mid I \in \hat{\mathcal{I}}\}$. (If there are many indices x such that $I \in \mathcal{I}_x$, choose one for $support(I)$.) Consider the following undirected (simple) graph $G = (V, E)$.

$$V = support(\hat{\mathcal{I}}), \text{ and}$$
$$E = \{\{x, x'\} \mid \exists I \in \hat{\mathcal{I}} : support(I) = x, \text{ and } J_{x'} \cap I \neq \emptyset\}.$$

Using the minimality of $\hat{\mathcal{I}}$, we can show the following property of G.

Claim 4 *Every subgraph of G has a vertex with degree at most $6\ell - 2$*

From Claim 4, we derive the crucial property of G.

Claim 5 *G is $6\ell - 1$-colorable. That is, there exists a partition $V_1, \ldots, V_r$ of V, where $r \leq 6\ell - 1$, such that every V_i forms an independent set in G. Furthermore, some polynomial-time algorithm computes the partition from a given G.*

Proof of Claim 5. G is colorable by a simple greedy algorithm that colors vertices in order of their degree (from the largest ones). This fact is provable by induction on the size of G. Let x be the vertex of G that is colored last by the algorithm, and let $\hat{G}$ be the subgraph of G obtained by deleting x from G. Then by induction, the algorithm colors $\hat{G}$ correctly; thus, the algorithm works correctly before coloring x. Now, since the degree of x is at most $6\ell - 2$, the algorithm will find a color for x. □ Claim 5

Now, for each i, where $1 \leq i \leq r$, define $X_i = V_i$. Let us see why $X_1, \ldots, X_r$ satisfy the condition of the lemma. Consider any $z \in J$. Since $\hat{\mathcal{I}}$ is a cover of J, there is some $I \in \hat{\mathcal{I}}$ containing z. Let $x = support(I)$, and let X_i be the subset containing x. Then from Claim 5, no other x' in X_i is adjacent to x. That is, $J_{x'} \cap I = \emptyset$. Therefore, there exists exactly one index (namely x) in X_i such that $z \in J_x$.

Finally, we note that $X_1, \ldots, X_r$ are polynomial-time computable (if $\preceq$ is polynomial-time decidable), which is clear from the above discussion. □

References

[AHH+93] V. Arvind, Y. Han, L. Hemachandra, J. Köbler, A. Lozano, M. Mundhenk, M. Ogiwara, U. Schöning, R. Silvestri, and T. Thierauf. Reductions to sets of low information content. *Recent Developments in Complexity Theory*. Cambridge University Press, 1993. (Also available as Technical Report TR-417, University of Rochester, Department of Computer Science, Rochester, NY, April 1992.)

[All86] E. Allender. The complexity of sparse sets in P. In *Proceedings 1st Structure in Complexity Theory Conference*, 1–11, IEEE Computer Society, 1986.

[BDG88] J. Balcázar, J. Díaz, and J. Gabarró. *Structural Complexity I*. EATCS Monographs on Theoretical Computer Science, Springer-Verlag (1988).

[BDG91] J. Balcázar, J. Díaz, and J. Gabarró. *Structural Complexity II*. EATCS Monographs on Theoretical Computer Science, Springer-Verlag (1991).

[Bei88] R. Beigel. NP-hard sets are P-superterse unless R = NP. Technical Report 88-04, Department of Computer Science, The John Hopkins University, 1988.

[CLR90] T. Corman, C. Leiserson, and R. Rivest. *Introduction to Algorithms*. The MIT Press, McGraw-Hill Book Company, 1990.

[ESY84] S. Evan, A. Selman, and Y. Yacobi. The complexity of promise problems with applications to public-key cryptography. *Information and Control*, 61:114–133, 1984.

[HHO+93] L. Hemachandra, A. Hoene, M. Ogiwara, A. Selman, T. Thierauf, and J. Wang. Selectivity. In *Proceedings of the 5th International Conference on Computing and Information*, 1993.

[HOW92] L. Hemachandra, M. Ogiwara, and O. Watanabe. How hard are sparse sets? In *Proc. 7th Structure in Complexity Theory Conference*, IEEE 222–238, 1992.

[JT93] B. Jenner and J. Torán. Computing functions with parallel queries to NP. In *Proc. 8th Structure in Complexity Theory Conference*, IEEE 280–291, 1993.

[Joc68] C. Jockusch. Semirecursive sets and positive reducibility. *Transactions of the AMS*, 131(2):420–436, 1968.

[KL82] R. Karp, R. Lipton. Turing machines that take advice. *L'Enseignement Mathématique*, 28:191-209, 1982.

[Ko83] K. Ko. On self-reducibility and weak P-selectivity. *Journal of Computer and System Sciences*, 26:209–221, 1983.

[LLS75] R. Ladner, N. Lynch, and A. Selman. A comparison of polynomial time reducibilities. *Theoretical Computer Science*, 1(2):103–124, 1975.

[Mah82] S. Mahaney. Sparse complete sets for NP: solution of a conjecture of Berman and Hartmanis. *Journal of Computer and System Sciences* 25:130-143, 1982.

[OW91] M. Ogiwara and O. Watanabe. On polynomial-time bounded truth-table reducibility of NP sets to sparse sets. *SIAM Journal on Computing*, 20(3):471–483, 1991.

[Sal92] S. Saluja. Relativized limitations of the left set technique and closure classes of sparse sets. Manuscript.

[Sch90] U. Schöning. The power of counting. In *Complexity Theory Retrospective* (A. Selman Ed.), Springer-Verlag (1990), 204–223.

[Sel79] A. Selman. P-selective sets, tally languages, and the behavior of polynomial time reducibilities on NP. *Mathematical Systems Theory*, 13:55–65, 1979.

[Sel82a] A. Selman. Analogues of semirecursive sets and effective reducibilities to the study of NP complexity. *Information and Control*, 52:36–51, 1982.

[Sel82b] A. Selman. Reductions on NP and P-selective sets. *Theoretical Computer Science*, 19:287–304, 1982.

[Sto77]   L. Stockmeyer. The polynomial-time hierarchy. *Theoretical Computer Science* 3:1−22, 1977.

[Tod91]   S. Toda. On polynomial-time truth-table reducibilities of intractable sets to P-selective sets. *Mathematical Systems Theory*, 24:69–82, 1991.

[Tor93]   J. Torán. Personal Communication.

[Val76]   L. Valiant. Relative complexity of checking and evaluating. *Information Processing Letters*, 5(1):20-23, 1976.

[VV86]   L. Valiant and V. Vazirani. NP is as easy as detecting unique solutions. *Theoretical Computer Science* 47:85−93, 1986.

[Wat90]   O. Watanabe. Unpublished note.

Two Refinements of the Polynomial Hierarchy

V.L.Selivanov *

Institute of Mathematics, Novosibirsk, Russia

Abstract

We introduce and study two classifications refining the polynomial hierarchy. Both extend the difference hierarchy over NP and are analogs of some hierarchies from recursion theory. We answer some natural questions on the introduced classifications, e.g. we extend the result of J.Kadin that the difference hierarchy over NP does not collapse (if the polynomial hierarchy does not collapse).

1 Introduction

Hierarchies are important tools for the classification of mathematical objects. E.g. in descriptive set theory (DST) they are used for the classification of subsets of the Baire space up to Wadge equivalence, in recursion theory (RT)—for the classification of sets of natural numbers up to m-equivalence, in complexity theory (CT)—for the classification of languages up to polynomial m-equivalence.

The most famous hierarchy in CT is the polynomial hierarchy $\{\Sigma_{n+1}^p\}_{n<\omega}$. It is the analog of the finite Borel hierarchy in DST and of the arithmetical hierarchy in RT. In the last years people actively investigate the difference (or Boolean) hierarchy over NP= Σ_1^p, which is also the analog of hierarchies studied in DST and RT. This hierarchy seems to be of some use for classification of languages which are in $\Sigma_2^p \cap \Pi_2^p$ but are harder than $\Sigma_1^p \cup \Pi_1^p$. More generally, people considered also the difference hierarchy over Σ_{n+1}^p, this is (hopefully) useful for the classification of some languages from $\Sigma_{n+2}^p \cap \Pi_{n+2}^p$.

For $n > 1$ there are natural sets nonclassifiable in the difference hierarchy over Σ_{n+1}^p. E.g. let

$$D = \{\langle a, b\rangle | (a \notin A \wedge b \in B) \vee (a \in A \wedge b \notin B)\},$$

where A, B are polynomially m-complete in Σ_1^p and Σ_2^p respectively, and $\langle a, b\rangle$ is the code of the pair of words a, b. It is easy to see that both the set D and its complement D'

---

*The work was done at the University of Heidelberg and was supported by the Alexander von Humboldt Foundation. I would like to thank K.Ambos-Spies and B.Borchert for discussions and pointing out to me some literature in complexity theory.

are differences of Σ_2^p-sets and are harder that Σ_1^p. In this paper we will show that D is polynomially m-incomparable with its complement (if the polynomial hierarchy does not collapse). So D is not classifiable up to polynomial m-equivalence in the difference hierarchy over Σ_2^p.

When one tries to classify not only isolated sets but sets from a class with some closure properties (e.g. closed under propositional connectives on corresponding unary predicates) then one meets a lot of easy "nonclassifiable" sets similar to that considered above. For the context of RT this was understood by me long ago, and was the reason for search of a new hierarchy extending known hierarchies and sufficient for classification of closed enough classes of sets. Such a fine hierarchy was found in 1983 and was applied in [7] and [8] for classification of some sets in RT. This hierarchy turned out to be a finite analog of the Borel Wadge hierarchy in DST.

The aim of this paper is to present some analogs of this hierarchy in CT and discuss their properties and possible applicability. We hope that analogies between problems in mentioned fields may be of some interest, in particular we hope that classes of our hierarchies are natural complexity classes which may be useful to classify some languages up to polynomial m-equivalence (because we think that the mentioned analogy with the classification of sets up to m-equivalence is natural and fruitful). Unfortunately the CT-world is less friendly than the RT-world, so we will see that some questions having nice solutions in RT lead to difficult open problems in CT.

Let 2^* be the set of all words in the alphabet $2 = \{0, 1\}$ and $P(2^*)$ be the class of all subsets of 2^*. Classes of our hierarchies will be subsets of $P(2^*)$, A' denotes the complement of $A \subseteq 2^*$ and co-$C = \{A' | A \in C\}$ is the dual of the class $C \subseteq P(2^*)$.

2 The Typed Boolean Hierarchy

Both our refinements extend the difference hierarchy over NP, so we start with reminding some information on this hierarchy. Let $B = (B; \cup, \cap, ', 0, 1)$ be a Boolean algebra and L be a sublattice of $(B; \cup, \cap, 0, 1)$. Let $D_k(k < \omega)$ be the set of all elements $\cup_i(a_{2i} \setminus a_{2i+1})$ where $a_i \in L$ satisfy $a_0 \supseteq a_1 \supseteq \cdots$ and $a_k = 0$. The sequence $\{D_k\}_{k<\omega}$ is called *difference hierarchy over L*. Note that the definition does not (modulo isomorphism) depend on B. Note also that by the Stone representation theorem we may without loss of generality think that L is a lattice of sets. It is well known that $D_k \cup$co-$D_k \subseteq D_{k+1}$ and $\cup_{k<\omega} D_k$ is the Boolean algebra generated by L.

Let T be the set of all Boolean terms from variables $v_0, v_1, \ldots$ (recall that these terms are expressions defined by induction as follows: any variable v_i is a term; constants $0,1$ are terms; if s, t are terms then so are the expressions $s', (s \cup t), (s \cap t)$). Relate to any $t = t(v_0, \ldots, v_n) \in T$ the set $t(L) = \{t(a_0, \ldots, a_n) | a_i \in L\}$ of all values of t when its variables range over L. We call the sets $t(L)$ *classes of the Boolean hierarchy over L*. From a result of K.Wagner and G.Wechsung in [9] follows that the classes of the difference hierarchy over NP coincide with the classes of the Boolean hierarchy over NP, i.e. $\{D_k, \text{co-}D_k | k < \omega\} = \{t(NP) | t \in T\}$. This result is a starting point of our investigation.

First we introduce a natural extension of the Boolean hierarchy over NP. Let T^* be the set of all Boolean terms from variables $v_i^n (n, i < \omega)$; we call $v_i^n (i < \omega)$ *variables of type n* and elements of T^* *typed Boolean terms*. Relate to any typed Boolean term t the class $t(L)$ of all its values when variables of type n range over Σ_{n+1}^p (L denotes here the sequence $\{\Sigma_{n+1}^p\}_{n<\omega}$). The classes $t(L)$ ($t \in T^*$) are called *classes of the typed Boolean hierarchy over* $\{\Sigma_{n+1}^p\}_{n<\omega}$. It is clear that among these classes are all levels of the polynomial hierarchy as well as all levels of the difference hierarchy over any Σ_{n+1}^p. But among them are also many more exotic classes, e.g. for the term $t = v_0^{0'} v_0^1 \cup v_0^0 v_0^{1'}$ the class $t(L)$ contains just sets $A'B \cup AB'$, where $A \in \Sigma_1^p$, $B \in \Sigma_2^p$ and AB abbreviates $A \cap B$. It is easy to see that the set D from the introduction is polynomially m-complete in this class $t(L)$. Let us prove an easy but important generalisation of this example.

2.1.Proposition. *The classes of the typed Boolean hierarchy are closed downwards under polynomial m-reducibility and have polynomially m-complete sets.*

Proof. Let $t = t(v_0^0, \ldots, v_n^0, \ldots, v_0^n, \ldots, v_n^n)$ be a typed Boolean term containing only the listed variables. Let $X \in t(L)$ and $Y \leq_m^p X$; we have to show that $Y \in t(L)$. Choose Σ_{k+1}^p-sets X_i^k with $X = t(X_0^0, \ldots, X_n^0, \ldots, X_0^n, \ldots, X_n^n)$ and a polynomially computable function f with $Y = f^{-1}(X)$. By induction on the term t we get $Y = t(f^{-1}(X_0^0), \ldots, f^{-1}(X_n^n))$. By the downword closedeness of the polynomial hierarchy $f^{-1}(X_i^k) \in \Sigma_{k+1}^p$. So $Y \in t(L)$.

It remains to show that $t(L)$ has a complete set. Let A^k be a polynomially m-complete set in Σ_{k+1}^p. Let $B_i^k = \{\langle a_0^0, \ldots, a_n^0, \ldots, a_0^n, \ldots, a_n^n \rangle | a_i^k \in A^k\}$ and $B = t(B_0^0, \ldots, B_n^n)$, where $\langle a_0^0, \ldots, a_n^n \rangle$ is a polynomially computable coding of all $(n+1)^2$-tuples of words. We have $B_i^k \leq_m^p A^k$, so $B_i^k \in \Sigma_{k+1}^p$ and $B \in t(L)$. We claim that B is $t(L)$-complete, i.e. every $t(L)$-set X represented as above is polynomially m-reducible to B. Choose polynomially computable functions f_i^k m-reducing X_i^k to A^k and define a polynomially computable function f by $f(a) = \langle f_0^0(a), \ldots, f_n^0(a), \ldots, f_0^n(a), \ldots, f_n^n(a) \rangle$. Then

$$f^{-1}(B) = t(f^{-1}(B_0^0), \ldots, f^{-1}(B_n^n)) = t(X_0^0, \ldots, X_n^n) = X.$$

So $X \leq_m^p B$ completing the proof.

2.2.Remark. Note that if the sets A^k code "natural" combinatorial problems then so does the set B. For this reason we believe that the typed Boolean hierarchy may be useful for the classification of some "natural" combinatorial problems.

Hierarchies in descriptive set theory and recursion theory usually have the following important property making them look as scales for measuring complexity: the structure of all their levels under inclusion is *almost well-ordered*, i.e. is well-founded and *almost linearly ordered* (the last term means that for any levels A, B either $A \subseteq B$ or co-$B \subseteq A$).

The main lack of the typed Boolean hierarchy is the fact that we cannot prove that the structure $(\{t(L)|t \in T^*\}; \subseteq)$ is almost well-ordered (indeed this seems to us to be one of the main open questions about this hierarchy). We will return to this structure later on after considering in the next section an alternative classification which is almost well-ordered and may be used as an instrument for investigation of the typed Boolean hierarchy.

3   The Fine Hierarchy

Let again $(B; \cup, \cap, ', 0, 1)$ be a Boolean algebra. By *a base* we mean any sequence $L = \{L_n\}_{n<\omega}$ of sublattices of $(B; \cup, \cap, 0, 1)$ satisfying $L_n \cup \text{co-}L_n \subseteq L_{n+1}$. In [7] and [8] we related to any base L a sequence $\{S_\alpha\}_{\alpha<\varepsilon_0}$ called *the fine hierarchy over* L. The class S_α is S_α^0, where classes $S_\alpha^n (n < \omega)$ (having for $n > 0$ only technical value) are defined as follows:

$S_0^n = \{0\}$, $S_{\omega^\gamma}^n = S_\gamma^{n+1}$ for $\gamma > 0$,

$S_{\alpha+1}^n = \{u_0 x_0 \cup u_1 x_1 | u_i \in L_n, \ x_0 \in S_\alpha^n, \ x_1 \in \text{co-}S_\alpha^n, \ u_0 u_1 x_0 = u_0 u_1 x_1\}$,

$S_{\alpha+\omega^\gamma}^n = \{u_0 x_0 \cup u_1 x_1 \cup u_0' u_1' y | u_i \in L_n, \ x_0 \in S_\alpha^n, \ x_1 \in \text{co-}S_\alpha^n, \ y \in S_{\omega^\gamma}^n, \ u_0 u_1 x_0 = u_0 u_1 x_1\}$ for $\alpha = \omega^\gamma \cdot \beta > 0$, $\gamma > 0$.

To see that this inductive definition is correct note that every nonzero ordinal $\alpha < \varepsilon_0 = sup\{\omega, \omega^\omega, \omega^{\omega^\omega}, \ldots\}$ is uniquely representable (see [6]) in the form

$\alpha = \omega^{\gamma_0} k_0 + \omega^{\gamma_1} k_1 + \cdots$ for $\gamma_0 > \gamma_1 > \cdots (\gamma_0 < \alpha)$ and $0 < k_i < \omega$.

So representing α as $\omega^{\gamma_0} + \omega^{\gamma_0} + \cdots + \omega^{\gamma_1} + \cdots$ and applying the appropriate points of the definition we subsequently get $S_{\omega^{\gamma_0}}^n, S_{\omega^{\gamma_0}\cdot 2}^n, \ldots, S_\alpha^n$.

We need the following properties of these classes taken from [7], [8] in which $\alpha(0, k) = k$ and $\alpha(n + 1, k) = \omega^{\alpha(n,k)}$:

3.1. Properties. (i) $S_{k+1}^n = S_{\alpha(n,k+1)}$ *is the* $(k + 1)$-*th level* $(k < \omega)$ *of the difference hierarchy over* L_n;

(ii) $S_{\alpha(n,1)} = L_n$ *for* $n < \omega$;

(iii) $S_\alpha \cup \text{co-}S_\alpha \subseteq S_\beta$ *for* $\alpha < \beta < \varepsilon_0$ *and* $\cup_{\alpha<\varepsilon_0} S_\alpha = \cup_{n<\omega} L_n$;

(iv) $S_{\alpha+2}^n = \{ux | u \in L_n, x \in \text{co-}S_{\alpha+1}^n\}$;

(v) $S_{\omega^\gamma(k+2)}^n = \{ux \cup u'y | u \in L_n, x \in \text{co-}S_{\omega^\gamma(k+1)}^n, y \in S_{\omega^\gamma}^n\}$ *for* $\gamma > 0$, $k < \omega$;

(vi) *if* $\{L_n\}$ *and* $\{\mathcal{L}_n\}$ *are bases in Boolean algebras* B *and* $\mathcal{B}$ *respectively and* $g : B \to \mathcal{B}$ *is a homomorphism satisfying* $g(L_n) \subseteq \mathcal{L}_n$ *for all* $n < \omega$, *then* $g(S_\alpha) \subseteq \mathcal{S}_\alpha$ *for all* $\alpha < \varepsilon_0$.

If L_n is the $(n + 1)$-th level of the Borel hierarchy, then the corresponding fine hierarchy is a finite version of the Wadge hierarchy of Borel sets playing a noticible role in descriptive set theory. If L_n is the $(n + 1)$-th level of the arithmetical hierarchy, then the corresponding fine hierarchy is a natural hierarchy having applications (see [7], [8]) to the classification of sets of natural numbers up to m-equivalence.

Having in mind the mentioned in the introduction analogy between the arithmetical and the polynomial hierarchies it seems natural and even instructive to consider the fine hierarchy $\{S_\alpha\}_{\alpha<\varepsilon_0}$ over $L = \{\Sigma_{n+1}^p\}$. By (i) this fine hierarchy extends the difference hierarchy over any level of the polynomial hierarchy. By (ii) it is a refinement of the polynomial hierarchy. By (iii) its classes are almost well-ordered by inclusion. This is its main advantage as compared with the typed Boolean hierarchy. The next result states another good property of the fine hierarchy.

3.2. Proposition. *The classes* S_α $(\alpha < \varepsilon_0)$ *are downward closed under the polynomial* m-*reducibility*.

Proof. Let $A \in S_\alpha$ and f be a polynomially computable function; we have to show that $f^{-1}(A) \in S_\alpha$. The map $X \mapsto f^{-1}(X)$ is a homomorphism of the Boolean algebra

$P(2^*)$ into itself preserving all classes $\Sigma_{n+1}^p = L_n$. So by (vi) $f^{-1}(A) \in S_\alpha$ completing the proof.

The main lack of the fine hierarchy is that we cannot prove (or disprove) that all its levels have polynomially complete sets, e.g. we cannot prove this for levels $S_{\omega+k+1}$ ($k < \omega$). Let us show that in some cases the situation is somewhat better if we consider relativized versions of these classes.

3.3.Theorem. *There is a recursive oracle modulo which all classes* $S_{\omega+k+1}$ ($k < 1$) *have polynomially m-complete sets.*

Proof. Take a recursive oracle modulo which Σ_2^p is different from Π_2^p and $\Sigma_2^p \cap \Pi_2^p$ is the class of all sets polynomially T-reducible to the NP-complete set (on the existence of such an oracle see theorem 7.16 from [3]). By definition $S_\omega = \Sigma_2^p$ and $S_{\omega+1}$ is the class of all sets $U_0 X_0 \cup U_1 X_1$ where $U_i \in \Sigma_1^p$, $X_0 \in \Sigma_2^p$, $X_1 \in \Pi_2^p$ and $U_0 U_1 X_0 = U_0 U_1 X_1$. An easy set-theoretic argument shows that $S_{\omega+1}$ is the class of all sets $V_0 V_1' Y_0 \cup V_0' V_1 Y_1 \cup V_0 V_1 Y_2$, where $V_i \in \Sigma_1^p$, $Y_0 \in \Sigma_2^p$, $Y_1 \in \Pi_2^p$, $Y_2 \in \Sigma_2^p \cap \Pi_2^p$.

According to [1] the class $\Sigma_2^p \cap \Pi_2^p$ has (for the choosen oracle) a polynomially m-complete set. Classes Σ_k^p also have complete sets. From the description of $S_{\omega+1}$ we now just as in the proof of 2.1 get that this class also has a polynomially m-complete set. For classes $S_{\omega+k+2}$ we again use the argument of the proof of 2.1 and the property (iv). This completes the proof.

In the next section we consider the relationship between the introduced hierarchies.

4 The Relationship Between the Hierarchies

Let us discuss the relationship between the typed Boolean and the fine hierarchies. First we consider this question for much easier recursive case, i.e. for the fine hierarchy $\{S_\alpha\}_{\alpha < \varepsilon_0}$ over the base $L = \{\Sigma_{n+1}^0\}$ formed by levels of the arithmetical hierarchy and for the typed Boolean hierarchy $\{t(L)\}_{t \in T^*}$ over L (note that the definition of the typed Boolean hierarchy in section 2 is applicable to any base). This recursive case is interesting in its own right because it gives a very simple and new description of the recursive fine hierarchy. Its proof uses some nontrivial earlier results from [8].

4.1. Theorem. *The classes of the fine hierarchy over* $L = \{\Sigma_{n+1}^0\}$ *coincide with the classes of the typed Boolean hierarchy over* L, *i.e.* $\{S_\alpha, \text{co-}S_\alpha | \alpha < \varepsilon_0\} = \{t(L) | t \in T^*\}$.

Proof. To prove the inclusion from left to right it clearly suffices to find typed Boolean terms t_α^n satisfying $S_\alpha^n = t_\alpha^n(L)$. Define $t_\alpha^n (n < \omega)$ by induction on $\alpha < \varepsilon_0$ as follows:

$t_0^n = 0$, $t_1^n = v$, $t_{\omega\gamma}^n = t_\gamma^{n+1}$ for $\gamma > 0$,

$t_{\lambda+1}^n = v_0 v_1' t_\lambda^n(\mathbf{x}) \cup v_0' v_1 t_\lambda^n(\mathbf{y})'$ for limit λ, $t_{\alpha+2}^n = t_{\alpha+1}^n(\mathbf{x})' v$,

$t_{\alpha+\omega\gamma}^n = v_0 v_1' t_\alpha^n(\mathbf{x}) \cup v_0' v_1 t_\alpha^n(\mathbf{y})' \cup v_0' v_1' t_{\omega\gamma}^n(\mathbf{z})$ for $\alpha = \omega^\gamma \cdot \beta > 0$, $\gamma > 0$.

Here v, v_0, v_1 are variables of type n and $\mathbf{x}, \mathbf{y}, \mathbf{z}$ are sequences of other different variables of appropriate types.

The equality $S_\alpha^n = t_\alpha^n(L)$ is checked by induction on α according to the definition of terms, the three first cases of the definition being trivial. Let $\alpha = \lambda + 1$, then by induction $S_\lambda^n = t_\lambda^n(L)$. Let $A \in t_\alpha^n(L)$, then

$$A = U_0 U_1' A_0 \cup U_0' U_1 A_1 \tag{1}$$

for some $U_i \in L_n$, $A_0 \in t_\lambda^n(L)$, $A_1 \in \text{co-}t_\lambda^n(L)$. Let $V_i \in L_n$ be reducing sets for U_i, i.e. sets satisfying

$$V_i \subseteq U_i, \quad V_0 V_1 = \emptyset, \quad V_0 \cup V_1 = U_0 \cup U_1. \tag{2}$$

Then

$$A = V_0 B_0 \cup V_1 B_1 \text{ and } V_0 V_1 = \emptyset, \tag{3}$$

where $B_0 = U_0 U_1' A_0$ and $B_1 = U_0' U_1 A_1$. By [7] $B_0 \in S_\lambda^n$ and $B_1 \in \text{co-}S_\lambda^n$, so $A \in S_\alpha^n$.

Conversely, let $A \in S_\alpha^n$, then by [7] we have (3) for some $V_i \in L_n$, $B_0 \in S_\lambda^n$, $B_1 \in \text{co-}S_\lambda^n$, $V_0 V_1 = \emptyset$. But then we have (1) for $U_i = V_i$ and $A_i = B_i$, so $A \in t_\alpha^n(L)$.

The case of an ordinal $\alpha + \omega^\gamma$ is considered in the same way. Finally, the case $\alpha = \beta + 2$ folows from 3.1.(iv).

It remains to prove that any $t(L)$ ($t \in T^*$) is one of S_α,co-$S_\alpha(\alpha < \varepsilon_0)$. By the recursive analog of 2.1 the class $t(L)$ has a m-complete set B, so it suffices to prove that the set B is m-complete in one of the levels of the fine hierarchy. In [8] we proved some sufficient conditions for this which we now apply. The set B is a Boolean combination of the sets $B_i^k(i, k < \omega)$ from the proof of 2.1, so by theorem 1 in [8] it suffices to check that the class $\mathcal{A} = \{B_i^k | i, k \leq n\}$ is universal and simple. By lemmas 4 and 5 in [8] it suffices to check that singletons $\mathcal{A}_k = \{A^k\}$ consisting of Σ_{k+1}^0-complete sets are universal and simple. But universality of such a singleton just means that A^k is Σ_{k+1}^0-complete. Simplicity of such a singleton by the definition from [8] means the following two conditions, in which $\mathcal{L}_n$ is the class of all Σ_{n+1}^0-sets from the Boolean algebra generated by $\mathcal{A}_k$ (k is fixed):

a) ω is not representable as a nontrivial union of $\mathcal{L}_0$-sets;

b) for any n every two disjoint co-$\mathcal{L}_{n+1}$-sets are separable by a Boolean combination of $\mathcal{L}_n$-sets.

Both properties are checked in an obvious way completing the proof.

4.2. Corollary. *The classes of the typed Boolean hierarchy over L are almost well-ordered by inclusion with the corresponding ordinal ε_0.*

It is natural to ask what properties of the base L are responsible for the coincidence of the classes of the typed Boolean and the fine hierarchies over L. An analysis of the above proof together with proofs of the corresponding assertions from [8] shows that if all classes L_n have the reduction property (i.e. for all $U_0, U_1 \in L_n$ there are $V_0, V_1 \in L_n$ satisfying (2)), then theorem 4.1 is true for the hierarchies over L.

But what about our main base $L = \{\Sigma_{n+1}^p\}$? If theorem 4.1 would be true for this base, then the main mentioned open questions on both our hierarchies would be automatically settled. Unfortunately the reduction property for the levels of the polynomial hierarchy is an open question, so we can prove none of the inclusions between $\{t(L) | t \in T^*\}$ and $\{S_\alpha,\text{co-}S_\alpha | \alpha < \varepsilon_0\}$. It is not even known is there an oracle modulo which the polynomial hierarchy does not collapse and for any n one of Σ_{n+1}^p, Π_{n+1}^p has the reduction property (for $n = 0$ this was asked already in [4]). In the opposite direction K.Ambos-Spies (private communication) constructed a recursive oracle modulo which $\Sigma_1^p \neq \Pi_1^p$ and none of these classes has the reduction (and even the separation) property.

The result of Wagner and Wechsung mentioned in section 2 is indeed true for any lattice L in place of NP. So may be theorem 4.1 is also true for any base? Unfortunately this is not the case.

4.3.Example. Let R and S be recursive sets for which all sets RS, RS', $R'S$, $R'S'$ are infinite. Let $L_0 = \{\emptyset, RS, R, S, R \cup S, 2^*\}$, $L_1 = \Sigma_1^0$, $L_{n+2} = P(2^*)$, $t_0 = u_0 u_1' v_0 \cup u_0' u_1 v_1'$, $t_1 = t_0 \cup u_0 u_1$ and $t_2 = t_0 \cup u_0' u_1'$, where variables u_i are of type 0 and v_i are of type 1. An easy computation shows that $t_i(L) \not\subseteq t_j(L) \cup t_k(L)$ for the base $L = \{L_n\}$ and all pairwise different $i, j, k < 3$. So the structure $(\{t(L) | t \in T^*\}; \subseteq)$ is not almost linearly ordered and *a fortiori* some of $t(L)$ is different from all levels of the corresponding fine hierarchy. It can also be shown that class $S_{\omega+1}$ over L is different from all $t(L)$ ($t \in T^*$).

So the structure of lattices L_n is essential for the relationship between the fine and the typed Boolean hierarchies over L. It seems that up to now there is not enough information on the classes Σ_{k+1}^p to state the relationship between our hierarchies over $\{\Sigma_{n+1}^p\}$.

We have seen that both introduced hierarchies have some positive as well as some negative properties. In the next section we consider a common part of our hierarchies which inherits the good properties of both of them.

5 A Common Fragment

Let Θ be the least set of ordinals such that $0 \in \Theta$ and if $\theta \in \Theta$ then $\omega^\theta \cdot k \in \Theta$ for $k < \omega$. By definition of the ordinals $\alpha(n, k)$ in section 3 all these ordinals are in Θ, i.e. by property 3.1.(i) the fragment $\{S_\theta\}_{\theta \in \Theta}$ of the fine hierarchy contains the levels of the difference hierarchy over any Σ_{n+1}^p. The ordinal type of $(\Theta; <)$ is ω^ω and that of $(\{\alpha(n, k) | n, k < \omega\}; <)$ is ω^2, so the fragment $\{S_\theta\}_{\theta \in \Theta}$ contains also many other classes. E.g. the class $S_{\omega \cdot 2}$ consists by the property 3.1.(v) just of the sets $A'X \cup AY'$, where $A \in \Sigma_1^p$ and $X, Y \in \Sigma_2^p$. Indeed this class has an easier description as the class of sets $A'B \cup AB'$, where $A \in \Sigma_1^p$ and $B \in \Sigma_2^p$ (to see this take $B = XA' \cup YA$, then $A'X \cup AY' = A'B \cup AB'$). So the set D from the introduction is m-complete in $S_{\omega \cdot 2}$.

Let us show that $\{S_\theta\}_{\theta \in \Theta}$ is a fragment of the typed Boolean hierarchy from section 2.

5.1.Proposition. *Any class $S_\theta (\theta \in \Theta)$ is a class of the typed Boolean hierarchy, and consequently contains a polynomially m-complete set.*

Proof. It suffices to prove by induction on $\theta \in \Theta$ that any S_θ^n is a class of the typed Boolean hierarchy. For zero ordinal this is trivial so let us have a nonzero ordinal θ of the form $\omega^\gamma \cdot k$. For $\gamma = 0$ the assertion follows from 3.1.(i) and the result of Wagner and Wechsung cited in section 2. For $\gamma > 0$ we use the induction on k: if $k = 1$, then $S_\theta^n = S_\gamma^{n+1}$ and the assertion is true by induction on θ; if $k = l + 2$, then it follows from 3.1.(v). This completes the proof.

5.2.Remark. Let $A \oplus B$ denotes the set C with the characteristic function c_C defined by $c_C(x) = c_A(x) \oplus c_B(x)$, where $\oplus$ is the addition modulo 2. For classes of sets $\mathcal{A}, \mathcal{B}$ let $\mathcal{A} \oplus \mathcal{B} = \{A \oplus B | A \in \mathcal{A}, B \in \mathcal{B}\}$. When I discussed this paper with K.Wagner he noted that $S_{\omega \cdot 2} = \Sigma_2^p \oplus \Sigma_1^p$ and asked what classes are obtained when one applies the operation $\oplus$ to the levels of polynomial hierarchy. It is not difficult to show that we get exactly the nonzero of our fragment. Namely, for any sequence $n_0, \ldots, n_k$ of natural numbers there is a nonzero $\theta \in \Theta$ with $S_\theta = \Sigma_{n_0+1}^p \oplus \cdots \oplus \Sigma_{n_k+1}^p$, and vice versa. This gives another natural description of our fragment using Boolean terms.

One of the main questions on any hierarchy is of course its nontriviality: is any level different from its dual? It is clear that we can hope to prove this in our case only under the assumption that the polynomial hierarchy does not collapse, i.e. that any of its levels is different from its dual. From 3.1.(i) and a theorem of J.Kadin (see e.g. [5]) follows that any $\alpha(n, k+1)$-th level of the fine hierarchy is different from its dual. We can extend this result to all levels of the introduced fragment.

5.3.Theorem. *If the polynomial hierarchy does not collapse, then* $S_\theta \neq co\text{-}S_\theta$ *for all* $\theta \in \Theta$.

Proof. For shortness and for a clearer presentation of the main idea let us consider only a typical particular case $\theta = \omega \cdot 2$ (and $n = 0$); the general case is by a straightforward induction. It suffices to show that the $S_{\omega \cdot 2}$-complete set D is not in co-$S_{\omega \cdot 2}$. Our proof is similar to that in [5].

By the remark before proposition 5.1 D looks as follows:

$$D = \{\langle a, b \rangle | (a \notin A \wedge b \in B) \vee (a \in A \wedge b \notin B)\},$$

where A and B are complete in Σ_1^p and Σ_2^p respectively. The set B is representable (see [2]) in the form

$$b \in B \leftrightarrow (\exists x)_{|x| \leq p(|b|)}(g(b, x) \notin A) \tag{4}$$

for a polynomial p and a polynomially computable function g. Let r be a polynomial such that $|g(b, x)| \leq r(|b|)$ for all words x of length at most $p(|b|)$.

Suppose that $D \in$ co-$S_{\omega \cdot 2}$, then

$$D = A_1' B_1' \cup A_1 B_1 \tag{5}$$

for some $A_1 \in \Sigma_1^p$ and $B_1 \in \Sigma_2^p$. Call a word c *hard* if for any word a of length at most $r(|c|)$ we have $\langle a, c \rangle \in A_1 \leftrightarrow a \notin A$. Note that if c is hard then by (4) for any word b of length $|c|$ we have

$$b \in B' \leftrightarrow (\forall x)_{|x| \leq p(|b|)}(\langle g(b, x), c \rangle \notin A_1). \tag{6}$$

Note also that if b is not hard then from (5) follows

$$b \in B' \leftrightarrow (\exists a)_{|a| \leq r(|b|)}((a \in A \leftrightarrow \langle a, b \rangle \in A_1) \wedge \langle a, b \rangle \in B_1). \tag{7}$$

Let f be a polynomially bounded advice function (cf. [5], p.14) which provides a hard word c of length n (if any) on the input 1^n or says that there is no such word (in the last case we write $f(1^n) = \perp$). Then

$$b \in B' \leftrightarrow (f(1^{|b|}) = c \wedge R6) \vee (f(1^{|b|}) = \perp \wedge R7),$$

where $R6$ and $R7$ are the righthandsides of (6) and (7) respectively. This shows that $B' \in \Sigma_2^p/poly$. But then by [10] the polynomial hierarchy collapses. This contradiction completes the proof.

We see that our fragment $\{S_\theta\}_{\theta \in \Theta}$ has very good properties: it extends known hierarchies and looks very natural, it is almost well-ordered, any level has a polynomially m-complete set, it does not collapse.

We do not know is any level of the fine hierarchy (or of the typed Boolean hierarchy) different from its dual or not.

6 Conclusion

We succeeded in proving positive results only for the fragment $\{S_\theta\}_{\theta \in \Theta}$ of the fine hierarchy. Outside this fragment most questions are open. Some of them were stated above. Among others we can mention the following: is the structure of the classes of the typed Boolean hierarchy under inclusion well-founded, is this structure (modulo some oracle) not almost linearly ordered? We hope that these questions are of some interest to complexity theory because the introduced classes (especially the classes of the typed Boolean hierarchy) seem to be very natural.

References

[1]   K.Ambos-Spies: A note on complete problems for complexity classes. Information Processing Letters, 23,227-230(1986)

[2]   J.L.Balcázar, J.Díaz, and Gabarró: Structural Complexity I, EATCS Monographs on Theoretical Computer Science, v.11. Berlin: Springer 1988

[3]   J.L.Balcázar, J.Díaz, and Gabarró: Structural Complexity II, EATCS Monographs on Theoretical Computer Science, v.22. Berlin: Springer 1990

[4]   A.Blass and Y.Gurevich: Equivalence relations, invariants, and normal forms. In: Logic and Machines: Decision Problems and Complexity. Lecture Notes in Computer Science 171. Berlin: Springer 1986, pp.24-42

[5]   R.Chang: On the structure of NP-computations under Boolean operators. Ph.D Thesis, Cornell University 1991

[6]   K.Kuratowski and A.Mostowski: Set Theory. Amsterdam: North Holland 1967

[7]   V.L.Selivanov: Fine hierarchies of arithmetical sets and definable index sets. Trans. Inst. Math., Novosibirsk 12,165-185(1989) (in Russian)

[8]   V.L.Selivanov: Fine hierarchies and definable index sets. Algebra and logic 30,705-725 (1991) (in Russian, there is an English translation)

[9]   K.Wagner and G.Wechsung: On the Boolean closure of NP. In: Proceedings of the 1985 Int. Conf. on Fundamentals of Computation theory. Lecture Notes in Computer Science 199. Berlin: Springer 1985, pp.485-493

[10]   C.Yap: Some consequences of non-uniform conditions on uniform classes. Theoretical Computer Science 26, 287-300(1983)

Current authors address: Victor Selivanov, Mathematisches Institut der Universität Heidelberg, Im Neuenheimer Feld 294, 69120 Heidelberg, Germany.

On Different Reducibility Notions for Function Classes

Heribert Vollmer

Theoretische Informatik, Universität Würzburg,
Am Exerzierplatz 3, D-97072 Würzburg, Germany

Abstract. This paper continues research of Toda (The Complexity of Finding Medians, 31st *Symposium on Foundations of Computer Science* (1990), pp. 778–787) on problems complete for function classes like $FP^{\#P}$ and Mid P under Krentel's metric reductions. We first show that metric reductions wipe out the difference between Mid P and other related classes of functions which are probably different from Mid P. In order to obtain a more detailed classification of naturally arising functional problems we then define and examine a stricter notion of reducibility and show that a number of problems, among them those proved by Toda to be hard for Mid P under metric reductions, are complete for different classes of median functions related to Mid P under our stricter reducibility. Finally, we use these results to exhibit new natural complete sets for the well studied classes of sets PP, PP^{NP}, and P^{PP}.

1   Introduction

In [9] Toda introduced the class of functions Mid P. It consists of those functions that yield the middle element in the set of output values of nondeterministic polynomial time Turing machines. This class is contained in $FP^{\#P}$, the class of all functions computable by a deterministic polynomial time Turing machine with oracle queries to Valiant's class $\#P$ [11]. Toda compared functions from these classes under metric reductions, first introduced by Krentel [6] in the context of the function class Opt P, and a characterization theorem for $FP^{\#P}$ allowed him to exhibit a number of natural complete problems for that class.

However, the power of a Turing machine performing a metric reduction is rather high. The class Mid P for instance is probably not closed under metric reductions but its closure is equal to $FP^{\#P}$. We consider two other classes of median functions: A class Med P which is defined to consist of those functions that yield the middle element in the ordered *sequence* (not *set*, as for Mid P) of output values of nondeterministic polynomial time Turing machines; this class is (under reasonable complexity theoretic assumptions) incomparable to Mid P (and there are oracles separating them) but it is also contained in $FP^{\#P}$; and a class $\overline{Med} P$ defined to yield the middle accepting path itself (in any reasonable encoding) of machines as above, a (probably strict) subclass of both other median classes. We then show that the closure of these classes under metric reductions is also equal to $FP^{\#P}$; and that all four classes of functions share the same hard problems under metric reductions. Thus this kind of reducibility wipes out the differences between the considered classes.

This is an unsatisfactory situation. For instance, the function yielding the middle satisfying assignment of a propositional formula seems to be dissimilar to the function yielding the middle weight of a knapsack. The first one is a typical element of $\overline{\text{Med}}\,\text{P}$, since by Cook's Theorem [3] a satisfying assignment corresponds directly to an accepting path of a Turing machine. The second one however is of another kind, since the contents of the knapsack corresponds to a path of a Turing machine while its weight is similar to the output on that path; thus this function is an element of Mid P (or Med P, depending on whether we are willing to count multiplicities), and we will see that it is not in $\overline{\text{Med}}\,\text{P}$ (unless the classes are equal). But *both* functions are complete for $\text{FP}^{\#\text{P}}$ under metric reductions and therefore also hard or complete for all three of the median classes. The equivalence class of these problems seems to be rather large and contains functions with differing properties. So what we have to look for when we want to classify these functions better is a different reducibility notion.

We propose a stricter notion of reducibility which we call functional many-one reducibility. This notion copies one of the strictest reducibilities between sets: the intuitively well-understood many-one reducibility. We observe that all three median classes are closed under this reducibility and possess complete problems. Thus, we conclude that—in contrast to metric reducibility—if the classes share the same hard problems under functional many-one reducibility then they are equal (contradicting relativized worlds). Then we present a number of natural complete problems for the median classes and we show that the problems considered by Toda or slight modifications of them are complete in different median classes under our stricter reducibility.

These results show that our reducibility is better suited for the examination of function classes in $\text{FP}^{\#\text{P}}$. We can show that the two functions from above, which in our intuition have dissimilar properties, are indeed of different complexity by proving them complete for different median classes under functional many-one reducibility. Our paper develops a means for the classification of functions and the complexity classes they define which in this context is superior to the comparison via metric reductions.

Eventually, we prove that a completeness result for a function class under functional many-one reducibility directly yields completeness results for corresponding classes of sets under usual many-one reducibility. Thus, we exhibit more natural complete problems for PP, PP^{PP}, and PP^{NP}. Wagner in [13] already presented problems complete for the last of these classes, but all of his problems were defined using so called *input languages*; i.e. problems of lower complexity become PP^{NP}-complete when its instances are presented in a succinct representation. Our problems are the (to our knowledge) first natural problems which are PP^{NP}-complete not because of the input representation but because of their intrinsic complexity.

2 Preliminaries

We assume the reader to be familiar with basic complexity theory notions. Our notation here is standard; see e.g. [1].

We start by defining the classes of median-functions we consider. Let FP denote the class of functions computable in deterministic polynomial time.

The following definition is equivalent to Toda's definition of the class Mid P [9]:

Definition 1. The class Mid P consists of those functions h, for which there exist $f, g \in$ FP, such that if the set of all values $f(x, y)$ for $0 \le y \le g(x)$ is

$$\{z_0, z_1, \ldots, z_k\}, \quad z_0 < z_1 < \cdots < z_k,$$

then $h(x) =_{\text{def}} z_{\lfloor k/2 \rfloor}$.

Our version of a median class where multiplicities are taken into account is made precise in the following definition (which is from [12]):

Definition 2. The class Med P consists of those functions h, for which there exist $f, g \in$ FP, such that if the ordered sequence of all values $f(x, y)$ for $0 \le y \le g(x)$ (with multiplicities) is

$$z_0 \le z_1 \le \cdots \le z_{g(x)},$$

then $h(x) =_{\text{def}} z_{\lfloor g(x)/2 \rfloor}$.

It is obvious, that Med P (Mid P, resp.) is the class of functions that yield the middle element in the sequence (set, resp.) of the outputs over all paths of a nondeterministic polynomial time Turing machine. If this relation holds between such a machine M and a function f from Med P or Mid P, we say that f is computed by M.

The third kind of median class we consider is the following, again introduced in [12]:

Definition 3. Let $\mathcal{K}$ be a class of sets. Then the class $\overline{\text{Med}}\, \mathcal{K}$ consists of those functions h, for which there exist $A \in \mathcal{K}$, $g_1, g_2 \in$ FP such that $h(x)$ is equal to the middle element of the set

$$\{\, y \mid g_1(x) \le y \le g_2(x) \wedge (x, y) \in A \,\}.$$

By nature of definiton, in this case only elements with multiplicity one can occur; and this makes it possible to show the following inclusionships [12]:

Proposition 4. $\overline{\text{Med}}\, \text{P} \subseteq \text{Med P}$ *and* $\overline{\text{Med}}\, \text{P} \subseteq \text{Mid P}$.

It was shown in [12] that under reasonable widely accepted complexity theoretic assumptions these inclusionships are strict: If $\overline{\text{Med}}\,P = \text{Mid}\,P$, then the second level of the polynomial time hierarchy is in PP (contradicting some relativized worlds [2]); and if $\overline{\text{Med}}\,P = \text{Med}\,P$, then the counting hierarchy [13, 10] collapses. Moreover, it was shown that under the same assumptions, Med P and Mid P are uncomparable: If $\text{Med}\,P \subseteq \text{Mid}\,P$, then the counting hierarchy collapses; and if $\text{Mid}\,P \subseteq \text{Med}\,P$, then PP contains the second level of the polynomial time hierarchy.

Additionally, it was shown that the operator $\overline{\text{Med}}$ allows a characterization of Toda's class: $\overline{\text{Med}}\,\text{NP} = \text{Mid}\,P$ [12].

Vollmer and Wagner proved an analogue to Toda's main theorem [9] also for the classes $\overline{\text{Med}}\,P$ and Med P. For a function f and a class of functions $\mathcal{F}$, $\text{FP}^f[k]$ ($\text{FP}^{\mathcal{F}}[k]$, resp.) denotes the class of functions computable by a deterministic Turing machine in polynomial time with k queries to f (a function from $\mathcal{F}$, resp.).

Proposition 5.

$$\begin{aligned} \text{FP}^{\text{PP}} &= \text{FP}^{\text{Mid}\,P} = \text{FP}^{\text{Mid}\,P}[1] \\ &= \text{FP}^{\text{Med}\,P} = \text{FP}^{\text{Med}\,P}[1] \\ &= \text{FP}^{\overline{\text{Med}}\,P} = \text{FP}^{\overline{\text{Med}}\,P}[1] \end{aligned}$$

(The first two equalities of this proposition were already proved by Toda [9].)

It was even shown in [12] that the $\text{P}^{\text{Mid}\,P}[1]$, $\text{P}^{\text{Med}\,P}[1]$, and $\text{P}^{\overline{\text{Med}}\,P}[1]$ computations can be further normalized. They can be arranged to consist only of asking for one value of the oracle function class and then giving as output the rest of the integer division of this function value by 2. That is, for every $A \in \text{P}^{\text{PP}}$, there exists some $h \in \text{Mid}\,P$ (or Med P, or $\overline{\text{Med}}\,P$) such that for all x, $c_A(x) \equiv h(x)$ (mod 2).

Thus, although the remarks above show that the three median classes are probably different, there are contexts in which all three classes have the same power. This duality will again come up when we talk about reducibilities in the next sections.

3   Metric Reductions

The reducibility notion we first examine is a well known one, introduced by Krentel [6].

Definition 6. A function f is metrically reducible to function h, in symbols: $f \leq^{\text{FP}}_{met} h$, if and only if there exist two functions $g, g' \in \text{FP}$ such that for all x, $f(x) = g'(x, h(g(x)))$.

Metric reductions were examined by Toda [9] in the context of the class Mid P. We now show that they wipe out the differences between our three median classes.

Lemma 7. *Let f and h be functions. Then $f \leq^{FP}_{met} h$ if and only if $f \in FP^h[1]$. Thus, for a class of functions $\mathcal{F}$, the closure of $\mathcal{F}$ under metric reductions is equal to the class $FP^{\mathcal{F}}[1]$.*

Proof. obvious. □

Corollary 8. *The closure of each of the classes $\overline{Med}\,P$, $Med\,P$, and $Mid\,P$ is equal to $FP^{\#P}$.*

Proof. Consequence of the previous lemma and Proposition 5. □

Corollary 9. *The classes $\overline{Med}\,P$, $Med\,P$, $Mid\,P$, and $FP^{\#P}$ have the same hard functions under $\leq^{FP}_m$-reducibility.*

Thus we get a number of natural problems to be hard under metric reductions for all three median classes, namely those shown to be complete for $FP^{\#P}$ by Toda [9], e.g. Lexical middle satisfying assignment of a boolean formula, Lexical middle Hamiltonian circuit of an undirected graph, and many others. We will later come back to these problems and give exact definitions of them.

4   Functional Many-one Reductions

Having seen that metric reductions are not sufficient to distinguish between the classes $\overline{Med}\,P$, $Med\,P$, and $Mid\,P$, we now proceed by introducing a stricter notion of reducibility which is similar in spirit to many-one reducibility between sets (see also [13, 5]).

Definition 10. A function f is polynomial time functionally many-one reducible to function h, in symbols: $f \leq^{FP}_m h$, if and only if there exists a function $g \in FP$ such that for all x, $f(x) = h(g(x))$.

The following is easy to verify:

Proposition 11. *$\overline{Med}\,P$, $Med\,P$ and $Mid\,P$ are closed under $\leq^{FP}_m$.*

Proof. Let h be a function from any of the considered classes and let h be computed by the Turing machine M, and let $f(x) =_{def} h(g(x))$ for some $g \in FP$. Then f is computed by the machine M' which on input x first computes $g(x)$ and then simulates the work of M on input $g(x)$. □

Complete problems can be constructed artificially:

Theorem 12. *$\overline{Med}\,P$, $Med\,P$ and $Mid\,P$ have $\leq^{FP}_m$ complete functions.*

Proof. The construction proceeds in a canonical way: Define

UNIV$_{\overline{Med}}(x, M, 0^j, 0^k)$ to be the middle y, $|y| \leq j$, such that the Turing machine encoded (in any reasonable way) by M on input (x, y) run for k steps accepts;

$\textsc{Univ}_{\text{Med}}(x, M, 0^k)$ to be the middle element in the sequence of outputs over all paths of the Turing machine encoded by M on input x run for k steps; and $\textsc{Univ}_{\text{Mid}}(x, M, 0^k)$ to be the middle element in the set of outputs over all paths of the Turing machine encoded by M on input x run for k steps.

$\textsc{Univ}_{\overline{\text{Med}}}$, $\textsc{Univ}_{\text{Med}}$, and $\textsc{Univ}_{\text{Mid}}$ are $\leq_m^{\text{FP}}$-complete for $\overline{\text{Med}}\,\text{P}$, $\text{Med}\,\text{P}$ and $\text{Mid}\,\text{P}$, resp. All proofs are completely analogously. We only sketch one: Let $f \in \text{Mid}\,\text{P}$ be computed by some nondeterministic Turing machine M. Let $\langle M \rangle$ be the encoding of M, and let p be a polynomial bounding the running time of M. Then the following function g reduces f to $\textsc{Univ}_{\text{Mid}}$:

$$g(x) =_{\text{def}} (x, \langle M \rangle, 0^{p(|x|)}).$$

$\square$

Corollary 13. *If a function hard for* $\text{Mid}\,\text{P}$ *under* $\leq_m^{\text{FP}}$ *is in* $\text{Med}\,\text{P}$, *then the second level of the polynomial time hierarchy is in* PP.
If a function hard for $\text{Med}\,\text{P}$ *under* $\leq_m^{\text{FP}}$ *is in* $\text{Mid}\,\text{P}$, *then the counting hierarchy collapses.*

Proof. Consequence of the closure of the considered classes under $\leq_m^{\text{FP}}$ and the remarks following Proposition 4. $\square$

Thus we have the following result which should be contrasted with Corollary 9:

Corollary 14. *If the classes* $\overline{\text{Med}}\,\text{P}$, $\text{Med}\,\text{P}$, $\text{Mid}\,\text{P}$, *and* $\text{FP}^{\#\text{P}}$ *have the same* $\leq_m^{\text{FP}}$-*hard functions, then the counting hierarchy collapses and* PP *includes the second level of the polynomial time hierarchy.*

Proof. Follows from Theorem 12 and Corollary 13. $\square$

So it turns out that the notion of functional many-one reducibility in contrast to metric reducibility is well-suited to elaborate the differences between the considered classes of median functions. We will do so in the following subsections by presenting a number of natural problems complete for these classes under $\leq_m^{\text{FP}}$.

4.1 Problems Complete for $\overline{\text{Med}}\,\text{P}$

We start with a problem concerning boolean circuits.

Problem: LexMidCVal

Input: a boolean circuit C with n inputs

Output: the lexicographic middle element of all strings of length n that given as input to C produce the output 1.

Theorem 15. LexMidCVal *is* $\leq_m^{\text{FP}}$-*complete for* $\overline{\text{Med}}\,\text{P}$.

Proof. Obviously, LEXMIDCVAL $\in$ MĒD P. We now have to show that UNIV$_{\overline{\text{Med}}}$ $\leq_m^{FP}$ LEXMIDCVAL:

If we want to evaluate UNIV$_{\overline{\text{Med}}}(x, \langle M \rangle, 0^j, 0^k)$, we produce the circuit C with j inputs that simulates the computation of M on input (x, y), were x is coded directly into the circuit and y corresponds to C's inputs. This construction can be performed in polynomial time (cf. e.g. [1]). Then the middle y of length at most j that is accepted by M if run for k steps is the middle input y that forces C to output 1. □

In the context of polynomial time complexity of sets, a problem defined using the notion of a circuit can most often be changed to a problem defined using the notion of a boolean formula without changing the complexity. For instance, given a circuit, to decide whether it has an input that produces output 1 is equivalent to the question whether a boolean formula has a satisfying assignment. In our context, this seems not to be the case because of the following:

Consider the proof of Cook's Theorem [3] saying that *SAT* is NP-complete: There, given a Turing machine M and an input x a boolean formula F is constructed such that there is a one-one relation between accepting paths of M and satisfying assignments for F. There are certain variables in F that correspond directly to the nondeterministic guesses of M and given an assignment of these variables the assignment of the other ones in a satisfying assignment can be computed in deterministic polynomial time.

If we want to describe the circuit from a LEXMIDCVAL-instance by a boolean formula, then the same phenomenon arises: We encode the circuit by a conjunction of small formulae describing local connectivity properties of the circuit. Each input and each gate of the circuit corresponds to a boolen variable. If we are given the values of the inputs of the circuits, then the values of the internal gates can be computed deterministically. Thus, if we know the values of the boolean variables corresponding to the inputs, then we can compute deterministically the values of the remaining variables in a satisfying assignment in an obvious step by step way, reflecting directly the level by level evaluation of the circuit.

We now make the following definition:

Definition 16. Given a boolean formula F with variables V then we say that a subset $V_0 \subseteq V$ is a set of *external variables* if for every satisfying assignment of F the assignment of the variables in $V_1 =_{\text{def}} V \setminus V_0$ (the so called *internal variables*) can be computed by the above described completion algorithm from the assignment of the variables V_0. An assignment of F with respect to V_0 is a mapping $b \colon V_0 \to \{\text{true}, \text{false}\}$. To determine the value of F under b, we first extend b to a mapping of all variables to truth values and then evaluate F as usual.

Thus, in the proof of Cook's theorem the given nondeterministic Turing machine M can be described by a boolen formula in such a way that the variables corresponding to the nondeterminism of M are *external variables*, the others are *internal*. This allows us to prove:

456

Problem: LEXMIDSAT

Input: a propositional formula F and a sequence V of distinguished variables of F

Output: the lexicographic middle satisfying assignment of F w.r.t. V, if V is external; and any assignment else

Theorem 17. LEXMIDSAT *is $\leq_m^{FP}$-complete for* $\overline{\text{Med}}\,P$.

Proof. As already mentioned, an argumentation following Cook's Theorem would do the proof. But it is simpler to observe LEXMIDCVAL $\leq_m^{FP}$ LEXMIDSAT: Given a cicuit C, build a boolean formula F with one variable for each gate of C as described above. The variables corresponding to C's inputs are chosen to be the set of distinguished variables. $\square$

An analogous problem LEXMID3SAT defined similar to the previous one, but only for conjunctive formulae with three literals per clause can by standard techniques be shown to be $\leq_m^{FP}$-complete for $\overline{\text{Med}}\,P$, too.

Next consider the problem of finding a Hamiltonian circuit in a given undirected graph G. Again, we make a distinction between *external edges* and *internal edges*, if G is such that a possible Hamiltonian circuit is already completely determined by the external edges. We describe a Hamiltonian circuit by ordering the external edges and then transforming the circuit into a sequence of bits, one for each external edge showing whether it is in or is not in the circuit. The ordering of Hamiltonian circuits is then defined to be the lexicographic ordering of their descriptions.

Problem: LEXMIDHAMC

Input: an undirected graph G and a set E of distinguished edges

Output: the lexicographic middle Hamiltonian circuit, if E is external; any sequence of edges else

Theorem 18. LEXMIDHAMC *is $\leq_m^{FP}$-complete for* $\overline{\text{Med}}\,P$.

Proof. Obviously, LEXMIDHAMC $\in \overline{\text{Med}}\,P$. We now reduce LEXMID3SAT to LEXMIDHAMC following a proof concerning a similar problem given in [9]. The details require a long explanation which can be found in [8]. We only remark that the absence or non-absence of certain edges in the Hamiltonian circuit corresponds directly to the assignment of certain variables in the given formula. The set of external edges can be determined directly from the given set of external variables of the formula. $\square$

4.2   Problems Complete for Med P

Our first problem is related to a problem proven Opt P-complete by Krentel [6].

Problem: MEDWEIGHTSAT

Input:	a propositional formula F with weights on its variables
Output:	the middle number in the sequence of the sums of the weights of variables assigned "true" over all satisfying assignments of F

Theorem 19. MEDWEIGHTSAT *is* $\leq_m^{FP}$*-complete for* Med P.

Proof. Obviously, MEDWEIGHTSAT $\in$ Med P. We now prove that UNIV$_{\text{Med}}$ $\leq_m^{FP}$ MEDWEIGHTSAT:

Given a Turing machine M, define a formula F such that there is a one-one correspondence between accepting paths of M and satisfying assignments for F. Give weight 2^{i-1} to the variable describing the i-th last bit of the output of M; and give weight 0 to all other variables. Then the weight of a satisfying assignment is equal to the value printed by M on the corresponding path. $\quad\square$

Problem:	MEDKNAPSACK
Input:	integers $x_1, \ldots, x_n, M, N$
Output:	the middle sum $\sum_{i \in S} x_i - M$ in the sequence of sums over all $S \subseteq \{1, \ldots, n\}$ that sum up to a value between 0 and $N - M$.

Problem:	MEDTSPTOUR
Input:	weighted undirected graph G
Output:	the length of the middle Travelling Salesperson Tour over the sequence of all possible round-trips in G.

Theorem 20. MEDKNAPSACK *and* MEDTSPTOUR *are complete for* Med P *under* $\leq_m^{FP}$*-reductions.*

Proof.

1. MEDWEIGHTSAT $\leq_m^{FP}$ MEDKNAPSACK can be shown similar to a proof found in [6] reducing Maximum Satisfying Assignment to Knapsack, using standard encoding tricks from other knapsack-style reductions (see [4]).
2. MEDWEIGHTSAT $\leq_m^{FP}$ MEDTSPTOUR can be shown using a reduction similar to Krentel's from Weighted Sat to TSP [6, 7].

$\quad\square$

4.3 Problems Complete for Mid P

In this subsection we will first consider again a problem from propositional logic, now concerning Σ_1-formulae, and then turn to problems which are defined similar to those examined in the previous subsection.

We define a restriction of *quantified boolean formulae* (see [1]) as follows: A Σ_1-*formula* is a boolean formula F where some of the variables appear within the scope of an $\exists$-quantifier. An assignment for F is a mapping of the variables not within the scope of any quantifier, the so called *free* variables, to boolean values. An assignment is satisfying if the mapping of the free variables can be extended in some way to a mapping of all variables which satisfies the formula $\hat{F}$ which is equal to F but with all quantifiers deleted.

Problem: LexMidΣ_1Sat

Input: a boolean Σ_1 formula F

Output: the lexicographic middle satisfying assignment of F.

Theorem 21. LexMidΣ_1Sat *is* $\leq_m^{\text{FP}}$*-complete for* Mid P.

Proof. LexMidΣ_1Sat $\in$ Mid P, since we can use the nondeterminism of the Turing machine to guess the assignment of the free variables *and* a value for the quantified variables. If such a guess leads to a satisfying assignment, then the machine prints the assignment of the free variables.

We now show Univ$_{\text{Mid}}$ $\leq_m^{\text{FP}}$ LexMidΣ_1Sat: Given a machine M and an input x, build a Σ_1-formula F with free variables $y_1, \ldots, y_m$ saying "there is an accepting path of M on input x with output $y_1 \cdots y_m$." Then, the middle y printed by M is equal to the middle satisfying assignment of F. □

Problem: MidWeightSat

Input: a propositional formula F with weights on its variables

Output: the middle number in the set of the sums of the weights of variables assigned "true" over all satisfying assignments of F

Problem: MidKnapsack

Input: integers $x_1, \ldots, x_n, M, N$

Output: the middle sum $\sum_{i \in S} x_i - M$ in the set of sums over all $S \subseteq \{1, \ldots, n\}$ that sum up to a value between 0 and $N - M$.

Problem: MidTSPTour

Input: weighted undirected graph G

Output: the length of the middle Travelling Salesperson Tour over the set of all possible round-trips in G.

Theorem 22. MidWeightSat, MidKnapsack, *and* MidTSPTour *are* $\leq_m^{\text{FP}}$*-complete for* Mid P.

Proof. All proofs are similar to the corresponding ones in the previous subsection. □

5 Completeness Results for Classes of Sets

In this section we will prove that completeness results for a median class as just given allow one to directly deduce completeness results for PP, PP^{NP} and P^{PP}. Thus using the results from the previous section we get a number of natural sets complete for these classes.

Theorem 23.

1. If f is $\leq_m^{FP}$-complete for $\overline{Med}\,P$ or $Med\,P$, then the set $\{\,(x,k)\mid f(x)\geq k\,\}$ is $\leq_m^P$-complete for PP.
2. If f is $\leq_m^{FP}$-complete for $Mid\,P$, then the set $\{\,(x,k)\mid f(x)\geq k\,\}$ is $\leq_m^P$-complete for PP^{NP}.

Proof. We give the proof for Statement 1. The proof for 2 is similar.

In [12] it was shown that the class PP is exactly equal to the class of sets A for which there exists an $f\in\overline{Med}\,P$ (or alternatively, $f\in Med\,P$) and a $g\in FP$ such that for all x, $x\in A$ if and only if $f(x)\geq g(x)$. Thus $\{\,(x,k)\mid f(x)\geq k\,\}$ is in PP for $f\in\overline{Med}\,P\cup Med\,P$.

Let now f be complete for $Med\,P$ (the proof for $\overline{Med}\,P$ is completely analogous) and A be some set from the class PP. Then by the remarks above there exists $h\in Med\,P$ and a $g\in FP$ such that for all x, $x\in A$ if and only if $h(x)\geq g(x)$. From the completeness of f we get the existence of some $g'\in FP$ such that for all x, $h(x)=f(g'(x))$. Thus,

$$x\in A \iff f(g'(x))\geq g(x)$$
$$\iff (g'(x),g(x))\in\{\,(x,k)\mid f(x)\geq k\,\}$$

Thus, the function $g''\in FP$, defined by $g''(x)=_{\mathrm{def}}(g'(x),g(x))$ reduces A to $\{\,(x,k)\mid f(x)\geq k\,\}$. □

Thus the problems from Subsections 4.1 and 4.2 yield a number of complete problems for PP and the problems from Subsection 4.3 yield natural complete probems for PP^{NP}; e.g. to determine whether the length of the middle element in the set of all TSP-tours of a graph G is greater than a given number k is complete for PP^{NP}.

The next theorem allows us to use the results from Section 4 to get completeness results for the class P^{PP}. Toda [9] proved a number of sets to be complete for this class, but he had to give an individual proof for each problem. Our result generalizes his work and it yields completeness results in a uniform more or less mechanical way. Toda showed that P^{PP} is exactly the class of sets A for which there exists an $f\in Mid\,P$ such that for all x, $x\in A \iff f(x)\equiv 1$ (mod 2). Proposition 5 shows that in this characterization, we might as well choose $f\in\overline{Med}\,P$ or $f\in Med\,P$. We now prove that the set obtained from a complete function f is itself complete for P^{PP}:

Theorem 24. If f is $\leq_m^{FP}$-complete for $\overline{Med}\,P$, $Med\,P$, or $Mid\,P$, then the set $\{\,x\mid f(x)\equiv 1\pmod 2\,\}$ is $\leq_m^P$-complete for P^{PP}.

Proof. For f from any of the considered classes of median functions, the set $\{\, x \mid f(x) \equiv 1 \pmod 2 \,\}$ is in P^{PP}, since we can determine the middle element by binary search and then check if it is odd. Let now f be complete for Med P (the proofs for $\overline{\text{Med}}\,P$ and Mid P are completely analogous) and let A be some set from P^{PP}. Then the characteristic function from A is in FP^{PP}. As consequence of the remarks following Proposition 5 we get the existence of a function $h \in$ Med P such that $x \in A$ if and only if $h(x)$ is odd. From the completeness of f we get the existence of some $g' \in FP$ such that for all x, $h(x) = f(g'(x))$. Thus,

$$x \in A \iff f(g'(x)) \equiv 1 \pmod 2$$
$$\iff g'(x) \in \{\, x \mid f(x) \equiv 1 \pmod 2 \,\}$$

Thus, g' reduces A to $\{\, x \mid f(x) \equiv 1 \pmod 2 \,\}$. $\qquad\square$

Acknowdledgement. Thanks to Klaus W. Wagner (Würzburg) for steady support and many helpful discussions. Thanks to Ulrich Hertrampf (Würzburg) for very carefully reading an earlier draft of this paper and for lots of helpful comments.

References

1. J. L. BALCÁZAR, J. DÍAZ, J. GABARRÓ, *Structural Complexity I and II;* Springer (Berlin – Heidelberg – New York, 1988 and 1990).
2. R. BEIGEL, Perceptrons, PP, and the polynomial time hierarchy; 7th *Structure in Complexity Theory Conference* (1992), pp. 14–19.
3. S. A. COOK, The complexity of theorem proving procedures; 3rd *Symposium on the Theory of Computing* (1971), pp. 151–158.
4. M. R. GAREY, D. S. JOHNSON, *Computers and Intractability: A Guide to the Theorey of* NP-*Completeness;* Freeman & Co. (New York, 1979).
5. J. KÖBLER, Strukturelle Komplexität von Anzahlproblemen, Dissertation, Fakultät für Informatik, Universität Stuttgart, 1989 .
6. M. W. KRENTEL, The complexity of optimization problems; *Journal of Computer and Systems Sciences* **36** (1988), pp. 490–509.
7. C. H. PAPADIMITRIOU, On the complexity of unique solutions; *Journal of the ACM* **31** (1982), pp. 392–400.
8. C. H. PAPADIMITRIOU, K. STEIGLITZ, *Combinatorial Optimization;* Prentice Hall (Englewood Cliffs, New Jersey, 1992).
9. S. TODA, The complexity of finding medians; 31st *Symposium on Foundations of Computer Science* (1990), pp. 778–787.
10. J. TORÁN, Complexity classes defined by counting quantifiers; *Journal of the ACM* **38** (1991), pp. 753–774.
11. L. G. VALIANT, The complexity of computing the permanent; *Theoretical Computer Science* **8** (1979), pp. 189–201.
12. H. VOLLMER, K. W. WAGNER, The complexity of finding middle elements; Technical report No. 53, University Würzburg; to appear in the *International Journal of Foundations of Computer Science.*
13. K. W. WAGNER, The complexity of combinatorial problems with succinct input representation; *Acta Informatica* **23** (1986), pp. 325—356.

Parallel Algorithms 2

Optimal Parallelization of Las Vegas Algorithms

Michael Luby[†]   Wolfgang Ertel[‡]

International Computer Science Institute
Berkeley, California

Abstract

We describe a parallel simulation strategy with optimal expected running time for Las Vegas Algorithms. This strategy has been implemented on a network of workstations and applied to a randomized automated theorem prover.

1   Introduction

Let A be a randomized algorithm of the *Las Vegas* type, i.e., an algorithm that uses a source of truly random bits and has the following properties. Let $A(x)$ denote algorithm A with respect to fixed input x and let the random bits used by A be called the *seed*. For any x, and for any setting of the seed, when (and if) $A(x)$ halts it produces a correct answer. However, the exact behavior of $A(x)$, and in particular its running time, $T_A(x)$, depends on the setting of the seed. For example, for some settings of the seed $A(x)$ could halt in one step whereas for other settings $A(x)$ could run forever.

In [1], the following problem was studied in the sequential setting: Find a sequential simulation strategy for $A(x)$ that minimizes the expected time required to get an answer. In this setting, $A(x)$ is viewed as a black box, and the only allowable use of $A(x)$ is the following: Choose at random a setting for the seed and run $A(x)$ for t_1 steps. If $A(x)$ halts within time t_1 then we are done, otherwise randomly and independently choose another seed and run $A(x)$ for t_2 steps, etc. Thus, a *sequential strategy S* consists of a sequence of positive integers $(t_1, t_2, \ldots)$, and $S(A(x))$ denotes the new Las Vegas algorithm that is obtained by applying S to $A(x)$.

Of special interest are sequential *repeating* strategies, i.e. strategies that consist of repetitions of the same experiment. For every positive integer t, we let $S_t = (t, t, t, \ldots)$ denote the repeating sequential strategy with experiments of length t. For notational convenience, we let S_∞ be the sequential strategy which when applied to an algorithm consists of running the algorithm as is, i.e., $S_\infty(A(x))$ is identical to $A(x)$.

[†]Research supported in part by NSF Grants CCR-9016468 & CCR-9304722 and grant No. 89-00312 & 92-00226 from the United States-Israel Binational Science Foundation (BSF), Jerusalem, Israel.

[‡]Research supported by an ICSI Postdoctoral Fellowship.

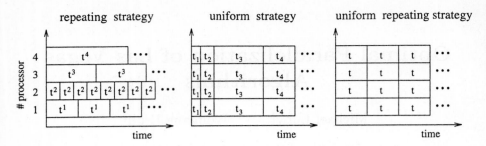

Figure 1: Three important subclasses of strategies.

In this paper, we consider parallel simulation strategies for this problem. Throughout, we let k denote the number of processors on which the parallel simulation is to be executed. A *parallel strategy* $\mathcal{S}^k$ is described by the k sequential strategies $(t_1^1, t_2^1, \ldots), \ldots, (t_1^k, t_2^k, \ldots).$[1] Strategy $\mathcal{S}^k$ applied to $A(x)$, $\mathcal{S}^k(A(x))$, consists of using the k processors to execute independently and in parallel each of the k sequential strategies applied to $A(x)$. The overall parallel algorithm successfully halts at the first point in time when one of the k sequential simulations halts, i.e., this can be viewed as a *competition* among the k sequential strategies.

The three subclasses of parallel strategies illustrated in Figure 1 will be of special interest for us. A strategy $\mathcal{S}^k$ is *repeating* if each of the k sequential strategies defining $\mathcal{S}^k$ is repeating; such a strategy can be described by a set of k positive integers.

A strategy $\mathcal{S}^k$ is *uniform* if each of the k sequential strategies defining $\mathcal{S}^k$ is identical, and thus when $\mathcal{S}^k$ is applied to any algorithm all k processors restart their experiments within their sequential simulations at exactly the same points in time. Any uniform strategy can be described as a composition of the following strategy $\mathcal{PAR}^k$ with a sequential strategy. $\mathcal{PAR}^k$ is the simple strategy which when applied to any algorithm consists of running the algorithm independently in parallel on k processors and stopping when the first of the k independent executions halts. Thus, $\mathcal{PAR}^k(A(x))$ consists of running $A(x)$ on k processors in parallel using independently chosen seeds. Any uniform strategy can be expressed as the composition of $\mathcal{PAR}^k$ and some sequential strategy $\mathcal{S}$, where the composed strategy is denoted $\mathcal{PAR}^k \circ \mathcal{S}$.[2]

We let $\mathcal{S}_t^k = \mathcal{PAR}^k \circ S_t$ denote the *uniform repeating* strategy which imposes the same fixed time bound t on all experiments executed by all processors.

This paper proves results about parallel simulations that are analogous to the sequential simulation results shown in [1]. If full knowledge is available about the distribution of $T_A(x)$, then it is possible to design a uniform repeating strategy $\mathcal{S}_*^k$ that is *close to optimal*, in the sense that for any fixed k it achieves the minimum expected running time within a constant factor amongst all strategies for $A(x)$. In Section 2 we will show that this is true for a carefully chosen value t_*^k that depends on the entire distribution of $T_A(x)$ and the number of processors k used. Let $\ell_A^k(x)$ be the expected running time of this strategy. Similar to the sequential setting [1], $\ell_A^k(x)$ is a natural and easily characterized quantity associated with the distribution of $T_A(x)$.

---

[1]In the following, we will use the general term *strategy* for parallel strategies ($k > 1$), but we will always use *sequential strategy* if a strategy is not parallel ($k = 1$).

[2]The composition of two strategies $\mathcal{S}$ and $\mathcal{R}$ yields a new strategy $\mathcal{R} \circ \mathcal{S}$, and when this new strategy is applied to $A(x)$ it defines a new algorithm $(\mathcal{R} \circ \mathcal{S})(A(x)) \equiv \mathcal{R}(\mathcal{S}(A(x)))$.

While the existence of an optimal strategy is an interesting theoretical observation, it is of little value in practice because it requires for its implementation detailed information about the distribution of $T_A(x)$. In practical applications, very little, if any, a priori information is available about this distribution, and its shape may vary wildly with x. Furthermore, since we only want the answer once for any x, there is no point in running experiments to gather information about the distribution: the only information that could be gathered from such a run is that $A(x)$ stops, in which case we also obtain the answer. Thus, the problem we address is that of designing an efficient *universal* strategy, i.e., one that is to be used for all distributions on running times.

In [1], a simple universal sequential strategy S_{univ} was introduced. In Section 3 we consider the simple universal parallel strategy $\mathcal{PAR}^k \circ S_{\text{univ}}$, which we hereafter call S^k_{univ}. We show that for any $A(x)$ and any k the expected running time of $S^k_{\text{univ}}(A(x))$ is $O(\ell^k_A(x) \log(\ell^k_A(x)))$,[3] which is only a logarithmic factor slower than an optimal strategy that assumes full information about the distribution. For a wide variety of distributions — esp. distributions with infinite or very long running times — even for $k = 1$ this represents a dramatic speedup over the naïve sequential strategy of running the algorithm till termination on one processor.

An important application area for this kind of parallelization of randomized algorithms is combinatorial search. Here, the algorithm $A(x)$ consists of random search of a (often highly unbalanced) tree. A straightforward way to parallelize such a randomized search algorithm is to use $\mathcal{PAR}^k(A(x))$. In [3] this strategy was called *random competition* and applied to randomized combinatorial search algorithms with various examples from automated theorem proving, some of which will be used here again. The distribution on the running time of the randomized theorem prover turned out to be wildly erratic for most of the examples.

We show in Section 2 for large classes of problems when the distribution is known that almost linear speedup can be achieved with an optimal uniform strategy. Even if the distribution is not known, for most examples the speedup (of S^k_{univ}) is close to linear. This is one of the benefits over [3] where $A(x)$ was parallelized without using a provably good universal strategy and therefore the speedup figures were hardly predictable.

Due to space restrictions most proofs had to be removed from this paper. They can be found in [2].

2 Known Distribution

In the remainder of this paper, we identify a Las Vegas algorithm A, together with an input x, with the probability distribution p on its running time $T_A(x)$. Thus p is a probability distribution over $\mathbb{Z}^+ \cup \{\infty\}$, and $p(t)$ denotes the probability that $A(x)$ stops after exactly t steps. We will always assume that p is non-trivial in the sense that $p(\infty) < 1$, so that there exists a finite earliest time, $t = t_{\min}$ say, for which $p(t) > 0$. Our main focus of attention is the expected running time of a strategy S^k on k processors when applied to an algorithm $A(x)$ described by distribution p, which we denote $E(S^k, p)$. We will always be considering a fixed distribution p, so we abbreviate $E(S^k, p)$ to $E(S^k)$.

The first question we ask is the following. Suppose that we have full knowledge of the distribution p; is there some strategy S^k that is *optimal* for p, in the sense that $E(S^k) = \inf_{S^k} E(S^k)$? In contrast to the sequential case [1], where the optimal sequential strategy is the repeating sequence $S_* = (t_*, t_*, t_*, \ldots)$ for a carefully chosen value of t_*, the optimal parallel strategy is not easy to describe. Although the best uniform strategy

---

[3] All logarithms in this paper are base 2.

is within a constant factor of optimal as we will see in Theorem 1 it turns out that this strategy is not necessarily optimal.

The uniform repeating strategy S_t^k can be viewed as a sequential repeating strategy, where each run consists of k parallel independent runs of $A(x)$ with the time bound t. Thus, we can apply the sequential results from [1] for computing the expected value of any uniform repeating strategy. However, we have to use a different probability density function $p^k(t)$, which denotes the probability that the shortest of k runs takes t steps.

The parallel density function p^k depends on p and k in the following way. If we define the cumulative distribution q^k (we will use the abbreviations $q = q^1$, $p = p^1$, $r = r^1$ for the sequential case) in the standard way and the tail probability as $r^k(t) \equiv 1 - q^k(t)$, it is easy to see that $r^k(t) = r(t)^k$. In [1] the expected value $\ell(t)$ of a sequential strategy $S_t = (t, t, t, \ldots)$ was shown to be

$$\ell(t) \equiv E(S_t) = \frac{1}{q(t)}\Big(t - \sum_{t'=0}^{t-1} q(t')\Big) = \frac{\sum_{t'=0}^{t-1} r(t')}{q(t)}. \tag{1}$$

In order to specify the optimal sequential strategy, we define

$$\ell_p = \inf_{t < \infty} \ell(t). \tag{2}$$

It is easy to see that ℓ is finite for any non-trivial distribution p. Let t_* be any finite value of t for which $\ell(t) = \ell$, if such a value exists, and $t_* = \infty$ otherwise. From [1] we know that for any distribution p, the sequential strategy $S_* \equiv S_{t_*} = (t_*, t_*, t_*, \ldots)$ is an optimal sequential strategy for p, and $E(S_*) = \ell_p$.

To formulate a similar theorem for the parallel case we define t_*^k as that value of t for which $\ell^k(t)$ is minimal, in the same way as above, where we now have

$$\ell_p^k = \inf_{t<\infty} \ell^k(t) \qquad \text{and} \qquad \ell^k(t) = E(S_t^k) = \frac{\sum_{t'=0}^{t-1} r^k(t')}{q^k(t)}. \tag{3}$$

The so defined strategy $S_*^k \equiv S_{t_*^k}^k$ is the *optimal uniform strategy*[4], which we will prove to be close to optimal.

Theorem 1 *The running time $E(S_*^k) = \ell_p^k$ of the optimal uniform strategy S_*^k is within a constant factor of the running time of an optimal strategy.*

To prove this theorem we develop a simplified intuitive model of execution which is mathematically easier to analyse.

2.1 The SIMD-Model

To simplify the analysis we restrict our general model of execution for uniform repeating strategies and define the *SIMD-model* as follows: A run of any uniform repeating strategy S_t^k in the SIMD-model is only allowed to stop at times which are integer multiples of the time bound t, i.e. S_t^k stops at the next multiple of t after the first processor stops, or more formally, S_t^k stops at mt iff one of the k instances of $A(x)$ terminates at any time t' where $(m-1)t < t' \le mt$. This makes mathematical analysis much easier since only complete runs of equal length have to be considered. In the following we use $E_{\text{SIMD}}(S^k)$ to denote that the expected value is computed in the SIMD-model. All other expected values are in the general model.

---

[4] Note that *optimal* in this term is relative to uniform strategies.

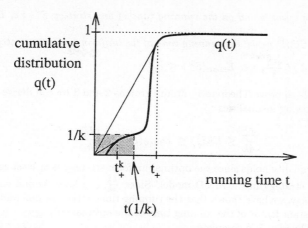

Figure 2: Graphical interpretation of $L_p(t)$ and construction of t_+.

It is immediately obvious that the expected execution time of any strategy in the *SIMD-model* is at least as big as its expected value in the general model. It will be helpful to introduce one further function associated with a distribution p. For finite values of $t \geq t_{\min}$, define $L_p(t) = t/q(t)$, where q is the cumulative distribution function of p as before, and by analogy with (2) define

$$L_p = \inf_{t<\infty} L(t). \tag{4}$$

and

$$L_p^k = \inf_{t<t(1/k)} L(t), \qquad \text{where} \quad t(x) = \inf\{t : q(t) \geq x\}. \tag{5}$$

Here $t(x)$ denotes the smallest value of t for which $q(t) \geq x$. Note that $\ell_p \leq L_p \leq 4\ell_p$; the first inequality is obvious, and the second may readily be checked. Furthermore, as can easily be verified, there are always some finite values $t = t_+$ and $t = t_+^k$ such that $L_p(t_+) = L_p$ and $L_p(t_+^k) = L_p^k$.

The quantity $L_p(t)$ is equal to the expected value of the running time of the sequential repeating strategy S_t in the SIMD-model, since in the average $\frac{1}{q(t)}$ runs of $A(x)$ with length t have to be made. The optimal sequential repeating strategy in the SIMD-model is $S_+ \equiv S_{t_+}$ since the minimum of the expected running time $L_p(t)$ is at $t = t_+$. The motivation for the above construction of the parallel time bound t_+^k is the following. If for any given k the value of $q(t)$ is less than $1/k$, then the amount of redundancy of the k parallel runs of $A(x)$ is negligible and $q^k(t)$ is close to $k\,q(t)$, i.e. the sum of the cumulative probabilities of all processors. To be a little more specific, if $q(t) = 1/k$, then $k\,q(t) = 1$ whereas we have $q^k(t) = 1 - (1 - 1/k)^k$ which is greater than $1 - \frac{1}{e} \approx 0.632$.[5]

A graphical interpretation of L_p and L_p^k is given in Figure 2 where the cumulative distribution function $q(t)$ is plotted vs. the time t. The point t_+ of minimal expected value of the sequential repeating strategy in the SIMD-model is that value of t for which the slope $(q(t)/t)$ of the straight line from the origin to the graph of $q(t)$ is maximal. In the same way t_+^k is constructed, but with the constraint that the point of maximal slope must be found within the shaded region ($q(t) \leq 1/k$).

To prove Theorem 1 we show a lower bound on the expected running time of any strategy and an upper bound for the running time in the SIMD-model.

---

[5] $e \approx 2.7182818$ is the Euler number.

Lemma 2 $\frac{L_p^k}{4k}$ *is a lower bound on the running time of any strategy* S^k, *i.e.* $E(S^k) \geq \frac{L_p^k}{4k}$.

Lemma 3 *In the SIMD-model the running time of the uniform repeating strategy* $S_+^k \equiv S_{t_+^k}^k$ *has an upper bound of* $\frac{eL_p^k}{k}$, *i.e.* $E_{\text{SIMD}}(S_+^k) \leq \frac{eL_p^k}{k}$.

We are now able to prove Theorem 1. From Lemmas 2 and 3 we can derive the first and the last of the following inequalities

$$\frac{L_p^k}{4k} \leq E(S_*^k) \leq E_{\text{SIMD}}(S_+^k) \leq \frac{eL_p^k}{k}$$

and the second inequality holds since the optimal uniform strategy is at least as good as any uniform repeating strategy in the SIMD-model. Since $\frac{L_p^k}{4k}$ is a lower bound on the running time of every strategy, we have shown that the running time of the optimal uniform strategy S_*^k is within a constant factor of the running time of the optimal strategy with k processors and the proof of Theorem 1 is complete.

2.2 The best Uniform Repeating Strategy is not Optimal

Unlike in the sequential case, the optimal uniform strategy is not optimal for all distributions $q(t)$. We demonstrate this with a counterexample, i.e. we show that there exists a distribution $q(t)$ for which there is a non-uniform strategy which has smaller expected value than the optimal uniform strategy.

Theorem 4 *The optimal uniform strategy* S_*^k *is not the best strategy for all distributions* $q(t)$.

Proof: The distribution $p(t)$ with $p(3) = p(7) = 1/2$ allows the algorithm $A(x)$ to stop only at the times $t = 3$ and $t = 7$. Thus, the only useful time bounds t_i^j in any strategy are 3 and 7. Any other time bound ($t \in \{1, 2, 4, 5, 6\}$) would waste at least part of the running time of $A(x)$ while waiting for the impossible event. If we use two processors, the running time of the uniform repeating strategy can be computed by equation (3) which results in the the same expected running time of 4 for the two strategies S_3^2 and S_7^2. This is not optimal, since the strategy

$$S = \begin{pmatrix} 3, 3 \\ 7 \end{pmatrix}$$

with the expected running time $E(S) = \frac{3}{4} \cdot 3 + \frac{1}{8} \cdot 6 + \frac{1}{8} \cdot 7 = \frac{31}{8}$ is better. $\quad\square$

Remarks: (a) S is better than S_3^2 since the guaranteed termination after 7 time-steps reduces the expected running time. S is better than S_7^2 since a second parallel run of 7 steps can not increase the probability to stop after 7 steps, since this is already 1 with only one processor. Starting a new run after 3 steps on one processor creates the chance to stop after 6 steps and therefore a shorter expected running time.

This and other similar counter-examples show that finding the optimal parallel strategy for a given distribution $q(t)$ is a complex optimization problem which is similar to bin packing. The task here is to assemble a set of time-bounds from the support of p into a strategy S^k such that the expected value $E(S^k)$ is minimal. Like in other optimization problems, a close to optimal solution can be found in time $O(|p|)$ where $|p|$ is the number of different running times with nonzero probability. Since the scheduling strategies in general consist of infinite sequences, it might even be impossible to give a finite description of the optimal strategy. It remains an open question whether an algorithm exists for that problem which is polynomial in the size of the distribution p for the case that full information about the distribution is available.

(b) For the case of more than 2 processors the optimal strategy is to execute one run of 7 steps on one processor and on the $k - 1$ remaining processors the same strategy $(3, 3)$.

2.3 Speedup of the Optimal Uniform Strategy

We have shown that the uniform repeating strategy S_*^k is close to optimal, i.e. no strategy can do much better. However, we do not know whether this strategy is efficient, i.e. if for a not too large number of processors k the speedup is linear (i.e. equal to k) or close to linear. We define the Speedup $Sp_{\mathrm{opt}}(k)$ of the strategy S_*^k by relating its expected running time to the optimal sequential strategy S_*.

$$Sp_{\mathrm{opt}}(k) \equiv \frac{E(S_*)}{E(S_*^k)} = \frac{\ell_p}{\ell^k}.$$

Since the sequential strategy S_* has optimal expected running time [1], the speedup $Sp_{\mathrm{opt}}(k)$ can at most be k. Unfortunately, it is not true that the speedup is almost linear for all distributions p. If for example $p(t) = 1$ for $t = t_0$ (i.e. $p(t) = 0$ for $t \neq t_0$) then no strategy – neither parallel nor sequential – can run faster than t_0 and in particular we have $Sp_{\mathrm{opt}}(k) \equiv 1$. However, the next Lemma says that for a large class of distributions, if the number of processors used is not too large, the speedup is close to linear.

Lemma 5 *If $k\, q(t_*) \ll 1$ then $Sp_{\mathrm{opt}}(k) \approx k$.*

The intuitition behind this is as follows. If $q(t_*)$ is small enough such that $k\, q(t_*)$ is well below 1 then the probability that some processor is successful is close to the sum of the individual success probabilities of the processors and thus their efficiency (speedup) is close to optimal. However, if $k \gg 1/q(t_*)$, then, since $1/q(t_*)$ processors running for t_* have about the same probability of success (close to probability 1) as k processors running for t_* time, and thus the speedup is clearly sublinear. The experimental speedup figures shown in Section 4 confirm these results and show that for almost all our examples close to linear speedup can be achieved with the optimal uniform strategy.

3 Unknown Distribution

The optimal uniform strategy S_*^k described in the previous section clearly requires detailed knowledge of the distribution p for its implementation. As we have already explained, however, in the applications we have in mind there will be no information available about p. We are therefore led to ask what is the best performance we can achieve in the absence of any a priori knowledge of p. Our next theorem says that, with no knowledge whatsoever about the distribution p, we can always come surprisingly close to the optimum value for the case of full knowledge given in Theorem 1. Moreover, this performance is achieved by a uniform strategy of a very simple form that is easy to implement in practice.

In [1] the universal sequential strategy $S_{\mathrm{univ}} = (1, 1, 2, 1, 1, 2, 4, \dots)$ was described and proven to be within a logarithmic factor of any optimal sequential strategy. One way to describe this sequential strategy is to say that for each processor all run lengths are powers of two, and that each time a pair of runs of a given length has been completed, a run of twice that length is immediately executed. For a more formal definition we give a recursive function s that computes any finite prefix of the sequence of running times for one processor up to the first run of length 2^{n+1}

$$\forall n \in \mathbf{N} \cup \{0\} : \quad s(n+1) = (s(n), s(n), 2^{n+1})$$
$$s(0) = (1)$$

where for all sequences a, b, c we define $((a), (b), c) = (a, b, c)$. Note that the sequential strategy is "balanced" in the sense that the total time spent on runs of each length is roughly equal.

Now, if k processors are available, we run this sequential strategy competitively on all processors and define $\mathcal{S}_{\text{univ}}^k \equiv \mathcal{PAR}^k(\mathcal{S}_{\text{univ}})$.

Theorem 6 *For all p and any strategy $\mathcal{S}^k$* : $E(\mathcal{S}_{\text{univ}}^k) = O(E(\mathcal{S}^k) \log(E(\mathcal{S}^k)))$.

4 Experimental Results

To get an impression of the relevance of the various strategies analysed, we computed the expected value of the running time for a number of different distributions. Each of these distributions is the result of a large number of sample runs of the randomized automated theorem prover SETHEO on a particular mathematical theorem. Thus, here SETHEO acts as the black box algorithm A and any particular theorem as its input x. SETHEO [4] does randomized depth first backtracking search for a first solution in an OR-search-tree. These search-trees usually are highly structured and the solutions are distributed non-uniformly. The resulting running time distributions reflect this complex structure and usually have high variance. As a consequence, in most cases the shortest possible running time $t_{\min}$ of SETHEO is much shorter than the expected running time $E(\mathcal{S}_\infty)$ when SETHEO is run until it stops. Therefore SETHEO is an ideal application of the strategies described above. Since $\mathcal{S}_\infty$ is the default sequential strategy used by SETHEO (and most other combinatorial search algorithms) we will use its expected value as a reference point to compare the sequential repeating strategy $\mathcal{S}_*$ and the sequential universal strategy $\mathcal{S}_{\text{univ}}$.

Two of the example theorems listed in Figure 3 (8-puzzle, queens10) are combinatorial puzzle problems which are easy to formalize in logic. All the other theorems have been selected randomly from a set of several hundred mathematical theorems which SETHEO is able to prove.

The offset time t_{off} for $\mathcal{S}_{\text{univ}}^k$ used for computing the figures in Figure 3 is 100 inferences, since the shortest running time of SETHEO varies between 10 and 100 inferences in most examples.[6] Since the performance of the sequential universal strategy shows only little dependence on t_{off}, we did no further tuning of this parameter for the sequential measurements. With this setting we computed the expected values of the default sequential strategy $\mathcal{S}_\infty$, the optimal sequential repeating strategy $\mathcal{S}_*$ and the sequential universal strategy $\mathcal{S}_{\text{univ}}$ for a number of theorem proving problems which are shown in Figure 3. Hereby we used (3) for $E(\mathcal{S}_*^k)$ and to compute $E(\mathcal{S}_{\text{univ}}^k)$ we used the generic formula

$$E(\mathcal{S}_{\text{univ}}^k) = \sum_{t=0}^{t_1} t\, p(t) + r(t_1) \left(t_1 + \sum_{t=0}^{t_2} t\, p(t) + r(t_2) \left(t_2 + \sum_{t=0}^{t_3} t\, p(t) + \ldots \right) \right)$$

$$= \sum_{i=1}^{\infty} \left(t_{i-1} + \sum_{t=0}^{t_i} t\, p(t) \right) \prod_{j=0}^{i-1} r(t_j)$$

---

[6] The time required for SETHEO to perform one inference step was used as time unit for our measurements.

SETHEO-example	$E(\mathcal{S}_\infty)$	t_*	$E(\mathcal{S}_*)$	$\frac{E(\mathcal{S}_*)}{E(\mathcal{S}_\infty)}$ $t_{\text{off}} = 100$	$E(\mathcal{S}_{\text{univ}})$	$\frac{E(\mathcal{S}_{\text{univ}})}{E(\mathcal{S}_\infty)}$
times4	1640888	160	95672	0.06	327462	0.20
mult3	1104297	88	151617	0.137	227442	0.206
s6-i14	4147714	125	591450	0.143	1870577	0.451
8-puzzle-d15	43533	95	12006	0.276	22071	0.507
i1-d7	4376	104	1992	0.455	3656	0.836
s5-i10	6184	2162	4524	0.732	5725	0.926
non-obvious	34567	1457	14742	0.426	36242	1.05
ip1-i19	1532500	12118	758128	0.495	1656073	1.08
queens10	732790	∞	732790	1.0	2092472	2.86
s8t1-i10	4998	∞	4998	1.0	14043	2.81

Figure 3: Empirical performance comparison of the two sequential strategies $\mathcal{S}_*^k$ and $\mathcal{S}_{\text{univ}}^k$ with the default sequential strategy $\mathcal{S}_\infty$ on a set of theorem proving examples. The table is ordered by the last column, i.e. by the relative expected time of the sequential universal strategy.

with $t_0 = 0$. This formula can be applied to any sequential strategy $\mathcal{S} = (t_1, t_2, \ldots)$. For parallel strategies $p(t)$ has to be replaced by $p^k(t)$.

Of special interest are the fourth and the last numeric columns in Figure 3, where the time ratios are given. As expected, $\mathcal{S}_*$ is always at least as good as $\mathcal{S}_\infty$ and often much better. The sequential universal strategy however is for two examples significantly worse than $\mathcal{S}_\infty$. The reason is that here $\mathcal{S}_\infty$ is already optimal and therefore the logarithmic overhead is reflected in an almost three times longer running time.

However, it must be noted that the distributions of the above examples are only partial. The real distributions for all these examples are infinite, i.e. due to infinite loops in certain branches of the computation[7] the running time can be infinite with finite probability. This means that the expected value of the default sequential strategy $\mathcal{S}_\infty$ for all real distributions would be infinite, whereas $\mathcal{S}_{\text{univ}}$ and $\mathcal{S}_*$ still have finite expected value for all these examples.[8] A detailed comparison of the sequential universal strategy with other sequential search strategies (e.g. iterative deepening search) that guarantee finite expected values is part of ongoing research and will be published separately.

Here we are mainly interested in speedup results of $\mathcal{S}_*^k$ and $\mathcal{S}_{\text{univ}}^k$ which are shown for four of the above examples in Figure 4. The uppermost diagram for each example shows $n(t)$, the frequency of the observed running times which is approximately proportional to $p(t)$ together with the mean running times of the different sequential strategies. The two lower graphs which have the same abscissae show the speedup curves Sp_{opt} and Sp_{univ} and the ratio of these two, which gives an estimate of how far $\mathcal{S}_{\text{univ}}^k$ is from optimal.

4.1 Speedup of the Optimal Uniform Strategy

For all examples except the last one in Figure 4 the speedup of the optimal uniform strategy is close to linear if the number of processors is not too large. This is the region

---

[7]The infinite loops are essentially due to the undecidability of first order predicate logic.

[8]Note that for all nontrivial distributions p, $\mathcal{S}_{\text{univ}}$ as well as $\mathcal{S}_*$ and $\mathcal{S}_+$ have finite expected running time.

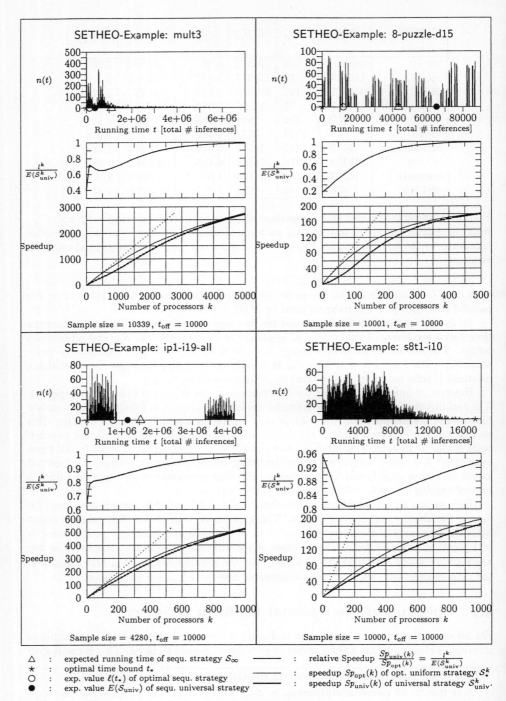

Figure 4: Empirical running time distribution and speedup of optimal repeating strategy and universal strategy computed for four examples.

where $k\, q(t_*) \ll 1$ and therefore Theorem 5 applies. We also see that at least in this region of few processors $\mathcal{S}_*^k$ is very close to optimal. For the example "mult3", even with 1000 processors a speedup of 870 can be achieved. Close to linear speedup has also been observed in all the other examples listed in Figure 3. For the last example "s8t1-i10" the speedup Sp_{opt} of $\mathcal{S}_*^k$ is clearly sublinear, even for a small number of processors. The reason for this is that $q(t_*) = 1$ and therefore $k\, q(t_*) \geq 1$, so the requirement for close to linear speedup is not fulfilled.

4.2   Speedup of the Universal Strategy

A drawback of the universal strategy is that all runs which are shorter than the shortest possible running time $t_{\min}$ of $A(x)$ are superfluous. An obvious way to improve $\mathcal{S}_{\text{univ}}^k$ is therefore to multiply all the time bounds t_i by an offset value t_{off}. The best value for t_{off} is close to t_*^k, but t_*^k is not known in practice. However, it is also helpful to have some knowledge about the shortest possible running time and use this to get a better offset value.

In all the parallel experiments we used $t_{\text{off}} = 10000$. For any fixed input x and fixed number of processors there is a value of t_{off} that minimizes the expected running time $E(\mathcal{S}_{\text{univ}}^k)$. Nevertheless, we always used $t_{\text{off}} = 10000$, since we are interested in a *universal* strategy, that works well for all examples without any knowledge of the distribution. Note that for $t_{\text{off}} = \infty$ the universal strategy is equal to the strategy $\mathcal{PAR}^k = \mathcal{S}_\infty^k$ which does nothing else than competition of k independent runs of $A(x)$.

In all the examples the speedup Sp_{univ} of $\mathcal{S}_{\text{univ}}^k$ is close to that of $\mathcal{S}_*^k$. As we observed, for a fixed probability distribution, if k is fixed large enough, then as t_{off} is getting bigger, the speedup of $\mathcal{S}_{\text{univ}}^k$ is increasing, asymptotically approaching the optimal possible speedup. In other words, for large (but fixed) number of processors the highest speedup can be achieved with $t_{\text{off}} = \infty$, i.e. if on all processors $A(x)$ is being executed without interrupt. If for example $k \gg 1/q(t_{\min})$ and $t_{\text{off}} \geq t_{\min}$ no processor is interrupted before $t_{\min}$ and with high probability one of the processors stops within the first $t_{\min}$ steps and thus the expected running time is close to $t_{\min}$. On the other hand no strategy can stop before $t_{\min}$ steps. Thus it makes no big difference if all processors run with the optimal time bound or without any time bound. If however the offset of $\mathcal{S}_{\text{univ}}^k$ is too small, the logarithmic overhead decreases performance drastically.

These results show that the simplest parallel strategy $\mathcal{PAR}^k = \mathcal{S}_\infty^k$ performs very well if the number of processors is really large. For small k however, in most cases $\mathcal{S}_{\text{univ}}^k$ is better than running $A(x)$ without interrupt. Therefore, at least for small k the universal strategy with a smaller offset value is extremely useful. We found that the performance of the sequential strategy $\mathcal{S}_{\text{univ}}$ does not depend strongly on t_{off} and that as a reasonable heuristic value t_{off} should be somewhat bigger than the shortest possible running time.

5   Implementation

An implementation of $\mathcal{PAR}^k$, which is identical to the parallel default strategy $\mathcal{S}_\infty^k$ for SETHEO has been performed on a network of 110 HP 9000/720 workstations

474

with a total raw performance of more than 6000 MIPS. The only overhead due to parallel implementation is caused by the broadcast used to start and stop the whole system and takes a total time between some milliseconds and 12 seconds, depending on the safety requirements on the communication protocol used. Therefore, for the hard theorem proving problems which require use of a parallel machine these times are negligible.

Since these values do not change if the universal strategy $\mathcal{S}^k_{univ}$ is used, the speedup figures computed in the previous section will with almost no change transfer to the 110 processor implementation. If a pure broadcast on the Ethernet is used, the communication time for starting and stopping is constant (i.e. it does not depend on the number of workstations used) and therefore, as many workstations as available can be used.

With this implementation of $\mathcal{S}^k_\infty$ it was possible to prove two new theorems, Sam's lemma (lattice theory) in 50.4 sec. and Ex5 (group theory) in 36.8 sec., which could both not be solved by SETHEO within several days. For more details on the implementation and results see [3].

References

[1] M. LUBY, A. SINCLAIR, D. ZUCKERMAN. Optimal speedup of las vegas algorithms. Information Processing Letters 47, 1993, 173-180.

[2] M. LUBY, W. ERTEL. Optimal Parallelisation of Las Vegas Algorithms. TR-93-041, International Computer Science Institute, Berkeley CA, 1993.

[3] W. ERTEL. OR-Parallel theorem proving with random competition. *In: Logic Programming and Automated Reasoning,* Springer LNAI 624, 1992, 226–237.

[4] R. LETZ, J. SCHUMANN, S. BAYERL, W. BIBEL. SETHEO, a high-performance theorem prover. Journal of Automated Reasoning 8(2), 1992, 183–212.

Efficient Parallel Algorithms for Geometric k-Clustering Problems *

(Extended Abstract)

Amitava Datta [†]

Abstract

We present efficient parallel algorithms for two geometric k-clustering problems in the CREW PRAM model of parallel computation. Given a point set P of n points in two dimensions, these problems are to find a k-point subset such that some measure for this subset is minimized. We consider the problems of finding a k-point subset with minimum L_∞ perimeter and minimum L_∞ diameter. For the L_∞ perimeter case, our algorithm runs in $O(\log^2 n)$ time and $O(n \log^2 n + nk^2 \log^2 k)$ work. For the L_∞ diameter case, our algorithm runs in $O(\log^2 n + \log^2 k \log\log k \log^* k)$ time and $O(n \log^2 n)$ work. The work done (processor-time product) by our algorithms is close to the time complexity of best known sequential algorithms. Previously, no parallel algorithm was known for either of these problems.

1 Introduction

Clustering problems are important in *pattern recognition* and *cluster analysis* [1, 9]. In this paper, we consider clustering problems of the following type. Given a point set P with n points, the problem is to compute a subset of k points such that some *closeness measure* is minimized. As an example, we may want to minimize the diameter of the k-point subset. Aggarwal *et al* [2] considered closeness measures like diameter, side length of the enclosing square, the perimeter of enclosing rectangle, etc. They gave algorithms for these problems on the plane based on higher order Voronoi diagrams. Eppstein and Erickson [7] gave a general framework for solving k point clustering problems based on computing rectilinear nearest neighbours for the points in the set P. The best known sequential algorithms for many of these problems were presented by Datta *et al* [6]. They improved upon the strategy of Eppstein and Erickson [7] by imposing a grid on the point set and solving the problems for smaller subsets of points.

The applications in pattern recognition and cluster analysis typically involve large sets of data. Hence, for solving these problems in real-time, it is important to study these problems in the domain of parallel algorithms. In this paper, we initiate the investigation of parallel complexity of these problems. Our model of computation is the *Parallel Random Access Machine (PRAM)* [10]. We are interested in the *Concurrent Read Exclusive Write (CREW)* PRAM. In this model, two or more processors can read from the same memory location simultaneously, but only one processor can write to a memory location at a time. For details of this model, see [10]. In this paper, we give efficient parallel algorithms for two of the k-clustering problems. In the first problem, we compute a minimum L_∞ diameter

---

*This work was done when the author was working as a Post Doctoral Fellow in Max Planck Institut für Informatik, Saarbrücken, Germany. This work was supported by the ESPRIT Basic Research Actions Program, under contract No. 7141 (project ALCOM II).

[†]Praktische Informatik VI, FernUniversität Hagen, Elberfelderstraße 95, D-58084 Hagen, Germany.

k point subset (or the minimum side-length square). In the second problem, we compute the minimum L_∞ perimeter k point subset (or the minimum perimeter rectangle). The best known sequential algorithms for these two problems were given in [6]. The sequential algorithm for the minimum L_∞ diameter k point subset problem runs in $O(n \log n + n \log^2 k)$ time. We present a parallel algorithm which runs in $O(\log^2 n + \log^2 k \log \log k \log^* k)$ time and $O(n \log^2 n)$ work. The sequential algorithm for the minimum L_∞ perimeter problem runs in $O(n \log n + n k^2)$ time. Our parallel algorithm for this problem runs in $O(\log^2 n)$ time and $O(n \log^2 n + n k^2 \log^2 k)$ work. So, the work complexities (processor-time product) of our algorithms compare favourably with the time complexities of the best sequential algorithms, both when k is small or $k = O(n)$.

We solve these problems by non-trivial parallelizations of the algorithms in [6]. For computing the minimum L_∞ perimeter k point subset, we use an optimal parallel construction of the well known geometric data structure of *range tree*. This construction takes $O(\log n)$ time and $O(n)$ processors in the EREW PRAM. Since range searching is an important geometric operation, this construction may be useful for solving other geometric problems in parallel. The rest of the paper is organized as follows. In section 2, we give the general strategy. In section 3, we discuss the construction of a degraded δ-grid in parallel. In section 4, we discuss the problem of range searching in parallel. In section 5, we present the parallel algorithm for finding the minimum L_∞ perimeter k point subset. Finally, in section 6, we present the parallel algorithm for computing minimum L_∞ diameter k point subset.

2 The general strategy

Let P be a set of n points on the plane. The points in the set P are represented by $p_1, p_2, \ldots, p_n$. The x (resp. y) coordinate of the point p_i is represented by x_i (resp. y_i). We use some terminology from [6]. Let k be an integer such that $1 \le k \le n$. By a *box*, we mean a 2 dimensional axes-parallel rectangle of the form $\Pi_{i=1}^{2}[a_i : b_i]$. If $b_i = a_i + \delta$ for $i = 1, 2$, then we call the box as a δ-box. The closure of a box, i.e., the product of 2 closed intervals $[a_i : b_i]$, $i = 1, 2$ is called a *closed box*.

- μ denotes a function which maps a set V of points in 2-space to a real number $\mu(V)$.

- $S(P, k)$ denotes the problem of finding a subset of P of size k whose measure is minimal among all k-point subsets.

- $\mu_{opt}(P)$ denotes the minimal measure.

- P_{opt} denotes a k- point subset of P such that $\mu(P_{opt}) = \mu_{opt}(P)$.

- $\mathcal{A}$ denotes a CREW PRAM algorithm that solves problem $S(P', k)$, where $P' \subset P$ and $|P'| = O(k)$.

- $T(P', k)$ (resp. $W(P', k)$) denotes the time (resp. work) complexity of algorithm $\mathcal{A}$.

For example, if $\mu(B)$ is the L_∞ diameter of set B, then $S(B, k)$ is the problem of finding a subset of size k whose L_∞ diameter is minimum among all k point subsets. We make the following assumptions about the measure μ which we prove later for each of the problems.

Assumption 2.1 *There exists a closed $\mu_{opt}(P)$ box that contains the optimal solution P_{opt}.*

Assumption 2.2 *There exists an integer constant c such that for any $\delta < \mu_{opt}(P)/c$, any closed δ box contains less than k points of P.*

The constant c will depend on the particular problem and we will fix this constant later for each problem. Our algorithms are based on the following

Lemma 2.1 *Let δ be a real number. Assume that there exists a closed δ box that contains at least k points of P. Then $\mu_{opt}(P) \leq c\delta$ and there exists a closed $(c\delta)$ box that contains the optimal solution P_{opt}.*

Proof: By Assumption 2.1, we know that the optimal solution is contained in a closed μ_{opt} box. From Assumption 2.2, we know if $c\delta < \mu_{opt}(P)$, any closed δ-box contains less than k points of P. Hence, the optimal solution cannot be found in such a closed δ-box. This proves that $\mu_{opt} \leq c\delta$. □

Our algorithms work in the following way. We reduce problem $S(P, k)$ to $O(n/k)$ subproblems $S(P', k)$ for subsets $P' \subset P$ of size $O(k)$. All the subproblems are solved simultaneously in parallel. Each subproblem is solved by a CREW PRAM algorithm $\mathcal{A}$. Before discussing the decomposition of our problem, we need some more definitions.

Definition 2.2 *Let δ be a positive real number, let $\alpha \leq \beta$ be positive integers, and let $\mathcal{R}$ be a collection of δ-boxes such that*

1. *each box in $\mathcal{R}$ contains at least one point of P,*

2. *each point of P is contained in exactly one box of $\mathcal{R}$,*

3. *there is a box in $\mathcal{R}$ that contains at least α points of P,*

4. *each box in $\mathcal{R}$ contains at most β points of P.*

Then $\mathcal{R}$ is called an $(\alpha, \beta; \delta)$-covering of P.

We give the generic algorithm $\mathcal{G}$ for both of our problems in Algorithm 1.

---

1. Compute a positive real number δ together with a $(k, 4k; \delta)$ -covering $\mathcal{R}$ of P. In the next section, we compute this covering in $O(\log^2 n)$ time using $O(n)$ processors in the CREW PRAM.

2. For each box $B \in \mathcal{R}$, do the following two substeps:

   (a) Find all boxes in $\mathcal{R}$ that overlap the $(2c + 1)\delta$-box that is centered at B. These boxes are found as follows:
   Let (b_1, b_2) be the lower-left corner of B. Then in the data structure for $\mathcal{R}$, we locate the $(2c + 1)^2$ points
   $$(b_1 + \epsilon_1 \delta, b_2 + \epsilon_2 \delta),$$
   $$\epsilon_i \in \{-c, -c + 1, \ldots, c - 1, c\}, i = 1, 2.$$

   (b) Let P' be the subset of points of P that are contained in the boxes that are found in the previous step. If $|P'| \geq k$, solve problem $S(P', k)$ using algorithm $\mathcal{A}$.

3. Find the optimal solution out of $O(n/k)$ solutions found in Step 2. Output μ_{opt} and P_{opt}.

Algorithm 1: The main steps in our generic algorithm $\mathcal{G}$.

Theorem 2.3 *The algorithm correctly solves the problem $S(P, k)$. Moreover, there is a constant c' such that the algorithm takes $O(\log^2 n + T(c'k, k))$ time and $O(n \log^2 n + (n/k)W(c'k, k))$ work.*

Proof: By Lemma 2.1, there is a closed $(c\delta)$-box that contains the optimal solution. It is clear that this box must be contained in the $(2c+1)\delta$-box that is centered at some box of the data structure $\mathcal{R}$. The algorithm checks all these $(2c+1)\delta$-boxes. If there are less than k points in such a box, then it does not contain the optimal solution. Hence, the correctness of Step 2(b) follows. Each box in $\mathcal{R}$ contains at most $4k$ points. Moreover, the point location queries in Step 2(a) find at most $(2c+1)^2$ boxes of $\mathcal{R}$. Therefore, the set P' in step 2(b) has size at most $(2c+1)^2 4k$. There are at most $(2c+1)^2(n/k)$ boxes $B \in \mathcal{R}$ that give rise to a subset P' of size at least k. Hence, the algorithm $\mathcal{A}$ is applied in parallel to at most $(2c+1)^2(n/k)$ different subsets. We will show in section 3 that a δ-covering $\mathcal{R}$ can be computed in $O(\log^2 n)$ time using $O(n)$ processors. Moreover, in $O(\log n)$ time and using $O(n)$ processors, $\mathcal{R}$ can be stored in a data structure such that a point location query can be answered by a single processor in $O(\log n)$ time. Hence, the correctness of the algorithm follows from the correctness of algorithm $\mathcal{A}$. In Step 3, we have to compute the maximum of $O(n/k)$ quantities. This can be easily done in $O(\log n)$ time using $O(n)$ processors [10] i.e., $O(n \log n)$ work. Also, μ_{opt} and P_{opt} can be reported within this time and work.

So, the running time of our algorithm is bounded by :

$$O(\log^2 n + T((2c+1)^2 4k, k)) \tag{1}$$

and the work done by the algorithm is :

$$O(n \log^2 n + (n/k)(2c+1)^2 W((2c+1)^2 4k, k)) \tag{2}$$

$\square$

3   Parallel algorithm for computing a $(k, 4k; \delta)$ covering

In a standard δ-grid, we divide the plane into slabs of width exactly δ. In such a grid, if we fix a lattice point, all other lattice points are automatically fixed. In a *degraded δ-grid*, the slabs do not start and end at integer multiples of δ. The slabs have width at least δ and the slabs that contain points have width exactly δ. The empty slabs can have arbitrary width. In other words, the degraded grid is defined by the point set it stores. We first give a formal definition of a degraded one-dimensional δ-grid.

Definition 3.1 *[6] Let P be a set of n real numbers and let δ be a positive real number. Let $a_1, a_2, \ldots, a_l$ be a sequence of real numbers such that,*

1. *for all $i \le j < l$, $a_{j+1} \ge a_j + \delta$,*

2. *for all $p \in P$, $a_1 \le p < a_l$,*

3. *for all $1 \le j < l$, if there is a point $p \in P$ such that $a_j \le p < a_{j+1}$, then $a_{j+1} = a_j + \delta$.*

The collection of intervals $[a_j, a_{j+1})$, $1 \le j < l$, is called a one-dimensional degraded δ-grid for P.

3.1   Construction of two-dimensional degraded δ-grid in parallel

We briefly discuss the construction of a one-dimensional δ-grid, given a real number δ. We first store the elements of P according to increasing x coordinates in an array X and associate a processor with each point. The processor associated with point p_i checks whether $|x_{i+1} - x_i| \ge \delta$. If this check succeeds (resp. fails), the processor marks the point p_{i+1} with 1 (resp. 0). The point p_{i+1} is the left boundary of a δ-slab when it is marked 1. The left-most element in the array X, i.e., x_1 is marked with 1. This step clearly can be done by $O(n)$ processors in $O(1)$ time. After this, for every point x_i, we find the nearest 1 to its left. This can be done by the algorithm for finding the *all nearest larger value* [3]. This computation takes $O(n/\log n)$ processors and $O(\log n)$ time in the CREW PRAM. Now, every processor knows the nearest marked element to its left. Suppose, for the point x_m, the nearest marked point to its left is the point x_n. The processor associated with x_m computes the quantity $c = x_n + \delta \times \lfloor |x_m - x_n|/\delta \rfloor$. Then, $c \le x_m \le c + \delta$. It is easy to see that c is the left boundary of the δ-slab to which x_m belongs. It is possible to do this computation without using the non-algebraic floor function. We omit the details in this version. After this step, every element knows the left boundary of its δ-slab. The elements within a δ-slab can be counted easily since we know the boundaries of the δ-slabs. The difference of indices of two consecutive boundaries is the number of points inside that δ-slab. This step also can be done within $O(\log n)$ time using $O(n)$ processors.

The two-dimensional δ-grid is constructed by applying the algorithm recursively within each δ-slab. We omit the details in this version.

Lemma 3.2 *Given a real number δ, a two-dimensional degraded δ-grid can be constructed in $O(\log n)$ time, using $O(n)$ processors in the CREW PRAM. Moreover, this grid can be stored in a data structure $\mathcal{R}$ of size $O(n)$, such that a single processor can answer point location queries in $O(\log n)$ time.*

3.2 Parallel construction of a degraded δ-grid with $O(k)$ points per cell

In this subsection, we discuss how to compute a real number δ and a parallel algorithm for constructing a $(k, 4k; \delta)$ covering. We first use some notations from [6] and prove the existence of such a δ.

Definition 3.3 *Suppose, P is a set of n points on the plane.*

- *Assume δ is a real number and $\mathcal{R}$ is a degraded δ-grid for P. We number the boxes arbitrarily from $1, 2, \ldots, r$, where the number of cells in $\mathcal{R}$ is r. We define n_i to be the number of points of P, that are contained in the ith box in $\mathcal{R}$. Then we denote $M(\mathcal{R}) = max_{1 \le i \le r} n_i$.*

- *Let P' be a subset of P of size $4k$ with minimal L_∞ diameter among all $(4k)$-point subsets. Then, δ^* denotes the L_∞-diameter of P'.*

Lemma 3.4 *Using the above notation, the following holds:*

1. *For any $\delta \ge \delta^*$ and any degraded δ-grid $\mathcal{R}$ for P, we have $M(\mathcal{R}) \ge k$.*

2. *For any $\delta \le \delta^*$ and any degraded δ-grid $\mathcal{R}$ of P, we have $M(\mathcal{R}) \le 4k$.*

Proof: See [6]. □

The parallel algorithm searches for a real number δ together with a degraded δ-grid $\mathcal{R}$ of P such that $k \le M(\mathcal{R}) \le 4k$.

Lemma 3.4 implies that there is at least one such δ for which such a covering exists, namely $\delta = \delta^*$. Notice that, such a δ is contained in all the L_∞ distances between pairs of points in P. Our search for such a δ is based on the sequential algorithm of Johnson and Mizoguchi [11]. A parallel algorithm based on the algorithm in [11] has been already used by Lenhof and Smid [12]. Their algorithm takes $O(\log^2 n \log \log n)$ expected time and

1. Store the points in the arrays X and Y according to sorted x and y coordinates. Initialize the intervals associated with $X[j]$ and $Y[j]$ $(1 \leq j \leq n)$ in the following way, $[a_{mj} : b_{mj}] = [j+1, n]$, where, $m = x, y$. This step can be done in $O(\log n)$ time using $O(n)$ processors.

2. For each $i \leq j < n$, if $a_{xj} \leq b_{xj}$, take the pair $X[\lfloor (a_{xj} + b_{xj})/2 \rfloor]$ and $X[j]$, and take the positive difference of their x coordinate. Give this difference weight $(b_{xj} - a_{xj} + 1)$. Do a similar computation for the elements in the array Y. This computation gives at most $2(n-1)$ weighted differences and can be done in $O(1)$ time using $O(n)$ processors.

3. Let $s_1, s_2, \ldots, s_r$ be the sequences of numbers obtained from Step 2. Note that, $r = O(n)$. We sort the s_i's according to increasing order and find a weighted median δ by using a prefix sum algorithm and equation (3). This can be done in $O(\log n)$ time, using $O(n)$ processors [5, 10].

4. Construct a δ-covering $\mathcal{R}$ of P by using the algorithm in Section 3.1 and compute $M(\mathcal{R})$ in $O(\log n)$ time, using $O(n)$ processors. There are three possible cases (which can be done in $O(\log n)$ time, using $O(n)$ processors):

   (a) $k \leq M(\mathcal{R}) \leq 4k$, then output δ and $\mathcal{R}$ and stop.

   (b) If $M(\mathcal{R}) < k$ then, for each pair $X[\lfloor (a_{xj} + b_{xj})/2 \rfloor]$ and $X[j]$ (resp. $Y[\lfloor (a_{yj} + b_{yj})/2 \rfloor]$ and $Y[j]$) selected in Step 2 such that the difference of their x (resp. y) coordinate is at most δ, set $a_{xj} := \lfloor (a_{xj} + b_{xj})/2 \rfloor + 1$ (resp. $a_{yj} := \lfloor (a_{yj} + b_{yj})/2 \rfloor + 1$). Goto Step 2.

   (c) If $M(\mathcal{R}) > 4k$, then for each pair $X[\lfloor (a_{xj} + b_{xj})/2 \rfloor]$ and $X[j]$ (resp. $Y[\lfloor (a_{yj} + b_{yj})/2 \rfloor]$ and $Y[j]$) selected in Step 2 such that the difference of their x (resp. y) coordinate is at least δ, set $b_{xj} := \lfloor (a_{xj} + b_{xj})/2 \rfloor - 1$ (resp. $a_{yj} := \lfloor (a_{yj} + b_{yj})/2 \rfloor - 1$). Goto Step 2.

Algorithm 2: Main steps in the algorithm for choosing $(k, 4k; \delta)$-covering

$O(n \log n \log \log n)$ work in the *randomized CRCW PRAM* model of parallel computation. We present a much simpler algorithm for computing a $(k, 4k; \delta)$ covering for the set P in the weaker CREW PRAM. We recall the notion of weighted medians from [11]. Let, $x_1, x_2, \ldots, x_n$ be a sequence of real numbers such that every element x_i has a weight w_i, and w_i is a positive real number. Let $W = \sum_{j=1}^{n} w_i$. Element x_i is called a weighted median if

$$\sum_{j:x_j < x_i} w_j < W/2 \quad and \quad \sum_{j:x_j \leq x_i} w_j \geq W/2 \qquad (3)$$

Lemma 3.5 *[11] The weighted median of a set of n weighted real numbers can be computed in $O(n)$ time.*

We use a simpler algorithm for computing weighted medians which requires $O(n \log n)$ work. We do not enumerate all candidate L_∞ differences since that will require $\Omega(n^2)$ work. We maintain the candidate differences in an implicit way. For details of the algorithm, see Algorithm 2. After the initialization, (Step 1 in Algorithm 2) $|x_s - x_r|$ is a candidate difference iff $a_{xj} \leq j' \leq b_{xj}$. Hence, the total number of candidate differences is equal to

$$\sum_{m=x,y} \sum_{j=1}^{n-1} (b_{mj} - a_{mj} + 1) \qquad (4)$$

Initially, this sum is $O(n^2)$. As in [11, 12], the parallel algorithm performs a sequence of iterations and in each iteration, the summation in equation (4) is decreased by a constant factor. The algorithm maintains the following invariant:

Invariant: *At each step of the iteration, the value δ^* is contained in the set of candidate differences.*

Lemma 3.6 *The algorithm makes at most $O(\log n)$ iterations and correctly maintains the invariant at every iteration.*

Proof: Omitted in this version. □

Lemma 3.7 *A $(k, 4k; \delta)$ covering for the set P can be constructed in $O(\log^2 n)$ time , using $O(n)$ processors in the CREW PRAM.*

Proof: It is clear from the description of Algorithm 2 that each step of the algorithm takes $O(\log n)$ time and $O(n)$ processors. From Lemma 3.6, we know that the algorithm terminates within $O(\log n)$ steps. Hence, the lemma follows. □

4 Constructing a range tree optimally in parallel

We briefly review the sequential version of the range tree [13]. First the points are sorted according to x coordinate and a skeletal *segment tree* [13] is built. Then for every internal node in this segment tree, the points in its subtree are sorted according to y coordinates. The array of points in the subtree of the node u is represented by $Y[u]$. The points in $Y[u]$ are sorted according to decreasing y coordinates. Consider an internal node u and its left and right children v and w. Consider a point $p_i \in u$. Notice that, p_i will occur either in $Y[v]$ or in $Y[w]$. We assume without loss of generality that p_i is a member of $Y[v]$. A pointer is kept from the occurance of p_i in $Y[u]$ to its occurance in $Y[v]$. Following the notation of [13], we call such a pointer as $LBRIDGE$. A similar pointer is kept to the element immediately above p_i in $Y[w]$. This pointer is called as $RBRIDGE$. Such pointers are maintained for every element in every internal node of the tree T. Finally, all the points in the root are kept in a balanced binary tree sorted according to y coordinates. We call this tree as $T[root]$. For details of the construction of this structure and range searching, see [13]. The count mode query can be performed in $O(\log n)$ time and the report mode query in $O(\log n + k)$ time, where k is the number of points in the query rectangle R.

4.1 Parallel construction of range tree

In our parallel construction of the range tree, we follow a strategy based on Cole's [5] optimal parallel merge sort algorithm. We first sort the points according to increasing x coordinate and establish them in the leaves of a complete binary tree T from left to right. We assume for simplicity that $n = 2^k$, for some $k > 1$. In the general case, the algorithm can be easily modified by introducing dummy leaves. Now, we build the primary segment tree according to x coordinates by the method of construction of plane sweep tree as described in [4, 10]. This construction takes $O(\log n)$ time and $O(n)$ processors in the CREW PRAM. The next step is to sort the points according to y coordinate. This sorting is done through a merge sort procedure as in [5] and described below. In Cole's algorithm, the merging in an internal node u is done by cross ranking the elements in its two children v and w, where v and w are respectively the left and right child of u. An element $p_i \in v$ is ranked in the array of w through the elements in their parent u. The merging is done through sampling in three phases and once all the elements in the array at u are sorted, the cross ranking pointers are destroyed. Notice that, at the time when all the elements in the array of u are sorted, the cross ranking pointers are exactly the pointers $LBRIDGE$ and $RBRIDGE$ in our above description. Suppose, an element $p_i \in v$ is ranked between two elements $p_j, p_k \in u$ and $y_j > y_k$. If p_j does not appear in $Y[v]$, then the element just below p_j in $Y[v]$ is p_i. So, this is the $LBRIDGE$ pointer in the reverse direction. We can easily keep a pointer in the other direction. So, in the y sorting stage, instead of destroying the cross ranking pointers after a node becomes saturated, we maintain them throughout the execution of the algorithm. At the end, we get a layered structure as in the sequential case. The time and processor requirement is exactly the same as in Cole's algorithm, i.e., $O(\log n)$ and $O(n)$ respectively. This construction can be done in the EREW PRAM [5]. The space requirement is $O(n \log n)$. If we want to do multiple range searching on this tree in parallel, we need the CREW PRAM model of parallel computation. Notice that, a single processor can answer an orthogonal count-mode range query in $O(\log n)$ time as in the sequential case. We summarize in the following

Lemma 4.1 *A range tree can be constructed in $O(\log n)$ time, using $O(n)$ processors and $O(n \log n)$ space in the CREW PRAM. A count-mode orthogonal range query can be answered by a single processor in this range tree in $O(\log n)$ time.*

In another version of range searching, given an orthogonal query range R, we want to find out the maximum x coordinate point in this range. This is the well-known range-maxima query. An algorithm is given in [10, pp.131-136] for preprocessing an array A for range-maxima queries. This takes $O(\log n)$ time and $O(n/\log n)$ processors in the CREW PRAM. After this preprocessing, given any two indices i, j in the array A, a single processor can find the maximum element in the subarray $A[i], \ldots, A[j]$ in $O(1)$ time. We preprocess the arrays present at every internal node of our range tree by using this algorithm. Since every element occurs in $O(\log n)$ nodes of the range tree, the overall processor and time requirements are $O(n)$ and $O(\log n)$ respectively. An orthogonal range-maximum query can be answered in the same way as the counting problem. The only difference is that, at a particular node of the tree, instead of counting the number of elements inside the query range, we do a range maximum query and update the current maximum if necessary. Since a range-maximum query takes $O(1)$ time, it is easy to see that the maximum element in the complete query range can be found in $O(\log n)$ time by a single processor.

Lemma 4.2 *A range tree can be preprocessed in $O(\log n)$ time using $O(n)$ processors in the CREW PRAM, such that given an orthogonal query range R, we can find the maximum element with respect to x coordinate inside R in $O(\log n)$ time, using a single processor.*

5 Parallel algorithm for computing minimum L_∞ perimeter k point subset

In this section, we discuss an algorithm for finding a k-point subset with minimum L_∞ perimeter from a set of $O(k)$ points. This will imply a solution for the problem $S(P, k)$ as discussed in Theorem 2.3. We first prove the following

Lemma 5.1 *For μ the L_∞ perimeter measure, Assumptions 2.1 and 2.2 hold with $c = 4$.*

Proof: If there is no closed $\mu_{opt}(P)$-box that contains the optimal solution P_{opt}, then the L_∞ perimeter of P_{opt} must be greater than $\mu_{opt}(P)$. This shows that Assumption 2.1 holds. For proving Assumption 2.2, let $\delta < \mu_{opt}(P)/4$. If there is a closed δ-box that contains at least k points, then there are k points that have L_∞ perimeter at most $4\delta < \mu_{opt}(P)$. This is clearly a contradiction. $\square$

We need the following simple property for our algorithm $\mathcal{A}$.

Property 5.1 *The four sides of the minimum L_∞ perimeter k-point subset pass through four points from the set.*

We first sort the points in the $O(k)$ subset according to increasing x coordinate and store them in an array X. This requires $O(\log k)$ time and $O(k)$ processors [5]. We also construct a range tree T as described in Section 4. In this range tree, one processor can perform an orthogonal range counting or a range maximum query in $O(\log k)$ time. If the left side of a rectangle passes through a point p_k, we say that p_k is the left support for the rectangle. Consider a pair of points (p_i, p_j) such that $x_i < x_j$ and $y_i > y_j$. Such a pair (p_i, p_j) fixes the bottom-left corner of a rectangle. We search for a k-point subset enclosed in a rectangle with the bottom-left corner fixed in this way. The left (resp. bottom) support of such a rectangle is the point p_i (resp. p_j). The top support is a point p_k such that $x_k > x_i$ and $y_k > y_i$. We associate $O(k)$ processors with every pair (p_i, p_j). One processor is associated with a point p_k which satisfies the condition above. Now, three supports of the rectangle are fixed and we have to fix the right support such that the rectangle contains k points. This is done in the following way. The processor associated with p_k does a binary search for finding the right support. Notice that, during this binary search, we should consider a point p_m as a candidate for the right support such that, $x_m > max(x_k, x_j)$ and $y_k > y_m > y_j$. But sorting these points for every such semi-unbounded rectangle requires too much work. Instead, we do the following. We do a binary search in the array X. Suppose, the current candidate for the right support is the point p_n. There are two possibilities. In the first case, $y_k > y_n > y_j$. We do a range search in the range tree T. The query range is a rectangle R such that its three sides are fixed as explained before and the right side is the point p_n. If the number of points inside this rectangle is k, we store this rectangle as a possible candidate rectangle. Otherwise, if the number of points is less than k (resp. greater than k), we shift the right support towards higher (resp. lower) x coordinate points. In the other case, y_n may not be inside the interval $[y_k, y_j]$. We do a range search again with the right side at the position x_n. If there are exactly k points inside this rectangle, we can find the right side of this rectangle by doing a range searching in the tree T and finding the maximum x coordinate point inside this rectangle.

There are $O(k^2)$ pairs like (p_i, p_j). For each such pair, we allocate $O(k)$ processors. So, the overall processor requirement is $O(k^3)$. The binary search takes $O(\log k)$ time and at every position during the binary search, we do a range searching which takes $O(\log k)$ time. So, the overall time is $O(\log^2 k)$. After this, there will be at most $O(k^3)$ candidate rectangles left and among them the minimum perimeter rectangle can be found easily in $O(\log k)$ time, using $O(k^3)$ processors. The main steps of the algorithm are given in Algorithm 3.

---

1. Sort the points according to increasing x coordinates and store them in an array X. This can be done in $O(\log k)$ time using $O(k)$ processors [5].

2. Construct a range tree T for answering orthogonal range counting and range maxima queries by the method in Section 4. This step takes $O(\log k)$ time and $O(k)$ processors.

3. For every pair of points (p_i, p_j) such that $x_i < x_j$ and $y_i > y_j$, we allocate $O(k)$ processors. This group of processors find the minimum L_∞ perimeter k point subset with p_i (resp. p_j) as the left (resp. bottom) support. This step takes $O(\log^2 k)$ time and $O(k^3)$ processors, as discussed above.

4. Among the possible $O(k^3)$ rectangles found in Step 3, find the minimum perimeter one. This can be done in $O(\log k)$ time, using $O(k^3)$ processors.

Algorithm 3: The main steps in the algorithm for finding a minimum L_∞ perimeter k point subset.

Lemma 5.2 *The overall time and work requirements of Algorithm 3 is $O(\log^2 k)$ and $O(k^3 \log^2 k)$.*

Algorithm 3 is applied simultaneously to all the (n/k) subsets of size $O(k)$ each. We state the result in the following

Theorem 5.3 *The minimum L_∞ perimeter k point subset can be computed in $O(\log^2 n)$ time using $O(n \log^2 n + nk^2 \log^2 k)$ work.*

Proof: We get the stated time and work bounds by plugging in the values from Lemma 5.2 into equations 1 and 2 in Theorem 2.3. The total time is $O(\log^2 n + \log^2 k)$,i.e., $O(\log^2 n)$, since $n \geq k$. $\qquad\square$

6 Parallel algorithm for computing a k point subset with minimum L_∞ diameter

In this section, we describe an algorithm for finding a k point subset with minimum L_∞ diameter. We apply this algorithm simultaneously in parallel on small sets of $O(k)$ points each. This will imply a solution for problem $S(P, k)$ by Theorem 2.3. First, we state the following

Lemma 6.1 *For μ the L_∞ diameter measure, Assumptions 2.1 and 2.2 hold with $c = 1$.*

Proof: Suppose, there is no closed $\mu_{opt}(P)$-box that contains the optimal solution. Then there must be two points in P_{opt} that have L_∞ distance greater than μ_{opt}, a contradiction. This shows that Assumption 2.1 holds. For proving Assumption 2.2, let $\delta < \mu_{opt}(P)$. Assume that there is a closed δ-box that contains k points. Then there is a subset of k points that have L_∞ diameter less than μ_{opt}. This is a contradiction. $\qquad\square$

Our algorithm is based on the following

Lemma 6.2 *The minimum L_∞ diameter of a k point subset is determined by the difference, either $|x_i - x_j|$ or $|y_i - y_j|$ for two points p_i, p_j in the set P. Moreover, two opposite sides of the minimum L_∞ diameter set must be supported by these two points.*

Proof: The first part of the Lemma is obvious. If two opposite sides are not supported by the pair of points determining the L_∞ diameter, the L_∞ diameter of the set can be decreased. $\qquad\square$

We also need the following result.

Lemma 6.3 *Given a point set P and a fixed size square Q, in $O(\log n)$ time and using $O(n)$ processors, we can find an axes-parallel placement of Q such that Q contains maximum number of points from the set P. This computation can be done in the CREW PRAM.*

Proof: We transform this problem in the following way. We replace each point in the set P by a square of size Q. The square Q_i corresponding to the point $p_i \in P$ is placed such that its bottom-left corner coincides with the point p_i and its sides are parallel to the axes. Consider the arrangement of this set of squares $Q_1, Q_2, \ldots, Q_n$. We define a graph $\mathcal{H}$ such that the set of vertices for this graph is the set of squares and two vertices are connected by an edge, if the two corresponding squares intersect. Consider the maximum clique in the graph $\mathcal{H}$. It is easy to see that all the squares in this clique has a common point p inside them. We place the square Q with its top-right corner at this point. This placement of Q will contain all the points in P which gave rise to the clique $\mathcal{H}$. For an algorithm, we can transform the point set into squares of size Q in $O(1)$ time, using $O(n)$ processors. Then we apply an algorithm by Chandran *et al* [4] for finding a maximum clique and a deepest point in this arrangement of squares. This algorithm takes $O(\log n)$ time and $O(n)$ processors in CREW PRAM. ☐

From Lemma 6.2, it is clear that the L_∞ diameter for the minimum k point subset is present in the set of all coordinate differences. In our algorithm, we search for the optimal such difference along each axis. We first sort the points along each coordinate axis x and y and store them in two arrays X and Y. Now, the difference in the coordinates along each axis can be represented as a triangular matrix. There are two $O(k) \times O(k)$ triangular matrices in our case. We represent them as M_x and M_y. The first row of M_x has the difference of x coordinate between the first point and all the other points. The matrix M_y is also defined in a similar way. Note that, both rows and columns are in sorted order in these matrices. For example, the first two elements in the jth column of matrix M_x actually denote the differences $|x_1 - x_j|$ and $|x_2 - x_j|$. Obviously, the first quantity is greater than the second, since the numbers $x_1, x_2, \ldots, x_{O(k)}$ are in sorted order. We do not actually construct the matrices M_x and M_y, since that will require $\Omega(k^2)$ work. But we can generate any element in $O(1)$ time from the sorted arrays X and Y. So, we can effectively assume as if the complete matrices are available. We have to repeatedly select elements from these matrices for doing a binary search to find an appropriate L_∞ diameter. An $O(k)$ time sequential algorithm was presented in [8] for selection from matrices with sorted rows and columns. The best known parallel algorithm for selecting an element with specified rank from sorted matrices is by Sarnath and He [14]. Their algorithm runs in $O(\log k \log \log k \log^* k)$ time using $O(k/\log k \log^* k)$ processors in the EREW PRAM. The work done by the algorithm is $O(k \log \log k)$. We use their algorithm for our binary search. At every step of our binary search, we select an L_∞ distance from the matrices M_x and M_y. We compute a placement of a square with side lengths equal to this L_∞ distance such that this square contains maximum number of points from the set. This computation can be done by the algorithm in Lemma 6.3, in $O(\log k)$ time and $O(k)$ processors. We stop the binary search when such a square contains k points. Clearly, the time for every step of the binary search is dominated by the complexity of the selection algorithm in [14]. The overall time requirement for the complete binary search is $O(\log^2 k \log \log k \log^* k)$. The total work done by the selection algorithm is $O(k \log k \log \log k)$ and that by the algorihm in Lemma 6.3 is $O(k \log^2 k)$. So, the overall work is $O(k \log^2 k)$. The main steps of the algorithm are given in Algorithm 4.

---

1. Sort the points according to increasing x and y coordinates and store them in two arrays X and Y.

2. Do a binary search in the matrices M_x and M_y as explained above. At each step of the binary search, find an optimal placement of the square with the current L_∞ distance as its side length. This is done by the algorithm in Lemma 6.3.

3. Stop when an L_∞ distance is found such that the corresponding square contains k points inside it.

Algorithm 4: The main steps in the algorithm for finding a k point subset with minimum L_∞ diameter

Lemma 6.4 *The minimum L_∞ diameter k point subset within a set of $O(k)$ points can be computed in $O(\log^2 k \log \log k \log^* k)$ time and $O(k \log^2 k)$ work in the CREW PRAM.*

As mentioned earlier, this algorithm is applied in parallel to all the $O(k)$ subsets in the grid. So, the overall complexity of the algorithm is stated in the following

Theorem 6.5 *The minimum L_∞ diameter k point subset within a set of n points can be found in $O(\log^2 n + \log^2 k \log\log k \log^* k)$ time and $O(n \log^2 n)$ work.*

Proof: We get the stated complexities by plugging in the values from Lemma 6.4 into equations 1 and 2 in Theorem 2.3. The total work is $O(n\log^2 n + n\log^2 k)$, i.e., $O(n\log^2 n)$, since $n \geq k$. $\qquad\qquad\qquad\qquad\qquad\qquad\qquad\qquad\qquad\qquad\qquad\qquad\qquad\qquad\qquad\Box$

Acknowledgement

The author would like to thank Michiel Smid for many interesting and helpful discussions on clustering problems.

References

[1] H. C. Andrews. *Introduction to Mathematical Techniques in Pattern Recognition.* Wiley-Interscience, New York, 1972.

[2] A. Aggarwal, H. Imai, N. Katoh and S. Suri. *Finding k points with minimum diameter and related problems.* J. Algorithms **12** (1991), pp. 38-56.

[3] O. Berkman, D. Breslauer, Z. Galil, B. Scheiber and U. Vishkin. *Highly parallelizable problems*, Proc. 21st Annual ACM Symp. on Theory of Computing, 1989, pp. 309-319.

[4] S. Chandran, S. K. Kim and D. M. Mount. *Parallel computational geometry of rectangles.* Algorithmica, **7**, (1992), pp. 25-49.

[5] R. Cole. *Parallel merge sort.* SIAM J. Comput. **17**, (1988), pp. 770-785.

[6] A. Datta, H. P. Lenhof, C. Schwarz and M. Smid. *Static and dynamic algorithms for k-point clustering problems.* Proceedings of WADS '93, Lecture Notes in Computer Science, Springer-Verlag, **Vol. 709**, pp. 265-276.

[7] D. Eppstein and J. Erickson. *Iterated nearest neighbours and finding minimal polytopes.* Proc. 4th ACM-SIAM Symp. on Discrete Algorithms, (1993), pp. 64-73.

[8] G. N. Frederickson and D. B. Johnson. *The complexity of selection and ranking in $X + Y$ and matrices with sorted columns.* Journal of Computer and System Sciences, **24**, (1982), pp. 197-208.

[9] J. A. Hartigan. *Clustering Algorithms*, John-Wiley, New York, 1975.

[10] J. JáJá. *An introduction to Parallel Algorithms.* Addison-Wesley, 1992.

[11] D. B. Johnson and T. Mizoguchi. *Selecting the Kth element in $X + Y$ and $X_1 + X_2 + \ldots + X_m$.* SIAM J. Comput. **7**, (1978), pp. 147-157.

[12] H. P. Lenhof and M. Smid. *Sequential and parallel algorithms for the k-closest pairs problem.* Max Planck Institut für Informatik, Technical Report, MPI-I-92-134, August 1992. A preliminary version appears in *Proc. 33rd Annual IEEE Symp. on Foundations of Computer Science*, pp. 380-386.

[13] F. P. Preparata and M. I. Shamos. *Computational Geometry : an Introduction.* Springer-Verlag, New York, 1985.

[14] R. Sarnath and X. He. *Efficient parallel algorithms for selection and searching on sorted matrices.* Proc. 6th International Parallel Processing Symposium, (1992), pp. 108-111.

A SIMPLE OPTIMAL PARALLEL ALGORITHM FOR REPORTING PATHS IN A TREE

Anil Maheshwari
Computer Systems and Communications Group
Tata Institute of Fundamental Research
Homi Bhabha Road, Bombay 400 005, India
manil@tifrvax.bitnet

Andrzej Lingas
Department of Computer Science
Lund University
Box 118, Lund. S-22 100, Sweden
Andrzej.Lingas@dna.lth.se

Abstract

We present optimal parallel solutions to reporting paths between pairs of nodes in an n−node tree. Our algorithms are deterministic and designed to run on an exclusive read exclusive write parallel random-access machine (EREW PRAM). In particular, we provide a simple optimal parallel algorithm for preprocessing the input tree such that the path queries can be answered efficiently. Our algorithm for preprocessing runs in $O(\log n)$ time using $O(n/\log n)$ processors. Using the preprocessing, we can report paths between k node pairs in $O(\log n + \log k)$ time using $O(k + (n + S)/\log n)$ processors on an EREW PRAM, where S is the size of the output. In particular, we can report the path between a single pair of distinct nodes in $O(\log n)$ time using $O(L/\log n)$ processors, where L denotes the length of the path.

1   Introduction

In many problems in computer science, the underlying structure is a tree. For several fundamental algorithmic problems on tree, optimal parallel algorithms are known. For example, computing Euler tour and several functions on tree [14], evaluating expression tree [2], lowest common ancestor [12], dictionaries on 2-3 trees [11], *etc.*

Enumerating paths between pairs of nodes is one of the fundamental operation on trees. For instance, a request for reporting a path from a vertex in a connected graph to another vertex in the graph can be reduced to the corresponding path query on any spanning tree of the graph [13]. Analogously, a request for a shortest path from a distinguished vertex v of a graph or a geometric structure to another vertex reduces to the corresponding query in the tree of shortest paths that is rooted at v [6]. Also, in computational geometry, dominance problems require enumerating paths between pairs of nodes as one of the basic routines [3, 5, 7]. In [4], Djidjev *et al.* used path queries for trees as subroutines in their parallel solutions to shortest path queries for planar digraphs. After an $O(\log n)$-time and $O(n/\log n)$ -processor preprocessing on an EREW PRAM they achieved $O(L)$ time for reporting a path of length L in the input tree on n nodes, using single processor.

In this paper we present new results on path queries in trees which yield substantial improvements over the aforementioned results. We provide a simple optimal (in the time-processor product sense, see [8]) logarithmic-time algorithm for preprocessing the input tree such that the path queries can be answered efficiently. Using the preprocessing, we can firstly reduce the time of reporting a path of length L to $O(\log n)$ by using the optimal number of EREW PRAM processors, i.e., $O(L/\log n)$. Our method avoids applying the standard concurrent-read pointer-jumping technique. This enables us to derive our main result on parallel path queries in the EREW PRAM model: we answer k path queries in parallel in $O(\log n + \log k)$ time using $O(k + (n + S)/\log n)$ processors on an EREW PRAM, where S is the size of the output.

In our algorithms, we assume the so-called adjacency list representation of the input tree. The paths are reported in an array.

Our algorithms use an output sensitive number of processors. The output size, i.e., S is not known in advance. We compute the size of the output on the fly and allocate the required number of processors in the spirit of [5]. The processors are 'spawned' depending on the output size. When new processors are allocated, a global array of pointers is created. A processor can know the exact location from where it should start working by accessing this array. For the details of this computation model, see Goodrich [5].

In our optimal parallel solutions, we use the following tools previously developed in the area of parallel computing: parallel merge-sort [1], list ranking and doubling, parallel prefix sums (e.g., see [8, 9, 10]), tree operations including the Euler tour technique [14], lowest common ancestor in a tree [12], searching in search trees [11].

The remainder of the paper is organized as follows. In Section 2, we prove several basic technical lemmas. In Section 3 we describe and analyze the tree preprocessing step and then provide the optimal algorithms for reporting paths relying on the preprocessing. In Section 4 we conclude with a few open problems.

2 Preliminaries

Let T denote the n-node rooted binary tree and let us further assume that T is represented in such a way that the Euler tour of T can be computed in $O(\log n)$ time using $O(n/\log n)$ processors [14] (e.g., adjacency list representation). Let $size(v)$, $postorder(v)$ and $level(v)$ respectively denote the number of vertices in the subtree rooted at v, postorder number of v in the postorder traversal and level number of v, where v is a node of T. To facilitate our discussion, we prove the following lemmas.

Lemma 2.1 *Let A be an array of $O(\log n)$ elements. We can make k copies of A in $O(\log n + \log k)$ time using $O(k)$ processors on an EREW PRAM.*

Proof: The proof uses the technique of *pipelining*. First compute a balanced binary tree on k nodes. Assume that there is a processor at each node of the tree.

Now copy the first element of the input array A into the zero level, i.e., the root of the tree. In the next step this element is copied into every node on the first level of the tree, and so on. Finally in $O(\log k)$ stages there are k copies of this element and each leaf of the tree contains one copy. While the first element of A is getting copied to nodes in the first level, we can initiate the process for the second element of A. Clearly in $O(\log n + \log k)$ stages, copy of each element of A will reside in every leaf of the binary tree. □

---

1. Construct an Euler tour of T for each node v of T compute $level(v)$ using the algorithm of Tarjan and Vishkin [14].

2. For each leaf node v of T, create a linear array A_v of size $level(v)$.

3. Label the leaves of T by distinct consecutive numbers.

4. For each node v of T, compute the interval, $range(v)$, of the labels of the leaves in its subtree.

5. For each $z \in range(v)$, $A_z[level(v)] := v$.

6. Stop.

Algorithm 1: An algorithm for reporting paths from all leaves to the root

---

Lemma 2.2 *Let T be a rooted binary tree on n-nodes. Algorithm 1 correctly computes all paths from leaves to the root in T in $O(\log n)$ time using $O(S/\log n)$ processors on an EREW PRAM, where S is the sum total of nodes in the paths from all leaves to the root (i.e., the size of the output).*

Proof: First we show the correctness of the algorithm and then we analyze its complexity. Clearly, for any leaf v of T, the path to the root is of length $level(v)$. For any internal node v of T, only leaves in its subtree are in $range(v)$. Hence, for any internal node v of T, we know precisely where v is going to appear in the paths from the leaves in $range(v)$ to the root.

Now we analyze the complexity stepwise.

Step 1 takes $O(\log n)$ time using $O(n/\log n)$ processors [14].

Consider Step 2. Let S be the sum of $level(v)$ over all v, where v is a leaf of T. The sum S can be computed in $O(\log n)$ time using $O(n/\log n)$ processors. Clearly S is $\Omega(n)$. Next, by using parallel prefix sums, the optimum number of processors to compute the arrays A_v corresponding to each leaf v of T can be respectively assigned. Hence this step can be performed in $O(\log n)$ time using $O(S/\log n)$ processors on an EREW PRAM.

Consider Step 3. We can label the leaves by using the Euler tour technique as follows. First compute the Euler tour of T. Then mark all leaves in the tour. Now compute the postorder numbering of only the marked nodes in the tree traversal. So, this step can be performed in $O(\log n)$ time using $O(n/\log n)$ processors.

Consider Step 4. We can compute $range(v)$ for every node v by using the Euler tour of T and parallel list ranking. Compute the leaf number of the leaf following v in postorder and $\#range(v)$. Hence this step requires $O(\log n)$ time using $O(n/\log n)$ processors.

Finally consider Step 5. Note that the total size of the output to be written is S. Using parallel prefix sums allocate $O(S/\log n)$ processors such that each processor, with only exclusive read capabilities, writes in the appropriate location of the arrays A_z in $O(\log n)$ time, where $z \in range(v)$. $\qquad\square$

Lemma 2.3 *Let T be a rooted binary tree on n-nodes and with $k \leq n$ distinct marked nodes. We can compute paths in T from all marked nodes to the root of T in $O(\log n)$ time using $O((n+S)/\log n)$ processors on an EREW PRAM, where S is the sum total of nodes in the paths from the marked nodes to the root (i.e., the size of the output).*

Proof: The algorithm and the proof are analogous to Algorithm 1 and Lemma 2.2, respectively. $\qquad\square$

Lemma 2.4 *A binary tree on n-nodes can be preprocessed in $O(\log n)$ time using $O(n/\log n)$ processors such that k lowest common ancestor queries can be answered in $O(\log k)$ time using $O(k)$ processors on the EREW PRAM.*

Proof: Schieber and Vishkin [12] have proposed an algorithm for preprocessing a binary tree in $O(\log n)$ time using $O(n/\log n)$ processors such that a single processor can answer a lowest common ancestor query in $O(1)$ time. Hence k queries can be answered in $O(1)$ time using $O(k)$ processors on a CREW PRAM. By using the standard simulation of the CREW PRAM on an EREW PRAM, we get the desired complexity. $\qquad\square$

Lemma 2.5 *(Paul, Vishkin and Wagener [11]) A sequence of k keys can be searched in an $n-$node binary search tree in $O(\log n + \log k)$ time using $O(k)$ processors on an EREW PRAM.*

3 The preprocessing and the queries

In this section first we state an algorithm (Algorithm 2) for preprocessing the n-node binary tree T. Then we show that the path queries can be answered efficiently using the data computed in the preprocessing step.

Lemma 3.1 *Algorithm 2 preprocesses an n-node binary tree in $O(\log n)$ time using $O(n/\log n)$ processors on an EREW PRAM and the resulting data structure is of linear size.*

Proof: Steps 1, 2 can be implemented in $O(\log n)$ time using $O(n/\log n)$ processors [12, 14].

1. Preprocess T for answering the lowest common ancestor queries.

2. Perform an Euler tour traversal of T and compute $postorder(v)$ and $level(v)$ for each node $v \in T$.

3. For each node v of T, compute the interval $range(v)$ of the postorder numbers of each vertex in its subtree.

4. Find $m_0 \in [0, \lceil \log n \rceil)$ such that there are $O(n/\log n)$ nodes v of T satisfying $level(v) = m_0 \bmod \lceil \log n \rceil$ and mark all such nodes.

5. Group the marked nodes according to their level number in T and let G_i denote the marked nodes at level i in T, where $i = m_0 \bmod \lceil \log n \rceil$.

6. For each group G_i, compute a binary search tree B_i, where the leaf nodes in B_i are the nodes at level i in T. The leaf nodes in B_i are sorted in the increasing order by $postorder(v)$.

7. Stop.

Algorithm 2: An algorithm for preprocessing a binary tree

To implement Step 3, for all nodes v in T, $range(v)$ is computed by using the Euler tour technique as discussed in Lemma 2.2.

The implementation of Step 4 proceeds further as follows. First, the set of nodes of T is divided into $O(n/\log n)$ subsets U kept in arrays of size $O(\log n)$, by applying the optimal EREW parallel prefix sums algorithm [8]. Next, for each subset U, the integers $level(v) \bmod \lceil \log n \rceil$ over nodes in U are bucket sorted by a single processor in $O(\log n)$ time. Then, for all integers m in $[0, \lceil \log n \rceil)$, the numbers $n_m(U)$ of the occurences of m in the sorted sequence for U are computed, again in $O(\log n)$ time using a single processor. Now, it is sufficient to compute the sums $\sum_U n_m(U)$ in parallel for all m in $[0, \lceil \log n \rceil)$ in order to set m_0 to an m minimizing $\sum_U n_m(U)$. It takes $O(\log n)$ time and totally $O(((n/\log n)/\log n)\log n)$ processors. Finally, the number m_0 is broadcasted to the $O(n/\log n)$ subsets in logarithmic time using $O(n/\log n)$ processors [8], and for each subset U, the single processor assigned to U marks the vertices in U satisfying $level(v) = m_0$ in $O(\log n)$ time.

To implement Step 5, the marked vertices are extracted using the optimal parallel prefix sums algorithm [10] and then sorted according to their level number. Since the number of marked nodes is at most $O(n/\log n)$, the sorting can be done in logarithmic time with $O(n/\log n)$ processors in the EREW PRAM model [1]. Thus the groups G_i can be computed in $O(\log n)$ time using $O(n/\log n)$ processors.

To implement Step 6, within each group G_i the nodes are sorted in the increasing order by $postorder(v)$. Analogously as in Step 5, the sorting takes logarithmic time and $O(n/\log n)$ processors totally. Further, binary search trees on $O(n/\log n)$ nodes are computed in $O(\log n)$ time using $O(n/\log n)$ processors.

We conclude that the algorithm can be implemented to run within the claimed time and processor bounds. Since each step of the algorithm requires only linear space, the space complexity follows. $\square$

First we discuss the problem of answering a path query and then present an algorithm for answering k path queries using the above preprocessing step.

Let the query be a pair of nodes (a, b) in T. We are asked to compute the path between nodes a and b, denoted as $path(a, b)$. In the following we show that $path(a, b)$ can be computed in $O(\log n)$ time using $O(max\{1, |path(a, b)|/\log n\})$ processors, where $|path(a, b)|$ denotes the number of nodes in $path(a, b)$.

First compute the lowest common ancestor node of a and b in T. Denote it by c. Now the problem reduces to reporting the paths $path(a, c)$ and $path(b, c)$. So, for simplicity assume that b is an ancestor of a.

---

1. Compute the level and the postorder numbers of nodes a and b in T.

2. Compute the set $index(a, b) = \{i | i = m_0 \bmod \lceil \log n \rceil$ and $level(b) \leq i \leq level(a)\}$. Locate the groups G_i, where $i \in index(a, b)$.

3. For each B_i, where $i \in index(a, b)$, locate the leaf l_i of B_i, such that $postorder(a) \in range(l_i)$.

4. Compute paths in T from each l_i to l_{i+1}. Further, compute $path(a, l_i)$ for the largest value of $i \in index(a, b)$ and analogously compute $path(l_i, b)$ for the smallest value of $i \in index(a, b)$.

5. Compose the paths computed in Step 4 to obtain $path(a, b)$.

6. Stop.

Algorithm 3: An algorithm for computing $path(a, b)$

Theorem 3.2 *Algorithm 3 computes the path between two query nodes a and b, $path(a, b)$, in $O(\log n)$ time using $O(max\{1, |path(a, b)|/\log n\})$ processors on the EREW PRAM, where b is an ancestor of a and $|path(a, b)|$ denotes the number of nodes in $path(a, b)$.*

Proof: The correctness is straightforward. The number of nodes in $path(a, b)$ is $|path(a, b)| = level(a) - level(b)$. So, we assign $O(max\{1, |path(a, b)|/\log n\})$ processors to compute $path(a, b)$ in $O(\log n)$ time. The set $index(a, b)$ can be computed in $O(\log n)$ time. Note that $|index(a, b)| \leq max\{1, |path(a, b)|/\log n\}$. Since the binary search trees are of height $O(\log n)$, the ith processor can search for the appropriate leaf node l_i in the binary search tree B_i in $O(\log n)$ time. Once the leaves l_i are located in each search tree B_i, where $i \in index(a, b)$, the remaining task is to compute the paths from nodes l_i to l_{i+1} for the appropriate values of i in T. Since the number of nodes in each path is at most $O(\log n)$, each of these paths can be computed in $O(\log n)$ time. Note that this method requires only exclusive read and write capabilities, since the nodes in each B_i are pairwise distinct. □

Now using the theory developed so far, we discuss the main result of this paper. The problem is to solve k-path queries simultaneously. Using Lemma 2.4, compute the lowest common ancestor of each query node. As before, we can now assume that each query is a pair of nodes a_i and b_i of T, where b_i is an ancestor of a_i, for $i = 1..k$.

---

1. For each query pair (a_i, b_i) compute $level(a_i)$, $level(b_i)$, $|path(a_i, b_i)|$, $postorder(a_i)$ and $postorder(b_i)$.

2. Compute $S = \sum_{i=1}^{i=k} |path(a_i, b_i)|$.

3. For each query pair (a_i, b_i), locate the binary search trees B_j such that $j = m_0$ mod $\lceil \log n \rceil$ and $level(b_i) \leq j \leq level(a_i)$. Let $index(a_i, b_i)$ be the set of values which j takes. For each $j \in index(a_i, b_i)$, generate a search pair (B_j, a_i).

4. For each search pair (B_j, a_i), mark the leaf l_j of B_j, such that $postorder(a_i) \in range(l_j)$.

5. For each query pair (a_i, b_i) compute paths in T from l_j to l_{j+1}, for all $j \in index(a_i, b_i)$.

6. Compose the paths computed in Step 5 to obtain $path(a_i, b_i)$.

7. Stop.

Algorithm 4: An algorithm for computing k-path queries.

Theorem 3.3 *Algorithm 4 correctly computes paths between k-query nodes in $O(\log n + \log k)$ time using $O(k + (n + S)/\log n)$ processors on an EREW PRAM, where S is the size of the output.*

Proof: The correctness is straightforward and follows from the fact that for any pair of query nodes a_i and b_i, first we compute every $O(\log n)$th node in the path and then compute the rest of the path.

Now we analyze the complexity of the algorithm. Using Lemma 2.4, the lowest common ancestors of k node pairs can be computed in $O(\log k)$ time using $O(k)$ processors.

Consider Step 1 of the algorithm. For each pair of query nodes, we can compute level and postorder information in $O(1)$ time on the CREW PRAM. Hence in $O(\log k)$ time using $O(k)$ processors, we can compute the required quantities in Step 1 on an EREW PRAM for all queries.

The sum of k numbers, in Step 2, can be computed in $O(\log k)$ time using $O(k/\log k)$ processors. Once we know the value of S, we assign $O(S/\log n)$ processors in $O(\log S)$ time to perform our task. Associate $max\{1, |path(a_i, b_i)|/\log n\}$ processors for each pair of query nodes (a_i, b_i).

Consider Step 3. Using a $max\{1, |path(a_i, b_i)|/\log n\}$ processors, we can compute the set $index(a_i, b_i)$ and generate the search pair (B_j, a_i) for each $j \in index(a_i, b_i)$ in $O(\log n)$ time.

Consider Step 4. We write $(B_j, a_i) \le (B_p, a_l)$ if and only if either $j < p$ or $j = p$ and $postorder(a_i) \le postorder(a_l)$. Sort all search pairs according to the lexicographic order by the algorithm of Cole [1]. We have at most $O(S/\log n)$ search pairs, since for any $path(a_i, b_i)$, $|index(a_i, b_i)| \le max\{1, |path(a_i, b_i)|/\log n\}$. Hence, sorting of the search pairs requires $O(\log S)$ time using $O(S/\log n)$ processors. Now the task is to mark the leaves in the search tree B_j corresponding to query nodes a_i, for all desired values of i and j. Consider one such search tree, say B_j and let there be l search pairs involving B_j. Using Lemma 2.5, we can mark the leaves corresponding to the search pairs in $O(\log |B_i| + \log l)$ time using $O(l)$ processors. Since we search for a total of at most $O(S/\log n)$ search pairs and the number of nodes in all the search trees is at most $O(n)$, the overall complexity of this step is $O(\log n + \log S)$ time using $O(S/\log n)$ processors.

Consider Step 5. We have several marked nodes in T, which are either the leaves l_j, marked in the previous step or the nodes a_i. The task is to report the path starting from each marked node x, upto a node y, such that i) y is in the path from x to the root of T ii) $level(y)$ mod $\lceil \log n \rceil = m_0$ and iii) $|path(x, y)| \le \log n$. We accomplish the task as follows. First partition the tree into subtrees T_i by cutting the tree at the m_0 level, and then at every $\lceil \log n \rceil$th level. The resulting subtrees have height at most $\lceil \log n \rceil$ and the root r_i of any subtree T_i, different from the top one rooted at the root of T, satisfies $level(r_i)$ mod $\lceil \log n \rceil = m_0$. Now the problem reduces to that of reporting all paths from the marked nodes in T_i to the root r_i of T_i, for every subtree T_i of T. Using Lemma 2.3, we can compute paths in each T_i from each marked node to r_i. Note that in all we have $O(n)$ vertices partitioned among T_is and the total number of nodes to be reported in all query paths is S. Hence the overall complexity of computing paths from each marked node to the root of its subtree will be $O(\log n)$ time using $O((n + S)/\log n)$ processors.

Consider Step 6. For each query path $path(a_i, b_i)$, we have computed subpaths consisting of at most $O(\log n)$ nodes. Note that a subpath may be common to several path queries. If a subpath is common to l path queries, we can replicate it l times using the results of Lemma 2.1. The number of times a subpath needs to be replicated can be computed as follows. While searching for the leaf nodes in the search tree in Step 4, we can compute how many times each leaf is marked. Since each leaf is marked once for each search query, the number of times it gets marked gives the number of times a subpath needs to be replicated. Once we know all the subpaths for a pair of query nodes, we can easily output the whole path.

All the steps of the algorithm use only exclusive read and exclusive write capabilities, which proves our result. □

4 Conclusion

In this paper we have presented optimal parallel solutions to reporting paths between pairs of nodes in a tree. Using our results we can also compute the weight of the path between query nodes in a weighted tree within the same complexity bounds. There are several related problems which might be of interest. One of them is to consider the dynamic version where insertions and deletions of tree nodes are possible. Other interesting problem is to study the lowest common ancestor query problem in the dynamic setting.

5 Acknowledgements

The authors thank unknown referees for valuable comments on Lemmata 2.1, 3.1.

References

[1] R. Cole. *Parallel merge sort.* SIAM J. Computing, **17**, (1988), pp. 770-785.

[2] R. Cole and U. Vishkin. *The accelerated centroid decomposition technique for optimal parallel tree evaluation in logarithmic time.* Algorithmica, **3** (1988), pp. 329-346.

[3] A. Datta, A. Maheshwari, J.-R. Sack. *Optimal parallel algorithms for direct dominance problems.* First Annual European Symposium on Algorithms, Lecture Notes in Computer Science, Vol. 726, pp. 109-120, Springer-Verlag, 1993.

[4] H.N. Djidjev, G.E. Pantziou and C.D. Zaroliagis. *Computing Shortest Paths and Distances in Planar Graphs.* Proceedings 18th ICALP, Madrid, 1991, LNCS 510, pp. 327-338, Springer Verlag.

[5] M. T. Goodrich. *Intersecting line segments in parallel with an output-sensitive number of processors.* SIAM J. Computing, **20**, (1991), pp. 737-755.

[6] L. J. Guibas and J. Hershberger. *Optimal shortest path queries in a simple polygon.* J. of Computer and System Sciences **39**, pp. 126-152, 1989.

[7] R. Güting, O. Nurmi and T. Ottmann. *Fast algorithms for direct enclosures and direct dominances.* J. Algorithms **10** (1989), pp. 170-186.

[8] J. JáJá. *An Introduction to Parallel Algorithms.* Addison-Wesley, 1992.

[9] R. M. Karp and V. Ramachandran, *Parallel Algorithms for Shared-Memory Machines,* Handbook of Theoretical Computer Science, Edited by J. van Leeuwen, Volume 1, Elsevier Science Publishers B.V., 1990.

[10] R. E. Ladner and M. J. Fisher. *Parallel prefix computation,* JACM, 27(4) (1980), pp. 831-838.

[11] W. Paul, U. Vishkin and H. Wagener. *Parallel dictionaries on 2-3 trees.* Proc. 10th ICALP, Lecture Notes in Computer Science, Vol. 154, pp. 597-609, 1983.

[12] B. Schieber and U. Vishkin. *On finding lowest common ancestors: Simplification and Parallelization.* SIAM. J. Computing, **17** (1988), pp. 1253-1262.

[13] R.E. Tarjan. *Data Structures and Network Algorithms.* SIAM, Philadelphia, 1983.

[14] R. E. Tarjan and U. Vishkin. *An efficient parallel biconnectivity algorithm.* SIAM J. Computing, **14** (1985), pp. 862-874.

Parallel Detection of all Palindromes in a String

Alberto Apostolico*   Dany Breslauer†   Zvi Galil‡

Abstract

This paper presents two efficient concurrent-read concurrent-write parallel algorithms that find all palindromes in a given string:

1. An $O(\log n)$ time, n-processor algorithm over general alphabets. In case of constant size alphabets the algorithm requires only $n/\log n$ processors, and thus achieves an optimal-speedup.

2. An $O(\log \log n)$ time, $n \log n/\log \log n$-processor algorithm over general alphabets. This is the fastest possible time with the number of processors used.

These new results improve on the known parallel palindrome detection algorithms by using smaller auxiliary space and either by making fewer operations or by achieving a faster running time.

1 Introduction

Palindromes are symmetric strings that read the same forward and backward. Palindromes have been studied for centuries as word puzzles and more recently have several important uses in formal languages and computability theory.

Formally, a string w is a palindrome if $w = w^R$, where w^R denotes the string w reversed. It is convenient to distinguish between even length palindromes that are strings of the form vv^R and odd length palindromes that are strings of the form vav^R, where a is a single alphabet symbol.

Given a string $\mathcal{S}[1..n]$, we say that there is an even palindrome of radius $\mathcal{R}$ centered at position k of $\mathcal{S}[1..n]$, if $\mathcal{S}[k-i] = \mathcal{S}[k+i-1]$ for $i = 1, \cdots, \mathcal{R}$. We say that there is an odd palindrome of radius $\hat{\mathcal{R}}$ centered on position k of $\mathcal{S}[1..n]$, if $\mathcal{S}[k-i] = \mathcal{S}[k+i]$

*Computer Science Department, Purdue University, West Lafayette, IN 47907 and Dipartimento di Elettronica e Informatica, Università di Padova, 35131 Padova, Italy. Partially supported by NSF Grants CCR-89-00305 and CCR-92-01078, by NATO Grant CRG 900293 and by the National Research Council of Italy.

†Istituto di Elaborazione della Informazione, Consiglio Nazionale delle Ricerche, Via S. Maria 46, 56126 Pisa, Italy. Partially supported by the European Research Consortium for Informatics and Mathematics postdoctoral fellowship. Part of this work was done while visiting at the Institut National de Recherche en Informatique et en Automatique, Rocquencourt, France.

‡Computer Science Department, Columbia University, New York, NY 10027 and Computer Science Department, Tel-Aviv University, Ramat-Aviv 69978, Israel. Partially supported by NSF Grants CCR-90-14605 and CISE Institutional Infrastructure Grant CDA-90-24735.

for $i = 1, \cdots, \mathcal{R}$. The radius $\mathcal{R}$ (or $\hat{\mathcal{R}}$) is maximal if there is no palindrome of radius[1] $\mathcal{R} + 1$ centered at the same position. In this paper we are interested in computing the maximal radii $\mathcal{R}[k]$ and $\hat{\mathcal{R}}[k]$ of the even and the odd palindromes which are centered at all positions k of $\mathcal{S}[1..n]$.

Manacher [17] discovered an elegant linear-time on-line sequential algorithm that finds all initial palindromes in a string. Galil [11] and Slisenko [18] presented real-time initial palindrome recognition algorithms for multitape Turing machines. It is interesting to note that the existence of efficient algorithms that find initial palindromes in a string was also implied by theoretical results on fast simulation [6, 10]. Knuth, Morris and Pratt [15] gave another linear-time algorithm that finds all initial palindromes in a string.

A closer look at Manacher's algorithm shows that it not only finds the initial palindromes, but it also computes the maximal radii of palindromes centered at all positions of the input string. Thus Manacher's algorithm solves the problem considered in this paper in linear time.

A parallel algorithm is said to be *optimal*, or to achieve an *optimal-speedup*, if its time-processor product, which is the total number of operation performed, is equal to the running time of the fastest sequential algorithm. Note that there exists a trivial constant-time CRCW-PRAM algorithm that finds all palindromes in a string using $O(n^2)$ processors. However, the large number of processors leaves much to be desired.

Fischer and Paterson [9] noticed that any string matching algorithm that finds all overhanging occurrences of a string in another can also find all initial palindromes. This observation has been used by Apostolico, Breslauer and Galil [1] to construct an optimal $O(\log \log n)$ time parallel algorithm that finds all initial palindromes in strings over general alphabets, improving an $O(\log n)$ time non-optimal algorithm of Galil [12]. Breslauer and Galil [5] show that any parallel algorithm that finds initial palindromes in strings over general alphabets requires $\Omega(\lceil n/p \rceil + \log \log_{\lceil 1+p/n \rceil} 2p)$ time using p processors. Thus, the fastest possible optimal parallel algorithm that finds initial palindromes must take $\Omega(\log \log n)$ time and this is the time required even with $n \log n$ processors.

Crochemore and Rytter [7] discuss a general framework for solving string problems in parallel. (Similar results have been discovered by Kedem, Landau and Palem [14].) Most problems they consider, including the problem of detecting all palindromes in a string, have $O(\log n)$ time, n-processor CRCW-PRAM algorithms. However, their method uses $O(n^{1+\epsilon})$ space and requires that the input symbols are drawn from an ordered alphabet, an unnecessary restriction in the palindrome detection problem.

This paper presents two new CRCW-PRAM algorithms for detecting all palindromes in a string. Both algorithms have the same time-processor product as the Crochemore-Rytter algorithm, use linear space and work under the general alphabet assumption, where the only access they have to the input symbols is by pairwise comparisons that determine if two symbols are equal.

1. The first algorithm takes $O(\log n)$ time using n processors. If the alphabet size is bounded by a constant, then the number of processors can be reduced to $n/\log n$, making the algorithm optimal.

---

[1] For the convenience of our notation, we sometimes refer to indices in $\mathcal{S}[1..n]$ that are out of the defined range. It is agreed that all undefined symbols are distinct and different from the symbols in $\mathcal{S}[1..n]$.

2. The second algorithm takes $O(\log \log n)$ time using $n \log n / \log \log n$ processors. This algorithm is the fastest possible with the number of processors used since it takes at least this time to find the initial palindromes.

The paper is organized as follows. Section 2 overviews some parallel algorithms and tools that are used in the new algorithms. Section 3 gives important properties of periods and palindromes. Sections 4 and 5 describe the new algorithms. Concluding remarks and open problems are listed in Section 6.

2   The CRCW-PRAM Model

The algorithms described in this paper are for the concurrent-read concurrent-write parallel random access machine model. We use the weakest version of this model called the *common CRCW-PRAM*. In this model many processors have access to a shared memory. Concurrent read and write operations are allowed at all memory locations. If several processors attempt to write simultaneously to the same memory location, it is assumed that they always write the same value.

Our palindrome detection algorithms use an algorithm of Fich, Ragde and Wigderson [8] to compute the minima of n integers from the range $1, \cdots, n$, in constant time using an n-processor CRCW-PRAM. The second algorithm uses Breslauer and Galil's [4] parallel string matching algorithm that takes $O(\log \log n)$ time using an $n / \log \log n$-processor CRCW-PRAM.

One of the major issues in the design of PRAM algorithms is the assignment of processors to their tasks. In this paper, the assignment can be done using standard techniques and the following general theorem.

Theorem 2.1 *(Brent [3]) Any synchronous parallel algorithm of time t that consists of a total of x elementary operations can be implemented on p processors in $\lceil x/p \rceil + t$ time.*

3   Periods and Palindromes

Periods are regularities of strings that are exploited in many efficient string algorithms.

Definition 3.1 *A string S has a period u if S is a prefix of u^k for some large enough k. The shortest period of a string S is called the period of S. Alternatively, a string $S[1..m]$ has a period of length π if $S[i] = S[i + \pi]$, for $i = 1, \cdots, m - \pi$.*

Lemma 3.2 *(Lyndon and Schutzenberger [16]) If a string of length m has two periods of lengths p and q and $p + q \leq m$, then it also has a period of length $\gcd(p, q)$.*

Throughout the paper, we discuss only the detection of even palindromes. If interested also in the odd palindromes, one can convert the input string $S[1..n]$ into a string $\hat{S}[1..2n]$ that is obtained by doubling each symbol of the original string. It is not difficult to verify that the string $\hat{S}[1..2n]$ has even palindromes that correspond to each odd and even palindrome of $S[1..n]$. Thus, the palindrome detection algorithms can be presented with the string $\hat{S}[1..2n]$ as their input, while their output is considered in the context of the original string $S[1..n]$. Note that an odd palindrome in $\hat{S}[1..2n]$ consist of equal symbols.

The palindrome detection algorithms use the following lemmas that allow them to handle efficiently long palindromes that are centered close to each other. The lemmas concern only even palindromes, but there exist similar versions for odd palindromes.

Lemma 3.3 *Assume that the string $S[1..n]$ contains two even palindromes whose radii are at least r centered at positions k and l, such that $k < l$ and $l - k \leq r$. Then the substring $S[k - r..l + r - 1]$ is periodic with period length $2(l - k)$.*

Proof: If $1 \leq i \leq r$, then

$$S[k - i] = S[k + i - 1] = S[l - (l - k) + i - 1] =$$
$$S[l + (l - k) - i] = S[k + 2(l - k) - i]$$

and

$$S[l + i - 1] = S[l - i] = S[k + (l - k) - i] =$$
$$S[k - (l - k) + i - 1] = S[l - 2(l - k) + i - 1],$$

establishing that $S[k - r..l + r - 1]$ is periodic with period length $2(l - k)$. $\square$

Lemma 3.4 *Assume that the string $S[1..n]$ contains an even palindrome whose radius is at least r centered at position k. Furthermore, let $S[\epsilon_L..\epsilon_R]$ be the maximal substring that contains $S[k - r..k + r - 1]$ and is periodic with period length $2r$. Namely, $S[i] = S[i + 2r]$ for $i = \epsilon_L, \cdots, \epsilon_R - 2r$, and $S[\epsilon_L - 1] \neq S[\epsilon_L + 2r - 1]$ and $S[\epsilon_R + 1] \neq S[\epsilon_R - 2r + 1]$.*

Then the maximal radii of the palindromes centered at positions $c = k + lr$, for integral positive or negative values of l, such that $\epsilon_L \leq c \leq \epsilon_R$, are given as follows:

- *If $c - \epsilon_L \neq \epsilon_R - c + 1$, then the radius is exactly $\min(c - \epsilon_L, \epsilon_R - c + 1)$.*

- *If $c - \epsilon_L = \epsilon_R - c + 1$, then the radius is larger than or equal to $c - \epsilon_L$. The radius is exactly $c - \epsilon_L$ if and only if $S[\epsilon_L - 1] \neq S[\epsilon_R + 1]$.*

Proof: By the periodicity of $S[\epsilon_L..\epsilon_R]$, $S[i] = S[j]$ if $\epsilon_L \leq i, j \leq \epsilon_R$ and $i \equiv j \pmod{2r}$. Combined with the existence of the even palindrome with radius r centered at position k, we get that $S[i] = S[j]$ if $\epsilon_L \leq i, j \leq \epsilon_R$ and $i + j \equiv 2k - 1 \pmod{2r}$.

Consider the even palindrome centered at some position $c = k + lr$, for integral positive or negative values of l, such that $\epsilon_L \leq c \leq \epsilon_R$. Since $(c-i)+(c+i-1) \equiv 2k-1 \pmod{2r}$, we get that $S[c - i] = S[c + i - 1]$ for $i = 1, \cdots, \min(c - \epsilon_L, \epsilon_R - c + 1)$, establishing that the radius of the palindrome centered at position c is at least $\min(c - \epsilon_L, \epsilon_R - c + 1)$.

If $c - \epsilon_L < \epsilon_R - c + 1$, then $S[c - (c - \epsilon_L + 1)] \neq S[c + (c - \epsilon_L + 1) - 1]$ since $S[\epsilon_L - 1] \neq S[\epsilon_L + 2r - 1]$ and $S[2c - \epsilon_L] = S[\epsilon_L + 2r - 1]$, establishing that the radius is exactly $c - \epsilon_L$. Similar arguments hold if $c - \epsilon_L > \epsilon_R - c + 1$.

Finally, if $c - \epsilon_L = \epsilon_R - c + 1$, then it is clear that the radius is larger than $c - \epsilon_L$ if and only if $S[\epsilon_L - 1] = S[\epsilon_R + 1]$. $\square$

4 An $O(\log n)$ time algorithm

Theorem 4.1 *There exists an algorithm that computes the radii of all even palindromes in a string $S[1..n]$ in $O(\log n)$ time using n processors.*

Proof: The algorithm consists of $\lfloor \log n \rfloor - 1$ steps. In step number η, $0 \leq \eta \leq \lfloor \log n \rfloor - 2$, the input string $S[1..n]$ is partitioned into consecutive blocks of length 2^η. (Only palindrome centers are partitioned. The palindromes themself may overlap.) The algorithm proceeds simultaneously in all $\lfloor n/2^\eta \rfloor$ blocks. It takes constant time and makes $O(2^\eta)$ operations in each block. Therefore, each step takes constant time using n processors.

The description below concentrates on a single block. The ideal situation is when the radii of all palindromes that are centered in the block are determined by the end of the step. However, this will not always be the case. The algorithm maintains the following invariant at the completion of step number η:

> The palindromes whose radii are determined are exactly those whose radii are smaller than $2^{\eta+2}$.

The main observation is that at the beginning of step number η, the position of all undetermined radii in the block form an arithmetic progression. Let $c_1 < c_2 < \cdots < c_l$ be the positions of palindromes whose radii are not determined. We show that if $l \geq 3$, then $c_{i+1} - c_i = c_i - c_{i-1}$ for $i = 2, \cdots, l-1$. By the invariant and Lemma 3.3, $S[c_{i-1} - 2^{\eta+1}..c_i + 2^{\eta+1}]$ is periodic with period length $2(c_i - c_{i-1})$ and $S[c_i - 2^{\eta+1}..c_{i+1} + 2^{\eta+1}]$ is periodic with period length $2(c_{i+1} - c_i)$. Therefore, by Lemma 3.2, $S[c_i - 2^{\eta+1}..c_{i+1} + 2^{\eta+1}]$ is periodic with period length $c = 2 \gcd(c_i - c_{i-1}, c_{i+1} - c_i)$. But by Lemma 3.4, if $c_i - c_{i-1} > c$, then the radius of the palindrome centered at position $c_i - c$ is larger than the radius of the palindrome centered at position c_{i-1} or the palindrome centered at position c_i, violating the invariant. Therefore, $c_i - c_{i-1} = c$ and similarly also $c_{i+1} - c_i = c$, establishing that the sequence of undetermined radii $\{c_i\}$ forms an arithmetic progression.

Note that an arithmetic progression can be represented by three integers: the start, the difference and the sequence length. If the undetermined radii in the two $2^{\eta-1}$-blocks that compose the current 2^η-block are represented this way, then the two representations are merged using a constant number of operations. This permits an efficient access to all palindromes whose radii are undetermined.

We show next how to maintain the invariant at the end of each step. The computation takes a constant time and $O(2^\eta)$ operations using symbol comparisons and the integer minima algorithm.

1. If the block contains a single undetermined radius, then the algorithm checks if the radius is at least $2^{\eta+2}$ or finds the radius exactly if it is shorter.

2. If the block contains a non-trivial arithmetic progression of undetermined radii $\{c_i\}$, $i = 1..l$, with difference c, then let $S[\epsilon_L..\epsilon_R]$ be the maximal substring that contains $S[c_1 - c..c_l + c - 1]$ and is periodic with period length $2c$. By Lemma 3.4, the radius of the palindrome centered at position c_i is exactly $\min(c_i - \epsilon_L, \epsilon_R - c_i + 1)$ except for at most one of the c_i's that satisfies $c_i - \epsilon_L = \epsilon_R - c_i + 1$.

The algorithm checks if $\mathcal{S}[c_1 - 2^{\eta+2}..c_l + 2^{\eta+2} - 1]$ is periodic with period length $2c$. If this substring is not periodic, then the algorithm has found at least one of ϵ_L and ϵ_R and it can determine all radii which are smaller than $2^{\eta+2}$ by Lemma 3.4. If the algorithm found both ϵ_L and ϵ_R and there is a palindrome with undetermined radius centered at position $(\epsilon_L + \epsilon_R + 1)/2$, then the algorithm checks if the radius of this palindrome is at least $2^{\eta+2}$ or finds the radius exactly if it is shorter.

Sometime the algorithm finds radii of longer palindromes but we prefer to leave these radii undetermined to maintain the invariant.

In the beginning of step number 0 there is a single undetermined radius in each block and the invariant is satisfied at the end of the step. At the end of step number $\lfloor \log n \rfloor - 2$ all radii have been determined. $\square$

4.1 Constant size alphabets

If the size of the alphabet is bounded by some constant, then the $O(\log n)$ time algorithm described above can be implemented using only $n/\log n$ processors, similarly to Galil's [12] string matching algorithm. This is achieved using the "four Russians trick" [2] of packing $\log n$ symbols into one number, in order to facilitate comparisons of up to $\log n$ symbols in a single operation.

5 An $O(\log\log n)$ time algorithm

Theorem 5.1 *There exists an algorithm that computes the radii of all even palindromes in a string $\mathcal{S}[1..n]$ in $O(\log\log n)$ time using $n \log n/\log\log n$ processors.*

Proof: The algorithm proceeds in independent stages which are computed simultaneously. In stage number η, $0 \le \eta \le \lfloor \log n \rfloor - 3$, the algorithm computes all entries $\mathcal{R}[i]$ of the radii array such that $4l_\eta \le \mathcal{R}[i] < 8l_\eta$, for $l_\eta = 2^\eta$.

Note that each stage computes disjoint ranges of the radii values and that all radii that are greater than or equal to 4 are computed by some stage. The radii between 0 and 3 are computed in a special stage that takes constant time and $O(n)$ operations. (The special stage assigns one processor to each entry of the radii array to check sequentially if the corresponding radius is between 0 and 3.)

We denote by T_η the time it takes to compute stage number η using O_η operations. In the next section we show that each stage η can be computed in $T_\eta = O(\log\log l_\eta)$ time and $O_\eta = O(n)$ operations. Since the stages are computed simultaneously, the time is $\max T_\eta = O(\log\log n)$. The total number of operation performed is $\Sigma_\eta O_\eta = O(n \log n)$. By Theorem 2.1, the algorithm can be implemented in $O(\log\log n)$ time using $n \log n/\log\log n$ processors. $\square$

5.1 A single stage

This section describes a single stage η, $0 \le \eta \le \lfloor \log n \rfloor - 3$, that computes all values of the radii array $\mathcal{R}[1..n]$ that are between $4l_\eta$ and $8l_\eta - 1$, in $O(\log\log l_\eta)$ time and $O(n)$ operations.

Partition the input string $S[1..n]$ into consecutive blocks of length l_η. Namely, block number k is $S[(k-1)l_\eta + 1..kl_\eta]$. Stage number η consists of independent sub-stages that are also computed simultaneously. There is a sub-stage for each block. The sub-stage finds the radii of all palindromes which are centered in the block and whose radii are in the range computed by stage η. Sometimes palindromes whose radii are out of this range can be detected, but these radii do not have to be written into the output array since they are guaranteed to be found in another stage.

The sub-stage that is assigned to block number k starts with a call to the string matching algorithm to find all occurrences of the four consecutive blocks $S[(k-4)l_\eta + 1..kl_\eta]$, reversed, in $S[(k-2)l_\eta + 1..(k+4)l_\eta - 1]$. Let p_i, $i = 1, \cdots, r$, denote the indices of all these occurrences. The sequence $\{p_i\}$ has a "nice" structure as we show next.

Lemma 5.2 *Assume that the period length of a string $A[1..l]$ is p. If $A[1..l]$ occurs only at positions $p_1 < p_2 < \cdots < p_k$ of a string B and $p_k - p_1 \leq \lceil \frac{l}{2} \rceil$, then the p_i's form an arithmetic progression with difference p.*

Proof: See the paper by Apostolico, Breslauer and Galil [1]. □

Lemma 5.3 *The sequence $\{p_i\}$, which is defined above, forms an arithmetic progression.*

Proof: The sequence $\{p_i\}$ lists the indices of all occurrences of a string of length $4l_\eta$ in a string of length $6l_\eta - 1$. By Lemma 5.2, the p_i's form an arithmetic progression. □

By the last lemma, the sequence $\{p_i\}$ can be represented by three integers: the start, the difference and the sequence length. This representation is computed from the output of the string matching algorithm in constant time and $O(l_\eta)$ operations using the integer minima algorithm.

The next lemma states that we essentially found all "interesting" palindromes.

Lemma 5.4 *There exists a correspondence between the elements of the $\{p_i\}$ sequence to all palindromes that are centered in block number k and whose radii are large enough.*

- *If $p_i + kl_\eta$ is odd, then p_i corresponds to an even palindrome which is centered at position $(p_i + kl_\eta + 1)/2$.*

- *If $p_i + kl_\eta$ is even, then p_i corresponds to an odd palindrome which is centered on position $(p_i + kl_\eta)/2$.*

Each palindrome whose radius is at least $4l_\eta - 1$ has some corresponding p_i, while palindromes that correspond to some p_i are guaranteed to have radii that are at least $3l_\eta$.

Proof: Assume that there is an even palindrome whose radius is at least $4l_\eta - 1$ which is centered at position c, such that $(k-1)l_\eta < c \leq kl_\eta$. That is, $S[c-i] = S[c+i-1]$ for $i = 1, \cdots, 4l_\eta - 1$. In particular, $S[c-i] = S[c+i-1]$ for $c - kl_\eta \leq i \leq c - (k-4)l_\eta - 1$, establishing that there is an occurrence of $S[(k-4)l_\eta+1..kl_\eta]$, reversed, starting at position $2c - kl_\eta - 1$.

Conversely, if there is an occurrence of $S[(k-4)l_\eta+1..kl_\eta]$, reversed, starting at position p_i, then $S[kl_\eta - j] = S[p_i + j]$ for $j = 0, \cdots, 4l_\eta - 1$. In particular, if $p_i + kl_\eta$ is odd, then

$S[kl_\eta - j] = S[p_i + j]$ for $j = (kl_\eta - p_i + 1)/2, \cdots, 4l_\eta - 1$, establishing that there is an even palindrome of radius $4l_\eta - (kl_\eta - p_i + 1)/2 \geq 3l_\eta$ centered at position $(p_i + kl_\eta + 1)/2$.

Similar arguments hold for odd palindromes. $\square$

We could design the algorithm to find the odd palindromes directly, but we rather use the reduction to even palindromes that was given in Section 3. Define the sequence $\{q_i\}$ for $i = 1, \cdots, l$, to list all centers of the even palindromes that correspond to elements in $\{p_i\}$. By the last lemma, if the difference of the arithmetic progression $\{p_i\}$ is even or if there is only a single element, then all the p_i's correspond either to odd or to even palindromes. If the difference of the arithmetic progression $\{p_i\}$ is odd, then every second element corresponds to an even palindrome. Thus, the sequence $\{q_i\}$ also forms an arithmetic progression and therefore it can be computed efficiently.

If the $\{q_i\}$ sequence does not have any elements, then there are no even palindromes whose radius is at least $4l_\eta$ that are centered in the current block. If there is only one element q_1, then we can find in constant time and $O(l_\eta)$ operations what is the radius of the palindrome that is centered at q_1 or we can conclude that it is too large to be computed in this stage.

If there are more elements, let q denote the difference of the arithmetic progression $\{q_i\}$. The next lemma shows how to find the radii of the palindromes centered at $\{q_i\}$ efficiently.

Lemma 5.5 *It is possible to find the radii of all palindromes centered at positions in $\{q_i\}$ in constant time and $O(l_\eta)$ operations.*

Proof: For each ζ, such that $q_1 - 8l_\eta \leq \zeta < q_1$, verify if $S[\zeta] = S[\zeta + 2q]$. Let ζ_L be the smallest such index ζ that satisfies $S[\zeta_L..q_1 - 1] = S[\zeta_L + 2q..q_1 + 2q - 1]$. Similarly, for each ζ, such that $q_l \leq \zeta < q_l + 8l_\eta$, verify if $S[\zeta] = S[\zeta - 2q]$. Let ζ_R be the largest such index ζ that satisfies $S[q_l - 2q..\zeta_R - 2q] = S[q_l..\zeta_R]$. ζ_L and ζ_R are computed in constant time and $O(l_\eta)$ operations using symbol comparisons and the integer minima algorithm.

By Lemma 5.4, the palindromes centered at the positions q_i have radii that are larger than q. Therefore, by Lemma 3.3, $\zeta_L < q_1 - q$ and $\zeta_R \geq q_l + q$ and by Lemma 3.4, the radius of the palindrome centered at position q_i is at least $\rho_i = \min(q_i - \zeta_L, \zeta_R - q_i + 1)$.

If $\rho_i \geq 8l_\eta$, then the radius of the palindrome centered at q_i is too large to be computed in this stage and it does not have to be determined exactly. Otherwise, the radius is exactly ρ_i except for at most one of the q_i's which satisfies $q_i - \zeta_L = \zeta_R - q_i + 1$. For this particular q_i, we can find in constant time and $O(l_\eta)$ operations what is the radius of the palindrome or we can conclude that it is too large to be computed in this stage. $\square$

Lemma 5.6 *Stage number η correctly computes all entries of the output array $\mathcal{R}[1..n]$ that are in the range $4l_\eta, \cdots, 8l_\eta - 1$. It takes $O(\log \log l_\eta)$ time and make a total of $O(n)$ operations.*

Proof: There are $\lfloor n/l_\eta \rfloor$ sub-stages in stage η, each uses $O(l_\eta)$ operations. Thus the number of operations used is $O(n)$. Breslauer and Galil's [4] parallel string matching algorithm takes $O(\log \log l_\eta)$ time to find the $\{p_i\}$ sequence and the rest of the work is done in constant time. $\square$

6 Conclusion

The question whether there exists an optimal $O(\log \log n)$ time parallel algorithm that finds all palindromes in strings over general alphabets remains open. It is possible that one could prove an $\Omega(n \log n)$ lower bound on the operation count of any $O(\log \log n)$ time algorithm and even for $O(\log n)$ time algorithms.

The recognition problem of *Palstar*, the language of strings that are obtained as concatenation of non-trivial palindromes, is an interesting related problem. In the sequential setting Knuth, Morris and Pratt [15] described a linear time algorithm that recognizes strings that are composed of even palindromes. Galil and Seiferas [13] solved the general problem by giving a linear-time on-line algorithm that recognizes *Palstar*.

In parallel, Crochemore and Rytter [7] designed an $O(\log n)$ algorithm for the case of even palindromes and composition of k palindromes, for $k = 2, 3, 4$. Their algorithm uses the radii of all palindromes, which are computed more efficiently by the new algorithms that were described in this paper. However, the other steps of their algorithms seem to require $O(\log n)$ time, and the question of fast parallel recognition of *Palstar* is still open.

7 Acknowledgments

We thank Roberto Grossi and Laura Toniolo for several discussions about palindromes and for comments on this paper.

References

[1] A. Apostolico, D. Breslauer, and Z. Galil. Optimal Parallel Algorithms for Periods, Palindromes and Squares. In *Proc. 19th International Colloquium on Automata, Languages, and Programming*, pages 296–307. Springer-Verlag, Berlin, Germany, 1992.

[2] V.L. Arlazarov, E.A. Dinic, M.A. Kronrod, and I.A. Faradzev. On economic construction of the transitive closure of a directed graph. *Soviet Math. Dokl.*, 11:1209–1210, 1970.

[3] R.P. Brent. Evaluation of general arithmetic expressions. *J. Assoc. Comput. Mach.*, 21:201–206, 1974.

[4] D. Breslauer and Z. Galil. An optimal $O(\log \log n)$ time parallel string matching algorithm. *SIAM J. Comput.*, 19(6):1051–1058, 1990.

[5] D. Breslauer and Z. Galil. Finding all Periods and Initial Palindromes of a String in Parallel. Technical Report CUCS-017-92, Computer Science Dept., Columbia University, 1992.

[6] S.A. Cook. Linear time simulation of deterministic two-way pushdown automata. In *Information Processing 71*, pages 75–80. North Holland Publishing Co., Amsterdam, the Netherlands, 1972.

[7] M. Crochemore and W. Rytter. Usefulness of the Karp-Miller-Rosenberg algorithm in parallel computations on strings and arrays. *Theoret. Comput. Sci.*, 88:59–82, 1991.

[8] F.E. Fich, R.L. Ragde, and A. Wigderson. Relations between concurrent-write models of parallel computation. In *Proc. 3rd ACM Symp. on Principles of Distributed Computing*, pages 179–189, 1984.

[9] M.J. Fischer and M.S. Paterson. String matching and other products. In R.M. Karp, editor, *Complexity of Computation*, pages 113–125. American Mathematical Society, Prividence, RI., 1974.

[10] Z. Galil. Two fast simulations which imply some fast string matching and palindrome-recognition algorithms. *Inform. Process. Lett.*, 4(4):85–87, 1976.

[11] Z. Galil. Palindrome Recognition in Real Time by a Multitape Turing Machine. *J. Comput. System Sci.*, 16(2):140–157, 1978.

[12] Z. Galil. Optimal parallel algorithms for string matching. *Inform. and Control*, 67:144–157, 1985.

[13] Z. Galil and J. Seiferas. A Linear-Time On-Line Recognition Algorithm for "Palstar". *J. Assoc. Comput. Mach.*, 25(1):102–111, 1978.

[14] Z. Kedem, G.M. Landau, and K. Palem. Optimal parallel suffix-prefix matching algorithm and applications. Manuscript, 1988.

[15] D.E. Knuth, J.H. Morris, and V.R. Pratt. Fast pattern matching in strings. *SIAM J. Comput.*, 6:322–350, 1977.

[16] R.C. Lyndon and M.P. Schutzenberger. The equation $a^m = b^n c^p$ in a free group. *Michigan Math. J.*, 9:289–298, 1962.

[17] G. Manacher. A new Linear-Time "On-Line" Algorithm for Finding the Smallest Initial Palindrome of a String. *J. Assoc. Comput. Mach.*, 22, 1975.

[18] A.O. Slisenko. Recognition of palindromes by multihead Turing machines. In V.P. Orverkov and N.A. Sonin, editors, *Problems in the Constructive Trend in Mathematics VI (Proceedings of the Steklov Institute of Mathematics, No. 129)*, pages 30–202. Academy of Sciences of the USSR, 1973. English Translation by R.H. Silverman, pp. 25–208, Amer. Math. Soc., Providence, RI, 1976.

Computational Complexity

On the Structure of Parameterized Problems in NP *
(Extended Abstract)

Liming Cai[1]   Jianer Chen[1]   Rodney Downey[2]   Michael Fellows[3]

[1]Dept. of Computer Science, Texas A&M Univ., College Station, TX 77843, USA
[2]Dept. of Mathematics, Victoria Univ., P.O. Box 600, Wellington, New Zealand
[3]Dept. of Computer Science, Univ. of Victoria, Victoria, B.C. V8W 3P6, Canada

Abstract. Fixed-parameter intractability of optimization problems in *NP* is studied based on computational models with limited nondeterminism. Strong evidence is shown that many *NP* optimization problems are not fixed-parameter tractable and that the fixed-parameter intractability hierarchy (the *W*-hierarchy) does not collapse.

1   Introduction

A theory of fixed-parameter tractability of *NP* optimization problems has been initialized recently by Downey and Fellows [1, 2, 15, 16] with the aim of refining the class of *NP* optimization problems and of solving *NP* optimization problems in practice. They have observed that many *NP* optimization problems can be parameterized, while the complexity of these problems may vary very differently with respect to the parameter. For example, the problem of finding a size k vertex cover in a graph can be solved in time $O(n^c)$, where c is a constant independent of the parameter k (in fact, $c = 1$ by [8]); while the problem of finding a size k dominating set in a graph has the contrasting situation where essentially no better algorithm is known than the "trivial" algorithm of time $O(n^{k+1})$ that just exhaustively tries all possible solutions.

In order to capture the fixed-parameter intractability of *NP* optimization problems, Downey and Fellows [15] have introduced a hierarchy (called the *W-hierarchy*)

$$FPT \subseteq W[1] \subseteq W[2] \subseteq \cdots \subseteq W[P]$$

Sitting at the bottom of the hierarchy is the class *FPT* of fixed-parameter tractable problems that can be solved for each fixed k in time $O(n^c)$ where c is a constant independent of the parameter k. Examples in the class *FPT* are

* Cai is supported in part by Engineering Excellence Award from Texas A&M University; Chen is supported in part by NSF Grant CCR-9110824; Downey is supported in part by a grant from the Victoria University IGC, by the United States/New Zealand Cooperative Science Foundation under grant INT 90-20558, and by the Mathematical Sciences Institute at Cornell and Cornell University; and Fellows is supported in part by the National Science and Engineering Research Council of Canada, and by the United States NSF under grant MIP-8919312.

Vertex-Cover and *Minimum-Genus* [3, 18, 23]. More than a dozen problems, including *Independent-Set*, have been shown to be complete for the class $W[1]$ [4], while *Dominating-Set* and a number of other problems are shown to be complete for the class $W[2]$. A typical complete problem for the "cap class" $W[P]$ of the hierarchy is the *Weighted Circuit Satisfiability* problem. It is conjectured that the W-hierarchy is infinite [15]. Therefore, the completeness of a problem at some level of the W-hierarchy indicates the computational difficulty of the problem with respect to the parameter. The completeness theory for parameterized computational complexity has been shown to have many applications in diverse problem domains including familiar graph-theoretical problems, VLSI layout, games, computational biology, cryptography, and computational learning [14, 17, 18, 19].

Another motivation of the study of fixed-parameter intractability is due to its close connection to the approximability of NP-hard optimization problems. As shown by Cai and Chen [10], with a minor restriction, the approximability of an optimization problem implies the fixed-parameter tractability of the problem. Therefore, the completeness study of the W-hierarchy provides a useful tool for proving the non-approximability of problems: showing an optimization problem to be hard for some level in the W-hierarchy implies that the problem is not approximable unless the W-hierarchy collapses.

Therefore, it has wide-ranging practical and theoretical significance to show that the W-hierarchy does not collapse. However, it may seem a bit ambitious to derive a direct proof since any separation result for the W-hierarchy would imply $P \neq NP$. Thus, it may be instead more feasible to show that the collapsing of the W-hierarchy implies unlikely results in classical complexity theory.

In the present paper we study the structural properties of the W-hierarchy based on computational models with limited nondeterminism [11]. By techniques of inverse functions, we are able to show that a parameterized problem is fixed-parameter tractable if and only if it can be solved by a polynomial time algorithm that is allowed to guess a string of length $f(k)$, while a parameterized problem is in the class $W[P]$ if and only if it can be solved by a polynomial-time algorithm that is allowed to guess a string of length $g(k) \log n$, where $f(k)$ and $g(k)$ are arbitrary recursive functions independent of the input length n. These characterizations of the classes FPT and $W[P]$ indicate a clear difference between the two classes. Therefore, to find a vertex cover of size k in a graph, we only need to guess a string of length $f(k)$, no matter how large the graph is, where $f(k)$ is a fixed recursive function depending only on the parameter k; while to find a weight k satisfying assignment for a circuit C, we *must* be able to guess a string whose length is of the form $g(k) \log |C|$ for some recursive function $g(k)$, which increases with the size $|C|$ of the circuit C.

We also derive a characterization for each level of the W-hierarchy by computations with limited nondeterminism, and show strong evidence supporting the conjecture that the W-hierarchy does not collapse. More specifically, for

---

[4] The completeness in the W-hierarchy is based on the reduction called "*uniform reduction*" that will be described precisely in Section 2.

each level $W[t]$ of the W-hierarchy, we introduce a computation model with the ability of making limited nondeterminism and show that this model defines a subclass of $W[t]$ that is equivalent to the class $W[t]$ up to the uniform reduction. Then we prove that the defined subclass of $W[t]$ and the defined subclass of $W[t+1]$ are distinct for all $t > 1$.

Another interesting question is whether approximability and fixed-parameter tractability are equivalent for computational optimization problems. Roughly speaking, approximability implies fixed-parameter tractability [10]. However, there are problems, such as *Longest Path*, which are fixed-parameter tractable [18] but not approximable [4]. Having observed this fact, we further refine the class FPT with the intention of specifying the approximability of the problems. We show that the class FPT can be further classified in term of the ability of guessing and the power of verifying. Strong evidence is given that these subclasses are distinct.

The paper is organized as follows. In Section 2 we introduce the necessary definitions and preliminaries. The characterizations of the classes FPT and $W[P]$ in terms of the computation models with limited nondeterminism are given in Section 3. The structural properties of the W-hierarchy are discussed in Section 4. Section 5 discusses the refinement of the class FPT. Conclusions are given in Section 6.

2 Preliminaries

We first give a brief review on the fundamentals of the theory of fixed-parameter tractability. For detailed description, see [1, 15, 16].

Definition 1. A *parameterized problem* L is a subset of $\Sigma^* \times N$, where Σ is a fixed alphabet. Therefore, each instance of the parameterized problem L is a pair $\langle x, k \rangle$, where the second component k will be called *the parameter*.

The complexity of a parameterized problem can be specified in terms of the two components of its instances.

Definition 2. A parameterized problem L is (*strongly*) *fixed-parameter tractable* if there is an algorithm to decide whether $\langle x, k \rangle$ is a member of L in time $f(k)|x|^c$, where $f(k)$ is a recursive function and c is a constant independent of the parameter k. Let FPT denote the class of fixed-parameter tractable problems.

Definition 3. Let L and L' be two parameterized problems. We say that L is (*uniformly*) *reducible* to L' if there is an algorithm M that transforms $\langle x, k \rangle$ into $\langle x', g(k) \rangle$ in time $f(k)|x|^c$, where f and g are recursive functions and c is a constant independent of k, such that $\langle x, k \rangle \in L$ if and only if $\langle x', g(k) \rangle \in L'$.

It is easy to observe that if L is reducible to L' and L' is fixed-parameter tractable, then so is L.

To define the W-hierarchy, we need the following notations similar to those introduced by Boppana and Sipser [6]. We say a circuit C is a Π_t^h-circuit if C is of unbounded fan-in and of depth at most $t + 1$ with an AND gate at the output and gates of fan-in at most h at the input level. Let t and h be two integers, we define a parameterized problem as follows:

$$WCS(t, h) = \{(C, k) \mid \text{The } \Pi_t^h\text{-circuit } C \text{ accepts an input vector of weight } k\}$$

Definition 4. A parameterized problem L belongs to the class $W[t]$ if L is reducible to the parameterized problem $WCS(t, h)$ for some constant h.

The class $W[P]$ is defined similarly as $W[t]$ with no restriction on the depth of the circuits. Formally,

Definition 5. A parameterized problem L belongs to the class $W[P]$ if L is reducible to the following *Weighted Circuit Satisfiability* (*WSC*) problem:

$$WCS = \{(C, k) \mid \text{The circuit } C \text{ accepts an input vector of weight } k\}$$

The above leads to an interesting hierarchy (called the *W-hierarchy*)

$$FPT \subseteq W[1] \subseteq W[2] \subseteq \cdots \subseteq W[P]$$

for which a wide variety of natural problems are now known to be complete or hard for various levels (under the uniform reduction) [15].

The structural properties of the W-hierarchy will be studied based on the following GC model (for "Guess-then-Check") introduced by Cai and Chen [11].

Definition 6. Let $s(n, k)$ be a recursive function on two variables. A parameterized problem L is in $GC(s(n, k), P)$ if there is a deterministic algorithm M and a polynomial q such that for all $z = \langle x, k \rangle$, $z \in L$ if and only if $\exists y \in \{0, 1\}^*$, $|y| \le s(|x|, k)$, and M accepts $z \# y$ in time $O(q(|z|))$.

Intuitively, the first component $s(n, k)$ in the GC model specifies the length of the guessed string y, which is the amount of nondeterminism allowed to make in the computation, while the second component P (polynomial time computation) specifies the power of verifying of the computation. Note that the complexity of the verifying algorithm M is measured by the size of z rather than the size of the input $z \# y$ to the algorithm M. Similarly, the GC model may also be defined by substituting the complexity class P by other complexity classes such as DL, NL, and R.

The GC model is quite robust. It can be shown that for many functions $s(n, k)$ and for many complexity classes $\mathcal{C}$, the class $GC(s(n, k), \mathcal{C})$ has natural complete languages [11]. We also point out that some restricted forms of the GC model have been studied recently in the literature [7, 13, 20, 25, 26].

Let $R(x_1)$ and $R(x_1, x_2)$ be the set of all recursive functions of one and two variables, respectively. Let $\mathcal{C}$ be an arbitrary complexity class, we will define

$$GC(R(n, k), \mathcal{C}) \qquad GC(R(k), \mathcal{C}) \qquad GC(R(k) \log n, \mathcal{C})$$

to be the following classes, respectively.

$$\bigcup_{f \in R(x_1, x_2)} GC(f(n, k), \mathcal{C}) \qquad \bigcup_{f \in R(x_1)} GC(f(k), \mathcal{C}) \qquad \bigcup_{f \in R(x_1)} GC(f(k) \log n, \mathcal{C})$$

Remark 1. Parameterized problems form a restricted subclass in the class of general problems. Therefore, we can talk about the complexity of a parameterized problem in terms of the instance size. For example, we say that a parameterized problem is in the class *NP* if there are a nondeterministic algorithm M and a polynomial r such that M can decide whether a given instance $z = \langle x, k \rangle$ is a member of L in time $r(|z|)$.

Remark 2. Since a parameterless problem can always be regarded as a parameterized problem with a dummy parameter, the model GC can also be used to define classes of general problems.

3 The characterizations of *FPT* and *W[P]*

We start with the following simple observation.

Theorem 7. *Every parameterized problem in NP is in the class $GC(R(n, k), P)$.*

Recall that a function $t(n)$ is *time-constructible* if there is a deterministic algorithm M of running time $O(t(n))$ such that given input 1^n, M gives as the output $1^{t(n)}$ [5]. We need to introduce the concept of log-space constructibility of functions.

Definition 8. A function $s(n)$ is *log-space constructible* if there is a deterministic algorithm M that runs in space $O(\log(s(n)))$ such that given input 1^n, M outputs $s(n)$ in binary form.

Lemma 9. *For any recursive function $r(n)$, there is a log-space constructible non-decreasing function $f(n) \geq n$ such that $f(n) \geq r(n)$ for all $n \geq 1$.*

Let f be an unbounded non-decreasing function. The *inverse function f^{-1}* of f is defined as follows:

$$f^{-1}(m) = \max\{n \mid f(n) \leq m\}$$

It is easy to see that f^{-1} is well-defined, unbounded, and non-decreasing.

Lemma 10. *Let $f(n)$ be an unbounded non-decreasing function and let k be an arbitrary integer. Then $f(k) \leq n$ if and only if $f^{-1}(n) \geq k$.*

Lemma 11. *Let $f(n) \geq n$ be an unbounded, non-decreasing and log-space constructible function. Then the inversion function $f^{-1}(n)$ of f is computable by a deterministic algorithm whose space is bounded by $O(\log n)$.*

Now we are ready for our main theorems in the section.

Theorem 12. *Let L be an arbitrary parameterized problem in NP. Then L is in $GC(R(k), P)$ if and only if L is in FPT.*

Proof. (Sketch) Let $L \in FPT$. Then there is a deterministic algorithm M_1 deciding whether $\langle x, k \rangle$ is in L in time $f(k)|x|^c$, where by Lemma 9, we can assume that $f(k)$ is an unbounded nondecreasing log-space constructible function and c is a constant independent of k. Moreover, since L is in NP, there is a nondeterministic algorithm M_2 that decides whether $z = \langle x, k \rangle$ is in L in time $q(|z|)$, where q is a polynomial.

Now construct a deterministic algorithm M as follows. Given an input of the form $z\#y$, where $z = \langle x, k \rangle$, the algorithm M first compares $f(k)$ with $|x|$. If $f(k) \leq |x|$ then M simulates the algorithm M_1 on input $z = \langle x, k \rangle$. If $f(k) > |x|$ then M simulates the algorithm M_2 on input $z = \langle x, k \rangle$ following the computation path specified by the string y.

We analyze the complexity of the algorithm M. By Lemma 10, $f(k) \leq |x|$ is equivalent to $f^{-1}(|x|) \geq k$. Moreover, according to Lemma 11, the function value $f^{-1}(|x|)$ can be computed in time $O(|x|^d)$ for some constant d. Therefore, in time $O(|x|^d) \leq O(|z|^d)$, the algorithm M can check whether $f(k) \leq |x|$. In case $f(k) \leq |x|$, the algorithm M simulates the algorithm M_1 on input $z = \langle x, k \rangle$, which runs in time $f(k)|x|^c \leq |x|^{c+1} \leq |z|^{c+1}$, while in case $f(k) > |x|$, the algorithm M simulates the algorithm M_2 on input z following the computation path specified by y, which is a deterministic computation of running time $q(|z|)$. In summary, the running time of the algorithm M is bounded by a polynomial of $|z|$.

The construction of M shows that the language L is in the class $GC(q(f(k) + \log k), P)$. In fact, for a given input $z = \langle x, k \rangle$, if $f(k) \leq |x|$, the algorithm M can decide whether $z \in L$ without consulting the guessed string y; while in case $f(k) > |x|$, the length $|z|$ of $z = \langle x, k \rangle$ is bounded by $f(k) + \log k$ and the length of the computation path of M_2 is bounded by $q(|z|) \leq q(f(k) + \log k)$. Therefore, a guessed string y of length at most $q(f(k) + \log k)$ is sufficient to specify an accepting computation path of M_2.

The other direction of the theorem is relatively easier. Let L be a problem in $GC(f(k), P)$, where f is a recursive function. Given an input $\langle x, k \rangle$, a deterministic algorithm M simply enumerates all strings y of length $f(k)$ and simulates the verifier on the input $\langle x, k \rangle \# y$. It is easy to see that the running time of the algorithm M is bounded by $g(k)n^c$, where g is a recursive function and c is a constant independent of the parameter k. ☐

The class $W[P]$ can also be characterized by the GC model. However, the proof technique is very different from that of Theorem 12.

Lemma 13. *The problem WCS is in the class $GC(k \log n, P)$.*

Lemma 14. $\qquad GC(R(k) \log n, P) \subseteq W[P]$.

Proof. (Sketch) Suppose that $L \in GC(f(k) \log n, P)$, where $f(k)$ is a recursive function. By the definition, there is a deterministic algorithm M such that for each instance $z = \langle x, k \rangle$, $z \in L$ if and only if there is a string y, $|y| \leq f(k) \log(|x|)$ such that $z \# y \in L(M)$ and the running time of M is bounded by a polynomial q of $|z|$. We show how the problem L can be uniformly reduced to the problem WCS.

Let $z = \langle x, k \rangle$ be an instance of L. Since the running time of M is bounded by $q(|z|)$, in time polynomial in $|z|$, we can construct a circuit C such that C accepts $z \# y$ if and only if the algorithm M does [21]. Assigning the input part corresponding to the string z by the value of z gives a circuit C' with $f(k) \log n$ input bits. Now construct another circuit C'' with $f(k)n$ input bits such that the circuit C'' accepts an input vector of weight $f(k)$ if and only if the circuit C' has a satisfiable assignment, which is in turn if and only if the algorithm M accepts the input $z \# y$ for some string y of length $f(k) \log n$. It can be shown that the above reduction can be done in time $h(k)n^c$, where h is a recursive function and c is a constant independent of k. This shows that the problem L is reducible to the problem WCS. Thus, L is in the class $W[P]$. $\square$

Theorem 15. *Let L be a parameterized problem in NP. Then L is in the class $GC(R(k) \log n, P)$ if and only if L is in the class $W[P]$.*

Proof. (Sketch) By Lemma 14, we only need to show that if L is in $W[P]$ then L is in $GC(R(k) \log n, P)$.

Since the problem L is in NP, there is a nondeterministic algorithm M_0 that decides whether $\langle x, k \rangle$ is in L in time $p(|x| + |k|)$, where p is a polynomial.

Suppose $L \in W[P]$, by definition L is reducible to the problem WCS, that is, there is a deterministic algorithm M_1 running in time $f(k)|x|^c$ that transforms a pair $\langle x, k \rangle$ into a pair $\langle C, g(k) \rangle$ such that $\langle x, k \rangle \in L$ if and only if the circuit C accepts an input vector of weight $g(k)$, here f and g are recursive functions and by Lemma 9, we may assume that the function f is unbounded, non-decreasing, and log-space constructible.

By Lemma 13, the problem WCS is in the class $GC(k \log n, P)$. Thus, there is a deterministic polynomial time algorithm M_2 such that $\langle C, k \rangle$ is in WCS if and only if there is a string y of length at most $k \log |C|$ and M_2 accepts $\langle C, k \rangle \# y$.

Now we construct a deterministic algorithm M as follows. Given an input of the form $z \# y$, where $z = \langle x, k \rangle$, M first check if $f(k) \leq |x|$. As indicated in the proof of Theorem 12, this checking can be done in time $|x|^d \leq |z|^d$ for some constant d. If $f(k) \leq |x|$, then M simulates the algorithm M_1, transforms the pair $z = \langle x, k \rangle$ into an instance $\langle C, g(k) \rangle$ of the problem WCS, and then simulates the algorithm M_2 on input $\langle C, g(k) \rangle \# y$. If $f(k) > |x|$, then M simulates the nondeterministic algorithm M_0 on input $\langle x, k \rangle$ following the computation path specified by y. It can be shown that $\langle x, k \rangle$ is in L if and only if M accepts an input $\langle x, k \rangle \# y$, where y is a string of length at most $\max\{p(f(k) + |k|), g(k) \log n\}$. Moreover, it can also be shown that the running time of M is bounded by a polynomial of $|z|$. Thus, L is in the class $GC(R(k) \log n, P)$. $\square$

Theorem 12 and Theorem 15 give strong evidence that the class FPT is a proper subclass of the class $W[P]$ and point out an intrinsic difference among various *NP*-hard optimization problems. For example, by Theorem 12, to find a vertex cover of size k in a graph G, which is a fixed-parameter tractable problem, we only need to guess a string of length $f(k)$, no matter how large the graph G is, where $f(k)$ is a fixed recursive function depending only on the parameter k; while according to Theorem 15, to find a weight k satisfying assignment for a circuit C, for which the corresponding problem *WCS* is complete for $W[P]$, we *must* be able to guess a string whose length is of the form $g(k) \log |C|$ for some recursive function $g(k)$, which increases with the size $|C|$ of the circuit C.

Formally, using these characterizations and padding techniques, we can show that $W[P] = FPT$ would imply a major breakthrough in complexity theory, as stated in the following theorem.

Theorem 16. *In the following, (1) and (2) are equivalent, and both implies (3).*
(1) $W[P] = FPT$;
(2) $GC(s(n) \log n, P) \subseteq P$ for some unbounded non-decreasing function $s(n)$;
(3) $NTIME(n) \subseteq DTIME(2^{o(n)})$.

4   The structure of the *W*-hierarchy

In this section, we will characterize the *W*-hierarchy by the *GC* model and show strong evidence that the *W*-hierarchy does not collapse.

Definition 17. Let $\mathcal{C}$ and $\mathcal{C}'$ be two classes of parameterized problems. The two classes are *equivalent up to the uniform reduction* if every problem in class $\mathcal{C}$ can be uniformly reduced to some problem in the class $\mathcal{C}'$ and vice versa.

Let Π_t (resp. Σ_t) denote the class of languages accepted by log-time alternating Turing machines of alternation depth at most t that must begin with $\wedge$ states (resp. $\vee$ states). For a more careful discussion of this kind of alternating Turing machines, the reader is referred to [9, 11].

Lemma 18. *The class $GC(R(k) \log n, \Pi_t)$ is a subclass of the class $W[t]$, for all $t > 1$.*

Proof. (Sketch) The proof is similar to that of Lemma 14. Suppose that L is a problem in the class $GC(f(k) \log n, \Pi_t)$, where f is a recursive function. Then there is an alternating Turing machine M of alternation depth t, such that $z = \langle x, k \rangle$ is in L if and only if there is a string y of length $f(k) \log(|x|)$ and M accepts the input $z\#y$ in $O(\log |z|)$ time. We show how to reduce the problem L to the problem $WCS(t, h)$ for some constant h.

Let $z = \langle x, k \rangle$ be an instance of L. By Theorem 5.3 in [9], a Π_t^h-circuit C can be constructed in time polynomial in $|z|$ such that the circuit C accepts the input $z\#y$ if and only if the alternating Turing machine M does, where y is a string of length $f(k) \log(|x|)$. Assigning the input part of C corresponding to the string z by the value of z results in a Π_t^h-circuit C' with $f(k) \log(|x|)$ input bits. Now by a technique similar to but more delicate than the proof of Lemma 14, we can construct a Π_t^h-circuit C'' of $f(k)|x|$ input bits *without increasing the depth* so that the circuit C' has a satisfiable assignment if and only if C'' accepts an input vector of weight $f(k)$. This gives the uniform reduction from the problem L to the problem $WCS(t, h)$. Thus, L is in the class $W[t]$. ∎

Lemma 19. *For fixed integers $t > 1$ and $h \geq 1$, the parameterized problem $WCS(t, h)$ is uniformly reducible to the parameterized problem $WCS(t, 1)$ that is contained in the class $GC(k \log n, \Pi_t)$.*

Proof. (Sketch) That the problem $WCS(t, h)$ is uniformly reducible to the problem $WCS(t, 1)$ is proved in [15]. To show that $WCS(t, 1)$ is contained in the class $GC(k \log n, \Pi_t)$, we construct a log-time alternating Turing machine M of alternation depth t as follows. On an input of form $\langle C, k \rangle \# y$, where C is a Π_t^1-circuit and $|y| = k \log |C|$, the machine M will interpret the string y as k input gate names and check whether the assignment that assigns all these k inputs 1 and all other inputs 0 is satisfiable. ∎

Theorem 20. *The classes $GC(R(k) \log n, \Pi_t)$ and $W[t]$ are equivalent up to the uniform reduction, for all $t > 1$.*

Proof. Follows directly from Lemma 18 and Lemma 19 and the definitions. ∎

Therefore, in some sense, the class $GC(R(k) \log n, \Pi_t)$ and the class $W[t]$ are of the same fixed-parameter complexity. Surprisingly enough, we show below that all classes $GC(R(k) \log n, \Pi_t)$ are distinct.

Theorem 21. *The class $GC(R(k) \log n, \Pi_t)$ is a proper subclass of the class $GC(R(k) \log n, \Pi_{t+1})$ for all $t \geq 1$.*

Proof. (Sketch) Suppose the theorem is not true so that

$$GC(R(k) \log n, \Pi_t) = GC(R(k) \log n, \Pi_{t+1})$$

Let A be a language in the class Π_{t+1}. Fix an integer k_0. Consider the following parameterized problem:

$$L_A = \{\langle x, k_0 \rangle \mid x \in A\}$$

Then clearly, $L_A \in GC(f(k) \log n, \Pi_{t+1})$ for some recursive function f (in fact, we can let $f(k) \equiv 0$). By our assumption, the problem L_A is in the class $GC(g(k) \log n, \Pi_t)$ for some recursive function g. Since the parameter k in the problem L_A is fixed to be k_0, the problem L_A is in the class $GC(g(k_0) \log n, \Pi_t)$. Thus, there is a log-time alternating Turing machine M of alternation depth t such that for any $z = \langle x, k_0 \rangle$, $z \in L_A$ if and only if there is a string y of length $g(k_0) \log(|x|)$ and M accepts $z \# y$. Construct a new log-time alternating Turing machine M' as follows: given an input x, M' first existentially guesses a string y of length $g(k_0) \log n$ then simulates the machine M on input $\langle x, k_0 \rangle \# y$. It is easy to see that M' accepts the language A. Moreover, the machine M' has alternation depth at most $t + 1$ and running time bounded by $O(\log n)$, and always starts with $\vee$ states. Thus, the language A is in the class Σ_{t+1}.

Since A is an arbitrary language in Π_{t+1}, we conclude that $\Pi_{t+1} \subseteq \Sigma_{t+1}$. However, this contradicts a result by Sipser [24] (see also [6] and [9]). ∎

Corollary 22. *For all $t \geq 1$, the class $GC(R(k)\log n, \Pi_t)$ is a proper subset of the class $GC(R(k)\log n, P)$.*

Another natural question for the W-hierarchy is whether the class $W[P]$ contains all parameterized problems in NP. Interesting enough, we show below that this question is closely related to the question whether the classes FPT and $W[P]$ are identical.

Lemma 23. *Let f, g be recursive functions and $h(n) = \omega(\log n)$ a polynomial time constructible function. If $GC(f(k)h(n), P) \cap NP = GC(g(k)\log n, P) \cap NP$, then $GC(h(n), P) = GC(\log n, P)$.*

Theorem 24. *If the class $W[P]$ contains all parameterized problems in NP, then $W[P] = FPT$.*

Proof. Let $h(n)$ be any polynomial-time constructible function such that $h(n) = \omega(\log n)$. Consider parameterized problems in $GC(R(k)h(n), P) \cap NP$. By the assumption of the theorem, $GC(R(k)h(n), P) \cap NP \subseteq W[P]$. By Theorem 15, $GC(R(k)h(n), P) \cap NP \subseteq GC(R(k)\log n, P) \cap NP$, which implies immediately $GC(h(n), P) \subseteq GC(\log n, P) = P$ by Lemma 23, which in turn leads to $W[P] = FPT$ by Theorem 16. $\square$

5 Subclasses in *FPT*

It has been observed that almost all known NP optimization problems with constant approximation ratio are fixed parameter tractable [10] (the proofs for some problems may involve nontrivial techniques used in [22]). This strong evidence suggests us to conjecture that approximability implies fixed parameter tractability for optimization problems. On the other hand, there are NP optimization problems that are fixed parameter tractable but not approximable. For example, *Longest Path* has been shown to have no constant approximation ratio [4] while it is fixed parameter tractable [18]. Thus, a further refinement of the class *FPT* is needed to capture the approximability of optimization problems in the class *FPT*.

A possible refinement has been considered recently, and a variety of practical problems have been shown to belong to various subclasses of *FPT* [12]. In the following, we discuss a refinement of the class *FPT* in terms of the GC models.

We first consider the GC models with guessing ability strictly limited.

Theorem 25. *(1) Vertex-Cover is in the class $GC(k, P)$;*
(2) MAX-3SAT is in the class $GC(3k, P)$.

We point out that the two problems above are approximable and they are in the class $GC(dk, P)$ for some constant d. A contrasting example is the problem *Longest Path*, which can be solved in deterministic $O(2^k k! n)$ time [18] and is unknown to be in the class $GC(dk, P)$ for any constant d. On the other hand, it is known that the problem *Longest Path* is not approximable to a constant ratio in polynomial time unless $P = NP$ [4].

We can also define subclasses of *FPT* by limiting the verifier in the GC model. By carefully examining the proofs of Theorems 1.1 and 2.7 in [12], we have

Theorem 26. *(1) Vertex-Cover is in the class $GC(k \log k, DL)$*
(2) k-Leaf Spanning Tree is in the class $GC(12k(k+1) \log k, NL)$

It is interesting to notice that separation of subclasses of $GC(R(k), P)$ defined by limiting the verifiers in the GC model implies separation of the corresponding subclasses in P, as shown in the following theorem.

Theorem 27. *(1) $GC(R(k), P) = GC(R(k), NL)$ if and only if $P = NL$*
(2) $GC(R(k), NL) = GC(R(k), DL)$ if and only if $NL = DL$
(3) $GC(R(k), P) = GC(R(k), DL)$ if and only if $P = DL$

6 Conclusions

We have characterized the classes in the W-hierarchy by the GC models. Our results give strong evidence that the W-hierarchy does not collapse. New techniques have been developed to separate the ability of guessing and the power of verifying in computations of practical problems. The class of fixed-parameter tractable problems have been further refined for possible classifications in order to capture the approximability of problems in the class FPT. These results should have important impact on the study of computational optimization problems, in particular for those studies based on the theory of completeness of parameterized problems.

References

1. K. ABRAHAMSON, R. G. DOWNEY AND M. R. FELLOWS, Fixed-parameter intractability II, *Lecture Notes in Computer Science (STACS'93)*, (1993), pp. 374-385.

2. K. R. ABRAHAMSON, J. A. ELLIS, M. R. FELLOWS, AND M. E. MATA, On the complexity of fixed parameter problems, *Proc. 30th Annual Symposium on Foundations of Computer Science*, (1989), pp. 210-215.

3. S. ARNBORG, J. LAGERGREN, AND D. SEESE, Problems easy for tree-decomposable graphs, *Lecture Notes in Computer Science 317 (ICALP'88)*, (1988), pp. 38-51.

4. S. ARORA, C. LUND, R. MOTWANI, M. SUDAN, AND M. SZEGEDY, Proof verification and intractability of approximation problems, *Proc. 33rd Annual Symposium on Foundations of Computer Science*, (1992), pp. 14-23.

5. J. BALCAZAR, J. DIAZ, AND J. GABARRO, *Structural Complexity I*, Springer-Verlag, 1988.

6. R. B. BOPPANA AND M. SIPSER, The complexity of finite functions, in *Handbook of Theoretical Computer Science, Vol. A*, J. van Leeuwen, ed., (1990), pp. 757-804.

7. J. F. BUSS AND J. GOLDSMITH, Nondeterminism within P, *SIAM J. Comput.* *22*, (1993), pp. 560-572.

8. S. BUSS, *Personal communication*, (1992).

9. L. CAI AND J. CHEN, On input read-modes of alternating Turing machines, *Technique Report 93-046*, Dept. Computer Science, Texas A&M University, (1993).

10. L. CAI AND J. CHEN, Fixed parameter tractability and approximability of *NP*-hard optimization problems, *Proc. 2rd Israel Symposium on Theory of Computing and Systems*, (1993), pp. 118-126.

11. L. CAI AND J. CHEN, On the amount of nondeterminism and the power of verifying, *Lecture Notes in Computer Science 711 (MFCS'93)*, (1993), pp. 311-320.

12. L. CAI, J. CHEN, R. G. DOWNEY, AND M. R. FELLOWS, Advice classes of parameterized tractability, *Proc. Asian Logic Conference*, (1993).

13. J. DIAZ AND J. TORAN, Classes of bounded nondeterminism, *Mathematical Systems Theory 23*, (1990), pp. 21-32.

14. R. G. DOWNEY, P. A. EVANS, AND M. R. FELLOWS, Parameterized learning complexity, *Proc. 6th ACM Workshop on Computational Learning Theory (COLT'93)*, (1993), pp. 51-57.

15. R. G. DOWNEY AND M. R. FELLOWS, Fixed-parameter intractability, *Proc. 7th Structure in Complexity Theory Conference*, (1992), pp. 36-49.

16. R. G. DOWNEY AND M. R. FELLOWS, Fixed parameter tractability and completeness, in *Complexity Theory: Current Research*, Ambos-Spies et al., ed., Cambridge University Press, (1993), pp. 191-225.

17. M. R. FELLOWS, M. T. HALLETT, AND H. T. WAREHAM, DNA physical mapping: three ways of difficult, *Proc. 1st European Symposium on Algorithms*, (1993), 157-168.

18. M. R. FELLOWS AND M. A. LANGSTON, On search, decision and the efficiency of polynomial-time algorithms, *Proc. 21st ACM Symp. on Theory of Computing*, (1989), pp. 501-512.

19. M. R. FELLOWS AND N. KOBLITZ, Fixed-parameter complexity and cryptography, *Lecture Notes in Computer Science (AAECC10)*, (1993).

20. C. H. PAPADIMITRIOU AND M. YANNAKAKIS, On limited nondeterminism and the complexity of the V-C dimension, *Proc. 8th Structure in Complexity Theory Conference*, (1993), pp. 12-18.

21. N. PIPPENGER AND M. J. FISCHER, Relations among complexity measures, *J. Assoc. Comput. Mach. 26*, (1979), pp. 361-381.

22. J. PLEHN AND B. VOIGT, Finding minimally weighted subgraphs, (1993), to appear.

23. N. ROBERTSON AND P. D. SEYMOUR, Graph minors XV. Wagner's conjecture, to appear.

24. M. SIPSER, Borel sets and circuit complexity, *Proc. 15th Ann. ACM Symp. on Theory of Computing*, (1983), pp. 61-69.

25. R. SZELEPCSENYI, β_k-complete problems and greediness, *Technique Report # 455*, Computer Science Department, University of Rochester, (1993).

26. M. J. WOLF, Nondeterministic circuits, space complexity, and quasigroups, *Theoretical Computer Science*, to appear, 1993.

On the Approximability of Finding Maximum Feasible Subsystems of Linear Systems

Edoardo Amaldi* and Viggo Kann**

Abstract. We consider the combinatorial problem MAXFLS which consists, given a system of linear relations, of finding a maximum feasible subsystem, that is a solution satisfying as many relations as possible. The approximability of this general problem is investigated for the three types of relations $=$, $\geq$ and $>$. Various constrained versions of MAXFLS where a subset of relations must be satisfied or where the variables take bounded discrete values, are also considered. We show that MAXFLS with $=$, $\geq$ or $>$ relations is NP-hard even when restricted to homogeneous systems with bipolar coefficients. The various NP-hard versions of MAXFLS belong to different approximability classes depending on the type of relations and the additional constraints. While MAXFLS with equations and integer coefficients cannot be approximated within p^ε for some $\varepsilon > 0$ where p is the number of relations, MAXFLS with strict or nonstrict inequalities can be approximated within 2 but not within every constant factor.

1 Introduction

We consider the general problem of finding maximum feasible subsystems of linear relations for the three types of relations $=$, $\geq$ and $>$. The basic versions, named MAXFLS$^{\mathcal{R}}$ with $\mathcal{R} \in \{=, \geq, >\}$, are defined as follows: Given a linear system $A\mathbf{x}\mathcal{R}\mathbf{b}$ with a matrix A of size $p \times n$, find a solution $\mathbf{x} \in \mathbb{R}^n$ which satisfies as many relations as possible.

Different variants of these combinatorial problems occur in various fields such as pattern recognition [16], operations research [8, 11] and artificial neural networks [1, 10].

Whenever a system of linear equations or inequalities is consistent, it can be solved in polynomial time using an appropriate linear programming method [13]. If the system is inconsistent, standard algorithms provide solutions that minimize the least mean squared error. But such solutions, which are appropriate in linear regression, are not satisfactory when the objective is to maximize the number of relations that can be simultaneously satisfied.

Previous works have focused mainly on algorithms for tackling various versions of MAXFLS. Surprisingly enough, only a few results are known on the

* Dep. of Mathematics, Swiss Federal Institute of Technology, CH-1015 Lausanne, E-mail: amaldi@dma.epfl.ch
** Dep. of Numerical Analysis and Computing Science, Royal Institute of Technology, S-100 44 Stockholm, E-mail: viggo@nada.kth.se, supported by grants from TFR.

complexity of solving some special cases of MAXFLS to optimality and none concerns their approximability.

Johnson and Preparata proved that the OPEN HEMISPHERE and CLOSED HEMISPHERE problems, which are equivalent to MAXFLS$^>$ and MAXFLS$^\geq$, respectively, with homogeneous systems and no pairs of colinear row vectors of A, are NP-hard [11]. Moreover, they devised a complete enumeration algorithm.

Greer developed a tree method for maximizing functions of systems of linear relations that is more efficient than complete enumeration but still exponential in the number of variables n [8]. This general procedure can be used to solve MAXFLS with any of the three types of relations.

Recently the problem of minimizing the number of errors of a perceptron, which is closely related to MAXFLS$^>$ and MAXFLS$^\geq$, has attracted a considerable interest in the artificial neural network literature [1, 10]. But, although maximizing the number of satisfied relations is equivalent to minimizing the number of unsatisfied ones, the approximability of such complementary problems can differ enormously.

Over the last few years new substantial progresses have been made in the study of the approximability of NP-hard optimization problems. Papadimitriou and Yannakakis defined the approximability class MAX SNP, thereby giving the possibility of characterizing a problem's approximability simply from the structure of its definition [15]. Reductions preserving approximability in different ways have been introduced and used to compare the approximability of optimization problems (see [12]).

Recently several striking results in the area of interactive proofs have been obtained and they have surprisingly been used to show strong bounds on the approximability of MAX SNP-hard problems, maximum independent set, graph colouring and minimum set cover [5, 14].

A remarkably well-characterized approximation problem is that relative to MAXFLS$^=$ over $GF(q)$ where the equations are degree 2 polynomials that do not contain any squares as monomials. Håstad, Phillips and Safra have shown that this problem can be approximated within $q^2/(q-1)$ but not within $q - \varepsilon$ for any $\varepsilon > 0$ [9].

This extended abstract is organized as follows. Section 2 recalls the important facts about the hierarchy of approximability classes. In Sect. 3 we focus on the complexity of solving the basic MAXFLS$^{\mathcal{R}}$ optimally and we determine their degree of approximability. Various constrained versions of these three problems are considered in Sect. 4 and 5. First we focus on variants where a subset of relations must be satisfied and the objective is to find a solution fulfilling all mandatory relations and as many optional ones as possible. Then we consider the particular cases in which the variables are restricted to take a finite number of discrete values. In Sect. 6 the various results are discussed and open questions are mentioned. Most of the proofs are omitted but can be found in the full paper [3].

2   Approximability Hierarchy

Definition 1. An NP optimization (NPO) problem over an alphabet Σ is a four-tuple $F = (\mathcal{I}_F, S_F, m_F, opt_F)$, where $\mathcal{I}_F \subseteq \Sigma^*$ is the space of *input instances*, $S_F(x) \subseteq \Sigma^*$ is the space of *feasible solutions* on input $x \in \mathcal{I}_F$, $m_F : \mathcal{I}_F \times \Sigma^* \to \mathbb{N}$, the *objective function*, is a polynomial time computable function, $opt_F \in \{\max, \min\}$ tells if F is a *maximization* or a *minimization* problem.

The set $\mathcal{I}_F$ must be recognizable by a Turing machine in polynomial time. The only requirement on S_F is that there exist a polynomial q and a polynomial time computable predicate π such that for all x in $\mathcal{I}_F$, S_F can be expressed as $S_F(x) = \{y : |y| \leq q(|x|) \wedge \pi(x, y)\}$ where q and π only depend on F.

Solving an optimization problem F given the input $x \in \mathcal{I}_F$ means finding a $y \in S_F(x)$ such that $m_F(x, y)$ is optimum, that is as large as possible if $opt_F = \max$ and as small as possible if $opt_F = \min$. Let $opt_F(x)$ denote this optimal value of m_F.

Approximating an optimization problem F given the input $x \in \mathcal{I}_F$ means finding any $y' \in S_F(x)$. How good the approximation is depends on the relation between $m_F(x, y')$ and $opt_F(x)$. The *performance ratio* of a feasible solution with respect to the optimum of a maximization problem F is defined as $R_F(x, y) = opt_F(x)/m_F(x, y)$ where $x \in \mathcal{I}_F$ and $y \in S_F(x)$.

Definition 2. An optimization problem F *can be approximated within c* for a constant c if there exists a polynomial time algorithm A such that for all instances $x \in \mathcal{I}_F$, $A(x) \in S_F(x)$ and $R_F(x, A(x)) \leq c$. More generally, an optimization problem F *can be approximated within $p(n)$* for a function $p : \mathbb{Z}^+ \to \mathbb{R}^+$ if there exists a polynomial time algorithm A such that for every $n \in \mathbb{Z}^+$ and for all instances $x \in \mathcal{I}_F$ with $|x| = n$ we have that $A(x) \in S_F(x)$ and $R_F(x, A(x)) \leq p(n)$.

Various reductions preserving approximability within constants have been proposed to relate optimization problems, but the L-reduction is the most easy to use and the most restrictive one (see [12]).

Definition 3. [15] Given two NPO problems F and G and a polynomial time transformation $f : \mathcal{I}_F \to \mathcal{I}_G$. f is an *L-reduction* from F to G if there are positive constants α and β such that for every instance $x \in \mathcal{I}_F$, $opt_G(f(x)) \leq \alpha \cdot opt_F(x)$, and for every solution y of $f(x)$ with objective value $m_G(f(x), y) = c_2$ we can in polynomial time find a solution y' of x with $m_F(x, y') = c_1$ such that $|opt_F(x) - c_1| \leq \beta\, |opt_G(f(x)) - c_2|$.

A *cost preserving transformation* is an L-reduction with no objective function amplification.

Definition 4. An NPO problem F is *polynomially bounded* if there is a polynomial p such that

$$\forall x \in \mathcal{I}_F \, \forall y \in S_F(x), \ m_F(x, y) \leq p(|x|).$$

The class of all polynomially bounded NPO problems is called NPO PB and the subclass of all polynomially bounded maximization problems MAX PB.

All versions of MAXFLS are included in MAX PB since their objective function is the number of satisfied relations.

Definition 5. Given an NPO problem F and a class C, F *is C-hard* if every $G \in C$ can be L-reduced to F. F *is C-complete* if $F \in C$ and F is C-hard.

The range of approximability of NPO problems stretches from problems which can be approximated within every constant in polynomial time, i.e. that have a *polynomial time approximation scheme*, to problems which cannot be approximated within n^ε for some $\varepsilon > 0$, where n is the size of the input instance, unless P = NP.

In the middle of this range we find the important class SYNTACTIC MAX SNP, which is syntactically defined, and the class MAX SNP defined as the closure of SYNTACTIC MAX SNP under L-reductions [15, 12]. All problems in MAX SNP can be approximated within a constant in polynomial time and several maximization problems such as MAX 2SAT have been shown to be complete in SYNTACTIC MAX SNP (and therefore also complete in MAX SNP). Hence SYNTACTIC MAX SNP $\subset$ MAX SNP $\subset$ APX, where APX is the class of NPO problems that can be approximated within a constant. The inclusions are strict.

Recently Arora, Lund, Motwani, Sudan and Szegedy proved, using results about interactive proofs, that it is impossible to find a polynomial time algorithm that approximates a MAX SNP-hard problem within every constant, unless P = NP [5]. Thus showing a problem to be MAX SNP-complete describes the approximability of the problem quite well: it can be approximated within a constant but not within every constant.

The results by Arora et al. also imply that the maximum independent set problem cannot be approximated within n^ε for some $\varepsilon > 0$, where n is the number of nodes in the input graph. If there is an approximation preserving reduction from MAX IND SET to an NPO problem F we say that F is MAX IND SET-hard, which means that it is at least as hard to approximate as the maximum independent set problem.

There exist natural problems that are complete in MAX PB, for example MAX PB $0-1$ PROGRAMMING [6]. These are the hardest problems to approximate in this class since every NPO PB problem can be reduced to them using an approximation preserving reduction.

Our purpose is to show where various versions of MAXFLS are placed in this hierarchy of approximability classes. We will see that the approximability of apparently similar variants can differ enormously.

3 Complexity of MAXFLS$^\mathcal{R}$ with $\mathcal{R} \in \{=, \geq, >\}$

In order to determine the complexity of solving MAXFLS$^\mathcal{R}$ to optimality, we consider the corresponding decision versions that are no harder than the original optimization problems. Given a linear system $A \mathbf{x} \mathcal{R} \mathbf{b}$ where A is of size $p \times n$ and an integer K with $1 \leq K \leq p$, does there exist a solution $\mathbf{x} \in \mathbb{R}^n$ satisfying at least K relations of the system?

In the homogeneous versions of MAXFLS$^\mathcal{R}$ we are not interested in the trivial solutions where all variables occurring in the satisfied relations are zero.

Theorem 6. MAXFLS$^\mathcal{R}$ with $\mathcal{R} \in \{=, \geq, >\}$ *is* NP-*hard even when restricted to homogeneous systems with bipolar coefficients in* $\{-1, 1\}$.

For MAXFLS$^\geq$ and MAXFLS$^>$, this result is stronger than that established in [11]. MAXFLS$^\mathcal{R}$ is intractable not only when the points corresponding to the rows of A lie on the n-dimensional hypersphere but also when they belong to the n-dimensional hypercube.

Since these problems are NP-hard for bipolar coefficients, they turn out to be strongly NP-hard, i.e. intractable even with respect to unary coding of the data. According to a well-known result concerning polynomially bounded problems [7], they do not have a fully polynomial time approximation scheme (an ε-approximation scheme where the running time is bounded by a polynomial in both the size of the instance and $1/\varepsilon$) unless P=NP.

It is worth noting that if the number of variables n is constant MAXFLS$^\mathcal{R}$ can be solved in polynomial time using Greer's algorithm. These problems are easy when all maximal feasible subsystems contain a maximum number of relations and trivial when the total number of relations p is constant.

The previous NP-hardness results make extremely unlikely the existence of polynomial time methods for solving the three basic versions of MAXFLS to optimality. But in practice optimal solutions are not always required and approximate algorithms providing solutions that are guaranteed to be a fixed percentage away from the actual optimum are often satisfactory.

According to the following theorems, MAXFLS$^\mathcal{R}$ with integer coefficients cannot be approximated within every constant unless P=NP.

Theorem 7. MAXFLS$^\mathcal{R}$ with $\mathcal{R} \in \{=, \geq\}$ *is* MAX SNP-*hard even when restricted to systems with ternary coefficients in* $\{-1, 0, 1\}$.

Proof. We only give the proof for MAXFLS$^=$. We proceed by L-reduction from the known MAX SNP-complete problem MAX 2SAT which is defined as follows [7]. Given a finite set X of variables and a set $C = \{C_1, \ldots, C_m\}$ of disjunctive clauses with at most 2 literals in each clause, find a truth assignment for X which satisfies as many clauses of C as possible. Let (X, C) with $C = \{C_1, \ldots, C_m\}$ be an arbitrary instance of MAX 2SAT. For each clause C_i, $1 \leq i \leq m$, containing two variables x_{j_1} and x_{j_2} we construct the following equations:

$$a_{ij_1} x_{j_1} + a_{ij_2} x_{j_2} = 2 \quad a_{ij_1} x_{j_1} + a_{ij_2} x_{j_2} = 0 \tag{1}$$

$$x_{j_1} = 1 \quad x_{j_1} = -1 \tag{2}$$

$$x_{j_2} = 1 \quad x_{j_2} = -1 \tag{3}$$

where $a_{ij} = 1$ if x_j occurs positively in C_i and $a_{ij} = -1$ if x_j occurs negatively. Thus we have a system with $6m$ equations.

Given a truth assignment that satisfies s clauses of the MAX 2SAT instance, we immediately get a solution $\mathbf{x}$ which satisfies $2m + s$ equations of the MAXFLS$^=$ instance. This is simply achieved by setting the variables x_j to 1 or -1 depending on whether the corresponding boolean variable is TRUE or FALSE in the assignment.

Consider any solution $\mathbf{x}$ of the MAXFLS$^=$ instance. For each i, $1 \leq i \leq m$, at most 3 equations can be simultaneously satisfied: at most one of (1), at most one of (2) and at most one of (3). If any component of $\mathbf{x}$ is neither 1 nor -1, we can set it to 1 without decreasing the number of satisfied equations. In other words, we can suppose that any solution $\mathbf{x}$ has bipolar components.

Consequently, we have a correspondence between solutions of the MAX 2SAT instance satisfying s clauses and solutions of the MAXFLS$^=$ instance fulfilling $2m + s$ equations. Since opt$_{\text{MAXFLS}=} \leq 3m$ and since there exists an algorithm providing a truth assignment that satisfies at least $\lceil \frac{m}{2} \rceil$ of the clauses in any MAX 2SAT instance (see for example [48]), we have opt$_{\text{MAXFLS}=} \leq 6 \cdot$ opt$_{\text{MAX 2SAT}}$.

Thus all conditions for an L-reduction are fulfilled and MAXFLS$^=$ is MAX SNP-hard since MAX 2SAT is MAX SNP-complete and L-reductions preserve approximability within constants. $\qquad\Box$

The question of whether MAXFLS$^=$ and MAXFLS$^\geq$ are also MAX SNP-hard when restricted to systems with bipolar coefficients is still open. However, the answer is affirmative for MAXFLS$^>$.

Theorem 8. MAXFLS$^>$ *is* MAX SNP-*hard even for systems with bipolar coefficients.*

The following results give a better characterization of the approximability of MAXFLS$^{\mathcal{R}}$. Although MAXFLS$^=$ can be approximated within $p/\min\{n-1, p\}$ where p is the number of equations and n the number of variables occurring in the system, it cannot be approximated within a constant factor[3].

Proposition 9. MAXFLS$^=$ *restricted to homogeneous systems with integer coefficients is not in* APX *unless* P$=$NP.

Proof. Suppose that MAXFLS$^=$ can be approximated within a constant $c > 1$ and consider an arbitrary instance with p homogeneous equations $e_1 = 0, \ldots,$ $e_p = 0$. Let s be the number of equations contained in a maximum feasible subsystem.

Construct a new problem with the equations $e_{i,j,k} = 0$ where $e_{i,j,k} = e_i + k \cdot e_j, 1 \leq i \leq p, 1 \leq j \leq p, 1 \leq k \leq T$ for an integer T. Since $e_{i,j,k} = 0$ for every value of k if both $e_i = 0$ and $e_j = 0$, the s satisfied equations of the original problem give $T \cdot s^2$ satisfied equations of the new problem. However,

---

[3] While completing this paper we discovered that the same type of result has been found independently by Arora, Babai, Stern and Sweedyk [4].

some additional equations may be satisfied when $e_i = -k \cdot e_j$ and $e_i \neq 0$. But no more than p^2 equations are fulfilled in such a way because there is at most one such equation for each pair (i, j).

Since the optimal solution contains at least $T \cdot s^2$ satisfied equations, the approximation algorithm provides a solution that fulfills at least $T \cdot s^2/c$ equations. We examine the satisfied equations and throw away every equation $e_i + k \cdot e_j$ where $e_i \neq 0$. This leaves us with at least $T \cdot s^2/c - p^2$ equations. Since there are at most T equations for every pair (i, j), we can obtain at least

$$\sqrt{\frac{T \cdot s^2/c - p^2}{T}} = \sqrt{\frac{s^2}{c} - \frac{p^2}{T}}$$

satisfied equations of the original problem. If we run the approximation algorithm directly on the original problem we are only guaranteed to find s/c satisfied equations.

By choosing T large enough, we always find more satisfied equations by applying the approximation algorithm to the $e_{i,j,k}$ problem than by applying it to the original problem. This can be done over and over again to get better constants in the approximation. But Theorem 7 states that MAXFLS$^=$ is MAX SNP-hard and thus there exists a constant $\varepsilon > 0$ such that it cannot be approximated within a smaller constant than $1 + \varepsilon$. Hence MAXFLS$^=$ is not in APX. □

By using tuples of $\log p$ equations instead of pairs of equations and by using walks on expander graphs in order to choose a polynomial number of these tuples it is possible to show a yet stronger result.

Theorem 10. *Unless* P$=$NP, *there is a positive constant ε such that homogeneous* MAXFLS$^=$ *cannot be approximated within p^ε, where p is the number of equations.*

MAXFLS$^\geq$ and MAXFLS$^>$ turn out to be much easier to approximate than MAXFLS$^=$.

Proposition 11. MAXFLS$^\mathcal{R}$ *with $\mathcal{R} \in \{\geq, >\}$ can be approximated within 2.*

Proof. Both problems can be approximated within 2 using the following simple algorithm.

Algorithm:

```
Input: An instance (A, b) of MAXFLS^R with R ∈ {≥, >}
Init:   X := {variables occurring in (A, b)}
        E := {inequalities in (A, b)}
 WHILE E ≠ ∅ DO
 IF there are inequalities in E containing a single variable THEN
    U := {x ∈ X | x occurs as a single variable in at least one
          inequality of E}
    Pick at random y ∈ U
    F(y) := {e ∈ E | e contains only the variable y}
```

```
    Assign a value to y satisfying as many inequalities in
    F(y) as possible
    E := E - F(y)
ELSE
    Pick at random a variable y and assign a random value to it
    Reevaluate the inequalities in E containing y
END IF
X := X - {y}
END WHILE
```

This algorithm is guaranteed to provide a 2-approximation because we can always assign to y a value which satisfies at least half of the inequalities in $F(y)$. Moreover, it runs in polynomial time since each variable and each inequality are considered only once. $\square$

Provided that P$\neq$ NP, the previous results describe the approximability of MAXFLS$^{\mathcal{R}}$ quite well. While MAXFLS$^{=}$ cannot be approximated within p^{ε} for some $\varepsilon > 0$ where p is the number of equations, MAXFLS$^{\geq}$ and MAXFLS$^{>}$ can be approximated within a factor 2 but not within every constant.

One can observe that MAXFLS$^{\geq}$ and MAXFLS$^{>}$ share a common property: a constant fraction of the relations can always be simultaneously satisfied. The above 2-approximation algorithm is optimal in the sense that no constant fraction larger than $1/2$ can be guaranteed. Of course no such a property holds for MAXFLS$^{=}$.

4   Approximability of Constrained MAXFLS

In this section we establish the complexity of several constrained versions of MAXFLS$^{\mathcal{R}}$ where some relations are mandatory and the others optional. The objective is to find a solution that satisfies all mandatory relations and as many optional ones as possible. Most of these problems, named C MAXFLS, turn out to be as hard to approximate as MAX IND SET.

When considering mixed variants of C MAXFLS with different types of mandatory and optional relations, C MAXFLS$^{\mathcal{R}_1;\mathcal{R}_2}$ with $\mathcal{R}_1, \mathcal{R}_2 \in \{=, \geq, >\}$ denotes the variant where the mandatory relations are of type $\mathcal{R}_1$ and the optional ones of type $\mathcal{R}_2$.

Theorem 12. C MAXFLS$^{>;>}$ *restricted to homogeneous systems with ternary coefficients is* MAX IND SET-*hard.*

Proof. The proof is by cost preserving polynomial transformation from MAX IND SET. Let $G = (V, E)$ be an arbitrary instance of MAX IND SET. For each edge $(v_i, v_j) \in E$ we construct the following mandatory inequality with $|V|$ variables

$$\mathbf{ax} > 0 \qquad (4)$$

where $a_i = a_j = -1$ and $a_l = 0$ for $1 \leq l \leq |V|$ with $l \neq i$ and $l \neq j$. For each $v_i \in V$ we consider the optional inequality

$$\mathbf{a}\mathbf{x} > 0 \tag{5}$$

where $a_i = 1$ and $a_l = 0$ for $1 \leq l \leq |V|$ with $l \neq i$. Thus we have a system with $|E| + |V|$ strict inequalities.

One can verify that the given graph G contains an independent set I of size s if and only if there exists a solution $\mathbf{x}$ satisfying all mandatory and s optional inequalities. $\square$

Theorem 13. C MAXFLS$^{\geq;\geq}$ *is* MAX IND SET*-hard even for systems with ternary coefficients and binary right hand side components.*

Thus forcing a subset of relations makes MAXFLS$^{\mathcal{R}}$ harder for $\mathcal{R} \in \{\geq, >\}$: MAXFLS$^{\mathcal{R}}$ are MAX SNP-hard and in APX while C MAXFLS$^{\mathcal{R};\mathcal{R}}$ are MAX IND SET-hard. This is not true for MAXFLS$^=$ since any instance of C MAXFLS$^{=;=}$ can be transformed in an equivalent instance of C MAXFLS$^{=;=}$ by eliminating variables in the set of optional equations using the set of mandatory ones.

The following results show that two simple variants of C MAXFLS$^{=;=}$ and MAXFLS$^=$ are very hard to approximate.

Proposition 14. C MAXFLS$^{\geq;=}$ *is* MAX IND SET*-hard even for systems with ternary coefficients and bipolar right hand side components.*

This proposition has an immediate consequence on the approximability of MAXFLS$^=$ with the natural nonnegativeness constraint.

Corollary 15. MAXFLS$^=$ *restricted to systems with ternary coefficients and nonnegative variables is* MAX IND SET*-hard.*

5 Approximability of MAXFLS with Bounded Discrete Variables

In this section we assess the approximability of MAXFLS$^{\mathcal{R}}$ when the variables are restricted to take a finite number of discrete values. Both extreme cases with binary variables in $\{0,1\}$ and bipolar variables in $\{-1,1\}$ are considered. The corresponding variants of MAXFLS are named BIN MAXFLS$^{\mathcal{R}}$ and BIP MAXFLS$^{\mathcal{R}}$ respectively.

Theorem 16. BIN MAXFLS$^{\mathcal{R}}$ *with* $\mathcal{R} \in \{=, \geq, >\}$ *is* MAX IND SET*-hard even for systems with ternary coefficients.*

Corollary 17. BIP MAXFLS$^{\mathcal{R}}$ *with* $\mathcal{R} \in \{=, \geq, >\}$ *is* MAX IND SET*-hard even for systems with ternary coefficients and integer right hand side components.*

The transformation used to prove the results above does not preserve homogeneity, but we know from the L-reductions used to prove Theorems 7–8 that homogeneous BIP MAXFLS$^{\mathcal{R}}$ is MAX SNP-hard. In fact, homogeneous BIP MAXFLS$^{\geq}$ and BIP MAXFLS$^{>}$ belong to APX.

Proposition 18. *Homogeneous* BIP MAXFLS$^{\geq}$ *can be approximated within 2 and homogeneous* BIP MAXFLS$^{>}$ *can be approximated within 4.*

Thus restricting the systems to be homogeneous makes BIP MAXFLS$^{\geq}$ and BIP MAXFLS$^{>}$ much easier to approximate. The situation is quite different for homogeneous BIP MAXFLS$^{=}$ with integer coefficients. According to the same arguments as in the proof of Theorem 10, this problem cannot be approximated within p^{ε} for some $\varepsilon > 0$.

The following result shows that the constrained variants of BIN MAXFLS$^{\mathcal{R}}$ with mandatory relations, named C BIN MAXFLS$^{\mathcal{R};\mathcal{R}}$, are at least as hard to approximate as every maximization problem with polynomially bounded objective function.

Proposition 19. C BIN MAXFLS$^{\mathcal{R};\mathcal{R}}$ *with* $\mathcal{R} \in \{=, \geq, >\}$ *is* MAX PB-*complete even for systems with ternary coefficients.*

Proof. We proceed by cost preserving transformations from MAX PB $0 - 1$ PROGRAMMING which is defined as follows [7]. Given an $m \times n$-matrix A and an m-vector $\mathbf{b}$, both with ternary components in $\{-1, 0, 1\}$, find a binary n-vector $\mathbf{x}$ that satisfies $A\mathbf{x} \leq \mathbf{b}$ and has as many 1 components as possible.

We only give the proof for C BIN MAXFLS$^{=;=}$. Let $(A, \mathbf{b})$ be an arbitrary instance of MAX PB $0 - 1$ PROGRAMMING. For every inequality

$$\sum_{j=1}^{n} a_{ij} x_j \leq b_i$$

we construct the following mandatory equation of the associated instance of C BIN MAXFLS$^{=;=}$:

$$\sum_{j=1}^{n} a_{ij} x_j + y_{i1} + y_{i2} + \ldots + y_{ik} = b_i$$

where $k = |\{j \mid a_{ij} = -1\}| + b_i$ and y_{ij} are additional binary variables. As optional equations we consider the equation $x_i = 1$ for each i, $1 \leq i \leq n$. Clearly, there exists a solution $\mathbf{x}$ of the $(A, \mathbf{b})$ instance with s components equal to 1 if and only if there exists a solution of the associated C BIN MAXFLS$^{=;=}$ that satisfies all mandatory equations and at least s optional ones. $\square$

Using the same type of transformation one shows that C BIN MAXFLS$^{\geq;>}$ and C BIN MAXFLS$^{\geq;=}$ are also MAX PB-complete. These results imply, using the same argument as in Corollary 17, that the corresponding bipolar versions C BIP MAXFLS$^{\mathcal{R};\mathcal{R}}$, C BIP MAXFLS$^{\geq;>}$ and C BIP MAXFLS$^{\geq;=}$ are MAX PB-complete for systems with ternary coefficients and integer right hand side components.

Corollary 20. BIN MAXFLS$^{=}$ *and* BIP MAXFLS$^{=}$ *are* MAX PB-*complete.*

6 Conclusions

The various versions of MAXFLS$^\mathcal{R}$ that we have considered are obtained by placing constraints on the coefficients (left and right hand sides), on the variables and on the relations that must be satisfied. Table 1 summarizes our main approximability results.

Table 1. The main approximability results.

	real variables	binary variables
MAXFLS$^=$	not within p^ε for some $\varepsilon > 0$	MAX PB-complete
MAXFLS$^\geq$	MAX SNP-hard (within 2)	MAX IND SET-hard
MAXFLS$^>$		
C MAXFLS$^{=;=}$	not within p^ε for some $\varepsilon > 0$	
C MAXFLS$^{\geq;\geq}$		
C MAXFLS$^{>;>}$	MAX IND SET-hard	MAX PB-complete
C MAXFLS$^{\geq;>}$		
C MAXFLS$^{\geq;=}$		

Although the approximability of similar variants of MAXFLS can differ enormously depending on the type of relations, there is some structure: all basic versions of MAXFLS$^\mathcal{R}$ are MAX SNP-hard, restricting the variables to binary (bipolar) values or introducing a set of relations that must be satisfied makes them harder to approximate, and if both restrictions are considered simultaneously all problems become MAX PB-complete.

We have also shown that MAXFLS$^=$ and C MAXFLS$^{=;=}$ restricted to nonnegative variables are MAX IND SET-hard and that some problems, like BIP MAXFLS$^>$ and BIP MAXFLS$^\geq$, are much easier to approximate when only homogeneous systems are considered.

Several interesting questions are still open. Are there better approximation algorithms for MAXFLS$^>$ and MAXFLS$^\geq$? Does MAXFLS$^=$ become harder when the variables are constrained to be nonnegative or is it already MAX IND SET-hard?

The approximability of the complementary minimization problems where the objective is to minimize the number of unsatisfied relations instead of maximizing the number of satisfied ones will be studied elsewhere [2].

Acknowledgments

The authors are grateful to Oded Goldreich, Mike Luby and most of all to Johan Håstad for their valuable suggestions concerning the proofs of Proposition 9 and Theorem 10. Edoardo Amaldi thanks Claude Diderich for helpful discussions.

532

References

1. E. Amaldi. On the complexity of training perceptrons. In T. Kohonen et al., editor, *Artificial Neural Networks*, pages 55–60, Amsterdam, 1991. Elsevier science publishing company.
2. E. Amaldi and V. Kann, 1993. Manuscript in preparation.
3. E. Amaldi and V. Kann. The complexity and approximability of finding maximum feasible subsystems of linear relations. Technical Report ORWP-11-93, Department of Mathematics, Swiss Federal Institute of Technology, Lausanne and Technical Report TRITA-NA-9313, Department of Numerical Analysis and Computing Science, Royal Institute of Technology, Stockholm, 1993.
4. S. Arora, L. Babai, J. Stern, and Z. Sweedyk. The hardness of approximate optima in lattices, codes, and systems of linear equation. In *Proc. of 34rd Ann. IEEE Symp. on Foundations of Comput. Sci.*, pages 724–733, 1993.
5. S. Arora, C. Lund, R. Motwani, M. Sudan, and M. Szegedy. Proof verification and hardness of approximation problems. In *Proc. of 33rd Ann. IEEE Symp. on Foundations of Comput. Sci.*, pages 14–23, 1992.
6. P. Berman and G. Schnitger. On the complexity of approximating the independent set problem. *Inform. and Comput.*, 96:77–94, 1992.
7. M. R. Garey and D. S. Johnson. *Computers and Intractability: a guide to the theory of NP-completeness.* W. H. Freeman and Company, San Francisco, 1979.
8. R. Greer. *Trees and Hills: Methodology for Maximizing Functions of Systems of Linear Relations*, volume 22 of *Annals of Discrete Mathematics*. Elsevier science publishing company, Amsterdam, 1984.
9. J. Håstad, S. Phillips, and S. Safra. A well-characterized approximation problem. *Inform. Process. Lett.*, 47:301–305, 1993.
10. K-U. Höffgen, H-U. Simon, and K. van Horn. Robust trainability of single neurons. Technical Report CS-92-9, Computer Science Department, Brigham Young University, Provo, 1992.
11. D. S. Johnson and F. P. Preparata. The densest hemisphere problem. *Theoretical Computer Science*, 6:93–107, 1978.
12. V. Kann. *On the Approximability of NP-complete Optimization Problems.* PhD thesis, Department of Numerical Analysis and Computing Science, Royal Institute of Technology, Stockholm, 1992.
13. N. Karmarkar. A new polynomial time algorithm for linear programming. *Combinatorica*, 4:373–395, 1984.
14. C. Lund and M. Yannakakis. On the hardness of approximating minimization problems. In *Proc. Twenty fifth Ann. ACM Symp. on Theory of Comp.*, pages 286–293, 1993.
15. C. H. Papadimitriou and M. Yannakakis. Optimization, approximation, and complexity classes. *J. Comput. System Sci.*, 43:425–440, 1991.
16. R. E. Warmack and R. C. Gonzalez. An algorithm for optimal solution of linear inequalities and its application to pattern recognition. *IEEE Trans. on Computers*, 22:1065–1075, 1973.

On the Acceptance Power of Regular Languages

Bernd Borchert
Universität Heidelberg

Im Neuenheimer Feld 294
69120 Heidelberg, Germany
bb@math.uni-heidelberg.de

Abstract

In [BCS92] it was shown that several well–known complexity classes which have a complete set for every relativization can be characterized by an acceptance language for the words of ouputs produced by a nondeterministic polynomial time computation. In [HL*93] some results were shown for classes for which this acceptance language is regular. Here a partial order on relativizable classes is presented which reflects the idea of oracle independent inclusion. The main result will be that this partial order on the classes characterized by regular languages is atomic and therefore not dense. The atoms correspond to the classes NP, co-NP and MOD_pP for p prime.

1 Introduction

Consider the relativized versions of the classes Σ_i^p and Σ_{i+1}^p. For all oracles the first class is a subset of the second but there is an oracle for which this inclusion is proper, see [BGS75, Sto77, Has86]. The same holds for the relativized versions of many pairs of complexity classes, for example for the relativized versions of the classes NP and PP or MOD_pP and MOD_{pq}P for p, q prime and $p \neq q$, see [Her90, Bei91, BG92]. Note that this concept can be formalized to define a partial order on relativizable complexity classes which in a way expresses that an inclusion is oracle independent, a notation for this concept was defined for example in [Za88].

There exist relativizable complexity classes which are in the above sense located properly between P and NP: for example UP or the classes of the low hierarchy and high hierarchy: for all oracles these classes are a superset of P and a subset of NP, but for each class there are oracles separating them from P and NP, see [BGS75, HH88, Ko91].

One result of this paper will be that such classes located properly between P and NP in the above weak sense do not exist if one only considers the following set of classes which were defined in [HL*93]: the set of classes for which there is a regular acceptance language for the words of output bits produced by nondeterministic computations. In

[HL*93] it was indicated that this concept of characterizing classes is quite powerful, for example the classes Σ_i^p, Π_i^p of the polynomial time hierarchy, the classes of the Boolean hierarchy, the classes MOD_kP, the classes investigated in [GW87] including 1–NP, and PSPACE can be characterized this way.

It will be shown that such classes characterized by a regular language do also not exist between P and co-NP, and between P and MOD_pP for p prime.

2 Preliminaries

In this report a *word* will be a word over the alphabet $\{0, 1\}$, a *language* and an *oracle* will be a set of words, and a *class* will be a set of languages. For relativized complexity classes the exponent notation like NP^X will be used. Often regular expressions will be used to describe languages, for example 1^* is the language which consists of the words which do not use the letter 0.

Consider the relativized version of the nondeterministic polynomial time Turing machines as described for example in [HL*93]. Such a machine M^X is supplied with an oracle X and outputs for a given input on every computation path in polynomial time either 0 for rejecting or 1 for accepting. Let $w(M^X, x)$ be the word consisting of the output bits produced by machine M^X on input x, read from left to right. Relativizing the concept of [BCS92, HL*93] define for an oracle X and a language A the class $[A]^X$ to be the set of languages L such that there is a nondeterministic polynomial time machine M^X for which the equivalence $x \in L \iff w(M^X, x) \in A$ holds. Note that with the notation from [BCS92] $[A]^X = \mathcal{C}^X(A, \overline{A})$ and with the notation from [HL*93] $[A]^\emptyset = \mathcal{R}_m^{p,\text{bit}}(A)$. In [BCS91, BCS92] it is shown that a lot of well–known complexity classes which have a complete language for every oracle can be described this way.

Let a *family* be a mapping which maps every oracle to a class of languages. For simplicity a family will here be notated just by parenthesis around the oracle variable, for example $\text{NP}^{(X)}$ denotes the family which maps an oracle X to the class NP^X. Say that A *accepts* the family $[A]^{(X)}$. As an example, 0^* accepts the same family as 1^*, namely co-$\text{NP}^{(X)}$.

Define the partial order $\to$ on the set of families which are accepted by some language: for two languages A, B define $[A]^{(X)} \to [B]^{(X)}$ iff $[A]^X \subseteq [B]^X$ holds for every oracle X. Let $\Rightarrow$ denote the corresponding irreflexive relation: $[A]^{(X)} \Rightarrow [B]^{(X)}$ iff $[A]^{(X)} \to [B]^{(X)}$ but not $[A]^{(X)} = [B]^{(X)}$.

Note that the partial order $\to$ corresponds to the idea of oracle independent inclusion of relativizable complexity classes. The concept and the notation is the same as in [Za88] though the definition is for families instead of classes, what is more precise.

The partial order $\to$ is an upper semi–lattice: given two languages A, B it is not difficult to show that $[A \oplus B]^{(X)}$ is a $\to$–supremum for $[A]^{(X)}$ and $[B]^{(X)}$, where $A \oplus B$ is the language $0A \cup 1B$.

Call the languages which can not distinguish any words $w(M^X, x)$ of outputs of nondeterministic computations *trivial*, these are the languages $T_1 := \emptyset, T_2 := \{\epsilon\}, T_3 := \{0, 1\}^*$ and $T_4 := \{0, 1\}^* - \{\epsilon\}$, note that $w(M^X, x)$ has at least length 1. It is easy to see that $[T_1]^{(X)} = [T_2]^{(X)}$ and $[T_3]^{(X)} = [T_4]^{(X)}$, that these two families are $\rightarrow$–incomparable, and that $[T_1]^{(X)}, [T_3]^{(X)} \Rightarrow [L]^{(X)}$ for every nontrivial language L.

3 Families accepted by regular languages

Consider the families accepted by regular languages over the alphabet $\{0, 1\}$. In [HL*93] it was pointed out that these families are just the families characterized by associative locally definable accptance types as defined in [Her92].

First some examples of families accepted by regular languages will be given. Define the following regular languages: $<\text{P}> := 1\{0, 1\}^*$, $<\text{NP}> := 0^*1\{0, 1\}^*$, $<\text{co-NP}> := 0^*$, $<\text{MOD}_n\text{P}> := \{\{0^*1\}^n\}^*0^*$ for every $n \geq 2$. The reason for this suggestive notion is that by simple observation $<\text{P}>$ accepts the family $\text{P}^{(X)}$ and that by definition $<\text{NP}>$, $<\text{co-NP}>$ and $<\text{MOD}_n\text{P}>$ accept the families $\text{NP}^{(X)}$, $\text{co-NP}^{(X)}$ and $\text{MOD}_n\text{P}^{(X)}$, respectively.

In [HL*93] it is mentioned that for every $i \in N$ there exist regular languages accepting the families $\Sigma_i^{p,(X)}$ and $\Pi_i^{p,(X)}$ of the polynomial hierarchy, and also there the existence of a regular language accepting the family $\text{PSPACE}^{(X)}$ is shown.

In order to state results with the help of well–known order theoretic notions the trivial languages (which are regular) will be ignored: let $\mathcal{R}$ be the set of families which are accepted by a nontrivial regular language. For the restriction of $\rightarrow$ to $\mathcal{R}$ the same symbol $\rightarrow$ is used.

Proposition 1 *The partial order $(\mathcal{R}, \rightarrow)$ is an upper semi–lattice which has a minimum, a maximum, an infinite chain and an infinite antichain.*

The upper semi–lattice part also holds for this restriction because when A and B are regular also $A \oplus B$ is regular. The minimum of the partial order is of course $\text{P}^{(X)}$ and the maximum is $\text{PSPACE}^{(X)}$ by the result in [HL*93]. The chain is given by the families $\Sigma_i^{p,(X)}$ for $i \in N$: $\Sigma_i^{p,(X)} \rightarrow \Sigma_{i+1}^{p,(X)}$ was shown in [Sto77], and $\Sigma_i^{p,(X)} \neq \Sigma_{i+1}^{p,(X)}$ by the result in [Has86]. To obtain an antichain consider the families $\text{MOD}_p\text{P}^{(X)}$ for p prime: by a result in [BG92] there exists for primes $p \neq q$ an oracle X such that MOD_pP^X is not a subset of MOD_qP^X, what is another way of saying that the families $\text{MOD}_p\text{P}^{(X)}$ for p prime are pairwise $\rightarrow$–incomparable.

The following extension of the antichain above will be used later, the incomparabilities were shown in [BGS75, Yao85, Bei91]:

Proposition 2 *The families $\text{NP}^{(X)}$, $\text{co-NP}^{(X)}$ and $\text{MOD}_p\text{P}^{(X)}$ for p prime are pairwise $\rightarrow$–incomparable, and (therefore) these families are different from the minimum $\text{P}^{(X)}$.*

Call a partial order to be *dense* iff for every comparable pair of elements there exists an element which is properly between them. For a partial order with a minimum m an *atom* is defined to be an element $a \neq m$ for which there exists no element properly between m and a. A partial order with a minimum is called *atomic* iff for every element

b which is neither the minimum nor an atom there exists an atom a such that a is below b.

A natural question for a given partial order is to ask about density, see for example [Lad75]. The main result of this report will be that $(\mathcal{R}, \rightarrow)$ is atomic and therefore not dense. The atoms will be the families listed in the previous proposition.

To get this result the following detour to formal language theory will be made.

4   A lemma about regular languages

Let an ϵ-*free homomorphism* be a mapping h which maps the letters 0 and 1 to non-empty words. An (ϵ-free) homomorphism is extended the usual way to words, see [HU79].

For two languages A and B the *o-h-reducibility* will be defined. The name stands for *offset–homomorphism*, the concept does not seem to be defined in the literature. A is *o-h-reducible* to B iff there exist two words y, z, called *offsets*, and an ϵ-free homomorphism h such that for all words x

$$x \in A \iff yh(x)z \in B.$$

It is easy to see that the o-h-reducibility relation is reflexive and transitive. The motivation for the definition of o-h-reducibility is the following proposition:

Proposition 3 *If A is o-h-reducible to B then* $[A]^{(X)} \rightarrow [B]^{(X)}$.

Proof.   Let M^X be a machine. Construct the machine M_0^X: it produces by nondeterminism the two offsets in the leftmost and rightmost paths and by simulating M^X it produces paths for h(0) or h(1) everytime M^X rejects or accepts, respectively. Obviously $w(M^X, x) \in A \iff w(M_0^X, x) \in B$, therefore $[A]^X \subseteq [B]^X$ for every oracle X. □

As an example one can see that co-NP$^{(X)} \rightarrow$ 1–NP$^{(X)}$ because 1^* accepts co-NP$^{(X)}$, 0^*10^* accepts by defintion 1–NP$^{(X)}$, and 1^* is o-h-reducible to 0^*10^* via the homomorphism h with $h(0) = 1, h(1) = 0$ and the offsets $y = 1$ and $z = \epsilon$.

Note that the opposite direction of the proposition above does not hold: 0^*10^* accepts 1–NP$^{(X)}$, $0^*10^*10^*$ accepts by definition 2–NP$^{(X)}$ and $0^*10^*10^*$ is obviously not o-h-reducible to 0^*10^*, but 1–NP$^{(X)}$ = 2–NP$^{(X)}$ was shown in [GW87].

For each number $k \geq 2$ let A_k be the set of nonempty and proper subsets of $\{0, \ldots, k-1\}$. For an $S \in A_k$ let $<S_k>$ be the regular language consisting of the words for which the number of 1's is equal modulo k to n, where n is an element of S. For example $<\text{MOD}_k\text{P}> = <\{0\}_k>$

Proposition 4   (a) *If* $S \in A_k$ *then there exists a prime p and a set $T \in A_p$ such that* $<T_p>$ *is o-h-reducible to* $<S_k>$.
(b) *If* $S \in A_p$ *for a prime p then* $<S_p>$ *accepts* $\text{MOD}_p\text{P}^{(X)}$.

(a) is shown by induction on factorization of k, and (b) is shown by the methods of [BG92].

Call the languages $<$NP$>$, $<$co-NP$>$ and $<S_p>$ for $S \in A_p$ with p prime the *atomic* languages. Call a language L to be *not determined at the ends* iff for every natural number n there exist four words x, y, v, w such that x and y have length $\geq n$ and xvy is in L but xwy is not in L. This is the two-sided version of the concept of not being *definite* defined in [Har65]. Note that a language determined at the ends is a regular language, but for example none of the regular languages $<$NP$>$, $<$co-NP$>$ and $<S_k>$ for $S \in A_k$ is determined at the ends.

The following is a lemma about regular languages, independent of questions about polynomial time computations:

Lemma 1 *A regular language R is not determined at the ends iff at least one of the atomic languages is o-h-reducible to R*

Proof. The direction $\Longleftarrow$ is easy to see. For the other direction assume that R is accepted by the deterministic finite automaton $(Q, \{0, 1\}, \{\delta_0, \delta_1\}, q_0, F)$ where Q is the set of states, $\delta_0, \delta_1 : Q \longrightarrow Q$ are the two transition functions, q_0 is the initial state and F is the set of accepting states. Assume w.l.o.g that every state is reachable from q_0.

Extend like usual the δ-notation to every word $w = x_1 \ldots x_n$ by defining $\delta_w : Q \longrightarrow Q$ to be the mapping $\delta_{x_n} \circ \ldots \circ \delta_{x_1}$, δ_ϵ stands for the identity function. The definition reflects the idea that δ_w is the function which starts with a state q and then follows the letters of w stopping in state $\delta_w(q)$.

Because Q is finite, for every word w the iteration of δ_w starting in a state q has to run into a cycle sometime, more formally: for every word w and every state q there exist two numbers $1 \leq m \leq n$ such that $c_1, \ldots, c_m, \ldots, c_n$ are different states, $c_1 = q$, $c_{i+1} = \delta_w(c_i)$ for $1 \leq i < n$ and $c_m = \delta_w(c_n)$. Assume that for some other word z the set $\{\delta_z(c_m), \ldots, \delta_z(c_n)\}$ has elements from both F and $Q \setminus F$. It is shown that in this case an atomic language is o-h-reducible to R: let $k := 1 + n - m$ and define $S \in A_k$ to be the set $\{j - m \mid m \leq j \leq n$ and $\delta_z(c_j) \in F\}$. Take a word z' for which $\delta_{z'}(q_0) = c_m$. Define the homomorphism h by $h(0) = w^k$ and $h(1) = w$. Now it is clear that for every word x: $x \in <S_k> \iff z'h(x)z \in R$, this means that the language $<S_k>$ is o-h-reducible to R, and by proposition 4(a) and by the transitivity of o-h-reducibility also an atomic language of the type $<T_p>$ with $T \in A_p$ for some prime p is o-h-reducible to R.

From now on assume that for all states q and for all words w, z like above the set $\{\delta_z(c_m), \ldots, \delta_z(c_n)\}$ consists of states which are either all in F or all in $Q \setminus F$.

Because R is not determined at the ends there exist words r, a, b, s such that r and s have length $\geq |Q|^{|Q|}$ and $ras \in R$ but $rbs \notin R$. There are at most $|Q|^{|Q|}$ mappings $Q \longrightarrow Q$, therefore there exist words s_1, s_2, s_3 such that $s = s_1 s_2 s_3$, $s_2 \neq \epsilon$ and $\delta_{s_1 s_2} = \delta_{s_1}$, i.e. δ_{s_2} is the identity function on the set of states reachable by δ_{s_1}.

Consider for some word u and a state q reachable by δ_{s_1} the set of states $\{c_1, \ldots, c_m, \ldots, c_n\}$ of the iteration of δ_{us_1} starting with $q = c_1$. By assumption the states

$\delta_{s_3}(c_m), \ldots, \delta_{s_3}(c_n)$ do belong either all to F or all to $Q \setminus F$. Consider the first case and assume that for some $c_j \in \{c_1, \ldots, c_{m-1}\}$ the state $\delta_{s_3}(c_j)$ is not in F. Then, taking a word z for which $\delta_z(q_0) = c_j$ and defining a homomorphism h by $h(0) = s_2$ and $h(1) = \{us_1\}^m$ it is easy to see that $x \in \text{<NP>} \iff zh(x)s_3 \in R$, i.e. <NP> is o-h-reducible to R. Likewise, <co-NP> is o-h-reducible to R if none of the states $\delta_{s_3}(c_m), \ldots, \delta_{s_3}(c_n)$ is in F and there is some $c_j \in \{c_1, \ldots, c_{m-1}\}$ such that $\delta_{s_3}(c_j)$ is in F.

So the only case left is that for each word u and each state q reachable by δ_{s_1} the following holds: $\delta_{s_3}(q) \in F \iff \delta_{us_1s_3}(q) \in F$.

Take the word r of above for which $ras \in R$ but $rbs \notin R$. Because r has length $\geq |Q|$ there exist three words r_1, r_2, r_3 such that $r = r_1r_2r_3$, $r_2 \neq \epsilon$ and $\delta_{r_1}(q_0) = \delta_{r_1r_2}(q_0)$. Define the homomorphism h by $h(0) = r_2$ and $h(1) = r_3as_1$. Then $x \in \text{<NP>} \iff r_1h(x)r_3bs \in R$, i.e. <NP> is o-h-reducible to R. The implication $\Leftarrow$ is obvious, and for $\Rightarrow$ consider a word $x = 0^*1y$: then the state $\delta_{r_1h(0^*1)}(q_0)$ is reachable by δ_{s_1} and $\delta_{r_1h(0^*1)s_3}(q_0) = \delta_{ras}(q_0) \in F$ but therefore by the above assumption applied to $u = h(y)r_3b$ also $\delta_{r_1h(0^*1y)r_3bs}(q_0) \in F$. $\square$

5 Applications to the density question

With the previous lemma it is easy to prove the following theorem:

Theorem 1 *The partial order $(\mathcal{R}, \rightarrow)$ is atomic. The atoms are the pairwise different families $NP^{(X)}$, $co\text{-}NP^{(X)}$ and $MOD_pP^{(X)}$ for p prime.*

Proof. Consider a nontrivial regular language A. If A is determined at the ends then it accepts the family $P^{(X)}$: of course $P^{(X)} \rightarrow [A]^{(X)}$, and to see $[A]^{(X)} \rightarrow P^{(X)}$ let a non-deterministic machine M^X be given: construct the deterministic machine M_0^X which for an input just visits deterministicly the constant number of leftmost and rightmost paths of the computation of M^X which compute the outputs A depends on, and then decides according to A.

If A is not determined at the ends then by the previous lemma 1 at least one of the atomic languages is o-h-reducible to A. Therefore by propositions 3 and 4(b) at least one of the relations $NP^{(X)} \rightarrow [A]^{(X)}$, $co\text{-}NP^{(X)} \rightarrow [A]^{(X)}$, $MOD_pP^{(X)} \rightarrow [A]^{(X)}$ holds.

By proposition 2 the families $NP^{(X)}$, $co\text{-}NP^{(X)}$ and $MOD_pP^{(X)}$ for p prime are in fact different from each other and are different from $P^{(X)}$. $\square$

539

Figure 1: The result shown as a diagram

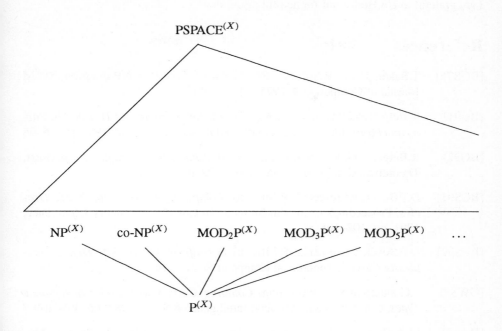

Corollary 1 *The partial order* $(\mathcal{R}, \rightarrow)$ *is not dense.*

The theorem allows to describe the regular languages accepting $P^{(X)}$:

Corollary 2 *A regular language accepts* $P^{(X)}$ *iff it is not trivial and is determined at the ends.*

6 Open Questions

In this paper only some properties of the upper semi–lattice $(\mathcal{R}, \rightarrow)$ were shown, other questions about it could not be solved, for example if it is distributive or if it is a lattice.

A possible extension of this paper may be to consider acceptance languages which are more powerful than regular languages, for example contextfree languages, note that by definition the families $PP^{(X)}$ and $C_=P^{(X)}$ are accepted by contextfree languages. Another possible extension may be to investigate the families accepted by locally definable acceptance types defined in [Her92]. In both cases the question if $NP^{(X)}$ is still an atom seems to be interesting.

540

7 Acknowledgements

I am grateful to Uli Hertrampf for helpful discussions.

References

[BGS75] T.Baker, J.Gill, R.Solovay. *Relativations of the* P =?NP *question*, SIAM Journal of Computing **4**, 1975, pp. 431–442

[Bei91] R.Beigel. *Relativized Counting Classes: Relations among Thresholds, Parity and Mods*, Journal of Computer and System Science **42**, 1991, pp. 76–96

[BG92] R.Beigel, J.Gill. *Counting Classes: thresholds parity, mods, and fewness*, Theoretical Computer Science **103**, 1992, pp. 3–23

[BCS91] D.P.Bovet, P.Crescenzi, R.Silvestri. *Complexity Classes and Sparse Oracles*, Proceedings of the 6th Structure in Complexity Theory Conference, 1991, pp. 102–108

[BCS92] D.P.Bovet, P.Crescenzi, R.Silvestri. *A Uniform Approach to Define Complexity Classes*, Theoretical Computer Science **104**, 1992, pp. 263–283

[GW87] T.Gundermann, G.Wechsung. *Counting Classes with Finite Acceptance Types*, Computers and Artificial Intelligence **6** No. 5, 1987, pp. 395–409

[Har65] M.A.Harrison. *Introduction to Switching and Automata Theory*, McGraw Hill, 1965

[HH88] J.Hartmanis, L.Hemachandra. *Complexity classes without machines: On complete languages fo UP*, Theoretical Computer Science **58**, 1988, pp. 129-142

[Has86] J.Hastad. *Almost Optimal Lower Bounds for Small Depth Circuits*, Proceedings of the 18th ACM Symposium on Theory of Computing, 1986, pp. 6–20

[Her90] U.Hertrampf *Relations among Mod–Classes*, Theoretical Computer Science **74**, 1990, pp. 325–328

[Her92] U.Hertrampf. *Locally Definable Acceptance Types for Polynomial Time Machines*, Proceedings 9th STACS, 1992, pp. 199–207

[HL*93] U.Hertrampf, C.Lautemann, Th. Schwentick, H.Vollmer, K.Wagner. *On the Power of Polynomial Time Bit-Computations*, Proceedings of the 8th Structure in Complexity Theory Conference, 1993, pp. 200–207

[HU79] J.E.Hopcroft, J.D.Ullman. *Introduction to Automata Theory, Languages, and Computation*, Addison-Wesley, 1979

[Ko91]   K.Ko. *Separating the low and high hierarchies by oracles*, Information and Computation **90(2)**, 1991, pp. 156–177

[Lad75]   R.E.Ladner. *On the structure of polynomial time reducibility*, Journal of the ACM **22**, 1975, pp. 155–171

[Sto77]   L.Stockmeyer. *The polynomial-time Hierarchy*, Theoretical Computer Science **3**, 1977, pp. 23–33

[Yao85]   A.Yao. *Separating the Polynomial time Hierarchy by Oracles*, Proceedings of the 26th Annual IEEE Symposium on Foundations of Computer Science, 1985, pp. 1-10

[Za88]   S.Zachos. *Probabilistic Quantifiers and Games*, Journal of Computer and System Sciences **36**,1988, pp. 433-451

Complexity Classes with Finite Acceptance Types[*]

Ulrich Hertrampf

Theoretische Informatik, Universität Würzburg,
Am Exerzierplatz 3, D-97072 Würzburg, Germany

Abstract. Complexity classes with finite acceptance types are those classes that can be obtained by nondeterministic machines, if the global acceptance condition is of the form: the number of accepting computation paths is in the set A, for some fixed finite set A. We study the relationships between such classes, exhibiting conditions, under which one class is contained in another one relative to all oracles, or conversely there is an oracle seperation. The proof technique uses a key lemma which transforms the inclusionship question for these classes into an existence question for certain hypergraphs.

1 Introduction

Recently, a lot of characterization results for many complextiy classes in the area between P and PSPACE have been obtained, using nondeterministic polynomial time Turing machines with some kind of global acceptance condition. A very general framework, allowing characterizations of nearly all introduced complexity classes in this area, has been developed by Bovet, Crescenzi, and Silvestri in [1, 2].

In [5] (see also [6]) a polynomial time machine scheme for such characterizations is introduced using a finite set of k-valued functions, the so called locally definable acceptance types. A special case of finite acceptance types appears, if we just add up the number of accepting paths, but mapping all numbers greater than k to k. Filtering out those cases where this number is in subset A of $\{1, \ldots, k\}$ results in counting classes of finite acceptance type. These classes were introduced by Gundermann, and Wechsung [3], see also [4].

In [3, 4] the inclusionship structure of such classes was investigated for cases where the used sets A consisted of intervals. In the current paper we are interested in the general case, where A may be any finite set of natural numbers. We give a translation of the question, whether a given class is contained in another one, to the question, whether a certain sequence of hypergraphs (or set systems)

---

[*] This research was supported by Deutsche Forschungsgemeinschaft, Grant number Wa 847/1-1, "k-wertige Schaltkreise". Part of this work was done while the author was an assistant at Universität Trier.

exists, or not. Using this translation, we prove and disprove the existence of oracle separations in a wide variety of cases.

The organization of the paper is as follows: In Section 2 we give the formal definition of a complexity class with finite acceptance type, and we recall the connection between this kind of complexity and the concept of leaf languages from [1, 2] (see also [7]). Section 3 introduces hypergraph sequences. We prove some easy facts on existence or non-existence of special types of such sequences. Section 4 connects the existence question for hypergraph sequences with the inclusionship question for certain counting classes. Finally, in Section 5, the results of the previous sections are applied to obtain a nearly complete solution of the question, whether two given classes $\{a,b\}P$ and $\{c,d\}P$ can be separated by an oracle.

2 Counting Classes and Leaf Languages

We now give the formal definition of a finite acceptance class and a co-finite acceptance class, resp. These classes are counting classes in a strong sense, since the acceptance condition merely depends on the number of accepting computations, and no computation is done except that we stop counting after reaching a certain maximal value. By $acc_M(x)$ we denote the number of accepting paths of machine M on input x.

Definition 1. A finite acceptance class $\mathcal{C}$ is a class of sets such that there exists a fixed finite set $A \subset \mathbb{N}$ with the following property:

$$L \in \mathcal{C} \iff \exists M \text{ (NTM) with } x \in L \leftrightarrow acc_M(x) \in A. \qquad (\star)$$

The finite acceptance class associated with set A is denoted by $(A)P$.

A co-finite acceptance class $\mathcal{C}$ is a class of sets such that the class $\mathcal{D} := co - \mathcal{C} = \{L \mid \Sigma^* - L \in \mathcal{C}\}$ is a finite acceptance class.

Clearly a class $\mathcal{C}$ is a co-finite acceptance class if and only if there is a fixed co-finite set $A \subset \mathbb{N}$ with property $(\star)$.

One can easily see that coNP is a finite acceptance class: take A to be $\{0\}$. Consequently, NP is the co-finite acceptance class $co-(A)P$. The class 1-NP is the finite acceptance class for $A = \{1\}$ (this class is sometimes also called US).

All (co-) finite acceptance classes are contained in the Boolean Hierarchy:

Proposition 2. Let $A \subset \mathbb{N}$ be a finite set, $|A| = k$. Then $(A)P \subseteq NP(2k)$.

Proof. Let $A = \{a_1, a_2, \ldots, a_k\}$. Let $L \in A$, and let M be a fixed machine such that $x \in L \leftrightarrow acc_M(x) \in A$. Define $L^{\leq c} := \{x \mid acc_M(x) \leq c\}$ and

$L^{\geq c} := \{x \mid acc_M(x) \geq c\}$. Obiously all sets $L^{\leq c}$ belong to coNP, all sets $L^{\geq c}$ belong to NP, and

$$L = (L^{\leq a_1} \cap L^{\geq a_1}) \cup \ldots \cup (L^{\leq a_k} \cap L^{\geq a_k}).$$

Thus, by definition of the classes in the Boolean Hierarchy, $L \in NP(2k)$.

Corollary 3. *All classes of the types $(A)P$ or co-$(A)P$ are subclasses of* BH, *the union of all classes of the Boolean Hierarchy.*

Complexity classes with finite acceptance types can also be characterized by their leaf languages. This depends on the fact that these classes can be described via nondeterministic polynomial time machines by a regular language in the following way:

- With every class $\mathcal{C} = (A)P$, where $A = \{a_1, \ldots, a_k\}$, the regular language

$$R_A = (0^*10^*)^{a_1} \cup \ldots \cup (0^*10^*)^{a_k}$$

  is associated.
- For every $L \in \mathcal{C}$ there is a polynomial time NTM M, such that on inputs from L, M's computation in its leaves, read from left to right yields a word from R_A, and on inputs from $\overline{L}$ a word from $\overline{R_A}$.

The leaf languages can be used to obtain oracle separations between two finite acceptance classes, or to prove the non-existence of such separations. This connection was given in [1, 2]. We need the following definition:

Definition 4. A language A is plt-reducible to B, $A \leq_m^{plt} B$, if there exist two functions f and g, each computable in polylogarithmic time on a deterministic machine with random access to the input, f is zero-one-valued, such that

$$x \in A \iff f(x,1)f(x,2)\ldots f(x,g(x)) \in B.$$

It follows from the work of [1, 2] that plt-reduction is the key to proving existence or non-existence of oracle separations between two finite acceptance classes. We restate their result as follows:

Theorem 5 (Bovet, Crescenzi, Silvestri). *Let $\mathcal{C}_1$ and $\mathcal{C}_2$ be two complexity classes with leaf languages A_1 and A_2, resp. Then A_1 is plt-reducible to A_2 if and only if $\mathcal{C}_1$ is contained in $\mathcal{C}_2$ in all relativizations.*

This allows us in the subsequent sections, to only consider leaf languages, when we talk about oracle separations.

3 Hypergraphs, Sequences, and Uniformity

In this section we will introduce our notion of hypergraphs, which are also called set systems in the literature. Various definitions are possible, e.g. sometimes the empty set is not allowed as a hyperedge, or each set is only allowed to occur at most once. We choose the most general definition.

Definition 6. A hypergraph H on the finite set X is a mapping $H : 2^X \longrightarrow I\!N$. The elements of X are called vertices of H. If for some $Y \subseteq X$ the value $H(Y)$ is greater than zero, then we call Y a hyperedge of multiplicity $H(Y)$.

Obviously, the structure of a hypergraph does not depend on the set X, but in fact only on the cardinality of X. So we will always assume X to be the set $\{x_1, x_2, \ldots, x_n\}$, when the cardinality of X is n.

In this paper we are mainly interested in sequences of hypergraphs:

Definition 7. A hypergraph sequence, also called H-sequence, is an infinite sequence of hypergraphs $H_1, H_2, \ldots$, such that for all $i \in I\!N$, H_i is a hypergraph on $\{x_1, \ldots, x_i\}$.

The hypergraph sequence $H_1, H_2, \ldots$ is a uniform H-sequence, if there exists a deterministic polynomial time algorithm, which on input $(n, j_1, \ldots, j_k)$ with $j_\nu \leq n, (1 \leq \nu \leq k)$, can compute $H_n(\{x_{j_1}, \ldots, x_{j_k}\})$.

The crucial property of (uniform) H-sequences, needed for the separations and inclusions in Section 5, is a correspondence between two sets of natural numbers:

Definition 8. We say that the H-sequence $(H_i)_{i \in I\!N}$ realizes the correspondence (A, B), where $A, B \subset I\!N$ are finite sets, if for all i with $i > \max(A)$, we have

$$\sum_{C' \subseteq C} H_i(C') \in B \quad \Longleftrightarrow \quad |C| \in A.$$

To understand the motivation for this definition, imagine a bitwise reduction, where every bit of the output merely depends on a fixed set of bits in the input, and it is set to 1 if and only if all these bits in the input are set to 1. Now we can, for each set of inputs, determine how many of the output bits depend exactly on that set. This number is H applied to the set of inputs. But if these input bits are all set to 1, then also all the output bits depending on proper subsets of this set of inputs, will be set to 1. So the number of outputs set to 1 for a given set of 1's in the input can be computed by a sum like the one in the above definition. We will return to this point in Section 4.

Now we derive some easy correspondences that can be realized by uniform H-sequences.

Lemma 9. *Let* $A = \{a_1, \ldots, a_k\}$*, where* $a_1 < a_2 < \ldots < a_k$*. Then the correspondence* $(A, \{a_1, \ldots, a_{k-1}, a_k+1\})$ *is realized by a suitable uniform H-sequence.*

Proof. Let for all i, $H_i(Y) = 1$, if $|Y| \in \{1, a_k\}$, and $H_i(Y) = 0$, in all other cases. Obviously this H-sequence is uniform, and it realizes the desired correspondence, since in sets with less than a_k elements, the only hyperedges are the ones with one element, but in sets with exactly a_k elements one additional hyperedge exists, consisting of all the a_k elements.

Lemma 10. *Let* $A = \{a_1, \ldots, a_k\}$*, where* $a_1 < a_2 < \ldots < a_k$*. Then the correspondence* $(A, \{a_1+1, \ldots, a_k+1\})$ *is realized by a suitable uniform H-sequence.*

Proof. Let for all i, $H_i(Y) = 1$, if $|Y| \in \{0, 1\}$, and $H_i(Y) = 0$, in all other cases. Obviously this H-sequence is uniform, and it realizes the desired correspondence, since in every set there is the hyperedge consisting of the empty set, plus as many one-element hyperedges as there are elements.

Lemma 11. *Let* $A = \{a, b\}$ *with* $a < b$*, and let* $B = \{1, \binom{b}{a}\}$*. Then there is a uniform H-sequence that realizes the correspondence* (A, B)*.*

Proof. Let for all i, $H_i(Y) = 1$, if $|Y| = a$, and $H_i(Y) = 0$, otherwise. This uniform H-sequence has the desired property.

We also need some non-existence results. To make them as general as possible, we will consider all (possibly non-uniform) H-sequences here.

Lemma 12. *Let* $A = \{a, b\}$ *with* $a < b$*, and let* $B = \{c, d\}$ *with* $c < d$*. If* $d - c < a - b$*, then there is no H-sequence that realizes the correspondence* (A, B)*.*

Proof. We assume that there is an H-sequence $(H_i)_{i \in \mathbb{N}}$ that realizes the correspondence (A, B). Define $\beta_i(C)$ to be the sum $\sum_{C' \subseteq C} H_i(C')$. Define further $X_{j,k} = \{x_j, \ldots, x_k\}$ for all pairs (j, k) such that $j < k$. From the definition of A and B, it is clear that

$$\beta_i(X_{1,a}) \in \{c, d\} \quad \text{and} \quad \beta_i(X_{2,a+1}) \in \{c, d\}$$

but since $\beta_i(X_{2,a}) \notin \{c, d\}$, then $\beta_i(X_{1,a})$, as well as $\beta_i(X_{2,a+1})$ have to differ from $\beta_i(X_{2,a})$. Consequently in the set $X_{1,a}$ there is a hyperedge involving vertex x_1, and in set $X_{2,a+1}$ there is a hyperedge involving vertex x_{a+1}, so

$$\beta_i(X_{1,a+1}) > \max(\beta_i(X_{1,a}), \beta_i(X_{2,a+1}))$$

and from $b \geq a + 1$ we conclude

$$\beta_i(X_{1,b}) > \max(\beta_i(X_{1,a}), \beta_i(X_{2,a+1})).$$

Thus $\beta_i(X_{1,a}) = c$ and $\beta_i(X_{1,b}) = d$, and the same argument yields $\beta_i(C) = c$, whenever $|C| = a$ and $\beta_i(C) = d$, whenever $|C| = b$.

Now we can start with $X_{1,a}$, which yields value c, and successively add x_{a+1}, x_{a+2}, ..., x_b. In every step, a simple argument as the one above shows, that the β_i-value has to increase at least by one, since an a-element subset of the new set always contains a hyperedge involving the newly added vertex. So after the $b - a$ addition steps, we arrive at a value that is at least $c + b - a > d$. That is a contradiction, since by assumption $\beta_i(\{x_1, \ldots, x_b\}) \in \{c, d\}$.

Lemma 13. *Let $A = \{a, b\}$ with $a < b$, and let $B = \{1, d\}$ with $d > 1$. If $d < \binom{b}{a}$, then there is no H-sequence that realizes the correspondence (A, B).*

Proof. We assume that there is an H-sequence $(H_i)_{i \in \mathbb{N}}$ that realizes the correspondence (A, B). Define $\beta_i(C)$ and $X_{j,k} = \{x_j, \ldots, x_k\}$ as above. We can derive as above that all a-element subsets C fulfill $\beta_i(C) = 1$, and all $(a - 1)$-element subsets C fulfill $\beta_i(C) = 0$. This means, that for a-element subsets C, we have $H_i(C) = 1$, and thus for b-element subsets C, $\beta_i(C) \geq \binom{b}{a}$, because these sets contain $\binom{b}{a}$ subsets of cardinality a, and all of these add a one to the sum for C. This contradicts the assumption.

Similar arguments show the following lemma:

Lemma 14. *Let $|A| > |B|$, and $0 \notin A$. Then there is no H-sequence that realizes the correspondence (A, B).*

4   The Main Lemma

In this section we want to link the concept of hypergraphs to the plt-reductions of Section 2. Recall that a plt-reduction in Section 2 was defined as a pair of functions f and g, and the result was the string $f(x, 0)f(x, 1) \ldots f(x, g(x))$. This latter string we will refer to as $h(x)$, thus viewing the reduction as a function h that takes a string x as argument and outputs another string $h(x)$. To make things easier we will talk of h as the plt-reduction.

We start with two technical lemmas. For strings $w \in \{0, 1\}^*$, we denote the number of 1-bits in w by $|w|_1$.

Lemma 15. *Let h be a plt-reduction, reducing L_1 to L_2 $(L_1, L_2 \subseteq \{0, 1\}^*)$. Let m and k be such that $|x|_1 \leq m \Rightarrow |h(x)|_1 \leq k$. Then there exists a plt-reduction h' such that*

$$|x|_1 \leq m \Rightarrow |h'(x)|_1 = |h(x)|_1$$

and

$$|x|_1 > m \Rightarrow k < |h'(x)|_1 \leq \binom{|x|_1}{m}k + \binom{|x|_1}{m+1}(k + 1)$$

(Note that the new reduction does not necessarily reduce L_1 to L_2 anymore, but on inputs with at most m 1-bits, it still behaves like h.)

Proof. Let $h(x) = f(x,1)f(x,2)\ldots f(x,g(x))$. So if $|x|_1 \leq m$ then at most k of the bits $f(x,j)$ have value one. Define g' as follows:

$$g'(x) = g(x) + \binom{|x|}{m+1}(k+1)$$

We understand each of the values $g(x)+1$, $g(x)+2$, $\ldots$, $g'(x)$ as an encoding of an $(m+1)$-tuple of bits from x, each $(m+1)$-tuple occuring exactly $k+1$ times.

Now we can define f':

$$f'(x,j) = \begin{cases} 1, & \text{if } j \leq g(x) \text{ and } f(x,j) = 1 \text{ and the computation} \\ & \text{of } f \text{ on input } (x,j) \text{ reads at most } m \text{ ones of } x \\ & \text{or } j > g(x) \text{ and the } (m+1)\text{-tuple of bits in } x \text{ encoded} \\ & \text{by } j \text{ consists entirely of bits of value one} \\ 0, & \text{otherwise} \end{cases}$$

We abbreviate the plt-reduction defined by f' and g' as $h'(x)$.

If $|x|_1 \leq m$ then $f'(x,j)$ has value one, if and only if $j \leq g(x)$ and $f(x,j) = 1$, thus $|h'(x)|_1 = |h(x)|_1$ in this case, as desired.

Now let $|x|_1 > m$. We have exactly $\binom{|x|_1}{m+1}$ different $(m+1)$-tuples that will cause bits of value one, each $(k+1)$ times. So the number of one bits produced by $f'(x,j)$ for $j > g(x)$ is exactly $\binom{|x|_1}{m+1}(k+1)$, and especially this value is greater than k. It remains to show that no more than $\binom{|x|_1}{m}k$ values of j with $j \leq g(x)$ result in $f'(x,j) = 1$: When $f'(x,j)$ has value one for such a j, then f must read at most m ones of x. This means that there is a word x' with at most m ones such that also $f(x',j) = 1$. Consequently, there exist at most k such values of j for any possible x'. Since the number of words x' with this property is bounded by $\binom{|x|_1}{m}$ and each x' can cause only k ones in $h(x)$ and thus also in $h'(x)$, we have the bound of $\binom{|x|_1}{m}k$ for the number of ones among the $f'(x,j)$ with $j \leq g(x)$. This completes the proof.

Lemma 16. *Let h be a plt-reduction with $|x|_1 \leq m \Rightarrow |h(x)|_1 \leq k$. Then for sufficiently large x there is a set of indices $I \subseteq \{1,\ldots,|x|\}$, such that*

1. $|I| = m$

2. $\forall J \subseteq I: \quad U(X_J) \cap I \subseteq J$

3. $J_1 \subseteq J_2 \subseteq I \quad \Rightarrow \quad U(X_{J_1}) \subseteq U(X_{J_2})$

Here, $X_J = z_1 z_2 \ldots z_n$ with $z_i = 1 \Leftrightarrow i \in J$, and $U(x)$ is the set of all indices j, such that there is a computation in $h(x)$ that outputs 1 and reads the j-th input bit.

Proof. We first prove the existence of a set I of cardinality m fulfilling condition 2:

There are $\binom{n}{m}$ different sets I, which is $\Theta(n^m)$. How many of these sets violate condition 2 because of a subset J of fixed cardinality j $(0 \le j \le m)$? Let J be fixed. Then

$$|X_J|_1 = j \le m \quad \Rightarrow \quad |h(X_J)|_1 \le k \quad \Rightarrow \quad |U(X_J)| \le k \cdot \log^c n$$

for some constant c. So to violate condition 2 I has to include at least one of the $k \cdot \log^c n$ elements of $|U(X_J)|$ which is not in J.

Now we have only $O(n^j)$ choices for J, and only $O(n^{m-j-1} \log^c n)$ possible extensions of J to a set I contradicting condition 2. So there are only $O(n^{m-1} \log^c n)$ choices of I where 2 is violated with a set J of size j. Summing up over all values of j gives us still only $O(n^{m-1} \log^c n)$ bad choices for I, but there are $\Theta(n^m)$ choices for I altogether. Thus we can choose an I fulfilling condition 2.

As to condition 3, consider the plt-reduction on X_{J_1} and X_{J_2}. Every one bit in the image of X_{J_1} depends only on bits from J_1 or from outside I, because of condition 2. But all bits in J_1 and outside I are the same for X_{J_1} and X_{J_2}. So the one bits in the image of X_{J_1} are one bits in the image of X_{J_2} too. Consequently $U(X_{J_1}) \subseteq U(X_{J_2})$.

Now we are ready to prove our main lemma:

Lemma 17. *Let A and B be two finite sets. If there exists a plt-reduction, reducing the leaf language of $(A)P$ to the leaf language of $(B)P$, then there exists an H-sequence $(H_i)_{i \in \mathbb{N}}$ that realizes the correspondence (A, B).*

Conversely, if a uniform H-sequence realizes the correspondence (A, B), then there is a plt-reduction, reducing the leaf language of $(A)P$ to the leaf language of $(B)P$.

Proof. By Lemma 15 we can modify the plt-reduction in a way that it still reduces the leaf language of $(A)P$ to the leaf language of $(B)P$, but for every number m we can give an explicit bound on the number of ones in images of inputs with m ones. So for every desired size we can apply Lemma 16 to get an input x with a set of indices I fulfilling the three conditions 1, 2, and 3. Thus these indices form a sort of monotonicity area:

When x is an input such that only bits with index from I can have value one, and if y is another input of that kind with $x_i = 1 \Rightarrow y_i = 1$, then also all one bits in the image of x remain one bits in the image of y. When the plt-reduction is h, we can formalize this by

$$x \le y \quad \Rightarrow \quad h(x) \le h(y)$$

where the ordering is meant bitwise.

We can exploit this by taking I as the basic set for a hypergraph H, and defining $H(J)$ = the number of bits in $h(X_I)$ that are ones already in $h(X_J)$, but are zero in all $h(X_{J'})$, when $J' \subset J$. Obviously $\beta(J) = |h(X_J)|_1$. So for all J with $|J| \in A$ we have $\beta(J) = |h(X_J)|_1 \in B$, since h maps all words x with $|x|_1 \in A$ to words $h(x)$ with $|h(x)|_1 \in B$ by definition. Thus the sequence of hypergraphs defined that way realizes the correspondence (A, B).

For the second part, note that the following pair (f, g) reduces the leaf language of $(A)P$ to the leaf language of $(B)P$:

$$g(x) = \max(B) \sum_{a \in A} \binom{|x|}{a}$$

Let every j $(1 \le j \le g(x))$ be the encoding of a pair consisting of an a-tuple of indices in x and a number from 1 to $\max(B)$. We can encode each such pair exactly once in a value j. Now define f as follows:

$$f(x, j) = \begin{cases} 1, & \text{if } j \text{ encodes the pair } (i, d) \text{ and the hyperedge associated} \\ & \quad \text{with } i \text{ exists and has multiplicity at least } d \\ 0, & \text{else} \end{cases}$$

5 Application: Results about Inclusion Relations

In this section we are going to combine Lemma 17 with the results of Section 3 to obtain separations and inclusions between several types of complexity classes with finite acceptance types.

In the following, speaking of pairs (a, b) we generally assume $a < b$. The first result in this line is derived directly from Lemma 9 and Lemma 10:

Theorem 18. *Let the pairs (a, b) and (c, d) be such that $a \le c$ and $b - a \le d - c$. Then $(\{a, b\})P \subseteq (\{c, d\})P$ in all relativizations.*

Combining Lemma 11 with Theorem 18 we get:

Theorem 19. *Let the pairs (a, b) and (c, d) be such that $c \ge 1$ and $d - c \ge \binom{b}{a} - 1$. Then $(\{a, b\})P \subseteq (\{c, d\})P$ in all relativizations.*

On the other hand, we conclude from Lemma 12:

Theorem 20. *Let the pairs (a, b) and (c, d) be such that $b - a > d - c$. Then there is an oracle, such that in the relativized world $(\{a, b\})P \not\subseteq (\{c, d\})P$.*

Finally, from Lemma 13 we see:

552

Theorem 21. *Let $d < \binom{b}{a}$. Then there is an oracle, such that in the relativized world we have $(\{a,b\})P \not\subseteq (\{1,d\})P$.*

These results are summarized in the following picture, where in the columns we fix the value a, $(a \geq 0)$, and in the rows we have b, $(b > a)$. For a given pair (a, b) the part in the upper right, looking like a "W" is known to include $(\{a,b\})P$, the parts on the left and on the bottom do not include $(\{a,b\})P$, (i.e. relative to an oracle), and for the finite part in the middle it is not known, which case applies.

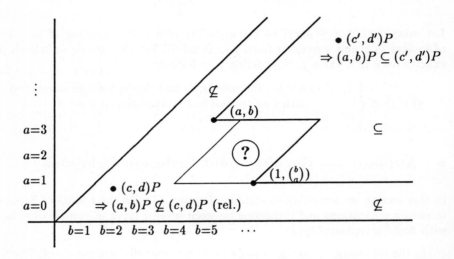

We proceed with a result about finite acceptance type classes, where the acceptance types have a different number of elements:

Theorem 22. *Let $|A| > |B|$, and $0 \notin A$. Then there is an oracle, such that in the relativized world $(A)P \not\subseteq (B)P$.*

Proof. This follows from Lemma 14.

A generalization of the technique used here also shows:

Theorem 23. *Let A and B be two finite sets of natural numbers. Then there is an oracle, such that in the relativized world co-$(A)P$ is not contained in $(B)P$, and there is an oracle such that in the relativized world $(A)P$ is not contained in co-$(B)P$.*

As a corollary of this result we obtain a well known fact:

Corollary 24. *There is an oracle, separating NP from coNP.*

Acknowledgement. I am grateful to Christoph Meinel for his support. Thanks are also due to Heribert Vollmer for fruitful discussions on the paper's subject.

References

1. D. P. BOVET, P. CRESCENZI, R. SILVESTRI, Complexity classes and sparse oracles; 6th *Structure in Complexity Theory Conference* (1991), pp. 102–108.
2. D. P. BOVET, P. CRESCENZI, R. SILVESTRI, A uniform approach to define complexity classes; *Theoretical Computer Science* **104** (1992), pp. 263–283.
3. T. GUNDERMANN, G. WECHSUNG, Counting Classes of finite acceptance types; *Computers and Artificial Intelligence* **6** (1987), pp. 395–409.
4. T. GUNDERMANN, N. A. NASSER, G. WECHSUNG, A survey on counting classes; 5th *Structure in Complexity Theory Conference* (1990), pp. 140–153.
5. U. HERTRAMPF, Locally definable acceptance types for polynomial time machines; 9th *Symposium on Theoretical Aspects of Computer Science* (1992), LNCS 577, pp. 199–207.
6. U. HERTRAMPF, Locally definable acceptance types – the three-valued case; 1st *Latin American Symposium on Theoretical Informatics* (1992), LNCS 583, pp. 262–271.
7. U. HERTRAMPF, C. LAUTEMANN, T. SCHWENTICK, H. VOLLMER, K. W. WAGNER, On the power of polynomial time bit-reductions; 8th *Structure in Complexity Theory Conference* (1993), pp. 200–207.

Theory of Parallel Computation

The Complete Axiomatization of Cs-congruence

Joachim Parrow[1, 2, 3] and Peter Sjödin[1]

[1] Swedish Institute of Computer Science, Box 1263, S-16428 Kista, Sweden
[2] Dept. of Teleinformatics, Royal Institute of Technology, Stockholm, Sweden
[3] Dept. of Computer Systems, Uppsala University, Sweden

Abstract. The coupled simulation equivalence is slightly larger than observation equivalence. Where observation equivalence is based on weak bisimulations, coupled simulation equivalence is based on pairs of simulations which coincide at stable states. We establish the corresponding congruence and provide a complete axiomatization by adding a new τ-law, $\tau.(\tau.P + Q) = \tau.P + Q$, to the axiomatization of observation congruence. We further indicate how the definition of the equivalence can be extended to divergent transition systems.

1 Introduction

A problem that naturally arises when working with transition system models of computation is to determine when two given transition systems should be regarded as "equivalent" in an abstract sense. Clearly, identity is too strong an equivalence since it does not equate transition systems that intuitively represent the same behaviour. Language equivalence (or trace equivalence), on the other hand, is often too weak since it equates transition systems that represent different deadlock properties.

We here treat a particular equivalence, *cs-equivalence*, that was introduced in our companion paper [6]. There we argued that cs-equivalence is suitable for implementation-oriented applications, and that it is practical even for large transition systems. The use of cs-equivalence was illustrated through a realistic example—a distributed algorithm for multi-process synchronization. The distributed algorithm was defined as a *distributed synchronizer*, which is a set of processes that cooperate to establish multi-process synchronizations. A *central* synchronizer was defined as an abstraction of the distributed synchronizer. The idea was that the central synchronizer should be simple and intuitively "correct," so the distributed algorithm could be verified by showing the central and distributed synchronizers to be equivalent. However, the two synchronizers select processes for synchronization in slightly different ways: the central synchronizer does this in a single internal step, while the distributed synchronizer gradually narrows down the possible combinations until only one remains.

In order to verify the distributed algorithm, we need an equivalence relation with two features: it should have a practical proof method, and it should not require an exact correspondence between all internal choices in equivalent transition systems. To our knowledge, cs-equivalence is unique in possessing these two desirable properties. The first property is important in any large-scale application, and the second is important in for example verification that a distributed system (which may resolve internal choices through negotiations between components) is equivalent to a non-distributed system (where internal choices are resolved atomically). We briefly explain these points below in comparison with two other popular equivalences: observation equivalence and testing equivalence.

Observation equivalence (originally suggested by Milner [4]) is based on the idea that two equivalent transition systems should be able to mimic each other indefinitely. Formally, it can be defined through the notion of *bisimulation*, which is a binary relation on the states of the systems. Two states are bisimilar if any transition from one of them can be mimicked by an appropriate sequence of transitions from the other, leading again to bisimilar states.

Not surprisingly, observation equivalence is a formally undecidable relation for most process formalisms that can define infinite-state transition systems. In spite of this there is a useful method for checking that a *particular* relation is a bisimulation, namely to go through all transitions in the systems, and for each find a simulating sequence. Although there are many transitions in non-trivial applications, it is often possible to find a structure to the transitions and perform a case analysis over them. The practical importance of this method is that the two systems to be compared for equivalence may be accompanied by some intuition—perhaps supplied by the designer of the systems—for *why* they are equivalent. A bisimulation is a convenient way to make this intuition explicit, and a case analysis over transitions will determine if the intuition is correct.

However, the bisimulation requirement is sometimes unnecessarily strong. If at one state a certain set of internal choices is resolved, at any bisimilar state exactly the same choices must be resolved. If we compare two transition systems which do not resolve internal choices in "lock step", we find that no bisimulation relation between their states exists, and that the systems consequently are not observation equivalent. Thus, although there is a nice method to establish observation equivalence, based on case analysis over transitions, it is inapplicable in some problem areas.

Testing equivalence [2] is a weaker equivalence which does not suffer from this problem. This equivalence presupposes some precisely defined class of *tests*, and two transition systems are equivalent if they can pass exactly the same tests; different classes of tests yield different equivalences. By including traces and deadlock potentials among the tests an interesting equivalence akin to the "failures" equivalence of CSP [3] is obtained. This equivalence does not require bisimilarity, so it can equate transition systems which differ in the way internal choices are resolved. However, to establish that testing equivalence holds it is necessary to perform a case analysis over all *sequences* of transitions, a much more difficult task than analyzing single transitions. Hence, testing equivalence is difficult to apply to large-scale problems.

Cs-equivalence is to our knowledge the only equivalence to combine the advantages of these equivalences. It is based on simulations, so a case analysis over single transitions suffices to verify a cs-equivalence. However, where observation equivalence requires bisimilarity at every state, cs-equivalence only requires bisimilarity at *stable* states (states where no further internal transitions are possible). So cs-equivalence equates more systems than observation equivalence (though less than testing equivalence) and is consequently applicable in areas where observation equivalence is inappropriate.

In the present paper we derive a complete axiomatization for cs-congruence. In brief, this means that we establish a small set of syntactic rewrite laws through which cs-equivalent transition systems can be transformed into each other. Such an axiomatization makes it possible to treat transition systems algebraically, and gives a better picture of how the equivalence relates to other equivalences.

The rest of the paper is structured as follows. In Section 2 we recapitulate the usual definitions of transition systems and observation equivalence, and in Section 3 we give the definition of cs-equivalence and establish its associated congruence. This is given a complete axiomatization in Section 4. Finally, in Section 5 we sum up the results, mention related work and indicate possible future work; in particular we demonstrate how the equivalence can be generalized to systems with divergences.

2 Preliminaries

We assume a set of *observable actions Act* ranged over by a, b. The *silent action* τ is not in *Act*, and we use α to range over $Act \cup \{\tau\}$. A silent action represents an internal computation step of an entity.

We use a simple language, in the lines of Milner's CCS [5], to describe transition systems. Thus, our *agents*, ranged over by $P, Q, \ldots$ are given by

$$P \quad ::= \quad 0 \quad | \quad \alpha.P \quad | \quad P + Q$$

Sometimes in examples we omit a trailing 0, so e.g. $a.0 + \tau.0$ is written $a + \tau$.

The family of transition relations $\xrightarrow{\alpha}$ on agents is defined inductively as follows. 0 is *inaction* and has no transitions. An *action prefix* expression $\alpha.P$ has the one transition $\alpha.P \xrightarrow{\alpha} P$. The *choice* expression $P + Q$ has all transitions from P and Q; i.e. if $P \xrightarrow{\alpha} R$ or $Q \xrightarrow{\alpha} R$ then $P + Q \xrightarrow{\alpha} R$. The *depth* of an agent is the maximal number of nested prefix operators; for example the depth of $a + \tau.b$ is 2. We do not include a parallel operator in our investigation. Although of undisputed practical value, parallel composition is easy to axiomatize with an expansion law as in [5].

We say that P is *unstable* if, for some P', $P \xrightarrow{\tau} P'$, otherwise P is *stable*. If P' is reachable by zero or more transitions from P we call P' a *state* of P.

Given a the transition relations $\xrightarrow{\alpha}$ we construct, in the standard way, the relations $\Longrightarrow$ meaning that α can be preceded and followed by internal steps. Thus, $P \stackrel{\alpha}{\Longrightarrow} P'$ means $P(\xrightarrow{\tau})^* \xrightarrow{\alpha} (\xrightarrow{\tau})^* P'$. Following Milner we write $\stackrel{\widehat{\alpha}}{\Longrightarrow}$ to mean $\stackrel{\alpha}{\Longrightarrow}$ if $\alpha \neq \tau$ and $\stackrel{\alpha}{\Longrightarrow} \cup \mathbf{Id}$ (where $\mathbf{Id}$ is the identity relation on agents) if $\alpha = \tau$.

We formulate equivalence and congruence relations through *simulation* relations between agents.

Definition 1 (simulation). A *(weak) simulation* is a binary relation S satisfying

$$\text{whenever } PSQ \text{ and } P \xrightarrow{\alpha} P' \text{ then } \exists Q' : Q \stackrel{\widehat{\alpha}}{\Longrightarrow} Q' \text{ and } P'SQ' \ .$$

Following Milner [5] we then define observation equivalence and congruence:

Definition 2 (observation equivalence). A binary relation S on agents is called a *(weak) bisimulation* if both S and S^{-1} are weak simulations. Two agents P and Q are *observation equivalent*, written $P \approx Q$, if they are related by a weak bisimulation.

Definition 3 (observation congruence). Two agents P and Q are *observation congruent*, written $P \approx^c Q$, if

$$\text{whenever } P \xrightarrow{\alpha} P' \text{ then } \exists Q' : Q \stackrel{\alpha}{\Longrightarrow} Q' \text{ and } P' \approx Q' \ ,$$
$$\text{whenever } Q \xrightarrow{\alpha} Q' \text{ then } \exists P' : P \stackrel{\alpha}{\Longrightarrow} P' \text{ and } P' \approx Q' \ .$$

Milner writes "=" for observation congruence but we prefer to use "=" as identity. It is a standard result that observation congruence is the largest congruence included in observation equivalence.

3 Coupled Simulations

3.1 Cs-equivalence

The coupled simulations from our companion paper we here call *S-coupled* (coupled by *stability*). The intuition is that two agents can simulate each other, and also bisimulate each other in the stable states (in contrast, observation equivalence requires bisimilarity in every state).

Definition 4 (S-coupled simulation). An *S-coupled* simulation is a pair (S_1, S_2), where S_1 and S_2^{-1} are weak simulations, that satisfies both of the following:

1. If $P S_1 Q$ and P is stable then $P S_2 Q$.
2. If $P S_2 Q$ and Q is stable then $P S_1 Q$.

Two agents are *cs-equivalent*, written $=_{cs}$, if they are related by both components of an S-coupled simulation.

Definition 5. P is *simulated* by Q, written $P \preceq Q$, if $P S_1 Q$ for some S-coupled simulation (S_1, S_2). P is *co-simulated* by Q, written $P \succeq Q$, if $P S_2 Q$ for some S-coupled simulation (S_1, S_2).

Lemma 6. 1. $(\preceq, \succeq)$ is the largest S-coupled simulation,
2. $\preceq = \succeq^{-1}$,
3. $=_{cs} = \preceq \cap \succeq$.

Proof

1. We prove that $(\preceq, \succeq)$ is an S-coupled simulation directly from the definitions. If $P \preceq Q$ then $P S_1 Q$ for some S-coupled simulation (S_1, S_2). Then if $P \xrightarrow{\alpha} P'$ it holds $Q \overset{\widehat{\alpha}}{\Longrightarrow} Q'$ for some Q' such that $P' S_1 Q'$, which implies $P' \preceq Q'$. Also if P is stable then $P S_2 Q$ whence $P \succeq Q$. With the symmetric argument for $\succeq$ this establishes that $(\preceq, \succeq)$ is an S-coupled simulation; since it includes all S-coupled simulations it must be the largest.
2. $\preceq = \succeq^{-1}$ follows from the fact that if (S_1, S_2) is an S-coupled simulation, then (S_2^{-1}, S_1^{-1}) is also an S-coupled simulation.
3. If $P =_{cs} Q$ then $P(S_1 \cap S_2)Q$ for some S-coupled simulation (S_1, S_2); this implies $P(\preceq \cap \succeq)Q$. Conversely, if $P(\preceq \cap \succeq)Q$ then $P =_{cs} Q$ since $(\preceq, \succeq)$ is an S-coupled simulation. $\qquad\square$

The relation $\preceq$ is not transitive, as evidenced by $0 \preceq \tau \preceq \tau + a$ and $0 \not\preceq \tau + a$. In spite of this $=_{cs}$ is transitive:

Proposition 7. $=_{cs}$ is an equivalence relation.

Symmetry and reflexivity are easy to establish but transitivity is more difficult. Rather than giving a direct proof here we refer to our technical report [7].

As a simple example, consider a system P consisting of one master process and one slave. The master can either perform an action a, or tell the slave to start execution. The slave, when started, performs some internal computation to determine whether it should perform b or c. The system thus has an externally observable behaviour described by

$$P = a + \tau.(\tau.b + \tau.c)$$

where the first τ represents the communication between master and slave, and the second and third τ represent the internal computation in the slave resolving the choice between b and c. A more abstract description of the system, Q, may employ only one process which either does an a or internally chooses between b and c:

$$Q = a + \tau.b + \tau.c \ .$$

So P has a state $\tau.b + \tau.c$ representing the fact that a has been preempted but b and c are still both possible. There is no bisimilar state in Q, so P and Q are not observation equivalent. But they are cs-equivalent; consider the transition $a+\tau.(\tau.b+\tau.c) \xrightarrow{\tau} \tau.b+\tau.c$. This is simulated by Q remaining in the initial state, and $\tau.b + \tau.c \preceq a + \tau.b + \tau.c$ as required. Note that $\tau.b + \tau.c \succeq a + \tau.b + \tau.c$ does not hold.

3.2 Cs-congruence

Since we aim at a complete axiomatization we next consider the congruence induced by $=_{\mathrm{cs}}$. It turns out to have an attractive characterization:

Definition 8. P and Q are *cs-congruent*, written $P =_{\mathrm{cs}}^c Q$, if

1. $P =_{\mathrm{cs}} Q$,
2. P is stable iff Q is stable.

It may be surprising that this defines a congruence since the corresponding property of observation equivalence fails: there are unstable observation equivalent agents which are not observation congruent, for example $\tau.(\tau + a)$ and $\tau + a$. We proceed to show that $=_{\mathrm{cs}}^c$ is indeed a congruence.

Lemma 9. If $P =_{\mathrm{cs}} Q$, then $\alpha.P =_{\mathrm{cs}}^c \alpha.Q$.

Proof Directly from the definitions. □

Lemma 10. $P =_{\mathrm{cs}}^c Q$ iff for all R, $P + R =_{\mathrm{cs}} Q + R$.

Proof For the direction $\Longrightarrow$, assume $P =_{\mathrm{cs}}^c Q$ and choose an arbitrary R. By symmetry it suffices to prove $P + R \preceq Q + R$. So assume $P + R \xrightarrow{\alpha} P'$. We must establish that $Q + R \xRightarrow{\widehat{\alpha}} Q'$ with $P' \preceq Q'$. If the transition from $P + R$ emanates from R, then also $Q + R \xrightarrow{\alpha} P'$ and $P' \preceq P'$. So assume it emanates from P. If $\alpha \neq \tau$ then from $P \preceq Q$ we get $Q \xRightarrow{\alpha} Q'$ and thus also $Q + R \xRightarrow{\alpha} Q'$ with $P' \preceq Q'$. So assume that P and thus also Q are unstable, and that $P \xrightarrow{\tau} P'$.

It is convenient to establish the more general result here that if $P \xRightarrow{\tau} P'$ there is a simulating sequence of transitions $Q + R \xRightarrow{\widehat{\tau}} Q'$ with $P' \preceq Q'$; the proof goes by induction of the depth of P'. First, from $P \preceq Q$ we get that Q can simulate $P \xRightarrow{\tau} P'$ with $Q \xRightarrow{\widehat{\tau}} Q'$ such that $P' \preceq Q'$. If this involves at least one τ-transition from Q, i.e. $Q \xRightarrow{\tau} Q'$, then also $Q + R \xRightarrow{\widehat{\tau}} Q'$ and we are done. So assume that $Q = Q'$, and thus $P' \preceq Q$.

If P' is stable, as in the base case of the induction, then also $P' \succeq Q$. But Q is unstable and thus has at least one τ-transition, and since Q is convergent $Q \xRightarrow{\tau} Q''$ for some stable Q''. So $P' \xRightarrow{\widehat{\tau}} P''$ with $P'' \succeq Q''$. But P' is stable so $P' = P''$, and Q'' is stable so $P' \preceq Q''$. In conclusion $Q + R \xRightarrow{\tau} Q''$ with $P' \preceq Q''$.

There remains the case where also P' is unstable; we will argue that then $P' \preceq Q + R$ and thus $Q + R \stackrel{\widehat{\tau}}{\Longrightarrow} Q + R$ is the required simulating transition. Let $P' \stackrel{\beta}{\longrightarrow} P''$ be any transition from P'. Thus $P \stackrel{\beta}{\Longrightarrow} P''$. If $\beta = \tau$ then by induction we get a simulating transition from $Q + R$. If $\beta \neq \tau$ then by $P' \preceq Q$ we get $Q \stackrel{\beta}{\Longrightarrow} Q'$ and thus also $Q + R \stackrel{\beta}{\Longrightarrow} Q'$ with $P'' \preceq Q'$.

For the direction $\Longleftarrow$, assume $P + R =_{cs} Q + R$ for all R. By choosing $R = 0$ we get that $P =_{cs} Q$. Assume that P is unstable and Q is stable; we will derive a contradiction and thus (by symmetry) $P =_{cs}^c Q$. Let the τ-transition from P be $P \stackrel{\tau}{\longrightarrow} P'$, and choose $R = \ell.0$, such that neither P nor Q has any ℓ-transitions. Since $P + R \stackrel{\tau}{\longrightarrow} P'$ there must be a simulating transition $Q + R \stackrel{\widehat{\tau}}{\Longrightarrow} Q'$ with $P' \preceq Q'$. But Q and R are stable, so $Q' = Q + R$. Since P' is convergent there is a P'' such that $P' \stackrel{\widehat{\tau}}{\Longrightarrow} P''$ where P'' is stable; again this must be simulated such that $P'' \preceq Q + R$. But P'' is stable so also $P'' \succeq Q + R$ must hold; this is impossible since $Q + R \stackrel{\ell}{\longrightarrow} 0$ and P'' has no ℓ-transition. $\square$

Lemma 11. If $P =_{cs}^c Q$ then for any R, $P + R =_{cs}^c Q + R$.

Proof Use the associativity of $+$ and Lemma 10 twice: $P =_{cs}^c Q$ implies that for all R' and R, $P + (R + R') =_{cs} Q + (R + R')$, i.e. $(P + R) + R' =_{cs} (Q + R) + R'$, which implies $P + R =_{cs}^c Q + R$. $\square$

We also get that $=_{cs}^c$ is an equivalence (from Lemma 10 and the fact that $=_{cs}$ is an equivalence), so collecting the results in this section we have:

Corollary 12. $=_{cs}^c$ is the largest congruence included in $=_{cs}$.

It should be mentioned that this result holds even if a parallel composition operator is added to the language. The relation between observation and cs-equivalence (congruence) is captured by the following two lemmas:

Lemma 13. If $P \approx Q$ then $P =_{cs} Q$

Proof Directly from the definitions, observing that $(\approx, \approx)$ is an S-coupled simulation. $\square$

Lemma 14. If $P \approx^c Q$ then $P =_{cs}^c Q$

Proof Directly from Lemma 10 and the corresponding result for observation congruence ([5, p. 153]), using Lemma 13: $P \approx^c Q$ implies $\forall R : P + R \approx Q + R$ implies $\forall R : P + R =_{cs} Q + R$ which implies $P =_{cs}^c Q$. $\square$

These implications are strict as seen by the following example:

$$a + \tau.(\tau.b + c) \stackrel{=_{cs}^c}{\underset{\not\approx}{}} a + \tau.b + c$$

However, for a special class of agents the converses of the last two lemmas hold, and we use this fact in the completeness proof in the next section.

4 Axiomatization

We base our axiomatization of cs-congruence on Milner's results on observation congruence; the following axiom system is sound and complete for observation congruence [5, p. 160]:

$$\text{Axioms } \mathcal{A}_2$$

A1 $P + Q = Q + P$
A2 $P + (Q + R) = (P + Q) + R$
A3 $P + P = P$
A4 $P + 0 = P$
A5 $\alpha.\tau.P = \alpha.P$
A6 $P + \tau.P = \tau.P$
A7 $\alpha.(P + \tau.Q) + \alpha.Q = \alpha.(P + \tau.Q)$

For cs-congruence we add a τ law and get axiom system $\mathcal{A}_{cs}$:

$$\text{Axioms } \mathcal{A}_{cs}$$

A1–A7
A8 $\tau.(P + \tau.Q) = P + \tau.Q$

A8 says that when a τ occurs immediately under another τ, then this outer τ can be removed. Thus, through this axiom agents can be reduced so that P is stable in any subagent of type $\tau.P$ (this is one of the key steps in the completeness proof below). Of course **A8** is sound for weaker congruences such as testing congruence, but these additionally satisfy further axioms such as $\alpha.P + \alpha.Q = \alpha.(\tau.P + \tau.Q)$, which do not hold for cs-equivalence in general.

Theorem 15. $\mathcal{A}_{cs}$ is sound for cs-congruence.

Proof All axioms are true if $=$ is replaced by $=_{cs}^c$. In view of Lemma 14 we only have to check **A8**. Note that $\tau.(P + \tau.Q) \xrightarrow{\tau} P + \tau.Q$ is simulated by $P + \tau.Q \overset{\widehat{\tau}}{\Longrightarrow} P + \tau.Q$ and that both sides of this axiom are unstable. □

The rest of this section is devoted to the proof that $\mathcal{A}_{cs}$ is complete. The proof contains several intricate points and it is substantially more complex than the corresponding result for observation congruence. The main idea is to show that each agent can be reduced to a normal form through $\mathcal{A}_{cs}$, and that equivalent normal forms are provably equal. In this respect the structure of our proof is similar to that for observation congruence, where Milner defines [5, p. 162] that P is a *full standard form* if

1. $P = \sum_{i=1}^{m} \alpha_i.P_i$, where each P_i is in full standard form,
2. Whenever $P \overset{\alpha}{\Longrightarrow} P'$ then $P \xrightarrow{\alpha} P'$,

and shows that for any P, there is a full standard form P' such that $\mathcal{A}_2 \vdash P = P'$ [5, pp. 163]. We have to introduce more requirements on full standard forms to obtain the normal forms suitable for our completeness proof.

Definition 16. $\widehat{P}$ is a *partial sum* of P if $P = \sum_{i \in I} \alpha_i.P_i$ and $\widehat{P} = \sum_{i \in J} \alpha_i.P_i$ and $J \subseteq I$.

Definition 17. P is a *normal form* if

1. $P = \sum_{i=1}^{m} \alpha_i.P_i$ where each P_i is a normal form,

2. Whenever $P \overset{\alpha}{\Longrightarrow} P'$ then $P \overset{\alpha}{\longrightarrow} P'$,
3. If $\tau.P'$ is a summand of P then P' is stable,
4. Whenever P has a summand of the form $\alpha.(\tau.P' + Q)$, then for any partial sum $\widehat{Q}$ of Q there is a summand $\alpha.R$ of P such that $R =^c_{cs} \tau.P' + \widehat{Q}$.

Below follows an example of an agent (left) and a normal form for it (right).

$$
\begin{aligned}
a.\tau.(\tau.b + \tau.c) =^c_{cs} \ & a.b + a.c + \\
& a.(\tau.b + b) + a.(\tau.c + c) + \\
& a.(\tau.b + b + c) + a.(\tau.c + b + c) + \\
& a.(\tau.b + \tau.c + b + c)
\end{aligned}
$$

Lemma 18. For any P there is a normal form N of equal or less depth such that $\mathcal{A}_{cs} \vdash N = P$.

Proof By induction on the depth of P. For the base case P has depth 0, then it is just a sum of 0, and **A3** suffices to rewrite P to 0, which is a normal form.

For the inductive step, Milner shows [5, pp. 163] how to rewrite any agent to a sum $\sum_{i=1}^{m} \alpha_i.P_i$ satisfying clause 2. (For this, axiom system $\mathcal{A}_2$ suffices.) By induction all P_i can be assumed to be normal forms. We next demonstrate that with the use of **A8**, P can be rewritten to satisfy clauses 3 and 4 and still satisfy clauses 1 and 2.

For clause 3, we show that any summand $\tau.P'$ of P where P' is unstable can be rewritten to P'. For such a summand $P' = \tau.P'' + R$ where $R = \sum_i \alpha_i.R_i$. Thus $\tau.P' = \tau.(\tau.P'' + R) =^c_{cs} \tau.P'' + R = P'$ by **A8**. So $\tau.P'$ can be replaced by the summands of P'; all these satisfy clause 3 since by induction P' is a normal form. Clearly this rewrite does not invalidate clause 2 since it does not introduce any new transitions $P \overset{\alpha}{\Longrightarrow} Q$. Also, it does not invalidate clause 1 since P'' and all R_i are, by induction, normal forms.

For clause 4, let a summand of P be $\alpha.(\tau.P' + Q + R)$. Then, by **A8** and **A7**,

$$
\begin{aligned}
\alpha.(\tau.P' + Q + R) &=^c_{cs} \alpha.(\tau.(\tau.P' + Q) + R) \\
&=^c_{cs} \alpha.(\tau.(\tau.P' + Q) + R) + \alpha.(\tau.P' + Q) \\
&=^c_{cs} \alpha.(\tau.P' + Q + R) + \alpha.(\tau.P' + Q)
\end{aligned}
$$

Thus the summand $\alpha.(\tau.P' + Q)$ can be added to P; in this way all required partial sums can be introduced. This operation does not invalidate clause 3 since it does not introduce new summands $\tau.P'$ where P' is unstable. Also, it does not invalidate clause 2 since any new transition $P \overset{\alpha}{\Longrightarrow} \widehat{Q}$ that it generates corresponds to one of the new summands $\alpha.\widehat{Q}$. However, it may invalidate clause 1 since in a new summand $\alpha.\widehat{Q}$ (where $\widehat{Q}$ is a partial sum), $\widehat{Q}$ is not necessarily a normal form—$\widehat{Q}$ may not satisfy clause 2 and 4. But by induction $\widehat{Q}$ is provably equivalent to a normal form. Rewriting all such summands to normal form produces the required normal form for P. This concludes the inductive step and the proof. $\square$

The reason for introducing clause 4 in the normal forms is to make possible the following lemma:

Lemma 19. Let P, Q be normal forms, $P \overset{\alpha}{\longrightarrow} P'$ and $Q \overset{\alpha}{\longrightarrow} Q'$, and $P' \preceq Q'$. Then there exists a U such that $Q \overset{\alpha}{\longrightarrow} U$ and $P' =_{cs} U$.

Proof The proof is by induction on the sum of the depths of P' and Q'. If P' is stable, as in the base case where $P' = Q' = 0$, then immediately $P' \succeq Q'$ whence $P' =_{cs} Q'$. So suppose P' is unstable. There are two cases:

1. For some P'', R it holds that $P' = \tau.P'' + R$ and $P'' \preceq Q'$. But P' is a normal form so P'' is stable; this implies $P'' \succeq Q'$, so $P'' =_{cs} Q'$, and we can write

$$P' =_{cs} \tau.Q' + R \ . \tag{$*$}$$

The idea in the following proof is to show that each summand $\beta.R'$ in R can be eliminated while preserving $(*)$. Put $R = \beta.R' + R''$. Because of $P' \preceq Q'$, there must exist a Q'' such that $Q' \stackrel{\widehat{\beta}}{\Longrightarrow} Q''$ and $R' \preceq Q''$. There are two sub-cases for this. The first sub-case is when $\beta = \tau$ and $R' \preceq Q'$. Then $P' =_{cs} \tau.Q' + \tau.R' + R''$. But P is in normal form so R' must be stable, and therefore $R' \succeq Q'$ and $R' =_{cs} Q'$ so

$$P' =_{cs} \tau.Q' + \tau.Q' + R'' =_{cs} \tau.Q' + R'' \ .$$

The second sub-case is when $Q' \stackrel{\beta}{\Longrightarrow} Q''$ such that $R' \preceq Q''$, and since Q is a normal form $Q' \stackrel{\beta}{\longrightarrow} Q''$. The depths of R' and Q'' are less than the depths of P' and Q', so by induction there exists a Q''' such that $Q' \stackrel{\beta}{\longrightarrow} Q'''$ and $R' =_{cs} Q'''$. Let $Q' = \beta.Q'''+T$. Then

$$P' =_{cs} \tau.(\beta.Q''' + T) + \beta.Q''' + R'' =_{cs} \tau.(\beta.Q''' + T) + R'' =_{cs} \tau.Q' + R''$$

where the middle equality follows from **A6** and **A3**.
In conclusion, we have shown that if $R = \beta.R' + R''$ then $P' =_{cs} \tau.Q' + R''$. By doing this repeatedly we find that $(*)$ holds if we replace R by 0, so $P' =_{cs} \tau.Q' =_{cs} Q'$, so we fulfil the lemma by $U = Q'$.

2. For no summand $\tau.P''$ of P' does it hold that $P'' \preceq Q'$. Then, because of $P' \preceq Q'$, for each $P' \stackrel{\beta}{\longrightarrow} P''$ there is a corresponding $Q' \stackrel{\beta}{\Longrightarrow} Q''$ (and since Q' is a normal form $Q' \stackrel{\beta}{\longrightarrow} Q''$) such that $P'' \preceq Q''$. Both P'' and Q'' are of less depth than P' and Q', respectively, so by induction there exists a Q''' such that $Q' \stackrel{\beta}{\longrightarrow} Q'''$ and $P'' =_{cs} Q'''$.
Let $\widehat{Q'}$ be the partial sum of Q' consisting of only such summands $\beta.Q'''$. That is, $\beta.Q'''$ is a summand of $\widehat{Q'}$ if and only if there exists a P'' such that $P' \stackrel{\beta}{\longrightarrow} P''$ and $P'' =_{cs} Q'''$. Then $P' \preceq \widehat{Q'}$, since for each transition of P' there is a simulating transition in $\widehat{Q'}$, and conversely $P' \succeq \widehat{Q'}$ since only summands which have simulating counterparts in P' are included in $\widehat{Q'}$. In other words, $P' =_{cs} \widehat{Q'}$.

Now P' is unstable, so Q' must also be unstable (since each transition $\stackrel{\beta}{\longrightarrow}$ from P' is simulated by Q'). Then also $\widehat{Q}$ is unstable (there is a $P' \stackrel{\tau}{\longrightarrow} P''$ so there must be a $Q' \stackrel{\tau}{\longrightarrow} Q''$ such that $P'' =_{cs} Q''$, and therefore $\tau.Q''$ is a summand of $\widehat{Q}$). Furthermore, $\widehat{Q}$ is a partial sum of Q' so, since Q is a normal form, there is a transition $Q \stackrel{\alpha}{\longrightarrow} R =_{cs} \widehat{Q} =_{cs} P'$. Thus we fulfil the lemma with $U = R$. $\square$

The lemma above enables the key result that observation congruence and cs-congruence coincide on normal forms. So our completeness proof goes through by a reduction to the completeness of $\mathcal{A}_2$ for observation congruence.

Lemma 20. Let P, Q be normal forms. Then $P =_{cs} Q$ iff $P \approx Q$, and $P =_{cs}^c Q$ iff $P \approx^c Q$.

Proof In view of Lemmas 13 and 14 it suffices to establish the directions $\Longrightarrow$. For the equivalences, we show that

$$\{(P,Q) : P =_{cs} Q \text{ and } P, Q \text{ normal forms}\}$$

is a weak bisimulation. So assume that P, Q are normal forms, $P =_{cs} Q$, and $P \xrightarrow{\alpha} P'$. Then $Q \xRightarrow{\hat{\alpha}} Q'$ with $P' \preceq Q'$. If $\alpha = \tau$ then P' must be stable, so we immediately get $P' \succeq Q'$, which implies $P' =_{cs} Q'$. Otherwise $Q \xRightarrow{\alpha} Q'$, and since Q is a normal form this means $Q \xrightarrow{\alpha} Q'$. Then Lemma 19 says that for some Q'', $Q \xrightarrow{\alpha} Q''$ with $P' =_{cs} Q''$ as required (P and Q are both normal forms, so P', Q' and Q'' must also be normal forms).

For the congruences, assume $P =_{cs}^c Q$ and $P \xrightarrow{\alpha} P'$. Then $Q \xRightarrow{\hat{\alpha}} Q'$ with $P' \preceq Q'$. If the transition involves at least one action, i.e. $Q \xRightarrow{\alpha} Q'$, then as above we get $Q \xrightarrow{\alpha} Q''$ with $P' =_{cs} Q''$ which, with the first part of this lemma, implies $P' \approx Q''$ as required. If not, then $\alpha = \tau$ and $Q' = Q$. Since P is a normal form P' must be stable, so $P' =_{cs} Q$. But P is unstable, so (by $=_{cs}^c$) Q must be unstable, i.e. $Q \xrightarrow{\tau} Q''$ for some Q''. Thus $P' \xRightarrow{\hat{\tau}} P''$ with $P'' \succeq Q''$; since P' is stable $P' = P''$, i.e. $P' \succeq Q''$; further Q'' is stable (because Q is a normal form) so $P' =_{cs} Q''$, and since these are normal forms $P' \approx Q''$ by the first part of the lemma. $\quad\square$

Theorem 21. $\mathcal{A}_{cs}$ is complete for cs-congruence.

Proof Assume $P =_{cs}^c Q$. By Lemma 18 there are normal forms P' and Q' such that $\mathcal{A}_{cs} \vdash P = P'$ and $\mathcal{A}_{cs} \vdash Q = Q'$. Since $\mathcal{A}_{cs}$ is sound, $P' =_{cs}^c Q'$, which with Lemma 20 gives that $P' \approx^c Q'$. Then by [5, p. 164] (Proposition 18) $\mathcal{A}_2 \vdash P' = Q'$. Since $\mathcal{A}_{cs}$ includes $\mathcal{A}_2$ we get $\mathcal{A}_{cs} \vdash P = Q$. $\quad\square$

5 Conclusion

We have provided a complete axiomatization of cs-congruence ($=_{cs}^c$) by adding a new τ-law,

$$\tau.(\tau.P + Q) = \tau.P + Q$$

to the axiomatization of observation congruence ($\approx^c$). Compared with the corresponding result for $\approx^c$ [5], our normal forms make more requirements on agents: No two τ may occur after each other (if so the first τ can be removed with the new law), and if $\alpha.(\tau.P + Q + R)$ is a summand then so is $\alpha.(\tau.P + Q)$ (this summand can be added with the new and old τ laws). We have shown that any agent can be rewritten to normal form, and that $\approx^c$ and $=_{cs}^c$ coincide on normal forms.

Our proofs are substantially different from any completeness result we know, and more complicated than the corresponding result for $\approx^c$. One reason is that induction arguments are harder in the absence of bisimulations. Completeness proofs for e.g. testing equivalence [2] are also complicated but their understanding are facilitated by the intuitive denotational models of processes as acceptance trees. We know of no such model for $=_{cs}^c$.

A natural question is whether our axiomatization can be extended to the *finite-state* agents obtained by adding recursion to the simple language with "." and "+". We conjecture that adding the laws **R1–R5** of [5] will provide a complete inference system, but the details of the proof remain to be worked out. In the presence of recursion a subtlety arises: Proposition 7 (that $=_{cs}$ is an equivalence relation) breaks down when we consider *divergent* agents (agents with infinite sequences of τ-transitions).

This can be demonstrated by the following small example, where Ω is a divergent agent (e.g. $\Omega \stackrel{\text{def}}{=} \tau.\Omega$):

$$a.b =_{cs} a.b + a.\Omega =_{cs} a.b + a$$

whereas

$$a.b \neq_{cs} a.b + a \ !$$

If we want to generalize $=_{cs}$ to divergent agents it appears that we lose one of its main advantages, namely a characterization admitting case analysis over single transitions. A possible generalization is the following: A *weakly coupled* (*W-coupled*) simulation is a pair $(\mathcal{S}_1, \mathcal{S}_2)$, where $\mathcal{S}_1$ and $\mathcal{S}_2^{-1}$ are simulations, that satisfies both of the following:

1. If $P\mathcal{S}_1 Q$ then $\exists Q' : Q \stackrel{\widehat{\tau}}{\Longrightarrow} Q'$ and $P\mathcal{S}_2 Q'$.
2. If $P\mathcal{S}_2 Q$ then $\exists P' : P \stackrel{\widehat{\tau}}{\Longrightarrow} P'$ and $P'\mathcal{S}_1 Q$.

Two agents are *cw-equivalent* if they are related by both components of a W-coupled simulation. As can be seen the notion of stability does not enter the definition. Where the S-coupled simulations were coupled at stable states, the weakly coupled simulations are coupled through the relation $\stackrel{\widehat{\tau}}{\Longrightarrow}$. This entails an equivalence which coincides with cs-equivalence for convergent agents. The proof is standard; in particular transitivity follows from the fact that the component-wise composition of two W-coupled simulations is a W-coupled simulation. For convergent agents, an S-coupled simulation can be built from a W-coupled, and vice versa. Essentially, to build a W-coupled simulation it is necessary to add pairs to the S-coupled simulation in order to achieve weak coupling (broadly speaking, the relation must be "closed" under $\stackrel{\widehat{\tau}}{\Longrightarrow}$). Conversely, to build an S-coupled simulation from a W-coupled it is necessary to remove some pairs which might invalidate the S-coupling. Note that these results imply Proposition 7. Full proof details can be found in [7].

A considerable number of alternative equivalences has been axiomatized by van Glabbeek [10]. These are however based on a framework without unobservable actions, and are thus not directly comparable to our work. Some of the equivalences have been generalized to cater for unobservables, the *stable bisimulation* equivalence [8] is one that is close to cs-equivalence[4]. A stable bisimulation is a binary relation $\mathcal{S}$ such that $P\mathcal{S}Q$ implies

$$\text{if } P \stackrel{s}{\Longrightarrow} P' \text{ and } P' \text{ is stable, then } \exists Q' : Q \stackrel{s}{\Longrightarrow} Q' \text{ and } P'\mathcal{S}Q'$$

and vice versa. Here s is a *sequence* of actions, so in order to verify that a relation is a stable bisimulation it is necessary to analyze all possible sequences of transitions from all states. This means that stable bisimulation equivalence can be difficult to establish for large examples. It lies between $=_{cs}$ and testing equivalence (the intersection of the two components of a coupled simulation is a stable bisimulation), and its distinguishing axiom (which does not hold for $=_{cs}$) is $\alpha.P+\alpha.Q = \alpha.(\tau.P+\tau.Q)$. For divergent processes stable bisimulation equivalence suffers from the same problem as $=_{cs}$: it is not transitive.

---

[4] This reference is hard to access; we base our exposition on personal communications from Rob van Glabbeek.

An alternative characterization in terms of *contrasimulations* remedies this: a relation S is a contrasimulation if PSQ implies

$$P \stackrel{s}{\Longrightarrow} P' \text{ implies } Q \stackrel{s}{\Longrightarrow} Q' \text{ and } Q'SP'$$

(note the reversed order in the consequent!), and P and Q are contrasimilar if PSQ and QSP for some contrasimulation S.

There are several other possible avenues of further work. Many other equivalences between observation equivalence and testing equivalence have recently been surveyed by van Glabbeek [9], and it remains to be seen if any of them is practically useful in the same way as cs-equivalence. Another idea is to implement a decision procedure for finite-state systems; an easy way would be to implement the normalization procedure, as sketched in the proof of Lemma 18, within the Concurrency Workbench [1] and then use the algorithm for observation equivalence. The algorithmic complexity of this is unclear—the normalization may generate an exponential blowup in the size of terms—and it would be interesting to determine whether there is a polynomial algorithm for cs-equivalence (observation equivalence has a polynomial algorithm but testing equivalence is PSPACE hard). However, the main practical motivation for cs-equivalence is in the method to verify that a pair of relations constitute a coupled simulation. We believe that tool development for support of this would be more rewarding (but also more time consuming).

Acknowledgement

We are grateful for extended discussions with Rob van Glabbeek on the axiomatization of stable bisimulation and similar equivalences. Rob also suggested the definition of weakly coupled simulations (in analogy with contrasimulations) to cater for divergent agents.

References

1. R. Cleaveland, J. Parrow, and B. Steffen. A semantics-based verification tool for finite-state systems. In E. Brinksma, G. Scollo, and C. A. Vissers, editors, *Protocol Specification, Testing, and Verification, IX*, pages 287–302. North-Holland, 1989.
2. M. Hennessy. *Algebraic Theory of Processes*. The MIT Press, 1988.
3. C. A. R. Hoare. *Communicating Sequential Processes*. Prentice-Hall International, 1985.
4. R. Milner. *A Calculus of Communicating Systems*, volume 92 of *Lecture Notes in Computer Science*. Springer-Verlag, Berlin, 1980.
5. R. Milner. *Communication and Concurrency*. Prentice Hall, 1989.
6. J. Parrow and P. Sjödin. Multiway synchronization verified with coupled simulation. In W. R. Cleaveland, editor, *Proceedings of CONCUR '92*, volume 630 of *Lecture Notes in Computer Science*, pages 518–533. Springer-Verlag, 1992.
7. J. Parrow and P. Sjödin. The complete axiomatization of cs-congruence. Research report, Swedish Institute of Computer Science, 1994. In preparation.
8. R. J. van Glaabeek. De semantiek van eidige, sequentiële processes met interne acties. Syllabus processemantieken, deel 2. Handwritten manuscript, in Dutch, 1988.
9. R. J. van Glaabeek. The linear time – branching time spectrum II. In E. Best, editor, *Proceedings of CONCUR '93*, volume 715 of *Lecture Notes in Computer Science*, pages 66–80. Springer-Verlag, 1993.
10. R. J. van Glabbeek. *Comparative Concurrency Semantics and Refinement of Actions*. PhD thesis, Free University of Amsterdam, The Netherlands, 1990.

Transition system specifications in stalk format with bisimulation as a congruence

V. van Oostrom & E.P. de Vink
Department of Mathematics and Computer Science, Vrije Universiteit
De Boelelaan 1081a, NL–1081 HV Amsterdam
oostrom@cs.vu.nl & vink@cs.vu.nl

Abstract A many-sorted variant, called stalk format, of the single sorted tyft-format for transition system specifications, introduced by Groote and Vaandrager, is proposed. The stalk format is shown to be a convenient formalism to express continuation-style transition systems for which the existing formats seem less adequate. Extending a similar result for the single sorted case, it holds that for an appropriate generalization of strong bisimilarity for the present many-sorted setting, bisimulation with respect to a transition system specification in stalk format, is a congruence. The present format is compared with several existing ones in the literature, viz. De Simone-, GSOS- and pure tyft-format.

Keywords and phrases semantics of programming languages, Structured Operational Semantics, transition system specifications, bisimulation equivalence

1 Introduction

In providing an operational semantics for programming language concepts the Structural Operational Semantics (SOS) or Plotkin-style approach based on labeled transition systems is likely to be the most widely used technique. The behavior of an abstract machine executing the language under consideration is described using a set of syntax-driven axioms and rules. The steps made by the abstract machine, transitions from one configuration to another, together with the performance of some externally observable action, are exactly those which can be derived from the axioms using the rules of this collection. Referring to the collection of steps as a *transition system* one may call the description itself, the axioms and rules, a *transition system specification*.

Presently, all core example languages for concurrency theory have been given an operational semantics using SOS, e.g., CCS, TCSP, ACP and Meije and many more variants and extensions. However, the general theory of transition system specifications has, compared to the bulk of the applications, attracted little attention. A small number of formats for transition system specifications have been proposed in the literature, [Sim84, BIM88, GV92, Gro90, Fok93], viz. so-called De Simone, GSOS, tyft/tyxt, ntyft/ntyxt and tree rule format, respectively. Main questions studied are the bisimulation and completed trace congruences induced by the type of transition system specifications.

In the present paper we propose yet another format for transition system specifications which is suitably expressive to describe continuation style transition systems, as has been frequently used in comparative (metric) semantics, e.g., [AB88, AR89, Bak91, EV93]. The transition system specifications of these papers do not fit in the formats mentioned above, but will fit into the format introduced by the present paper, that we will call the *stalk* format. One can view it as a many sorted extension of the single sorted tyft-format without lookahead, but allowing a restricted type of contexts, so-called smooth stalks, in the rules of a specification. It will be illustrated that a transition system specification for such a concept as process creation fit neatly within the stalk format. As will be discussed below in Section 4, the stalk format does not precisely generalize the tyft format of [GV92] due to the absence of lookahead. A technical condition on variable occurrences, necessitated by the proof of the congruence theorem, prohibits the stalk format of having such a facility. However, there is, to our opinion, convincing evidence for the stalk format to be an appropriate vehicle for defining continuation style transition systems (cf. the report version [OV93] of this paper).

In order to advocate the further adequacy of the stalk format we have shown strong *bisimilarity,* translated to the many sorted setting of the format, to be a *congruence* for transition systems induced by specification adhering to the stalk format. (See the technical report [OV93].) Such a result is desired for the familiar reasons. Firstly, identification based on observations may not be dependent upon the incidental details of a particular transition system specification. Equivalent terms should yield the same behavior in all contexts. Secondly, in the presence of a general theorem ad hoc maneuvers for particular instances of transition systems can be avoided. Checking that the transition system fits into the format will give bisimulation as a congruence for free!

It is argued in this paper that the stalk format is suited for the operational modeling of intricate (abstract) programming concepts. On syntactical grounds the present format can be considered an extension of GSOS without negative premises and of tyft without lookahead. However, further investigation should clarify the relative position of the expressiveness of the stalk format. In particular a characterization of completed trace congruences in terms of a special bisimulation would facilitate the comparison with general GSOS and pure tyft.

On the other hand, for particular cases it seems possible, following [BV92a] to discard the many sortedness of the format. It therefore may very well be the case that the restrictions of the format (contexts in the shape of smooth stalks) can be relaxed. Also, if the congruence result of the paper can be generalized (which seems to require amendments as just indicated) to cope with lookahead as for tyft, an even more general format may be obtained.

The structure of the remainder is now as follows. After mathematical preliminaries in the next section, in Section 3 the stalk format will be introduced and its convenience and expressiveness is illustrated, the notion of contextual bisimilarity is defined and it is stated that this observational equivalence is substitutive. In conclusion, Section 4, the comparison of the stalk format and De Simone, GSOS and tyft together with open problems are discussed.

2 Mathematical preliminaries

A *many-sorted signature* Σ is a triple $\Sigma = (\mathcal{S}, \mathcal{F}, \mathcal{V})$ where $\mathcal{S}$ is the non-empty set of sorts or types, $\mathcal{F}$ is the set of function symbols with associated functionality and $\mathcal{V}$ is the set of $\mathcal{S}$-sorted variables. We let $\mathbb{T}(\Sigma)$ denote the collection of well-sorted (not necessarily closed) terms over Σ, and let $T(\Sigma)$ denote the collection of all closed well-sorted terms. A substitution $\sigma{:}\mathcal{V} \to \mathbb{T}(\Sigma)$ is called closed iff $\sigma(v) \in T(\Sigma)$ for all $v \in \mathcal{V}$. The notions of a one-hole context $C[\cdot]{:}S \to S'$ and of a multi-hole context $C[\cdot]{:}S_1 \times \cdots \times S_k \to S$ are defined as usual.

Definition 2.1 Let Σ be a many-sorted signature and $\mathcal{A}$ be a set, of the elements are referred to as actions or labels. A *transition system specification* $\mathcal{T}$ for Σ over $\mathcal{A}$ is a triple $\mathcal{T} = (\Sigma, \mathcal{A}, \mathcal{R})$ where $\mathcal{R}$ is a collection of rules of the form

$$\frac{t_i \overset{a_i}{\to} t_i' \quad (i \in I)}{t \overset{a}{\to} t'}$$

with I some index-set and, for all $i \in I$, $t_i, t_i', t, t' \in \mathbb{T}(\Sigma)$, $a_i, a \in \mathcal{A}$.

Example 2.2 (Basic Process Algebra with δ and ϵ, [GV92] Example 3.4) Let a be a typical element of a set Act of so-called actions. Put $Act_{\checkmark} = Act \cup \{\checkmark\}$ where $\checkmark$ is some new symbol. $Act_{\checkmark}$ is ranged over by α. The signature Σ_{bpa} is single-sorted, with only sort S, say, and the following function symbols:

$$a, \delta, \epsilon{:}S, \text{ for } a \in Act \qquad \text{'}\cdot\text{', '+'}{:}S \times S \to S$$

employing infix notion for '$\cdot$' and '+'. The transition system specification $\mathcal{T}_{bpa}$ for Σ_{bpa} over Act has as its axioms and rules the schemes $(\text{Act})_a$, (Eps), $(\text{Seq})_1$, $(\text{Seq})_2$, $(\text{Alt})_1$ and $(\text{Alt})_2$ given as follows:

$$a \overset{a}{\to} \epsilon \qquad (\text{Act})_a \qquad\qquad \epsilon \overset{\checkmark}{\to} \delta \qquad (\text{Eps})$$

$$\frac{x \overset{a}{\to} x'}{x \cdot y \overset{a}{\to} x' \cdot y} \quad (\text{Seq})_1 \qquad \frac{x \overset{\checkmark}{\to} x' \quad y \overset{\alpha}{\to} y'}{x \cdot y \overset{\alpha}{\to} y'} \quad (\text{Seq})_2$$

$$\frac{x \overset{\alpha}{\to} x'}{x + y \overset{\alpha}{\to} x'} \quad (\text{Alt})_1 \qquad \frac{y \overset{\alpha}{\to} y'}{x + y \overset{\alpha}{\to} y'} \quad (\text{Alt})_2$$

with x, x', y, y' variables in Σ_{bpa}.

3 The stalk format and contextual bisimulation

In this section we introduce a special kind of many-sorted signatures, called layered signature, in which the set of sorts is partially ordered. On the basis of the ordering of the sorts, one can distinguish certain one-hole contexts, referred to as smooth stalks. This type of contexts is, together with restrictions on variables, the main ingredient in the formulation of the notion of a transition system specification in so-called stalk format. After having introduced the appropriate notion of bisimilarity, referred to as contextual bisimulation, we are in a position to state that for transition system specifications in stalk format bisimulation is a congruence.

Definition 3.1 A pair $(\Sigma, \leq)$ is called a *layered* signature iff Σ is a many-sorted signature and $\leq$ a partial ordering, with a least element, of the sorts of Σ. We refer to the least sort of $(\Sigma, \leq)$ as the root type, notation S_{rt}. With $\mathrm{T}_{rt}(\Sigma)$ we denote the collection of closed terms over Σ of type S_{rt}.

Examples 3.2

(1) Clearly, every single-sorted signature can be considered a layered signature with sort S and $\{S\}$ trivially ordered. In particular, the signature Σ_{bpa} of Example 2.2 is layered.

(2) (uniform language with process creation, cf. [AB88, AR89]) Let $\mathcal{A}$ and $\mathcal{X}$ be fixed sets. $\mathcal{A}$ can be thought of as a collection of *atomic actions*, $\mathcal{X}$ can be thought of as a collection of *procedure names*. The many-sorted signature Σ_{pc} has two sorts, viz. S_r and S_s. The function symbols of Σ_{pc} are summarized as follows:

$$\text{E}\colon S_r \qquad `:'\colon S_s \times S_r \to S_r \qquad (\cdot,\cdot)\colon S_r \times S_r \to S_r$$
$$a, X\colon S_s \qquad \mathbf{new}(\cdot)\colon S_s \to S_s \qquad `;', `+'\colon S_s \times S_s \to S_s$$

(for each $a \in \mathcal{A}$, $X \in \mathcal{X}$). Σ_{pc} is made a layered signature $(\Sigma_{pc}, \leq_{pc})$ if we put $S_r <_{pc} S_s$.

In Examples 3.5 and 3.6 below we will present transition systems in so-called stalk format for the layered signatures just given.

Definition 3.3 Let $(\Sigma, \leq)$ be a layered signature.

(a) A *stalk* is a context $C[\cdot]$ with function symbols only from the root to the hole (considering a term as a downward branching tree).

(b) A stalk is called *proper* iff every function symbol has type strictly less than the type of the hole.

(c) A stalk is called *smooth* iff it is proper and the type of the function symbols is strictly ascending from the root to the hole.

(d) A one-hole context $C[\cdot]$ is called *proper* iff it is a closed (variable) instance of a proper stalk, i.e., $C[\cdot] \equiv \sigma(C'[\cdot])$ for some proper stalk $C'[\cdot]$ and closed substitution σ.

So a proper context $C[\cdot]$ with a hole of sort S, admits, on the path from the hole to the root only function symbols $f:S_1 \times \cdots \times S_k \rightarrow S'$ such that $S' < S$ with respect to the ordering of the layered signature $(\Sigma, \leq)$. There are no restrictions on other function symbol appearances. For a smooth stalk we demand that the function symbols appear *only* from the root to the hole. In addition the sorts of the function symbols and the hole should be strictly descending going up from the hole to the root.

We are now ready to give the definition of the stalk format for many-sorted transition system specifications. It turns out that, for a appropriate notion of bisimulation, bisimilarity with respect to a transition system specification in stalk format is a congruence.

Definition 3.4 Let $(\Sigma, \leq)$ be a layered signature. A transition system specification $\mathcal{T} = (\Sigma, \Lambda, \mathcal{R})$ over Σ is said to be in *stalk format*, with respect to $(\Sigma, \leq)$, iff every rule in $\mathcal{R}$ is of the format

$$\frac{B_i \xrightarrow{a_i} \gamma_i \quad (i \in I)}{B[g(x_1, \ldots, x_\ell)] \xrightarrow{a} B'}$$

where

(1) B_i, γ_i, $B[g(x_1, \ldots, x_\ell)]$, B' are of the root type

(2) $\mathrm{var}(B_i) \subseteq \mathrm{var}(B[g(x_1, \ldots, x_\ell)])$ $(i \in I)$

(3) every variable occurs at most once in $B[g(x_1, \ldots, x_\ell)]$

(4) γ_i, $i \in I$ are pairwise distinct variables

(5) $\mathrm{var}(B[g(x_1, \ldots, x_\ell)]) \cap \{\gamma_i \mid i \in I\} = \emptyset$

(6) $B[\cdot]$ is a *smooth* stalk

The first condition (1) captures the idea that transitions model the steps taken by some abstract machine executing the (abstract) language under consideration. Terms of the root sort represent the configurations of this machine. The last condition (6) means, intuitively, that the rules are not allowed to look inside the structure further than the first occurrence of a sort, i.e., deeper than the function symbol g. The remaining conditions, (2)–(5), are of a technical nature.

The second clause for the stalk format, viz. $var(B_i) \subseteq var(B[g(x_1, \ldots, x_\ell)])$ $(i \in I)$, is crucial for the set-up of the proof as is given for Theorem 3.8 in [OV93]. (Incorporation of this condition implies that the stalk format does not strictly subsumes the tyft-format for the single-sorted case. See Section 4.)

In [GV92] various counter examples (Examples 5.11.1 through 5.11.5) are constructed which show that, generally, for the single-sorted tyft-format, bisimulation is no longer a congruence in case *any* of the conditions (3) through (6) in Definition 3.4 is omitted. We observe that the transition system specification of $P(BPA_\delta^\epsilon)$, on which the counter examples are based, fits into the stalk format (cf. Example 3.5 below). Therefore the examples given in [GV92] illustrate that also for the present format, the conditions are essential for Theorem 3.8 to hold. With respect to condition (2) of Definition 3.5, Groote and Vaandrager show, translated to the presentation here, the necessity of

$$var(B_i) \subseteq var(B[g(x_1, \ldots, x_\ell)]) \cup \{\, \gamma_i \mid i \in I \,\} \qquad (3.1)$$

(in combination with a non-circularity condition that we suppress here). As pointed out above, we need, for technical reasons, a stronger requirement. At the moment, it is an open question whether or not the more liberal version, equation (3.1), can be used instead. We will not copy the counter examples of [GV92] but refer the reader to the particular paper.

Example 3.5 The transition system specification $\mathcal{T}_{bpa}$ over the single-sorted signature Σ_{bpa} of Example 2.2 is in stalk format. The only stalk involved is the empty context. (In fact, $\mathcal{T}_{bpa}$ is in the so-called De Simone format of [Sim84], which is a special subcase of a transition system specification in stalk format. See Section 4.)

Example 3.6 For a more illustrative example we turn to a simple uniform language with process creation. This language is a prominent example of an (abstract) imperative programming language, for which the use of a many-sorted signature in describing its transitional behavior is pivotal when aiming for a comparison with an equivalent continuation-style denotational semantics. We base our treatment on the presentation of [AB88, BV91] and refer to these papers for a more detailed explanation of the various transition schemes.

The transition system specification $\mathcal{T}_{pc}$ is given by $\mathcal{T}_{pc} = (\Sigma_{pc}, \mathcal{A}, \{\,(\text{Act})_a, (\text{Rec})_X, (\text{Seq}), (\text{Alt})_1, (\text{Alt})_2, (\text{New}), (\text{Par})_1, (\text{Par})_2 \mid a \in \mathcal{A}, X \in \mathcal{X}\,\})$. Thus the configurations are terms of the layered signature Σ_{pc} of type S_r, the labels are taken from the pre-assumed set $\mathcal{A}$, ranged over by α. Furthermore, we have besides the transition schemes (Seq), (New), (Alt)$_1$, (Alt)$_2$, (New), (Par)$_1$ and (Par)$_2$, a rule (Act)$_a$ and a rule (Rec)$_X$ for each constant $a \in \mathcal{A}$ and $X \in \mathcal{X}$. The set of rules (Rec)$_X$ for $X \in \mathcal{X}$, is based on some given declaration, that determines a body D_X, i.e., a closed term of sort S_s, for the procedure name X. This scheme models the usual body replacement rule. Below s, s_1, s_2 (r, r', r_1, r_1', r_2, r_2') are variables of type S_s (S_r).

$$a : r \xrightarrow{a} r \qquad \text{(Act)}_a \qquad \qquad \frac{D_X : r \xrightarrow{\alpha} r'}{X : r \xrightarrow{\alpha} r'} \qquad \text{(Rec)}_X$$

$$\frac{s_1 : (s_2 : r) \xrightarrow{\alpha} r'}{(s_1 ; s_2) : r \xrightarrow{\alpha} r'} \qquad \text{(Seq)} \qquad \qquad \frac{(s : \mathrm{E}, r) \xrightarrow{\alpha} r'}{\mathbf{new}(s) : r \xrightarrow{\alpha} r'} \qquad \text{(New)}$$

$$\frac{s_1 : r \xrightarrow{\alpha} r'}{(s_1 + s_2) : r \xrightarrow{\alpha} r'} \qquad \text{(Alt)}_1 \qquad \qquad \frac{s_2 : r \xrightarrow{\alpha} r'}{(s_1 + s_2) : r \xrightarrow{\alpha} r'} \qquad \text{(Alt)}_2$$

$$\frac{r_1 \xrightarrow{\alpha} r_1'}{(r_1, r_2) \xrightarrow{\alpha} (r_1', r_2)} \qquad \text{(Par)}_1 \qquad \qquad \frac{r_2 \xrightarrow{\alpha} r_2'}{(r_1, r_2) \xrightarrow{\alpha} (r_1, r_2')} \qquad \text{(Par)}_2$$

Note that we have both rules for the S_s-type (viz. the schemes (Act) through (New)) as well as for the S_r-type (viz. the schemes (Par)$_1$ and (Par)$_2$). Most striking are the rules for procedures, sequential composition and the **new**-construct, for which the left-hand side of the premise is not structurally simpler than the left-hand side of the conclusion. For the constant E, representing termination, there is no rule or axiom.

Next we turn to the notion of so-called contextual bisimulation, the observational equivalence for the stalk format that generalizes the usual notion of bisimilarity.

Definition 3.7 Let $(\Sigma, \le)$ be a layered signature, $\mathcal{A}$ a set and $\to\; \subseteq \mathrm{T}_{rt}(\Sigma) \times \mathcal{A} \times \mathrm{T}_{rt}(\Sigma)$.

(a) A binary relation $[*] \subseteq \mathrm{T}(\Sigma)^2$ is called a *contextual bisimulation* with respect to ' $\to$ ' iff

   (i) '$[*]$' is sort consistent, i.e., if $u \, [*] \, v$ then u, v are of the same sort;

   (ii) $u \, [*] \, v$ for $u, v \in \mathrm{T}(\Sigma)$ of sort S, implies for all proper contexts $C[\cdot]{:}S \to S_{rt}$ and all $a \in \mathcal{A}$

$$C[u] \xrightarrow{a} D \Rightarrow \exists E {:} \bigl(C[v] \xrightarrow{a} E\bigr) \wedge \bigl(D \, [*] \, E\bigr) \; \& $$
$$C[v] \xrightarrow{a} E \Rightarrow \exists D {:} \bigl(C[u] \xrightarrow{a} D\bigr) \wedge \bigl(D \, [*] \, E\bigr)$$

(b) Two elements $u, v \in \mathrm{T}(\Sigma)$ are called *contextual bisimilar*, notation $u \, [\leftrightarrow] \, v$, iff $u \, [*] \, v$ for some contextual bisimulation '$[*]$'.

The main result of the paper, generalizing the congruence result of [GV92], stating that contextual bisimulation for transition system specifications in stalk format is substitutive, now follows.

Theorem 3.8 Let $\mathcal{T} = (\Sigma, A, \mathcal{R})$ be a transition system specification over the layered signature $(\Sigma, \le)$ in stalk format. Then it holds that contextual bisimulation $[\leftrightarrow]$ with respect to $\mathcal{T}$ is a congruence for Σ.

Proof See the technical report [OV93]. □

4 Comparison and future work

In positioning the proposed stalk format, let us first describe, translated to our present setting, the De Simone, GSOS and tyft format.

The De Simone format [Sim84] which is historically the first format introduced, allows rules of the form

$$\frac{x_i \xrightarrow{a_i} y_i \quad (i \in I)}{f(x_1, \ldots, x_\ell) \xrightarrow{a} t}$$

where the variables x_k, y_i ($1 \leq k \leq \ell, i \in I$) are all distinct, $I \subseteq \{1, \ldots, \ell\}$ and the term t is a so-called architectural expression (the definition of which does not matter for the discussion here), which amongst others, imposes a linearity condition on the variables of t, and, more particularly, satisfies $var(t) \subseteq \{z_1, \ldots z_\ell\}$ where $z_k \equiv x_k$ if $k \notin I$ and $z_k \equiv y_k$ otherwise.

The form of a GSOS rule or, as it is called in [BIM88], a Structured Transition Rule is the following

$$\frac{x_k \xrightarrow{a_{ij}} y_{ij} \quad (i \in I, j \in J) \qquad x_k \overset{b_{ik}}{\nrightarrow} (i \in I', k \in K)}{f(x_1, \ldots, x_\ell) \xrightarrow{a} t}$$

where x_i, y_{ij} ($1 \leq k \leq \ell, j \in J$) are all different variables $I, I' \subseteq \{1, \ldots, \ell\}$ and $var(t) \subseteq \{x_i, y_{ij} \mid 1 \leq i \leq \ell, j \in J\}$. The antecedents $x_i \overset{b_{ik}}{\nrightarrow}$ are so-called *negative* premises and express the *absence* of any transition $x_i \xrightarrow{b_{ik}} t_{ik}$ (for the current instance of x_i).

Finally, a tyft rule of [GV92] fits into the format

$$\frac{t_i \xrightarrow{a_i} y_i \quad (i \in I)}{f(x_1, \ldots, x_\ell) \xrightarrow{a} t}$$

where the variables x_k, y_i ($1 \leq k \leq \ell, i \in I$) are all distinct, and following from an additional well-foundedness and freeness condition, $var(t) \subseteq \{x_k, y_i \mid 1 \leq k \leq \ell, i \in I\}$. The auxiliary condition demands that a variable may occur as right-hand side of a premise only if any variable in the left-hand side of the premise is either one of the variables $x_1, \ldots, x_\ell$ or, otherwise, may already have occurred as right-hand side of a premise. (This is a rephrasing of the inductivity requirement in the presentation of the tyft format in [Rut92].) Thus a rule of the form, taken from [BK88],

$$\frac{x \xrightarrow{a_1} x_1 \qquad x_1 \xrightarrow{a_2} x_2 \qquad \ldots \qquad x_n \xrightarrow{a_n} \mathrm{E}}{[x] \xrightarrow{a} \mathrm{E}}$$

where $x, x_1, \ldots, x_n$ are variables, E is a constant and $[\cdot]$ is unary function symbol, is permitted in the tyft format. This feature, referred to as lookahead, is not allowed by the stalk-format (for otherwise the present proof of Theorem 3.8 would not hold). In the transition system specifications of [GV92] also rules in the so-called tyxt-format are allowed. Since such rules can be replaced using rules in tyft-format only without changing the induced set of transitions, we do not consider them in the comparison below.

A first difference, in comparing the stalk format to the three formats given above, concerns the many-sortedness of the former vs. the single-sortedness of the latter three. The many-sortedness is not an essential distinction, since following [BV92a], many-sortedness can be, so to speak, coded into the transition schemes by ensuring the well-sortedness of the $x_1, \ldots, x_\ell$ by adding extra premises $x_i \xrightarrow{\checkmark} sort(S_i)$ and rules

$$\frac{x_i \xrightarrow{\checkmark} sort(S_i) \quad (1 \leq i \leq k)}{f(x_1, \ldots, x_k) \xrightarrow{\checkmark} sort(S)}$$

for $f{:}S_1 \times \cdots \times S_k \rightarrow S$, where $\checkmark$ is a new symbol and the $sort(S')$ are new constants, one for each $S' \in \mathcal{S}$. However, the many-sortedness is natural in the context of continuation-style operational semantics. In fact, main inspiration for the formulation of a transition system specification in stalk format for which bisimulation is a congruence are the studies in comparative semantics dealing with resumptions/continuations. Cf., e.g., [AB88, AR89, Bak91, BV92b, EV93]. There transition system specifications not fitting in the De Simone, GSOS and tyft formats are used as a basis for an operational semantics to be compared with a denotational one.

A second, more decisive, difference between the stalk formats and the others concerns the function symbols allowed to occur in the left-hand side of the conclusion of a rule. Note that the De Simone, GSOS and tyft format only allow flat expressions $f(x_1, \ldots, x_\ell)$ with a *single* function symbol to occur, whereas the proposed format admits more general contexts, viz. smooth stalks (from which the format inherits its name). Several function symbols in the left-hand side of the conclusion of rules are the main attraction of the stalk format in that they facilitate a convenient description of a transition system, e.g., for the programming concepts discussed in the papers cited above. Thus, from a syntactic point of view, the stalk format is incomparable to the GSOS and tyft format and subsumes the De Simone format, as can be directly verified from the definitions.

In [GV92] it is argued that, from the semantic point of view of completed trance congruences, the tyft format is more distinctive then GSOS, which, in turn, is more distinctive than the De Simone format. By characterizing trace congruence by a specialized (bi)simulation one can classify (restricting to image finite transition system specifications) the various formats: completed trace congruence for De Simone format corresponds to failure equivalence $\equiv_F$ [Sim84, BKO88], for GSOS it corresponds to $\frac{2}{3}$-bisimulation equivalence $\underline{\leftrightarrow}_{\frac{2}{3}}$ [BIM88, LS89], while for the tyft format it corresponds to 2-nested simulation equivalence $\underline{\leftrightarrow}^2$ [GV92]. Since $\equiv_F \subseteq \underline{\leftrightarrow}_{\frac{2}{3}} \subseteq \underline{\leftrightarrow}^2$ the result then follows. In the perspective of such a relationship, future work includes the characterization of completed trace congruence for the stalk format. In order to see whether expressiveness is added, with respect to the GSOS and tyft formats, by the feature of multiple function symbols such a specialized (bi)simultion should be compared to $\frac{2}{3}$-bisimulation and 2-nested simulation equivalence.

Further research spawning off now involves the incorporation of negative premises along the lines of the ntyft/ntyxt format [Gro90, BG91] and of predicates as done in [BV93] and [Ver93] for the panth format. One might be optimistic about incorporation of the GSOS format by the stalk-format with negative premises, if such can be achieved. More detailed re-examination of the mere shape of a stalk (and the proof of Theorem 4.8) may lead to certain tree-like contexts replacing smooth stalk in the definition of the format. Also, such questions as finite vs. infinite expressibility and axiomatisations as is an issue in comparing the tree rule and tyft format in [Fok93] should be considered. Furthermore, questions concerning decidabliblity and termrewriting aspects should be addressed.

A final direction into which to extend the research concerns the derivation of denotational semantics from transition system specifications. In [Rut90] such a construction is achieved in a setting of metric spaces for the De Simone format. In [Rut92] this is extended, in a setting of non-wellfounded sets, to the (image finite) tyft-format. In both cases, the denotational semantics obtained is of a direct nature. The stalk format is inspired by continuation style models. It is open how to adapt the method of Rutten to deal with the stalk format in general and to deal, in particular, with the resumption/continuation operational and denotational meanings referred to above.

Acknowledgments The second author is grateful to Jaco de Bakker, Franck van Breugel, Jan Rutten, Frits Vaandrager and Herbert Wiklicky for their comments on the draft of this paper. We acknowledge also the comment of one of the STACS'94 referees.

References

[AB88]   P. America and J.W. de Bakker. Designing equivalent models for process creation. *Theoretical Computer Science*, 60:109–176, 1988.

[AR89]   P.H.M. America and J.J.M.M. Rutten. A parallel object-oriented language: Design and semantic foundations. In J.W. de Bakker, editor, *Languages for Parallel Architectures: Design, Semantics, Implementation Models*, pages 1–49. Wiley, 1989.

[Bak91] J.W. de Bakker. Comparative semantics for flow of control in logic programming without logic. *Information and Computation*, 91:123–179, 1991.

[BG91]   R. Bol and J.F. Groote. The meaning of negative premises in transition system specifications. In J. Leach Albert, B. Monien, and M. Rodríguez Artalejo, editors, *Proc. ICALP'91*, pages 481–494. LNCS 510, 1991.

[BIM88] B. Bloom, S. Istrail, and A.R. Meyer. Bisimulation can't be traced. In *Proc. Principles of Programming Languages*, pages 229–239. San Diego, 1988.

[BK88] J.W. de Bakker and J.N. Kok. Uniform abstraction, atomicity and contractions in the comparative semantics of Concurrent Prolog. In *Proc. of the International Conference on Fifth Generation Computer Systems*, pages 347–355. Institute for New Generation Computer Technology, 1988.

[BKO88] J.A. Bergstra, J.W. Klop, and E.-R. Olderog. Readies and failures in the algebra of communicating processes. *SIAM Journal on Computing*, 17:1134–1177, 1988.

[BV91] J.W. de Bakker and E.P. de Vink. CCS for OO and LP. In S. Abramsky and T.S.E. Maibaum, editors, *Proc. TAPSOFT'91, volume 2*, pages 1–28. LNCS 494, 1991.

[BV92a] J.C.M. Baeten and F.W. Vaandrager. An algebra for process creation. *Acta Informatica*, 29:303–334, 1992.

[BV92b] J.W. de Bakker and E.P. de Vink. Bisimulation semantics for concurrency with atomicity and action refinement. Technical Report CS–R9210, CWI, 1992.

[BV93] J.C.M. Baeten and C. Verhoef. A congruence theorem for structured operational semantics with predicates. In E. Best, editor, *Proc. CONCUR'93*, pages 477–492. LNCS 715, 1993.

[EV93] A. Eliëns and E.P. de Vink. Asynchronous rendez-vous in Distributed Logic Programming. In J.W. de Bakker, W.-P. de Roever, and G. Rozenberg, editors, *Semantics: Foundations and Applications*, pages 174–203. LNCS 666, 1993.

[Fok93] W.J. Fokkink. The tyft/tyxt format reduces to tree rules. Technical report, CWI, 1993. Draft. Extended abstract to appear in proc. Theoretical Aspects of Computer Science'94.

[Gro90] J.F. Groote. Transition system specifications with negative premises. In J.C.M. Baeten and J.W. Klop, editors, *Proc. CONCUR'90, Theories of Concurrency: Unification and Extension*, pages 332–342. LNCS 458, 1990.

[GV92] J.F. Groote and F.W. Vaandrager. Structured operational semantics and bisimulation as a congruence. *Information and Computation*, 100:202–260, 1992.

[LS89] K.G. Larsen and A. Skou. Bisimulation through probabilistic testing. In *Proc. Principles of Programming Languages*, pages 344–352, 1989.

[OV93]   V. van Oostrom and E.P. de Vink. Transition system specifications in stalk format with bisimulation as a congruence. Technical Report IR–332, Vrije Universiteit, 1993. Obtainable through anonymous ftp from `ftp.cs.vu.nl` as `/pub/oostrom/stalk.ps.Z`.

[Rut90]   J.J.M.M. Rutten. Deriving denotational models for bisimulation from Structured Operational Semantics. In M. Broy and C.B. Jones, editors, *Programming concepts and methods, proc. of the IFIP Working Group 2.2/2.3 Working Conference*, pages 155–177. North-Holland, 1990.

[Rut92]   J.J.M.M. Rutten. Processes as terms: non-well-founded models for bisimulation. *Mathematical Structures in Computer Science*, 2:257–275, 1992.

[Sim84]   R. de Simone. *Calculabilité et Expressivité dans l'Algèbre de Processus Parallèles MEIJE*. PhD thesis, Thèse de 3eme cycle, Université de Paris VII, 1984.

[Ver93]   C. Verhoef. A congruence theorem for structured operational semantics with predicates and negative premises. Report CSN-93/18, Eindhoven University of Technology, Eindhoven, 1993.

Decidability Questions for Bisimilarity of Petri Nets and Some Related Problems*

Petr Jančar

Dept. of Computer Science, University of Ostrava

Dvořákova 7, 701 00 Ostrava 1, Czech Republic

e-mail: jancar@oudec.osu.cz

Abstract

The main result is undecidability of bisimilarity for labelled (place / transition) Petri nets. The same technique applies to the (prefix) language equivalence and reachability set equality, which yields stronger versions with simpler proofs of already known results. The paper also mentions decidability of bisimilarity if one of the nets is deterministic up to bisimilarity. Another decidability result concerns semilinear bisimulations and extends the result of [CHM93] for Basic Parallel Processes (BPP).

1   Introduction

The relation of bisimulation plays an important role in the theory of parallelism and concurrency (cf. e.g.[M89]). An interesting question concerns decidability of bisimilarity for various classes of (models of) processes (see e.g. [CHS92],[CHM93] for recent results). In fact, BPP of [CHM93] are a special subclass of Petri nets. For the general (place/transition labelled) Petri nets, the problem was mentioned as open e.g. in [ABS91].

Using the halting problem for Minsky counter machines, this paper shows undecidability of the problem even if restricted to labelled Petri nets with a fixed static structure and 2 unbounded places.

The proof also shows undecidability of (prefix) language equivalence for the mentioned Petri nets with 2 unbounded places. This problem for (unrestricted) Petri nets is known to be undecidable due to Hack ([H75]); Valk and Vidal-Naquet ([VV81]) showed that nets with 4 and 5 unbounded places are sufficient for the undecidability.

---

*Partly supported by the Grant Agency of Czech Republic, Grant No. 201/93/2123

A similar technique applies also to equality of reachability sets, which yields undecidability of the problem even if restricted to Petri nets with 5 unbounded places. The known proofs in [B73], [H76] (see also [P81]) use Hilbert's 10th problem and Petri nets weakly computing polynomials; they do not put any bound on the number of unbounded places.

In this sense, the technique of the proof for bisimilarity also yields stronger versions of some known results. In addition, it shows them in a significantly simpler way.

This paper also contains some decidability results. The decidability of bisimilarity for one-to-one labelled (or "unlabelled") Petri nets is clear due to reducibility of (prefix) language equivalence of these nets to the reachability problem (cf. [H75], [M84]).
We mention here another reduction, the details of which are given in [J93], allowing an easy generalization for the nets which are deterministic up to bisimilarity.

Another subclass of labelled Petri nets for which the decidability of bisimilarity has been known is the above mentioned BPP of [CHM93] (isomorphic to Petri nets where each transition has one input place only). The proof employs a technique (suggested by Y.Hirshfeld) which is, in fact, more general – it implies decidability for the subclass where the bisimulation equivalence is a congruence w.r.t. (nonnegative vector) addition.
Here the result is further extended: we show that the existence of a semilinear bisimulation is sufficient for the decidability. It is completed by the fact, known from [ES69], that any congruence is semilinear.

Section 2 contains basic definitions, Section 3 the undecidability results, Section 4 the decidability results. Section 5 contains additional remarks (e.g. the relation to vector addition systems) and some hints for further work.

The paper is based on the report [J93].

2 Definitions

$\mathcal{N}$ denotes the set of nonnegative integers, A^* the set of finite sequences of elements of A.

A *(labelled) static net* is a tuple (P,T,F), (P,T,F,L) respectively, where P and T are finite disjoint sets of *places* and *transitions* respectively, $F : (P \times T) \cup (T \times P) \longrightarrow \mathcal{N}$ is a *flow function* (for $F(x,y) > 0$, there is an *arc* from x to y with *multiplicity* $F(x,y)$) and $L : T \longrightarrow A$ is a *labelling* (attaches an action name – from a set A – to each transition). By L we also denote the homomorphic extension $L : T^* \longrightarrow A^*$.

A *(labelled) Petri net* is a tuple $N = (S, M_0)$, where S is a (labelled) static net and M_0 is an *initial marking*, a *marking* M being a function $M : P \longrightarrow \mathcal{N}$. (A marking gives the number of *tokens* for each place). A transition t is *enabled* at a marking M, $M \xrightarrow{t}$, if $M(p) \geq F(p,t)$ for every $p \in P$. An enabled transition t may *fire* at a marking M yielding marking M', $M \xrightarrow{t} M'$, where $M'(p) = M(p) - F(p,t) + F(t,p)$ for all $p \in P$. In the natural way, the definitions can be extended for sequences of transitions $\sigma \in T^*$.

The *reachability set* of a Petri net N is defined as
$\mathcal{R}(N) = \{M \mid M_0 \xrightarrow{\sigma} M \text{ for some } \sigma \in T^*\}$.
A *place* $p \in P$ is *unbounded* if for any $k \in \mathcal{N}$ there is $M \in \mathcal{R}(N)$ s.t. $M(p) > k$.

The *(prefix) language* of a labelled Petri net N is defined as
$\mathcal{L}(N) = \{w \in A^* \mid M_0 \xrightarrow{\sigma} \text{ for some } \sigma \text{ with } L(\sigma) = w\}$.

Given two labelled static nets (P_1, T_1, F_1, L_1), (P_2, T_2, F_2, L_2), a binary relation $R \subseteq \mathcal{N}^{P_1} \times \mathcal{N}^{P_2}$ is a *bisimulation* if for all $(M_1, M_2) \in R$:

– for each $t_1 \in T_1$, $M_1 \xrightarrow{t_1} M_1'$, there is $t_2 \in T_2$ s.t. $L_1(t_1) = L_2(t_2)$ and $M_2 \xrightarrow{t_2} M_2'$, where $(M_1', M_2') \in R$
and conversely
– for each $t_2 \in T_2$, $M_2 \xrightarrow{t_2} M_2'$, there is $t_1 \in T_1$ s.t. $L_1(t_1) = L_2(t_2)$ and $M_1 \xrightarrow{t_1} M_1'$, where $(M_1', M_2') \in R$.

Two labelled Petri nets N_1, N_2 are *bisimilar* if there is a bisimulation relating their initial markings.

Notice that $\mathcal{L}(N_1) = \mathcal{L}(N_2)$ for bisimilar nets N_1, N_2.

3 Undecidability Results

A *counter machine* C with nonnegative counters $c_1, c_2, ..., c_m$ is a program

$$1 : COMM_1; \; 2 : COMM_2; \; ...... ; \; n : COMM_n$$

where $COMM_n$ is a $HALT$-command and $COMM_i$ ($i = 1, 2, ..., n - 1$) are commands of the following two types

1/ $c_j := c_j + 1$; *goto* k

2/ *if* $c_j = 0$ *then goto* k_1 *else* $(c_j := c_j - 1$; *goto* $k_2)$

assuming $1 \leq k, k_1, k_2 \leq n$, $1 \leq j \leq m$.

The set BS of *branching states* is defined as $BS = \{i \mid COMM_i$ is of the type 2$\}$.

It is well-known (cf. [M67]) that there is a fixed ("universal") counter machine C with two counters c_1, c_2 such that it is undecidable for given input values x_1, x_2 of c_1, c_2 whether C halts or not.

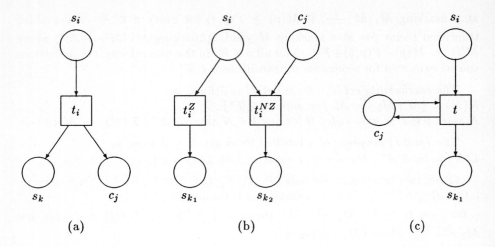

Figure 1:

Consider a counter machine C, with input values $x_1, x_2, ..., x_m$, in the above notation. We describe a construction of the *basic net* N_C which simulates C in a weak sense. By adding (x, y) we mean increasing $F(x, y)$ by 1 (mostly it means from 0 to 1 – adding one arc), unless otherwise stated. If $F(x, y)$ is not mentioned explicitly, it is equal to 0.

Construction of N_C

1. Let $c_1, c_2, ..., c_m$ (the counter part) and $s_1, s_2, ..., s_n$ (the state part) be places of N_C .

2. For $i = 1, 2, ..., n - 1$ add new transitions and arcs depending on the type of $COMM_i$:

Case 1: $COMM_i$ is $c_j := c_j + 1$; *goto* k :
   Add t_i with (s_i, t_i), (t_i, c_j), (t_i, s_k) (cf. Fig.1(a))

Case 2: $COMM_i$ is *if* $c_j = 0$ *then goto* k_1 *else* $(c_j := c_j - 1$; *goto* $k_2)$:
   add t_i^Z (Z for zero) with (s_i, t_i^Z), (t_i^Z, s_{k_1}), and
   t_i^{NZ} (NZ for non-zero) with (s_i, t_i^{NZ}), (c_j, t_i^{NZ}), (t_i^{NZ}, s_{k_2}) (cf. Fig.1(b)).

3. The initial marking will consist of the input values $x_1, x_2, ..., x_m$ in places $c_1, c_2, ..., c_m$, 1 token in s_1, 0 in the other places, which completes the construction.

N_C can simulate C in a natural way but (only) transitions t_i^Z can "*cheat*", i.e. fire although the relevant c_j is not 0.

Adding a *dc-transition* (*dc* for "definitely cheating") to N_C for some $i \in BS$ means adding a new transition t with (s_i, t), (c_j, t), (t, c_j), (t, s_{k_1}), j, k_1 taken from $COMM_i$ (cf Fig.1(c)).

Notice that such t has the same effect as t_i^Z but firing it always means cheating.

Now we establish the main theorems.

Theorem 3.1. *Bisimilarity as well as language equivalence are undecidable for labelled Petri nets, even if restricted to nets with a fixed static structure and 2 unbounded places.*

Proof. Let C be a (fixed) universal counter machine, with input values x_1, x_2, and N_C the basic net in the notation as above. Let us construct nets N_1, N_2 as follows.

Construction of N_1, N_2

1. To N_C, add new places p, p' and a new transition x with arcs (s_n, x), (p, x).

2. Take any any one-to-one labelling L of transitions.

3. For each $i \in BS$, add two *dc*−transitions t_i', t_i'' (with the relevant arcs) and additional arcs (p, t_i'), (t_i', p'), (p', t_i''), (t_i'', p) and put $L(t_i') = L(t_i'') = L(t_i^Z)$ (cf Fig.2).

4. Now take two copies of the arised net.
   In one copy put 1 token in p and 0 in p' (elsewhere the initial marking coincides with that of N_C); the resulting marking will be denoted by M_1, the whole net by N_1.
   In the other copy put 1 token in p' and 0 in p; the resulting marking will be denoted by M_2, the whole net by N_2.

Notice that only c_1, c_2 are (possibly) unbounded.

Now we show that the following conditions are equivalent

a) C does not halt (for the given inputs x_1, x_2)

b) N_1, N_2 are bisimilar

c) $\mathcal{L}(N_1) \subseteq \mathcal{L}(N_2)$

d) $\mathcal{L}(N_1) = \mathcal{L}(N_2)$

which proves the theorem. Thus we also directly show the undecidability of the language containment problem, although it follows from the undecidability of the language equivalence problem.

If C halts (for input x_1, x_2): $L(\sigma)$ where σ is the correct (non-cheating) sequence ended by x belongs to $\mathcal{L}(N_1)$ and not to $\mathcal{L}(N_2)$. (Firing σ in N_2 we

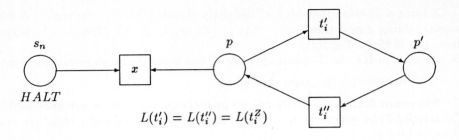

$$L(t_i') = L(t_i'') = L(t_i^Z)$$

Figure 2:

have no possibility to fire a dc−transition; hence we can not move the token from p' to p and x will remain disabled.)

Hence $\mathcal{L}(N_1) \not\subseteq \mathcal{L}(N_2)$ which implies that $\mathcal{L}(N_1) \neq \mathcal{L}(N_2)$ and that N_1, N_2 are not bisimilar.

If C does not halt: Consider the set $\mathcal{M}$ of all couples (M', M'') where M', M'' are reachable without cheating from M_1, M_2 respectively and $M'(p) = 1, M'(p') = 0, M''(p) = 0, M''(p') = 1$.

$\mathcal{D}$ will denote the diagonal, the set of all couples (M, M).

We show that the union $\mathcal{D} \cup \mathcal{M}$ is a bisimulation containing (M_1, M_2) (notice that $(M_1, M_2) \in \mathcal{M}$).

As the static nets underlying N_1 and N_2 are the same, the condition from the definition of bisimulation is clear for any couple $(M, M) \in \mathcal{D}$.

As regards a couple $(M', M'') \in \mathcal{M}$:

− for any noncheating firing in M' (M'') there is the same noncheating firing in M'' (M') yielding again a couple of markings from $\mathcal{M}$,

− for any cheating firing of t_i^Z or t_i' in M', firing of t_i'' or t_i^Z respectively is possible in M'' resulting in a couple $(M, M) \in \mathcal{D}$. Similarly for t_i^Z, t_i'' in M'' and t_i', t_i^Z in M'.

Hence N_1, N_2 are bisimilar, which implies $\mathcal{L}(N_1) = \mathcal{L}(N_2)$ and $\mathcal{L}(N_1) \subseteq \mathcal{L}(N_2)$. □

Remark. Considering only language equivalence, we could use a simpler, "nonsymmetric", construction: N_1 without p' and dc−transitions, N_2 with only one set of dc−transitions moving the token from p' to p. Recently Hirshfeld [Hi93] modified the construction showing undecidability of language equivalence even for labelled Petri nets equivalent to BPP (each transition has one input place only).

Theorem 3.2. *The containment and the equality problems for reachability sets of Petri nets are undecidable, even if restricted to nets with one of two fixed static structures and 5 unbounded places.*

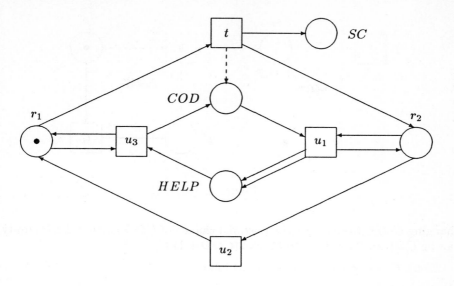

Figure 3:

Proof. Let C and N_C be as in Proof of Theorem 3.1. Let us perform the following construction of a net N.

Construction of N

1. Take N_C and add a dc−transition t'_i for each $i \in BS$.

2. Add places $COD, HELP, SC$ (step counter) and r_1, r_2; put 1 token in r_1, 0 in the others.

3. Add arcs $(r_1, t), (t, r_2), (t, SC)$ for each (so far constructed) transition t and (t_i^{NZ}, COD) for each t_i^{NZ}.

4. Add transitions u_1, u_2, u_3 and arcs (COD, u_1), (r_2, u_1), (u_1, r_2), $(u_1, HELP)$ with $F(u_1, HELP) = 2$, (r_2, u_2), (u_2, r_1), $(HELP, u_3)$, (r_1, u_3), (u_3, r_1), (u_3, COD) (cf. Fig.3).

5. The arised net is denoted by N.

Hence each "non-u_i" transition in N "moves" the token from r_1 to r_2 and adds a token to SC; each transition t_i^{NZ}, in addition, adds a token to COD. Before next firing of a non-u_i transition, a sequence from $u_1^* u_2 u_3^*$ is performed (possibly)

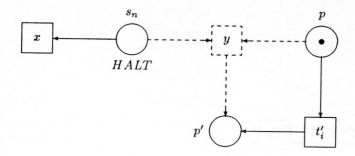

Figure 4:

changing COD. Notice that the maximal change of COD (with $HELP$ empty) can be $COD := 2.COD$ or $COD := 2(COD + 1)$ (for t_i^{NZ}).

Using N, let us construct N_1, N_2 as follows.

Construction of N_1, N_2

1. Take N and add a place p with 1 token and a place p' with 0 tokens.

2. Add a transition x with the arc (s_n, x) and the arcs (p, t_i'), (t_i', p') for each $i \in BS$.

3. The arised net will be denoted by N_2. N_1 arises from N_2 by adding a transition y and the arcs (s_n, y), (p, y), (y, p') (cf. Fig.4).

Trivially $\mathcal{R}(N_2) \subseteq \mathcal{R}(N_1)$. Also notice that only places $c_1, c_2, COD, HELP, SC$ are (possibly) unbounded.

Now we show that the following conditions are equivalent

a) C does not halt (for the given inputs x_1, x_2)

b) $\mathcal{R}(N_1) \subseteq \mathcal{R}(N_2)$

c) $\mathcal{R}(N_1) = \mathcal{R}(N_2)$

which proves the theorem.

If C halts (for input x_1, x_2): N_1 can perform the correct (non-cheating) sequence finished by y with the maximal intermediate changes of COD. If N_2 "wants" to reach the same marking, it must fire the same number of transitions counted in SC; but, not having y, it must digress from the path of N_1 (N_2 cheats, i.e. uses some t_i^Z or t_i' instead of t_i^{NZ}) and can not reach at the same time the same value of COD (it is clear from the idea of COD as a binary number). Hence $\mathcal{R}(N_1) \not\subseteq \mathcal{R}(N_2)$ implying $\mathcal{R}(N_1) \neq \mathcal{R}(N_2)$.

If C does not halt : N_1 and N_2 only differ in the transition y. If N_1 uses it in some firing sequence (it can be only once – at the end of the sequence) it means that no t'_i has been fired and a token has been put in the $HALT$ place s_n; hence at least one firing of t_i^Z was cheating. After performing the same sequence with one t'_i instead of t_i^Z, N_2 reaches the same marking by firing x (instead of y).

Hence $\mathcal{R}(N_1) \subseteq \mathcal{R}(N_2)$ and $\mathcal{R}(N_1) = \mathcal{R}(N_2)$. $\qquad\qquad\qquad\qquad\square$

Remark. The construction can be slightly modified so that also the reachability sets restricted to unbounded places have the same properties.

4   Decidability Results

4.1   Deterministic Nets

First we consider one-to-one labelled (or "unlabelled") Petri nets. It is clear that the bisimilarity problem is the same as the language equivalence problem in that case; the latter is known to be recursively equivalent to the reachability problem (cf. [H75]) which is known to be decidable from [M84]. (The *reachability problem* is to decide for a given Petri net N and a marking M whether $M \in \mathcal{R}(N)$.)

We do not give details here but [J93] shows another reduction of the language equivalence to the reachability problem. The reduction is simpler than that in [H75] and allows a straightforward generalization.

This generalization shows decidability of bisimilarity for *deterministic nets*, which are nets where no reachable marking enables two different transitions with the same labels. We can even allow the nets to be *deterministic up to bisimilarity* – in such a net, different transitions with the same labels can be enabled simultaneously but their firings have to lead to bisimilar results. It even suffices when *one* of the nets is deterministic up to bisimilarity.

Hence we have the following theorem (the proof is shown in [J93]).

Theorem 4.1. *Bisimilarity is decidable for two labelled Petri nets, supposing one of them is deterministic up to bisimilarity (hence if one of them is deterministic, hence if one of them is one-to-one labelled).*

[J93] also contains the following technical complexity results.

Lemma.
1. The bisimilarity problem for one-to-one labelled Petri nets is at least as hard as the reachability problem (and can be reduced to it).
2. The problem, whether a given net is deterministic, can be reduced to the coverability problem and is at least as hard.
3. The problem, whether a given net is deterministic up to bisimilarity, can be reduced to the reachability problem and is at least as hard.

The *coverability problem* is to decide for a given Petri net N and a marking M whether there is $M' \in \mathcal{R}(N)$ such that $M' \geq M$ ($\geq$ taken componentwise).

4.2 Semilinear Bisimulations

For our aims, we can suppose nets where each transition t has at least one input place p ($F(p,t) \geq 1$); if not, we can always add such p with 1 token and arcs (p,t), (t,p). Also notice the obvious fact that if we add to a net N another net N' with the zero initial marking (we simply put N and N' beside each other) then the resulting net is bisimilar to N (N' has no effect).

Hence it is clear that, without loss of generality, we can only consider bisimilarity for the case of both nets having the same static structure (they differ in initial markings only).

Then a bisimulation is, in fact, a relation on $\mathcal{N}^n$ for the relevant n. An equivalence relation R on $\mathcal{N}^n$ will be called a *congruence* if $(u,v) \in R$ implies $(u+w, v+w) \in R$ for any $w \in \mathcal{N}^n$ (addition taken componentwise).

As we already mentioned, the recent result of [CHM93] shows, in fact, that bisimilarity is decidable for the class of Petri nets where the bisimulation equivalence (the greatest bisimulation) is a congruence.

We extend this result using the notion of semilinear sets (cf. e.g. [GS66]).

Definition. A *set* $B \subseteq \mathcal{N}^k$ of k-dimensional nonnegative vectors is *linear* if there are vectors b (*basis*), $c_1, c_2, ..., c_n$ (*periods*) from $\mathcal{N}^k$ such that
$B = \{b + x_1 c_1 + x_2 c_2 + ... + x_n c_n \mid x_i \in \mathcal{N}, 1 \leq i \leq n\}$.
B is a *semilinear set* if it is a finite union of linear sets.

Labelled Petri nets are a special case of finitely branching transition systems. Generally, non-bisimilarity is semi-decidable for such systems. (cf. e.g. [M89], [CHS92]). Hence semi-decidability of bisimilarity is sufficient to show decidability.

Theorem 4.2. *For the class of (couples of) labelled Petri nets where bisimilarity implies the existence of a semilinear bisimulation relating the initial markings, bisimilarity is decidable.*

Proof. Due to decidability of Presburger arithmetic (theory of addition) (see e.g. [O78]), it can be verified whether a given semilinear set is a bisimulation (w.r.t. two given nets); it is not difficult to verify that the conditions from the definition of bisimulation can be then expressed by a Presburger formula.
Semi-decidability (and hence decidability) of bisimilarity is then clear: generate successively all semilinear sets and verify for each of them if it relates the initial markings and is a bisimulation (deciding the relevant Presburger formula). □

Remark. The theorem could be generalized in an obvious way: "a semilinear bisimulation" is replaced by "a bisimulation from $\mathcal{C}$" where $\mathcal{C}$ is an effectively generable class of relations and where it is decidable for a given relation from $\mathcal{C}$ whether it is a bisimulation relating the initial markings (states).

591

The fact that Theorem 4.2. is really an extension of the mentioned result of [CHM93] follows from a theorem proved in [ES69].

Theorem.(Th.II in [ES69]) *Every congruence in a finitely generated commutative monoid M is a rational (or semilinear) subset of $M \times M$.*

The monoid in our case is the set $\mathcal{N}^n$ with (vector) addition.

5 Additional remarks

Recall that (*n-dimensional*) *vector addition systems* (*VASs*) are isomorphic to (reachability sets of) Petri nets (with n places) without self-loops (without both (p,t),(t,p) as arcs). Hopcroft and Pansiot in [HP79] introduce also *VASSs* (*VASs* with an additional finite state control); $n - dim\ VASS$ are, in fact, Petri nets with (at most) n unbounded places. They show that any $2 - dim\ VASS$ (unlike $3 - dim$) and any $5 - dim\ VAS$ (unlike $6 - dim$) is an effectively computable semilinear set; hence the equality problem is decidable for them. (The complexity of the problem for $2 - dim\ VASSs$ is studied in [HRHY86].) [HP79] also show how any $n - dim\ VASS$ can be simulated by an $(n+3) - dim\ VAS$; it can be done by a Petri net with $n+2$ places (using self-loops).

The proof of Theorem 3.2. can be easily modified to show undecidability for (very restricted subclasses of) $5 - dim\ VASS$ and $8 - dim\ VAS$ (leaving the dimensions 3,4, resp. 6,7, open).

For bisimilarity and (prefix) language equivalence we have undecidability for (a very restricted subclass of) Petri nets with 2 unbounded places. My conjecture is that it is decidable for the case of 1 unbounded place. E.g. I think that in that case bisimulation equivalence is semilinear.

It might be also interesting to find out the relation betweeen the deterministic nets and "semilinear bisimulations" and, in the whole, better explore the "decidability border" for bisimilarity.

Acknowledgements.
I would like to thank J.Bradfield, P.Čížek, Y.Hirshfeld and C.Stirling for helpful discussions; special thanks to S.Christensen whose observation helped to simplify the construction used in the undecidability proof.
I also thank to the STACS program committee member who drew my attention to the paper [ES69].

References
[ABS91] Autant C., Belmesk Z., Schnoebelen Ph.: Strong bisimilarity on nets revisited; PARLE'91, LNCS 506, 295-312
[B73] Baker H.: Rabin's proof of the undecidability of the reachability set inclusion problem of vector addition systems; MAC - Memo 79, MIT (1973)
[CHS92] Christensen S., Hüttel H., Stirling C.: Bisimulation equivalence is

decidable for all context-free processes; CONCUR'92, LNCS 630, 138-147

[CHM93] Christensen S., Hirshfeld Y., Moller F.: Bisimulation equivalence is decidable for all Basic Parallel Processes; CONCUR'93, LNCS 715, 143-157

[ES69] Eilenberg S., Schützenberger M.: Rational sets in commutative monoids; J. of Algebra 13, 1969, 173-191

[GS66] Ginsburg S.,Spanier E.: Semigroups, Presburger formulas, and languages; Pacific J.of Mathematics, 16(2),1966, 285-296

[H75] Hack M.: Decision problems for Petri nets and vector addition systems; MAC Tech.Memo 53, MIT (1975)

[H76] Hack M.: The equality problem for vector addition systems is undecidable; TCS 2, 1976, 77-95

[Hi93] Hirshfeld Y.: Petri nets and the equivalence problem; to appear in Proc. of Computer Science Logic '93; Swansea, Wales, September 13-17, 1993.

[HP79] Hopcroft J., Pansiot J.: On the reachability problem for 5-dimensional vector addition systems; TCS 8, 1979, 135-159

[HRHY86] Howell R., Rosier L., Huynh D., Yen H.: Some complexity bounds for problems concerning finite and 2-dimensional vector addition systems with states; TCS 46, 1986, 107-140

[J93] Jančar P.: Decidability questions for bisimilarity of Petri nets and some related problems; Techn. rep. ECS-LFCS-93-261, Univ. of Edinburgh, UK, April 1993

[M84] Mayr E.: An algorithm for the general Petri net reachability problem; SIAM J.Comput. 13(3), 1984, 441-460

[M67] Minsky M.: *Computation: Finite and Infinite Machines*; Prentice Hall, 1967

[M89] Milner R.: *Communication and Concurrency*; Prentice Hall 1989

[O78] Oppen D.C.: A $2^{2^{2^{pn}}}$ upper bound on the complexity of Presburger Arithmetic; JCSS 16, 1978, 323-332

[P81] Peterson J.L.: *Petri Net Theory and the Modeling of Systems*; Prentice Hall 1981

[VV81] Valk R., Vidal-Naquet G.: Petri nets and regular languages; JCSS 23, 1981, 299-325

Formal Languages
and Complexity

The Variable Membership Problem: Succinctness Versus Complexity

Gerhard Buntrock[1] and Krzysztof Loryś[*2]

[1] Institut für Informatik, Universität Würzburg, D-97072 Würzburg, Germany.
[2] Instytut Informatyki, Uniwersytet Wrocławski, 51-151 Wrocław, Poland.

A rule in a grammar is quasi growing if it is growing with respect to given weights of the symbols. Using this definition several types of grammars similar to context sensitive grammars are defined. In this paper we examine the variable membership problem for different types of grammars, namely context-sensitive grammars (CSG), quasi context-sensitive grammars (QCSG), growing context-sensitive grammars (GCSG), quasi growing context-sensitive grammars (QGCSG), and quasi growing grammars (QGG). We show the completeness of these problems in appropriate complexity classes (PSPACE, NEXPTIME). Interestingly the complexity of the variable membership problem differs even when the grammars define the same language class.

1 Introduction

Usually for automata the universal problem is defined as follows: Given an automaton and an input string — does the automaton accept the input?

Sometimes the device solves the universal problem itself. In this case this problem is called complete for the problem class defined by this type of device. Correspondingly in formal language theory the universal problem is called the variable membership problem: Given a grammar and a string — does the grammar produce the string?

Of course the most investigated problem for language classes defined by grammars is the membership problem. The complexity of this problem represents the relationship between language classes defined by grammars and complexity classes.

The complexity of the membership problem yields a lower bound for the variable membership problem. On the other hand for different types of machines or grammars this problem may be of different complexity. If the complexity is of the same complexity as the membership problem, it makes sense to use a universal machine, say an interpreter. If it is higher we should use a compiler since the interpreter would consume higher resources.

The difference in complexity of these problems may be caused by several reasons. The descriptions of the different devices may be of different length. In this case we speak of a difference in the succinctness of the language representation. The number of derivation steps may differ as well.

---

* This research was partly supported by Humboldt Foundation.

Goldschlager gave an example of two different types of grammars, both characterizing CFL, which are of different variable membership complexity [Gol81]. Precisely, in [JL77] it is proved that the variable membership problem is P-complete. On the other hand for the characterization of CFL by ε-free grammars the variable membership problem is of the same complexity as the membership problem, namely it is in AC^1 [Ruz80].

For regular languages we have different variable membership problems for deterministic, nondeterministic and two-way automata. For example, in the case of deterministic automata this problem is complete for deterministic logarithmic space and in the case of nondeterministic automata it becomes complete for nondeterministic logarithmic space. For related results see [DHL92].

In 1986 Elias Dahlhaus and Manfred Warmuth introduced growing context-sensitive grammars and proved that the membership problem is efficiently solvable (i.e. contained in LOGCFL [DW86]). In [Bun93] it is shown that GCSL is contained in the closure of CFL under one-way logarithmic space bounded reductions. Also important is the automaton characterization of GCSL in [Bun93]. The complexity of the variable membership problem for growing context-sensitive grammars is shown to be NP-complete in [NK87, CH90, BL92].

In [BL92] we introduced the notion of a quasi growing grammar, i.e. a grammar for which weights exist for the terminal and non-terminal symbols such that the rules are growing only with respect to the weights. We proved that this type of grammars characterizes the growing context-sensitive languages. We were convinced that these grammars are somewhat more easy to handle, since it is often more complicate and troublesome to construct a growing context-sensitive grammar. Perhaps one reason for this may be that in growing context-sensitive grammars we cannot bound the length of the rules. For quasi growing grammars we have the Kuroda normal form [BL92]. Here we will prove that the variable membership for these types of grammars varies between NP and NEXPTIME.

In Theorem 9 we show that the variable membership problem for quasi growing context-sensitive grammars is PSPACE-complete under a logarithmic space bounded reduction. The first complete problems for this class were found in automata theory (*Linear Bounded Automaton Acceptance* [Kar72]) and logic (*Quantified Boolean Formulas* and *First Order Theory of Equality*) [SM73]).

In Theorem 10 we strengthen our completeness result and show that this problem is CSL-complete under a reduction with the same space bound and an additional linear bound on its output.

For quasi growing grammars, i.e. grammars that have not to be context-sensitive, we show that the variable membership problem is NEXPTIME-complete (see Theorem 11). Even this type of grammars characterizes the class of growing context-sensitive languages [BL92].

We interpret our results as a way to get information about the succinctness of language representation. The most succinct representation will have certainly the highest complexity.

In Corollary 12 we get that for the class of context-sensitive languages the characterizing quasi context-sensitive grammars have a NEXPTIME-hard variable membership problem. This again gives us a hint that this new type of grammars may be more succinct than the context-sensitive ones.

2 Grammars with weight functions

We assume the reader to be familiar with elementary formal language theory and computational complexity theory, and use the standard notations according to [HU79, BDG88, BDG90].

Sometimes there exists confusion on definitions, e. g. of exponential time-bounded complexity classes. Therefore we recall some important notations. By NEXPTIME we denote the class of languages acceptable in nondeterministic time $O(2^{n^{O(1)}})$. A grammar is a quadruple $\langle N, T, S, P \rangle$, where N and T are finite, disjoint alphabets of nonterminal and terminal symbols, respectively; $S \in N$ is a start symbol and P is a finite set of productions of the form $\alpha \to \beta$, with $\alpha, \beta \in (N \cup T)^*$, where α contains at least one nonterminal symbol. The grammars with $|\alpha| \leq |\beta|$ for all productions from P are called *context-sensitive grammars* (CSG). By replacing the above inequality by a sharp one we obtain growing context-sensitive grammars.

Definition 1 *A context-sensitive grammar* $G = \langle N, T, S, P \rangle$ *is growing if S does not appear on the right side in any rule and*

$$\forall (\alpha \to \beta) \in P : \alpha \neq S \Longrightarrow |\alpha| < |\beta|.$$

We denote the growing grammars by GCSG and the class of languages generated by such grammars by GCSL.

We distinguish two types of grammars which are growing with respect to a weight function, namely those, which are in addition context-sensitive, and those, which are not. We define a weight function to be a homomorphism from words with concatenation to the positive integers $(\mathbb{N}_+)$ with addition:

Definition 2 *We call a function $f : \Sigma^* \to \mathbb{N}_+$ a weight function if $\forall w, v \in \Sigma^* : f(w) + f(v) = f(wv)$.*

It has been proven that weight functions for grammars are a good tool to restrict grammars such that they characterize CSL or GCSL. Such grammars are often more easy to construct than context sensitive or growing ones. Here we give the definitions:

Definition 3 *Let $G = \langle N, T, S, P \rangle$ be a grammar and $f : (N \cup T)^* \to \mathbb{N}$ a weight function.*

1. *We call G quasi growing if $f(\alpha) < f(\beta)$ for all productions $(\alpha \to \beta) \in P$. We denote the set of quasi growing grammars by QGG.*
2. *We call G quasi growing context-sensitive if it is quasi growing and a context-sensitive grammar. We denote the set of quasi growing context-sensitive grammars by QGCSG.*

3. We call G quasi context-sensitive if $f(\alpha) \leq f(\beta)$ for all productions $(\alpha \to \beta) \in P$. We denote the set of quasi context-sensitive grammars by QCSG.

There exist normal forms for context-sensitive grammars as well as for the last two types of weighted grammars (Def. 3(2), 3(3)). A context-sensitive grammar is in *Cremers' normal form* if all productions are of the forms

$$AB \to CD$$
$$A \to CD$$
$$A \to a$$

where A, B, C, D are nonterminals and a is a terminal [Cre73]. Obviously such a normal form is not growing. But it is not difficult to show that every QGG or QGCSG can be transformed into an equivalent one in Cremers' normal form. We will need the following proposition:

Proposition 4 *For every context-sensitive (quasi context-sensitive, quasi growing, quasi growing context-sensitive) grammar an equivalent grammar in Cremers' normal form can be constructed in polynomial time [Cre73, BL92].*

We will extend Cremers' normal form in such a way that we allow all rules of the form $(\alpha \to \beta)$ with $|\alpha|, |\beta| \leq 2$. Then we can conclude:

Proposition 5 *For every grammar $G = \langle N, T, S, P \rangle \in$ QGG with weight function f there exists a grammar in Cremers' normal form with weight function f' which fulfills*

$$\forall x \in N \cup T : f'(x) \leq \max\{|\alpha| + |\beta| - 2 \mid (\alpha \to \beta) \in P\} \cdot \max\{f(x) \mid x \in N \cup T\}$$

For a proof see [BL92].

To get an upper bound for the complexity of variable membership problems sometimes we need to estimate the values of the weight function. For this we define minimal weight functions and minimal grammars for minimal weight functions.

Definition 6 *A weight function f is called* minimal *for a quasi growing grammar G if for all weight functions f' for G we have*

$$\sum_{x \in N \cup T} f(x) \leq \sum_{x \in N \cup T} f'(x)$$

We are interested in a minimal weight function for a grammar. At first we will extract the set of rules which are responsible for the highest size of the values of a minimal weight function. This extraction leads to a notion of *minimal grammar* for a minimal weight function.

Definition 7 *Let $G = \langle N, T, S, P \rangle$ be a quasi growing grammar and f a minimal weight function for G. We call a quasi growing grammar $G' = \langle N', T', S, P' \rangle \neq G$ smaller for (f, G) if the following conditions are fulfilled:*

- $N' \subseteq N, T' \subseteq T$
- f is a minimal weight function for G'
- G' is free of repetitions; i. e. in no rule a symbol occurs on both sides.
- A maximal element will remain in G':

$$\max\{f(x) \mid x \in N \cup T\} = \max\{f(x) \mid x \in N' \cup T'\}$$

- $\forall (A'_1 A'_2 \cdots A'_{q'_1} \rightarrow B'_1 B'_2 \cdots B'_{q'_2}) \in P'$:
  $\exists (A_1 A_2 \cdots A_{q_1} \rightarrow B_1 B_2 \cdots B_{q_2}) \in P$ and a mapping
  $\sigma_i : \{1, \ldots, q_i\} \rightarrow \{0, 1, \ldots, q_i\}, \sigma_i(j) \in \{0, j\}$:

$$A'_1 A'_2 \cdots A'_{q'_1} = A_{\sigma_1(1)} A_{\sigma_1(2)} \cdots A_{\sigma_1(q_1)}$$
$$B'_1 B'_2 \cdots B'_{q'_2} = B_{\sigma_2(1)} B_{\sigma_2(2)} \cdots B_{\sigma_1(q_2)}$$

where A_0 and B_0 denote the empty string ε. In other words σ is deleting some symbols in a rule of the grammar.

If there is no smaller grammar for (f, G'), then G' is called minimal for (f, G). Note that a construction of a smaller grammar may modify the language.

A grammar which is minimal for (f, G), where G is in Cremers' normal form, is called in minimal normal form. Note that such a minimal grammar is in Cremers' normal form.

Proposition 8 For every quasi growing grammar $G = \langle N, T, S, P \rangle$ there is a polynomial p and a minimal weight function f such that for all $x \in N \cup T$ the following holds

$$f(x) \leq 2^{p(|N|+|T|)}.$$

Proof. Let $G' = \langle N', T', S, P' \rangle$ a grammar in minimal normal form for f. Let $N' \cup T' = \{x_1, x_2, \ldots, x_m\}$ such that $f(x_i) \leq f(x_{i+1})$ for $i = 1, \ldots, m-1$. Now we partition the rules P' into the sets $P_0, P_1, \ldots, P_m$ such that $P_0 = \emptyset$ and for $i > 0$:

$$P_i = \{(\alpha \rightarrow \beta) \in P' \mid \forall j < i : (\alpha \rightarrow \beta) \notin P_j, \ \alpha, \beta \in \{x_1, x_2, \ldots, x_i\}^*\}$$

Let j be the smallest index of all nonempty sets P_i. From the minimal condition of G' we conclude that $f(x_j)$ is bounded by $2 \cdot j$. In general we have in the worst case in P_{i+1} a rule of the form $x_i x_i \rightarrow x_{i+1}$. It is easy to see that in this case the weight for x_{i+1} can be bounded by $2f(x_i) + 1$. In this way we can conclude that the maximal weight is bounded by $2^{(|N'|+|T'|)} - 1$. Since the construction of G' is polynomial time-bounded (see Proposition 4) the number of elements in N' is also polynomial bounded. Let p be the polynomial bound of $|N'|$, then we have a bound of $2^{p(|N|+|T|)}$ for the maximal weight for G'. Note that the maximal weight of a minimal weight function for G is bounded by the maximal weight of every minimal weight function for G'. $\qquad \square$

3 Completeness results

In this section the main results of this paper will be presented. In Theorem 9 we show that for QGCSG the variable membership problem is PSPACE-complete. For the next result, Theorem 10, we can use the proof of Theorem 9 to show that the same problem is also complete for CSL under a stronger reduction type. Finally, in Theorem 11, we show in a similar manner that the same problem for a more general type of grammars becomes NEXPTIME-complete. These results may somehow surprise. They tell us that for GCSL we have three different types of grammars which characterize the same language class and all these grammar types are of different variable membership complexity (unless NP = PSPACE or PSPACE = NEXPTIME).

Clearly, derivations in GCSG are bounded by the length of the derived words. It is easy to see that derivations in QGCSG and QGG have a length linearly depending on the length of derived words. An appropriate factor for this linear bound can be obtained from the maximum value of the minimal weight function. This fact will be important to get the upper complexity bound of the variable membership problem of QGG.

In the first proof the idea is to construct a grammar for a deterministic linearly space-bounded Turing machine such that the grammar will produce a certain very simple tally string iff the machine will accept its input. It will be shown that this construction can be done within logarithmic space. A similar method will work for the third theorem. But instead of the space-bounded machines we have nondeterministic exponentially time-bounded machines.

Theorem 9 *The variable membership problem for* QGCSG *is PSPACE-complete.*

Proof. The upper bound of this problem is the same as for context-sensitive grammars. Here we have Kuroda's classical result: context-sensitive languages are characterized by linear automata [Kur64]. This result is proven by a transformation which can be done in polynomial space. This result carries over to the variable membership problem, i.e. the variable membership problem for all types of context-sensitive grammars belongs to PSPACE.

The hardness will be shown by a generic reduction from the class DCSL. This is sufficient since the closure under any reasonable reduction (e.g. polynomial time-bounded, logarithmically space-bounded) of DCSL yields the class PSPACE. Without loss of generality we can assume that each language L from DCSL will be given by a deterministic single tape Turing machine M such that each word w of L will be accepted in space $|w|$ and time $t := 2^{c|w|}$ for some constant c.

We construct for every pair (M, w) a pair (G, w') such that M accepts w iff we can derive w' from G. Here $M = \langle Q, \Sigma, \Gamma, \delta, q_0, \flat, F \rangle$ is the space-bounded machine as mentioned above. We use Q for the states, Σ and Γ are the input and work tape alphabets, respectively, δ is the transition function, q_0 is the initial state, by $\flat$ we denote the blank symbol, F contains the accepting states. We will assume that $\Sigma \subseteq \Gamma$. $G = \langle N, T, P, S \rangle$ will be a QGCSG with weight function f. The set given by G will be a tally language over the single letter alphabet $T := \{0\}$.

Our transformation will produce the following fact: Each phrase in a derivation of the grammar that we will present here, will encode a configuration of the computation of the machine M on input $w = w_1 w_2 \cdots w_{|w|}$, whereat every nonterminal describing a part of the configuration (see N_1) encodes one symbol on the tape, and possibly the state, if the considered symbol is scanned by the head of the machine. With the rules we will simulate the computation. To be growing with respect to a weight function in every step some value will occur, which will be moved to the left, where it will be collected in a kind of a counter. This counting we do with the nonterminals from N_2.

We define the set of nonterminals N which are partitioned into $N_0 \cup N_1 \cup N_2$:

$$N_0 := \{S, \#\}$$
$$N_1 := (Q \times \Gamma \times \{1, 2\}) \ \cup \ (\{\cdot\} \times \Gamma \times \{1, 2, \ldots, |w| - 1\})$$
$$N_2 := \{0, 1, 2\} \ \times \ \{3^0, 3^1, \ldots, 3^{c|w|}\}$$

The last component of a nonterminal in N_1 encodes the weight of this nonterminal. With the symbols from N_2 we encode the position and the digit in a ternary number that will represent a weight collector.

$$f((r, b, j)) := j$$
$$f((k, 3^i)) := (k + 1) \cdot 3^i \cdot |w|$$

for $j \in \{1, \ldots, |w| - 1\}$, $i \in \{0, \ldots, |w|\}$, $k \in \{0, 1, 2\}$, $r \in \{\cdot\} \cup Q$, $b \in \Gamma$. For the nonterminals S and $\#$ we define $f(S) := f(\#) := 1$. And for the only terminal symbol 0 we define $f(0) := |w| \cdot 3^{c|w|+1} + 1$, such that it is the heaviest symbol in our grammar.

The set of productions P is partitioned into the set consisting of the starting rule (P_1), the simulation rules (P_2), the weight moving rules (P_3), the weight collecting rules (P_4), and the terminal rules (P_5):

$$P := P_1 \cup P_2 \cup P_3 \cup P_4 \cup P_5$$

With the starting rule we produce the initial configuration and the symbol $\#$ initializes the counter:

$$P_1 := \{S \longrightarrow \#(q_0, w_1, 1)(\cdot, w_2, 1) \ldots (\cdot, w_{|w|}, 1)\}$$

Without loss of generality we assume that in the calculation of M only right and left moves occur, i. e.

$$\delta : Q \times \Gamma \longrightarrow Q \times \Gamma \times \{L, R\}$$

For every right move $\delta(q, a) = (q', a', R)$ and all $b \in \Gamma$ we put the rule

$$(q, a, 1)(\cdot, b, 1) \rightarrow (\cdot, a', 2)(q', b, 1)$$

into P_2. For every left move $\delta(q,a) = (q', a', L)$ and all $b \in \Gamma$ we put the rule

$$(\cdot, b, 1)(q, a, 1) \to (q', b, 2)(\cdot, a', 1)$$

into P_2.

The set P_3 consists of the rules which transport the weights to the left. For all $q \in Q$, $a, b \in \Gamma$, and $i = 2, 3, \ldots, |w| - 2$, we put the rules

$$(\cdot, a, 1)(q, b, 2) \to \quad (\cdot, a, 3)(q, b, 1)$$
$$(\cdot, a, 1)(\cdot, b, i) \to (\cdot, a, i+1)(\cdot, b, 1)$$

into P_3. Note that since the length of all configurations is $|w|$, the weights encoded in these nonterminals cannot exceed $|w| - 1$.

The next part consists of the rules which will in some sense collect the weights produced by P_2 and transported by P_3. For all $(r, j) \in (Q \times \{2\}) \cup (\{\cdot\} \times \{2, 3, \ldots, |w| - 1\})$, $a \in \Gamma$, $3^i \in \{3^0, 3^1, \ldots, 3^{c|w|-1}\}$ the following rules belong to P_4:

$$\#(r, a, j) \to \#(1, 3^0)(r, a, 1)$$
$$(0, 3^0)(r, a, j) \to (1, 3^0)(r, a, 1)$$
$$(1, 3^0)(r, a, j) \to (2, 3^0)(r, a, 1)$$
$$\#(2, 3^i) \to \#(1, 3^{i+1})(0, 3^i)$$
$$(0, 3^{i+1})(2, 3^i) \to (1, 3^{i+1})(0, 3^i)$$
$$(1, 3^{i+1})(2, 3^i) \to (2, 3^{i+1})(0, 3^i)$$

A computation of M will halt and accept if a configuration will contain a final state. In the last part P_5 of the rules the nonterminal that encodes a final state will give the possibility to apply the terminal rules: For all $q \in F$, $a \in \Gamma$ the rules

$$(q, a, 1) \to 0$$

belong to P_5. Moreover, for all nonterminals $X \in N$ we have in P_5 :

$$X0 \to 00$$
$$0X \to 00$$

To check whether the grammar is growing with respect to the weight function we check only the rules in P_4, since in all other cases it is obvious:

$$\#(r, a, j) \to \#(1, 3^0)(r, a, 1)$$
$$1 + j < 1 + |w| < 2|w| + 2 = 2 \cdot 3^0 \cdot |w| + 2$$

$$(0, 3^0)(r, a, j) \to (1, 3^0)(r, a, 1)$$
$$3^0 \cdot |w| + j < 2 \cdot 3^0 \cdot |w| + 1$$

$$(1, 3^0)(r, a, j) \to (2, 3^0)(r, a, 1)$$
$$2 \cdot 3^0 \cdot |w| + j < 3 \cdot 3^0 \cdot |w| + 1$$

$$\#(2, 3^i) \to \#(1, 3^{i+1})(0, 3^i)$$
$$1 + 3 \cdot 3^i \cdot |w| < 1 + 2 \cdot 3^{i+1} \cdot |w| + 3^i \cdot |w|$$

$$(0, 3^{i+1})(2, 3^i) \to (1, 3^{i+1})(0, 3^i)$$
$$3^{i+1} \cdot |w| + 3 \cdot 3^i \cdot |w| < 2 \cdot 3^{i+1} \cdot |w| + 3^i \cdot |w|$$

$$(1, 3^{i+1})(2, 3^i) \to (2, 3^{i+1})(0, 3^i)$$
$$2 \cdot 3^{i+1} \cdot |w| + 3 \cdot 3^i \cdot |w| < 3 \cdot 3^{i+1} \cdot |w| + 3^i \cdot |w|$$

To get the polynomial time bound, we estimate the length of the grammar G. At first we count the number of nonterminals:

$$|N| = |\Gamma \times (\{\cdot\} \times \{1, 2, \ldots, |w| - 2\} \cup Q \times \{1, 2\})|$$
$$+ 3 \cdot |\{3^0, 3^1, \ldots, 3^{c|w|}\}| + |\{S, \#\}|$$
$$= |\Gamma| \cdot (|w| - 2 + 2 \cdot |Q|) + 3 \cdot (c|w| + 1) + 2$$
$$< d \cdot |\Gamma| \cdot (|w| + |Q|) \quad \text{for some constant } d.$$

We count the number of rules:

$$|P| = |P_1| + |P_2| + |P_3| \qquad\qquad +|P_4| \qquad\qquad\qquad +|P_5|$$
$$\leq \quad 1 \quad + \quad |\delta| \quad +(|Q| + |w|) \cdot |\Gamma|^2$$
$$+3(|\Gamma| \cdot (|w| - 1) + c|w|)$$
$$+|F| \cdot |\Gamma| + 2|N|$$
$$< |\delta| + d'|\Gamma|^2 \cdot (|w| + |Q|) \quad \text{for some constant } d'.$$

This number is clearly polynomially bounded in the length of (M, w).

It is easy to see that G will produce a tally string of polynomial length iff the machine M will accept the input w. From this and the easyness of the construction we can conclude that in the construction of the grammar and the tally string, only logarithmic space is needed. Moreover, to simplify the computation of the length of the tally string we add the rule

$$0 \to 00$$

In this way it is sufficient to compute an upper bound of this number. $\square$

Meyer and Stockmeyer introduced the stronger reduction type of logarithmically space-bounded reductions: reductions with the same space bound but additionally with linearly length-bounded output [MS72]. Note that the class CSL is closed under this type of reductions.

Theorem 10 *The variable membership problem for* QGCSG *is* CSL-*complete under logarithmically space-bounded and linearly length-bounded reductions.*

Proof. We can use the proof of Theorem 9. First we note that the changes needed for nondeterministic machines can be easily done. Now, without loss of generality we can assume that all Turing machines work on the same alphabet. For this case we have to enlarge the space bound such that M can use $c' \cdot |w|$ tape cells for some constant c'. One can easily verify that the length of the output of the reduction in this way is linearly bounded. $\square$

Theorem 11 *The variable membership problem for* QGG *is* NEXPTIME-*complete.*

Proof. An upper bound of the complexity can be obtained in the following way. For a given quasi growing grammar with the minimal weight function f and a string w we have to decide if w is derivable by the grammar. Let $\&_x$ for every symbol x in the grammar be a new symbol. We substitute all symbols x in the grammar by the string $x\&_x^{f(x)}$. In this way the grammar becomes growing and membership can nondeterministically be checked in polynomial time. Since the blow-up by this substitution is bounded exponentially in the length of the grammar (see Proposition 8), it is bounded exponentially also in the length of the input of the variable membership problem for QGG. Therefore we can conclude that the latter problem can be solved nondeterministically in exponential time.

The hardness can be shown by a similar construction as in Theorem 9. The main changes consist in how the counter is organized. $\square$

From this result we get the corresponding theorem for context-sensitive languages.

Corollary 12 *The variable membership problem for* QCSG *is* NEXPTIME-*hard.*

Proof. Obviously the reduction from Theorem 11 works for this type of grammars too. $\square$

If we try to find an upper bound for QCSG with the method from Theorem 11 we will find exponential space. It may be the case that this problem is exponential-space complete.

Wagner investigated the complexity of combinatorial problems under different input languages. He shows that in several cases more succinctness of the input languages causes a blow-up of the complexities [Wag86]. Our results give us a hint that the grammars from QGG, QGCSG, and QCSG are somewhat more succinct than the corresponding grammars from GCSG and from CSG, respectively.

Acknowledgement

Thanks go to Ronald Book, Diana Rooß, Ulrich Hertrampf, Markus Holzer, Clemens Lautemann, Gundula Niemann, Carmen Schwenkel, Heribert Vollmer, and Klaus Wagner for several discussions and hints.

References

[BDG88] José L. Balcázar, Josep Díaz, and Joaquim Gabarró. *Structural Complexity Theory I*. Springer, 1988.

[BDG90] José L. Balcázar, Josep Díaz, and Joaquim Gabarró. *Structural Complexity Theory II*. Springer, 1990.

[BL92] Gerhard Buntrock and Krzysztof Loryś. On growing context-sensitive languages. In *Proc. of 19th ICALP*, volume 623 of *LNCS*, pages 77–88. Springer, 1992.

[Bun93] Gerhard Buntrock. Growing context-sensitive languages and automata. Technical Report 69, Universität Würzburg, Institut für Informatik, Am Exerzierplatz 3, D-97072 Würzburg, November 1993.

[CH90] Sang Cho and Dung T. Huynh. The complexity of membership for deterministic growing context-sensitive grammars. *International Journal of Computer Mathematics*, 37:185–188, 1990.

[Cre73] A. B. Cremers. Normal forms for context-sensitive grammars. *Acta Informatica*, 3:59–73, 1973.

[DHL92] Carsten Damm, Markus Holzer, and Klaus-Jörn Lange. The parallel complexity of iterated morphisms and the arithmetic of small numbers. In *Proc. of 17th MFCS*, volume 629 of *LNCS*, pages 227–235. Springer, 1992.

[DW86] Elias Dahlhaus and Manfred K. Warmuth. Membership for growing context-sensitive grammars is polynomial. *Journal of Computer and System Sciences*, 33:456–472, 1986.

[Gol81] Leslie M. Goldschlager. ε-productions in context-free grammars. *Acta Informatica*, 16(3):303–308, 1981.

[HU79] John E. Hopcroft and Jeffrey D. Ullman. *Introduction to Automata Theory, Languages and Computation*. Addison-Wesley, 1979.

[JL77] Neil D. Jones and William T. Laaser. Complete problems for deterministic polynomial time. *Theoretical Computer Science*, 3:105–117, 1977.

[Kar72] Richard M. Karp. Reducibility among combinatorial problems. In R. E. Miller and J. W. Thatcher, editors, *Complexity of Computer Computations*. Plenum Press, New York, 1972.

[Kur64] S.-Y. Kuroda. Classes of languages and linear-bounded automata. *Information and Control*, 7:207–223, 1964.

[MS72] Albert R. Meyer and Larry J. Stockmeyer. The equivalence problem for regular expressions with squaring requires exponential space. In *Proc. of the 13th Annual IEEE Symposium on Switching and Automata Theory*, pages 125–129, 1972.

[NK87] Paliath Narendran and Kamela Krithivasan. On the membership problem for some grammars. COINS Technical Report CAR-TR-267 & CS-TR-1787 & AFOSR-86-0092, Center for Automaton Research, University of Maryland, College Park, MD 20742, March 1987.

[Ruz80]   Walter L. Ruzzo. Tree-size bounded alternation. *Journal of Computer and System Sciences*, 21:218–235, 1980.

[SM73]   Larry J. Stockmeyer and Albert R. Meyer. Word problems requiring exponential time: preliminary report. In *Proc. of 5th STOC*, pages 1–9, 1973.

[Wag86]   Klaus W. Wagner. The complexity of combinatorial problems with succinct input representation. *Acta Informatica*, 23:325–356, 1986.

Economy of Description
for Single-valued Transducers[*]

Andreas Weber[†] and *Reinhard Klemm*[‡]

Fachbereich Informatik, Johann Wolfgang Goethe–Universität
Postfach 111932, D–60054 Frankfurt am Main, Germany

Abstract. Questions of economy of description are investigated in connection with single-valued finite transducers. The following results are shown. (1) Any single-valued real-time transducer M with n states can be effectively transformed into an equivalent unambiguous real-time transducer having at most 2^n states. (2) Let M be a single-valued real-time transducer with n states and output alphabet Δ which is equivalent to some deterministic real-time or subsequential transducer M'. Then, M can be effectively transformed into such an M' having at most $1 + 2^n \cdot \max\{2, \#\Delta\}^{2n^3 l}$ states where l is a local structural parameter of M. (3) For any single-valued real-time transducer M it is decidable in deterministic polynomial time whether or not it is equivalent to some deterministic real-time transducer (to some subsequential transducer, respectively). The results (1)–(3) can be extended to the case that M is not real time. The upper bound in (1) is at most one state off the optimal upper bound. Any improvement of the upper bound in (2) is greater or equal than 2^n.

0   Introduction

The semantic meaning of a description is the object it describes. Two descriptions are equivalent if they have the same semantic meaning. The complexity of a description is intended to reflect its size. Having this terminology in mind, the basic question of economy of description can be informally stated as follows. Given two classes D_1 and D_2 of descriptions each having its semantic meaning and given a description in class D_1 of a certain complexity — what is the minimal complexity of an equivalent description in class D_2? In other words, we would like to transform a description in class D_1 describing a certain object into a description in class D_2 describing the same object, and we would like to ask for the increase/decrease of complexity of the descriptions caused by this transformation.

Let us illustrate this concept by considering different types of finite automata describing (recognizing) regular languages where the complexity of an automaton is assumed to be the number of its states. Using the well-known subset construction (see, e.g., [HU79]), a given nondeterministic finite automaton (NFA) with n states can be transformed into an equivalent deterministic finite automaton (DFA) having at most

---

[*]A part of this research was done while the first author was supported by a Postdoctoral Fellowship of the Japan Society for the Promotion of Science

[†]E-mail: weber@psc.informatik.uni-frankfurt.de

[‡]This author's present affiliation is: 331 Pond Lab., Dept. of Computer Science and Engineering, Pennsylvania State University, University Park, PA 16802, U.S.A., e-mail: klemm@cse.psu.edu

2^n states. In certain cases this increase of complexity (from n to 2^n) is unavoidable because there are NFAs with n states such that every equivalent DFA has at least 2^n states ([M71], [MF71]). By means of the above-mentioned subset construction an NFA with n states is being transformed into an equivalent unambiguous finite automaton (UFA) having at most $2^n - 1$ states. Again, this increase of complexity (from n to $2^n - 1$) is unavoidable because there are NFAs with n states such that every equivalent UFA has at least $2^n - 1$ states [L93].

Up to now, questions of economy of description have been studied for various types of automata, regular expressions, pushdown automata, context-free grammars, etc., describing certain families of formal languages (see [M71], [MF71], [Sdt78], [KW80], [SH85], [A87], [RI89], [KPW93], [L93], etc.). For a general framework on descriptional (or Kolmogorov) complexity the reader is referred to the survey [U92].

This paper is apparently the first one *explicitly* dealing with questions of economy of description for finite transducers describing (realizing) rational relations. Some implicit previous work on this topic will be pointed out below. For a general background on transducers we refer to the textbooks [B79] and [G89] and to the survey [CC83]. The transducers being involved here are single-valued (or functional), unambiguous, subsequential, and deterministic ones. Single-valued and unambiguous transducers are known to have the same descriptive power ([E74, Thm. IX.8.1], see [B79, §IV]), but they are more powerful than subsequential transducers which are again more powerful than deterministic ones. Morphic characterizations of the relations realized by all these transducers are given in [HKL92a] and [HKL92b]. Subsequential transducers are also motivated in [CS86] and [R91].

Our main results are as follows.

(1) Any single-valued real-time transducer M with n states can be effectively transformed into an equivalent unambiguous real-time transducer having at most 2^n states (see §2).

(2) Let M be a single-valued real-time transducer with n states and output alphabet Δ which is equivalent to some deterministic real-time or subsequential transducer M'. Then, M can be effectively transformed into such an M' having at most $1 + 2^n \cdot \max\{2, \#\Delta\}^{2n^3 l}$ states where l is a local structural parameter of M (see §3).

(3) For any single-valued real-time transducer M it is decidable in deterministic polynomial time whether or not it is equivalent to some deterministic real-time transducer (to some subsequential transducer, respectively, see §4).

The results (1)–(3) can be extended to the case that M is not necessarily real time. From results about automata ([M71], [MF71], [L93]) it follows that the upper bound in (1) is at most one state off the optimal upper bound and that any possible improvement of the upper bound in (2) is greater or equal than 2^n (see §§2–3). The result (3) may be used in order to decide whether one of the transformations in (2) can be applied to a given single-valued real-time transducer. Note that it is decidable in deterministic polynomial time whether or not a given transducer is single valued ([GI83], [HW93]).

Our proof of (1) employs an "unambiguous subset construction" for single-valued transducers which is apparently new even for automata. This method is entirely different from previous work by M.P. Schützenberger ([Sbr76], see [B79, §IV] and [HKL92a]) which yields an unambiguous transducer with $n \cdot 2^{n-1}$ states (see §2).

In order to prove result (2) we generalize the above-mentioned "deterministic" subset construction from automata to single-valued transducers. The new construction allows to transform every "balanced" single-valued real-time transducer M into an equivalent subsequential transducer M' of exponential size. If M also preserves prefixes, then M' can be furthermore transformed into an equivalent deterministic real-time transducer. On the other hand, every single-valued real-time transducer M which lacks the former (latter) property is not equivalent to any subsequential (deterministic real-time) transducer.

Another characterization of the relations realized by subsequential transducers involves the concept of "twinned" states. Our efficient algorithms proving (3) are based on structural properties of transducers which are mainly related to a "combinatorial" formulation of this concept. An "algebraic" formulation of the same concept appears in work by C. Choffrut and is used there in order to obtain an (inefficient) construction of a subsequential transducer in (2) and an (inefficient) algorithm deciding the second property mentioned in (3) ([C78], see [B79, §IV]). A definition of a balanced transducer similar to ours is used in [CS86, Lem. 5] (see §§3–4).

After a first version of this paper was distributed in 1991, H. Seidl extended our results (1)–(3) and some of our proof methods for (2) to bottom-up tree transducers [Se93].

1 Preliminaries

We use the following notations. $\mathbb{N}$ and $[n]$ denote the sets $\{1, 2, 3, \ldots\}$ and $\{1, \ldots, n\}$, respectively. A partial function $\varphi: U \hookrightarrow V$, where U and V are sets, is just a function $\varphi: U \longrightarrow 2^V$ which maps every element of U to a subset of V having cardinality at most 1.

Let Δ be some nonempty finite set. Let $y \in \Delta^*$ and $j \in [|y|]$, then $y(j) \in \Delta$ denotes the jth letter of y. Let $y_1, y_2 \in \Delta^*$, and let $j \in [\min\{|y_1|, |y_2|\}]$. We say that y_1 and y_2 differ at position j if $y_1(j)$ and $y_2(j)$ are distinct. We write $y_1 \sqsubseteq y_2$ if y_1 is a prefix of y_2, i.e., $|y_1| \le |y_2|$ and, for all $j \in [|y_1|]$, $y_1(j) = y_2(j)$. The greatest common prefix of a nonempty set $U \subseteq \Delta^*$, denoted by $\mathrm{gcp}(U)$, is the uniquely determined longest word in Δ^* which is a prefix of every word in U.

The free group generated by Δ (see [LS77, §I]), denoted by $\mathrm{FG}(\Delta)$, is defined as the quotient of the free monoid $(\Delta \cup \Delta^{-1})^*$, where $\Delta^{-1} := \{b^{-1} \mid b \in \Delta\}$, by the congruence generated by the relations $bb^{-1} = b^{-1}b = \varepsilon$ for every $b \in \Delta$. A word $y \in (\Delta \cup \Delta^{-1})^*$ is called reduced if it contains no factor of the form bb^{-1} or $b^{-1}b$ where $b \in \Delta$. It can be seen that every element of $\mathrm{FG}(\Delta)$ has a unique reduced representative in $(\Delta \cup \Delta^{-1})^*$. We can therefore identify in an obvious way $\mathrm{FG}(\Delta)$ with the set of reduced words in $(\Delta \cup \Delta^{-1})^*$. Let $y = b_1^{\gamma_1} \ldots b_m^{\gamma_m} \in \mathrm{FG}(\Delta)$ where $b_1, \ldots, b_m \in \Delta$ and $\gamma_1, \ldots, \gamma_m \in \{1, -1\}$. Then, the inverse of y, denoted by y^{-1}, is $b_m^{-\gamma_m} \ldots b_1^{-\gamma_1}$. The length of y, denoted by $|y|$, is defined to be m. Δ^* and $(\Delta^{-1})^*$

are submonoids of $FG(\Delta)$. The *sign* of a word $y \in \Delta^* \cup (\Delta^{-1})^*$, denoted by $\operatorname{sign}(y)$, is 1, -1, or 0, depending on whether this word is in $\Delta^* \backslash \{\varepsilon\}$, $(\Delta^{-1})^* \backslash \{\varepsilon\}$, or in $\{\varepsilon\}$, respectively. For any $y, y' \in \Delta^*$, $y \sqsubset y'$ or $y' \sqsubset y$ if and only if $y^{-1}y'$ is in $\Delta^* \cup (\Delta^{-1})^*$.

A *finite transducer* is a 6-tuple $M = (Q, \Sigma, \Delta, \delta, Q_I, Q_F)$ where Q, Σ, and Δ denote nonempty finite sets of states, input symbols, and output symbols, respectively, $Q_I, Q_F \subseteq Q$ denote sets of initial and final (or accepting) states, respectively, and δ is a finite subset of $Q \times \Sigma^* \times \Delta^* \times Q$. Σ (Δ) is called the input (output) alphabet, δ is called the transition relation. Each element of δ denotes a *transition*.[1] In general, of course, M will be *nondeterministic*. Since we only deal with transducers of the above type, the adjective "finite" is omitted from now on. M is called *normalized* (*real time*[2]) if δ is a finite subset of $Q \times (\Sigma \cup \{\varepsilon\}) \times \Delta^* \times Q$ ($Q \times \Sigma \times \Delta^* \times Q$, respectively). If δ is a subset of $Q \times \Sigma \times \{\varepsilon\} \times Q$, then M is called a *finite automaton*, where we again omit the adjective "finite." The latter definition is, of course, isomorphic to the usual one of a nondeterministic finite automaton.

The mode of operation of M is described by paths. A *path* π (of length m) is a word $(q_1, x_1, z_1) \ldots (q_m, x_m, z_m) q_{m+1} \in (Q \times \Sigma^* \times \Delta^*)^m \cdot Q$ such that $(q_1, x_1, z_1, q_2), \ldots, (q_m, x_m, z_m, q_{m+1})$ are transitions. π is said to lead from q_1 to q_{m+1}, to consume $x := x_1 \ldots x_m \in \Sigma^*$, to produce $z := z_1 \ldots z_m \in \Delta^*$, and to realize $(x, z) \in \Sigma^* \times \Delta^*$. π is called *accepting* if q_1 is an initial and q_{m+1} is a final state. Whenever convenient we identify a transition (p, x, z, q) with the path $(p, x, z)q$ of length 1 and vice versa. We define $\hat{\delta}$ to be the set of all $(p, x, z, q) \in Q \times \Sigma^* \times \Delta^* \times Q$ such that (x, z) is realized by some path in M leading from p to q. If M is real time, then δ equals $\hat{\delta} \cap Q \times \Sigma \times \Delta^* \times Q$. In this case we rename $\hat{\delta}$ by δ. A state of M is called *useful* if it appears on some accepting path. If all states of M are useful, then M is called *trim*.

The *transduction* (or *relation*) *realized* by M, denoted by $T(M)$, is the set of pairs (in $\Sigma^* \times \Delta^*$) realized by the accepting paths in M. If $(x, z) \in \Sigma^* \times \Delta^*$ belongs to $T(M)$, then z is called a *value* for x in M. The *language recognized* by M, denoted by $L(M)$, is the domain of $T(M)$, i.e., the set of words (in Σ^*) consumed by the accepting paths in M. Two transducers are *equivalent* if the transductions realized by them coincide.

Next we define some local structural parameters and the size of M. $\operatorname{diff}(\delta)$ denotes the minimal nonnegative k such that, for all pairs $((p, x, z, q), (p', x, z', q'))$ of transitions consuming the same $x \in \Sigma^*$, $||z'| - |z||$ is at most k. $\operatorname{im}(\delta)$ is the set of ε and of all words (in Δ^*) produced by any transition. We set $\operatorname{iml}(\delta) := \max\{|z| \mid z \in \operatorname{im}(\delta)\}$. The *size* of δ, denoted by $\|\delta\|$, is defined as 1 plus the sum of $1 + |x| + |z|$ over all transitions (p, x, z, q). The *size* of M, denoted by $\|M\|$, is defined as $\#Q + \#\Sigma + \#\Delta + \|\delta\|$. Note that $\operatorname{diff}(\delta) \leq \operatorname{iml}(\delta) \leq \|\delta\| - 1$.

M is called *deterministic*[3] if it has exactly one initial state, if the words consumed by any two distinct transitions starting from the same state differ at some position, and if every transition consuming ε does not start from a final state. M is called

---

[1] M may be isomorphically seen as a finite automaton with two one-way input tapes, but then many of the subsequent notations have another intuitive meaning.

[2] Real-time transducers are sometimes called nondeterministic generalized sequential machines.

[3] Deterministic real-time transducers are sometimes called deterministic generalized sequential machines.

unambiguous if every word in Σ^* is consumed by at most one accepting path. M is called *single valued* if every word in Σ^* has at most one value. Obviously, every deterministic transducer is unambiguous and every unambiguous transducer is single valued. In order to avoid trivial cases we demand from now on that in a single-valued transducer the empty word has no value other than ε.

For any transducer M it is straightforward to construct an equivalent normalized transducer M' such that $\|M'\| \in \Theta(\|M\|)$. The following proposition shows that the real-time transducer, not just the normalized one, can be used as a "normal form" (see, e.g., [HKL92a, §3] and [HKL92b, Lem. 4.1]) for a single-valued, unambiguous, or deterministic transducer.

Proposition 1.1 *Let $M = (Q, \Sigma, \Delta, \delta, Q_I, Q_F)$ be a single-valued transducer with n states. Then, there is an equivalent real-time transducer M' having at most $\|M\|$ states and size at most $3 \cdot (1 + n^2) \cdot (1 + \mathrm{iml}(\delta)) \cdot \|M\|$. M' inherits from M the property of being unambiguous or deterministic. M' can be constructed in deterministic time polynomial in $\|M\|$.*

Following [B79], a transducer $M = (Q, \Sigma, \Delta, \delta, Q_I, Q_F)$ is called *sequential* if it is deterministic and real time and if all its states are final. M is called *subsequential* if either M is deterministic and real time or there is a deterministic real-time transducer $M' = (Q', \Sigma, \Delta, \delta', Q_I, Q'_F)$, a partial function $\zeta : Q' \hookrightarrow \Delta^*$ with domain Q'_F, and a state q_F such that $Q = Q' \,\dot\cup\, \{q_F\}$, $Q_F = \{q_F\}$, and $\delta = \delta' \cup \bigcup_{p \in Q'}\{p\} \times \{\varepsilon\} \times \zeta(p) \times \{q_F\}$. A subsequential transducer M as above can be easily transformed into an equivalent unambiguous real-time transducer of size at most $\|M\| \cdot (2 + \mathrm{iml}(\delta))$. By definition, any sequential transducer is deterministic and real time and any deterministic real-time transducer is subsequential. Note that our definitions of deterministic and unambiguous automata are isomorphic to the usual ones.

Having in mind Proposition 1.1 and the remark before that, a relation $R \subseteq \Sigma^* \times \Delta^*$ is called *sequential* (*deterministic rational, subsequential, unambiguous rational*, a *rational function, real time rational, rational*) if it is realized by some sequential (deterministic real-time, subsequential, unambiguous real-time, single-valued real-time, real-time, normalized) transducer.

2   Unambiguous Transducers

In this section we investigate the transformation of a single-valued into an equivalent unambiguous transducer. For this transformation the following exponential upper and lower bounds are known.

Proposition 2.1 ([HKL92a, Lem. 3.2], [Sbr76], [B79, Thm. IV.4.5])
For any single-valued real-time transducer M with n states there is an equivalent unambiguous real-time transducer M' having at most $n \cdot 2^{n-1}$ states and size at most $\|M\| \cdot 2^{n-1}$. M' can be constructed in deterministic time polynomial in $\|M\| \cdot 2^n$.

Proposition 2.2 ([L93]) *Let $n \in \mathbb{N}$. There is an automaton M having n states, two input symbols, and $c \cdot n$ transitions, for some constant c, such that any equivalent unambiguous automaton has at least $2^n - 1$ states. When seen as a transducer every such M is single valued and real time and any equivalent unambiguous real-time transducer has at least $2^n - 1$ states.*

The purpose of this section is to present an apparently new "unambiguous subset construction" for single-valued transducers. This construction yields an upper bound on the increase of the number of states in the above transformation which is at most one state off the optimal upper bound. The outcome is stated in the following theorem.

Theorem 2.3 *For any single-valued real-time transducer M with n states there is an equivalent unambiguous real-time transducer M' having at most 2^n states and size at most $\|M\|^5 \cdot 2^n$. M' can be constructed in deterministic time polynomial in $\|M\| \cdot 2^n$.*

Note that Theorem 2.3 improves the upper bound on the number of states of M' in Proposition 2.1 from $n \cdot 2^{n-1}$ to 2^n. It remains open whether this or the lower bound $2^n - 1$ stated in Proposition 2.2 is optimal. Using Proposition 1.1, Proposition 2.1 and Theorem 2.3 can be automatically extended from real-time to general transducers. Since every unambiguous transducer is single valued, Proposition 2.1 (or Theorem 2.3) directly implies that the class of rational functions coincides with the class of unambiguous rational relations. The first proof of this result is due to S. Eilenberg ([E74, Thm. IX.8.1], see [B79, Thm. IV.4.2]). It uses the cross-section theorem and is different from the proofs of Proposition 2.1 and Theorem 2.3. Note that the automaton M in Proposition 2.2 recognizes the language $L_n := (\{0\} \cup (\{0\}\{1\}^*)^{n-1}\{0\})^*$ using $2n$ transitions.

In the remainder of this section we will establish Theorem 2.3.

Proof of Theorem 2.3: Let $M = (Q, \Sigma, \Delta, \delta, Q_I, Q_F)$ be a single-valued real-time transducer with n states. We are going to construct an unambiguous real-time transducer M' having at most 2^n states and being equivalent to M. Our basic idea is to employ an "unambiguous subset construction" for single-valued transducers. Given any subset of Q and any input symbol in Σ, M' *nondeterministically* moves to a "next subset" which is a connected component in a certain "usefulness graph." We furthermore develop the notion of a "lead" of one state in Q over another in order to handle the output in M'.

We may assume that M is trim. Let "$<$" be some fixed complete order on Q. A pair of states $(q_1, q_2) \in Q^2$ is called *useful* if there are pairs of states $(r_1, r_2) \in Q_I^2$ and $(s_1, s_2) \in Q_F^2$ and words $u, w \in \Sigma^*$ and $y_1, y_2, z_1, z_2 \in \Delta^*$ such that, for each $i \in \{1, 2\}$, $(r_i, u, y_i, q_i) \in \delta$ and $(q_i, w, z_i, s_i) \in \delta$. Since M is single valued, $y_1^{-1}y_2$ is in $\Delta^* \cup (\Delta^{-1})^*$. Moreover, for any pair of states $(\tilde{r}_1, \tilde{r}_2) \in Q_I^2$ and for any words $\tilde{u} \in \Sigma^*$ and $\tilde{y}_1, \tilde{y}_2 \in \Delta^*$ such that for each $i \in \{1, 2\}$ $(\tilde{r}_i, \tilde{u}, \tilde{y}_i, q_i) \in \delta$, we observe that $\tilde{y}_1^{-1}\tilde{y}_2$ coincides with $y_1^{-1}y_2$. The latter word is called the *lead* of q_2 over q_1, denoted by $\lambda(q_1, q_2)$. Since the length of the above $\tilde{u}$ can be chosen to be at most $n^2 - 1$, we obtain that the length of $\lambda(q_1, q_2)$ is at most $n^2 \cdot \text{diff}(\delta)$. Note that if (q_1, q_2) is useful then so is (q_2, q_1).

The *usefulness graph* of M is the undirected graph G with all states of M as vertices and all unordered useful pairs of states as edges. A subset B of Q is called *connected* if the graph G restricted to B is connected. B is said to be a *connected component* of a subset C of Q if it is a nonempty, connected component of the graph G restricted to C. Finally, Q' is defined to be the smallest subset of $2^Q \setminus \{\emptyset\}$ such that every connected component of Q_I is in Q' and if B is in Q' then, for each $a \in \Sigma$, every connected component of $C := \{s' \in Q \mid \exists s \in B \, \exists z' \in \Delta^* : (s, a, z', s') \in \delta\}$ is in Q'. Q' is the designated set of nonfinal states of M'.

Let us consider any $B \in Q'$. By definition of Q' there is a word $u \in \Sigma^*$ such that B is a connected subset of $\{q \in Q \mid \exists r(u, q) \in Q_I \, \exists y(u, q) \in \Delta^* : (r(u, q), u, y(u, q), q) \in \delta\}$. Let $p, q \in B$. Consider any path $q_1, q_2, \ldots, q_{l+1}$ in G restricted to B leading from p to q. Then,

$$
\begin{aligned}
|y(u, q)| - |y(u, p)| &= \sum_{j=1}^{l} (|y(u, q_{j+1})| - |y(u, q_j)|) \\
&= \sum_{j=1}^{l} \operatorname{sign}(\lambda(q_j, q_{j+1})) \cdot |\lambda(q_j, q_{j+1})|,
\end{aligned}
$$

i.e., $|y(u, q)| - |y(u, p)|$ only depends on p, q, and B. We can therefore define the *base* of B, denoted by $\beta(B)$, to be the minimal $p \in B$ — with respect to "$<$" — such that, for all $q \in B$, $|y(u, q)| - |y(u, p)| \geq 0$. Set $p := \beta(B)$, and let $q \in B$. Consider any path $q_1, q_2, \ldots, q_{l+1}$ in G restricted to B leading from p to q. It can be seen by induction on k that, for all $k \in \{0, \ldots, l\}$, $\prod_{j=1}^{k} \lambda(q_j, q_{j+1}) = y(u, q_1)^{-1} y(u, q_{k+1}) \in \Delta^*$. Thus, $y(u, p)^{-1} y(u, q)$ is a word in Δ^* which only depends on q and B. It is called the *lead* of q over the base of B, denoted by $\lambda_B(q)$. Since the above l can be chosen to be at most $n - 1$, we obtain that the length of $\lambda_B(q)$ is at most $n^3 \cdot \operatorname{diff}(\delta)$. Since M is single valued, we have for any $q, q' \in B \cap Q_F$ that $\lambda_B(q)$ and $\lambda_B(q')$ coincide. If B is a subset of Q_I, then $\lambda_B(q) = \varepsilon$ for all $q \in B$.

Recall the above definition of Q'. A path in the new transducer M' leading from an initial state (of M') to some state $B \in Q'$ is designated to simulate the input/output behavior of a path in M leading from an initial state (of M) to the base of B. Following this intention, we now construct the real-time transducer $M' = (Q' \cup \{q'_F\}, \Sigma, \Delta, \delta', Q'_I, \{q'_F\})$ by setting

$$
Q'_I := \{B \in Q' \mid B \text{ is a connected component of } Q_I\} \cup \{q'_F \mid (\varepsilon, \varepsilon) \in T(M)\}
$$

and $\delta' := \delta'_1 \cup \delta'_2$ where

$$
\begin{aligned}
\delta'_1 := \{&(B, a, z, B') \in Q' \times \Sigma \times \Delta^* \times Q' \mid B' \text{ is a connected component} \\
&\text{of } C := \{s' \in Q \mid \exists s \in B \, \exists z' \in \Delta^* : (s, a, z', s') \in \delta\} \quad \& \\
&\exists s_0 \in B \, \exists z_0 \in \Delta^* : (s_0, a, z_0, \beta(B')) \in \delta \, \& \, z = \lambda_B(s_0) \cdot z_0\}
\end{aligned}
$$

and

$$
\begin{aligned}
\delta'_2 := \{&(B, a, z, q'_F) \in Q' \times \Sigma \times \Delta^* \times \{q'_F\} \mid \exists s'_0 \in Q_F \, \exists s_0 \in B \, \exists z_0 \in \Delta^* : \\
&(s_0, a, z_0, s'_0) \in \delta \, \& \, z = \lambda_B(s_0) \cdot z_0\}.
\end{aligned}
$$

It is easy to see that $\#(Q' \cup \{q'_F\}) \leq 2^n$, $\#\delta' \leq \#\delta \cdot 2^n$, $\|\delta'\| \leq \|\delta\| \cdot n^3 \cdot (1 + \operatorname{diff}(\delta)) \cdot 2^n$, $\|M'\| \leq n^3 \cdot (1 + \operatorname{diff}(\delta)) \cdot \|M\| \cdot 2^n \leq \|M\|^5 \cdot 2^n$, and M' can be constructed in

Figure 1: Definition of the automaton M (the output ε is omitted).

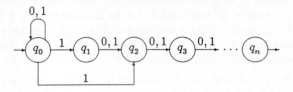

Figure 2: Unambiguous automaton M' (the output ε is omitted).

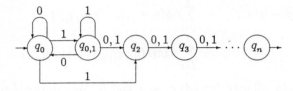

deterministic time polynomial in $\|M\| \cdot 2^n$. Let $B_0 \in Q'_I \cap Q'$, $B \in Q'$, $u \in \Sigma^*$, and $y \in \Delta^*$ such that $(B_0, u, y, B) \in \delta'$. Then, it is easy to show by induction on the length of u that B is contained in the set $\{q \in Q \mid \exists\, r(u,q) \in B_0 \colon (r(u,q), u, y \cdot \lambda_B(q), q) \in \delta\}$. Let moreover $a \in \Sigma$ and $z \in \Delta^*$ such that $(B, a, z, q'_F) \in \delta'$. Then there are $s \in Q_F$, $q \in B$, and $z_0 \in \Delta^*$ such that $(q, a, z_0, s) \in \delta$ and $z = \lambda_B(q) \cdot z_0$, i.e., $(ua, yz) = (ua, y \cdot \lambda_B(q) \cdot z_0) \in T(M)$. By this we have verified that $T(M')$ is included in $T(M)$. On the other hand, it is easy to show that $L(M)$ is included in $L(M')$. Since M is single valued, this altogether implies that M and M' are equivalent. It remains to be shown that M' is unambiguous.

Since M' is single valued, each accepting path of this machine is uniquely determined by the sequence of its states and by the word it consumes. Let us now assume that M' is ambiguous. Then there must be states $B_1, B_2 \in Q'_I \cap Q'$ and $B'_1, B'_2 \in Q'$ and words $u, w \in \Sigma^*$ such that each $(q_1, q_2) \in B'_1 \times B'_2$ is useless and for each $i \in \{1,2\}$ there are paths π_i and π'_i in M' consuming u and w, respectively, and leading from B_i to B'_i and from B'_i to q'_F, respectively. By going through π'_1, π'_2 and π_1, π_2 from right to left, it is straightforward to find a useful pair of states $(q_1, q_2) \in B'_1 \times B'_2$. (Contradiction!) Hence, M' is unambiguous. $\square$

Note that if in the proof of Theorem 2.3 M is an automaton, then the base of any $B \in Q'$ is just its minimal element and the leads are all ε. The size of M' is at most $\|M\| \cdot 2^n$ in this case. In certain cases of M, M' has exponentially fewer states than the automaton obtained from M by the well-known "deterministic" subset construction for automata (see, e.g., [HU79]). In order to demonstrate this let us consider, for any fixed $n \geq 2$, the language $L_n := \{0,1\}^*(\{1\}\{0,1\}^{n-1} \cup \{1\}\{0,1\}^{n-2})$ being recognized by the automaton M shown in Figure 1. The usefulness graph of M has exactly one edge, which connects its vertices q_0 and q_1. The unambiguous subset construction of Theorem 2.3 applied to M yields the unambiguous automaton M' shown in Figure 2. Note that in any automaton recognizing L_n each accepting path consuming the word

10^{n-1} consists of $n + 1$ different states. Thus, M and M' are both minimal automata for L_n. Note that another minimal unambiguous automaton can be obtained from M by removing the transition $(q_1, 1, \varepsilon, q_2)$ from that machine. On the other hand, applying the deterministic subset construction to M it is a routine exercise to show that the minimal deterministic automaton recognizing L_n has at least $2^{n/2}$ states.

3 Deterministic Transducers

In this section we investigate the transformation of a single-valued into an equivalent subsequential or deterministic transducer if such a transducer exists. For this transformation the following exponential lower bound is well-known.

Proposition 3.1 ([M71], [MF71]) *Let $n \in \mathbb{N}$. There is an automaton M having n states, two input symbols, and $c \cdot n$ transitions, for some constant c, such that any equivalent deterministic automaton has at least 2^n states. When seen as a transducer every such M is single valued and real time and any equivalent deterministic real-time or subsequential transducer has at least 2^n states.*

The purpose of this section is to announce a subset construction for "balanced" single-valued transducers which yields an exponential upper bound on the increase of the number of states and the size in the above transformation. The outcome is stated in Theorems 3.2–3.3. These theorems also give efficiently testable characterizations for a rational function to be subsequential or deterministic rational. In order to formulate these characterizations we need the following definitions.

Let $M = (Q, \Sigma, \Delta, \delta, Q_I, Q_F)$ be a real-time transducer with n states. Two states $q_1, q_2 \in Q$ are said to be *twinned* if, for all states $p_1, p_2 \in Q_I$ and for all words $u, v \in \Sigma^*$ and $y_1, y_2, z_1, z_2 \in \Delta^*$ such that $(p_1, u, y_1, q_1), (q_1, v, z_1, q_1) \in \delta$ and $(p_2, u, y_2, q_2), (q_2, v, z_2, q_2) \in \delta$, it follows that (∗) either $z_1 = z_2 = \varepsilon$ or $|z_1| = |z_2| \neq 0$ and $y_1 \sqsubset y_2$ or $y_2 \sqsubset y_1$. Using [B79, Prop. IV.6.2], it is not difficult to see that the above definition remains unchanged if the "combinatorial" assertion (∗) is replaced by the "algebraic" equation $y_1 z_1 y_1^{-1} = y_2 z_2 y_2^{-1} \in \Delta^*$. Thus, it is equivalent to the definition of twinned states in [B79, p. 128].

Let $k_1 := (n^2 - 1) \cdot \mathrm{diff}(\delta)$ and $k_2 := n^2 \cdot \mathrm{iml}(\delta)$. M is called *balanced* if, for all useful states $p_1, p_2 \in Q_I$ and $r_1, r_2 \in Q$ and for all words $u \in \Sigma^*$ and $z_1, z_2 \in \Delta^*$ such that $(p_1, u, z_1, r_1) \in \delta$ and $(p_2, u, z_2, r_2) \in \delta$, it follows that $||z_1| - |z_2|| \leq k_1$ and $\min\{|z_i| - |\mathrm{gcp}\{z_1, z_2\}| \,|\, i \in \{1, 2\}\} \leq k_2$. Note that a similar condition appears in [CS86, Lem. 5].

The domain of a relation $R \subseteq \Sigma^* \times \Delta^*$, i.e., the set of all $w \in \Sigma^*$ such that $(w, z) \in R$ for some $z \in \Delta^*$, is called *prefix closed* if it contains all prefixes of all its elements. We say that R (or any transducer realizing R) *preserves prefixes* if, for all $(w_1, z_1), (w_2, z_2) \in R$, $w_1 \sqsubset w_2$ implies that $z_1 \sqsubset z_2$. Note that if M preserves prefixes, then it is single valued. In contrast to [B79, p. 97], we do not require here that the domain of a prefix preserving relation is prefix closed.

Theorem 3.2 *Let $M = (Q, \Sigma, \Delta, \delta, Q_I, Q_F)$ be a single-valued real-time transducer with n states. The following assertions are equivalent.*

(i) $T(M)$ is subsequential.

(ii) Any two useful states of M are twinned.

(iii) M is balanced.

If $T(M)$ is subsequential, then it can be realized by a subsequential transducer M' having at most $1 + 2^n \cdot \max\{2, \#\Delta\}^{2n^3 \cdot \mathrm{iml}(\delta)}$ states and size at most $2^{n+1} \cdot \max\{2, \#\Delta\}^{2n^3 \cdot \mathrm{iml}(\delta)} \cdot \|M\|^4$. M' can be constructed in deterministic time polynomial in $2^n \cdot \max\{2, \#\Delta\}^{n^3 \cdot \mathrm{iml}(\delta)} \cdot \|M\|$.

Theorem 3.3 A relation $R \subseteq \Sigma^* \times \Delta^*$ is deterministic rational if and only if it is subsequential and preserves prefixes. R is sequential if and only if it is subsequential, preserves prefixes, and has a prefix-closed domain. For every single-valued real-time transducer $M = (Q, \Sigma, \Delta, \delta, Q_I, Q_F)$ with n states such that $T(M)$ is deterministic rational (sequential) there is an equivalent deterministic real-time transducer (sequential transducer) M' having at most $1 + 2^n \cdot \max\{2, \#\Delta\}^{2n^3 \cdot \mathrm{iml}(\delta)}$ states and size at most $2^{n+3} \cdot \max\{2, \#\Delta\}^{2n^3 \cdot \mathrm{iml}(\delta)} \cdot \|M\|^7$. M' can be constructed in deterministic time polynomial in $2^n \cdot \max\{2, \#\Delta\}^{n^3 \cdot \mathrm{iml}(\delta)} \cdot \|M\|$.

Using Proposition 1.1, the transformation parts of Theorems 3.2 and 3.3 can be automatically extended from real-time to general transducers. The equivalence of the assertions (i) and (ii) of Theorem 3.2 was shown by C. Choffrut ([C78], see [B79, Thm. IV.2.7 and Prop. IV.6.4], see also [R91, Thm. 3]) using the notion of bounded variation which does not appear in this paper. In our proof of Theorem 3.3 the characterization of sequential relations turns out to be a by-product of the characterization of deterministic rational relations. A direct proof of the former result also appeared in [B79, Prop. IV.2.6].

As pointed out by H. Leung [L91] the language recognized by the automaton M in Proposition 3.1 can be chosen as $L_n := (\{0\} \cup \{0,1\}^{n-1}\{0\})^*$. In this case M has $2n$ transitions. Due to the good choice of L_n, this M has fewer transitions than the automaton in [MF71] and is "easier" than the automaton in [M71].

The proofs of Theorems 3.2 and 3.3 are omitted here. Our basic idea for the proof of the implication "$(iii) \Longrightarrow (i)$" in Theorem 3.2 is to generalize the well-known subset construction (see, e.g., [HU79]) from automata to balanced single-valued transducers.

4 Polynomial-time Algorithms

Recall the definition of twinned states and of the prefix preserving property of a real-time transducer at the beginning of §3. In this section we state the two following lemmas.

Lemma 4.1 Given a real-time transducer M, it is decidable in deterministic time polynomial in its size whether or not any two useful states of M are twinned.

Lemma 4.2 Assume that any two useful states of a given real-time transducer M are twinned. It is decidable in deterministic time polynomial in the size of M whether or not this machine preserves prefixes.

Using Proposition 1.1 and the characterizations stated in Theorems 3.2 and 3.3, Lemmas 4.1 and 4.2 directly imply the main result of this section.

Theorem 4.3 *Given any single-valued transducer M, it is decidable in deterministic time polynomial in its size whether or not*

(i) $T(M)$ is subsequential.

(ii) $T(M)$ is deterministic rational.

It is easy to obtain a nondeterministic polynomial-space algorithm deciding whether or not the language recognized by a given automaton is prefix closed. Therefore, employing Theorems 3.3 and 4.3, it can be decided in polynomial space whether or not a given single-valued transducer realizes a sequential relation. Using different methods, C. Choffrut obtained inefficient algorithms deciding the property (i) of Theorem 4.3 and the problem of the last sentence ([C78], see [B79, Thm. IV.6.1]).

Our basic approach for the proofs of Lemmas 4.1 and 4.2 is to use graph characterizations of structural properties of transducers (see, e.g., [W90, §3] or [P92, §6]) which are related to the concepts of twinned states and of preserved prefixes. These proofs are omitted here.

Acknowledgment. We thank Detlef Wotschke for suggesting us to extend the first author's previous unpublished work about deterministic and unambiguous transducers and to combine it with new work by the second author in order to present it in the context of economy of description. We thank Kosaburo Hashiguchi, Juhani Karhumäki, Hing Leung, and Helmut Seidl for discussions about the former topics.

References

[A87]   K. Abrahamson, Succinct representation of regular sets using gotos and Boolean variables, J. Computer and System Sciences 34 (1987) 129–148.

[B79]   J. Berstel, Transductions and Context-Free Languages, Teubner, Stuttgart, 1979.

[C78]   C. Choffrut, Contribution à l'étude de quelques familles remarquables de fonctions rationnelles, thèse de doctorat d'état, Université Paris VII, 1978.

[CC83] C. Choffrut and K. Culik II, Properties of finite and pushdown transducers, SIAM J. Computing 12 (1983) 300–315.

[CS86] C. Choffrut and M.P. Schützenberger, Décomposition de fonctions rationnelles, Proc. 3rd STACS 1986, in: Lecture Notes in Computer Science 210, Springer, Berlin, Heidelberg, 1986, pp. 213–226.

[E74]   S. Eilenberg, Automata, Languages, and Machines, Volume A, Academic Press, New York, NY, 1974.

[G89]   E. Gurari, An Introduction to the Theory of Computation, Computer Science Press, Rockville, MD, 1989.

[GI83] E. Gurari and O. Ibarra, A note on finite-valued and finitely ambiguous transducers, Mathematical Systems Theory 16 (1983) 61–66.

618

[HKL92a]   T. Harju, H.C.M. Kleijn, and M. Latteux, Compositional representation of rational functions, RAIRO Informatique théorique et Applications 26 (1992) 243–255.

[HKL92b]   T. Harju, H.C.M. Kleijn, and M. Latteux, Deterministic sequential functions, Acta Informatica 29 (1992) 545–554.

[HW93]   T. Head and A. Weber, Deciding code related properties by means of finite transducers, in: Sequences II, (R. Capocelli, A. De Santis, and U. Vaccaro, eds.), Springer, New York, NY, Berlin, Heidelberg, 1993, pp. 260–272.

[HU79]   J. Hopcroft and J. Ullman, Introduction to Automata Theory, Languages, and Computation, Addison-Wesley, Reading, MA, 1979.

[KPW93]   C. Kintala, K.-Y. Pun, and D. Wotschke, Concise representations of regular languages by degree and probabilistic finite automata, Mathematical Systems Theory 26 (1993) 379–395.

[KW80]   C. Kintala and D. Wotschke, Amounts of nondeterminism in finite automata, Acta Informatica 13 (1980) 199–204.

[L91]   H. Leung, personal communication, 1991.

[L93]   H. Leung, Separating exponentially ambiguous NFA from polynomially ambiguous NFA, Proc. 4th ISAAC 1993, in: Lecture Notes in Computer Science, Springer, Berlin, Heidelberg, to appear.

[LS77]   R. Lyndon and P. Schupp, Combinatorial Group Theory, Springer, Berlin, Heidelberg, New York, NY, 1977.

[MF71]   A. Meyer and M. Fischer, Economy of description by automata, grammars, and formal systems, Proc. 12th SWAT 1971, pp. 188–191.

[M71]   F.R. Moore, On the bounds for state-set size in the proofs of equivalence between deterministic, nondeterministic, and two-way finite automata, IEEE Transactions on Computers 20 (1971) 1211–1214.

[P92]   J.-E. Pin, On reversible automata, Proc. 1st LATIN 1992, in: Lecture Notes in Computer Science 583, Springer, Berlin, Heidelberg, 1992, pp. 401–416.

[RI89]   B. Ravikumar and O. Ibarra, Relating the type of ambiguity of finite automata to the succinctness of their representation, SIAM J. Computing 18 (1989) 1263–1282.

[R91]   C. Reutenauer, Subsequential functions: characterizations, minimization, examples, Proc. 6th IMYCS 1990, in: Lecture Notes in Computer Science 464, Springer, Berlin, Heidelberg, 1991, pp. 62–79.

[Sdt78]   E.M. Schmidt, Succinctness of descriptions of context-free, regular, and finite languages, Ph.D. thesis, Cornell University, 1978.

[Sbr76]   M.P. Schützenberger, Sur les relations rationnelles entre monoïdes libres, Theoretical Computer Science 3 (1976) 243–259.

[Se93]   H. Seidl, When is a functional tree transduction deterministic? Proc. 4th TAPSOFT 1993, in: Lecture Notes in Computer Science 668, Springer, Berlin, Heidelberg, 1993, pp. 251–265.

[SH85]   R. Stearns and H. Hunt III, On the equivalence and containment problems for unambiguous regular expressions, regular grammars and finite automata, SIAM J. Computing 14 (1985) 598–611.

[U92]   V.A. Uspensky, Complexity and entropy: an introduction to the theory of Kolmogorov complexity, in: Kolmogorov Complexity and Computational Complexity, (O. Watanabe, ed.), Springer, Berlin, Heidelberg, 1992, pp. 85–102.

[W90]   A. Weber, On the valuedness of finite transducers, Acta Informatica 27 (1990) 749–780.

Automaticity: Properties of a Measure of Descriptional Complexity
(Extended Abstract)

Jeffrey Shallit[*][1] and Yuri Breitbart[**][2]

[1] Department of Computer Science, University of Waterloo, Waterloo, Ontario,
Canada N2L 3G1 (shallit@graceland.uwaterloo.ca)
[2] Department of Computer Science, University of Kentucky, Lexington, KY 40506
USA (yuri@s.ms.uky.edu)

Abstract. Let Σ and Δ be nonempty alphabets with Σ finite. Let f be a function mapping Σ^* to Δ. We explore the notion of *automaticity*, which attempts to model how "close" f is to a finite-state function. Formally, the automaticity of f is a function $A_f(n)$ which counts the minimum number of states in any deterministic finite automaton that computes f correctly on all strings of length $\leq n$ (and its behavior on longer strings is not specified). The same or similar notions were examined previously by Trakhtenbrot, Grinberg and Korshunov, Karp, Breitbart, Gabarró, Dwork and Stockmeyer, and Kaneps and Freivalds.

1 Introduction

Suppose x is a finite or infinite string. There have been many attempts to associate with x some measure of its "descriptional complexity"— the most famous being, of course, Kolmogorov(-Chaitin-Solomonoff) complexity $K(x)$, where the complexity of a string x is measured by the length of the shortest program to compute x. While this measure is extremely productive and useful, it suffers from the defect that $K(x)$ is not partial recursive.

There have been many other suggestions for more computable measures of "descriptional complexity". To name just a few: boolean circuit complexity, shortest straight-line program (using operations such as union, concatenation, and intersection), "rational index", description by context-free grammars, etc.

In this paper, we will examine the properties of another measure, which we call *automaticity*. The automaticity of a function f (or language L) measures how close f (or L) is to a finite state function (or language). Although the concept of automaticity is not new (see §3), we claim that it has many properties that have not been previously studied.

---

[*] Research supported in part by NSERC.
[**] Research supported in part by NSF grant #IRI-9221947.

2 Automaticity Defined

We will use the following notation: $\Sigma^{\leq n} = \epsilon + \Sigma + \Sigma^2 + \cdots + \Sigma^n$.

We will be concerned with finite automata that can compute functions. A *deterministic finite automaton with output* (DFAO) is a sextuple

$$M = (Q, \Sigma, \delta, q_0, \Delta, \tau),$$

where Q is a finite nonempty set of states, Σ (the input alphabet) and Δ (the output alphabet) are finite nonempty sets, δ is the transition function mapping $Q \times \Sigma$ into Q, q_0 is the initial state, and τ is an output function mapping Q into Δ. We emphasize that δ is *complete*; i.e., it is defined for all members of $Q \times \Sigma$. The machine M computes a function g_M from Σ^* to Δ as follows: $g_M(w) = \tau(\delta(q_0, w))$.

In the case where $\Delta = \{0, 1\}$, this flavor of automaton coincides with the ordinary notion of automaton and acceptance/rejection. In this case we can associate a set of *final states* F such that $F = \{q \in Q : \tau(q) = 1\}$. The language accepted by M is then $L(M) = \{w \in \Sigma^* : \delta(q_0, w) \in F\}$.

There is another possible model of finite automata with outputs that has appeared in the literature. In this model, the output function τ maps $Q \times \Sigma \to \Delta$, so that outputs are associated with transitions, not states. In this case, the machine M computes a function h_M from Σ^+ to Δ as follows: $h_M(w_1 w_2 \cdots w_n) = \tau(\delta(q_0, w_1 w_2 \cdots w_{n-1}), w_n)$. Note that $h_M(\epsilon)$ is undefined in this model. We will not examine this model further in this paper.

By $|M|$ we will mean the "size" of the automaton M, which we define to be the cardinality of the set Q of states in M. Another measure of size is $\| M \|$, the number of transitions in M.

Let Σ and Δ be alphabets, with $0 < |\Sigma|, |\Delta| < \infty$ and $|\Delta| > 0$. Let f be a map from Σ^* to Δ. Then the *(deterministic) automaticity* of f is a function $A_f(n)$ defined as follows:

$$A_f(n) = \min \{|M| : M \in \text{DFAO and } \forall \, w \in \Sigma^{\leq n} \; f(w) = g_M(w)\}.$$

Roughly speaking, $A_f(n)$ counts the minimum number of states in any DFAO M that simulates f correctly on all strings of length $\leq n$; how M behaves on longer strings is unspecified. In general, there may be many different automata for which the number of states is a minimum.

If $L \subseteq \Sigma^*$ is a language, then we write $A_L(n)$ for the automaticity of the characteristic function $\chi_L(w)$, defined as follows:

$$\chi_L(w) = \begin{cases} 1, & \text{if } w \in L; \\ 0, & \text{otherwise.} \end{cases}$$

In this case, $A_L(n) = \min \{|M| : M \in \text{DFA and } L(M) \cap \Sigma^{\leq n} = L \cap \Sigma^{\leq n}\}$.

There is also a *nondeterministic* analogue of automaticity $N_L(n)$, which we define only for languages L:

$$N_L(n) = \min \{|M| : M \in \text{NFA and } L(M) \cap \Sigma^{\leq n} = L \cap \Sigma^{\leq n}\}.$$

The implied constant in the big-O, big-Ω, and little-o bounds in this paper may depend on $k = |\Sigma|$ and $\ell = |\Delta|$, but not on n.

3 Previous Work

The history of automaticity goes back thirty years. During this time, the basic results were re-proved two or more times by different investigators who did not know about previous work. Some of the earliest results only appeared in Russian in obscure Soviet journals, and were never widely disseminated in the West. For this reason, we reprise the history of the field below, in the hope that future investigators will not have to begin anew.

The first result related to automaticity appears to be that of Trakhtenbrot in 1964 [21]. However, he used the second model of finite-state function computation we discussed above in §2, that is, the model based on Mealy machines. He called the minimum number of states the "weight of a finite tree". He proved an upper bound, similar to our Theorem 5 below, and constructed an example with high automaticity. He also gave a lower bound similar to our Theorem 6. Trakhtenbrot's results are summarized in English in [22, p. 144].

In 1965, Kuz'min [17] examined the smallest Mealy machine that computes a Boolean function of n variables; this is similar to the deterministic initial index $da_L(n)$ discussed below. He obtained results similar to our Theorems 5 and 6.

Trakhtenbrot's results on the Mealy model were improved in 1966 by Grinberg and Korshunov [11]. (Prof. Grinberg has kindly informed us that, due to printing errors in that paper, the direction of the inequality is reversed in Lemma 2 and the second half of Corollary 3. These errors appear in both the Russian original and English translation.)

The first person to study the concept of automaticity exactly as we have defined it was R. M. Karp. In [16], he proved Theorem 3 given below.

In 1971, Breitbart [3] studied the automaticity of the characteristic function f of the kth powers, expressed in a prime base p. He proved that for this f the estimate $A_f(n) = \Omega(p^{n/k})$ holds. In his Ph. D. thesis [4], published in 1973, Breitbart gave an example of a language $L \subseteq (0+1)^*$ such that $A_L(n) \geq 2^{n+2}/n$ for infinitely many n. He also gave an example of a language $L \subseteq (0+1)^*$ such that $A_L(n) \geq 2^n/n - 1$ for all $n \geq 1$. Additional results appeared in [5].

In 1977, Paredaens and Vyncke [18] studied some measures on formal languages. In the first sentence of their paper, they implied they would study the quantity

$$d\mu_L(n) = \min \{|M| \ : \ M \in \text{DFA and } L(M) = L \cap \Sigma^{\leq n}\}.$$

However, the rest of the paper deals with another quantity, which they called $f_L(n)$. Write $x \sim y$ if for all $w \in \Sigma^*$ we have $xw \in L$ exactly when $yw \in L$, the Myhill-Nerode equivalence relation. Then $f_L(n)$ was defined to be the number of distinct equivalence classes induced by $\sim$ on Σ^n. However, these two measures are not the same, and neither of them are the same as $A_L(n)$.

Other measures were introduced in 1983 by J. Gabarró [9, 10]. In [9], he defined a function $\mu_L(n)$ which he called the "initial index" of L:

$$\mu_L(n) = \min \{|M| \ : \ M \in \text{NFA and } L(M) = L \cap \Sigma^{\leq n}\}.$$

He also discussed (but did not name) a notion that coincides with what we called $d\mu_L(n)$ above. Again, neither of these two definitions are the same as $A_L(n)$.

In 1985, Balcázar, Díaz, and Gabarró [1] defined a slightly different notion of "initial index" which they denoted by $a_L(n)$. Here $a_L(n)$ was defined as follows:

$$a_L(n) = \min \{ |M| \ : \ M \in \text{NFA and } L(M) = L \cap \Sigma^n \}.$$

They also defined "deterministic initial index" $da_L(n)$; this was defined by

$$da_L(n) = \min \{ |M| \ : \ M \in \text{DFA and } L(M) = L \cap \Sigma^n \}.$$

Also see [2, §5.9].

In 1988, Ibarra and Ravikumar [12, p. 2] defined a notion of nonuniform space complexity for two-way deterministic finite automata (2-dfa's) that is very similar to our $A_L(n)$.

In 1989, Serna [20] introduced a complexity measure similar to Gabarró's "initial index"; however, instead of counting the minimum number of *states* in a nondeterministic machine, she counted the minimum number of *transitions*. Formally, she considered the quantity

$$\min \{ \| M \| \ : \ M \in \text{NFA and } L(M) = L \cap \Sigma^n \}.$$

She obtained theorems similar in some ways to Theorems 5 and 6 below.

In a 1989 conference paper, Dwork and Stockmeyer [7] introduced what they called a "measure of nonregularity". Given a language $L \subseteq \Sigma^*$, they called two words $w, w' \in \Sigma^*$ n–dissimilar if $|w|, |w'| \leq n$ and there exists v with $|wv|, |w'v| \leq n$ and $wv \in L$ iff $w'v \notin L$. Their measure of nonregularity, as a function of n, was defined to be the maximum number of distinct words that are pairwise n–dissimilar. (The same idea had been introduced previously by Karp [16] and Breitbart [4], but they only proved that the number of n-dissimilar words was a lower bound on $A_L(n)$.) Although it is perhaps not immediately obvious, Dwork and Stockmeyer's nonregularity measure coincides with $A_L(n)$ (in fact this was proved by Kaneps and Freivalds; see below). They also proved a weak version of Karp's theorem (Theorem 3) discussed below. They used their measure to show that if a two-way probabilistic finite automaton M recognizes a nonregular language with probability $1/2 + \delta$ for some fixed $\delta > 0$, then there is a constant b such that M uses at least 2^{n^b} expected time for infinitely many n. The journal paper containing proofs of these results is [8], where Theorem 2, Part 2, is also proved.

In 1990, independently of Dwork and Stockmeyer, Kaneps and Freivalds [13] introduced a measure they called $r_{\text{sim}}(L, \Sigma^{\leq n})$, which counts the number of distinct pairwise n–dissimilar words; their definition was the same as that of Dwork and Stockmeyer. They proved the following theorem:

Theorem 1 (Kaneps & Freivalds) *We have* $r_{\text{sim}}(L, \Sigma^{\leq n}) = A_L(n)$.

They also proved a weaker version of Theorem 3 below. They used their measure to show that any language recognized by a probabilistic Turing machine in $o(\log \log n)$ space is regular. In a later paper [14] they also proved (independently) a result on two-way probabilistic finite automata similar to that of Dwork and Stockmeyer mentioned above.

Recently, Condon et al. showed that deterministic automaticity is related to one-directional deterministic communication complexity. Consider two cooperating communicating parties, Alice and Bob, who know a language L and who are trying to determine membership in L for a word w with $|w| \leq n$. Alice knows w_A and Bob knows w_B, where $w = w_A w_B$. Bob must determine if $w \in L$ by making use of bits sent by Alice over a one-directional communication line. Let $C(n)$ denote the maximum number of bits required by the best possible strategy. Condon et al. showed [6] that $C(n) = \log_2 A_L(n)$.

4 Basic Properties of Automaticity

In this section we state some of the basic properties of deterministic and nondeterministic automaticity. The proofs are omitted.

Theorem 2 *Let $f : \Sigma^* \to \Delta$ and $L \subseteq \Sigma^*$. Then*

1. *For all $n \geq 0$ we have $A_f(n) \leq A_f(n+1)$ and $N_L(n) \leq N_L(n+1)$.*
2. *(Dwork-Stockmeyer; Kaneps-Freivalds) The language L is regular if and only if $A_L(n) = O(1)$. (The same statement holds for $N_L(n)$.)*
3. *For all $n \geq 0$ we have $N_L(n) \leq A_L(n) \leq 2^{N_L(n)}$. If $L \subseteq 0^*$, then there exists a constant c such that $A_L(n) \leq ce^{\sqrt{N_L(n) \log N_L(n)}}$.*
4. *For all $n \geq 0$ we have $A_L(n) = A_{\overline{L}}(n)$. (Here $\overline{L}$ denotes the complement of L.)*
5. *For all $n \geq 0$ we have*

$$A_L(n) \leq 2 + \sum_{w \in L \cap \Sigma^{\leq n}} |w| \leq 2 + n|L \cap \Sigma^{\leq n}|$$

and

$$N_L(n) \leq 1 + \sum_{w \in L \cap \Sigma^{\leq n}} |w| \leq 1 + n|L \cap \Sigma^{\leq n}|.$$

Theorem 3 (Karp) *Let $L \subseteq \Sigma^*$ be a nonregular language. Then $A_L(n) \geq (n+3)/2$ for infinitely many n.*

Theorem 4 *The bound in Theorem 3 is best possible, in the sense that the result is not true if the "2" in the denominator is replaced by any smaller positive real number, nor if the "3" is replaced by any larger real number.*

Proof. To prove Theorem 4, we demonstrate the existence of a nonregular language L_s for which $A_{L_s}(n) = \lfloor (n+3)/2 \rfloor$ for all $n \geq 0$.

Our L_s is most easily described by using a deterministic automaton with infinitely many states:

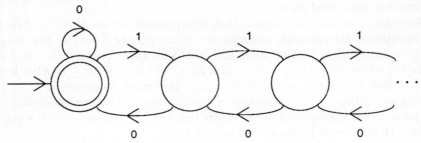

It is easy to see that L_s is not regular, since

$$L \cap 1^+ 0^+ = \{1^m 0^n \;:\; 1 \leq m \leq n\}.$$

(In fact, L_s is context-free, as it is generated by the following context free grammar: $G = (V, T, P, S) = (\{S, A, M\}, \{0, 1\}, P, S)$, where P, the set of productions is given as follows: $S = (S \rightarrow SAM \mid \epsilon, \quad A \rightarrow 0A \mid \epsilon, \quad M \rightarrow 1M0M \mid \epsilon)$.)

First we show that $A_{L_s}(n) \leq \lfloor (n+3)/2 \rfloor$. To do this, we observe that that we can simulate L_s on strings of length $\leq n$ with a finite automaton of $r + 1 = \lfloor (n+3)/2 \rfloor$ states, as follows:

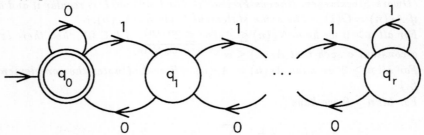

To prove the bound, $A_{L_s}(n) \geq \lfloor (n+3)/2 \rfloor$, observe that the strings 1^i for $0 \leq i \leq \lfloor (n+1)/2 \rfloor$ are pairwise n–dissimilar. It follows that $A_{L_s}(n) = \lfloor (n+3)/2 \rfloor$.

Now we show that Theorem 3 is best possible, in the sense described above. Suppose that for all nonregular L we have $A_L(n) \geq (n+c)/d$ infinitely often, where $0 < d < 2$. (Note that c could conceivably be negative.) Choose k large enough so that $d \leq 2 - 1/k$. Then for all $n > 6k - 2kc$ we have $k(n+c)/(2k-1) > (n+3)/2$; hence for infinitely many n and all nonregular L we have

$$A_L(n) \geq \frac{n+c}{d} \geq \frac{n+c}{d} \geq \frac{n+c}{2 - 1/k} > \frac{n+3}{2},$$

a contradiction when $L = L_s$.

Similarly, suppose that for all nonregular L we have $A_L(n) \geq (n + c)/2$ infinitely often, where $c > 3$. But then for all n we have

$$A_{L_s}(n) = \lfloor (n + 3)/2 \rfloor < (n + c)/2,$$

a contradiction. ∎

Some comments are in order. At first glance, our example of the language L_s with $A_{L_s}(n) = \lfloor (n + 3)/2 \rfloor$ might seem to contradict Theorem 3! But in fact, it does not, since $\lfloor (n + 3)/2 \rfloor \geq (n + 3)/2$ for infinitely many n (namely, all odd n). Second, to prove that the constant "3" in Theorem 3 is best possible, it does *not* suffice to give an example achieving the bound $\lfloor (n+4)/2 \rfloor$ for all sufficiently large n. This is because, for example, a stronger (but incorrect) lower bound of $(n + 4)/2$ for infinitely many n would be compatible with an example of a language L with $A_L(n) = \lfloor (n + 4)/2 \rfloor$ for all n sufficiently large.

This is a subtle point which was pointed out to us by S. Pottle after reading a draft of this paper, and previous investigators have also fallen into this trap. For example, Karp [16] proved that $A_L(n) > n/2 + 1$ infinitely often, and then attempted to show that the constant 1 is best possible by exhibiting a nonregular language L_k which satisfies $A_{L_k}(n) = \lfloor (n + 4)/2 \rfloor$ for $n \geq 1$. However, this example is actually consistent with the stronger (false) bound "for all nonregular L we have $A_L(n) > n/2+3/2$ for infinitely many n", and is therefore not sufficient to prove the claim.

5 Bounds on Deterministic Automaticity

We are interested in bounding $A_f(n)$ as a function of n. We state several theorems without proof.

Theorem 5 *Let $|\Sigma| = k$ and $|\Delta| = \ell$. Then if $2 \leq k, \ell < \infty$, we have $A_f(n) \leq \frac{Ck^{n+2}}{n}(1 + o(1))$, where $C = \frac{\log_k \ell}{(k - 1)^2}$.*

The upper bound provided by Theorem 5 cannot be substantially improved, because for each $k \geq 2$ and $\ell \geq 2$ there is a function f such that $A_f(n) \geq \frac{Ck^{n+2}}{n}(1 - o(1))$ for infinitely many n. The construction of L for $k = \ell = 2$ is given in [4].

We can find a nearly matching lower bound for "almost all" functions f. Phrasing the construction in the language of probability, we assume the space of functions is described by choosing the value of f at each word $w \in \Sigma^*$ randomly and uniformly to be $a \in \Delta$ with probability $1/|\Delta|$.

Theorem 6 *Let $k = |\Sigma| \geq 2$, $l = |\Delta| \geq 2$, and $C = (\log_k \ell)/(k - 1)^2$. Then for almost all functions $f : \Sigma^* \to \Delta$ and any $\epsilon > 0$, we have $A_f(n) > (1-\epsilon)Ck^{n+1}/n$ for all sufficiently large n.*

The lower bound in Theorem 6 cannot substantially be improved, because we have the following result:

Theorem 7 *Let $k = |\Sigma| \geq 2$ and $\ell = |\Delta| \geq 2$, and $C = (\log_k \ell)/(k-1)^2$. Then for all $f : \Sigma^* \rightarrow \Delta$ we have $A_f(n) \leq \frac{Ck^{n+1}}{n}(1 + o(1))$ for infinitely many n.*

6 Bounds on Deterministic Automaticity: The Unary Case

Some very interesting questions arise when one attempts to determine automaticity of functions over a 1–letter alphabet, say $\Sigma = \{0\}$. Oddly enough, this case does not seem to have been investigated previously.

Let us introduce some notation. We say that the string x is a *factor* of a string y if there exist strings w, z such that $y = wxz$. If $\Sigma = \{0\}$, and $f : \Sigma^* \rightarrow \Delta$, we define $w = w(f) = f(\epsilon)f(0)f(0^2)f(0^3)\cdots$. We call $w(f)$ the *characteristic word* of f.

Lemma 8 *Let $\Sigma = \{0\}$, $\ell = |\Delta| \geq 2$, and let $f : \Sigma^* \rightarrow \Delta$ be any function. Let $w = w(f) = w_0 w_1 w_2 \ldots$ be the characteristic word of f, so $w_i = f(0^i)$. Then $A_f(n) = n + 1 - t$, where t is the length of the longest (possibly empty) suffix of $w_0 w_1 \ldots w_n$ that is also a factor of $w_0 w_1 \ldots w_{n-1}$.*

It is easy to see that $A_f(n) \leq n + 1$; in fact, this bound can be attained for any *particular* value of n by setting $f(0^i) = 0$ for $0 \leq i < n$, and $f(0^n) = 1$.

A more interesting question is to ask about the behavior of $A_f(n)$ for any fixed f, as $n \rightarrow \infty$.

Theorem 9 *Let $\Sigma = \{0\}$ and $\ell = |\Delta| \geq 2$. Then for any function $f : \Sigma^* \rightarrow \Delta$ the inequality $A_f(n) \leq n + 1 - \lfloor \log_\ell n \rfloor$ holds for infinitely many n.*

Theorem 10 *Suppose $\Sigma = \{0\}$ and $|\Delta| = \ell$. Then for almost all functions $f : \Sigma^* \rightarrow \Delta$ we have $A_f(n) > n - 2\log_\ell n - 2\log_\ell \log_\ell n$ for all sufficiently large n.*

7 Bounds on Nondeterministic Automaticity

In this section we give some bounds on nondeterministic automaticity, $N_L(n)$.

Theorem 11 *Let $k = |\Sigma| \geq 2$ and let $L \subseteq \Sigma^*$. Then*

$$N_L(n) \leq \begin{cases} \dfrac{2(k^{n/2+1} - 1)}{k - 1}, & n \text{ even}; \\[2ex] \dfrac{k^{(n+1)/2} + k^{(n+3)/2} - 2}{k - 1}, & n \text{ odd}; \end{cases}$$
$$= O(k^{n/2}).$$

We now give an almost matching lower bound on nondeterministic automaticity.

Theorem 12 *Let* $k = |\Sigma| \geq 2$, *and let* $L \subseteq \Sigma^*$. *Then for almost all* L *and every* $\epsilon > 0$ *we have* $N_L(n) > (1 - \epsilon)k^{n/2}/\sqrt{k-1}$ *for all sufficiently large* n.

8 Lower Bounds for Nonregular Languages when $k = 1$

The statement of Karp's theorem, that if L is not regular then $A_L(n) \geq (n+3)/2$ for infinitely many n, does not depend on k (the size of the input alphabet), and hence is true if $k = |\Sigma| = 1$. It follows that if $L \subseteq 0^*$ is not regular, then

$$\limsup_{n \to \infty} \frac{A_L(n)}{n} \geq \frac{1}{2}.$$

However, this bound does not seem attainable for $k = 1$. We make the following

Conjecture 13 *If* $L \subseteq 0^*$ *is not regular, then*

$$\limsup_{n \to \infty} \frac{A_L(n)}{n} \geq \frac{\sqrt{5}-1}{2} \doteq .61803.$$

Using Lemma 8, we can rephrase this conjecture in a purely combinatorial fashion:

Conjecture 13' *Let* $w = w_0 w_1 w_2 \ldots$ *be an infinite word over a finite alphabet that is not ultimately periodic. Define* $s_w(n)$ *to be the length of the longest suffix of* $w_0 w_1 \ldots w_n$ *that is also a factor of* $w_0 w_1 \ldots w_{n-1}$. *Then*

$$\liminf_{n \to \infty} \frac{s_w(n)}{n} \leq \frac{3 - \sqrt{5}}{2} \doteq .38197.$$

J.-P. Allouche has kindly informed us that Conjecture 13' is related to a similar one of G. Rauzy [19, §5.2]. This paper also mentions that Rauzy's conjecture has been proved by C. Rauzy in the case of the so-called Sturmian words.

We do not know how to prove Conjecture 13. However, we can prove that *if* the conjecture is true, then the constant $(\sqrt{5}-1)/2$ is best possible. In fact, this bound is achieved for an L related to f, the famous *Fibonacci word*.

One possible definition of f is as follows: define $h_1 = 1$, $h_2 = 0$, and $h_n = h_{n-1}h_{n-2}$. Thus, for example, $h_3 = 01$, $h_4 = 010$, $h_5 = 01001$, etc. Clearly h_n is a prefix of h_{n+1} for all $n \geq 2$, and hence we can define $f = \lim_{n \to \infty} h_n$. We write the individual bits of f as $f_0, f_1, \ldots$, and we have

$$f = f_0 f_1 f_2 \cdots = 0100101001001 \cdots.$$

Notice that $|h_i| = F_i$, where F_i is the i'th Fibonacci number, defined by $F_0 = 0$, $F_1 = 1$, and $F_i = F_{i-1} + F_{i-2}$ for $i \geq 2$.

We define the *unary Fibonacci language*, L_F, as follows:

$$L_F = \{0^i \ : \ f_i = 0\} = \{\epsilon, 0^2, 0^3, 0^5, 0^7, 0^8, \ldots\}.$$

It is known that f is not ultimately periodic (this follows, for example, from Karhumäki's result [15] that f is fourth-power-free), and hence L_F is not regular.

Theorem 14 *Let* $L = L_F$, *the unary Fibonacci language. Suppose* $F_n - 2 \leq k \leq F_{n+1} - 3$. *Then* $A_L(k) = F_{n-1}$.

Corollary 15 *If* $L = L_F$, *then*

$$\limsup_{k \to \infty} \frac{A_L(k)}{k} = (\sqrt{5} - 1)/2.$$

9 Lower bounds for nondeterministic automaticity for nonregular languages

As we have seen, if L is not regular, then $A_L(n) \geq (n + 3)/2$ infinitely often. We can ask if there is a similar theorem for the nondeterministic case. The best lower bound we know is the following:

Theorem 16 *Suppose* $L \subseteq \Sigma^*$. *If* L *is not regular, then* $N_L(n) \geq \log_2((n+3)/2)$ *infinitely often.*

We do not know if Theorem 16 is best possible. The following example was suggested to us by B. Ravikumar. The bound was obtained in a conversation with J. Buss.

Theorem 17 *Let* $L = \{0^i 1^j \mid i \neq j\}$. *Then* L *is not a regular language, and*

$$N_L(n) = O((\log n)^2/(\log \log n)).$$

For the unary case we can obtain a better lower bound:

Theorem 18 *There exists a constant* c' *(which does not depend on* L*) such that if* $L \subseteq 0^*$ *is not regular, then* $N_L(n) \geq c'(\log n)^2/(2 \log \log n)$ *infinitely often.*

We do not know a unary language that achieves this lower bound, but assuming some reasonable conjectures, we can get close.

Theorem 19 *Let* $L = \{0^{n^2} \ : \ n \text{ odd}, \geq 1\}$. *Then* $\overline{L}$ *is not a regular language. Assuming Conjecture 20 below, we have* $N_{\overline{L}}(n) = O((\log n)^2(\log \log n))$. *Assuming the Extended Riemann Hypothesis (ERH), we have* $N_{\overline{L}}(n) = O((\log n)^4/(\log \log n))$.

For m a positive integer $\equiv 1 \pmod{8}$ that is not a square, define $J(m)$ to be the least odd prime p such that the Jacobi symbol $\left(\frac{m}{p}\right) = -1$.

Conjecture 20 *We have* $J(m) = O((\log m)(\log \log m))$.

We can also give an example of a nonregular unary language with poly-logarithmic nondeterministic automaticity where the bound does not depend on unproved hypotheses. The theorem below was obtained in a discussion with L. Hellerstein:

Theorem 21 *Let p_j denote the j'th prime number (with $p_1 = 2$). Define $L = \{0^{2 \cdot 3 \cdot 5 \cdots p_i} : i \geq 1\}$. Then $\overline{L}$ is not a regular language, and*

$$N_{\overline{L}}(n) = O((\log n)^5/(\log \log n)^2).$$

10 Acknowledgments

We would like to thank Anne Condon for telling us about the papers of Kaneps and Freivalds [13], and Dwork and Stockmeyer [7, 8]. We are grateful to Larry Stockmeyer for telling us about the papers of Gabarró [9] and Balcazar, Díaz, and Gabarró [1]. We would also like to thank Joaquim Gabarró, who kindly sent us a copy of his thesis [10] and told us about the paper of Serna [20]. Our thanks also go to Jean-Camille Birget, who told us about the paper of Ibarra and Ravikumar [12]. We thank B. Ravikumar for telling the first author about the work of the second author [5]. The first author would like to thank David Barrington and Howard Straubing for graciously helping him discover how wrong his initial ideas about automaticity were. Ming Li and Marek Chrobak made several useful comments. Eric Bach read a draft of this paper and made several useful suggestions. We are very grateful to Sam Pottle for finding some embarrassing gaps in our original discussion of Theorems 3 and 4. Finally, we would like to thank Dean Gaudet for his assistance with programming.

References

1. J. L. Balcázar, J. Díaz, and J. Gabarró. Uniform characterizations of non-uniform complexity measures. *Inform. and Control* **67** (1985), 53–89.
2. J. L. Balcázar, J. Díaz, and J. Gabarró. *Structural Complexity I*, Vol. 11 of *EATCS Monographs on Theoretical Computer Science*. Springer-Verlag, 1988.
3. Y. Breitbart. On automaton and "zone" complexity of the predicate "to be a kth power of an integer". *Dokl. Akad. Nauk SSSR* **196** (1971), 16–19. In Russian. English translation in *Soviet Math. Dokl.* **12** (1971), 10–14.
4. Y. Breitbart. *Complexity of the calculation of predicates by finite automata*. PhD thesis, Technion, Haifa, Israel, June 1973.
5. Y. Breitbart. Some bounds on the complexity of predicate recognition by finite automata. *J. Comput. System Sci.* **12** (1976), 336–349.
6. A. Condon, L. Hellerstein, S. Pottle, and A. Wigderson. On the power of finite automata with both nondeterministic and probabilistic states. Manuscript in preparation, 1993.

7. C. Dwork and L. Stockmeyer. On the power of 2-way probabilistic finite state automata. In *Proc. 30th Ann. Symp. Found. Comput. Sci.*, pages 480–485. IEEE Press, 1989.

8. C. Dwork and L. Stockmeyer. A time complexity gap for two-way probabilistic finite-state automata. *SIAM J. Comput.* **19** (1990), 1011–1023.

9. J. Gabarró. Initial index: a new complexity function for languages. In J. Díaz, editor, *ICALP '83: 10th International Colloquium on Automata, Languages, and Programming*, Vol. 154 of *Lecture Notes in Computer Science*, pages 226–236. Springer-Verlag, 1983.

10. J. Gabarró. *Funciones de complejidad y su relación con las familias abstractas de lenguajes.* PhD thesis, Facultdad de Informatica, Universidad Politecnica de Barcelona, 1983. In Spanish.

11. V. S. Grinberg and A. D. Korshunov. Asymptotic behavior of the maximum of the weight of a finite tree. *Problemy Peredachi Informatsii* **2** (1966), 96–99. In Russian. English translation in *Problems of Information Transmission* **2** (1966), 75–78.

12. O. H. Ibarra and B. Ravikumar. Sublogarithmic-space Turing machines, nonuniform space complexity, and closure properties. *Math. Systems Theory* **21** (1988), 1–17.

13. J. Kaneps and R. Freivalds. Minimal nontrivial space complexity of probabilistic one-way Turing machines. In B. Rovan, editor, *MFCS '90 (Mathematical Foundations of Computer Science)*, Vol. 452 of *Lecture Notes in Computer Science*, pages 355–361. Springer-Verlag, 1990.

14. J. Kaneps and R. Freivalds. Running time to recognize nonregular languages by 2-way probabilistic automata. In J. Leach Albert, B. Monien, and M. Rodríguez Artalejo, editors, *ICALP '91 (18th International Colloquium on Automata, Languages, and Programming)*, Vol. 510 of *Lecture Notes in Computer Science*, pages 174–185. Springer-Verlag, 1991.

15. J. Karhumäki. On cube-free ω-words generated by binary morphisms. *Disc. Appl. Math.* **5** (1983), 279–297.

16. R. M. Karp. Some bounds on the storage requirements of sequential machines and Turing machines. *J. Assoc. Comput. Mach.* **14** (1967), 478–489.

17. V. A. Kuz'min. Realization of functions of the algebra of logic by means of automata, normal algorithms, and turing machines. *Problemy Kibernetiki* **13** (1965), 75–96. In Russian.

18. J. Paredaens and R. Vyncke. A class of measures on formal langauges. *Acta Informatica* **9** (1977), 73–86.

19. G. Rauzy. Suites à termes dans un alphabet fini. *Sém. de Théorie des Nombres de Bordeaux* (1982–1983), 25–01–25–16.

20. M. J. Serna. Asymptotical behaviour of some non-uniform measures. *RAIRO Informatique Théorique et Applications* **23** (1989), 281–293.

21. B. A. Trakhtenbrot. On an estimate for the weight of a finite tree. *Sibirskiĭ Matematicheskiĭ Zhurnal* **5** (1964), 186–191. In Russian.

22. B. A. Trakhtenbrot and Ya. M. Barzdin'. *Finite Automata: Behavior and Synthesis*, Vol. 1 of *Fundamental Studies in Computer Science*. North-Holland, Amsterdam, 1973.

Invited Lecture

Towards a Theory of Recursive Structures

David Harel*

Abstract: In computer science, one is interested mainly in finite objects. Insofar as *infinite* objects are of interest, they must be computable, i.e., recursive, thus admitting an effective finite representation. This leads to the notion of a recursive graph, or, more generally, a recursive structure or data base. In this paper we summarize our recent work on recursive structures and data bases, including (i) the high undecidability of many problems on recursive graphs, (ii) somewhat surprising ways of deducing results on the classification of NP optimization problems from results on the degree of undecidability of their infinitary analogues, and (iii) completeness results for query languages on recursive data bases.

1 Introduction

This paper provides a summary of some of the work we have carried out recently on infinite recursive (i.e., computable) structures and data bases, and attempts to put it in perspective. The work itself is contained in three papers [H, HH1, HH2], which we summarize, respectively, in Sections 2, 3 and 4.

When computer scientists become interested in an infinite object, they require it to be computable, i.e., recursive, so that it possesses an effective finite representation. Given the prominance of finite graphs in computer science, and the many results and open questions surrounding them, it would seem appropriate to investigate recursive graphs too. Moreover, insight into finite objects can often be gleaned from results about infinite recursive variants thereof. An infinite recursive graph can be thought of simply as a recursive binary relation over the natural numbers. Recursive graphs can be represented by the (finite) algorithms, or Turing machines, that recognize their edge sets, so that it makes sense to investigate the complexity of problems concerning them. Indeed, a significant amount of work has been carried out in recent years regarding the complexity of problems on recursive graphs. Some of the first papers were written in the 1970s by Manaster and Rosenstein [MR] and Bean [B1, B2]. Following that,

*Dept. of Applied Mathematics and Computer Science, The Weizmann Institute of Science, Rehovot, Israel. Email: harel@wisdom.weizmann.ac.IL. The author holds the William Sussman Chair of Mathematics.

a variety of problems were considered, including ones that are NP-complete for finite graphs, such as k-colorability and Hamiltonicity [B1, B2, BG2, Bu, GL, MR] and ones that are in P in the finite case, such as Eulerian paths [B2, BG1]

In most cases (including the above examples) the problems turned out to be undecidable. This is true even for highly recursive graphs [B1], i.e., ones for which node degree is finite and the set of neighbors of a node is computable. Beigel and Gasarch [BG1] and Gasarch and Lockwood [GL] investigated the precise level of undecidablity of many such problems, and showed that they reside on low levels of the arithmetic hierarchy. For example, detecting the existence of an Eulerian path is Π_3^0-complete for recursive graphs and Π_2^0-complete for highly recursive graphs [BG1].

The case of Hamiltonian paths seemed to be more elusive. In 1976, Bean [B2] had shown that the problem is undecidable (even for planar graphs), but the precise characterization was not known. In our first paper [H], summarized in Section 2, we prove that Hamiltonicity is in fact *highly* undecidable, *viz*, Σ_1^1-complete. The result holds even for highly recursive graphs with degree bounded by 3, and for planar graphs too. Hamiltonicity is thus an example of an interesting graph problem that becomes highly undecidable in the infinite case.

The question then arises as to what makes some NP-complete problems highly undecidable in the infinite case, while others (e.g., k-colorability) remain on low levels of the arithmetical hierarchy. This was the starting point of our second piece of work [HH1], summarized in Section 3. We provide a general definition of the infinite recursive version of an NP optimization problem, in such a way that MAX CLIQUE, for example, becomes the question of whether a recursive graph contains an infinite clique. Two results are proved, one enables using knowledge about the infinite case to yield implications to the finite case, and the other enables implications in the other direction. Put very generally, the results establish a connection between the descriptive complexity of (finitary) NP optimization problems, particularly the syntactic class MAX NP, and the computational complexity of their infinite versions, particularly the class Σ_1^1. Taken together, the two results yield many new problems whose infinite versions are highly undecidable and whose finite versions are outside MAX NP. Examples include MAX CLIQUE, MAX IND SET, MAX SUBGRAPH, and MAX TILING.

In our third piece of work [HH2], summarized in Section 4, the idea of infinite recursive relational data bases is put forward. Such a data base can be defined simply as a finite tuple of recursive relations (not necessarily binary) over some countable domain. We thus obtain a natural generalization of the notion of a finite relational data base. This is not an entirely wild idea: Tables of trigonometric functions, for example, can be viewed as a recursive data base, since we might be interested in the sines or cosines of infinitely many angles. Instead of keeping them all in a table, which is impossible, we keep rules for computing the values from the angles, and vice versa, which is really just to say that we have an effective way of telling whether an edge is present between nodes i and j in an infinite graph — the precise notion of a recursive graph.

Recursive data bases appear to constitute a fertile area for research, raising theoretical and practical questions concerning the computability and complexity of queries and update operations, and the power and flexibility of appropriate query languages. We have attempted to initiate such research, by investigating the class of computable queries over recursive data bases, the motivation being borrowed from [CH]. Since the set of computable queries on such data bases is not closed under even simple relational operations, one must either make do with a very humble class of queries or considerably restrict the class of allowed data bases. We define two query languages, one for each of these possibilities, and prove their completeness. The first is quantifier-free first-order logic, which is shown to be complete for the non-restricted case. The second is an appropriately modified version of the complete language QL of [CH], which is proved complete for the case of "highly symmetric" data bases, i.e., ones whose set of automorphisms is of finite index for each tuple-width.

2 Hamiltonicity in recursive graphs

This section describes the main parts of [H].

A *recursive directed graph* is a pair $G = (V, E)$, where V is recursively isomorphic to the set of natural numbers $\mathcal{N}$, and $E \subset V \times V$ is recursive. G is *undirected* if E is symmetric. A *highly recursive graph* is a recursive graph for which there is a recursive function H from V to finite subsets of V, such that $H(v) = \{u \mid \langle v, u \rangle \in E\}$.

A *one-way* (respectively, *two-way*) *Hamiltonian path* in G is a 1-1 mapping p of $\mathcal{N}$ (respectively, $\mathcal{Z}$) onto V, such that $\langle p(x), p(x+1) \rangle \in E$ for all x.

Bean [B2] showed that determining Hamiltonicity in highly recursive graphs is undecidable. His reduction is from non-well-foundedness of recursive trees with finite degree, which can be viewed simply as the halting problem for (nondeterministic) Turing machines. Given such a tree T, Bean constructs a graph G, such that infinite paths in T map to Hamiltonian paths in G. The idea is essentially to make the nodes of G correspond to those of T, but with all nodes that are on the same level being connected in a cyclic fashion. In this way, a Hamiltonian path in G simulates moving down an infinite path in T, but at each level it also cycles through all nodes on that level. A fact that is crucial to this construction is the finiteness of T's degree, so that the proof does not generalize to trees with infinite degree, Thus, Bean's proof only establishes that Hamiltonicity is hard for Π_1^0, or co-r.e.

We have been able to show that the problem is actually Σ_1^1-complete. Hardness is proved by a reduction from the non-well-foundedness of recursive trees with possibly *infinite* degree, which is well-known to be a Σ_1^1-complete problem [R]:

Theorem: *Detecting (one-way or two-way) Hamiltonicity in a (directed or undirected) highly recursive graph is Σ_1^1-complete, even for graphs with $H(v) \leq 3$ for all v.*

Sketch of Proof. In Σ_1^1 is easy: With the $\exists f$ quantifying over total functions from $\mathcal{N}$ to $\mathcal{N}$, we write

$$\exists f \; \forall x \; \forall y \; \exists z \; (\langle f(x), f(x+1)\rangle \in E \wedge (x \neq y \rightarrow f(x) \neq f(y)) \wedge f(z) = x).$$

This covers the case of one-way paths. The two-way case is similar.

We now show Σ_1^1-hardness for undirected recursive graphs with one-way paths. (The other cases require more work, especially in removing the infinite branching from the graphs we construct, in order to obtain the result for highly recursive graphs. The details can be found in [H].)

Assume a recursive tree T is given, with nodes $\mathcal{N} = 0, 1, 2, 3, \ldots$, and root 0, and whose *parent-of* function is recursive. T can be of infinite degree. We construct an undirected graph G, which has a one-way Hamiltonian path iff T has an infinite path.

Figure 1.

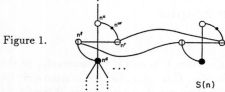

S(n)

For each element $n \in \mathcal{N}$, G has a cluster of five internal nodes, n^u, n^d, n^r, n^l and n^{ur}, standing, respectively, for *up, down, right, left* and *up-right*. For each such cluster, G has five internal edges (see Fig. 1):

$$n^l \;\text{——}\; n^d \;\text{——}\; n^u \;\text{——}\; n^{ur} \;\text{——}\; n^r \;\text{——}\; n^l$$

For each edge $n \longrightarrow m$ of the tree T, $n^d \;\text{——}\; m^u$ is an edge of G. For each node n in T, let $S(n)$ be n's distance from the root in T (its *level*). Since $S(n) \in \mathcal{N}$, we may view $S(n)$ as a node in T. In fact, in G we will think of $S(n)$ as being n's *shadow node*, and the two are connected as follows:[1]

$$n^r \;\text{——}\; S(n)^r \quad \text{and} \quad S(n)^l \;\text{——}\; n^l$$

To complete the construction, there is one additional root node g in G, with an edge $g \;\text{——}\; 0^u$.

Since T is a recursive tree and S, as a function, is recursive in T, it is obvious that G is a recursive graph. To complete the proof we show that T has an infinite path from 0 iff G has a Hamiltonian path.

(*Only-if*) Suppose T has an infinite path p. A Hamiltonian path p' in G starts at the root g, and moves down G's versions of the nodes in p, taking detours to the right to visit n's shadow

---

[1]Clearly, given T, the function $S : \mathcal{N} \to \mathcal{N}$ is not necessarily one-one. In fact, Figs. 1 and 2 are somewhat misleading, since there may be infinitely many nodes with the same shadow, so that the degree of both up-nodes and down-nodes can be infinite. Moreover, $S(n)$ itself is a node somewhere else in the tree, and hence has its own T-edges, perhaps infinitely many of them.

node $S(n)$ whenever $S(n) \notin p$. The way this is done can be seen in Fig. 2. Since p is infinite, we will eventually reach a node of any desired level in T, so that any $n \notin p$ will eventually show up as a shadow of some node along p and will be visited in due time. It is then easy to see that p' is Hamiltonian.

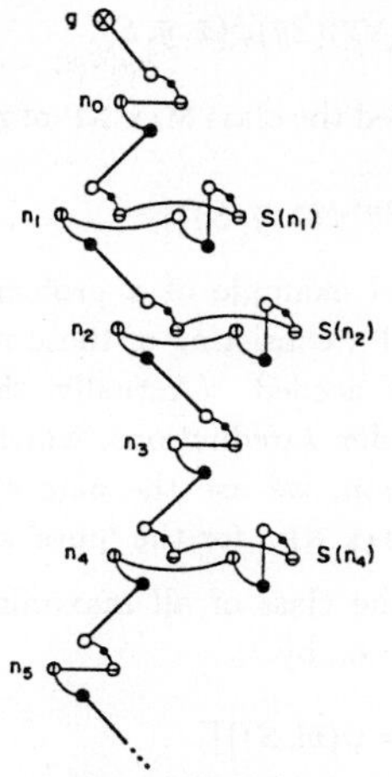

Figure 2.

(*If*) Suppose G has a Hamiltonian path p. It helps to view the path p as containing not only the nodes, but also the edges connecting them. Thus, with the exception of the root g, each node in G must contribute to p exactly two incident edges, one incoming and one outgoing.

We now claim that for any n, if p contains the T-edge incident to the up-node n^u, or, when $n = 0$, if it contains the edge between g and 0^u, then it must also contain a T-edge incident to the down node n^d.

To see why this is true, assume p contains the T-edge incident to n^u (see Fig. 1). Consider n^{ur}. It has exactly two incident edges, both of which must therefore be in p. But since one of them connects it to n^u, we already have in p the two required edges for n^u, so that the one between n^u and n^d cannot be in p. Now, the only remaining edges incident to n^d are the internal one connecting it to n^l, and its T-edges, if any. However, since p must contain exactly two edges incident to n^d, one of them must be one of the T-edges. $\triangle$

In fact, Hamiltonicity is Σ_1^1-complete even for planar graphs [HH1].

3   From the finite to the infinite and back

This section describes the main parts of [HH1].

Our approach to optimization problems focuses on their descriptive complexity, an idea that started with Fagin's [F] characterization of NP in terms of definability in second-order logic on finite structures. Fagin's theorem asserts that a collection C of finite structures is NP-computable if and only if there is a quantifier-free formula $\psi(\overline{x}, \overline{y}, S)$, such that for any finite structure A:

$$A \in C \Leftrightarrow A \models (\exists S)(\forall \overline{x})(\exists \overline{y})\psi(\overline{x}, \overline{y}, S).$$

Papadimitriou and Yannakakis [PY] introduced the class MAX NP of maximization problems that can be defined by

$$\max_{S} |\{\overline{x}: \ A \models (\exists \overline{y})\psi(\overline{x}, \overline{y}, S)\}|,$$

for quantifier-free ψ. MAX SAT is the canonical example of a problem in MAX NP . They also considered the subclass MAX SNP of MAX NP , consisting of those maximization problems in which the existential quantifier above is not needed. (Actually, the classes MAX NP and MAX SNP of [PY] contain also their closures under L-reductions, which preserve polynomial-time approximation schemes. To avoid confusion, we use the names MAX Σ_0 and MAX Σ_1, introduced in [KT], rather than MAX SNP and MAX NP , for the 'pure' syntactic classes.)

Kolaitis and Thakur [KT] then examined the class of all maximization problems whose optimum is definable using first-order formulas, i.e., by

$$\max_{S} |\{\overline{w}: \ A \models \psi(\overline{w}, S)\}|,$$

where $\psi(\overline{w}, S)$ is an arbitrary first-order formula. They first showed that this class coincides with the collection of polynomially-bounded NP-maximization problems on finite structures, i.e., those problems whose optimum value is bounded by a polynomial in the input size. They then proved that these problems form a proper hierarchy, with exactly four levels:

$$\text{MAX } \Sigma_0 \subset \text{MAX } \Sigma_1 \subset \text{MAX } \Pi_1 \subset \text{MAX } \Pi_2 = \bigcup_{i \geq 2} \text{MAX } \Pi_i$$

Here, MAX Π_1 is defined just like MAX Σ_1 (i.e., MAX NP), but with a universal quantifier, and MAX Π_2 uses a universal followed by an existential quantifier, and corresponds to Fagin's general result stated above. The three containments are known to be strict. For example, MAX CLIQUE is in MAX Π_1 but not in MAX Σ_1.

We now define a little more precisely the class of optimization problems we deal with[2]:

Definition: (See [PR]) An NPM problem is a tuple $F = (\mathcal{I}_F, S_F, m_F)$, where

- $\mathcal{I}_F$, the set of *input instances*, consists of finite structures over some vocabulary σ, and is recognizable in polynomial time.

---

[2]We concentrate here on maximization problems, though the results can be proved for appropriate minimization ones too.

- $S_F(I)$ is the space of *feasible solutions* on input $I \in \mathcal{I}_F$. The only requirement on S_F is that there exists a polynomial q and a polynomial time computable predicate p, both depending only on F, such that $\forall I \in \mathcal{I}_F$, $S_F(I) = \{S: |S| \leq q(|I|) \wedge p(I, S)\}$.

- $m_F: \mathcal{I}_F \times \Sigma^* \to \mathcal{N}$, the *objective function*, is a polynomial time computable function. $m_F(I, S)$ is defined only when $S \in S_F(I)$.

- The following decision problem is required to be in NP: Given $I \in \mathcal{I}_F$ and an integer k, is there a feasible solution $S \in S_F(I)$, such that $m_F(I, S) \geq k$?

This definition (with an additional technical restriction that we omit here; see [HH1]) is broad enough to encompass most known optimization problems arising in the theory of NP-completeness.

We now define infinitary versions of NPM problems, by evaluating them over infinite recursive structures and asking about the existence of an infinite solution:

Definition: Let $F = (\mathcal{I}_F, S_F, m_F)$ be an NPM problem. Define $F^\infty = (\mathcal{I}_F^\infty, S_F^\infty, m_F^\infty)$ as follows:

- $\mathcal{I}_F^\infty$ is the set of *input instances*, which are infinite recursive structures over σ.

- $S_F^\infty(I^\infty)$ is the set of *feasible solutions* on input $I^\infty \in \mathcal{I}_F^\infty$.

- $m_F^\infty: \mathcal{I}^\infty \times S_F \to \mathcal{N} \cup \{\infty\}$ is the *objective function,* satisfying

$$\forall I^\infty \in \mathcal{I}_F^\infty, \forall S \in S_F^\infty(I^\infty) \ (m_F^\infty(I^\infty, S) = |\{\overline{x}: \psi_F(I^\infty, S, \overline{x})\}|).$$

- The decision problem is: Given $I^\infty \in \mathcal{I}_F^\infty$, does there exist $S \in S_F^\infty(I^\infty)$, such that $m_F^\infty(I^\infty, S) = \infty$? Put another way:

$$F^\infty(I^\infty) = \text{TRUE} \quad \text{iff} \quad \exists S(|\{\overline{x}: \psi_F(I^\infty, S, \overline{x})\}| = \infty).$$

Due to the conditions on NPM problems, F^∞ can be shown not to depend on the Π_2-formula representing m_F. This is important, since, if some finite problem F could be defined by two different formulas ψ_1 and ψ_2 that satisfy the condition but yield different infinite problems, we could construct a finite structure for which ψ_1 and ψ_2 determine different solutions.

Here is our first main result:

Theorem: If $F \in \text{Max } \Sigma_1$ then $F^\infty \in \Pi_2^0$.

We like to view the theorem in its dual formulation:

Corollary: For any NPM problem F, if F^∞ is Σ_1^1-complete then F is not in Max Σ_1.

It follows that Hamiltonicity, which is Σ_1^1-complete and thus completely outside the arithmetical hierarchy, cannot be in MAX Σ_1. Obviously, the corollary is valid not only for such problems but for all problems that are above Π_2^0 in the arithmetical hierarchy. For example, since detecting the existence of an Eulerian path in a recursive graph is Π_3^0-complete [BG1], its finite variant cannot be in MAX Σ_1 either.

In order to be able to state our second main result, we define a special kind of *monotonic* reduction between finitary NPM problems, an *M-reduction*. We then show that *M*-reductions preserve the Σ_1^1-hardness of the corresponding infinitary problems.

Definition: Let $\mathcal{A}$ and $\mathcal{B}$ be sets of structures. A function $f\colon \mathcal{A} \to \mathcal{B}$ is *monotonic* if $\forall A, B \in \mathcal{A}$ $(A \leq B \Rightarrow f(A) \leq f(B))$. (Here, $\leq$ denotes the substructure relation.) Given two NPM problems: $F = (\mathcal{I}_F, S_F, m_F)$ and $G = (\mathcal{I}_G, S_G, m_G)$, an *M-reduction* g from F to G is a tuple $g = (t_1, t_2, t_3)$, such that:

- $t_1 \colon \mathcal{I}_F \to \mathcal{I}_G$, $t_2 \colon \mathcal{I}_F \times S_F \to S_G$, and $t_3 \colon \mathcal{I}_G \times S_G \to S_F$, are all monotonic, polynomial time computable functions..

- m_F and m_G grow monotonically with respect to t_1, t_2 and t_3.

We denote the existence of an *M*-reduction from F to G by $F \propto_M G$. Here is our second main result:

Theorem: Let F and G be two NPM problems, with $F \propto_M G$. If F^∞ is Σ_1^1-hard, then G^∞ is Σ_1^1-hard too.

We now list several NPM problems and their infinitary versions (more appear in [HH1]). For each, it is possible to prove that the infinitary versions are all Σ_1^1-complete. Mostly, this is done by establishing monotonic reductions on the finite level, and applying the second theorem above. From the first theorem it will then follow that the finitary versions must be outside MAX Σ_1.

1. MAX CLIQUE: I is an undirected graph, $G = (V, E)$.

$$S(G) = \{Y\colon Y \subseteq V,\ \forall y, z \in Y\ (y, z) \in E\}$$
$$m(G, Y) = |Y|$$

The maximization version is:

$$\max_{Y \subseteq V} |\{x\colon x \in Y \land \forall y, z \in Y\ (y, z) \in E\}|$$

MAX CLIQUE$^\infty$: I^∞ is a recursive graph G.

Q: Does G contain an infinite clique?

2. MAX IND SET: I is an undirected graph $G = (V, E)$.

$$S(G) = \{Y: Y \subseteq V, \forall y, z \in Y \ (y, z) \notin E\}$$
$$m(G, Y) = |Y|$$

$$\max_{Y \subseteq V} |\{x: x \in Y \wedge \forall y, z \in Y \ (y, z) \notin E\}|$$

MAX IND SET$^\infty$: I^∞ is a recursive graph G.

Q: Does G contain an infinite independent set?

3. MAX SET PACKING: I is a collection C of finite sets, represented by pairs (i, j), where the set i contains j.

$$S(C) = \{Y \subseteq C: \forall A, B \in Y \ A \cap B = \emptyset\}$$
$$m(C, Y) = |Y|$$

MAX SET PACKING$^\infty$: I^∞ is a recursive collection of infinite sets C.

Q: Does C contains infinitely many disjoint sets?

4. MAX SUBGRAPH: I is a pair of graphs, $G = (V_1, E_1)$ and $H = (V_2, E_2)$, with $V_2 = \{v_1, \ldots, v_n\}$.

$$S(G, H) = \{Y: Y \subseteq V_1 \times V_2, \forall (u, v), (x, y) \in Y, u \neq x \wedge v \neq y \wedge$$
$$(u, x) \in E_1 \Leftrightarrow (v, y) \in E_2\}$$
$$m(G, Y) = k \text{ iff } v_1, \ldots, v_k \text{ appear in } Y, \text{ but } v_{k+1} \text{ doesn't appear in } Y.$$

MAX SUBGRAPH$^\infty$: I^∞ is a pair of recursive graphs, H and G.

Q: Is H a subgraph of G?

5. MAX TILING: I is a grid D of size $n \times n$, and a set of tiles $T = \{t_1, \ldots, t_m\}$. (We assume the reader is familiar with the rules of tiling problems.)

$$S(D, T) = \{Y: Y \text{ is a legal tiling of some portion of } D \text{ with tiles from } T\}$$
$$m(\{D, T\}, Y) = k \text{ iff } Y \text{ contains a tiling of a full } k \times k \text{ subgrid of } D.$$

MAX TILING$^\infty$: I^∞ is a recursive set of tiles T.

Q: Can T tile the positive quadrant of the infinite integer grid?

4 Completeness for recursive data bases

This section describes the main parts of [HH2].

It is easy to see that recursive relations are not closed under some of the simplest accepted relational operators. For example, if $R(x, y, z)$ means that the yth Turing machine halts on input z after x steps (a primitive-recursive relation), then the projection of R on columns 2 and 3 is the nonrecursive halting predicate. This means that even very simple queries, when applied to general recursive relations, do not preserve computability. This difficulty can be overcome in essentially two ways. The first is to accept the situation as is; that is, to resign ourselves to the fact that on recursive data bases the class of computable queries will necessarily be very humble, and then to try to capture that class in a (correspondingly humble) complete query language. The second is to restrict the data bases, so that the standard kinds of queries *will* preserve computability, and then to try to establish a reasonable completeness result for these restricted inputs. The first case will give rise to a rich class of data bases but a poor class of queries, and in the second these will be reversed. In both cases, of course, in addition to being Turing computable, the queries will also have to satisfy the consistency criterion of [CH], more recently termed *genericity*, whereby queries must preserve isomorphisms.

Definition: Let D be a countable set, and let $R_1, \ldots, R_k$, for $k > 0$, be relations, such that for all $1 \leq i \leq k$, $R_i \subseteq D^{a_i}$. $B = (D, R_1, \ldots, R_k)$ is a *recursive relational data base* (or an r-db for short) of type $a = (a_1, \ldots a_k)$, if each R_i, considered as a set of tuples, is recursive.

Definition: Let $B_1 = (D_1, R_1, \ldots, R_k)$ and $B_2 = (D_2, R'_1, \ldots, R'_k)$ be two r-db's of the same type, and let $u \in D_1^n$ and $v \in D_2^n$, for some n. Then (B_1, u) and (B_2, v) are *isomorphic*, written $(B_1, u) \cong (B_2, v)$, if there is an isomorphism between B_1 and B_2 taking u to v. (B_1, u) and (B_2, v) are *locally isomorphic*, written $(B_1, u) \cong_l (B_2, v)$, if the restriction of B_1 to the elements of u and the restriction of B_2 to the elements of v are isomorphic.

Definition: An *r-query* Q (i.e., a partial function yielding, for each r-db B of type a, an output (if any) which is a recursive relation over $D(B)$) is *generic*, if it preserves isomorphisms; i.e. for all B_1, B_2, u, v, if $(B_1, u) \cong (B_2, v)$ then $u \in Q(B_1)$ iff $v \in Q(B_2)$. It is *locally generic* if it preserves local isomorphisms; i.e., for all B_1, B_2, u, v, if $(B_1, u) \cong_l (B_2, v)$ then $u \in Q(B_1)$ iff $v \in Q(B_2)$.

The following key lemma is used in the proof of our first theorem:

Lemma: If Q is a recursive r-query, then Q is generic iff Q is locally generic.

Definition: A query language is *r-complete* if it expresses precisely the class of recursive generic r-queries.

Theorem: The language of first-order logic without quantifiers is r-complete.

Thus, the class of computable queries on recursive data bases is indeed extremely poor. We now prepare for our second result, which insists on the full set of computable queries of [CH], but drastically reduces the allowed data bases in order to achieve completeness.

Definition: Let $B = (D, R_1, \ldots, R_k)$ be a fixed r-db. For each $u, v \in D^n$, u and v are *equivalent*, written $u \cong_B v$, if $(B, u) \cong (B, v)$. B is *highly symmetric* if for each $n > 0$, the relation $\cong_B$ induces only a finite number of equivalence classes of rank n.

Highly symmetric graphs consist of a finite or infinite number of connected components, where each component is highly symmetric, and there are only finitely many pairwise non-isomorphic components. In a highly symmetric graph, the finite degrees, the distances between points and the lengths of the induced paths are bounded. A grid or an infinite straight line, for instance, are not highly symmetric, but the full infinite clique is highly symmetric. Here is an example of another highly symmetric graph:

Figure 3.

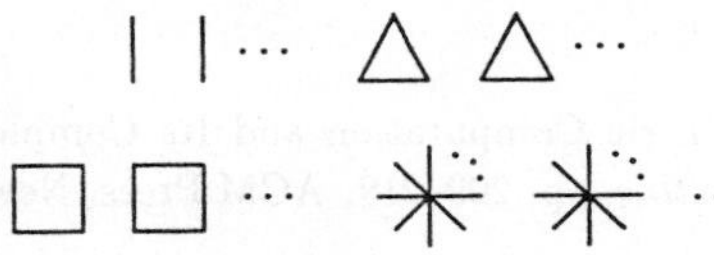

A *characteristic tree* for B is defined as follows. Its root is Λ, and the rest of the vertices are labelled with elements from D, such that the labels along each path from the root form a tuple that is a representative of an equivalence class of $\cong_B$. The whole tree covers representatives of all such classes. No two paths are allowed to form representatives of the same class. We represent a highly symmetric data base B by a tuple

$$C_B = (T_B, \cong_B, C_1, \ldots, C_k),$$

where T_B is some characteristic tree for B, and each C_i is a finite set of representatives of the equivalence classes constituting the relation R_i. We also require that $\cong_B$ be recursive, and that T_B be highly recursive (in the sense of Section 2).

We say that a query Q is *recursive* if the following version of it, that is applied to the representation C_B, rather than to the data base B itself, is partial recursive: Whenever $Q(C_B)$ is defined, it yields a finite set of representatives of the equivalence classes representing the relation $Q(B)$.

We now describe the query language QL_s. Its syntax is like that of the QL language of Chandra and Harel [CH], with the following addition: For any variable Y and any program P, **while** $|Y| = 1$ **do** P is a program. The semantics of QL_s is the same as the semantics of QL, except for some minor technical adaptations that are omitted here. As in [CH], the result of applying a program P to C_B is undefined if P does not halt; otherwise it is the contents of some fixed variable, say X_1.

Definition: A query language is *hs-r-complete* if it expresses precisely the class of recursive generic queries over highly symmetric recursive data bases.

Theorem: QL_s is hs-r-complete.

The proof follows four main steps, which are analogous to those given in the completeness proof for QL in [CH]. The details, however, are more intricate.

In the forthcoming journal version of [HH2] we have considered a number of additional issues, including the restriction to finite/co-finite recursive data bases, adding an oracle for the emptiness of a relation, completeness of the generic machines of [AV], and BP-completeness.

References

[AV]   S. Abiteboul and V. Vianu, "Generic Computation and Its Complexity", *Proc. 23rd ACM Symp. on Theory of Computing*, pp. 209–219, ACM Press, New York, 1991.

[AMS]   R. Aharoni, M. Magidor and R. A. Shore, "On the Strength of König's Duality Theorem", *J. of Combinatorial Theory (Series B)* **54**:2 (1992), 257–290.

[B1]   D.R. Bean, "Effective Coloration", *J. Sym. Logic* **41** (1976), 469–480.

[B2]   D.R. Bean, "Recursive Euler and Hamiltonian Paths", *Proc. Amer. Math. Soc.* **55** (1976), 385–394.

[BG1]   R. Beigel and W. I. Gasarch, unpublished results, 1986-1990.

[BG2]   R. Beigel and W. I. Gasarch, "On the Complexity of Finding the Chromatic Number of a Recursive Graph", Parts I & II, *Ann. Pure and Appl. Logic* **45** (1989), 1–38, 227–247.

[Bu]   S. A. Burr, "Some Undecidable Problems Involving the Edge-Coloring and Vertex Coloring of Graphs", *Disc. Math.* **50** (1984), 171–177.

[CH]   A. K. Chandra and D. Harel, "Computable Queries for Relational Data Bases", *J. Comp. Syst. Sci.* **21**, (1980), 156–178.

[F]   R. Fagin, "Generalized First-Order Spectra and Polynomial-Time Recognizable Sets", In *Complexity of Computations* (R. Karp, ed.), SIAM-AMS Proceedings, Vol. 7, 1974, pp. 43–73.

[GL]   W. I. Gasarch and M. Lockwood, "The Existence of Matchings for Recursive and Highly Recursive Bipartitie Graphs", Technical Report 2029, Univ. of Maryland, May 1988.

[H]   D. Harel, "Hamiltonian Paths in Infinite Graphs", *Israel J. Math.* **76**:3 (1991), 317–336. (Also, *Proc. 23rd ACM Symp. on Theory of Computing,* New Orleans, pp. 220–229, 1991.)

[HH1] T. Hirst and D. Harel, "Taking it to the Limit: On Infinite Variants of NP-Complete Problems", *Proc. 8th IEEE Conf. on Structure in Complexity Theory,* IEEE Press, New York, 1993.

[HH2] T. Hirst and D. Harel, "Completeness Results for Recursive Data bases", *12th ACM Symp. on Principles of Database Systems,* ACM Press, New York, 1993, 244–252.

[KT]   P. G. Kolaitis and M. N. Thakur, "Logical definability of NP optimization problems", *6th IEEE Conf. on Structure in Complexity Theory,* pp. 353–366, 1991.

[MR]   A. Manaster and J. Rosenstein, "Effective Matchmaking (Recursion Theoretic Aspects of a Theorem of Philip Hall)", *Proc. London Math. Soc.* **3** (1972), 615–654.

[NR]   A. Nerode and J. Remmel, "A Survey of Lattices of R. E. Substructures", In *Recursion Theory,* Proc. Symp. in Pure Math. Vol. 42 (A. Nerode and R. A. Shore, eds.), Amer. Math. Soc., Providence, R. I., 1985, pp. 323–375.

[PR]   A. Panconesi and D. Ranjan, "Quantifiers and Approximation", *Theor. Comp. Sci.* **107** (1993), 145–163.

[PY]   C. H. Papadimitriou and M. Yannakakis, "Optimization, Approximation, and Complexity Classes", *J. Comp. Syst. Sci.* **43**, (1991), 425–440.

[R]   H. Rogers, *Theory of Recursive Functions and Effective Computability,* McGraw-Hill, New York, 1967.

Strings, codes, combinatorics

Finding Minimal Generalizations for Unions of Pattern Languages and Its Application to Inductive Inference from Positive Data

Hiroki ARIMURA   Takeshi SHINOHARA   Setsuko OTSUKI

Department of Artificial Intelligence
Kyushu Institute of Technology
Kawazu 680-4, Iizuka 820, JAPAN
{arim, shino, otsuki}@ai.kyutech.ac.jp

Abstract

A pattern is a string of constant symbols and variables. The language defined by a pattern p is the set of constant strings obtained from p by substituting nonempty constant strings for variables in p. In this paper we are concerning with polynomial time inference from positive data of the class of unions of a bounded number of pattern languages. We introduce a syntactic notion of minimal multiple generalizations (mmg for short) to study the inferability of classes of unions. If a pattern p is obtained from another pattern q by substituting nonempty patterns for variables in q, q is said to be more general than p. A set of patterns defines a union of their languages. A set Q of patterns is said to be more general than a set P of patterns if for any pattern p in P there exists a more general pattern q in Q than p. Clearly more general set of patterns defines larger unions. A k-minimal multiple generalization (k-mmg) of a set S of strings is a minimally general set of at most k patterns that defines a union containing S. The syntactic notion of minimality enables us to efficiently compute a candidate for a semantically minimal concept. We present a general methodology for designing an efficient algorithm to find a k-mmg. Under some conditions an mmg can be used as an appropriate hypothesis for inductive inference from positive data. As results several classes of unions of pattern languages are shown to be polynomial time inferable from positive data.

1   Introduction

Inductive learning or inductive inference is a process to find general concepts from their concrete examples. As such a process, we can think of program synthesis from examples, grammatical inference, knowledge discovery in databases, etc. Studies on inductive learning vary from theories to practices. One of the most important objectives might be to find frameworks for inductive learning that are well founded by theories and suitable for practical applications. A framework of polynomial time PAC (probably approximately correct) learning [Val84] has been paid much attention from both sides of theory and practice. In this paper, we adopt another framework called *polynomial time inference from positive data* based on identification in the limit [Gol67] which has also been considered as a useful model for practical applications [Shi82b, Shi82a, Nix83, TY92].

As concepts to be learned, in this paper, we are mainly concerned with pattern languages. A pattern is a string consisting of constant symbols and variables. For example, $p = 0x1x$ is a pattern, where 0 and 1 are constant symbols and x is a variable. The language defined by a pattern is the set of constant strings obtained from the pattern by substituting nonempty constant strings for each variable. The language defined by a pattern $p = 0x1x$ is $L(p) = \{ 0w1w \mid w \in \Sigma^+ \}$.

The class of pattern languages was introduced by Angluin [Ang79] as a class inferable from positive data. Although the class of pattern languages is so simple, it has been considered as a very important class for studies on inductive learning [LW91, Muk92]. For example, elementary formal systems (EFSs for short), which were introduced by Smullyan [Smu61] and proposed as a unifying framework for language learning by Arikawa et. al. [ASY92], can be considered as natural extensions of patterns. Even from the viewpoint of practical applications, pattern languages have been paid much attention. Miyano et. al. [MSS91] considered the PAC learnability of EFS languages, and showed considerably successful experiments on some identification problems in Molecular Biology [AKM+92]. languages.

The weakness of inductive learning from positive data relative to that from positive and negative data is well known since the seminal study by Gold [Gol67]. However, there might be so many cases where only positive data are available. Although the class of pattern languages is inferable from positive data indeed, it is too restricted to be applied to practical problems. Fortunately, unions of a bounded number of pattern languages construct a richer class inferable from positive data [Shi83, Wri89b]. In this paper, we consider several subclasses of unions of pattern languages for which an efficient learning algorithm exists.

One of the most important problems for algorithms to infer concepts from positive data is how to avoid *overgeneralizations*. A straightforward way to solve this is to find the least or minimal concepts (minl for short) containing a given examples. It is not the case that such a way results in a correct identification in the limit. If, however, the class in problem has a property called "finite thickness" or "finite elasticity", then we can construct an inference algorithm utilizing minl. We say a class has finite thickness when it has finitely many concepts containing an arbitrarily given example. For example, it is easy to see that the class of ground instances of first-order terms has finite thickness. In this paper first-order terms are called tree patterns and sets of their ground instances tree pattern languages. Since a minl of first-order terms can be uniquely determined as the least generalization in polynomial time [Plo70], the class of tree pattern languages is polynomial time inferable from positive data. On the other hand, for the class of pattern languages there are possibly many minl's. It should be noticed that the computability of finding one of the minl's does not always require the decidability of containment for the class. In reality, although the containment for pattern languages is undecidable [SSY93], minl is computable but NP-hard [Ang79]. For some subclasses of pattern languages both containment and minl are polynomial time computable. A pattern is said to be one-variable if it contains at most one variable. A pattern is said to be regular if each variable appears at most once. Both the class of one-variable pattern languages and the class of regular pattern languages have a polynomial time minl algorithm.

Let us consider the class $C = R_1, R_2, \ldots$ of sets of positive integers, where $R_i = \{i \times n \mid n = 1, 2, \ldots\}$. Clearly C has finite thickness. If a set of integers $S = \{2, 3, 4\}$ is given, the minimal set containing S within C is $R_1 = \{1, 2, 3, 4, 5, \ldots\}$. On the other hand, if we consider within the class of unions of two sets taken from C, then $R_2 \cup R_3 = \{2, 3, 4, 6, \ldots\}$ is minimal. In this paper we consider the minl of this kind using unions of concepts instead of single concept. More precisely, we consider inductive learning and minl for the class of unions $C^n = \{R_1 \cup R_2 \cup \ldots \cup R_n \mid R_i \in C\}$ for some class C and some integer n. Wright introduced the notion of finite elasticity which is a natural extension of finite thickness. He showed that finite elasticity is a sufficient condition for a class to be inferable from positive data and it is closed under unions [Wri89b]. From his study we know the class C^n is inferable for any n if C has finite thickness. Note that the class C^* of unions of unbounded finitely many concepts is out of the scope of Wright's theorem.

In this paper the class, from which unions are taken, is assumed to be constructed by using a generalization. We call such a framework a generalization system. A generalization system has a set D of descriptions partially ordered by an effectively decidable relation $\preceq$ with the greatest element $\top$. When $p \preceq q$, we say q is a generalization of p or p is an instance of q. The set U of minimal descriptions can be used as a universe of concepts. A member of U is also called an object. A description p in D represents a concept $L(p)$ consisting of objects that are instances of p. For example, the class of pattern languages, the class of tree pattern languages, and the class of integer multiples above can be considered as classes constructed by generalization systems. Clearly from the definitions, the more general description defines the

Pattern Language Class $\mathcal{C}$	$\mathcal{C}^1$		$\mathcal{C}^2$		$\mathcal{C}^k$	
patterns	D	[Ang79]	D	[Shi83]	D	[Wri89b]
one-variable patterns	P	[Ang79]	P/2	[Wri89a]	P/k	this work
regular patterns	P	[Shi82b]		—	P/2km	this work
						(m-variable regular)
tree patterns	P	[Plo70]	P/2	[ASO92]	P/k	[ASO93]

Figure 1: Summary of known results for inferability of unions of a bounded number of pattern languages from positive data, where D and P denote Effective and Polynomial time inferability, respectively, and P/c means that P holds when $\sharp\Sigma > c$.

larger concept, that is, $p \preceq q \Longrightarrow L(p) \subseteq L(q)$. In general the converse does not hold. If the converse holds, the generalization system is called complete. In many cases to find a minimal common generalization (mcg for short) is much easier than to find a minimal concept itself. For example, when we can make descriptions less general step by step, a simple greedy search method which starts from the greatest element $\top$ and tries to make it as specific as possible works as a correct mcg algorithm. We call such operations to make descriptions less general step by step a stepwise refinement. Clearly, if the generalization system is complete, then any mcg algorithm can be used as a minl algorithm. Our main purpose in this paper is to extend the scope of the mcg algorithm using generalization to the class of unions and establish a general method to design efficient inductive learning algorithms.

The most important thing is how to extend the generalization relation $\preceq$ to the unions. A set P consisting of at most k descriptions is called a k-multiple description. The concept $L(P)$ defined by a multiple description P is the union $\cup_{p \in P} L(P)$. In this paper we deal with the Hoare powerset ordering $\sqsubseteq$. For multiple descriptions P and Q, $P \sqsubseteq Q$ iff for any $p \in P$, $p \preceq q$ for some $q \in Q$. Clearly $P \sqsubseteq Q$ implies $L(P) \subseteq L(Q)$. The converse does not hold in general, even in a complete generalization system. A k-minimal multiple generalization (k-mmg for short) for a set S of objects is a k-multiple description P such that $S \subseteq L(P)$ and for no k-multiple description $Q \sqsubset P$, $S \subseteq L(Q)$. We can show that k-mmg for a class $\mathcal{C}$ is computable if $\mathcal{C}$ is an effective generalization system. However, it is not easy to find a k-mmg in polynomial time, even if mcg is polynomial time computable. Fortunately for the class of unions of tree pattern languages we already know an efficient k-mmg algorithm [ASO93]. When $L(p) \subseteq L(q_1) \cup \ldots \cup L(q_m)$ implies $L(p) \subseteq L(q_i)$ for some i, we say that the class of unions has compactness with respect to containment. The class of tree pattern languages is a complete generalization system and the class of unions of at most k tree pattern languages has compactness with respect to containment under the condition that the number of function symbols is more than k. Therefore using the k-mmg algorithm for tree pattern languages we can construct an efficient inference machine that infers unions of k tree pattern languages from positive data.

In this paper, we extract the essence of the efficiency of the polynomial time k-mmg algorithm for tree patterns to establish a general methodology of designing efficient k-mmg algorithms for generalization systems. Our algorithm searches multiple descriptions in the direction from the most general $\{\top\}$ to more specific ones. We say a multiple description P is reduced with respect to a finite set S of objects, if $L(P)$ contains all objects in S but $L(P')$ cannot contain some objects in S for any proper subset P' of P. In other words, reduced description has no redundancy in covering all the given objects. First we try to find a reduced multiple description P consisting of at most k descriptions. Then we try to refine P to be more specific as long as consistency with given examples is maintained. Furthermore, if the number of descriptions in P is less than k, we try to divide some component of P as long as the total number of descriptions does not exceeds the bound k.

Our method extracted from the k-mmg algorithm for tree patterns is not easily applied to patterns. In general, the relation $\preceq$ on patterns including the membership problem for patterns is NP-complete. Furthermore $L(p) \subseteq L(q)$ does not always imply $p \preceq q$. Some subclasses such as one-variable patterns and regular patterns comprise an efficient and complete generalization system. Even such a subclass does not have compactness with respect to containment in general. However we can compute an mmg in polynomial time for both classes by using stepwise refinement. If the alphabet contains more than $2km$ constant symbols, then the class of unions of k regular pattern languages with at most m variables has compactness with respect to containment, and the k-mmg algorithm can work as a correct minl algorithm for unions. Therefore, the class of unions of at most k m-variable regular pattern languages is identifiable in the limit from positive data with consistent and conservative polynomial time update, if the number of constant symbols is greater than $2km$. Also a similar result can be obtained for the class of unions of one-variable pattern languages.

2 Preliminaries

First we introduce the class of pattern languages [Ang79], which is one of the most important generalization systems dealt with in this paper, and give the notion of identification in the limit from positive data [Gol67], which we adopt as a mathematical model of inductive learning. Furthermore we present generalization systems to capture properties common to systems such as patterns and tree patterns.

2.1 Pattern languages

For a set A of symbols, we denote by A^+ the set of nonempty finite strings over A, by $\sharp A$ the number of the elements in A. For a string w, we denote by $|w|$ the length of w. For a finite set S of strings, we denote by $|S|$ the total length of the strings in S. For $a \in A$, $A \setminus a$ denotes the set $\{x \in A \mid x \neq a\}$.

Let Σ be a finite set of *constant* symbols and X be a countable set of *variables* disjoint from Σ. A *pattern* is an elements in $(\Sigma \cup X)^+$. We denote the set of all patterns by $\mathcal{P}$. A *substitution* is a homomorphism from $\mathcal{P}$ to $\mathcal{P}$ that maps every constant symbol to itself. A set of replacements $\{x_1 := p_1, \ldots, x_n := p_n\}$ denotes the substitution that maps variable x_i to pattern p_i and any other variable to itself. By $p\theta$ we denote the image of a pattern p by a substitution θ. We define a binary relation $\preceq$ on $\mathcal{P}$ by $p \preceq q \Longleftrightarrow p = q\theta$ for some substitution θ. The language defined by a pattern p is the set $L(p) = \{w \in \Sigma^+ \mid w \preceq p\}$. Clearly $p \preceq q \Longrightarrow L(p) \subseteq L(q)$. If a language L is defined by some pattern p, then it is called a *pattern language*. A *one-variable pattern* is a pattern containing at most one variable. A *regular pattern* is a pattern where each variable occurs at most once [Shi82b]. Clearly a regular pattern defines a regular language. We denote by $\mathcal{P}$, $\mathcal{P}_1$, $\mathcal{P}_{\text{reg}}$ the sets of patterns, one-variable patterns, regular patterns, respectively, and by $\mathcal{PL}$, $\mathcal{PL}_1$, $\mathcal{PL}_{\text{reg}}$ the classes of pattern languages, one-variable pattern languages, regular pattern languages, respectively.

For example, let $\Sigma = \{0, 1\}$, $X = \{x, y, z, \ldots\}$. Then $p = xx1y1$ is a pattern that defines $L(p) = \{vv1w1 \mid v, w \in \Sigma^+\} = \{00101, 11101, 00001001, 01011011, \ldots\}$. Pattern p is neither one-variable nor regular. Pattern $q = xx1x1$ is a one-variable pattern, and $r = xy1z1$ is a regular pattern. Note that $L(q) \subsetneq L(p) \subsetneq L(r)$, because for substitutions $\theta_1 = \{y := x\}$ and $\theta_2 = \{y := x, z := y\}$, we have $q = p\theta_1$ and $p = r\theta_2$.

2.2 Inductive inference from positive data

Let U be a recursively enumerable set of *objects*. A *concept* is a subset of U. U is called the *universe* of concepts. An *indexed family of recursive concepts* or simply a *concept class* is a triple $\mathcal{C} = (C, D, L(\cdot))$, where C is a class of concepts, D is a recursively enumerable set of *descriptions*, $L(\cdot)$ is a mapping from D to C such that $C = \{L(p) \mid p \in D\}$, and there exists a total computable function $f : U \times D \to \{0,1\}$ such that $f(w,p) = 1$ iff $w \in L(p)$. The function f is called a *membership* function. We sometimes do not distinguish $\mathcal{C}$ and C from each other.

Let $\mathcal{C} = (C, D, L(\cdot))$ be a concept class. A *positive presentation* of a concept $L \in \mathcal{C}$ is an infinite sequence $w_1, w_2, \ldots$ of objects drawn from a concept L such that $L = \{ w \mid w = w_i$ for some $i \}$. An *inference machine* is an effective procedure M that runs in stages $1, 2, \ldots,$ where M requests an *example* and computes a *hypothesis* based on the examples so far received. Let M be an inference machine and $h_i \in D$ be the hypothesis produced by M at stage i ($i = 1, 2, \ldots$) when objects $w_1, w_2, \ldots$ are fed to M in this order. M is *consistent* if $L(h_i) \supseteq \{w_1, \ldots, w_i\}$ for any i. M is *conservative* if $h_{i-1} \neq h_i$ only if $w_i \notin L(h_{i-1})$. M is *polynomial time updating* if after receiving w_i M produces h_i within a polynomial time in $|w_1| + \ldots + |w_i|$. M on input $\sigma = w_1, w_2, \ldots$ *converges* to $p \in D$ iff after some finitely many stages it always produces p. M *identifies in the limit* or *infers* a concept L *from positive data* iff for any positive presentation σ of L, M on input σ converges to p with $L = L(p)$. M *infers* a concept class $\mathcal{C}$ *from positive data* iff M infers any concept L in $\mathcal{C}$. A concept class $\mathcal{C}$ is *inferable from positive data* when there exists an inference machine that infers $\mathcal{C}$.

Definition A concept class $\mathcal{C}$ is *polynomial time inferable from positive data* iff there exists a consistent, conservative and polynomial time updating inference machine M that infers $\mathcal{C}$ from positive data.

A concept class $\mathcal{C}$ has *finite thickness* iff $\sharp\{L \in \mathcal{C} \mid w \in L\}$ is finite for any object $w \in U$. A concept class $\mathcal{C}$ has *infinite elasticity* iff there exist infinite sequences $w_0, w_1, w_2, \ldots$ of objects and $p_1, p_2, \ldots$ of descriptions such that $\{w_0, \ldots, w_{i-1}\} \subseteq L(p_i)$ but $w_i \notin L(p_i)$ for any $i = 1, 2, \ldots$. A concept class $\mathcal{C}$ has *finite elasticity* iff $\mathcal{C}$ does not have infinite elasticity. Clearly from the definitions finite thickness implies finite elasticity. The *minl* problem is to find a description representing a minimal concept containing a given finite set of objects. Consider the following inference machine INFER utilizing minl, which receives an infinite sequence $w_1, w_2, \ldots$ of objects and produces an infinite sequence $p_1, p_2, \ldots$ of descriptions.

Algorithm INFER:

Stage 0. Set $S := \phi$, $h_0 := $ "none", and $i := 1$. Goto stage 1.

Stage i. Receive the next example w_i and add w_i into S. If h_{i-1} is inconsistent with S, that is, $S \not\subseteq L(h_{i-1})$, then set h_i to be a description representing a minimal concept containing S. Otherwise, set $h_i := h_{i-1}$. Output h_i. Set $i := i + 1$. Goto Stage i.

Theorem 2.1 ([Ang79, ASO92]) *If a concept class $\mathcal{C}$ has finite elasticity and the minl problem for $\mathcal{C}$ are computable, then the procedure INFER shown above infers $\mathcal{C}$ from positive data consistently and conservatively. Furthermore, if the membership function and the minl problem are polynomial time computable, then $\mathcal{C}$ is polynomial time inferable from positive data by INFER.*

2.3 Generalization systems

A *generalization system* (*GS* for short) is a partially ordered set $(D, \preceq)$ with the greatest element $\top$. Elements in D are called *descriptions*. If $p \preceq q$ then we say p is a *refinement* of q, q is a *generalization* of p, p is more *specific* than q, or q is more *general* than p. We write $p \prec q$ if $p \preceq q$ but $q \not\preceq p$. In case where $(D, \preceq)$ is not partially ordered set but $\preceq$ is transitive, we take the set $D_\equiv$ of representatives of the equivalence classes of D modulo $\equiv$, where $p \equiv q \iff p \preceq q$ and $q \preceq p$. Hereafter we identify descriptions which are equivalent to each other, and do not distinguish $(D, \preceq)$ and $(D_\equiv, \preceq)$ from each other. For any GS $(D, \preceq)$ we assume that the relation $\preceq$ is decidable and there exists recursive function $size : D \to N$ such that

- $p \prec q \implies size(p) > size(q)$ for any $p, q \in D$,
- for almost all $p \in D$, $size(p) \leq h(|p|)$ and $|p| \leq h'(size(p))$ for some recursive functions h and h', and
- $\{p \in D \mid size(p) \leq n\}$ is finite and computable for any $n \geq 0$,

where $|p|$ is the *length* of p as a representation. A GS $(D, \preceq)$ defines a concept class $(C, D, L(\cdot))$ such that

- The universe U of objects is the set of minimal elements in D.
- $C = \{L(p) \mid p \in D\}$, where the concept defined by $p \in D$ is $L(p) = \{w \in U \mid w \preceq p\}$.

Let S be a subset of D. If $q \preceq p$ holds for any $q \in S$, then p is called a *common generalization* (or *covering*) of S. If p is a common generalization of S and there is no common generalization of S that is properly more specific than p, then p is called a *minimal common generalization* (*mcg* for short) of S. The *mcg problem* is to find a minimal (with respect to $\preceq$) description covering a given finite set. Recall that the *minl problem* is to find a description that represents a minimal (with respect to $\subseteq$) concept. Clearly $p \preceq q \implies L(p) \subseteq L(q)$ for any $p, q \in D$ but the converse does not hold in general. We say a GS $(D, \preceq)$ is *complete* iff $p \preceq q \Longleftrightarrow L(p) \subseteq L(q)$.

If p is a covering of S, then $\text{size}(p) \leq \min\{\text{size}(w) \mid w \in S\}$. Therefore, we can effectively find mcgs of S, for any finite set $S \subseteq D$, because there exist only finitely many coverings of S whose sizes are bounded by $\min\{\text{size}(w) \mid w \in S\}$ and the relation $\preceq$ is decidable. We say a GS $(D, \preceq)$ is *efficient* iff

- $\preceq$ is polynomial time computable,
- for almost all $p \in D$, $\text{size}(p) \leq h(|p|)$ and $|p| \leq h'(\text{size}(p))$, for some polynomials h and h', and
- mcg is polynomial time computable.

Theorem 2.2 *Let $(D, \preceq)$ be an efficient GS and $(C, D, L(\cdot))$ be the concept class defined by $(D, \preceq)$. Then*

- *C has finite thickness, and*
- *there exists a polynomial time computable function which decides "$w \in L(p)$" or not.*

Furthermore, if $(D, \preceq)$ is complete, then

- *any mcg algorithm works as a correct minl algorithm, and*
- *C is polynomial time inferable from positive data.*

3 Multiple Generalization Systems

In this section we introduce multiple generalization systems by which unions of concepts are represented.

For a set D of descriptions, we define the set of *k-multiple descriptions* by $D^k = \{P \subseteq D \mid \sharp P \leq k\}$. A *k-multiple generalization system* (*k-MGS* for short) *derived from* a GS $(D, \preceq)$ is a partially ordered set $(D^k, \sqsubseteq)$, where the powerset ordering $\sqsubseteq$ is defined by $P \sqsubseteq Q$ iff for any $p \in P$, $p \preceq q$ for some $q \in Q$, $\text{size}(P) = \Sigma_{p \in P} \text{size}(p)$, and $|P| = \Sigma_{p \in P} |p|$. A *k-MGS* $(D^k, \sqsubseteq)$ defines a concept class $(C^k, D^k, L(\cdot))$ such that

- the universe U is the set of objects taken from D,
- $L(P) = \cup_{p \in P} L(p)$, and
- $C^k = \{L(P) \mid P \in D^k\}$.

A multiple description P is of *canonical form* if P contains no q such that $q \prec p$ for some $p \in P$. For any $P \in D^k$ there exists a unique $\hat{P}$ of canonical form such that $P \equiv \hat{P}$. Hereafter any multiple description is assumed to be of canonical form. Note that *k-MGS* $(D^k, \sqsubseteq)$ is a partially ordered set in this case.

A *k-multiple covering* of a finite set S of objects is a *k*-multiple description P such that $S \subseteq L(P)$. A *k-minimal multiple generalization* (*k-mmg* for short) is a *k*-multiple covering P of S such that $Q \not\sqsubseteq P$ for any *k*-multiple covering Q of S. In other words, the *k*-mmg is an mcg within a *k-MGS* $(D^k, \sqsubseteq)$. A *k-minl* is a minl for a concept class $(C^k, D^k, L(\cdot))$. A concept class $(C^k, D^k, L(\cdot))$ has *compactness with respect to containment* iff for any $p, q_1, \ldots, q_m$ $(1 \leq m \leq k)$, $L(p) \subseteq L(q_1) \cup \ldots \cup L(q_m)$ implies $L(p) \subseteq L(q_i)$ for some $1 \leq i \leq m$. Here we should note that compactness with respect to containment for unions and completeness for generalization guarantee $P \sqsubseteq Q \Longleftrightarrow L(Q) \subseteq L(P)$.

$$S = \left\{ \begin{array}{ll} 000, & 002 \\ 001, & 00011 \\ 011, & 02211 \end{array} \right\}, \qquad P = \left\{ \begin{array}{l} 00x \\ 0y1 \end{array} \right\}, \qquad p = 0x$$

Figure 2: A finite set S of strings over $\Sigma = \{0, 1, 2\}$, 2-minimal multiple generalization P of S for pairs of regular patterns, and a minimal common generalization p of S for regular patterns

Recall that in a GS $(D, \preceq)$ there exist only finitely many coverings of S for any finite set S of objects. On the other hand, usually in a k-MGS $(D^k, \sqsubseteq)$ there are infinitely many k-multiple coverings of S, that is, the concept class of unions does not have finite thickness. However, we can effectively find a k-mmg of S by restricting candidates for k-mmg to have no redundant description. A k-multiple covering $P \in D^k$ of S is said to be *reduced*, if $S \subseteq L(P)$ but $S \not\subseteq L(P')$ for any $P' \subsetneq P$.

Lemma 3.1 *Let S be a finite set of objects and P be a k-multiple covering of S that is of canonical form. If P is a k-mmg of S, then P is a reduced covering of S.*

Proof. Assume P is a k-multiple covering of S but not reduced. Then there exists a proper subset $Q \subsetneq P$ such that $S \subseteq L(Q)$. Since both P and Q are of canonical form, $Q \sqsubset P$. Therefore P cannot be a k-mmg of S. $\qquad \Box$

From Lemma 3.1, any k-mmg of S can be found out of reduced k-multiple coverings of S. If P is a reduced k-multiple covering of S, then for any $p \in P$ there exists at least one object $w \in S$ such that $w \preceq p$. Therefore the set of reduced multiple coverings of S is finite and computable. In fact, it is a subset of a finite set G^k, where $G = \{p \in D \mid w \in L(p)$ for some $w \in S\}$. Thus, a simple algorithm that searches for a minimal element in G^k with respect to $\sqsubseteq$ can effectively find a k-mmg of any finite set S. However, this algorithm belongs to exhaustive search methods and it cannot run so efficiently, even if a GS $(D, \preceq)$ is efficient. To realize a polynomial time algorithm to find a k-mmg, we need a stronger lemma than Lemma 3.1 which will be presented in the next section.

Theorem 3.2 *Let $(D^k, \sqsubseteq)$ be a k-MGS derived from an efficient and complete GS $(D, \preceq)$. Then*

- *$\sqsubseteq$ is polynomial time computable,*
- *for almost all $P \in D^k$, size$(P) \le h(|P|)$ and $|P| \le h'($size$(P)))$ for some polynomials h and h',*
- *k-mmg is computable, and*
- *$(C^k, D^k, L(\cdot))$ has finite elasticity.*

Furthermore, if the concept class C^k has compactness with respect to containment and k-mmg is polynomial time computable, then

- *any k-mmg algorithm for $(D^k, \sqsubseteq)$ works as k-minl for C^k, and*
- *C^k is polynomial time inferable from positive data.*

4   Polynomial time minimal multiple generalization algorithm

In this section we present a characterization of the possible forms of k-mmgs and polynomial time algorithm to find a k-mmg based on a greedy search.

First we show a necessary and sufficient condition for a k-multiple description P consisting of *just* k descriptions to be a k-mmg of a finite set of objects. A k-multiple covering P of a finite set S of objects is said to be *tightest* iff any $p \in P$ is an mcg of $S - L(P \setminus p)$. Clearly, if P is a tightest covering of S, then P is of canonical form and reduced covering of S.

Theorem 4.1 *Let S be a finite set of objects, P be a reduced k-multiple covering of S, and $\sharp P = k$. Then P is a tightest k-multiple covering of S iff P is a k-mmg for S.*

Proof. If part is obvious. Let $P = \{p_1, \ldots, p_k\}$ be a tightest k-multiple covering of S and Q be a k-multiple covering of S such that $Q \sqsubseteq P$. Let $S_i = S - L(P \setminus p_i)$ for each $i = 1, \ldots, k$. Note that $S_i \neq \phi$ and $i \neq j \implies S_i \cap S_j = \phi$.

Claim 1. For each $q \in Q$, $L(q)$ can have a nonempty intersection with at most one of S_1, $S_2, \ldots, S_k$. If $L(q)$ has a nonempty intersection with S_i, then $q \preceq p_i$.

(Proof of Claim 1) Since $Q \sqsubseteq P$, $q \preceq p_i$ for some $i = 1, \ldots, k$. Assume that $L(q)$ has a nonempty intersection with S_j. Then $\phi \subsetneq S_j \cap L(q) \subseteq S_j \cap L(p_i)$ because $L(q) \subseteq L(p_i)$. If $i \neq j$, then $S_j \cap L(p_i) = \phi$. Therefore we have $i = j$.

Claim 2. For each $i = 1, \ldots, k$, S_i has a nonempty intersection with $L(q)$ for some $q \in Q$.

(Proof of Claim 2) Clear from the condition $S \subseteq L(Q)$.

From these two claims we have $\sharp Q \geq \sharp P = k$. Since we assume $\sharp Q \leq k$, $\sharp Q = \sharp P = k$. For each $q \in Q$, $L(q)$ has a nonempty intersection with some unique S_i. For any $q' \in Q$ other than q, such S_i does not have nonempty intersection with $L(q')$. Therefore q should cover whole S_i. From Claim 1, $q \preceq p_i$. Since p_i is a mcg of S_i, $q \not\prec p_i$. Therefore $q = p_i$. Thus we have $Q \equiv P$. $\square$

Theorem 4.1 does not fully characterize k-mmgs because the number of descriptions in some k-mmgs may be less than k. To explain such phenomena we introduce the notion of divisibility. Assume a GS $(D, \preceq)$ and a k-MSG $(D^k, \sqsubseteq)$ for some $k > 1$. Let S be a finite set of objects and p be a covering of S. For $k > 1$, a k-*division* of p *with respect to* S is a reduced k-multiple covering P of S such that $\sharp P > 1$ and $P \sqsubset \{p\}$. We say p is k-*divisible with respect to* S if there exists a k-division of p with respect to S. Note that k-divisibility implies k'-divisibility if $k \geq k'$ but it does not hold in general if $k < k'$. For example, consider a pattern $p = xy$ that covers a set $S = \{01, 12, 20\}$. Then p is not 2-divisible with respect to S. However, p is 3-divisible because S itself is a 3-division of p.

Theorem 4.2 *Let S be a finite set of objects, P be a reduced k-multiple covering of S. Then P is a k-mmg for S iff P is a tightest covering of S and any $p \in P$ is not Δk-divisible with respect to $S - L(P \setminus p)$, where $\Delta k = (k - \sharp P + 1)$.*

From Theorem 4.2 we see that there are *two* key problems to find a k-mmg; how to find a division of a description with respect to a finite set of objects, and how to get a tightest covering from a division.

Let $p \in D$ be a covering of a finite set S. A *partial covering* of S relative to p is a refinement q of p such that p is not a covering of S but $L(p)$ has a nonempty intersection with S, that is, $\phi \subsetneq S \cap L(p) \subsetneq S$. A *complete set of partial covering* (*cspc* for short) *of S relative to* a covering p is a set P of partial coverings of S relative to p such that for any partial covering q of S relative to p, there is some $q' \in P$ satisfying that $S \cap L(q) \subseteq S \cap L(q')$. We denote an arbitrary cspc of S relative to p by $\mathrm{cspc}(S, p)$. The following lemma is obvious from the definitions, which asserts that whenever a description p is a k-divisible covering of a finite set S of objects, we can effectively find a reduced k-multiple covering P of S.

Lemma 4.3 *Let $(D, \preceq)$ be a complete GS, S be a finite set of objects and p be a covering of S. Assume that Q is any cspc of S relative to p. Then p is k-divisible iff there exists a k-division P that is a subset of Q.*

A *tightest refinement* (*tr* for short) of a description p with respect to a finite set S of objects is a refinement of p that is an mcg of S. Suppose an algorithm that computes a tightest refinement of p with respect to S and denote by $\mathrm{tr}(p, S)$ the answer computed by the algorithm. Then, the following procedure, given a reduced k-multiple covering P of S, computes a tightest k-multiple covering of S by taking a tightest refinement of each member p in P. Hereafter, we denote by $\mathrm{TC}(S, P)$ the tightest covering computed by the procedure.

begin /* Computing the tightest covering of S less general than P */
$\quad Q := P$;
$\quad$**while** there exists some $q \in Q$ that is not marked **do**
$\quad\quad r := \mathrm{tr}(q, S - L(Q \setminus q))$, and mark r;
$\quad\quad Q := Q \setminus q \cup \{r\}$;
$\quad$**endwhile**;
$\quad$output Q;
end

Now, we have the algorithm MMG shown below to find a k-mmg of a finite set S of objects. Starting with the greatest multiple description $P = \{\top\}$, the algorithm MMG refines P by alternately applying two operations *dividing* at Line 4 and *tightening* at Line 5 to P. We claim that whenever it enters the while loop at Line 3, P is a tightest covering of S. If $P = \mathrm{TC}(T, Q)$ for some set T and a multiple covering Q of T, P is a tightest covering of T with just $\sharp Q$ members. Thus, P is a tightest covering of S when MMG enters the while loop at the first time. If P is a tightest covering of S and some $p \in P$ is Δk-divisible for some $\Delta k > 1$, then MMG finds a tightest covering Q of the set $S - L(P \setminus p)$ such that $Q \sqsubset \{p\}$, where $S - L(P \setminus p)$ is the set of strings in S that are covered by p but not by any other members in P. Then, we can show that the set $P \setminus p \cup Q$ obtained at Line 5 is also a tightest covering of S. Therefore P is being a tightest covering of S during the execution of the while loop. On the other hands, the number $\sharp P$ of members of P properly increases every time MMG executes the while loop, while $\sharp P$ cannot exceed k because Δk is defined as $\Delta k = k - \sharp P + 1$. Thus, MMG executes the loop at most $k - 1$ times and eventually terminates. Then, no member of P must be Δk-divisible for any $\Delta k > 1$ and P is a tightest covering of S. Hence, we have the correctness and the efficiency of the algorithm MMG from Theorem 4.2.

Theorem 4.4 *If $\mathrm{cspc}(S, p)$ and $\mathrm{tr}(p, S)$ are polynomial time computable for an efficient and complete GS $(D, \preceq)$, then a k-mmg of a finite set S of objects is computable in polynomial time in $|S|$ for the k-MGS $(D^k, \sqsubseteq)$.*

Algorithm $\mathrm{MMG}(k, S)$;
input: a positive integer k and a finite set S of objects;
output: a k-mmg P of S;
method:
$\quad$**begin**
1 $\quad\quad P := \mathrm{TC}(S, \{\top\})$;
2 $\quad\quad \Delta k := k$;
3 $\quad\quad$**while** $\Delta k \geq 2$ and there exists some $p \in P$ that is
$\quad\quad\quad\quad \Delta k$-divisible with respect to $S - L(P \setminus p)$ **do**
4 $\quad\quad\quad$find Δk-division ΔP of p with respect to $S - L(P \setminus p)$; $\quad$ /* dividing */
5 $\quad\quad\quad P := P \setminus p \cup \mathrm{TC}(\Delta P, S - L(P \setminus p))$; $\quad\quad\quad\quad\quad$ /* tightening */
6 $\quad\quad\quad \Delta k := k - \sharp P + 1$;
7 $\quad\quad$**endwhile**
8 $\quad\quad$output P;
$\quad$**end**

5 Refinement operators

In the previous section, we show a sufficient condition for a concept class to have a polynomial time k-mmg algorithm. If we can design polynomial time algorithms to compute cspc and tr, then we construct a polynomial time k-mmg algorithm. In this section, we show algorithms for cspc and tr using refinement operators.

First we introduce the notion of refinement operator [Sha81, Lai88]. For a binary relation R, we denote the set $\{b \mid (a,b) \in R\}$ by $R(a)$ and the transitive closure of R by R^+. Let $(D, \preceq)$ be an efficient GS. A *refinement operator* is a subrelation of $\prec$. A refinement operator ρ is *complete* if $p \prec q \Longleftrightarrow p \in \rho^+(q)$ for any $p, q \in D$. A refinement operator ρ is *efficient* if $\rho(p)$ is polynomial time computable.

Clearly from the definitions, if ρ is a complete refinement for a complete GS, then the set $\{p \in \rho(p) \mid S \cap L(p) \neq \phi\}$ is the complete set of partial covering of S relative to p. Therefore if an efficient and complete refinement operator are available, a cspc is computable in polynomial time.

To compute $\mathrm{tr}(p, S)$, we can adopt a simple greedy search using a complete refinement operator. Consider the procedure shown below that, given a finite set S of objects and a covering p of S, computes a tightest refinement $\mathrm{tr}(p, S)$:

begin /* Computing a tightest refinement of p with respect to S */
    $q := p$;
    while there exists some $r \in \rho(q)$ such that $S \subseteq L(r)$ **do**
        $q := r$;
    output q
end

Let $n = \min\{\mathrm{size}(w) \mid w \in S\}$. Note that n is polynomial order of $|S|$ if the GS is efficient. If $r \in \rho(q)$ then $\mathrm{size}(r) > \mathrm{size}(q)$. If $\mathrm{size}(p) > n$ then $L(p)$ cannot contain any w such that $\mathrm{size}(w) \leq n$. Therefore the number of iterations on while loop in the procedure shown above is at most $n - \mathrm{size}(p)$. Hence, the procedure runs in polynomial time when both of GS and ρ are complete and efficient. From these observations we have the following theorem.

Theorem 5.1 *Let $(D, \preceq)$ be an efficient and complete GS, ρ be an efficient and complete refinement operator for $\prec$, S be a finite set of objects, and p be a covering of S. Then $cspc(S, p)$ and $\mathrm{tr}(p, S)$ are computable in polynomial time in $|p|$ and $|S|$.*

6   Applications to pattern languages

First we present an efficient and complete refinement operator ρ for regular patterns [ASY92]. We define the *size* of a pattern p by $\mathrm{size}(p) = 2 \times |p| - \sharp v(p)$, where $v(p)$ is the set of variables appearing in p. Clearly $\mathrm{size}(p) \leq 2 \times |p|$ and $|p| \leq \mathrm{size}(p)$ for any p. A substitution θ is said to be *basic* for a regular pattern p, if θ satisfies one of the following:

- $\theta = \{x := a\}$, where $x \in v(p)$ and $a \in \Sigma$.
- $\theta = \{x := yz\}$, where $x \in v(p)$ and y, z are distinct variables not appearing in p.

We define ρ by $\rho(p) = \{q \mid q = p\theta, \theta \text{ is basic for } p\}$. Then we can show that ρ is an efficient and complete refinement for regular patterns. If $\sharp\Sigma > 2$, GS $(\mathcal{P}_{\mathrm{reg}}, \preceq)$ is efficient and complete [Shi82b, Muk92]. The following theorem is direct from Theorem 5.1.

Theorem 6.1 *If $\sharp\Sigma > 2$, then a k-mmg of a finite set S of strings is computable in polynomial time in $|S|$ for the k-MGS $(\mathcal{P}_{\mathrm{reg}}^k, \sqsubseteq)$.*

We cannot use our k-mmg algorithm as a k-minl for regular pattern languages, since $\mathcal{PL}_{\mathrm{reg}}^k$ does not have compactness with respect to containment. By a similar discussion as in [Muk92], we can show the compactness for the subclass $\mathcal{PL}_{\mathrm{reg}(m)}^k$ of unions of k m-variable regular pattern languages under $\sharp\Sigma > 2km$.

Lemma 6.2 *Let $k \geq 1$ and $m \geq 0$. If $\sharp\Sigma > 2km$, then for any m-variable regular patterns $p, q_1, \ldots, q_k$, $L(p) \subseteq L(q_1) \cup \ldots \cup L(q_k) \Longrightarrow L(p) \subseteq L(q_i)$ for some $1 \leq i \leq k$.*

However, we cannot use ρ as it is for $\mathcal{P}_{\text{reg}}$ for m-variable regular patterns, because some $q \in \rho(p)$ contains more than m variables. To avoid this problem, we slightly modify ρ as ρ_m.

Let m be a positive integer. A substitution θ is said to be m-basic for a regular pattern p, if $\sharp v(p\theta) \leq m$ and θ satisfies one of the following:

- $\theta = \{x := a\}$, where $x \in v(p)$ and $a \in \Sigma$.
- $\theta = \{x := yz\}$, where $x \in v(p)$ and y, z are distinct variables not appearing in p.
- $\theta = \{x := ax\}$ or $\theta = \{x := xa\}$, where $x \in v(p)$ and $a \in \Sigma$.

We define ρ_m by $\rho_m(p) = \{q \mid q = p\theta, \theta \text{ is } m\text{-basic for } p\}$. Then we can show that ρ_m is an efficient and complete refinement for m-variable regular patterns.

Theorem 6.3 If $\sharp\Sigma > 2km$, then the class $\mathcal{PL}_{\text{reg}(m)}^k$ of unions of k m-variable regular pattern languages is polynomial time inferable from positive data.

An Example : Let S be the set { 0000, 00000, 0002, 000222, 00122, 002222, 00222, 1211, 112111, 2221 } of strings over $\Sigma = \{0, 1, 2\}$ and $k = 4$. The following table illustrates how the computation of a k-mmg of S for regular patterns proceeds, where a pattern underlined in some step indicates that it is selected to be divided at the step. Starting with the most general set $\{x\}$ at Step 1, the algorithm MMG refines the set of patterns step by step applying tightening and dividing operations alternately.

1: Tightening	{ x }		4: Dividing	{ $\underline{00zu}$, $x2z1$ }
2: Dividing	{ $\underline{xyzu}$ }		5: Tightening	{ $000u$, $00z2$, $x2z1$ }
3: Tightening	{ $0yzu$, $xyz1$ }		6: Solution	{ $000u$, $00y22$, $x2z1$ }

At Step 6, the algorithm terminates. Then, $\{000u, 00y22, x2z1\}$ is a k-mmg of S because the set is a tightest cover of S and none of $000u, 00y22, x2z1$ are Δk-divisible for $\Delta k = 4 - 3 + 1 = 2$.

7   Discussions

The main subject of this paper is to find an appropriate subclass of pattern languages whose unions form a class polynomial time inferable from positive data. We have generalized our former results for tree pattern languages [ASO93]. For inductive inference we need a description of a minimal concept explaining given the examples. Instead of the problem of finding minimal concept, we consider the problem of finding a syntactically minimal common generalization. Taking this approach we can show a uniform method to design efficient generalization algorithms. We also showed a condition for our algorithm finding a syntactically minimal description to be used as an algorithm finding a description of a minimal concept. As an application, we showed a class of unions consisting of at most k regular pattern languages with at most m variables is polynomial time inferable from positive data under the condition that the number of constant symbols is greater than $2km$.

For one-variable patterns, it seems to be hard to find an efficient and complete refinement operator. For example, the most general pattern x has infinitely many refinements xx, xxx, $xxxx$, ... Therefore if ρ is a complete refinement for $\mathcal{P}_1$, then $\rho(x)$ should contains these infinitely many refinements. However, we do not need all elements in $\rho(p)$ to compute a complete set of partial covering and a tightest refinement. For instance, we do not need any pattern q whose size is larger than the minimum size in S. To compute a tightest refinement, we can use a minl algorithm based on one-variable pattern automata [Ang79]. In reality we can efficiently compute both cspc and tr for $\mathcal{P}_1$. Therefore we can show that a k-mmg for one-variable patterns is also polynomial time computable for any $k \geq 1$. Angluin [Ang79] and Wright [Wri89a] showed the same result just for $k = 1, 2$, respectively. We can also show the compactness of unions of one-variable pattern languages under a similar condition on the number of constant symbols and the number of components of unions [Wri89a]. We will report more details on one-variable patterns elsewhere.

Theorem 7.1 If $\sharp\Sigma > k$, then the class $\mathcal{PL}_1^k$ of unions of k one-variable pattern languages is polynomial time inferable from positive data.

References

[AKM⁺92] S. Arikawa, S. Kuhara, S. Miyano, A. Shinohara, and T. Shinohara. A learning algorithm for elementary formal systems and its experiments on identification of transmembrane domains. In *Proc. of the 25th Hawaii International Conference on System Sciences*, pp. 675–684, 1992.

[Ang79] D. Angluin. Finding patterns common to a set of strings. In *Proceedings of the 11th Annual Symposium on Theory of Computing*, pp. 130–141, 1979.

[ASO92] H. Arimura, T. Shinohara, and S. Otsuki. Polynomial time inference of unions of two tree pattern languages. *IEICE Trans. Inf. & Syst.*, E75-D, pp. 426–434, 1992.

[ASO93] H. Arimura, T. Shinohara, and S. Otsuki. A polynomial time algorithm for finding finite unions of tree pattern languages. In *Proceedings of the Second International Workshop on Nonmonotonic and Inductive Logic*, pp. 118–131. LNAI 659, Springer, 1993.

[ASY92] S. Arikawa, T. Shinohara, and A. Yamamoto. Learning elementary formal systems. *Theoretical Computer Science*, Vol. 95, pp. 97–113, 1992.

[Gol67] E.M. Gold. Languages identification in the limit. *Information and Control*, Vol. 10, pp. 447–474, 1967.

[Lai88] P. D. Laird. *Learning from good and bad data*. Kluwer Academic, 1988.

[LW91] S. Lange and R. Wiehagen. Polynomial-time inference of arbitrary pattern languages. *New Generation Computing*, Vol. 8, No. 4, pp. 361–370, 1991.

[MSS91] S. Miyano, A. Shinohara, and T. Shinohara. Which classes of elementary formal systems are polynomial-time learnable? In S. Arikawa, A. Maruoka, and T. Sato, editors, *Proceedings of the Second Workshop on Algorithmic Learning Theory*, pp. 139–150, 1991.

[Muk92] Y. Mukouchi. Characterization of pattern languages. *IEICE Trans. Inf. and Syst.*, Vol. E75-D, No. 7, 1992.

[Nix83] R. Nix. Editing by example. Technical Report 280, Department of Computer Science, Yale University, 1983.

[Plo70] G. Plotkin. A note on inductive generalization. In B. Meltzer and D. Mitchie, editors, *Machine Intelligence*, volume 5, pp. 153–163. Edinburgh Univ. Press, 1970.

[Sha81] E. Y. Shapiro. Inductive inference of theories from facts. Technical Report 192, Yale University, Department of Computer Science, 1981.

[Shi82a] T. Shinohara. Polynomial time inference of extended regular pattern languages. In *RIMS Symposia on Software Science and Engineering*, pp. 115–127. LNCS 147, Springer, 1982.

[Shi82b] T. Shinohara. Polynomial time inference of pattern languages and its applications. In *Proceedings of the 7th IBM Symposium on Mathematical Foundations of Computer Science*, pp. 191–209, 1982.

[Shi83] T. Shinohara. Inferring unions of two pattern languages. *Bulletin of Informatics and Cybernetics*, Vol. 20, pp. 83–88, 1983.

[Smu61] R. M. Smullyan. *Theory of Formal Systems*. Princeton Univ. Press, 1961.

[SSY93] A. Salomaa, K. Salomaa, and Sheng Y. Inclusion is undecidable for pattern languages. In *Proc. 20th ICALP*, 1993.

[TY92] N Tanida and T. Yokomori. Polynomial-time identification of strictly regular languages in the limit. *IEICE Trans. Inf. and Syst.*, Vol. E75-D, No. 1, pp. 125–132, 1992.

[Val84] L. G. Valiant. A theory of the learnable. *Comm. ACM*, Vol. 27, No. 11, pp. 1134–1142, 1984.

[Wri89a] K. Wright. *Inductive Inference of Pattern Languages*. PhD thesis, University of Pittsburgh, 1989.

[Wri89b] K. Wright. Identification of unions of languages drawn from an identifiable class. In *Proceedings of the 2nd Annual Workshop on Computational Learning Theory*, pp. 328–333, 1989.

Nondeterminism in Patterns

Alexandru Mateescu   Arto Salomaa

Academy of Finland and Department of Mathematics,
University of Turku, SF-20500 Turku, Finland

Abstract. The paper investigates nondeterminism and degrees of nondeterminism in representing words according to a pattern given a priori. The issues involved belong to the basic combinatorics of words. Our main results concern decidability and construction of finite degrees of nondeterminism.

Topics : automata and formal languages

1. Introduction

There has been much interest recently in *patterns* and *pattern languages*. (See, for instance, [3], [5], [6], [8] and their references.) Indeed, a natural way of describing a given sample of words is to exhibit a common pattern for the words. Such an approach is especially appropriate if the sample is growing, for instance, through some *learning* process. Finding patterns for a sample sets is, thus, a typical problem of *inductive inference*.

Pattern languages in the sense understood in this paper were introduced in [1]. The essential difference between the two cases, where the empty word λ can or cannot be substituted for the variables, was studied in [5]. It was also observed that many problems in combinatorics of words, ranging from the classical ones discussed in [11] to the more recent ones discussed in [2] and [7], can be expressed in terms of the inclusion problem for pattern languages. The same holds true for certain problems in term rewriting, [8]. From this point of view it is not surprising that the inclusion problem turned out to be undecidable, [6].

Given a terminal word w and a pattern α, it may happen that w "follows" the pattern α in several ways. In other words, there are several assignments for the variables in α, each of which gives rise to w. This kind of *nondeterminism* or *ambiguity* in patterns will be investigated in this paper. Indeed, the classical language-theoretic notions of *unambiguity, inherent ambiguity* and *degrees of ambiguity* (see [10]) find their natural counterparts in the context of patterns. The proofs make use of various aspects in combinatorics of words. The case of a finite degree of ambiguity greater than one turns out to be rather involved. In decidability issues, modifications of the result by Makanin, [9], can be used.

* Research supported by the Academy of Finland, Project 11281. All correspondence to Arto Salomaa.

2. Definitions and preliminary results

Let Σ be an alphabet (of *terminals*) and V an alphabet (of *variables*) such that $\Sigma \cap V = \emptyset$. Let $H(\Sigma, V)$ (resp. $H_+(\Sigma, V)$) be the set of all morphisms (resp. nonerasing morphisms)

$$h : (\Sigma \cup V)^* \to \Sigma^*$$

such that $h(a) = a$ for all $a \in \Sigma$.

Nonempty words α over $\Sigma \cup V$ are referred to as *patterns*. A pattern $\alpha \in (\Sigma \cup V)^+$ defines the *languages* :

$$L_E(\alpha) = \{w \mid h(\alpha) = w, \text{ for some } h \in H(\Sigma, V)\}$$
$$L_{NE}(\alpha) = \{w \mid h(\alpha) = w, \text{ for some } h \in H_+(\Sigma, V)\}.$$

The language $L_E(\alpha)$ and $L_{NE}(\alpha)$ are referred to as *pattern languages*. Sometimes we speak of *E-patterns* and *NE-patterns* ("erasing" and "nonerasing") to indicate which of the languages we are interested in. Also the alphabet Σ may be indicated in the notation : $L_E(\alpha, \Sigma)$ or $L_{NE}(\alpha, \Sigma)$. This is the case especially if Σ is not visible from α, that is, all letters of Σ do not occur in α.

We now come to the central notions of this paper. It may happen that a word w in $L_E(\alpha)$ or $L_{NE}(\alpha)$ has several "representations", that is, there are several morphisms h satisfying $w = h(\alpha)$. For instance, the terminal word $w = a^7 b a^7$ possesses 8 representations in terms of the pattern $\alpha = xyx$. (The number is 7 if α is viewed as an NE-pattern.) We express this by saying that the *degree of ambiguity* of w with respect to α equals 8. Whenever important, we indicate whether we are dealing with the E- or NE- case.

The *degree of ambiguity of a pattern* α equals the maximal degree of ambiguity of words w in the language of α, or infinity (∞) if no such maximal degree exists. More formally, we associate to a pattern α over $\Sigma \cup V$ and a word $w \in \Sigma^+$ the subset $S(\alpha, w, \Sigma)$ of $H(\Sigma, V)$, consisting of morphisms h such that $h(\alpha) = w$. The *cardinality* of this subset is denoted by $card(\alpha, w, \Sigma)$. (We make here the *convention* that morphisms differing only on variables not present in α are not counted as different.) The *degree of ambiguity* of α equals $k \geq 1$ iff

$$card(\alpha, w, \Sigma) \leq k, \text{ for all } w \in L_E(\alpha),$$

and

$$card(\alpha, w', \Sigma) = k, \text{ for some } w' \in L_E(\alpha).$$

If there is no such k, then the *degree of ambiguity* of α equals ∞. For $k = 1$, α is also termed *unambiguous* and, for $k > 1$, α is termed *ambiguous*.

Remark. The terminals actually appearing in α constitute a subset Σ', maybe empty, of Σ. Indeed, any pattern over $\Sigma' \cup V$ is a pattern also over $\Sigma \cup V$, where $\Sigma' \subseteq \Sigma$. In the definition of the degree of ambiguity we actually specified the pair (α, Σ). However, it is pleasing to observe that, in fact, it suffices to specify only α because the degree is independent of the choice of Σ. The following argument justifies this observation.

If α contains no terminals (that is, Σ' is empty), then the degree of ambiguity of α is 1 or ∞, depending on whether α contains occurrences of one or more than one variable. If Σ' contains at least one terminal a, we denote by $g : \Sigma^* \to \Sigma'^*$ the morphism keeping the letters of Σ' fixed and mapping the letters of $\Sigma - \Sigma'$ into a. Clearly, the degree of ambiguity does not decrease if the terminal alphabet Σ' is replaced by Σ. But it does not increase either because, whenever w has m representations according to α, then $g(w)$ has at least m representations according to α. $\qquad\square$

By the above remark, we speak of the degree of ambiguity of a pattern α (without specifying the alphabet). The above definitions were carried out in the E- case. The NE- case is analogous.

The notions are now naturally extended to concern languages. We do this in the E- case. A *pattern language* L is *ambiguous of degree* $k \geq 1$ if $L = L_E(\alpha)$, for some pattern α ambiguous of degree k, but there is no pattern β of degree less then k such that $L = L_E(\beta)$. Here k is a natural number or ∞. Again, if $k = 1$ we say that L is *unambiguous*. Otherwise, L is *(inherently) ambiguous*.

It was shown in [1] that two NE-patterns are *equivalent* (in the sense that they generate the same language) exactly in the case they are identical up to a possible renaming of variables. This yields immediately the following result :

Theorem 1. *The degree of ambiguity of an NE-pattern α equals the degree of ambiguity of the pattern language $L_{NE}(\alpha)$.*

Theorem 1 does not hold for E-patterns : $L_E(X) = L_E(XY)$ but the degrees of ambiguity of the patterns X and XY are 1 and ∞, respectively.

Theorem 2. *For every E-pattern (containing at least one variable), there is an equivalent E-pattern whose degree of ambiguity is ∞. Conversely, there are E-patterns (for instance, $XYYX$) such that the degree of ambiguity of every equivalent E-pattern, and hence also the degree of ambiguity of the generated language, equals ∞.*

Proof. To prove the first sentence, it suffices to replace all occurrences of a variable X in the pattern with $X_1 X_2$. The second sentence follows by a simple case analysis concerning patterns equivalent to $XYYX$. $\qquad\square$

In what follows we do not make any distinction between E- and NE-patterns because the results hold in both cases.

Theorem 3. *Every pattern containing occurrences of only one variable X is unambiguous. Every pattern containing occurrences of at least two variables X and Y but of at most one terminal a is ambiguous of degree ∞.*

Proof. The first sentence follows by a length argument : for every w, the value $h(X)$ is uniquely determined. To prove the second sentence, we first replace in the given pattern the other variables (if any) with a. The resulting pattern contains $m \geq 1$ X's, $n \geq 1$ Y's and $p \geq 0$ a's. Given any k, we can find a z_k such that

$$mx + ny + p = z_k$$

has more that k positive solutions (x, y). This means that a^{z_k} has more than k represetations according to the given pattern. ☐

3. Determinism and nondeterminism

We now continue the study begun in the preceding section and characterize some basic cases of ambiguity and nonambiguity.

Theorem 4. *Every pattern α satisfying the following two conditions is of ∞ degree of ambiguity. (i) α contains occurrences of at least two variables. (ii) Some variable occurs in α only once.*

Proof. Let Z be the variable that has only one occurrence in α. We'll consider the following two possibilities :

Case 1. The pattern α starts or ends with Z. Assume that α ends with Z (the situation α starts with Z is symmetric). Hence, $\alpha = \beta Z$, where β is a pattern that contains at least one variable, but Z does not occur in β. Let X be the leftmost variable in β, i.e. $\beta = X\gamma$, where γ is a pattern. (We assume without loss of generality that β starts with a variable.) Therefore, $\alpha = X\gamma Z$ and Z does not occur in $X\gamma$.

Now, assume to the contrary that α has the degree of ambiguity k, where $k < \infty$. Let w be a terminal word that has k different decompositions with respect to α. Let u be a fixed terminal word. Consider the morphism f, defined as : $f(X) = w$ and $f(Y) = u$, for any variable Y, $Y \neq X$. We obtain $f(\alpha) = t = wv$.

The terminal word t has one decomposition with respect to α corresponding to the morphism f and, moreover, t has k other decompositions with respect to α, corresponding to the k possible decompositions of w, each such decomposition being modified as follows : if Z was substituted by r in the originally considered decomposition of w, then Z is substituted by rv, in order to obtain t, and any other variable Y continues to be substituted as in the originally considered decomposition of w. Thus, t has $k + 1$ different decompositions with respect to α, contrary to the assumption that α has the degree of ambiguity k.

Case 2. The variable Z has only one occurrence in α and this occurrence is neither the leftmost nor the rightmost occurrence of a variable in α. Hence, $\alpha = X\beta Z\gamma Y$, where β, γ are patterns, X, Y, Z variables (possibly $X = Y$) and Z does not occur in $X\beta\gamma Y$. Again, assume to the contrary that α has the degree of ambiguity k, where $k < \infty$, and let w be a terminal word that can be decomposed in k different ways with respect to α. Hence, there are p_i, q_i, r_i, $i = 1, \ldots, k$, such that $w = p_i r_i q_i$ and Z was substituted by r_i. Consider the morphism f, such that : $f(X) = w$, $f(Y) = w$, and $f(Q) = u$, for any Q, $Q \neq X$, $Q \neq Y$, and u is a fixed, arbitrary terminal word. (Note that, if $X = Y$, then f continues to be well-defined.) Let t be the terminal word $f(\alpha)$. Hence, $t = wsw$, where $s = f(\beta Z\gamma)$. Note that t has one decomposition, with respect to α, corresponding to the morphism f. Moreover, $t = p_i r_i q_i s p_i r_i q_i$, for $i = 1, \ldots, k$. Each such decomposition of t is corresponding to the substitution of Z in α with the terminal word $r_i q_i s p_i r_i$, and the remaining variables are substituted as in the original decomposition of w. Therefore, altogether, t has $k + 1$ different decompositions with respect to α, contrary to the assumption that the degree of ambiguity of α is k.

$\square$

Theorem 3 and 4 determine the degree of ambiguity of all patterns except patterns α satisfying each of the following three conditions : (i) α contains occurrences of at least two variables. (ii) α contains occurrences of at least two terminals. (iii) Every variable occurs in α at least twice. Indeed, all tricky cases fall among such patterns α. Let us consider patterns with two occurrences of two variables, separated by terminal words. Such patterns belong to one of the three types

$$X w_1 Y w_2 X w_3 Y, \qquad X w_1 Y w_2 Y w_3 X, \qquad X w_1 X w_2 Y w_3 Y.$$

We mention without proof that the first two types are always of degree of ambiguity 1 or ∞ , whereas a finite degree $\neq 1$ is possible in the third type. We will return to this matter in Section 5.

The following theorem serves as a basis in many constructions.

Theorem 5. *The pattern* $XaYXbY$ *is unambiguous.*

Proof. Assume that for some terminal words u_1, v_1, u_2, v_2 there is the equality :

$$u_1 a v_1 u_1 b v_1 = u_2 a v_2 u_2 b v_2 \qquad (1)$$

Note that $|u_i a v_i| = |u_i b v_i|$, $i = 1, 2$. Thus, the equality (1) leads to the next two equalities :

$$u_1 a v_1 = u_2 a v_2 \quad \text{and} \quad u_1 b v_1 = u_2 b v_2 \qquad (2)$$

Without loss of generality, we can assume that $|u_1| \leq |u_2|$ and, consequently, $|v_1| \geq |v_2|$. Thus, there are terminal words u_3 and v_3 such that $u_2 = u_1 u_3$ and $v_1 = v_3 v_2$. Hence, from (2) we deduce that :

$$av_3 = u_3 a \qquad \text{and} \qquad bv_3 = u_3 b .$$

The above system of equations has the unique solution $u_3 = v_3 = \lambda$. Therefore, we obtain $u_1 = u_2$ and $v_1 = v_2$ and thus, the pattern is unambiguous.

$\square$

Composition can be applied to patterns in the natural fashion : variables are uniformly substituted by patterns. If in the pattern of Theorem 5 the variable X is replaced by $X_1 a Y_1 X_1 b Y_1$ (that is, the original pattern with renamed variables) and the variable Y is left unchanged, we obtain the pattern

$$X_1 a Y_1 X_1 b Y_1 a Y X_1 a Y_1 X_1 b Y_1 b Y.$$

Clearly, also this pattern is unambiguous, by Theorem 5. In fact, the next theorem is a corollary of Theorem 5.

Theorem 6. *Compositions of unambiguous patterns are unambiguous. Unambiguous patterns of arbitrarily many variables can be effectively constructed.*

4. Decidability

Using the general theorem of Makanin, [9], the following results can be obtained quite independently of our other results.

Theorem 7. *The following problems are decidable, given a pattern α and a natural number k. Is the degree of ambiguity of α equal to k, greater than k or less than k? Consequently, it is decidable whether or not α is unambiguous.*

Proof. It was shown in [4] how Makanin's decidability result can be extended to concern systems of equations and *inequalities*. Inequalities $x \neq x'$ are essential in expressing that a given equation possesses two solutions. The details of the argument are left to the reader. □

Theorem 7 does not yield a method of deciding whether or not the degree of ambiguity of α is ∞. Indeed, this is an open decision problem. As regards decision methods for pattern languages, the results of Theorems 1 and 7 can be combined for NE-patterns. The situation is trickier for E-patterns. In fact, even the decidability of the equivalence problem is open for E-patterns.

We mention, finally, that Theorem 6 gives a simple way of going from a system of equations to a single equation. Consider a system of equations

$$(*) \qquad\qquad \alpha_i = \beta_i, \qquad\qquad i = 1, \ldots, n,$$

where α_i and β_i may contain variables and constants (that is, terminals). Choose an unambiguous pattern $P(X_1, \ldots, X_n)$ of n variables X_i. Then (*) has a solution exactly in the case the equation

$$P(\alpha_1, \ldots, \alpha_n) = P(\beta_1, \ldots, \beta_n)$$

has a solution.

5. Finite degree of ambiguity

It is a rather difficult to exhibit patterns with the degree of ambiguity $k > 1$, where k is finite. Indeed, it was our conjecture for a long time that 1 and ∞ are the only possible degrees.

Theorem 8. *Explicit examples of patterns with degrees of ambiguity 2 and 3 can be given.*

Proof. A rather long argument (to appear in a forth coming paper), based on combinatorics of words. Our example of a pattern of degree 3 has length 324 and the shortest word that actually has 3 different decompositions with respect to this pattern has length 1018. On the other hand, our example of a pattern of degree 2 given in Corollary B of the Appendix is rather simple : $XabXbcaYabcY$. □

By forming compositions and using Theorem 6, our last result is obtained as a corollary of Theorem 8.

Theorem 9. *For any* $m \geq 0$ *and* $n \geq 0$, *a pattern with the degree of ambiguity* $2^m 3^n$ *can be effectively constructuded.*

It is worth mentioning that we have not been able to find any inductive way of going from the degree of ambiguity k to the degree $k + 1$. Thus, we cannot exhibit patterns with an arbitrarily given finite degree of ambiguity.

6. Conclusion. Open problems.

Our results deal with patterns and pattern languages and, thus, are interconnected with all related areas, as already indicated in the Introduction. However, the results can also be viewed to concern the basic theory of word equations as follows.

Let $P(X_1, \ldots, X_n)$ be a pattern of n variables X_i. The pattern P defines infinitely many individual equations

$$(*) \qquad P(X_1, \ldots, X_n) = Z,$$

where Z ranges over Σ^+. For given P and Z, we denote by $N(P, Z)$ the number of solutions of $(*)$, that is, the number of n-tuples of words $(w_1, \ldots, w_n)$ over Σ^* satisfying $(*)$. For each pair (P, Z), $N(P, Z)$ is a nonnegative integer. For a *fixed* P, there are three possibilities.

(i) $N(P, Z) \leq 1$, for all Z.
(ii) There is a Z' such that $N(P, Z') > 1$ but the numbers $N(P, Z)$ possess an upper bound, that is, for some k, $N(P, Z) \leq k$ for all Z.
(iii) The numbers $N(P, Z)$ possess no upper bound, that is, for every k, $N(P, Z') > k$ holds for some Z'.

We have been able to exhibit extensive classes of patterns for which (i) or (iii) holds. For instance, (i) holds if the number of variables $n = 1$, and (iii) holds if $n > 1$ and P is "linear" with respect to some variable (see Theorems 3 and 4). According to our main results (Theorems 8 and 9), also (ii) is possible. However, it is an open problem, and in our estimation very fundamental one in the theory of word equations, whether *all finite degrees* of ambiguity can actually be constructed. By theorem 6, it suffices to carry out the construction for prime degrees. We conjecture that such a construction is possible. Since arbitrarily large degrees can be obtained (Theorem 9), it would seem rather strange if some degrees were "missing".

The most interesting open decision problem is the decidability status of (iii). "Almost all" patterns seem to satisfy (iii), and yet Makanin's Theorem is not directly applicable to this case.

References

1. D. Angluin, *Finding patterns common to a set of strings*, Journal of Computer and System Sciences 21(1980) 46-62.
2. J. Bean, A. Ehrenfeucht, G. McNulty, *Avoidable patterns in strings of symbols*, Pacific Journal of Mathematics 85(1979) 261-294.

3. J. Cassaigne, *Unavoidable binary patterns*, Acta Informatica 30 (1993) 385-395.
4. K. Culik II, J. Karhumäki, *Systems of equations over a free monoid and Ehrenfeucht's conjecture*, Discrete Mathematics 43 (1983) 139-153.
5. T. Jiang, E. Kinber, A. Salomaa, K. Salomaa, S. Yu, *Pattern languages with and without erasing*, to appear in International Journal of Computer Mathematics.
6. T. Jiang, A. Salomaa, K. Salomaa, S. Yu, *Inclusion is undecidable for pattern languages*, ICALP-93 Proceedings, Springer Lecture Notes in Computer Science 700 (1993) 301-312.
7. V. Keränen, *Abelian squares can be avoided on four letters*, Springer Lecture Notes in Computer Science 623 (1992) 41-52.
8. G. Kucherov, M. Rusinowitch, *On ground reducibility problem for word rewriting systems with variables*, Centre de Recherche en Informatique de Nancy, Report CRIN 93-R-012.
9. G.S. Makanin, *The problem of solvability of equations in a free semigroup* (in Russian), Matematiceskij Sbornik 103 (145) (1977) 148-236.
10. A. Salomaa, *Formal Languages*, Academic Press, 1973.
11. A. Thue, *Über unendliche Zeichenreihen*, Norske Vid. Selsk. Skr., I Mat. Nat. Kl., Kristiania 7(1906) 1-22.

Upper bounds for the expected length of a longest common subsequence of two binary sequences

Vlado Dančík [*]   and   *Mike Paterson* [**]

Department of Computer Science, University of Warwick,
Coventry, CV4 7AL, England.
{vlado,msp}@dcs.warwick.ac.uk

Abstract. Let $f(n)$ be the expected length of a longest common subsequence of two random binary sequences of length n. It is known that the limit $c = \lim_{n \to \infty} f(n)/n$ exists. Improved upper bounds for c are given using a new method.

Classification: computational complexity, average-case analysis, string-matching.

1   Introduction and notation

Let $a, b \in \{0, 1\}^*$ be two binary sequences. The sequence c is a *common subsequence* of a and b if c is both a subsequence of a and a subsequence of b. A *longest common subsequence* of a and b is any common subsequence of maximal possible length and $v(a, b)$ is this length. The expected length $f(n)$ of the longest common subsequence of two random binary strings of length n is the average value of $v(a, b)$ over all pairs a, b. It is known that there is a constant c such that $c = \lim_{n \to \infty} f(n)/n$ (Chvátal, Sankoff [1]). The best known bounds were $0.7615 \leq c \leq 0.8575$ (Deken [2, 3]). In this paper we describe a new method for upper bounds for this constant and derive the upper bound 0.837623. We start with some definitions.

Let $\Sigma = \{0, 1\}$ be the binary alphabet, let Σ^* be the set of all binary sequences and $\Pi = \Sigma^* \times \Sigma^*$ the set of all pairs of binary sequences. Let $l(u)$ denote the length of a sequence u, and $l\binom{u}{v} = l(u) + l(v)$ the length of a pair $\binom{u}{v}$. Let t and b be the projections of a pair $\binom{u}{v}$ to its members: $t\binom{u}{v} = u$ and $b\binom{u}{v} = v$. Let $\operatorname{cat}(p, q) = \binom{t(p)t(q)}{b(p)b(q)}$ be the *concatenation* of pairs p, q. The definitions of concatenation, projections, and length are naturally extended to sequences of

---

[*] This author was supported by an East European Scholarship from the University of Warwick and an ORS Award from the CVCP.

[**] This author was partially supported by the ESPRIT II BRA Programme of the EC under contract 7141 (ALCOM II).

pairs:

$$\mathrm{cat}(p_1, p_2, \ldots, p_n, p_{n+1}) = \mathrm{cat}(\mathrm{cat}(p_1, p_2, \ldots, p_n), p_{n+1}),$$
$$t(p_1, p_2, \ldots, p_n) = t(\mathrm{cat}(p_1, p_2, \ldots, p_n)),$$
$$b(p_1, p_2, \ldots, p_n) = b(\mathrm{cat}(p_1, p_2, \ldots, p_n)),$$
$$l(p_1, p_2, \ldots, p_n) = l(\mathrm{cat}(p_1, p_2, \ldots, p_n)).$$

The pair $p = \binom{u}{v}$ is a *match* if u and v have the same last symbol, and let $c(p)$ be this symbol. A sequence $\mathbf{p} = p_1, p_2, \ldots, p_n, p_{n+1}$ of pairs is called a *collation of order* n if pairs $p_1, p_2, \ldots, p_n$ are matches, and $c(\mathbf{p}) = c(p_1)c(p_2)\cdots c(p_n)$ denotes the sequence of matching symbols. The collation $\mathbf{p}$ *generates* the pair $\binom{a}{b}$ if $\mathrm{cat}(\mathbf{p}) = \binom{a}{b}$. The positions of pairs of matching symbols form the *collation key* $L(\mathbf{p})$, where $L(\mathbf{p}) = L(p_1, p_2, \ldots, p_{n+1}) = l(p_1), l(p_1, p_2), \ldots, l(p_1, p_2, \ldots, p_n)$.

We shall use a partial order '$\prec$' on collations, based on a "*reverse* lexicographical" ordering of their collation keys. For integer sequences $\mathbf{x} = x_1, \ldots, x_k$ and $\mathbf{y} = y_1, \ldots, y_k$, we define $\mathbf{x} \prec \mathbf{y}$ if and only if, for some i, $1 \le i \le k$, $x_i < y_i$ and, for all j, $i < j \le k$, $x_j = y_j$. Now, for any two collations $\mathbf{p}$, $\mathbf{q}$, of the same order and such that $\mathrm{cat}(\mathbf{p}) = \mathrm{cat}(\mathbf{q})$, we say $\mathbf{p} \prec \mathbf{q}$ if and only if $L(\mathbf{p}) \prec L(\mathbf{q})$. Note that it may happen that $\mathrm{cat}(\mathbf{p}) = \mathrm{cat}(\mathbf{q})$ and $L(\mathbf{p}) = L(\mathbf{q})$ but $\mathbf{p} \ne \mathbf{q}$. Collation $\mathbf{p}$ *dominates* collation $\mathbf{q}$ if $\mathrm{cat}(\mathbf{p}) = \mathrm{cat}(\mathbf{q})$ and $\mathbf{p} \prec \mathbf{q}$. Collation $\mathbf{q}$ is *dominated*, if there exists a collation $\mathbf{p}$ such that $\mathbf{p}$ dominates $\mathbf{q}$.

We see that the sequence c is a common subsequence of a, b if and only if there is a collation $\mathbf{p}$ such that $\mathbf{p}$ generates $\binom{a}{b}$ and $c = c(\mathbf{p})$. The expected length $f(n)$ of a longest common subsequence of two random binary strings of length n is given by

$$f(n) = \frac{1}{2^{2n}} \sum_{|a|=|b|=n} v(a, b).$$

Let $F(n, i)$ be the number of pairs of sequences, both of length n, with a longest common subsequence of length i, i.e., $F(n, i) = |\{(a, b) : |a| = |b| = n \ \& \ v(a, b) = i\}|$. Let $\mathcal{G}(m, i)$ be the set of pairs of strings of total length m with a longest common subsequence of length i, i.e., $\mathcal{G}(m, i) = \{(a, b) : |a| + |b| = m \ \& \ v(a, b) = i\}$, and define $G(m, i) = |\mathcal{G}(m, i)|$. We have

$$f(n) = \sum_{i=0}^{n} \frac{iF(n, i)}{2^{2n}}, \quad \sum_{i=0}^{n} F(n, i) = 2^{2n} \text{ and } F(n, i) \le G(2n, i).$$

2 Preliminary results

The following lemma uses a standard truncation technique to obtain upper bounds for the expected length of a longest common subsequence.

Lemma 1. *Let $H(m, i)$ be any upper bound for $G(m, i)$, i.e., $G(m, i) \le H(m, i)$ for all m, i. If y is such that $\sum_{i=\lceil yn \rceil}^{n} H(2n, i) = o(2^{2n})$, then $c = \lim_{n \to \infty} f(n)/n \le y$.*

Proof.

$$\frac{f(n)}{n} = \frac{1}{n2^{2n}} \sum_{i=0}^{n} iF(n,i)$$

$$= \frac{1}{n2^{2n}} \left(\sum_{i=0}^{\lceil yn \rceil - 1} iF(n,i) + \sum_{i=\lceil yn \rceil}^{n} iF(n,i) \right)$$

$$\leq \frac{1}{n2^{2n}} \left(yn \sum_{i=0}^{n} F(n,i) + n \sum_{i=\lceil yn \rceil}^{n} H(2n,i) \right) = y + o(1) \qquad \square$$

We can use the following fact to prove that some function is $o(2^{2n})$. All logarithms used in this paper have base 2.

Fact 1. *If* $\lim\limits_{n \to \infty} \frac{1}{2n} \log g_n < 1$ *then* $g_n = o(2^{2n})$.

Previous methods for an estimate of $G(m, i)$ counted the number of all possible pairs that have a specific sequence as a common subsequence. To improve the upper bound we must avoid counting any one pair too many times. To do so we will use the dominance partial order defined above. We will not count a pair $\binom{a}{b}$ in association with subsequence c when we know that there is some common subsequence c' of $\binom{a}{b}$ such that the collation based on c' dominates that of c.

The first way to reduce overcounting is to consider "minimal" matches. The match p is *minimal* if there is no match q such that $p = \text{cat}(q, r)$ for some $r \in \Pi$ with $l(r) > 0$. In the binary alphabet the only minimal matches are in $\binom{0^*1}{1}$, $\binom{0}{0^*1}$, $\binom{1^*0}{0}$, and $\binom{0}{1^*0}$. These matches are symmetric: there is one symmetry between the top and bottom sequences of the pair, another symmetry between 0's and 1's. The symmetries form an equivalence relation between pairs and we can split all pairs into equivalence classes according to this relation. The equivalence class associated with a pair $\binom{a}{b}$ is denoted by $\begin{bmatrix} a \\ b \end{bmatrix}$. This notation is naturally extended to sequences of matches and sets of sequences of matches. Thus all minimal matches are in $\begin{bmatrix} 1^*0 \\ 0 \end{bmatrix}$.

Fact 2. *Let* $\mathbf{p}$ *be a collation with at least one nonminimal match. Then* $\mathbf{p}$ *is dominated.*

To improve the upper bound further we take advantage of the following idea. The collation $\binom{01}{1}\binom{0}{01}\binom{0}{0}$ generates a pair $\binom{0110}{1010}$ and has the collation key $3, 6, 8$. But having the match $\binom{01}{1}$ followed by the match $\binom{0}{01}$ is not optimal, because it is possible to arrange matches in a better way, namely $\binom{0}{10}\binom{1}{1}\binom{10}{0}$, with the collation key $3, 5, 8$. This idea is generalized and made precise in Fact 3. (Note that 0^+ denotes a string of one or more 0's.)

Fact 3. *Let* **p** *be a collation containing matches of the form* $\left[\binom{0\,+\,1}{1}\binom{1}{0\,+\,1}\right]$. *Then* **p** *is dominated.*

These inefficient collations from Facts 2 and 3 are said to be *rejected*. Collations that are not rejected, are *accepted*.

Let $\mathcal{H}(m, i)$ be the set of all accepted collations **p** of order i generating pairs of total length m and let $H(m, i)$ be the number of pairs in $\mathcal{H}(m, i)$. Clearly, for every pair $\binom{a}{b}$ from $\mathcal{G}(m, i)$ there is a collation generating $\binom{a}{b}$ in $\mathcal{H}(m, i)$ and therefore $G(m, i) \leq H(m, i)$.

To count $H(m, i)$ we can split $\mathcal{H}(m, i)$, $i \geq 1$, into two sets $\mathcal{H}_1(m, i)$ and $\mathcal{H}_2(m, i)$ such that all collations beginning with a match of type $\begin{bmatrix} 0 \\ 0 \end{bmatrix}$ will form $\mathcal{H}_1(m, i)$ and all collations beginning with a match of type $\begin{bmatrix} 1\,+\,0 \\ 0 \end{bmatrix}$ will form $\mathcal{H}_2(m, i)$. For $i = 0$ we set $\mathcal{H}_1(m, 0) = \mathcal{H}(m, 0)$ and $\mathcal{H}_2(m, 0) = \emptyset$.

We build the sets $\mathcal{H}_1(m, i)$ and $\mathcal{H}_2(m, i)$ by induction on i. All collations of order 0 (forming the set $\mathcal{H}_1(m, 0)$) are those in $\left[\begin{smallmatrix} \{0, 1\}^* \\ \lambda \end{smallmatrix}\right] \cup \left[\begin{smallmatrix} 0\,+ \\ 1\,+ \end{smallmatrix}\right]$. (Here λ denotes the sequence of length 0.) Now let us suppose we have the sets $\mathcal{H}_1(m, i - 1)$ and $\mathcal{H}_2(m, i - 1)$ for all m. To get all accepted collations from $\mathcal{H}(m', i)$ we will extend the collations from $\mathcal{H}(m, i - 1)$ to the *left* by one match. The extensions by the matches from $\begin{bmatrix} 0 \\ 0 \end{bmatrix}$ form $\mathcal{H}_1(m', i)$. The situation in the case of extensions by the matches from $\begin{bmatrix} 1\,+\,0 \\ 0 \end{bmatrix}$ is a bit more complicated. When the collation from $\mathcal{H}_2(m, i - 1)$ begins with a match from $\binom{1\,+\,0}{0}$, the extension by a match from $\binom{0}{1\,+\,0}$ does not create an accepted collation. Therefore $\mathcal{H}_2(m', i)$ is formed by the extensions of collations from $\mathcal{H}_1(m, i - 1)$ by the matches from $\begin{bmatrix} 1\,+\,0 \\ 0 \end{bmatrix}$, and by the extensions of collations from $\mathcal{H}_2(m, i - 1)$ beginning with a match from $\binom{1\,+\,0}{0}$ by matches from $\binom{1\,+\,0}{0} \cup \binom{0\,+\,1}{1} \cup \binom{1}{0\,+\,1}$, and similarly for the symmetric cases. The containments between the sets $\mathcal{H}_1(m, i)$ and $\mathcal{H}_2(m, i)$ can be described by the diagram in Figure 1.

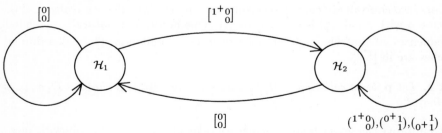

Fig. 1. The containments between the sets $\mathcal{H}_1(m, i)$ and $\mathcal{H}_2(m, i)$.

Let $H_j(m, i)$ be the number of collations in $\mathcal{H}_j(m, i)$, $j = 1, 2$. From the definitions of $\mathcal{H}_1(m, 0)$ and $\mathcal{H}_2(m, 0)$ we have

$$H_1(0,0) = 1,$$
$$H_1(m,0) = 2^{m+1} + 2m - 2 \quad \text{for } m > 0,$$
$$H_2(m,0) = 0.$$

For convenience we take $H_1(m,i) = H_2(m,i) = 0$ for $m < 0$ and all $i \geq 0$. Now we can transform the containments from the diagram into the following recurrences.

$$H_1(m,i) = 2H_1(m-2,i-1) + 2H_2(m-2,i-1),$$
$$H_2(m,i) = 4\sum_{j=3}^{m} H_1(m-j,i-1) + 3\sum_{j=3}^{m} H_2(m-j,i-1).$$

We can express these recurrences more compactly in terms of the generating functions $h_1^{(i)} = \sum H_1(m,i)z^m$, $h_2^{(i)} = \sum H_2(m,i)z^m$, and $h^{(i)} = h_1^{(i)} + h_2^{(i)} = \sum H(m,i)z^m$. The contribution of each pair from $\binom{0}{0}$ is z^2 and the total contribution of the pairs from $\binom{1+0}{0}$ is $\frac{z^3}{1-z}$, etc. The resulting recurrences are the following.

$$h_1^{(0)} = \frac{1+2z}{1-2z} + \frac{2z^2}{(1-z)^2},$$
$$h_2^{(0)} = 0,$$
$$h_1^{(i)} = 2z^2 h_1^{(i-1)} + 2z^2 h_2^{(i-1)},$$
$$h_2^{(i)} = \frac{4z^3}{1-z} h_1^{(i-1)} + \frac{3z^3}{1-z} h_2^{(i-1)}.$$

To solve the system of the linear recurrences we can use the following well known lemma.

Lemma 2. Let $\left\{ \mathbf{x}^{(r)} = \mathbf{Q}\mathbf{x}^{(r-1)}; \mathbf{x}^{(0)} = (x_1^{(0)}, \ldots, x_k^{(0)})^T \right\}$ be a system of k linear recurrences. Let $\lambda_1, \ldots, \lambda_l$ be the characteristic values of the matrix $\mathbf{Q}$ and let $e_1, \ldots, e_l$ be their multiplicities. Then there are constants $s_{111}, \ldots, s_{kle_l}$ such that, for sufficiently large r,

$$x_t^{(r)} = \sum_{j=1}^{l} \left(s_{tj1} + s_{tj2}r + \ldots + s_{tje_j}r^{e_j-1} \right) \lambda_j^r, \quad 1 \leq t \leq k.$$

Let $\lambda_1(z), \ldots, \lambda_l(z)$ be the characteristic values of the matrix $\mathbf{Q}(z)$ corresponding to our recurrences and let $\lambda(z) = \max_{j=1,\ldots,l} |\lambda_j(z)|$.

Corollary 3. There is some $s(z)$, independent of i, such that

$$h^{(i)}(z) \leq ki^k s(z) (\lambda(z))^i.$$

From $h^{(i)}(z)$, we can easily get bounds on $H(m,i)$. Let $Z \subseteq (0,1)$ be the set of all $z \in (0,1)$ such that $\lambda(z) < 1$.

Fact 4. *If $Z \neq \emptyset$ then*

$$H(m, i) = [z^m]h^{(i)}(z) \leq \inf_{z \in Z} \frac{h^{(i)}(z)}{z^m}.$$

Knowing bounds for $H(m, i)$, we can find when $\sum_{i=\lceil yn \rceil}^{n} H(2n, i)$ is vanishing with respect to 2^{2n}.

Lemma 4. *Let $z_0 \in (0, 1)$ be such that $\lambda(z_0) < 1$ and let y be such that $y > \frac{\log 4z_0^2}{\log \lambda(z_0)}$. Then $\sum_{i=\lceil yn \rceil}^{n} H(2n, i) = o(2^{2n})$.*

Proof.

$$\frac{1}{2n} \log \sum_{i=\lceil yn \rceil}^{n} H(2n, i) \leq \frac{1}{2n} \log \sum_{i=\lceil yn \rceil}^{n} \inf_{z \in Z} \frac{h^{(i)}(z)}{z^{2n}}$$

$$\leq \frac{1}{2n} \inf_{z \in Z} \log \sum_{i=\lceil yn \rceil}^{n} \frac{ks(z)i^k(\lambda(z))^i}{z^{2n}}$$

$$\leq \frac{1}{2n} \inf_{z \in Z} \log \frac{nks(z)n^k(\lambda(z))^{yn}}{z^{2n}}$$

$$\leq \frac{y}{2} \log \lambda(z_0) - \log z_0 + \frac{\log ks(z_0) + (k+1)\log n}{2n} .$$

Therefore

$$\lim_{n \to \infty} \frac{1}{2n} \log \sum_{i=\lceil yn \rceil}^{n} H(2n, i) \leq \frac{y}{2} \log \lambda(z_0) - \log z_0 < 1,$$

and, using Fact 1, we get $\sum_{i=\lceil yn \rceil}^{n} H(2n, i) = o(2^{2n})$. □

3 Main results

Lemma 4 and Lemma 1 together give us the main theorem.

Theorem 1. *Let $\lambda(z)$ be maximum of the characteristic values of the matrix of the recurrences of the estimate. Let $z_0 \in (0, 1)$ be such that $\lambda(z_0) < 1$ and let $y = \frac{\log 4z_0^2}{\log \lambda(z_0)}$. Then $\lim_{n \to \infty} f(n)/n \leq y$.*

This yields an upper bound $c \leq 0.853173$, with $z_0 = 0.185199$ and $\lambda(z_0) = 0.0974715$. To improve this bound we can find other cases where specific collations are not efficient enough, for example, when **p** is a collation containing any of the following patterns:

$$\left[\binom{1}{01}\binom{0}{0}\left(\binom{1}{1}\binom{0}{0}\right)^{*}\binom{10}{0}\right], \qquad \left[\binom{0}{10}\left(\binom{1}{1}\binom{0}{0}\right)^{*}\binom{10}{0}\right],$$

$$\left[\binom{0}{110}\binom{1}{1}\left(\binom{1}{1}\binom{0}{0}\right)^{*}\binom{10}{0}\right], \qquad \left[\binom{0}{110}\binom{0}{0}\binom{110}{0}\right].$$

Again, in each case, the collation **p** is dominated.

We split set $\mathcal{H}(m,i)$ into more than just two sets. We also refine the classification of matches into 10 sets: $\binom{0}{0}$, $\binom{10}{0}$, $\binom{1^{+}10}{0}$, and their symmetric variants, as shown at the top of Figure 2. Each of these sets contains collations that have prefixes with similar properties.

To specify which prefixes have similar properties we introduce the notion of reducibility between sequences of matches. We say that the sequence of matches $r_1 \ldots r_j$ is *reducible to* the sequence of matches $s_1 \ldots s_j$ if for any sequence of matches $p_1 \ldots p_j$ such that $p_1 \ldots p_l \binom{\lambda}{\lambda}$ is not dominated and $p_1 \ldots p_l s_1 \ldots s_j \binom{\lambda}{\lambda}$ is dominated, the collation $p_1 \ldots p_l r_1 \ldots r_j \binom{\lambda}{\lambda}$ is dominated. We define reducibility of sequences with nonequal length in the following way: the sequence of matches $r_1 \ldots r_l$ is *reducible to* the sequence of matches $s_1 \ldots s_j$ if $j \leq l$ and $r_1 \ldots r_j$ is reducible to $s_1 \ldots s_j$. Reducibility of collations to sequences of matches is defined in the same way.

The set characterized by the prefix $p_1 \ldots p_j$ is denoted by $[p_1 | \ldots | p_j]$. The collation can appear in the set $[p_1 | \ldots | p_j]$ only if it is equivalent to a prefix reducible to $p_1 \ldots p_j$.

Now we split set $\mathcal{H}(m,i)$ into the eight (disjoint) sets $\mathcal{H}_1(m,i), \ldots, \mathcal{H}_8(m,i)$, represented by $\begin{bmatrix}0\\0\end{bmatrix}$, $\begin{bmatrix}10\\0\end{bmatrix}$, $\begin{bmatrix}110\\0\end{bmatrix}$, $\begin{bmatrix}1\\1\end{bmatrix}\begin{bmatrix}10\\0\end{bmatrix}$, $\begin{bmatrix}10\\0\end{bmatrix}\begin{bmatrix}10\\0\end{bmatrix}$, $\begin{bmatrix}1\\01\end{bmatrix}\begin{bmatrix}10\\0\end{bmatrix}$, $\begin{bmatrix}0\\0\end{bmatrix}\begin{bmatrix}110\\0\end{bmatrix}$, and $\begin{bmatrix}0\\10\end{bmatrix}\begin{bmatrix}1\\1\end{bmatrix}\begin{bmatrix}10\\0\end{bmatrix}$. Using reducibilities of prefixes, we can establish containments among the sets $\mathcal{H}_1(m,i)$, $\ldots, \mathcal{H}_8(m,i)$ as shown in Figure 2.

To do this we have to show that if the entry in row $[p_1 | \ldots | p_l]$ and column q is $[r_1 | \ldots | r_j]$ then $q p_1 \ldots p_l$ is reducible to $r_1 \ldots r_j$. Not all of these containments are "pure", i.e., obtained by prepending the match in the front of the description of the set and (possibly) erasing some symbols or removing matches from the back of this description (and so easily proved correct). The correctness of the containment in row $\begin{bmatrix}0\\0\end{bmatrix}\begin{bmatrix}110\\0\end{bmatrix}$ and column $\binom{0}{10}$ is proved in Lemma 5. Correctness of the other containments marked with a "◁" can be proved in a similar way.

Lemma 5. $\binom{0}{10}\binom{0}{0}\binom{110}{0}$ *is reducible to* $\binom{0}{10}\binom{1}{1}\binom{10}{0}$.

Proof. Let $\mathbf{p} = p_1 \ldots p_j$ be any sequence of matches such that $p_1 \ldots p_j \binom{\lambda}{\lambda}$ is not dominated. Let collation $\mathbf{q} = q_1 \ldots q_{j+4}$ dominate $p_1 \ldots p_j \binom{0}{10}\binom{1}{1}\binom{10}{0}\binom{\lambda}{\lambda}$. According to Fact 2, we can suppose that all matches in **p** and **q** are minimal. The collation **p** is not dominated and therefore either $t(q_{j+4}) = \lambda$ or $b(q_{j+4}) = \lambda$. If $b(q_{j+4}) = \lambda$, then $p_1 \ldots p_j \binom{0}{10}\binom{\lambda}{\lambda}$ is dominated by $q_1 \ldots q_{j+1} q$, where q is a suitable pair, and therefore $p_1 \ldots p_j \binom{0}{10}\binom{0}{0}\binom{110}{0}\binom{\lambda}{\lambda}$ is dominated. If $t(q_{j+4}) = \lambda$

	$\binom{0}{0}$	$\binom{1}{1}$	$\binom{10}{0}$	$\binom{0}{10}$	$\binom{01}{1}$	$\binom{1}{01}$	$\binom{1+10}{0}$	$\binom{0}{1+10}$	$\binom{0+01}{1}$	$\binom{1}{0+01}$
$\left[\begin{smallmatrix}0\\0\end{smallmatrix}\right]$	$\left[\begin{smallmatrix}0\\0\end{smallmatrix}\right]$	$\left[\begin{smallmatrix}1\\1\end{smallmatrix}\right]$	$\left[\begin{smallmatrix}10\\0\end{smallmatrix}\right]$	$\left[\begin{smallmatrix}0\\10\end{smallmatrix}\right]$	$\left[\begin{smallmatrix}01\\1\end{smallmatrix}\right]$	$\left[\begin{smallmatrix}1\\01\end{smallmatrix}\right]$	$\left[\begin{smallmatrix}110\\0\end{smallmatrix}\right]$	$\left[\begin{smallmatrix}0\\110\end{smallmatrix}\right]$	$\left[\begin{smallmatrix}001\\1\end{smallmatrix}\right]$	$\left[\begin{smallmatrix}1\\001\end{smallmatrix}\right]$
$\left[\begin{smallmatrix}10\\0\end{smallmatrix}\right]$	$\left[\begin{smallmatrix}01\\1\end{smallmatrix}\right]$◄	$\left[\begin{smallmatrix}1&10\\1&0\end{smallmatrix}\right]$	$\left[\begin{smallmatrix}10&10\\0&0\end{smallmatrix}\right]$	×	$\left[\begin{smallmatrix}01\\1\end{smallmatrix}\right]$	$\left[\begin{smallmatrix}1&10\\01&0\end{smallmatrix}\right]$	$\left[\begin{smallmatrix}10&10\\0&0\end{smallmatrix}\right]$	×	$\left[\begin{smallmatrix}001\\1\end{smallmatrix}\right]$	$\left[\begin{smallmatrix}1\\001\end{smallmatrix}\right]$
$\left[\begin{smallmatrix}110\\0\end{smallmatrix}\right]$	$\left[\begin{smallmatrix}0&110\\0&0\end{smallmatrix}\right]$	$\left[\begin{smallmatrix}1&10\\1&0\end{smallmatrix}\right]$	$\left[\begin{smallmatrix}10&10\\0&0\end{smallmatrix}\right]$	×	$\left[\begin{smallmatrix}0&110\\0&0\end{smallmatrix}\right]$◄	$\left[\begin{smallmatrix}1&10\\01&0\end{smallmatrix}\right]$	$\left[\begin{smallmatrix}10&10\\0&0\end{smallmatrix}\right]$	×	$\left[\begin{smallmatrix}0&110\\0&0\end{smallmatrix}\right]$◄	$\left[\begin{smallmatrix}1\\001\end{smallmatrix}\right]$
$\left[\begin{smallmatrix}1&10\\1&0\end{smallmatrix}\right]$	$\left[\begin{smallmatrix}0\\0\end{smallmatrix}\right]$	$\left[\begin{smallmatrix}1\\1\end{smallmatrix}\right]$	$\left[\begin{smallmatrix}10\\0\end{smallmatrix}\right]$	$\left[\begin{smallmatrix}0&1&10\\10&1&0\end{smallmatrix}\right]$	$\left[\begin{smallmatrix}01\\1\end{smallmatrix}\right]$	$\left[\begin{smallmatrix}1\\01\end{smallmatrix}\right]$	$\left[\begin{smallmatrix}110\\0\end{smallmatrix}\right]$	×	$\left[\begin{smallmatrix}001\\1\end{smallmatrix}\right]$	$\left[\begin{smallmatrix}1\\001\end{smallmatrix}\right]$
$\left[\begin{smallmatrix}10&10\\0&0\end{smallmatrix}\right]$	$\left[\begin{smallmatrix}01\\1\end{smallmatrix}\right]$◄	$\left[\begin{smallmatrix}1&10\\1&0\end{smallmatrix}\right]$◄	$\left[\begin{smallmatrix}10&10\\0&0\end{smallmatrix}\right]$	×	$\left[\begin{smallmatrix}01&01\\1&1\end{smallmatrix}\right]$◄	×	$\left[\begin{smallmatrix}10&10\\0&0\end{smallmatrix}\right]$	×	$\left[\begin{smallmatrix}01&01\\1&1\end{smallmatrix}\right]$◄	×
$\left[\begin{smallmatrix}0&1&10\\01& &0\end{smallmatrix}\right]$	$\left[\begin{smallmatrix}0&01\\0&1\end{smallmatrix}\right]$◄ $\left[\begin{smallmatrix}10&10\\0&0\end{smallmatrix}\right]$◄	$\left[\begin{smallmatrix}0&1\\10&01\end{smallmatrix}\right]$	$\left[\begin{smallmatrix}10\\0\end{smallmatrix}\right]$	$\left[\begin{smallmatrix}0&1&10\\10&1&0\end{smallmatrix}\right]$◄	$\left[\begin{smallmatrix}01&01\\1&1\end{smallmatrix}\right]$◄	×	$\left[\begin{smallmatrix}110\\0\end{smallmatrix}\right]$	×	$\left[\begin{smallmatrix}01&01\\1&1\end{smallmatrix}\right]$◄	×
$\left[\begin{smallmatrix}0&110\\0&0\end{smallmatrix}\right]$	$\left[\begin{smallmatrix}0&01\\0&1\end{smallmatrix}\right]$◄ $\left[\begin{smallmatrix}10&10\\0&0\end{smallmatrix}\right]$◄	$\left[\begin{smallmatrix}0&1\\10&01\end{smallmatrix}\right]$	$\left[\begin{smallmatrix}10\\0\end{smallmatrix}\right]$	$\left[\begin{smallmatrix}0&1&10\\10&1&0\end{smallmatrix}\right]$◄	$\left[\begin{smallmatrix}01&01\\1&1\end{smallmatrix}\right]$◄	×	×	$\left[\begin{smallmatrix}0&01\\10&10\end{smallmatrix}\right]$	$\left[\begin{smallmatrix}01&01\\1&1\end{smallmatrix}\right]$◄	×
$\left[\begin{smallmatrix}0&1&10\\10&1&0\end{smallmatrix}\right]$	$\left[\begin{smallmatrix}01\\1\end{smallmatrix}\right]$◄	$\left[\begin{smallmatrix}1&10\\01&0\end{smallmatrix}\right]$◄	×	$\left[\begin{smallmatrix}0&1\\10&10\end{smallmatrix}\right]$	$\left[\begin{smallmatrix}01&01\\1&1\end{smallmatrix}\right]$◄	×	×	$\left[\begin{smallmatrix}0&0\\10&10\end{smallmatrix}\right]$	$\left[\begin{smallmatrix}01&01\\1&1\end{smallmatrix}\right]$◄	×

Fig. 2. The containments between the sets $\mathcal{H}_1(m, i), \ldots, \mathcal{H}_8(m, i)$.

(and $b(q_{j+4}) = a10$ for some $a \in \Sigma^*$) then $p_1 \ldots p_j \binom{0}{10}\binom{0}{0}\binom{110}{0}\binom{\lambda}{\lambda}$ is dominated by $q_1 \ldots q_j q'_{j+1} q'_{j+2} q_{j+3} \binom{\lambda}{a00}$, where q'_{j+1} and q'_{j+2} are the same as q_{j+1} and q_{j+2} but one of them has an extra 0. □

Hence we can create a system of eight linear recurrences $\mathbf{x}^{(i)} = \mathbf{Q}\mathbf{x}^{(i-1)}$; $\mathbf{x}^{(0)} = \left(\frac{2z^2}{(1-z)^2} + \frac{1+2z}{1-2z}, 0, 0, 0, 0, 0, 0, 0 \right)^T$, where

$$\mathbf{Q} = \begin{pmatrix}
2z^2 & 0 & 0 & 2z^2 & 0 & 0 & 0 & 0 \\
4z^3 & z^2+z^3 & 0 & 3z^3 & z^2 & z^2 & z^3 & 2z^2 \\
\frac{4z^4}{1-z} & \frac{2z^4}{1-z} & \frac{z^4}{1-z} & \frac{3z^4}{1-z} & z^2 & \frac{z^4}{1-z} & \frac{z^4}{1-z} & 0 \\
0 & z^2 & z^2 & 0 & 0 & z^2 & z^2 & 0 \\
0 & \frac{z^3}{1-z} & \frac{z^3}{1-z} & 0 & \frac{2z^3}{1-z} & \frac{z^3}{1-z} & \frac{z^2}{1-z} & \frac{2z^3}{1-z} \\
0 & z^3 & z^3 & 0 & 0 & z^3 & 0 & 0 \\
0 & 0 & \frac{z^2}{1-z} & 0 & 0 & 0 & 0 & 0 \\
0 & 0 & 0 & z^3 & 0 & z^3 & z^3 & 0
\end{pmatrix}.$$

Using Theorem 1 with $z_0 = 0.228424$, we get $\lambda(z_0) = 0.155602 < 1$ and $c \le y = 0.842166$. For our best bound we split $\mathcal{H}(m, i)$ into 52 sets, build a system of 52 linear recurrences and use Theorem 1 with $z_0 = 0.252652$. As a result we get $\lambda(z_0) = 0.195960 < 1$ and $c \le y = 0.837623$. The transition diagram is given in Figure 3. There are two peculiarities among these containments. First, the set $\mathcal{H}_9$ has to be described by a pair $\binom{00}{1}$ that is not a match and, second, the containment between sets $\mathcal{H}_{25}$ and $\mathcal{H}_{32}$ is valid only for the match $\binom{0}{110}$, not the whole of $\binom{0}{1+10}$, and the contribution of this match is only z^4 instead of $z^4/(1-z)$. The numerical computations in this paper were performed with the help of Mathematica.

		$\binom{0}{0}$	$\binom{1}{1}$	$\binom{10}{0}$	$\binom{0}{10}$	$\binom{01}{1}$	$\binom{1}{01}$	$\binom{1+10}{0}$	$\binom{0}{1+10}$	$\binom{0+01}{1}$	$\binom{1}{0+01}$
1	$\left[\begin{smallmatrix}0\\0\end{smallmatrix}\right]$	1	1	2	2	2	2	3	3	3	3
2	$\left[\begin{smallmatrix}10\\0\end{smallmatrix}\right]$	2	4	5	×	6	7	18	×	23	20
3	$\left[\begin{smallmatrix}110\\0\end{smallmatrix}\right]$	8	29	10	×	45	41	52	×	19	20
4	$\left[\begin{smallmatrix}1&10\\1&0\end{smallmatrix}\right]$	21	25	2	11	2	2	3	×	3	3
5	$\left[\begin{smallmatrix}01\\1\end{smallmatrix}\right]$	3	2	12	×	5	×	12	×	18	×
6	$\left[\begin{smallmatrix}10&01\\0&1\end{smallmatrix}\right]$	2	24	5	×	47	32	18	×	23	×
7	$\left[\begin{smallmatrix}10&1\\0&1\end{smallmatrix}\right]$	14	33	15	×	26	7	35	×	×	20
8	$\left[\begin{smallmatrix}1&001\\1&1\end{smallmatrix}\right]$	5	24	13	×	47	32	13	×	23	×
9	$\left[\begin{smallmatrix}00\\1\end{smallmatrix}\right]$	9	21	8	7	2	11	19	20	3	×
10	$\left[\begin{smallmatrix}01&001\\1&1\end{smallmatrix}\right]$	18	2	13	×	5	×	13	×	18	×
11	$\left[\begin{smallmatrix}01&1&0\\0&1&10\end{smallmatrix}\right]$	16	16	15	×	×	15	35	×	×	35
12	$\left[\begin{smallmatrix}01&10&10\\0&0&0\end{smallmatrix}\right]$	19	5	12	×	13	×	12	×	13	×
13	$\left[\begin{smallmatrix}10&1&001\\0&1&1\end{smallmatrix}\right]$	13	3	13	×	12	×	13	×	12	×
14	$\left[\begin{smallmatrix}1&01&0\\1&1&10\end{smallmatrix}\right]$	38	27	17	×	40	39	×	×	20	19
15	$\left[\begin{smallmatrix}01&01&0\\1&1&10\end{smallmatrix}\right]$	3	14	17	×	15	×	×	×	35	×
16	$\left[\begin{smallmatrix}1&0&1&10\\1&10&1&0\end{smallmatrix}\right]$	38	4	17	×	6	7	×	×	23	20
17	$\left[\begin{smallmatrix}01&0&10&1\\1&0&0&01\end{smallmatrix}\right]$	51	16	×	×	15	×	×	×	35	×
18	$\left[\begin{smallmatrix}0&01&001\\0&1&1\end{smallmatrix}\right]$	3	8	12	×	10	×	12	×	52	×
19	$\left[\begin{smallmatrix}1&10&01&01\\1&0&1&01\end{smallmatrix}\right]$	12	29	13	×	45	32	13	×	19	×
20	$\left[\begin{smallmatrix}110&1\\0&01\end{smallmatrix}\right]$	31	29	49	×	30	41	35	×	×	20
21	$\left[\begin{smallmatrix}1&0&01\\1&0&1\end{smallmatrix}\right]$	22	1	2	34	2	28	3	3	3	20
22	$\left[\begin{smallmatrix}0&1&0&01\\0&1&0&1\end{smallmatrix}\right]$	4	1	6	7	2	34	23	20	3	3
23	$\left[\begin{smallmatrix}110&01\\0&1\end{smallmatrix}\right]$	8	29	10	×	45	32	52	×	19	×
24	$\left[\begin{smallmatrix}1&1&001\\1&1&1\end{smallmatrix}\right]$	42	25	2	26	2	28	3	×	3	20
25	$\left[\begin{smallmatrix}1&1&10\\1&1&0\end{smallmatrix}\right]$	43	1	2	36	2	2	3	32	3	3
26	$\left[\begin{smallmatrix}10&01&0&\\0&0&1&10\end{smallmatrix}\right]$	16	16	15	×	×	17	15	×	×	×
27	$\left[\begin{smallmatrix}0&0&0&01\\0&0&10&1\end{smallmatrix}\right]$	9	21	8	7	11	11	19	20	×	×
28	$\left[\begin{smallmatrix}10&0&1&0\\0&0&1&10\end{smallmatrix}\right]$	2	33	5	×	26	7	18	×	×	20
29	$\left[\begin{smallmatrix}0&001\\01&1\end{smallmatrix}\right]$	9	21	8	7	2	30	19	20	3	×
30	$\left[\begin{smallmatrix}1&0&001\\1&1&10\end{smallmatrix}\right]$	5	16	13	×	×	17	13	×	×	×
31	$\left[\begin{smallmatrix}1&001&0\\1&1&10\end{smallmatrix}\right]$	5	27	17	×	40	30	×	×	20	×
32	$\left[\begin{smallmatrix}110&1&1&0\\0&1&1&10\end{smallmatrix}\right]$	50	14	49	×	×	15	52	×	×	35
33	$\left[\begin{smallmatrix}1&10&1\\1&0&01\end{smallmatrix}\right]$	22	25	34	11	28	2	3	×	20	3
34	$\left[\begin{smallmatrix}10&1&0&1\\0&1&0&01\end{smallmatrix}\right]$	16	4	15	×	6	7	35	×	23	20
35	$\left[\begin{smallmatrix}001&01&0\\1&1&10\end{smallmatrix}\right]$	3	31	12	×	49	×	×	×	52	×
36	$\left[\begin{smallmatrix}10&1&1&0\\0&1&1&10\end{smallmatrix}\right]$	2	4	5	×	6	7	35	×	23	20
37	$\left[\begin{smallmatrix}1&0&01&0&10&0\\1&0&1&0&0&01\end{smallmatrix}\right]$	5	33	×	×	40	32	×	×	20	×
38	$\left[\begin{smallmatrix}1&0&10&01\\1&0&1&01\end{smallmatrix}\right]$	2	4	5	×	6	7	18	×	20	20
39	$\left[\begin{smallmatrix}10&0&0&01\\0&0&10&1\end{smallmatrix}\right]$	5	24	13	×	26	32	13	×	×	×
40	$\left[\begin{smallmatrix}10&0&0&01\\0&0&0&01\end{smallmatrix}\right]$	14	33	15	×	26	32	35	×	×	×
41	$\left[\begin{smallmatrix}10&001\\0&01\end{smallmatrix}\right]$	14	33	15	×	30	7	35	×	×	20
42	$\left[\begin{smallmatrix}0&1&0&001\\0&1&1&1\end{smallmatrix}\right]$	24	22	47	32	2	34	23	×	3	3
43	$\left[\begin{smallmatrix}1&0&0&01\\1&0&0&0\end{smallmatrix}\right]$	1	1	2	2	2	2	3	3	3	44
44	$\left[\begin{smallmatrix}110&0&01&\\0&0&1&10\end{smallmatrix}\right]$	8	29	10	×	30	41	52	×	×	20
45	$\left[\begin{smallmatrix}10&001\\0&1\end{smallmatrix}\right]$	5	24	13	×	6	46	13	×	23	×
46	$\left[\begin{smallmatrix}1&1&10&001\\01&0&1&1\end{smallmatrix}\right]$	12	14	13	×	×	17	13	×	×	×
47	$\left[\begin{smallmatrix}10&01&10\\0&1&0\end{smallmatrix}\right]$	2	48	5	×	47	32	18	×	23	×
48	$\left[\begin{smallmatrix}1&10&01&10\\1&0&1&0\end{smallmatrix}\right]$	42	24	2	26	47	32	3	×	23	×
49	$\left[\begin{smallmatrix}01&001&0\\1&1&10\end{smallmatrix}\right]$	18	14	17	×	15	×	×	×	35	×
50	$\left[\begin{smallmatrix}1&001&0&0&01\\1&0&0&0&01\end{smallmatrix}\right]$	5	24	17	×	47	32	×	×	23	×
51	$\left[\begin{smallmatrix}1&10&1&01&0\\1&0&1&0&0\end{smallmatrix}\right]$	37	27	×	×	39	40	×	×	19	20
52	$\left[\begin{smallmatrix}001&001\\1&1\end{smallmatrix}\right]$	18	8	13	×	10	×	13	×	52	×

Fig. 3. The containments between 52 sets.

4   Conclusion

We have described a new approach to providing upper bounds for one of the basic constants of string theory. With it we have substantially improved the previous upper bounds. While we have concentrated exclusively on binary strings the method is immediately applicable to larger alphabets.

There is statistical evidence [1] that the limit constant for binary strings may be approximately 0.81. While our bound may be further improved by using even finer partitions, we believe that the method itself requires further development before bounds converging on the true value of the constant can be obtained.

References

1. Václav Chvátal and David Sankoff. Longest common subsequence of two random sequences. *Journal of Applied Probability*, 12:306–315, 1975.
2. Joseph G. Deken. Some limit results for longest common subsequences. *Discrete Mathematics*, 26:17–31, 1979.
3. Joseph G. Deken. Probabilistic behavior of longest-common-subsequence length. In D. Sankoff and J. B. Kruskal, editors, *Time Warps, String Edits, and Macromolecules: The theory and practice of sequence comparison*, chapter 16, pages 359–362. Addison-Wesley, Reading, Mass, 1983.

The Ambiguity of Primitive Words*

H. Petersen

Fachbereich Informatik, Universität Hamburg
e-mail: petersen@informatik.uni-hamburg.de

Abstract

A word is primitive if it is not a proper power of a shorter word. We prove that the set Q of primitive words over an alphabet is not an unambiguous context-free language. This strengthens the previous result that Q cannot be deterministic context-free. Further we show that the same holds for the set L of Lyndon words. We describe 2DPDA accepting Q and L which imply efficient decidability on the RAM model of computation and we analyse the number of comparisons required for deciding Q. Finally we give a new proof showing a related language not to be context-free, which only relies on properties of semi-linear and regular sets.

1   Introduction

The notion of primitivity plays a central role in algebraic coding theory [23] and combinatoric theory of words [20, 19]. Recently attention has been drawn to the language Q of all primitive words over an alphabet with at least two symbols and questions concerning Q as well as certain subsets of Q were solved using methods from formal language theory in [8]. This language resisted even very strong iteration theorems, see [8], and should it be non-context-free it will be useful for studying the exactness of such theorems.

In [7] the authors conjecture that Q is not context-free and prove that Q cannot be deterministic context-free by exploiting the closure of the class of deterministic context-free languages under complementation. Clearly this technique cannot readily be generalized to larger classes such as unambiguous context-free languages or the full class of context-free languages.

Our approach therefore employs a totally different method for showing that Q, should it be context-free, is ambiguous. The technique, which is based on a result by Chomsky and Schützenberger, was shown to be a valuable tool for solving problems in the theory of formal languages by Flajolet [9]. The main idea is the construction of analytical models for combinatorial problems. Further we make use of classical results from number theory that surprisingly turn out to be applicable to our problem.

---

*Supported by the ESPRIT Basic Research Action WG 6317: Algebraic and Syntactic Methods in Computer Science (ASMICS 2)

In [17] Q has been studied in relation to finite automata. We will investigate another aspect namely automata recognizing the sets Q and L. The proofs will reveal the close connection of these languages with pattern matching problems (see the historical remarks in [18]).

The outline of this paper is as follows: Section 2 recalls some elementary definitions. Section 3 presents four lemmas on primitive words which are of importance in several parts of this work, and Section 4 prepares for our main result by summarizing facts from number theory, mathematical theory of context-free languages and about algebraic functions. Section 5 is dedicated to the generating function of Q and two observations on its properties. Section 6 proves that Q and L cannot be unambiguous context-free. In Section 7 we present 2DPDA accepting Q and L with an application. Section 8 gives a new proof showing that the set of words remaining primitive under arbitrary permutations is not context-free. Section 9 concludes the paper with a short summary and some open problems.

2 Definitions

Throughout this paper we will use a fixed alphabet Σ of size $k \geq 2$. For standard definitions of formal language theory (free monoid, Kleene star, empty word λ etc.) see [14, 19].

The set Q of *primitive words* consists of all words over Σ which are not proper powers of a single word. More formally we characterize Q as (see [19]):

$$Q = \{w \mid w \in \Sigma^*, \forall z \in \Sigma^* : (w \in z^* \Longrightarrow w = z)\}$$

Since $\lambda \in z^*$ for every z we have $\lambda \notin Q$.

Two words $w, v \in \Sigma^*$ are called *conjugate* if there are words $r, s \in \Sigma^*$ such that: $w = rs \wedge v = sr$. Conjugacy is easily seen to be an equivalence relation on the free monoid Σ^*. The *class of conjugates* of a word w is the set $c(w) = \{v \mid v \text{ and } w \text{ are conjugate}\}$.

A primitive word w is called a *Lyndon word* if it is the smallest word in $c(w)$ with respect to the usual lexicographic ordering on Σ^* induced by a total ordering on Σ. The set L of Lyndon words is thus specified:

$$L = \{w \mid w \in Q, \forall u, v \in \Sigma^* : w = uv \Longrightarrow w \leq vu\}$$

3 Basic Properties of Primitive Words

This section presents some simple and mostly well-known results concerning primitive words that we will make use of in the rest of the paper.

The first lemma is proved as Proposition 1.3.2 in [19] and is due to Lyndon and Schützenberger [20]:

Lemma 1 *Two words u and v commute if and only if they are powers of the same word:*

$$uv = vu \quad \Longleftrightarrow \quad \exists z \in \Sigma^* : u, v \in z^*$$

Our next lemmas are straightforward consequences of Lemma 1 and the proofs will be omitted. We give an alternative condition for primitivity:

Lemma 2 *A non-empty word $w \in \Sigma^+$ is primitive if and only if it cannot be factored into two non-empty commuting words:*

$$w \in Q \iff w \neq \lambda \wedge \forall u, v \in \Sigma^* : (w = uv = vu \implies \lambda \in \{v, u\})$$

The following lemma will be used to derive a structural description of Q:

Lemma 3 *The cardinality of the class of conjugates of a primitive word w of length n is n: $|c(w)| = n$.*

The last lemma provides an easily checked criterion for Lyndon words. Note that the condition of primitivity is made implicit by Lemma 4. It appears as Proposition 5.1.2 in [19] where the proof may be found:

Lemma 4 *A word $w \in \Sigma^*$ is a Lyndon word if and only if it is smaller (w.r.t. lexicographic order) than each of its proper right factors:*

$$w \in L \iff \forall v \in \Sigma^+ : (w \in \Sigma^+ v \implies w < v)$$

4 Definitions and Results for the Proof of Ambiguity

We will briefly review some facts from number theory that we need in the sequel. For more details see [1, 13].

If d divides a number h we write $d \mid h$, if not we write $d \nmid h$. By $d = (h, k)$ we denote the *highest (greatest) common divisor* of h and k, the largest natural number d such that both $d \mid h$ and $d \mid k$ hold. If $(h, k) = 1$ we call h and k *coprime (relatively prime)*.

The following classical result shows an important property of arithmetic progressions of a certain kind. It is proved as Theorem 7.9 in [1] on pages 148–154.

Theorem 5 (Dirichlet) *If $k > 0$ and h, k are coprime there are infinitely many primes in the arithmetic progression $ik + h$, $i = 0, 1, 2, \ldots$.*

A given system of congruences with coprime moduli allows a unique solution modulo the product of the moduli (Theorem 5.26 in [1], Theorem 121 in [13]):

Theorem 6 (Chinese Remainder Theorem) *If $m_1, m_2, \ldots m_r$ are pairwise coprime numbers and $b_1, \ldots b_r$ arbitrary integers then the system*

$$n \equiv b_1 \pmod{m_1}, \quad \ldots, \quad n \equiv b_r \pmod{m_r}$$

has a unique solution modulo $a = m_1 \cdots m_r$.

Based on the unique solution n modulo a we get an infinity of larger solutions of the form $ia + n$, $i = 1, 2, \ldots$.

Further we need the notion of the *generating function* for an infinite language $L' \subseteq \Sigma^*$. We define l_n as the number of words of length n in L':

$$l_n = |L' \cap \Sigma^n|$$

From this sequence we obtain the generating function of L' as a function in the variable z:

$$l(z) = \sum_{n \geq 0} l_n z^n$$

Now we recall a central result from [3], see also [9]:

Theorem 7 (Chomsky, Schützenberger) *Let $l(z)$ be the generating function of a context-free language L. If L is unambiguous then $l(z)$ is an algebraic function over the rationals Q.*

Recall that a function $y = f(x)$ is algebraic if it satisfies an equation

$$p_d(x)y^d + p_{d-1}(x)y^{d-1} + \cdots + p_0(x) = 0$$

where the $p_i(x)$ are polynomials.

Reversing the above argument a language with a non-algebraic generating function cannot be unambiguous context-free. In order to certify that a function is non-algebraic Flajolet supplied several criteria of which we will use his Criterion E [9]:

Lemma 8 *Let $l(z)$ be an algebraic function. Then there exists a finite sequence of polynomials $q_0(u), \ldots, q_m(u)$ such that for $n \geq n_0$*

$$\sum_{j=0}^{m} q_j(n) l_{n-j} = 0 \tag{1}$$

The criterion is based on a result by Comtet [4], see also Theorem 5.1 in [24]. This very general statement will be applied to the field of rationals here and therefore w.l.o.g. all coefficients may be integers. Further the sequence of polynomials is assumed to be nontrivial, i.e. $q_0 \not\equiv 0$, $q_m \not\equiv 0$, and $m > 0$.

5 The Generating Function of Q

For an alphabet of size k we follow [19] and denote by $\psi_k(n)$ the number of classes of conjugates of primitive words of length n. This function is the key to our result, and we will briefly recall its development.

Since every nonempty word can be uniquely written as a (possibly trivial) power of a primitive word (see Corollary 4.2 in [20]) we conversely obtain all k^n words of length n as conjugates of appropriate powers of primitive words. From Lemma 3 we know that $|c(w)| = n$ for primitive w of length n.

This is expressed in the formula:

$$k^n = \sum_{d|n} d\, \psi_k(d)$$

683

(Remark: The respective formula (1.3.6) in [19] contains a misprint.)

Recall the Möbius inversion formula (Theorem 266 in [13]):

For two functions f and g

$$g(n) = \sum_{d|n} f(d)$$

if and only if

$$f(n) = \sum_{d|n} \mu(d)\, g\left(\frac{n}{d}\right)$$

where μ is the Möbius function defined by

$$\mu(d) = \begin{cases} (-1)^i & d \text{ is the product of } i \text{ distinct primes} \\ 0 & d \text{ is divisible by a square} \end{cases}$$

Note that $\mu(1) = 1$. We set $g(n) = k^n$, $f(d) = d\,\psi_k(d)$ and obtain

$$\psi_k(n) = \frac{1}{n} \sum_{d|n} \mu(d)\, k^{n/d}$$

Since $|c(w)| = n$ for a primitive word of length n by Lemma 3 the generating function $l(z)$ of Q satisfies:

$$l_n = n\,\psi_k(n) = \sum_{d|n} \mu(d)\, k^{n/d} \tag{2}$$

Note that for prime p we have $l_p = k^p - k$ and observe the following:

Lemma 9 *If p is a prime and u a positive number then*

$$k^2 \nmid l_p \tag{3}$$

$$k^p \mid l_{p^2 u} \tag{4}$$

Proof: (3) is immediate since $l_p = k^p - k = k(k^{p-1} - 1)$. For (4) we note that in every nonzero term of (2) the exponent of k is a proper multiple of p because $\mu(p^2 m) = 0$ for each factor m of u. This excludes any d divisible by p^2. □

6 The Ambiguity of Q and L

Theorem 10 *The set Q of primitive words is not unambiguous context-free.*

Proof: By Theorem 6.4.1 of [14] (closure under intersection with regular sets) it is sufficient to show that $Q \cap \{a, b\}^*$ is not unambiguous, and we may assume $k = 2$ for this proof. We will suppose there are polynomials as specified in Lemma 8 and deduce a contradiction.

Suppose that Q is unambiguous context-free and therefore a finite sequence of polynomials satisfying Equation (1) with integer coefficients exists. From any such nontrivial sequence we can obtain a sequence of polynomials with an additional property:

Lemma 11 *For a nontrivial sequence of polynomials $q_0, \ldots, q_m$ with integer coefficients satisfying Equation (1) there is a sequence $q_0', \ldots, q_{m'}'$, still satisfying Equation (1) with the property that an odd index $d > 0$ exists, such that the constant term of q_d' is nonzero, i.e. $q_d'(0) \neq 0$.*

Proof: If the initial sequence has the desired property the statement is trivial.
Otherwise we consider the equations

$$\sum_{j=0}^{m} q_j(n - \delta)\, l_{n-\delta-j} = 0$$

for fixed numbers δ. The $q_i(n - \delta)$ are to be understood as functions in the variable n. Every equation is satisfied for $n > n_0 + \delta$. It is plainly true that the constant term of $q_0(n - \delta)$ is equal to $q_0(-\delta)$. Since $q_0 \not\equiv 0$ we know that $q_0(-\delta) \neq 0$ for almost all δ, hence for some $\delta > m$ with δ odd. By adding the new equation for this δ to the initial equation we obtain a system with the desired property, in which $d = \delta$ and $m' = m + \delta$, $q_i'(n) = q_i(n)$ for $0 \leq i \leq m$, $q_i'(n) = q_{i-\delta}(n - \delta)$ for $\delta \leq i \leq m'$, while all other polynomials are zero. $\square$

From now on we will assume that Equation (1) satisfies the property expressed in Lemma 11 for the index d.

Let 2^r be the largest power of 2 that divides $q_d(0)$ and t the index of a prime $p_t > \max(2, r + 1, m)$ in the sequence of primes $p_1 = 2, p_2 = 3, \ldots$. As above the number m is the largest index of a polynomial.

The system of congruences

$$
\begin{array}{lllll}
u & \equiv & 0 & & (\bmod\ 2^{r+1}(p_t)^2) \\
u & \equiv & 1 & & (\bmod\ (p_{t+1})^2) \\
u & \equiv & 2 & & (\bmod\ (p_{t+2})^2) \\
\vdots & \vdots & \vdots & & \\
u & \equiv & d-1 & & (\bmod\ (p_{t+d-1})^2) \\
u & \equiv & d+1 & & (\bmod\ (p_{t+d})^2) \\
\vdots & \vdots & \vdots & & \\
u & \equiv & m-1 & & (\bmod\ (p_{t+m-2})^2) \\
u & \equiv & m & & (\bmod\ (p_{t+m-1})^2)
\end{array}
$$

has an infinity of solutions $ia + u$, $i = 0, 1, 2 \ldots$ due to Theorem 6 where a is the product of the moduli. Now $(u - d)$ and a are coprime because each of the primes $p_t, p_{t+1}, \ldots p_{t+m-1}$ involved in the construction divides at most one of the $m+1$ consecutive numbers $u - m, u - m + 1, \ldots, u$ (remember that $p_t > m$), u is even, d is odd, hence $(u - d)$ is also odd.

From Theorem 5 we conclude that the sequence $ia + (u - d)$, $i = 0, 1, 2 \ldots$ contains a prime p large enough such that Equation (1) holds at the point $n = (p + d)$:

$$s = \sum_{j=0}^{m} q_j(p + d)\, l_{p+d-j} = 0$$

All terms of the sum are divisible by 2^{r+2}, with one exception. For all $i \neq p$ we have $2^{r+2} \mid l_i$ because each i is divisible by the square of a prime $p' \geq r+2$ (by the choice of the moduli in the above system of congruences) and according to (4) of Lemma 9, $2^{r+2} \mid 2^{p'} \mid l_i$. Further $2^{r+2} \mid (q_d(p+d) - q_d(0)) \, l_p$ because $2^{r+1} \mid (p+d)$ and $2 \mid l_p$. We conclude that $s \equiv q_d(p+d)l_p \equiv q_d(0)l_p \equiv 0$ (mod 2^{r+2}). But by construction $2^{r+1} \nmid q_d(0)$ and $2^2 \nmid l_p$ by (3) of Lemma 9, so $q_d(0)l_p \not\equiv 0 \pmod{2^{r+2}}$. Contradiction. $\qquad\square$

As an immediate consequence we have

Corollary 12 *The set L of Lyndon words is not unambiguous context-free.*

Proof: Let $y(z)$ be the generating function of L. Clearly $l_n = ny_n$ and therefore $zy'(z) = l(z)$ where $y'(z)$ is the derivative of $y(z)$. $\qquad\square$

7 Automata Accepting Q and L

In [7] the authors remark that Q is accepted by a deterministic linear bounded automaton (DLBA) (the same trivially holds for L) and Diekert observed that $Q \in \mathrm{DSPACE}(\log)$ [6]. We will show that deterministic two-way pushdown automata (2DPDA), which originally were introduced in [25], are also sufficient for this task. This result makes it possible to apply Cook's result [5] yielding an efficient recognition-algorithm.

We just recall that 2DPDA are defined like ordinary DPDA (accepting with final state) with the additional ability to move their input head in both directions. Apart from the bottom pushdown symbol $\perp$ there are two distinguished input symbols $\vdash$ and $\dashv$ marking the left and right end of the input string.

There are many modifications of the 2DPDA model in the literature, most of which are known to be equivalent. For a short discussion see [22].

Theorem 13 *The sets Q and L are accepted by 2DPDA.*

Proof: First we will informally describe how a 2DPDA A decides Q. Let $\vdash w \dashv$ be the input word augmented with endmarkers. If $w = \lambda$ automaton A rejects. Otherwise it advances its input head to $\dashv$. Then A skips the last symbol of w and pushes the remainder of w onto its pushdown store. Finally it moves its head to $\dashv$ again, pushes all of w onto its store, and pops one symbol.

If we write the input $w = xw'y$ with $x, y \in \Sigma$ (assuming $|w| \geq 2$) the pushdown looks as follows (we write the topmost symbol on the left side avoiding the usual reversal):

$$w'yxw'\perp$$

A compares w with the pushdown contents symbol by symbol. If the symbols match, the head moves right and A pops the pushdown. If in this way w is completely scanned ($\dashv$ is under the input-head of A) A rejects.

If a mismatch is encountered A moves the input head back to $\vdash$ and pushes the symbols scanned during this move. Then A pops one symbol and repeats the process. Should the pushdown become empty A accepts.

For the correctness we note that acceptance occurs if and only if w is not a factor of $w'yxw'$. But this is equivalent to the second part of Lemma 2.

Next we describe an automaton B accepting L. Let $\vdash w \dashv$ be an input as above. B first moves its input head to $\dashv$ and stores w onto the pushdown. Then it pops one symbol and compares the pushdown contents with w. Should B encounter a symbol a in the pushdown and b in w with $a < b$ or reach the bottom symbol in the pushdown it rejects.

In case of equality between the symbols B pops and moves its input head one position to the right. If the symbol on the pushdown is greater than the symbol in the input B returns to $\vdash$ and restores its pushdown by pushing the symbols scanned during this move. Finally one symbol is popped and if the pushdown is empty B accepts. This procedure is then repeated.

Evidently B correctly checks that w is lexicographically smaller than any of its right factors. By Lemma 4 B accepts L. $\square$

Our next results use the unit-cost RAM (random access machine) model of computation and we should discuss one subtlety before proceeding. In [5] a RAM is equipped with an input tape that is read sequentially during the computation. The machine may accept without reading the entire input and we have the counter-intuitive situation that the regular language $a\{a,b\}^*$ is recognized in $O(1)$ steps, but its mirror image requires $\Omega(n)$ steps. Contemporary texts on algorithms require the input as well as its length to be present in memory cells at the start of the RAM computation. The same applies to [18], and it seems to be the natural model when call by reference is possible.

Trivially the latter RAM model simulates the former without overhead and the above example shows that the former is weaker. We may therefore take advantage of the result in [5] while considering the stronger model.

Theorem 13 now admits an immediate corollary. The statement about L also follows from [2] where an algorithm for computing the Lyndon word in the class of conjugates of a given word is directly developed. We note that recently this problem has been investigated on the model of the CRCW PRAM [16].

Corollary 14 *The sets L of Lyndon words and Q of primitive words are accepted by a RAM in linear time. This is optimal for the worst case.*

Proof: In [5] it has been shown that a k-head 2DPDA with an input of length n can be simulated in time $O(n^k)$ on a RAM. For the 1-head machine of Theorem 13 this proves the claimed $O(n)$ time bounds.

To show optimality we use well-known adversary arguments. Initially the input w ($|w| = n$) is stored in an array text[1], text[2]...text[n].

For Q consider $w = a^n$ and suppose w is rejected without reading text[i] for an i with $1 \le i \le n$. Now we take as input $w' = a^{(i-1)}ba^{(n-i)}$. Since the RAM works deterministically it incorrectly rejects w'. Therefore at least $|w|$ operations are necessary in the worst case.

For L we let $\{a,b,c,d\} \subseteq \Sigma$ with $a < b < c < d$ and consider $w \in \{b,c\}^p \setminus \{b^p, c^p\}$ for prime p. Apparently w is primitive and membership in L only depends on minimality. Suppose w is accepted without checking symbol i. If

$i = 1$ we replace the first symbol with d, otherwise we replace symbol i with a. In any case the resulting word is not in L and should not be accepted. Again $|w|$ operations are necessary in the worst case. □

The structure of its generating function shows that only a small fraction of all possible strings are excluded from Q. This observation can be generalized to show that on the average an amazingly small amount of information suffices for recognizing primitive words.

First we specify what is meant by 'average' in this case. For a fixed input length n we simply suppose that all k^n words appear with equal frequencies. For the asymptotical behavior we adopt the notion of *normal order* from [13] where $f(n)$ has normal order $F(n)$ when for every given ϵ and n' the relation $(1-\epsilon)F(n) < f(n) < (1+\epsilon)F(n)$ is satisfied for all $n \le n'$ with $o(n')$ exceptions. So the the number of irregularities can never be large asymptotically.

Theorem 15 *There is a RAM program deciding Q such that the normal order of the average number of references to the input string w is $c \cdot \log\log(|w|)$ for a constant c.*

Proof: We will below supply a RAM program that obeys the claimed bound in a self-explanatory pseudo-code.

The program checks for every prime $p \mid n$, where $n = |w|$, if w is of the form z^p. The comparison of symbols is aborted as soon as possible.

```
function primitive(n: integer; var text: string): boolean;
var    is_primitive, is_power: boolean;
       p, index: integer;
begin
       is_primitive := true;
       for every prime divisor p of n do
       begin
              is_power := true;
              index := 1;
              while (is_power ∧ (index ≤ n − n/p)) do
              begin
                     is_power := is_power ∧ (text[index] = text[n/p + index]);
                     index := index + 1
              end;
              is_primitive := is_primitive ∧ ¬is_power
       end;
       primitive := is_primitive
end;
```

Let $D_n = \{\frac{n}{p} \mid p$ is a prime divisor of $n\}$ be the set of maximal elements in the set of proper divisors of n with respect to the partial order induced by divisibility. For correctness we observe that whenever **is_primitive** becomes false there must be a factoring $w = z^p$ where p is a prime. Conversely suppose that $w = z^k$ with arbitrary $k \geq 2$ and let $h = |z|$. Then $h \neq n$, $h \mid \frac{n}{p}$ for some $\frac{n}{p} \in D_n$. Now $w = z^k = \left(z^{\frac{n}{ph}}\right)^p$ and a factoring will be found by the program.

For the bound on the references and hence on comparison operations note that the cardinality of D_n is $\omega(n)$, the number of *distinct* prime divisors of n as defined in [13]. Theorem 431 of [13] tells us that the normal order of $\omega(n)$ is $\log\log(n)$. For every fixed divisor the average number of comparisons is at most $1 + \frac{1}{k} + \frac{1}{k^2} + \cdots = \frac{k}{k-1}$ which supplies the constant c of the statement. $\quad\square$

By counting only comparisons we have eliminated the computation of prime divisors from consideration and shifted it to an unspecified oracle. This can be justified because factoring is of a totally different nature than the combinatorial questions of deciding primitivity, and is certainly beyond the scope of this paper. Further we can argue that the input length is really a unary parameter, the work done for factoring n depends on $\log(n)$, and can be distributed between k^n possible inputs if prime factors are tabulated.

8 A Related Non-Context-Free Language

A non-context-free subset of Q is investigated in Theorem 3 of [8]. The proof given there is based on the non-empty variant of the Bader-Moura condition. We provide a different argument which employs well-known closure properties of semi-linear (abbr. s.l.) sets. For details see [10].

Theorem 16 ([8]) *The following set $L' \subset Q$ is not context-free:*

$$L' = \{w \mid w \in \Sigma^+ \text{ and every permutation of } w \text{ is primitive}\}$$

Proof: It is sufficient to consider $|\Sigma| = 2$. Suppose L' is context-free. Then the Parikh-image $\varphi(L')$ is a s.l. vector-set by Parikh's Theorem (see Theorem 5.2.1 in [10]). We will write vectors with angular brackets. As noted in [8], $\varphi(L') = \{\langle m, n\rangle \mid (m, n) = 1\}$ where (m, n) denotes the highest common divisor. Now $G = \{\langle 2, 1\rangle + i\langle 1, 1\rangle + j\langle 1, 0\rangle \mid i, j \geq 0\}$ is s.l. and therefore $C = G \setminus \varphi(L') = \{\langle m, n\rangle \mid m > n > 0, (m, n) > 1\}$, as the difference of s.l. sets, would be s.l. too (see Theorem 5.6.2 in [10]). Note that the basis vector $\langle 2, 1\rangle$ avoids anomalies concerning the divisibility of 0. The first components of vectors in C are exactly the composite numbers, for all $m \geq 1$:

$$\exists n : \langle m, n\rangle \in C \iff \exists n : 0 < n < m \wedge (m, n) > 1 \iff$$
$$\exists n, d : 0 < n < m \wedge d > 1 \wedge d \mid n \wedge d \mid m \iff$$
$$\exists d : d > 1 \wedge d < m \wedge d \mid m$$

The projection of C onto its first component would remain s.l. but the primes and hence the composites are not s.l., as can be verified by combining the non-regularity of the primes written in unary (Problem 6b of 2.2 in [14]) with the equivalence between Parikh-images of regular sets and s.l. vector-sets (Theorem 6.9.1 in [14]). Contradiction. $\quad\square$

Remark: The original research on which this proof is based is due to Parikh, Ginsburg and Spanier [21, 11]. A careful compilation of results on s.l. sets including new developments (Petri Nets, complexity) was done by Haas [12].

9 Summary and Open Problems

The structure of Q and L has been approached in two ways: By showing that a certain mechanism—unambiguous context-free grammars—cannot generate them, but 2DPDA as deterministic devices accept them. The conjecture in [7] that Q is not context-free remains an open problem. As observed by Diekert [6] the same conjecture for L can be no harder to prove, since the context-free languages are closed under cyclic permutation (Exercise 6.4 in [15]).

The strong number-theoretical flavor of this subject is not only exhibited by our main result but also by the new proof we found for Theorem 16. It should provide deeper insights into the structural properties of the formal languages we deal with.

Complexity issues have only partially been covered and might provide a different way of attacking the open questions.

Acknowledgement: The author is indebted to S. Horváth and V. Diekert for discussions and corrections which improved the paper. Thanks also go to the anonymous referees and to D. Hauschildt.

References

[1] T. M. Apostol: *Introduction to Analytic Number Theory,* Springer-Verlag, New York, Berlin, Heidelberg, Tokyo (1976, 3rd printing 1986).

[2] K.S. Booth: *Lexicographically least circular substrings,* Inform. Process. Lett. 10 (4) (1980) pp. 240–242.

[3] N. Chomsky, M. P. Schützenberger: *The algebraic theory of context-free languages,* Computer Programming and Formal Systems (P. Brafford, D. Hirschberg eds.), North-Holland, Amsterdam (1963), pp. 118–161.

[4] L. Comtet: *Calcul pratique des coefficients de Taylor d'une fonction algébrique,* L'Enseignement Mathématique 10 (1964) pp. 267–270.

[5] S. A. Cook: *Linear time simulation of deterministic two-way pushdown automata,* Inf. Proc. 71, North-Holland (1972) pp. 75–80.

[6] V. Diekert, personal communication (1993).

[7] P. Dömösi, S. Horváth, M. Ito: *Formal languages and primitive words,* Publ. Math., Debrecen 42 3–4 (1993) pp. 315–321.

[8] P. Dömösi, S. Horváth, M. Ito, L. Kászonyi, M. Katsura: *Formal languages consisting of primitive words,* Proc. FCT93, LNCS 710, Springer-Verlag, Berlin, Heidelberg, New York (1993) pp. 194–203.

[9] Ph. Flajolet: *Analytic models and ambiguity of context-free languages*, TCS 49 (1987) pp. 283–309.

[10] S. Ginsburg: *The Mathematical Theory of Context-Free Languages*, McGraw-Hill, New York (1966).

[11] S. Ginsburg, E. H. Spanier: *Bounded Algol-like languages*, Trans. AMS 113 (1964) pp. 333–368.

[12] J.-P. Haas: *Theorie und Anwendungen Semilinearer Vektormengen*, Universität Hamburg, Fachbereich Informatik, Bericht Nr. 130 (1987).

[13] G. H. Hardy, E. M. Wright: *An Introduction to the Theory of Numbers*, Oxford University Press, London (1938, reprinted 1968).

[14] M. A. Harrison: *Introduction to Formal Language Theory*, Addison-Wesley, Reading Mass. (1978).

[15] J. E. Hopcroft, J. D. Ullman: *Introduction to Automata Theory, Languages, and Computation*, Addison-Wesley, Reading Mass. (1979).

[16] C. S. Iliopoulos, W. F. Smyth: *Optimal algorithms for computing the canonical form of a circular string*, TCS 92 (1992) pp. 87–105.

[17] M. Ito, M. Katsura, H. J. Shyr, S. S. Yu: *Automata accepting primitive words*, Semigroup Forum 37 (1988) pp. 45–50.

[18] D. Knuth, J. Morris, V. Pratt: *Fast pattern matching in strings*, SIAM J. Comp. 6 (1977) pp. 323–350.

[19] M. Lothaire: *Combinatorics on Words*, Addison-Wesley, Reading Mass. (1983).

[20] R. C. Lyndon, M. P. Schützenberger: *The equation $a^M = b^N c^P$ in a free group*, Michigan Math. J. 9 (1962) pp. 289–298.

[21] R. J. Parikh: *On context-free languages*, JACM 13 (1966) pp. 570–581.

[22] H. Petersen: *Remarks on the power of 2-DPDA*, Universität Hamburg, Fachbereich Informatik, Bericht Nr. 162.

[23] H. J. Shyr, G. Thierrin: *Disjunctive languages and codes*, Proc. FCT77, LNCS 56, Springer-Verlag, Berlin, Heidelberg, New York (1977) pp. 171–176.

[24] R. P. Stanley: *Generating functions*, MAA Studies in Math. (G.-C. Rota ed.), Vol. 17: Studies in Combinatorics, MAA (1978) pp. 100–141.

[25] R. Stearns, J. Hartmanis, P. M. Lewis II: *Hierarchies of memory limited computations*, in: Proc. 6th Annual Symp. on Switching Circuit Theory and Logical Design (1965) pp. 179–190.

ON CODES HAVING NO FINITE COMPLETION

BY NGUYEN HUONG LAM

Hanoi Institute of Mathematics
P.O.Box 631, Bo Ho, 10 000 Hanoi, Vietnam

Abstract. For each natural number $n \geq 5$ we propose a class of finitely incompletable codes that contain a^n on a binary alphabet $\{a,b\}$. The construction is essentially based on unambiguous pairs unembeddable to a factorization of $\mathbf{Z}_n$.

1 Introduction

In this article, we deal with the notion of maximal code, which plays an important role in the theory of variable length codes. For background we refer to the book of Berstel and Perrin [1].

A typical result about codes is that every code is embedded into a maximal one i.e., a code any proper superset of which is no longer a code. Proving existence of such a maximal code is a standard technique by application of Zorn's lemma. Similarly, the problem of embedding a code into a maximal one is raised for special families of codes, which often requires more elaborate constructions than a simple application of Zorn's lemma. We mention two major results. First, Ehrenfeucht and Rozenberg proved that each regular code is embedded into a maximal code which is also regular [5]. Second, for the family of regular codes with finite deciphering delay, V. Bruyère, Limin Wang and Liang Zhang have recently showed that every such code is included in a regular maximal code with the same delay [2].

For finite codes, the situation is different. In [11], Restivo proposed a class of finite codes not contained in any finite maximal code. As the smallest among them one can take the code $\{a^5, a^2b, ba, b\}$ on a binary alphabet $\{a, b\}$. The very same example can be found in an earlier work of Al. A. Markov [10]. Further, some extensions and other constructions are presented in [4]. All of them are codes in $a^* \cup a^*b \cup ba^*$, containing $\{a^n, b\}$, but the constructions work only in case n is a prime larger than 3 or $n - 1$ is a composite larger than 6. In this paper, basing on simple multiplication properties of integers, we propose some constructions yielding finite codes with no finite completion covering all the existing classes in [10], [11], [4]. In fact, we prove that for any integer $n \geq 5$, there exist a code in $a^* \cup a^*ba^*$ containing $\{a^n, b\}$ having no finite completion. The cases of $n = 2, 3, 4$ remain open. Codes of the form $a^* \cup a^*ba^*$ are closely connected with the notion of factorization of the group $\mathbf{Z}_n$ of residues modulo n.

2 Notations and Main Results

Let $A = \{a, b\}$ be a binary alphabet and A^* the set of words on A with the catenation as product. A subset C of A^* is a code if whenever a word is expressed as a product of words from C, it is so uniquely i.e.,

$$c_1 \ldots c_n = c_1' \ldots c_m'$$

then $m = n$ and $c_1 = c_1', \ldots, c_m = c_m'$. A code is said to be *maximal* if it is not a proper subset of any other code. An application of Zorn's lemma shows that every code is contained in a maximal one, called a *completion* of it. If a code has a finite completion, we say also it is *finitely completable*; otherwise, we say that it is *finitely incompletable*. For more background information and definitions we refer to [1].

Let $\mathbf{N}$ denote the set of nonnegative integers and for $n \geq 1$, $\mathbf{N}_n = \{i : 0 \leq i \leq n - 1\}$, $\mathbf{Z}_n$ the residue class group modulo n. We recall a notion from [12]. A pair (H, K) of subsets of $\mathbf{N}$ is called an *unambiguous pair* provided, whenever

$$h + k = h' + k'$$

for $h, h' \in H$ and $k, k' \in K$, then $h = h', k = k'$. More specifically, we say that (H, K) is an *unambiguous pair for* a subset S if it is an unambiguous pair and $H + K = \{i + j : i \in H, j \in K\} \subseteq S$. Likewise, we introduce the following

DEFINITION 1. *The pair (H, K) of subsets of $\mathbf{Z}_n$ is called an* unambiguous pair *of $\mathbf{Z}_n$ if for any $s \in S$ there exists at most one pair $(i, j) \in (H, K)$ such that $s = i + j$.*

The classical notion of *factorization* of $\mathbf{Z}_n$ [7] is that of unambiguous pair such that $H + K = \mathbf{Z}_n$.

Since $\mathbf{N}_n$ is a complete residue system to the modulus n, we usually identify each element of $\mathbf{Z}_n$ by its representative in $\mathbf{N}_n$. By this convention, every unambiguous pair of $\mathbf{Z}_n$ is an unambiguous pair and, vice versa, every unambiguous pair for $\mathbf{N}_n$ can be viewed as that of $\mathbf{Z}_n$. In particular, an unambiguous pair (H, K) for $\mathbf{N}_n$ with $H + K = \mathbf{N}_n$ is obviuosly a factorization of $\mathbf{Z}_n$ and is called in [12] an *elementary factorization* of $\mathbf{Z}_n$.

From now on, for our purposes, the summands of unambiguous pairs of $\mathbf{Z}_n$ are supposed to contain 0, if we do not specify otherwise. We say that an unambiguous pair is *nontrivial* if each summand contains more than one element.

For any subset $C \subseteq A^*$, let us define the pair of subsets of $\mathbf{N}$ [12]

$$\mathrm{L}(C) = \{i : b^+ a^i \cap C \neq \emptyset\}, \quad \mathrm{R}(C) = \{j : a^j b^+ \cap C \neq \emptyset\}.$$

and for any pair of subsets (L, R) of $\mathbf{Z}_n$ let define the following language

$$\mathrm{C}(L, R) = \{a^n, b\} \cup \{ba^i : i \in L\} \cup \{a^j b : j \in R\}.$$

The following assertion is straightforward [12].

PROPOSITION 1. *If $C \subseteq A^*$ is a code such that $\{a^n, b\} \subseteq C, n \geq 1$, then*

(i) $(L(C), R(C))$ *is an unambiguous pair of* $\mathbf{Z}_n$;

(ii) *for any unambiguous pair* (L, R) *of* $\mathbf{Z}_n$, $C = C(L, R)$ *is a code and* $L(C) = L, R(C) = R$.

The following statement is simple but important for our consideration [12].

PROPOSITION 2. *Let C be a code such that $\{a^n, b\} \subseteq C$ then C has a finite completion only if there exists a factorization (H, K) of $\mathbf{Z}_n$ such that $L(C) \subseteq H$ and $R(C) \subseteq K$.*

Proof. Suppose that C has a finite completion X. Clearly, $L(C) \subseteq L(X), R(C) \subseteq R(X)$. To prove that $(L(X), R(X))$ is a factorization of $\mathbf{Z}_n$, by Proposition 1, it suffices to show that for any $s \in \mathbf{Z}_n$, there exist $(i, j) \in (L(X), R(X))$ such that $s \equiv i + j \bmod n$. Let d be any integer larger than the maximal length of the words of X and congruent to s modulo n. Consider the word $w = b^d a^d b^d$. Since X is maximal, it is *complete* [1], hence there are $u, v \in A^*, x_1, \ldots, x_m \in X$ such that

$$ub^d a^d b^d v = x_1 \ldots x_m \in X^*.$$

Let p be the largest and q the smallest integer such that $|ub^d| \leq |x_1 \ldots x_p| \leq |vb^d a^d| \leq |x_1 \ldots \ldots x_q|$. Since $d \geq |x_q|$ we have

$$x_p \in b^* a^i, x_{p+1} = \ldots = x_{q-1} = a^n, x_q \in a^j b^*$$

and thus $s \equiv d \equiv i + j \bmod n$. By Proposition 1, $(L(X), R(X))$ is a factorization of $\mathbf{Z}_n$. The proof is complete.

Now we attend to the construction of finitely incompletable codes. The following observation is crucial: for any factorization (H, K) of $\mathbf{Z}_n$, $|H||K| = n$, where $|H|$ denotes the cardinality of H. The argument in [4] and [11] requires the existence of a nontrivial factorization of $\mathbf{Z}_{n-1}$ which is possible only in case $n - 1$ is a composite number. For these values of n, as direct consequences of Proposition 2, we have already known results. First, if $n = p$ is a prime number, there is no nontrivial factorization of $\mathbf{Z}_n$. So, we have [12]

COROLLARY 1. *Let p be a prime and (L, R) a nontrivial unambiguous pair of* $\mathbf{Z}_p$, *then* $C(L, R)$ *has no finite completion.*

Remark. In particular, when (L, R) is a nontrivial unambiguous pair for $\mathbf{N}_{p-1}$ $(p \geq 5)$, we obtain the class of codes of Restivo [11], [12].

Proof. If $C = C(L, R)$ has a finite completion then there is a factorization (H, K) of $\mathbf{Z}_p$ such that $L = L(C) \subseteq H, R = R(C) \subseteq K$, by Proposition 2. Then $|H| \geq |L(C)| \geq 2, |K| \geq |R(C)| \geq 2$ and $p = |\mathbf{Z}_p| = |H||K|$, which is impossible as p is prime.

EXAMPLE 1. For a prime $p > 3$, $(H = \{0,1\}, K = \{0,2\})$ is a nontrivial unambiguous pair of $\mathbf{Z}_p$. Then $C(H,K) = \{a^p, ba, a^2b, b\}$ is a finitely incompletable code. If we take $H = \{0, p+1\}, K = \{0, p-2\}$, (H,K) is again a nontrivial unambiguous pair of $\mathbf{Z}_p$, thus $\{a^p, ba^{p+1}, a^{p-2}b, b\}$ has no finite completion.

Exploiting once again Proposition 2, we have the following assertion for odd composite numbers > 5.

COROLLARY 2. *Let $n > 5$ be an odd composite; then there exists a code containing $\{a^n, b\}$ and having no finite completion.*

Proof. Let p be the least prime divisor of n, say, $n = ps$. As n is odd composite, p, s are odd and $n > s \geq p \geq 3$. Consider $L = \{0,1\}, R = \{0,2,\ldots,2s\}$. Evidently, (L,R) is an unambiguous pair of $\mathbf{Z}_n$. If (L,R) could be completed to a factorization (H,K) of $\mathbf{Z}_n$, then $|H| \geq |L|$ and $|H|$ would be a divisor of n, which would imply $|H| \geq p$. Since $|K| \geq |R| = s + 1$, we get $n = |H||K| \geq p(s+1) > ps = n$, which is a contradiction showing that $C(L,R)$ is finitely incompletable.

In the following proposition, we extend the construction of [4].

PROPOSITION 3. *Let (L,R) be an unambiguous pair of $\mathbf{Z}_n$ such that $\min\{|L|,|R|\} > n - |L||R| > 0$. Then the code $C(L,R)$ has no finite completion.*

Proof. Suppose on the contrary that $C(L,R)$ has a finite completion. By Proposition 2, $L \subseteq H$, $R \subseteq K$ for some factorization (H,K) of $\mathbf{Z}_n$. Since $|L||R| < n$, either $|H| > |L|$ or $|K| > |R|$. Say, $|H| > |L|$, then $n = |H||K| \geq (|L|+1)|K| \geq (|L|+1)|R| = |L||R| + |R| > |L||R| + n - |L||R| = n$: a contradiction.

Remark. For any nontrivial unambiguous pair (L,R) of $\mathbf{Z}_n$ with $|R||L| = n-1$, as (L,R) is an unambiguous pair for the set $S = \{i+j : i \in L, j \in R\} \equiv \{0,1,\ldots,n-1\} - \{t\}$ modulo n for some $t : 0 < t \leq n-1$, we get the Corollary 2.3 of [4].

EXAMPLE 2. (a) Let n be an odd integer $\geq 5, n-1$ is even and ≥ 4. It is easy to obtain a nontrivial unambiguous pair for $\mathbf{N}_{n-1}$, for instance, let $n-1 = 2s, s \geq 2$, we set $H = \{0,1\}, K = \{0,2,\ldots,2(s-1)\}$. Therefore, the code $C(H,K)$ has no finite completion. It is another proof of Corollary 2.

(b) For some even integers, the construction of Proposition 3 is straightforward. Let $n = 14$, the subsets $H = \{0,1,2\}$ and $K = \{0,3,6,9\}$ constitute an unambiguous pair of $\mathbf{Z}_{14}$ with $|K| > |H| = 3 > 14 - 12 = 2$. Analogously proceeded for $n = 18$.

Note that for many values of n, Proposition 2 or 3 cannot be applied readily as above, the smallest one is $n = 8$. However, we have the following proposition which will give rise to a construction yielding the desired code for all $n \geq 5$ and $n \neq 6$.

PROPOSITION 4 *Let n, d, t, j be integers such that d does not divide n and $n = td + j$ with $t \geq 2, 0 < j \leq d-1$. If (L,R) is an unambiguous pair of $\mathbf{Z}_n$ such that $|R| = t$ and either of the following conditions*

(i) $t \nmid j$ and $|L| = d$,

(ii) $\{0, 1, \ldots, d-1\} = L$ and $d \in R$

holds then $C(L, R)$ has no finite completion.

Proof. Suppose on the contrary that $C(R, L)$ has a finite completion, therefore $L \subseteq H, R \subseteq K$ for some factorization (H, K) of $\mathbf{Z}_n$. For $|L| \geq d$, we have $|K| = |R|$, otherwise it follows $n = |K||H| \geq (|R|+1)|L| \geq (t+1)d > dt + j = n$. So in both cases (i) and (ii), $K = R$.

Let now (i) hold. Since $n = |H||K| = (|H| - d)t + dt$, it follows $j = (|H| - d)t$ which contradicts the assumption $t \nmid j$. Therefore, $C(L, R)$ has no finite completion in this case.

Next, suppose that (ii) holds. Let $K = R = \{k_0, k_1 \ldots, k_{t-1}\}$, where $k_0 = x_0 d + j_0, \ldots, k_{t-1} = x_{t-1}d + j_{t-1}$ with $0 \leq j_0, \cdots, j_{t-1} < d$ and $x_0 \leq x_1 \leq \cdots \leq x_{t-1} \leq t$. Since $\{0, 1, \ldots, d-1\} = L$ and (L, R) is an unambiguous pair, we have

$$0 \leq x_0 < x_1 < \cdots < x_{t-1} \leq t.$$

If $x_{t-1} = t$, as $k_{t-1} < n$, then $j_{t-1} < j$, which implies

$$0 \equiv n = k_{t-1} + (j - j_{t-1}) \bmod n$$

that is impossible, since $0 \neq j - j_{t-1} \in L$ and $k_{t-1} \in R$. Consequently, we have

$$x_0 = 0, x_1 = 1, \ldots, x_{t-1} = t - 1.$$

As is supposed $0, d \in R$, hence $j_0 = 0, j_1 = 0$. It can be seen also that

$$0 \leq j_2 \leq j_3 \leq \ldots \leq j_{t-1} \leq j.$$

In fact, for example, $j_3 < j_2$ implies

$$2d + j_2 + d - (j_2 - j_3) = 3d + j_3$$

with $0 < d - (j_2 - j_3) < d$ that contradicts the uniqueness of the presentation $L + R$. Further, if $j_0 = j_1 = \cdots = j_{t-1} = 0$, any element of $H - L$ must have the form $td + j', j' < j$. Hence the congruence

$$td + j' + d \equiv d - j + j' \bmod n$$

with $0 < d - j + j' < d$ implies that (H, K) is not a factorization: a contradiction. Thus, otherwise, let s be the minimal number such that $j_s \neq 0$, hence $t - 1 \geq s \geq 2$. Consider the number sd. Clearly $sd \notin K$; sd cannot belong to H, since $sd + d = sd + j_s + (d - j_s)$ with $d - j_s \in L \subseteq H$ and $d \in K$. Consequently, $sd \equiv h + k, h \in H - \{0\}, k \in K - \{0\}$. We show that this possibility also leads to a contradiction. We have two cases

(1) $sd = h + k \Rightarrow k < sd \Rightarrow k = ld \ (0 < l < s) \Rightarrow h = md \ (m > 0)$. As $d \in K$, we have $m > 1$, which implies $l < s - 1$. But then

$$(s + 1)d = sd + j_s + (d - j_s) = md + (l + 1)d,$$

where $l + 1 < s \Rightarrow (l + 1)d \in K$ that violates the assumption.

(2) $sd + n = h + k$. Set $h = xd + j' \Rightarrow x \le t$ (by convention $h < n$), $k = id + j_i \Rightarrow 0 < i \le t - 1$. We have

$$(s + t)d + j = (x + i)d + (j' + j_i).$$

Since $j_i \le j$, then $j = j' + j_i, x + i - t = s$. Hence $0 < i - s + 1 \le i$ and $j' + j_{i-s+1} \le j' + j_i = j$. But then

$$xd + j' + (i - s + 1)d + j_{i-s+1} = n + d - j + j' + j_{i-s+1} \equiv d - j + j' + j_{i-s+1} \bmod n$$

with $0 < d - j + j' + j_{i-s+1} \le d$. This is a contradiction with the assumption (H, K) a factorization of $\mathbf{Z}_n$, since $xd + j' > 0, (i - s + 1)d + j_{i-s+1} > 0$. This concludes the proof.

It turns out that, for all $n \ge 5, n \ne 6$, we can find a pair (L, R) satisfying (i) or (ii) of Proposition 4:

If n is odd, we have $n = \frac{n-1}{2} \cdot 2 + 1$, where $d = \frac{n-1}{2} > 1, t = 2, j = 1$ and $t \nmid j$ and any nontrivial unambiguous pair (L, R) with $|L| = d$ will do (for instance $L = \{0, \ldots, d - 1\}, R = \{0, d\}$). If n is even, $n = \frac{n-2}{2} \cdot 2 + 2$; $d = \frac{n-2}{2} \ge 3$ (as $n > 6$), $t = 2, j = 2$. We set $L = \{0, 1, \ldots, d - 1\}, R = \{0, d\}$ and see that (L, R), being a nontrivial factorization of $\mathbf{Z}_n$, satisfies (ii) of Proposition 4. Thus, we have proved

COROLLARY 3. *For every $n \ge 5, n \ne 6$ there exists a code containing $\{a^n, b\}$ having no finite completion.*

EXAMPLE 3. Let $n = 8$, we choose $d = 3, t = 2, j = 2$ and set $L = \{0, 1, 2\}, R = \{0, 3\}$; so $C(L, R) = \{a^8, ba, ba^2, a^3b, b\}$ is finitely incompletable. For $n = 10$, beside $d = 4, t = 2, j = 2$, we can take also $d = 3, t = 3, j = 1$. As $t \nmid j$ for $L = \{0, 1, 2\}, R = \{0, 3, 7\}$, $C(L, R) = \{a^{10}, ba, ba^2, a^3b, a^7b, b\}$ is finitely incompletable.

Now we propose a slightly modified technique intended to cover the case $n = 6$. We need one technical lemma.

LEMMA 1. *Given (L, R) a nontrivial factorization of $\mathbf{Z}_n$ with $|L| \ge 3$ and $|L| \ge |R|$. For any $x \in L$ let (H, K) be a factorization of $\mathbf{Z}_n$ such that $L - x \subseteq H$ and $R \subseteq L$. Then $K = R$ and $H = (L - x) \cup y$ for some $y \in x + R$.*

Proof. Suppose $K - R = \{a_1, \ldots, a_k\} \ne \emptyset$. If $k \ge 2$ then $n = |H||K| \ge (|L| - 1)(|R| + k) \ge (|L| - 1)(|R| + 2) = |L||R| + 2|L| - |R| - 2 = n + 2|L| - |R| - 2$. That is $2|L| \le |R| + 2$, thus $|L| \le 2$: contradiction. If $k = 1$, set $R = \{r_0, \ldots, r_{s-1}\}, s = |R| \ge 2$. We have the representation in $H + K$ for $x + r_0 = a_1 + l_0$ and $x + r_1 = a_1 + l_1$, where $l_0, l_1 \in L - x = H$

in this case. Hence $r_0 + l_1 = r_1 + l_0$ contradicting (L, R) a factorization. So $K = R$. Consequently, $|H| = |L|$ and thus $H = (L - x) \cup y$, which immediately implies $y = x + r$ for some $r \in R$.

For the following unambiguous pair (L, R):

$$L = \{0, 1, ..., l - 1\}, \quad R = \{l, 2l, ..., (s - 1)l\}$$

with s even, $s = 2t$, satisfying $s \geq 2$ if $l = 3$ and $s \geq 4$ if $l > 3$, we consider the subset defined as

$$C_1 = \{a^n, b, ba, ..., ba^{l-2}, a^l b, ..., a^{(s-1)l} b\} \cup \{a^{l-1} ba^r\} \cup \{a^{2(l-1)+jl} ba^r : 0 \leq j < t\}$$

with $n = ls$ and $r \in L$. A direct (by definition) verification (which we reserve for concrete examples below) shows that C_1 is a code. The condition on s is merely a technicality to ensure that.

PROPOSITION 5. C_1 is a finitely incompletable code.

Proof. If C_1 has a finite completion C then

$$L(C_1) = \{0, 1, ..., l - 2\} = L - \{l - 1\} \subseteq L(C)$$
$$R(C_1) = \{0, ..., (s - 1)l\} \subseteq R(C)$$

with $(L(C), R(C))$ a factorization of $\mathbf{Z}_n$. By Lemma 1, $L(C) = L - \{l-1\} \cup \{(l-1)+il\}$ for some $0 \leq i \leq s-1$. If $i < t$, using Sardinas–Patterson test [1], we have $a^{l-1+il} \in U_0(C)$, therefore $(a^{l-1+il})^{-1}(a^{2(l-1)+il} ba^r) = a^{(l-1)} ba^r \in U_1 \cap C_1 \subseteq U_1 \cap C$. Hence C is not a code. If $i \geq t$, as $a^{(l-2)} \in U_0(C)$ we get $a^{1+il} = (a^{l-2})^{-1}(a^{l-1+il}) \in U_1$ and $a^{l-1+(n-i-1)l} = (a^{1+il})^{-1} a^n \in U_2$ with $n - i - 1 < t$. As above, that means $U_3 \cap C \neq \emptyset$: C is not a code: a contradiction. The proof is complete.

Since every natural number n divided by 6 or every natural number divided by 4 and not less than 16 has a factorization $n = ls$ with $l = 3, s \geq 2$ or $l > 3, s = 4$, which evidently yields unambiguous pairs satisfying the foregoing proposition. Thus we have proved

COROLLARY 4. *For every n divided by 6 or divided by 4 and not less than 16, there exists a code containing $\{a^n, b\}$ having no finite completion.*

EXAMPLE 4. Consider $n = 6 = 3.2$. Set $L = \{0, 1, 2\}, l = 3; R = \{0, 3\}, s = 2, t = 1$ and $C_1 = \{a^6, b, ba, a^3 b, a^2 ba, a^4 ba\}$ with $r = 1$. We verify for sure that it is a code: $U_0 = \{a\}, U_1 = \{a^5, aba, a^3 ba, a^2 b\}, U_2 = \{a\}$, ect.

EXAMPLE 5. For the case $n = 16 = 4.4$, we proceed: $L = \{0, 1, 2, 3\}, l = 4; R = \{0, 4, 8, 12\}, s = 4, t = 2$ and $C_1 = \{a^{16}, b, ba, ba^2, ba^3, a^4 b, a^8 b, a^{12} b, a^3 ba, a^6 ba, a^{10} ba\}$ with $r = 1$. Calculation: $U_0 = \{a, a^2, a^3\}, U_1 = \{a^{15}, a^2 ba, a^5 ba, a^9 ba, a^3 b, a^7 b, a^{11} b, a^{14}, aba, a^8 ba, a^4 ba, a^2 b, a^6 b, a^1 0b\}, U_2 = \{a, a^2, a^3\}$, ect.

Summarizing Corollaries 3 and 4, we have

THEOREM 1. *For all* $n \geq 5$, *there exists a code containing* $\{a^n, b\}$ *having no finite completion.*

Remark. It is of an interest to search for a method to generate factorizations of $\mathbf{Z}_n$, but the problem of determining all factorazations of $\mathbf{Z}_n$ is very hard and is still open [7], [9]. However, the structure of elementary factorizations is described completely (see Krasner and Ranulac [8], Hajós [6] or De Felice [3]).

Acknowledgements

I would like to thank the referees for their useful information and suggestions, and Do Long Van for critically reading the manuscript and helping improve the presentation.

References

[1] J. Berstel, D. Perrin: Theory of Codes. New York: Academic Press 1985

[2] V. Bruyère, Limin Wang, Liang Zhang: On Completion of Codes with Finite Deciphering Delay. European Journal of Combinatorics 11, 513–521 (1990)

[3] C. De Felice: Construction of a Family of Finite Maximal Codes. Theoretical Computer Science 63, 157–184 (1989)

[4] C. De Felice, A. Restivo: Some Results On Finite Maximal Codes. RAIRO Informatique théorique 19, 383–403 (1985)

[5] A. Ehrenfeucht, G. Rozenberg: Each Regular Code Is Included In a Regular Maximal Code. RAIRO Informatique théorique 20, 89–96 (1986)

[6] G. Hajós: Sur le problème de factorisation de groupes cycliques. Acta Mathematica Acad. Sci. Hungaricae 1, 189–195 (1950)

[7] L. Fuchs: Abelian Groups. Budapest: Akadémiai kiadó 1958; Oxford–London–New York–Paris: Pergamon Press 1960

[8] M. Krasner, B. Ranulac: Sur une propriété des polynomes de la division du cercle. Comptes Rendus Acad. Sci. Paris 240, 297-299 (1937)

[9] G. Lallement: Semigroups and Combinatorial Applications. New York: John Wiley and Sons 1979

[10] Al. A. Markov: An Example of Independent System of Words Which Cannot Be Included into a Finite Complete System. Matematicheskie Zametki 1, 87–90 (1967), no 1 (in Russian)

[11] A. Restivo: On Codes Having No Finite Completions. Discrete Mathematics 17, 309–316 (1977)

[12] A. Restivo, S. Salemi, T. Sportelli: Completing Codes. RAIRO Informatique théorique 23, 135–147 (1989)

A New Approach To Information Theory

Richard J. Lipton[†]

Princeton University

Princeton, NJ 08544

rjl@princeton.edu

1. Introduction

Our contribution is to suggest a new way to view the problem of sending information over a noisy channel. Ever since Shannon's classic 1948 [9] paper, we have known that it is possible to send information at high rates over noisy channels provided we use an "error correcting code". Such a method assigns to each message a code word so that no two messages have code words that are "near" one another. In this way we can tell which message was sent provided only that the channel changes few bits of the code word. The requirement on the coding method is that no two code words be too close in their "Hamming" distance, i.e. no two code words agree in more than d bit positions. If this is true, then it is easy to see that as long as the channel makes less than $d/2$ changes to the code word, the correct message can be decoded. Currently, there is a vast literature on the construction of such codes [2,7,8].

Our insight is that Shannon's model of communication is *unrealistic*. The point is that the channel is allowed to be a very powerful adversary. The channel is only constrained to make less than $d/2$ errors: *as long as this is true the correct message is decoded*. The channel is not constrainted in how much computing power it has, only in how many bits of the code word it can change. This is an unrealistic assumption.

Our model only allows the channel to perform a "feasible" computation in determining which bits of the code word to change. This simple modification dramatically changes the whole situation. Once the channel is restricted in this way it is easy to construct coding methods that are both fast to encode/decode and have the ability to handle many errors. For example, we are able to prove the following: There is an explicit code that takes $O(n \log(n))$ to encode and $O(n^{1+\epsilon})$ to decode. Further, the decoder is highly likely to correctly decode the code word provided only that the channel was restricted to be a feasible computation and that it changed at most λn of the bits where $\lambda < 0.5$. Finally, the rate of the code, i.e. the ratio of useful bits to total bits is lower bounded by a nonzero constant. Such a code is

[†] Supported in part by NSF CCR-9304718

often called a "good" code [7]. We do not suggest that this code is optimal, only that it is an example of the way that our new model is much easier to work with. Constructing a code that matches this bound in the classic Shannon model appears to be difficult. (See [1] for a recent weaker result in the classic Shannon model.)

How do we restrict the channel? The answer is that we insist that it is a random polynomial-time computation. A central thesis of modern complexity theory is that we can model a feasible computation by one that makes at most a polynomial number of steps. Thus, a computation that takes time n^2 where n is the size of the input is considered feasible while one that takes 2^n is not. We also allow our computations to have access to random numbers. Thus, our computations can use the random numbers to decide what to do next. One of the exciting insights of the last few years in complexity theory is that allowing computations to be random may greatly improve their performance.

Thus, in our model we restrict the channel to be a random polynomial-time computation. Note, we are not claiming that real channels are this powerful: we are claiming since no feasible computation can do more it is a reasonable restriction. A real channel may be much weaker. For example, a real channel may be just a finite Markov process. The critical point, of course, is that if the channel is this weak it still is a feasible computation.

It is interesting to note that restricting the channel to a feasible computation has long been done in cryptography [4]. It appears to not have been done in the context of sending information over noisy channels.

Another way to view our results is that we are able to show that constructing a code that has large "average" distance is enough. In the classic case one must construct a code that has large worst case distance. In our model we only need to construct codes that have good average distance. Not surprising this is easier.

2. Basic Complexity Models and Results

We need a number of standard concepts from computational complexity. The first is that of a *polynomial time algorithm*. This is an algorithm that takes at most a polynomial number of steps for all its inputs. The exact model of "step", as usual, is not criticial. When such an algorithm is allowed to make decisions based on random numbers we will call it a *random polynomial time algorithm*. We also need the concept of circuit. A *circuit C_n* is made of *and*, *or*, and *not* gates, has n inputs, and computes a boolean function f in the standard way. The *size* of a circuit is the number of its gates. See [10] for details. A sequence of circuits $\{C_n(x)\}$ is *polynomial size* provided there is a constant c so that each is size at most n^c.

We also need the concept of a "Secure Pseudo-Random Number Generator". Consider G a family of boolean functions $G_n : \{0,1\}^{f(n)} \to \{0,1\}^n$ where $f(n) = O(n^{1/d})$ for some fixed $d > 1$. The family G is a *nonuniform secure pseudo-random number generator* provided: (1) There is a polynomial time algorithm that computes $G_n(s)$ given (n, s) as input. (2) For any polynomial size sequence of circuits $\{T_n(x)\}$, and any $c > 1$,

$$|Pr_z[T_n(z)] - Pr_s[T_n(G_n(s))]| < \epsilon$$

where ϵ is $\frac{1}{n^c}$. Intuitively, the "generator G passes all polynomial time statistical tests". Note, we have defined the family G so that $G_n(s)$ is n bits long. The input s is called the *seed*. The seed has many fewer bits than the generated pseudo-random output.

We will assume that a nonuniform secure pseudo-random number generator exists. It is widely believed that such generators exist. See [3,6,10] for additional results concerning such generators and possible candidate generators. In proving our results we will actually need a stronger but equivalent definition of pseudo-random number generator. See the appendix for details.

3. Codes and Channels

In order to present our results we need definitions of the notions of codes and channels. A *code* (E, D) consists of two parts: the *encoder* E and the *decoder* D. The first is a mapping from n-bit numbers to $m(n)$-bit numbers. The second is a mapping from $m(n)$-bit numbers to n-bit numbers. An n number x is called the *message* and the value $E(x)$ is called the *code word*. We always insist that for all x, $D(E(x)) = x$, i.e. in the presence of no errors the decoder gets the the correct message.

In order to avoid technical issues we assume that our codes are defined for all n. In many situations this may not be possible, i.e. the code may exist only when n is a number of some special type. All our results generalize to this and so we will concentrate on the easier situation where they exist for all n. Note, our codes are really "families" of codes in the usual sense [7,8]. The reason we need families is that arguments from computational complexity usually require asymptotic analysis. However, while our results are asymptotic they are practical; the implied constants are quite small.

A *channel* C with error probablity $p < 0.5$ is a random mapping from $m(n)$-bit numbers to $m(n)$-bit numbers. For each x, $C(x)$ is the result of sending x through the channel C. The only constraint on the channel is that the Hamming distance from x to $C(x)$ have binomial distribution, i.e. the probabilty that k bits of x are changed is distributed according to the binomial distribution. The places that are changed are the *errors*. Note, a channel is restricted to select the *number* of errors randomly, it is not restricted to select the places it changes randomly. It could select a random location and change k consecutive positions. It particular, we do not assume that a channel is memoryless.

A famous example of a channel is the *Binary Symmetric Channel* (BSC): For each bit i it flips an independent biased coin. With probability p it changes the ith bit and with probability $1 - p$ it does not. Clearly, the BSC is a channel in our sense

A channel is called *feasible* if its mapping is computable by a random polynomial-time computation. Clearly, the BSC is feasible for any fixed rational p: a random polynomial-time computation can simulate the flip of any biased coin. We will assume that p is rational from now on.

If (E, D) is a code and C is a channel, then the *success probability* is the minimum over all messages x of $Pr[D(C(E(x))) = x]$. This is the probability that the decoder correctly decodes messages. We of course are looking for a code (E, D) so that this probability is always near 1 for *any* feasible channel. Note, this is the new idea: in the classic situation one is looking for codes that work for any channel. We only are interested in feasible channnels.

Finally, the *rate* of a code is the ratio $n/m(n)$. Clearly, this is the measure of how many useful bits are contained in each code word.

4. Code Scrambling

Our goal in this section is to show how to transform any code that works for a BSC channel into one that works for feasible channels. The new code will be almost as easy to encode/decode as the original. This will be done by a method that we call "code scrambling". The idea of code scrambling is to "scramble" the bits in the code word so that it is difficult for the channel to tell which bits it should change. Essentially, the code words "look" random to a feasible channel; hence, its best strategy will be to randomly decide where to put its errors, i.e. act like a BSC.

In order to present our results we will first make the following assumption: we assume that the encoder and the decoder have access to a *common* source of random bits. That is, they both have access to the same sequence of random bits which the channel does not get to see. Of course in practice this is difficult to do, but it is a convenient way to initially present our results.

Suppose that (E, D) is a code. The *scrambled code* (E^*, D^*) is a new code that operates as follows: The encoder and decoder both select a random permutation π of $m(n)$ bits and a random vector r of $m(n)$ bits. Then, $E^*(x)$ is equal to $\pi(E(x)) + r$ where as usual the addition is modulo 2. Also $D^*(z)$ is equal to $D(\pi^{-1}(z + r))$. This works since both the encoder and the decoder know the permutation π and the vector r. Note, the time to encode the scrambled code is at most the time of the original code plus $O(m(n)\log(m(n)))$. The same is true for the decoder. Thus, if a code is easy to encode and decode, then so is its scrambled version. The scrambled code also, clearly, has the same rate as the original code.

The following theorem shows that the success probability of a scrambled code is easy to determine.

Theorem 1: *If (E, D) has success probability q for the BSC with error probability p, then the scrambled code (E^*, D^*) has success probability q for any channel with error probability p.*

Proof: Let C be any channel. Let x be a message. The channel is given z where $z = \pi(E(x)) + r$ and π is a random permutation and r is a random bit vector. Let $w(z)$ be the bit vector that corresponds to the error positions, i.e. $C(z) = z + w(z)$. Now the decoder receives this vector and computes

$$D(\pi^{-1}(z + w(z) + r)).$$

This is the same as

$$D(E(x) + \pi^{-1}(w(z))).$$

The key observation is that π and z are independent random values: fix π, clearly since each bit of z is flipped independently by r it is independent. Thus, $w(z)$ takes on patterns with the correct number of changes and π randomly permutes them. Therefore, the decoder essentially receives a value that has gone through a BSC. ∎

We next plan to remove the assumption that the encoder and the decoder share a common random coin by using pseudo-random number generators. However, it may be interesting to note that there *are* ways to share a random coin. For example, it is possible today to arrange for the encoder and the decoder to each have a CD-ROM filled with tens of billions of random bits. In this way we could construct codes that actually work for any channel at all. If messages are 100,000 bits long, then we could send tens of thousands of messages with a single CD-ROM.

Suppose that (E, D) is a code. The *pseudo-scrambled* code is (E^*, D^*) where now the permutation π and the vector r are generated by a pseudo-random number generator $G(s)$ where s is the seed. We further insist that the encoder/decoder both are polynomial time computations.

Theorem 2: *If (E, D) has success probability q for the BSC with error probability p, then pseudo-scrambled code (E^*, D^*) has success probability of $q + O(\epsilon)$ for any feasible channel with error probability p and any $\epsilon > 0$, for n large enough.*

Proof: Suppose that (E, D) is a code with success probability q and C is a feasible channel with error probability p. We need to carefully keep track of the uses of random bits. So let the encoder actually be $e(u, x)$ where u is all the random bits used and x is the message; let $d(u, z)$ be the decoder where u again is the random bits and z is the code word; and let $c(t, z)$ be the channel where t is the random bits and z is the code word. The random bits u encode both the permutation π and the vector r. Now conside the following predicate $A(u, t, x)$ defined as:

$$d(u, c(t, e(u, x))) = x.$$

$A(u, t, x)$ is true if and only if the message x is received correctly when the encoder/decoder use the random bits u and the channel uses the random bits t. We know that when the bits are all truly random by theorem 1, for all x

$$Pr[A(u,t,x)] = q.$$

Now replace the random bits used by the encoder/decoder by pseudo-randomly generated bits $G(s)$ where s is the random seed. Since the channel is feasible and so are the encoder/decoders, the predicate $A()$ is polynomial-time computable. Then, it must be the case for any $\epsilon > 0$ and large n,

$$Pr[A(G(s),t,x] = q + O(\epsilon).$$

If this was not true, the predicate $A(u,t,x)$ would be a pseudo-random test on which the generator fails. Note, we have used the stronger definition found in the appendix. ∎

Even with the use of a pseudo-random number generator, the encoder and decoder still need to select a random seed for each message. The point of the generator is that this seed is much smaller than the number of random bits they use. Note, also the ϵ is this theorem can actually be made to go to zero as $\frac{1}{n^c}$ for any $c > 1$.

We can do even better. Suppose that the encoder and decoder continue to use the same random seed for k messages in a row. That is, they continue to run the pseudo-random generator and get more pseudo-random bits from it. Then, provided k is at most polynomial in n, the conclusion of Theorem 2 is still valid. Thus, the probability of success for any feasible channel remains approximately q. The key to this is that the predicate $A()$ now becomes,

$$d(u^k, c(t, e(u^1, x^1), \ldots, e(u^k, x^k))) = x^k$$

where $x^1, \ldots, x^k$ are the k messages that are being sent. Note, the channel can now "remember" all the $k-1$ previous code words, and it can use this information in deciding what to do with the kth code word. Therefore, now the predicate $A()$ is true if and only if the kth message is received correctly even if the channel can remember all the previous $k-1$ messages. As long as k is not more than polynomial in n, the assumption that the pseudo-random number generator works implies that this predicate must be true with about probability q.

How many bits do the encoder and decoder need to agree on? The usual assumption allows the encoder and decoder to agree on n random bits as a seed and then send n^c messages without changing the seed where c is arbitrarily large. In practice one would expect that very small amounts of random bits would allow the encoder and decoder to operate essentially "forever".

5. A Good Code for Feasible Channels

In this section we show how to construct efficient codes that work well for any BSC. These codes all have good rates and are easy to encode and decode. Therefore, by Theorem 2, their pseudo-scrambled versions will be excellent codes for any feasible channel.

These codes are simple combination of known codes. They are not very interesting by themselves. The reason we present them is that they demonstrate the power of our theory. They are easy to construct codes that have good properties yet would normally not be considered interesting. While they work well with BSC's, they work poorly with arbitrary channels. Thus, without our new view of limiting consideration to feasible channels they would be of little interest. However, with our new model they are powerful codes.

Fix an error probability $p < 0.5$. We will now define our code. Note, we will not attempt to get the best bounds in order to avoid hiding the essential ideas. Let n be given and set k equal to $\alpha \log(n)$ where α is a constant to be determined. We further assume that k divides n: this is done to avoid technical statements. Our plan is to divide the message x of length n into n/k blocks of size k. We will encode each of them separately by the same code (E, D). This will be our code (E', D').

In order to complete the description of our code we need only supply the definition of the code (E, D). Before we do this however it may be helpful to make a few observations that hold for any (E, D). First, the encoding cost of our code is the cost of encoding n/k messages of length $\alpha \log(n)$. The same is true for the decoding cost. Thus, even if (E, D) is expensive to encode or decode since we are using it on very short messages the cost is much smaller for our code (E', D'). Second, if the code (E, D) has rate lower bounded by $r > 0$, then so does our code.

Finally, there is the question of the success probability of our code (E', D'). Suppose that (E, D) has a success probability of q for the BSC with error probability p. Then, it is *not* the case that our code has the same success probability q. The problem is that in order for our message to be correctly decoded *all* the blocks must be decoded correctly. The probability that all blocks are correctly decoded is $q^{n/k}$. Thus, in order for our code to work correctly we must have q quite close to 1.

There are many choices for the code (E, D). We will use the following. Let (E, D) be the code that corresponds to the usual Shannon method of a randomly selected block code [7,8]. Then, the encoding time for our code (E', D') is $O(n \log(n))$. Also we will decode our code by using the "brute force" decoder for the Shannon code: just try all the possible messages and take the most likely one. Since our blocks are $\alpha \log(n)$ long, this takes $n^{O(\alpha)}$ for each block. Thus, the total decoding time is at most $n^{1+O(\alpha)}$. For α small this is the bound claimed in the introduction. Of course the Shannon code has rate bounded below by $r > 0$ for some constant r.

It remains to discuss the success probability of our code. For the Shannon code the success can be arranged to be at least $1 - c^{-n}$ for any fixed $c > 1$. Thus, the probability that we make no errors in any blocks is

$$(1 - c^{-k})^{n/k}$$

which is upper bounded by $O(e^{-n/c^k})$. Since $k = \alpha \log(n)$, for any α and c large enough this is arbitrarily small as desired.

It may be interesting to note that the code (E', D') can be decoded in $O(\log\log(n))$ steps in parallel. This follows since each of the message bits depends only on $O(\log(n))$ bits.

A final remark about this code (E', D'). This code is very weak for a worst case channel. It can only handle $O(\log(n))$ worst case errors. Yet when it is scrambled, it can handle order n errors. This demonstrates the power of our whole approach. We have taken a simple code that usually would be considered weak and shown how to use it against any feasible channel.

6. Conclusions

The fundamental contribution of this work is to show that it is possible to change the way that we view the basic question of sending information over channel. In particular we can show that codes that are only good on "average" suffice for worst case performance provided the channel is restricted to be a feasible one. These methods have recently been used to show that one can give a "constructive" proof to Shannon's Theorem for any feasible channel [5].

Acknowledgement: I would like to thank Dan Boneh for many helpful conversations about this work.

References

[1] Babai, L., Fortnow L., Levin, L.A., Szegedy M. Checking computations in polylogarithmic time, in Proc. of the 23rd Annual Symp. on Theory of Computing, 21-31, 1991.

[2] Berelekamp, E.R. *Algebraic Coding Theory*. New York: McGraw-Hill, 1968.

[3] Blum, M. and Micali, S. How to generate cryptographically strong sequences of pseudo-random bits. IEEE FOCS 23,112-117, 1982.

[4] Diffie, W. and Hellman, M.E. New directions in cryptography. IEEE Trans. Info. Theory 22, 644-654, 1976.

[5] Lipton, R. On Coding for Noisy Feasible Channels, unpublished manuscript, 1993.

[6] Lagararias, J. C. *Pseudorandom Numbers* in Probability and Algorithms, National Research Council, 1992.

[7] MacWilliams, J., and Sloane, N.J.A. *The Theory of Error Correcting Codes.* (Elsevier, American ed.) Amsterdam: North-Holland, 1977.

[8] McEliece, R.J. *The Theory of Information and Coding.* Reading, Mass: Addison Wesley, 1977.

[9] Shannon, C.E. A mathematical theory of communication. Bell System Tech. J. 27,379-423 and 623-656, 1948.

[10] Dominic, W. *Codes and Cryptography* Oxford, 1988.

Appendix

In the proof of theorem 2 we argued that the predicate $A()$ was a pseudo-random test. However, the exact form of this test is not the same as the one used to define a pseudo-random number generator. What is needed is the following defintion. Let $T(x, y, z)$ be a circuit of size at most n^c for some constant $c > 0$. Each input x, y, z is n-bits long. Then, for n large enough, for all n-bit x,

$$|Pr_{y,z}[T(x,y,z)] - Pr_{y,s}[T(x,y,G(s))]| < \epsilon.$$

Here ϵ equals $\frac{1}{n^c}$. This is the defintion that is needed to prove the theorem. It appears to be stronger than the usual definition of a pseudo-random number generator. It is different in two ways. First, the test T is allowed to depend uniformly on x: in a sense it is not one test but a family of tests. Second, the test itself is allowed to be random. However, it is equivalent. Consider the following statements about a pseudo-random number generator. (In each we assume that ϵ equals $\frac{1}{n^c}$.)

Property 1: For each $c > 0$ and each family of circuits T_n of size at most n^c, for n large enough,

$$|Pr_z[T_n(z)] - Pr_s[T_n(G(s))]| < \epsilon.$$

Property 2: For each $c > 0$ and each n large enough, for all circuits T of size at most n^c,

$$|Pr_z[T(z)] - Pr_s[T(G(s))]| < \epsilon.$$

Property 3: For each $c > 0$ and each n large enough, for all circuits T of size at most n^c, for all n-bit x,

$$|Pr_z[T(x,z)] - Pr_s[T(x,G(s))]| < \epsilon.$$

Property 4: For each $c > 0$ and each n large enough, for all circuits T of size at most n^c, for all n-bit x,

$$|Pr_{y,z}[T(x,y,z)] - Pr_{y,s}[T(x,y,G(s))]| < \epsilon.$$

The usual definition of a pseudo-random number generator is of course property 1. We will now show that all the above are equivalent.

Suppose that the generator satisfies (1). Then, we first will prove that it satisfies (2). Suppose that it does not. Then, for each k there would be a circuit T_{n_k} with $n_k > k$ so that

$$|Pr_z[T_{n_k}(z)] - Pr_s[T_{n_k}(G(s))]| > \epsilon.$$

It is easy to see this implies that there is a family of circuits that contradicts (1).

Now assume that (2) is true and we will prove that (3) is true. Assume that (2) is true for all $n > k$. Then, if T does not satisfy (3), there must be an x so that

$$|Pr_z[T(x,z)] - Pr_s[T(x,G(s))]| > \epsilon.$$

But $T'(w) = T(x,w)$ is a circuit of size at most $n^c + n$ and so by (2), it follows that we have a contradiction.

We will now argue that if the generator satisfies (3) it must also satisfy (4). Let p_x be equal to $Pr_{y,z}[T(x,y,z)]$ and let q_x be equal to $Pr_{y,s}[T(x,y,G(s))]$. Then, by (3) for any $c > 0$ and n large enough, $|p_x - q_x| < \epsilon$. Now, (4) is equivalent to the following:

$$\frac{1}{2^n} \sum_x |p_x - q_x| < \epsilon.$$

But $|p_x - q_x| < \epsilon$ implies that this is true. Therefore (3) implies (4). Finally it is trivial to see that (4) implies (1) and so they all are equivalent as claimed.

Efficient Algorithms

On Voronoi Diagrams in the L_p-Metric in Higher Dimensions

Ngọc-Minh Lê [*]

Praktische Informatik VI, FernUniversität Hagen
D-58084 Hagen, Germany

Abstract

We prove upper bounds on the number of L_p-spheres passing through $D+1$ points in general position in D-space, and on the sum of the Betti numbers of the intersection of bisectors in the L_p-metric, where p is an even positive integer. The bounds found, surprisingly, do not depend on p. The proofs for these bounds involve the techniques of Milnor [14] and Thom [20] for finding bounds on the sum of the Betti numbers of algebraic varieties, but instead of the usual degree of polynomials we use their additive complexity, and apply results of Benedetti and Risler [2, 16]. Furthermore, using the theory of degree of mappings in D-space we prove that for even p the number of L_p-spheres passing through $D+1$ points in general position is odd. Combined with results in [10, 11], our results clarify the structure of Voronoi diagrams based on the L_p-metric (with even p) in 3-space.

1 Introduction

Voronoi diagrams based on the Euclidean metric in any dimension are well understood (see e.g. [6], an extensive survey and bibliography on this fundamental data structure can be found in [1]), but not much is known when more general distance functions, namely convex distance functions, are considered. An exception are planar Voronoi diagrams: Since in this case bisectors behave fully analogous to those in the Euclidean metric, they can still be computed with the same techniques [12, 4]. Recently, geometrical properties of bisectors based on smooth strictly convex distance functions, and their intersections, in 3-space have been clarified [10, 11].

The reason for the success in solving problems related to standard Voronoi diagrams in higher dimensions lies in their *linearity*: Bisectors are linear spaces, and so are their intersections. The situation in smooth strictly convex distance functions is much more different: Bisectors are no more linear spaces, and their intersections need not be connected [10, 11].

In this paper we consider smooth stricly convex distance functions, but we will devote more attention to the L_p-metrics with even $p \geq 2$, since these are immediate

---
[*]Email: ngoc-minh.le@fernuni-hagen.de. This work was partially supported by Deutsche Forschungsgemeinschaft, grant Kl 655/2-1.

generalization of the usual Euclidean metric. For odd p analogous results on upper bounds in the L_p-metric can also be obtained in a similar way.

First Problem. We want to estimate the complexity of Voronoi diagrams in the L_p-metric in $\mathbf{R}^D$. To simplify the discussion, take $D = 3$ and even p. Then the distance between two points x and y is given by $d_p(x, y) = ((x_1 - y_1)^p + \cdots + (x_3 - y_3)^p)^{1/p}$. Assume that the point sites are in general position. We must bound the number of vertices of the Voronoi diagram for four sites, or equivalently the number of L_p-spheres passing through the given points. Taking the p-powers of the distance functions above we reduce the problem to that of bounding the number of real solutions of a system of three polynomials of order $p - 1$. Our goal is to find a bound that is more favourable than the one of $(p - 1)^3$ derived from the Bézout's theorem, see e.g. [2, p. 299].

Second Problem. Given $D + 1$ points in general position in D-space, then one knows that there exists exactly one standard sphere passing through the given points. Does the analogy hold in the L_p-metric?

Our Results to the First Problem. We will show that for points in general position there is an upper bound *independent of p* to the number of L_p-spheres passing through them. In fact, we will prove more general results in D-space by using another kind of measure for complexity, namely the *Betti numbers*. Let us take a closer look to these.

The Betti numbers have their origin in the so-called "connectivity number" for a compact surface. Consider a closed curve C in a compact surface M. If the curve C equals the boundary of a face contained in M, then we say that C *bounds* in M. Now let $C_1, \ldots, C_k$ be closed curves in M. If the *sum*, i.e. the union, of $C_1, \ldots, C_k$ is identical to the boundary of a face or a union of faces in M, then we say like above that the sum of $C_1, \ldots, C_k$ *bounds* in M. Let n be the maximal number of closed curves $C_1, \ldots, C_n$ such that no C_i bounds in M, but for any other curve C' either C' itself or the sum of C' and some of $C_1, \ldots, C_n$ bounds in M. Then the number n is called the *connectivity number* of M. Examples: The connectivity number of a disk with h holes is h, and of a torus is 2.

For topological spaces or manifolds with dimension ≥ 2 one generalizes the connectivity number to k^{th} Betti number by replacing curves by appropriate k-dimensional submanifolds. Of course, the 1st Betti number is just the connectivity number. See [9] for further details.

The kth Betti number is the number of appropriate k-dimensional submanifolds ("k-cycles") of M that do *not* bound in M, it is therefore a kind of measure for the geometric complexity of M.

We will show that the Betti number of intersections of L_p-bisectors for point sites in general position is bounded above by a constant that depends only on the space dimension. Our proofs involve results of Milnor and Thom [14, 20] in algebraic geometry, and results of Benedetti and Risler [16, 2] on additive complexity of multivariate polynomials. The results of Benedetti and Risler substantially improve and generalize the results of Borodin and Cook [3].

In particular, our results imply that in D-space the complexity of the Voronoi diagram of n point sites in general position in the L_p-metric can be bounded by $O(n^c)$ — independent of p — for some $c \in \mathsf{N}$ (depending on D).

Our Results to the Second Problem. We will show that an analogy to the Euclidean metric holds, namely, the number of L_p-spheres (with even p) passing through $D + 1$ points in general position in $\mathbf{R}^D$ is an *odd* number. To this end, we compute the *algebraic number* of such spheres. This number seems to have some impact on algorithms for computing Voronoi diagrams in the L_p-metric, because the algebraic number mentioned is a numerical *invariant*; see Subsection 4.2 for a geometrical interpretation.

Let us briefly describe the algebraic number or *degree* associated to a continuous mapping $f : \Omega \to \mathbf{R}^D$. Assume that f is differentiable and y is a regular value of f, then the *degree of f (on Ω over y)* is defined to be the number of points in $f^{-1}(y)$ at which the linearization of f, i.e. the Jacobian matrix of f, preserves the orientation minus the number of points in $f^{-1}(y)$ at which the linearization reverses the orientation. The degree is therefore also called the *algebraic number* of solutions of the equation $f(x) = y$. One important property of degree is that whenever the degree of f (over y) differs from 0 then the equation $f(x) = y$ has at least one solution. For this reason the degree is one important tool widely used in nonlinear analysis for proving the existence of solutions of the equation $f(x) = y$, see [17].

Related Works. Deep results of Sharir [18, 19] imply that the combinatorial complexity of the Voronoi diagram in the L_p-metric of a set of n points sites in D-space is $O(n^{D+\epsilon})$, for any $\epsilon > 0$. But the constant in this bound tends to ∞ as $p \to \infty$. Thus, keeping n fixed our bound is more favourable for large p.

Makeev [13] has shown in a context quite different from ours that, given $D + 1$ linear independent points and a smooth convex body in D-space, there exists always a body homothetic to the given one so that its boundary passes through the given points. His proof is geometrical and is based on a similar kind of degree of mapping.

Implications. In particular, our results provide a clear picture of the geometrical structure of bisectors and their intersections based on the L_p-metric in 3-space: (1) Bisectors are homeomorphic to a plane (indeed, bisector is graph of a smooth real-valued function defined on a plane). They intersect in a single curve homeomorphic to a line [10, 11]. (2) The number N of L_p-spheres passing through 4 points in general position is odd — N may be > 1, see [10]. There exists a constant C that does not depend on p such that $N \leq C$.

The rest of this paper is organized as follows. Section 2 introduces the basic definitions, among them the important notion of "in general position" for points sites with respect to a smooth convex distance function, further we state there a key result needed in Sections 3 and 4. Section 3 is devoted to the upper bounds for the Betti number of L_p-bisector intersections. In Section 4 we compute the algebraic number of L_p-spheres passing though points in general position. Conclusions and open problems are discussed in Section 5.

2   Preliminaries

We now recall the definition of the L_p-metric in D dimensions. Let p be a real number with $1 \leq p < \infty$, and let x, $y \in \mathbf{R}^D$ with coordinates $(x_1, \ldots, x_D)$ and $(y_1, \ldots, y_D)$, respectively. Then the distance between x and y in the L_p-metric, denoted by $d_p(x, y)$, is defined to be $d_p(x, y) = (|x_1 - y_1|^p + \cdots + |x_D - y_D|^p)^{1/p}$. The L_p-*sphere* with center y and radius $R > 0$ is the set of all $x \in \mathbf{R}^D$ such that $d_p(x, y) = R$.

Let $d(\cdot, \cdot)$ denote a smooth strictly convex distance function in D-space. The concept of *Voronoi diagram* for convex distance functions in D dimensions can be defined analogously to the case of L_2-metric, see [4, 6]. For any two distinct points s and t in $\mathbf{R}^D$ we call the *bisector* of s and t the set $B(s, t) = \{x \in \mathbf{R}^D \mid d(x, s) = d(x, t)\}$. In the special case of the L_p-metric with even p, one can easily prove that $B(s, t)$ is a $(D-1)$-dimensional submanifold of $\mathbf{R}^D$. In fact, the gradient (with respect to x) of the polynomial $d_p(x, s)^p - d_p(x, t)^p$, whose zero set yields the bisector $B(s, t)$, does not vanish whenever $s \neq t$. Therefore the zero set of $d_p(x, s)^p - d_p(x, t)^p$ is a $(D-1)$-dimensional manifold. More generally, it can be shown [11] that for smooth strictly convex distance functions in D dimensions bisectors are $(D-1)$-dimensional hypersurfaces homeomorphic to a hyperplane, and that they intersect in a smooth surface homeomorphic to a $(D-2)$-dimensional linear space.

Let S be a finite set of points in D-space. For each $s \in S$ the set $VR(s) = \{x \in \mathbf{R}^D \mid d(x, s) < d(x, t) \text{ for each } t \in S \setminus \{s\}\}$ is called the *Voronoi region* of s. Now let $S = \{s^{(1)}, \ldots, s^{(N)}\}$, then the tuple $(s^{(1)}, \ldots, s^{(N)}) \in (\mathbf{R}^D)^N$ is called an N-*configuration*; note that another indexing of the N given points will yield another N-configuration, all N-configurations having the same set of components are considered as being equivalent. Let $T = \{t^{(1)}, \ldots, t^{(M)}\}$ be a subset of S. By $B(T)$ or $B(t^{(1)}, \ldots, t^{(M)})$ we denote the set of all $x \in \mathbf{R}^D$ having equal distances to the points of T, i.e., $B(T) = \{x \in \mathbf{R}^D \mid d(x, t^{(1)}) = \cdots = d(x, t^{(M)})\}$. We say that the points $s^{(1)}, \ldots, s^{(N)}$ are *in general position* or *non-degenerate (with respect to the metric d)*, if for any subsets T of S, any $q \in S$ but $\notin T$, and any $t \in T$ the sets $B(T)$ and $B(t, q)$ intersect *transversely* in $\mathbf{R}^D$, i.e., at every point of $B(T) \cap B(t, q)$ the tangents to $B(T)$ and $B(t, q)$ span the whole $\mathbf{R}^D$. Note that if $B(T)$ is a finite set of points, then its tangents are 0-dimensional vector spaces, so the only way for $B(T)$ and $B(t, q)$ to intersect transversely is that $B(T) \cap B(t, q) = \emptyset$.

In the L_2-metric in 3-space the usual definition of points being in general position is that no five points are cospherical and no four points are cocircular. Our definition of points being in general position generalizes this definition to smooth strictly convex distance functions. This claim follows by observing that in the L_2-metric the bisector of two points p and q is the plane passing through the middle of the segment pq and perpendicular to pq. But in the general case of metrics different from the L_2-metric, our definition of "in general position" still needs a formal justification: The sets of configurations of N distinct points $\in \mathbf{R}^D$ being "in general position" should be very large. Indeed, the following result [11] justifies our definition:

Theorem 1 *Let d be a smooth strictly convex distance function in $\mathbf{R}^D$. Then the set $\mathcal{G} \subset (\mathbf{R}^D)^N$ of N-configurations being in general position (with respect to the metric d) is dense in $(\mathbf{R}^D)^N$. Moreover, the complementary set of $\mathcal{G}$ in $(\mathbf{R}^D)^N$ has measure zero, if it is measurable.*

The result above says that "almost all" sets of N distinct points in $\mathbf{R}^D$ have the property of being in general position. Note that if only $D + 1$ points (among the N points being in general position) are considered, then we can in addition assume that they are linear independent.

Let S be a set of points in general position, and let $T \subset S$ with $|T| \geq 2$. The following claims follow directly from the definition of general position. If $|T| \leq D + 1$ then $B(T)$ is either a manifold with the dimension $D + 1 - |T|$ or an empty set. If

$|T| > D + 1$ then $B(T) = \emptyset$. A *K-face* of the Voronoi region of s is a K-dimensional maximal connected subset of $B(T)$ with $|T| = D + 1 - K$ that bounds $VR(s)$. We use *vertex* and *edge* to denote 0- and 1-face, respectively. Clearly, vertices of the Voronoi diagram $V(S)$ are contained in $B(T)$ for $|T| = D + 1$, edges of $V(S)$ are subsets of $B(T)$ for $|T| = D$. Thus, if we assume that the points of S are in general position, then by the discussion above, in order to construct the faces of a Voronoi region we need to investigate only the sets $B(T)$ with $|T| \leq D + 1$.

We restrict our investigation to the L_p-metrics with even p, because for odd $p > 2$ analogous results on upper bounds can be derived in a similar manner. In fact, in that case — although we must deal with *semi*-algebraic sets — the additional number of polynomials to be considered depends only on D but not on p.

For simplicity, from now on we will write d to denote the L_p-metric — instead of d_p. Let $S = \{s^{(1)}, \ldots, s^{(K+1)}\}$ be a set of $K + 1$ points in $\mathbf{R}^D$ (where $K \geq 1$). Define $f_1(x) = d(x, s^{(1)})^p - d(x, s^{(K+1)})^p, \ldots, f_K(x) = d(x, s^{(K)})^p - d(x, s^{(K+1)})^p$. Then clearly $B(s^{(1)}, \ldots, s^{(K+1)})$ is the zero set of the polynomial system $f_1 = 0, \ldots, f_K = 0$. Using the definition of $d(\cdot, \cdot)$ we obtain

$$
\begin{aligned}
f_1(x) \quad = \quad & (x_1 - s_1^{(1)})^p + \cdots + (x_D - s_D^{(1)})^p \\
& - (x_1 - s_1^{(K+1)})^p - \cdots - (x_D - s_D^{(K+1)})^p.
\end{aligned}
\tag{1}
$$

We obtain analogous expressions for $f_2, \ldots, f_K$.

3 Bounding the Complexity of Voronoi Diagrams in the L_p-Metric

3.1 Additive Complexity of Multivariate Polynomials

The notion of "additive complexity" of a real multivariate polynomial was generalized from the univariate case (Borodin and Cook [3]) by Risler [16] as follows — see also [2, Definition 4.3.1].

Let P be a real polynomial in D variables. If P is a monomial then the *additive complexity* of P is defined to be zero. Otherwise we can find a positive integer k and expressions $S_1, \ldots, S_{k+1}$ having the following form

$$
\left\{
\begin{aligned}
S_1 \quad &= \quad c_1 \quad + \quad x^{\alpha_1} \\
S_2 \quad &= \quad c_2 \quad + \quad x^{\alpha_2} S_1^{a_{1,2}} \\
&\quad \vdots \\
S_k \quad &= \quad c_k \quad + \quad x^{\alpha_k} \prod_{i=1}^{k-1} S_i^{a_{i,k}} \\
S_{k+1} \quad &= \quad c_{k+1} \quad \times \quad x^{\alpha_{k+1}} \prod_{i=1}^{k} S_i^{a_{i,k+1}}
\end{aligned}
\right.
\tag{2}
$$

with real numbers c_i, integers $a_{i,j}$, and multi-indices $\alpha_i \in \mathbf{Z}^D$ such that $P = S_{k+1}$ after successive eliminating the S_i for $i = 1, \ldots, k$. Then we define the *additive complexity* of P to be the minimum of such k's, and denote it by $L_+(P)$.

The following theorem was proved by Benedetti and Risler, see [16] and [2, Proposition 4.3.3]. It is a substantial improvement and generalization of results of Borodin and Cook [3], it shows that the notion of additive complexity is as useful as the ordinary degree used in the Bézout's theorem for bounding the number of solutions of polynomial systems.

Theorem 2 *Let* $P_1, \ldots, P_D$ *be real polynomials in* D *variables* $x_1, \ldots, x_D$. *Let* N *be the number of non-degenerate solutions of the system*

$$P_1(x_1, \ldots, x_D) = 0, \quad \ldots, \quad P_D(x_1, \ldots, x_D) = 0 .$$

Then we have $N \leq 2^A(A+1)^B 2^{B(B-1)/2}$ *where* $A = D + \sum_{i=1}^{D} L_+(P_i)$ *and* $B = D + 2\sum_{i=1}^{D} L_+(P_i)$. $\quad\square$

In order to apply Theorem 2 we have to estimate the additive complexity of polynomials defining bisectors in the L_p-metric. The following lemma provides useful rules for getting bounds on additive complexity of expressions that are composed of polynomials whose additive complexities are known.

Lemma 3 *Let* $P, P_1, \ldots, P_n$ *and* Q *be real polynomials. Let* m *be a non-negative integer. Then* $L_+(P_1 + \cdots + P_n) \leq n - 1 + L_+(P_1) + \cdots + L_+(P_n)$, $L_+(P^m) \leq L_+(P)$, *and* $L_+(PQ) \leq L_+(P) + L_+(Q)$.

Proof. The claims follow immediately from the definition of additive complexity. $\quad\square$

Given $u, v \in \mathbf{R}^D$ with $u \neq v$, we know that the bisector $B(u,v)$ of u and v in the L_p-metric is the zero set of the following polynomial having the same form as (1):

$$f = (x_1 - u_1)^p + \cdots + (x_D - u_D)^p - (x_1 - v_1)^p - \cdots - (x_D - v_D)^p . \tag{3}$$

Lemma 4 *The additive complexity of* f *is at most* $4D - 1$.

Proof. From Lemma 3 and the fact that the additive complexity of a constant or a monomial is zero, we have $L_+((x_i - u_i)^p) \leq 1$ and $L_+(-(x_i - v_i)^p) \leq 1$. The claim follows by applying the first rule of Lemma 3 to f. $\quad\square$

3.2 L_p-Metric

We point out that the assumption of non-degeneracy in the following theorem — which is required in order to apply Theorem 2 — is meaningful by Theorem 1.

Theorem 5 *For any* $D+1$ *points in* $\mathbf{R}^D$ *being in general position the number of* L_p-*spheres passing through the given points is bounded by a constant depending only on the dimension* D *but not on* p.

Proof. Let $s^{(1)}, \ldots, s^{(D+1)}$ be the given points. Then the centers of the L_p-spheres passing through them are the solutions of the following system of polynomial equations:

$$f_1(x_1, \ldots, x_D) = 0, \quad \ldots, \quad f_D(x_1, \ldots, x_D) = 0 \tag{4}$$

where each f_i has the same form as the polynomial (3). Let N_1 be the number of solutions of (4), then by Theorem 2 we have $N_1 \leq 2^A(A+1)^B 2^{B(B-1)/2}$ where $A = D + \sum_{i=1}^{D} L_+(P_i) \leq 4D^2$, and $B = D + 2\sum_{i=1}^{D} L_+(P_i) \leq D(8D-1)$. $\quad\square$

From the result above, combined with results in [11], it follows that in D-space the complexity of the Voronoi diagram of n points in general position in the L_p-metric is bounded by $O(n^c)$ where the exponent c and the factor do not depend on p (but on D). We omit the details.

Theorem 6 *For any set of $K+1$ points $s^{(1)}, \ldots, s^{(K+1)}$ in $\mathbf{R}^D$ the sum of the Betti numbers of $B(s^{(1)}, \ldots, s^{(K+1)})$ is bounded by a constant depending only on K and the space dimension D but not on p.*

Proof. In deriving the equation system whose number of zeros determine the upper bound to the sum of the Betti numbers to the algebraic variety $B(s^{(1)}, \ldots, s^{(K+1)})$, we will essentially follow [14] and [2]. For $i = 1, \ldots, K$ let f_i be the polynomial defining the bisector $B(s^{(i)}, s^{(K+1)})$, see (1). We assign to $f_1, \ldots, f_K$ the function $F = f_1^2 + \cdots + f_K^2 + \alpha(x_1^2 + \cdots + x_D^2) - \beta$. For any line L let π_L denote the orthogonal projection from $\mathbf{R}^D$ onto L. Then (see [14]) there exist $\alpha, \beta > 0$ and a line L such that the zero-set $F^{-1}(0)$ of F is a compact hypersurface in $\mathbf{R}^D$, and such that the restriction of π_L to $F^{-1}(0)$ is a Morse function, i.e., all its critical points are non-degenerate. (A critical point p of a function φ is *non-degenerate* if there are coordinates near p such that $\varphi(x_1, \ldots, x_D) = \varphi(p) - x_1^2 - \cdots - x_k^2 + x_{k+1}^2 + \cdots + x_D^2$ for some k.)

Let N_2 denote the sum of the Betti numbers of $B(s^{(1)}, \ldots, s^{(K+1)})$, then it can be shown [14] that $N_2 \leq (\# \text{ critical points of } \pi_L)/2$. Let $\lambda^{(1)}, \ldots, \lambda^{(D-1)}$ denote linear independent vectors orthogonal to the line L. Then clearly the critical points of π_L are solutions of the system

$$\begin{cases} F & = & 0 \\ G_1 & := & \lambda^{(1)} \operatorname{grad} F & = & 0 \\ & & \vdots \\ G_{D-1} & := & \lambda^{(D-1)} \operatorname{grad} F & = & 0 \end{cases}$$

where $\operatorname{grad} F$ denotes the gradient of F. This system is equivalent to

$$\begin{cases} F & = & f_1^2 + \cdots + f_K^2 + \alpha(x_1^2 + \cdots + x_D^2) - \beta & = & 0 \\ G_1 & = & \lambda_1^{(1)} \partial F/\partial x_1 & + \cdots + & \lambda_D^{(1)} \partial F/\partial x_D & = & 0 \\ & & \vdots \\ G_{D-1} & = & \lambda_1^{(D-1)} \partial F/\partial x_1 & + \cdots + & \lambda_D^{(D-1)} \partial F/\partial x_D & = & 0 \end{cases} \tag{5}$$

Since π_L is a Morse function, solutions of (5) are non-degenerate. Thus we can apply Theorem 2 to get an explicit upper bound for the number of solutions of (5). We need estimates for the additive complexity of F and $G_1, \ldots, G_{D-1}$.

To estimate $L_+(F)$ we first bound the additive complexity of each term of the expression for F in (5). From $L_+(f_i) \leq 4D - 1$ we see that $L_+(f_i^2) \leq 4D - 1$. Using Lemma 3 and these estimates we easily get $L_+(f_1^2 + \cdots + f_K^2) \leq 4KD - 1$. Further, $L_+(\alpha(x_1^2 + \cdots + x_D^2)) \leq D - 1$. Therefore $L_+(F) \leq 2 + L_+(f_1^2 + \cdots + f_K^2) + L_+(\alpha(x_1^2 + \cdots + x_D^2)) + L_+(\beta) \leq 4KD + D$.

Next we bound the additive complexity of $G_1, \ldots, G_{D-1}$ in (5). To this end, we compute the partial derivative of F with respect to x_i with $i = 1, \ldots, D$, and obtain $\partial F/\partial x_i = 2f_1 \partial f_1/\partial x_i + \cdots + 2f_K \partial f_K/\partial x_i + 2\alpha x_i$ where $f_1, \ldots, f_K$ have the same form as (3). Thus

$$\begin{aligned} \partial F/\partial x_i = \quad & 2f_1 \cdot \left(p(x_i - s_1^{(1)})^{p-1} - p(x_i - s_1^{(K+1)})^{p-1} \right) \\ + \quad & \vdots \\ + \quad & 2f_K \cdot \left(p(x_i - s_1^{(K)})^{p-1} - p(x_i - s_1^{(K+1)})^{p-1} \right) \\ + \quad & 2\alpha x_i \, . \end{aligned}$$

From this expression, using the additive complexity bounds for $f_1, \ldots, f_K$ derived before, we obtain $L_+(\partial F/\partial x_i) \leq K(4D+3)$ for $i = 1, \ldots, D$.

Using the estimates for $L_+(\partial F/\partial x_1), \ldots, L_+(\partial F/\partial x_D)$ just derived and the expression for G_i in (5) we find that $L_+(G_i) \leq KD(4D+3) + (D-1)$ for $i = 1, \ldots, D-1$. By Theorem 2 we obtain $N_2 \leq 2^A(A+1)^B 2^{B(B-1)/2}/2$ where

$$A = D + L_+(F) + \sum_{i=1}^{D-1} L_+(G_i) \quad \leq KD(4D^2 - D + 1) + D^2 + 1, \quad \text{and}$$

$$B = D + 2L_+(F) + 2\sum_{i=1}^{D-1} L_+(G_i) \leq KD(8D^2 - 2D + 2) + 2D^2 - D + 2. \qquad \square$$

Corollary 7 *For any set of $K+1$ points $s^{(1)}, \ldots, s^{(K+1)}$ in $\mathbf{R}^D$ the number of connected components of $B(s^{(1)}, \ldots, s^{(K+1)})$ is bounded by a constant depending only on K and D but not on p.*

Proof. The claim follows from Theorem 6 and the fact that the 0th Betti number of a topological space is the number of its connected components [9]. $\qquad \square$

Remark. The bound to N_1 given in the proof of Theorem 5 is much sharper than that obtained by using the bound for N_2 (with $K = D$) in the proof of Theorem 6.

4 Existence of L_p-Spheres Passing Through $D+1$ Points of D-Space

4.1 Degree of Continuous Mappings

Let Ω be an open and bounded subset of $\mathbf{R}^D$. Let $C(\overline{\Omega})$ denote the set of all continuous functions $f : \overline{\Omega} \to \mathbf{R}^D$. Let $C^k(\Omega)$ denote the set of all k-times continuous differentiable functions $f : \Omega \to \mathbf{R}^D$. Further we set $\overline{C}^k(\Omega) = C(\overline{\Omega}) \cap C^k(\Omega)$. If $f \in C^1(\Omega)$, then $f'(x)$ denotes the Jacobian matrix of f at $x \in \Omega$. The determinant of f' — the Jacobian determinant of f — is denoted by $J_f(x)$. Let N_f denote the set of critical points of f, i.e., points at which the Jacobian of f vanishes.

In the special case when $f \in \overline{C}^1(\Omega)$ and $y \notin f(\partial\Omega \cup N_f)$ at each $x \in f^{-1}(y)$ the Jacobian $J_f(x)$ does not vanish, so the *degree of f on Ω over y* is the integer

$$\deg(f, \Omega, y) := \sum_{x \in f^{-1}(y)} \text{sign } J_f(x), \quad \text{with the convention } \sum_{\emptyset} = 0. \qquad (6)$$

In the general case when $f \in C(\overline{\Omega})$ the *degree of f on Ω over y* is defined by reducing to the special case as follows. First we approximate f by functions $g \in \overline{C}^2(\Omega)$ that are sufficient close to f. If $y \notin N_g$ then we define $\deg(f, \Omega, y) = \deg(g, \Omega, y)$ where $\deg(g, \Omega, y)$ is given by Formula (6). Otherwise $y \in N_g$. We take $z \in \Omega$ sufficiently close to y and such that $z \notin N_g$. We then define $\deg(f, \Omega, y) = \deg(g, \Omega, z)$ where $\deg(g, \Omega, z)$ is defined by (6).

The degree defined above does not depend on the approximating g and z, see [17].

Lemma 8 *If the mapping $\Phi : [0,1] \times \overline{\Omega} \to \mathbf{R}^D$ is continuous and $y \notin \Phi(t, \partial\Omega)$ for every $t \in [0,1]$. Then $\deg(\Phi(t, \cdot), \Omega, y)$ is constant on $[0,1]$.*

Proof. See e.g. [17, Theorem 3.16(1)]. $\qquad \square$

For the proofs of the main results of the next subsection we need the following lemmas.

Lemma 9 *Let Ω be an open and bounded subset of* $\mathbf{R}^D$. *Let* $h, \delta \in C(\overline{\Omega})$ *such that* $|\delta(x)| < |h(x)|$ *for all* $x \in \partial\Omega$. *Then* $\deg(h + \delta, \Omega, 0) = \deg(h, \Omega, 0)$.

Proof. The lemma follows from Lemma 8. □

Lemma 10 *If y and z belong to the same connected component of* $\mathbf{R}^D \setminus f(\partial\Omega)$, *then* $\deg(f, \Omega, y) = \deg(f, \Omega, z)$.

Proof. See [17, Theorem 3.16(4)]. □

4.2 The Algebraic Number of L_p-Spheres Passing Through $D + 1$ Points of D-Space

For convenience we fix $D = 3$. But all results hold for arbitrary D, the proofs for the general case are similar to that for the special case. Let $S = \{s, t, u, v\}$ be a set of points in $\mathbf{R}^3$ being in general position. The bisectors $B(s, v)$, $B(t, v)$ and $B(u, v)$ are the zero sets of the following polynomials (analogous to polynomial (1)), respectively: $f_1(x) = d(x, s)^p - d(x, v)^p$, $f_2(x) = d(x, t)^p - d(x, v)^p$, and $f_3(x) = d(x, u)^p - d(x, v)^p$.

The degree of $f = (f_1, f_2, f_3)$ over 0 can be given a geometrical interpretation as follows. Consider the system $f_1 = 0, f_2 = 0$, and $f_3 = 0$ whose zeros yield the set $B(s, t, u, v)$. Observe that the bisector $B(s, v)$ is the zero set of $f_1 = 0$, and that $B(t, u, v)$ is the zero set of the system $f_2 = 0, f_3 = 0$. Hence $B(s, t, u, v)$ is the intersection of the bisector surface $B(s, v)$ and the curve $B(t, u, v)$. Let us see how the orientation of $B(s, v)$ and $B(t, u, v)$ are related to the Jacobian determinant used in the definition of degree. At each point in $B(s, v) \cap B(t, u, v)$ the Jacobian determinant of f is the scalar product of the tangent vector to $B(t, u, v)$ and the normal to $B(s, v)$. By the general position assumption these scalar products do not vanish. Hence the degree is the algebraic number of points in $B(s, v) \cap B(t, u, v)$, where each point is counted with appropriate signs determined by orientations of $B(s, v)$ and $B(t, u, v)$.

Wlog assume that $v = 0$. Expanding f_1 and because the monomials with exponents p cancel out, we obtain $f_1(x) = \sum_{\nu=1}^{p} b_\nu(s_1^\nu x_1^{p-\nu} + s_2^\nu x_2^{p-\nu} + s_3^\nu x_3^{p-\nu})$ where we put the binomial coefficient $(-1)^\nu \binom{p}{\nu} = b_\nu$. We have analogous expressions for f_2 and f_3.

Theorem 11 *The algebraic number of L_p-spheres passing through $D + 1$ points in general position is either* 1 *or* -1.

For simplicity we fix $D = 3$. The proof for the general case is analogous. The idea of the proof is as follows. We decompose each f_i (with $i = 1, 2, 3$) into the sum of a term h_i consisting of monomials having highest exponent $p - 1$ and a remainder δ_i containing monomials having exponents $< p - 1$. The polynomials h_i are given by

$$
\begin{aligned}
h_1(x) &= b_1(s_1 x_1^{p-1} + s_2 x_2^{p-1} + s_3 x_3^{p-1}) \\
h_2(x) &= b_1(t_1 x_1^{p-1} + t_2 x_2^{p-1} + t_3 x_3^{p-1}) \\
h_3(x) &= b_1(u_1 x_1^{p-1} + u_2 x_2^{p-1} + u_3 x_3^{p-1})
\end{aligned}
\tag{7}
$$

and the polynomials δ_i are given by

$$
\begin{aligned}
\delta_1(x) &= \sum_{\nu=2,\ldots,p} b_\nu(s_1^\nu x_1^{p-\nu} + s_2^\nu x_2^{p-\nu} + s_3^\nu x_3^{p-\nu}) \\
\delta_2(x) &= \sum_{\nu=2,\ldots,p} b_\nu(t_1^\nu x_1^{p-\nu} + t_2^\nu x_2^{p-\nu} + t_3^\nu x_3^{p-\nu}) \\
\delta_3(x) &= \sum_{\nu=2,\ldots,p} b_\nu(u_1^\nu x_1^{p-\nu} + u_2^\nu x_2^{p-\nu} + u_3^\nu x_3^{p-\nu})
\end{aligned}
\tag{8}
$$

Now the mapping f on $\mathbf{R}^3$ can be considered as the perturbation of a principal term $h : \mathbf{R}^3 \to \mathbf{R}^3$ with $h(x) := (h_1(x), h_2(x), h_3(x))$ by a "small" term $\delta : \mathbf{R}^3 \to \mathbf{R}^3$ given by $\delta(x) = (\delta_1(x), \delta_2(x), \delta_3(x))$. Here "small" is understood in a sense such that Lemma 9 is applicable. We need two lemmas for proving the theorem above.

Lemma 12 *For each $\rho > 0$ we have $|deg\,(h, B_\rho, 0)| = 1$.*

Proof. We will compute $|\deg\,(h, B_\rho, 0)|$ by using (6) and Lemma 10. To this end, we prove first that the mapping h is a homeomorphism on $\mathbf{R}^D$.

Clearly h is continuous. We prove that h is bijective. For each $y = (y_1, y_2, y_3) \in \mathbf{R}^3$ the equation $h(x) = y$ can be solved uniquely as follows. We first consider this equation as a linear equation system for the unknowns x_1^{p-1}, x_2^{p-1} and x_3^{p-1}. Now the matrix corresponding to this linear equation system is

$$\mathcal{D} = \begin{pmatrix} s_1 & s_2 & s_3 \\ t_1 & t_2 & t_3 \\ u_1 & u_2 & u_3 \end{pmatrix} \tag{9}$$

By the general position assumption we have $\det \mathcal{D} \neq 0$. Therefore this linear system is uniquely solvable. Moreover, since x_1^{p-1}, x_2^{p-1} and x_3^{p-1} have odd exponents, we can uniquely compute x_1, x_2 and x_3. Thus the mapping h is bijective. Applying the Domain Invariance Theorem, see e.g. [17, Corollary 3.22], the mapping h is a homeomorphism.

We are applying Lemma 10. Take y with $|y|$ sufficiently small such that y and 0 are still contained in the same connected component of $\mathbf{R}^3 \setminus h(\partial B_\rho)$ and such that none of the coordinates of $x = h^{-1}(y)$ vanishes; since h is a homeomorphism, such a y exists. By Lemma 10 we have

$$\deg\,(h, B_\rho, 0) = \deg\,(h, B_\rho, y). \tag{10}$$

From (7) we see that $h'(x) = (p-1)^3 b_1^3 x_1^{p-2} x_2^{p-2} x_3^{p-2} \mathcal{D}$. Because of the special choice of y the Jacobian matrix $h'(x)$ is non-singular. Thus the right hand side of (10) can be computed by using (6), it follows that $\deg\,(h, B_\rho, y) = \text{sign}\,J_h(x)$. □

Remark. Since B_ρ is symmetric and h is an odd mapping, i.e. $h(x) = -h(-x)$, Borsuk's theorem (see e.g. [17, Theorem 3.23]) implies that $\deg\,(h, B_\rho, 0)$ is an odd number. But we need the exact value of $\deg\,(h, B_\rho, 0)$.

Lemma 13 *For all sufficient large $\rho > 0$ we have $deg\,(h + \delta, B_\rho, 0) = deg\,(h, B_\rho, 0)$.*

Proof. For nonzero $x \in \mathbf{R}^3$ we can write uniquely $x = |x|(x/|x|)$, thus we may define the transformation $x = \rho n$ where $\rho > 0$ and $n = (n_1, n_2, n_3) \in \mathbf{R}^3$ with $|n| = 1$. After replacing in (7) x_1 by ρn_1, x_2 by ρn_2, and x_3 by ρn_3 the components of h become

$$\begin{aligned} h_1(x) &= b_1 \rho^{p-1}(s_1 n_1^{p-1} + s_2 n_2^{p-1} + s_3 n_3^{p-1}) \\ h_2(x) &= b_1 \rho^{p-1}(t_1 n_1^{p-1} + t_2 n_2^{p-1} + t_3 n_3^{p-1}) \\ h_3(x) &= b_1 \rho^{p-1}(u_1 n_1^{p-1} + u_2 n_2^{p-1} + u_3 n_3^{p-1}) \end{aligned} \tag{11}$$

Analogously, after applying the transformation $x = \rho n$ to δ given by (8) we obtain

$$\begin{aligned} \delta_1(x) &= \sum_{\nu=2,\ldots,p} b_\nu \rho^{p-\nu}(s_1^\nu n_1^{p-\nu} + s_2^\nu n_2^{p-\nu} + s_3^\nu n_3^{p-\nu}) \\ \delta_2(x) &= \sum_{\nu=2,\ldots,p} b_\nu \rho^{p-\nu}(t_1^\nu n_1^{p-\nu} + t_2^\nu n_2^{p-\nu} + t_3^\nu n_3^{p-\nu}) \\ \delta_3(x) &= \sum_{\nu=2,\ldots,p} b_\nu \rho^{p-\nu}(u_1^\nu n_1^{p-\nu} + u_2^\nu n_2^{p-\nu} + u_3^\nu n_3^{p-\nu}) \end{aligned} \tag{12}$$

To apply Lemma 9, we will show that $|\delta| < |h|$, or equivalently that $h^2 - \delta^2 > 0$ for all points on the sphere with center 0 having sufficient large radius ρ. First we compute h^2 from (11) and get $h^2(x) = b_1^2 \rho^{2(p-1)}((\sum_{1 \leq i \leq 3} s_i n_i^{p-1})^2 + (\sum_{1 \leq i \leq 3} t_i n_i^{p-1})^2 + (\sum_{1 \leq i \leq 3} u_i n_i^{p-1})^2)$. Next observe that $h^2 - \delta^2$ is a polynomial in ρ, and that the monomial in $h^2 - \delta^2$ having highest exponent — which is $2(p-1)$ — is exactly h^2. Hence the coefficient for $\rho^{2(p-1)}$ in $h^2 - \delta^2$ is $b_1^2((\sum_{1 \leq i \leq 3} s_i n_i^{p-1})^2 + (\sum_{1 \leq i \leq 3} t_i n_i^{p-1})^2 + (\sum_{1 \leq i \leq 3} u_i n_i^{p-1})^2)$. We will show that it does not vanish. Suppose the contrary. Then each term of the sum in the expression above would vanish, i.e., $s_1 n_1^{p-1} + s_2 n_2^{p-1} + s_3 n_3^{p-1} = 0$, $t_1 n_1^{p-1} + t_2 n_2^{p-1} + t_3 n_3^{p-1} = 0$, and $u_1 n_1^{p-1} + u_2 n_2^{p-1} + u_3 n_3^{p-1} = 0$. Since $\det \mathcal{D} \neq 0$ we obtain $n_1^{p-1} = n_2^{p-1} = n_3^{p-1} = 0$. Thus we have $n_1 = n_2 = n_3 = 0$, which contradicts the relation $|n| = 1$. We conclude that for sufficiently large ρ, say $\rho > \rho_0$, the relation $|\delta(x)| < |h(x)|$ holds for all x with $|x| = \rho$. Applying Lemma 9 we obtain $\deg(h + \delta, B_\rho, 0) = \deg(h, B_\rho, 0)$ where $\rho > \rho_0$. □

Proof. (of Theorem 11) From Lemma 13 we have $\deg(f, B_\rho, 0) = \deg(h + \delta, B_\rho, 0) = \deg(h, B_\rho, 0)$. Using Lemma 12 we obtain $|\deg(f, B_\rho, 0)| = 1$. □

Corollary 14 *Let K be a natural number $\leq D$. Then for any set of $K + 1$ points $s^{(1)}, \ldots, s^{(K+1)} \in \mathbf{R}^D$ being in general position the set $B(s^{(1)}, \ldots, s^{(K+1)})$ is nonempty. In particular, for $K = D$ the set $B(s^{(1)}, \ldots, s^{(D+1)})$ consists of an odd number of points that is bounded by a constant depending only on the dimension D but not on p.*

Proof. (a) From $\deg(f, B_\rho, 0) \neq 0$ we conclude that $B(s^{(1)}, \ldots, s^{(D+1)})$ is nonempty. Therefore $B(s^{(1)}, \ldots, s^{(K+1)})$ must also be nonempty. (b) Since $|\deg(f, B_\rho, 0)| = 1$, using the definition of degree we see that the number of points in $B(s^{(1)}, \ldots, s^{(D+1)})$ must be odd. This fact together with Theorem 5 imply the claim. □

5 Concluding Remarks

We have given upper bounds to the number of L_p-spheres passing through $D+1$ points in general position in $\mathbf{R}^D$, and to the sum of the Betti numbers of $B(s^{(1)}, \ldots, s^{(K+1)})$. These bounds do not depend on p. We have determined the parity of the number of L_p-spheres passing through $D + 1$ points in general position in D-space. Our results raise some open problems: (1) Determine the exact value of the maximum number of L_p-spheres passing through $D + 1$ points (in general position) in D-space. (2) Compute the algebraic number of spheres (induced by a smooth strictly convex distance function) passing through $D + 1$ points in general position in D-space.

Acknowledgement. The author thanks Rolf Klein for many helpful discussions. Thanks to Tomas Recio and Francisco Santos for valuable comments on an earlier draft of this paper.

References

[1] F. Aurenhammer: *Voronoi Diagrams — A Survey of a Fundamental Data Structure.* ACM Computer Surveys 23(3), 1991.

[2] R. Benedetti and J.-J. Risler: *Real algebraic and semi-algebraic sets.* Actualités mathématiques, Hermann, Paris 1990.

722

[3] A. Borodin and S. Cook: *On the number of additions to compute specific polynomials.* SIAM J. Comput. 5(1976), pp. 146–157.

[4] L. P. Chew and R. L. Drysdale: *Voronoi diagrams based on convex distance functions.* Proc. ACM Symposium on Comp. Geom., pp. 235–244, 1985.

[5] R. Drysdale and B. Schaudt: *Higher Dimensional Delaunay Diagrams for Convex Distance Functions.* Proc. 4th Canad. Conf. on Comp. Geom., pp. 274–279, 1992.

[6] H. Edelsbrunner: *Algorithms in Combinatorial Geometry.* Springer-Verlag, New York 1987.

[7] P. E. Ehrlich and H.-C. Im Hof: *Dirichlet regions in manifolds without conjugate points.* Comment. Math. Helvetici 54 (1979), pp. 642–658.

[8] M. Golubitsky and V. Guillemin: *Stable Mappings and Their Singularities.* Springer-Verlag, New-York 1973.

[9] M. J. Greenberg: *Lectures on algebraic topology.* Benjamin, 1967.

[10] C. Icking, R. Klein, N.-M. Lê, L. Ma: *Convex Distance Functions in 3-Space are Different.* Proc. 9th ACM Symposium on Comp. Geom., pp. 116–123, 1993.

[11] N.-M. Lê: *On general properties of smooth strictly convex distance functions in R^D.* Proc. 5th Canadian Conf. on Comp. Geom., pp. 375–380, 1993.

[12] D. T. Lee: *Two-dimensional Voronoi diagrams in the L_p-metric.* J. ACM 27(4) (1980), pp. 604–618.

[13] V. V. Makeev: *The degree of a mapping in some problems in combinatorial geometry.* J. of Soviet Mathematics 51(5), Plenum Publ. Corp., Oct. 1990.

[14] J. Milnor: *On the Betti numbers of real varieties.* Proc. Amer. Math. Soc. 15 (1964), pp. 275–280.

[15] J. L. Montaña, L. M. Pardo, T. Recio: *The Non-Scalar Model of Complexity in Computational Geometry.* Effective Methods in Algebraic Geometry, edited by T. Mora and C. Traverso, Birkhäuser, Boston 1991.

[16] J. J. Risler: *Additive complexity and zeros of real polynomials.* SIAM J. Comput. 14(1985), pp. 178–183.

[17] J. T. Schwartz: *Nonlinear Functional Analysis.* Gordon and Breach Science Publishers, New York 1969.

[18] M. Sharir: *Arrangements of surfaces in higher dimensions: envelopes, single cells, and other recent developments.* Proc. 5th Canadian Conf. on Comp. Geom., pp. 181–186, 1993.

[19] M. Sharir: *Almost tight upper bounds for lower envelopes in higher dimensions.* Manuscript, 1993.

[20] R. Thom: *Sur L'Homologie des Variétés Algébriques Réelles.* Differential and Combinatorial Topology, edited by S. S. Cairns, Princeton University Press, 1965.

Total Protection of Analytic Invariant Information in Cross Tabulated Tables

Ming-Yang Kao*

Abstract

To protect sensitive information in a cross tabulated table, it is a common practice to suppress some of the cells in the table. An *analytic invariant* is a power series in terms of the suppressed cells that has a unique feasible value and a convergence radius equal to $+\infty$. Intuitively, the information contained in an invariant is not protected even though the values of the suppressed cells are not disclosed. This paper gives an optimal linear-time algorithm for testing whether there exist nontrivial analytic invariants in terms of the suppressed cells in a given set of suppressed cells. This paper also presents NP-completeness results and an almost linear-time algorithm for the problem of suppressing the minimum number of cells in addition to the sensitive ones so that the resulting table does not leak analytic invariant information about a given set of suppressed cells.

1 Introduction

Cross tabulated tables are used in a wide variety of documents to organize and exhibit information, often with the values of some cells suppressed in order to conceal sensitive information. Concerned with the effectiveness of the practice of cell suppression [9], statisticians have raised two fundamental issues and developed computational heuristics to various related problems [2, 4, 5, 6, 7, 8, 19, 20, 21, 22]. The *detection* issue is whether an adversary can deduce significant information about the suppressed cells from the published data of a table. The *protection* issue is how a table maker can suppress a small number of cells in addition to the sensitive ones so that the resulting table does not leak significant information.

This paper investigates the complexity of how to protect a broad class of information contained in a two-dimensional table that publishes (1) the values of all cells except a set of sensitive ones, which are *suppressed*, and (2) an upper bound and a lower bound for each cell, and (3) all row sums and column sums

---

*Department of Computer Science, Duke University, Durham, NC 27706. Supported in part by NSF grants MCS-8116678, DCR-8405478, and CCR-9101385. Part of this work was done while the authors were at the Department of Computer Science, Yale University, New Haven, Connecticut 06520.

of the complete set of cells. The cells may have real or integer values. They may have different bounds, and the bounds may be finite or infinite. The upper bound of a cell should be strictly greater than its lower bound; otherwise, the value of that cell is immediately known even if that cell is suppressed. The cells that are not suppressed also have upper and lower bounds. These bounds are necessary because some of the unsuppressed cells may later be suppressed to protect the information in the sensitive cells. (See Fig. 1 and 2 for an example of a complete table and its published version.)

An *unbounded feasible assignment* to a table is an assignment of values to the suppressed cells such that each row or column adds up to its published sum. An *bounded* feasible assignment is an unbounded one that also obeys the bounds of the suppressed cells. An *analytic function* of a table is a power series of the suppressed cells, each regarded as a variable, such that the convergence radius is ∞ [17, 18]. An *analytic invariant* is an analytic function that has a unique value at all the bounded feasible assignments. If an analytic invariant is formed by a linear combination of the suppressed cells, then it is called a *linear invariant* [13, 15]. Similarly, a suppressed cell is called an *invariant cell* [11, 12] if it is an invariant by itself. For instance, in the published table in Fig. 2, let $X_{p,q}$ be the cell at row p and column q. $X_{6,i}$ is an invariant because it is the only suppressed cell in row 6. $X_{2,c}$ and $X_{3,c}$ are invariant cells because their values are between 0 and 9.5, their sum is 19, and both cells are forced to have the same unique value 9.5. Consequently, $(X_{3,c} \cdot X_{2,c} + 0.5 \cdot X_{2,c} - 95)^2 \cdot X_{1,b} + \sin(X_{2,c} \cdot X_{2,a} - 9.5 X_{2,a})$ is also an invariant.

Intuitively, the information contained in an analytic invariant is unprotected because its value can be uniquely deduced from the published data. In this paper, a set of suppressed cells is *totally protected* if there exists no analytic invariant in terms of the suppressed cells in the given set, except the trivial invariant that contains no nonzero terms. As the analytic power series form a very broad family of mathematical functions, total protection conceals from the adversary a very large class of information. This paper gives a very simple algorithm for testing whether a given set of suppress cells is totally protected. When a graph representation, called the *suppressed graph*, of a table is given as input, this algorithm runs in optimal $O(m + n)$ time, where m is the number of suppressed cells and n is the total number of rows and columns. This paper also considers the problem of computing and suppressing the minimum number of additional cells so that a given set of original suppressed cells becomes totally protected. This problem is shown to be NP-complete. For a large class of tables, this optimal suppression problem can be solved in $O((m+n) \cdot \alpha(n, m+n))$ time, where α is an Ackerman's inverse function and its value is practically a small constant [1, 3]. Moreover, for this class of tables, every optimal set of cells for additional suppression forms a spanning forest of some sort. As a consequence, at most $n - 1$ additional cells need to be suppressed to achieve the total protection of a given set of original suppressed cells. As the size of a table may grow quadratically in n, the suppression of $n - 1$ additional cells is a negligible price to pay for total protection for a reasonably large table.

row column index	a	b	c	d	e	f	g	h	i	row sum
1	9.5	4.5	1.5	7	1.5	1.5	5.5	2	3	36.0
2	4.5	9.5	9.5	4.5	4.5	9.5	9.5	9.5	4.5	65.5
3	6	1.5	9.5	0	9.5	6	5.5	2	5.5	45.5
4	2	1.5	4	7	1.5	4.5	9.5	5.5	2	37.5
5	1.5	5.5	4	6	5.5	0	0	4.5	9.5	36.5
6	2	3	3	4	6	5.5	2	2	9.5	37.0
column sum	25.5	25.5	31.5	28.5	28.5	27.0	32.0	25.5	34.0	

Figure 1: A Complete Table.

Previously, four other levels of data security have been considered that protect information contained, respectively, in individual suppressed cells [11, 12], in a row or column as a whole, in a set of k rows or k columns as a whole, and in a table as a whole [14]. These four levles of data security and total protection differ in two major aspects. First, these four levels of data security primarily protect information expressible as linear invariants, whereas total protection protects the much broader class of analytic invariant information. Second, these four levels of data security emphasize protecting regular regions of a table, whereas total protection protects any given set of suppressed cells and is more flexible. These four levels of data security and total protection share some interesting similarities. As total protection corresponds to spanning forests in suppressed graphs, these four levels of data security are equivalent to some forms of 2-edge connectivity [11, 12], 2-vertex connectivity, k-vertex connectivity and graph completeness [14]. In this paper, the NP-completeness results and efficient algorithms for total protection rely heavily on its graph characterizations. Similarly, the equivalence characterizations of these four levels of data security have been key in obtaining efficient algorithms [11, 12, 14] and NP-completeness proofs [14] for various detection and protection problems.

This paper is organized as follows. Section 2 reviews basic concepts and important previous results about two-dimensional tables. Section 3 formally defines the notion of total protection and gives a linear-time algorithm to test for this notion. Sections 4 and 5 give NP-completeness results and efficient algorithms for optimal suppression problems of total protection.

row column index	a	b	c	d	e	f	g	h	i	row sum
1			1.5	7	1.5	1.5	5.5	2	3	36.0
2										65.5
3	6	1.5				6	5.5	2	5.5	45.5
4	2	1.5	4	7	1.5			5.5	2	37.5
5	1.5	5.5	4	6	5.5					36.5
6	2	3	3	4	6	5.5	2	2		37.0
column sum	25.5	25.5	31.5	28.5	28.5	27.0	32.0	25.5	34.0	

Note: Let $X_{p,q}$ denote the cell at row p and column q. The lower and upper bounds for all suppressed cells except $X_{2,c}$ and $X_{3,c}$ are $-\infty$ and $+\infty$. The lower and upper bounds for $X_{2,c}$ and $X_{3,c}$ are 0 and 9.5.

Figure 2: A Published Table.

2 Basics of Two-Dimensional Tables

Mixed Graphs. A *mixed* graph is one that may contain both undirected and directed edges. A *traversable* cycle or path in a mixed graph is one that can be traversed along the directions of its edges. A *direction-blind* cycle or path is one that can be traversed if the directions of its edges are disregarded. The word direction-blind is often omitted for brevity. A mixed graph is *connected* (respectively, *strongly connected*) if each pair of vertices are contained in a direction-blind path (respectively, traversable cycle). A *connected component* (respectively, *strongly connected component*) of a mixed graph is a maximal subgraph that is connected (respectively, strongly connected). A set of edges in a mixed graph is an *edge cut* if its removal disconnects one or more connected components of that graph. An edge cut is a *minimal* one if it has no proper subset that is also an edge cut.

The Total and Suppressed Graphs of a Table. From this point onwards, let $\mathcal{T}$ be a table, and let $\mathcal{H}' = (A, B, E')$ and $\mathcal{H} = (A, B, E)$ be the bipartite mixed graphs constructed below. $\mathcal{H}'$ and $\mathcal{H}$ are called the *total graph* and the *suppressed graph* of $\mathcal{T}$, respectively [12]. For each row (respectively, column) of $\mathcal{T}$, there is a unique vertex in A (respectively, B). This vertex is called a *row*

row column index	a	b	c	row sum
1	0	9	1	10
2	9	9	0	18
3	6	0	5	11
column sum	15	18	6	

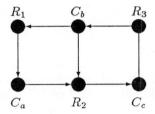

In the above 3×3 table, the number in each cell is the value of that cell. A cell with a box is a suppressed cell. The lower and upper bounds of the suppressed cells are 0 and 9. The graph below the table is the suppressed graph of the table. Vertex R_p corresponds to row p, and vertex C_q to column q.

Figure 3: A Table and Its Suppressed Graph.

(respectively, *column*) vertex. For each cell $X_{i,j}$ at row i and column j in T, there is a unique edge e in E between the vertices of row i and column j. If the value of $X_{i,j}$ is strictly between its bounds, then e is undirected. Otherwise, if the value is equal to the lower (respectively, upper) bound, then e is directed towards to its column (respectively, row) endpoint. Note that $\mathcal{H}'$ is a *complete bipartite mixed graph*, i.e., there is exactly one edge between each pair of vertices from the two vertex sets of the graph. The graph $\mathcal{H}$ is the subgraph of $\mathcal{H}'$ whose edge set consists of only those corresponding to the suppressed cells of T. Fig. 3 illustrates a table and its suppressed graph. For convenience, a row or column of T will be regarded as a vertex in $\mathcal{H}$ and a cell as an edge, and vice versa. The next theorem demonstrates part of the relationship between a table and its suppressed graph.

Theorem 1 ([12]) *A suppressed cell of T is an invariant cell if and only if it is not contained in a traversable cycle of $\mathcal{H}$.*

728

Effective Areas of Analytic Functions. The *effective area* of an analytic function F of $\mathcal{T}$, denoted by $EA(F)$, is the set of variables in the nonzero terms of F. The function F is called *nonzero* if $EA(F) \neq \emptyset$. Note that because the convergence radius of F is ∞, $EA(F)$ is independent of the point at which F is expanded into a power series.

Theorem 2 ([13]) *For every minimal edge cut Y of a strongly connected component of $\mathcal{H}$, $\mathcal{T}$ has a linear invariant F with $EA(F) = Y$.*

The Kernels of a Table. The *bounded kernel* (respectively, *unbounded kernel*) of $\mathcal{T}$, denoted by $BK(\mathcal{T})$ (respectively, $UK(\mathcal{T})$), is the real vector space consisting of all linear combinations of $x - y$, where x and y are arbitrary bounded (respectively, unbounded) feasible assignments of $\mathcal{T}$.

Theorem 3 ([15]) $UK(\mathcal{T}) = BK(\mathcal{T})$ *if every connected component of $\mathcal{H}$ is strongly connected.*

Direction-Blind Labeling. Because $\mathcal{H}$ is bipartite, every cycle of $\mathcal{H}$ is of even length. Thus, the edges of an edge-simple direction-blind cycle of $\mathcal{H}$ can be alternately labeled with $+1$ and -1. Such a labeling is called a *direction-blind labeling*. A direction-blindly labeled cycle is regarded as an assignment to the suppressed cells of $\mathcal{T}$. If the corresponding edge of a suppressed cell is in the given cycle, then the value assigned to that cell is the label of that edge; otherwise, the value is 0.

Lemma 4 *Every direction-blindly labeled cycle of $\mathcal{H}$ is a vector of $UK(\mathcal{T})$.*

3 Total Protection

A set Q of suppressed cells of $\mathcal{T}$ is *totally protected* in $\mathcal{T}$ if there is no nonzero analytic invariant F of $\mathcal{T}$ with $EA(F) \subseteq Q$. The goal of total protection can be better understood by considering Q as the set of suppressed cells that contain sensitive data. The total protection of Q means that no precise analytic information about these data, not even their row and column sums, can be deduced from the published data of $\mathcal{T}$. As analytic power series form a very large class of functions in mathematical sciences, this notion of protection requires a large class of information about Q to be concealed from the adversary.

The next lemma and theorem characterize the notion of total protection in graph concepts.

Lemma 5 *If F is a nonzero analytic invariant of $\mathcal{T}$ such that the edges in $EA(F)$ are contained in the strongly connected components of $\mathcal{H}$, then for some strongly connected component D of $\mathcal{H}$, $EA(F) \cap D$ is an edge cut of D.*

Proof. Let $\mathcal{T}_s$ be the table constructed from $\mathcal{T}$ by also publishing the suppressed cells that are not in the strongly connected components of $\mathcal{H}$. By Theorem 1, F remains a nonzero analytic function of $\mathcal{T}_s$. Also, the connected components of the suppressed graph $\mathcal{H}_s$ of $\mathcal{T}_s$ are the strongly connected components of $\mathcal{H}$. Thus, to prove the lemma, it suffices to prove it for $\mathcal{T}_s$, $\mathcal{H}_s$, and F. Let x_0 be a fixed bounded feasible assignment of $\mathcal{T}_s$. Let $K = \{x - x_0 | x$ is a bounded feasible assignment of $\mathcal{T}_s\}$. Since F is an analytic invariant of $\mathcal{T}_s$, the function $G(x) = F(x) - F(x_0)$ is an analytic invariant of $\mathcal{T}_s$ with $EA(G) = EA(F)$ and its value is zero over $x_0 + K$. Because K contains a nonempty open subset of $BK(\mathcal{T}_s)$, Gp is zero over $x_0 + BK(\mathcal{T}_s)$. By Theorem 3 and the strongly connectivity of the connected components of $\mathcal{H}_s$, $BK(\mathcal{T}_s) = UK(\mathcal{T}_s)$ and G is zero over $x_0 + UK(\mathcal{T}_s)$. Thus, it suffices to show that if $D - EA(F)$ is connected for all connected components D of $\mathcal{H}_s$, then $G(x_0 + z_0) \neq 0$ for some $z_0 \in UK(\mathcal{T}_s)$. To construct z_0, let $EA(G) = \{e_1, \ldots, e_k\}$. Let D_i be the connected component of $\mathcal{H}_s$ that contains e_i. By the connectivity of $D_i - EA(F)$, there is a vertex-simple path P_i in $D_i - EA(F)$ between the endpoints of e_i. Let C_i be the vertex-simple cycle formed by e_i and P_i. Next, direction-blindly label C_i with e_i labeled $+1$. Since G is a nonzero power series, $G(x_0 + y_0) \neq 0$ for some vector y_0. Note that y_0 is not necessarily in $UK(\mathcal{T}_s)$. So, let $z_0 = \sum_{i=1}^{k} h_i \cdot C_i$, where h_i is the component of y_0 at variable e_i. Then, by Lemma 4, $z_0 \in UK(\mathcal{T}_s)$. Because P_i is in $\mathcal{H}_s - EA(F)$, e_i appears only in the term C_i in $\sum_{i=1}^{k} h_i \cdot C_i$. Thus z_0 and y_0 have the same component values at the variables in $EA(G)$. Since the variables not in $EA(G)$ do not appear in any expansion of G, $G(x_0 + z_0) = G(x_0 + y_0) \neq 0$, proving the lemma. $\square$

Theorem 6 *A set Q of suppressed cells is totally protected in T if and only if the edges in Q are contained in the strongly connected components of $\mathcal{H}$ and for each strongly connected component D of $\mathcal{H}$, the graph $D - Q$ is connected.*

Proof. Follows from Lemma 5, and Theorems 1 and 2. $\square$

This paper investigates the following two problems concerning how to achieve total protection.

Problem 1 (Protection Test)
Input: The suppressed graph $\mathcal{H}$ and a set Q of suppressed cells of a table T.
Output: Is Q totally protected in T?

Theorem 7 *Problem 1 can be solved in linear time in the size of $\mathcal{H}$.*

Proof. Use Theorem 6 and linear-time algorithms for computing connected components and strongly connected components [1, 3]. $\square$

Problem 2 (Optimal Suppression)
Input: A table T, a subset Q of E, and an integer $p \geq 0$, where E is the set of all suppressed cells in T.
Output: Is there a set P consisting of at most p published cells of T such that Q is totally protected in the table $\overline{T}$ formed by T with the cells in P also suppressed?

This problem is clearly in NP. Section 4 shows that this problem with $Q = E$ is NP-complete. Section 5 proves that if the total graph of T is undirected, then this problem with general Q can be solved in almost linear time.

4   NP-Completeness of Optimal Suppression

Throughout this section, the total graph of T may or may not be undirected.

Theorem 8 *Problem 2 with $Q = E$ is NP-complete.*

The proof of this theorem first transforms Problem 2 with $Q = E$ to the following graph problem and then establishes the latter's NP-completeness.

Problem 3
Input: A complete bipartite mixed graph $\mathcal{H}' = (A, B, E')$, a subgraph $\mathcal{H} = (A, B, E)$, and an integer $p \geq 0$.
Output: Is there a set P of at most p edges in $E' - E$ such that every connected component of $(A, B, E \cup P)$ is strongly connected and the vertices of each connected component of $\mathcal{H}$ are connected in (A, B, P)?

Both Problem 2 with $Q = E$ and Problem 3 are clearly in NP. It follows from Theorem 6 that these two problems can be reduced to each other in linear time. Thus, to prove their NP completeness, it suffices to reduce the following NP-complete problem to Problem 3.

Problem 4 (Hitting Set [10])
Input: A finite set S, a nonempty family W of subsets of S, and an integer $h \geq 0$.
Output: Is there a subset S' of S such that $|S'| \leq h$ and S' contains at least one element in each set in W?

Given an instance $S = \{s_1, \ldots, s_q\}$, $W = \{S_1, \ldots, S_r\}$, h of Problem 4, an instance $\mathcal{H}' = (A, B, E'), \mathcal{H} = (A, B, E), p$ of Problem 3 is constructed as follows: Let $A = \{a_0, a_1, \ldots, a_q\}$. The vertices $a_1, \ldots, a_q$ correspond to $s_1, \ldots, s_q$, but a_0 corresponds to no s_i. Let $B = \{b_0, b_1, \ldots, b_r\}$. The vertices $b_1, \ldots, b_r$ correspond to $S_1, \ldots, S_r$ of S, but b_0 corresponds to no S_j. Let $E = \{a_0 \to b_1, \ldots, a_0 \to b_r\}$. Let $p = h + r + 1$. Let $E' = \{b_0 \to a_0\} \cup \{a_0 \to b_j \mid \forall\, j \text{ with } 1 \leq j \leq r\} \cup \{a_i \to b_0 \mid \forall\, i \text{ with } 1 \leq i \leq q\} \cup \{b_j \to a_i \mid \forall\, s_i \text{ and } S_j \text{ with } s_i \in S_j\} \cup \{a_i \to b_j \mid \forall\, s_i \text{ and } S_j \text{ with } s_i \notin S_j\}$.

5   Optimal Suppression in Almost Linear-Time

Under the assumption that the total graph of T is undirected, this section considers the following optimzation version of Problem 2.

Problem 5 (Optimal Suppression)
Input: The suppressed graph $\mathcal{H} = (A, B, E)$ of a table T and a set $Q \subseteq E$.
Output: A set P consisting of the smallest number of published cells in T such that Q is totally protected in the table $\overline{T}$ formed by T with the cells in P also suppressed.

For all positive integers n and m, let α denote the best known function such that $m + n$ unions and finds of disjoint subsets of an n-element set can be performed in $O((m+n)\cdot\alpha(n, m+n))$ time [1, 3].

Theorem 9 *Problem 5 can be solved in $O((m+n)\cdot\alpha(n, m+n))$ time, where m is the number of suppressed cells and n is the total number of rows and columns.*

To prove Theorem 9, Problem 5 is first converted to the next problem.

Problem 6

Input: An undirected bipartite graph $\mathcal{H} = (A, B, E)$ and a set $Q \subseteq E$.

Output: A forest P formed by the smallest number of undirected edges between A and B but not in E such that the vertices of each connected component of (A, B, Q) are connected in $(A, B, (E - Q) \cup P)$

Lemma 10 *Problems 5 and 6 can be reduced to each other in linear time.*

The above lemma follows from Theorem 6. It has several significant implications. Since P is a forest, it has at most $n - 1$ edges. Thus, for a table with an undirected total graph, no more than $n-1$ additional cells need to be suppressed to achieve total protection. This is a small number compared to the size of the table, which may grow quadratically in n. Moreover, when $\mathcal{H}$ is connected and $E = Q$, (A, B, P) is a spanning tree. In this case, many well-studied tree-related computational concepts and tools, such as minimum-cost spanning trees, can be apllied to consider other optimal suppression problems for total protection.

Note that because $Q \subseteq E$, the vertices of each connected component of (A, B, Q) are connected in $(A, B, (E - Q) \cup P)$ if and only if the vertices of each connected component of $\mathcal{H}$ are connected in $(A, B, (E - Q) \cup P)$. Using this equivalence, the next stage of the proof of Theorem 9 further reduces Problem 6 to another graph problem with the steps below:

A1. Compute the connected components $D_1, \cdots, D_r$ of $\mathcal{H}$.

A2. For each D_i, compute a maximal forest K_i over the vertices of D_i using only the edges in $E - Q$.

A3. For each D_i, extend K_i to a maximal forest L_i over the vertices of D_i using additional edges only from the complement graph D_i^c of D_i.

A4. Construct a graph $\hat{\mathcal{H}}$ from $\mathcal{H}$ by contracting each tree in each L_i into a single vertex.

A5. For each D_i, compute its contracted version $\hat{D}_i$ in $\hat{\mathcal{H}}$.

A6. Divide the vertices of $\hat{\mathcal{H}}$ into three sets, V_A, V_B, V_{AB}, where a vertex in V_A (respectively, V_B) consists of a single vertex from A (respectively, B), and a vertex in V_{AB} contains at least two vertices (thus with at least one from each of A and B).

A set of undirected edges between vertices in V_A, V_B, V_{AB} is called *semi-tripartite* if every edge in that set is between two of the three sets or is between two vertices in V_{AB}. Note that the set of edges in $\hat{\mathcal{H}}$ is semi-tripartite.

Problem 7

Input: Three disjoint finite sets V_A, V_B, V_{AB}, and a partition $\hat{D}_1, \ldots, \hat{D}_r$ of $V_A \cup V_B \cup V_{AB}$.

Output: A semi-tripartite set $\hat{P}$ consisting of the smallest number of edges such that no edge in $\hat{P}$ connects two vertices in the same D_i and the vertices in each D_i are connected in the graph formed by is $\hat{P}$.

Lemma 11 *Problem 6 can be reduced to Problem 7 in $O((m+n)\cdot\alpha(n, m+n))$ time, where m is the number of edges and n is the number of vertices in $\mathcal{H}$.*

Proof. The key idea is that an optimal P for Problem 6 can be obtained by connecting the vertices of each D_i first with edges in $E - Q$, which can be used for free, next with edges in D_i^c, and then with edges outside $D_i \cup D_i^c$. Let P' be a set of $|\hat{P}|$ edges in the complement of $\mathcal{H}$ that becomes $\hat{P}$ after Step A4. Then, $P' \cup (L_1 - K_1) \cup \cdots \cup (L_r - K_r)$ is a desired output P for Problem 6, showing that Steps A1–A6 can indeed reduce Problem 6 to Problem 7. Step A3 is the only step that requires more than linear time. It is important to avoid directly computing D_i^c at Step A3. Computing these complement graphs takes $\Theta(|A|\cdot|B|)$ time if some D_i contains a constant fraction of the vertices in $\mathcal{H}$. In such a case, if $\mathcal{H}$ is sparse, then the time spent on computing D_i^c alone is far greater than the desired complexity. Instead of this naive approach, Step A3 uses efficient techniques recently developed for complement graph problems [16] and takes the desired $O((m+n)\cdot\alpha(n, m+n))$ time. $\square$

The last stage of the proof of Theorem 9 is to give a linear-time algorithm for Problem 7. A component $\hat{D}_i$ is *good* if it has at least two vertices with at least one from V_{AB}; it is *bad* if it has at least two vertices with none from V_{AB} (and thus with at least one from each of V_A and V_B). The goal is to use as few edges as possible to connect the vertices in each of these components. Let w_g and w_b be the numbers of good and bad components, respectively. There are three cases based on the value of w_g.

Case 1: $w_g = 0$. If $w_b = 0$, then let $\hat{P} = \emptyset$ because no $\hat{D}_i$ needs to be connected. If $w_b > 0$ and $|V_{AB}| > 0$, then include in $\hat{P}$ an edge between each vertex in the bad components and an arbitrary vertex in V_{AB}. If $w_b > 0$ and $|V_{AB}| = 0$, then there does not exist a desired $\hat{P}$ and the given instance of Problem 7 has no solution.

Case 2: $w_g = 1$. Let $\hat{D}_j$ be the unique good component.

If $w_b > 0$, then find a bad component $\hat{D}_k$, and three vertices $u \in V_{AB} \cap \hat{D}_j$, $v_1 \in V_A \cap \hat{D}_k$, $v_2 \in V_B \cap \hat{D}_k$. Next, include in $\hat{P}$ an edge between v_2 and each vertex in $(\hat{D}_j \cap (V_A \cup V_{AB})) - \{u\}$, an edge between v_1 and each vertex in $\hat{D}_j \cap V_B$, and an edge between u and each vertex in the bad components.

If $w_b = 0$ and $V_{AB} - \hat{D}_j \neq \emptyset$, then include in $\hat{P}$ an edge between every vertex in $\hat{D}_j$ and an arbitrary vertex in $V_{AB} - \hat{D}_j$.

If $w_b = 0$ and $V_{AB} - \hat{D}_j = \emptyset$, then there are sixteen subcases depending on whether $V_A \cap \hat{D}_j = \emptyset$, $V_A - \hat{D}_j = \emptyset$, $V_B \cap \hat{D}_j = \emptyset$, $V_B - \hat{D}_j = \emptyset$. If $V_A \cap \hat{D}_j \neq \emptyset$, $V_A - \hat{D}_j \neq \emptyset$, $V_B \cap \hat{D}_j \neq \emptyset$, $V_B - \hat{D}_j \neq \emptyset$, then include in $\hat{P}$ an edge between each vertex in $V_A \cap \hat{D}_j$ and a vertex $v_2 \in V_B - \hat{D}_j$, an edge between each vertex in $V_B \cap \hat{D}_j$ and a vertex $v_1 \in V_A - \hat{D}_j$, and an edge between v_1 and each vertex in $V_{AB} \cup \{v_2\}$. The other fifteen subcases are handled similarly.

Case 3: $w_g \geq 2$. Let d be the total number of vertices in the good and bad components. Let w' be the number of connected components in $\hat{P}$ that contain the vertices of at least one good or bad $\hat{D}_i$; let d' be the number of vertices in these connected components of $\hat{P}$ that are not in any good or bad $\hat{D}_i$. By its minimality, $\hat{P}$ forms a forest and $|\hat{P}| = d' + d - w'$. The techniques for Cases 1 and 2 can be used to show that there exists an optimal $\hat{P}$ with $d' = 0$. Thus, to minimize $|\hat{P}|$ is to maximize w'. Because two bad components cannot be connected by edges between them alone, the strategy for maximizing w' is to pair a good component with a bad one, whenever possible, and include in $\hat{P}$ edges between them to connect their vertices into a tree. After this step, if there remain unconnected bad components but no unconnected good ones, then add to P an edge between each vertex in the remaining bad components and an arbitrary vertex in the intersection of V_{AB} and a good component. On the other hand, if there remain good components but no bad ones, then pair up these good components similarly. After this step, if there remains a good component, then add to $\hat{P}$ an edge between each vertex in this last good component and an arbitrary vertex in the intersection of V_{AB} and another good component. (As a result, if $w_g \leq w_b$, then $|\hat{P}| = d - w_g$; otherwise, $|\hat{P}| = d - \lfloor \frac{w_g + w_b}{2} \rfloor$.)

The above discussion yields a linear-time algorithm for Problem 7. This finishes the proof of Theorem 9.

Acknowledgements. The author is deeply grateful to Dan Gusfield for his constant encouragement and help.

References

[1] A. V. AHO, J. E. HOPCROFT, AND J. D. ULLMAN, *The Design and Analysis of Computer Algorithms*, Addison-Wesley, 1974.

[2] G. J. BRACKSTONE, L. CHAPMAN, AND G. SANDE, *Protecting the confidentiality of individual statistical records in Canada*, in Proc. the Conference of the European Statisticians 31st Plenary Session, Geneva, 1983.

[3] T. H. CORMEN, C. L. LEISERSON, AND R. L. RIVEST, *Introduction to Algorithms*, The MIT Press, Cambridge, Massachusetts, 1991.

[4] L. H. COX, *Disclosure analysis and cell suppression*, in Proc. the American Statistical Association, Social Statistics Section, 1975, pp. 380–382.

[5] ——, *Suppression methodology in statistics disclosure*, in Proc. the American Statistical Association, Social Statistics Section, 1977, pp. 750–755.

[6] ——, *Automated statistical disclosure control*, in Proc. the American Statistical Association, Survey Research Method Section, 1978, pp. 177–182.

[7] ——, *Suppression methodology and statistical disclosure control*, Journal of the American Statistical Association, Theory and Method Section, 75 (1980), pp. 377–385.

[8] L. H. COX AND G. SANDE, *Techniques for preserving statistical confidentiality*, in Proc. the 42nd Session of the International Statistical Institute, the International Association of Survey Statisticians, 1979.

[9] D. DENNING, *Cryptography and Data Security*, Addison-Wesley, 1982.

[10] M. GAREY AND D. JOHNSON, *Computers and Intractability: A Guide to the Theory of NP-Completeness*, W. H. Freeman and Company, 1979.

[11] D. GUSFIELD, *Optimal mixed graph augmentation*, SIAM J. Comput., 16 (1987), pp. 599–612.

[12] ——, *A graph theoretic approach to statistical data security*, SIAM J. Comput., 17 (1988), pp. 552–571.

[13] M. Y. KAO, *Efficient detection and protection of information in cross tabulated tables II: Minimal linear invariants*. Submitted, 1992.

[14] ——, *Efficient detection and protection of information in cross tabulated tables III: Data security equals graph connectivity*. Submitted, 1992.

[15] M. Y. KAO AND D. GUSFIELD, *Efficient detection and protection of information in cross tabulated tables I: Linear invariant test*, SIAM Journal on Discrete Mathematics, 6 (1993), pp. 460–476.

[16] M. Y. KAO AND S. H. TENG, *Simple and efficient compression schemes for dense and complement graphs*. Submitted, 1993.

[17] S. LANG, *Complex Analysis*, Springer-Verlag, 1985.

[18] H. ROYDEN, *Real Analysis*, Macmillan, 1988.

[19] G. SANDE, *Towards automated disclosure analysis for establishment based statistics*, tech. rep., Statistics Canada, 1977.

[20] ——, *A theorem concerning elementary aggregations in simple tables*, tech. rep., Statistics Canada, 1978.

[21] ——, *Automated cell suppression to preserve confidentiality of business statistics*, Statistical Journal of the United Nations, 2 (1984), pp. 33–41.

[22] ——, *Confidentiality and polyhedra, an analysis of suppressed entries on cross tabulations*, tech. rep., Statistics Canada, unknown date.

Dominating Cliques in Graphs with Hypertree Structure

Feodor F. Dragan [1] and Andreas Brandstädt [2]

[1] Dept. of Math. and Cybern. Moldavian State University A. Mateevici str. 60 Chisinau
277009 Moldova
[2] Universität –GH– Duisburg FB Math. FG Inf. D 47048 Duisburg Germany

Abstract. The use of (generalized) tree structure is one of the main topics in the field of efficient graph algorithms. The well–known partial k–tree approach belongs to this kind of research and bases on the tree structure of constant size–bounded maximal cliques. Without size bound on the cliques the tree structure remains helpful in some cases. We consider here graphs with this tree structure as well as a dual variant (in the sense of hypergraphs) of it which turns out to be useful for designing linear–time algorithms.

Elimination orderings of vertices are closely related to tree structures. Recently in several papers ([1], [4], [12], [21], [23]) graphs with maximum neighbourhood orderings were introduced and investigated. These orderings have some algorithmic consequences ([1], [9], [11]). Our aim in this paper is to carry over these techniques also to the dominating clique problem and to improve and generalize some recent results concerning this problem ([19], [20], [1]):

1) The dominating clique problem is generalized to r–domination (where each vertex has its "personal" domination radius).

2) We show that even for Helly graphs there exists a simple necessary and sufficient condition for the existence of dominating cliques, and the condition known from [20] on chordal graphs is shown to be valid also in the more general case of r–domination.

3) We give a linear–time algorithm for the r–dominating clique problem on graphs with maximum neighbourhood orderings.

4) We investigate some related problems on chordal graphs and on dually chordal graphs.

1 Introduction

One of the most important and useful example for generalizing trees in order to use the tree–structure for the design of efficient algorithms are the chordal graphs which are characterized by a tree structure of maximal cliques and the special case of k–trees where the size of maximal cliques is additionally bounded by $k + 1$. The well–known partial k–tree approach uses this structure for the design of efficient dynamic programming algorithms.

Without size bound on the cliques i.e. for chordal graphs the tree structure remains helpful in some cases. These graphs and their corresponding hypergraphs of maximal cliques which are α-acyclic turned out to be of importance.

We consider here graphs with this tree structure as well as a dual variant (in the sense of hypergraphs) of it which turns out to be useful. Elimination orderings of vertices are closely related to tree structures. They simply reflect the repeated deletion of leaves in trees which in chordal graphs is generalized by the repeated deletion of simplicial vertices – a generalization of leaves which will be defined below.

Recently in several papers ([1], [4], [12], [21], [23]) graphs with maximum neighbourhood orderings were introduced and investigated. It turned out that these graphs have a tree structure which is dual (in the sense of hypergraphs) to that of chordal graphs – a reason to call them *dually chordal graphs* [4]. The tree and elimination ordering properties of dually chordal graphs have some algorithmic consequences ([1], [9], [11]).

We describe here another application namely finding a minimum r–dominating clique in linear–time (or indicating that there is no such clique) which will be described subsequently after introducing the basic graph classes.

2 Notions and Basic Properties

Throughout this paper all graphs $G=(V,E)$ are finite, simple (i.e. without self-loops and multiple edges) and undirected.

Chordal, dually chordal and strongly chordal graphs are defined as follows: Let $G = (V, E)$ be a graph with vertex (node) set $V = \{v_1, ..., v_n\}$ and edge set E.

$N(v) = \{u : uv \in E\}$ is the *open neighbourhood* of v and $N[v] = N(v) \cup \{v\}$ is the *closed neighbourhood* of v.

For $U \subseteq V$ let $G(U)$ be the subgraph induced by U. Let $G_i = G(\{v_i, v_{i+1}, ..., v_n\})$ and $N_i[v](N_i(v))$ be the closed (open) neighbourhood of v in G_i.

A vertex v is *simplicial* iff N[v] induces a clique. A vertex v is *simple* iff $\{N[u] : u \in N[v]\}$ is linearly ordered by set inclusion.

An ordering $(v_1, ..., v_n)$ of the vertex set V is a *perfect elimination ordering* iff for all $i = 1, ..., n$ v_i is simplicial in G_i.

This ordering is a *simple elimination ordering* iff for all $i = 1, ..., n$ v_i is simple in G_i.

The graph G is *chordal (strongly chordal)* iff G has a perfect elimination ordering (simple elimination ordering). Equivalently, a graph is chordal iff it does not contain any induced cycle C_k of length $k \geq 4$.

Chordal graphs are a "classical" graph class (cf. [17]) and admit some nice algorithmic applications (cf. e.g. [22]). On the other hand there are several problems remaining NP–complete even on subclasses of chordal graphs as it is the case for domination.

Strongly chordal graphs are an algorithmically useful subclass of chordal graphs which leads to the efficient solution of further problems which are NP–complete on chordal graphs (cf. e.g. [14], [6]). The special structure of a strongly chordal graph G is reflected by its simple elimination ordering , the linear ordering of neighbourhoods $\{N_i[u] : u \in N_i[v_i]\}$, $i = 1, ..., n$ however, can be generalized by only demanding that each of these sets of neighbourhoods has a maximum. In some cases this is enough to obtain an efficient algorithm. This leads to graphs with a maximum neighbourhood ordering recently introduced and characterized in several papers ([1], [4], [12], [23]). [21] also introduces maximum neighbourhoods but only in connection with chordal graphs (chordal graphs with maximum neighbourhood ordering are called there *doubly chordal graphs*).

A vertex $u \in N[v]$ is a *maximum neighbour of v* iff for all $w \in N[v]$ $N[w] \subseteq N[u]$ holds (note that $u = v$ is not excluded).
A linear ordering $(v_1, v_2, ..., v_n)$ of the vertex set V of a graph G is a *maximum neighbourhood ordering* of G iff for all $i \in \{1, ..., n\}$ v_i has a maximum neighbour in G_i: for all $w \in N_i[v_i]$ $N_i[w] \subseteq N_i[u_i]$ holds.

There is a close connection between chordality and the existence of a maximum neighbourhood ordering which can be expressed in terms of hypergraphs (for hypergraph notions we follow [2]).

Let $\mathcal{N}(G) = \{N[v] : v \in V\}$ be the *neighbourhood hypergraph* of G.
Let $\mathcal{C}(G) = \{C : C$ is a maximal clique in G $\}$ be the *clique hypergraph* of G.
Let v be a vertex of G. The *disk* centered at v with radius k is the set of all vertices having distance at most k to v: $N^k[v] = \{u : u \in V$ and $dist(u, v) \leq k\}$.
Let $\mathcal{D}(G) = \{N^k[v] : v \in V$, k a positive integer $\}$ be the *disk hypergraph* of G.
Now let $\mathcal{E}$ be a hypergraph with underlying vertex set V. The *dual hypergraph* $\mathcal{E}^*$ has $\mathcal{E}$ as its vertex set and $\{e \in \mathcal{E} : v \in e\}$ $(v \in V)$ as its edges. The *line graph* $L(\mathcal{E}) = (\mathcal{E}, E)$ of $\mathcal{E}$ is the intersection graph of $\mathcal{E}$, i.e. $ee' \in E$ iff $e \cap e' \neq \emptyset$.

A hypergraph $\mathcal{E}$ has the *Helly property* iff any subfamily $\mathcal{E}' \subseteq \mathcal{E}$ of pairwise intersecting edges has a nonempty intersection.

A hypergraph $\mathcal{E}$ with underlying vertex set V is a *hypertree* iff there is a tree $T = (V, E)$ such that for all $e \in \mathcal{E}$ the induced subgraph $T(e)$ is connected i.e. a subtree of T. A hypergraph $\mathcal{E}$ is a *dual hypertree* iff $\mathcal{E}^*$ is a hypertree.

It is well–known that a hypergraph $\mathcal{E}$ is a hypertree iff it has the Helly property and its line graph is chordal (cf. [13], [16]) and, as a consequence, G is chordal iff $\mathcal{C}(G)$ is a dual hypertree (cf. [17] for further sources).

We mainly use the following characterization of graphs with maximum neighbourhood ordering :

Theorem 1 *([12], cf. also [4]) Let $G=(V,E)$ be a graph. Then the following conditions are equivalent:*

(i) G has a maximum neighbourhood ordering .

(ii) $\mathcal{N}(G)$ is a dual hypertree.

(iii) $\mathcal{N}(G)$ is a hypertree.

(iv) $\mathcal{C}(G)$ is a hypertree.

(v) $\mathcal{D}(G)$ is a hypertree.

Part (iv) of this theorem also justifies the name "dually chordal graphs" for graphs with maximum neighbourhood ordering : a graph G is *dually chordal* iff $\mathcal{C}(G)$ is a hypertree. (Note that unlike chordal graphs graphs with a maximum neighbourhood ordering are in general not perfect.) It should be remarked that it can be recognized in linear time whether a given graph is dually chordal.

Section 5 recalls an algorithm for the construction of a maximum neighbourhood ordering of a given dually chordal graph.

A graph G is a *Helly* graph (sometimes called *disk–Helly graph*) iff $\mathcal{D}(G)$ has the Helly property. Several of our results even hold for Helly graphs.

Now to a description of the special algorithmic problem investigated here: A subset $D \subseteq V$ is a *dominating set in G* iff for all $v \in V \setminus D$ there is a $u \in D$ with $uv \in E$. It is a *dominating clique in G* iff D is a dominating set in G and a *clique* (i.e. for all $u, v \in D$ $uv \in E$).

There are many papers investigating the problem of finding minimum dominating sets in graphs with (and without) additional requirements to the dominating sets. The problems are in general NP–complete. For more special graphs the situation is sometimes better (for a bibliography on domination cf. [18], for a recent survey on special graph classes cf. [3]).

In [6] efficient solutions of the following generalized domination problem (r–*domination*) on strongly chordal graphs are studied: Let $(r(v_1), ..., r(v_n))$ be a sequence of positive integers $r(v_i) \geq 0$ which is given together with the input graph. For any two vertices u, v denote by $dist(u, v)$ the length (i.e. number of edges) of a shortest path between u and v in G. A subset $D \subseteq V$ is an r–*dominating set* in G iff for all $v \in V \setminus D$ there is a $u \in D$ with $dist(u, v) \leq r(v)$. It is an r–*dominating clique* in G iff D is additionally a clique.

[19] and [20] investigate the dominating clique problem on strongly chordal and chordal graphs. We show that

1) even for Helly graphs there exists a simple necessary and sufficient condition for the existence of dominating cliques, and the condition known from [20] on chordal graphs is shown to be valid also in the more general case of r–domination.

2) We give a linear–time algorithm for the r–dominating clique problem on graphs with maximum neighbourhood orderings which improves and generalizes the results of [20] for strongly graphs since for strongly chordal graphs as a part of the input a simple elimination ordering is assumed for which no linear time construction is known if only the graph is given.

3) We investigate some related problems on chordal graphs and on dually chordal graphs.

3 The Existence of r-Dominating Cliques in Helly and in Chordal Graphs

It is known from [5] that the problem whether a given graph has a dominating clique is NP–complete even for weakly chordal graphs (a graph G is *weakly chordal* iff G does not contain induced cycles C_k of length $k \geq 5$ and no complements $\overline{C_k}$ of such cycles).

In this section we give a simple necessary and sufficient condition for the existence of an r–dominating clique in a given graph, if the graph is Helly or chordal. Note, however, that this condition does not yield an efficient solution for finding a minimum size r–dominating clique if one exists.

Theorem 2 *Let $G = (V, E)$ be a Helly graph with n-tuple $(r(v_1), ..., r(v_n))$ of positive integers and $M \subseteq V$ be any subset of V. Then M has an r-dominating clique C iff for every pair of vertices $v, w \in M$, the inequality*

$$dist(v, w) \leq r(v) + r(w) + 1$$

holds. Moreover such a clique C can be determined within time $O(|M| \cdot |E|)$.

Proof: 1) "$\Longrightarrow$": If such a clique C exists for M then obviously the inequality is fulfilled.

2) "$\Longleftarrow$": Consider the set
$X_M = \{x : x \in V$ and $dist(x, v) \leq r(v) + 1$ for all $v \in M\} = \bigcap_{v \in M} N^{r(v)+1}[v]$.
Since the disks of the family $\mathcal{M} = \{N^{r(v)+1}[v] : v \in M\}$ have pairwise nonempty intersection and G is Helly there is a common vertex of all these disks i.e. $X_M \neq \emptyset$.

Consider a maximal (w.r.t set inclusion) clique $C \subseteq X_M$. We show that C is r-dominating. Assume to the contrary that there is a vertex $y \in V$ such that $dist(y, C) = r(y) + 1$. Then the disks $\{N[v] : v \in C\} \cup \{N^{r(v)+1}[v] : v \in M\} \cup \{N^{r(y)}[y]\}$ pairwise intersect and thus there is a vertex $x \in X_M$ which has an edge to all vertices of C and distance r(y) to y. Thus C is not maximal – a contradiction.

3) *Time bound:* First determine within $O(|M| \cdot |E|)$ steps the distances of every vertex $v \in M$ to all other vertices of the graph.
Then X_M can be found within time $O(|M| \cdot |V|)$ which is bounded by $O(|M| \cdot |E|)$. A maximal clique $C \subseteq X_M$ can be found within time $O(|E|)$. $\qquad\square$

If in Theorem 2 "Helly" is replaced by "chordal" then the theorem remains true but the proof is somewhat longer. We need the following notion: A subset $S \subseteq V$ is m-convex iff S contains every vertex on every chordless path between vertices of S.
We use the following well-known properties:

Lemma 1 *[15] Any disk $N^r[v]$ of a chordal graph $G = (V, E)$ is m-convex.*

Lemma 2 *([7], [25]) Let $G = (V, E)$ be a chordal graph. If all vertices v_i of a clique $C = \{v_1, ..., v_k\}$ have the same distance from a vertex $v \in V$ then there is a common neighbour u of all elements of C which has distance $dist(v, C) - 1$ to v.*

Furthermore we need the following notion:
For a subset $S \subseteq V$ and a vertex $v \in V$ let $dist(v, S) = min\{dist(v, w) : w \in S\}$ and

$$proj(v, S) = \{u \in S : dist(v, u) = dist(v, S)\}$$

(the *metric projection* of v to S).
For a subset $X \subseteq V$ let $proj(X, S) = \bigcup\{proj(v, S) : v \in X\}$.
From the definition of m-convexity the following properties immediately follow:

Lemma 3 *The metric projection proj(C,S) of any clique C to an m-convex set S of the graph G is a clique.*

Lemma 4 *For any m-convex set S and vertices $v \in V, u \in S$ of the graph G there is a vertex $w \in proj(v, S)$ such that $dist(v, u) = dist(v, w) + dist(w, u)$ i.e. w lies on a shortest path between v and u.*

Theorem 3 *Let $G=(V,E)$ be a chordal graph with n-tuple $(r(v_1), ..., r(v_n))$ and $M \subseteq V$ be any subset of V. Then M has an r-dominating clique iff for every pair of vertices v and w, $v, w \in M$, the inequality*

$$dist(v, w) \leq r(v) + r(w) + 1$$

holds. Moreover such a clique can be determined within time $O(|M| \cdot |E|)$.

Proof: 1) "$\Longrightarrow$": Obvious.

2) "$\Longleftarrow$": Assume that $v_1, ..., v_n$ is an ordering of V such that M consists of the first $|M|$ vertices of this ordering. Let i be the largest index such that for all vertices $v_j \in M, 1 \leq j \leq i$, there is a clique C with property $dist(v_j, C) \leq r(v_j)$. If $i < |M|$ then for $v_{i+1} \in M$ $dist(v_{i+1}, C) \geq r(v_{i+1}) + 1$ holds.

Now consider the projection of C to the set $N_{r(v_{i+1})+1}[v_{i+1}]$. Due to the m-convexity of disks in chordal graphs the projection $proj(C, N_{r(v_{i+1})+1}[v_{i+1}])$ induces a clique C' according to Lemma 3.

For all j, $j \leq i$, consider a vertex $u_j \in C \cap N_{r(v_j)}[v_j]$ and $w_j \in N_{r(v_j)}[v_j] \cap N_{r(v_{i+1})+1}[v_{i+1}]$.

According to Lemma 4 there is a vertex $u'_j \in C'$ such that

$$dist(u_j, w_j) = dist(u_j, u'_j) + dist(u'_j, w_j)$$

holds. Due to the m-convexity of disks for all j, $j \leq i$, $u'_j \in N_{r(v_j)}[v_j]$ is fulfilled. Furthermore $dist(u'_j, v_{i+1}) = r(v_{i+1}) + 1$ holds for all $j \leq i$. But then according to Lemma 2 there is a vertex u'_{i+1} which is a common neighbour of all vertices of C' and which has the distance $r(v_{i+1})$ from v_{i+1}. This is a contradiction to the maximality of i.

3) *Time bound:* As in the proof of Theorem 2 first determine within $O(|M| \cdot |E|)$ steps the distances of every vertex $v \in M$ to all other vertices of the graph.

i-th step: If the distances of v_{i+1} to all other vertices are known in advance then the projection of clique C to the disk $N_{r(v_{i+1})+1}[v_{i+1}]$ can be determined within $O(|E|)$ steps. The vertices u'_{i+1} can be determined also within $O(|E|)$ steps. There are at most $|M|$ such steps, and each step requires at most $O(|E|)$ time. □

Corollary 1 *Let $r(v)=k$ for all $v \in V$. Then a Helly (a chordal) graph G has a k-dominating clique iff $diam(G) \leq 2k + 1$.*

Corollary 2 *Let G be a Helly or a chordal graph. Then G has a dominating clique iff $diam(G) \leq 3$.*

(For the case of chordal graphs Corollary 2 occurs already in [20].)

4 A Relation Between the r-Domination and the r-Dominating Clique Problem

Let $\gamma_r(G) = min\{|D| : D$ an r–dominating set in $G\}$, $\gamma_{r-conn}(G) = min\{|D| : D$ a connected r–dominating set in $G\}$, and $\gamma_{r-clique}(G) = min\{|D| : D$ an r–dominating clique in $G\}$. It is clear that for every graph G which has an r–connected dominating set and an r–dominating clique

$$\gamma_r(G) \leq \gamma_{r-conn}(G) \leq \gamma_{r-clique}(G)$$

holds but in general the parameters do not coincide. The next theorem shows the coincidence for Helly graphs which have an r–dominating clique.

Theorem 4 *Let D be a minimum r–dominating set of a Helly graph G which has an r–dominating clique. Then there is an r–dominating clique D' with $|D'| = |D|$.*

Corollary 3 *Let G be a Helly graph which has an r–dominating clique. Then*

$$\gamma_r(G) = \gamma_{r-conn}(G) = \gamma_{r-clique}(G)$$

(For the case of strongly chordal graphs this is contained already in [20].)

For the next corollary we have to introduce some more graph classes. A graph $G = (V, E)$ is a *bridged graph* iff each cycle C of length at least 4 contains two vertices whose distance from each other in G is strictly less than their distance in C.

An induced subgraph G' in a graph G is an *isometric subgraph* in G iff the distance of any two vertices in G' is equal to their distance in G.

Furthermore we need the notion of a *k-sun* S_k which is a graph with $2k$ vertices consisting of two disjoint sets $W = \{w_1, ..., w_k\}$, $U = \{u_1, ..., u_k\}$ such that W is independent, U forms a clique and for each i and j w_i is adjacent to u_i iff $i = j$ or $i \equiv j + 1 (mod k)$.

Corollary 4 *The r–dominating clique problem is solvable in polynomial time for any class of Helly graphs for which the r–domination problem is solvable in polynomial time.*
In particular, the r–dominating clique problem is solvable in polynomial time for graphs with a maximum neighbourhood ordering and for Helly graphs without C_4, $\overline{S_3}$ (and hence for bridged graphs without isometric sun S_k, $k \geq 3$, bridged graphs without S_3, $\overline{S_3}$, doubly chordal graphs and strongly chordal graphs).
Moreover, the r–domination problem is NP-complete for any subclass of Helly graphs for which the r–dominating clique problem is NP-complete.

Corollary 5 *Let $\mathcal{G}$ be a class of Helly graphs G for which the minimum size of an r–dominating clique in G is equal to the maximum number of pairwise disjoint r–neighbourhoods in G for any n–tuple $(r(v_1), ..., r(v_n))$. Then any r–dominating clique problem is solvable in polynomial time on $\mathcal{G}$.*

These corollaries base on results of [10].

Note that not for all chordal graphs G with a dominating clique $\gamma_r(G) = \gamma_{r-clique}(G)$ holds. This means that this equality for strongly chordal graphs (given also in Corollary 5 of [20]) is not due to chordality but to the Helly property.

5   A Linear-time Algorithm for Finding Minimum r-Dominating Cliques in Graphs with Maximum Neighbourhood Ordering

In the subsequent linear–time algorithm for the mimimum r–dominating clique problem on dually chordal graphs (i.e. graphs with maximum neighbourhood ordering) the special kind of a maximum neighbourhood ordering of G turns out to be of importance.

For graphs G with maximum neighbourhood ordering such an ordering can be determined in linear time $O(|V| + |E|)$ if the input is the graph G. [11] contains the following algorithm for this purpose. The algorithm bases on the maximum cardinality search (MCS) algorithm of [24] for finding a perfect elimination ordering of chordal graphs and constructs the ordering from right to left. (Perhaps the duality between chordal graphs and graphs with maximum neighbourhood orderings makes it more transparent why the MCS approach is successful for chordal graphs. For graphs with maximum neighbourhood ordering this approach is almost straightforward.)

Algorithm MNO (Find a maximum neighbourhood ordering of G)

Input: A dually chordal graph $G = (V, E)$
Output: A maximum neighbourhood ordering of G.

0)   Initially all $v \in V$ are unnumbered and unmarked;
1)   Choose an arbitrary $v \in V$, number v with n i.e. $v_n := v$ and $mn(v_n) := v$;
repeat
2)   among all unmarked vertices select a numbered vertex u such that $N[u]$ contains a maximum number of numbered vertices;
3)   number all unnumbered vertices x from N[u] consecutively with maximal possible numbers between 1 and $n - 1$ which are still free;
     for all of them let $mn(x) := u$;
4)   mark u;
until all vertices are numbered.

It should be stressed that in 3) the numbers (i.e. positions) for vertices are the largest possible ones among the numbers between 1 and n which are still free. The meaning of $mn(x)$ is a maximum neighbour of x.

In [11] it is shown that this algorithm MNO is correct i.e. it yields a maximum neighbourhood ordering of G iff G has such an ordering.

Note that the algorithm also yields a maximum neighbour for each vertex and all vertices of $N[v_n]$ occur consecutively in the ordering on the left of v_n and have v_n as their maximum neighbour. Furthermore for all v_i, $i \leq n - 1$, $mn(v_i) \neq v_i$. This will be used in the subsequent algorithm which has a structure similar to corresponding algorithms for the case of strongly chordal graphs in [6].

Algorithm DC (Find a minimum r–dominating clique of a dually chordal graph if there is one, and answer NO otherwise)

Input: A dually chordal graph $G=(V,E)$ and an n–tuple $(r(v_1), ..., r(v_n))$ of positive integers

Output: A minimum r–dominating clique of G if there is one and answer NO otherwise.

(1) $D := \emptyset$;
(2)   **if for all** $v \in V$ $r(v) > 0$ **then**
(3)   **begin**
(4)   with algorithm MNO find a max. neighb. ordering $(v_1, ..., v_n)$ of V;
(5)   **for** $i := 1$ **to** n **do**
(6)   **begin**
(7)   for max. neighb. $v_j = mn(v_i)$ $r(v_j) := min\{r(v_j), r(v_i) - 1\}$;
(8) $G := G - v_i$; $\{\ v_i \neq mn(v_i)$ for $i \leq n - 1\ \}$
(9)   **if** $r(v_j) = 0$ **then goto** *outloop*
(10)   **end**
(11)   **end**
(12)   **if for all** $v \in V$ $r(v) \neq 0$ **then** STOP with output $D := \{v_n\}$
(13) $\{v_n$ is an r–dominating vertex for G$\}$;
(14)   **else** $\{$ now r(v)=0 for some $v \in V$; suppose that G has now p vertices $\}$
outloop:
(15)   **begin**
(16)   with algor. MNO find a max. neighb. ordering $(v'_1, ..., v'_p)$ of the
(17)   rest graph G with $r(v'_p) = 0$;
(18)   **for** $i := 1$ **to** p **do**
(19)   **begin**
(20)   **if** $r(v'_i) = 0$ **then** $D := D \cup \{v'_i\}$
(21)   **else if for all** $x \in N[v'_i]$ $r(x) > 0$ **then**
(22)   for max. neighb. $v'_j = mn(v'_i)$ $r(v'_j) := min\{r(v'_j), r(v'_i) - 1\}$
(23)   **end**;
(24)   **if** D is no clique **then** output "there is no r–dom. clique in G"
(25)   **else** D is a minimum r–dominating clique of G
(26)   **end**

Lemma 5 *Assume that the graph G has an r–dominating clique and let $N[v] \subseteq N[u]$ for some vertices u and v. Then G has a minimum r–dominating clique D with $v \notin D$ iff $r(v) \neq 0$.*

Lemma 6 *(Reduction Lemma)*
Let u be a maximum neighbour of a vertex v in G with $r(v) > 0$. A subset $D \subseteq V \setminus \{v\}$ is a minimum r-dominating clique (set) of G if D is a minimum r'-dominating clique (set) of $G - v = G(V \setminus \{v\})$ with $r'(x) = r(x)$ when $x \neq u$, $r'(u) = r(u)$ when $r(w) = 0$ for some $w \in N[v]$ and $r'(u) = min\{r(u), r(v) - 1\}$ otherwise. In particular, the graph G has an r-dominating clique iff the graph $G - v$ has an r'-dominating clique.

Lemma 7 *If the label "outloop" is never reached by a goto command then $\{v_n\}$ is r-dominating for G.*

Theorem 5 *Algorithm DC is correct and works in linear time $O(|V| + |E|)$.*

6 r-Domination by Cliques and r-Dominant Cliques

Since a graph does not necessarily have a dominating clique it is natural to consider the following weaker *r-domination by cliques* problem: Given an undirected graph $G=(V,E)$ with weight function $(r(v_1), ..., r(v_n))$ of positive integers find a minimum number of cliques $C_1, ..., C_k$ such that $\bigcup_{i=1}^k C_i$ r-dominates G. Note that for the special case $r(v_i) = 0$ for all $i \in \{1, ..., n\}$ this is the well-known problem *clique partition*.

Another problem closely related to that is to find a clique in G which r-dominates a maximum number of vertices – we call this the *r-dominant clique* problem. For the special case $r(v_i) = 0$ for all $i \in \{1, ..., n\}$ this is again a well-known problem namely the *maximum clique* problem.

It is obvious that these two problems are NP-complete. The following results show that for chordal graphs the problems are solvable in polynomial time whereas they are NP-complete on dually chordal graphs.

For a graph $G=(V,E)$ with disks $\mathcal{N} = \{N_k[v] : v \in V$ and $k \geq 0$ a positive integer$\}$ let $\Gamma(G)$ be the following graph whose vertices are the disks of G and two disks $N_p[v]$, $N_q[w]$ are adjacent iff $N_{p+1}[v] \cap N_q[w] \neq \emptyset$ (or, equivalently, $N_p[v] \cap N_{q+1}[w] \neq \emptyset$ i.e. $0 < dist(v, w) \leq p + q + 1$).

By $l(G)$ we denote the length (number of edges) in a longest induced cycle of G.

Lemma 8 *For each graph G $l(G) = l(\Gamma(G))$ holds.*

A consequence of this lemma is that for chordal graphs G the graph $\Gamma(G)$ is also chordal. This together with Theorem 3 will be used in the following.

Theorem 6 *The problem r-domination by cliques can be solved for chordal graphs within time $O(|V| \cdot |E|)$.*

Theorem 7 *The r-dominant clique problem can be solved for chordal graphs within time $O(|V| \cdot |E|)$.*

Now we consider the same problems on dually chordal graphs.

Theorem 8 *The problems r–domination by cliques and r–dominant clique are NP– complete on dually chordal graphs even for r(v)=1 for all vertices v.*

References

[1] H. BEHRENDT and A. BRANDSTÄDT, Domination and the use of maximum neighbourhoods, TECHNICAL REPORT SM–DU–204, University of Duisburg 1992

[2] C. BERGE, Hypergraphs, *North Holland*, 1989

[3] A. BRANDSTÄDT, Special graph classes – a survey, *Technical Report SM–DU–199*, University of Duisburg 1993

[4] A. BRANDSTÄDT, F.F. DRAGAN, V.D. CHEPOI, and V.I. VOLOSHIN, Dually chordal graphs, *Technical Report SM–DU–225*, University of Duisburg 1993

[5] A. BRANDSTÄDT and D. KRATSCH, Domination problems on permutation and other graphs, *Theoretical Computer Science* 54 (1987) 181–198

[6] G.J. CHANG, Labeling algorithms for domination problems in sun–free chordal graphs, *Discrete Applied Mathematics* 22 (1988/89), 21–34

[7] G.J. CHANG and G.L. NEMHAUSER, The k–domination and k–stability problem on sun–free chordal graphs, *SIAM J. Alg. Discr. Meth.* 5 (1984), 332–345

[8] F.F. DRAGAN, Domination in Helly graphs without quadrangles, (in Russian), in press

[9] F.F. DRAGAN, Centers of graphs and the Helly property, (in Russian) Ph.D. Thesis, Moldova State University 1989

[10] F.F. DRAGAN, Dominating and packing in triangulated graphs, (in Russian), *Meth. of Discrete Analysis* (Novosibirsk), 1991, N. 51, 17–36

[11] F.F. DRAGAN, HT-graphs: centers, connected r–domination and Steiner trees, manuscript 1992, to appear in *Comput. Sci. J. of Moldova*, Kishinev 1993

[12] F.F. DRAGAN, C.F. PRISACARU, and V.D. CHEPOI, Location problems in graphs and the Helly property (in Russian), *Diskretnaja Matematika, Moscow*, vol. 4, 4 (1992), 67–73

[13] P. DUCHET, Propriete de Helly et problemes de representation, *Colloqu. Intern. CNRS 260*, Problemes Combin. et Theorie du Graphes, Orsay, France 1976, 117–118

[14] M. FARBER, Domination, independent domination and duality in strongly chordal graphs, *Discrete Applied Mathematics* 7 (1984), 115–130

[15] M. FARBER, and R.E. JAMISON, Convexity in graphs and hypergraphs, *SIAM J. Alg. Discr. Meth.* 7 (1986), 433–444

[16] C. FLAMENT, Hypergraphes arbores, *Discrete Mathematics* 21 (1978), 223–227

[17] M.C. GOLUMBIC, Algorithmic Graph Theory and Perfect Graphs, *Academic Press*, New York 1980

[18] S.C. HEDETNIEMI and R. LASKAR, (eds.), Topics on Domination, *Annals of Discr. Math.* 48, North–Holland, 1991

[19] D. KRATSCH, Finding dominating cliques efficiently, in in strongly chordal graphs and undirected path graphs, *Annals of Discrete Mathematics 48*, Topics on Domination, (S.L. Hedetniemi, R.C. Laskar, eds.), 225–238

[20] D. KRATSCH, P. DAMASCHKE and A. LUBIW, Dominating cliques in chordal graphs, to appear in Discrete Mathematics

[21] M. MOSCARINI, Doubly chordal graphs, Steiner trees and connected domination, *Networks, Networks*, 23(1993), 59–69

[22] D.J. ROSE, R.E. TARJAN and G.S. LUEKER, Algorithmic aspects of vertex elimination on graphs, *SIAM J. Comput.*, 1976, Vol. 5, No. 2, 266–283

[23] J.L. SZWARCFITER and C.F. BORNSTEIN, Clique graphs of chordal and path graphs, manuscript 1992

[24] R.E. TARJAN and M. YANNAKAKIS, Simple linear time algorithms to test chordality of graphs, test acyclicity of hypergraphs, and selectively reduce acyclic hypergraphs, *SIAM J. Comput.* 13,3 (1984), 566–579

[25] V.I. VOLOSHIN, On properties of triangulated graphs, (in Russian), *Oper. Res. and Programming* (Kishinev), 1982, 24-32

On Vertex Ranking for Permutation and Other Graphs[*]

J.S. Deogun[1], T. Kloks[2], D. Kratsch[3][**] and H. Müller[3]

[1] Department of Computer Science and Engineering
University of Nebraska – Lincoln
Lincoln, NE 68588-0115, USA
[2] Department of Mathematics and Computing Science
Eindhoven University of Technology
P.O.Box 513
5600 MB Eindhoven, The Netherlands
[3] Fakultät für Mathematik und Informatik
Friedrich-Schiller-Universität
Universitätshochhaus
07740 Jena, Germany

Abstract. In this paper we show that an optimal vertex ranking of a permutation graph can be computed in time $O(n^6)$, where n is the number of vertices. The demonstrated minimal separator approach can also be used for designing polynomial time algorithms computing an optimal vertex ranking on the following classes of well-structured graphs: circular permutation graphs, interval graphs, circular arc graphs, trapezoid graphs and cocomparability graphs of bounded dimension.

1 Introduction

In this paper we give a polynomial time algorithm which solves the vertex ranking problem on permutation graphs. The vertex ranking problem is also called the *ordered coloring problem* [15]. The problem has received much attention lately because of the growing number of applications. For example, the problem of finding an optimal vertex ranking is equivalent with the problem of finding the minimum height elimination tree of a graph. This measure is of importance in computing Cholesky factorizations of matrices in parallel [3, 9, 18]. Other applications lie in the field of VLSI-layout [17, 22]. Yet other applications can be found in scheduling problems of assembly steps in manufacturing systems [13, 14, 19, 21, 24].

Much work has been done in finding optimal rankings of trees. For trees there is now a linear time algorithm finding an optimal vertex ranking [20]. For the closely related edge ranking problem on trees an $O(n^3)$ algorithm was given

---

[*] This research was supported in part by the Office of Naval Research under Grant No. N0014-91-J-1693 and by Deutsche Forschungsgemeinschaft under Kr 1371/1-1.
[**] Currently under CHM contract at IRISA Rennes (France). Email: `kratsch@irisa.fr`

in [7]. This problem has also been considered in [24]. Efficient vertex ranking
algorithms were known for very few other classes of graphs. The vertex ranking
problem is trivial on split graphs and it is solvable in linear time on cographs [21].
Recently a $O(n^4)$ algorithm for vertex ranking of interval graphs was presented
in [1]. Our approach allows to design a $O(n^3)$ algorithm computing an optimal
vertex ranking for interval graphs.

The decision problem 'Given a graph G and a positive integer k, has G a
vertex ranking with at most k colors' is NP-complete, even when restricted to
cobipartite or bipartite graphs [2]. In view of this it is interesting to notice that
for each *constant* t, the class of graphs with vertex ranking number at most t
is recognizable in linear time [2].

In [15], among other things, an $O(\sqrt{n})$ bound is given for the vertex ranking
number of a planar graph and the authors describe a polynomial time algorithm
which finds a ranking using only $O(\sqrt{n})$ colors. For graphs in general there is
an approximation algorithm known with factor $O(\log^2 n)$ [3, 16]. In [3] it is also
shown that one plus the *pathwidth* of a graph is a lower bound for the vertex
ranking number of the graph (hence a planar graph has pathwidth $O(\sqrt{n})$, which
is also shown in [16] using different methods).

One of the most well-known and well-studied classes of perfect graphs is the
class of *permutation* graphs. Permutation graphs are exactly the comparability
graphs of posets of dimension at most two. They can also be characterized as
the graphs that are comparability and cocomparability graphs. It follows that
there is also a characterization in terms of forbidden induced subgraphs [8, 11].

Many problems, including DOMINATING SET, CLIQUE, INDEPENDENT SET,
PATHWIDTH, TREEWIDTH and MINIMUM FILL-IN can be solved efficiently for
permutation graphs [4, 5, 10, 16, 26].

For definitions and properties of classes of well-structured graphs not given
here we refer to [6, 8, 12].

In this paper we show that the vertex ranking problem can be solved efficiently for permutation graphs. Furthermore, our minimal separator approach
can also be used to design polynomial time algorithms solving the vertex ranking problem on circular permutation graphs, interval graphs, circular arc graphs,
trapezoid graphs and cocomparability graphs of bounded dimension.

2 Preliminaries

Throughout the paper the number of vertices of a graph is always denoted by n.
In this section we start with some definitions and easy lemmas on vertex rankings
and on permutation graphs. We start with some preliminaries on rankings.

2.1 Preliminaries on rankings

Definition 1. Let $G = (V, E)$ be a graph and let t be some integer. A *(vertex)*
t-ranking is a coloring $c : V \to \{1, \ldots, t\}$ such that for every pair of vertices x

and y with $c(x) = c(y)$ and for every path between x and y there is a vertex z on this path with $c(z) > c(x)$. The *vertex ranking number* of G, $\chi_r(G)$, is the smallest value t for which the graph admits a t-ranking.

By definition a vertex ranking is a proper coloring. Hence $\chi_r(G) \geq \chi(G)$ for every graph G. We call a $\chi_r(G)$-ranking of G an optimal ranking. Clearly, $\chi_r(K_n) = n$, where K_n is a complete graph on n vertices. Furthermore, the vertex ranking number of a disconnected graph is equal to the maximum vertex ranking number of its components.

Lemma 2. *Let $G = (V, E)$ be connected, and let c be a t-ranking of G. Then there is at most one vertex x with $c(x) = t$.*

Proof. Assume there are two vertices with color t. Since G is connected, there is a path between these two vertices. By definition this path must contain a vertex with color at least $t + 1$. This is a contradiction. □

Remark. Notice that if c is a t-ranking of a graph G and H is a subgraph of G, then the restriction c' of c to the vertices of H is a t-ranking for H.

This observation together with Lemma 2 leads to the following lemma which appeared in [15]. If $G = (V, E)$ is a graph and $X \subseteq V$ is a subset of vertices, then we denote by $G[X]$ the subgraph of G induced by X.

Lemma 3. *A coloring $c : V \to \{1, \ldots, t\}$ is a t-ranking for a graph $G = (V, E)$ if and only if for each $1 \leq i \leq t$, each connected component of the subgraph $G[\{x \mid c(x) \leq i\}]$ of G has at most one vertex y with $c(y) = i$.*

A concept called elimination tree, or separator tree, is closely related to ranking.

Definition 4. Let $G = (V, E)$ be a connected graph. An *elimination tree* for G is a rooted tree T with vertex set V defined recursively as follows. If $V = \{x\}$ then T is the rooted tree containing only one vertex x. Otherwise choose a vertex $r \in V$ as the root of T. Let $C_1, \ldots, C_p$ be the connected components of $G[V \setminus \{r\}]$. For each component C_i let T_i be an elimination tree. T is defined by making each root r_i of T_i adjacent to r.

The *height* of a rooted tree T is the maximal length of a path from the root to a leaf. The following result appeared, in different form, also in an earlier version of [2].

Lemma 5. *Let G be connected. Let $h(G)$ be the smallest height of an elimination tree of G. Then $\chi_r(G) = h(G) + 1$.*

Proof. Consider a $\chi_r(G)$-ranking c of G. We show that there is an elimination tree T of G with height at most $\chi_r(G) - 1$. If G has only one vertex, this is obvious. Otherwise, there is exactly one vertex with color $\chi_r(G)$. Make this vertex the root r of T. For each connected component of $G[V \setminus \{r\}]$, the restriction of

c is a $(\chi_r(G)-1)$-ranking. By induction, for each connected component there is an elimination tree of height at most $\chi_r(G) - 2$.

Now let T be an elimination tree of height h. Make a coloring of G by coloring the vertices level by level: Color the root (at level h+1) with color $h + 1$. All vertices of level i $(1 \le i \le h+1)$ get color i. Now let x and y be two vertices at the same level. Consider the set S of vertices at higher levels. By definition of an elimination tree, x and y are in different connected components of $G[V \setminus S]$. Since S contains only vertices with larger colors, every path between x and y must have a vertex of larger color. $\qquad\square$

Remark. Given an elimination tree with height h, a ranking can be obtained by coloring the vertices according to the level in which they appear in T, where the highest level of T is the level containing the root.

Remark. Using results of [3, 16] it follows that there exists an $O(\log^2 n)$ approximation algorithm to determine the vertex ranking number of a graph.

Definition 6. A subset $S \subseteq V$ is an a, b-separator for nonadjacent vertices a and b of a graph $G = (V, E)$, if the removal of S separates a and b in distinct connected components. If no proper subset of S is an a, b-separator then S is a minimal a, b-separator. A minimal separator S is a set of vertices such that S is a minimal a, b-separator for some nonadjacent vertices a and b.

The following theorem is our main tool for designing efficient vertex ranking algorithms on permutation and other graphs.

Theorem 7. *Let $G = (V, E)$ be a connected graph which is not complete. Then*

$$\chi_r(G) = \min_S \max_C \left(\chi_r(C) + |S| \right),$$

where S is a minimal vertex separator in G and C is a connected component of $G[V \setminus S]$.

Proof. First let S be a minimal separator such that each component of $G[V \setminus S]$ has vertex ranking number at most $\chi_r(G) - |S|$. Create an elimination tree of G by choosing first all vertices of S. Clearly this takes at most $|S|$ levels. For each component of $G[V \setminus S]$ choose an elimination tree with height at most $\chi_r(G) - |S| - 1$, hence the total height of this elimination tree of G is at most $\chi_r(G) - 1$.

Let T be an elimination tree of height $\chi_r(G) - 1$, and consider the coloring c given by the levels (see Remark 1 given after Lemma 5). Let $\chi_r(G) - s$ be the highest level in the tree containing more than one vertex. Let S be the set of vertices at higher levels. Hence $|S| = s$. Notice that $s < |V|$ since G is not a clique. Then $G[V \setminus S]$ is disconnected. Hence there is a minimal separator $S' \subseteq S$. The coloring c is such that all vertices of S have a unique color from $\{\chi_r(G), \ldots, \chi_r(G) - s + 1\}$. Obviously, we may permute these colors such that the vertices of S' all have a unique color from $\{\chi_r(G), \ldots, \chi_r(G) - |S'| + 1\}$. Then all vertices of $G[V \setminus S']$ have colors of $\{1, \ldots, \chi_r(G) - |S'|\}$, and hence each component has vertex ranking number at most $\chi_r(G) - |S'|$. $\qquad\square$

Remark. Notice that if S is a minimal separator of a graph $G = (V, E)$ such that all components C of $G[V \setminus S]$ have vertex ranking number at most $\chi_r(G) - |S|$, then there is a vertex ranking of G such that all vertices of S have a unique color from $\{\chi_r(G), \ldots, \chi_r(G) - |S| + 1\}$ and all other vertices have a smaller color.

Remark. The formula in Theorem 7 holds just as well if we replace 'minimal separator' by 'separator' or by 'inclusion minimal separator' (i.e., a minimal separator that is not properly contained in any other minimal separator).

Since subsets S which are not even a separator will not influence the minimum of the formula in Theorem 7 we get the following useful modification.

Corollary 8. *Let $G = (V, E)$ be a connected graph which is not complete. Then*

$$\chi_r(G) = \min_{S \in \mathcal{S}} \max_{C} \left(\chi_r(C) + |S| \right),$$

where $\mathcal{S}$ is any collection of subsets of V containing all inclusion minimal separators of G and C is a connected component of $G[V \setminus S]$.

Our algorithm relies on Theorem 7 and Corollary 8, which justifies that we do not have to check all subsets whether they are indeed minimal separators. It suffices that we make sure that all minimal separators will be considered.

2.2 Preliminaries on permutation graphs

Let π be a permutation of the numbers $1, \ldots, n$. We think of it as the sequence $\pi = [\pi(1), \ldots, \pi(n)]$.

Definition 9. If π is a permutation of the numbers $1, \ldots, n$, we can construct a graph $G[\pi] = (V, E)$ with vertex set $V = \{1, \ldots, n\}$ and edge set E:

$$(i, j) \in E \Leftrightarrow (i - j)(\pi^{-1}(i) - \pi^{-1}(j)) < 0.$$

($\pi^{-1}(i)$ denotes the position of i in $\pi = [\pi(1), \ldots, \pi(n)]$.)
An undirected graph G is a *permutation graph* if there is a permutation π such that $G \cong G[\pi]$.

The graph $G[\pi]$ is sometimes called the inversion graph of π. Given a permutation graph G, a permutation π with $G \cong G[\pi]$ can be computed in $O(n^2)$ time [23]. In this paper we assume that the permutation π is given and we identify the permutation graph with the inversion graph $G[\pi]$. A permutation graph is an intersection graph, which is illustrated by the permutation diagram [12].

Definition 10. Let π be a permutation of $1, \ldots, n$. The permutation diagram can be obtained as follows. Write the numbers $1, \ldots, n$ horizontally from left to right. Underneath, write the numbers $\pi(1), \ldots, \pi(n)$, also horizontally from left to right. Draw straight line segments, henceforth called *line segments*, joining the two 1's, the two 2's, etc.

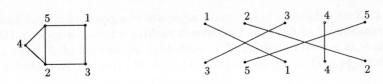

Fig. 1. permutation graph and permutation diagram

Notice that two vertices i and j of $G[\pi]$ are adjacent if and only if the corresponding line segments intersect. In Figure 1 we give an example.

Definition 11. A *scanline* in the diagram is any straight line segment with one end vertex on each horizontal line, such that the end points of the scanline do not coincide with end points of line segments in the diagram. A scanline s is *between* two non crossing line segments x and y if the top point of s is in the open interval between the top points of x and y and the bottom point of s is in the open interval between the bottom points of x and y.

If a scanline s is between line segments x and y then the intersection of each pair of the three straight line segments is empty. Consider two nonadjacent vertices x and y. The line segments in the diagram corresponding to x and y do not cross in the diagram. Hence we can find a scanline s between the lines x and y. Take out all the lines that cross the scanline s. Clearly this set of line segments corresponds to an x, y-separator in the graph. The next lemma, which appeared in [4, 16], shows that we can find all minimal x, y-separators in this way.

Lemma 12. *Let G be a permutation graph, and let x and y be nonadjacent vertices in G. For every minimal x, y-separator S there is a scanline s, which lies between the line segments corresponding to x and y, such that S is the set of all vertices of which the corresponding line segments cross the scanline s.*

If s is a scanline, then we denote by S the set of vertices of which the corresponding line segments cross s. We call two scanlines s_1 and s_2 equivalent, $s_1 \equiv s_2$, if they have the same position in the diagram relative to every line segment; i.e., the set of line segments with the top (or bottom) end point to the left of the top (or bottom) end point of the scanline is the same for s_1 and s_2.

Corollary 13. *The number of minimal separators of a permutation graph with n vertices is bounded by n^2.*

3 Pieces

Now we are going to define the main concept for designing polynomial time ranking algorithms via minimal separators. First we introduce some more notations for scanlines. We remind the reader that we may restrict the set of scanlines to a set of pairwise non-equivalent scanlines. Therefore, we are able to denote them by the position of their endpoints.

Definition 14. Let s be a scanline in a permutation diagram. Then we denote by $t(s)$ the number of line segments with top endpoint left of the top endpoint of s. By $b(s)$ we denote the number of line segments with bottom endpoint left of the bottom endpoint of s.

Hence, the ordered pair $(t(s), b(s))$ uniquely determines the scanline s.

Definition 15. The scanline s_1 is *left* of the scanline s_2 if $t(s_1) < t(s_2)$ and $b(s_1) < b(s_2)$ hold. A *piece* $P = \mathcal{P}(s_1, s_2)$ is a subgraph of G induced by all line segments that are *between* the two scanlines s_1 and s_2 where s_1 is left of s_2.

We identify the piece $P = \mathcal{P}(s_1, s_2)$ with the permutation diagram containing s_1, s_2 and all line segments corresponding to vertices of P. (If the vertex set of P is empty then P is an empty piece and $\chi_r(P) = 0$.)

Corollary 16. *The number of pieces of a permutation graph on n vertices is bounded by n^4.*

Pieces are of interest for designing a vertex ranking algorithm (on permutation graphs) for the following reason. Suppose we use recursively the formula of Theorem 7 for computing the vertex ranking number of a given graph G. Then we will have to compute the vertex ranking number of all those induced subgraphs H of G which may arise from G by iteratively repeating the following procedure until the current graph is H itself:

1. remove a minimal separator of the current graph and then
2. choose a connected component to be the new current graph and remove all the other components.

It is not hard to show that if G is a permutation graph then each such induced subgraph H is indeed a piece.

Definition 17. Let $P = \mathcal{P}(s_1, s_2)$ be a piece. A scanline s is *cutting* for P if $t(s_1) < t(s) < t(s_2)$ and $b(s_1) < b(s) < b(s_2)$ hold.

Cutting scanlines of pieces are similar to nice scanlines of candidate components, a concept used in [4]. The following lemma and its proof is very similar to a lemma on nice scanlines and minimal separators in [4].

Lemma 18. *Let S be a minimal separator of a piece $P = \mathcal{P}(s_1, s_2)$ of a permutation graph $G = (V, E)$. Then there is a cutting scanline s for P such that S is exactly the set of those line segments of P crossing s.*

Proof. Consider the permutation diagram of $P = \mathcal{P}(s_1, s_2)$. Let S be a minimal separator of P and let C_a and C_b be components of $P[V(P) \setminus S]$ such that every vertex $s \in S$ has a neighbour in C_a and a neighbour in C_b. Then there is a scanline s such that the scanline s does not cross any line segment corresponding to a vertex of $V(P) \setminus S$ and s is between C_a and C_b, i.e. for every line segment corresponding to a vertex of C_a and every line segment corresponding to a vertex of C_b holds that the scanline s is between these two line segments. Such a scanline s is cutting and the set of line segments crossing s is exactly S. $\square$

Let $P = \mathcal{P}(s_1, s_2)$ be a piece of a permutation graph G and let s be a cutting scanline of P. We denote by $A(s_1, s, s_2)$ the set of line segments of $P = \mathcal{P}(s_1, s_2)$ crossing the scanline s. Hence, the line segments belonging to $A(s_1, s, s_2)$ are exactly those which in the diagram of G cross s but cross neither s_1 nor s_2.

The following theorem gives a recursion formula for pieces of permutation graphs similar to Theorem 7.

Theorem 19. *Let $P = \mathcal{P}(s_1, s_2)$ be a piece of a permutation graph $G = (V, E)$ and let P have at least one cutting scanline. Then*

$$\chi_r(\mathcal{P}(s_1, s_2)) = \min_s \left\{ |S \setminus (S_1 \cup S_2)| + \max\left(\chi_r(\mathcal{P}(s_1, s)), \chi_r(\mathcal{P}(s, s_2))\right) \right\},$$

where the minimum is taken over all cutting scanlines s for P. S, S_1 and S_2 are the sets of vertices of which the corresponding line segments in the permutation diagram of G cross the scanline s, s_1 and s_2, respectively.

Proof. By Lemma 18 the collection of all sets $A(s_1, s, s_2)$, where s is a cutting scanline for $P = \mathcal{P}(s_1, s_2)$, contains all minimal separators of P. Therefore Theorem 7 and Corollary 8, when applied to the piece P, imply immediately that the following formula holds:

$$\chi_r(\mathcal{P}(s_1, s_2)) = \min_s \max_C \left(\chi_r(C) + |A(s_1, s, s_2)|\right),$$

where the minimum is taken over all cutting scanlines for P and the maximum is taken over all components C of $P[V(P) \setminus S]$.

Since the ranking number of a disconnected graph is equal to the maximum ranking number of its components and since each connected component C is either completely contained in $P(s_1, s)$ or in $P(s_2, s)$ we have

$$\max\{\chi_r(C) \mid C \text{ component of } P[V(P) \setminus S]\} = \max\left(\chi_r(\mathcal{P}(s_1, s)), \chi_r(\mathcal{P}(s, s_2))\right).$$

$\square$

4 Computing the vertex ranking number of a permutation graph

In this section we describe an algorithm to compute the vertex ranking number of a permutation graph. The advantage of this algorithm is that it will only deal with scanlines and pieces. It never has to check whether the set of line segments crossing a certain scanline is indeed a minimal separator, it never really computes connected components and it never computes the vertex set of a piece $\mathcal{P}(s_1, s_2)$. Instead it maintains pieces by their defining scanlines s_1 and s_2. Hence, we do not compute all pieces at the beginning of the algorithm and we do not have to sort the pieces by increasing size which is usually a typical part of similar algorithms.

The algorithm computes the vertex ranking number of all pieces according to the distance of their defining scanlines:

1. In a preprocessing compute the values $|A(s_1, s, s_2)| = |S \setminus (S_1 \cup S_2)|$ for all triples (s_1, s, s_2) with $t(s_1) < t(s) < t(s_2)$ and $b(s_1) < b(s) < b(s_2)$.
2. Compute the vertex ranking number of the 'small' pieces $P = \mathcal{P}(s_1, s_2)$, i.e. those with either $t(s_2) - t(s_1) \leq 1$ or $b(s_2) - b(s_1) \leq 1$ by the following formula:

$$\chi_r(\mathcal{P}(s_1, s_2)) = \begin{cases} 1 & \text{if there is one line segment between } s_1 \text{ and } s_2 \\ 0 & \text{otherwise} \end{cases}$$

3. Sort all remaining 'large' pieces $P = \mathcal{P}(s_1, s_2)$ according to the increasing value of $(t(s_2) - t(s_1)) + (b(s_2) - b(s_1))$.
4. Compute the vertex ranking number of the large pieces in this order using the formula of Theorem 19:

$$\chi_r(\mathcal{P}(s_1, s_2)) = \min_s \left\{ |A(s_1, s, s_2)| + \max\left(\chi_r(\mathcal{P}(s_1, s)), \chi_r(\mathcal{P}(s, s_2))\right) \right\}.$$

Notice that the largest piece has a scanline which lies totally to the left of all line segments and a scanline which lies totally to the right of all line segments. Hence, this piece is the graph G itself and the ranking number of this piece is exactly the ranking number of G, i.e. the output of the algorithm.

Theorem 20. *There is a $O(n^6)$ algorithm computing the vertex ranking number of a permutation graph.*

Proof. The number of pieces is at most n^4 since each is determined by two scanlines s_1 and s_2 where s_1 is left of s_2, see Corollary 16. The most time consuming steps of the algorithm are clearly Step 1 and 4.

Let us first consider step 4. The ranking number of a piece $P = \mathcal{P}(s_1, s_2)$ is computed by minimizing $|A(s_1, s, s_2)| + \max(\chi_r(\mathcal{P}(s_1, s)), \chi_r(\mathcal{P}(s, s_2)))$ over all scanlines s with $t(s_1) < t(s) < t(s_2)$ and $b(s_1) < b(s) < b(s_2)$. How often is this value computed?

There are at most n^2 cutting scanlines s for a piece $P = \mathcal{P}(s_1, s_2)$. Consequently, this computation is done at most n^6 times. The values $|A(s_1, s, s_2)|$, $\chi_r(\mathcal{P}(s_1, s))$ and $\chi_r(\mathcal{P}(s, s_2))$ can be determined by a table look-up in constant time. Hence, the overall running time of the algorithm is $O(n^6)$ if the preprocessing in step 1 can also be done in time $O(n^6)$.

Indeed the preprocessing can be done in time $O(n^5)$ by computing all values $a(s_1, s; t(s_2), b(s_2)) = |A(s_1, s, s_2)|$ for fixed scanlines s_1 and s and all possible values of $t(s_2)$ and $b(s_2)$ in time $O(n)$. We start with $a(s_1, s; t(s), b(s)) = 0$ and use the following formulas:

$$a(s_1, s; i+1, j) = \begin{cases} a(s_1, s; i, j) + 1 & \text{if } b(s_1) < \pi^{-1}(i+1) < b(s) \\ a(s_1, s; i, j) & \text{otherwise} \end{cases}$$

$$a(s_1, s; i, j+1) = \begin{cases} a(s_1, s; i, j) + 1 & \text{if } t(s_1) < \pi(j+1) < t(s) \\ a(s_1, s; i, j) & \text{otherwise} \end{cases}$$

where $t(s) \leq i \leq n$ and $b(s) \leq j \leq n$ is supposed.

The method used for the preprocessing is a standard method for computing these kind of values using the permutation diagram (see e.g. [4]). $\qquad\square$

Remark. An optimal vertex ranking of a given permutation graph can also be computed in time $O(n^6)$. Whenever $\chi_r(\mathcal{P}(s_1, s_2))$ has been computed by table look-up to smaller pieces we add pointers to a pair $\mathcal{P}(s_1, s)$ and $\mathcal{P}(s, s_2)$ giving raise to the value $\chi_r(\mathcal{P}(s_1, s_2))$. After finding $\chi_r(G)$ a backtracking using these pointers will produce an optimal vertex ranking or a minimum elimination height tree of G.

5 Other well-structured graphs

We described a simple algorithm to compute the vertex ranking number of a permutation graph.

The demonstrated 'dynamic programming on pieces' does not rely much on the structure of permutation graphs. Indeed, the key properties a graph class should have for using this approach are:

1. there is a polynomial p in n such that the number of minimal separators of every graph on n vertices, belonging to the class, is bounded by $p(n)$ and
2. there is a polynomial time algorithm listing all pieces of an input graph belonging to the class.

However, how to define the pieces? Let us consider a class $\mathcal{G}$ of graphs. The set of pieces of a graph has naturally to be chosen using the structural properties of $\mathcal{G}$. Furthermore, for every graph $G = (V, E)$ of $\mathcal{G}$ it contains G itself and all induced subgraphs H of G which may arise from G by iteratively repeating the procedure described below Corollary 16: first remove a minimal separator of the current graph and then choose a connected component to be the new current graph and remove all the other components. Thus, using the recursion formula of Theorem 7 one can compute then the vertex ranking number of G by 'dynamic programming on the pieces' of G. (If our approach is used for a certain class of well-structured graphs, then typically a preprocessing determining auxiliary data is necessary to reach the best time bound.)

The following classes of well-structured graphs have both properties which is always based on an intersection model (sometimes a 'circular' extension of a 'linear' model). Using dynamic programming on pieces an optimal vertex ranking can be computed in time $O(n^3)$ for interval graphs, in time $O(n^6)$ for trapezoid graphs, in time $O(n^3)$ for circular arc graphs and in time $O(n^6)$ for circular permutation graphs.

We can also show that there is $O(n^{3d})$ algorithm computing an optimal vertex ranking for cocomparability graphs of dimension at most d, if the intersection model is part of the input. A graph G is a *cocomparability graph of dimension at most d* if there is a poset P of dimension at most d and G is the complement of the comparability graph of P. Therefore, the recognition problem of cocomparability graphs of dimension at most d is NP-complete for every fixed $d \geq 3$ since it is equivalent to the partial order dimension problem which was shown to be NP-complete for every fixed $d \geq 3$ in [25].

However, an optimal vertex ranking can also be computed in polynomial time for cocomparability graphs of dimension at most d if the intersection model is not part of the input.

6 Open problems

We like to mention the following open problems:

- It is not known whether the vertex ranking can be done in polynomial time for other classes of well-structured graphs like chordal graphs and circle graphs.
- It is surprising that the algorithmic complexity of edge ranking on graphs in general is still open.

References

1. B. Aspvall and P. Heggernes, Finding minimum height elimination trees for interval graphs in polynomial time, Technical Report No 80, Department of Informatics, University of Bergen, Norway, 1993.
2. H. Bodlaender, J.S. Deogun, K. Jansen, T. Kloks, D. Kratsch, H. Müller and Z. Tuza, Rankings of graphs, in preparation.
3. H.L. Bodlaender, J.R. Gilbert, H. Hafsteinsson and T. Kloks, Approximating tree-width, pathwidth and minimum elimination tree height, *Proc. 17th International Workshop on Graph-Theoretic Concepts in Computer Science WG'91*, Springer-Verlag, Lecture Notes in Computer Science 570, 1992, pp. 1–12.
4. H. Bodlaender, T. Kloks and D. Kratsch, Treewidth and pathwidth of permutation graphs, *Proceedings of the 20th International Colloquium on Automata, Languages and Programming*, Springer-Verlag, Lecture Notes in Computer Science 700, 1993, pp. 114–125.
5. A. Brandstädt and D. Kratsch, On domination problems for permutation and other graphs, *Theoretical Computer Science* 54 (1987), 181-198.
6. A. Brandstädt, Special graph classes — a survey, Schriftenreihe des Fachbereichs Mathematik, SM-DU-199, Universität Duisburg Gesamthochschule, 1991 .
7. J.S. Deogun and Y. Peng, Edge ranking of trees, *Congressius Numerantium* 79 (1990), 19-28.
8. P. Duchet, Classical perfect graphs, in: *Topics on Perfect Graphs*, C. Berge and V. Chvátal, (eds.), Annals of Discrete Mathematics 21, 1984, pp. 67–96.
9. I.S. Duff and J.K. Reid, The multifrontal solution of indefinite sparse symmetric linear equations, *ACM Transactions on Mathematical Software* 9 (1983), 302–325.
10. M. Farber and M. Keil, Domination in permutation graphs, *Journal of Algorithms* 6 (1985), 309–321.
11. T. Gallai, Transitiv orientierbare Graphen, *Acta Mathematica Scientiarum Hungaricae* 18 (1967), 25–66.
12. M.C. Golumbic, *Algorithmic Graph Theory and Perfect Graphs*, Academic Press, New York, 1980.
13. A.V. Iyer, H.D. Ratliff and G. Vijayan, Parallel assembly of modular products–an analysis, Technical Report 88-06, Georgia Institute of Technology, 1988.

14. A.V. Iyer, H.D. Ratliff and G. Vijayan, On edge ranking problems of trees and graphs, *Discrete Applied Mathematics* **30** (1991), 43–52.

15. M. Katchalski, W. McCuaig and S. Seager, Ordered colourings, Manuscript, University of Waterloo, 1988.

16. T. Kloks, *Treewidth*, Ph.D. Thesis, Utrecht University, The Netherlands, 1993.

17. C.E. Leiserson, Area efficient graph layouts for VLSI, *Proceedings of the 21st Annual IEEE Symposium on Foundations of Computer Science*, 1980, pp. 270–281.

18. J.W.H. Liu, The role of elimination trees in sparse factorization, *SIAM Journal of Matrix Analysis and Applications* **11** (1990), 134–172.

19. J. Nevins and D. Whitney, (eds.), *Concurrent Design of Products and Processes*, McGraw-Hill, 1989.

20. A.A. Schäffer, Optimal node ranking of trees in linear time, *Information Processing Letters* **33** (1989/1990), 91–96.

21. P. Scheffler, Node ranking and Searching on Graphs (Abstract), in: U. Faigle and C. Hoede, (eds.), *3rd Twente Workshop on Graphs and Combinatorial Optimization*, Memorandum No.1132, Faculty of Applied Mathematics, University of Twente, The Netherlands, 1993.

22. A. Sen, H. Deng and S. Guha, On a graph partition problem with application to VLSI layout, *Information Processing Letters* **43** (1992), 87–94.

23. J. Spinrad, On comparability and permutation graphs, *SIAM Journal on Computing* **14** (1985), 658–670.

24. P. de la Torre, R. Greenlaw and A. A. Schäffer, Optimal ranking of trees in polynomial time, *Proceedings of the 4th Annual ACM-SIAM Symposium on Discrete Algorithms*, Austin, Texas, 1993, pp. 138–144.

25. M. Yannakakis, The complexity of the partial order dimension problem, *SIAM Journal on Algebraic and Discrete Methods* **3** (1982), 351–358.

26. M.-S. Yu, L.Y. Tseng and S.-J. Chang, Sequential and Parallel algorithms for the maximum-weight independent set problem on permutation graphs, *Information processing Letters* **46** (1993), 7–11.

Finding all minimal separators of a graph

T. Kloks[1]* and D. Kratsch[2]

[1] Department of Mathematics and Computing Science
Eindhoven University of Technology
P.O.Box 513
5600 MB Eindhoven, The Netherlands
[2] Fakultät für Mathematik und Informatik
Friedrich-Schiller-Universität
Universitätshochhaus
07740 Jena, Germany

Abstract. In this paper we give an efficient algorithm to find all minimal vertex separators of an undirected graph. The algorithm needs polynomial time per separator that is found.

1 Introduction

Given a graph, one is often interested in finding subsets of vertices, or their cardinality, which possess a certain property. For example the CLIQUE NUMBER of a graph G is the maximum cardinality of a subset S such that $G[S]$ is complete. Similar questions are the INDEPENDENCE NUMBER, the DOMINATION NUMBER or the CHROMATIC NUMBER. For many of these problems, it would be convenient if one could use a decomposition of the graph by means of certain *separators*.

This is perhaps best illustrated by the recent results for classes of graphs of bounded treewidth. For these classes, linear time algorithms exist for many NP-complete problems *exactly* because a decomposition can be made using *separators of bounded size* [1, 2, 3, 4, 11]. A decomposition of this type can be found in linear time [5, 11], however the huge constants involved in these algorithms do not make them of much practical use. Our results show that for many classes of graphs *efficient* decomposition algorithms exist, i.e., the size of the separators is of no importance.

A closely related, but somewhat different approach was surveyed in [15]. In this paper (see also [7]) it is shown that for many classes of graphs (for example chordal graphs, clique separable graphs and edge intersection graphs of paths in a tree or EPT-graphs) a decomposition by *clique separators* is possible, and it is illustrated that such a decomposition can also be used to solve efficiently many NP-complete problems like MINIMUM FILL-IN, MAXIMUM CLIQUE, GRAPH COLORING and MAXIMUM INDEPENDENT SET. In [16] an algorithm is given for finding clique separators efficiently (the algorithm uses $O(nm)$ time to find one clique separator). Our results generalize the above mentioned results in the sense that at least some of these NP-complete problems are solvable for much more graph classes, i.e., graph classes for which the number of minimal separators is polynomial bounded ([6, 12, 13, 14]).

---

* Email: ton@win.tue.nl.

In [10] an algorithm is given which finds all, what the authors call *minimum size separators*. By this they mean that given a graph which is k-connected, the algorithm finds all separators with k vertices. Moreover, they show in this paper that the number of these separators is bounded by $O(2^k \frac{n^2}{k})$. Their algorithm which lists all minimum size separators runs in time $O(2^k n^3)$. We call a subset of vertices S a minimal separator if there are non adjacent vertices x and y such that the removal of S separates x and y into disjoint connected components in such a way that no proper subset of S also does this (see Definition 1). A closely related concept which we call *inclusion minimal separators* lies more or less between the minimum size separators and the minimal separators, i.e., all minimum size separators are inclusion minimal and all inclusion minimal separators are minimal separators.

The following example shows that the minimum size separators and the inclusion minimal separators are only of limited use. Consider any graph G. Take a new vertex x and make this adjacent to all vertices of G. Take another new vertex y and make this adjacent to x. Call this new graph H. The only inclusion minimal separator which is also the only minimum size separator of H is $\{x\}$. However if S is some minimal separator of G, then $S \cup \{x\}$ is a minimal separator in H. Hence H has at least as many minimal separators as G.

In [6, 11, 12, 13, 14] it is shown that many important classes of graphs have a polynomial number of minimal vertex separators. These graph classes include permutation graphs, circular permutation graphs, trapezoid graphs, circle graphs, circular arc graphs, distance hereditary graphs, chordal bipartite graphs, cocomparability graphs of bounded dimension and weakly triangulated graphs. In this paper we present an algorithm to compute all minimal vertex separators. Notice that, in general, the number of separators can be exponential, as the following example shows. Consider the graph consisting of two non adjacent vertices s and t, and a set of $\frac{n-2}{2}$ (internally) vertex disjoint paths of length 3 from s to t. The number of minimal s,t-separators in this graph is $2^{(n-2)/2}$.

For listing other types of combinatorial structures we refer to [8].

2 Preliminaries

If $G = (V, E)$ is a graph and $W \subseteq V$ a subset of vertices then we use $G[W]$ as a notation for the subgraph of G *induced* by the vertices of W. For a vertex $x \in V$ we use $N(x)$ to denote the neighborhood of x.

The following definition can be found for example in [9].

Definition 1. Given a graph $G = (V, E)$ and two non adjacent vertices a and b, a subset $S \subset V$ is an a,b-*separator* if the removal of S separates a and b in distinct connected components. If no proper subset of S is an a,b-separator then S is a *minimal a,b-separator*. A *(minimal) separator* is a set of vertices S for which there exist non adjacent vertices a and b such that S is a (minimal) a,b-separator.

The following lemma appears for example as an exercise in [9]. It provides an easy test whether a given set S of vertices is a minimal separator or not.

Lemma 2. *Let S be a separator of the graph $G = (V, E)$. Then S is a minimal separator if and only if there are two different connected components of $G[V - S]$ such that every vertex of S has a neighbor in both of these components.*

Proof. Let S be a minimal a, b-separator and let C_a and C_b be the connected components containing a and b respectively. Let $x \in S$. Since S is a *minimal a, b-separator*, there is a path between a and b passing through x but using no other vertex in S. Hence x must have a neighbor in C_a and in C_b.

Now let S be a separator and let C_a and C_b be two connected components such that every vertex of S has a neighbor in C_a and in C_b. Let $a \in C_a$ and $b \in C_b$. Then clearly S is a minimal a, b-separator, for if $x \in S$, then there is a path between a and b which uses no vertices of $S \setminus \{x\}$. $\qquad\square$

Notice that this also proves the following. Let S be a minimal separator and let C_1 and C_2 be two connected components of $G[V - S]$ such that every vertex of S has a neighbor in both C_1 and C_2. If a is a vertex of C_1 and b is a vertex of C_2 then S is a minimal a, b-separator.

It may be a bit surprising at first sight that it is very well possible for one minimal separator to be contained in another one. An example of this can be found in [9]. However, for minimal a, b-separators things are different, since by definition one minimal a, b-separator cannot be contained in another one.

We now show that at least some of the minimal separators are easy to find.

Definition 3. Let a and b be non adjacent vertices. If S is a minimal a, b-separator which contains only neighbors of a then S is called *close to a*.

Lemma 4. *If a and b are non adjacent then there exists exactly one minimal a, b-separator close to a.*

Proof. Let S be a minimal a, b-separator close to a. For every vertex in S there is a path to b which does not use any other neighbors of a, since S is minimal. On the other hand, if x is a neighbor of a such that there is a path to b without any other neighbors of a, then x must be an element of S, otherwise there is a path between x and b which avoids S and this is a contradiction since x is in the component of $G[V - S]$ that contains a. $\qquad\square$

Notice that a minimal separator close to a can easily be computed as follows. Start with $S = N(a)$. Clearly, since a and b are non adjacent S separates a and b. Let C_b be the connected component of $G[V - S]$ containing b. Let $S' \subseteq S$ be the set of those vertices of S which have at least one neighbor in C_b. By Lemma 2 S' is a minimal a, b-separator, and since it only contains neighbors of a, it is close to a.

Lemma 5. *Let S be a minimal a, b-separator close to a and let C_a and C_b be the connected components containing a and b respectively. Let $S^* \neq S$ be another minimal a, b-separator. Then $S^* \subset S \cup C_b$.*

Proof. Since S^* is a minimal a, b-separator $S^* \subset C_a \cup C_b \cup S$. Assume S^* has a vertex $x \in C_a$. $S^* \setminus \{x\}$ does not separate a and b hence there is a path P between a and b using x but no other vertex of S^*. Since S is a minimal separator, P goes through a vertex $y \in S$. Since S is close to a, y is adjacent to a. Hence there is a path $P' \subset P$ between a and b that does not contain x. This is a contradiction since P' contains no vertex of S^*. □

In the next two sections we show how to obtain new minimal a,b-separators from a given one using so called minimal pairs. A minimal pair is in some sense the smallest step to go from one minimal a,b-separator to the next one. The main difficulty is to prove that we indeed obtain all minimal separators by using small steps only.

In section 5 we describe an algorithm that computes all minimal a,b-separators for a given pair of non adjacent vertices a and b in a breadth-first-search manner, we prove that it is correct and we analyse its time complexity. We end with some concluding remarks and some open problems.

3 Good pairs

Let $G = (V, E)$ be a graph and let a and b be non adjacent vertices in G. Let S be a minimal a,b-separator and let C_a and C_b be the connected components containing a and b respectively.

Definition 6. Let $\Delta \subseteq C_a \setminus \{a\}$ and let C'_a be the connected component of $G[C_a - \Delta]$ that contains a. Let $N \subseteq S$ be the set of vertices in S that do not have a neighbor in C'_a. The pair (Δ, N) is called *good* for S if the following conditions are satisfied.

1. $N \neq \emptyset$.
2. Each $\delta \in \Delta$ has at least one neighbor in C'_a.
3. Each $\delta \in \Delta$ either has a neighbor in N or there exists a vertex $x \in N$ and a connected component D of $G[C_a - \Delta]$ such that both x and δ have at least one neighbor in D.

Lemma 7. *If S is close to a then there is no good pair.*

Proof. Assume (Δ, N) is a good pair. Hence $\Delta \subseteq C_a \setminus \{a\}$. Let C'_a be the connected component of $G[C_a - \Delta]$ that contains a. The set N is defined as the subset of S that does not contain any neighbor in C'_a. Then $N = \emptyset$ since S contains only neighbors of a. But by definition $N \neq \emptyset$. □

Theorem 8 shows that a good pair defines a new separator. In Theorem 9 we show that each minimal a,b-separator can be obtained by a good pair for the separator that is close to b. In section 4 we show that only a restricted type of good pairs, called minimal pairs, have to be considered.

Theorem 8. *Let (Δ, N) be a good pair. Define $S^* = (S \cup \Delta) \setminus N$. Then S^* is a minimal a,b-separator.*

Proof. Let C'_a be the connected component of $G[C_a - \Delta]$ that contains a. Clearly, S^* separates a and b, since vertices of N do not have neighbors in C'_a. Let C'_b be the connected component of $G[V - S^*]$ that contains b. Notice that $C_b \subset C'_b$, and since each vertex of N has a neighbor in C_b, $N \subset C'_b$.

Each vertex of S^* has at least one neighbor in C'_a by definition of a good pair, and each vertex of $S^* \setminus \Delta$ has at least one neighbor in C'_b since it has at least one neighbor in C_b. The only thing left to show is that each vertex of Δ has a neighbor in C'_b. Let $\delta \in \Delta$. By definition, either δ has a neighbor in N (and hence in C'_b) or there is a vertex $x \in N$ and a connected component D of $G[C_a - \Delta]$ such that both δ and x have a neighbor in D. D is also connected in $G[V - S^*]$ and since x has a neighbor in D, $D \subset C'_b$. $\qquad \square$

Theorem 9. *Assume S is close to b. Let $S^* \neq S$ be a minimal a, b-separator. There exists a good pair (Δ, N) such that $S^* = (S \cup \Delta) \setminus N$.*

Proof. Let C^*_a and C^*_b be the connected components of $G[V - S^*]$ containing a and b respectively.

First notice that $S^* \subset C_a \cup C_b \cup S$, since S^* is minimal. Since S is close to b, by Lemma 5, $S^* \subset S \cup C_a$. Let $\Delta = S^* \cap C_a$ and $N = S \setminus S^*$. We show that (Δ, N) is a good pair.

Since $S^* \neq S$ and both are minimal a, b-separators: $N \neq \emptyset$.

Let C'_a be the connected component of $G[C_a - \Delta]$ containing a. We show that N is exactly the set of vertices in S which do not have a neighbor in C'_a. In order to do this we claim that $C'_a = C^*_a$. Since C'_a is a connected component of $G[V - (\Delta \cup S)]$ and since $S^* \subset \Delta \cup S$, $C'_a \subseteq C^*_a$. Now assume there is a vertex $x \in N$ which has a neighbor $y \in C'_a$. Since S is close to b, x is a neighbor of b. This is a contradiction since there would be a path between a and b which does not use any vertex of S^*. This shows that $C'_a = C^*_a$. Since S^* is minimal, N is exactly the set of vertices in S that do not have a neighbor in C'_a, and every vertex of $\Delta \cup (S \setminus N)$ has at least one neighbor in C'_a.

To prove the last item first notice that $N \subset C^*_b$ and that C^*_b contains exactly those connected components D of $G[C_a - \Delta]$ for which there is a vertex $y \in N$ which has a neighbor in D. Now let $\delta \in \Delta$. Since S^*_a is minimal, δ has a neighbor x in C^*_b. Since δ only has neighbors in $C_a \cup S$, x must be an element of N or of some component D of $G[C_a - \Delta]$. In this second case, there must also be a vertex $y \in N$ which has a neighbor in D. $\qquad \square$

4 Minimal pairs

Again let $G = (V, E)$ be a graph and let a and b be non adjacent vertices in G. Let S be a minimal a, b-separator and let C_a and C_b be the connected components of $G[V - S]$ containing a and b respectively. In this section we show how to find some good pairs.

Definition 10. Let $x \in S$ be non adjacent to a. Let $C_a(x)$ be the subgraph induced by $C_a \cup \{x\}$. Let Δ be the minimal x, a-separator in $C_a(x)$ close to x, and let C'_a be the connected component containing a. Now let N be the set of vertices of S which do not have a neighbor in C'_a. The pair (Δ, N) is called the *minimal pair* for S and x.

Lemma 11. *A minimal pair is good.*

Proof. Notice that $x \in N$, hence $N \neq \emptyset$.

Now, Δ is a minimal x, a-separator in $C_a(x)$ and hence every vertex of Δ has a neighbor in C'_a.

Finally, if $\delta \in \Delta$ then δ is adjacent to x since Δ is close to x. Hence each vertex of Δ has a neighbor in N. $\qquad\square$

We want to prove that we can find every minimal a, b-separator by starting with the minimal a, b-separator that is close to b and by recursively using minimal pairs. The following technical lemma proves this.

Lemma 12. *Let (Δ, N) be a good pair for S. Let $x \in N$ and let (Δ^*, N^*) be the minimal pair for S and x. Let $S^* = (S \cup \Delta^*) \setminus N^*$. Define $\overline{\Delta} = \Delta \setminus \Delta^*$ and $\overline{N} = (N \setminus N^*) \cup (\Delta^* \setminus \Delta)$. Then:*

1. *if $\overline{N} = \emptyset$ then $(S \cup \Delta) \setminus N = S^*$, and if*
2. *$\overline{N} \neq \emptyset$ then $(\overline{\Delta}, \overline{N})$ is a good pair for S^* and $(S \cup \Delta) \setminus N = (S^* \cup \overline{\Delta}) \setminus \overline{N}$.*

Proof. We start with some easy observations. Let C'_a be the connected component of $G[C_a - \Delta]$ that contains a and let C^*_a be the connected component of $G[C_a - \Delta^*]$ that contains a. Let $\Delta' = N(x) \cap \Delta$.

– $C'_a \subseteq C^*_a$ since Δ^* contains no vertices of C'_a.
– $\Delta' \subseteq \Delta^*$ since every vertex of Δ' has a neighbor in C'_a.
– $\Delta \setminus \Delta' \subseteq C^*_a$ since every vertex of Δ has a neighbor in C'_a.
– $N^* \subseteq N$, since $C'_a \subseteq C^*_a$.
– C'_a is exactly the connected component of $G[C^*_a - (\Delta \setminus \Delta')]$ containing a since $C^*_a - (\Delta \setminus \Delta')$ contains all vertices of C'_a but no vertex of Δ.
– The set of vertices in S^* without a neighbor in C'_a is exactly $\overline{N}$, which is easy to check.

Assume $\overline{N} = \emptyset$. Then $\Delta^* \subseteq \Delta$ and $N = N^*$ (since $N^* \subseteq N$). Now clearly, also $\Delta^* = \Delta$, otherwise S^* and $(S \cup \Delta) \setminus N$ are two minimal a, b-separators of which one is properly contained in the other which is impossible by definition. Hence $S^* = (S \cup \Delta) \setminus N$.

Now assume $\overline{N} \neq \emptyset$. We show that $(\overline{\Delta}, \overline{N})$ is good for S^*. Notice that every vertex of $\overline{\Delta}$ has a neighbor in C'_a, since this holds for every vertex of Δ.

Let $\delta \in \overline{\Delta}$ and assume that δ has no neighbors in $\overline{N}$. Since $\delta \in C^*_a$, δ has no neighbor in N^*. Hence δ has no neighbor in N. Now (Δ, N) is a good pair, hence there is a vertex $z \in N$ and a connected component D of $G[C_a - \Delta]$ such that δ and z have a neighbor in D. Assume by way of contradiction that for no vertex of $\overline{N}$ there is a connected component in $G[C^*_a - \overline{\Delta}]$ such that this vertex and δ both have a neighbor in this component. The following observations lead to a contradiction.

– $N(\delta) \cap D \subseteq C^*_a$. Otherwise, since $\Delta^* \setminus \Delta' \subset \overline{N}$, δ has a neighbor in $\overline{N}$.
– $G[D \setminus \Delta^*]$ is connected. Since otherwise every connected component has a vertex with a neighbor in $\Delta^* \setminus \Delta$, and hence there is a connected component and some vertex in $\overline{N}$ such that this vertex and δ both have a neighbor in this component.
– D contains no vertices of Δ^*, by the same argument.

This shows that $D \subset C_a^*$. If $z \in N^*$ then z can have no neighbors in D, since z has no neighbors in C_a^*. Hence $z \in N \setminus N^*$. This is a contradiction, since now there is a connected component D in $G[C_a^* - \overline{\Delta}]$ and a vertex $z \in \overline{N}$ such that z and δ both have a neighbor in D.

The fact that $(S \cup \Delta) \setminus N = (S^* \cup \overline{\Delta}) \setminus \overline{N}$ is obvious. □

By Lemma 12 and Theorem 9 we obtain the following result.

Corollary 13. *Let S be a minimal a, b-separator and let S_1 be the minimal a, b-separator close to b. There exists a sequence $(\Delta_1, N_1), \ldots, (\Delta_t, N_t)$ such that*

1. *(Δ_1, N_1) is a minimal pair for S_1 and some vertex $x_1 \in N_1$.*
2. *For $i = 2, \ldots, t$, (Δ_i, N_i) is a minimal pair for $S_i = (S_{i-1} \cup \Delta_{i-1}) \setminus N_{i-1}$ and some vertex $x_i \in N_i$.*
3. *For $i = 1, \ldots, t$, Δ_i and a are in the same connected component of $G[V - S_i]$.*
4. *$S = (S_t \cup \Delta_t) \setminus N_t$.*

5 An algorithm finding minimal separators

In this section we give an algorithm that, given a graph G and two non adjacent vertices a and b finds all minimal a, b-separators. This algorithm is displayed in figure 1.

Theorem 14. *Let S be the minimal a, b-separator that is close to b and let $\mathcal{T} = \{S\}$ and $\mathcal{Q} = \{S\}$. Then a call separators$(G, a, b, \mathcal{T}, \mathcal{Q})$ determines a set $\mathcal{Q}$ containing all minimal a, b-separators.*

Proof. By Corollary 13 the set $\mathcal{Q}$ contains all minimal a, b-separators. By Lemma 11 and Theorem 8 all sets in $\mathcal{Q}$ are minimal separators. □

Remark. If we let $\mathcal{T} = \{\{b\}\}$ and $\mathcal{Q} = \emptyset$ then a call separators$(G, a, b, \mathcal{T}, \mathcal{Q})$ has the same result.

Theorem 15. *Let R be the number of minimal a, b-separators (for non adjacent vertices a and b). The algorithm to determine all minimal a, b-separators can be implemented to run in time $O(n^4 R)$.*

Proof. Assume that the graph is given with an adjacency matrix. The minimal separator S that is close to b can easily be found in $O(n^2)$ time as follows. Initialize $S = N(b)$. Determine the connected component C_a of $G[V - S]$. Remove vertices from S that do not have a neighbor in C_a.

First we show that the outermost loop of the procedure separators is executed at most n times. If the outer loop is executed for the ith time, for each separator S in the set $\mathcal{T}$, the connected component of $G[V - S]$ that contains a has at most $n - i$ vertices.

Since the set $\mathcal{T}$ contains only different minimal separators, the second loop is executed at most R time. Clearly, each separator has at most $O(n)$ elements.

```
procedure separators(G, a, b, T, Q)
input: Graph G and non adjacent vertices a and b and
       sets T and S of minimal a, b-separators.
output: Set Q of all minimal a, b-separators in G.
begin
       T' := ∅;
       for each S ∈ T do
       begin
              Determine C_a;
              { C_a is the connected component of G[V − S] that contains a.}
              for each x ∈ S which is not adjacent to a do
              begin
                     Determine Δ;
                     {Δ is the minimal x, a-separator in C_a(x) that is close to x.}
                     Determine C'_a;
                     { C'_a is the connected component of G[C_a − Δ] that contains a.}
                     Determine N;
                     {N is the set of vertices in S that do not have a neighbor in C'_a.}
                     S* := (S ∪ Δ) \ N;
                     T' := T' ∪ {S*}
                     {Add S* to T' only if not yet present!}
              end for
       end for;
       Q := Q ∪ T';
       separators(G, a, b, T', Q)
end.
```

Fig. 1. Algorithm finding minimal separators

Determining Δ again takes at most $O(n^2)$ time. Also computing C'_a and N can clearly be done in $O(n^2)$ time. We have to make sure that the new set T' contains no duplicate separators. We can do this by keeping it in a suitable data structure, allowing an update in $O(n \log R) = O(n^2)$ time.

This shows that the algorithm can be implemented to run in $O(n^4 R)$ time. $\square$

Corollary 16. *The set of all minimal separators of a graph can be found in $O(n^6 R)$ time, where n is the number of vertices in the graph and R is the total number of minimal separators.*

6   Conclusions

In this paper we have presented an algorithm to determine a list of all minimal vertex separators of a graph. The algorithm needs only polynomial time per separator that is found. We like to mention some open problems.

First of all, we feel that it should be possible to improve the running time of the algorithm presented here.

A related concept is that of an *inclusion minimal separator*. This is a minimal separator with the additional constraint that no proper subset is also a minimal separator. The following lemma shows that our algorithm can be used to find all inclusion minimal separators. However, the example given in the introduction illustrates that this may not be the most efficient way to do this.

Lemma 17. *A separator S of a graph $G = (V, E)$ is inclusion minimal if and only if every vertex of S has a neighbor in every connected component of $G[V - S]$. .*

It follows that a list of all inclusion minimal separators can easily be obtained from the list of all minimal separators. Until now, we have not been able to find an efficient algorithm which finds all inclusion minimal separators.

7 Acknowledgement

We thank B. Monien for drawing our attention to this important problem.

References

1. Arnborg, S., Efficient algorithms for combinatorial problems on graphs with bounded decomposability – A survey, *BIT* **25**, (1985), pp. 2–23.
2. Arnborg, S., J. Lagergren and D. Seese, Easy problems for tree-decomposable graphs, *J.Algorithms* **12**, (1991), pp. 308–340.
3. Arnborg, S. and A. Proskurowski, Linear time algorithms for NP-hard problems restricted to partial k-trees, *Disc. Appl. Math.* **23**, (1989), pp. 305–314.
4. Bodlaender, H., A tourist guide through treewidth, Technical report RUU-CS-92-12, Department of Computer Science, Utrecht University, Utrecht, The Netherlands, (1992).
5. Bodlaender, H., A linear time algorithm for finding tree-decompositions of small treewidth, *Proceedings of the 25th Annual ACM Symposium on Theory of Computing*, (1993), pp. 226–234.
6. Bodlaender, H., T. Kloks and D. Kratsch, Treewidth and pathwidth of permutation graphs, *Proceedings of the 20th International Colloquium on Automata, Languages and Programming*, Springer-Verlag, Lecture Notes in Computer Science 700, (1993), pp. 114–125.
7. Gavril, F., Algorithms on clique separable graphs, *Discrete Math.* **19** (1977), pp. 159–165.
8. Goldberg, L. A., *Efficient algorithms for listing combinatorial structures*, Cambridge University press, 1993.
9. Golumbic, M. C., *Algorithmic Graph Theory and Perfect Graphs*, Academic Press, New York, 1980.
10. Kanevsky, A., On the number of minimum size separating vertex sets in a graph and how to find all of them, *Proceedings of the First Annual ACM-SIAM Symposium on Discrete Algorithms*, pp. 411–421, (1990).
11. Kloks, T., *Treewidth*, Ph.D. Thesis, Utrecht University, The Netherlands, 1993.
12. Kloks, T., Treewidth of circle graphs, To appear in: proceedings ISAAC'94.
13. Kloks, T. and D. Kratsch, Treewidth of chordal bipartite graphs, *10th Annual Symposium on Theoretical Aspects of Computer Science*, Springer-Verlag, Lecture Notes in Computer Science 665, (1993), pp. 80–89.

14. Kloks, T., Minimum fill-in for chordal bipatite graphs, Technical report RUU-CS-93-11, Department of Computer Science, Utrecht University, Utrecht, The Netherlands, (1993).
15. Tarjan, R. E., Decomposition by clique separators, *Discrete Mathematics* **55** (1985), pp. 221–232.
16. Whitesides, S. H., An Algorithm for finding clique cut-sets, *Information Processing Letters* **12** (1981), pp. 31–32.

On the Complexity of the Maximum Cut Problem

Hans L. Bodlaender[1]*, Klaus Jansen[2]

[1] Department of Computer Science, Utrecht University,
P.O.Box 80.089, 3508 TB Utrecht, The Netherlands.
[2] Fachbereich 11 - Mathematik, FG Informatik,
Universität Duisburg, 47 048 Duisburg, Germany.

Abstract. The complexity of the SIMPLE MAXCUT problem is investigated for several special classes of graphs. It is shown that this problem is NP-complete when restricted to one of the following classes: chordal graphs, undirected path graphs, split graphs, tripartite graphs, and graphs that are the complement of a bipartite graph. The problem can be solved in polynomial time, when restricted to graphs with bounded treewidth, or cographs. We also give large classes of graphs that can be seen as generalizations of classes of graphs with bounded treewidth and of the class of the cographs, and allow polynomial time algorithms for the SIMPLE MAX CUT problem.

1 Introduction

One of the best known combinatorial graph problems is the MAX CUT problem [10]. In this problem, we have a weighted, undirected graph $G = (V, E)$ and we look for a partition of the vertices of G into two disjoint sets, such that the total weight of the edges that go from one set to the other is as large as possible. In the SIMPLE MAX CUT problem, we take the variant where all edge weights are one.

Whereas the problems where we look for a partition with a *minimum* total weight of the edges between the sets are solvable in polynomial time with flow techniques, the (decision variants of the) MAX CUT, and even the SIMPLE MAX CUT problems are NP-complete [13, 10]. This motivates the research to solve the (SIMPLE) MAX CUT problem on special classes of graphs.

In [12] Johnson gives a table of the known results on the complexity of SIMPLE MAX CUT restricted to several classes of graphs. The most notable of the results listed there, is perhaps the fact that SIMPLE MAX CUT can be solved in polynomial time on planar graphs. Several cases however remain open. In this paper we resolve some of the open cases.

This paper is mostly concerned with the SIMPLE MAX CUT problem. In section 4 we comment on the MAX CUT problem (i.e., the problem where edges do not necessarily have unit weights.) Some applications of the MAXCUT problem are given in the references [5, 6, 15].

This paper is organized as follows. In section 2 we consider the chordal graphs, and the undirected path graphs. Next, we consider the split graphs, tripartite graphs,

---

* The work of this author was partially supported by the ESPRIT Basic Research Actions of the EC under contract 7141 (project ALCOM II).

and complements of bipartite graphs. In section 3.1, we consider cographs. An algorithm to solve SIMPLE MAX CUT on graphs with bounded treewidth is described in section 3.2. In section 3.3, the results of sections 3.1 and 3.2 are generalized. Finally, in section 4 we comment on the problem with arbitrary edge weights.

We conclude this introduction with some definitions. We first give a precise description of the SIMPLE MAX CUT problem.

Problem: SIMPLE MAX CUT
Input: Undirected graph $G = (V, E)$, $k \in \mathbb{N}$.
Question: Does there exist a set $S \subset V$, such that $|\{(s, u) \in E | s \in S, u \in V - S\}| \geq k$?

If we have a partition of V into sets $S \subseteq V$, and $V - S$, then an edge $(u, v) \in E$ with $u \in S$, $v \in V - S$ is called a *cut edge*.

2 NP-completeness results

In this section we analysed the SIMPLE MAX CUT problem for chordal graphs, split graphs, tripartite graphs, and complements of bipartite graphs.

2.1 Graphs, related to chordal graphs

A graph is chordal, if and only if it does not contain a cycle of length at least four as an induced subgraph. Alternatively, a graph is chordal, if and only if there exists a tree $T = (W, F)$ such that one can associate with each vertex $v \in V$, a subtree $T_v = (W_v, E_v)$ of T, such that $(v, w) \in E$ iff $W_v \cap W_w \neq \emptyset$. This is equivalent to stating that all maximal cliques of G can be arranged in a tree T, such that for every vertex v, the cliques that contain v form a connected subtree of T. (In other words: chordal graphs are the intersection graphs of subtrees of trees.)

We will show that SIMPLE MAX CUT is NP-complete for chordal graphs. Hereto, we use the MAX 2-SAT problem, described below.

Problem: MAX 2-SAT
Input: A set of p disjunctive clauses each containing at most two literals and an integer $k \leq p$.
Question: Is there a truth assignment to the variables which satisfies at least k clauses ?

MAX 2-SAT was proven to be NP-complete by Garey, Johnson and Stockmeyer [10]. (In [10] also a transformation from MAX 2-SAT to the SIMPLE MAX CUT problem for undirected graphs was given.) We note [9] that 3-SAT remains NP-complete if for each variable there are at most five clauses that contain either the variable or its complement. Using the reduction of Garey, Johnson and Stockmeyer [10] we can obtain a similar result for MAX 2-SAT such that for each variable there are at most 20 clauses containing the variable or its complement. It is possible to replace the number 20 by the smaller constant six using a different construction. In this construction each literal (variable or its complement) occurs at most three times.

Theorem 1. SIMPLE MAX CUT *is NP-complete for chordal graphs.*

Proof. (We will omit in this and all later proofs the statement that the problems are in NP.)

We give a transformation from MAX 2-SAT to SIMPLE MAX CUT for chordal graphs. Let $X = \{x_1, \ldots, x_n, \overline{x_1}, \ldots, \overline{x_n}\}$ be a variable set, let $(a_1 \vee b_1), \ldots, (a_p \vee b_p)$ denote a set of clauses.

Let $m = 2p$. First we define a number of sets:

(1) for each $i \in \{1, \ldots, n\}$ take $C^{(i)} = \{c_1^{(i)}, \ldots, c_{m+1}^{(i)}\}$, $D^{(i)} = \{d_1^{(i)}, \ldots, d_{m+2}^{(i)}\}$, $E^{(i)} = \{e_1^{(i)}, \ldots, e_{m+2}^{(i)}\}$.

(2) take for each $i \in \{1, \ldots, p\}$, the set $T^{(i)} = \{t_1^{(i)}, \ldots, t_{m+2}^{(i)}\}$, and take the sets $R = \{r_1, \ldots, r_p\}$, $Q = \{q_1, \ldots, q_p\}$, $Y = \{y_1, \ldots, y_p\}$ and $S = \{s_1, \ldots, s_{m+1}\}$.

(3) take $U = \{u_1, \ldots, u_p\}$, $V = \{v_1, \ldots, v_p\}$, $W = \{w_1, \ldots, w_p\}$, and $Z = \{z_1, \ldots, z_p\}$.

In the following we define an input graph $G' = (V', E')$ and want to partition the vertex set V' into sets V_1 and V_2 where V_1 gets literals with truth value *true* and V_2 gets literals with value *false*. The sets in (1) are used to place x_i into V_1 or V_2 and the complement $\overline{x_i}$ into the other set. Furthermore, the sets in (2) place R and Q into the first set V_1 which contains the literals with value *false*. For all values to a_i, b_i with $(a_i \vee b_i) = true$ we want to have the same number of generated cut edges and for $(a_i \vee b_i) = false$ a smaller number of cut edges. To obtain this we use the sets in (3) and the set $Q = \{q_1, \ldots, q_p\}$.

We now define the input graph $G' = (V', E')$ for the SIMPLE MAX CUT problem. V' is the disjoint union of all sets: X, $C^{(i)}$ ($1 \le i \le n$), $D^{(i)}$ ($1 \le i \le n$), $E^{(i)}$ ($1 \le i \le n$), S, R, Q, $T^{(i)}$ ($1 \le i \le p$), U, V, W, and Z. There is an edge between a pair of vertices in G', if and only if at least one of the following sets contains both vertices, i.e. each of the following sets forms a clique in G':

- for each $i \in \{1, \ldots, n\}$:
  - $\{x_i\} \cup C^{(i)} \cup E^{(i)}$,
  - $\{x_i\} \cup C^{(i)} \cup D^{(i)}$,
  - $\{x_i, \overline{x_i}\} \cup C^{(i)}$,
- for each $j \in \{1, \ldots, m+1\}$, take a set (clique) $R \cup \{s_j\}$.
- $X \cup R \cup Y$.
- for each $i \in \{1, \ldots, p\}$, and each $j \in \{1, \ldots, m+2\}$, take a set (clique) $\{r_i, q_i, t_j^{(i)}\}$.
- for each $i \in \{1, \ldots, p\}$: if the ith clause is $(a_i \vee b_i)$, then take sets (cliques)
  - $\{a_i, b_i, r_i, q_i\}$
  - $\{a_i, b_i, v_i, w_i\}$
  - $\{a_i, u_i, v_i\}$
  - $\{b_i, v_i, z_i\}$

First, we claim that the graph G', formed in this way is chordal. This follows because we can arrange all cliques in a tree T, such that every vertex belongs to a set of trees that forms a connected subtree of T. (Alternatively, one can check by tedious case analysis that G' does not contain an induced cycle of length more than 3.)

In order to count the maximum number of possible cut edges, we consider six types of edges:

1. Edges between vertices in $C^{(i)} \cup D^{(i)} \cup E^{(i)} \cup \{x_i\}$, for some $i \in \{1, \ldots, n\}$.
2. Edges of the form $(\overline{x_i}, c_j^{(i)})$.
3. Edges between vertices in $X \cup R \cup Y$.
4. Edges of the form (r_i, s_j).
5. Edges of the form (r_i, q_i), $(r_i, t_j^{(i)})$, $(q_i, t_j^{(i)})$, for some $i \in \{1, \ldots, n\}$.
6. Edges of the form (q_i, a_i), (q_i, b_i), (a_i, u_i), (a_i, v_i), (a_i, w_i), (b_i, v_i), (b_i, w_i), (b_i, z_i), (u_i, v_i), (v_i, w_i), (w_i, z_i), for some $i \in \{1, \ldots, n\}$, where the ith clause is $(a_i \vee b_i)$.

Note that each edge of G' has exactly one type.

Write $B = 2n \cdot (m+2)^2 + n \cdot (m+1) + (n+p)^2 + p \cdot (m+1) + 2p \cdot (m+2) + 6p$. We now claim that G' has a partition with at least $B + 2k$ cut edges, if and only there is a truth assignment, that verifies at least k clauses.

Suppose we have a truth assignment, that verifies at least k clauses. We construct a partition $V' = V_1 \cup V_2$, $V_1 \cap V_2 = \emptyset$ in the following way:

$$
\begin{aligned}
V_1 = \ & R \cup Q \cup \{x_i, c_j^{(i)} | x_i \text{ false }\} \\
& \cup \{\overline{x_i}, d_j^{(i)}, e_j^{(i)} | x_i \text{ true }\} \\
& \cup \{u_i, z_i | a_i \text{ false } \wedge b_i \text{ false }\} \\
& \cup \{v_i, z_i | a_i \text{ false } \wedge b_i \text{ true }\} \\
& \cup \{u_i, w_i | a_i \text{ true } \wedge b_i \text{ false }\} \\
& \cup \{v_i, w_i | a_i \text{ true } \wedge b_i \text{ true }\} \\
V_2 = \ & V \setminus V_1.
\end{aligned}
$$

We have $2n \cdot (m+2)^2$ cut edges of type 1, $n \cdot (m+1)$ cut edges of type 2, $(2n+p)^2$ cut edges of type 3, $p \cdot (m+1)$ cut edges of type 4, and $2p \cdot (m+2)$ cut edges of type 5. For a clause that is true, the number of type 6 cut edges corresponding to that clause is eight, and for a clause that is false, this number is six. Hence, the total number of cut edges of type 6 is $6p + 2k$. The total number of cut edges of all types is precisely $B + 2k$.

We can show, that when we have a partition of V' in sets V_1, V_2 with at least $B + 2k$ cut edges, then there must be a truth assignment with at least k true clauses. We consider for each type of edges the maximum number of cut-edges. We compare these numbers with the numbers obtained in the partition formed above. For the details, we refer to our full paper. NP-hardness of the problem follows, because G' can be constructed in polynomial time. □

Now we analyse a subclass of the chordal graphs, the undirected path graphs. A graph is an undirected path graph, if it is the intersection graph of paths in an (unrooted, undirected) tree. In other words, $G = (V, E)$ is an undirected path graph, if and only if there exists a tree $T = (W, F)$, and for every vertex $v \in V$ a path P_v in T, such that for all pairs of vertices $v, w \in V$, $v \neq w$: $(v, w) \in E$, if and only if P_v and P_w have at least one vertex in common.

Theorem 2. SIMPLE MAX CUT *is NP-complete for undirected path graphs.*

Proof. We can show this by changing the construction from the proof above. We use that MAX 2-SAT remains NP-complete, when for each variable, the number of clauses that contains the variable is bounded by the constant 3. Then, we replace each variable x_i by $x_{i,1}, \ldots, x_{i,3}$ and $\overline{x_i}$ by $\overline{x_{i,1}}, \ldots, \overline{x_{i,3}}$ and enlarge the sets $D^{(i)}$ and $E^{(i)}$ by two vertices.

A graph $G = (V, E)$ is a split graph, if and only if there is a partition of the vertices V of G into a clique C and an independent set U. Another necessary and sufficient condition for a graph G to be a split graph is that G and its complement G^c are chordal graphs, see also Földes and Hammer [8]. We analyse now a subclass of the split graphs, namely the class of those split graphs where each vertex of the independent set U is incident to exactly two vertices of the clique C. We call these graphs the 2-split graphs.

Theorem 3. SIMPLE MAX CUT *is NP-complete for 2-split graphs.*

Proof. We use a transformation from the (unrestricted) SIMPLE MAX CUT problem. Let a graph $G = (V, E)$ be given. Let $G^c = (V, E^c)$ be the complement of G. Let $H = (V \cup E^c, F)$, where $F = \{(v, w) \mid v, w \in V, \ v \neq w\} \cup \{(v, e) \mid v \in V, \ e \in E^c, \ v$ is an endpoint of edge $e\}$. In other words, we take a vertex in H for every vertex in G and every edge in the complement of G. V forms a clique, E^c forms an independent set in H. Every edge-representing vertex is connected to the vertices, representing its endpoints. We can show that G allows a partition with at least K cut edges, if and only if H allows a partition with at least $2 \cdot |E^c| + K$ cut edges.

2.2 Graphs, related to bipartite graphs

Bipartite graphs are graphs $G = (V, E)$ in which the vertex set can be partitioned into two sets V_1 and V_2 such that no edge joins two vertices in the same set. Simple MAXCUT is trivial for bipartite graphs. Thus, it is interesting to look at related graph classes. We consider the tripartite graphs, and the graphs that are the complement of a bipartite graph. The latter graphs we call the co-bipartite graphs.

A generalization of bipartite graphs are the tripartite graphs $G = (V, E)$. A graph is tripartite, if and only if the vertex set can be partitioned into three independent sets V_1, V_2 and V_3. In other words, a graph is tripartite if its chromatic number is at most three.

Theorem 4. SIMPLE MAX CUT *is NP-complete for tripartite graphs.*

Proof. By transformation from SIMPLE MAX CUT for split graphs to tripartite graphs. Let $G = (V, E)$ be a split graph, where the vertex set is partitioned into a clique C and an independent set U, and define a graph $\overline{G} = (\overline{V}, \overline{E})$. For each pair $c_i, c_j \in C$ with $i \neq j$ define a graph $G_{\{i,j\}}$ with vertex set

$$
\begin{aligned}
V_{\{i,j\}} &= \{c_i, c_j, , w_{\{i,j\}}, x_{\{i,j\}}, y_{\{i,j\}}, z_{\{i,j\}}\} \\
E_{\{i,j\}} &= \{(x_{\{i,j\}}, c_i), (z_{\{i,j\}}, c_i), (y_{\{i,j\}}, c_i), \\
&\quad (z_{\{i,j\}}, c_j), (y_{\{i,j\}}, c_j), (w_{\{i,j\}}, c_j), \\
&\quad (x_{\{i,j\}}, y_{\{i,j\}}), (z_{\{i,j\}}, y_{\{i,j\}}), (z_{\{i,j\}}, w_{\{i,j\}})\}
\end{aligned}
$$

and replace the edge (c_i, c_j) by the graph $G_{\{i,j\}}$. Then, $\overline{V}$ is the union of vertex sets $V_{\{i,j\}}$ and the independent set U. The edge set $\overline{E}$ is given as union of the edge sets $E_{\{i,j\}}$ and the set $\{e = \{c, u\} \in E | c \in C, u \in U\}$. The resulting graph is tripartite and we can show that G allows a partition with at least k cut edges if and only if $\overline{G}$ allows a partition with at least $k + 3|C|(|C| - 1)$ cut edges.

Theorem 5. SIMPLE MAX CUT *is NP-complete for co-bipartite graphs.*

Proof. We use a transformation from the SIMPLE MAX CUT problem, restricted to split graphs. Suppose $G = (C \cup U, E)$ is a split graph, U forms an independent set, and C forms a clique in G. Take a set U', disjoint from $C \cup U$, with $|U'| = |U|$. Let $H = (C \cup U \cup U', E \cup \{(v, w) \mid v \neq w, v, w \in U \cup U'\})$. In other words, H is obtained from G by adding the vertices in U', and putting a clique on $U \cup U'$. Clearly, H is a co-bipartite graph. We can show that G has a partition with at least K cut edges, if and only if H has a partition with at least $|U|^2 + K$ cut edges.

3   Composition of graphs

In this section we show that SIMPLE MAX CUT can be solved efficiently on a class of graphs that includes the graphs with bounded treewidth and the cographs. Independently, Wanke [18] has found a polynomial time algorithm for a class of graphs that includes the cographs. We first show the ideas of the method on cographs and on graphs with bounded treewidth.

3.1   Cographs

Definition 6. Let $G_1 = (V_1, E_1)$, $G_2 = (V_2, E_2)$ be two graphs, with V_1 and V_2 disjoint sets. The disjoint union of G_1 and G_2 is the graph $G_1 \cup G_2 = (V_1 \cup V_2, E_1 \cup E_2)$. The product of G_1 and G_2 is the graph $G_1 \times G_2 = (V_1 \cup V_2, E_1 \cup E_2 \cup \{(v, w) \mid v \in V_1, w \in V_2\})$.

Definition 7. The class of cographs is the smallest set of graphs, fulfilling the following rules:

1. Every graph $G = (V, E)$ with one vertex and no edges ($|V| = 1$ and $|E| = 0$) is a cograph.
2. If $G_1 = (V_1, E_1)$ is a cograph, $G_2 = (V_2, E_2)$ is a cograph, and V_1 and V_2 are disjoint sets, then $G_1 \cup G_2$ is a cograph.
3. If $G_1 = (V_1, E_1)$ is a cograph, $G_2 = (V_2, E_2)$ is a cograph, and V_1 and V_2 are disjoint sets, then $G_1 \times G_2$ is a cograph.

Alternatively, a graph is a cograph, if it does not contain a path with four vertices P_4 as an induced subgraph. Many NP-complete problems are polynomial time solvable on cographs; there are only a few notable expections, e.g. achromatic number [2] and list coloring [11] are NP-complete for cographs.

To each cograph G one can associate a corresponding rooted binary tree T, called the *cotree* of G, in the following way. Each non-leaf node in the tree is labeled with either "∪" (union-nodes) or "×" (product-nodes). Each non-leaf node has exactly two children. Each node of the cotree corresponds to a cograph. In [7], it is shown that one can decide in $O(n + e)$ time, whether a graph is a cograph, and build a corresponding cotree.

Our algorithm has the following structure: first find a cotree for the input graph G, which is a cograph. Then for each node of the cotree, we compute a table, called $maxc_H$, where H is the cograph corresponding to the node. These tables are computed 'bottom-up' in the cotree: first all tables of leaf-nodes are computed, and in general a table of an internal node is computed after the tables of its two children are computed.

Let $H = (V', E')$ be a cograph. The table $maxc_H$ has entries for all integers i, $0 \le i \le |V'|$, that denote the maximum size of a cut of H into a set of size i and a set of size $|V'| - i$, in other words:

$$maxc_H(i) = \max\{|\{(v,w) \mid v \in W_1,\ w \in W_2\}| \mid W_1 \cup W_2 = V',\ W_1 \cap W_2 = \emptyset,\ |W_1| = i\}$$

Clearly, the size of the maximum cut of G is $\max_{0 \le i \le |V|} maxc_G(i)$, hence, when we have the table $maxc_G$, i.e., the table of the root node of the cotree, then we know the size of the maximum cut. The tables can be computed efficiently, starting with the tables at the leaves, and computing tables in an order such that when we compute the table a node, then the tables of its children have already been computed.

The tables associated with leaf nodes are clearly all of the form: $maxc_H(0) = 0$, $maxc_H(1) = 0$. The following lemma shows how a table $maxc_{G_1 \cup G_2}$ or a table $maxc_{G_1 \times G_2}$ can be computed, after the tables $maxc_{G_1}$ and $maxc_{G_2}$ are computed. A more general result will be shown in section 5.3.

Lemma 8. *Let $G_1 = (V_1, E_1)$ and $G_2 = (V_2, E_2)$ be graphs, with V_1 and V_2 disjoint sets. Then:*
(i) $maxc_{G_1 \cup G_2}(i) = \max\{maxc_{G_1}(j) + maxc_{G_2}(i - j) \mid 0 \le j \le i,\ j \le |V_1|,\ i - j \le |V_2|\}$.
(ii) $maxc_{G_1 \times G_2}(i) = \max\{maxc_{G_1}(j) + maxc_{G_2}(i - j) + j \cdot (|V_2| - (i - j)) + (|V_1| - j) \cdot (i - j) \mid 0 \le j \le i,\ j \le |V_1|,\ i - j \le |V_2|\}$.

It directly follows that one can compute the table $maxc_{G_1 \cup G_2}$ and $maxc_{G_1 \times G_2}$ in $O(|V_1| \cdot |V_2|)$ time. By standard arguments, the following result now can be derived:

Theorem 9. *There exists an $O(n^2)$ algorithm for* SIMPLE MAX CUT *on cographs.*

It is easy to modify this algorithm such that it also *yields a partition* with the maximum number of cut edges, and uses also $O(n^2)$ time.

3.2 Graphs with bounded treewidth

It is well know that the SIMPLE MAX CUT problem can be solved in linear time on graphs with bounded treewidth (see e.g. [19]). We sketch the method here, as it will be generalized hereafter. The notion of treewidth of a graph was introduced by Robertson and Seymour [16], and is equivalent to several other interesting graph theoretic notions, for instance the notion of partial k-trees (see e.g., [1, 4]).

Definition 10. A tree-decomposition of a graph $G = (V, E)$ is a pair $(\{X_i \mid i \in I\}, T = (I, F))$, where $\{X_i \mid i \in I\}$ is a collection of subsets of V, and $T = (I, F)$ is a tree, such that the following conditions hold:

1. $\bigcup_{i \in I} X_i = V$.
2. For all edges $(v, w) \in E$, there exists a node $i \in I$, with $v, w \in X_i$.
3. For every vertex $v \in V$, the subgraph of T, induced by the nodes $\{i \in I \mid v \in X_i\}$ is connected.

The treewidth of a tree-decomposition $(\{X_i \mid i \in I\}, T = (I, F))$ is $\max_{i \in I} |X_i| - 1$. The treewidth of a graph is the minimum treewidth over all possible tree-decompositions of the graph.

It is not difficult to make small modifications to a tree-decomposition, without increasing its treewidth, such that one can see T as a rooted tree, with root $r \in I$, and the following conditions hold:

1. T is a binary tree.
2. If a node $i \in I$ has two children j_1 and j_2, then $X_i = X_{j_1} = X_{j_2}$.
3. If a node $i \in I$ has one child j, then either $X_j \subset X_i$ and $|X_i - X_j| = 1$, or $X_i \subset X_j$ and $|X_j - X_i| = 1$.

We will assume in the remainder that a tree-decomposition of G of this type is given, with treewidth at most k, for some constant k. Note that a tree-decomposition of G with treewidth $\leq k$ can be found, if it exists, in $O(n)$ time [3].

For every node $i \in I$, let Y_i denote the set of all vertices in a set X_j with $j = i$ or j is a descendant of i in the rooted tree T. Our algorithm is based upon computing for every node $i \in I$ a table $maxc_i$. For every subset S of X_i, there is an entry in the table $maxc_i$, fulfilling

$$maxc_i(S) = \max_{S' \subseteq Y_i, \; S' \cap X_i = S} |\{(v, w) \in E \mid v \in S', \; w \in Y_i - S'\}|.$$

In other words, for $S \subseteq X_i$, $maxc_i(S)$ denotes the maximum number of cut edges for a partition of Y_i, such that all vertices in S are in one set in the partition, and all vertices in $X_i - S$ are in the other set in the partition.

The tables are again computed in a bottom-up manner: start with computing the tables for the leaves, then always compute the table for an internal node later than the tables of its child or children are computed. The following lemma, which is easy to proof, shows how the tables can be computed efficiently:

Lemma 11. *(i) Let i be a leaf in T. Then for all $S \subseteq X_i$, $maxc_i(S) = |\{(v, w) \in E \mid v \in S, \; w \in X_i - S\}|$.*
(ii) Let i be a node with one child j in T. Suppose $X_i \subseteq X_j$. Then for all $S \subseteq X_i$, $maxc_i(S) = \max_{S' \subseteq X_j, \; S' \cap X_i = S} maxc_j(S')$.
(iii) Let i be a node with one child j in T. Suppose $X_j \cup \{v\} = X_i$, $v \notin X_j$. For all $S \subseteq X_i$, if $v \in S$, then $maxc_i(S) = maxc_j(S - \{v\}) + |\{(s, v) \mid v \in X_i - S\}|$, and if $v \notin S$, then $maxc_i(S) = maxc_j(S) + |\{(s, v) \mid v \in S\}|$.
(iv) Let i be a node with two children j_1, j_2 in T, with $X_i = X_{j_1} = X_{j_2}$. For all $S \subseteq X_i$, $maxc_i(S) = maxc_{j_1}(S) + maxc_{j_2}(S) - |\{(v, w) \in E \mid v \in S, \; w \in X_i - S\}|$.

It follows that computing a table $maxc_i$ can be done in $O(1)$ time. So, in $O(n)$ time, one can compute the table of the root r. The size of the maximum cut is $\max_{S \subseteq X_r} maxc_r(S)$.

Theorem 12. SIMPLE MAX CUT *can be solved in $O(n)$ time on graphs with constant bounded treewidth.*

Again, it is possible to modify the algorithm, such that it also yields a partition with the maximum number of cut edges.

3.3 Composition of graphs

We now generalize and combine the previous results in this section.

Definition 13. Let $H_0 = (V_0, E_0)$ be a graph with r vertices; $V_0 = \{v_1, v_2, \cdots, v_r\}$. Let $H_1 = (V_1, E_1), H_2 = (V_2, E_2), \ldots, H_r = (V_r, E_r)$ be r disjoint graphs. The factor graph $H_0[H_1, H_2, \cdots, H_r]$ is the graph, obtained by taking the disjoint union of H_1, $H_2, \ldots, H_r$, and adding all edges between pairs of vertices v, w, with $v \in V_i$, $w \in V_j$, and $(i,j) \in E_0$: $H_0[H_1, H_2, \cdots, H_r] = (\bigcup_{1 \le i \le r} V_i, \bigcup_{1 \le i \le r} E_i \cup \{(v,w) \mid \exists i,j : 1 \le i,j \le r, v \in V_i, w \in V_j, (i,j) \in E_0\})$.

It often is useful to try to write a graph $G = (V, E)$ as a factor graph $G = H_0[H_1, H_2, \cdots, H_r]$, for some suitable choice of $H_0, \ldots, H_r$. Such a 'factorization', where H_0 is as small as possible, $r \ge 2$, can be found in polynomial time [14]. (Clearly, a trivial factorization, where $G = H_0$ and all graphs $H_1, \cdots, H_n$ consist of one vertex always exists, but is not really useful.) Then, it is often useful to factorize the graphs $H_1, H_2, \ldots, H_r$ again, and then possibly factorize the formed parts of these graphs again, etc.

In this way, one can associate with a graph a factor tree. A factor tree is a rooted tree, where every non-leaf node is labeled with a graph. We call this graph a *label graph*. The number of vertices in a label graph equals the number of children of the node to which the graph is labeled; these vertices are always numbered 1,2,... To each node of the factor tree, one can associate then a graph, called the *factor graph*, in the following way. To a leaf node, associate a graph with one vertex and no edges. To a non-leaf node, with label graph $H_0 = (\{1, 2, \cdots, r\}, E_0)$, associate the graph $H_0[H_1, \cdots, H_r]$, where for all i, $1 \le i \le r$, H_i is the factor graph associated to the i'th child of the node. The factor graph associated to the root of the tree is the graph, represented by this factor tree.

The notion of factor tree generalizes the notion of cotree: in a cotree the only label graphs are K_2 (a graph with two vertices and one edge — the label of product nodes), and K_2^c (a graph with two vertices and no edges — the label of union nodes).

The following result generalizes the results of the previous two sections.

Theorem 14. *For all constants k, the SIMPLE MAX CUT problem is solvable in polynomial time for graphs, with a factor tree, where every label graph has treewidth at most k.*

The first step of the algorithm is to find the factor tree. By using the results from [14], it follows that the factor tree can be found in polynomial time, such that the size and also the treewidth of label graphs are minimal. Also, a tree-decomposition of treewidth at most k of the type as described in the previous section is computed for every label graph.

For each factor graph $H = (V', E')$, associated with a node of the factor tree, we compute — just as we did for cographs — a table $maxc_H$, which has entries for all integers i, $0 \le i \le |V'|$, that denote the maximum size of a cut of H into a set of size i and a set of size $|V'| - i$, in other words:

$$maxc_H(i) = \max\{|\{(v,w) \mid v \in W_1, \ w \in W_2\}| \mid W_1 \cup W_2 = V', \ W_1 \cap W_2 = \emptyset, \ |W_1| = i\}$$

These tables are easily computed for factor graphs, associated with leaves. Again, the tables are computed bottom up in the factor tree.

Suppose we want to compute the table for a factor graph $H = H_0[H_1, \cdots, H_r]$, $(H_0 = (\{1, 2, \cdots, r\}, E_0)$ is the label graph of some non-leaf node of the factor tree, and $H_1 = (V_1, E_1)$, ..., $H_r = (V_r, E_r)$ are the factor graphs, associated with the children of that node.) We have already computed all tables $maxc_{H_1}, \ldots, maxc_{H_r}$.

As in the previous section, for every node $\alpha \in I$, let Y_α denote the set of all vertices in a set X_β with $\beta = \alpha$ or β is a descendant of α in the rooted tree T.

For $\alpha \in I$, let $H_\alpha = (Z_\alpha, F_\alpha)$ denote the graph, obtained by removing all vertices from H, that are not in a graph H_i, with $i \in Y_\alpha$, or in other words, H_α is the subgraph of H, induced by all vertices in $Z_\alpha = \bigcup_{i \in Y_\alpha} V_i$.

In order to compute the table $maxc_H$, we compute now for every node $\alpha \in I$ of the tree-decomposition $(\{H_\alpha \mid \alpha \in I\}, T = (I, F))$ of label graph H_0 a table $maxc'_\alpha$, which has an entry for every function $f : X_\alpha \to \{0, 1, 2, \ldots\}$, such that $f(i) \le |V_i|$, where for all such functions f:

> $maxc'_\alpha(f, s)$ denotes the maximum cut size of a partition of Z_α into two disjoint sets W_1, W_2, such that for all $i \in X_\alpha$, $|W_1 \cap V_i| = f(i)$, and $|W_1| = s$.

In other words, we look for the maximum cut of H_α, such that f describes for all graphs H_i with i an element of the set X_α, how many vertices of H_i are in the set W_1.

We compute the tables $maxc'_\alpha$ bottom up, in the tree-decomposition. The next lemma shows how this can be done. The proof of this result is given in the full paper. Note that we are working with two types of trees: we have one factor tree, and with every node of this factor tree, we have associated a tree-decomposition.

Lemma 15. *(i) Let α be a leaf in T. Then for all $f : X_\alpha \to \{0, 1, 2, \ldots\}$, with for all $i \in X_\alpha : f(i) \le |V_i|$, $s = \sum_{i \in X_\alpha} f(i)$:*

$$maxc'_\alpha(f, s) = \sum_{i \in X_\alpha} maxc_{H_i}(f(i)) + \sum_{(i,j) \in E_0, \ i,j \in X_\alpha} (f(i) \cdot (|V_j| - f(j)) + f(j) \cdot (|V_i| - f(i)))$$

For all other values of s,

$$maxc'_\alpha(f, s) = -\infty$$

(ii) Let α be a node with one child β in T. Suppose $X_\alpha \subseteq X_\beta$. Then for all $s \geq 0$, $f : X_\alpha \to \{0, 1, 2, \ldots\}$ with for all $i \in X_\alpha : f(i) \leq |V_i|$:

$$maxc'_\alpha(f, s) = \max\{maxc'_\beta(f', s) \mid \forall i \in X_\alpha : f(i) = f'(i) \land \forall i \in X_\beta : f'(i) \leq |V_i|\}$$

(iii) Let α be a node with one child β in T. Suppose $X_\beta \cup \{i_0\} = X_\alpha$, $i_0 \notin X_\beta$. Then for all $s \geq 0$, $f : X_\alpha \to \{0, 1, 2, \ldots\}$ with for all $i \in X_\alpha : f(i) \leq |V_i|$: let f' be the function f restricted to X_β. Then

$$maxc'_\alpha(f, s) = maxc'_\beta(f, s-f(i_0)) + \sum_{(i_0,j) \in E_0, j \in X_\alpha} (f(i_0) \cdot (|V_j| - f(j)) + (|V_{i_0}| - f(i_0)) \cdot f(j))$$

(iv) Let α be a node with two children β_1, β_2 in T, with $X_\alpha = X_{\beta_1} = X_{\beta_2}$. Then for all $s \geq 0$, $f : X_\alpha \to \{0, 1, 2, \ldots\}$ with for all $i \in X_\alpha : f(i) \leq |V_i|$:

$$maxc'_\alpha(f, s) = \max_{s_1, s_2 \geq 0,\ s_1 + s_2 - \sum_{i \in X_\alpha} f(i) = s} maxc'_{\beta_1}(f, s_1) + maxc'_{\beta_2}(f, s_2)$$
$$- \sum_{(i,j) \in E_0, i, j \in X_\alpha} (f(i) \cdot (|V_j| - f(j)) + (|V_i| - f(i)) \cdot f(j))$$

From lemma 15, it follows directly how all tables $maxc'$ can be computed in a bottom up manner, given all tables $maxc_{H_i}$. The time, needed per table is linear in the size of the table, plus the sizes of the tables of its children, hence is polynomial in n (but exponential in k.) When we have the table $maxc'_\gamma$ with γ the root-node of the tree-decomposition, then we can compute the table $maxc_H$ (remember that $H = H_0[H_1, \cdots, H_r]$), using the following lemma.

Lemma 16. *For all $r \geq 0$, $r \leq |V_H|$, $maxc_H(r) = \max\{maxc'_\gamma(f, r) \mid \forall i \in X_\gamma : f(i) \leq |V_i|\}$.*

Proof. Note that $H = H_\gamma$. We just take the maximum over all possible numbers of vertices in W_1 that are in each of the sets V_i with $i \in X_\gamma$. $\square$

We now are one level higher in the factor tree. The processes are repeated until the table $maxc_G$ is obtained, from which the answer to the simple max cut problem can be determined. As each table computation can be done in polynomial time, and a linear number of tables must be computed, the whole algorithm takes time, polynomial in n, when k is a fixed constant. We now have proved theorem 14.

It is also possible to construct the partition which gives the maximum number of cut edges, without increasing the running time of the algorithm by more than a constant factor.

4 Weighted Max Cut

We conclude this paper with some small observations on the weigthed variant of the problem. First, observe that MAX CUT is NP-complete, when restricted to cliques, when only edge weigths 0 and 1 are allowed. (The problem in this form is equivalent to the SIMPLE MAX CUT problem.) So, MAX CUT is NP-complete for all classes of graphs that contain all cliques, (e.g., for the class of cographs.) Secondly, as first shown by Wimer [19], MAX CUT can be solved in linear time on graphs given with a tree-decomposition of bounded treewidth. (It is possible to modify the results of section 3.2 and obtain an algorithm, quite similar to the algorithm of Wimer.)

References

1. Arnborg, S.: Efficient algorithms for combinatorial problems on graphs with bounded decomposability — A survey. BIT **25** (1985) 2–23.
2. Bodlaender, H.L.: Achromatic Number is NP-complete for cographs and interval graphs. Information Processing Letters **31** (1989) 135–138.
3. Bodlaender, H.L.: A linear time algorithm for finding tree-decompositions of small treewidth. In: Proceedings of the 25th Annual Symposium on Theory of Computing, pages 226–234. ACM Press, 1993.
4. Bodlaender, H.L.: A tourist guide through treewidth. Technical Report RUU-CS-92-12, Department of Computer Science, Utrecht University, Utrecht, 1992. To appear in: Acta Cybernetica.
5. Chang, K., Du, D.: Efficient algorithms for the layer assignment problem. IEEE Trans. CAD **6** (1987) 67–78.
6. Chen, R., Kajitani, Y., Chan, S.: A graph theoretic via minimization algorithm for two layer printed circuit boards. IEEE Trans. Circuit Syst. (1983) 284–299.
7. Corneil, D.G., Perl, Y., Stewart, L.K.: A linear recognition algorithm for cographs. SIAM J. Comput. **4** (1985) 926–934.
8. Földes, S., Hammer, P.L.: Split graphs. In: Proceedings of the 8th Southeastern Conf. on Combinatorics, Graph Theory and Computing, pages 311–315. Louisiana State University, Baton Rouge, Louisiana, 1977.
9. Garey, M.R., Johnson, D.S.: Computers and Intractability, A Guide to the Theory of NP-Completeness. W.H. Freeman and Company, New York, 1979.
10. Garey, M.R., Johnson, D.S., Stockmeyer, L.: Some simplified NP-complete graph problems. Theoretical Computer Science **1** (1976) 237–267.
11. Jansen, K., Scheffler, P.: Some coloring results for tree like graphs. Workshop on Graph Theoretic Concepts in Computer Science. LNCS **657** (1992) 50–59.
12. Johnson, D.S.: The NP-completeness column: an ongoing guide. J. Algorithms **6** (1985) 434–451.
13. Karp, R.M.: Reducibility among combinatorial problems. in: Miller and Thatcher (eds.): Complexity of Computer Computations, Plenum Press (1972) 85–104.
14. Muller, J.M., Spinrad, L.: Incremental modular decomposition. J. ACM. **36** (1989) 1–19.
15. Pinter, R.: Optimal layer assignment for interconnect. In: Proc. Int. Symp. Circuit Syst. (ISCAS) (1982) 398–401.
16. Robertson, N., Seymour, P.D.: Graph minors. II. Algorithmic aspects of tree-width. J. Algorithms **7** (1986) 309–322.
17. Trotter, W.T.Jr., Harary, F.: On double and multiple interval graphs. J. Graph Theory **3** (1979) 205–211.
18. Wanke, E.: k-NLC graphs and polynomial algorithms. Bericht. Reihe Informatik 80. Universität Paderborn, 1991.
19. Wimer, T.V.: Linear algorithms on k-terminal graphs. PhD thesis. Department of Computer Science. Clemson University, 1987.

Index of Authors

Springer-Verlag
and the Environment

We at Springer-Verlag firmly believe that an international science publisher has a special obligation to the environment, and our corporate policies consistently reflect this conviction.

We also expect our business partners – paper mills, printers, packaging manufacturers, etc. – to commit themselves to using environmentally friendly materials and production processes.

The paper in this book is made from low- or no-chlorine pulp and is acid free, in conformance with international standards for paper permanency.